DATE DUE

ENCYCLOPEDIA OF THE
DEVELOPING WORLD

ENCYCLOPEDIA OF THE
DEVELOPING
WORLD

Volume 2
F–N
INDEX

THOMAS M. LEONARD
EDITOR

Routledge
Taylor & Francis Group
New York   London

Published in 2006 by
Routledge
Taylor & Francis Group
270 Madison Avenue
New York, NY 10016

Published in Great Britain by
Routledge
Taylor & Francis Group
2 Park Square
Milton Park, Abingdon
Oxon OX14 4RN

International Standard Book Number-10: 1-57958-388-1 (set) 0-415-97662-6 (Vol 1) 0-415-97663-4 (Vol 2) 0-415-97664-2 (Vol 3)
International Standard Book Number-13: 978-1-57958-388-0 (set) 978-0-415-97662-6 (Vol 1) 978-0-415-97663-3 (Vol 2) 978-0-415-97664-0 (Vol 3)
Library of Congress Card Number 2005049976

Library of Congress Cataloging-in-Publication Data

Encyclopedia of the developing world / Thomas M. Leonard, editor.
   p. cm.
  Includes bibliographical references and index.
   ISBN 1-57958-388-1 (set : alk. paper) -- ISBN 0-415-97662-6 (v. 1 : alk. paper) -- ISBN 0-415-97663-4 (v. 2 : alk. paper) -- ISBN 0-415-97664-2 (v. 3 : alk. paper)
   1. Developing countries--Encyclopedias. I. Leonard, Thomas M., 1937-

HC59.7.E52 2005
909'.09724'03--dc22

2005049976

Taylor & Francis Group is the Academic Division of T&F Informa plc.

Visit the Taylor & Francis Web site at
http://www.taylorandfrancis.com

and the Routledge Web site at
http://www.routledge-ny.com

BOARD OF ADVISORS

LIST OF CONTRIBUTORS

Rafis Abazov
Columbia University

Alfia Abazova
Dag Hammarskjöld Library

Janet Adamski
Southwestern University

Ali Ahmed
University of Birmingham

Nadine Akhund
Columbia University

Adam Allouba
McGill University

Samuel K. Andoh
Southern Connecticut State University

Anne Androuais
CNRS/FORUM/University Paris X

Christien van den Anker
University of Birmingham

Gasser Auda
University of Wales

Louis Augustin-Jean
University of Waseda

Rémi Bachand
Université Paris 1 (Panthéon-Sorbonne)

Josiah R. Baker
University of Central Florida

Mina Baliamoune
University of North Florida

Assefaw Bariagaber
Seton Hall University

John H. Barnhill
Yukon, Oklahoma

Graham Barrigan
La Trobe University

Greg Barton
Deakin University

Bob Beatty
Washburn University

Derek A. Bentley
Armstrong Atlantic State University

Mark T. Berger
University of New South Wales

Brian J. L. Berry
University of Texas at Dallas

Charles Boewe
Pittsboro, North Carolina

Valentin Boss
McGill University

Laura E. Boudon
American University

Lawrence Boudon
Library of Congress

Viviane Brachet-Márquez
El Colegio de México

Jillian Brady
Bayswater, Victoria, Australia

Susan Love Brown
Florida Atlantic University

Jürgen Buchenau
University of North Carolina at Charlotte

LIST OF CONTRIBUTORS

Ralf Buckley
Griffith University

Melissa Butcher
University of Sydney

Laura M. Calkins
Texas Tech University

David H. Carwell
Eastern Illinois University

James Chalmers
United Nations Development Programme,
Papua New Guinea

Frederick B. Chary
Indiana University Northwest

Dawn Chatty
University of Oxford

Janet M. Chernela
University of Maryland

James Chin
Universiti Malaysia Sarawak

George Cho
University of Canberra

Cristina Cielo
University of California at Berkeley

Katherine Cinq-Mars
McGill University

Andrew F. Clark
University of North Carolina at Wilmington

John F. Clark
Florida International University

Sharon C. Cobb
University of North Florida

Chris Coney
University of Melbourne

Daniele Conversi
London, England

Jose da Cruz
Armstrong Atlantic State University

Cecil B. Currey
Lutz, Florida

Robert L. Curry, Jr.
California State University at Sacramento

Kamran M. Dadkhah
Northeastern University

Kishore C. Dash
Thunderbird, The Garvin School of
International Management

Ansu Datta
Calcutta, India

Kusum Datta
Calcutta, India

Craig Davis
Point of Rocks, Maryland

Alan Dearling
Devon, England

Mahinda Deegalle
Bath Spa University College

Neil Denslow
Poole, Dorset, England

Linus digim'Rina
University of Papua New Guinea

Barbara J. Dilly
Creighton University

Steven C. Dinero
Philadelphia University

Thomas P. Dolan
Columbus State University

Manochehr Dorraj
Texas Christian University

David Dorward
LaTrobe University

Beth K. Dougherty
Beloit College

Emma Dowling
University of Birmingham

Mark A. Drumbl
University of Arkansas, Little Rock

Whitney D. Durham
Oklahoma State University

Mohammad Ehsan
University of Dhaka

Susana A. Eisenchlas
Griffith University

Nilly Kamal El-Amir
Cairo University

Mikhael Elbaz
Laval University

Nader Entessar
Spring Hill College

Jo-Anne Everingham
The University of Queensland

Mark Everingham
University of Wisconsin

Nicholas Farrelly
Australian National University

Mario D. Fenyo
Bowie State University

José Fernandez
University of Central Florida

Volker Frank
University of North Carolina at Asheville

Doris Fuchs
University of Munich

Mobo C. F. Gao
University of Tasmania

Andy Gibson
Griffith University

Brian J. Given
Carleton University

Arthur Goldschmidt, Jr.
The Pennsylvania State University

Michael Goldsmith
University of Waikato

Robert F. Gorman
Southwest Texas State University

Gustavo Adolfo Guerra Vásquez
University of California at Berkeley

Audrey Guichon
University of Birmingham

Juan-Carlos Gumucio Castellon
University of Uppsala

Alexander Gungov
Emory University

Michael M. Gunter
Tennessee Technological University

Michael M. Gunter, Jr.
Rollins College

Baogang Guo
Dalton State College

Michael R. Hall
Armstrong Atlantic State University

Reuel R. Hanks
Oklahoma State University

W. John Hansen
Ann Arbor, Michigan

Syed Hassan
Claflin University

Jonathan Haughton
Beacon Hill Institute for Public Policy

William P. Head
Warner Robins Air Logistics Center

Joseph Held
South Yarmouth, Massachusetts

Sirkku K. Hellsten
University of Birmingham

Anil Hira
Simon Fraser University

LIST OF CONTRIBUTORS

Frank J. Hoffman
West Chester University

Ha Thi Thu Huong
TMC Academy

Sylvanus Ikhide
University of Namibia

International Commission on Irrigation and Drainage
New Delhi, India

Muhammad Muinul Islam
University of Dhaka

Serguey Ivanov
American University in Bulgaria

M. R. Izady
New York, New York

B. M. Jain
Rajasthan University

Uzma Jamil
McGill University

Ho-Won Jeong
George Mason University

Helen Johnson
The University of Queensland

Rebecca R. Jones
Widener University

Nantang Jua
University of Buea

Lars v. Karstedt
University of Hamburg

Husain Kassim
University of Central Florida

John Keep
Bern, Switzerland

Kembo-Sure
Moi University

Kenneth Keulman
Harvard University

Arne Kislenko
Ryerson University

Reinhard Klein-Arendt
University of Cologne

Wm. Gary Kline
Georgia Southwestern State University

Yoshie Kobayashi
Gunma Prefectural Women's University

Laszlo Kocsis
Covasna, Romania

Charles C. Kolb
National Endowment for the Humanities

Waldemar Koziol
Warsaw University

Alisa Krasnostein
The University of Western Australia

Wanda C. Krause
University of Exeter

Krum Krumov
Sofia University

Chi-Kong Lai
University of Queensland

George M. Lauderbaugh
Jacksonville State University

Robert Lawless
Wichita State University

David M. Lawrence
J. Sargeant Reynolds Community College

Michael C. Lazich
Buffalo State College

Lavina Lee
University of Sydney

Keith A. Leitich
Seattle, Washington

Hal Levine
Victoria University of Wellington

Jonathan H. L'Hommedieu
University of Turku

Yianna Liatsos
Rutgers University

Tracy L. R. Lightcap
LaGrange College

Natasha J. Lightfoot
New York University

John Lodewijks
University of New South Wales

Staffan Löfving
Stockholm University

Roger D. Long
Eastern Michigan University

P. Eric Louw
University of Queensland

Ludomir Lozny
Hunter College

Ronald Lukens-Bull
University of North Florida

Christopher Lundry
Arizona State University

Carmela Lutmar
New York University

Paul J. Magnarella
Warren Wilson College

Plamen Makariev
Sofia University

Arman Manukyan
Central European University

Richard R. Marcus
University of Alabama in Huntsville

Ross Marlay
Arkansas State University

Daniel M. Masterson
United States Naval Academy

Dee F. Matreyek
Restorative Justice Center of the Inland Empire

Jean F. Mayer
Concordia University

John Mukum Mbaku
Weber State University

Tamba E. M'bayo
Michigan State University

William McBride
Purdue University

Grant McCall
University of New South Wales

Christopher McDowell
Macquarie University

Elisabeth McMahon
Indiana University

Joseph Mensah
York University

Nasser Momayezi
Texas A&M International University

Waltraud Q. Morales
University of Central Florida

Ishmael Irungu Munene
State University of New York at Albany

Ruth Murbach
Université du Québec à Montréal

Norman H. Murdoch
University of Cincinnati

Diego I. Murguía
Universidad de Buenos Aires

Loretta Napoleoni
London, England

Caryn E. Neumann
Ohio State University

Stephan E. Nikolov
Bulgarian Academy of Sciences

James A. Norris
Texas A&M International University

Milena Novakova
National Assembly of Republic of Bulgaria

P. Godfrey Okoth
Maseno University

Clémentine Olivier
National University of Ireland

Jorge Ortiz Sotelo
Peruvian Institute of Economy and Politics

Lazarus F. O'Sako
Ohio University

Patrick L. Osborne
International Center for Tropical Ecology,
University of Missouri at St. Louis

Tony Osborne
American University in Bulgaria

Úrsula Oswald S.
CRIM-UNAM and Diverse Women for Diversity

Charlene T. Overturf
Armstrong Atlantic State University

Steven Paulson
University of North Florida

Zoran Pavlović
Oklahoma State University

William D. Pederson
Louisiana State University in Shreveport

Carlos Pérez
California State University at Fresno

J. E. Peterson
University of Arizona

María Luisa Pfeiffer
Universidad de Buenos Aires

Aaron Z. Pitluck
University of Konstanz

Vincent Kelly Pollard
University of Hawai'i at Manoa

Nancy J. Pollock
Victoria University

Peter R. Prifti
San Diego, California

Lesley J. Pruitt
Arkansas State University

Ilie Rad
Babes-Bolyai University

Edward A. Riedinger
Ohio State University

Leonora Ritter
Charles Sturt University

Benjamin Rivlin
City University Graduate Center

Paul Rivlin
Tel Aviv University

Bruce D. Roberts
Minnesota State University Moorhead

Magaly Rodríguez García
Vrije Universiteit Brussel

David Romano
McGill University

Horacio N. Roque Ramirez
University of California at Santa Barbara

Stéphanie Rousseau
University of North Carolina at
Chapel Hill

Paul S. Rowe
University of Western Ontario

Werner Ruf
University of Kassel

Tom Ryan
University of Waikato

Arvee S. Salazar
San Fernando, Philippines

Steven S. Sallie
Boise State University

Amandeep Sandhu
University of California at Santa Barbara

L. Natalie Sandomirsky
Southern Connecticut State University

Christopher Saunders
University of Cape Town

Christian P. Scherrer
Ethnic Conflict Research Project

Ulrike Schuerkens
Ecole des Hautes Etudes en Sciences Sociales

Alexander Hugo Schulenburg
Corporation of London

Stephen R. Schwalbe
Air War College

David Schwam-Baird
University of North Florida

James D. Seymour
Columbia University

Rodger Shanahan
University of Sydney

Scott E. Simon
University of Ottawa

Amrita Singh

Udai Bhanu Singh
Institute for Defence Studies

Carl Skutsch
The School of Visual Arts

E. Valerie Smith
Florida Gulf Coast University

Subhash R. Sonnad
Western Michigan University

Radhamany Sooryamoorthy
University of Kwazulu-Natal

Paul Spoonley
Massey University

Jeffrey W. Steagall
University of North Florida

Jason E. Strakes
Claremont Graduate School

Mira Sucharov
Carleton University

Tadeusz Swietochowski
Columbia University

Joseph Takougang
University of Cincinnati

Mary Ann Tétreault
Trinity University

Daniel S. Tevera
University of Zimbabwe

Amos Owen Thomas
Maastricht School of Management

Marius Tita
Bucharest, Romania

Brian Turner
Randolph-Macon College

Ufo Okeke Uzodike
University of KwaZulu-Natal

Cheryl Van Deusen
University of North Florida

John M. VanderLippe
State University of New York at New Paltz

Carlos Velásquez Carrillo
York University

Iain Walker
University of Sydney

John Walsh
Shinawatra International University

Yosay Wangdi
Grand Valley State University

Fredrick O. Wanyama
Maseno University

LIST OF CONTRIBUTORS

Susanne Weigelin-Schwiedrzik
University of Heidelberg

Roland J. Wenzlhuemer
Salzburg University

Bruce M. Wilson
University of Central Florida

James E. Winkates
Air War College, Maxwell Air Force Base

Pamela A. Zeiser
University of North Florida

Eleanor Zelliot
Carleton College

Xinjun Zhang
Tsinghua University

Verónica M. Ziliotto
Universidad de Buenos Aires

Evert van der Zweerde
University of Nijmegen

TABLE OF CONTENTS

List of Entries A–Z   *xvii*

Thematic List of Entries   *xxvii*

Introduction   *xxxv*

Entries A–Z   *1*

Index   *11*

LIST OF ENTRIES A–Z

A

Acid Precipitation
Afghanistan
African Development Bank (ADB)
African Diaspora
African Monetary Fund (AfMF)
African National Congress (ANC)
Agriculture: Impact of Globalization
Agriculture: Impact of Privatization
Ahidjo, Ahmadou
Albania
Algeria
All-African People's Conference (AAPC)
Allende Gossens, Salvador
Alliance for Progress
All-India Muslim League (AIML)
Amin, Idi
Amnesty International
Andean Community
Andean South America: History and
    Economic Development
Andean South America: International Relations
Anglican Communion
Anglo-Iranian Oil Company (AIOC)
Angola
Anguilla
Antigua and Barbuda
Apartheid
Aprismo
Aquino, Benigno, and Corazón
Arab Economic Unity Council
Arab Maghreb Union (AMU)
Arab Nationalism
Arabian American Oil Company (ARAMCO)
Arab–Israeli Wars (1948, 1956, 1967, 1973)
Arafat, Yasser
Árbenz Guzmán, Jacobo
Argentina
Arias Sanchez, Oscar
Aristide, Jean-Bertrand
Armed Forces of the People
Armenia
Arms and Armaments, International Transfer of
Arms Industry

ASEAN Free Trade Association
ASEAN Mekong Basin Development
    Cooperation (Mekong Group)
Asian Development Bank (ADB)
Asian "Economic Miracle"
Asian Monetary Fund
Asian Tigers
Asia-Pacific Economic Cooperation (APEC)
Association of Caribbean States (ACS)
Association of Southeast Asian Nations (ASEAN)
Aswan High Dam and Development in Egypt
Aung San Suu Kyi
Authoritarianism
Awami League
Ayub Khan, Muhammad
Azerbaijan
Azikiwe, Benjamin Nnamdi

B

Ba'ath Party
Baghdad Pact
Bahamas
Bahrain
Balfour Declaration
Balkan Wars of the 1990s
Bandung Conference (1955)
Bangladesh
Bank for International Settlements (BIS)
Banking
Bantustans
Barbados
Basic Human Needs
Batista y Zaldívar, Fulgencio
Bedouin
Begin, Menachem
Belarus
Belize
Ben Bella, Ahmed
Ben-Gurion, David
Benin
Berbers
Berlin Wall (1961–1989)

Betancourt, Rómulo
Bhutan
Bhutto, Benazir
Biafra
Biodiversity Conservation
Bishop, Maurice
Black Market/Shadow Economy
Black Sea Economic Cooperation
    Organization (BSEC)
Bolivia
Bosch, Juan
Bosnia and Herzegovina
Botha, P. W.
Botswana
Boumédiènne, Houari
Bourguiba, Habib
Bracero Program
Brain Drain
Brazil
Brunei
Buddhism
Bulgaria
Bunche, Ralph
Bureaucratic Authoritarianism
Burkina Faso
Burma
Burundi
Buthelezi, Mangosuthu Gatsha

C

Cabral, Amilcar
Cambodia
Cameroon
Camp David Accords (1979)
Canadian International Development
    Agency (CIDA)
Capital Flight
Capitalist Economic Model
Cardoso, Fernando Henrique
CARE
Caribbean Basin Initiative (CBI)
Caribbean Community and Common
    Market (CARICOM)
Caribbean Development Bank (CDB)
Caribbean Free Trade Association (CARIFTA)
Caribbean: History and Economic Development
Caribbean: International Relations
Cartels
Caste Systems
Castro, Fidel
Cayman Islands
Ceausescu, Nicolae

Central Africa: History and Economic Development
Central Africa: International Relations
Central African Republic
Central America: History and
    Economic Development
Central America: International Relations
Central American Common Market (CACM)
Central and Eastern Europe: History
    and Economic Development
Central and Eastern Europe: International
    Relations
Central Asia: History and Economic Development
Central Asia: International Relations
Central Intelligence Agency (CIA)
Central Treaty Organization (CENTO)
Chad
Chávez, Hugo
Chiang Ching-kuo
Chiang Kai-shek
Children and Development
Chile
China: Cultural Revolution
China, People's Republic of
Chinese Communist Party (CCP)
Chinese Revolution
Christianity
Christians in the Middle East
Chuan Leekpai
Civic Education
Civil Disobedience
Civil Rights
Civil Society
Collectivism
Colombia
Colombo Plan
Colonialism: History
Colonialism: Legacies
Common Market for Eastern and Southern
    Africa (COMESA)
Commonwealth (British)
Commonwealth of Independent States: History
    and Economic Development
Commonwealth of Independent States:
    International Relations
Communist Economic Model
Comoros
Congo, Democratic Republic of the
Congo, Republic of the
Constitutionalism, Definition
Contras
Coptic Church (Copts)
Corruption, Governmental
Costa Rica
Cote d'Ivoire (Republic of the Ivory Coast)
Counterinsurgency

Countertrade
Coup d'Etat
Croatia
Cuban Revolution
Cultural Perceptions
Currency Devaluations
Currency Regimes
Cyprus
Czech Republic

D

da Silva, Luiz Inácio "Lula"
Dalits
DAWN (Development Alternatives with
    Women for a New Era)
De Klerk, Frederik W.
Debt: Impact on Development
Debt: Relief Efforts
Deforestation
Democratization
Deng Xiaoping
Desertification
De-Stalinization (1953–1956)
Development History and Theory
Development, Measures of
Dictatorships
Disaster Relief
Djibouti
Doctors Without Borders/Médecins Sans Frontières
Doi Moi
Dominica
Dominican Republic
Domino Theory
Draft Declaration on the Rights of Indigenous Peoples
Drug Trade
Drug Use
Druze
Dubcek, Alexander
Duvalier, François

E

East Africa: History and Economic Development
East Africa: International Relations
East African Community
East Asia: History and Economic Development
East Asia: International Relations
East Timor
Economic and Customs Union of
    Central Africa (ECUCA)

Economic Commission for Africa (ECA)
Economic Community of Central African
    States (ECCAS)
Economic Community of West African
    States (ECOWAS)
Economic Cooperation Organization (ECO)
Ecotourism
Ecuador
Education
Egypt
807 Industries
El Salvador
Elections
Energy: Alternative Development
Energy: Impact on Development
Entrepreneurship
Environment: Government Policies
Environmentalism
Equatorial Guinea
Eritrea
Eritrean Liberation Front (ELF)
Erosion, Land
Estonia
Ethiopia
Ethnic Conflicts: Caribbean
Ethnic Conflicts: Central Africa
Ethnic Conflicts: Central and Eastern Europe
Ethnic Conflicts: Central Asia
Ethnic Conflicts: Commonwealth of
    Independent States
Ethnic Conflicts: East Africa
Ethnic Conflicts: East Asia
Ethnic Conflicts: Mexico and Central America
Ethnic Conflicts: Middle East
Ethnic Conflicts: North Africa
Ethnic Conflicts: Oceania
Ethnic Conflicts: Southeast Asia
Ethnic Conflicts: Southern Africa
Ethnic Conflicts: Southern Cone (Latin America)
Ethnic Conflicts: West Africa
Ethnicity: Impact on Politics and Society
Eurocentrism
European Bank for Reconstruction and Development
Evangelical Protestantism
Export-Oriented Economies
Extractive Industries

F

Family Planning and Structure
Fanon, Frantz
Farabundo Martí National Liberation
    Front (FMLN)

Fiji
Food and Nutrition
Foreign Direct Investment (FDI)
Fox, Vicente
Francophonie Institutionnelle
Free Market Economy
Free Trade Area of the Americas (FTAA)
Frei, Eduardo
FRELIMO (Front for the Liberation
  of Mozambique)
French Guiana
Fujimori, Alberto
Fulbright Program

G

Gabon
Gambia, The
Gandhi, Indira
Gandhi, Mohandas
Gandhi, Rajiv
General Agreement on Tariffs and Trade (GATT)
Georgia
Ghana
Glasnost and Perestroika
Global Climate Change
Globalization: Impact on Development
Goh Chok Tong
Gorbachev, Mikhail
Great Leap Forward
Greek Orthodox Church
Green Revolution
Grenada
Group of 77
Guadeloupe
Guam
Guatemala
Guerrilla Army of the Poor (EGP)
Guerrilla Warfare
Guevara, Ernesto "Che"
Guinea
Guinea-Bissau
Gulf Cooperation Council
Gus Dur
Guyana

H

Haile Maryam, Mengistu
Haiti
HAMAS

Hassan II, King (Morocco)
Havel, Václav
Haya de la Torre, Víctor Raúl
Health Care
Helsinki Final Act on Human Rights (1975)
Hezbollah
Hinduism
Hirschman, Albert
HIV/AIDS
Ho Chi Minh
Honduras
Hong Kong
Houphouët-Boigny, Félix
Hoxha, Enver
Human Resource Development
Human Rights as a Foreign Policy Issue
Human Rights: Definition and Violations
Humanitarian Relief Projects
Hun Sen
Hungarian Crisis of 1956
Hungary
Hussein, King of Jordan
Hussein, Saddam

I

Import Substitution Industrialization
Income Distribution
India
Indian–Pakistani Wars
Indigenous Medical Practices
Indonesia
Industrialization
Infant Mortality
Infanticide
Infectious Diseases
Intellectual Property Rights
Inter-American Development Bank (IDB)
International Air Transport Association (IATA)
International Atomic Energy Agency (IAEA)
International Bank for Reconstruction and
  Development (IBRD) (World Bank)
International Center for Settlement
  of Investment Disputes (ICSID)
International Cocoa Organization (ICCO)
International Coffee Organization (ICO)
International Committee of the Red Cross (ICRC)
International Criminal Police
  Organization (INTERPOL)
International Development Association (IDA)
International Finance Corporation (IFC)
International Maritime Organization (IMO)
International Monetary Fund (IMF)

International Organization for Migration (IOM)
International Planned Parenthood Federation (IPPF)
International Rice Research Institute (IRRI)
International Telecommunication Union (ITU)
Inter-Religious Relations
Intifada
Iran
Iran–Iraq War, 1980–1988
Iraq
Irrigation
Islam
Islamic Fundamentalism
Israel
Itaipú Dam

J

Jagan, Cheddi
Jamaica
Jaruzelski, Wojciech
Jiang Zemin
Jihād
Jordan
Judaism

K

Kashmir Dispute
Kaunda, Kenneth
Kazakhstan
Kenya
Kenyatta, Jomo
Khama, Sir Seretse
Khmer Rouge
Khomeini, Ayatollah Ruhollah
Khrushchev, Nikita
Kiribati
Korea, North
Korea, South
Kubitschek, Juscelino
Kurdistan
Kurds
Kuwait
Kuwait Fund for Arab Economic Development
Kyrgyzstan

L

Laar, Mart
Labor

Lake Chad Basin Commission
Land Distribution Patterns
Landsbergis, Vytautas
Language, Influence on Development
Language, Influence on Politics
Laos
Latin American Integration Association (ALADI)
Latvia
Lebanon
Lee Kuan Yew
Legal Systems
Lesotho
Liberation Theology
Liberia
Libya
Libyan Cultural Revolution
Lithuania
Lomé Convention
Lumumba, Patrice
Luthuli, Albert

M

Macau/Macao
Macedonia
Machel, Samora
Madagascar
Maghrib Peoples
Magsaysay, Ramon
Mahathir bin Mohammed, Dato Seri
Malan, D. F.
Malaŵi
Malaysia
Maldives
Mali
Malvinas/Falklands
Malvinas/Falklands War, 1982
Mandela, Nelson
Mao Zedong
Maquiladora Program
Marcos, Ferdinand
Marshall Islands, Republic of
Martinique
Marxism
Mau Mau
Mauritania
Mauritius
Mbeki, Thabo
Meir, Golda
Menchú Túm, Rigoberta
Menem, Carlos
Mental Health
Mexico: History and Economic Development

Mexico: International Relations
Micronesia, Federated States of
Middle East: History and Economic Development
Middle East: International Relations
Migration
Military and Civilian Control
Military and Development
Military and Human Rights
Milošević, Slobodan
Minorities/Discrimination
Mixed Economy
Modernization
Moldova
Monarchic Government
Money Laundering
Mongolia
Montenegro
Montoneros
Montserrat
Morocco
Mossaddeq, Muhammed
Mozambique
Mubarak, Hosni
Mugabe, Robert
Mujahedin
Mujibar Rahman, Sheikh
Multinational Corporations and Development
Muslim Brotherhood
Muslim League
Myanmar

N

Namibia
Nasser, Gamal Abdel
Nation Building
National Action Party
National Front for the Liberation of South Vietnam
    (NFLSV)/National Liberation Front (NLF)
National Liberation Army (ELN) (Colombia)
Natural Disasters
Ndi, Ni John Fru
Nehru, Jawaharlal
Neocolonialism
Neoliberalism
Nepal
Netherlands Antilles
New Economic Policy (Malaysia)
New International Economic Order (NIEO)
New Jewel Movement
New People's Army
Newly Industrialized Economies (NIEs)
Nicaragua

Nicaraguan Revolution
Niger
Nigeria, The Federal Republic of
Niue
Nkrumah, Kwame
Nonaligned Movement
Non-Governmental Organizations (NGOs)
North Africa: History and Economic Development
North Africa: International Relations
North American Free Trade Agreement (NAFTA)
North Atlantic Treaty Organization (NATO)
Northern South America: History and
    Economic Development
Northern South America: International Relations
Nyerere, Julius

O

Oceania: History and Economic Development
Oceania: International Relations
Okello, John
Oman
Operation Bootstrap
Organization of African Unity (OAU)
Organization of American States (OAS)
Organization of Arab Petroleum Exporting
    Countries (OAPEC)
Organization of Eastern Caribbean States (OECS)
Organization of Petroleum Exporting
    Countries (OPEC)
Organization of the Islamic Conference (OIC)
Overseas Private Investment Corporation (OPIC)
Oxfam

P

Pacific Islands Forum
Pahlavi, Shah Muhammed Reza
Pakistan
Palau, Republic of
Palestine
Palestine Liberation Organization (PLO)
Palestinian Diaspora
Pan-Africanism
Panama
Panama Canal Treaties, 1977
Papua New Guinea
Paracel and Spratly Islands
Paraguay
Park Systems, National
Party of the Institutionalized Revolution (PRI)

Pathet Lao
Peacekeeping Operations, Regional and
  International
Peasants, Impact of Development on
People's Liberation Armed Forces (PLAF)
Pérez Jiménez, Marcos
Perón, Juan Domingo
Persian Gulf War, 1991
Persian Gulf War, 2003
Peru
Petrodollars
Philippines
Pinochet Ugarte, Augusto
Plan Colombia
Poland
Political Culture
Pollution, Agricultural
Pollution, Industrial
Popular Movement for the Liberation
  of Angola (MPLA)
Popular Sectors
Population Growth: Impact on Development
Populism
Poverty: Definition and Trends
Poverty: Impact on Development
Prague Spring, 1968
Prebisch, Raúl
Private Property Rights
Privatization
Public Health
Public Sector Reform
Puerto Rico

Q

Qaddafi, Muammar
Qatar
Quality of Life: Definition

R

Rafsanjani, Ali Akbar
Rahman, Tunku Abdul
Rain Forest, Destruction of
Ramos, Fidel
Rastafarianism
Refugees
Religion
Revolutionary Armed Forces of Colombia (FARC)
Revolutionary Army of the People
Revolutionary Democratic Front (FDR)
Rhee, Syngman

Rockefeller Foundation
Roman Catholic Church
Romania
Russia
Russian Orthodox Church
Rwanda

S

Sadat, Anwar
Salinas de Gortari, Carlos
Salvation Army
Samoa
Sanctions, Economic
Sandinista National Liberation Front (FSLN)
Saudi Arabia
Selassie, Emperor Haile
Self-Determination
Senegal
Sénghor, Leopold
Serbia
Sex Trade/Trafficking
Seychelles
Shining Path/*Sendero Luminoso*
Siad Barre, Mohammed
Sierra Leone
Sihanouk, Norodom
Sikhism (Sikhs)
Silva, Luiz Inácio "Lula" da
Singapore
Single-Party States
Slovakia
Slovenia
Smaze
Social Revolution
Socialism
Socialist Economic Model
Solidarity Union
Solomon Islands
Somalia
Somoza Debayle, Anastasio
Somoza García, Anastasio
Soros Foundations Network
South Africa
South Asian Association for Regional
  Cooperation (SAARC)
South West Africa People's Organization (SWAPO)
Southeast Asia: History and Economic
  Development
Southeast Asia: International Relations
Southeast Asia Treaty Organization (SEATO)
Southern Africa: History and Economic
  Development

Southern Africa: International Relations
Southern African Customs Union (SACU)
Southern African Development
    Community (SADC)
Southern Cone Common Market (MERCOSUR)
Southern Cone (Latin America): History
    and Economic Development
Southern Cone (Latin America): International
    Relations
Soviet Bloc
Sri Lanka
St. Christopher and Nevis
St. Helena
St. Lucia
St. Vincent and the Grenadines
Stalin, Joseph
State-Directed Economy
Stroessner, Alfredo
Structural Adjustment Programs (SAPs)
Subsistence Living
Sudan
Sufism
Sukarno
Suriname
Sustainable Development
Swaziland
Syria

T

Taiwan
Tajikistan
Taliban
Tanzania
Technology: Impact on Development
Territorial Disputes
Terrorism
Thailand
Third World
Three Gorges Dam
Tibet
Tiananmen Square Massacre
Tito, Josip Broz (Marshall Tito)
Togo
Tonga
Torrijos Herrera, Omar
Totalitarianism
Touré, Sékou
Trade Policies and Development
Trading Patterns, Global
Transparency
Trinidad and Tobago
Trujillo, Rafael Leonidas

Tudjman, Franjo
Tunisia
Tupamaros
Turkey
Turkmenistan
Tutu, Bishop Desmond
Tuvalu
26th of July Movement

U

Uganda
Ukraine
Ulmanis, Guntis
Um-Nyobe, Reuben
Underdevelopment
United Arab Emirates (UAE)
United Arab Republic (UAR)
United Malays National Organization (UMNO)
United Nations Center for Human
    Settlements (UNCHS)
United Nations Children's Fund (UNICEF)
United Nations Commission on Crime Prevention
    and Criminal Justice (CCPCJ)
United Nations Conference on Trade and
    Development (UNCTAD)
United Nations Development Program (UNDP)
United Nations Economic and Social Commission
    for Asia and the Pacific (ESCAP)
United Nations Economic and Social
    Council (ECOSOC)
United Nations Economic Commission for Latin
    America and the Caribbean (ECLAC)
United Nations Food and Agriculture
    Organization (FAO)
United Nations High Commissioner for
    Refugees (UNHCR)
United Nations Industrial Development
    Organization (UNIDO)
United Nations International Court of
    Justice (ICJ)
United Nations International Drug Control
    Program (UNDCP)
United Nations International Fund for
    Agricultural Development (IFAD)
United Nations International Institute on
    Aging (UNIIA)
United Nations International Research and
    Training Institute for the Advancement
    of Women (INSTRAW)
United Nations Permanent Forum on
    Indigenous Peoples
United Nations Population Fund (UNFPA)

United Nations Relief and Works Agency
 for Palestine (UNRWA)
United Nations Trusteeship Council
United Nations University (UNU)
United States Agency for International
 Development (USAID)
United States–Dominican Republic–Central
 American Free Trade Agreement
Universal Declaration of Human Rights
Untouchables (Dalits)
Urbanization: Impact on Development
Urbanization: Impact on Environment
Uruguay
Uzbekistan

V

Vähi, Tiit
Vanuatu
Vargas, Getúlio
Velvet Revolutions
Venezuela
Verwoerd, Hendrik
Viet Cong
Viet Minh
Vietnam
Vietnam War
Virgin Islands (British)
Virgin Islands (United States)
Virtual Water Trade
Visehrad Group

W

Wałęsa, Lech
War and Development
Waste Management
Water Resources and Distribution

West Africa: History and Economic Development
West Africa: International Relations
West African Economic and Monetary
 Union (WAEMU)
West African Monetary Union (WAMU)
White Community in Africa
Wildlife Preservation
Williams, Eric
Wojtyła, Karol (John Paul II)
Women: Legal Status
Women Living Under Muslim Laws (WLUML)
Women: Role in Development
World Bank
World Confederation of Labor (WCL)
World Council of Churches
World Federation of Trade Unions (WFTU)
World Food Program
World Health Organization (WHO)
World Meteorological Organization (WMO)
World Trade Organization (WTO)
Wyszyński, Cardinal Stefan

Y

Yahya Khan, Agha Muhammad
Yemen
Yugoslavia

Z

Zaire
Zambia
Zapatista National Revolutionary Army (EZLN)
Zhou Enlai
Zia ul-Haq, Muhammed
Zimbabwe
Zionism

THEMATIC LIST OF ENTRIES

Countries and Regions

Afghanistan
Albania
Algeria
Andean South America: History and Economic
  Development
Andean South America: International Relations
Angola
Anguilla
Antigua and Barbuda
Argentina
Armenia
Azerbaijan
Bahamas
Bahrain
Bangladesh
Barbados
Belarus
Belize
Benin
Bhutan
Biafra
Bolivia
Bosnia and Herzegovina
Botswana
Brazil
Brunei
Bulgaria
Burkina Faso
Burundi
Cambodia
Cameroon
Caribbean: History and Economic Development
Caribbean: International Relations
Cayman Islands
Central Africa: History and Economic Development
Central Africa: International Relations
Central African Republic
Central America: History and Economic
  Development
Central America: International Relations

Central and Eastern Europe: History and
  Economic Development
Central and Eastern Europe: International Relations
Central Asia: History and Economic Development
Central Asia: International Relations
Chad
Chile
China, People's Republic of
Colombia
Commonwealth of Independent States: History
  and Economic Development
Commonwealth of Independent States:
  International Relations
Comoros
Congo, Democratic Republic of the
Congo, Republic of the
Costa Rica
Cote d'Ivoire (Republic of the Ivory Coast)
Croatia
Cyprus
Czech Republic
Djibouti
Dominica
Dominican Republic
East Africa: History and Economic Development
East Africa: International Relations
East Asia: History and Economic Development
East Asia: International Relations
East Timor
Ecuador
Egypt
El Salvador
Equatorial Guinea
Eritrea
Estonia
Ethiopia
Fiji
French Guiana
Gabon
Gambia, The
Georgia
Ghana

Grenada
Guadeloupe
Guam
Guatemala
Guinea
Guinea-Bissau
Guyana
Haiti
Honduras
Hong Kong
Hungary
India
Indonesia
Iran
Iraq
Israel
Jamaica
Jordan
Kazakhstan
Kenya
Kiribati
Korea, North
Korea, South
Kurdistan
Kuwait
Kyrgyzstan
Laos
Latvia
Lebanon
Lesotho
Liberia
Libya
Lithuania
Macau/Macao
Macedonia
Madagascar
Malaŵi
Malaysia
Maldives
Mali
Malvinas/Falklands
Marshall Islands, Republic of
Martinique
Mauritania
Mauritius
Mexico: History and Economic Development
Mexico: International Relations
Micronesia, Federated States of
Middle East: History and Economic Development
Middle East: International Relations
Moldova
Mongolia
Montenegro
Montserrat
Morocco

Mozambique
Myanmar
Namibia
Nepal
Netherlands Antilles
Nicaragua
Niger
Nigeria, The Federal Republic of
Niue
North Africa: History and Economic Development
North Africa: International Relations
Northern South America: History and
    Economic Development
Northern South America: International Relations
Oceania: History and Economic Development
Oceania: International Relations
Oman
Pakistan
Palau, Republic of
Palestine
Panama
Papua New Guinea
Paracel and Spratley Islands
Paraguay
Peru
Philippines
Poland
Puerto Rico
Qatar
Romania
Russia
Rwanda
Samoa
Saudi Arabia
Senegal
Serbia
Seychelles
Sierra Leone
Singapore
Slovakia
Slovenia
Solomon Islands
Somalia
South Africa
Southeast Asia: History and Economic
    Development
Southeast Asia: International Relations
Southern Africa: History and Economic
    Development
Southern Africa: International Relations
Southern Cone (Latin America): History and
    Economic Development
Southern Cone (Latin America): International
    Relations
Soviet Bloc

Sri Lanka
St. Christopher and Nevis
St. Helena
St. Lucia
St. Vincent and the Grenadines
Sudan
Suriname
Swaziland
Syria
Taiwan
Tajikistan
Tanzania
Thailand
Tibet
Togo
Tonga
Trinidad and Tobago
Tunisia
Turkey
Turkmenistan
Tuvalu
Uganda
Ukraine
United Arab Emirates (UAE)
United Arab Republic (UAR)
Uruguay
Uzbekistan
Vanuatu
Venezuela
Vietnam
Virgin Islands (British)
Virgin Islands (United States)
West Africa: History and Economic Development
West Africa: International Relations
Yemen
Yugoslavia
Zambia
Zimbabwe

Organizations

African Development Bank (ADB)
African Monetary Fund (AfMF)
African National Congress (ANC)
All-African People's Conference (AAPC)
Alliance for Progress
All-India Muslim League (AIML)
Amnesty International
Andean Community
Anglican Communion
Anglo-Iranian Oil Company (AIOC)
Arab Economic Unity Council
Arab Maghreb Union (AMU)

Arabian American Oil Company (ARAMCO)
Armed Forces of the People
ASEAN Free Trade Association
ASEAN Mekong Basin Development
  Cooperation (Mekong Group)
Asian Development Bank (ADB)
Asian Monetary Fund
Asia-Pacific Economic Cooperation (APEC)
Association of Caribbean States (ACS)
Association of Southeast Asian Nations (ASEAN)
Awami League
Ba'ath Party
Baghdad Pact
Bank for International Settlements (BIS)
Black Sea Economic Cooperation Organization (BSEC)
Canadian International Development
  Agency (CIDA)
CARE
Caribbean Community and Common
  Market (CARICOM)
Caribbean Development Bank (CDB)
Caribbean Free Trade Association (CARIFTA)
Central American Common Market (CACM)
Central Intelligence Agency (CIA)
Central Treaty Organization (CENTO)
Chinese Communist Party (CCP)
Common Market for Eastern and Southern
  Africa (COMESA)
Commonwealth (British)
Contras
DAWN (Development Alternatives with
  Women for a New Era)
Doctors Without Borders/Médecins
  Sans Frontières
East African Community
Economic and Customs Union of Central
  Africa (ECUCA)
Economic Commission for Africa (ECA)
Economic Community of Central African
  States (ECCAS)
Economic Community of West African
  States (ECOWAS)
Economic Cooperation Organization (ECO)
Eritrean Liberation Front (ELF)
European Bank for Reconstruction and
  Development
Farabundo Martí National Liberation
  Front (FMLN)
Francophonie Institutionnelle
Free Trade Area of the Americas (FTAA)
FRELIMO (Front for the Liberation
  of Mozambique)
Greek Orthodox Church
Group of 77
Guerrilla Army of the Poor (EGP)

Gulf Cooperation Council
HAMAS
Hezbollah
Inter-American Development Bank (IDB)
International Air Transport Association (IATA)
International Atomic Energy Agency (IAEA)
International Bank for Reconstruction and
    Development (IBRD) (World Bank)
International Center for Settlement of
    Investment Disputes (ICSID)
International Cocoa Organization (ICCO)
International Coffee Organization (ICO)
International Committee of the Red Cross (ICRC)
International Criminal Police
    Organization (INTERPOL)
International Development Association (IDA)
International Finance Corporation (IFC)
International Maritime Organization (IMO)
International Monetary Fund (IMF)
International Organization for Migration (IOM)
International Planned Parenthood Federation (IPPF)
International Rice Research Institute (IRRI)
International Telecommunication Union (ITU)
Khmer Rouge
Kuwait Fund for Arab Economic Development
Lake Chad Basin Commission
Latin American Integration Association (ALADI)
Mau Mau
Montoneros
Mujahedin
Muslim Brotherhood
Muslim League
National Action Party
National Front for the Liberation of South
    Vietnam (NFLSV)/National Liberation
    Front (NLF)
National Liberation Army (ELN) (Colombia)
New Jewel Movement
New People's Army
North American Free Trade
    Agreement (NAFTA)
North Atlantic Treaty Organization (NATO)
Organization of African Unity (OAU)
Organization of American States (OAS)
Organization of Arab Petroleum Exporting
    Countries (OAPEC)
Organization of Eastern Caribbean States (OECS)
Organization of Petroleum Exporting
    Countries (OPEC)
Organization of the Islamic Conference (OIC)
Overseas Private Investment Corporation (OPIC)
Oxfam
Pacific Islands Forum
Palestine Liberation Organization (PLO)
Party of the Institutionalized Revolution (PRI)

Pathet Lao
People's Liberation Armed Forces (PLAF)
Popular Movement for the Liberation
    of Angola (MPLA)
Revolutionary Armed Forces of Colombia (FARC)
Revolutionary Army of the People
Revolutionary Democratic Front (FDR)
Rockefeller Foundation
Roman Catholic Church
Russian Orthodox Church
Salvation Army
Sandinista National Liberation Front (FSLN)
Shining Path/Sendero Luminoso
Solidarity Union
Soros Foundations Network
South Asian Association for Regional
    Co-operation (SAARC)
South West Africa People's Organization
    (SWAPO)
Southeast Asia Treaty Organization (SEATO)
Southern African Customs Union (SACU)
Southern African Development
    Community (SADC)
Southern Cone Common Market (MERCOSUR)
Taliban
26th of July Movement
Tupamaros
United Malays National Organization (UMNO)
United Nations Center for Human
    Settlements (UNCHS)
United Nations Children's Fund (UNICEF)
United Nations Commission on Crime
    Prevention and Criminal Justice
United Nations Conference on Trade and
    Development (UNCTAD)
United Nations Development Program (UNDP)
United Nations Economic and Social Commission
    for Asia and the Pacific (ESCAP)
United Nations Economic and Social
    Council (ECOSOC)
United Nations Economic Commission for
    Latin America and the Caribbean (ECLAC)
United Nations Food and Agriculture
    Organization (FAO)
United Nations High Commissioner for
    Refugees (UNHCR)
United Nations Industrial Development
    Organization (UNIDO)
United Nations International Court of Justice (ICJ)
United Nations International Drug Control
    Program (UNDCP)
United Nations International Fund for
    Agricultural Development (IFAD)
United Nations International Institute on
    Aging (UNIIA)

United Nations International Research and
    Training Institute for the Advancement of
    Women (INSTRAW)
United Nations Permanent Forum on
    Indigenous Peoples
United Nations Population Fund (UNFPA)
United Nations Relief and Works Agency for
    Palestine (UNRWA)
United Nations Trusteeship Council
United Nations University (UNU)
United States Agency for International
    Development (USAID)
Viet Minh
Visehrad Group
West African Economic and Monetary
    Unoin (WAEMU)
West African Monetary Union (WAMU)
Women Living Under Muslim Laws (WLUML)
World Bank
World Confederation of Labor (WCL)
World Council of Churches
World Federation of Trade Unions (WFTU)
World Food Program
World Health Organization (WHO)
World Meteorological Organization (WMO)
World Trade Organization (WTO)
Zapatista National Revolutionary
    Army (EZLN)

Persons

Ahidjo, Ahmadou
Allende Gossens, Salvador
Amin, Idi
Aquino, Benigno, and Corazón
Arafat, Yasser
Árbenz Guzmán, Jacobo
Arias Sanchez, Oscar
Aristide, Jean-Bertrand
Aung San Suu Kyi
Ayub Khan, Muhammad
Azikiwe, Benjamin Nnamdi
Batista y Zaldívar, Fulgencio
Begin, Menachem
Ben Bella, Ahmed
Ben-Gurion, David
Betancourt, Rómulo
Bhutto, Benazir
Bishop, Maurice
Bosch, Juan
Botha, P. W.
Boumédiènne, Houari
Bourguiba, Habib

Bunche, Ralph
Buthelezi, Mangosuthu Gatsha
Cabral, Amilcar
Cardoso, Fernando Henrique
Castro, Fidel
Ceausescu, Nicolae
Chávez, Hugo
Chiang Ching-kuo
Chiang Kai-shek
Chuan Leekpai
De Klerk, Frederik W.
Deng Xiaoping
Dubcek, Alexander
Duvalier, François
Fanon, Frantz
Fox, Vicente
Frei, Eduardo
Fujimori, Alberto
Gandhi, Indira
Gandhi, Mohandas
Gandhi, Rajiv
Goh Chok Tong
Gorbachev, Mikhail
Guevara, Ernesto "Che"
Gus Dur
Haile Maryam, Mengistu
Hassan II, King (Morocco)
Havel, Václav
Haya de la Torre, Víctor Raúl
Hirschman, Albert
Ho Chi Minh
Houphouët-Boigny, Félix
Hoxha, Enver
Hun Sen
Hussein, King of Jordan
Hussein, Saddam
Jagan, Cheddi
Jaruzelski, Wojciech
Jiang Zemin
Kaunda, Kenneth
Kenyatta, Jomo
Khama, Sir Seretse
Khomeini, Ayatollah Ruhollah
Khrushchev, Nikita
Kubitschek, Juscelino
Laar, Mart
Landsbergis, Vytautas
Lee Kuan Yew
Lumumba, Patrice
Luthuli, Albert
Machel, Samora
Magsaysay, Ramon
Mahathir bin Mohammed, Dato Seri
Malan, D. F.
Mandela, Nelson

Mao Zedong
Marcos, Ferdinand
Mbeki, Thabo
Meir, Golda
Menchú Túm, Rigoberta
Menem, Carlos
Milošević, Slobodan
Mossaddeq, Muhammed
Mubarak, Hosni
Mugabe, Robert
Mujibar Rahman, Sheikh
Nasser, Gamal Abdel
Ndi, Ni John Fru
Nehru, Jawaharlal
Nkrumah, Kwame
Nyerere, Julius
Okello, John
Pahlavi, Shah Muhammed Reza
Pérez Jiménez, Marcos
Perón, Juan Domingo
Pinochet Ugarte, Augusto
Prebisch, Raúl
Qaddafi, Muammar
Rafsanjani, Ali Akbar
Rahman, Tunku Abdul
Ramos, Fidel
Rhee, Syngman
Sadat, Anwar
Salinas de Gortari, Carlos
Selassie, Emperor Haile
Sénghor, Leopold
Siad Barre, Mohammed
Sihanouk, Norodom
Silva, Luiz Inácio "Lula" da
Somoza DeBayle, Anastasio
Somoza García, Anastasio
Stalin, Joseph
Stroessner, Alfredo
Sukarno
Tito, Josip Broz (Marshall Tito)
Torrijos Herrera, Omar
Touré, Sékou
Trujillo, Rafael Leonidas
Tudjman, Franjo
Tutu, Bishop Desmond
Ulmanis, Guntis
Um-Nyobe, Reuben
Vähi, Tiit
Vargas, Getúlio
Verwoerd, Hendrik
Wałęsa, Lech
Williams, Eric
Wojtyła, Karol (John Paul II)
Wyszyński, Cardinal Stefan
Yahya Khan, Agha Muhammad

Zhou Enlai
Zia ul-Haq, Muhammed

Topics

Acid Precipitation
African Diaspora
Agriculture: Impact of Globalization
Agriculture: Impact of Privatization
Apartheid
Aprismo
Arab Nationalism
Arab–Israeli Wars (1948, 1956, 1967, 1973)
Arms and Armaments, International Transfer of
Arms Industry
Asian "Economic Miracle"
Asian Tigers
Aswan High Dam and Development in Egypt
Authoritarianism
Balfour Declaration
Balkan Wars of the 1990s
Bandung Conference (1955)
Banking
Bantustans
Basic Human Needs
Bedouin
Berbers
Berlin Wall (1961–1989)
Biodiversity Conservation
Black Market/Shadow Economy
Bracero Program
Brain Drain
Buddhism
Bureaucratic Authoritarianism
Camp David Accords (1979)
Capital Flight
Capitalist Economic Model
Caribbean Basin Initiative (CBI)
Cartels
Caste Systems
Children and Development
China: Cultural Revolution
Chinese Revolution
Christianity
Christians in the Middle East
Civic Education
Civil Disobedience
Civil Rights
Civil Society
Collectivism
Colombo Plan
Colonialism: History
Colonialism: Legacies

Communist Economic Model
Constitutionalism, Definition
Coptic Church (Copts)
Corruption, Governmental
Counterinsurgency
Countertrade
Coup d'État
Cuban Revolution
Cultural Perceptions
Currency Devaluations
Currency Regimes
Debt: Impact on Development
Debt: Relief Efforts
Deforestation
Democratization
Desertification
De-Stalinization (1953–1956)
Development History and Theory
Development, Measures of
Dictatorships
Disaster Relief
Doi Moi
Domino Theory
Draft Declaration on the Rights of
    Indigenous Peoples
Drug Trade
Drug Use
Druze
Ecotourism
Education
807 Industries
Elections
Energy: Alternative Development
Energy: Impact on Development
Entrepreneurship
Environment: Government Policies
Environmentalism
Erosion, Land
Ethnic Conflicts: Caribbean
Ethnic Conflicts: Central Africa
Ethnic Conflicts: Central and Eastern Europe
Ethnic Conflicts: Central Asia
Ethnic Conflicts: Commonwealth of
    Independent States
Ethnic Conflicts: East Africa
Ethnic Conflicts: East Asia
Ethnic Conflicts: Mexico and Central America
Ethnic Conflicts: Middle East
Ethnic Conflicts: North Africa
Ethnic Conflicts: Oceania
Ethnic Conflicts: Southeast Asia
Ethnic Conflicts: Southern Africa
Ethnic Conflicts: Southern Cone (Latin America)
Ethnic Conflicts: West Africa
Ethnicity: Impact on Politics and Society

Eurocentrism
Evangelical Protestantism
Export-Oriented Economies
Extractive Industries
Family Planning and Structure
Food and Nutrition
Foreign Direct Investment (FDI)
Free Market Economy
Fulbright Program
General Agreement on Tariffs and Trade (GATT)
Glasnost and Perestroika
Global Climate Change
Globalization: Impact on Development
Great Leap Forward
Green Revolution
Guerrilla Warfare
Health Care
Helsinki Final Act on Human Rights (1975)
Hinduism
HIV/AIDS
Human Resource Development
Human Rights as a Foreign Policy Issue
Human Rights: Definition and Violations
Humanitarian Relief Projects
Hungarian Crisis of 1956
Import Substitution Industrialization
Income Distribution
Indian–Pakistani Wars
Indigenous Medical Practices
Industrialization
Infant Mortality
Infanticide
Infectious Diseases
Intellectual Property Rights
Inter-Religious Relations
Intifada
Iran–Iraq War, 1980–1988
Irrigation
Islam
Islamic Fundamentalism
Itaipú Dam
Jihad
Judaism
Kashmir Dispute
Kurds
Labor
Land Distribution Patterns
Language, Influence on Development
Language, Influence on Politics
Legal Systems
Liberation Theology
Libyan Cultural Revolution
Lomé Convention
Maghrib Peoples
Malvinas/Falklands War, 1982

Maquiladora Program
Marxism
Mental Health
Migration
Military and Civilian Control
Military and Development
Military and Human Rights
Minorities/Discrimination
Mixed Economy
Modernization
Monarchic Government
Money Laundering
Multinational Corporations and Development
Nation Building
Natural Disasters
Neocolonialism
Neoliberalism
New Economic Policy (Malaysia)
New International Economic Order (NIEO)
Newly Industrialized Economies (NIEs)
Nicaraguan Revolution
Nonaligned Movement
Non-Governmental Organizations (NGOs)
Operation Bootstrap
Palestinian Diaspora
Pan-Africanism
Panama Canal Treaties, 1977
Park Systems, National
Peacekeeping Operations, Regional and International
Peasants, Impact of Development on
Persian Gulf War, 1991
Persian Gulf War, 2003
Petrodollars
Plan Colombia
Political Culture
Pollution, Agricultural
Pollution, Industrial
Popular Sectors
Population Growth: Impact on Development
Populism
Poverty: Definition and Trends
Poverty: Impact on Development
Prague Spring, 1968
Private Property Rights
Privatization
Public Health
Public Sector Reform

Quality of Life: Definition
Rain Forest, Destruction of
Rastafarianism
Refugees
Religion
Sanctions, Economic
Self-Determination
Sex Trade/Trafficking
Sikhism (Sikhs)
Single-Party States
Smaze
Social Revolution
Socialism
Socialist Economic Model
State-Directed Economy
Structural Adjustment Programs (SAPs)
Subsistence Living
Sufism
Sustainable Development
Technology: Impact on Development
Territorial Disputes
Terrorism
Third World
Three Gorges Dam
Tienanmen Square Massacre
Totalitarianism
Trade Policies and Development
Trading Patterns, Global
Transparency
Underdevelopment
United States–Dominican Republic–Central
    American Free Trade Agreement
Universal Declaration of Human Rights
Untouchables (Dalits)
Urbanization: Impact on Development
Urbanization: Impact on Environment
Velvet Revolutions
Vietnam War
Virtual Water Trade
War and Development
Waste Management
Water Resources and Distribution
White Community in Africa
Wildlife Preservation
Women: Legal Status
Women: Role in Development
Zionism

INTRODUCTION

Historically identified by various terms, the "Developing World" has always existed, but it came into vogue as a concept immediately after the close of World War II in 1945. For the next generation, the "Third World" was the most commonly used term, followed for the next two decades by the "Underdeveloped World." Influenced by trade liberalization, globalization, and the policy agenda known as the Washington Consensus, the term "Developing World" came into prominence in the 1980s. In response, at least one professional organization, the Association of Third World Studies, briefly considered changing its name.

The most commonly asked questions about the "Developing World" focus upon the countries and residents that comprise it, the status of its economy, its political and social characteristics, and its cultural components. At the end of World War II, analysts identified Africa, Asia, and Latin America as the most underdeveloped global regions. Within each were numerous sub-regions, such as South Asia, sub-Saharan Africa, and Latin America's Southern Cone. Over time, the Middle East was added to the mix and the regions were further subdivided. Although the Soviet Union and its East European Bloc often demonstrated advances in scientific achievement, industrial output, or military hardware, it remained an underdeveloped area in terms of the low quality of life for its inhabitants and the lack of civil and human rights, factors that became glaringly apparent with the end of the Cold War in 1991.

Today's conventional wisdom suggests that all but the Group of Seven, or G-7, nations and their periphery fall into the so-called "Developing World." The G-7 is comprised of the world's seven largest industrial nations: United States, Japan, Great Britain, France, Germany, Italy, and Canada, though the industrialized world also includes the other Western European nations, Australia, and New Zealand. By the 1990s Singapore, South Korea, and Taiwan became prosperous nations. The inclusion of the latter three countries suggests that an economic definition of the "Developing World" remains too simplified.

Beyond economic development, analysts came to consider the extent of public participation in the political process. How democratic and representative of its people is any given government? Are human and civil rights secured and protected? What is the availability of basic human services such as education and health care? Are there environmental protections? The assumption is that developed nations are representative democracies where the rights of people are guaranteed, basic human needs are satisfied, and the environment secured from various forms of pollution. Although several of the developed nations fall short in some of these categories, the absence of most is a characteristic of the "Developing World."

The logo map used in the publications of the Association of Third World Studies substantiates the given economic, political, and social definitions of the "Developing World." The G-7 nations and their periphery are absent from that map.

The assistance programs sponsored by the developed world since 1945 reflect the changing definition of the "Developing World." Immediately after World War II, assistance focused upon improvement in infrastructure—roads, ports, electricity, water supplies, and the like—to provide for increased opportunities to export primary products, including raw materials. By the late 1950s and into the early 1960s, assistance programs shifted direction. The end of colonialism, the independence of India and Indonesia, the emergence of new and independent nations in Africa, and Fidel Castro's Revolution in Cuba brought an awareness of the need to focus upon economic opportunities for the general population, improvement in quality of life, and the right of a nation's people to political participation and civil and human rights. These goals remained the objectives of programs sponsored by government and non-government organizations that continued into the 1980s when world politics again shifted. Identified best by the Washington Consensus, a set of suggested reforms set forth for Latin America by the economist John Williamson in 1989, this change in policy by developed nations cut back on their international assistance programs and, instead, called upon the nations of the "Developing World" to remove their protective barriers against foreign investment, provide for the privatization of state owned industries and for increased exports, particularly of so-called niche products. As they invited developing nations to enter the global arena, developed nations increased their pressure on developing nations to democratize the political process, protect civil and human rights, and encourage environmentalism. International agreements since the 1980s often contain provisons for the implementation of plans to address these human needs.

Despite the good intentions, the "Developing World" persists. Poverty, with its concomitant shortcomings in education, health care, housing, and other basic human needs, remains a reality for a disproportionate number of the world's inhabitants. Political democracy and civil and human rights are not universally guaranteed. Environmental pollution continues to go unchecked, taking its most devastating toll upon the "Developing World."

As the twenty-first century dawned, many analysts queried the advisability of imposing the developed world's criteria for modernization upon the "Developing World." The histories of the world's regions varied with their own political experiences, their own ethnic and religious conflicts, and their political, religious, and social traditions that resist and in some cases, outright defy modernization as envisioned by the developed world.

The *Encyclopedia of the Developing World* provides a ready reference work for understanding the issues that affect approximately three quarters of the globe's residents. The *Encyclopedia* is unique because of its focus upon the post 1945 period when the old colonial structures in Africa, Asia, and the Middle East crumbled and elsewhere, as in China, Japan, and Latin America the traditional elite structure has been replaced by something new. During the same time period, the "Developing World" began to demand a greater share of the world's economy and an improvement in quality of life, along with social justice, political participation, and individual liberties.

How to Use This Book

The *Encyclopedia of the Developing World* is composed of almost 800 free-standing entries of 500 to 5000 words in length. They range from factual narratives, such as country descriptions and biographies, to thematic interpretations and analytical discussions of timely topics like global trading patterns, and a combination of all three, such as overview articles on the history and economic development of a particular region. As much as possible, the encyclopedia covers the history, economic development, and politics of the developing world from 1945 to the present, providing the reader with a reliable, up-to-date view of the current state of scholarship on the developing world.

Perhaps the most significant feature of the encyclopedia is the easily accessible **A to Z format**. Cross-referencing in the form of **See Alsos** at the end of most entries refers the reader to other related entries. Each article contains a list of **References and Further Reading**, including sources used by the writer and editor as well as additional items that may be of interest to the reader. Most books or articles cited are easily available through interlibrary loan services in libraries. **Blind Entries** direct readers to essays listed under another title. For example, the blind entry "World Bank" refers the reader to the article entitled with that institution's official name, "International Bank for Reconstruction and Development." A thorough, analytical **index** complements the accessibility of the entries, easing the reader's entry into the wealth of information provided. A **thematic list of entries** is also included to assist readers with research in particular subjects.

Each country has a stand-alone entry, but also is included in larger regional studies. For example, discussion of Chile can be found under the country's entry, but its place in regional matters can be found in "Southern Cone (Latin America): History and Economic Development"; "Southern Cone (Latin America): International Relations"; and "Ethnic Conflicts: Southern Cone (Latin America)." There are stand-alone entries for important individuals, like Jomo Kenyatta, but for context readers should also refer to the country entry on Kenya and the topical entries, such as "Colonialism: History" and "Colonialism: Legacies," to more fully understand Kenyatta's philosophy and objectives. The discussion of "Development History and Theory" is augmented by the entry "Development, Measures of." Both are enhanced by the discussions of the various economic models: capitalist, communist, socialist, and so on. The cross-references will lead readers from stop to stop on such paths throughout the encyclopedia, and the index is another good starting place to find the connected discussions.

A total of 251 authors have contributed the entries to this encyclopedia. They are based around the world, in both developing and developed nations, including Argentina, Australia, Austria, Belgium, Bulgaria, Cameroon, Canada, China, Egypt, France, Germany, Hungary, India, Israel, Japan, Kenya, Malaysia, Mexico, the Netherlands, New Zealand, the Philippines, Poland, Romania, Singapore, South Africa, Sweden, Switzerland, Thailand, the United Arab Emirates, the United Kingdom, the United States, and Zimbabwe. In keeping with the global and interdisciplinary nature of this encyclopedia, contributors represent a variety of fields, among them finance, religion, anthropology, geography, environmental science, and law, with subspecialties such as global business, human rights, ethics, and refugee studies. The expertise of a wide-ranging and diverse group of contributors will provide the reader with a broad-based overview of issues, events, and theories of the developing world.

Acknowledgments

Several people helped to bring this work to its completion. A special thanks goes to Lorraine Murray of Fitzroy Dearborn Publishers, who kindly provided me the opportunity to undertake this project and to Mark L. Georgiev at the Taylor and Francis imprint of Routledge, for directing its completion following Routledge's acquisition of the project from Fitzroy Dearborn. The guidance offered by the Board of Advisors—Ade Adefuye, Akwasi B. Assensoh, Nader Entessar, Stephen Fischer-Galati, Alexander Gungov, Harold Isaacs, Gary Kline, Paul J. Magnarella, John Mukum Mbaku, Alojzy Z. Nowak, Philip Oxhorn, Paul A. Rodell, Houman A. Sadri, Barbara Tenenbaum and Pamela A. Zeiser—ensured the *Encyclopedia's* comprehensiveness. The expertise of each author made possible the accuracy and completeness of the 762 entries. The editorial efforts by Mark O'Malley and particularly Rachel Granfield made this a more readable work. As always, Yvonne offered the encouragement, support, and understanding that only a wife could. This work is dedicated to her.

Thomas M. Leonard

F

FAMILY PLANNING AND STRUCTURE

Demographic Challenges and Family Planning

The reproductive function of the family is just one of the factors that impact the demographic characteristics of a given country or region. The demographic explosion or the demographic slump correlates to a myriad other factors, of which the following stand out: political crisis and wars, the state of the economy, emigration, and a high mortality rate.

Conversely, each of these factors contains a multiplicity of triggers that determine the power of its effect. So, for example, the high mortality rate is defined by the existence of four underlying drivers—income levels, state of development of the health care system, living conditions, and the environment. The comprehensive interplay of the said factors, coupled with the reproductive function of the average statistical family defines the "demographic map" of every country, of every region of the world during the various stages in their development.

As a result, the twentieth century experienced interesting dynamics in demographic trends that may be illustrated by the following facts. In 1950, one-third of the world's population was living in the developed countries, in 2000—less than one-fifth. While

in the early twentieth century Africa was sparsely populated, in the twenty-first century, the continent is well ahead of Europe by population figures. As a result of migration and primarily because of the intensity with which population reproduces in some parts of the world, the continents are ranked by population density in the early twenty-first century in the following order: Asia, Africa, Europe, Latin America, North America, and Oceania. The maximum natural population growth rate (3% per year) was registered in Afghanistan, Angola, and Uganda, whereas the maximum population loss is recorded by Bulgaria, the Czech Republic, Hungary, Romania, Russia, Ukraine, Latvia, and Belarus. The disparity in the average size of families in different regions is rather drastic: in Europe and America, it is three persons; in Asia and Africa, more than five; in Iraq, Algeria, and most of the African countries, more than seven; in Sweden, Norway, and Denmark, it stands at 2.3 persons. The imbalance that existed in the early twenty-first century in natural population growth in the different regions of the world has forced the governments of twenty countries to refocus their demographic policy on increasing the birth rate, while the governments of eighty-five countries have trained their policy on reducing the birth rate. Family planning has emerged as a tangible factor that plays a substantive role in balancing demographic processes and tempering the birth rate.

The Nature of Family Planning

The term "family planning" appears in the official papers of several international organizations—the United Nations (UN), the UN Organization for Education, Science and Culture (UNESCO), the World Health Organization (WHO), etc. According to the official position of the UN, family planning is a blend of actions aimed at protecting the parents' right to freely and responsibly discharge their reproductive function. Family planning encompasses activities that support parents in adequately exercising their reproductive functions and is conducive to the following results: preventing undesirable pregnancies, the delivery of wanted children, regulating interim periods between pregnancies, age control in childbearing, and control over the number of children in a family.

One of the major goals of family planning is associated with the avoidance of accidental or unplanned pregnancies. In practical terms, this means that to avoid unplanned pregnancies, the use of contraceptives has to be managed effectively, inclusive of the use of modern and reliable contraception methods. In order for parents to freely and responsibly exercise their reproductive functions, the following conditions ought to be met: effective and adequate legislation; a proper health insurance system; the presence of positive attitudes and willingness on the part of general practitioners to engage in the prevention of unwanted pregnancies; availability of information about the ways to prevent unwanted pregnancies; availability, accessibility, and reliability of means to prevent unwanted pregnancies; an operational sexual education system; and a system for marital and family counseling. The very essence of family planning is centered on providing all of the above conditions.

The Ideological Aspect: Pros and Cons of Family Planning

This issue has been hotly debated since the early twentieth century. Advocates of family planning believe it is necessary in order to strictly regiment the birth rate and population growth in the world. A range of disconcerting facts are furnished in support of this premise. So, for instance, in the early twenty-first century, the world population reached 6 billion, and human population grows at the rate of almost 80 million people annually. If the pace is kept, the world will suffer from a deficit in resources to feed mankind by the year 2025. To avoid this scenario, the mean birth rate ratio (the average number of children born by a single woman) that would ensure a stable population growth rate worldwide should be 2.1.

The case for family planning can be argued very strongly by pinpointing the growth in sexually transmitted infections, and first and foremost, of persons infected with AIDS. In the early twenty-first century, there were more than 40 million people infected with the immune deficiency virus, the majority of them in the developing world. An estimated 2.5 million AIDS victims are children under the age of fifteen. In 2003 alone, 3 million people died of AIDS and another 5 million were infected. The absence of family planning or its unsatisfactory state is believed to lead to the lack of use of contraception by women, resulting in abortions or the bearing of unwanted children. So, for example, empirical studies show that while people in the developing world need family planning, it has not yet reached a satisfactory state of advancement. In developing countries, over 100 million married women of reproductive age—an estimated one in five women outside China—has an "unmet need" for family planning. Unmet need, which is estimated from survey data, refers to married women who say that they would prefer to avoid or postpone childbearing but who are not using any method of contraception.

Family planning opponents support their position with three major ideological arguments. The first rests on the theory launched by Thomas Malthus in 1798—namely that population has an inherent tendency to uninhibited procreation that ultimately leads to economic deprivation, famine, war, and plagues. This invited the conclusion that if mankind desired prosperity, the birth rate ought to be contained artificially. The second argument relates to Charles Darwin's theory of the origin of the species, published in 1859. According to family planning opponents, Darwin transposed the principles of natural selection and the survival struggle, intrinsic to the animal world, to human society, thereby pronouncing man an integral part of the animal kingdom and releasing him of moral obligations. The third argument relates to the science of eugenics that gained popularity in the late nineteenth century. Eugenics pursues the perfection of man's biological nature by means of selection, something achieved in Germany and the USA in the 1920s and 1930s, primarily through the sterilization of inferior individuals. Serious historical facts also have been furnished, mainly in relation to the Bolsheviks in Russia and the Nazis in Germany, among which we could list the legitimization of abortions, sterilization of inferior persons, planned numbers of the Slav population in the occupied territories, and others. In the postmodern age, the opponents of family planning find correlations between the latter and euthanasia, cloning, sex-change surgery, and the death penalty, to mention but a few. To them, it is an expression of bigotry and a refined means to kill people for the sake of personal comfort.

Family Planning Structures

Family planning first appeared at the beginning of the twentieth century, and its structure evolved over the first fifty years of the century, mainly in the USA and Western Europe. In the USA it is associated with the first standard certificate of death issued in 1900 and above all with the name of Margaret Stanger, who broke the law in 1916, having set up the first family planning clinic in Brooklyn, N.Y. The following important events took place in the USA over the same period: in 1937 the American Medical Association endorsed birth control; in 1937, the first state (North Carolina) included birth control in a public health program; and in 1942, the Planned Parenthood Federation of America was established. In the first half of the twentieth century Nazis in Germany were the most active among Western Europeans to carry out family planning, associating its initiatives with the pure "Aryan race" and the need to sterilize inferior individuals.

Family planning also aroused vivid discussions as far back as the 1920s in the UK. Empirical research into family planning and the fertility of women in this country started in 1938, the first study being an opinion poll inquiring into the ideal number of children in a British family. Special attention also was paid to this issue in France—in 1947, the first study on issues of family planning and the reproductive behaviour of French women was carried out. Important operations and the intense development of international and national family planning structures, however, began in the second half of twentieth century after the establishment of the International Planned Parenthood Federation (IPPF). IPPF was founded in Bombay in 1952 by representatives of eight countries—India, Germany, Hong Kong, the Netherlands, Singapore, Sweden, the United Kingdom, and the United States.

From this point on, family planning became the focus of attention on a global scale, and in individual countries, the establishment of national autonomous Family Planning Associations (FPAs) began, their number being more than 180 as of the end of twentieth century. Additional structures also were set up to deal with control over reproductive family functions; a number of empirical studies were carried out, looking into the reproductive behaviour of women; a number of international forums on family planning

issues were held; legislation in individual countries was amended to legalize abortions and the use of contraceptive drugs; and various periodicals began publication, etc. The following facts relevant to the USA may be cited to illustrate the above occurrences: 1955, the first national fertility survey was conducted; 1960, the birth control pill was approved by the Food and Drug Administration (FDA); 1965, Supreme Court (*Griswold vs. Connecticut*) declared unconstitutional state laws prohibiting contraceptive use by married couples; 1972, Medicaid funding for family planning services was authorised; 1973, Supreme Court (*Roe vs. Wade*) legalized abortion; 1973, the first National Survey of Family Growth conducted; 1993, the female condom was approved by the FDA; 1997, the emergency use of oral contraceptive pills was approved by the FDA.

Over the same period, Western European countries also were extremely active in the field of family planning. It was a focus of attention in France, where the relevant legal foundations were laid down, the necessary organisational structures were set up, and a large number of sociological and social/psychological surveys also were carried out. For example, in 1954, 1956, and 1960 the *French Institut National d'Etudes Demographiques* (INED) began research on the ideal French family model. In 1966, a new study was carried out, delineating the specifics in the reproductive behaviour of French women and the formative mechanisms operating inside French families. Until 2000, INED implemented a number of studies in France, the outcomes of which served to complete the picture of the family planning situation in Europe. In the UK, in 1967, a second Family Intentions Survey was conducted, offering representative data about the ideal family according to the UK population. Parallel to it, public opinion polls were carried out in relation to contraceptive pills, abortions, etc.

The important contributions of Scandinavian countries and especially of the Netherlands need to be noted here. By the end of twentieth century, a solid family planning system was set up in all Western European countries, comprised of governmental and nongovernmental structures. Similar structures also were established (mainly after the political changes of 1989) in Central and Eastern European countries, including the following: the Russian Family Planning Association (RFPA), the Bulgarian Family Planning Association (BFPA), the Lithuanian Family Planning and Sexual Education Association (LFPSEA), the Albania Family Planning Association (AFPA), the Czech Society for Family Planning and Sex Education (CSFPSE), the Family Planning Association of Estonia (FPAE), and the Slovak Association for Family Planning and Parenthood Education

(SAFPPE), etc. Structures set up in individual countries and, as a rule, national family planning associations, are all IPPF members and work to further its objectives, both nationally and internationally.

Family Planning Goals and Objectives

Family planning goals and objectives have been specified in IPPF official documents and in national autonomous Family Planning Associations' (FPAs) documentation. The main goals of family planning are as follows:

1. Meet the demand and unmet need for quality services;
2. Promote sexual and reproductive health for people;
3. Eliminate unsafe abortion;
4. Organize affirmative action to gain equity, equality and empowerment for women;
5. Help young people understand their sexuality and provide services that meet their demands; and
6. Maintain the highest standards of care in the countries all over the world throughout the IPPF.

The achievement of these goals requires the implementation of the following practical objectives:

1. Family planning structures need to actively work to impose standards of contraceptive safety, program management, service provision and gender equity.
2. All family planning structures need to campaign locally, regionally and internationally, through policymakers, opinion leaders, professionals, and the media, to increase support for reproductive health and family planning worldwide.
3. Individuals working for the family planning system defend women's reproductive rights, both at the national, advocacy level and, at the individual level, by focusing on quality of care in the provision of family planning services specifically designed to meet women's needs.
4. Individuals working for the family planning system make available reproductive health services, including counseling, information, and a choice of family planning methods and providers.
5. Family-planning system decision makers advocate before governments and policymakers to improve national health services.
6. Family planning structures work to prepare adolescents for responsible parenthood by

offering services, such as infertility treatment, premarital counseling, pregnancy testing, and breast and cervical cancer screening.

Family Planning Methods

Family planning methods are mainly distinguished through the criterion of control over either conception or birth. There are, therefore, two main methods of family planning: contraception and abortion.

Contraception appears as a chief element in family planning, since it plays a significant role in protecting women's lives. It is a preliminary method for control over the process of conception, whereas abortion is a method for the artificial disruption of pregnancy.

The contraceptive method, in principle, does not give rise to any vivid discussions or harsh controversies. However, abortion makes the object of acute debate and controversial statements in individual countries. Even now, abortion is an illicit method in many countries across the world. In Europe, it was first legalized in Russia in 1920 and then in Germany in 1934. Subsequently, this method was legalized in a number of other countries: United Kingdom (1967), Finland (1970), the United States (1973), Denmark (1973), France (1975), Sweden (1975), Family Rights Group (FRG) (1976), Norway (1976), Italy (1978), Luxembourg (1978), The Netherlands (1984), Portugal (1984), Spain (1985), and Belgium (1990).

Important differences are observed in relation to family planning methods used in developed and in developing countries, as well as between Eastern and Western European countries. In developed countries, the emphasis is placed on taking contraceptive pills, whereas in Eastern Europe (former socialist countries, including Russia) and in developing countries, abortion is heavily relied upon. The following information about the use of contraceptives is available: in developed industrialized nations, 70%; in developing countries, 46%. The largest share of women using contraceptives is in the Netherlands, between the ages of fifteen and forty-four. According to researchers, the low level of contraceptive use in developing countries is attributed to its unavailability and high cost.

Family Planning: General Trends in Developing Countries

Some general trends, but also important differences, are characteristic for family planning in developing countries. A general trend stems from reduced birth rates, and it is a globally valid one. Over the past few decades, as fertility rates have fallen, world population growth has slowed. Population is growing at an annual rate of 1.3%, estimated in 1998, compared with 2.1% in the 1960s. Nevertheless, the world's population is growing by almost 80 million per year—about 1 billion every thirteen years. In the beginning of the twenty-first century, fertility fell to or below replacement level in sixty-one countries, thirteen of them in the developing world. In 123 countries, fertility is still above replacement level. In most countries, couples still have at least three children. About 1.7 billion people live in forty-seven countries, where fertility averages between three and five children per woman. Another 730 million people live in forty-four countries in which the average woman has five children or more.

Overall fertility declined by approximately one-third from the 1960s through the 1980s, from an average of six to four children per woman, with dramatic decreases occurring in some parts of the world (e.g., 24% decline in fertility in Asia and Latin America, approximately 50% in Thailand, and approximately 35% in Colombia, Jamaica, and Mexico). As fertility declined in developing countries, the infant mortality rate decreased from approximately one hundred fifty deaths per one thousand live births in the 1950s to approximately eighty per one thousand in the early 1990s. Among married women of reproductive age in developing countries, 53% plan the size of their families; 90% of these women report using modern birth control methods.

Many countries in Asia and the Pacific successfully implemented family planning programs. Their success is evidenced by data indicating a reduction in the fertility rate, increased life expectancy, lower infant death rate, and the delayed growth of the population. From 1960 to 1970, the general fertility rate in the region was 5.65 children per woman, life expectancy was 51.9 years, the infant death rate was 120.5 per 1,000 newborns, and the population growth was 2.29% per year. From 1970 to 1980, the general birth rate was 4.5 children per woman, life expectancy was 67.9 years, the infant death rate was ninety-four per one thousand newborns, and the population growth was 2.03% per year.

The birth rate in the region is decreasing, which is evidenced by a comparison of the following data sets: the general fertility rate in 1992 was 3.1 children per woman, which is an estimated 38% lower, compared with 5.0 children per woman during 1970–1975. This trend is even more apparent once data about individual countries, valid as of 1980 and 1991–1992, are compared: in India, the general fertility rate was 5.3 children per woman in 1980 vs. 3.9 in 1991. Almost half of couples use birth control. In Indonesia, the fertility

rate was 4.6 children per woman in 1980 vs. 3.0 in 1992. In the Philippines, the fertility rate was 5.0 children per woman in 1980 vs. 4.1 in 1991. The Catholic Church opposes family planning, and only 22% of couples use modern contraception. In Morocco, the fertility rate was 6.9 children per woman in 1980 vs. 4.2 in 1992. Nurses deliver contraceptives to secluded Muslim women. In Egypt, the fertility rate was 4.6 children per woman in 1965 vs. 4.4 in 1992. Egypt's population grows by a million people every year. In Saudi Arabia, the fertility rate was 7.2 children per woman in 1980 vs. 7.2 in 1991. The above data illustrate that success has been registered in reducing the birth rate in developing countries, which of course relates to the implementation of an overall family planning strategy, also aiming to popularize contraceptives. Their use in the region has grown, even though certain differences exist between individual countries. Data from 1989–1993 about the use of contraceptives is as follows: the use of contraceptives is higher in East and Southeast Asia. China, Hong Kong, the Republic of Korea, and Singapore achieved contraceptive prevalence levels of 70%–74%, while Sri Lanka and Thailand attained levels between 62% and 68%. Countries having prevalence levels of 43%–53% were India, Indonesia, Malaysia, the Philippines, and Vietnam. The remaining countries in the region had prevalence levels of 25% or less.

In most general terms, as of the end of the twentieth century, contraceptives have become an exceptionally popular regulator of the birth rate in developing countries. Statistical data indicate that in developing countries, the percentage of married couples using contraception has risen substantially, from less than 10% in the 1960s to 55% in 1998, and it continues to rise. Of course, the reduced birth rate in developing countries correlates to a reduction in the mortality rate. The country's maternal mortality rate has declined from 397 per 100,000 live births in 1994 to 307 in 2004, compared with Thailand, which has only 44 deaths per 100,000, the Philippines (200), Vietnam (130), Malaysia (41), and Singapore (30). Family planning programs have played a key role in this process.

Family Planning at the Beginning of Twenty-First Century

In order to better understand family planning at the beginning of twenty-first century, it is necessary to outline in brief some statistical information about developing countries, including the countries with the largest populations, China and India.

In 2003, the population in China was 1.3 billion people, and the growth index was 0.6%. Life expectancy is 72.22 years (overall): 70.33 years for males and 74.28 years for females. Because China is the most populated country in the world, family planning is at an exceptionally high level of development. Based on scientific analyses, owing to its perfect family planning over the past two decades, China has managed to reduce its population by 300 million people. Government policy provides incentives for later marriages and for implementing the "one-child family" model, while, under favorable conditions, the two-child model is also allowed. There are plans for the number of population not to exceed 1.4 billion by 2010, assuming that by the middle of the twenty-first century, the population in this country will steady at 1.6 billion. A special government policy is implemented to this effect, to prevent high birth rates and to promote the use of contraceptives. Data from 1991 indicate that 88.85% of Chinese couples of reproductive age use contraceptives.

India is the second country in the world in terms of population numbers; however, forecasts indicate that in a few decades it will surpass China due to its high birth rate. If absolute population growth levels remain unchanged, which equaled 161 million people during 1981–1991, the population in this country will double every thirty years. That is why, in 1951, the National Family Welfare Programme was set up in India with the objective of reducing the birth rate to make it compatible with the constraints of national economy. In 2000, a new National Programme for Demographic Policy was issued, whose objective is to reach a fertility rate by 2010 complying with the simple replacement level of the population, and by 2045—to stabilize its number. In general terms, there is progress in reducing the birth rate, which in 1991 was 3.9 children per woman. This is attributable to the use of contraceptives, which in the 1990s was over 40%. Weaker outcomes of India's demographic policy in comparison to China are due to social and economic factors: the existence of significant levels of poverty among the larger share of the population (one-third of Indians live below the poverty threshold), poor education (in 2000, the level of education among women was 54%, compared with 76% among men).

Special attention is being paid in Bangladesh to family planning, but birth rates remain high and there is strong resistance to the use of contraceptives. The unwillingness to use contraceptives is associated with the desire for more children, religious attitudes, the opposition shown by male spouses and mothers-in-law, and the fear of potential side effects. Almost 100% of deliveries are carried out at home, and only 5% of births are assisted by trained personnel. The percentage of sexually transmitted infections is quite high. Young people have no or only limited access to information about sexual or reproductive health. *Essential statistic data*: Bangladesh is the most densely populated in the world—it has a total population of 133 million, with 36% aged ten to twenty-four years. Population growth is 2.2% per year. Human development index ranking for 2002 is: 145 out of 173 countries. Sociodemographic and health indicators are well below the South Asia average. Average life expectancy at birth is fifty-nine years. The infant mortality rate is high at sixty-six per one thousand live births.

The maternal mortality rate is very high at six hundred per one hundred thousand live births. The contraceptive prevalence rate among married women (ages fifteen to forty-nine) is 54%. The number of women per one hundred men is ninety-four.

Individuals involved in family planning in Ghana have actively fought against AIDS and advocated for the use of contraceptives. An important number of the population define condoms as a form of protection against AIDS. Empirical research reported an increase in modern contraceptive use from 10.5% to 36.4%. The largest increase is among fifteen- to nineteen-year-olds. *Essential statistic data:* Population is 20.2 million, with 33% aged ten to twenty-four years. Human Development Index ranking: 129 out of 173 countries. Average life expectancy at birth is fifty-eight years. The infant mortality rate is fifty-six per one thousand live births. The maternal mortality rate is 590 per 100,000 live births. The total fertility rate is estimated at 4.3. Only 22% of married women aged fifteen to forty-nine years are included in the family planning. Only 44% of all births are assisted by trained personnel. The population living with HIV/AIDS (ages fifteen to forty-nine) was 3% at the end of 2001. The literacy rate among adults is 63% for women and 80% for men.

Special attention is paid in Ethiopia to the provision of information about family planning among young people. A large number of youth centers have been opened for them, where they can obtain family counseling or information about protection from AIDS, etc. *Essential statistic data:* The population is 67.7 million, with 32% aged ten to twenty-four years. Human Development Index ranking: 168 out of 173 countries. Average life expectancy at birth is fifty-two years. The infant mortality rate is very high at ninety-seven per one thousand live births. The maternal mortality rate is very high at 1,800 per 100,000 live births. The total fertility rate is estimated at 5.9, with only 8% of married women aged fifteen to forty-nine years practicing family planning. Only 10% of births are assisted by trained personnel. The population living with HIV/AIDS (ages fifteen to forty-nine years) is 6.4%. The literacy rate among adults is low at 33% for women and 44% for men.

Before 1989, Kenya enjoyed the dubious distinction of having the highest fertility rate and, consequently, the highest population growth in the world. At its height, the population growth rate was 4%, and the total fertility rate was eight children. Research has revealed that since the late 1980s and early 1990s, the once-high fertility rate is declining, and Kenya is now among the nations that are experiencing fertility transitions. *Essential statistic data*: The population is 31.1 million, with 37% aged ten to twenty-four years. Human Development Index ranking: 134 out of 173 countries. The average life expectancy at birth is forty-eight years. The infant mortality rate is high at seventy-four per one thousand live births. The maternal mortality rate is very high at 1,300 per 100,000 live births. The total fertility rate is estimated at 4.4, with only 39% of married women aged fifteen to forty-nine years practicing family planning. Only 44% of all births are assisted by trained personnel. The population living with HIV/AIDS (aged fifteen to forty-nine years) is 15%. The literacy rate among adults is high at 76% for women and 89% for men.

The population of the Philippines is 81.6 million, with 32% aged ten to twenty-four years. Human Development Index ranking: eighty-five out of 175 countries. Average life expectancy at birth is seventy years. The infant mortality rate is twenty-six per one thousand live births. The maternal mortality rate is 240 per 100,000 live births. The total fertility rate is estimated at 3.5 with only 49% of married women aged fifteen to forty-nine practicing family planning. Only 56% of all births are assisted by trained personnel. The population living with HIV/AIDS (ages fifteen to forty-nine years) is 0.05%. The literacy rate among adults is high at 95% for women and 96% for men.

The population of Vietnam is 80.8 million, with 32% aged ten to twenty-four years. Human Development Index ranking: 109 out of 175 countries. Average life expectancy at birth is seventy-two years. The infant mortality rate is twenty-six per thousand live births. The maternal mortality rate is ninety-five per hundred thousand live births. The total fertility rate is estimated at 2.3 with 77% of married women aged fifteen to forty-nine practicing family planning. 77% of all births are assisted by trained personnel. Population living with HIV/AIDS (fifteen to forty-nine) is 0.3%. The literacy rate among adults is high at 91% for women and 96% for men.

The population of Sudan is 32.6 million, with 33% aged ten to twenty-four years. Human Development Index ranking: 139 out of 173 countries. Average life expectancy at birth is fifty-six years. The infant mortality rate is high at eighty-two per one thousand live births. The maternal mortality rate is very high at 1,500 per 100,000 live births. The total fertility rate is estimated at 4.9, with only 10% of married women aged fifteen to forty-nine years practicing family planning. An estimated 86% of all births are assisted by trained personnel. The population living with HIV/AIDS (aged fifteen to forty-nine years) is 2.6%. The literacy rate among adults is 46% for women and 70% for men.

KRUM KRUMOV

References and Further Reading

Back, K. *Family Planning and Population Control: Tthe Challenges of a Successful Movement*. Boston: Twayne Publishers, 1989.
Bulatao, R.A. *The Value of Family Planning Programs in Developing Countries*. Santa Monica, CA: RAND, Population Matters, 1998.
Conly, S.R., Chaya, N., and Helsing, K. *Family Planning Expenditures in 79 Countries: A Current Assessment*. Washington, DC: Population Action International, 1995.
Dixon-Mueller, R. *Population Policy & Women's Rights: Transforming Reproductive Choice*. Westport, CT and London: Praeger, 1993.
Glasier, A., Gebbie, A. and N. Loudon. *Handbook of Family Planning and Reproductive Health Care*. Churchill Livingstone, 2000.
Huston, P. *Motherhood by Choice: Pioneers in Women's Health and Family Planning*. The Feminist Press, 1992.
Senanayake, P., and R. Kleinman, eds. *Family Planning: Meeting Challenges, Promoting Choices*. New York: The Parthenon Publishing Group, 1993.
Wolff, J.A., Suttenfield, L.J., and S. C. Binzen. *The Family Planning Manager's Handbook. Basic Skills and Tools for Managing Family Planning Programs*. West Hartford, CT: Kumarian Press, 1991.

WWW Sites

http://www.questia.com/popularSearches/family_planning.jsp
http://www.ippf.org/resource/index.htm

FANON, FRANTZ

Frantz Fanon lived only thirty-six years, but he became widely known as an active revolutionary, a psychiatrist, and a political theorist. Fanon was embittered by racism, and he passionately supported anticolonial revolutions. He is best known for his ideological justification of revolutionary violence.

Fanon was born on July 20, 1925, in Fort-de-France, Martinique (then the French Antilles). His lifelong preoccupation with the psychological damage of racism may be traced to his home, where he was the most dark-skinned of eight children in a Caribbean household. His middle-class family made sure that he received a good French education in Martinique, and he imagined himself as part of a universal French culture based on language, not race. He called himself a "Frenchman," and at age eighteen, he joined Free French forces to fight the Germans in North Africa and France. But he found that white Frenchmen regarded him as inferior.

After World War II, Fanon studied medicine at the University of Lyon. He specialized in psychiatry and began to interpret European imperialism in terms of psychological dominance: the colonized (Algerians, Africans, Vietnamese, etc.) were crippled by their induced sense of racial inferiority and could only regain their psychological health by fighting their oppressors. Fanon's first book, *Black Skin, White Masks* (1952) expressed his personal frustration with racism, yet in October of that year, he married Marie-Josephe Dublé, a white Frenchwoman.

In 1953, having completed his medical training, Fanon was appointed chief of the psychiatric ward at a French government hospital in Algeria. The Algerian revolution began in 1954. Dr. Fanon secretly helped Algerian rebels of the Front de Libération Nationale (FLN) for the next two years. In 1956, he resigned from the French medical service and joined the FLN at their base in Tunis, editing the rebel newspaper *El Moudjahid* and later taking to the field.

The year 1959 marked a turning point in Fanon's life. His analysis of the Algerian revolution, *Studies in a Dying Colonialism*, was published. He was severely wounded when his Jeep hit a landmine on the border of Algeria and Morocco. He was evacuated to Rome for medical treatment and there escaped two murder attempts, presumably orchestrated by French colonial gangs. Also, he was diagnosed with leukemia. These setbacks did not prevent him from assuming the post of ambassador to Ghana for the Algerian Provisional Government and making a 1,200-mile trek across the Sahara Desert in an effort to open up a southern supply route for the Algerian revolutionaries.

By 1961, Fanon was gravely ill. In an odd twist of Cold War politics, he was brought to the United States by a CIA agent, Ollie Iselin. Fanon died in Bethesda, Md., on December 6, 1961. Iselin accompanied his body back to FLN-controlled territory in eastern Algeria, where he was buried. His last book, *The Wretched of the Earth*, was published by his friend Jean-Paul Sartre. Algeria achieved full independence in 1962.

Fanon was a Marxist, but he emphasized psychological rather than economic factors in colonialism. His writings anticipated the ideas of Edward Said— that artificial racial and cultural concepts underlie imperialism. Fanon glorified violence, which he saw as a cleansing force, but he believed that after the collective catharsis of revolution, a new and better society could be created.

Ross Marlay

See also Algeria; Colonialism: History; Colonialism: Legacies; Ethnicity: Impact on Politics and Society; Eurocentrism

References and Further Reading

Caute, David. *Frantz Fanon*. New York: Viking, 1970.

Gendzier, Irene. *Frantz Fanon: A Critical Study*. New York: Random House, 1973.

Macey, David. *Frantz Fanon: A Biography*. New York: Picador, 2000.

FARABUNDO MARTÍ NATIONAL LIBERATION FRONT (FMLN)

The history of the Farabundo Martí National Liberation Front (FMLN) is grounded in the life and death of Agustín Farabundo Martí. Martí was born in 1893 in the department of La Libertad, El Salvador, where he grew up among the rural poor. As a young man, he made contact with the Communist International in Mexico and became active in recruitment in Central America. Outraged at the military intervention of the United States in Nicaragua, he joined Augusto César Sandino's Defending Army of the National Sovereignty of Nicaragua in June 1928. Sandino wanted Martí to recruit more foreign volunteers for his struggle for independence, but the Communist International expected him to draw Sandino closer to its ideological cause. This contradiction strained the relationship between the two men until they parted ways in early 1930. Martí then returned to El Salvador in the midst of a coffee depression. In 1932, he led a mass rebellion against plantation owners that culminated in the massacre of thirty thousand peasants and the subsequent public execution of Martí and several other peasant leaders. This tragic episode of Salvadoran history, known as the *matanza*, was merely the beginning of six decades of state repression and revolutionary resistance.

The emergence of the Popular Forces of Liberation "Farabundo Martí" in 1970 and the People's Revolutionary Army in 1972 was the precursor of a political and armed struggle against the Salvadoran oligarchy and army. The Sandinista revolution in Nicaragua in July 1979 facilitated the unification of five separate guerrilla organizations in El Salvador. Shortly after Archbishop Oscar Romero was assassinated by military officers on March 24, 1980, the FMLN formed to carry out an insurrection against the governmental and military establishment. In January 1981, the FMLN launched a guerrilla strategy known as the "final offensive" and called for a general strike that never materialized. The massacre of more than one thousand peasants at El Mozote in December 1981 marked the onset of a full-scale bloody civil war. The unprovoked attack on the village by the government's Atlacatl Battalion, whose members trained at the School of the Americas in the United States, manifested a chilling counterinsurgency campaign. The United States government under the Reagan administration spent $6 billion in an attempt to destroy the FMLN and prevent another Cuban-Soviet foothold in the Americas.

In late 1989, the FMLN launched a major offensive on San Salvador, occupying one-third of the capital including several wealthy neighborhoods and the heavily populated working class district of Santa Marta. The government bombed Santa Marta, causing the FMLN to retreat, but lost support from citizens in urban areas. On November 16, 1989, in retaliation for the FMLN attacks, military officers of the Atlacatl Battalion murdered six Jesuit priests, their housekeeper, and her daughter at the Central American University.

These events brought the antagonists under pressure to intensify negotiations for a peace agreement. The secretary-general of the United Nations received a formal request from the government of El Salvador in September 1989 to start talks with the FMLN. The first breakthrough was achieved in 1990 when the parties agreed to ensure respect for human rights. To verify this and future agreements, the Security Council established the United Nations Observer Mission in El Salvador (ONUSAL) in 1991.

Further intense negotiations were brokered by the representative of the UN Secretary General and culminated in a series of the peace accords on December 31, 1991, in New York. A formal signing ceremony was held on January 16, 1992, in Mexico City. The conflict claimed more than seventy-five thousand lives, disabled more than three hundred thousand people, and created five hundred thousand refugees. The FMLN cooperated with ONUSAL in an investigation of crimes against humanity and human rights violations. Many accused military officers and guerrillas were granted amnesty in 1993.

The FMLN became a legal political party, holding its first convention in early 1994. The national elections of March 1994 resulted in the FMLN's defeat at the presidential level. However, the revolutionaries-cum-politicians secured sixty-two municipalities, fifteen mayoral posts, and twenty-one seats in the national legislature out of a total of eighty-four for an equivalent of 21.4% of the valid votes. In the wake of the transition to democracy and the 1994 polls, the FMLN developed political factions and ideological tendencies that expressed different modes of thinking and caused serious disputes in the party leadership. This situation affected the party's ability to coordinate an effective political strategy to compete in the 1999 elections. The electoral victory of conservative and neoliberal parties caused a permanent fracture in the FMLN's structure along revolutionary socialist and social democratic lines. The main party apparatus is now controlled by a group of leaders known as the "renovators."

While unable to win the presidency, the factions of the FMLN continue to garner support in legislative and municipal elections throughout the country. The March 2000 elections gave the FMLN block the largest single portion of the Legislative Assembly and control of eighty municipal councils in seven of the fourteen largest cities, including the greater San Salvador metropolitan area.

MARK EVERINGHAM

See also Mexico: International Relations; Central America: International Relations; Central America: History and Economic Development

References and Further Reading

Constable, Pamela. "At War's End in El Salvador," *Current History*, 92: 576 (1993).
Dunkerley, James. *Power in the Isthmus*, New York: Verso, 1988.
Farabundo Martí National Liberation Front, official web site: www.fmln.org.sv.
Fitzsimmons, Tracy and Mark Anner. "Civil Society in a Postwar Period: Labor in the Salvadoran Democratic Transition," *Latin American Research Review*, 34:3 (1999).
Jackson, David, John Dodson, and Laura O'Shaughnessy. "Protecting Human Rights: The Legitimacy of Judicial System Reforms in El Salvador," *Bulletin of Latin American Research*, 18: 4 (1999).
"NACLA: A 35-Year Retrospective on Central America," *NACLA Report on the Americas*, 36:3 (2002).

FIJI

The Fiji Islands consist of approximately 300–350 islands (depending on high tide) in the South Pacific, of which approximately two hundred are inhabited. The total land area is 7,056 square miles, roughly the size of the state of New Jersey. It is located northeast of Australia and New Zealand, while slightly southwest of Hawaii in the Oceania region. Viti Levu, where the capital city Suva is located, and Vanua Levu are the two largest islands where most business activity occurs. Vanua Levu is primarily developed around a sugar mill, and the rest is hardwood forests, much sought after by Western economies. Viti Levu is cosmopolitan by comparison, with industry, commerce, government, and agriculture. The economy is based on tourism, sugar, copra, apparel, gold, fishing, and lumber. The tropical climate is temperate year round, and the Fiji Islands have primarily developed their land in the old custom of "nothing taller than a coconut tree." Coconuts and fish remain staples of the village economy, supplemented by tourism.

The ancestors of present-day Fijians were Austronesian-speaking explorers whose early civilizations have been dated at 3,200 years ago (Geraghty 1994). In 1874, the ruling Fijian chief, Cakobau, ceded the Fiji Islands to the British Crown in a political maneuver designed to quell opposition between European settlers and village tribes (Lotherington 1998). This move changed the ethnic makeup of Fiji in that the British colonial government recruited indentured laborers from the Indian subcontinent to do the hard work in the sugar cane fields. In 1970, Fiji achieved independence, although the country retains friendly relations with England. However, the almost century of colonial rule changed the islands from a network of tribal villages into a multiracial nation. Still, the village system is still firmly entrenched in the Fijian society today. The *Ratu* (village chief) and *vanua* (land owning with a common ancestor) are the focus of hereditary authority and decision-making (Tuimaleali'ifano 2000). The *Ratu* is the eldest in line and may be either a male or female. Traditional ceremonies occur regularly and educational values are passed on in community life through a strong oral tradition. Storytelling and singing are part of the fabric of village life (Lotherington 1995), along with *kava* (also known as *yaqona*), a brown nonalcoholic drink made of water and the crushed roots of a pepper plant. *Kava* is drunk from a coconut cup.

By most standards, Fiji is one of the most successful of the Pacific Island nations. The literacy rate is over 92%, although it was not until 1956 that Fijians other than the village chiefs were provided with secondary education. As of 1986, over 95% of the teachers were trained, reflecting the Fijian government's efforts to professionalize its teaching force (Tavola 1991).

Medical care is available on the two main islands, but the outer islands have a shortage of clinics.

Fiji is an independent and multicultural republic, with English, Fijian, and Hindi spoken by the ethnic makeup of 51% Fijians, 44% Indo-Fijians, and 4% of mixed heritage (Vaughan 1995). The remaining populations are other Pacific Islanders, Europeans, Chinese, and people of mixed races. According to 2004 estimates, Fiji has approximately 880,000 inhabitants.

This mixture of indigenous Fijians and the Indians has led to racial stress and conflict over the past fifteen years. In 1987, the democratically elected multiracial government was overthrown in two coups, in which the balance of power shifted back to the traditional Fijian hierarchy (Lotherington 1998). The coups stimulated a huge exodus of Indo-Fijians, many who migrated to Australia, New Zealand, Canada, and the USA. It was the professional people in top positions who could most easily migrate, thus resulting in a brain drain of the country.

In general, crime has been relatively low in Fiji. There is only one prison, which is located in the capital city of Suva. Currently, there is a small but active women's rights movement. In 1997, the Constitution was amended to become more equitable. Women now enjoy equal rights; however, wage inequalities still exist—especially in the garment industry, where female workers are subject to a special minimum wage that is considerably lower than in other industries. In general, women in the Fijian community are more likely to rise to prominence in their own right than are women of Indian or Indo-Fijian descent.

In 2000, the people of Fiji endured an armed takeover of parliament and a hostage crisis lasting fifty-six days (Tarte 2001). Martial law was declared, and there was mutiny in the armed forces, which raised the specter of civil war and economic collapse and international ostracism. Again, this coup was based on the election of an Indian leader of the government being ousted. The group of rebels overthrowing the government were arrested after almost two months and charged with treason. An interim government was sworn in. The interim government was later elected democratically by popular vote and continues on its path to long-term recovery. Two coups in quick succession were disturbing to the neighbors of Fiji (Swarts 2000), and the political developments since the last elections had led to erosion of the commitment to build cross-community bridges (Chand 2001).

Tourism, which dropped off after the coup, is slowing drawing back people to the magic of the island. Some concern exists over global warming and its effects on the Fiji Islands.

CHERYL VAN DEUSEN

See also Ethnic Conflicts: Oceania; Oceania: History and Economic Development; Oceania: International Relations

References and Further Reading

Chand, Satish. "Confronting Fiji futures" in *Confronting Fiji Futures*, edited by A. Haroon Akramlodhi. Asia Pacific Press, ANU, 2000.

Lotherington, Heather. "Language Choices and Social Reality: Education in Post-Colonial Fiji," in *Journal of Intercultural Studies*, 19: 1, (1998).

Swarts, Will. "Island Coups" in *World Press Review*, 47: 8, (2000).

Tarte, Sandra. "*The Contemporary Pacific*," University of Hawaii Press, 13: 2, 2001.

Tavola, H. "Secondary Education in Fiji: A Key to the Future," *Suva, Institute of Pacific Studies*, University of the South Pacific, 1991.

Tuijmaleai'fano, Morgan, "Current developments in the Pacific," *Journal of Pacific History*, 35: 3 (2000).

FOOD AND NUTRITION

Some Preliminary Comments

Food serves three basic functions for most living beings. Firstly, food creates energy required in the absorption and translocation of nutrients necessary for growth, sustenance, and biological and physical activities of the organism. Secondly, food supplies reducing agents indispensable in synthetic processes inside of cells. Thirdly, food purveys the materials—structural and catalytic chemical components of living cells—that are built through anabolism. When one of these functions is absent, living organisms substitute the deficiency with the others.

Nutrition is the process through which food substances are absorbed and used by living organisms. Commencing with the act of feeding, the process continues with digestion, where proteins are broken down into aminoacids. Subsequently, intestines absorb nutrients, which once integrated, are then distributed throughout the body for assimilation and metabolic transformation within each cell. The last stage is excretion of waste and toxins.

Food and nutrition are often confused, since both are intertwined. It is the nourishment found in food that after consumption is assimilated through the process of nutrition, in order to sustain life. *Food* is a generic term to cognate vegetal and animal organisms as a whole, in parts or secretions: flowers, fruits, leaves, shoots, roots, sheaths, milk, eggs, and muscles and inner organs, such as liver or kidneys.

Nutritional requirements of living organisms that enable the proper functioning of cells, maintaining their structure and controlling their metabolism, are approximately one hundred substances found in the environment. Generally, nutrients are chemical compounds of heavy molecular weight (starch, proteins, sugars, fibers, salts). Nutrients travel via the blood's circulation, to be absorbed by cells.

Eating is a biological necessity, determining life quality and health status of human beings. However, eating is a holistic human experience, representing pleasure for the senses, culinary aesthetics, communication and social cohesion tools, moral etiquette, core components of ceremonial and mourning rituals, and channels to strengthen *cultural and territorial identity*.

A Brief Diagnosis of the World's Food Situation

Nutritional dietary requirements of each individual vary according to age, gender, height, body complexion, physical activities, physiological state (growth, pregnancy, breast-feeding), health, and genetic and climatic factors. Throughout the history of humanity, portentous changes have occurred. From a culture of hunting and gathering, consuming mainly raw food, the agricultural revolution triggered a culinary revolution. After the domestication of plants and animals in different regions, more complex alimentary patterns emerged, engendering various culinary traditions.

Food extraction, processing, and presentation relate to cultural, environmental, and epidemiological conditions, as well as to habits, income and access to markets. Adverse conditions or imbalances of essential nutrients, such as proteins, carbohydrates, vitamins, and minerals occasion *dietary deficiencies*, which result in malnutrition, diseases, and in extreme cases, death. *Overconsumption* of calories produces obesity.

Malnutrition affects health and well-being of more than one third of the world's population. Two billion people are anemic, 3.7 billion suffer from iron deficiencies, and 24,000 die daily from hunger (FAO 2000b). Around 80% of estimated *hunger* concentrates in rural areas, especially among women and children, where it is more frequent and severe. Complex malnutrition cases are recurrent within adolescent mothers, whose conditions negatively affect their health and that of the fetus. Similar adverse malnutrition befalls fertile mothers, becoming pregnant while still breast-feeding.

Developing countries are increasingly dependent on food importation, which increased from 28% to 37% during 1970 and 1997. In the poorest countries, food imports account for more than 50% of consumption. An estimated 55 million people are malnourished in Latin America. Hunger is linked to poverty and deficient job opportunities. Discontinued rural policies and increasing dependency on food imports push peasant populations out of their lands into urban slums.

In the Third World as a whole, urbanization processes, reduction in social spending, and poor economic growth linked to high levels of population growth, have impeded improvement in living conditions. Latin America can be taken as an example for other developing countries. Periodic economic crises since the 1980s have produced two lost decades of development (CEPAL 2004). Poverty has increased in numbers and conditions defining this condition have worsened. Although food disposal has risen from 2,485 kcl to 2,570 kcl in twenty of the twenty-four countries belonging to the region, income inequalities translate to differential food conditions: Between 1990 and 2000, Haiti, Cuba, El Salvador, Venezuela, Guatemala, Mexico, and Argentina have increased their hunger rate. Guatemala, Honduras, Mexico, Haiti, Bolivia, Peru, Nicaragua, El Salvador, and Guyana are the countries with the highest chronic malnutrition and low economic growth.

Food production has improved during the last decades, but poverty, hunger, and preventable illnesses have simultaneously increased. Overall global consumption reached $24 billion in 1998. In 1996, the daily ingestion of calories per person in high human developed countries was 3,347 (11.6% more compared with 1976), with 102.7g of proteins (13% more); in medium developed countries, it was 2,696 calories (26.9% more) with 69.6g of proteins (33.7% more); and in low developed countries, 2,145 calories (1% less) with 51.0 g of proteins (4.4% less). Another indicator of undernourishment is infant low birth weight, which was 7% in high, 17% in medium, and 20% in low developed countries (UNDP 1999).

The lowest income quintile met only 72% of the minimal nutritional requirements in sub-Saharan Africa, 78% in Latin America, and 80% in the new independent states. The gap in Asia and sub-Saharan Africa is predicted to deteriorate, and only the highest of five income groups is projected to meet minimal nutritional requirements, given present food policies.

Over the next decade, the food gap is expected to widen. In thirty-five poor countries, nutritional requirements will fall short, and forty-seven countries are projected to reduce per capita consumption. This means new subsidies for agricultural surplus production and greater food power for the USA compared with the rest of the world.

Food Sovereignty Versus Food Security

Food sovereignty represents both a social and a personal right of individuals and communities to healthy, culturally appropriate food. Food security, on the other hand, means sufficient food for disposal by individuals or nations, once subtracting unused food. At a national level, it represents the sum of domestic produced food and imported food minus nonconsumed food.

The first definition represents a basic human right and an obligation to states and world networks to provide it. The second definition is a technical one, as it gives no responsibility to governments at any level. Furthermore, food security is defined as the balanced daily intake of proteins, carbohydrates, vitamins, and minerals necessary to sustain a healthy life. Food safety is also linked to hygiene and the prevention of food-borne diseases. The World Health Organization has confirmed that bacteria are the greatest threat to food safety, occurring in professional and domestic food handling.

The US Department of Agriculture evaluates national food security by "measuring the gaps between actual food consumption (domestic production, plus commercial imports, minus unused food and consumption targets)." The nutritional gap also measures minimal daily nutritional requirements, in relation to age and activities.

Purchasing power exacerbates food insecurity within the sixty-six poorest countries, given resource-access differentials. The richest fifth of the world population today accounts for 86% of global consumption, compared with the poorest fifth left with 1.3%. This means also that the remaining 60% only consume 12.7%. Africa disposes today 20% less food than twenty-five years ago and per capita consumption in industrialized countries is still rising (United Nations Developing Program 1998–2001).

For this reason, food insecurity resulting from extreme poverty is better defined as perverse poverty (Oswald 1990). Perversity lies in the fact that infants are condemned to be second-class citizens before birth, given irreversible brain damages and low birth weight, caused by mother's chronicle undernourishment.

Causes of Food Insecurity in Developing Countries

Hunger is not due to the gap between food production and population rates. Enough food is produced worldwide: 4.3 pounds of food per person a day; 2.5 pounds of grains, beans and nuts; about a pound of meat, milk, and eggs, and another pound of fruits and vegetables (Lappe 1998). Increasing food insecurity within countries and continents on the one hand, and greater production with fewer consumers on the other hand, are two sides of the same process: corporate agriculture.

Multinational companies (MNC) induce individual farmers to technological innovation and capital-intensive production processes, only feasible by undergoing heavy debts. As an example, an average poultry producer raises 240,000 birds each year. After paying its costs, "this prodigious (and inhumane) production earns the farmer only $12,000, or five cents per bird" (Gorelick). Only bigger farms can survive under these conditions. Such corporations monopolize almost every stage of processing, distribution, trade, and inputs of food production (seeds, fertilizers, pesticides, medicines, equipment, processors, transportation, marketing, and banking), and increasingly control natural resources (water, gas and oil).

Corporate agriculture also affects human health and the environment. Not enough is known about the human health effects caused by ingestion of controversial genetically modified organisms (GMO food) or cattle fed with these grains. However, hormones are used extensively with livestock, such as Bovine Somatropin, known to stimulate the hormone insulin-like growth factor 1. These hormones are linked to an increased incidence of breast cancer in premenopausal women and prostate cancer (180%) in men (Epstein), and greater vulnerability of the immune system.

The conjunction of these processes leads to an exclusive globalization, in economic, communicative and political terms, surpassing national borders and capacity of nation-states. The integration of regions into commercial blocks—the European Union, North American Free Trade Agreement (NAFTA), Mercado Común Sur (MERCOSUR), Asian-Pacific Economic Cooperation (APEC)—protects above all free circulation of commodities, intellectual property rights (TRIPS, an agreement on trade-related aspects of intellectual property rights, including trade in counterfeit goods, defended by the World Trade Organization [WTO]) and regulates potential commercial conflicts in favor of the industrialized nations. Additionally, the International Monetary Fund imposes structural adjustment policies in highly indebted countries, truncating agrarian reforms and substantially reducing subsidies and technological support for food production, given debt service payments. Cheap prices for food and primary products in world markets are artificially dropped, and most technological innovations are profit-driven rather than need-oriented.

In Third World countries, corporate agriculture reduces national food sovereignty and diminishes food security at local level, as well as pushing peasants off the land. Today in Latin America and North Africa, food imports represent around 40% of consumption. Food aid, increasing imports of basic grains, substitution of food by export crops, and technology-linked agribusinesses destroy rural policies in the South. Countries are exposed to foreign food power, depending on international markets and prices. Unequal terms of trade—low raw material prices and high input costs—clearly prevent poor people from buying food.

Malnutrition and hunger are both part of a complex and interrelated system of social, agricultural, economic, political, and ecological realities. In poor countries, hunger is exacerbated by high indebtedness and debt servicing; the substitution of local foodstuffs with export commodities—vegetables, tropical fruits and flowers—in order to earn foreign currency to service debts; the raising of livestock instead of subsistence crops; the submission of local and regional markets to the interests of international monopolies; forced bankruptcy of small farmers and peasants facing high interest rates, constant increases in agro-chemical and other products; and the falling prices of peasant's agricultural products because of international artificial prices (dumping). In addition, natural disasters and global warming, as well as food aid to countries south of the Sahara, which prolongs their situation of dependency, turns peasants into migrants, furthers dependency, and generalizes a deficient transnational food culture.

Unless there is food sovereignty at the local and national level, no country in the world will be immune to food power and starvation. Food self-sufficiency is only possible when integrating private and public enterprises, economic, social, commercial, productive, political, and human ethics with gender and social equity, under a clear defined sustainable framework to overcome inequality.

ÚRSULA OSWALD S.

References and Further Reading

Binswanger, Hans, and Ernst Lutz. "Agricultural Trade Barriers, Trade Negotiations, and the Interests of Developing Countries." Washington, DC: World Bank, 2000.

CEPAL. *Balance Preliminar de la Economía en América Latina*. Santiago de Chile: CEPAL, 2004.

Epstein, Samuel S. *The Cancer Prevention Coalition*, Washington, DC: 1998, and *Science*, January 23, 1999.

FAO. *A Millennium without Hunger*. Rome: FAO, 2000a.

Gorelick, Steven. "Solution for a Farming Future." *The Ecologist*, 30:4, 2000.

Lappe, F.M., J. Collins, and P. Rosset. *World Hunger: Twelve Myths*. New York: Grove Press, 1998.

Mosley, Henry. "An Analytical Framework for the Study of Child Survival in Developing Countries," *Population and Development Review*, 10 Suppl.: 25–45, 1984.

Newman, Lucile F., ed. *Hunger in History, Food Shortage, Poverty, and Deprivation*. Cambridge and Oxford: Basil Blackwell, 1990.

Olweny, C. "Bioethics in Developing Countries: Ethics of Scarcity and Sacrifice." *Journal of Medical Ethics*, 20:3:169–174, 1994.

Oswald, Úrsula, Estrategias de Supervivencia en la Ciudad de México (Survival Strategies in Mexico City). Cuernavaca, Mexico: CRIM-UNAM, 1990.

Oswald Spring, Úrsula, "Sustainable Development with Peace Building and Human Security," in: EOLSS/ UNESCO, *Our Fragile World: Challenges and Opportunities for Sustainable Development, Encyclopedia on Life Support System (EOLSS)*. London: UNESCO: Section 2, 2001.

Sen, Amartya. *Inequality Reexamined*. New York: Russell Sage Foundation and Harvard University Press, 1992.

Shiva, Vandana, Asfar H. Jafri, Gitanjali Bedi, and Radha Holla-Bhar. *The Enclosure of the Commons, Biodiversity, Indigenous Knowledge, and Intellectual Property Rights*. New Delhi: Research Foundation for Science, Technology, and Ecology, 1997.

UNDP. *Human Development Report, 1997–2004*. London: UNDP, 1997–2004.

World Bank. *Assault on World Poverty*. Baltimore, MD, and London: John Hopkins University Press, 1995

FOREIGN DIRECT INVESTMENT (FDI)

Introduction

In the post–World War II era, foreign direct investment (FDI) by multinational (or transnational) corporations has increased greatly. During the colonial era, multinationals corporations (MNCs) from colonial powers had set up subsidiaries and factories, particularly in regions endowed with natural resources such as silver, gold, and, later on, oil and other minerals. The abundance and proximity of raw materials, coupled with cheap labor, meant high profits for parent companies. In those days, FDI consisted mainly of firms from colonial countries doing business in overseas colonies and territories. Thus, FDI was considered as a form of exploitation of developing—but resource-endowed—nations

In the modern era, FDI has, in general, been viewed more favorably. From the standpoint of transnational corporations, the focus is no longer exclusively on labor costs and raw materials. From the viewpoint of host countries, FDI is seen as a source of finance and a much-needed channel to access advanced technology. However, it was not until the early 1970s that policymakers began considering FDI as a potentially important contributor to economic development. In the 1970s and early 1980s, developing nations employed tax incentives (exemptions) and protectionary measures to attract FDI.

Many of the early projects targeted import substitution. In the late 1980s and early 1990s, most developing nations have come to realize that tax incentives were not sufficient long-term measures. Advised and/ or pressured by international lending institutions such as the International Monetary Fund (IMF) and the World Bank, many developing countries have undertaken significant reforms including trade and financial liberalization. A number of countries have liberalized current and capital accounts and introduced flexible exchange rate regimes, with the view to attract more FDI. While the reforms have been viewed as factors that fostered inward FDI into these countries, the experiences of emerging countries in Southeast Asia and Latin America in the 1990s points to the potential dangers of increased openness to foreign capital.

FDI has increasingly been considered a major indicator of globalization. Yet, a number of scholars and policymakers still view the effects of inward FDI as a combination of positive and costly (if not negative) effects.

There are two major reasons for the growing interest in FDI in the last decade. First, the influence of MNCs has been increasing over the last three decades of the twentieth century. This influence was strengthened by the ability of MNCs to have large, integrated operations around the world. Second, the role of FDI as a source of capital and a major tool in the fight against poverty began to be emphasized due to the decline in official development aid. While FDI to developing countries has increased, official aid has been falling.

Definition and Terminology

FDI—also called direct foreign investment (DFI)— refers to the acquisition and control of foreign assets. FDI includes activities that are organized and controlled by firms abroad; i.e., outside their country of origin (where their headquarters and their main decision-making centers are located). The extent of control or ownership may depend on the country. The World Trade Organization (WTO) defines FDI as follows: "[FDI] occurs when an investor based in one country (the home country) acquires an asset in another country (the host country) with the intent to manage the asset." Thus, FDI can be divided into three categories. The first is "equity capital," which is the value of the MNC's investment in the shares of an enterprise in a foreign country. The second comprises "reinvested earnings," which are the MNC's share of affiliate earnings not distributed as dividends or remitted to the MNC. The third category is labeled "other capital" and includes short- or long-term borrowing and lending of funds between the MNC and the affiliate. The establishment of "new" production or distribution facilities in a foreign country is called Greenfield FDI. If the MNC acquires a foreign company (entirely or partially), it is referred to as FDI by acquisition. Currently, most FDI comprises mergers, acquisitions, or takeovers.

The US government defines FDI as "the ownership, or control of 10% or more of an enterprise's voting securities, or the equivalent interest in an unincorporated business." Some countries place an upper limit to foreign ownership of home businesses, but the 10% minimum is widely used around the world. The country where these activities are located is referred to as the host country, while the country of origin is referred to as home country. When FDI flows from one country to another, it is referred to as inward FDI for the host country and outward FDI (also called "direct investment abroad") for the home country. The investor is typically referred to as the parent firm and the asset owned (totally or partially) abroad as the affiliate or subsidiary.

FDI can serve either as an export replacement (import substitution from the standpoint of the host country) or export platform; production in the host country is exported to other countries. FDI is one of the main components of the capital account of a country's balance of payment. The United Nations Conference on Trade and Development (UNCTAD) is the principal source of data and commentary on the state and trends of world FDI. It produces an annual report, the World Investment Report (WIR), which includes figures, tables, and charts depicting the behavior of world FDI and often focuses its analysis on a specific topic. For example, WIR 2001 ("Promoting Linkages") focused on the issue of linkages between foreign affiliates of multinational enterprises and local companies in developing countries; while WIR 1999 ("Foreign Direct Investment and the Challenge of Development") emphasized the impact of FDI on key objectives of economic development. These effects included increasing financial resources for investment, enhancing technological capabilities, boosting export competitiveness, generating and upgrading employment, and protecting the environment.

The impact of FDI is often contrasted with the effect of foreign portfolio investment (FPI). FPI comprises the holding of financial assets but does not involve control or participation in management operations of the firm issuing the securities. The main motivations for FPI are risk diversification and high returns; whereas FDI is motivated by different factors and is regarded as a less volatile, hence less destabilizing, form of foreign capital. FDI tends to be quite resilient during financial crises and thus may be a more desirable form of capital inflow to developing countries.

Theories of FDI

Modernization School

This school includes the neoclassical (perfect market approach), Ownership, Location, and Internalization (OLI) paradigm, and industrial organization theories (imperfect market approach). The neoclassical theory posits that free trade and free markets would lead to higher growth and increased FDI flows, and that developing countries will be able to grow through this channel by implementing the liberalization policies of developed countries (natural order of development stages). The neoclassical theory stresses the link between free trade and FDI. The industrial organization theory argues that market imperfections (such as the existence of oligopolies) lead to horizontal or vertical integration, and hence FDI is more likely to take place in oligopolies. The OLI paradigm (= O + L + I), developed by John Dunning, represents a mix of three distinct FDI theories. Each theory emphasizes a different focus. The "O" represents "ownership" advantages. These are firm specific advantages that address the question of "Why go abroad?" The "L" refers to "location" advantages and addresses the issue of "Where should the MNC locate?" Finally, the "I" refers to "internalization" advantages and focuses on the question of "How will the firm go abroad?" The OLI paradigm is an eclectic theory of FDI that focuses on FDI determinants from the perspective of the firm.

The Dependency School (Dependencia/Neo-Marxist and Structuralist Theories)

The neo-Marxist theory postulates that the repatriation of profits from developing countries worsens these countries' terms of trade; and the structuralist theory claims that countries or regions on the periphery are marginalized since their resources are being exploited by prosperous centers. Thus, dependency theories view FDI as a cause of increased spatial inequality in economic development within and across countries.

The Integrative School (Institutional Theories)

This school includes the bargaining theory, integrative theory, and "institutional FDI fitness" theory. The bargaining and integrative approaches focus on the determinants of FDI from the viewpoint of both host countries and foreign investors. The institutional fitness theory, formally outlined by Saskia K.S. Wilhelms (1998), is an integrative theory that emphasizes macro-, micro-, and meso-economic variables. Where the meso-economic variables include institutions linking the host economy and the foreign firm. This theory focuses on the public and private sector interaction. In general, institutional theories focus on FDI in developing economies and provide analyses useful to researchers of the topics of economic growth and development.

Another way to distinguish among theories is to group them into macro-level and micro-level approaches. At the macro level, early mainstream theories included the neoclassical and the dependency theories discussed above. The three early conventional micro-level theories used approaches that focused on different dimensions of the firm behavior. First, there was an emphasis on the ownership advantage and market structure (Hymer 1960). Hymer tried to solve the puzzle as to why firms would prefer FDI, which is more costly than exports or licensing, by highlighting the fact that MNCs do not operate in perfectly competitive industries. Then, the focus was directed to the location advantage (Vernon, 1966). Finally, there was an emphasis on the internalization advantage (Buckley and Casson 1976). These conventional approaches emphasized FDI from the viewpoint of the firm and examined the reasons firms invest in foreign countries. Additional theories focused on market structure (monopolistic or oligopolistic) and highlighted the rivalry aspects in global markets. Oligopolistic industries tend to undertake the bulk of FDI as they compete in the global market. The micro theories of FDI also include industrial organization theories and the OLI paradigm, which nicely combines the three conventional firm-focused theories.

A more recent strand of the literature emphasizes the issues from the standpoint of host countries, particularly developing nations. In general, three broad areas are examined. The first is whether developing nations should welcome FDI. The second area concerns the study of what host countries have to offer foreign investors. In other words, it focuses on the determinants of inward FDI, including sociopolitical and economic variables, and policy indicators (incentives, markets, and prices). The third area focuses on evaluating the effects of FDI on a wide range of macroeconomic and microeconomic indicators in host countries.

Determinants of FDI

Until recently, most developing countries have had a negligible share of outward FDI. Thus, economists and policymakers tend to focus mainly on the effects of inward FDI on economic development and growth. To study the determinants of FDI, researchers first specify the dependent variable. FDI (as a dependent variable) may be net—inward minus outward FDI—or simply inward FDI flows. Second, depending on what we want to test, the focus may be on FDI flows or FDI stocks. Models examining the behavior of inward FDI to developing economies have used a wide spectrum of variables including market size, economic growth, human capital, physical capital, financial and trade reforms, geography, and institutions. Perhaps the most encompassing model is that studied by Wilhelms (1998), who developed an integrative model to test the determinants of net inflows of FDI in emerging economies. The model includes four main dimensions (concepts). The first concept represents government fitness, which in turn includes several variables. The variables included in this dimension are a measures of economic openness (parallel market exchange rate premium, export marketing board, and import quotas), and legal and administrative impartiality and transparency (country risk, rule of law, and corruption). The second dimension is market fitness. It includes "overall market fitness" that covers several variables. These variables are gross domestic product (GDP) to proxy for economic development, total population to proxy for market size, an indicator of rural infrastructure and linkages represented by population density in rural areas, trade volume, and tax revenues to measure taxation of the private sector. Market fitness also comprises "capital market fitness," which includes domestic credit provided by the banking sector (relative to GDP). In addition, this dimension includes a measure of market linkages represented by an indicator for development of energy infrastructure. The third component is educational fitness, which covers indicators of basic education. The last dimension refers to sociocultural fitness. It includes a dummy variable for the region and a dummy for time changes. The empirical tests reveal that most of these variables are important determinants of FDI. Economic openness, a strong rule of law, and low corruption foster inward FDI. While FDI does not seem to respond to the level of per capita income, implying that countries with low levels of economic development have succeeded in attracting FDI. As argued by Wilhelms, this is consistent with the fact that FDI tolerates low economic development while portfolio investment targets mainly developed countries. Taxes deter investors and hence have a negative effect on FDI; whereas the volume of trade, domestic credit provided by the banking sector, and market linkages fitness attract inward FDI. The sociocultural dimension also is a significant determinant of FDI.

Numerous other studies have focused on particular countries or regions. A study that examined the macroeconomic impact of FDI flows to China following the implementation of the "open-door policy" in late 1978 shows that FDI had significantly contributed to economic growth in China; through its contribution to domestic capital formation, export enhancement, and job creation. The findings also indicate that, thanks to its technology transfer component, export promoting and enabling of more intersectoral flows of capital and labor, inward FDI to China had improved the productive efficiency of domestic industries (Haishun Sun [1998], Foreign Investment and Economic Development in China, 1979–1996, Ashgate Publishing). In the same line of research, tests of the FDI-led growth hypothesis in Brazil, Chile, Colombia, Mexico, and Venezuela (these countries received most of the FDI to the region in 1970–1991) provide evidence that trade regimes and domestic policy variables are major determinants of FDI and economic growth (De Melo 1999). Some studies have investigated the role of corruption and non-transparency (Kaufman et al. 1999) on inward FDI. In general, the findings indicate that corruption and nontransparency deter FDI. The geography of international investments also has been examined by a number of studies. One important study found that, after adjusting for market share, a substantial share of FDI remains close to the home country. After adjusting for distance, the results show that the main determinant of FDI is market size. It also is shown that FDI is more geographically concentrated than exports or production as a whole (Schatz and Venables 2000).

In view of the diversity of the determinants of FDI, it had become necessary to have a simple index that can serve as a "rough-and-ready" indicator of the country's ability to attract inward FDI. In 2001, United Nations Conference on Trade and Development (UNCTAD) introduced the inward FDI index (World Investment Report 2001). This index measures foreign direct investment relative to a country's share of global GDP, exports, and employment. Index values exceeding unity indicate countries that are particularly attractive to foreign investors. As stated by the UNCTAD, the index "captures the ability of countries to attract FDI after taking into account their size and competitiveness." The index confirms the wide disparities among countries. For example, in 1998–2000, fifty-three countries had an inward FDI index higher than unity. Five countries had an inward FDI index value of one. On the other hand, more than half (seventy-nine) of the countries included in the study had an index lower than one. This comprised countries with negative indexes (for example, Yemen had an index equal to −0.8). Belgium and Luxembourg had the highest index (17.3). However, while the index may serve as a tool of benchmarking country attractiveness of FDI, the UNCTAD warns that the index must be supplemented by other elements such as policy and economic variables.

In sum, although the empirical literature on the determinants of FDI does not always provide definite conclusions, it does tend to support the following claims. First, the impact of liberalization (trade openness and export orientation) as a determinant of FDI can be quite significant. Countries that have liberalized trade and markets tend to attract higher FDI. Second, to attract FDI into developing countries, economic growth is not a major determinant provided other indicators—such as transparency, rule of law human capital, and political stability—are strong. Third, market size is important (the case of China) when other elements are weak. Fourth, the influence of geography remains important. Fifth, cultural links and colonial heritage can play a major role. For example, in 1992–1994, the United Kingdom invested $1.3 billion in South Africa and only $90 million in Morocco, whereas France invested $287 million in Morocco and only $56 million in South Africa. It is important to remember that the list of the determinants of FDI can be large and vague and tends to change over time. In 1998, the UNCTAD dedicated a major part of the annual World Investment Report to the study of the determinants of inward FDI. It concluded that the main determinants are "the policy framework, business facilitation measures, and economic factors." Obviously, this could involve more than a dozen variables.

FDI and Economic Development in the Host Country

The theoretical literature on the influence of inward FDI on economic development suggests that there are significant benefits but also some potential costs. The benefits include positive effects on economic growth, exports, firm productivity, human capital, and other spillover effects to the economy of the host country.

The role of FDI as purveyor of technology, knowledge, and other intangible assets has been acknowledged by many scholars and policymakers. It is through this channel that FDI is thought to have the most significant effect on economic growth. Thanks to FDI, a developing country may be able to access advanced technology from industrialized countries, adopt this technology, and perhaps even adapt it to country-specific realities. At least in theory, the diffusion of advanced technologies could allow developing countries to leapfrog to a higher stage of economic development. After all, Japan's early stages of industrialization were not based on inventing new technologies but on adopting and adapting existing technologies from more industrially advanced countries. Some theoretical studies have found that licensing and joint ventures with local firms lead to technology transfer to the host country as this implies sharing of know-how and experiences. However, empirical evidence in support of this claim is rather weak. In addition, studies show that FDI will more likely benefit the host country if one or more of the following conditions are fulfilled. First, there is a large cost of communication between the headquarters and the production plant (located in the host country). Second, there are substantial intermediate goods in the final product being produced in the host country. Third, the variety of intermediate goods in home and host country is not very different. Host countries will more likely be harmed if reverse conditions prevailed (Rodriguez-Clare 1996).

The theoretical literature suggests that the potential costs include worsening of the balance of payments and negative effects on tax revenue collection due to transfer pricing. There may also exist adverse effects on domestic firms when the competition effect—domestic firms competing against foreign firms—is stronger than the technology effect. This may deprive the host country from the opportunity to develop its own (domestic) know-how and technologies. FDI may also cause a damaging effect to sociocultural values due to possible abuse of host country's traditions. In addition, governments tend to be concerned about the destabilizing effect of FDI when there is divestment. Though FDI is less volatile than portfolio investment, there are cases where divestment by MNCs exacerbated financial and macroeconomic crises. In addition, researchers and NGOs have recently begun to focus on the impact of FDI on labor standards (including the issue of child labor) and the environment in developing countries.

On the empirical side, many studies have examined the effects of FDI on economic growth and on the components of income or GDP. FDI contributes assets such as capital to create new businesses or expand existing ones, and technology transfer. It also provides the host country with intangible assets such as know-how, managerial skills, and spillovers to other industries. Due to linkages and spillovers, other industries can benefit from new opportunities created in export sectors as a result of linking to foreign markets and MNCs. FDI can also promote research and development activities in the host countries. The indirect benefits to domestic firms, however, are not automatic. The positive effects on economic growth have been proclaimed by international institutions such as the UNCTAD and the World Bank. A comprehensive World Bank study (Klein et al. 2001) argues that FDI "remains among the most effective tools in the fight against poverty." Another study that examined the impact of capital inflows on investment in fifty-eight developing nations for the 1978–1995 period has shown that a one-dollar increase in FDI leads to a one-dollar increase in domestic investment while portfolio inflows had only a negligible influence on domestic investment (Bosworth and Collins 1999).

Some empirical studies have focused on specific regions. Studies of the experiences of Indonesia, Malaysia, and the Philippines indicate that, although the experiences have varied, FDI constituted a vital ingredient in export-led growth. The role of foreign firms in the electronic sector—which was the fastest growing sector—was quite important. However, because FDI promotion was on a selective basis, other industries did not develop at the same pace. Thus, these countries could not take full advantage of spillovers from foreign firms to domestic firms. Other empirical work focused on specific projects. Encarnation and Wells (1986) analyzed the impact of fifty FDI projects on national income and have found that not all projects were income enhancing. Overall, 55%–75% of the projects had a positive effect on income, while 25%–45% had a negative effect on national income. The main reason for the negative impact was protectionist measures granted to the firms undertaking the FDI projects.

Consequently, it is not always wise to assume that there is an automatic positive effect of FDI on economic growth. Empirical findings indicate that human capital (education and other skills) as well as institutions are key ingredients to attract FDI and also to ensure a positive effect of FDI on income. A study that examined the way FDI affects economic growth (Borensztein et al. 1998) argues that the stock of human capital in the host country limits the absorptive capability of a developing country. Other researchers have found that the benefits are contingent upon certain features of the host country. In particular, trade and financial liberalization are crucial. Additionally, domestic firms may be harmed by increased FDI inflows. For example, empirical research has found that inward FDI may have negative effects on productivity in domestic firms in Morocco. Similar findings were reported for firms in Venezuela. This suggests that when the negative competition effect dominates the positive technology effect, productivity in the domestic sector may fall.

A line of research that has been growing in the 1990s focuses on the impact of FDI on wages and labor standards in developing countries. While wages for skilled labor often increase as a result of higher FDI, the inequality between skilled and unskilled labor earnings has widened. FDI into China, for example, has contributed to the worsening of the environment, an increase in interregional inequality, and increased round-tripping of the capital of Chinese firms. Domestic firms would send funds outside China and bring them back as foreign capital to take advantage of FDI-promoting incentives (Sun 1998). Thus far, there has been no empirical finding in support of a relationship between FDI and worsening in labor standards in developing countries. Moreover, researchers at the World Bank as well as UNCTAD have investigated the effect of inward FDI on the environment. In general, empirical studies have found fairly weak support for the "pollution haven" hypothesis.

Recent Trends

From an economic theory standpoint, we would expect to see countries with lower levels of capital, and hence higher marginal returns on capital, attract foreign capital. One of the channels through which FDI enhances growth is productivity and efficiency. Economic theory stipulates that capital would flow to where it is scarce: i.e., where there are higher marginal returns. This would enhance global efficiency. However, the facts are not in support of this assertion. Africa is quite rich in natural resources and low-cost labor. Capital tends to be scarce implying a higher marginal return on investment. Yet, Africa in general has not been very successful in attracting foreign capital. In fact, the data published by UNCTAD clearly show that Africa's share of global FDI inflows has actually fallen over time.

The share of Africa in world FDI inflows fell from an average of 2.13% in the first half of the 1980s to 1.23% in the second half of the 1990s, while the shares of Asia and Latin have increased substantially (particularly emerging economies in Asia). In addition, the share of industrial countries remained at an average of two-thirds of world inward FDI. Inward FDI going to developing countries nearly doubled in the early 1990s (1991–1993) relative to the second half of the 1980s (UNCTAD). While these surges of FDI inflows could indicate that developing countries can be successful in attracting FDI, the concentration of FDI remains regional. For most of the 1990s, Asia received the largest share of FDI, and Latin America received the second largest share, while Africa, has remained quite, marginalized. Thus, in terms of promoting economic growth and alleviating poverty in Africa, FDI is not a main contributor, as Africa receives very little amounts. On the other hand, inward FDI to some Asian and Latin American emerging countries was sizeable and is believed to have promoted human development and economic growth. Equally important is the concentration of FDI in specific sectors. In Africa, most FDI is concentrated in the exploitation of natural resources (raw materials). According to some researchers (including those at the World Bank), the effects of such foreign investment on the economy of the host country are not clear. In addition to the potential effect on the environment, the depletion of natural resources constitutes a cost to the developing country that is not properly incorporated in the computation of GDP and economic growth.

FDI outflows from developing economies in Asia doubled in 2000. This is a new trend that indicates a significant change in the origin of FDI, which in the past was almost exclusively from developed countries. It also suggests that countries receiving of FDI from developing countries may not be able to access advanced technology usually associated with FDI from industrial countries such as the G-7 countries. According to UNCTAD (2001), when comparing inward FDI in 2000 and 1985, we observe that in 2000, FDI reached more countries and involved higher amounts. In 2000, twenty-three developing countries received an average amount of FDI greater than $1 billion each, compared with only six countries in 1985. Outward FDI experienced a similar trend. In 1985, only one developing country had outward FDI flows of more than $1 billion. At the end of the 1990s, this number increased to thirteen countries.

Since the 1970s, world FDI flows have been growing and the share of developing countries has increased during recent years. In the 1980s and 1990s, FDI flows have risen in absolute terms and relative to trade and GDP. Between 1984 and 1987, FDI outflows have almost tripled, to surpass the growth rate of world GDP and world trade. While in the 1970s and 1980s, FDI had been mainly targeting developed countries; the flows to developing countries have grown to reach about 40% in 1996. Yet, the bulk of FDI flowing to developing countries is limited to a group of countries in Southeast Asia and Latin America.

In the 1970s, outward FDI came mainly from developed countries. But in the 1990s, there were significant amounts coming from developing countries. In 1970, 99% of world outward FDI came from developed countries, with about 91% from what became known as the G-7 countries, with the US leading the group in terms of the volume of FDI outflows (60% of the total). In 1993, the share of FDI originating from developed countries fell to 94%. Asian countries contributed the bulk of the remaining 6%. The US share fell from 60% in 1970 to about 30% in 1993. In 2000, the average share of Africa in total world FDI was 0.6%, much lower than its average share in the 1980s. The shares of developing Asian countries and Latin America were 11.3% and 6.8%, respectively. The share of industrial countries has been around two-thirds of total FDI for both periods the downward trend in the growth rate of FDI received by Africa is a disturbing phenomenon.

In 2000, the share of developed countries in world FDI inflows was slightly above 79%. China has had the lion's share of FDI inflows to developing countries. In 1978, China introduced the open-door policy to many coastal provinces, and the result has been a significant inflow of foreign capital and expansion of Chinese exports.

MINA BALIAMOUNE

See also Globalization: Impact on Development

References and Further Reading

Borensztein, Eduardo, José De Gregorio, and Jong-Wha Lee."How Does Foreign Direct Investment Affect Growth?" *Journal of International Economics*, Vol. 45, pp. 115–135, 1998.

Bosworth, Barry P., and Susan M. Collins. "Capital Flows to Developing Economies: Implications for Saving and Investment," Brookings Papers on Economic Activity:1. Washington, DC: Brookings Institution, pp. 143–169, 1999.

Buckley, P. J., and M. C. Casson. *The Future of Multinational Enterprise*. London: Macmillan, 1976.

De Mello, Luiz R. Jr., *Foreign Direct Investment-Led Growth: Evidence from Time Series and Panel Data*. Oxford Economic Papers, 51–81, 1999.

Drabek, Zdenek, and Warren Payne. "The Impact of Transparency on Foreign Direct Investment," Staff Working Paper ERAD-99-02, Geneva: World Trade Organization, 1999.

Dunning, J. H. "Trade, Location of Economic Activity and the MNE: A Search for an Eclectic Approach." In *The International Allocation of Economic Activity*, B. Ohlin, P.O., 1977.

Encarnation, Dennis, and Louis T. Wells, in *Investing in Development: New Roles for Private Capital?* Theodore Moran, ed. Washington, DC: Overseas Development Council, 1986.

Hymer, S.H. *The International Operations of National Firms: A Study of Direct Foreign Investment*. Cambridge, MA: MIT Press, 1960; republished 1976.

Kaufman, Daniel, and Shang-Jin Wei. "Does Grease Money Speed Up the Wheels of Commerce?", Policy Research Working Paper 2254. Washington, DC: World Bank, 1999.

Klein, M. C. Aaron, and B. Hadjimichael. "FDI and Poverty Reduction," Policy Research Working Paper 2613, Washington, DC: World Bank, 2001.

Maskus, Keith E., and Guifang Yang. "Intellectual Property Rights, Foreign Direct Investment, and Competition Issues in Developing Countries," in *International Journal of Technology Management*, 10:22–34, 2000.

Rodriguez-Clarke, A. "Multinationals, Linkages, and Economic Development," *American Economic Review*, 86:4, pp. 852–873, 1996.

Shatz, H. J., and A. J. Venables. *The Geography of International Investment: The Oxford Handbook of Economic Geography*, eds. Gordon L. Clarke, Maryann P. Feldman, and Meric S. Gertler. Oxford: Oxford University Press, 2000.

Vernon, Raymond. "International Investment and International Trade in the Product Cycle," *Quarterly Journal of Economics*, 83:190–207, 1966.

Wilhelms, Saskia K. S. "Foreign Direct Investment and Its Determinants in Emerging Economies," African Economic Policy Discussion Paper No. 9. Washington, DC: United States Agency for International Development, 1998.

FOX, VICENTE

Vicente Fox Quesada was born in Mexico City on July 2, 1942. While he was still a boy, his parents returned to the family ranch of his Irish-born grandfather. Raised in a comfortable, traditional rural environment and educated in private schools, he graduated in business administration from the Jesuit Iberoamericana University in 1964. His first job was with the American multinational corporation, Coca-Cola de Mexico.

Offered a promotion that would have required him to move to the US, he chose to remain in Mexico. Fox left Coca-Cola and returned to Guanajuato. He joined his family's agricultural and industrial enterprise, the Grupo Fox. A business and civic leader, he joined the Partido Acción Nacional (National Action Party, PAN). It was the traditional conservative opposition party to the Partido Revolucionario Institucional (Institutionalized Revolutionary Party, PRI). Firmly in power throughout the twentieth century, PRI considered itself the guardian of the Mexican

Revolution. At the beginning of the century that movement had overthrown repressive, elite political forces representing foreign economic and domestic cultural and religious interests.

PRI was committed to national development through government control. Nationalist and secular, it was hostile to business. This nationalist and nationalizing policy reached a height during 1970s and early 1980s. However, consequent debt, recession, and unemployment, together with chronic corruption and repression, brought PRI under severe criticism. It attempted to generate development and the growth of jobs through policies more open to foreign, private enterprises and investment. Thereby the appeal of PAN rose in this atmosphere more favorable to its ideology and goals.

In 1988, Fox successfully ran for Congress. In 1995, he was elected governor of Guanajuato and became a rising national political star. Eyeing the Mexican presidential race for 2000, he presented encouraging private enterprise and international investment. He focused on education and the provision of microloans to support widespread development of small businesses. He worked to prosecute political corruption, reforming the police and judicial systems.

In 2000, Fox became the first opposition party member to be elected president of Mexico in seventy-one years. His victory, in alliance with the Green Party of Mexico, was an extraordinary political and ideological reversal in Mexican history. However, his presidency has not seen unmitigated success. Unemployment continues to be high along with crime and corruption. The US even cut off the hope of employment through emigration as it further restricted its borders subsequent to the events of September 11, 2001. Worldwide recession during the first years of the twenty-first century reduced investment in Mexico. The PRI continues in power with a majority of state governorships and seats in Congress, blocking much of PAN's program of economic and government reforms.

EDWARD A. RIEDINGER

See also Mexico; Mexico: History and Economic Development; Mexico: International Relations; Party of the Institutionalized Revolution (PRI)

References and Further Reading

Beer, Caroline C. *Electoral Competition and Institutional Change in Mexico*. Notre Dame, IN: University of Notre Dame Press, 2003.
Domínguez, Jorge I., and Chappell H. Lawson, eds. *Mexico's Pivotal Democratic Election: Candidates, Voters, and the Presidential Campaign of 2000*. Stanford, CA: Stanford University Press, 2004.
Grayson, George W. *Mexico: Changing of the Guard*. New York: Foreign Policy Association, 2001.
Preston, Julian, and Samuel Dillon. *Opening Mexico: The Making of a Democracy*. New York: Farrar, Straus, and Giroux, 2004.

FRANCOPHONIE INSTITUTIONNELLE

The Francophonie Institutionnelle was established to enhance cooperation between the French language native-speaking and foreign learners and their countries. The Francophonie Institutionnelle is an intergovernmental organization with forty-nine members states in addition to four associated states and ten observer states. The institution is composed of nine main bodies and subsidiary organs: the Summit of Heads of States and Governments, Permanent Council for Francophonie, Ministerial Conference for Francophonie, Secretary General, International Governmental Agency for Francophonie, and Parliamentary Association for Francophonie. Subsidiary organs are: International Association for Francophonie specialists, Senghor University, TV5 Channel, and University Agency for Francophonie.

The secretary general is appointed by the foreign ministers conference for a period of four years. As the highest authority of the general secretariat and subsidiary organs, the secretary general is responsible for implementing the international policies of the institution and supporting multilateral cooperation. He is also responsible for carrying out action plans adopted by the institution and the secretary general, in addition to supervising the implementation of the resolutions and recommendations of the summits and the Francophonie conferences of foreign ministers.

The general secretary of the institution is Abdou Diouf, the former prime minister (1970–1981) and president (1981–2000) of Senegal. He succeeded Francophonie Institutionnelle's first general secretary, Boutros Boutros-Ghali. Francophonie Institutionnelle's six major fields of interests are: education, economics and development, cultural diversification, peace, democracy, and human rights.

Francophonie Institutionnelle is keen to cooperate with the major regional and international organizations in the world. For example, it cooperates with League of Arab States in the cultural and educational aspects as well as with the United Nations specialized organizations and agencies for crisis management and peacekeeping in the member states.

Francophonie Institutionnelle has four permanent missions to the United Nations headquarters in New York and Geneva, in addition to a mission to the

European Union in Belgium, the African Union, and the Economic Committee for Africa in Addis Ababa in Ethiopia.

NILLY KAMAL EL-AMIR

References and Further Reading

Ghali, Boutros Boutros, *et.al. Francophonie and the Arab World*. Paris: Institute of Arab World, 2002.

Marchal, Roland. (France and Africa: The Emergence of Essential Reforms) *International Affairs*, 47:2 (April 1998).

Olsen, Gorm Rye, "Western Europe's Relations with Africa since the End of the Cold War," *Journal of Modern African Studies*, Vol. 2 (1997).

Shalabi, Ibrahim. *International Organization: The International Regional and Specialized Organization*, Beirut: El-Dar El-Gamia, 1992.

FREE MARKET ECONOMY

A free market economy is one in which individual economic agents make voluntary decisions based upon their own self-interest. Economic agents include consumers, taxpayers, firms, employers, employees, lobbies, trade unions, government workers, etc. Although agents freely make decisions based upon purely internal incentives, Adam Smith (1776) first demonstrated that such self-interested choices can, under plausible circumstances, guide the economy as if by an "invisible hand" to socially optimal production and consumption patterns.

The Gains from Trade

Why does economic activity generate benefits? Consider an economy in which two agents produce and consume just two goods. If each individual possesses "absolute advantage" in producing a different good, meaning that each can produce one good using fewer resources than the other, the gains from specialized production and trade are clear. However, even if one individual has absolute advantage in the production of both goods, both individuals can still benefit from specialization and exchange. This reality obtains because even with absolute advantage in producing both goods, the production advantage is relatively larger in one good than in the other. Given limited time and energy, each individual must forgo producing some amount of one good, its "opportunity cost," in order to generate a unit of the other product. Opportunity costs of the two goods are reciprocals, so each agent has a lower opportunity cost in precisely one

of the goods—the "comparative advantage" product. Specialized production therefore maximizes aggregate output. Moreover, neither agent would accept less consumption with specialization vis-à-vis through self-sufficiency, each individual must be better off under specialization. Note that this analysis applies equally well to individuals, firms, and even nations. Nations that trade are better off than they could be in isolation.

One can, therefore, consider the free market economy to generate the same outcome as a benign social planner whose interest is solely in maximizing the well-being of the society. However, in order to accomplish this task, the social planner would have to know the incentive structure, abilities, resources, etc., of every economic agent in the society. The infeasibility of that requirement is the reason that alternative economic models that rely on social planning, such as socialism and communism, have failed to generate strong economies. Attaining the knowledge requisite for coordination of all economic activities is impossible.

The free market has its own way of achieving economic coordination—through market prices. The price of any good or service is determined by the interactions among relevant economic agents. The information contained in the price must therefore summarize all of the individual demand functions for all consumers, including relative valuations of similar and alternative goods or services and all information about producers of the good or service, including resource prices, transaction costs, technologies, etc. Furthermore, the free market summarizes this tremendous amount of information with a single number, the price, which consumers and producers compare with prices for other goods and service. From those comparisons, economic agents glean the information relevant to their decision-making processes without ever collecting or analyzing the (unknowable) raw data.

Assumptions of the Model

Several assumptions are required to generate the socially optimal resource allocation described above. In order to understand the applicability of the model to economic development, it is critical to understand these assumptions, the validity of which varies significantly across countries. First, the rule of law must characterize the economy. Second, property rights must be well defined and enforceable. In particular, property ownership must be clear, and the owner must have the exclusive rights to develop and profit from (or not) ownership and to transfer ownership to another agent. This pair of assumptions ensures that agents pay the costs and receive the benefits of their actions. Third, exchanges between economic agents must be voluntary. Thus, any exchange implies that both agents are better off than they had been before the exchange, so that each trade raises the welfare of the society by reallocating resources in a socially preferred manner.

Two types of problems can cause the free market economy to fail to deliver the socially optimal resource allocation. First, when making economic decisions, an economic agent considers only the costs and benefits of the choice to himself. However, some products (and services) generate spillover effects that accrue to those other than the two agents engaged in the transaction. These "externalities" may be either beneficial or costly to the society. For example, suppose that a farmer wished to build a road from his home to the nearest city. Although he would pay the entire cost of the roadway, others would benefit from the road's existence. Roads generate social benefits beyond those private benefits that accrue to the builder. Since the builder weighs only private costs against private benefits in determining whether to build the road, the free market generates too few roads from a societal viewpoint. Alternatively, consuming the services of one's automobile generates social costs in the form of increased pollution and traffic congestion. Since drivers ignore these costs when deciding whether to drive, the free market generates more driving than would a social planner.

Second, the benefits of the free market derive from the competition inherent among firms and among consumers, but some industries lack adequate competition, implying excessive market power for a few firms. This might be the result of either private sector issues (e.g., large capital outlays to enter the industry, technological threshold) or public sector sponsorship (e.g., patents, copyrights, trademarks, local utility monopolies). The lack of competition restricts the choices available to the consumer, whereas a social planner would also consider consumer welfare in determining production patterns.

A Role for Government Intervention in the Economy

The problems of externalities and lack of competition are inherent in the incentive system of the free market. The economic agent capable of providing remedies is the government. With externalities, the traditional economic view was that governments should provide or subsidize goods and services that exhibit social benefits in excess of private benefits. In transferring the social benefits from society at large to politicians, who reap the benefits of increased votes due to higher social welfare, the nation considers both social costs and benefits in determining output levels. The government provides more such goods than would the private sector acting alone. Analogously, the government can restrict, regulate, or tax the negative externalities in order to decrease the amount produced or consumed. Once again, the methodology equates private costs to social costs, so that the agent makes the socially optimal decision. The key is that the decision makers (politicians) internalize the social benefits, ensuring that they consider all costs and benefits, both private and social, just as the social planner would. The rather significant drawback of this approach is the same one that has destroyed all attempts at central planning: bureaucrats, being economic agents themselves, act according to their incentives as individuals, rather than as benign representatives of society, thereby recreating the original problem that decisions are not based on social costs and benefits.

More recently, economists have recommended the alternative solution proposed by 1991 Nobel Laureate Ronald Coase (1960), who recognized that the inequality of social and private benefits and costs derives from a lack of clearly defined and enforceable property rights. If the farmer could restrict access to his road, then those wishing to use the road would have to pay for the benefits they receive. Because he cannot do so, others use his road for free, reaping a benefit without paying for it. The problem of pollution is more complex, as pollution is a "bad" rather than a "good." The producer should pay its cost, if pollution is to be kept to its socially optimal level. Coase's solution is for the government to issue pollution vouchers, each valid for a maximum output of pollution, making illegal the production of pollution without adequate vouchers. Vouchers thus become the "good" for which polluters will be willing to pay in order to generate legally the "bad" of pollution. Once these property rights have been clearly defined by using the Coasean approach, the market determines their proper prices according to social costs and benefits. Thus, the Coasean solution to externalities is creating the appropriate property rights, then allowing the market to function unfettered by natural bureaucratic tendencies. Coasean solutions could also deal with excessive market power by creating a market for the rights to these lucrative markets, although regulatory efforts have typically been used in practice.

By allowing economic agents to make their own choices, the free market also gives them the right to succeed as well as the opportunity to fail. Moreover, whether one succeeds or fails can often be due to factors beyond one's control, whether due to genetic makeup, environmental factors, or simple luck. The free market can generate misery. Therefore, another legitimate role of government is the redistribution of wealth. This can occur through taxation of income and wealth, subsidization of goods and services for the poor, unemployment compensation, and a host of other means. Diverse perspectives on the extent to which governments should be involved in such efforts have generated widely varying versions of the market economy across countries, each of which has advantages and disadvantages.

Free Markets and Economic Development

Despite its potential problems, the empirical evidence on economic growth overwhelmingly supports the free market economic model. The wealthiest nations have had and still have the freest markets in the world. This can be no coincidence. Economic development in low- and middle-income nations often has been slow due to the lack of a truly free market. This section considers three factors that have contributed to the lack of free markets in such countries—corruption, a tilted playing field for trade, and the slow implementation of Coasean solutions.

Arguably, the most pervasive problem facing developing nations is that of corruption, which prevents them from fulfilling the assumptions necessary to generate a truly free market. Corrupt law enforcement institutions destroy the rule of law. The bribes often required by bureaucrats for providing services such as providing official documentation undermine property rights. Corruption that restricts business opportunities to the relatives or cronies of those with power steals the rights of others to make mutually beneficial exchanges in the marketplace, reducing social welfare. Therefore, when countries with endemic corruption have attempted to introduce market-oriented reforms and institutions, the result has typically been to sour the people's attitude toward free markets, because the market cannot work and individuals thus cannot reap its benefits under such regimes.

Rich countries also have implemented numerous policies that restrict the ability of developing nations to create free markets. The United States and Western Europe have virtually dictated trade rules, despite the multilateral mission of the World Trade Organization (WTO), under whose auspices such rules are negotiated. Indeed, the main benefits of the Uruguay Round (1986–1994) of global trade talks held by the WTO's predecessor organization, the General Agreement on Tariffs and Trade (GATT), accrued in services, intellectual property, subsidization, and agriculture. The majority of developing nations are uncompetitive in these sectors. Worse, trade in those goods in which developing nations hold the strongest comparative advantages, including unskilled-labor-intensive production and agriculture, have long been kept outside the various rounds of international trade liberalization. Similarly, rules on international investment have been designed to benefit chiefly the donor nations, rather than the recipients. Although the developing world continues to be better off trading in this unfavorable environment than they would be if they abstained from trade, such rules and exceptions have deprived it of its best chances for engaging in mutually beneficial voluntary exchanges. India has taken a leadership role, supported by a large proportion of developing nations, in demanding that such issues be negotiated in good faith during the Doha Round of WTO negotiations, which were commencing at the time of this writing (2002).

Finally, pollution, insufficient economic infrastructure, and firms with significant market power are problematic in developing countries. Powerful environmental lobbies attempt to hold developing countries to standards to which rich nations never adhered during analogous stages of development. Coasean solutions exist for these problems. Some, like property rights for rain forest preservation, would likely be highly demanded by the world's wealthy, channeling additional resources for development. Unfortunately, developed countries have only begun to implement Coasean solutions. Developing nations will tarry even longer.

Jeffrey W. Steagall

See also Capitalist Economic Model; Communist Economic Model; General Agreement on Tariffs and Trade (GATT); Mixed Economy; Socialist Economic Model

References and Further Reading

Alchian, Armen A., and Harold Demsetz. "The Property Rights Paradigm," *Journal of Economic History*, 33:1 (1973).

Coase, Ronald H. "The Problem of Social Cost," *Journal of Law and Economics*, 3 (1960).

Friedman, David. *Hidden Order: The Economics of Everyday Life*. Harper Business (1996)

Friedman, Milton, and Rose Friedman. *Free to Choose: A Personal Statement*. New York: Harcourt Brace Jovanovich (1980).

Hayek, Friedrich A., "The Use of Knowledge in Society," *American Economic Review*, 35:4 (1945).

Klamer, Arjo, Donald N. McCloskey, and Robert M. Solow. *The Consequences of Economic Rhetoric*,

Cambridge, U.K., and New York: Cambridge University Press (1988).

Landsburg, Steven E. *The Armchair Economist.* Free Press (1993).

Okun, Arthur M. *Equality and Efficiency: The Big Trade of.*, Washington, DC: The Brookings Institution (1975).

Roberts, Russell. *The Choice*, 2nd Ed. Englewood Cliffs, NJ: Prentice Hall, (2000).

Scully, Gerald W. "The Institutional Framework and Economic Development," *Journal of Political Economy*, 96:3 (1988).

Smith, Adam. *An Inquiry into the Nature and Causes of the Wealth of Nations.* New York: The Modern Library (1776).

FREE TRADE AREA OF THE AMERICAS (FTAA)

Introduction

The Free Trade Area of the Americas (FTAA) agreement is an ambitious plan to create a free trade zone throughout the Western Hemisphere by 2005. The FTAA grew out of a statement by George H. W. Bush in 1990 of the Enterprise for the Americas Initiative (EAI) to crate a hemispheric free trade zone in response to Latin American governments who felt left out of the 1992 North American Free Trade Agreement (NAFTA). The EAI was an important object of discussion throughout the 1990s.

The First Summit of the Americas was held in Miami in 1994, where a joint declaration was issued by the participating countries, at the instigation of the US Clinton administration. The declaration stated that the countries of the Western Hemisphere were dedicated to democracy, economic growth sustainable development, and wiping out poverty. It goes on to say that free flows of trade and investment are a "key to prosperity," economic growth. The declaration stated that negotiations for an FTAA would be concluded by 2005.

However, serious negotiations did not begin until 2001 under the Clinton administration. Like other trade treaties and globalization generally, the FTAA has sparked a great deal of opposition among student activists, labor organizations, and nongovernmental organizations. The closed nature of the negotiations; the lack of enforceable labour standards to ensure reasonably safe working conditions and basic collective bargaining rights, and of environmental safeguards; and concerns about local control over key economic issues are the issues put forward most often by opponents to such a treaty in the North

about free trade agreements everywhere. These issues were adopted as part of the platform of several Democratic candidates in the 2004 presidential election campaign. In Latin America, on the other hand, the more important issue seems to be a perceived failure of neoliberal economic policies, including free trade, on the one hand, and a continuing strong opposition to perceived US imperialism. For example, Cuba has been excluded in the negotiations. The FTAA is, therefore, seen by many in Latin America as the latest instrument of external dominance and exploitation. Latin American politicians have been able to take advantage of this sentiment; the issue was featured prominently in the 2002 Brazilian presidential campaign.

Strategic Context

In discussing a potential FTAA, it is important to keep the general context of international trade in mind. First, almost all international trade and investment occurs among the US, Canada, the European Union (EU), and Japan. Second, the US economy is by far the largest in the world and dwarfs those of every other economy in the world with the exceptions of the EU and Japan. Third, among Latin American countries as well, there is a great deal of variety in terms of the overall size of the market, with Brazil and Mexico reaching a par in terms of gross domestic product with Canada (though still about one-quarter the size of the US economy), and Argentina as about half of the size of Brazil. Venezuela is fourth largest economy in the region and is about half the size of Argentina's. After that, the size of the economy varies from fairly small by world standards, such as Colombia, to tiny, if we consider some of the smaller islands of the Caribbean. Fourth, on the other hand, for most countries in Latin America, with the notable exceptions of the Southern Cone countries of Chile, Argentina, Uruguay, and Brazil, close to 90% of imports and exports are with the US. There is relatively little intra–Latin American trade. Moreover, key trading partners Canada and Mexico already have access to the US market through NAFTA, and so may wish to preserve this advantage. Fifth, almost every Latin American nation has a huge external debt (in some cases, as high as 70% of the value of annual exports) with recurring interest payments on the one hand, and an extremely weak financial and taxation system on the other. As a result, there is a strong thirst for external finance and investment. Sixth, both as a part of the conditions for international finance and as a result of current thinking in economics, Latin American countries have moved towards rolling back the role of the state (see entry on neoliberalism) in the economy, including privatization of state-owned enterprises, and embracing foreign investment by multinational corporations.

From these facts, we can better understand the strategic context of the negotiations. We can conclude foremost that the FTAA is part of the global process of bargaining between the US and her major trading partners, the EU and Japan. It is extremely unlikely that the US would agree to an FTAA that compromised its position at the multilateral rounds of the General Agreement on Trade and Services Negotiations or the World Trade Organization. In fact, it might be better to say that the FTAA is one chip that the US is using in attempting to extract better terms from the EU.

We can also conclude that there are strong asymmetries in the negotiations. The desire to gain access to the US market and the generally dire economic circumstances of the region explain the willingness of Latin American governments and the private sectors to resist their historical tendency against imperialism and US interference. Similarly, among Latin American countries there is an asymmetry between the larger economies and the medium and small ones in the region. It is no surprise, therefore, that Brazil has emerged as the leader in terms of regional bargaining with the US. However, within the regional structure, there is potential for alliances, not just along lines of striking a stronger bargain with the US, but also within particular issue areas. For example, the petroleum exporters in the region, including Mexico, Ecuador, Venezuela, Colombia, and Trinidad and Tobago, will all surely pay close attention to provisions that affect that economic sector. On the other side, the US has stepped up its efforts to reduce a possible anti-US negotiating coalition by signing or putting in motion a number of bilateral agreements, including ones with Chile (2003) and Central America (in negotiations). In turn, the smaller economies of the Caribbean and Central America have attempted to create tighter free trade agreements within their respective subregions in order to approach the FTAA with a more unified position, but, because of internal differences and competition among their economies, have found negotiations difficult. Finally, both business proponents and opponents, and the aforementioned anti–free trade groups, have all attempted to develop cross-border alliance networks.

Finally, it is important to note that there is growing weariness of free trade not only in the US as a result of its current war, but throughout Latin America. A string of new leaders in the region, including Gutierrez in Ecuador, Lula in Brazil, Chavez in Venezuela, and Kirchner in Argentina, were elected in good part because of their anti-imperialist credentials and statements. With the financial meltdown in Argentina and continued stagnation through much of the continent, the familiar onus of International Monetary Fund and US culpability has become part of a concerted public questioning of the neoliberal policies of market liberalization and free trade. Thus, it will be tough for these leaders to sell an FTAA at home unless they can extract some clear concessions from the US.

Timeline of the Negotiations

There were several important organizing meetings among the countries in the 1990s. The first was the December 1994 Summit of the Americas meeting in Miami. At this meeting, the 2005 date was set as the target date for the signing of the treaty, as well as the important provision that the negotiations would be "a single undertaking." By *single undertaking*, trade negotiators refer to the idea that compromises would be reached to produce one final document that could then be ratified or rejected by each member country. The advantage is that it may push compromises among countries that see a balance between overall gains and gains in one area and losses in another. The disadvantage could be that the potential bargaining power of smaller economies in one area, such as Ecuador in oil, could be dampened by the need to be included in the wider agreement. In 1995, the first ministerial meeting was held in Denver. This meeting created the main media for negotiations—ministerial and vice-ministerial meetings and working groups—and enlisted the Organization of American States, the Inter-American Development Bank, and the United Nations Economic Commission for Latin America for support. In addition, seven negotiating groups were set up along the following lines: market access, customs procedures and rules of origin, investment, standards and technical barriers to trade, sanitary and phytosanitary measures, subsidies, antidumping and countervailing duties, and smaller economies. The second ministerial meeting was held in Cartagena in March 1996. At this meeting, four additional working groups were started: government procurement, intellectual property rights, services, and competition policy. The third ministerial meeting in Belo Horizonte in May 1997 led to the development of a new working group on dispute settlement. These efforts culminated with the signing of the Declaration of San Jose at the fourth ministerial in Costa Rica in 1998. That meeting also set up three non-negotiating special committees:

the consultative group on smaller economies, the committee of government representatives on the participation of civil society, and a joint government–private sector committee of experts on electronic commerce. The meeting also set up an administrative secretariat to coordinate future summits. Although several other ministerials and a third Summit of the Americas have been held, the main formal progress was an agreement on business facilitation and information harmonization measures signed at the Toronto Ministerial in November 1999.

Structure of the Negotiations

At least in formal terms, the FTAA negotiating process is fairly straightforward. The sites of the ministerials are rotated every eighteen months, with the host serving as the chair of negotiations for that particular round. The actual foreign trade ministers of each country therefore act as the top negotiators. Below them, the vice ministers form the trade negotiations committee and meet at least twice a year. In addition, there are the ongoing negotiating groups, as noted above, as well as an ad hoc business facilitation group. In practice, the probable functioning of the negotiations are for the ministers to come in and sign the final agreements that have been negotiated at lower levels, in many cases in an informal fashion in the working groups. As with other trade negotiations, this could raise considerable difficulties for smaller countries without the budget, personnel, or technical expertise to handle all of these issues simultaneously. They can rely upon the technical support agencies noted above, but it is still a disadvantage vis-à-vis the larger countries. In addition, while the committee for the participation of civil society has held a few meetings, it has hardly served to satisfy the demands for greater transparency and participation by civil society groups.

Potential Obstacles and Prognosis

From the outset, there were major obstacles to actually creating free trade in the hemisphere that mirror those in the international arena. Besides the need to fit within a US strategy of interlocking trade agreements, and the ongoing opposition of civil society, labour, and environmental groups, there are important differences in terms of the potential economic gains and losses of domestic groups and nations. Although liberalizing agriculture could lead to enormous benefits for Latin American producers, agriculture has been the most contentious sector for international trade negotiations. While Northern countries subsidize their agriculture industries to the tune of millions of dollars, for many developing countries, agricultural exports are their mainstay. Moreover, the EU and Japan have particularly strong domestic agricultural lobbies, which leads to a general reticence to agree to any major cuts in subsidies or protection. Secondly, developing countries generally have felt disappointed with the results of the last (Uruguay) multilateral trading round. They are, therefore, especially reluctant to further liberalize services and investment sectors, which are the main areas of US interest. Indeed, by 2004, Brazil has emerged as the opposition leader to the US in the FTAA negotiations. As in its stance in multilateral talks, Brazil is attempting to create a coalition of states that hold fast for US concessions in agriculture, and a reduction of US demands in terms of market and investment access. Thirdly, developing country governments, including those in Latin America, have steadfastly refused the demands for international labor and environmental standards, which they see as not only another external imposition, but also creating an unfair competitive advantage for Northern countries.

Another problem has been the unclear US position on the FTAA. President Clinton sent the Export Expansion and Reciprocal Trade Agreements Act of 1997 to the Congress for consideration, which included consideration of "fast track" authority for the FTAA. This is considered a vital element of negotiations because it allows the president to force to the Congress to pass or reject a whole trade agreement (without the possibility of amendment). However, fast track failed in the House. With the US declaration of a war on terrorism in 2001, a continuing severe recession in the US, and other developments, the whole international scenario for free trade shifted, creating considerable doubt as to whether there can be free trade in the Americas in the foreseeable future. The renewed emphasis on the Middle East and energy security have increased the United States' interest in gaining secure access to oil suppliers within the hemisphere, particularly Canada, Mexico, Venezuela, Ecuador, and Colombia, though the possible restoration of Iraqi oil to the market might dampen it. President Bush was granted fast-track authority on 2002. The "trade promotion authority" included built-in trade adjustment assistance and notes that consultation with the Congress on sensitive sectors must take place. The sensitive sectors include agriculture, fishing, textiles, and apparel.

However, other than ongoing anti-guerrilla narcotrafficking support to the Colombian government the Bush (Jr.) Administration seems to have largely forgotten about Latin America. In addition, the Argentine financial meltdown, continuing US protection of the steel industry against Brazilian imports, and devastation of the Mexican agricultural sector, all in 2001–2003, created considerable challenges for hemispheric economic relations. New presidents Lula in Brazil and Kirchner in Argentina, with leftist and populist support among their core constituencies, have pronounced their opposition to any "caving in" on US demands for an FTAA. Amid growing outsourcing of US professional jobs, including the key telecommunications and information technology sectors, it remains to be seen whether even the US still has a strong appetite for a substantial FTAA.

As a result, the FTAA negotiations, like multilateral talks on trade, seemed to be relatively stagnant. In recognition of the emergence of Brazil as the key leader of one bloc, Brazil and the US were made the joint chairs of the final round of negotiations. It remains to be seen whether Brazil can hold its alliance together to extract more concessions out of the US or whether the United States' successful efforts to conclude separate agreements with other countries, including Chile and Central America, will melt away any opposition.

ANIL HIRA

References and Further Reading

Avery, William ed. *World Agriculture and the GATT.* Boulder, CO: Lynne Rienner, 1993.

Bergsten, C. Fred. "A Renaissance for US Trade Policy?" *Foreign Affairs*, 81:6 (Nov/Dec), pp. 86–99, 2002.

Cameron, Maxwell A., and Brian W. Tomlin. *The Making of NAFTA: How the Deal Was Done.* Ithaca, NY: Cornell University Press, 2000.

Council of the Americas. *FTAA: Blueprint for Prosperity: Building on NAFTA's Success.* Washington, DC: September 2001.

Free Trade Agreement of the Americas (http://www.ftaa-alca.org.).

Grinspun, Ricardo, and Maxwell A. Cameron. "Restructuring North America: The Impact of Unequal Integration," in Theodore Georgakopoulos, Christos C. Paraskevopoulos, and John Smith, eds., *Economic Integration between Unequal Partners.* Brookfield, VT: Edward Elgar. 1994.

Keohane, Robert. *International Institutions and State Power.* Boulder, CO: Westview, 1989.

Kerremans, Bart, and Bob Switky. *The Political Importance of Regional Trade Blocs.* Aldershot, UK: Ashgate, 2000.

Mace, Gordon, Louis Belanger, et al., eds. *The Americas in Transition: The Contours of Regionalism.* Boulder, CO: Lynne Rienner, 1999.

Mayer, Frederick W. *Interpreting NAFTA: The Science and Art of Political Analysis.* New York: Columbia University Press, 1998.

Robert, Maryse. *Negotiating NAFTA: Explaining the Outcome in Culture, Textiles, Autos, and Pharmaceuticals.* Toronto: University of Toronto Press, 2000.

Robert, Maryse, and Jose Manuel Salazar-Xirinachs, eds. *Toward Free Trade in the Americas.* Washington, DC: Organization of American States, 2001.

Stephen, Roland Stephen, Thomas Oatley, and Chris Harrisan. "Three Logics of an International Bargain: Exchange, Domestic Politics, and Coercion in the Uruguay Round," conference paper, American Political Science Convention, Atlanta, Sept. 1–6, 1999.

Tirado Mejía, Alvaro. *Integración y democracia en América Latina y el Caribe*, Intal Documento de Divulgación 1. Washington, DC: Inter-American Development Bank, November 1997.

Wise, Carol, ed. *The Post-NAFTA Political Economy: Mexico and the Western Hemisphere.* University Park, PA: Pennsylvania State University Press, 1998.

FREI, EDUARDO

Eduardo Frei (1911–1982) was the president of Chile from 1964–1970. He was married to Maria Ruiz-Tagle in 1935, and had seven children, among them Eduardo Frei Ruiz-Tagle (president of Chile, 1994–2000) and Carmen Frei Ruiz-Tagle (senator of the Christian Democratic Party since 1990). Frei was a first-generation Chilean: his father was of Swiss-German origin. Frei obtained a law degree from the Universidad Católica de Chile in 1932. In 1938, dissatisfied with the Conservative Party—seen as too hierarchical and too doctrinaire in its views of poverty, injustice, and social concerns—Frei and his friends created the Falange Nacional. A meeting with the French philosopher Jacques Maritain had left a profound impression on the young Frei, and Maritain's Social-Christian philosophy became a leading principle of Frei's political thinking.

The final separation of the Falange from the Conservative party came about in the 1938 presidential election, when the Falange chose to rally behind the Popular Front candidate Pedro Aguirre Cerda, who went on to win the presidency. In 1945, Frei became Minister of Public Works under President Juan Antonio Ríos. In the parliamentary elections of 1949, Frei became the Falange's first senator.

Frei's (and the Falange's) shifting allegiance from the Right to the Left indicates to what degree the new movement was caught up in a search for political identity. Frei saw the advantages of pragmatism as exemplified by his participation in governments that included Socialists and Communists.

Eduardo Frei provided the intellectual leadership during the 1950s to transform the Falange from a small, internally divided party to the Christian Democratic party that emerged in 1957. Barely one year later, the Christian Democrats managed to not only replace the Radicals as the major center party, they had also become a viable "third option" to the political Right and Left.

Frei was able to exert sufficient influence to prevent the Falange from moving too close to the Left while at the same time allowing the Falange to identify with issues such as workers' welfare and social legislation. However, beginning in the early 1950s, when internal divisions threatened the Falange's future, Frei's views prevailed. Radical thinkers in the Falange sought explicit worker and peasant support (e.g., Jacques Chonchol). Opposing such a move, Frei countered that capitalism, social reform, equality, justice, development, and democracy were compatible; he believed that workers and capitalists did not have to be "natural enemies."

The other alternative to reform—revolution—was increasingly advocated by Latin America's Left and thus contributed to the radicalization of Chilean politics, reaching its climax in the election of Socialist Salvador Allende and the rise to power of the Unidad Popular (1970–1973). Frei realized that if it ever wanted to seize political power, the Falange needed to grow, and for that, it was necessary to reach out to the moderate wing of the Conservative Party (the so-called Social Christians) who at the time were skeptical about a coalition with the Falange. However, the two groups joined in 1953, creating the Social Christian Federation. This paved the way for the creation of the Christian Democratic Party six years later. By 1957, Frei had become a national political figure and his influence over Chilean politics in general and over the moderate political Center in specific, was evident. Between his first presidential bid in 1958 and his successful election in 1964, Frei and the Christian Democratic Party continued to gain popular support as its leaders convinced the public that the new party was the best vehicle to deliver social reform and to avoid the risks of Communism.

Frei's "Revolution in Liberty" was meant to be a gradual though profound change of Chilean society, brought about democratically. He hoped to gain enough electoral strength to implement his "Revolution" without the need for political concessions to other parties in Congress. Frei's social programs were geared towards rural as well as urban populations. Early on in his tenure, he initiated "promoción popular" (popular promotion), an ambitious project to give the urban and marginal poor a greater voice by lending legal, technical as well as financial support. The program benefitted from the Christian Democratic Party's proximity to the Catholic Church, but ultimately it was short-lived and failed in part because of an ineffective state bureaucracy.

Frei's record with organized labor was mixed. Attempting to overcome a decades-old hostility between a largely Leftist labor movement and anything to the political Right of that, the Frei government was nonetheless known for its open hostility towards the national union federation Central Unitaria de Trabajo (CUT). Yet through his economic policies, Frei also sought to improve the standard of living of the working class. In addition, housing and health conditions improved for many. In education, the Frei government built schools, raised teacher salaries, increased student enrollment, and decreased the illiteracy rate.

The two outstanding projects of the Frei government were the agrarian reform, initiated in 1967, and the nationalization of copper. Frei pursued three interrelated goals with the reform: improve agricultural output and productivity, raise the standard of living of rural areas by giving land to peasants, and facilitate unionization of the countryside. Although the reform fell far short of the government's as well as peasants' expectations (out of an estimated one hundred thousand land titles, only about a tenth of that were actually granted), it did help establish the Christian Democratic Party in the countryside. Christian Democrat–controlled peasant unions remain a fixture in Chile. The idea to incrementally nationalize Chile's copper—criticized by Left and Right alike—was perhaps Frei's most ambitious project. The Chilean state did not expropriate foreign copper companies outright but instead purchased partial ownership, in some cases acquiring up to 51% (e.g., Kennecott). Ironically, this piecemeal approach to nationalization made it easier for Salvador Allende to propose complete national ownership later.

Frei was convinced that the state's role in the economy and society needed to be modernized and reformed, but kept prominent. Frei's "Revolution in Liberty" faced pressures from the Left and Right, as well as from within the Christian Democratic Party. He managed to hold the Center, though popular support was beginning to erode towards the end of his term. Overall, Frei's economic record was mixed, and economic growth had stagnated and inflation increased, giving rise to frequent strikes. The country was polarizing as a Socialist president was about to gain control of the government.

Frei's role in the rise of Christian Democracy in Chile and the influence of his party on Chilean politics is crucial for an understanding of twentieth century Chile. The social and economic impact of his programs and reforms were hampered by the party composition in Congress. Following the presidential election, the Christian Democratic Party was in the minority, but this changed in 1965 when they obtained a majority in the Chamber of Deputies, though they still did not control the Senate. Hence, the need to compromise with the Left and Right. In the 1969 Congressional elections, the party lost dramatically, further evidencing that the Christian Democrats' ideas and policies were too little for the Left and perhaps too much for the Right. His wait-and-see attitude towards the Marxist Allende government ultimately gave way to an unyielding opposition that supported Pinochet's military coup of September 11, 1973. Frei would come to deeply regret this later in life, and his opposition to the dictator's 1980 plebiscite is evidence of that. Frei helped modernize Chile, and unwittingly directed a Nation onto the "socialist road" of Allende's Popular Unity.

VOLKER FRANK

See also Allende Gossens, Salvador; Chile

References and Further Reading

Alexander, Robert. *Agrarian Reform in Latin America*. New York: Macmillan, 1974.
Fisher, Kathleen B. *Political Ideology and Educational Reform in Chile, 1964–1976*. Los Angeles: Latin American Center, University of California, Los Angeles, 1979.
Fleet, Michael. *The Rise and Fall of Chilean Christian Democracy*. Princeton, NJ: Princeton University Press, 1985.
Frei, Eduardo M. *Latin America: The Hopeful Option*. Maryknoll, NY: Orbis Books, 1978.
Frei, Eduardo M. *The Mandate of History and Chile's Future*. Athens, OH: Center for International Studies, Ohio University, 1977.
Kaufman, Robert K. *The Politics of Land Reform in Chile, 1950–1970. Public Policy, Political Institutions and Social Change*. Cambridge, MA: Harvard University Press, 1972.
Scully, Timothy R. *Rethinking the Center. Party Politics in Nineteenth and Twentieth Century Chile*. Stanford, CA: Stanford University Press, 1992.
Stallings, Barbara. *Class Conflict and Economic Development in Chile 1958–1973*. Stanford, CA: Stanford University Press, 1978.

FRELIMO (FRONT FOR THE LIBERATION OF MOZAMBIQUE)

FRELIMO is the acronym of the principal movement for the independence of Mozambique from Portugal. Beginning in the sixteenth century, Mozambique became a crucial outpost for the Portuguese in their global empire. The Portuguese controlled the rich trade in this region for a century but later lost dominance to larger European countries. As Portugal's empire withered, the only significant colonies that remained for it were Angola and Mozambique. By mid-twentieth century, both of these were in ferment for independence.

After World War II, a wave of African colonies sought and achieved independence. Much of the political rhetoric and strategy for these movements occurred within a wider Cold War tension of communist and noncommunist states and of developed and developing nations. Portugal, through one of the longest surviving authoritarian regimes in Europe, fought desperately to hold on to its mineral rich African colonies. The dictatorship of Portuguese Prime Minister António de Oliveira Salazar lasted from 1928 until his death in 1968. His fascist regime continued after his death, using increasing military force to maintain control of its colonies.

This force had increased in response to the mounting organization of armed independence movements in Portuguese Africa. These were based on socialist ideology and encouraged by Soviet support. By 1962, three such movements joined, the União Democrática Nacional de Moçambique (UDENAMO, National Democratic Union of Mozambique), the União Nacional Africana para Moçambique Independente (National Democratic Union for an Independent Mozambique, UNAMI), and the Kenya-modeled Mozambique African National Union (MANU). They formed the Marxist-Leninist Frente de Libertação de Moçambique (FRELIMO, Mozambique Liberation Front). It was led by a Harvard Ph.D. in anthropology, Eduardo Chivambo Mondlane, and committed to armed struggle for independence. He succeeded in liberating the northern part of Mozambique, but because he was assassinated in 1969, he did not live to see the final and complete liberation of the country.

Samora Machel, head of FRELIMO's guerilla forces, assumed command of the movement. In 1974, a rebellion of the Portuguese armed forces overthrew the fascist regime in Portugal, and that country eventually assuming a socialist government. The following year, all remaining Portuguese colonies were granted independence. Samora Machel thereby became the first president of an independent Mozambique.

Mozambique's powerful capitalist, white-dominated neighbors, Rhodesia and South Africa, formed and financially backed an anti-Communist movement, the Resistência Nacional Moçambicana (RENAMO, Mozambican National Resistance). It was vigorously backed by US President Gerald Ford and Secretary of State Henry Kissinger. FRELIMO, meanwhile, received support from the Soviet Union.

RENAMO maneuvered against FRELIMO throughout Mozambique, attacking in the south and occupying strongholds in the highlands. FRELIMO held the capital in the south, and RENAMO raided there and in the north. The conflict assumed a north–south character. Everywhere, it left hundreds of thousands dead, wounded, or displaced. Landmines left over from this conflict remain one of the war's deadliest legacies.

Conflict endured throughout the late 1970s and into the early 1990s, only ending as the forces backing each side collapsed. In 1980, the white-ruled government of Rhodesia fell, and the independent black government of Zimbabwe was declared. The Berlin Wall came down in 1989, and the Soviet Union ended two years later. By 1990, white dominance in South Africa began to unravel. A peace of exhaustion reconciled FRELIMO and RENAMO, officially recognized through accords finalized in Rome in 1992. Machel himself did not see this final peace. He was killed under suspicious circumstances in an airplane crash in 1986.

Joaquim Chissano, foreign minister in the Samora government, succeeded him as leader of FRELIMO and president of Mozambique. In national elections in 1994 and 1998, he continued as president, defeating the candidates of RENAMO, which became the official opposition party. Corruption and scandals so marred the Chissano government, however, that in 2004, it chose a different presidential candidate, Armando Guebuza, who had earlier negotiated the Rome Peace Accords.

With the collapse of the Soviet Union, it was Guebuza who perceived that Mozambique would have to redirect its policy for economic development to reflect a market focus, thereby obtaining the approval of world banking institutions. He fostered the idea of developing private ownership of property and a bourgeois class. By overseeing the privatization of government companies and resources, he himself became one of, if not the largest holders of property and wealth in Mozambique.

EDWARD A. RIEDINGER

See also Angola; Mozambique; Southern Africa: History and Economic Development; Southern Africa: International Relations

References and Further Reading

Alden, Chris. *Mozambique and the Construction of the New African State: From Negotiations to Nation Building.* New York: Palgrave, 2001.
Cabrita, João M. *Mozambique: The Tortuous Road to Democracy.* New York: Palgrave, 2000.
Cravinho, João Titterington Gomes. *Modernizing Mozambique: Frelimo Ideology and the Frelimo State.* Doctoral dissertation, Oxford University, 1995.
Friedland, Elaine A. *A Comparative Study of the Development of Revolutionary Nationalist Movements in Southern Africa–FRELIMO (Mozambique) and the African National Congress of South Africa.* Vols. 1 and 2. Doctoral dissertation, City University of New York, 1980.
Macel, Samora. *Frelimo and the Transitional Government of Mozambique.* Braamfontein: South African Institute of International Affairs, 1974.
Newitt, M. D. D. *A History of Mozambique.* Bloomington, IN: Indiana University Press, 1995.
Nwafor, Azinna. *FRELIMO and Socialism in Mozambique.* Roxbury, MA: Omenana, 1983.

FRENCH GUIANA

After more than five centuries of European colonialism in the Americas, French Guiana, which lies between Brazil and Suriname, remains the only nonindependent state on the South American mainland. Over 90% of French Guiana's 91,000 square kilometers are covered by tropical forest. Most of French Guiana's two hundred thousand inhabitants live along the 378-km-long coastline. The majority of these inhabitants, who enjoy the economic benefits of the French social security system, are content to remain a part of France.

The original inhabitants of northern South America were the Carib and Arawak Indians. By 1650, the Dutch, British, and French had all established colonies in the region. The French had established Cayenne, the capital of French Guiana, at the mouth of the Cayenne River on a small island in 1634. Sugar and rainforest timber became the colony's economic mainstays. Slaves brought from Africa worked the sugar plantations, although their success was limited by tropical diseases and the hostility of the local Indians. By 1776, there were only 1,300 whites and 8,000 slaves in the colony. Thousands of slaves escaped into the interior of the colony and established runaway slave communities. The sugar plantations' output never matched that of Haiti and other French Caribbean colonies, and after the abolition of slavery in 1848, the sugar industry virtually collapsed.

At about the same time that slavery was abolished, Emperor Napoleon III decided that penal settlements in the colony would reduce the cost of prisons in France and contribute to the development of the colony. Between 1852 and 1938, over fifty-six thousand prisoners, including Alfred Dreyfus, were sent to Devil's Island. Prisoners sentenced to a term of less than eight years had to spend an equal period of time living in the colony after their release from prison. Prisoners whose sentence was more than eight years had to remain in the colony permanently. Regardless, since 90% of the prisoners died of disease and abuse, the prison population did little to augment the colony's struggling population. The most atrocious activities on Devil's Island occurred in the timber camps on the mainland. The underfed, naked convicts were forced to work in water up to their waist. Although escape was arduous, and the punishment for a failed escape attempt quite severe, prisoners, such as Henri "Papillon" Charrière, frequently tried to escape. In 1938, the government ceased sending prisoners to Devil's Island, and the penal settlement was eventually closed in 1945. Unfortunately, French Guiana has never fully escaped its negative image as a former penal colony with an unhealthy climate and an impenetrable hinterland.

In 1946, after more than three centuries as a French colony, French Guiana was transformed into an overseas department—*département d'outremer*—of France. Unlike the peoples of other European colonies in the Caribbean who loudly clamored for independence during the post-1945 era, the people of French Guiana wanted to remain part of the French nation. In theory, French Guiana was to be equal and identical to any other French department. As a result of their nonindependent status, the people of French Guiana enjoy a standard of living vastly superior to the people of the former Dutch and British Guianas. The people of French Guiana receive generous social security and medical benefits, wages are higher than in the rest of the Eastern Caribbean, and the infrastructure is vastly superior. With its mineral resources and potential for hydroelectric energy, especially the Petit-Saut dam project on the Sinnamary River, French Guiana has great potential to develop its economy.

During French President Charles De Gaulle's Fourth Republic, the power of the *Préfet*—the local representative in French Guiana of the central government—was increased, giving him total responsibility for defense and security, as well as a central role in economic affairs. Thus, beginning in 1958, and culminating in the 1970's, French Guiana underwent a significant economic transformation. The traditional agriculture-based productive economy of the colonial era was replaced by a skewered consumer-oriented economy based on massive cash infusions from France. By 2000, over three-fourths of the population was involved in the service sector. Between 1958 and 1978, food production declined by over 50%. As a result, today most foodstuffs are imported from France. Although cattle-raising and rice cultivation have been introduced, the most dynamic sector of French Guiana's economy is the fishing industry. By 2000, shrimp exports represented 60% of French Guiana's total exports. Gold, timber, and rice exports each account for about 10% of total exports. Regardless, exports remain minimal when compared with the substantial imports.

Since 1982, the French government has encouraged French immigration to the territory. Many of these recent immigrants, who make up 25% of the population, are working for the European Space Agency, which launches its communication satellites from Kourou. At the same time, political parties supporting greater autonomy—such as the Parti Socialiste Guyanais (PSG)—began to attract more support. Since 1982, Marie-Claude Verdan's PSG has dominated local politics. Since the 1980s, the French government has granted greater autonomy to the local government. The small but vocal independence movement led by Jean-Victor Castor has earned less than 5% of the vote in recent elections. Residents of French Guiana, who witnessed economic and political chaos in neighboring Suriname after independence from the Netherlands, are unwilling to give up their high standard of living based on generous subsidies from the French government.

MICHAEL R. HALL

See also Suriname

References and Further Reading

Burton, Richard D. E., and Fred Reno. *French and West Indian: Martinique, Guadalupe, and French Guiana Today*. Charlottesville. VA: University of Virginia Press, 1995.

Charrière, Henri. *Papillon*. New York: Perennial, 2000 (reprint).

Crane, Janet. *French Guiana*. Santa Barbara, CA: ABC-Clio, 1999.

Davis, Hassoldt, and Ruth Davis. *The Jungle and the Damned*. Lincoln, NE: University of Nebraska Press, 2000.

Miles, Alexander. *Devil's Island: Colony of the Damned*. Berkeley, CA: Ten Speed Press, 1988.

Redfield, Peter. *Space in the Tropics: From Convicts to Rockets in French Guiana*. Berkeley, CA: University of California Press, 2000.

FUJIMORI, ALBERTO

Alberto Fujimori (1938–) was the highly polarizing president of Peru from 1990 to 2000. His dramatic and controversial decade in power featured spectacular accomplishments in defeating murderous communist insurgents and taming hyperinflation. But the country paid a price. Fujimori trampled Peru's democratic institutions while embezzling astronomical sums of money.

Fujimori's father emigrated from Japan to Peru in 1920. He returned home to find a wife, whom he took to Peru 1934. Alberto was born in Lima on July 28, 1938. Although the parents kept their Japanese culture, they had their son baptized as a Catholic and sent him to a Catholic high school, from which he graduated as valedictorian. The youth earned a bachelor's degree in agricultural engineering from Agricultural National University in Peru and a master's degree in mathematics from the University of Wisconsin (1969). During the 1970s, while Peru was ruled by military regimes, Fujimori rose in the academic ranks at La Molina National University.

In 1980, democracy returned to Peru, but in that same year, an obscure philosophy professor named Abimael Guzmán founded a revolutionary movement he named *Sendero Luminoso* (Shining Path). Guzmán believed that the Khmer Rouge had done things well in Cambodia, and he planned a similar future for Peru. Under the inept presidency of Fernando Belaunde (1980–1985), Peruvian poverty deepened, especially in the Indian villages in the Andes where the *Sendero* was quietly organizing its insurgency. Alan Garcia of the APRA (socialist) party followed Belaunde as president. During his term (1985–1990), Peru reached the verge of collapse. Real income had declined by 63% between 1988 and 1990. The government was printing money to pay its civil servants and soldiers. The inflation rate in 1990 was 7,650%. And the Shining Path controlled over half the territory of Peru.

Fujimori, who had become president of the National Commission of Peruvian University Rectors, is not known to have had political ambitions before he began hosting a television talk show, which gave him a chance to analyze politics in a direct way that appealed to the common people. In 1989, he formed his own political party, *Cambio 90* (Change 90), and campaigned for president on the simple slogan: "Honesty, technology, and work." Observers considered this political unknown a long shot against the famous author Mario Vargas Llosa, but Fujimori survived the first round and won the runoff. The Spanish-speaking urban elite opposed Fujimori, as did the Catholic Church. But Fujimori cheerfully accepted the (inaccurate) nickname *el chino* (the Chinaman), knowing that the Quechua- and Aymara-speaking Indians distrusted the light-skinned traditional politicians. In his campaign Fujimori presented himself as "a president like you." The diminutive son of Japanese immigrants was sworn in as president of Peru on his fifty-second birthday, July 28, 1990.

President Fujimori immediately implemented a program of severe austerity and privatization programs. This economic shock therapy hit the poor the hardest, but brought inflation down to 139% in 1991 and 57% in 1992. In 1999, Fujimori's last full year in power, inflation was only 3.7%. The free-market privatization programs raised an estimated $9 billion, but it is not clear where all that money went.

Fujimori was even more successful in his war against the Shining Path, though here, too, his methods do not stand close scrutiny. The *Senderistas* financed their revolution by exporting coca leaves from the Huallaga Valley, where the Peruvian Army rarely ventured. They armed the peasants and taught them that Fujimori was a "genocidal hyena." Fujimori and his sinister henchman, Vladimiro Montesinos, organized death squads to eliminate *Senderistas* and their supporters. Arguing that the war against the communists was hindered by the apparatus of democracy, Fujimori, with army backing, mounted an *autogolpe* (self-coup) on April 5, 1992. He put tanks around the parliament, dismissed thirteen of twenty-three Supreme Court justices, and suspended the constitution. These drastic moves met with much popular approval.

Fujimori's popularity reached new heights when Guzmán, the Shining Path leader, was arrested on September 12, 1992. Guzmán was dressed in prison stripes and publicly displayed in a cage before being sent to prison for life. Without his leadership, the *Sendero Luminoso* withered.

Gradually reintroducing democracy, Fujimori promulgated a new constitution and began preparing for reelection. His wife, Susan Higuchi, with whom he had four children, left him and threatened to run for president against him. Fujimori settled that problem by passing a law forbidding relatives of the president from running for office and refusing to divorce Higuchi until after the 1995 election. Fujimori easily defeated his opponent, Javier Pérez de Cuéllar, the former Secretary General of the United Nations.

Early in his second term, Fujimori faced a threat from a different guerrilla group, the Tupac Amaru. On December 17, 1996, Tupac guerrillas seized 452 hostages at a reception at the Japanese ambassador's home. There followed a four-month standoff during which most hostages were gradually released. On April 22, 1997, Peruvian special forces raided the building, freed the remaining seventy-two hostages, and killed all the Tupac Amaru guerrillas present.

With these triumphs, Fujimori began to float the idea of a third term, which his own constitution explicitly forbade. But Fujimori argued that his 1990 election had been under the old constitution and that therefore he should be eligible to run again in 2000. The Supreme Court disagreed until Fujimori dismissed three of its judges, and then changed its mind. Fujimori shut down an opposition TV station and gained control of the tabloid newspapers. The 2000 election was widely regarded as fraudulent. Fujimori's men were alleged to have forged over a million signatures. His main opponent, Alejandro Toledo, dropped out in disgust. Fujimori narrowly won the May 28 election with 51% of the vote, against 18% for Toledo. Thirty-one percent of the voters spoiled their ballots. Only two other Latin American leaders attended his inauguration on July 28.

Within two months the Fujimori government came undone. The immediate catalyst was the broadcast of a one-hour videotape showing Montesinos bribing an opposition congressman to defect for $15,000. Faced with a crisis of legitimacy, Fujimori offered to call a new election, but he was engulfed in a tidal wave of unpopularity. Demonstrations swept the country. Montesinos went into hiding, and Fujimori's failure to find him led Peruvians to conclude that Fujimori could no longer count on full control of the army. In November 2000, Fujimori attended a summit meeting of Asian and Pacific leaders in Brunei, and then flew on to Japan, where he was granted Japanese citizenship. Conveniently, Peru has no extradition treaty with Japan. Fujimori contemptuously faxed a letter of resignation to the Peruvian Congress on November 20, 2000. The Congress refused to accept the fax, and instead voted the next day by a margin of sixty-two to nine to declare Fujimori "permanently morally unfit" to govern.

In exile, Fujimori has opened his own web site, which justifies his every act in Spanish, English and Japanese. Interpol has issued two international arrest warrants for Fujimori, charging him with "crimes against humanity," but Fujimori still dreams of returning to lead Peru. He may have the wherewithal: Transparency International, a watchdog group, estimated that Fujimori had embezzled $600 million during the decade he ruled Peru. In 2003, he launched a new political party, *Si Cumple* ("He keeps his word"), to prepare the ground for his comeback.

ROSS MARLAY

See also Andean South America: History and Economic Development; Peru

References and Further Reading

Crabtree, John. *Fujimori's Peru*. London: University of London, 1998.
Kimura, Rei. *Alberto Fujimori of Peru: The President Who Dared to Dream*. New York: Beekman, 1998.

FULBRIGHT PROGRAM

Signed into law on August 1, 1946, by President Harry S. Truman, the Fulbright Act merely provided that foreign credits from the sale of war material left overseas after World War II could be used for the educational exchange of teachers, students, professors, and research scholars between the United States and participating countries.

A Rhodes Scholar and president of the University of Arkansas before he entered politics, Senator Fulbright himself never referred to development as a purpose of the program that made his name familiar throughout the world. From its inception, the Fulbright Program focused on the exchange of academic persons, the mix of disciplines and ranks being determined through consultation between the United States and the host countries. To this end, nonprofit binational commissions or foundations (whichever term better suited the host country) were established in fifty-one nations; the program eventually operated in eighty-nine others directly out of the US embassy when there was no binational commission. At the American end, though funded through appropriations to the Department of State, the program's administration was delegated originally to two nongovernment agencies, the Institute of International Education (for students), the Council for the International Exchange of Scholars (for professors), and the government's own Office of Education (for teachers, and later certain categories of students and researchers). Later, other nongovernment bodies such as the Social Science Research Council and American Friends of the Middle East undertook the administration of appropriate portions of the program.

The earliest of the binational agreements was signed with China in 1947. Under it, the first American to profit from the program was Derk Bodde, a Sinologist at the University of Pennsylvania, who translated Chinese philosophical texts during his grant and on his return recounted his experiences in *Peking Diary: A Year of Revolution* (New York: Henry Schuman, 1950). Signed a month later the same year, the second binational agreement, with Burma, brought the first foreign participants to the United States, among them students from renowned "Burma Surgeon" Gordon Seagrave's hospital and nursing school.

As these early examples imply, the Fulbright Program could only develop people by means of educational exchange. Unlike government programs such as those of the United States Agency for International Development (USAID) or those in the private sector such as the Ford Foundation's, it never could contribute to physical infrastructure.

In 1948, Representative Karl E. Mundt (South Dakota) and Senator H. Alexander Smith (New Jersey) collaborated on legislation that became second only to Fulbright's in shaping the dimensions of America's involvement in international educational exchange. This was their P.L. 402, the so-called Smith-Mundt Act. For one thing, this legislation broadened the mandate of the program to include countries where there was no surplus property. For another, it provided for the Congressional appropriation of dollar funds to maintain foreign participants in the United States where, because of currency controls in many of the developing countries, foreign funds could not support them. It also established for the first time an American propaganda organization, the United States Information Agency (USIA).

Throughout his long Senate career, Fulbright continued to defend the intellectual integrity of his program and maintain its level of funding. In 1952, in anticipation of the early exhaustion of overseas surplus property, he also got implemented an amendment that authorized the use of foreign currencies arising from *any* source. This was a particular boon for programs in South Asia, because by the 1950s the United States was making massive shipments of wheat to both India and Pakistan for which payment was accepted in nonconvertible rupees. The availability of these funds led to the Indian Fulbright program being the world's largest for a short time. However, the Rabaut Amendment to the appropriations act the next year required that such foreign currencies had to be "bought" with appropriated dollars from the US Treasury, with the result that an effective ceiling was placed on program growth in India and elsewhere.

In 1961, with Representative Wayne Hays (Ohio), Senator Fulbright sponsored legislation to further strengthen the program, which since has operated under this Fulbright–Hays Act. One section of the act, administered by the US Office of Education, provided overseas training in languages that had been little studied in the United States. Another section established a special visa category for foreign students coming to the United States, because there had been much concern at the time about the "brain drain" from developing countries. Even though holders of these visas were required to return to their home countries on completion of their studies and to remain there at least two years before applying for immigrant visas, the brain drain was little diminished by them. A study conducted in India in 1981 showed that 78% of Indian students in the United States managed to change their visa status to stay in the country.

There is no way to quantify the impact of the Fulbright Program on developing nations, but it may be noted that among the 146,000 people from foreign countries who participated during the first fifty years of its existence were such persons as those who later became a Moroccan Ambassador (Mohamed Benaissa), President of Brazil (Fernando Cardoso), Prime Minister of Poland (Wlodziemierz Cimoszewicz), United Nations General Secretary (Boutros Boutros Ghali), Jordanian Minister of Education (Khalid Omari), Korean Minister of Trade (Jae Yoon Park), Prime Minister of Greece (Andreas Papandreou), Peruvian Minister of Education (Alberto Varilla), and Hungarian Minister of Foreign Affairs (Geza Jeszenszky). During the same period, among the eighty-eight thousand Americans receiving grants under the program were four people who became Nobel Laureates—in physics, medicine, and economics. Moreover, presidents of Harvard University, New York University, University of Chicago, and Georgetown University all had Fulbright grants early in their careers, as did the Librarian of Congress and four American ambassadors.

By fiscal year 2000, foreign governments, principally those in Western Europe, were making direct contributions of $28 million to it, while several of the developing countries made contributions in kind, such as housing for visiting professors. In the same fiscal year the congressional appropriation amounted to $105.7 million. However, in constant dollars, the Fulbright Program has suffered a 43% reduction in funding since 1994, when the congressional appropriation amounted to $126 million.

CHARLES BOEWE

References and Further Reading

Arndt, Richard T., and David Lee Rubin, eds. *The Fulbright Difference, 1948–1992*. New Brunswick, NJ: Transaction Publishers, 1993.

Byrnes, Robert Francis. *Soviet-American Academic Exchanges, 1958–1975*. Bloomington, IN, and London: Indiana University Press, 1977.

Dudden, Arthur Power, and Russell Rowe Dynes, eds. *The Fulbright Experience: Encounters and Transformations*. New Brunswick, NJ: Transaction Books, 1987.

Gayner, Jeffrey B. *The Fulbright Program after 50 Years: From Mutual Understanding to Mutual Support*. Washington, DC: Capital Research Center, 1994.

Glazer, Nathan, ed. *The Fulbright Experience and Academic Exchanges*. Newbury Park, CA: Sage Publications, 1987.

Mohanty, Sachidananda. *In Search of Wonder, Understanding Cultural Exchange: Fulbright Program in India*. New Delhi: Vision Books, 1997.

Salamone, Frank A., ed. *Fulbright Experience in Benin*. Williamsburg, VA: College of William and Mary, 1994.

Tysse, Agnes N., compiler. *International Education: Tthe American Experience, a Bibliography*. Metuchen, NJ: Scarecrow Press, 1974.

G

GABON

The Republic of Gabon lies on the Atlantic Ocean. It borders on Equatorial Guinea and Cameroon (north), and on the Republic of the Congo (east and south). The climate is tropical, hot, and humid, with little seasonal variation. Heavy rains fall from October to May.

The country is covered by dense forests, except for a narrow coastal zone. A geographic feature important for Gabon's development is the Ogooué River flowing through its eastern two-thirds into the Atlantic Ocean, near Port-Gentil. The river is navigable for 114 miles upstream all year and is used to ship goods, especially lumber, to the coast.

Gabon was populated first by Pygmies in the forest, then over centuries by forty diverse Bantu groups that migrated from the interior. Now, half of Gabon's 1.2 million inhabitants live in the two principal cities: Libreville, the administrative and commercial capital, and Port-Gentil, the center of wood and petroleum industries.

The first Europeans at the Gabon estuary bartered for hardwood and ivory along coastal rivers. Commercial trade turned into slave trade (1760–1840) as interior peoples sent their undesirables and war prisoners to the coastal Mpongwe and Orungu, who acted as slave brokers.

Gradually (1855–1880), the French took over along the coast and sent explorers into the interior. Subsequent occupation of the interior met with little opposition, but interference with the slave trade, imposition of head taxes, and forced labor aroused substantial resistance. Unwilling to shoulder the expenditures required by development, the French divided the area into parcels, which they leased to private companies (1898). These parcels ruthlessly exploited both human and natural resources, devastating the Gabonese population. After failure of the concessionary system, France created the Federation of French Equatorial Africa, uniting Gabon with Congo-Brazzaville, Oubangui-Chari (Central African Republic), and Chad (1910). With ivory and rubber depleted, France neglected Gabon. After World War II, Gabon's progress towards independence (1960) paralleled that of other French sub-Saharan colonies.

At independence, Léon M'ba (1902–1967), head of the Gabonese Democratic Bloc, was elected president of the parliamentary republic of Gabon. He consolidated his personal power and limited freedom of speech and political assembly. In 1964, he provoked a military coup by decreeing a one-party system. He was overthrown and jailed, but was rescued and reinstated by French paratroopers. Under M'ba's rule, Gabon began prospecting for petroleum and exploiting its mineral resources, and further developed its lumber trade. French firms provided investment capital and, along with a small Gabonese elite, reaped most of the benefits. With French backing, M'ba remained president until his death.

Beginning in 1967 and up to the present, Gabon has been ruled by Omar Bongo. The original 1961 constitution was revised in 1991. It instituted political pluralism, but in reality, Bongo, who serves both as president of Gabon and secretary general of the

Gabonese Democratic Party (PDG)—offshoot of the Gabonese Democratic Bloc—rules autocratically. For thirty-five years, he has allowed just enough democracy to stay in power but has reverted to autocracy whenever he deemed it feasible.

He faced his greatest challenge when declining oil prices and a weakening US dollar produced a prolonged economic crisis (1986). Gabon was unable to service its foreign debt, and the International Monetary Fund forced it to implement austerity programs. The patronage system that had propped up Bongo's regime collapsed. Unemployment rose, affecting mainly the poor. Popular discontent erupted. Riots in Libreville and Port-Gentil led Bongo to call upon French troops to intervene. Then, in 1990, he reached a compromise with opposition leaders, only to resume harassing them as the 1993 presidential elections approached. Bongo's subsequent victory at the polls caused rioting to resume. Compromising once more, Bongo agreed to form a transitional coalition government, revise the electoral code, and schedule legislative elections for 1996. Divisions in the opposition enabled the PDG to win these elections and the presidential ones that followed (1998). As before, the losers denounced fraud and refused to serve in Bongo's government, but the regime survived.

Over the years, Bongo did improve social services, education, and public health. The country as a whole has a relatively high doctor-to-population ratio. Nonetheless, tropical diseases remain endemic, and infant mortality rates and life expectancy are about average for sub-Saharan Africa. Recently, AIDS has been spreading so rapidly that demographers' projections take into account the excess mortality it causes. Education is now compulsory between the ages of six and sixteen, and about 75% of this age group attend school. The literacy rate at 63.2% is high for the region. Bongo also has made investments in transportation—such as the Transgabonal Railroad—and in social service. Gabon is relatively stable. Inflation has dropped in recent years. Real GDP has continued to grow.

However, there are problems. Because oil exports still represent 60% of the government's total revenues, Gabon remains vulnerable to volatility in international oil markets. The apparent availability of better economic opportunity in cities has led to urban overcrowding and unemployment. Population growth outstrips job creation. Although the government attempts to diversify the economy by encouraging foreign investment in fisheries, light industry, and construction of port facilities, and although it has undertaken gradual privatization of key industries such as water and electricity and post and telecommunications, economic inequities persist unchanged.

Nor do plans to help the poorest seem to be in place. For instance, agriculture, which employs about two-fifths of the workforce, accounts for less than 10% of the GDP and is not attracting noticeable governmental attention, although subsistence farming is insufficient to meet domestic demand.

The IMF recently deemed Gabon's performance "broadly satisfactory" but required Gabon to continue diversification and privatization, implement anticorruption laws, "improve the transparency of public finances," and adopt "a participatory poverty reduction strategy."

A much-discussed aspect of Gabon's current development is its environmental cost. Gabon's forests are threatened by powerful timber interests. Conservationists fear the extinction of forms of animal and plant life. Epidemiologists express concern that the stress to which the forest ecosystem is subjected and increasing human exposure to forest animals could unleash new infectious diseases. Meteorologists caution against the consequences of deforestation on climate.

L. NATALIE SANDOMIRSKY

See also Central Africa: History and Economic Development; Central Africa: International Relations

References and Further Reading

Adams, Adrian. *La Terre et Les Gens du Fleuve: Salons, Balise.* Paris: L'Harmattan, 1985.
Barnes, James F. *Gabon Beyond the Colonial Legacy.* Boulder, CO: Westview Press, 1992.
De Saint-Paul, Marc A. *Gabon:,The Development of a Nation.* New York: Routledge, 1989.
Gardinier, David E. *Gabon.* Santa Barbara, CA: ABC-CLIO, 1993.
———. *Historical Dictionary of Gabon.* Lanham, PA: Scarecrow Press, 1994.
Gaulme, Francois. *Le Gabon et Son Ombre.* Paris: Karthala, 1988.
Weinstein, Brian. *Gabon: Nation-Building on the Ogooué.* Cambridge, MA: MIT Press, 1967.
Yates, Douglas A. *The Rentier State in Africa, Oil Rent Dependency & Neocolonialism in the Republic of Gabon.* Lawrenceville: Africa World Press, 1996.

GAMBIA, THE

The Republic of the Gambia, situated on the western coast of Africa, is the smallest nation on the continent. The country is a relatively flat strip of land fifteen to thirty miles wide on either side of the Gambia River, and almost two hundred miles long. Except for its small Atlantic coastline, the nation is entirely surrounded by the Republic of Senegal. The climate is tropical, with a rainy season lasting from June to

October, followed by a cool dry season. About forty inches of rain falls near the coast each year, whereas inland areas receive even less precipitation. Mangrove and scrub forest line the river banks, whereas sandy soil covers the rest of the country. The population is estimated at approximately 1.3 million, with an estimated annual growth rate of 3.5%. The capital, Banjul, known as Bathurst until 1973, is located where the Gambia River flows into the Atlantic Ocean and has a population of about seventy-five thousand.

The nation's peculiar shape and size are the result of territorial compromises made during the colonial period of the nineteenth century by Britain, which controlled the Gambia River, and France, which ruled the neighboring colony of Senegal. Prior to European colonial rule, the Gambia River region was dominated by a series of small Muslim Mande and Fulbe kingdoms. Agriculture and fishing dominated the local economy. The first Europeans to arrive in the area were the Portuguese in the 1440s, followed by the English, French, and Dutch, all of whom traded with the kingdoms on the river, seeking agricultural products and also slaves. By the eighteenth century, the British dominated trade that was centered on slave exports along the river. After the abolition of the slave trade in the early nineteenth century, the British encouraged the production and export of peanuts, which grew well in the local soils and climate. Peanut cultivation dominated the colonial economy of The Gambia, which was the poorest and smallest colony in British West Africa. Because of its small size and weak economy, moves toward self-rule in The Gambia lagged behind other West African nations, and independence was granted in February 1965. The Gambia became a republic in 1970, and Dawda Jawara, initially elected in 1965 as prime minister, became president. Jawara ruled until his ouster by a military coup in 1994. The military, headed by Yaha Abdul Jammeh, permitted elections in late 1996 and early 1997. Jammeh, who retired from the military to run for office, was elected president, and his political party, the Alliance for Patriotic Reorientation and Construction, won a slim majority in the national assembly. Opposition groups and some foreign observers accused the military government of fraud and intimidation to influence voters. Jammeh and his party won the most recent elections in 2001, again amidst allegations of intimidation.

The Gambian economy has consistently and overwhelmingly been based on the production and export of peanuts. During the 1970s and 1980s, the Gambian environment and economy were seriously affected by the Sahelian drought, which devastated much of Western Africa along the Sahara Desert, from which it has never completely recovered. Approximately

85% of residents make a living primarily from agriculture, with peanuts being the only significant cash crop. Farmers also grow millet and sorghum. The country continues to be highly dependent on imports of rice and other staple grains. Fisheries and tourism are also foreign exchange earners, although tourism as well as foreign aid declined precipitously after the 1994 military coup. Neither the Jawara or Jammeh regimes have made serious efforts to diversify the economy. The government submitted to International Monetary Fund pressure by cutting back its large civil service and drastically devaluing the local currency, but the efforts have done little to improve the nation's economic prospects. Per capita gross domestic product was $1,170 in 2002, making the Gambia one of the poorest countries in the world, and 62% of the population lives at or below the poverty line. The country also has an overall trade deficit. Further, smuggling between The Gambia and Senegal remains a serious problem and attempts to curtail it have failed.

The Jawara regime was characterized by corruption, nepotism, and mismanagement. The country relied primarily on foreign assistance for survival. The Gambia did, however, have relatively strong respect for individual liberty and human rights until the military takeover in 1994. The Jammeh regime has imposed serious restrictions on freedom of speech and assembly. In recent years, the population of the capital, Banjul, has been augmented by refugees from the civil wars in Sierra Leone and Liberia, two other English-speaking nations in a largely francophone region. Senegal has periodically accused the Gambia of harboring separatists from the southern Senegalese region of the Casamance, heightening differences between the two countries. Historically, there have been no serious tensions in the country among the different ethnic groups. Over 90% of the population is Muslim, but no militant Islamic movement exists.

The Gambia has very little economic infrastructure. The river is the country's main transportation route. There are no bridges across the river, so passengers and goods passing from the river's northern and southern banks have to be ferried across the river on antiquated boats. There are no railroads and only one main airport, located near Banjul. The adult literacy rate is approximately 40% and, despite free elementary education, many children, especially girls, never attend school. There is no institution of higher learning. Beyond some primary health care, most Gambians do not have access to modern medical care. There are approximately two physicians and twenty-five nurses for every ten thousand people. Life expectancy for males is fifty-two years for males and fifty-six years for females. The population growth rate (3.09% annually) and infant mortality (76.3 per 1,000 live births) are among the highest in the region. The government has continually promised improvements in education, health, transportation, and economic infrastructure yet most of the plans have yet to be realized. Unemployment, especially among secondary school graduates, is extremely high, and many secondary school graduates migrate overseas for employment.

ANDREW F. CLARK

References and Further Reading

Gailey, Harry. *A History of the Gambia.* New York: Prager, 1965.

———. *Historical Dictionary of the Gambia.* Metuchen, NJ: Scarecrow Press, 1987.

Gamble, David, compiler. *A General Bibliography of the Gambia.* Boston: G. K. Hall, 1988.

Gray, J. M. *A History of the Gambia.* London: Frank Cass, 1965.

Hughes, Arnold, ed. *The Gambia: Studies in Society and Politics.* Birmingham, AL: University African Studies Series, 1991.

McPherson, Malcolm, and Steven Radelet, eds. *Economic Recovery in the Gambia: Insights for Adjustment in Sub-Saharan Africa.* Cambridge, MA: Harvard Institute for International Development, 1995.

Wiseman, John. "Military Rule in the Gambia: An Interim Assessment." *Third World Quarterly,* 17:5 (1996).

Wright, Donald. *The World and a Very Small Place in Africa,* Armonk, NY: M.E. Sharpe, 1997.

GANDHI, INDIRA

Indira Priyadarshini Gandhi (1917–1984) was the only child of Jawaharlal Nehru, the first prime minister of India. She was not related to Mohandas (Mahatma) Gandhi, but the Gandhi name had a halo effect in Indian elections, especially among the many illiterate rural voters. Schooled at home, she later attended Oxford University. After graduating in 1939, she worked as a volunteer for the Red Cross in Europe. After she returned to India in 1941, she married Feroze Gandhi (1913–1960) who also was politically active. Indira Gandhi and her husband were both put in prison by the British authorities for one year.

Since her mother had died earlier, she acted as her father's help and official hostess. In 1959, she was selected as President of the All India National Congress party (then the Congress party). After her father's death, she became Minister of Information and Broadcasting in Prime Minister Lal Bahadur Shastri's cabinet. In 1966, after Shastri's unexpected death of a heart attack, she was nominated by the party powerful for that position, because it was believed that she could be easily manipulated and controlled. That was clearly a misjudgment on their part. She was sworn in as the third prime minister of India in 1966 and served the country in that capacity from 1966 to 1977, and again from 1980 to 1984. During her tenure in office, she consolidated her powers a great deal and continued the political dynasty begun by Nehru. Among her initiatives was the nationalization of banks and insurance companies in 1967.

In addition to the usual complex Indian political problems, she faced other problems during her first term of office that included famines for two years in a row and an influx of about 10 million refugees from East Bengal. Additionally, a split occurred in the Congress party in 1969; this would occur again in 1978. In 1971, the Third Indo-Pakistan War brought the defeat of the Pakistani army and the creation of Bangladesh via the secession of the Pakistani state of East Bengal. That event made Gandhi enormously popular and powerful in India. The explosion of a nuclear device in 1974 by the Indian government enhanced her popularity even more.

In 1975, the Allahabad High Court found her guilty of corrupt election practices on a technicality, and she was asked to step down from power and resign her seat. To avoid such a harsh outcome, she convinced the president of India to proclaim a national emergency. During the emergency rule, approximately one hundred thousand individuals, including well-known political opponents, were jailed, and the freedom of the Indian press was muzzled. The emergency was highly resented throughout India and resulted in her loss of a seat in the Loka Sabha in the next general election conducted after the emergency rule was lifted. She was sentenced to prison twice for short periods of time in 1977 and 1978 for the violation of election rules and for obstructing an official inquiry into one of the industrial projects of her second son. Nonetheless, she was sworn in again as prime minister in 1980, as her party won in the national general elections due to the overwhelming support from poor people and minorities, especially poor and illiterate women.

A group within the minority community of Sikhs in India demanded a separate independent state for the Sikhs to be named Khalistan and initiated terrorist activities toward the achievement of that goal. In June 1984, Indira Gandhi ordered a military attack on the Golden Temple, which is the holiest site of the Sikhs, as the terrorists had taken refuge there. The attack shocked and stunned the Sikh minority as well as the rest of the minorities. The raid on the Golden Temple proved to be the last major misjudgment of her career: two of her Sikh bodyguards assassinated her before the end of that year. Her son, Rajiv Gandhi was sworn in as prime minister that evening.

Toward the end of her career, Gandhi had been isolated from the party leaders and did not trust anyone completely except her family. During her administration, corruption and nepotism proliferated and spread into most sectors of the public arena on a large scale.

She was a charming person with highly developed diplomatic skills. She also continued to be one of the most important figures in the Third World movements throughout her life. She wielded great power in a highly patriarchal society. Unfortunately, many of her significant accomplishments have been overshadowed by the declaration of emergency and, later on, by her raid on the Golden Temple.

SUBHASH R. SONNAD

See also Gandhi, Mohandas; Gandhi, Rajiv; India; Nehru, Jawaharlal

References and Further Reading

Damodaran, A.K., ed. *Indian Foreign Policy, the Indira Gandhi Years.* India: Radiant Publishers, 1990.

Dhar, P. N. *Indira Gandhi, the "Emergency," and Indian Democracy.* New Delhi: Oxford University Press, 2000.

Frank, Katherine. *Indira: the Life of Indira Nehru Gandhi.* Boston: Houghton Mifflin Company, 2002.

Gupte, Pranay. *Mother India: A Political Biography of Indira Gandhi.* New York: Maxwell Macmillan International, 1992.

Jayakar, Pupul. *Indira Gandhi: an Intimate Biography.* New York: Pantheon Books, 1992.

Sahgal, Nayantara. *Indira Gandhi's Emergence and Style.* Durham, NC: Carolina Academic Press, 1978.

GANDHI, MOHANDAS

Mohandas Karamchand Gandhi (1869–1948), also called *Mahatma*, which means "great soul," was one of the most admired world leaders of the twentieth century. His popularity and sway over the Indian masses was unparalleled. Known as the father of the Indian freedom movement, he was its undisputed leader from 1920 onward. Although his major goal of freedom for India was achieved in 1947, Gandhi was saddened by the partition of India into India and Pakistan and the strife that ensued between Hindus and Muslims.

Gandhi was born in an affluent family in the state of Gujarat, India, in 1869. He was married in 1883. He sailed to England for legal studies and returned to India to practice law in 1891. He accepted a position in South Africa in 1893 and stayed there until 1914. He championed the causes of the Indian community there, protesting in particular the compulsory registration certificates policy directed against them. He was imprisoned twice in South Africa, and his experiences there turned out to be a starting point for many of his ideas and actions such as the practice of nonviolence, noncooperation and civil disobedience.

He initiated and led three major political movements through the National Indian Congress party (called Congress party) against the British rule in India. The first, a mass anti-imperialist movement occurred in 1921, the first of its kind in India, but Gandhi called it off in 1922 because of mob violence. The next movement he led was in 1930 in protest to the colonial law that Indians could not produce their own salt and thus had to pay taxes on it. The movement picked up steam and spread all over India. Gandhi was jailed but was released in 1931 to attend a Round Table Conference wherein he made a pact with the administration and called off the civil disobedience movement. He attended a second conference in London later that year, yet it yielded mostly negative results. Gandhi decided to fast until death to stop the granting of separate electorates for the depressed classes. Gandhi broke his fast only after that provision was rescinded. India gradually started participating in a democratic process under the British rule, and Gandhi spent much of the 1930s engaged in activities aimed at the elimination of untouchability.

The third and last major movement launched by Gandhi was in 1942 during World War II and was called the "Quit India" movement, which demanded immediate withdrawal of the British from India. He was arrested again that year but released in 1944 on grounds of poor health. His wife died that same year while she was in detention. Off and on, Gandhi spent more than six years in jails and prisons.

Whenever Gandhi was out of jail, he was engaged in different types of social reforms and movements. These included the economic and educational uplift of members of the untouchable caste, empowerment of women, utilization of village handicrafts, and economic betterment of rural areas and boycotting of British goods. Between 1944 and 1947, he had ongoing talks with leaders of the Muslim league and the British Government to bring about unity between the Hindu and Muslim communities, but without much success. He toured Bihar state and fasted in Bengal to reduce the incidence and intensity of communal violence between the Hindu and Muslim communities.

The methods he used to achieve his political and social goals included, for example, *satyagraha* (holding on to truth or asserting truth), civil disobedience, nonviolent noncooperation, development of village handicrafts such as homespun clothing (*khadi*), and undertaking fasts. Particularly in that era, these strategies were quite unorthodox. His movements directed against the British also had at their core a moral and spiritual essence; his philosophy and practice taught the people to rely on themselves and their own, moral, spiritual, economic, and political strengths.

Gandhi was a nondogmatic religious liberal and an activist reformer as well. He was open to the positive aspects of different religions and cultures. Gandhi was deeply affected by the Indian religious traditions and the Jain religious principles and practice of nonviolence. Thinkers from other countries such as Leo Tolstoy, John Ruskin, and Henry David Thoreau also made a profound impression on his mind. He did not hate the British categorically and volunteered to help the British in the Boer War and World War I.

Despite his overwhelming successes in some arenas, he was not successful in either addressing the problems of the untouchables or maintaining peace between Hindus and Muslims. Many Indians today think of his visions as outdated, impractical, too idealistic, naive, and irrelevant in the modern world. Gandhi, however, left many positive and enduring legacies, not just for India, but also for other countries, applicable to other times and other contexts as well. Indian independence was a catalytic event on the colonial scene from 1947 onward, as it demonstrated that colonial rule could be overthrown nonviolently without traditional weapons and armor. Gandhi's legacy has left its mark on the anticolonial and minority struggles and movements spanning four continents—Asia, Africa, Europe and North America. His principles of nonviolence were a major influence on the American civil rights activist Martin Luther King, Jr. In 1948, a Hindu religious militant assassinated Gandhi, who was en route to a prayer meeting.

SUBHASH R. SONNAD

See also India

References and Further Reading

Chadha, Yogesh. *Gandhi: A Life.* New York: John Wiley, 1997.
Coward, Harold, ed. *Indian Critiques of Gandhi.* Albany, NY: State University of New York Press, 2003.
Jack, Homer A. *Gandhi Reader: A Source Book of His Life and Writings.* Bloomington, IN: Indiana University Press, 1956.
Mehta, Ved. *Mhatma Gandhi and His Apostles.* New Haven, CT: Yale University Press, 1977.
Nanda, Bal Ram. *In Search of Gandhi: Essays and Reflections.* New Delhi and New York: Oxford University Press, 2002.
———. *Gokhale, Gandhi, and the Nehrus: Studies in Indian Nationalism.* New York: St. Martin's Press, 1974.
Terchek, Ronald. *Gandhi: Struggling for Autonomy.* Lanham, MD: Rowman & Littlefield Publishers, 1998.

GANDHI, RAJIV

Rajiv Gandhi (1944–1991) was a reluctant heir to the role of a politician. He was born in Bombay in 1944. His grandfather, Jawaharlal Nehru, was the first prime minister of India. His mother, Indira Gandhi, was the third prime minister of India. He studied engineering at Trinity College, Cambridge, but later transferred to Imperial College of London. In London, he met and married Sonia Maino who was an Italian citizen. They had two children. He also took flying lessons while he was in London, and upon his return to India in 1968 started an apprenticeship with Indian Airlines, where he became a pilot.

Rajiv Gandhi was drafted into politics in 1980 by his mother after the death of his brother. He resigned from his job as a pilot and was elected to the Lok Sabha (lower house of the Indian parliament) in 1981. He was sworn in as the sixth prime minister of India in 1984 after the assassination of his mother.

Rajiv Gandhi was young and energetic and had the reputation of being honest and noncorrupt. In 1985, he won his first national election with an unexpected landslide majority larger than his mother or grandfather had received. During the initial phase of his administration, he enjoyed great popularity, especially among the educated population. He opened the economy to foreign investments and bolstered India's technology, education, environmental policies, and agricultural production. He was comfortable with the leaders outside India and conducted successful diplomatic missions to the USSR and the People's Republic of China as well as negotiating treaties with Pakistan and improving relations with Sri Lanka.

On the other hand, riots among the Sikhs and Hindus broke out immediately after he assumed office. He had inherited the cabinet from his mother, and as problems kept surfacing, the cabinet kept being reshuffled. His party kept losing in the state elections, and Gandhi was not widely popular among the rural population.

Despite his initial reputation for honesty and transparency, he got muddied in the Borfous scandal starting in 1987 about purchase of arms from Sweden with the rights to manufacture them in India and later on the purchase of submarines from Germany. Many politicians from his party were involved in the kickbacks. Although he was cleared of the corruption charges later, it came too late to help him in the 1989 elections.

While in office, he succeeded in brokering a peace accord between the government of Sri Lanka and the Liberation Tigers of Tamil Elam. Indian troops were stationed in Sri Lanka as a peacekeeping force.

Unfortunately, many actions of the Indian military totally enraged the Tamil group, who felt betrayed. This resentment culminated in the assassination of Rajiv Gandhi during a comeback campaign in India.

SUBHASH R. SONNAD

See also Gandhi, Indira; India; Nehru, Jawaharlal

References and Further Reading

Hazarika, Sanjoy. *Bhopal, The Lessons of a Tragedy.* New Delhi: Penguin Books India, 1987.

Mehta, Ved. *Rajiv Gandhi and Rama's Kingdom.* New Haven, CT: Yale University Press, 1994.

Sen Gupta, Bhabani. *Rajiv Gandhi, a Political Study.* New Delhi: Konrak Publishers, 1989.

Sharma, Rajeev. *Beyond the Tigers: Tracking Rajiv Gandhi's Assassination.* New Delhi: Kaveri Books, 1998.

GENERAL AGREEMENT ON TARIFFS AND TRADE (GATT)

At a meeting in 1947, the major powers of the world devised as a comprehensive plan to set up mechanisms to deal with international trade, investment, and foreign exchange. This "system" produced the International Monetary Fund (IMF), the International Bank for Reconstruction and Development (IBRD, or the World Bank) and an International Trade Organization (ITO). The ITO however never materialized, and its intended functions were taken over by the General Agreement on Tariffs and Trade (GATT).

The GATT/World Trade Organization (WTO)

In the following, the text refers to GATT for developments up till 1994 and to WTO after 1995 when the latter came into being. While originally intended only as an interim agreement to the ITO, GATT has become the dominant organization and body of rules dealing with intergovernmental trading relationships. The original agreement was signed on October 30, 1947. The signatories agreed to the application of GATT under a Protocol of Provisional Application from January 1, 1948.

GATT developed its institutional structure over time and found a permanent home in Geneva. Modifications of the Agreement are made through negotiated "rounds." In general, the Agreement's central principle is nondiscrimination, whereby contracting parties made mutual promises that any trading advantage offered to one country would be freely available to all other contracting parties. There are exceptions in the area of customs unions and free trade areas and developing countries. The Agreement promoted tariffs as the only legitimate means of protection and encouraged tariff reductions. Import quotas and other nontariff barriers are proscribed. GATT also developed a dispute settlement function to adjudicate disputes.

Background and Evolution

In February 1946, the United Nations (UN) Economic and Social Council (ECOSOC) called for an International Conference on Trade and Employment with a view to drafting an ITO. A UN Conference on Trade and Employment was held in Havana between November 1947 and March 1948, and a text was adopted known as the Havana Charter.

As work progressed to establish the ITO, some countries were anxious to immediately bring down trade barriers and sought to create an interim tariff reduction agreement. On October 30, 1947 the GATT Agreement was signed by twenty-three countries.

A Protocol of Provisional Application was signed at the same time, whereby signatories agreed that the GATT Agreement would be applied from January 1, 1948, on a provisional basis. As events proved, GATT developed into a permanent and central institution. How this came about stems from the protocol. A provision in the protocol stated that Part Two of GATT need only be applied "to the fullest extent not inconsistent with existing legislation." Known as the "grandfather clause," this allowed many signatories to maintain existing protectionist measures inconsistent with GATT Agreement. Subsequently, negotiations within GATT ("rounds") involved attempts to have countries relinquish these measures.

As an interim device, GATT did not establish any institutional framework necessary for an ongoing international trade-regulating organisation. When the ITO failed to eventuate, GATT developed its institutional and dispute settlement elements.

Operations of GATT

GATT worked on two levels—first, on a day-to-day level, where existing rules sought to circumscribe protectionist government activity, disputes were sought to be resolved, and discussions could be held on general issues. A second level involved negotiating "rounds," or lengthy multilateral trade negotiations aimed at improving liberalization and the general structure of the Agreement. Early rounds focused on the promotion of further tariff reductions on a reciprocal negotiating basis. Later rounds dealt with other trade rules and protectionist barriers beside tariff. The rounds were as follows: Geneva Round (1947), Annecy Round (1948), Torquay Round (1950), Geneva Round (1956), Dillon Round (1960–1961), Kennedy Round (1964–1967), Tokyo Round (1973–1979), and the Uruguay Round (1986–1994).

GATT Rounds: Summary Table

Round	Participating Countries	Result Summary
1947 Geneva	23	Agreement on 20 schedules covering 45,000 tariff concessions. Manufacturing tariff in industrialized countries dropped from average of 40% to 25% over a decade.
1948 Annecy	13	An additional 5,000 tariff concessions exchanged to continue the tariff cutting momentum.
1950 Torquay	38	8,700 tariff concessions exchanged.
1956 Geneva	26	About US$2.5 billion worth of tariff reductions.
1960–1961 Dillon	26	4,400 tariff concessions covering US$4.9 billion worth of trade.
1964–1967 Kennedy	62	Introduced across-the-board rather than product-by-product approach to cutting tariffs. Concessions covering US$40 billion worth of trade. Antidumping rules introduced. By end of decade, industrial tariffs to average about 17%.
1973–1979 Tokyo	99	Tariff reductions covering US$300 billion of trade. Preferential treatment for developing countries. Codes agreed on subsidies, counter-vailing measures and other nontariff-barriers. Progressive lowering of industrial tariffs to current level of 4.7%.
1986–1993 Uruguay	116	Changes to a range of trading areas: agriculture, services, intellectual property rights and investment. The GATT to become the WTO with revamped rules and dispute-setting machinery.

The Uruguay Round

The Uruguay Round is the most significant to date because it spawned the establishment of the WTO. However, there are many reasons why the Uruguay Round took place. Other than the perceived irrelevance of GATT to world trade relations and the need for significant modifications for the 1990s and beyond, the following reasons may be tabulated.

- The significant departures from the nondiscrimination principles of GATT to add to the exemptions, special rules for developing countries and free trade areas, and other side agreements.
- The development of three key "players"—the United States, the European Union, and Japan—and the inclusion of nonmarket economies into GATT system added to trade problems.
- The role of multinational corporations (MNCs) having immense economic power and control over trade but not subject to GATT.
- The growing attitude among some governments that managed trade as opposed to free trade can lead to significant benefits, which in turn lessens the promotion of GATT norms.
- The use of nontariff barriers in response to years of low growth and recession. Subsidies also were used to defend the competitiveness of local industries leading in some cases to over-production and, in turn, to subsidising the export of surplus production. Another nontariff barrier is the voluntary export restraint—to prevent the threat of protectionist measures in an importing country. Arguably, these measures were deemed to be outside GATT and therefore permissible.
- Dispute resolution mainly stemming from procedural issues were rife.

The above issues prompted many countries to press for a new round of trade talks. There was a need to revitalize the organizational and dispute settlement functions and to broaden substantive rules. Further, the GATT Agreement only dealt with trade in goods, yet more than half of the workforce in industrialized countries was involved in the services sector.

The Uruguay Round was protracted for a number of reasons. First, a major recession was experienced during the trade talks, giving rise to higher levels of unemployment and calls for higher protectionism, thereby leading to a lesser likelihood of consensus among members. Second, major political events took higher priority—the collapse of the Soviet Union, the reunification of Germany, and the integration of the European market in 1992 meant that it was extremely difficult to get key political leaders to focus on the immediate and more long-term needs. Further, changes in government in key European countries and the US meant that support from the leaders in these countries were not readily forthcoming.

The GATT/WTO Agreement

It also is important to note that GATT is not a single agreement. It involves many primary documents, including the initial 1947 agreement, protocols, and accession agreements in which new countries joined GATT and the codes were negotiated during the Kennedy and Tokyo Rounds. To understand its rules and principles, it is necessary to consider the elements of the GATT Agreement and the related documents and modifications made in the Uruguay Round.

The WTO came into being on January 1, 1995. However, the basis of the multilateral trading system that governs the WTO was established in 1948. One of the agreements annexed to the WTO Agreement is GATT1994, which incorporates the basic principles of GATT1948.

Annex 1A to the WTO Agreement is a general interpretative note that gives a statement of an "understanding"—that is, how certain provisions are to be interpreted. Where there is a conflict between what was the old GATT and an agreement in Annex 1A, the new agreement prevails. In all other cases, the WTO is guided by the decisions, procedures, and customary practices followed under GATT1948. The new agreements on trade in services and trade-related aspects of intellectual property and transfer of technology are found in Annexes IB and IC—General Agreement on Trade in Services (GATS) and TRIPS, an agreement on trade-related aspects of intellectual property rights, including trade in counterfeit goods, respectively. Both have important implications for trade in both goods as well as services. There also are agreements that include trade-related investment measures (TRIMS), trade-related environmental management (TREM), and regional trade agreements (RTAs).

GEORGE CHO

See also International Bank for Reconstruction and Development (IBRD) (World Bank); International Monetary Fund (IMF)

References and Further Reading

Burnett, R. *International Business Transactions*, 2nd ed. Sydney: The Federation Press, 1999, pp. 204–214.

Cho, G. *Trade, Aid and Global Interdependence*. London and New York: Routledge, 1995, pp. 123–153.
Hoeckman, B. and M. Kostecki. *The Political Economy of the World Trading System: From GATT to WTO*. New York: Oxford University Press, 1995.
Islam, M. R. *International Trade Law*. Sydney: LBC Information Services, 1999. pp. 23–161, 183–202, 398–414, and 432–438.
LeQuesne, C. *Reforming World Trade: The Social and Environmental Priorities*. Oxford: Oxfam Publications, 1996.
The George Washington University. *A Three-Year Review of the World Trade Organization*. Washington, DC: The Elliott School of International Affairs, 1998.
Treblicock, M. and R. Howse. *The Regulation of International Trade*. New York: Routledge, 1997.

GEORGIA

The Republic of Georgia is a Eurasian country located in the Caucasus region where the somewhat arbitrary line between Europe and Asia is drawn. Its total landmass is approximately 69,875 square kilometres (26,979 square miles), with the landscape being dominated by the Caucasus Mountains to the north and west and the remainder of the country primarily constituting lowland plains. Rivers and lakes are found throughout the country, and coniferous forests dominate roughly one-third of the landscape, leaving about 9% of the country available for agricultural purposes. Best described as having a mild alpine climate, Georgia only receives snowfall at the highest elevations, and the average annual rainfall is one thousand to two thousand millimetres per year, while temperature averages range from 5°C (41°F) during the winter to 22°C (72°F) during the summer. Georgia shares borders with the Russian Federation to the north, Turkey to the southwest, Armenia to the south, and Azerbaijan to the southeast, with the Black Sea comprising Georgia's western edge. According to a 2004 United Nations estimate, the population of Georgia is approximately 5 million and has been declining at a rate of –0.36% per year. Georgia's capital is Tblisi, and it also is the largest city with a population of over 1 million. The name Georgia, as used by the West, is derived from an ancient Persian term for the country, *Gurj*. The native Georgians refer to their country as *Sakartvelo*.

The population of Georgia is dominated by a variety of native Caucasian peoples and other groups. The Georgians, known as the *Kartvelebi* in Georgian, comprise the largest group with 70% of the population. Various ethnic minorities include Armenians (8%), Russians (roughly 6%), Azerbaijanis (6%), Ossetians (3%), Abkhazians (1.8%), and others including the Adjarians (whose language is virtually identical to Georgian), Ukrainians, Kurds, and other smaller groups constitute the remainder (5.2%). Religion in Georgia displays a similar eclectic situation and includes Georgian Orthodox Christians (65%), Muslims (11%), Russian Orthodox Christians (10%), Armenian Apostolics (8%), and others (6%). The impact of official atheism, during the many decades of Soviet rule, also has had an impact upon the largely secular society of Georgia.

The Caucasus region is, in many ways, as fractured as the Balkans with overlapping peoples and, often, capricious borders being drawn by the ebb and flow of empires throughout history. Georgians are primarily descendents of Ibero-Caucasian peoples, who are believed to be the oldest natives of the Caucasus region. In fact, Georgian is part of a family of languages classified as a language isolate group that is not related to the Indo-European languages of the Russians, Armenians, and Ossetians (speakers of an Iranian language) or the Altaic tongue of Azeri Turkish. The Georgian language has borrowed many words and other characteristics from the aforementioned languages as well as Turkish and Farsi (Persian). Georgian is part of the South Caucasian branch of the Ibero-Caucasian family of languages (with its own unique script), whereas Abkhaz is part of the North Caucasian group.

The Caucasus region has been invaded on numerous occasions by the Greeks, Persians, Romans, Arabs, Mongols, Turks, and Russians, all of whom have left their impressions upon the local population in a variety of ways. In addition, Georgia has one of the oldest continuous Christian communities on earth, dating back to 317 CE Christianity has managed to remain the predominant faith in spite of centuries of Islamic domination and the number of Georgians (such as the Adjarians) who have converted to Islam over the centuries. After centuries of Persian rule, modern Georgian history began with Russian annexation in 1801. During this period, Georgia became an integral part of the Russian Empire and attempts at russification were met with local resistance. An influx of Russians as well as Armenian merchants relegated the Georgian population to a secondary on their own lands. Georgian intellectuals increasingly mimicked Russian and Western European philosophical models, and Marxism gained a foothold among some local activists just as it was spreading in other parts of the Russian Empire. Russian reforms in 1905 had the same impact that they had in other parts of the empire as the Mensheviks gained prominence, but the Bolsheviks, led by the young Ioseb Jughashvili, a.k.a. Josef Stalin, agitated against them. Following Russia's involvement in World War I and the Russian Revolution, Georgia managed to gain independence for a brief period under the rule of local Mensheviks in 1918. Georgian independence ended in 1921 with the invasion of the Red Army, which annexed Georgia into the newly formed Union of Soviet Socialist Republics. Josef Stalin, possibly Georgia's most well-known native son, gained control of the USSR several years after the death of Lenin. Georgia suffered along with the rest of the USSR during Stalin's reign, but did gain some cultural autonomy. Georgia would not regain independence until 1991 with the fall of communism. After independence, Georgia suffered from various internal struggles, including secessionist movements in the outer provinces of Abkhazia, South Ossetia, and Adjaria. These regions remain somewhat problematic, and Russian intervention on behalf of the agitating provinces has prompted the Georgian government to seek closer ties with the United States.

Politically, Georgia has had democratic elections since independence and has managed to retain this democratic plurality with the peaceful changing of its leadership. Most notably, there was the ascension of former Soviet notable Eduord Shevardnadze in 1995, who then voluntarily resigned after allegations of fraudulent elections in 2003. This relatively bloodless passing of power, dubbed the Velvet Revolution of 2003, and continued elections have made Georgia politically stable in spite of regional civil strife. Unlike some parts of the former Soviet Union, Georgia is tolerant of its free press; however, journalists face dangers when covering Georgia's regional conflicts, corruption, and organized crime.

The economy has not met with the same success as the electoral process, and Georgia remains one of the poorest countries of the former Soviet Union. Early strikes, heightened defence spending, and civil conflict have ravaged Georgia's economic prospects throughout the 1990s. In addition, the economic downturn that has impacted the West has also had a ripple effect in Georgia, which has been exacerbated by incompetent leadership and economic mismanagement. Price controls were set by politicians to gain public support in the early 1990s but have been reversed in favor of market-oriented reforms. Tourism and agriculture (including a renowned viniculture industry) remain the most significant sources of income along with a limited manufacturing capacity. The abundance of rivers makes hydroelectricity plentiful but insufficient to compensate for the loss of energy resources that Georgia enjoyed during the Soviet era. Georgian leaders are optimistic that they will be able to benefit from an oil pipeline running from Baku in Azerbaijan to the port of Batumi in Adjaria, but civil unrest there may prompt the pipeline to be diverted to Georgia's other main port of Poti. In recent years, the Georgian government has done its part to curtail inflation (still hovering around 19%) and formulate a more stable free market-oriented economy. These measures have improved economic conditions, along with substantial guidance and assistance from the International Monetary Fund and the World Bank. Investments from the European Union and the United States also have helped local development, but it has not been enough to modernize Georgia's fledgling infrastructure or meet its energy needs. Georgia has cut its debt and deficit with great effort, but widespread tax evasion and rampant corruption have led to disappointing tax revenues. Per capita income has increased, but remains very low by European standards. According to the World Bank, the annual per capita income of Georgia is only $2,300. The Georgian currency, introduced in 1998, is the *lari* and has remained relatively stable since its inception. However, with nearly 60% of Georgians living at or below the poverty line, there is much more work to be done. The unemployment rate has been reduced in recent years and tends to hover around 15%, but the quality of jobs has not met with the expectations of many Georgians. Future prospects look promising for Georgia if its internal turmoil and regional conflicts can be resolved. Otherwise, Georgia will continue to suffer from a population outflow as more and more young Georgians move to Russia, the EU, and the US in search of better prospects.

ALI AHMED

See also Commonwealth of Independent States: History and Economic Development; Commonwealth of Independent States: International Relations

References and Further Reading

Chervonnaya, Svetlana. *Conflict in the Caucasus: Georgia, Abkhazia, and the Russian Shadow.* Glastonbury: Gothic Image, 1994.

Curtis, Glenn E. *Armenia, Azerbaijan, and Georgia Country Studies (Area Handbook Studies).* Washington DC: Federal Research Division Library of Congress, 1995.

Central Intelligence Agency. *The World Factbook.* Washington DC, 1998.

Rosen, Roger. *The Georgian Republic.* Lincolnwood, Ill.: Passport Books, 1992.

Salia, Kalistrat. *History of the Georgian Nation.* (Trans., Katharine Vivian.), 2nd ed. Paris: Académie Française, 1983.

Shevardnadze, Eduard. *The Future Belongs to Freedom.* New York: Free Press, 1991.

Suny, Ronald G. *The Making of the Georgian Nation,* 2nd ed. Indianapolis, IN: Indiana University Press, 1994.

GHANA

Geography

Ghana, formerly Gold Coast, is situated along the Atlantic coast of West Africa. It is bordered by three Francophone nations: Côte d'Iviore on the west, Togo on the east, and Burkina Faso on the north. Ghana is in close contact with both the equator and the prime meridian; the latter passes through the port city of Tema in the southeast. Ghana has a coastline of about 572 kilometers and extends some 840 kilometers in the north–south direction. With an estimated landmass of 238,533 square kilometers, Ghana is about the size of Great Britain. The nation is divided into ten administrative regions: Greater Accra, Central, Eastern, Western, Volta, Ashanti, Brong-Ahafo, Northern, Upper West, and Upper East.

Ghana has a network of streams and rivers; the largest river is the Volta, which starts from Burkina Faso and drains to the Gulf of Guinea. Other major rivers include the Pra, Tano, and Ankobra. Only the Volta, Ankobra, and Tano rivers are navigable by launches and lighters. Ghana's topography is mostly low plains, with the exception of the east where the Akwapim-Togo Ranges peak at 885 meters on Mt. Afadjato, the highest point in the country. Lowlands dominate the southern part of the country. To their immediate north are the Volta basin (to the east) and the Ashanti Uplands (to the west). Northern Ghana is dominated by dissected plateaus, which range between 150 and 460 meters in height.

Ghana has a warm tropical climate, with mean annual temperatures ranging between 26°C and 29°C. The weather is generally warm and dry in the southeast; warm and humid in the southwest; and hot and dry in the north. Ghana's climate is influenced by three main air masses: the hot and dry tropical continental winds (the *harmattan*), from the northeast; the cool and moist tropical maritime winds (the southwest monsoon), from the Gulf of Guinea; and the warm equatorial easterlies. The northern half of the country has one rainy season (May to October) and one dry season (November to April). Southern Ghana, however, has two rainy seasons and two dry seasons. The major rainy season is from May to June, whereas the minor is from September to November. The minor and major dry seasons last from July to August and from December to April, respectively. The heaviest rainfalls occur in the southwestern corner, where the mean annul rainfall reaches 2,230 millimeters. The amount of rainfall generally reduces northward.

People and Ethnic Groups

Ghana has a population of 18.4 million people (2000 census). Like most tropical African nations, Ghana's population is predominantly Black, with enormous ethno-linguistic diversity. The major ethnic groups include Akan (44%), Mole-Dagomba (16%), Ewe (13%), Ga (8%), and others (0.2%); each of which has several subgroups. The Akans are predominant in southwestern and central Ghana, the Ewes and Gas are mostly in the southeast, and the Mole-Dagombas are mainly in the north. More than fifty different languages and dialects are spoken in Ghana, but the official language is English. Islam and Christianity are the main non-African religions in the north and south, respectively. With a high fertility rate (five pregnancies per woman), a high birth rate (forty-four births per one thousand), and a high infant mortality rate (eighty-four deaths per one thousand live births), Ghana's demographic characteristics are not much different from those of other West African countries. However, Ghanaians are relatively well-educated; the nation's literacy rate of about 65% is surpassed only by Cape Verde's, in the West African context.

Whereas the majority of Ghanaians live in rural areas, there has been an increase in urbanization in recent years. In 1948, the urban share of the nation's population of 4.4 million was only 13%. By 1960, the urban share of the national population of 6.7 million had reached 23%; by the 1990s, more than a third of Ghanaians live in cities (Chamlee-Wright 1997). The main cities include Accra, the national capital; Tema, Kumasi, Cape Coast, and Temale. Accra is a typical primate city with a population of about 1.2 million. It is home to nearly all national government ministries, all the regional administrative offices of the Accra Metropolitan Area, and almost all international organizations and embassies in Ghana.

History and Politics

The ancestors of the people of Ghana are believed to have migrated from Mauritania and Mali in the thirteenth century. The work of James Anquandah (1982) suggests that by the end of the sixteenth century, most of the ethnic groups of contemporary Ghana had settled in their present location. Portuguese traders were the first Europeans to come to Ghana in the early 1470s; they named the area the Gold Coast because it was rich in minerals, particularly gold. The Portuguese established the first European fort at Elmina in 1482 to assert control over the gold, ivory, and timber trade. The British arrived in 1553, followed by the Dutch in 1595, the Swedes and Danes in 1640, and the Germans in 1683. These imperial powers competed for control of the Gold Coast, until it became a British colony in the 1874. The British colonial administration ended on March 6, 1957, when the Gold Coast became the first Black African nation to gain independence under the leadership of Kwame Nkrumah and changed its name to Ghana. The nation became a republic in 1960.

Several development analysts, including David Apter (1972), Mohammed Huq (1989), and Kwadwo Konadu-Agyemang have noted that in the immediate years following Ghana's independence, her economy was among the richest in Africa, with a relatively high annual gross domestic product (GDP) growth rate of about 6%; a substantial foreign exchange reserve; a well-educated and skilled workforce; and a strong civil service. Also, Ghana was the world's leading producer and exporter of cocoa and exported some 10% of the world's gold by the early 1960s. Nkrumah's socialist government instituted a policy of free education and health care, initiated mass industrialization and electrification,and established several state corporations to compete with private and foreign enterprises. By 1964, Nkrumah had resorted to autocratic rule and moved Ghana into a one-party state, by consolidating power in his Convention People's Party (CPP). Human right abuses by the government, economic mismanagement, corruption, and the consequent economic decline led to massive anti-government demonstrations across the country and, ultimately, Nkrumah's overthrow in 1966.

Unfortunately, the fall of Nkrumah did little to improve the well-being of Ghanaians, as political instability and economic mismanagement continued unabated. By 2000, Ghana's postcolonial political pendulum had swung intermittently between four military dictatorships and four democratic governments. The National Liberation Council (NLC), which overthrew Nkrumah, was replaced by the democratic government of K. A. Busia and his Progress Party in 1969, only to be toppled by the National Redemption Council (NRC) in 1972. Jerry Rawlings and his Armed Forces Revolutionary Council (AFRC), in turn, overthrew the NRC in 1979. In 1979, Rawlings handed over power to the democratic government of Hilla Limann, only to come back with his Provincial National Defence Council (PNDC) in yet another coup in 1981. Rawlings ruled Ghana as an elected civilian president from 1992 until 1999, when his National Democratic Congress (NDC) party was defeated in a general election by the current New Patriotic Party (NPP) headed by J.A. Kuffour.

Development Experience

Ghana's economy is dominated by agriculture, mining, and forestry. The leading exports are cocoa, timber, gold, bauxite, and diamonds. In the 1960s and 1970s, Ghana produced nearly a third of the world's cocoa, but in recent decades, cocoa output has declined as a result of factors such as increased drought and forest fire, lower producer prices, and increased smuggling to neighbouring Côte d'Iviore. Since the early 1990s, gold has surpassed cocoa in export earnings, and diamond output also has increased significantly. Ghana currently produces about 10% of the world's gold and a substantial amount of diamond, bauxite, and hardwood. Ghana has ample supply of arable land and a favourable climate for faming and human settlement. The nation's education, health, transportation, and communication facilities are also among the best in Sub-Saharan Africa. Nonetheless, "by the time Ghana could celebrate the silver jubilee of its independence, the most promising economy in Sub-Saharan Africa had atrophied, with all the conventional socioeconomic indicators of well-being pointing down" (Dzorgbo 2001). Whereas exogenous factors, such as the OPEC crisis of the 1970s, rising interest rates on foreign loans, and unfavorable terms of trade contributed to Ghana's decline, the main explanatory factors are internal: bad governance characterized by corruption, political arbitrariness, and the lack of development vision.

During the early 1980s, Rawlings and his PNDC government plunged Ghana into political extremism. With the support of radical students, the PNDC engaged in what Dzorgbro (2001) calls "Robin Hood" politics, involving extortion, detention, confiscation of property, abduction, and sometimes murder of the "enemies" of the revolution—that is, the rich. The violence-soaked socialist revolution pushed Ghana into a virtual economic coma. By 1982, it was clear that the revolution only exacerbated the nation's economic woes, because chronic food shortages, mass poverty, and astronomical inflation were prevalent.

The situation worsened in 1982–1983 with Ghana's worst drought of the twentieth century, resulting in high incidences of bush fire and hunger. Worse still, in 1983, more than 1 million Ghanaians were repatriated from Nigeria, putting additional pressure on the nation's economy. Things got so bad that Rawlings and his socialist revolutionaries were compelled to turn to capitalist nations including the United States and the United Kingdom for food and medical aid. In 1983, with pressure from the IMF and the World Bank, the Rawlings' government adopted a

Structural Adjustment Program (SAP), locally dubbed the Economic Recovery Program (ERP). As with IMF/World Bank packages elsewhere, Ghana's SAP entailed trade liberalization; public-sector retrenchment; removal of subsidies on food, petrol, and social services, including health and education, increased taxes, privatization, adoption of flexible foreign exchange regime, and devaluation of the nation's currency—the *cedi*.

Ghana's SAP received mixed reviews in the available literature. The IMF and World Bank touted Ghana's SAP as a success because of Ghana's improved economic growth rates; resuscitated cocoa, mining, and forestry industries; and restored confidence of international financial institutions in the nation's economy. Official reports suggest that Ghana registered an average GDP growth rate of about 5% annually under the program. However, some observers, notably UNICEF (1986) and Konadu-Agyemang (2001), have criticized Ghana's SAP for increasing the nation's dependence on foreign aid and imposing significant economic hardships on vulnerable groups such as women, children, and the poor through higher taxation, public sector retrenchment, and the removal of subsidies. Critics also contend that Ghana's SAP was geared toward growth, as measured by quantitative yardsticks such as income per capita and GDP, rather than development which generally entails a qualitative improvement in human welfare.

In response to these criticisms, the government embarked on its Program of Action to Mitigate the Social Costs of Adjustment (PAMSCAD) in 1987, to reduce mass poverty by providing training, work, and income through community development projects for targeted groups such as retrenched workers, women, and poor households. Several community development projects (e.g., construction of roads, schools, and health centres) were undertaken under PAMSCAD. However, critics contend that the PAMSCAD did little to alleviate the economic hardships faced by the truly disadvantaged, notably women. It is argued that most of the resources, credit, and construction projects initiated under the PAMSCAD favoured men over women. Brydon and Legge (1996) note that the section of the PAMSCAD designed to enhance the opportunity for women in development (PAMSCAD WID) "was the last to get off the ground." Furthermore, most of the income-generating activities funded for women only reinforced women's traditional roles of cooking, child care, and petty trading, rather than empowering them in new and more lucrative sectors of the economy.

Since 1992, Ghana has become politically stable, enjoying its longest spell of democratic government with no military intervention. The nation has embarked on several poverty-reduction programs under its Vision 2020 program, which seeks to alleviate poverty by 2020. Nonetheless, mass poverty, unemployment, corruption, and bureaucratic ineffi-ciencies persist. If true development entails the mobilization of human and natural resources to achieve better living standards for all (Dzorgbo 2001), then what Ghana really needs is a clearly de-fined, culturally informed development goal as well as good governance, couched in efficiency, transparency, public safety, and a respect for property rights, the rule of law, and environmental sustainability.

JOSEPH MENSAH

See also Nkrumah, Kwame; Structural Adjustment Program

References and Further Reading

Anquandah, James. *Rediscovering Ghana's Past.* Essex: Longman, 1982.

Apter, David E. *Ghana in Transition.* Princeton, NJ: Prin-ceton University Press, 1972.

Aryeetey, Ernest, Jane Harrigan, and Machiki Nissanke, eds. *Economic Reforms in Ghana: The Miracle and the Mirage.* Oxford: James Currey; Accra: Woeli Pub-lishing Services; and Trenton, NJ: Africa World Press, 2000.

Berry, LaVerle, ed. *Ghana: A Country Study.* Washington, DC: Federal Research Division, Library of Congress, 1995.

Brydon, Lynne, and Katen Legge. *Adjusting Society: The World Bank, the IMF and Ghana,* London and New York: I.B. Tauris Publishers, 1996.

Chamlee-Wright, Emily. *The Cultural Foundations of Eco-nomic Development: Urban Female Entrepreneurship in Ghana.* London and New York: Routledge, 1997.

Dzorgbo, Dan-Bright S. *Ghana in Search of Development: The Challenge of Governance, Economic Management, and Institutional Building.* Aldershot, UK; Burlington, Singapore, and Sydney: Ashgate, 2001.

Donkor, Kwabena. *Structural Adjustment and Mass Pover-ty in Ghana.* Aldershot, UK, Brookfield, Singapore, and Sydney: Ashgate, 1997.

Huq, M.M. *The Economy of Ghana: The First 25 Years Since Independence.* New York: St. Martin's Press, 1989.

Konadu-Agyemang, Kwadwo, ed. *IMF and World Bank Sponsored Structural Adjustment Programs in Africa: Ghana's Experience, 1983–1999.* Aldershot, UK, Bur-lington, Singapore, and Sydney: Ashgate, 2001.

Pereira, Sérgio *et al., Ghana: Economic Development in a Democratic Environment.* Washington, DC: Internation-al Monetary Fund, 2000.

Ray, Donald I. *Ghana: Politics, Economics and Society.* London: Frances Pinter Publishers, 1989; Boulder, CO: Lynne Rienner Publishers, 1989.

United Nations Economic Commission for Africa (ECA). *Africa's Alternative Framework to Structural Adjustment Programmes for Socio-Economic Recovery and Growth in the 1980s.* Addis Ababa: ECA, 1989.

UNICEF. *Ghana: Adjustment Policies and Programmes to Protect Children and Other Vulnerable Groups.* Accra: UNICEF, 1986.

World Bank. *Sub-Saharan Africa: From Crisis to Sustain-able Growth. A Long-Term Perspective Study.* Washing-ton, DC: World Bank, 1989.

GLASNOST **AND** PERESTROIKA

The twin notions of *glasnost* and *perestroika*, asso-ciated most of all with the name of Mikhail Gorbachev, mark a crucial episode in the late twentieth century: the attempt at serious reform of the political, economic, and social system called the Soviet Union, with far-reaching effects both in the USSR and beyond. This episode started in 1986 and lasted until August 1991, when a half-hearted reactionary coup put an end to Gorbachev's power and yielded, with winner Boris Yeltsin, a situation of which the crushing of the power of the Communist Party of the Soviet Union (CPSU) and the dismantling of the Soviet empire were inevitable consequences.

As notions, *glasnost* and *perestroika* are not Gor-bachev's inventions. *Perestroika* means rebuilding or reconstruction; *glasnost* means publicity or "being open to the public." While *perestroika* is really an ordinary word, *glasnost* has always had political con-notations, and the call for more *glasnost* in Russia dates back to Vladimir Lenin and Alexander Herzen (Laqueur 1989). Gorbachev launched *perestroika* and *glasnost* in 1987, and he became immensely popular in the West when he gave up the very idea of the Soviet block: the arms race slowed down abruptly, Velvet and other "soft" revolutions took place, and Ger-many was reunified after the fall of the Berlin Wall in 1989. The call for independence grew louder in most Soviet republics, especially in the Baltic states, and one after another split off in years to come. Countries west of Russia quickly left the idea of state socialism, reformed or not: instead of *perestroi-ka,* they opted—with the exception of Belarus—for liberal democracy, free market, and closer ties to Western Europe.

At home, Gorbachev was increasingly perceived as the person who "sold out" Soviet Russia to the West. *Glasnost* was a success, and a pluralistic free press was quickly established. But it proved a lot easier to point out what was wrong with a politically, economically, and socially bankrupt system than to lead the way to a better one. Reforms were started—for example, the acceptance of small private business, a relaxation of censorship, the introduction of real elections, rehabil-itation of many figures from the Russian and Soviet past, increased academic freedom, and allowance for Russian citizens to travel abroad. But it is easier to lift restrictions than it is to implement new policies such as the introduction of a "socialist market economy," the establishment of rule of law, or the top-down creation of a "civil society." As a popular Russian joke explained: "It is easy to turn an aquarium into a bowl of fish soup, but much more difficult to make an aquarium out of fish soup."

Support for the new policy came from various sides. Within the party, there was widespread recognition of the fact that the Soviet system had to reform itself if it wanted to survive, and the *nomenklatura* feared for its own position. From within the economic establishment, so-called technocrats who knew that the system was highly inefficient supported Gorbachev's policy of putting an end to fake statistics, "overfulfilling" of plans, corruption, and financial irresponsibility. From the side of the liberal-minded intelligentsia, there was a strong call for *glasnost*, academic freedom, and civil rights, many still cherishing the 1968 Dubček dream of a "socialism with a human face" (Scherrer 1996). Among the population at large, there was support from the victims of repression, in particular from relatives of people who had died in the Gulag. Finally, a strong impulse came from youth culture, which was interested in freedom rather than politics (Troitsky 1987).

Gorbachev's major slogan was an essentially weak variant of the TINA argument: "There Is No Alternative" (Afanas'ev 1988). While it was obvious to everybody that things had to change, a clear idea of what had to be was absent, and lack of alternative is never a lasting motivation. Once academia and public opinion had been liberated, an intensive search for alternatives began (Chernyshev 1995), which stimulated a "renaissance" of Russian national consciousness and the search for a new "national idea." Commentators have concluded, with the advantage of hindsight, that Gorbachev was too hesitant and inconsistent in his policies, and that he might have been more successful had he abolished, or at least left the Party at an early stage, and organized himself a populist platform—as Boris Yeltsin did with instant success in 1991.

Soviet-style communism was a twentieth century social experiment that failed (Furet 1995; Walicki 1995). This experiment included the attempt to create a New Man, the *Homo sovieticus* (Kharkhordin 1999). One of the burning questions for post-Soviet Russia still is whether *Homo post-sovieticus* is capable of forming the human material for a new, prosperous, and democratic Russia. The Russian word for experiment is *opyt*, which also means experience, and one thing is clear: all thinking about alternatives will have to take into account the Soviet *opyt*.

Ultimately, *perestroika* has lost its meaning because there no longer is a "system" that needs reform in order to survive, but *glasnost* has not lost its political relevance.

EVERT VAN DER ZWEERDE

See also Gorbachev, Mikhail

References and Further Reading

Cnernyshev, Sergei B., ed. *Inoe: Khrestomatiia Novogo Rossiiskogo Samosoznaniia.* Moskva: Argus, 1995.
Furet, François. *Le Passé d'une Illusion : Essai sur l'Idée Communiste au XXe Siècle.* Paris: Robert Laffont/ Calmann-Lévy, 1995.
Kharkhordin, Oleg. *The Collective and the Individual in Russia: A Study of Practices.* Berkeley, CA, Los Angeles, and London: University of California Press, 1999.
Sakwa, Richard. *Russian Politics and Society.* London and New York: Routledge, 1993.
Scherrer, Jutta. *Requiem für den Roten Oktober: Russlands Intelligenzija im Umbruch 1986–1996.* Leipzig: Leipziger Universitätsverlag, 1996.
Walicki, Andrzej. *Marxism and the Leap to the Kingdom of Freedom: The Rise and Fall of the Communist Utopia.* Stanford, CA: Stanford University Press, 1995.

GLOBAL CLIMATE CHANGE

In 1988, climatologist James Hansen of the National Aeronautics and Space Administration's Goddard Institute of Space Studies warned, in testimony before the US Senate, that human activities were altering the world's climate. The statement ignited a scientific and policymaking controversy—not everyone agreed that humans were changing the climate, and even if humans were changing the climate, not everyone agreed that the change was such a bad thing.

What Hansen told the Senate was that combustion of fossil fuels, by increasing the concentration of the gas carbon dioxide in the Earth's atmosphere, was creating a "greenhouse effect." Greenhouses allow farmers and gardeners to grow plants through the cold months of the year by allowing sunlight to shine through the walls and ceiling to warm the contents, but then trapping the heat inside so that it cannot be lost to the outside environment.

The same thing happens in the greenhouse effect, except the effect is global—carbon dioxide and other "greenhouse" gases replace glass and plastic in trapping heat radiation that would otherwise be lost to space, thus raising the temperature of the Earth's surface.

The science behind Hansen's testimony was not new. Svante Arrhenius, a Swedish scientist who was awarded the Nobel Prize in Chemistry in 1903, began a side project in the 1890s investigating the cause of the ice ages, prolonged periods of below normal temperatures and extensive glaciation lasting thousands—even millions—of years. In 1895, Arrhenius presented a paper at a meeting of the Stockholm Physical Society entitled "On the Influence of Carbonic Acid in the Air upon the Temperature of the Ground," which explained how changes in atmospheric carbon dioxide concentrations affected the heat balance of the Earth.

Change in the Wind

Arrhenius's work focused on carbon dioxide, a major by-product of combustion of fossil fuels. But the suite of greenhouse gases includes naturally occurring compounds such as water vapor, methane (a major component of natural gas), nitrous oxide (also known as laughing gas), and ozone; and man-made compounds such as chlorofluorocarbons, fluorocarbons, and sulfur hexafluoride.

While the ozone layer at the top of the atmosphere is destroyed by chlorofluorocarbons, the fact is that human activities have increased the concentrations of carbon dioxide, nitrous oxide, and, of course, the man-made greenhouse gases. The concentrations of some of the naturally occurring greenhouse gases, such as water vapor and methane, may increase as the climate warms, for example, increasing the water holding capacity of the atmosphere or increasing release of methane from "cold" storage in wetland or marine sediments.

Climate Changes

Based on fundamental physics, it is natural to predict that an increase in the concentration of greenhouse gases in the atmosphere would lead to warming at the Earth's surface. And if the concentration of greenhouse gases was the only factor that changed, the prediction would likely be accurate.

But the Earth-ocean-atmosphere system is much more complicated. Many things affect global temperatures. Albedo (reflectivity) of the Earth's surface can affect the amount of solar radiation absorbed or reflected—the more that is absorbed, the warmer the Earth's surface, whereas the more that is reflected, the cooler. Warmer temperatures can lead to increased precipitation—more snow, particularly in the Arctic and Subarctic regions, may paradoxically increase albedo and lead to lower global temperatures overall!

Particulate matter in the atmosphere can reflect solar radiation away from the Earth's surface, thus making the surface cooler. Volcanic eruptions, by spewing ash, dust, and small particulates into high levels of the atmosphere, can cool the Earth's climate. Mt. Pinatubo in the Philippines erupted in 1991 and cooled global temperatures by as much as 0.5°C (about 0.9°F). The 1815 eruption of Tambora, on the island of Sumbawa in what is now Indonesia, was one of the largest volcanic explosions in history, blasting fifty cubic kilometers (about eleven cubic miles) of material as high as forty-three kilometers (twenty-six miles) above the Earth's surface. The average drop in global temperatures was 1°C (1.8°F). Changes in volcanic activity can thus affect global climate.

Higher concentrations of carbon dioxide can lead to greater plant growth, which in turn would slow the increase of carbon dioxide in the atmosphere. Likewise, the oceans can, and probably have, absorbed a lot of the excess carbon dioxide released into the atmosphere since the dawn of the Industrial Revolution. But warmer temperatures may lead to more fires, which would release more carbon dioxide into the atmosphere and possibly produce more surface warming.

If warmer global temperatures trigger massive melting of glaciers and the Arctic and Antarctic icecaps, sea levels will rise. This would be disastrous for island nations and other regions that are barely above sea level now. Bangladesh, a densely populated, low-lying country that borders the Indian Ocean, is one of the most vulnerable to sea level rise. The average elevation of the nation is three meters (about ten feet) above sea level. Tropical cyclones (otherwise known as hurricanes or typhoons) periodically batter the country, and storm surges—walls of water pushed forward by storm winds—can inundate large swaths of the Ganges River Delta, where much of the country lies. In 1970, at least three hundred thousand people died when a twelve-meter (forty-foot) surge swept the country.

Major climate changes can occur relatively suddenly. Temperature changes as much as 10°C (about 18°F) may occur in as little as a couple of decades. Such abrupt changes would give human societies and plant and animal populations no warning and little time to respond, possibly triggering societal collapses and mass extinctions.

While the concern is over the deleterious effects of climate change, some regions may benefit. Growing seasons may lengthen in the middle and high latitudes, and some arid areas may receive more rainfall, thus increasing food production. Minimum daily temperatures are rising, which may reduce heating costs for human societies living in areas of strongly developed cold seasons.

But these beneficial effects are not without cost. Ecological systems adapted to cold conditions, such as high-elevation forests and tundra communities, may disappear completely as they are replaced by species adapted to warmer conditions. Formerly arid areas that experience an increase in rainfall may be subjected to increased flooding and soil erosion. Warmer temperatures and longer growing seasons may affect fire frequency, which would lead to increased destruction of forests and grasslands. Also, longer growing seasons may increase the pressure to convert natural systems to agriculture, thus causing a net loss of available habitat for native plants and animals and driving some species to extinction.

Past Extremes

The Earth has been through worse climate extremes in its history. For example, between about 550 million and 800 million years ago, the Earth experienced several prolonged cold snaps—so cold that land-based glaciers reached to within ten degrees latitude of the equator. During these "Snowball Earth" episodes, much of the ocean surface froze, although there is debate over whether the oceans were completely covered in ice or whether the oceans were more of a "slushball" than a "snowball." During another significant glaciation that occurred about 450 million years ago, the Earth may have had atmospheric carbon dioxide concentrations ten times higher than those today.

The Earth has had its share of warm spells, too. One of the warmest periods in Earth's history was between 50 million and 55 million years ago, when there was little or no ice at the Earth's poles, and tropical conditions extended to midlatitude regions.

Prognostication and Observation

The Intergovernmental Panel on Climate Change (IPCC) was established by the United Nations Environment Program (UNEP) and the World Meteorological Organization (WMO) in 1988 to coordinate international efforts to assess the likelihood and effects of climate change. The IPCC has issued several reports—the IPCC Third Assessment Report, the most recent at the time of publication of this encyclopedia, was released in 2001.

The IPCC, in its *Third Assessment Report*, concluded that the decade of the 1990s was the warmest since instrumental records began being systematically kept in the 1860s. The panel also concluded that human activity is responsible for most of the warming that has been observed in the second half of the twentieth century.

The *Third Assessment Report* predicts that global temperatures will rise between 1.4° and 5.8°C (2.5–10°F) over the 1990 average by the year 2100. Sea levels are predicted to rise between 0.09 to 0.88 meters (0.3 to 2.9 feet) over 1990 levels by 2100.

Warming and sea level rises already have been observed the last few decades. But other changes in the Earth's climate have been recorded. The extent of Arctic sea ice has decreased, and the ice cap has melted at the North Pole in the summer. Glaciers are receding worldwide, with mountain glaciers in the tropics and midlatitudes most seriously affected. Precipitation patterns have changed, with increases in some regions and decreases in others.

Changes have been observed in come cyclical climate phenomena. For example, El Niño episodes— in which a buildup of warm surface waters off the west coast of South America disrupts climate in the tropics, subtropics, and midlatitudes—appear to have grown more frequent and more intense since the 1970s.

Regional Outlooks

Developing nations, already stressed to meet the needs of growing populations, will be hard-pressed to cope with the changing climate. All have limited resources and technological capability that will limit their ability to respond. What follows are predictions given in the IPCC *Third Assessment Report* for Africa, Asia, Latin America, the Polar Regions, and small island states.

- **Africa**. Africa will be especially vulnerable to climate change. Food production will decrease, and infectious disease outbreaks will increase. Many native plant and animal species will be pushed over the brink of extinction. Recurring droughts will be even more of a problem than they are today. Deserts will likely increase in extent in the subtropical portions of the continent. In the tropical, particularly the equatorial portion, larger and more frequent floods will result as rainfall patterns change. Also, along the coasts, higher sea levels and more intense storms will place coastal areas at greater risk.
- **Asia**. Developing nations in Asia have to face some of the same challenges faced by Africa in coping with climate change. Temperate and tropical regions have and will continue to be beset by more extreme climate events, ranging

from fires and droughts to floods and tropical storms. Low-lying countries, such as Bangladesh, will be hit hard by rising sea levels and resulting increase in the height of storm surges. The Asian monsoon will strengthen, increasing rainfall and flooding along the rivers draining into the Indian and Pacific Oceans. In addition, northern portions of Asia will warm, disrupting the boreal forest and tundra regions as well as the populations that depend on the resources of the far north.

- **Latin America**. Mexico and the Caribbean, and Central and South American states have rapidly growing populations but limited resources to fuel the growth needed to keep up with the increase. Many localities depend on Sierran and Andean mountain glaciers to supply their water, but with the observed retreat and loss of alpine glaciers, the dependability of the once-reliable source is questionable. Agriculture will suffer, as well as the diversity of the regions rich plant and animal communities. Extreme events, such as floods, droughts, and storms, will become even more extreme. Coastal and island states will be even more vulnerable to tropical storms than in the past.

- **Polar Regions**. Polar regions are just as likely to affect the global climate as be affected by it. Warming is shrinking the extent of glaciers as well as the thickness of sea-ice. Permafrost, a layer of ice in the soil that normally never melts, will do just that—melt. Polar and subpolar ecosystems will be disrupted as species migrate north with rising atmospheric temperatures. On the other hand, higher temperatures will force methane—a more powerful greenhouse gas than carbon dioxide—out of cold storage in wetland and marine sediments and into the atmosphere. This would trigger even more atmospheric warming. As glaciers and sea-ice melt, more fresh water will flow into the ocean. This influx of fresh water may disrupt ocean currents that moderate the climate, much as the Gulf Stream moderates the climate of eastern North America and western Europe, thus triggering abrupt climate changes.

- **Small Island States**. Most small island states lay in the tropical and subtropical Pacific Ocean, the Indian Ocean, and the Caribbean Sea. They have limited land surface—migration off the islands will be almost impossible for most plants and animals. People may be able to move, but in that case, many of the island populations affected will be forced off homelands their ancestors have occupied for centuries.

Rising sea levels and increasing storm frequency and intensity are a major problem for these nations. Water supplies may be disrupted, and vital ecological systems may be damaged. For example, coral bleaching—in which the animals that build up the coral reefs die—is largely caused by warm ocean temperatures. Fish stocks may decline, endangering the food supplies of these nations, many of which have few options for food and agricultural development.

DAVID M. LAWRENCE

See also Deforestation; Desertification; Disaster Relief; Environment: Government Policies; Environmentalism; Erosion, Land; Global Climate Change; Infectious Diseases; Irrigation; Natural Disasters; Rain Forest, Destruction of; United Nations Environmental Program (UNEP); United Nations Food and Agriculture Organization (FAO); Urbanization: Impact on Environment; Water Resources and Distribution; Wildlife Preservation; World Health Organization (WHO)

References and Further Reading

Field, Christopher B., and Michael R. Rapauch, eds. *Global Carbon Cycle: Integrating Humans, Climate, and the Natural World*. New York: Island Press, 2004.

Intergovernmental Panel on Climate Change. *Climate Change 2001: Impacts, Adaptation, and Vulnerability. A Contribution of Working Group II to the Third Assessment Report of the Intergovernmental Panel on Climate Change*. New York: Cambridge University Press, 2001. (http://www.grida.no/climate/ipcc_tar/wg1/index.htm).

Intergovernmental Panel on Climate Change. *Climate Change 2001: The Scientific Basis. A Contribution of Working Group I to the Third Assessment Report of the Intergovernmental Panel on Climate Change*. New York: Cambridge University Press, 2001. (http://www.grida.no/climate/ipcc_tar/wg2/index.htm).

Intergovernmental Panel on Climate Change. *Climate Change 2001: Synthesis Report. A Contribution of Working Groups I, II, and III to the Third Assessment Report of the Intergovernmental Panel on Climate Change*. New York: Cambridge University Press, 2001. (http://www.ipcc.ch/pub/syreng.htm).

Markandya, Anil, and Kirsten Halsnaes. *Climate Change and Sustainable Development: Prospects for Developing Countries*. London: Earthscan Publications Ltd., 2003.

McMichael, A. J., D. H. Campbell-Lendrum, C. F. Corvalán, K. L. Ebi, A. Githeko, J. D. Scheraga, and A. Woodward, eds. *Climate Change and Human Health: Risks and Responses*. Geneva, Switzerland: World Health Organization, 2003.

National Research Council. *Abrupt Climate Change: Inevitable Surprises*. Washington, DC: National Academy Press, 2002. (http://www.nap.edu/books/0309074347/html/).

Okonski, Kendra. *Adapt or Die: The Science, Politics, and Economics of Climate Change*. London: Profile, 2003.

Ravindranath, N. H. and Jayant A. Sathaye. *Climate Change and Developing Countries.* Boston: Kluwer Academic Publishers, 2002.

Weart, Spencer. *The Discovery of Global Warming.* Cambridge, MA: Harvard University Press, 2003.

GLOBALIZATION: IMPACT ON DEVELOPMENT

From the early 1990s onward, globalization has become the central topic of debate in social science and in both developed and developing societies, due to the movement of money, goods, people, technology, and ideas across national borders at an accelerating pace. Globalization refers to the transformation of much of the world into a single-market economy where national borders are decreasingly serving as a barriers to the free flow of goods, services, information, and money. Globalization also refers to the relationships between nations and societies and the influences that developments in one society have on others. The driving idea behind globalization is free-market capitalism, meaning that the more market forces rule and the more open the economy to free trade and competition, the more efficient and flourishing the economy will be. Globalization means the spread of free-market capitalism to virtually every country in the world. It also has its own set of economic rules—rules that revolve around opening, deregulating, and privatizing your economy. The privatization of state-owned enterprises, the liberalization and deregulation of markets—especially for services—and the removal of a bevy of structural distortions, have all worked to stimulate cross-border corporate integration, both within transnational corporations and between independent firms or group of firms.

Globalization is more than the internationalization of commerce and manufacturing; it represents a new development paradigm that creates new links among corporations, international organizations, governments, communities, and families. As markets have spread, tying populations together, environmental, military, social, and political interdependence have increased proportionately. The forces of globalization—the relentless expansion of market forces and the constant search for greater economic efficiencies—influence everything from indigenous cultures to environmental and labor standards to patterns of productivity. Although globalization has been taking place for decades, if not centuries, the incorporation of the world into a single capitalist economic system began after the World War II. After the war, the General Agreement on Tariffs and Trade (GATT) was created by the international community, along with the International Monetary Fund (IMF), the World Bank, and other international organizations.

Liberals had long believed that unhampered trade would result not only in maximum economic welfare for the participant states but also in more peaceful relations among states. Each state would benefit from such trade and have a vested interest in its continuance, uninterrupted by war. Based on the principles of multilateral cooperation, GATT had a mandate to roll back tariffs from their pre-war peaks and to gradually reduce them in the future. GATT was extremely successful in 1947 during the first Geneva Round in reducing tariffs by 35%. Successive rounds in the 1950s, 1960s, and 1970s, and the recent Uruguay Round have virtually eliminated tariffs on manufactured goods. In 1994, 117 nations agreed to the following: (1) reduce tariffs 38% for developed countries; (2) eliminate certain nontariff barriers and subsidies; (3) broaden GATT principles to areas such as trade in services, investment, and intellectual property rights; and (4) apply more effective disciplines to agricultural trade. Negotiators established long-term rules and reduced national policies that distorted and hindered access to the market. Nevertheless, agricultural subsidies remain obstacles to free trade; farmers in each of the developed countries wield too much political power to allow anything but minimal face-saving formulas to be reached.

By cutting tariffs substantially in successive rounds of negotiations, GATT could claim much of the credit for the postwar growth of the world trade and production. Its framework is based on the principle of reciprocity—that one state's lowering of trade barriers to another should be matched in return—and of nondiscrimination. The latter principle is embodied in the "most-favored nation" (MFN) concept, which says that trade restrictions imposed by a GATT member must be applied equally to all GATT members. That is, every member is entitled to the same treatment that a state gives its most-favored trading partner. If Australia applies a 20% tariff on auto parts imported from France, it is not supposed to apply a 40% tariff on auto parts from the United States. In this way, GATT does not remove barriers to trade altogether but equalizes them in global framework in order to create a level playing field for all member states. States are not prevented from protecting their own industries by a variety of means but cannot play favorites among their trading partners.

An exception to the MFN system is the Generalized System of Preference (GSP) through which industrialized states began in the 1970s to give trade concessions to third world states to help the latter's economic development. These preferences amount to a promise by wealthy states to allow imports from less developed ones under even lower tariffs than those imposed under MFN.

In 1995, GATT members began to operate at a higher level of institutionalization, becoming the World Trade Organization (WTO). The WTO has enlarged its membership, and 135 countries that have agreed to adhere to its free-trade rules are spread across the globe.

Regional free-trade areas are also very important in the structure of world trade. In such areas, groups of neighboring states agree to clear away the entire structure of trade barriers within their area. The most important free-trade area is in Europe; it is connected with the European Union but with a somewhat larger membership. Europe contains a number of small industrialized states living close together, so the creation of a single integrated market allows states to gain economic advantages that come inherently to a large state such as the United States. In October 1992, the North American Free Trade Agreement (NAFTA) was signed between the United States, Canada, and Mexico. NAFTA, which went into effect on January 1, 1994, created a free-trade area of some 370 million consumers by linking the United States to its largest (Canada) and third-largest (Mexico) trading partners.

During the Cold War, the Soviet bloc maintained its own trading bloc, the Council for Mutual Economic Assistance (CMEA), also known as COMECON. After the Soviet Union collapsed, the members scrambled to join up with the world economy, from which they had been largely cut off.

The Globalization of the Trade and Finance

Globalization has developed dramatically since the Cold War. It now encompasses economic interaction, ideas and information technology, culture, and even labor force. Distance ceases to be a decisive factor in the overall competition for market share. The worldwide movement of production, capital, and information has become easier and more widely used. Globalization can be seen most clearly in the quickening pace and scope of international commerce. Global exports as a share of global domestic product have increased from 14% in 1970 to 24% today, and the growth of trade has consistently outpaced growth in global output. In the United States, the ratio of two-way trade and investment income flows as a share of gross domestic product has roughly tripled since the 1960s. Annual global flows of

foreign direct investment surged to a record $827 billion in 1999, with 25% directed to less developed countries (LDCs), up from 17% in 1990. Indeed, by 2005, international trade is expected to account for 40% of national output in industrial countries and more than 50% in developing countries. International financial flows, only $20 billion per day fifteen years ago, are now more than $1.5 trillion per day, or $548 trillion a year; by 2015, they may reach $30 trillion per day. About two-thirds of this moves through the banking centers in just four countries: Germany, Japan, the United Kingdom, and the United States. To accommodate the globalization of money, there has been a parallel globalization of banking and other financial services. In a relatively short period of time, banks have grown from hometown to national to multinational enterprises. One result of increased international trade and both financial and monetary interchange is that the subjects of national economic health and international economics have become increasingly enmeshed. Domestic economics, employment, inflation, and overall growth are heavily dependent on foreign markets, imports of resources, currency exchange rates, capital flows, and other international economic factors. The rise in trade is both a cause and a result of this increased international economic interdependence. The health of the United States economy depends increasingly on the prosperity of its trading partners and on the smooth flow of trade and finance across borders. For better or worse the trend toward global economic integration has gained enormous momentum.

The expansion of international trade and foreign investment has not been the result of some grand design imposed on the global economy. It has resulted from two developments of the 1980s: the collapse of global communism and the demise of the Third World's romance with import substitution. The fall of the Berlin Wall and the final disintegration of the Soviet empire two years later released 400 million people from the grip of centrally commanded and essentially closed economic systems. Meanwhile, the debt crisis of 1982 and the resulting "Lost Decade" of the 1980s imposed a painful hangover on many Third World nations that had tried and failed to reach prosperity by shunning foreign capital and by protecting and subsidizing domestic "infant" industries. Beginning with Chile in mid-1970s and China later that decade, LDC from Mexico and Argentina to India more recently have been opening their markets and welcoming foreign investment. The globalization of the last decade has not been the result of a blind faith in markets imposed from above, but of the utter exhaustion of any alternative vision.

Global Communication

In addition to trade, globalization is also widely associated with the technological revolution in transport, communications and data processing. These developments have changed what is produced and how it is produced. In this light many observers have characterized the global economy as an informational, knowledge-based, postindustrial or service economy. The Internet is the most prominent and visible of networking technologies. It is credited with holding extravagant promise for the entire globe. An increasing body of research, as well as firsthand observations, suggest that the Internet has the capacity to change nearly every aspect of social, political, and economic life. In the business world, it is an enabling technology that makes possible new products and services and new ways of organizing markets, connecting with customers, managing relations with suppliers, structuring the corporation, and designing business processes.

The World Wide Web is a borderless world with access available to anyone, from anywhere, at anytime. If one has Internet access, one suffers no limitation because of distance or location. The Internet was developed in the late 1960s at the initiative of the US Department of Defense. Its intent was to enable scientists and engineers working on military contracts to share computers, resources, and ideas. The popularity of the Internet spread slowly through the academic world, which by the mid-1980s was its principal user. In 1994, commercial companies surpassed universities as the leading users of the Internet. Today, the sharply plummeting price of personal computers has fueled the growth of Internet popularity. The boundary of the consumer's market space is the World Wide Web. Furthermore, for businesses, the value chain can be managed from anywhere in the world with the rich and deep exchange of information available with digital networks. Cellular phones are becoming available worldwide, enabling many in the world who have never before made a phone call to communicate instantly with others. The "wireless world" of cellular phones which uses radio waves rather than installed lines is growing by almost 50% yearly, allowing communication between rural areas in developing countries with wired developed countries where connected telephone lines are already abundant. According to the *The Economist,* "the death of distance as a determinant of the cost of communications will probably be the single most important economic force shaping society in the first half of the twenty-first century" (*The Economist* September 1995).

Communication technology set this era of globalization apart from any other. Communication technology has drastically transformed the way people communicate with each other.

Globalization and Democracy

Such revolutionary changes in communication have invariably had profound effects on the quality and vitality of democracy. There is evidence that globalization can enhance democracy in the United States and abroad. For example, the globe-spanning Internet allows people everywhere to gain access to information that makes them more informed and gives them the tools to form alliances with people around the world who share similar interests and concerns, such as environmental protection and human rights. With imperfect control over the information that crosses their national borders, moreover, nondemocratic regimes become less stable as their people gain access to ideas about self-governance and individual rights. This assisted in toppling regimes in the Soviet Union and Eastern Europe and has threatened the Communist regime in China. Also, many nations that have successfully joined the burgeoning global market economy, including South Korea and Taiwan, have recently become more democratic. Scholars believe this comes about because of the fact that people in economically successful nations tend to become much more demanding of their governments, eventually insisting on better service and more citizen participation in decision making. Furthermore, by raising the general standard of living, free trade allows people to achieve higher levels of education and to gain access to alternative sources of information. It helps to create a larger and more independent minded middle class that can form the backbone of more representative forms of government. The wealth created from expanded trade can help to nurture and sustain civil institutions that can offer ideas and influence outside government. Involvement in the global economy exposes citizens to new arrangements.

In his book *Business as a Calling*, Michael Novak explains the linkage with what he calls the "wedge theory," wherein capitalism brings the ideals of free societies to repressive regimes, "wedg[ing] a democratic camel's nose under the authoritarian tent" (Novak 1996).

Globalization also poses some threats to democracy. Globalization has the potential to undermine the degree of political equality in society as it alters the relative power of individuals, groups, and organizations. In a highly competitive, globalized economy, for instance, labor unions tend to lose political influence while large business enterprises gain it. Low-skilled manual workers, with little to offer global enterprises—such as the inner-city poor—suffer declining incomes and lose their ability to sway government officials. Also, economic globalization can undermine popular sovereignty to the extent that it decreases the ability of government to make and enforce policies that control the destinies of their jurisdictions or protect the well-being of their citizens. More broadly, many analyst have linked the growth of global relations to diminishing nation-state, the decline of the nation-state and retreat of state. Such assertions have triggered a host of rebuttals. For example, certain authors insist that globalization has done nothing to undermine sovereign statehood. According to this view, the increased flow of global communications may in some cases such as ecology—strengthen the state rather than undermine it.

Globalization and Its Impact on Developing Countries

Does globalization benefit most people and most countries, or only a few? On that, the evidence is mixed. It is argued that for the poorer developing countries, most of which are far removed from the critical nodes of growth, the impact of globalization and alliance capitalism is likely to be marginal—except in so far as they may benefit from "trickle down" affect through some manners of subcontracting. The historical growth of trade, it is suggested, has not occurred evenly throughout the world. On the whole, the decreased importance of territorial geography has gone markedly further in North America, the Pacific Rim, and Western Europe than in Sub-Saharan Africa and Central Asia. Phenomena such as global companies and electronic mail have been primarily concentrated in the so-called North. Trade is overwhelmingly dominated by the countries of the Northern Hemisphere. These countries amass 67% of the merchandise exports and 76% of the exports in goods and services combined. The percentage of the world trade shared by LDCs is relatively small, especially in per capita figure. Only a small percentage of global commerce occurs among LDCs. The merchandise trade among LDCs in 1999 accounted for a scant 14% of the world total. Moreover, the handful of developed countries bought 54% of all LDC exports. The pattern of trade leaves the LDCs heavily dependent on the developed countries for export earning

and, thus, places them in a vulnerable position. Finally, it has been argued that developed countries predominantly export manufactured and processed products. LDCs export mostly primary products, such as food, fiber, fuels, and minerals. Developing countries also face the challenge of competing for what is called "foreign direct investment" (FDI) against the developed countries, which— possessing more advanced human and physical infrastructures—offer more attractive locations for international production. Indeed, the early signs of globalization brought forth warnings of a marginalization of developing countries. Analysts pointed to a concentration of investment in the triad of Europe, Japan, and the United States.

On the other hand, some analysts believe that LDCs have the most to gain from engaging in the global economy. First, they gain access to much larger markets, both for imports and exports. On the import side, consumers gain access to a dramatically larger range of goods and services, raising their real standard of living. Domestic producers gain access to a wider range and better quality of intermediate inputs at lower prices. On the export side, domestic industries can enjoy a quantum leap in economies of scale by serving global markets rather than a confined and underdeveloped domestic market only.

Second, LDCs that open themselves up to international trade and investment gain access to a much higher level of technology. This provides LDCs the most needed technology without bearing the cost of expensive, up-front research and development. Poor countries can import the technology off the shelf, much of it embodied in imported capital equipment—that is, machinery that raises the productive capacity of the country.

Third, engagement in the global economy provides capital to fuel future growth. Most LDCs are people rich and capital poor. In a few countries in Asia, the level of domestic savings has been high enough to finance domestic investment, but typically the domestic pool of savings in an LDC is inadequate. Global capital markets can fill the gap, allowing poor nations to accelerate their pace of growth.

Fourth, engagement in global economy encourages governments to follow more sensible economic policies. Sovereign nations remain free to follow whatever economic policies their government chooses, but globalization has raised the cost that must be paid for bad policies. With capital more mobile than ever, countries that insist on the following anti-market policies will find themselves being dealt out of the global competition for investment. As a consequence, nations have a greater incentive to choose policies that encourage foreign investment, and domestic, market-led growth.

Fifth, engagement in the global economy encourages governments to follow more sensible economic policies. Sovereign nations remain free to follow whatever economic policies their governments choose, but globalization has raised the cost that must be paid for bad policies (Griswold 2001).

History suggests that the probable winners are likely to be those developing countries which open their markets to trade and tend to be more prosperous that nations that are relatively closed. The wealthiest nations and regions of the world—Western Europe, the United States, Canada, Japan, Hong Kong, Taiwan, South Korea, Singapore—are all trade-oriented. Their producers, with a few notable exceptions, must compete against other multinational producers in the global marketplace. In contrast, the poorest regions of the world—the Indian subcontinent and Sub-Saharan Africa, for example remain the least friendly to foreign trade. Meanwhile, those countries that have moved decisively toward openness—Chile, China, and Poland, among others—have reaped tangible in their standard of living.

In practice, when states have relied on a policy of autarky (to avoid trading altogether and instead try to produce everything one needs by oneself) they have eventually lagged behind others. China's experience illustrates the problems with autarky. China's economic isolation in the 1950s and 1960s resulted from an economic embargo imposed by the United States and its allies and was deepened during its own Cultural Revolution in the late 1960s when it broke ties with the Soviet Union. In that period, all things foreign were rejected. For instance, Chinese computer programmers were not allowed to use foreign software such as AssemblerLanguage and Fortran—standards in the rest of the world. Instead, they had to create their own software; China would not depend on foreigners for goods, services, or technology. As a result, the computer industry lagged far behind, reinventing the wheel, as the world's computer industry sped ahead. When China opened up to the world economy in the 1980s, the pattern was reversed. The rapid expansion of trade, along with market-oriented reforms in its domestic economy, resulted in rapid economic growth, which continued into the mid-1990s.

Globalization is making it easier to transfer capital and technology across borders, thereby giving lower-wage developing countries access to improved production techniques and so strengthening their economies. Likewise, it is not unreasonable to expect that as productivity rises in developing countries, so too will wages or the real exchange rate. As this happens, those countries become significant markets for goods from more developed countries.

In order for every country to benefit from global markets, wealthier economies must assist the developing world to ride the wave of globalization. If the benefits are to be reaped, then domestic policy settings of developing nations need to encourage and sustain the development of an efficient and competitive economy. Furthermore, the international community must work to develop rules that are trade enhancing, which clear away trade distortions and restrictions including those behind the national borders, and which are consistent with imperatives of sustainable development. Only by working together can the international community address these issues of common interest.

NASSER MOMAYEZI

See also Agriculture: Impact of Globalization; Debt: Impact on Development; Energy: Impact on Development; Industrialization; Poverty: Impact on Development

References and Further Reading

Charles W. Kegley, Jr., and Eugene R. Wittkopf. *The Global Agenda: Issues and Perspectives*, 4th ed. New York: McGraw Hill, 2001.

Falk, Richard "State of Siege: Will Globalization Win Out?," *International Affairs*, 73 (January 1997).

Friedman, Thomas L. *The Lexus and the Olive Tree: Understanding Globalization.* New York: Farrar, Straus & Giroux, 1999.

Keohane, Robert O., and Joseph S. Nye, Jr. "Globalization: What's New? What's Hot? (And So What)." *Foreign Policy*, 118 (Spring 2000).

Klab, Don, Marco Van der Land, Richard Staring, Bart Van Steenbergen, and Nico Wilterdink. *The Ends of Globalization: Bringing Society Back In.* New York and Oxford: Rowman & Littlefield Publishers, 2000.

Mandle, Jay R. "Trading Up: Why Globalization Aids the Poor," *Commonweal* (June, 2000).

Maswood, Javed. *International Political Economy and Globalization*, Hackensack, NJ, and London: World Scientific Publishing, 2000.

Mittelman, James H., ed. *The Globalization Syndrome; Transformation and Resistance.* Princeton, NJ: Princeton University Press, 2000.

Rodrik, Dani. *Has Globalization Gone Too Far?* Washington, DC: Institute for International Economics, 1997.

Rosenau, James N. "The Complexities and Contradictions of Globalization," in *Global Issues: 98/99*, Robert M. Jackson, ed. Sluice Dock, Guilford, CT: Dushkin/McGraw Hill, 1999.

Sachs, Jeffrey. "International Economics: Unlocking the Mysteries of Globalization," *Foreign Policy*, 110 (Spring 1998).

Schaeffer, Robert K. *Understanding Globalization*, Oxford: Rowman & Littlefield, 1997.

Scholte, Jan A. *Globalization: A Critical Introduction*, New York: St. Martin's Press, 2000.

Scott, Gregory M., Louis Furmanski, and Randal Jones, Jr. *21 Debated Issues in World Politics.* Upper Saddle River, NJ: Prentice Hall, 2000.

Spanier, John, and Robert L. Wendzel, *Games Nations Play*, 9th ed. Washington, DC: Congressional Quarterly, 1996.
Waters, M. *Globalization.* London: Routledge, 1995.

GOH CHOK TONG

Goh Chok Tong, Senior Minister of Singapore, was born on May 20, 1941, and graduated in 1964 from the University of Singapore with a bachelor's degree in Economics. He went on to pursue a master's degree in economics at Williams College in the United States. After returning to Singapore in 1967, he worked in the Ministry of Finance and served as an executive at several private transportation companies. His political career started in 1976 when he joined the People Action's Party and became a member of Parliament. From 1977 through 1985, Goh held various ministerial positions in the Singaporean government, and was appointed first deputy prime minister in 1985.

Due to Goh's less aggressive personality and weak communication skills in English, Prime Minister Lee Kuan Yew reluctantly chose Goh as his successor. However, Lee let his fellow cabinet members vote, and the unanimous vote was for Goh. On November 28, 1990, Goh was appointed as the prime minister of Singapore.

Although there was rumor that Goh was only the seat warmer for Lee Hsien Long (Lee Kuan Yew's son), Goh proved an effective leader in his own right. Under Goh's leadership, the Singapore economy recovered after the economic crisis and the severe acute respiratory syndrome (SARS) outbreak. Goh's other achievements include a high economic growth rate, education and medical initiatives, free trade agreements, stable labor relations within Singapore, and peaceful relationships with neighboring countries. Goh became the senior minister of Singapore when Lee Hsien Long, on Goh's advice, was appointed prime minister on August 12, 2004. As senior minister, Goh remains active in Singapore's economic and political leadership.

HA THI THU HUONG

See also Singapore; Southeast Asia: History and Economic Development

References and Further Reading

Chong, Alan. *Goh Chok Tong, Singapore's New Premier.* Malaysia: Pelanduk Publications, 1991.
Goh, Chok Tong. *Agenda for Action: Goals and Challenges: A Green Paper Presented to Parliament.* Singapore: Singapore National Printers, 1988.
Lee, Kuan Yew (2001). "Personal Reflections on Leadership, Conversations on Leadership, 2000–2001."
President and Fellows of Harvard College. http://www.ksg.harvard.edu/leadership/personal_reflections_on_leadership.html (8/8/2004).
Nonis, George. *From Kuan Yew to Chok Tong and Beyond: The Untold Singapore Story 2.* Singapore: Angsana Book, c2001.
Shin Min Daily News (ed.), translated by Lee, Seng Giap. *From Lee Kuan Yew to Goh Chok Tong.* Singapore: Shing Lee Publishers, 1991.

GORBACHEV, MIKHAIL

Mikhail Sergeevich Gorbachev was born in 1931 in a Stavropol village in the foothills of the northern Caucasus. His father, a tractor driver, was arrested during collectivization but survived. Gorbachev owed his relatively unencumbered rise to power to his early connection with the Stavropol Young Communist League and the support he received to study law at Moscow University. After graduating in 1956 and witnessing the onset of Khrushchev's destalinisation campaign at the Twentieth Party Congress that year, Gorbachev returned home and after eight years as a party secretary was promoted to membership of the Central Committee. Thanks to the patronage of Yurii Andropov he became a member of the Politburo in 1980. After Chernenko's death in 1985, Gorbachev was chosen as general secretary.

Perestroika and *Glasnost*

In April 1986, the thermonuclear accident in Chernobyl—and the irresponsible way Gorbachev appeared to handle it—added to the public disdain first felt for the new Soviet leader. But his image began to change radically with his release from exile at the end of that year of Andrei Sakharov, father of the Soviet H-bomb and Russia's best-known dissident, who had been deported on Brezhnev's orders six years earlier.

A year later, Gorbachev published his book *Perestroika and New Thinking for Russia and the Entire World*. It announced that people were "tired of tension and confrontation"; they wanted a world in which "everyone would preserve their own . . . way of life." To lead his *perestroika* campaign, Gorbachev unleashed the ideologically sophisticated Alexander Yakovlev. This strategy required a return to the road taken by Khrushchev—the hero of Gorbachev's youth—in again discrediting Stalin. With Khrushchev, this attempt ended with his defeat and disgrace. In the spring of 1988, it seemed to the public that *perestroika* was about to fizzle out in the same way.

However, at the Party's Nineteenth Conference in the summer, Gorbachev proposed a presidential system for the Soviet Union, a new parliament, an increase in the power of local Soviets at the expense of the Communist Party, and the removal of the Party from state economic management.

This was followed at the end of the year by Gorbachev's visit to the United Nations in New York, where he announced the unilateral reduction of half a million military personnel within two years as well as the withdrawal of six tank divisions from Eastern Europe, and called for a new world order based on the United Nations and the renunciation of force.

Annus Mirabilis

During the summer of 1989, a few weeks after elections in Poland resulted in an overwhelming victory by Solidarity candidates over the Communists, the proceedings of the Congress of People's Deputies were televised live throughout the USSR. Gorbachev was elected chairman, and he and its members exchanged uncensored views about the country's present and future. Gorbachev declared that the Warsaw Pact countries were free to choose their own road to socialism.

In September, Hungary opened its borders with the West. Thousands of East Germans emigrated to West Germany. In October, Gorbachev came to East Berlin, where he was cheered as he told the German crowds that "life punishes those who fall behind." Erich Honecker, the German Democratic Republic (GDR) leader, fell from power, and the Berlin Wall was dismantled. This led in turn to a "Velvet Revolution" in Prague and the resignation of its Communist government at the end of the year.

In Romania, the rioting in Timosoara evoked a more bloody response—the execution of President Ceausescu and his wife. Astutely, Gorbachev would use such excesses to persuade reluctant Communists in Moscow to support the constitutional amendment which ended the Party's monopoly of power. On October 3, the two Germanies united with the support of Gorbachev, who was awarded the Nobel Peace Prize for 1990.

The Communist Coup

The hard-line communists waited for their moment to strike back. It came the following year on August 18–21, while Gorbachev was on holiday with his family in the Crimea. In March, he had organized a referendum that showed a majority in favor of a reformed and democratic Soviet Union. Gorbachev then began negotiations with republican leaders. In retaliation, the so-called "Gang of Eight" struck. Because they had widespread support within the cabinet, the secret police, and the military, it was widely assumed around the world and inside the Soviet Union that it would succeed.

At a hastily convened press conference the vice president of the USSR, Yanaev, announced that Gorbachev had suddenly been taken ill. It was therefore Yanaev's constitutional duty to take over. The plot began to unravel after the conspirators flew to the Crimea to get Gorbachev to resign. He refused despite threats. But the failure of the putsch was largely because of Yeltsin's leadership in Moscow where, as President of the Russian Federation, he also was in danger from the Gang of Eight. Yeltsin, standing theatrically on a tank next to the headquarters of the Russian republican government, summoned the capital's citizens to the defense of freedom.

When Gorbachev flew back to Moscow, he returned (as he memorably observed) to "a different country." Yeltsin was now powerful enough to compel Gorbachev to disband the Communist Party. Yeltsin then seized its republican assets and ousted the KGB from the Russian Federation. Two of the plot's leaders committed suicide, while the rest were placed under arrest.

Estonia, Latvia, and Lithuania, which the Soviet Union had annexed in 1939, declared their independence before the attempted putsch. Some dozen other republics making up the USSR were prepared, their leaders said, to negotiate the new union with Gorbachev. With the coup, this prospect vanished, and they followed Baltic states to independence.

Yeltsin's Plot and the End of the Soviet Union

The Russian Republic's elected president, Yeltsin, had said all along that in principle he, too, was for the retention of a reformed Soviet Union. However, at the beginning of December, he met the leaders of Ukraine and Belarus, and on December 8 they declared that the USSR would be replaced by a Commonwealth of Independent States (CIS).

On Christmas Day 1991, a sad and somber-looking Gorbachev addressed the citizens of the USSR on television for the last time. On this occasion, his resignation as President of the Soviet Union was authentic. On December 31, the USSR formally ceased to exist.

The Gorbachev Revolution

Gorbachev failed to foresee the pent-up forces released by *perestroika* and *glasnost*. Additionally, he was unwilling to take the drastic measures needed to transform or abolish a systemically underperforming centralized planned economy. Nor did Gorbachev anticipate the re-emergence of nationalism and inter-ethnic strife that dictatorship had kept under control.

But he did contribute mightily towards the democratization of a society, which before he came to power, did not tolerate religion, did not enjoy a free press or freedom of assembly, the right to travel abroad, genuine multiparty elections, or the right to private property. It also is to Gorbachev's credit that, following his recall of Soviet troops from Afghanistan, the USSR managed to avoid the kind of civil war that tore Yugoslavia apart. Indeed, Gorbachev was legally entitled to use force to crush Yeltsin's plot, but Gorbachev's reluctance to resort to violence marked the crucial distinction between him and earlier Soviet rulers. The change into a physically smaller but more civil and humane society—which is still going on—will be seen as the most significant outcome of what most Russian historians have now come to call the Gorbachev Revolution.

VALENTIN BOSS

See also *Glasnost* **and** *Perestroika*; **Russia; Soviet Bloc**

References and Further Reading

Arbatov, Georgi. *The System: An Insider's Life in Soviet Politics.* New York: Times Books, 1992.
Boldin, Valery. *Ten Years that Shook the World.* New York: Basic Books, 1994.
Dobrynin, Anatoly. *In Confidence: Moscow's Ambassador to America's Six Cold War Presidents.* New York: Random House, 1995.
Gorbachev, Mikhail. *On My Country and the World.* New York: Columbia University Press, 2000.
———. *Perestroika: New Thinking for Our Country and the World.* New York: Harper & Row, 1987.
———, and Zdenek Mlynar. *Conversations with Gorbachev: On Perestroika, the Prague Spring, and the Crossroads of Socialism.* New York: Columbia University Press, 2002.
Ligachev, Yegor. *Inside Gorbachev's Kremlin.* New York: Pantheon, 1993.
Matlock, Jack F., Jr. *Autopsy on an Empire: The American Ambassador's Account of the Collapse of the Soviet Union.* New York: Random House, 1995.
———. *Reagan and Gorbachev: How the Cold War Ended.* New York: Random House, 2004.

GREAT LEAP FORWARD

In 1958, the Chinese Communist Party launched the Great Leap Forward (GLF) campaign, which reflected Maoist radical thinking in social engineering and utopian revolutionary values. Its primary motive was to catapult China ahead of the western nations in a remarkably short time—in 1958, it was claimed that China, through the GLF, would be able to surpass Great Britain in steel production within fifteen years, effectively making up a hundred years of economic development.

One of the most important concepts behind the GLF was the idea of a move away from the Soviet centralized bureaucracy model to a decentralized, Chinese-specific mode of economic development. It was believed that a "red over expert" approach should be adopted. Although party leaders appeared generally satisfied with the accomplishments of the First Five-Year Plan, they believed that more could be achieved in the Second Five-Year Plan (1958–1962) if the mass could be ideologically aroused and if domestic resources could be utilized more efficiently for simultaneous development of industry and agriculture. The GLF was aimed at accomplishing the economic and technical development of the country at a vastly faster pace with greater results for China's transition from socialism to communism. The slogan "More, Better, Faster," appeared throughout China. Another slogan that emerged through the GLF was "Walk on Two Legs." Mao believed that if the people's ideological awareness was increased, resulting revolutionary fervor could transform social institutions. On an ideological level, collectivization would prevent the re-emergence of wealth inequality.

The GLF centered on a new socioeconomic and political system created in 1958 in the countryside and in a few urban areas—the people's communes. Each commune was placed in control of all the means of production and was to operate as the sole accounting unit; it was subdivided into production brigades and production teams. Each commune was planned as a self-supporting community for agriculture, small-scale local industry, marketing, security, education, administration, common kitchens, and childcare units. The system was based on the assumption that it would release additional manpower for development.

Problems soon emerged with many aspects of the GLF. First, many of the labor-intensive industries that were set up by the communes proved to be unable to meet the most basic needs of the communes. Many of the backyard furnaces, which used to produce iron and steel from thousands of small units, ended as a colossal waste of materials and labour.

More fundamentally, communization of the countryside did not go as planned. Many cadres showed themselves to be overzealous in communizing the countryside, simply choosing to forcibly confiscate the property of the peasant's right down to the cookware and small farm tools. Across the nation, peasants responded to this initiative by slaughtering their animals to avoid handing them over to the collectives. More important was the lack of material rewards offered by the commune system, which proved to be a serious disincentive to many peasants—negating the advantages offered by the economy of scale.

The GLF ended in famine as exaggerated grain levels and decreased Soviet aid took their toll. Water conservancy programs and infrastructure construction were undertaken in terrible conditions. Drought turned into famine in both the cities and the countryside and took the lives of between 15 million and 20 million people in the three years from 1959 to 1961.

The GLF was no longer bringing China to modernization but further away, this thought was echoed by the party meeting in Lushan in August 1959, where the official acknowledgment of the GLF failure occurred. Following the failure of the GLF, the CCP was forced to reorientate its economic planning to include a great emphasis on agricultural growth which, although slowing the rate of industrialization, was a more sustainable policy.

However, GLF was not without its positives. The mass mobilization of people on projects such as irrigation, terracing, and construction opened up previously infertile regions, bringing increased prosperity. It was during this period that total arable land in China reached its peak. During the GLF, hundreds of thousands of folk tales and songs were collected which might otherwise have remained inaccessible and lost to the culture.

CHI-KONG LAI

See also China, People's Republic of; Chinese Communist Party; Mao Zedong

References and Further Reading

Chan, Alfred. "Campaign for Agricultural Development in the Great Leap Forward: A Study of Policy-Making in Liaoning." *The China Quarterly* (May 1992): 52–71.
Domenach, Jean-Lug. *The Origins of the Great Leap Forward.* Boulder, CO: Westview Press, 1995.
Eckstein, Alexander. *China's Economic Revolution.* Cambridge, MA: Cambridge University Press, 1977.
Joseph, William A. "A Tragedy of Good Intentions: Post-Mao Views of the Great Leap Forward." *Modern China* (October 1986): 419–457.

GREEK ORTHODOX CHURCH

Greek Orthodox Church, originally Orthodox Catholic Church, usually (Eastern) Orthodox Church of Greece, Bulgaria, and so forth. Also, the state church of Greece. Greek or Eastern Orthodoxy is one of the three institutionalized branches of Christianity. Its adherents live mostly in the Balkans, Russia, Ukraine, Belarus, Georgia, and the Middle East. The Orthodox Church of America unites many but not all English-speaking communities of Orthodox Christians in the United States. Some churches technically differ from Eastern Orthodoxy but nevertheless adopted the name.

Eastern Orthodoxy asserts its spiritual continuity with the original apostolic faith of Christianity (by contrast to heretical heterodoxy).

Historically, it is an offshoot of the Greek-speaking Byzantine imperial church, hence the common Western term Greek Orthodox Church. The introduction of Eastern Orthodoxy virtually orientated people toward the Byzantine cultural sphere. Three centers of Eastern Orthodox culture were dominant: Byzantium, with surviving Ecumenical patriarchate of Constantinople, from the sixth until the late nineteenth century; slavic Bulgaria (the initial cultural mediator) from the late ninth until the fourteenth century; and Russia. The latter has been the most influential, especially after the inauguration of the imperial doctrine *Moscow: The Third Rome* and of the patriarchate of Moscow and all Russia in the sixteenth century.

Eastern Orthodoxy formally is viewed as monolithic, preserving Byzantine heritage in theology, liturgy, sacraments, hierarchy and canon law, all basic festal rites and lists of saints, vestments, and architecture. Local vernacular has always been liturgical language.

Relations with Christian West

After centuries of disputes (e.g., the notorious ninth-century "Photius schisms"), Greek Orthodox Church finally broke communion with Rome in 1014, when the dual procession of the Holy Spirit from God the Father and God the Son (*filioque*) rather than from the Father alone was introduced into the Western Creed. Rome was officially anathematized in 1054 (*Great Schism*). Despite a number of bilateral attempts to restore ecclesiastical union (1274, 1369, and 1439), in 1755, the Greek Orthodox Church proclaimed all Western baptismal rites invalid. In 1965, patriarch Athenagoras I and Pope Paul VI nullified the excommunications (reconciliation was reaffirmed in 2004). However, Eastern Orthodoxy remains isolated from Rome, emphasizing its full unity and holding that the Roman Catholic and Protestant Churches have seriously strayed from original Christianity. This issue strongly influences Greek Orthodox

Churches' external relations, including participation in the Ecumenical movement and reaction to the Pope's attempts to reunite all Christians. John Paul II visited two of traditionally Orthodox countries (Romania in 1999 and Bulgaria in 2002) for the first time in modern history on official governmental invitation and with a final consent of the local churches. In contrast to this, the all-Russian patriarch Alexis II in August 2004 emphasized once again that a Pope's visit to his country seemed meaningless.

Origin, Evolution, and Teaching

The bipolar division of European Christendom has deep roots in the cultural, linguistic, and political history of the Western and Eastern Mediterranean world. Eastern Orthodoxy's specific history can be traced back mainly to the final split between Roman West and East (395), to the first Seven Ecumenical councils (325–787), Iconoclastic controversy (726–843), and to the period of the Byzantine cultural Commonwealth (after 1054–1204).

Despite forceful dogmatic and ecclesiological statements (e.g. condemnation of religious nationalism in 1872), Eastern Orthodoxy is a fellowship of national and/or territorial autocephalous churches. A patriarch, considered equal in rank to the Roman Pope and other patriarchs leads bigger (of Russia, Bulgaria, Romania, Serbia, etc.) or original (of Jerusalem, Antioch, etc.) church bodies. A metropolitan/archbishop leads lesser (of Cyprus, etc.) or national (of Athens and all Greece, etc.) bodies. Both are aided by an episcopal synod. The Ecumenical patriarch nowadays enjoys solely a primacy of honor. No patriarch or metropolitan/archbishop can claim infallibility or interfere with another church's affairs, but jurisdiction of lesser bodies in Eastern Orthodoxy is oftentimes controversial (the short but intensive dispute between the Church of Greece and the Ecumenical Patriarchate on archbishop appointments in 2004). Salient trait was *caesaropapism*, the duality of power of patriarch and king. The latter often prevailed in all matters, being considered the "preserver of Orthodoxy" (the "Orthodoxy, monarchy, nation" thesis in Russia).

Greek Orthodoxy differs from Western Christianity by acceptance of white (married) and black (celibate) priesthood (bishops are always celibate or widowed clerics), denial of Roman papal primacy, Mary's Immaculate Conception, and purgatory. The emphasis is on Jesus' Resurrection rather than His Crucifixion. God the Father is the sovereign and the sole source of both the Word and the Spirit. Original sin is an inherited frailty due to Adam's transgression, rather than human's state of guilt. Thus, all nature is graceful, and man's choice is to strive for intimate personal encounter of God. Liturgy is centered upon Jesus' birth, Ministry and Resurrection and is the core and criterion of all religious life. Veneration of icons is Eastern Orthodoxy's strongest distinctive feature. Dogmatically, icon is a pictorial expression of faith. Only those who have lived bodily life can be depicted (Jesus, Mary, Apostles, and saints above all), and solely the prototype is really adored. Images of God the Father, the Holy Spirit, and bodiless creatures are widespread but have been proclaimed unsupported theologically, as intended solely for the laity's edification.

Theological and liturgical consistency with the past (i.e., Scripture, Tradition, liturgy, and the canons of the first seven ecumenical councils) is the measure of all.

In ethics, little stress is put on social involvement. Ascetics are not organized in orders and rather flee from the world to acquire individual contemplative experience than to educate, proselytize. Mount Athos monasteries, in Greece, are considered the ideal spiritual center of all Orthodoxy.

Eastern Orthodoxy, icon veneration, vernacular liturgy, and local (Greek, Armenian, Cyrillic, Georgian) alphabet often are viewed as signs of ethnicity in all "traditionally Orthodox" countries, which originates in medieval identification of religious affiliation with ethnic origin. Thus, in 2001, 83.8% of ethnic Bulgarians, including agnostics, claimed to be "traditionally Orthodox."

The Greek Orthodox Church Prior to and After the Fall of Communist Totalitarianism

The Church in Greece has always remained a national and state institution. The former Communist regimes in the "traditionally" Eastern Orthodox countries differed as to their acceptance of the church: from deprivation of legal rights, rude intervention in internal affairs, and harsh persecutions (Soviet Russia till ca. 1943) to a loose political control with almost no intervention in internal church affairs (Romania). Some Communist regimes extensively used local Orthodoxy for nationalistic propaganda, severely controlling all church activity and portraying it as an important, but a mere cultural heritage from the past (e.g., in Bulgaria, the Orthodox Church was acclaimed as the basic preserver of national identity in the times of Ottoman domination). In return, it avoided all confrontation with the Communist government.

Since the early 1990s, some churches have been split as to the flock's acceptance of the acting patriarch, retaining yet a complete unity in doctrine and liturgy (schism). He is either silently accepted by the flock's majority or extensively criticized by dissidents for the former Communist government's uncanonical intervention in his election and for his collaboration with the regime. The split however seems to have also a financial flavor (e.g., legal disputes over management of profitable candle-producing facilities). Political and social involvement of Greek Orthodox Churches increases and a similar trend is observable in the new democratic governments' support of Eastern Orthodoxy: in July 2004, some two hundred Bulgarian "alternative" synod's churches were stormed by police and reassigned to the "traditional" patriarch's synod. Thus, the wish for a "better state law of religious communities" in all Orthodox countries seems logical.

SERGUEY IVANOV

See also Armenia; Belarus; Bulgaria; Christianity; Cultural Perceptions; Ethnic Conflicts: Central and Eastern Europe; Ethnicity: Impact on Politics and Society; Georgia; Religion; Roman Catholic Church; Romania; Russia; Serbia; Totalitarianism; Ukraine; World Council of Churches

References and Further Reading

Arseniev, Nicholas. *Revelation of Life Eternal: An Introduction to the Christian Message.* Crestwood, NY: St Vladimir's Seminary Press, 1964.

Cronk, George. *The Message of the Bible: An Orthodox Christian Perspective.* Crestwood, NY: St Vladimir's Seminary Press, 1982.

Hopko, Thomas. *The Orthodox Faith,* Vol. 1–4. New York: Orthodox Church in America, Department of Religious Education, 1973–1976.

John Meyendorff. *The Orthodox Church: Its Past and Its Role in the World Today.* New York, Pantheon Books, 1962.

Lossky, Vladimir. *Orthodox Theology: An Introduction.* Translated by Ian and Ihita Kesarcodi-Watson, Crestwood, NY: St Vladimir's Seminary Press, 1978.

———. *The Mystical Theology of the Eastern Church,* translated from the French by members of the Fellowship of St. Alban and St. Sergius. Crestwood, NY: St. Vladimir's Seminary Press, 1976.

Ouspensky, Leonid. *Theology of the Icon,* Vol. 1 and 2, translated by Anthony Gythiel with selections translated by Elizabeth Meyendorff. Crestwood, NY: St. Vladimir's Seminary Press, 1992.

Shmemann, Alexander. *The Historical Road of Eastern Orthodoxy,* translated by Lydia W. Kesich. New York: Holt, Rinehart, & Winston, 1963.

The Orthodox Study Bible: New Testament and Psalms, New King James Version. Project Director, Peter E. Gillquist, managing editor, Allan Wallerstedt, general editors Joseph Allen, *et al.* Nashville, TN: Thomas Nelson Publishers, 1993.

Ware, Kallistos (Timothy). *The Orthodox Church.* London and New York: Penguin Books, 1963.

———. *The Orthodox Way.* Oxford: A. R. Mowbray & Co., 1979.

GREEN REVOLUTION

The term "Green Revolution" refers to the incorporation of scientific approaches in plant breeding to produce high-yielding varieties (HYVs) of rice, maize (corn), and wheat that increase yields considerably over indigenous varieties. The Green Revolution began in the 1940s when American agronomists financed by the Rockefeller Foundation introduced short-stemmed, disease-resistant wheat and maize varieties in Mexico that effectively converted fertiliser and controlled water inputs into high yields. The Mexican programme inspired similarly successful rice, sorghum, maize, cassava, and beans research efforts in many developing countries. By the mid-1970s, the HYVs had replaced the indigenous varieties previously used by farmers in Latin America, Asia, and Africa. The high-yielding hybrid rice grown in West Africa is an early maturing, drought- and disease-tolerant cross-breeding of Asian and African varieties that has increased yields by 150% over traditional varieties.

Trends in Yields and Production

The impact of the Green Revolution is best demonstrated by changes in cereal production in developing countries, especially Mexico, Sri Lanka, Bangladesh, India, Pakistan, and the Philippines, where dramatic increases in yields per hectare of wheat, rice, and maize have been recorded. The Green Revolution enabled Mexico to shift from being a wheat-importing country to an exporter within twenty years. In 1944, Mexico was importing half its wheat; by 1956, it was self-sufficient in wheat production; and by 1964, it was exporting half a million tons of wheat.

In China, Pakistan, and India, the HYVs increased the opportunity for double cropping by making it possible for farmers to plant rice in summer and wheat in winter where previously they were only able to do so once a year because of the short growing season. Consequently, in India, where the new HYVs take up over 75% of the wheat acreage, production increased from 12 million tons in 1966 to 47 million tons in 1986. After importing 10 million tons of wheat annually in the mid-1960s, by the mid-1980s, the country had a surplus of several million tons. By the early 1980s, the Green Revolution had contributed to the achievement of food security in several developing countries mainly by inducing a long-term decline in the price of food grains thereby making it possible for consumers to afford more of the cheaper food.

However, after two decades of impressive harvests, many countries began reporting crop failures. For example, long-term experiments indicate that yields and total-factor productivity of irrigated rice and maize have declined over time. For example, in sub-Saharan Africa, per capita food production declined by 14% during the same period. The general lack of success of the Green Revolution in Africa can be attributed to the continent's predominantly poor soils, erratic water resources, prevalence of pests and disease, and general environmental degradation.

Green Revolution critics, however, argue that it has created many socioeconomic and ecological problems in developing countries that have not been given adequate policy attention. Problems with the Green Revolution relate to specific practices and their adverse effects on the agroecosystem or other ecosystems.

Socioeconomic Impacts

The Green Revolution has had mixed socioeconomic impacts. On the positive side, millions of farmers who have successfully grown the new wheat, rice, and maize varieties have greatly increased their income. The Green Revolution has stimulated the growth of agroindustry by increasing the demand for fertiliser, pumps, machinery, and other materials and services. Also, given the high productivity of the new technology, both land and labour have been released from crop production, and these have been reabsorbed in other sectors of the economy.

However, despite its success at increasing yields and augmenting aggregate food supplies, the Green Revolution, as a development approach, has not translated into benefits for the rural poor in terms of greater food security or greater economic opportunity and well-being. Despite three decades of rapidly expanding global food supplies, there were about 800 million hungry people in the world in the late 1990s. In India, despite the increased wheat and rice, five thousand children die from malnutrition every day. The fact that many people are still starving in developing countries brings to the fore a paradoxical situation whereby, despite its resounding success in terms of agricultural production, the Green Revolution has failed in its overall social objectives. Under-nutrition and poverty are still prevalent, and the

distribution of food remains skewed, with families in landless, small-scale farming households and farm workers as high-risk groups. Also, in India, the Green Revolution has had mixed effects on women in small-cultivator households. For many, the adoption of the HYV package has either forced them to work as farm workers or to increase their work burden of farming activities in an effort to avoid the use of paid labourers.

In the late 1960s, Mexico began to export its Green Revolution wheat at a time when 80% of its rural population was malnourished. Also, the Green Revolution has had differential impacts on rural populations by both class and gender. The better-off strata of rural society have gained access to better incomes generated by the introduction of technology, whereas the poorest strata have lost incomes they previously enjoyed. Thus, the Green Revolution has helped to create a landscape of large commercial farms alongside fewer and smaller peasant plots.

Furthermore, the Green Revolution has had dis-equalizing effects on the bigger and smaller farmers within developing countries through increases in the amount of inputs purchased by the farmers, and thus sharply raises the cost of farming. Even in areas where the "Green Revolution" has been technologically successful, it has not benefited large numbers of hungry people who are unable to buy the newly produced food. However, it has benefited mainly the bigger and generally wealthy farmers who have better access to subsidised loans and foreign exchange required to buy the patented technical inputs.

As a result, the more commercialised farmers have tended to buy out small-scale producers and evict small tenants who are unable to buy inputs. Striking effects of labour-displacing machinery and the purchase of additional land by rich farmers include agricultural unemployment, increased landlessness, rural-urban migration, and increased malnutrition for those unable to purchase food produced by the Green Revolution.

Ecological Impacts

While the Green Revolution was clearly an agricultural success, many argue that it is ecologically unsustainable and has been a social disaster. It depends on large-scale, monocrop farming that is ecologically unstable because of its chemical dependency. It also depends on controlled water supplies, which have been instrumental in increasing the incidence of human diseases such as malaria and schistosomiasis.

After the dramatic increases in the early stages of the technological transformation, yields subsequently began falling due to long-term soil degradation. The new strains need large quantities of chemical fertilisers, which are both expensive and polluting, and they also require frequent pesticide applications because they lack natural resistance to local plant diseases and insects. In Central Luzon, Philippines, rice yields increased by 13% during the 1980s, but this was achieved at a cost of a 21% increase in fertiliser use. Use of chemical fertilisers and pesticides pollutes the environment and harms wildlife. Also, use of HYVs causes genetic erosion and genetic vulnerability.

The large fertiliser and pesticide inputs cause problems with water quality when they run off into rivers or percolate into groundwater. The increasing use of agrochemical-based pest and weed control has adversely affected the surrounding environment through significant genetic erosion as well as human health. Widespread irrigation has resulted in increased salinization and acidification of the land.

The Green Revolution has resulted in farmers planting fewer crop varieties so that they can focus on use of high yielding varieties. In addition, the varieties that are planted have been bred to a high degree of genetic uniformity within each variety. There have been problems in India, Afghanistan, and Pakistan with epidemics in new HYVs of wheat. Annual fluctuations in yields have increased since the introduction of Green Revolution varieties because of their vulnerability to disease and climatic variations. The traditional varieties were not as high-yielding, but were less vulnerable to pathogens or climatic anomalies.

Technological Impacts

A dramatic consequence of Green Revolution agriculture has been the loss of wage labor opportunities due to the introduction of technology. For example, the mechanisation of post-harvest practices has reduced the availability of wage work for women. The introduction of a subsidised scheme for motorised rice hullers in Java (Indonesia) is estimated to have resulted in employment for more than 1 million landless women, who were previously employed in the hand-pounding of rice.

The Green Revolution requires a large and rapid expansion in the irrigation services to be provided. Water control is difficult in the conditions which characterise the traditional rice-exporting countries of Southeast Asia, where the main crop is grown in the wet season in flood plains and where it is not economical for the farmer to apply fertiliser because it will simply be washed away.

The new rice varieties offer a real opportunity for intensive use of available land by growing at least two crops a year instead of a single crop. This has necessitated changes in cropping patterns and harvesting methods. Mechanical drying and bigger storage facilities will be required for harvesting rice during the wet season. There is need for research on plant protection and diversified breeding to reduce the risks of large-scale crop failure through disease. However, in many developing countries the required political, social, and economic environments that encourage farmers to adopt improved practices and support their efforts to employ them in a sustainable way have not been adequate.

Green Revolution agriculture has had a narrow focus on production increasing technologies that have not adequately addressed the issue of food security in developing countries. Perhaps, what these countries need is a pro-poor alternative agriculture that is self-reliant, small-scale, and highly productive and yet environmentally friendly. The evolution of development thinking is now pointing to a post–Green Revolution phase characterised by "sustainable agriculture."

DANIEL S. TEVERA

See also Pollution, Agricultural

References and Further Reading

Bayliss-Smith, Tim, and Sudhir Wanmali, eds. *Understanding Green Revolution.* New York: Cambridge University Press, 1984.
Byerlee, Derek, and Carl K. Eicher, eds. *Africa's Emerging Maize Revolution.* Boulder, CO: Lynne Reinne Publishers, 1997.
Conway, Gordon R., and Edward B. Barbier. *After the Green Revolution: Sustainable Agriculture for Development.* London: Earthscan, 1990.
Jiggins, Janice. *Gender-Related Impacts and the Work of the International Agricultural Research Centers.* Washington, DC: World Bank, 1986.
Madeley, J. Food for All: The Need for a New Agriculture. London: ZED Books, 2002.
Meier, G. M. *Leading Issues in Economic Development.* New York: Oxford University Press, 1976.
Mittal, Anuradha, and Peter Rosset. *There Is Food for All: Access Is the Problem.* Oakland, CA: Food First/Institute of Food and Development Policy, 2000. http://www.foodfirst.org/media/opeds/2000/12-access.html.
Rosset, Peter, Joseph Collins, and Frances Moore Lappé. *Lessons from the Green Revolution: Do We Need New Technology to End Hunger?* Oakland, CA: Food First/Institute for Food and Development Policy, 2000. http://www.foodfirst.org/media/opeds/2000/4-greenrev.html.

GRENADA

The island of Grenada is located in the Caribbean Sea, north of Trinidad and Tobago. It consists of three islands: Grenada, Carriacou, and Petit Martinique. The climate is tropical, with a hurricane season from June to November. The population is 89,357 (CIA July 2004 estimate). The capital is St. George's, on Grenada, with a population of about 33,000. Originally inhabited by the Carib Indians, who resisted settlement by the Europeans, the island was eventually conquered by the French in the mid-1600s. Great Britain also had interests in the Caribbean. France gave up Grenada to Great Britain through the 1783 Treaty of Versailles.

Because of French support of the American cause during its revolution, the French settlers on Grenada, St. Vincent, and Dominica were denied many rights of citizenship, and properties on those islands held by the Catholic Church were confiscated. These actions led to rebellions by the French and native islanders against the British in 1795.

To stabilize the situation on the islands, the British government prosecuted many Frenchmen and non-British islanders. Great Britain also called for its soldiers in the islands to be returned for its wars in Europe and for the formation of a corps of natives for defense. This was met with objection by the British settlers, but was done nevertheless.

With the end of the war with France, trade from the British islands in the Caribbean dropped significantly, and property values dropped as well. This led the colonial legislatures there to push for reductions in British tariffs, and Grenada asked for permission to trade directly with America in 1823.

In 1833, Grenada joined St. Vincent, Tobago, and Barbados under the control of the Governor of the Windwards. Slavery was abolished in Grenada the next year. Barbados became its own colony in 1876, and in 1877, Grenada also became a Crown Colony. The island became an associate state of Great Britain in 1967, and gained full independence in 1974. The modern history of Grenada has every bit as much intrigue and excitement as its earlier years.

The first modern political leader of Grenada was Eric Gairy. Born in Grenada, he was active in politics and became the prime minister of Grenada when Grenada shed its Crown Colony status. He had been the leader of the Grenada Union Labor Party (GULP) since 1950. Other parties were in opposition to the GULP, the most significant of which were the Movement for the Assemblies of People (MAP) and the Movement for the Advance of Community (MACE). These parties joined with another opposition group, the Joint Endeavor for Welfare, Education, and Liberation (JEWEL), to form the "New JEWEL Movement" in 1973. One of the opposition leaders was Maurice Bishop, a Grenadan who had returned from England after studying law there.

Prime Minister Gairy sought to hold on to power through a program often put into place by revolutionary governments, that of land redistribution. His "Land for the Landless" program did in fact provide small plots of land to some Grenadans, but these half-acre plots were too small for development as farms. A more successful effort was in developing Grenada as a tourist attraction; in 1973, the number of tourists increased and the average tourist stay doubled. Land prices for tourist development increased (even as land was being given to Grenadans), and the economic future for the island was promising. Unfortunately, political events would bring this to an end.

In 1973, Gairy was able to convince Great Britain to grant full independence, which was to take place in 1974. However, opposition parties, labor unions, and the Catholic Church in Grenada called for a general strike and protest march in January 1974, which was put down with violence. The father of Maurice Bishop was killed by government forces.

The path for Grenadan independence from Great Britain did continue nevertheless, and with its independence imminent, Grenada was eligible for membership in the Caribbean Free Trade Agreement (CARIFTA) organization, and with its independence, Grenada joined the organization, which had by that time been renamed the Caribbean Community and Common Market (CARICOM).

The first five years of independence were marked by corruption and violence. In March 1979, while Prime Minister Gairy was attending a United Nations conference, opposition leader Maurice Bishop seized power and brought order to the island. Bishop favored a policy of nonalignment, and instead of fully participating with the capitalist economies of the region, sought and gained support from Cuba. Bishop's People's Revolutionary Government (PRG) called for a "workers' government" and seemed to have all the components of a new socialist regime in the Caribbean. Bishop himself was overthrown and executed in October 1983.

This concerned its neighbors and more importantly, US President Ronald Reagan, who had begun his showdown with the Soviet Union, a confrontation which would end with the collapse of the Soviet bloc.

Two trends had emerged from the time of Bishop's seizure of power: the value of exports from Grenada dropped (which may have been due to a surplus of those products on the world market), and tourism fell as well. One response to the latter was that between

1980 and 1982, Grenada undertook a substantial program of construction, which included a major expansion for its airport at St. Georges. Because this was being done with funding and expertise from Cuba, the United States saw this as a potential military facility.

With the cooperation of the governments of Grenada's neighboring islands, the United States invaded Grenada on October 12, 1983, on the premise that American medical students there were at risk. The massive invasion did locate and protect the students, as well as free the governor-general of the island, who was being held by Grenadan forces at his residence. The invading forces also captured Cuban, Libyan, East German, North Korean, and Bulgarian forces as well as Grenadan military personnel.

With Bishop dead and the military government eliminated, the United States worked with the existing nonrevolutionary parties to establish a postrevolutionary government. The parties joined to form the New National Party, and Herbert Blaize was elected president. The NNP has been the dominant party since that time, and with the support of the US, Grenada's economy and tourist industry were steadily rebuilt. The deep-water harbors that had always been assets to shipping benefitted the tourist industry as well, and exports included textiles, food and beverages, and light industry products.

However, in September 2004, most of the island's buildings were damaged or destroyed when Hurricane Ivan hit the island, killing dozens of people. Recovery of the island's service infrastructure (electricity and water) was accomplished rapidly, but repair of public buildings, including churches, will take years.

THOMAS P. DOLAN

See also Caribbean: History and Economic Development; Caribbean: International Relations; Ethnic Conflicts: Caribbean

References and Further Reading

Alonso, Irma T. ed. *Caribbean Economies in the Twenty-First Century*. Gainesville, FL: University Press of Florida, 2002.
Cole, Ronald H. *Operation Urgent Fury: The Planning and Execution of Joint Operations in Grenada, October 12–November 2, 1983*. Washington, DC: Joint History Office, Office of the Chairman of the Joint Chiefs of Staff, 1997.
Chernick, Sidney E. *The Commonwealth Caribbean: The Integration Experience*. Baltimore, MD: The Johns Hopkins University Press, 1978.
Payne, Anthony. *The Politics of the Caribbean Community, 1961–1979: Regional Integration among New States*. New York: St. Martin's Press, 1980.
Ragatz, Lowell Joseph. *The Fall of the Planter Class in the British Caribbean, 1763–1833: A Study in Social and Economic History*. New York: Octagon Books, 1977.
Thornedike, Tony. "Grenada: The New Jewel Revolution" in *Dependency under Challenge: The Political Economy of the Commonwealth Caribbean*. Payne, Anthony and Paul Sutton, eds. Manchester: Manchester University Press, 1984.
———. *Grenada: Politics, Economics, and Society*. Boulder, CO: Lynne Reinner Publishers, Inc., 1985.

GROUP OF 77

The Group of 77 (G77) is an informal association of now more than 130 countries that was established following the first United Nations Conference on Trade and Development (UNCTAD 1) in 1964. The Group consisted of the developing nations of Africa, Asia, Latin America, and the Caribbean and has subsequently grown as more nations in those regions have joined. The purpose of the Group is to represent the interests of the Global South —that is, those nations that are among the least economically developed. The Group shares a general belief that the rules of world trade and investment are structurally and systematically unfair to the Global South and works to promote awareness of this in the developed world (that is, the Global North), while campaigning to change those rules. The Group also works to promote economic and social development within its member countries through sponsoring economic and technical cooperation among developing countries (Economic Cooperation for Developing Countries [ECDC]/Technical Cooperation for Developing Countries [TCDC]).

Its operations are closely tied to the workings of the United Nations (UN), and it makes use of networks created in that organisation. Chapters of the Group have been established in leading diplomatic capitals, and its activities are coordinated by the New York chapter. Contributions to the organisation are made by member governments to finance operations. Executive decisions are made at regular ministerial meetings.

The "Joint Declaration of 77 Developing States" was issued on June 15, 1964, and called, in part, for the establishment of a New International Economic Order. This call was influenced by the success in the early 1970s of oil-producing countries drastically to improve the terms of trade in their favour. The Group of 77 was unable to wield an equivalent level of economic power, but their campaign was successful in raising awareness of the situation that they faced and in modifying the ways in which international development assistance has flowed and is organised. The stable alliance of the Group of 77 countries in successive UNCTAD negotiations has proved an effective tool in ensuring a number of small but definite improvements in the management of world trade.

The Group of 77, together with China, has subsequently adopted the "Charter of Algiers" in 1967 and the "Caracas Plan of Action" in 1997 (originally planned in 1981). This latter plan explicitly recognised the importance of liberalization and globalisation as forces in the world, as well as the increasing emergence of the information economy, which further negatively impacted upon the commodity trades upon which some members of the Global South continue to rely. The Group also has explicitly noted the importance of creating partnerships between the private and public sectors. The Caracas Declaration stated in part:

> The creation of the Group of 77, 25 years ago, was the result of the collective perception of developing countries that their problems are shared and common and originate in the inherently inequitable pattern of international economic relations. It represented their resolve to remedy this situation through international co-operation based on a mutuality of interests. In its objectives, the Group of 77 reflected the principles and purposes of the Charter of the United Nations and the conviction that maintaining international peace and security requires the resolution of international economic social and humanitarian problems. The Group therefore reaffirms the validity and supreme necessity of restructuring international economic relations on a just and equitable basis. It shall continue to place abiding faith in multilateral co-operation in the forums of the United Nations.

With the informal joining of China to the Group of 77, a stable bloc of countries has coalesced desiring to work through the institutions of the UN and to reform rather than destroy those aspects that appear inequitable, such as the membership of the permanent Security Council. A commitment to multilateral negotiations means that agreements are more likely to be favorable rather than otherwise to Group of 77 nations but at the expense of increased transaction costs (i.e., the time and cost necessary to reach agreements).

Within the Group of 77, an initiative known as the Generalised System of Trade Preferences among Developing Nations (GSTP) has attracted the initial support of forty-four members and may achieve more in the future. The GSTP follows free trade models of development that attune Group of 77 members more closely to the current development model of the Western countries. Consequently, it represents something of a commitment to complying with existing rules of international trade, despite the wish to reform those rules.

With the breakdown of talks in the World Trade Organisation and the willingness of some leading Western countries to negotiate bilateral rather than multilateral agreements, as well as the willingness of China to make common cause, the Group of 77 has become a more important organisation representing the interests of the poor. It represents perhaps the largest and most stable international grouping in the world economy and is a vital source of solidarity for the South. However, its achievements have been limited in scope and the nations within remain, internationally, tarred with a similar brush for being corrupt, driven by internal wars and schisms, and needlessly susceptible to diseases such as HIV/AIDS. Poverty and low levels of education preclude most people within the Group of 77 countries themselves from being able to understand and to participate in discourse or debate on those issues that have such a great impact on their lives.

JOHN WALSH

See also United Nations Conference on Trade and Development (UNCTAD); World Trade Organization (WTO)

References and Further Reading

Denis Benn. *Multilateral Diplomacy and the Economics of Change: The Third World and the New International Economic Order.* Kingston and Miami: Ian Randle Publishers, 2003.

Sauvant, Karl P. and Joachim W. Muller, eds. *The Third World Without Superpowers: The Collected Papers of the Group of 77*, Vols. 1–15. New York and London: Oceana Publications, 1981.

———. *Group of 77: Evolution, Structure, Organization.* New York: Oceana Publications, 1981.

The Group of 77's official web site may be found at www.g77.org. The Caracas Declaration is located at: http://www.g77.org/Docs/Caracas%20Declaration.html.

Williams, Marc. *Third World Cooperation : The Group of 77 in UNCTAD.* London and Pinter; NY: St. Martin's Press, 1991.

GUADELOUPE

Guadeloupe is a French *département d'outre-mer* (overseas department) in the Caribbean. It is an archipelago of five principal islands—Basse-Terre, Grande-Terre, La Désirade, Les Saintes, and Marie Galante—in the Leeward Islands. Guadeloupe, which occupies 1,704 square kilometers of territory, is located between Montserrat to the north and Dominica to the south. A narrow channel divides Guadeloupe proper—Basse-Terre and Grande-Terre—into two islands. The resulting land mass is butterfly-shaped. The capital, Basseterre, is located on the western island of Basse-Terre, which is volcanic and mountainous. The largest city, Pointe-à-Pitre, is located on the eastern island of Grande-Terre, which is a limestone plateau surrounded by coral reefs. The highest point in Guadeloupe, Soufrière de Guadeloupe, which is 1,484 meters high, is an active volcano on the island of Basse-Terre. Guadeloupe has abundant cultivable land and sandy beaches. Most of Guadeloupe's 445,000 people are French-speaking Roman Catholics of African descent.

Guadeloupe administers St. Martin and St. Barthélemy, which are located in the northern Leeward Islands. The French and Dutch divided the eighty-eight-square-kilometer island of St. Martin/St. Maarten in 1648. The northern part of the island is controlled by the French, whereas the southern part of the island is controlled by the Dutch. Tourism is the main economic activity. The twenty-square-kilometer island of St. Barthélemy, commonly called St. Barts, is the home to seven thousand people, but receives over two hundred thousand day visitors from cruise ships annually. Although St. Barts has been a French possession since 1648, it was occupied by Sweden from 1785 to 1878. Today, the island has a very pronounced US cultural footprint. In 2003, the people of both islands voted for secession from Guadeloupe. The majority of the people on both islands feel virtually no cultural affinity toward the people of Guadeloupe proper and resent the possibility of ever becoming a dependency of an independent Guadeloupe.

When Christopher Columbus discovered Guadeloupe in 1493, it was occupied by hostile Carib Indians. Spain's attempts to settle the island during the sixteenth century were frustrated by fierce resistance from the Indians. In 1635, a group of French entrepreneurs established the first permanent settlement on Guadeloupe at Basseterre. The French successfully removed the Indian population from the island and established a successful sugar-producing colony based on African slave labor. From 1759 to 1763, during the latter stages of the French and Indian War (1754–1763), the British occupied Guadeloupe. The British expanded the commercial importance of Pointe-à-Pitre, which had a natural harbor. The ability to trade with the thirteen British colonies in North America proved to be quite lucrative for the French colonists on the island.

In the Treaty of Paris (1763), which ended the French and Indian War, France agreed to surrender Canada to the British in return for the resumption of French control over Guadeloupe. In 1794, during the French Revolution, the British once again invaded Guadeloupe. Many of the wealthiest colonists were French royalists who supported the stability provided by British intervention. The revolutionary French government, however, sent a contingent of troops led by black nationalist Victor Hughes, who not only forced the British to flee, but also freed the slaves, killed hundreds of loyalists, and unleashed a wave of violence that threatened to destroy the political economy. Once Napoleon Bonaparte came to power, French troops were sent to the island to end the black nationalist uprising and restore slavery. The British temporarily took control of Guadeloupe in 1810, but relinquished control to the Swedes in 1813, who ultimately returned the island to France in 1815. During the nineteenth century, after the loss of Haiti, Guadeloupe was France's most valuable sugar-producing colony in the Caribbean. Once slavery was abolished in 1848, plantation owners imported laborers from India to supplement the labor force.

In 1946, Guadeloupe, Martinique, and French Guiana officially became French overseas departments. Although the overwhelming majority of Guadeloupe's people prefer continued association with France, albeit for economic reasons, a small, violent secessionist movement has resorted to terrorism to make its viewpoint heard. As an overseas department of France, Guadeloupe is entitled to elect two representatives to the French Senate and four representatives to the French National Assembly, The French president, on the advice of the French Minister of Interior, appoints a governor, known as a prefect, to represent the interests of the French government in Guadeloupe. The power of the prefect—Paul Girot de Langlade since 2004—is largely ceremonial. Local power is vested in a General Council consisting of forty-two members and a Regional Council consisting of forty-one members. The presidents of the General and Regional Councils are elected by their respective members. Jacques Gillot was elected president of the General Council in 2001. Victorin Lurel was elected president of the Regional Council in 2004.

Agriculture is the single most important economic activity in Guadeloupe. Bananas, however, have replaced sugarcane as the most important crop. Over 50% of the revenue from agricultural exports comes from bananas. Revenue from tourism, which was enhanced from a large increase in the number of US cruise ships visiting Guadeloupe, was hurt by the tragic events of September 11, 2001. Hurricanes have had a negative impact on both agriculture and tourism. France continues to provide huge subsidies. Guadeloupe is still dependent on imported food, mostly from France.

MICHAEL R. HALL

See also Caribbean: History and Economic Development; Caribbean: International Relations; French Guiana; Martinique

References and Further Reading

Burton, Richard D. E., and Fred Reno, eds. *French and West Indian: Martinique, Guadeloupe, and French Guiana*

Today. Charlottesville, VA: University Press of Virginia, 1995.

Gaspar, David Barry, and David Patrick Geggus. *A Turbulent Time: The French Revolution and the Greater Caribbean.* Bloomington, Ind.: Indiana University Press, 1997.

Jennings, Eric. *Vichy in the Tropics: Petain's National Revolution in Madagascar, Guadeloupe, and Indochina, 1940–1944.* Stanford, CA: Stanford University Press, 2002.

Sutton, Paul. *Dual Legacies in the Contemporary Caribbean: Continuing Aspects of British and French Dominion.* London: Frank Cass Publishers, 1986.

GUAM

The island of Guam is the largest and most southerly in the Marianas chain, located in the Pacific Ocean east of the Philippines and north of New Guinea. It is an unincorporated territory of the United States and falls under the management of the Department of the Interior's Office of Insular Affairs.

Prior to the arrival of Europeans, Guam was the most populous of the Marianas, with approximately half of the overall population of the indigenous people, the Chamorros, living there. The Chamorros had a typical Polynesian culture that included farming and fishing. Although some stone was used in construction, metals were unknown.

Europeans first came to the Marianas in 1521 with the voyage of Ferdinand Magellan. At the time of Magellan's visit, some of the islands were uninhabited, but records of his exploration note that a small boat from one of his ships was stolen, leading him to name the southernmost two of the islands as *Los Ladrones* (The Thieves). The Chamorros people were described by the early Spanish explorers as physically attractive but lacking in any but primitive weapons, and the first landing of Europeans on Guam was to reclaim the stolen boat, burn many houses, and kill several men.

Except for voyages of exploration, most ocean navigation at the time was accomplished through the technique of "parallel sailing," in which a ship would proceed along a line of latitude (which was relatively easy to determine through celestial navigation). For this reason, significant landmarks were important, and Guam's size made it an important point of navigation for Spanish ships making the voyage from western North America to the Philippines. Although Guam had been mapped, it was not necessary for ships to actually land there during the transits.

Although Magellan had mapped Guam and the Marianas, competition between Portugal and Spain limited travel through that part of the Pacific Ocean. Not until the Spanish consolidation of power in western North America would Spanish ships attempt to navigate the western Pacific, with the first expedition departing from Mexico in late 1564. This expedition formally claimed Guam as a Spanish possession. Unfortunately, as with the Magellan expedition, conflict broke out between the natives and Spaniards, with one Spaniard and several natives being killed.

Spain had exclusive control over the Marianas from 1668 to 1898. Under Spanish control the native population was nearly eliminated, and by the end of the eighteenth century fewer than two thousand Chamorros remained on Guam.

The American acquisition of Guam came as a result of the American victory in the Spanish-American War, but was a continuation of American interest in the Pacific which by that time had led to the purchase of Alaska from Russia, the claiming of Midway Island in the Pacific, the initiation of relations with (and eventual annexation of) Hawaii, and the forced entry into Korea. The war with Spain resulted in America obtaining Guam and the Philippine Islands in this region.

At first there was no consensus within the government as to what to do with Guam. The Philippines had more territory, resources, and facilities than Guam, but technological advances in shipping and communications (the shift from sailing ships to propulsion by coal, and the development of the telegraph) did give Guam's location some utility to the Americans. The US Navy foresaw use of Guam as a coaling station and ship repair facility, but the natural harbor would need substantial improvements (including dredging), and fortifications would be needed. In the years between the Spanish-American War and World War I, however, the relatively small military budgets restricted development.

Technological developments continued to undermine Guam's usefulness to the Navy, as wireless radio reduced the need for underwater transoceanic cables and ship propulsion shifted from coal to oil, giving ships much longer ranges. Additionally, the availability of Hawaii as a major naval base was seen as more appealing than having to deal with the problems of pacifying the population of the Philippines.

A bigger problem for the Americans in the early twentieth century was the increasing power and presence of Japanese military forces in the Pacific. During Japan's military expansion in the years before and after World War I, it became apparent to American military commanders that the Philippines would be more vulnerable to a Japanese attack than Guam would be, so military development of Guam came back under consideration. This vulnerability proved true; following the Japanese attack on Pearl Harbor which involved America in the War in the Pacific, it was evident that Guam could not be defended for long. As was the case with other American possessions, Guam, the Philippines, Wake Island, and Midway Island came under attack, and the larger islands were captured. The end of the war brought about a return to American control, and Guam became a strategic location for the basing of naval ships, submarines, and long-range bomber aircraft.

The current population of Guam, other than US military personnel and civilian government workers (and families), is descended at least in part from a mixture of the native Chamorro people, Spaniards, Japanese, and other island people. They are properly referred to as Guamanian. In 2004, the population was estimated by the US Census bureau to be 166,090, with moderate growth predicted for the next fifty years.

Guam's economy in the early years of the twenty-first century was undergoing a transition, with a reduction in US government personnel (military and civilian), and an increase in tourism. In the 1990s, approximately 90% of tourists came from Japan.

THOMAS P. DOLAN

See also Oceania: History and Economic Development; Oceania: International Relations

References and Further Reading

Bahrenburg, Bruce. *The Pacific: Then and Now*. New York: G. P. Putnam's Sons, 1971.
Carano, Paul, and Pedro C. Sanchez. *A Complete History of Guam*. Rutland, VT: Charles E. Tuttle Co., 1964.
Dudden, Arthur Power. *The American Pacific: From the Old China Trade to the Present*. New York: Oxford University Press, 1992.
Oliver, Douglas L. *The Pacific Islands* (revised edition). Honolulu: University Press of Hawaii, 1962.
Thompson, Robert Smith. *Empires on the Pacific: World War II and the Struggle for the Mastery of Asia*. New York: Basic Books, 2001.

GUATEMALA

The Republic of Guatemala is situated on the Central American isthmus between Mexico in the north, Belize and Honduras to the east, and El Salvador to the southeast. It has an extensive Pacific Ocean coast on the south and a very small Caribbean coastline in the Gulf of Honduras. At 108,890 square miles, Guatemala is the largest country in Central America (approximately the size of Ohio). It also has the largest population in the region with 14.3 million people; more than 2.5 million people live in the capital, Guatemala City. Over 50% of Guatemalans are descendents of the ancient Maya, the remaining population are *mestizo* (mixed Indian and European

heritage). Although Spanish is the official language, twenty-four indigenous languages also are spoken. Roman Catholicism is the dominant religion, but Guatemala has been the most receptive country in Central America for evangelical Protestantism, which is now practiced by more than 40% of the population.

As the rest of Central America, Guatemala received its independence from Spain in 1821 and joined the ill-fated Mexican Empire and then the violence-ridden United Provinces of Central America before it became a sovereign state in the early 1840s. In the post-independence period, Guatemalan history is replete with undemocratic, repressive governments that took power by force with only occasional periods of representative government. And although significant strides toward democratic governance have taken place since the 1980s, political violence has not been completely eradicated.

Guatemala's economy is dominated by the agro-export sector (coffee, sugar, bananas), which makes up 22% of gross domestic product (GDP) and 75% of all its exports. Exports are concentrated on two principal trading partners: 39% of Guatemalan exports go to the countries of the Central American Common Market (CACM), and another 30% to the United States. The country's industrial sector is relatively small (13% of GDP). Unlike many countries in Central America, Guatemala's economy has very little government involvement. According to the US State Department, the private sector accounts for more than 85% of GDP. In May 2004, Guatemala signed the CAFTA free trade agreement with the other Central American countries and the United States. The treaty has not yet been ratified by the US Congress.

Although the GDP is relatively large ($23 billion in 2002), income distribution is among the most uneven in Latin America; the top 20% of income earners receive two-thirds of all income. A significant consequence of this inequality is the very high incidence of poverty in the country. It has been estimated that 80% of the population lives in poverty, while over 50% of the total population endures extreme poverty.

The failure of economic and social policy in Guatemala can be seen in two partially related measures. The first measure of the impact of social policy is life expectancy, which in Guatemala is approximately sixty-six years, the lowest in Central America. The next lowest life expectancy is a full three years higher (Honduras), which is still nine years lower than Costa Rica's seventy-eight years and five years lower than the Central American average. The second index reflecting the failure of social and economic development policy in Guatemala is the United Nations Development Program's Human Development Index (HDI) rankings. The HDI is a composite measure of Human development taking into account life expectancy, health, education, and standard of living. Guatemala ranks lowest of all Central American countries at position 119th, which compares very unfavorably with Costa Rica, which earned the 42nd position in the world rankings.

Political life in Guatemala has been difficult, with its transition to democracy being fitful, late, and incomplete. Post-independence Guatemala was governed by a series of *caudillos* and military dictators. This use of violence for political ends was briefly broken in 1944 when the military dictatorship of General Jorge Ubico was overthrown by junior military officers. Following the democratic election of a civilian president in 1945, the new government implemented a series of social reforms. The subsequent democratic election of Jacobo Arbenz allowed the reforms to be continued and expanded. His attempt to implement land reform, though, caught the wrath of US banana companies that would lose land as a consequence of the reform. The political reforms that included permitting some communists to participate in the government caught the attention of the US embassy, which then fermented and fostered a military coup by Col. Carlos Castillo Armas in 1954. With Castillo Armas's assassination in 1958, General Miguel Ydigoras Fuentes took office.

The return of the military in 1954 led to a series of coups and counter-coups and military governance for more than thirty years until a civilian president was elected in 1986. A second important impact of the return of the military to government was the start of one of the longest and the bloodiest civil war in Latin America, which resulted in the deaths of over two hundred thousand people. In the early 1980s, after another military coup by junior officers designed to prevent yet another general from taking office, the level of state repression increased still further.

As a result of this coup, General José Efraín Ríos Montt, an evangelical lay preacher, became head of a military *junta*. He eventually dismissed the rest of the junta, became president, and unleashed a wave of repression against the rural, largely indigenous population of Guatemala. The general's counterinsurgency tactics militarized the country forcing indigenous peoples in the countryside to join self-defense militias. Ríos Montt's bloody repression was furthered by the existence of right-wing death squads, most notably the *Mano Blanca* (White Hand).

In the mid-1980s, a region-wide peace process, brokered by President Oscar Arias of Costa Rica, was signed by leaders of Central American republics calling for an end to the civil wars in Nicaragua, El Salvador, and Guatemala and the installation of democratic governance. The human rights situation also was brought to international attention with the publication of Rigoberta Menchu's *testimonio*, *I Rigoberta* in 1983.

The Peace Process and a new constitution facilitated the return to democratic politics in the late 1980s and the 1990s. New governmental institutions were created or strengthened including the Supreme Court and a Human Rights Ombudsman's office. But even with most recent elected government, which took office in January 2004, the democracy remains incomplete. Crime and violence against human rights workers remain a persist problem for governance.

BRUCE M. WILSON

See also Central America: History and Economic Development; Central America: International Relations; Ethnic Conflicts: Mexico and Central America

References and Further Reading

Christopher Chase-Dunn, Susanne Jonas, and Nelson Amaroeds. *Globalization on the Ground: Postbellum Guatemalan Democracy and Development*. Lanham, MD: Rowman & Littlefield Publishers, 2001.

Hall, Carolyn, Héctor Pérez Brignoli, and John V. Cotter (cartographer). *Historical Atlas of Central America*. Norman, OK: University of Oklahoma Press. 2003.

Perez-Brignoli, Hector. *A Brief History of Central America*. Berkeley, CA: California University Press, 1989.

Rachel M. McCleary. *Dictating Democracy: Guatemala and the End of Violent Revolution*. Gainesville, FL: University Press of Florida, 1999.

Robert H. Trudeau. 1993. *Guatemalan Politics: The Popular Struggle for Democracy*. Boulder, CO: Lynne Rienner, 1993.

Roland H. Ebel. *Misunderstood Caudillo: Miguel Ydigoras Fuentes and the Failure of Democracy in Guatemala*. Lanham, MD: Tulane Studies in Political Science and University Press of America, 1998.

United Nations Development Programme. *Human Development Report 2004*. (http://hdr.undp.org).

GUERRILLA ARMY OF THE POOR (EGP)

The Guerrilla Army of the Poor (EGP) was founded on January 19, 1972, when a group of fifteen combatants entered the Guatemalan jungle area known as Ixcán. On February 7, 1982, it joined the other three major Guatemalan insurgency groups in forming the National Revolutionary Unity of Guatemala (URNG) but remained one separate military organization until the demobilization process of 1997 when URNG was transformed into a legitimate political party.

Like the other guerrilla formations in Guatemala in the 1970s, EGP represented a second phase of an insurgency with roots in the 1960s and in an armed opposition to the CIA-monitored overthrow of President Jacobo Árbenz in 1954. The Guatemalan rebels of the second phase are best characterized by an ideological affinity for Cuba and Fidel Castro, and they designated the United States, not the Guatemalan government, as their principal enemy. The EGP drew their tactics from doctrines first formulated by its leader Rolando Morán, alias Ricardo Arnoldo Ramirez de Leon, in 1964, explicitly focusing on the poor segments of the population for a slow process of mobilization with the ultimate goal of defeating the national army and take national power. But it staged an insurgency that differed from its roots in the 1960s in that it rejected *foquismo* strategies of revolutionary warfare—that is, the idea that a few committed militants could become a catalyst for revolution, without the process of first organizing the population—and instead prepared for a prolonged war in the highlands. The geographical transition from the northeast to the northwest, brought about by the establishment of the EGP, also implied a movement from areas populated by Guatemala's nonindigenous minority to the Maya majority of the western highlands. By the early 1970s, the Ixcán jungle area had recently been colonized by an ethnic mix of landless peasants. As the slow process of mobilization gradually moved south and into the Maya-Quiché and Maya-Ixil inhabited highland regions of the country, the EGP confronted a more rooted local political system, more difficult to infiltrate than the settler cooperatives of Ixcán. The high extent to which people welcomed, voluntarily supported, and also joined the men in olive green uniforms testifies to a prior mobility of seasonal workers in the highland areas of Guatemala. Even though based in indigenous communities, many were already accustomed to trade union organizing on coastal plantations, peasant league formations among workers on local estates, and members of a politically radicalized Catholic Church influenced by the era's theology of liberation.

In its heydays prior to the military defeat of 1981 to 1983, EGP was organized in an hierarchical structure in which the governing body, *Dirección Nacional* (DN) ruled by assembling representatives of each of the different (four to eight) military divisions, known as *frentes*. The four most prominent ones were Frente Guerrillero comandante Ernesto Guevara of the Huehuetenango and Ixcán regions, Frente Guerrillero Ho Chi Minh of the Ixil and central Quiché regions, Frente Guerrillero Luis Augusto Turcios Lima of the provinces of the western pacific coast, and finally Frente Guerrillero Otto René Castillo of the metropolitan region. Each division, in turn, collaborated on the local level with local irregular forces (FIL) where

mobilized villagers served on and off depending on the war's level of intensity. Finally, also the nonarmed civilian population was politically organized into something called local clandestine committees (CCL) in an intricate system of intelligence, education, and health attendance.

While successful in tying large sectors of the rural population to its relatively small military core—the number of armed rebels reached a maximum of about four hundred in 1983—this system proved to be vulnerable to military setbacks, and with the defeat of the early 1980s, it never regained its former strength. Incidences of internal guerrilla violence and of guerrilla massacres have been attributed to the lack of control on behalf of the leadership in the DN when the goal of bridging the different levels of its organization could not be achieved.

EGP also made propagandistic efforts to gain the support of the international community, a front that it even claimed to be of equal importance to that of the local masses. While it is clear that this accounts for the endurance of the Guatemalan insurgency until the peace agreement of December 29, 1996, the extent to which the indigenous population actually supported the rebellion, and how to assess the nature of that support, is an ongoing controversy within social movements in Guatemala and among historiographers of its civil war.

The Accord on the Definitive Cease-Fire was signed on December 16, 1996. It set out the procedures for the concentration and disarming of the URNG under UN supervision. The reincorporation of former guerrillas involved the concentration and demobilization of ex-combatants in eight camps across the country. Due to the fear of registering under an original name, the attraction of economic compensation for surrendering arms and the long history of civil war, conflict emerged over the right to be recognized as a former rebel. The cease-fire entered into force on March 3, 1997—535,102 weapons and rounds of ammunition were handed over to MINUGUA, the UN verification mission to Guatemala. In all, 2,928 URNG combatants were demobilized and issued temporary identification cards in the spring of 1997.

In favor of the recomposition of the URNG in a single party structure, the EGP officially dissolved during the demobilization process of 1997. As a political party, the URNG has downplayed its previous emphasis on ideology, casting itself as a democratic representative of the nation's class and ethnic diversity. The compliance with the Peace Accords has replaced older doctrines.

EGP founder and chief commander Rolando Morán died from a heart attack on September 11,

1998, then holding the post of secretary general of the URNG. Despite his efforts to present the insurgency of which he had been an integral part since 1964 in terms of an ethnic national struggle, just as important as the class-based revolution, it was primarily the voices of the indigenous movement in Guatemala that during the latter part of the 1990s and the beginning of the 2000s undermined the popular support of the URNG, claiming that its revolution was more akin to Western and racist ideology than to the culturally egalitarian vision of the new organizations of the Maya majority of Guatemala.

STAFFAN LÖFVING

See also Árbenz Guzmán, Jacobo; Central America: History and Economic Development; Counterinsurgency; Guatemala; Liberation Theology

References and Further Reading

Castañeda, Jorge G. *Utopia Unarmed: The Latin American Left after the Cold War.* New York: Knopf, 1993.

CEH. *Guatemala: Memoria del silencio.* Informe de la Comisión para el Esclarecimiento Histórico. Guatemala City: UNOPS, 1999.

Le Bot, Yvon. *La Guerra en Tierras Mayas: Comunidad, Violencia y Modernidad en Guatemala (1970–1992).* Mexico D.F.: Fondo de Cultura Económica, 1995.

Löfving, Staffan. "Silence, and the Politics of Representing Rebellion. On the Emergence of the Neutral Maya in Guatemala" in *No Peace, No War: An Anthropology of Contemporary Armed Conflict,* edited by Paul Richards, pp. 77–97. Oxford and Athens, OH: James Currey and Ohio University Press, 2005.

Vinegrad, Anna. "From Guerrillas to Politicians: the Transition of the Guatemalan Revolutionary Movement in Historical and Comparative Perspective" in *Guatemala after the Peace Accords,* edited by Rachel Sieder, pp. 207–227. London: Institute of Latin American Studies, University of London, 1998.

Wickham-Crowley, Timothy. *Guerrillas & Revolution in Latin America: A Comparative Study of Insurgents and Regimes Since 1956.* Princeton, NJ: Princeton University Press, 1992.

GUERRILLA WARFARE

Guerrilla warfare is an ancient military strategy and/or tactic of fighting by irregular and autonomous armed forces that dates to millennia before Christ and persists in essentially the same form today. In contemporary insurgency cases guerrillas generally have represented nonstate or substate entities, such as freedom fighters or revolutionary insurgents, conducting an undeclared war or rebellion against an established government or state. As a tactic or strategy, however, regular or uniformed military forces of a state or states also may employ guerrilla fighting styles, such as in low-intensity conflict or low-intensity warfare, in both a declared and conventional, as well as an undeclared and unconventional, war setting.

One of the earliest proponents of guerrilla war tactics is the Chinese master of warfare, Sun Tzu, whose *Art of War* is the source of many often quoted Chinese proverbs on terrorism and guerrilla struggle. Perhaps one of the best known dictums on guerrilla warfare is that of the twentieth century Chinese Marxist revolutionary, Mao Zedong: "The guerrilla is of the people as the fish is of the sea." In other terms, support of the local population is critical to success in guerrilla warfare. Ho Chi Minh, the guerrilla strategist and father of the Marxist Vietnamese revolution, had a more prescient aphorism: "You will kill ten of our men, and we will kill one of yours, and in the end, it will be you who tire of it." The basic military concept of guerrilla war, therefore, is the use of irregular troops or units to harass a powerful enemy in a "war of the flea," until the enemy is exhausted or wiped out. Both quotations emphasize the two central tenets of twentieth-century guerrilla warfare—a protracted, popular, indigenous struggle against a foreign enemy and its domestic allies—or wars of national liberation.

In modern times, especially since the rise of urban guerrilla movements, it has become more difficult to distinguish classic, rural-based guerrilla warfare from terrorism. Historically, there has always been a close link between these two forms of limited and unconventional warfare, both in practice and in contemporary and nineteenth century manuals such as *On War* by Karl von Clausewitz, the noted German war theoretician. Some theorists have argued that terrorism intends to create a psychological state of despair and hopelessness among the civilian population and regime forces, as expressed in the popular Chinese maxim: "Kill one; frighten ten thousand." Guerrilla war, on the other hand, is intended to induce a psychology of hope through successful armed struggle, that is, the belief that an armed popular and irregular force can defeat a professional army. According to military historians, guerrilla warfare has traditionally been seen as a people's struggle against a more powerful enemy, often an occupying power. Among notable historical examples are the confrontations between the Romans and the Hebrews, and the Romans and the Gauls; the British and the American colonists; the US Army and the American Indians; and the Turkish Empire and T.E. Lawrence of Arabia. More contemporary examples include indigenous rebellions in Malaysia, the Philippines, Algeria, and East Timor.

The term *guerrilla warfare*, is derived from the Spanish word for war or *guerra*, and "guerilla" literally means "little war." Military historians date the use of the term to the popular insurgency by Spanish resistance forces against the invasion of Napoleon and his French troops in 1808. The subsequent usurpation of the Spanish throne launched both pro- and anti-royalist forces in Spain's colonies in the New World and ultimately culminated in a wave of independence revolts and guerrilla struggles in nineteenth century Latin America. This form of warfare not only has been closely linked to the rise of modern nationalism in Europe, but also nationalism's diffusion to the Third World developing nations as a reaction against European imperialism and colonialism. Thus, from the outset, guerrilla war has been understood as a people's war, peasant war, or war of national liberation and resistance. In addition to the fundamental component of nationalism, modern guerrilla war has been motivated by a struggle for social reform and/or revolutionary change. In this sense, guerrilla war combines both the elements of a war against external aggression and of a revolution against a domestic class enemy and/or repressive government.

War, especially guerrilla war, has always been intimately linked with politics. In the nineteenth century, for example, Clausewitz insisted that "war is not merely a political act, but also a political instrument." Indeed, most military historians note that while the military components of guerrilla warfare have remained the same for millennia, the most important contemporary contributions have been psychological and political. Perhaps among the most noteworthy contributors to the politicization of guerrilla warfare have been Mao Zedong, Ho Chi Minh, and Ernesto "Che" Guevara. In turn, contemporary counterinsurgency doctrine has had to devise effective political and psychological strategies to "win hearts and minds" and deny guerrilla movements the popular support essential to success.

Mao Zedong especially took the Clausewitzian maxim to heart when he founded the People's Liberation Army (or Red Army) and launched a protracted people's war that culminated in the Chinese Marxist revolution of 1949. Employing the phrase, "the party controls the gun," Mao emphasized the critical role of political education and indoctrination by his Chinese Communist Party in their war of national liberation against the Japanese invaders and the subsequent civil war against the "traitorous" Guomindang Nationalists. People's war, the central concept of Mao's form of guerrilla struggle and the basis for his peasant-based, rural, socialist revolution in China, had several key components. First was the importance of the peasantry as a base of widespread popular support as both combatants and noncombatants. Unlike classical Marxist and Leninist thought which had concluded that peasants were ignorant clods and

unreceptive to revolution, Mao argued that the peasant masses, and not the urban proletariat (of which feudal China had very few), could be energized into a popular revolutionary force by nationalism, Maoism, and the indoctrination of the communist party. Second was the creation of a politicized military force of peasants, the People's Liberation Army, which began as a small irregular guerrilla army living the ideals of the socialist revolution and diffusing these in everyday society. By 1945, however, the Red Army had grown into a large conventional force between a half and a million strong.

The Chinese model of guerrilla warfare was a rural model based in the countryside and its purpose was to encircle the cities—the bastions of government control—and force the class enemy's capitulation. Mao had rejected the Stalinist path to Marxist revolution in 1938 and was denounced as a heretic and fool. Nevertheless, Mao argued that China was different. It was "a semicolonial and semifeudal country" and not "an independent democratic state," where the communist party could join a united front of democratic and bourgeois forces, and carry out a protracted legal struggle. Unlike the Russian experience, it was necessary for Chinese communists' to take the opposite road and first seize the countryside and then the big cities.

Mao's guerrilla strategy was summarized in his dictum: "The enemy advances, we retreat; the enemy camps, we harass; the enemy tires, we attack; the enemy retreats, we pursue." Warfare had several strategic stages; the first was a defensive stage which focused on establishing a secure base area or liberated zone where the party cadres could safely engage in organization and political indoctrination. In the intermediate stage, guerrilla forces emphasized mobility, the creation of supply lines, winning popular support, and engaging in successful hit and run and ambush tactics. They sought to expand military control over the countryside and weaken government forces. In the final offensive stage, the guerrillas completely encircled and choked off the cities from the rest of the country. At this point, the insurrectionary force was powerful and large enough to operate as a regular army and to conduct a conventional war.

Mao also developed extensive rules of protracted guerrilla struggle which were studied and, in some cases, followed by later revolutionaries. One rule was to defeat the enemy through attrition and demoralization and to limit military confrontations to quick engagements that destroyed the government's fighting ability. Second, guerrilla units should emphasize mobility, avoid fixed battle lines, and develop self-sufficient intelligence and supply systems. Third, the army must never terrorize or plunder the local population: "Oppose bandit ways, and uphold strict political discipline." Finally, the party must control the military.

In Vietnam, the revolutionary Marxist leaders Ho Chi Minh and Vo Nguyen Giap systematized their theory of modern people's war and the political-military rules for wars of national liberation. They established a similar political-military infrastructure and implemented Maoist strategies to mobilize and ensure peasant support, such as land reform and direct political control in local villages. Also, as in the Chinese Marxist case, the Vietnamese national liberation struggle was a revolutionary war, that is, an anti-colonial war against foreign imperialists, and a socialist revolution against internal class enemies. Thus, the Vietnamese also melded the ideologies of nationalism and Marxism into a powerful justification for protracted guerrilla warfare first against the French in the First Indochinese War (1946–1954), and then against the United States in the Second Indochinese War (1964–1975).

Ernesto "Che" Guevara realized that foreign intervention and the fusion of revolution and war were indispensable for successful guerrilla warfare. Guevara accepted the view of Mao and Ho that class conflict without a nationalist insurgency against foreign intervention could be insufficient to spark revolution. Therefore, Che Guevara and other guerrilla leaders of the 1960s and 1970s sought to provoke US intervention in Latin America and the Third World. Guevara and Fidel Castro's writings on guerrilla warfare describe this strategy as one of creating "many Vietnams" in Latin America.

Their Latin model of guerrilla warfare also attempted to reconcile theoretical disputes over revolutionary strategy. Should revolution arise from above or below? Should it be by workers or by peasants? And is the rural or urban-based struggle primary? In his 1963 treatise, *Guerrilla War*, Guevara underlined the importance of guerilla action as the "central axis of the struggle." And like Castro, he ridiculed Latin revolutionaries who struggled in capital cities and underestimated the rural guerrilla movement. Distilling from the Cuban revolutionary experience (often incorrectly), Guevara rejected urban guerrilla warfare, and the urban insurrections, terrorism, student demonstrations and general strikes sweeping Latin America in the 1960s and 1970s. Marxist laborite, Peronist, and Tupamaro guerrilla movements in Venezuela, Brazil, Uruguay, and Argentina in particular viewed urban warfare as the right recipe for revolution. In most cases, however, urban guerrilla warfare failed and created or further entrenched existing military dictatorships.

In the urban setting guerrilla warfare was often indistinguishable from outright acts of terrorism.

For example, Carlos Marighella, a Brazilian communist militant who wrote the *Minimanual of the Urban Guerrilla*, held that "Terrorism is an arm the revolutionary can never relinquish." In his view, rebellion originated in the cities and spread to the countryside. The urban guerrilla's principal task is "to distract, to wear out, to demoralize" the military dictatorship and "to attack and destroy the wealth and property of the North Americans . . . and the Brazilian upper class." In this way, the urban guerrilla supports the emergence and survival of rural guerrilla warfare. In the 1980s, Peru's *Sendero Luminoso* or Shining Path guerrilla movement dispensed with these distinctions altogether and inflicted terrorism and guerrilla warfare on both city and countryside.

By and large, urban guerrilla movements failed, according to experts, because of the absence of outside support and/or a mortal internal crisis. In *The Urban Guerrilla* (1969 p. 95), Martin Oppenheimer concluded that paramilitary activities in urban areas would succeed "in overturning the established order only where that order is already so decayed that a mere push will suffice." Nevertheless, urban guerrilla warfare and its close association with terrorism may have achieved a new lease on life in the chaos of the United States–Iraq War and Islamic–al Quaeda insurgencies in Samara and Fallujah.

Che Guevara developed the guerrilla *foco* theory of revolution, in which he favored rural-based insurgency because he believed that in the modern age the advanced military technology, firepower, and efficient counterinsurgency training of regime forces could easily crush an urban insurgency. At best, urban insurrection may serve as a distraction and tie up enemy soldiers, but it is subordinate to the fundamental struggle. Guevara also rejected the Stalinist united front strategy, the Leninist and Maoist emphasis on the communist party and the Maoist strategy of fixed base areas, arguing that one cannot slavishly imitate past revolutions. The conditions which favored these models were simply not present in the Americas. Instead, he proposed Cuba as the model for successful Latin American guerrilla warfare.

In 1961, Guevara published the article "Cuba: Exception or Vanguard?" wherein he argued that Latin America was ripe for revolution and that a guerrilla-led peasant struggle would begin in the countryside and spread to engulf the cities of the continent. Guevara believed that existing socioeconomic conditions favored revolution and that the introduction of a guerrilla force into the region would introduce important subjective conditions for revolution: "The most important is the consciousness of the possibility of victory by violent means in the face of the imperialist powers and their internal allies." He developed this theory further in his 1963 work, *Guerrilla Warfare*. The Cuban Revolution, he wrote, had made "three fundamental contributions to the laws of the revolutionary movement" in the Americas: the people's forces could win a war against the army; revolutionary conditions can be created by insurrection; the battle-ground in the region's underdeveloped countries was in the countryside.

In the 1967 treatise *Revolution in the Revolution?* the French revolutionary theorist Regis Debray presented Guevara's guerrilla *foco* model as a revolution in revolutionary thought and a "third way" for Latin American revolutions. The guerrilla *foco* was described as a "center of guerrilla operations" and initially operated as a "mobile strategic force" and the "nucleus of a people's army" in a future socialist state. Guerrilla warfare in this model progressed through three stages: establishment of an independent and clandestine guerrilla force, and its supply lines and exploration of the terrain; development and defensive engagement with the enemy; and the revolutionary offensive that included a political and military phase.

The central logic of the *foco* model was the political and psychological impact of armed propaganda (or the "consciousness of victory by violent means"), which was to occur between the second and the third stage. Politicization prior to this, especially by established Marxist-Leninist parties, Guevara considered dangerous. Action not speeches would shake the peasantry out of its repressed and "colonial" mentality. Only when the guerrilla force was able to demonstrate "that a soldier and a policeman are no more bulletproof than anyone else," would the peasants be willing to support the guerrillas. Insurrectional activity, therefore, served as "the number one political activity." Guevara and Debray also rejected the leadership or vanguard role of existing Marxist-Leninist parties. The guerrillas were the "fighting vanguard of the people." And the true revolutionary party must arise out of the guerrilla movement and the future People's Army (as occurred in Cuba); or in Debray's words: "Essentially, the party is the army."

In 1967, Che Guevara exported his *foco* model of guerrilla warfare to Bolivia, located in the heart of South America and bordering his homeland of Argentina. Guevara reasoned that the conditions were not only ripe in Bolivia, but that revolution in the Andes would spread, provoke US intervention and eventually create "many Vietnams" throughout the continent. Bolivia, in Guevara's words, would be a "sacrificial lamb to be offered on the altar of continental revolution." None of these assumptions proved correct. Bolivia's revolution in 1952 made the population unreceptive to Guevara, and indeed his small band of Cuban guerrillas had few Bolivian recruits. The *foco* itself was viewed as a form of foreign intervention, whereas the assistance of US Army Rangers in destroying the insurgency was welcomed by the Bolivian Army, government, and population generally.

Critiques would later conclude that Guevara was blinded by his idealization of the Cuban experience, overgeneralization of the Latin American condition, and a populist understanding of revolutionary causality. And, most important, he miscalculated the US response and misinterpreted the Bolivian situation. In short, the *foco* model of guerrilla warfare failed both in theory and practice. And although Central American revolutionaries in Nicaragua, El Salvador, and Guatemala would be inspired by Guevara's guerrilla warfare theories, none would implement them as Guevara envisioned, and only the Sandinista National Liberation Movement in Nicaragua would achieve success through rural guerrilla warfare.

WALTRAUD Q. MORALES

See also Counterinsurgency; War and Development

References and Further Reading

Chaliand, Gerard (ed.). *Guerilla Warfare: From the Long March to Afghanistan*. Berkeley, CA: University of California Press, 1982.

Clausewitz, Karl von. *On War*. Book I, Chapter I., Trans. J. J. Graham. London, (1874) 1909.

Debray, Regis. *Revolution in the Revolution?* New York: Monthly Review Press, 1967.

Giap, Vo Nguyen. *People's War, People's Army*. Praeger: New York, 1964.

Gott, Richard. *Rural Guerrillas in Latin America*. Harmondsworth, UK: Penguin, 1973.

Guevara, Ernesto Che. *The Bolivian Diary of Ernesto Che Guevara*. New York: Pathfinder, 1994.

———. *Guerrilla Warfare: Selected Case Studies*. Brian Loveman and Thomas M. Davies, Jr., eds. Lincoln, NE: University of Nebraska Press, 1985.

———. "Cuba: Exception or Vanguard?" *Verde Olivo* (Havana), 1961.

Laqueur, Walter Z. *Guerrilla: A Historical and Critical Study*. Boston: Little, Brown, 1976.

Mao Ze-dong. "Problems of Strategy in the Guerrilla War Against Japan."; "On Protracted War"; "Problems of Strategy in China's Revolutionary War"; in *Selected Works*. Vol. 1–4. Vol. 2: 79–254. Beijing: Foreign Languages Press, 1965.

Marighela, Carlos. "Minimanual of the Urban Guerrilla." in *Terror and Urban Guerrillas*. Jay Mallin, ed. Coral Gables, FL: University of Miami Press, 1971.

Oppenheimer, Martin. *The Urban Guerrilla*. Chicato: Quadrangle Books,1969.

Pomeroy, William J. (ed.). *Guerrilla Warfare and Marxism*. New York: International Publishers, 1968.

Wickham-Crowley, Timothy P. *Guerrillas and Revolution in Latin America: A Comparative Study of Insurgents and Regimes Since 1956*. Princeton, NJ: Princeton University Press, 1992.

GUEVARA, ERNESTO "CHE"

Born June 14, 1928, into a blue-blooded aristocratic family in Argentina, Che Guevara became a communist leader and twentieth-century icon fighting in Cuba, Africa, and South America. Throughout his life, Guevara was racked by asthma, which contributed to his enormous will as well as to his desire to study medicine. He completed his studies at the University of Buenos Aires in three years (instead of the usual six), interspersed with extensive journeys around South America. These trips greatly influenced Che as he recognised how poverty was linked to the economic system that was greatly benefiting the United States. However, he only later linked this to a deep understanding of Marxism. While traveling in Guatemala, he witnessed the overthrow of Jacobo Arbenz's radical government by US-backed Castillo Armas. Guevara fled to Mexico, where he met Fidel Castro in 1954 and joined Castro's group of exiles planning for an invasion of Cuba. The group landed in 1956, and during two years of guerrilla warfare Che cemented his position as one of their leaders. His camps became a model of organisation, and he greatly reformed the areas under his control, by, for instance, creating schools, clinics, and hospitals. He also gave interviews to foreign journalists and gained a reputation as the most radical of the Cuban guerrillas. Once the guerrillas seized power, Che served in various economic positions in Castro's government and oversaw land redistribution and the nationalisation of most Cuban and foreign companies. He combined his economic work inside with extensive foreign travel visiting countries throughout the world.

Che led a Cuban delegation to the Punta del Este conference in Uruguay in August 1961, where the US government presented the details of President Kennedy's Progress for Alliance. The plan was a major change in US policy, but Che denounced it and the "weak and sycophantic" Latin American governments who welcomed it. He saw the plan as an attempt to stifle social revolutions in the region, and he instead presented a Third World agenda, a list of economic and trade reforms including lower tariffs and fixed prices. This more global perspective reflected how Che was beginning to hope to replicate the Cuban Revolution elsewhere in Latin America. However, his dreams were blocked by a lack of encouragement from the USSR and resistance among native Communist leaders. Instead, he continued developing theories about guerrilla warfare and writing pamphlets which inspired a later generation of revolutionaries.

Frustrated in Latin America, Che turned to Africa, which he saw as virgin soil not yet divided up into Cold War spheres of influence. He went on a three-month tour of the continent starting in December 1964, during which time he decided to become actively involved in the civil war in the Congo. He arrived in April 1965, but by then the war was all but over as Belgian paratroopers and mercenaries from Rhodesia and South Africa, aided by American aeroplanes, had crushed the rebels. Che and his Cubans fought until November, but they achieved little and were forced to leave the country under fear of capture. Unwilling to return to Havana following an ideological break with Castro, Che instead went to Bolivia in 1966, which seemed the most promising country in South America for guerrilla warfare. He traveled in disguise to Bolivia and fought skirmishes with the Bolivian army. However, the Bolivian military overcame the poorly trained group he led into the country, and Guevara was captured and executed near Vallegrande, Bolivia, on October 8, 1967.

NEIL DENSLOW

See also Castro, Fidel; Cuban Revolution

References and Further Reading

Anderson, Jon Lee. *Che Guevara: A Revolutionary Life.* London: Bantam Press and New York: Grove Press, 1997.

Castañeda, Jorge. *Vida en Rojo: Una Biografía Del Che Guevara.* Alfaguara, Mexico: Alfaguara, 1997; as *Compañero: The Life and Death of Che Guevara*, translated by Marina Castañeda. London: Bloomsbury, and New York: Vintage Books, 1998.

James, Daniel. *Ché Guevara: A Biography.* New York: Stein and Day, 1969; London: Allen, 1970; 2nd ed., New York: Cooper Square Press, 2001.

Taibo, Paco Ignacio II. *También Conocido Como el Che*, Mexico, D.F.: Editorial Planeta Mexicana, 1997; as *Guevara: Also Known As Che*, translated by Martin Michael Roberts. New York: St. Martin's Press, 1997.

GUINEA

The Republic of Guinea is a coastal West African country, bordered by Senegal, Mali, Guinea-Bissau, Sierra Leone, Liberia, and Cote d'Ivoire (Ivory Coast). It has about 250 miles of Atlantic coastline. The country, sometimes called Guinea-Conakry to distinguish it from its much smaller neighbor, Guinea-Bissau, consists of a flat, largely swampy, coastal plain that rises to a hilly and mountainous interior. The Gambia, Niger, and Senegal Rivers have their sources in the Fouta Djallon highlands of interior Guinea, and there are numerous smaller rivers in the area. The climate is tropical, with annual rainfall averaging from seventy-five to one hundred inches, with coastal areas receiving the most precipitation.

Several ethnic groups, including Mande, Fulbe, and Sosso, inhabit Guinea which is 85% Muslim. French is the official language. The population is approximately 8 million, with an annual growth rate of 2.5%. About 1.6 million people live in the capital, Conakry, a port on the Atlantic coast. Agriculture, based on cereal crops and tropical fruit, dominates the economy. The country has considerable mineral deposits of bauxite, diamonds, and iron ore. Despite its economic potential and an annual gross domestic product growth rate of 3.3%, Guinea ranks as one of the poorest countries in the world, with an annual per capita income of $1,900.

Prior to colonial rule, several peoples and kingdoms controlled various parts of the region. Coastal and interior peoples and states had little contact, especially after interior groups adopted Islam, whereas coastal peoples retained traditional religions. The Fulbe dominated the Futa Djallon highlands, forming the center of a powerful Islamic state in the eighteenth and nineteenth centuries, which incorporated much of the interior highlands. The coastal region experienced early but minimal trading contacts with Europeans. Because of its lack of good harbors and the presence of noncentralized, coastal peoples, the trans-Atlantic slave trade had little impact on the region, and trade was sporadic. French conquest of the region in the late nineteenth century met with serious resistance from local groups, especially the forces of the ruler Samori Toure in the interior, which resisted occupation for over twenty years. By 1900, the colony of French Guinea became part of the Federation of French West Africa. The French established rubber and tropical fruit plantations, worked by local forced labor, and also exploited the area's rich mineral deposits.

By the early 1950s, Sekou Toure, a labor organizer who claimed descent from Samori Toure, was calling for independence. Because of the harshness of colonial rule and the colony's grinding poverty, Toure's message appealed to most Guineans. In 1958, when President Charles de Gaulle of France called for a referendum on continued ties or immediate independence for the colonies in French West Africa, only Guinea, at the urging of Toure, voted for independence, which was granted on October 2, 1958. The French withdrew quickly, sabotaging much of the area's infrastructure, ending all economic and military aid, and completely severing diplomatic links. Toure defiantly turned to the Soviet Union and the Eastern bloc for assistance, further isolating Guinea from the West and its West African neighbors, especially Senegal and the Cote D'Ivoire (Ivory Coast), whose independent governments relied heavily on French aid and expertise. Toure blamed the country's

worsening economic woes on colonialism, the lack of Western aid, and purported French attempts to overthrow his regime. He crushed all dissent, and as many as 2 million people fled into exile. Thousands were imprisoned, and many disappeared in detention, as Toure became increasingly dictatorial and paranoid. In the early 1980s, Toure made some overtures to France and the West, but he died suddenly in March 1984, throwing the government into turmoil, until the military, headed by General Lansana Conte, seized power. Conte remains the president of Guinea.

Neither Conte nor his regime found an effective solution to Guinea's overwhelming economic woes. Overtures were made to France and to the West for assistance, especially after the collapse of the Soviet Union, but foreign donors were reluctant to help the repressive military government. Conte faced several coup attempts, all brutally crushed. Despite its rich deposits of bauxite, iron ore, and diamonds, and a harsh structural adjustment program imposed by foreign donors in the late 1980s, including devaluation of the currency, elimination of many civil service jobs, and a general dismantling of many of the socialist structures established by the previous government, the country experienced little economic improvement. Unlike its neighbors, the nation has good soils and climate for agriculture, but only 3% of land is cultivated. Blame for the poor agriculture performance rests largely on the Toure regime, which instituted a corrupt and highly inefficient state-controlled system of marketing and distribution. The Conte government has tried to dismantle the system, but with little success. Much of the mineral wealth was and continues to be smuggled out of the country. Corruption is rampant in Guinea, especially among the ruling military elite. Much of the country's paltry export revenue was used to pay interest on the country's massive foreign debt, estimated at $3.5 billion. In the 1990s, more than half a million refugees from the civil wars in Sierra Leone and Liberia flooded into Guinea. Refugees have drained the country's scarce resources and there have been periodic clashes between Guineans and refugees. There have recently been serious border clashes between Guinea and Liberia, prompting fears that Guinea will be dragged into a wider regional conflict.

In 1992, the government did institute a program of multiparty politics, yet the 1993 and 2002 elections were marked by widespread fraud and intimidation. Periodically, sections of the military have rioted, and there has been serious unrest among the urban population, but all dissent is immediately and harshly crushed. Human rights abuses are rampant. The government faces constant threats of a military coup. Economic conditions have worsened in the past few years with increased smuggling, influxes of refugees, and mismanagement. Inadequate transportation systems hinder economic development. Most of the country's roads are unpaved and in poor condition. The railroads linking the interior to the coast, built by the French for exploitation of mineral deposits, are in serious disrepair. Education and health services are sorely neglected, with an adult literacy rate of 36%. Infant mortality, at 127 per 1,000 live births, is among the highest in the world. Life expectancy for males is forty-three years and forty-eight years for females. The Guinea's political and economic future is uncertain at best.

ANDREW F. CLARK

See also Colonialism: Legacies; West Africa: History and Economic Development; West Africa: International Relations

References and Further Reading

Barry, Boubacar. *Senegambia and the Atlantic Slave Trade,* Cambridge: Cambridge University Press, 1998.
Nelson, Harold D. *Area Handbook for Guinea,* Washington, DC: Government Printing Office, 1975.
O'Toole, Thomas. *Historical Dictionary of Guinea.* Metuchen, NJ: Scarecrow Press, 1987.
Riviere, Claude. *Guinea: The Mobilization of a People.* Ithaca, NY: Cornell University Press, 1977.
Rodney, Walter. *A History of the Upper Guinea Coast, 1545–1800,* Oxford, Clarendon Press, 1970.
Suret-Canale, Jean. *La Republique de Guinee.* Paris: Editions Sociales, 1970.

GUINEA-BISSAU

The Republic of Guinea-Bissau, situated on the northwestern coast of Africa between Senegal and Guinea, is one of the smallest nations on the continent, comprising about fourteen thousand square miles. The country is mostly a low coastal marshplain rising to savanna in the east, with a tropical climate consisting of a monsoonal rainy season from June to November and a hot dry season. More than 80% of the population is engaged in rice, cashew nut, bean, and cassava cultivation. With 217 miles of coastline, several small islands, and numerous meandering rivers and streams, fishing forms an important economic sector. The population is estimated at approximately 1.4 million, with an annual growth rate of 2.2%. The capital, Bissau, is located on the coast and had a population of anywhere between two hundred thousand and three hundred thousand in 2002 and 2003. The figure has varied widely in the last three years, owing to periodic influxes of rural refugees with unrest in the interior, and then considerable decreases when violence has engulfed the capital. Current population figures are impossible to estimate. Portuguese is the official language, with numerous ethnic languages, including Krioko, widely spoken. Ethnic groups include the Balante, Fula, and Mandinka; religious affiliation is almost evenly divided between Muslims and indigenous religions, with about 5% Christian.

The area was long part of a series of largely decentralized kingdoms, and then, from the thirteenth century onwards, the Empire of Mali, centered in the Western Sudan. In the mid-fifteenth century, the Portuguese began exploring, trading, and fort-building in the region. Soon the area became a major slave exporter to Brazil. By the mid-seventeenth century, the Portuguese had established some administrative control over the coast and near interior to protect their slave trading from the French and British who were also active in slave trading nearby. Some Portuguese traders settled permanently in the Bissau area and intermarried with indigenous women, creating a highly influential and comparatively wealthy *metis* population that influenced local language, society, and culture. With the abolition of the Atlantic slave trade in the mid-nineteenth century, the area, known as the *Rios de Guine* (Rivers of Guinea), became a commercial center for the export of fish as well as agricultural and forest products.

At the Berlin Conference of 1885–1886, Portuguese Guinea, consisting of both the mainland and the Cape Verde islands, was formally recognized by the European colonial powers. Under colonial rule, the colony was neglected by the Portuguese in favor of their larger and richer possessions in Angola and Mozambique. In 1952, Portuguese Guinea, like other Portuguese controlled territories in Africa, officially became an overseas province of Portugal. This action soon led to an independence movement that in 1961, developed into a prolonged armed struggle, jointly waged by Cape Verde islanders and mainlanders. The insurgency was led by Amilcar Cabral, a Cape Verdian, who soon established control over most of the interior, whereas the coast and Bissau, remained under Portuguese control. The liberation war was brutal and costly to the colony's population and limited infrastructure, which was virtually destroyed in the fighting. Cabral was assassinated in early 1973, and in September 1974, Guinea-Bissau formally achieved its complete independence. Civilian rule was initially established but in 1980, General Joao Vieira, a mainlander, led a coup and installed a military regime. In 1981, the Cape Verde Islands renounced their mainland ties.

The change from civilian to military rule did little to improve the country's poor economic development. Amid growing unrest over an increasingly authoritarian regime and lack of economic progress, a constitution was approved in 1984 that, with amendments, has remained in force. Vieira was elected in 1984 and again in 1989, surviving several coup attempts. A multiparty system was announced in 1991, but Vieira remained in power, indefinitely postponing presidential elections. In 1999, Vieira was driven into exile and replaced as head of state by General Ausmane Mane, who called for presidential elections in January 2000. Mane lost to Kumba Yala, who ruled until September 2003 when he was overthrown by the current military regime that promises elections and a return to civilian rule. No progress has been made in that regard because, the regime claims, continuing unrest and outside military intervention by neighboring Senegal threatens the country.

Guinea-Bissau's internal political unrest, which intensified in 2003 and 2004, is one factor in its dismal economic performance. Relations with neighboring Senegal and nearby Gambia have been marred since the early 1990s by disputes over offshore oil drilling and fishing rights, conflicting land border claims, military incursions, and reported external support for coup attempts. Refugees fled into the capital as well as from the country. Economic production was seriously disrupted by the continued turmoil and upheaval. Any infrastructure that existed in the 1990s has been destroyed. In addition, the lack of developed natural resources, little international aid, virtually no foreign investment, widespread corruption, systemic mismanagement, and considerable emigration have all contributed to Guinea-Bissau being consistently ranked as one of the world's ten poorest countries. A structural adjustment program, implemented in 1987, sought to move the country from a centrally planned economy, cut public spending, eliminate many civil servant positions, and accelerate privatization. It has not, however, significantly helped to improve economic performance. Substantial amounts of rice and other foodstuffs are now being imported. External debt in 2000 was estimated at $950 million. Education has been sorely neglected, with an adult literacy rate of about 35% in 2003. Despite compulsory, free education, most children, especially girls, never attend schools, and there is no institution of higher learning. Beyond some primary health care and traditional medicine, most citizens have no access to modern medical care. The infant mortality rates has been estimated at 109 deaths per 1,000 live births; life expectancy for men is forty-five years; forty-eight years for women. The gross domestic product is approximately $900, one of the lowest in the world. Both the political and economic situation of Guinea-Bissau remain perilous.

ANDREW F. CLARK

See also Ethnic Conflicts: West Africa; West Africa: History and Economic Development; West Africa: International Relations

References and Further Reading

Adebajo, Adekeye. *Building Peace in West Africa: Liberia, Sierra Leone, and Guinea-Bissau.* Boulder, CO: Lynne Riener, 2002.

Brooks, George. *Landlords and Strangers: Ecology, Society, and Trade in Western Africa, 1000–1630.* Boulder, CO: Westview, 1993.

Cabral, Amilcar. *Revolution in Guinea: Selected Texts.* New York: Monthly Review, 1969.

Davidson, Basil. *The People's Cause: A History of Guerrillas in Africa.* Essex: Longman, 1981.

Guinea-Bissau Country Study Guide. Washington, DC: International Business Publications, 2004.

Hawthorne, Walter. *Planting Rice and Harvesting Slaves: Transformations along the Guinea-Bissau Coast, 1400–1900.* Portsmouth, NH: Heinemann, 2003.

Lobban, Richard. *Historical Dictionary of the Republics of Guinea-Bissau and Cape Verde.* London: Scarecrow, 1979.

Mark, Peter. *Portuguese—Style and Luso-African Identity: Precolonial Senegambia, Sixteenth–Nineteenth Centuries.* Bloomington, Ind.: Indiana University, 2002.

GULF COOPERATION COUNCIL

Officially known as the Cooperation Council for the Arab States of the Gulf, the Gulf Cooperation Council (GCC) was officially established after a meeting held in Abu Dhabi on May 25, 1981. The GCC comprises Saudi Arabia, the United Arab Emirates, Kuwait, Oman, Bahrain, and Qatar. The objectives of the GCC, as encapsulated in its Charter, emphasise the desire of the member states to achieve commonality in a wide range of areas. These include common regulatory frameworks for finance, trade, and customs, as well as cooperative ventures in both private investment and scientific and technical ventures. The Supreme Council of the GCC comprises the heads of state of each of the member states, a Ministerial Council, a Secretariat, and an Advisory Commission for the Supreme Council.

Although the commencement of the Iran-Iraq war had prompted these nations to examine their relative vulnerabilities, security issues have by no means dominated the affairs of the Council. That having been said, a Comprehensive Security Strategy was approved by the member states, and a security agreement was concluded in 1994. The agreement sees each member of the GCC considering an attack on a member as an attack on all member states. The most concrete example of security cooperation has been the establishment of the Peninsula Shield Force, a combined arms grouping from each of the member states that has a standing headquarters and exercises its forces a number of times a year.

In a region where the history of multilateral cooperation has not been encouraging, the GCC has stood out as a relative success story. While its security achievements have been relatively limited, it can point out a number of examples where long-term negotiations have led to the signing of binding multilateral agreements. In particular, the GCC has striven for cooperative arrangements in economic affairs. This has led to the freedom of labour movement of GCC nationals between member states (although some professions in some member states remain restricted to those nationals only). Effective January 1, 2003, a Customs Union introduced a standard tariff on all goods imported from outside the GCC and allowed freedom of movement within GCC countries once they had arrived. This had originally been planned for 2005 but was brought forward two years, illustrating the degree of cooperation that member states have been able to achieve. Joint institutions such as the Gulf Investment Authority and a Commercial Arbitration Centre for all GCC members have also been established. The GCC also has sought to institute a common GCC currency by the year 2010.

RODGER SHANAHAN

See also Middle East: History and Economic Development; Middle East: International Relations

References and Further Reading

Gulf Cooperation Council web site: www.gcc-sg.org.
Ramazani, Rouhollah K. *The Gulf Cooperation Council: Record and Analysis.* Charlottesville, VA: University Press of Virginia, 1988.

GUS DUR

Well before becoming Indonesia's first democratically elected president in October 1999, Kiai Haji Abdurrahman Wahid's influence within Indonesian public life was felt in the spheres of religion, politics, civil society, and intellectual exchange. In the religious sphere, his influence was, and continues to be, unrivalled. Indeed, it is fair to say that during the fifteen years (1984–1999) that Wahid was the chairman of *Nahdlatul Ulama* (NU), he was one of the world's most important Islamic leaders. After all, with an estimated 35 million members and extensive grassroots support, NU is not only Indonesia's largest Islamic organization but also the largest in the world.

Similarly, in the political realm, as leader of NU, Wahid occupied a unique position; since taking up the chairmanship of NU in 1984, he oversaw the official withdrawal of NU from party politics and the opening up of vigorous debate regarding many issues previously considered sacrosanct. In the 1990s, while no longer a political party NU arguably represented the single most politically important grouping of people outside of the government's party GOLKAR and the army. Moreover, Wahid now also headed Forum Demokrasi, a small but very important intellectual lobby group, which he established in 1990 to be an independent nonsectarian vehicle to lobby publicly for democratic reform.

Finally, in the arena of intellectual debate and the public exchange of ideas, Wahid was always a figure of no mean ability. An astute and highly influential public figure, Wahid is controversial but generally well-liked, particularly by the younger generation, as is evidenced by the universal preference for affectionately referring to him by his sobriquet "Gus Dur."

Despite his well-established position as a reform-minded liberal intellectual, Wahid's traditional Islamic credentials are thoroughly sound. Born in Jombang, East Java, in 1940, Wahid studied at a number of *pesantren*, traditional Islamic boarding schools, in Java before undertaking tertiary level studies at the Al-Azhar Islamic university in Cairo, Egypt in 1964. From Al-Azhar in 1966, he went on to further studies in the field of literature at the University of Baghdad in Iraq, graduating from there in 1970. Encouraged by news of interesting developments in the *pesantren* scene in Indonesia and unable to study in Europe, Wahid returned home in 1971. He immediately immersed himself in the *pesantren* world, holding a number of positions at various *pesantren*.

In 1989, he was resoundingly re-elected for a second term as NU Chairman despite considerable opposition from the Soeharto regime. He again emerged victorious in November 1994, having been elected to a third five-year term in the face of a concerted and vigorous campaign directed against him by Soeharto, who was angrier than ever at his outspoken dissent.

In late 1996, in the wake of Soeharto's dramatic ouster of Megawati Sukarnoputri from the leadership of the Democratic Party of Indonesia (PDI) when further opposition seemed futile, Wahid sought and achieved a rapprochement of sorts with Soeharto. But when the Asian Economic Crisis began to pummel the Indonesia economy a year later and calls for Soeharto's resignation grew steadily more strident, the public looked to Abdurrahman Wahid, Megawati Sukarnoputri and Amien Rais (leader of NU's counterpart, the 25-million-strong modernist Muslim organization Muhammadiyah) to lead the push to topple the Soeharto regime. Fearing bloody confrontation, all three leaders urged restraint. Then, in January 1998, Wahid suffered a near-fatal stroke and the loss of what was left of his failing eyesight. He was still bedridden four months later when Soeharto finally resigned on May 21. By June, however, he recovered sufficient strength to oversee the formation of the National Awakening Party (PKB), a non-Islamist party formed to mobilize the NU masses for the June 7, 1999 elections, Indonesia's first free and fair elections since 1955. Despite the fact that PKB won less than 13% of the vote in the parliamentary elections, on October 20, 1999, the Peoples Consultative Assembly (MPR) Electoral College voted Wahid president. Megawati, whose party had achieved almost 34% of the vote, was elected vice president in the June elections. The relationship between the two leaders and their supporters, which had been deteriorating since mid-May, never recovered, and as a result, Wahid failed to gain the backing of parliament. His maverick leadership style and overly ambitious push for sweeping reforms on multiple fronts exacerbated antipathy towards him in the legislature, the bureaucracy, and the military; and the MPR finally ended his term on July 23, 2001, through moving what was effectively a vote of no-confidence against him.

The broadly based popularity and respect that he continues to enjoy, despite his tumultuous presidency, is hard-earned, but it can be attributed in part to his perceived spiritual linage, something of great value in traditional Islamic circles where mystical power, often inherited, is more important than head knowledge. His grandfather, KH Hasyim Asy'ari, helped found NU in 1921, and his father, KH Wahid Hasyim, also led NU and was Minister of Religious Affairs in the early 1950s.

Today, Wahid stands together with other progressive Indonesian Islamic intellectuals such as Nurcholish Madjid as representing a new kind of *ulama* (Islamic scholar) and a new movement of thought, sometimes referred to as Neo-Modernism, which goes beyond both Islamic modernism and Islamic traditionalism, breaks the bounds of conventional jurisprudential reasoning, and brings together the core teachings of Islam and the insights of modern "western" scholarship.

Under the influence of a new generation of thinkers such as Wahid, Indonesian Islamic thought has become steadily more cosmopolitan and open, confidently embracing the pluralism of modern Indonesian society. The acceptance of a sophisticated position on the separation of "church" and state combined with a profound appreciation of the core values of Islam to enable, and indeed encourage, the growth of pluralist liberal thought as rich and broad as that found anywhere in the world. Abdurrahman is but one of a number of Islamic intellectuals who have contributed to the emergence of what is now commonly referred to as Islamic liberalism. Without his contribution, however, this movement might not have developed the broad support it now enjoys within the youth of NU and mainstream Muslim society in Indonesia.

GREG BARTON

See also Indonesia; Southeast Asia: History and Economic Development

References and Further Reading

Barton, Greg. *Abdurrahman Wahid, Indonesian President, Muslim Democrat: A View from the Inside.* Honolulu: University of Hawaii Press, 2002.
———. "The Wahid Presidency in Context: Regime Change, Inflated expectations, Islam and the Promise of Democracy" in *Indonesia Matters: Unity, Diversity and Stability in Fragile times,* edited by Thang D. Nguyen and Frank-Jürgen Richter. Singapore: Times Editions, 2003.
Barton Greg, and Greg Fealy, eds. *Nahdlatul Ulama, Traditional Islam, and Modernity in Indonesia.* Clayton: Monash Asia Institute, 1996.
Hefner, Robert W. *Civil Islam: Muslims and Democratization in Indonesia.* Princeton, NJ: Princeton University Press, 2000.
Ramage, Douglas E. *Politics in Indonesia: Democracy, Islam, and the Ideology of Tolerance.* London: Routledge, 1995.

GUYANA

Guyana, a country about the size of Idaho, is located above Brazil and east of Venezuela on the north coast of South America. The capital is Georgetown. Its population in 2004 was 705,803 and does not grow because so many of its residents immigrate to the United States, Canada, and other islands in the Caribbean. Guyana also has a very high mortality rate for infants and deaths due to AIDS.

"Guiana" was first visited by the English, but it was the Dutch who established the first fortified settlement on an island in the Essequibo River just off the coast of Guyana with Amerindian trading partners in 1616. After changing hands between the British and the Dutch several times, it was a British colony from 1803 until 1966, when it became an independent republic of the British Commonwealth. As a former British colony, the official language of Guyana is English, but most Guyanese speak Creole in informal communication. Amerindians maintain many dialects, and Hindi and Urdu also are spoken.

Except for the small number of Amerindian communities in the interior, the Guyanese population is largely urban and coastal. The people of Guyana are comprised of Indo-Guyanese (50%), Amerindians

(7%), Afro-Guyanese (6%), English, Dutch, Portuguese, Chinese, and other Asian immigrants of multiple national origins There are many racially mixed Guyanese as well. Their primary religions are Christian, Hindu, and Muslim, in that order. They came as colonists, slaves, and indentured servants to manage and work on sugar cane plantations. Modern Guyanese are engaged in industry and commerce, agriculture, and public-sector service labor. The current economy slowed in 2003 as a result of a shortage of skilled labor and the underdevelopment of the infrastructure. The government also is plagued with the need to balance public investment and the unemployment of unskilled labor with high external debt payments.

Guyana has had racial strife, largely between its Indo-Guyanese and Afro-Guyanese populations. Due to the plantation labor history of Guyana, these conflicts were both racially motivated and class-based. As the new democracy emerged, these two dominant groups engaged in violent political rivalry. It was not until 1992 that Guyana's political elections were widely recognized as free and fair. The current democratic government defends human rights and supports the expansion of the private economic sector through global networks with other democracies. Despite the racial conflicts of their early national independence, the Guyanese are primarily peaceful people. Along with cricket, the Guyanese enjoy basketball, soccer, and volleyball, among other team sports.

With the collapse of the sugar market, which precipitated independence from Britain, Guyana's developing economy is based primarily on the extractive industries of fishing, logging, and mining. It exports bauxite, gold, diamonds, hardwoods, rum, rice, molasses, and shrimp. However, there is strong national desire and international support for the protection of Guyana's rain forest reserves.

The people of Guyana gave Iwokrama, a 1-million-acre preserve of virgin rainforest in the Amazonian region of the interior, to the people of the Commonwealth for scientific research and sustainable management. Funds from Great Britain, Canada, and the United Nations maintain a research camp visited by biologists, anthropologists, and other scholars from around the world. The Iwokrama Rain Forest works with local Amerindians and international partners to project local ecosystems and cultures. It is the homeland of the Makushi people, who work with anthropologists from the University of Guyana Amerindian Research Unit and the United States to develop ecotourism in the region. A local Makushi Research Unit is involved in collaborative ethnobotany research with international pharmaceutical development agencies.

The topography of Guyana is diverse. In addition to Iwokrama's rain forest, Guyana offers ecotourists and adventurers breathtaking pristine natural beauty. It features 450 miles of Atlantic coastline; millions of acres of rain forest; the Pakaraima Mountains; mighty rivers like the Essequibo, Demerara, Berbice, and the Potaro; and the Rupununi savannah in the south. Kaieteur Falls, accessible by private plane, drops four times the length of Niagara Falls. Visitors to the rain forest can see jaguars, caiman, the Harpy Eagle, Giant River Otter, and Arapaima freshwater fish. Including macaws, toucans, and parrots, there are more than seven hundred species of indigenous birds. The rich biodiversity of the rain forest also is home to exotic plants and butterflies.

In Georgetown, visitors will see St. George's Cathedral. Built in the 1800s of Guyana's indigenous hardwoods, it is the tallest wooden building in the world. Green heart and purple heart hardwoods also were used to build ships because of their resistance to moisture. They are still exported as luxury building and craft materials.

BARBARA J. DILLY

See also Northern South America: History and Economic Development; Northern South America: International Relations

References and Further Reading

Baines, Stephen Grant, and Stephen Nugent. "Makuxi and Wapishana Indians on the Brazil: Guyana Border," in *Critique of Anthropology* (December 2003) 23:4, p. 339.

Dilly, Barbara J. "Gender, Culture, and Ecotourism: Development Policies and Practices in the Guyanese Rain Forest," in *Women's Studies Quarterly* (Fall/Winter 2003) 31: 3–4, p. 58.

Forte, Janette, and Ian Melville. Amerindian Testimonies. Boise, ID: Boise State University Press, 1989.

Fredericks, Marcel, et al. *Society and Health in Guyana: The Sociology of Health Care in a Developing Nation*. Durham, NC: Carolina Academic Press, 1986.

Hintzen, Percy C. "Creoleness and Nationalism in Guyanese Anticolonialism and Postcolonial Formation," in *Small Axe: A Caribbean Journal of Criticism* (March 2004) Issue 15, p. 106.

Lehman, S. M. "Distribution and Diversity of Primates in Guyana: Species-Area Relationships and Riverine Barriers," in *International Journal of Primatology* (February 2004) 25:1, p. 73.

Mistry, Jayalaxshmi, Matthew Simpson, Andrea Berardi, and Yung Sandy. "Exploring the Links Between Natural Resource Use and Biophysical Status in the Waterways of the North Rupununi, Guyana," in *Journal of Environmental Management*. (September 2004) 72:3, p. 117.

Rose, Euclid A. Dependency and Socialism in the Modern Caribbean: Superpower Intervention in Guyana, Jamaica, and Grenada, 1970–1985.

H

HAILE MARYAM, MENGISTU

Mengistu Haile Maryam, a ruthless army officer with Marxist leanings, dominated Ethiopia from 1974 to 1991. He was born in 1937, but little else is publicly known about his background or his private life. His regime murdered thousands of political opponents and private citizens before he fled the country in 1991.

Ethiopia under Emperor Haile Selassie (1892–1975) was a feudal country in which the imperial family was estimated to have owned 42% of the land and the Coptic Church another 18%. Numerous ethno-linguistic groups in the provinces felt themselves exploited by Amhara-speakers who lived in and around the capital, Addis Ababa. Discontent turned into revolt after a great famine in 1973. On January 12, 1974 the army mutinied, led by the Dergue, a committee of 120 officers, including Major Mengistu. Seven months later the Dergue arrested the Emperor, suspended the constitution, and proclaimed a provisional military government.

The Dergue's nominal leader was executed on orders of Mengistu in November 1974. In December the Dergue proclaimed a socialist program for Ethiopia. Foreign businesses and banks were nationalized. Students and teachers were to be sent into the countryside to help collectivize farms. Mengistu promoted himself from major to lieutenant colonel in 1976. The next year he named himself head of state after another bloody internal purge of the officer corps.

All this was taking place in the context of Cold War rivalry that focused on the Horn of Africa. The United States had supported Ethiopia in its territorial dispute with Somalia, which was armed by the Soviet Union. But after Mengistu proclaimed himself a Marxist the superpowers switched sides: Mengistu signed a treaty of friendship and cooperation with the USSR. East German security police and ten thousand Cuban troops were sent to help Mengistu control the situation. Washington, therefore, approved of Somalia's invasion of Ethiopia in July, 1977.

Col. Mengistu, fearing internal enemies, launched the so-called Red Terror in 1977. To show citizens what he wanted he called a huge rally in the capital at which he threw bottles filled with blood onto the pavement. The killing began in Addis Ababa, where the Dergue distributed weapons to neighborhood associations, which kept meticulous records of their executions. Bodies of victims were left in streets for three days as a warning to others, and relatives who wished to claim them had to pay for the bullets expended. At least five thousand people were killed in the initial phase of the terror. Many of these were students resisting forced conscription.

A far greater toll was exacted by the famine of 1984–1985 in Tigre Province, bordering Eritrea. Mengistu's solution was to forcibly relocate Tigreans to the distant south. As many as five hundred thousand of these internal refugees died. Internal opposition to Mengistu spread in the late 1980s, and the Ethiopian army grew demoralized. The new Soviet leader, Mikhail Gorbachev, warned Mengistu to negotiate an end to the ethnic wars.

With few options left, Mengistu fled Ethiopia on May 21, 1991, to live in a heavily-guarded mansion in

Harare, Zimbabwe. He is being tried *in absentia* on 209 counts of crimes against humanity.

ROSS MARLAY

See also East Africa: History and Economic Development; East Africa: International Relations; Ethiopia; Ethnic Conflicts: East Africa; Selassie, Emperor Haile

Bibliography

Halliday, Fred, and Maxine Molyneax, *The Ethiopian Revolution.* Norton, 1982.
Human Rights Watch, *Evil Days: 30 Years of War and Famine in Ethiopia* (1991).
"Interview With Former President of Ethiopia, Colonel Mengistu Haile Mariam," (January 2003) http://www.ethiopis.com/modules.php?op=modload&name=News&file=article&sid=55&newlang=eng

HAITI

History and Economic Development

Haiti occupies the western third of the Caribbean island of Hispaniola and lies between 19° and 20° N and 72° and 74° W. Ninety kilometers southeast of Cuba, 187 kilometers northeast of Jamaica, and about one thousand kilometers from Florida, it contains 27,750 square kilometers (10,714 square miles). Haiti's topography ranges from flat, semiarid valleys to densely forested mountains, and about one third of its area reaches between two hundred and five hundred meters above sea level. The remaining two-thirds is divided into three mountain ranges with the highest elevation at about 2,680 meters (8,793 feet). The average daytime temperature usually remains between 24°C and 27°C. The main variation in temperature is due to elevation with three-quarters of a degree decrease for each one hundred-meter increase in elevation. The northern mountains receive about two hundred centimeters (eighty inches) of rain annually; the southern coast receives less than one hundred centimeters (forty inches) annually.

Demographic information is highly unreliable, but the total population is estimated to be 8.5 million with the capital of Port-au-Prince containing about 1.5 million people. According to various studies, the birth rate is probably around 35.5 per 100,000, and the annual growth rate somewhere just less than 2% per annum; the mortality per 1,000 is approximately 13; infant mortality per 1,000 is just less than 120; and life expectancy at birth is about 56 years.

Haitians speak a language that is usually referred to as Haitian Creole. For most of its history, however, the official language of government, business, and education has been French. Nevertheless, only about 8% of the population speaks French with any appreciable fluency. This educated elite has traditionally used the requirement of French to exclude the masses from competing for positions in government and business. Haitian Creole is currently becoming more widely accepted, and the prestige of French is rapidly declining in Haiti. Article Five of the 1987 constitution, which was distributed in both French and Creole, stated, "All Haitians are united through one common language: Creole. Creole and French are the official languages of the Republic." Due to the recent flood of Haitian migrants to Florida, the international decline of the French language, and the economic and cultural trends in the Caribbean, English is increasingly learned and used by Haitians.

The second oldest independent nation in the Western Hemisphere, the Republic of Haiti is the only one with a French-Creole background as well as the only one with an overwhelmingly African culture. Also, large numbers of Haitians live outside Haiti, especially in the Dominican Republic, on other Caribbean islands, in the countries of Central America, northern South America, and in North America. After Port-au-Prince the second largest Haitian community is in New York City.

The economic life of much of Haiti can be understood as a product of various historical factors. After having defeated the colonial government of the French slave-owners in a bloody war ending in 1804 the newly independent nation faced the threat of a French army returning to re-enslave them. The government of the newly independent nation confiscated private land, imposed forced labor (which was unworkable and quickly abandoned), and attempted to develop an export agriculture to obtain the importation of war material. These actions led to the fragmentation of land holdings, the peasantization of Haiti, and the alienation of the masses from the government and the ruling elites. Haiti is, indeed, one of the most peasantified of all countries with about 65% of the labor force in agriculture. Currently 60% to 80% of the rural population owns their own land, though the plots are fragmented and small. A typical Haitian family feeds itself on beans, corn, rice, and yams. Despite the importance of agriculture, however, the countryside is about 95% deforested and about 25% of the soil is undergoing rapid erosion.

Coffee, sugar, rice, and cocoa are traditionally Haiti's primary export products. Shoes, soap, flour, cement, and domestic oils comprise its light manufacturing products. Haiti also has a few cotton mills. Offshore industries have traditionally produced garments, toys, baseballs, and electronic goods for the US market, but due to the current chaotic political situation few offshore industries are functioning. The oil crises of 1973–1974 and 1980 were great shocks to the Haitian economy. In 1980, a horrific hurricane devastated the coffee industry. Many people engage in part-time craft work, particularly in the manufacture of small items and tools, but the annual per capita income is estimated at only $380 US dollars.

Most of the internal economic activity occurs in open-air markets; in rural areas men generally handle the agricultural production and women handle the products of agriculture.

International Relations

Haiti is closely tied to the United States with a majority of its exports coming to North America and a goodly portion of its economy dependent on government and non-government aid from the United States. October 2001 marked the seventh anniversary of President Jean-Bertrand Aristide's return to power after thirty-six months in exile following a 1991 military coup d'etat. He was reinstalled in 1994 through the military intervention of twenty-two thousand US soldiers, though his socialist and anti-American rhetoric meant that influential sectors in the US government would continue to oppose his administration.

Since May 2000, when the party of twice-elected President Aristide won approximately 80% of the seats in a parliamentary election and the US-backed opposition front Democratic Convergence alleged that the election was rigged, Haiti has been in a political and economic crisis. Largely under pressure from the United States, over $500 million US dollars in international aid has been frozen until the government and the opposition reach an agreement to hold new elections. In May 2002, when Aristide addressed the United Nations in New York City about the worldwide exploitation of children, a thousand or so people demonstrated against this decision by the international community, and especially by the United States, to withhold assistance to Haiti.

ROBERT LAWLESS

See also Caribbean: History and Economic Development; Caribbean: International Relations; Duvalier, François

References and Further Reading

Arthur, Charles. *Haiti: A Guide to the People, Politics and Culture*. New York: Interlink, 2002.
Dash, J. Michael. *Culture and Customs of Haiti*. Westport, CT: Greenwood, 2001.
DeWind, Josh, and David H. Kinley III. *Aiding Migration: The Impact of International Development Assistance on Haiti*. Boulder, CO: Westview, 1988.
Diederich, Bernard. "Swine Fever Ironies: The Slaughter of the Haitian Black Pig," *Caribbean Review* 14(1):16–17,41 (1985).
English, E. Philip. *Canadian Development Assistance to Haiti*. Ottawa: North-South Institute, 1984.
Latortue, Paul R. "The External Debt Situation of Haiti," in Foreign Debt and Latin American Economic Development, edited by Antonio Jorge, Jorge Salazar-Carillo, and Rene P. Higonnet. New York: Pergamon, 1983.
Lawless, Robert. *Haiti's Bad Press: Origins, Development, and Consequences*. Rochester, VT: Schenkman, 1992.
Maguire, Robert. *Bottom-Up Development in Haiti*, 2nd edition. Rosslyn, VA: Inter-American Foundation, 1981.
Rotberg, Robert I. editor, *Haiti Renewed: Political and Economic Prospects*. Washington, DC: Brookings Institution, 1997.

HAMAS

HAMAS (the acronym for the Arabic *Harakat al-Muqawamah al-Islamiyya*, also meaning "zeal" or "bravery") is the Islamic Resistance Movement that developed in the Israeli-Occupied Palestinian Territories of the West Bank and Gaza Strip in late 1987 to early 1988 during the height of the first Palestinian *intifada*. The Movement is an offshoot of the Muslim Brotherhood. According to the HAMAS Covenant, the goals and objectives of this nationalist movement are to liberate Palestine through jihad, ridding it of all Zionist and other foreign non-Muslim influences. This entails, specifically, the need for all Believers to strive to destroy and then replace the State of Israel, the West Bank, and the Gaza Strip with a Palestinian State, which is to be governed by the precepts of *shariah* (Muslim) law.

The liberation ideology and theology of the Movement is based almost entirely upon a very strict interpretation of the teachings of the Qur'an. As such, the Movement takes its guidance, most especially with regard to relations with Jews, from the concept that Muslims can coexist peacefully with *dhimmi* communities (that is, Jews and Christians) so long as these communities live under the protective "wing" of Muslim governance. Within such a Qur'anic context, foreign rule of Muslim lands (*dar al-Islam*) by Jews or other non-Muslims cannot be tolerated.

In addition, classically anti-Semitic texts coming from pre-Holocaust Christian Europe, such as the *Protocols of the Elders of Zion,* also inform the ideals and philosophy of HAMAS members and their views of Jews and Judaism. Such texts mesh well with HAMAS ideology, further validating the insidious nature of the Zionist movement, and its desires to take over the entire world. Thus, HAMAS equates Zionism with Nazism and imperialism, and contends that any and all means of striving to rid the Muslim Middle East of what it sees as a "vicious," invalid movement—if necessary, while losing one's life in the process—are legitimate acts when the objective is the liberation of Palestine from Jewish control.

A Brief History of HAMAS

HAMAS was founded in the late 1980s as an offshoot of the Muslim Brotherhood. Led by the blind paraplegic Sheikh Ahmad Yassin, the movement began to gather Palestinian followers immediately, as those discouraged and angered by years of an unsuccessful secular liberation movement headed by Yasser Arafat's Palestine Liberation Organization (PLO) were offered renewed hope that the HAMAS alternative might succeed where others before them had failed.

During the first *intifada*, HAMAS's military wing, the Izz ed-Din al-Qassam Brigades, were instrumental in attacking Israeli settlers and soldiers as a part of the armed struggle against the Zionist control of Palestine. The strategy of seeking out and attacking Israeli civilians, the Movement contends, began only after the mass murder of Muslim worshippers in Hebron by an Israeli West Bank settler, Baruch Goldstein, in early 1994. Thereafter, the Movement determined that *all* Zionists were acceptable targets in its efforts to liberate Palestine from non-Muslim control.

Although HAMAS has stated its support for the PLO and its President, Yasser Arafat, on numerous occasions, it has long opposed the PLO with regard to any sort of compromise with the Israeli/Zionist government. When, for example, Arafat signed the Oslo Accords with Israel effectively ending the Palestinian-Israeli conflict in 1993, HAMAS announced its refusal to accept the Accords, and its unwillingness to recognize any sort of agreement that would suggest an acceptance or recognition of Zionist claims in the region. That said, some HAMAS supporters ran as independents in the Palestinian elections held in 1996 that resulted from the Oslo agreements.

Since the onset of the *al-Aqsa intifada* in September 2000, HAMAS has played a central role in opposing what the Movement perceives to be Israeli crimes against the Palestinian people. HAMAS views its suicide bombers, for example, not as terrorists but rather as martyrs who are employed to fight an incredibly powerful enemy for a just and righteous cause condoned—if not, required—by the tenets of Islam.

In response to the rise in suicide attacks throughout the West Bank, Gaza, and Israel, the Israeli authorities began to target the HAMAS leadership in March 2004. HAMAS leader and founder Sheikh Ahmad Yassin was the first to be assassinated by the Israeli authorities; his replacement, Abdel Aziz Rantisi, was assassinated in a similar fashion only a few weeks thereafter in April 2004. While the Israelis contend that the assassinations of these and other al-Qassam commanders thereafter are all legitimate in light of ongoing attacks against civilians and others by HAMAS operatives, the HAMAS leadership asserts that such killings of these significant individuals only strengthen the resolve of the Palestinian people as a whole. Moreover, they state that each killing simply encourages HAMAS leaders to call on its members to undertake further acts of revenge and retaliation, and not the surrender that the Israeli authorities seek to achieve.

The Role of HAMAS as an Evolving Regional Player

Although viewed by the United States and West as a solely terrorist organization infamous for its numerous suicide attacks and other violent acts against Israel and its interests, HAMAS also successfully operates numerous charitable and community aid programs in mosques, community centers, schools, and health clinics throughout the Palestinian Territories. Increasingly, such programs serve to attract a broad political spectrum of Palestinian supporters, who contend that HAMAS has proven able to provide them with various basic services in areas where the Palestinian Authority has long failed.

Thus HAMAS, since its founding in the late 1980s, has begun to supplant the role of the Palestine Liberation Organization and its post-Oslo counterpart, the Palestinian Authority (PA), throughout the West Bank and Gaza Strip. As a viable alternative to the ineffectual PLO/PA, HAMAS offers the Palestinian people hope, while simultaneously challenging the PLO as the standard bearer of the Palestinian liberation movement through its violent acts of retribution against the Israeli government, military, and civilian interests.

STEVEN C. DINERO

See also Arafat, Yasser; Balfour Declaration; Intifada; Israel; Middle East: History and Economic Development; Middle East: International Relations; Palestine; Palestine Liberation Organization; Palestinian Diaspora; Zionism

References and Further Reading

Abu-Amr, Ziad. *Islamic Fundamentalism in the West Bank and Gaza: Muslim Brotherhood and Islamic Jihad (Indiana Series in Arab and Islamic Studies)*. Bloomington, IN: Indiana University Press, 1994.

Alexander, Yonah. *Palestinian Religious Terrorism: Hamas and Islamic Jihad*. Ardsley, NY: Transnational Publishers, 2002.

Hroub, Khaled. *Hamas: Political Thought and Practice* Washington, DC: Institute for Palestine Studies, 2000.

Mishal, Shaul and Avraham Sela. *The Palestinian Hamas.* New York: Columbia University Press, 2000.

Nusse, Andrea. *Muslim Palestine: The Ideology of Hamas.* London: Routledge, 1998.

HASSAN II, KING (MOROCCO)

King Hassan II, full name Moulay Hassan Ben Mohammed, was born in Rabat, Morocco, on July 9, 1929, the son of King Mohammed V of the *Alaouite* dynasty. He received his education in Rabat and the extension school of the University of Bordeaux in Rabat, obtained a *diplôme des Etudes Supérieures* (equivalent to a master's degree) in public law in 1952. He was invested as crown prince and became commander in chief of the Moroccan army in 1957, served as minister of defense and vice premier from 1960 to February 26, 1961, when he was crowned as the king of Morocco upon his father's death.

Upon his crowning, King Hassan started building dams throughout most of the country, but the goal of helping provide water for farmers and urban areas in periods of drought remains only partly achieved. His politics emphasized market economy and capitalism but were relatively conservative. In the mid-1980s, he authorized the gradual liberalization of deposit interest rates in an attempt to increase private domestic savings. During the last decade of his reign he implemented several other reforms that are widely viewed as conducive to economic development. In 1991, he initiated a number of privatization programs. In 1993, he introduced partial convertibility of the local currency (the dirham) by allowing full convertibility of current accounts. In general, he maintained a good rapport with USAID, IMF, and World Bank. Hassan pursued the most Western friendly politics in North Africa, and tried to bring Arab countries and Israel closer to peace.

The Green March, which took place in 1975, remains the most important national event in the Reign of Hassan II. On November 6, 1975, 350,000 Moroccan volunteers crossed the artificial borders between the main land and the Sahara. On November 14, 1975, the Madrid Accords whereby Morocco restored its sovereignty over the Sahara were signed. During Hassan's reign, income and gender inequalities were high. The Ominium Nord African (ONA) which is owned mainly by the royal family is said to own about 20% of Morocco's gross domestic product (GDP). Women's rights were not addressed until the late 1980s and early 1990s. There has been no tangible advancement in this area, as the Dahir (law) that is intended to enhance women's right had not been signed when Hassan died.

Primarily due to a corrupt administration, this world leader's attempts to reduce poverty and illiteracy among Moroccans produced little results. Illiteracy and unemployment rates in Morocco were no lower in 2001 than when he became king in 1961. Frustrated groups often rioted against austere stabilization and structural adjustment programs and human rights abuses. However, many blamed the poor human rights record and economic problems on his long time minister of interior, Driss Basri.

King Hassan died in Rabat of a heart attack on July 23, 1999.

MINA BALIAMOUNE

See also Morocco; North Africa: History and Economic Development; North Africa: International Relations

References and Further Reading

Coupe, Jeffrey. "Courting His Majesty: USAID in King Hassan's Morocco," *Middle East Policy*, 5 (1997).

El Alaoui, Issa Babana. *La Dimension d'un Roi - Hassan II.* Paris: Fabert, 1999.

Hughes, Stephen. *Morocco Under King Hassan*. Garnet Publishing, 2000.

White, Gregory. *A Comparative Political Economy of Tunisia and Morocco*. State University of New York Press, 2001.

HAVEL, VÁCLAV

Václav Havel was born in 1936 in Prague, in a free Czechoslovakia, but spent most of his life under dictatorships. Czechoslovakia had only been created in 1918 after the collapse of the old Austro-Hungarian Empire. A Nazi invasion in 1939 ended its freedom, and "liberation" by the Soviet Union in 1945 only placed Czechoslovakia under a different kind of oppression. The Soviets imposed a communist dictatorship on the country, backed by an occupying army.

Havel began his career working with Prague theater companies as a stagehand. He had been considered too "bourgeois" by the communist government to be allowed to get a university education, but he persevered on his own, working as a lab technician during the day while studying at night. By the 1960s, he was writing plays for Prague theaters. His plays were avant garde and surreal in conception, but from the beginning they were strongly critical of the Communist Party's rule in Czechoslovakia. "The Memorandum," for example, was about a government officials' inability to obey a government memo because they could not understand its convoluted language. Havel became a more active dissident after the 1968 Czechoslovakian uprising against the Soviets, known as the Prague Spring.

In spite of government censorship, Havel continued to write plays critical of totalitarian governments in general and, by implication, his own government in particular. His plays during this period include "Audience" (1975) and "Protest" (1978). His anti-government activities increased after the 1977 government trial of a Czech rock band called "The Plastic People of the Universe." Havel signed a document protesting against the unjust persecution of the Plastic People and other artists. This became the beginning of what was known as the Charter 77 Movement. For his resistance, he was sent to prison from 1979 to 1983.

The situation in Czechoslovakia, as in the rest of Communist Europe, began to shift with the coming to power of Mikhail Gorbachev, the new premier of the Soviet Union. Gorbachev believed that communism needed to be reformed with *Glasnost* (Openness) and *Perestroika* (Restructuring). Czechoslovakian dissidents believed that these ideas should be applied to their country as well and began to agitate more aggressively for change.

On January 15, 1989, thousands of demonstrators gathered in Prague to protest against Communist Party policies and oppression. The government reacted by arresting Havel and other dissidents. Havel was sentenced to nine months in prison. However, instead of backing the Czechoslovakian Communist government, Gorbachev began to withdraw Soviet troops from the country. Without the backing of Soviet soldiers, and with the citizenry rallying against them, the government's position became increasingly untenable.

In May, Havel, along with other dissidents, was released from prison. He and others, including many artists, formed the Civic Forum, a political group opposed to Communist one-party rule. By mid-November 1989 tens of thousands of people were demonstrating in Prague, demanding the government's overthrow.

Rather than face a possibly violent revolution, the Communist leaders of Czechoslovakia negotiated a peaceful transfer of power to the leaders of the Civic Forum, of whom Havel was the most prominent. On December 29, 1989, Havel was chosen to be President of new Czechoslovakian government.

As president, Havel successfully oversaw the dismantling of the old Communist system. With remarkable speed, he and his colleagues ended one-party rule and created a democratic society where freedom of speech was the law of the land. Some have criticized his leniency towards former government officials, but one of Havel's primary goals was to avoid the bloodshed that had characterized transfers of power in countries like Romania. His success gave the transfer of power in Czechoslovakia the label "The Velvet Revolution."

As leader of a free Czechoslovakia, Havel's success was mixed. He was the most popular politician in the country, but by the time he stepped down his popularity had waned. Many saw him as an impractical dreamer who did not understand the realities of political office. His ambivalent attitude towards his own authority led some to criticize him for not being sufficiently presidential (to get around the long hallways of the presidential palace, for example, he sometimes used a child's toy scooter). He was never a nationalist. For instance, on the occasion of the Czech hockey team's victory in 1999, rather than lauding its victory Havel took the opportunity to lecture his fellow countrymen on the dangers of excessive nationalism. He also worked with limited success to reduce prejudice against the Rom (Gypsy) population of Czechoslovakia.

A lifelong opponent of communism, Havel was also a critic of Western-style capitalism. In his writings, he argued that capitalism's emphasis on soulless consumption could be as dangerous as communist oppression. In spite of this criticism (or perhaps unaware of it), Havel was awarded the United States Presidential Medal of Freedom by President George W. Bush in 2003.

Havel's greatest failure in his own eyes was the split of the Czechoslovakian state in 1992. Havel had opposed the split, but ethnic Czech nationalists allied themselves with ethnic Slovak nationalists and succeeded in tearing the country apart. Havel resigned as Czechoslovakia's president only to be elected the first president of the new Czech Republic in 1993, serving until 2003.

CARL SKUTSCH

See also Central and Eastern Europe: History and Economic Development; Czech Republic; Velvet Revolutions

References and Further Reading

Havel, Václav (trans. Paul Wilson). *The Art of the Impossible: Politics as Morality in Practice.* New York: Knopf, 1997.
Keane, John. *Václav Havel.* New York: Basic Books, 2001.
Shepherd, Robin E.H. *Czechoslovakia : The Velvet Revolution and Beyond.* New York: St. Martin's Press, 2000.
Sire, James. *Vaclav Havel: The Intellectual Conscience of International Politics: An Introduction, Appreciation & Critique.* Downers Grove, IL: InterVarsity Press, 2001.

HAYA DE LA TORRE, VÍCTOR RAÚL

Víctor Raúl Haya de la Torre (1895–1979) was a charismatic Peruvian populist who led a native Indian movement that advocated and somewhat achieved wide ranging transformations in the politics of Spanish America. His indigenist ideas for national development and native cultures were rooted in numerous social and economic reforms.

He was born in the northern coastal Peruvian town of Trujillo on February 22, 1895. As he matured he witnessed significant socio-economic changes in his region. Foreign business interests were supplanting traditional landowners. He was from an established family that confronted uncertain economic prospects and status.

As a student in Lima, Haya de la Torre became a leader in the university reform movement, which had an agenda of broad educational and social changes. Spearheading demonstrations against the dictatorial government of President *Augusto Leguía*, Haya was exiled from Peru in 1923.

Going to Mexico, he witnessed the heady early days of the Mexican Revolution. The innovative Mexican education and cultural leader, José Vasconcelos, fostered during the 1920s many of the cultural goals of the indigenist movement. Haya de la Torre led a group of young Latin American reformers in founding a political party, the *Alianza Popular Revolucionaria Americana* (APRA = American Revolutionary Popular Alliance). They believed that the Indian races of the region and the mystical force of their history would be the basis for developing their countries. They referred to the region collectively as Indo America. They intended to establish APRA in all countries of Indo America.

The proud cultures of the Aztecs and Mayas in Mexico and Central America and of the Incas in the Andean countries had been defeated and marginalized in the sixteenth century by the invading Spanish conquistadors. Since then native peoples, their numbers decimated, had become impoverished and despised. The elites of European descent who ruled over them and their former territories considered the native an inferior race. Haya de la Torre and the Aprista (adjective in Spanish for APRA) movement sought to re-assert the dignity and accomplishment of historic Indian cultures. They sought to strengthen the nations of Latin America by more fully integrating native populations into social, economic, and political life. Physically, Haya de la Torre bore Indian features and appeared himself to be of Inca descent.

The movement also believed an alliance of intellectuals, laborers, and peasants was necessary to oppose United States economic domination. It supported economic nationalization, unification of Latin America, and solidarity with all oppressed peoples. Living in various countries of Europe and the United States, he came to know many of the leading intellectual and cultural figures of his time. Travel in the Soviet Union made him conclude that communism would not be an adequate political system for the reforms he sought.

In 1930, Leguía was overthrown by a military uprising led by Luis M. Sánchez Cerro, and the following year Haya returned to Peru. Before his return, his followers organized APRA in Peru, designating it the Partido Aprista Peruano (PAP = Peruvian Aprista Party). Over the next half century, the party would elaborate a vast social system parallel to the government, organizing educational, cultural, and welfare programs into the furthest reaches of the country. In 1931, Haya ran as the Aprista presidential candidate against Sánchez Cerro but was defeated.

Followers of Haya believed he lost the election due to fraud. He advocated the overthrow of the traditional elite that had always ruled Peru and was arrested and sentenced to prison. An Aprista uprising occurred in Trujillo that culminated in the assassination of Sánchez Cerro. The new president, General Oscar Benevides, freed Haya and allowed the Apristas to resume political activity. Nonetheless, Benevides reverted to repression of the party, causing Haya to go into hiding until 1945.

In that year, the Aprista party became crucial in electing President José Luis Bustamante y Rivero and was able to manipulate Bustamente's government. The party supported a massive transfer of economic and political power from the wealthy to the native majority, advocating land reform that expropriated massive private estates. After the party provoked a military uprising in Callao, the port city of Lima, the new president once again suppressed it.

Haya entered into hiding, later obtaining asylum in the Colombian embassy in Lima, where he remained until 1954. He then went again into exile in Mexico and Europe until 1956. In 1962, the Aprista party, despite military opposition, nominated Haya as its candidate for the presidency. He did not obtain sufficient votes to be elected. Nonetheless, the armed forces staged a coup to prevent negotiations that might lead to Aprista influence in a new government.

Presidential elections were again conducted in 1963, with Haya a candidate. However, with the electorate assuming the military would never allow him to assume office, he was defeated by Fernando Belaúnde Terry, who proceeded to carry out significant social and economic reforms based on the Aprista program. To better integrate Indians into national life, he inaugurated a networked system of roads and highways, thereby also facilitating marketing of agricultural produce from native lands. He also established basic education and training programs for Indians.

In 1968, a military coup led by Juan Velasco Alvarado overthrew Belaúnde and inaugurated a regime that, while once again proscribing the Aprista party, proceeded to carry out further parts of its reform program. He brought about land reform by expropriating large estates of the traditional landed elite.

The last public act of Haya before he died in 1979 was to preside over the constituent assembly that returned Peru to democratic government the following year. Never married, Haya was accompanied throughout his life by his secretary companion, Jorge Idiáquez.

Only in Peru did the party achieve political significance, operating extensive social, cultural, and educational programs. Frequently repressed during Haya's lifetime, it finally obtained power during the ill-fated presidency of Alan García Pérez (1985–1990). It has declined since then.

EDWARD A. RIEDINGER

See also Peru

References and Further Reading

Ciccarelli, Orazio Andrea. *Militarism, Aprismo, and violence in Peru: The Presidential Election of 1931*. Buffalo, NY: Council on International Studies, State University of New York at Buffalo, 1973.

Graham, Carol. *Peru's APRA: Parties, Politics, and the Elusive Quest for Democracy*. Boulder, CO: L. Riener Publishers, 1992.

Haya de la Torre, Víctor Raúl. *Aprismo: The Ideas and Doctrines of Víctor Raúl Haya de la Torre*. Translated and edited by Robert J. Alexander. Kent, OH: Kent State University Press, 1973.

Hilliker, Grant. *The Politics of Reform in Peru: The Aprista and Other Mass Parties of Latin America*. Baltimore, MD: Johns Hopkins University Press, 1971.

Klarén, Peter F. *Modernization, Dislocation, and Aprismo: Origins of the Peruvian Aprista Party, 1870–1932*. Austin, TX: University of Texas Press, 1973.

Pike, Frederick B. *The Politics of the Miraculous in Peru: Haya de la Torre and the Spiritualist Tradition*. Lincoln, NE: University of Nebraska Press, 1986.

Stein, Steve. *Populism in Peru: The Emergence of the Masses and the Politics of Social Control*. Madison, WI: University of Wisconsin Press, 1980.

HEALTH CARE

Health care in the developing world since World War II is not easy to treat under a single heading. It refers to many dimensions, notably to the health care services provided in times of mostly infectious diseases and in those of epidemiological transition. It also refers to the organizational structure and components of the systems delivering them, to socio-political choices, limited resources as well as to international cooperation and constraints. Considerable regional and local differences prevail; cultural traditions are numerous while geopolitical situations and socio-economic dependence, brought by economic crises and structural adjustment programs, vary in space and time. Many authors have recognized that health of both populations and individuals is bound up with development, although there is no simple correlation between 'more' development and better health. Developmental improvements are rather linked to 'different' health and changes in prevailing health patterns, from persistent infectious diseases to cancers, cardiovascular and chronic afflictions. They also mean environmental change, demographic ageing of the populations and more complex health issues. Longer average life expectancy brings with it other health and social care problems but also new demands for social support.

Health and health care figures still show tremendous inequality between developed and developing countries in terms of life expectancy at birth (80 years in Sweden against 40.7 years in Rwanda, 48.0 in Ethiopia, 48.6 in Chad, in 2001), under five mortality rate per 1,000 life births (4 in Sweden against 198 in Chad, in 1998), doctors per 100,000 people (299 in Sweden against 2 in Chad, 4 in Ethiopia and Tanzania, in 1993) and nurses per 100,000 people (1,048 in Sweden against 6 in Chad, 8 in Ethiopia, 46 in Tanzania, in 1993). In 1996, 30% of Chad's population had access to health care services, 42% in Tanzania, and 46% in Ethiopia.

Most authors agree that there is an association between a country's redistribution level of resources, the distribution of health services, and the accessibility of health care. "A common consensus in the redistribution debate is that, while economic growth is necessary for improvement of living standards and social services, countries emphasizing redistribution as a major development objective (and not only socialist countries) are characterized by better education, lower infant mortality, and higher life expectancy than countries choosing growth alone" (Kloos p. 210). The poorest countries' health care systems can be usefully presented using Roemer's four tier typology, reaching from the entrepreneurial system to welfare-oriented, comprehensive, and socialist systems. In health care systems following entrepreneurial policies, most physicians work in private (urban) practice and medical schools as well as hospitals are predominantly private (examples are Kenya, Ghana, Zaire, Pakistan, Indonesia). Welfare oriented health care systems are part of a larger welfare state, offer better access to health care and egalitarian social services (for example the State of Kerala, India). In socialist systems finally, such as China, the role of the state is overwhelming, large numbers of auxiliary health personnel ascertain primary health care for the largest numbers and traditional health practices and practitioners are integrated into modern medical services.

Introduced during the colonial era, Western health services were originally operated by the colonial administrators and the missions. After independence, some newly established national health services continued in the same way, while more radical governments adopted socialist approaches. During the initial post-colonial period, urban curative systems expanded up to a certain point while rural areas lacked access to basic care. The health systems of the newly independent states were unable to attain objectives even close to those set for the colonial period. By the 1980s, many countries adopted systems based on the primary health care approach (PHC) proposed at the Alma-Ata conference in 1978 as a means to attain the World Health Organization's "Health for All by the Year 2000" goal (see later discussion). But PHC has not produced the hoped for miracles and health care systems are still hesitating between dependency, accentuated by financial crises, and integration. The HIV/AIDS pandemic puts them under additional strain. Most of the poorest countries have pluralistic medical systems with elements of traditional healing systems, lay practice, household remedies, quakes, and Western biomedicine. Traditional medicine is widely used, and may even constitute the only health resource in some places, although it has not yet been integrated nor recognized by modern medicine, particularly in Africa. With a few exceptions, traditional birth attendants are still the only component of traditional medicine that is widely used and recognized in national health care systems.

After a general and chronological overview of the development of health care systems and the situation in Africa and Latin America, follows a brief discussion of the primary health care strategy adopted to reach WHO's ambitious goal of "Health for All," of the role of traditional medical practices and their integration into modern medicine and of the attention given to women and health care.

Development of Health Care Systems

Group consciousness for the need of health care can be traced back to earliest societies, from the high esteem in which medicine men or shamans were held in tribal societies, to the dietary and sanitary rules of the Hebrews and to the policy to appoint physicians for the poor in classical Greece or to attend to the slaves in Rome's *latifundia*. In medieval Europe, the sick turned for help to the Church and its monasteries. The rise of universities in the growing cities and the training of physicians during the Renaissance established independent practitioners. Health care had a price and the guilds introduced the idea of insurance as a collective aid to the sick, before humanitarianism became a social doctrine with the beginning of industrialization and the first public health laws appeared in mid-nineteenth century. They brought gradual access to health care services but also increased sanitary control of individuals and populations.

Czarist Russia established the *Zemstvo* system by 1865, which offered health care to the peasant population and was financed through taxes, levied at the district level. In Bismarck's Germany, compulsory insurance for medical care and disability for those on the labor market was introduced in 1883, a model followed by other countries and gradually extended towards social security and employer liability for industrial accidents. In Africa and Asia, the colonial medical systems created first for the European settlers and the military were later also directed either towards workers in particular fields or, at minimal expenditures, to the native populations.

At the time of World War I, the basic structure of health care services was in place. During the interwar period, the conception of a social responsibility for health care is reinforced by the International Labor Organization's call for peace through social justice. Medical advances lead to increased specialization and the proliferation of hospitals. After the Great Depression, social insurance expanded in European countries. In the United States, the Social Security Act was adopted in 1935, accompanied by the Blue Cross movement for voluntary insurance.

After World War II, Britain's Beveridge model, based on national taxes and intended to protect those in greatest need, led to complete health coverage for all and access to health care was considered a citizen's right. France followed, although with a different indemnity payment system, while Germany and other countries maintained the model of compulsory insurance through *Krankenkassen,* introduced by Bismarck. Australia and New Zealand adopted similar models and Canada went stepwise from compulsory insurance and special programs to universal hospital care coverage. The Eastern European countries slowly converted to the soviet model.

In the developing countries, India first considered public health coverage in 1946; but progress was slow except for insurance plans for certain workers in the urban centers of Bombay, Delhi, and Calcutta, while rural areas were left behind. In the post-war years, there were efforts in other parts of Asia and in Africa towards collective organization of health care. Physicians and other health personnel need to be trained, hospitals built, but resources are extremely scarce. In Latin America, health insurance for miners and certain groups of industrial workers covered during this period was only a small fraction of the population.

The creation of the World Health Organization (WHO) in 1948 was a major event. From the beginning, its mandate of "the attainment by all peoples of the highest possible level of health" marks a new era in international public health policy. The multiple functions related to WHO's goal of preventing, controlling the spread, and curing disease follow a new conception of health. As outlined in its Constitution, health is not only the absence of disease or infirmity but depends on many interrelated social, economic, and environmental factors that have to be considered. WHO is a major player among the development agencies, notwithstanding frequent political controversies and funding problems with member states. Among many other activities, WHO offers technical assistance to governments in strengthening effective national health care services.

Health Care Systems in Africa

Health indicators for Africa still show an alarming situation. After independence and during the 1960s, the eradication of epidemic and endemic diseases mobilizes WHO, UNICEF, and different nongovernmental organizations (NGOs) whose actions have a stimulating impact on health care development in most countries. Health care services become a political priority during election campaigns, a factor that amplifies the unequal distribution of health facilities left by the colonial administrations, in spite of egalitarian programs stated in national plans (Iyun). During the 1970s, promising developments such as the training of health care workers and the establishment

of new facilities are under way, with an emphasis on mother and child care. Several countries (Benin, Ghana, Nigeria, Sudan, and Zambia) provide for free health care for children and experiment with "flying doctors" to reach rural areas. The health care systems are however weak. They dramatically lack the needed resources and most of the allocated funds are used to cover salaries, leaving little for medicines and other essential material. By the end of the 1980s, faced with high population growth rates, African governments could not cope with the increasing health care demands and costs. At the same time, the structural adjustment programs imposed by the IMF and the World Bank forced African countries to reduce their public expenditures, which translated into even less funding for health care and other social programs. This context was far from favorable to implement WHO's primary health care approach, even more so as the economic crisis causes a "brain drain" of qualified health personnel and the HIV/AIDS pandemic takes catastrophic proportions. The result is that "health care is in shambles in Africa" (Iyun 259).

Health Care Systems in Latin America

Latin American countries such as Argentina, Brazil, Chile, and Uruguay have had social and health care services for specific groups since the 1920s. Under the pressure of labor unions and political movements, expensive privileges held by a few were gradually eliminated by the 1960s, the health care systems were unified and the health care coverage extended. Social security programs were also promoted as a factor of social stabilization. In Mexico, Columbia, Peru, and Venezuela, the health care systems were introduced during the 1940s, influenced by the British Beveridge model of universal coverage. Different types of health care systems can interact in Latin America. Private health care services, paid directly or by private insurance for those who can afford it, exist along with public health services financed by the state through taxes, for those who are not covered by the social security system. The social security health care approach, based on Bismarck's model and financed by contributions from the state, employees and employers, is less adapted to the Latin American situation where most workers are independent or in agriculture. In Cuba, Nicaragua, Haiti, and the English speaking Caribbean, the public health care system prevails, while Argentina, Brazil, Costa Rica, Mexico, Panama, Uruguay, and Venezuela have work-related social security benefits for the majority.

Examples of countries with mixed systems are Bolivia, Colombia, Ecuador, El Salvador, Guatemala, Honduras, Paraguay, Peru and the Dominican Republic. In many countries, however, the financial stability of the health care systems is fragile, due to high unemployment or lack of political will. The economic crisis and the related reduction of public expenditures since the 1980s have affected the health care systems and the health of the populations. Noteworthy is a particularity of the Latin American health care situation: physicians outnumber nurses (Curta de Casas). The number of private hospitals increases continuously since the 1960s and expensive curative medicine and an excessive use of medicines predominate.

Health-for-All and the Primary Health Care Approach

The joint WHO and UNICEF conference held at Alma-Ata (USSR) in 1978 established the principles of primary health care (PHC), which was adopted as the major strategy to achieve WHO's then called "Health for All by the Year 2000" goal. The time limit "by the year 2000" was obviously too ambitious, but the general policy of Health-for-All has been revised and reaffirmed by WHO in 1998. The proposed strategy was considered revolutionary as it recognized explicitly that health promotion could not be attained without improving socio-economic conditions and alleviating poverty. It enlarged the dominant medical perspective to environmental, social, political, and economic determinants of the health of individuals and populations. The PHC proposition was inspired by successful local and national initiatives such as in China, Cuba, and Kerala State, India. They were evidence that higher levels of health are achievable when political will is committed to egalitarian principles of social justice and equity rather than to economic growth alone. The Chinese model in particular showed the importance of preventive measures, community participation, and decentralized health care services, with the famous "bare foot doctors" bringing health care to rural communities.

PHC is neither the equivalent of primary medical care nor of health services for all. Its purpose is to reach every human being, particularly those in greatest need, by establishing a continuous relationship between the health sector, individuals, and families. The PHC approach, as adopted at Alma-Ata, aims at the equitable distribution of resources and access to essential care for everyone. It recognizes that in order

to attain the highest level of health, a concerted effort in all fields of human activity is needed. Health promotion and disease prevention are considered as essential as curative care, which has to be based on scientifically sound technology within the limits of the affordable. Individual and community participation in the local development of health care is a right as well as an obligation. Community development is viewed as both a management tool to reform health service delivery systems and a means of empowerment. Although the latter might seem rhetoric to some authors (see Asthana), numerous successful health promotion experiences and advocacy initiatives in developing countries are documented (see Dillon and Philip), supported by communities, the media, NGOs, university researchers, and the international organizations.

It is difficult to evaluate PHC and the Health-for-All strategy in general, as there are social, economic, ecological, political, biomedical, and management aspects relevant to many countries on the six continents with countless cultures and communities. The strategy has without doubt brought achievements and provoked fundamental changes if not a social revolution in health care development. Equity as its essential feature calls for positive developments in education, agriculture but also employment, environmental protection and absence of war and civil strife. Female education and increased autonomy in some places show the possible synergy between health care and education, although the overall illiteracy and poverty indicators are still alarming. In Latin America, the primary health care approach adopted also by the Pan-American Health Organization (PAHO) has led to the emergence of a new model of local health systems, *systemas locales de salud* (SILOS), where the community participates in planning, implementation and evaluation. SILOS are conceived for geographically defined populations. PHC in Latin America has however to cope with large indigenous populations distinguished by ethnic, religious, and economic differences (Curta de Casas). Another example is India, which preceded the Alma-Ata declaration with its 1975 Report on Health and Family Planning in which it rejected the Western medical perspective, because of its over-professionalization and excessive costs. India opted rather for a primary health care approach with locally chosen semi-professional community health workers and trained volunteers. Their numerical increase, from 67 in the 1950s, to 23,000 in the 1990s gives a measure of the impact of primary health care. But great differences still exist from state to state, with the state of Kerala often being singled out as the most successful example, despite economic difficulties.

It should also be noted that critiques addressed to the primary health care strategy—and they are numerous—have exposed the approach's condescendence as well as the emphasis placed on prevention, which leaves numerous unpreventable illnesses without necessary treatments.

Integrating Traditional Medicine

The 1978 Alma-Ata declaration insisted on the essential contribution of traditional medical knowledge and practices to primary health care, but the debate about integrating traditional medicine and its practitioners into modern national health care systems is ongoing. The contemptuous colonial attitude towards traditional medical practices considered as unscientific is still perceptible, even if they are in many parts of the world the only affordable health care available. Medical schools continue to offer training oriented towards the scientific medical model in which cultural variations have little room. The result is that professional and political acceptability of traditional medicine goes from outright prohibition over some tolerance to exceptionally formal recognition with state support. This is the case for example in China and to a lesser degree in India. The Indian Congress party indeed recommended early on, in 1918, to secure the advantages of the traditional Ayuveda, Unani, and Siddha systems, but the preferences of Nehru for the Western scientific health care indicate that the official position was debated for some time. The primary health care approach adopted during the 1970s integrated a combination of allopathic and traditional Indian systems of medicine, based on Ayuveda, Unani, Siddha and homeopathy to provide affordable and culturally acceptable care in rural areas. The professional position of traditional practitioners stays nevertheless inferior. They are perceived by medical practitioners as auxiliaries to be supervised rather than as professionals, although they are trusted and esteemed in the communities they serve. In most countries, the two systems coexist and integration is limited to obstetrics. China is the best example of a real institutional integration of traditional and modern medicine through national health care services, with professionalization and training of practitioners in both fields. WHO has developed guidelines and principles covering a wide range of activities in order to better integrate traditional medicine, such as ways to improve the protection of patients from charlatans and encouraging research to assess the quality of traditional medicines and treatment.

Health Care and Women

International policies about health care for women have traditionally been oriented towards reproductive health and maternal and child care and welfare, as expressed since 1946 in the Constitution of the World Health Organization. Many programs have been developed to reduce maternal and infant mortality and morbidity and such activities include family planning, training of traditional birth attendants, nutrition, and health education. WHO has dedicated the 2005 World Health Day to the theme "Make every mother and child count." The vulnerability of women during pregnancy and childbirth in developing countries is still a major preoccupation and cause of illness and death. Yet women also play a crucial role as health care providers in their families and communities and there is a growing awareness about the central contribution of women to economic development and environmental protection, beyond their reproductive lives. As such, women in the developing world are also exposed to hazards from working conditions in the formal and informal sectors where they try to make a living. They are confronted with domestic, traditional (female genital mutilation), sexual and political violence, migration, with sexually transmissible diseases, particularly HIV/AIDS, with changing family structures and "post-reproductive" or widowhood discrimination. The Fourth World Conference on Women in Beijing, in 1995, contributed to raise public awareness about health and health care problems of women in the developing world. Many authors suggest that research is needed to better understand women's multiple health related roles in developing countries.

Perspectives

Health implies complex interactions between humans and their social, physical, and biological environment. The impacts of environmental changes as determinants of health have to be assessed. Health care systems in developing countries are not only challenged by the "pervasive factor of poverty" (Phillips and Verhasselt 310) due to the consequences of economic crises and structural adjustment programs. They also have to face threats from the resurgence of infectious diseases, aggravated by the HIV/AIDS pandemic, and the epidemiological transition to more chronic diseases. Children, women, the handicapped, the mentally ill, and the elderly continue to be the most vulnerable groups. Growing numbers of refugees or internally displaced persons and of victims of conflict or political violence have particular health care needs. The international agencies have recognized the right to essential health care for all human beings and adopted strategies to attain this goal, with varying results.

RUTH MURBACH AND MIKHAEL ELBAZ

See also Doctors Without Borders/Médecins sans Frontières; HIV/AIDS; Infant Mortality; Infectious Diseases; Public Health; World Health Organization (WHO)

References and Further Reading

Asthana, S. "Primary Health Care and Selective PHC" in D.R. Phillipps and Y. Verhasselt (eds.). *Health and Development*. New York: Routledge, 1994, 182–196.

Burci, C.L., and C.H. Vignes. *World Health Organization*. The Hague: Kluwer Law International, 2004.

Conrad, P. *Health and Health Care in Developing Countries: Sociological Perspectives*. Philadelphia, Temple University Press, 1993.

Curto de Casas, S.I. "Health Care in Latin America" in D.R. Phillipps and Y. Verhasselt (eds.). *Health and Development*. New York: Routledge, 1994, 234–248.

Dillon, H.S., and L. Philip. *Health Promotion and Community Action for Health in Developing Countries*. Geneva: WHO, 1994.

Dror, D.M. and A.S, Preker (eds.) *Social Reinsurance: A New Approach to Sustainable Community Health Financing*. Washington/Geneva: World Bank/ILO, 2002.

Kloos, H. "The Poorer Third World: Health and Health Care in Areas that have yet to Experience Substantial Development" in D.R. Phillipps and Y. Verhasselt (eds.). *Health and Development*. New York: Routledge, 1994, 199–215.

Leon, D.A. *Poverty, Inequality and Health : An International Perspective*. New York, Oxford University Press, 2001.

Phillips, D.R. *et al.* "Health, Environment and Development: Issues in Developing and Transitional Countries" (1998) 44:2 *Geography Journal*, 97.

Phillips, D.R., and Yola Verhasselt (eds.). *Health and Development*. New York: Routledge, 1994.

Preker, A.S., and G. Carrin (eds.). *Health Financing for Poor People: Resource Mobilization and Risk Sharing*. Washington/Geneva: World Bank/WHO, 2004.

Roemer, M.I. *National Health Systems of the World*. Cambridge: Oxford University Press, 1991.

SAPRIN. *Structural Adjustment: the SAPRI Report. The Policy Roots of Economic Crisis, Poverty, and Inequality*. London: Zed Books, 2004.

WHO. *The World Health Report*. 2001–2005. http://www. who.int/whr/en/.

WHO. *The World's Women 1970–1990: Trends and Statistics*. New York: United Nations organization, 1991.

HELSINKI FINAL ACT ON HUMAN RIGHTS (1975)

The Helsinki Conference on European Security was signed on August 1, 1975, by the High Representatives of Austria, Belgium, Bulgaria, Canada, Cyprus, former Czechoslovakia, Denmark, Finland, France, the former German Democratic Republic (GDR), the former Federal Republic of Germany, Greece, the Holy See, Hungary, Iceland, Ireland, Italy, Liechtenstein, Luxembourg, Malta, Monaco, the Netherlands, Norway, Poland, Portugal, Romania, San Marino, Spain, Sweden, Switzerland, Turkey, the former Union of Soviet Socialist Republics, the United Kingdom, the United States of America, and the former Yugoslavia.

Today, a total of fifty-four nations are signatories to the Final Act and as such are members of the Organization for Security & Cooperation in Europe (OSCE), a leading international organization promoting democracy and human rights, among them the Democratic and Popular Republic of Algeria, the Arab Republic of Egypt, Israel, the Kingdom of Morocco, the Syrian Arab Republic, and Tunisia.

The document was at the time considered a milestone of detente between the East and the West. It was perhaps the most influential international agreement since the establishment of the United Nations (UN), which continues to have an influence on international politics. Envisioned as a conference to recognize the existing borders and to institutionalize the peaceful coexistence then present in the world, the Conference's accomplishments included recognizing those borders, assuring the Soviet bloc that the West harboured no aggressive designs against them, establishing a mechanism to resolve disputes, and encouraging ongoing arms control talks. Perhaps the most significant of the accomplishments was the elevation of basic human rights to treaty status, thus placing human rights and fundamental freedoms on the international agenda and also creating a framework for bringing world attention on human rights abuses. In 1982, in order to maintain a control on the implementation of Human Rights, the representatives of a number of the Helsinki committees held an International Citizens Helsinki Watch Conference. These committees played an important role at defending the human rights in the communist countries, but haven't been active since the Berlin Wall was destroyed in 1989. This act has two main purposes: the achievement of peace and security.

The document establishes as a condition for all member-countries "the promotion of fundamental rights, economic and social progress and well-being for all people." The acts claims that peace cannot be achieved without increasing common and effective efforts towards the solution of major world economic problems such as food, energy, commodities, monetary and financial problems, and therefore emphasizes the need for promoting stable and equitable international economic relations, thus contributing to the continuous and diversified economic development of all countries. If peace and security are the *ends*, then solidarity and cooperation are the *means*. This means to have a critical perspective upon competition and, fundamentally, the market as a means.

The Act's most significant objectives are:

- To respect each other's right to determine its laws and regulations, irrespective of their political, economic or social systems as well as of their size, geographical location or level of economic development;
- To settle disputes by peaceful means in such a manner that does not endanger international peace and security;
- To refrain from any intervention, direct or indirect, individual or collective, in the internal or external affairs falling within the domestic jurisdiction of another participating State, regardless of their mutual relations;
- To refrain from making each other's territory the object of military occupation or other direct or indirect measures of force. No such occupation or acquisition will be recognized as legal.
- To promote and to encourage the effective exercise of civil, political, economic, social, cultural and other rights and freedoms, all of which derive from the inherent dignity of the human person and are essential for his free and full development. This means that the member States have recognized their obligations to assure their inhabitants the right to receive health, education, decent housing, in sum, a human future.

The respect for the human rights is an essential factor to achieve peace, justice and well being. It is also necessary to ensure the development of friendly relations and cooperation *among the member States as well as among all States*. As a matter of fact, if human rights were, not only among the member States but worldwide respected, there would probably be no danger of wars. This is desirable and also possible as the Final Act established that the States commit themselves to constantly respect these rights and freedoms in their mutual relations and endeavour jointly and separately, including in co-operation with the UN, to promote universal and effective respect for them. The States that signed the Act realized that the benefits resulting from increased mutual knowledge and the achievements in the economic, scientific, technological, social, cultural, and humanitarian fields were not enough if they were not obtained worldwide. The authentic peace and security would only be accomplished whenever those benefits gained a worldwide

range. Therefore, the member States claimed that they would take steps to promote conditions favourable to making these benefits available to all and also that they would take into account the interest of all in the narrowing of differences in the levels of economic development, and in particular the interest of developing countries throughout the world.

The recognition that this is an obligation as for governments, institutions, organizations, and persons has a relevant and positive role to play in contributing towards the achievement of these aims for cooperation.

One of the most important results of this Act was its contribution to the strengthening of peace and security in the world by the treaties of *disarmament*. Leaving the conventional aspects of military security aside for the moment, the Final Act of Helsinki was then a unique document inasmuch as it featured issues relating to economic development, environmental and cultural affairs, specifically recognising that human rights and fundamental freedoms formed one of the core issues of the Act's comprehensive concept of European security. However, the environmental situation has worsened, wars still occur and take many innocent lives, human rights still suffer violations not only in non-developed countries. We therefore need to have the statements of declarations such as this one are effectively put into practice.

MARÍA LUISA PFEIFFER

See also Human Rights as a Foreign Policy Issue; Human Rights: Definition and Violations

References and Further Reading

Fry, John. *The Helsinki Process: Negotiating Security and Cooperation in Europe.* Washington, DC: National Defense University Press, 1993.

Green, William C. "Human Rights and Détente", on *The Ukrainian Quarterly*, Volume XXXVI, No 2 (Summer), 1980.

Kavass, Igor, Paquin Granier Jacqueline and Mary Frances, Dominick, eds. *Human Rights, European Politics and the Helsinki Accord: the documentary evolution of the Conference on Security and Cooperation in Europe, 1973–1975.* Buffalo, NY: W.S. Hein, 1981.

Thomas, Daniel C. *Helsinki Effect: International Norms, Human Rights, and the Demise of Communism.* Princeton, NJ: Princeton University Press, 2001.

HEZBOLLAH

An exact date for the emergence of Hezbollah (Party of God) is impossible to verify, however, its origins lie intellectually in the 1979 Iranian revolution and practically in the 1982 Israeli invasion of Lebanon. In response to the latter event, a group of like-minded Shi'a coalesced around a nine-man committee of members from Islamic Amal (an Islamist faction of the parent Amal movement), the Da'wa party (an international Shi'a group that emerged from the legal schools of Najaf in the 1960s) and independent Shi'a jurists. The influence of Iran on the organisation was then, and remains, significant. Iranian Revolutionary Guards trained the original Hezbollah militia, has funded Hezbollah, and the party defers to the Iranian Supreme Leader on all matters of Islamic jurisprudence. Originally acting as an umbrella organisation for the founding Shi'a groups, Hezbollah did not officially announce its existence until the production of its political manifesto in February 1985. The manifesto stated that the organisation "was convinced of Islam as an ideology and a system and (we) call on everyone ... to adopt it as a religion and to abide by its teachings whether on the personal, political or community level." In addition to this, it denied the right of Israel to exist, and claimed that the United States was Israel's spearhead into the Islamic world.

Hezbollah's political outlook has evolved from its initial advocacy of the requirement for a revolutionary systemic change to create an Islamic state within Lebanon along Iranian lines, to a position today where it publicly acknowledges the unique social makeup of Lebanon and seeks a transition to an Islamic state by political evolution. Central to this pragmatic approach was the decision, following discussions with Iranian officials in Tehran in 1989, to begin a dialogue with the other Lebanese communal groups and to enter mainstream Lebanese politics. As a consequence, they contested the 1992 parliamentary elections and have done so ever since. Whilst electorally successful, in a parliament where political representation is distributed according to religious identity, their ability to capture the twenty-seven parliamentary seats on offer to the Shi'a community is limited by the fact that Syria directs them to run on joint electoral tickets with Amal, the other Shi'a sectarian political party.

Hezbollah is best known for its military wing, the Islamic Resistance, which was instrumental in forcing the withdrawal in 2000 of the Israeli forces occupying the south of Lebanon. The military wing has received generous financial and logistical assistance from Iran and general encouragement from Syria. The success of the Islamic Resistance was also assisted by the fact that, unlike the other party militias from the civil war era, Hezbollah was allowed to remain armed to continue the fight against Israeli forces. In the formative years of the organisation, Hezbollah was also linked to the kidnapping and detention of Western hostages,

a claim that the party denies. More recently, it has been accused of having links with a number of militant Palestinian movements.

Hezbollah's non-military operations include a wide range of welfare services for the poorer Shi'a areas, which may experience shortfalls in government services. Through its Islamic Health Committee it operates hospitals and clinics, and it also runs schools and supports agricultural enterprises amongst and for the Shi'a community. These social welfare initiatives, as well as providing practical benefits to its recipients, have also been a way of establishing a client base from amongst the larger Shi'a population. The party understands well the power of information and as a consequence it is also active in all forms of the media—it runs the *al-Manar* television station, the *al-Nour* radio station, as well as newspapers and magazines.

Despite Hezbollah's parliamentary performance, its support nationally is limited to the three areas where Shi'a dominate—the Biqa' Valley, South Lebanon, and the southern suburbs of Beirut. Its limited geographic support base, as well as its Islamist character, provides the party with a dilemma in achieving wider popular political support.

Hezbollah represents an important step in the political development of the Shi'a Muslims of Lebanon. It has illustrated how a sectarian political party with allegiances outside the country can successfully transition from a purely military organisation to become a responsible domestic political player. In doing so it has ensured its long-term viability as a political entity by adopting a pragmatic political course of action, so that it can survive once the justification for its armed wing diminishes, or political pressure forces it to disband this element. Its avowedly sectarian composition, as well as its refusal to renounce totally its desire for an Islamic state, however, will continue to limit its popular appeal amongst Lebanese of all religious persuasion for the foreseeable future.

RODGER SHANAHAN

See also Islam; Islamic Fundamentalism; Lebanon

References and Further Reading

Abu-Khalil, As'ad. 'Ideology and Practice of Hizballah in Lebanon: Islamisation of Leninist Organisational Principles', *Middle Eastern Studies*, vol. 27, no. 3, July 1991.
Hamzeh, A. Nizar. 'Lebanon's Hezbollah: From Islamic Revolution to Parliamentary Accommodation', *Third World Quarterly*, vol. 14, no. 2, 1993.
Jaber, Hala. *Hezbollah: Born with a Vengeance*. New York : Columbia University Press, 1997.
Saad-Ghorayeb, Amal. *Hezbollah: Politics & Religion*. London : Pluto Press, 2002.

HINDUISM

Hinduism is one of the major religions of the world and one of the oldest. It is speculated that the rudiments of the religion were introduced from migrants around 1500 BCE, it probably adopted and assimilated some features of the local religions and supplanted them. Hinduism later spread to other parts of South East Asia and significantly influenced their cultures. Later, during the British regime, many Hindu migrated to other colonies as indentured laborers and settled there permanently. Recently, some Hindus have migrated to the United States, United Kingdom, and other parts of the Western world. Many Hindus have migrated to India from Pakistan and Bangladesh as refugees. According to the Indian Census of 2001, 80% of the Indian population or 827 million were classified as Hindus. It is estimated that approximately an additional 30 million or so reside outside India.

Hinduism is often aptly described as a way of life rather than a religious doctrine. Of all the major religions of the world, Hinduism is the least prescriptive or demanding, though there are many injunctions, inter-caste marriage is one example. Hinduism is all-pervasive and a major influence in all facets of social and political life in India. Unlike other major religions, Hinduism is basically non-hierarchical and structurally flexible. It does not have a single religious text or an individual as the authoritative source on which the religion is based, thus giving rise to a high level of multiplicity and complexity of views. Unfortunately, there are many myths about the religion. Proselytizing is not one of it tenets, and there are few conversions to Hinduism.

The ancient Hindu religious literature was written in Sanskrit and includes the Vedas and Upanishads, probably dating from 1500–300 BCE, which are considered as divinely revealed. Interpretations and commentaries continue to be written on this literature pertaining to the nature of ultimate reality and nature of the *atman* (self or soul) and their confluence, with three major variant themes. The other segments of the religious literature include two epics, Ramayana and Mahabharata, which describe the life and adventures of divine heroes and *Puranas* and *Sutras* that contain religious mythologies and deal with social and religious issues.

Hinduism can be depicted as a polytheistic religion in practice because thousands of gods, goddesses, deities (divine beings), animate, inanimate sacred symbols, and even ancestors are offered prayers and homage, though some scholars argue that basically the religion is monotheistic. Creation and destruction are among the two major functions of the gods and deities.

There have been many efforts to reform or break away from Hinduism for three millennia and have resulted in the birth of new religions such as Buddhism, Jainism, and Sikhism. Many other social and religious reform movements are of much more recent origin. Often the new movements were incorporated within the fold of the Hindu religion as new sects, castes, or branches. Hinduism has withstood the conquests from Alexander, the Moguls, Portuguese, French, and the British, as well as influx of other religions such as Islam and Christianity and conversions to those religions. The religion has proved to be rather resilient in the face of many historical challenges from within and without and is also currently facing new and serious challenges and transformations because of urbanization, higher levels of education, secularization, democratic process of government, Westernization, globalization and technological developments in India and abroad. Consequently, ministers, governors, and presidents of India have been recruited from the ranks of women, lower castes, and other minorities.

Hinduism abounds with festivals or celebrations associated with different deities, saints (sometimes from a different religion), mythical or actual events, seasons, occupations, and regions. Though temples were scarce in the Vedic period, now there are a large number of temples or places of worship in India, from the very modest makeshifts to the most magnificent architectures. Hindus observe many *Sanskaras* or sacraments, which are rites of passage and marriage is considered the most important one. The essence of Hinduism is interpreted in various ways and it is generally agreed that there is more than one *marga* (road or path) to attain the religious goal of Moksha (liberation, salvation) from the cycle of birth and death as Hindu religion subscribes to the idea of rebirth or reincarnation. Soul is eternal and takes on different forms of life. Human beings are not born sinful but can commit *papa* (sin) and also accumulate *punya* (merit), thus, the higher the merit, the higher the level of rebirth in the order of life. Similarly, moral and spiritual values are emphasized throughout the Hindu religion. The Hindu cosmology and worldview are also quite varied and complex. The life cycle of the planet is usually divided into different *Yugas* (eons) and life renews itself anew from the destruction in each of the cycles.

Everyone is expected to abide by and uphold their Dharma (literally translated as religion), the term has broader connotations that include cosmic and spiritual laws that are enjoined. Karma (action or result of actions, preordained or otherwise) refers to the types of deeds that one is engaged in or accumulation of the result of our deeds. The traditional Hindu social structure and the social order were based on the division of Hindus into four *varnas* and term *jati* (caste) is tantamount to a subdivision of the original *varnas*. The term *caste* is a European description of the Hindu social order. Caste is ascribed at birth and traditionally the lifelong occupations and expected duties of each individual are based on the caste into which one is born and is perpetuated by caste endogamy. The caste of an individual can be rarely changed and was rigidly adhered. Traditionally, someone from the upper castes was not supposed to accept food from the lowest caste members as it affected their purity.

The practice of Hinduism has significantly changed over the centuries. The British codified Hindu law in the nineteenth century. Missionary activities in India started from 1813 on and have been a major source of threat and friction, especially in tribal areas. Hindu religion is also gaining more importance and a political party affiliated with it has been in power in some states and at the federal level. The Hindus in India still have to overcome the social inequality between the two genders, face the egregiousness of the caste system in practice, injustices against the tribal groups, and surmount communal disharmony.

Hinduism has been basically tolerant of other religions and cultures because it is non-dogmatic, non-violent at the core, and based on moral and spiritual values. The impact of the religion is evident in all walks of Hindu life. Hinduism has provided a very rich heritage for humanity in many facets of life and learning in spite of its many drawbacks, and continues to do so.

SUBHASH R. SONNAD

See also Caste Systems; India

References and Further Reading

Bhaskarananda. The essentials of Hinduism: A comprehensive overview of the world's oldest religion. Seattle: Viveka Press, 1994.

Chaudhuri, Nirad C., Madeleine Biardeau., D.F. Pocock., and T.N. Madan. *The Hinduism Omnibus*. Oxford: Oxford University Press, 2003.

Flood, Gavin. Ed. *The Blackwell Companion to Hinduism*. Oxford: Blackwell Publishing, 2003.

Klostermaier, Klaus K. *A Survey of Hinduism*. Albany, NY: State University Of New York Press, 1989.

Knott, Kim. *Hinduism: A Very Short Introduction*. Oxford: Oxford University Press, 1998.

Michaels, Alex. *Hinduism, Past and Present*. Trans. Barbara Harshav. Princeton, NJ: Princeton University Press, 2004.

Radhakrishnan, S. *The Hindu View of Life*. London: G. Allen & Unwin, Ltd., 1927.

——. *Bhagavadgita*. Trans. S. Radhakrishnan. New York: Harper, 1948.

HIRSCHMAN, ALBERT

Albert Otto Hirschman's ideas on economic development in the Third World influenced generations of scholars, students, and policymakers in the post-World War II world. Hirschman argued that broad theories of economic development were not applicable to the nations in the developing world. Rather than applying conventional theories of economic development to the developing nations, Hirschman argued that economic development should be analyzed on a case-by-case basis.

Born in Berlin in 1915, Hirschman was educated at the University of Berlin (1932–1933), the Sorbonne (1933–1935), the London School of Economics (1935–1936), and the University of Trieste (1936–1938), where he was awarded his doctorate in economics. In 1940, Hirschman joined the French Army. In 1941, after the Germans defeated France, he fled to the United States. He was a research fellow in international economics at Berkeley from 1941 to 1943. In 1943, he joined the US Army. From 1946 to 1952 he was an economist for the Federal Reserve in Washington, DC. He served as an economic advisor and consultant in Bogotá, Colombia, from 1952 to 1956. After leaving Colombia, he taught at Yale (1956–1958), Columbia (1958–1964), Harvard (1964–1974), and Princeton (1974–1985). Since 1985, Hirschman has held emeritus status at Princeton.

In his first book, *National Power and the Structure of Foreign Trade* (1945), Hirschman explained the correlation between economic and political power. He argued that economic policy was often controlled by political exigencies. As such, his book caused many to question the implementation of the Marshall Plan in Europe. It was in Colombia, however, that Hirschman began to formulate his theories on Third World development. In *The Strategy of Development* (1958), Hirschman criticized previous theories of economic development that had been applied to Latin America. He argued that imposing broad economic development theories on the developing nations was inappropriate. Rather, developing nations should develop individual development strategies that utilize their own unique resources and structures. Hirschman also emphasized the importance of forward and backward linkages to national development strategies.

In recognition of his extensive scholarship and teaching, Hirschman has been granted honorary degrees from Rutgers (1978), University of Southern California (1986), University of Turin (1987), Free University of Berlin (1988), University of Paris (1989), University of Buenos Aires (1989), University of Campinas (1990), Georgetown (1990), Yale (1990), University of Tier (1990), Universidad Internacional

Menéndez Pelayo, Santander (1992), University of Coimbra (1993), University of Paris-Nanterre (1993), Williams College (1993), University of Naples (1999), University of Complutense (2001), and Harvard (2002). In addition, he has been awarded the Order of San Carlos from Colombia and the Order of the Southern Cross from Brazil.

MICHAEL R. HALL

See also Development History and Theory; Development, Measures of

References and Further Reading

Hirschman, Albert. *Crossing Boundaries: Selected Writings.* Cambridge, MA: Zone Books, 1999.
Hirschman, Albert. *The Strategy of Development.* New Haven, CT: Yale University Press, 1958.

HIV/AIDS

The global spread of the human immunodeficiency virus (HIV), which causes a breakdown of the immune system, has increased to an alarming stage. In 2003 alone over 5 million people were newly infected with HIV worldwide. Of these 4.2 million were adults and 700,000 children below the age of 15 years. This brings the number of people living with HIV/AIDS around the world to over 40 million. In the same year, more than 3 million people died of AIDS worldwide. Out of these, half a million were children below the age of 15 years. All in all, after its classification in 1981, HIV/AIDS has killed over 20 million people worldwide. While HIV/AIDS is resident in humans in every region of the globe, infections are concentrated largely in countries least able to afford the care for infected people. More than 95% of people with HIV live in poor countries, and the World Health Organization (WHO) estimates that by the end of 2020 HIV will be responsible for 37% of all adult deaths from infectious diseases in the developing world.

While the number of people living with HIV/AIDS continues to increase across the globe, sub-Saharan Africa is still registering the highest prevalence. In 2003, an estimated 3 million people in the region became newly infected, 26.6 million in this region were living with the virus, and AIDS killed approximately 2.3 million. The estimated number of deaths by the end of the decade is 20 million. This region also has 50 million orphaned children, and more than a third will have lost one or both parent to AIDS.

The fastest and most recent epidemics are experienced in Asia, the Pacific, Eastern Europe and Central Asia, China, Indonesia, Papua New Guinea, Viet Nam, as well as in several Central Asian Republics, the Baltic States, and North Africa. In Russia, which has a population of 145 million, there are millions of people infected and it has the world's fastest-growing infection rate. India has more than 5 million people living with the virus, and it will likely soon overtake South Africa as the country with the greatest number of cases in the world.

HIV/AIDS and Development: Impact on Social Order, Economy, and Politics

HIV/AIDS has an impact not only on individuals and communities but also on politics and economy, and thus, on development as a whole. The AIDS pandemic is destroying the lives and livelihoods of millions of people around the world, and the situation is worst in regions and countries where poverty is extensive, gender inequality pervasive, and public services weak. Thus, HIV/AIDS threatens development achievements that local and donor governments, citizens, non-governmental organization, and international agencies have worked to achieve. In many sub-Saharan countries, AIDS has increased infant mortality and reduced life expectancy to levels not seen since the 1960s. Infant and child mortality are expected to double and even triple early in the next century. The AIDS pandemic overwhelms underfunded and inadequate health delivery systems in much of the developing world, and it could undo health, social, and economic gains by nations across the world. It also represents a significant increase in government costs. Its increased incidence among military populations threatens security, and its impact on the widening gap between "haves" and "have nots" (in local and global context, in first-world/third-world relations, and in gender relations) challenges the values of democracy as well as the principles of human rights, which are all inextricable elements of policy development and implementation.

Africa, for example, provides ample proof that AIDS impacts economics. The disease claims adults in their most productive working years. The price in lost productivity in training replacements and care provision once a worker falls sick is crippling. When tens of millions of working-age adults become sick and die, the economic outputs and productivity of many countries' suffer. Because HIV is still predominantly transmitted sexually, AIDS afflicts many people in their 20s, 30s, and 40s, during their childbearing as well as their most economically productive years. In Zambia and South Africa, income in households of

AIDS sufferers has declined by 66 to 80%. The International Monetary Fund (IMF) predicts that AIDS may exact an annual toll of as much as 2% on economic growth in sub-Saharan Africa. The World Bank cautions that South Africa's economy could collapse in a few generations if the AIDS crisis is not averted. AIDS could take a similarly heavy toll on China's economy as well as other Asian economies. Similarly grim economic outlooks are predicted for Eastern Europe. Regionally, a severe HIV/AIDS epidemic will worsen poverty and increase inequality because low-income households will be more adversely affected by an HIV/AIDS related illness and death. Decisions made at the household level to reallocate resources (such as time, labor, housing, and land) to meet costs related to the disease may alter the distribution of income in society and create new groups of poverty. AIDS also exacerbates poverty and inequality by increasing the number of children who lose one or both parents. Embattled populations are becoming progressively less productive and are burdened with increasing numbers of children orphaned by AIDS. As a result, development in these countries is adversely affected, and they will require an increase in economic and medical assistance from the community of developed nations and create additional pressures on transfers of resources, cooperation, and bilateral relations between developing and developed nations.

AIDS in Africa, Asia, and Eastern Europe is taking a center stage also in the global political arena as Western governments became increasingly concerned that the epidemic could lead to the emergence of radicalism and the undermining of newly adopted democratic systems. HIV/AIDS will breed suffering, want, and resentment that can lead into social and economic instability. In Africa, military HIV infections rates are much higher than in the civilian population and as the disease progresses, militaries will suffer from inability to meet their commitments and may be indifferent for their responsibilities. The epidemic may also threaten security in countries like Russia, China, and India, which all have nuclear weapons.

HIV/AIDS hinders development because it (as well as other infectious diseases) causes poverty, intrastate violence, and political insecurity, all of which have long-term negative effects on regional, and global economic, political, and social stability. Instability, for its part, damages international relations and hinders international political and economic cooperation and national development efforts particularly in the poor countries. HIV/AIDS has then most negative effects on social, economic, and political development in the third world countries. It not only decreases economic productivity by impeding the formation and consolidation of human capita, and by chocking the households as well as the private sector and the public sector with the increase in morbidity and mortality rates, but it also leads into income inequalities by stigmatization and in general to marginalization of large segments of society. All this leads into a gradual erosion of social capacity of the poor nations. It also brings degeneration of the state capacity and even further increases poverty. This enforces the vicious circle of poverty and HIV/AIDS. The combination (lack of resources, malnutrition, vulnerability to other diseases, ignorance), for its part, contributes to increasing governance problems and social development in affected states and regions. In extreme cases it can contribute to political destabilization and thus, have even wider political impacts on human security. When disease takes over all aspects of our daily lives, and in the end our whole lives, when there is no effective treatment, cure, or care available, people lose their hope for life and for better future. People are more easily led into offences against humanity, when they have no expectations to live long enough to be brought before the law, to trial and punishment or compensation.

The spread of AIDS, particularly in poor societies, on the one hand, can lead to anarchy, but on the other hand, its control in the name of public health can sometimes be seen as paternalist and/or totalitarian manipulation of people's freedom. In relation to AIDS, there is still a tendency to isolate the infected and ill in order to protect the society as a whole, to avoid public panic, and to prioritize scarce resources available the danger is in wider inequality, discrimination, and violation of human rights. This brings problems particularly to the ability of transitional states to consolidate democratic and effective systems of governance needed to deal with the problems to start with. However, the same tendencies are also present in the international relations related to the issue of global, distributive justice.

HIV/AIDS, Human Rights, and Gender

HIV/AIDS is probably the most challenging health problem of our time. In addition to the challenges posed by limited resources, the current scientific knowledge about HIV infection and AIDS is incomplete and many research findings are controversial and inconclusive. Moreover, lack of a vaccine and fully effective treatment, as well as the difficulties in preventing modes of transmission, have accentuated the magnitude and severity of the HIV/AIDS epidemic. This epidemic has created not only difficult socio-economic and medical issues, but also ethical and legal questions in relation to global and local development and national and international issues of cooperation and social justice.

In general HIV/AIDS is related to the human rights issues in international development. Not only are the "right to life" and "right to health" violated by the infection, but also other human rights principles such as right to equality are affected. The main human rights principles relevant to HIV/AIDS epidemic are life; the highest attainable standard of physical and mental health; non-discrimination; equal protection and equality before the law; liberty and security of person; freedom of movement; privacy; freedom of opinion and expression and the right to freely receive and impart information; freedom of association; to work, marry, and found a family; an adequate standard of living; social security, assistance and welfare; to share in scientific advancement and its benefits; to participate in public and cultural life; to be free from torture and cruel, inhuman, or degrading treatment or punishment. While these principles should protect those infected by HIV/AIDS, many of them are violated particularly in the poor countries, which are hardest hit by the epidemic. The lack of respect for human rights in general continues to increase vulnerability of individuals as well as particular groups of people to the virus. Individuals or groups who suffer from discrimination to start with and whose rights are not protected are both more vulnerable to becoming infecting and less able to cope with the burdens of HIV/AIDS. Refugees, migrants, prisoners, sex workers, and sexual minorities may be more vulnerable because in many parts of the world they often are unable to realize their civil, political, economic, social, and cultural rights. Gender inequalities spur on the spread of the epidemic and its disproportionate impact on women. Also the response to the HIV epidemic is hindered due to lack of enjoyment of freedom of speech and association, the right to information and education by infected and affected groups, and the civil society at large due to authoritarian and/or fundamentally religious governments.

From the point of view of development ethics, the moral and legal dilemmas related to HIV/AIDS and development can then be roughly grouped in two categories: (1) those which contain local and global resource allocation dimensions and are thus related to questions of distributive justice; and (2) those which deal with conflicting claims and rights in relation to our social responsibilities. Unresolved issues within the first group include the difficult issues of resource distribution between the competing demands of prevention among the still-uninfected and medical treatment and support for those already infected and/or impacted by HIV. An additional angle in the relationship between HIV/AIDS and development is the question of the role of international donor agencies and governments. When these groups are called upon for financial support by recipient governments, to what extent is it legally and ethically appropriate for these agencies to dictate conditions, policies, and priorities for the resources, which they provide to the countries most severely hit by HIV/AIDS?

The ethical and legal dilemmas that emerge in the second group of conflicting claims, rights, and responsibilities include the important problem of balancing individual and collective rights, most specifically between one's right to privacy and the public health imperative to control the spread of the disease. In relation to this, another difficult problem within this category deals with process—to what extent are affected governments obligated to include representation of people living with HIV/AIDS and vulnerable populations (women in general, but also including particularly orphans and widows) in the formulation and implementation of policies that strongly affect their lives?

The issues of human rights protection and democratic participation become most relevant in poor countries in relation to HIV/AIDS. This includes gender inequality, which had led to growing "feminization" of HIV/AIDS. The number of women infected is increasing yearly. Globally, nearly half of all persons infected between the ages of fifteen and forty-nine are women. In Africa, the proportion is reaching 60% and women are considerably at least 1.2 times more likely to be infected with HIV than men. Among young people aged fifteen to twenty-four this ratio is highest. These discrepancies have been attributed to several factors including the biological fact that HIV is more easily transmitted from men to women (than vice versa). As well, sexual activity tends to start earlier for women, and young women tend to have sex with much older partners. Frequently women also have less agency in regards with whom, when, and on what condition to have sex. In many cultures there are also sociocultural traditions (such as female genital mutilation (FGM), polygamy, widow inheritance, conjugal bonds, and/or few social sanctions on premarital or extramarital sex) which all contribute further to the spread of HIV/AIDS, particularly among women. Because of gender inequality women have less influence in policies concerning HIV/AIDS and women living with HIV/AIDS often also experience greater stigma and discrimination.

Global Response to HIV/AIDS

Since the HIV/AIDS endemic cannot be solved or even seriously tackled within the borders of one nation-state only, the discussion and action has to be in a global scope with local focus for implementation policies that work in combating AIDS. Most national policies are not or cannot be comprehensive enough, though they cover a variety of issues from gender inequality to prevention of prenatal transmission, employment, and HIV infection, and political/social empowerment. The biggest challenge for legislators is to adopt policies that can effectively limit the spread of HIV without undermining the rights and needs of an infected individual. Such a difficult balance can be achieved only in consultation with policymakers, professional ethicists, medical and health care professional, and representatives of communities that will be most heavily impacted by these policies.

Thus, combating HIV/AIDS in the world scale will require the combined effort of all those able to respond, namely; governments, donors, non-governmental organizations (NGOs), faith based organizations (FBOs), the private sector and the community groups already struggling on the forth line responses. However, initially the international response to HIV/AIDS has been slow and there was a lack of ethical response from the affluent countries with knowledge and resources. Instead the rich countries let the pharmaceutical companies block the access to medicine, and denied the scale of the problem. There was the question of who is the most responsible for the global HIV/AIDS crisis. What is the global responsibility and responsibility of the individual governments of the rich and the poor countries to deal with the epidemic? How to rationalize and prioritize the use of scarce resources available? How to extend the prevention and treatment programs to poor countries, where there may be no dispensaries, hospitals, clinics, professional health care personnel or even clean water?

Recently the United Nations system and partners have endorsed a framework of action to provide guidance to both donor nations and affected governments to respond to the urgent needs of those affected by the pandemic and the global response has expanded widely in the past few years. Domestic and external spending on HIV/AIDS programmes in low- and middle-income countries increased again in 2003, notably in sub-Saharan Africa. Dozens of national AIDS coordinating bodies are now in operation, and growing number of countries (many of them in Africa) have begun extending antiretroviral and other AIDS-related medications to their citizens (UNAIDS/

WHO 2003 and 2004). The cost of antiretroviral (ARV) drugs have fallen by 98% in the past few years, with the result that a life can be saved for less than a dollar a day. Simultaneously political commitment is growing stronger and grassroots mobilization is becoming more dynamic, and prevention efforts are being expanded locally, nationally, and internationally. Nevertheless, ARV treatment coverage remains dismal in sub-Saharan Africa overall, despite recent efforts in countries such as Botswana, Cameroon, Nigeria, and Uganda. The decision by pharmaceutical companies to withdraw their patent suit in South Africa after the mid-April 2001 world protests was an important step toward wider global access to HIV/AIDS treatment. Nevertheless, the drugs are still very expensive for most poor countries and do not reach most of those infected. Thus, WHO (World Health Organization)—the convening programme for HIV care in the UNAIDS, that is, the Joint United Nations programme (with partners such as UNICEF, WFP, UNDP, UNFPA, UNODC, ILO, UNESCO, WHO, World Bank)—is developing a comprehensive global strategy to bring antiretroviral treatment to 3 million people by 2005.

HIV/AIDS is not simply about mustering resources, technological know-how, and collective will to manage and eventually stop the spread of diseases. The political and economic reverberations of HIV/AIDS demand yet broader international and local responses. While the global response to HIV/AIDS is moving into a new phase, the current pace and scope of the world's response to HIV/AIDS falls far short of what is required. Increases in resources and political commitment (both international and those in hard-hit countries themselves) are needed to ensure equitable access to treatment that benefits the poor and marginalized section of societies, especially women. Alongside that huge challenge stands the urgent need to boost prevention programmes. Prevention and wider treatment have to go hand in hand with attempts to increase social justice and gender equality.

SIRKKU K. HELLSTEN

See also Health Care; World Health Organization (WHO)

References and Further Reading

Barnett, T. 'The social and economic impact of HIV/AIDS on development' in V. Desai and R.B. Potter (eds) *The Companion to Development Studies*. London: Arnord/Hodder Headline Group, 2002.
Baylies, C. "Perspectives on Gender and AIDS in Africa", in C. Baylies and J. Bujira (eds.), *AIDS, Sexuality and Gender in Africa*. London: Routledge, 2000.

Holden, S. *AIDS on the Agenda*. An Oxfam publication in association with ActionAid and Save the Children UK. Eynsham: Information Press, 2003.

Human Rights Watch. *HIV/AIDS and Human Rights*. 2004. http://hrw.org.

Irwin, A., Millen, J., and Fallows, D. *Global AIDS: Myths and Facts. Tools for Fighting the AIDS Pandemic*. Cambridge, South End Press, 2003.

Price-Smith, A. *The Health of Nations; Infectious Disease, Environmental Change and Their Effects on National Security and Development*. Cambridge, MA and London: The MIT Press, 2003.

UNICEF *Africa's Orphaned Generations*. UNICEF's HIV/AIDS Unit, UNICEF. New York, 2003.

USAID *U.S. International Response to HIV/AIDS*. Washington, DC: Department of State Publication, 2003.

HO CHI MINH

Ho Chi Minh (1890–1969) was the primary founder of the Vietnamese Communist Party and the first President of the Democratic Republic of Vietnam (DRV) (1945–1969). Most scholars credit Ho as being the father of the Vietnamese revolution and the most influential political figure in modern Viet Nam. The youngest of three children, the man who would become Ho Chi Minh was born Nguyen Sinh Cung on May 19, 1890, in a small village in the central Vietnamese province of Nghe Tinh. He was given the name Nguyen That Thanh at ten.

His father, Nguyen Sinh Sac, was a Confucian scholar who had served as an official in the Vietnamese imperial bureaucracy but resigned his post and became an itinerant teacher in protest against French occupation following the Treaty of Protectorate in 1884. Out of hatred for the French, Sac refused to learn French, but he had his son educated at the prestigious National Academy (Quoc Hoc) in Hue. Here Ho learned to speak French fluently. The area was indirectly ruled by the French through a puppet emperor. Its peasants led by traditional dissidents, actively opposed the French presence. In 1908, inheriting his father's rebellious spirit, Ho participated in a series of tax protests, acquiring a reputation as a rabble rouser. It was this experience that left him frustrated with a system that made him a second-class citizen in his own country.

Thoroughly imbued with the French ideals of liberty, equality, and fraternity he yearned to see them in practice in France. He also determined to find out why Western nations had become predominate in the world. He signed on as a cook's helper with a French steamship company and traveled to Europe. In 1911, he arrived in Marseilles as a galley boy aboard a passenger liner. Not long after he briefly took up residence in London. At the end of World War I, he settled in Paris. He soon became caught up in the whirlwind of Socialist political activities coursing through post-war Europe. Assuming the pseudonym Nguyen Ai Quoc (Nguyen the Patriot), he gained credibility within the local Vietnamese community by coauthoring a petition sent to Allied leaders gathered at Versailles demanding self-determination for all colonial peoples. The rejection of the petition made Ho believe that Western "liberalism" was bankrupt and so, in 1920, he joined the French Communist Party as one of its founding members.

Ho soon gained the reputation as a gifted and hard-working party organizer and, in 1923, was invited to Moscow to be part of the Communist International (Comintern). When Chinese nationalist revolutionary Sun Yat-sen, formed an alliance with the Communist Chinese Party (CCP), Ho and others were sent to Sun's headquarters in Canton in late 1924. Ho received instructions to recruit members from Indochina to act as the basis for an Indochinese Marxist revolutionary party.

In 1925, Ho formed the Vietnamese Revolutionary Youth League comprised mainly of radical Indochinese nationals living in south China. The new group was to train members to be future communist leaders. The League reflected the Leninist strategy of first embracing national independence to gain power and then implementing Communist ideology. For three years, the League focused the Vietnamese revolution on demands for national independence and social justice. In 1925 Dr. Sun had died and two years later, Ho Chi Minh had been forced to flee China and return to the Union of Soviet Socialist Republics (USSR) in the aftermath of Chiang Kai-shek's purge of the CCP from the Kuo Min Tang (KMT) (Nationalist Party) in China. In 1928, the Comintern revised its policy to emphasize class struggle and Marxist proletarian leadership concepts. This split the League into two rival factions.

In 1930, Ho traveled to Hong Kong via Thailand. Here he unified the rival faction into the Vietnamese Communist Party (VCP). In October, Ho and others changed the name to Indochinese Communist Party (ICP) to reflect the Comintern view that small nations could only liberate themselves by banning together in larger alliances.

In June 1931, Ho was arrested by the British in Hong Kong. After languishing in jail for nearly two years, he was released on a legal technicality and soon fled to the USSR. In Moscow he came under suspicion from Soviet leader Joseph Stalin, who did not trust independent-minded communists. To survive, Ho spent most of the rest of the 1930s in obscurity hiding from the watchful eye of "Uncle Joe" and the West.

With the advent of the Sino-Japanese war in July 1937 and the retreat of Chiang Kai-shek's KMT forces into the western Chinese hinterland in 1938, Ho was allowed to return to China to resume his organizing activities. After several months serving with the CCP in central and south China, he reestablished contact with ICP leaders in Viet Nam. With the fall of France to German forces in June 1940 and the collaboration of the Vichy French government, the pro-fascist French colonial government allowed the Japanese access to important natural resources and military installations in Indochina. This angered most indigenous Indochinese and provided fuel to independence movements.

In May 1941, Ho and ICP led the formation of a broad-based nationalist alliance called the League for the Independence of Viet Nam better known as the Viet Minh. Much like the Youth League, the Viet Minh soft-peddled Marxist ideology and class struggle and disguised the ICP role in the Front. Instead, they focused on nationalist issues such as anti-imperialism, land reform, independence, social justice, and civil liberties. This soon won the general support of almost all political elements and social classes against French colonialism and Japanese occupation.

With no other real nationalist anti-Japanese force in place the Viet Minh became the main symbol of national resistence. General Vo Nguyen Giap soon built a well-trained partisan army. The Viet Minh's political and military headquarters were centered in the mountains north of the Red River Delta, near an region known as Viet Bac.

Ho constantly traveled between Viet Nam and China building up the Viet Minh base inside Viet Nam. Throughout the war, in China, the CCP and KMT maintained an uneasy anti-Japanese "United Front." During one trip, KMT authorities arrested Ho but later released him because his anti-Japanese activities were so effective. At the same time, he established contacts with US Office of Special Services (OSS) agents who supported him with some small arms and even life-saving medical supplies and treatment in turn for information on Japanese troop movements and operations in Indochina. During the war, the Viet Minh anti-Japanese activities proved highly successful.

Even as the Japanese announced their surrender on August 14, 1945, the Viet Minh marched into Ha Noi, where Ho announced Vietnamese independence and the establishment of the Democratic Republic of Viet Nam (DRV). It was during this time he adopted the name Ho Chi Minh or "he who enlightens." This was apparently an effort to calm moderate fears of the famous radical Nguyen Ai Quoc. Ho also placated Nationalist Chinese occupying forces in the north by agreeing to guarantee at least seventy seats in the national assembly to his main rival party Viet Nam Quoc Dan Dang during the January 1946 elections.

Concurrently, he held delicate negotiations with the chief Free French representative in Indochina, Jean Saiteny, in an effort assure a peaceful resolution of disputes about the future of Viet Nam. In March 1946, the two came to a tentative agreement allowing Viet Nam to be a "free state" within the French Union. As part of the agreement, they agreed that the status of the colony of Cochin China (a region in present-day Viet Nam) would be determined by a future plebiscite. Ho also agreed to assure the protection of French economic and cultural interests in Indochina. He also acceded to allow French troops to be stationed in the north.

That summer Ho went to Paris as an observer while representatives of the DRV negotiated with the newly elected conservative French government. When talks broke down, the official representatives returned to Ha Noi in protest. Ho stayed behind and worked out a compromise that called for further discussion to be held in January of 1947. Many DRV leaders were angered by Ho's interference but he convinced them the delay was necessary to prepare for war.

In the meantime, tensions between French and Viet Minh troops in northern Viet Nam reached a breaking point. In December, Vietnamese forces attacked French government installations and residence in Ha Noi. Unable to sustain open combat at this point, Ho and Giap removed the core of the Viet Minh to their mountain stronghold of Viet Bac, where they had resisted the Japanese. Once again embracing national liberation and submerging Marxist revolution, Ho formulated political policy and Giap carried out a guerilla campaign waiting for the right moment to strike. Supported with aid from the USSR and People's Republic of China (PRC) (founded in 1949), the Viet Minh finally cornered a major French unit in Dien Bien Phu and after weeks of siege forced their surrender. The defeat led to negotiation at Geneva in 1954. While Ho was again not an official representative, he was active behind the scenes and was instrumental in getting the DRV to accept a compromise peace and division of the country along the seventeenth parallel in July. With the restoration of the DRV government in Ha Noi in October, Ho returned to lead it and played a role in its move toward a socialist society. However, by the end of the decade his health had begun to deteriorate and such leaders as General Secretary Troung Chinh were making key domestic decisions.

Ho Chi Minh's position as president of the DRV was confirmed in the Constitution of 1959, but his health was failing, and after the mid-1960s, his role in decision making became primarily ceremonial. He died on September 3, 1969. In a testament that he dictated during his final days, he asked to be cremated and asked that taxes be lowered to reduce the burden of the war on the people. Both requests were ignored. Instead, a mausoleum was erected on Ba Dinh Square in Ha Noi. After his death, Ho was officially bestowed the status of a revolutionary saint and hailed as the beloved "Uncle Ho" of the Vietnamese people.

Ho's life and career have long been shrouded in controversy. To some, he was a heroic figure and the symbol of the struggle of the Vietnamese people for national independence and reunification. To others, he was a hardened revolutionary who disguised his commitment to proletarian internationalism behind a mask of patriotism. To this day many still wonder if he was primarily a nationalist or a communist. They ponder whether he was a secret moderate surrounded by militant radicals, as some have alleged and he himself often implied. The answers to these questions are not readily available from the evidence and, like the life of most "founding fathers," are often obscured by legend and socio-political partisanship.

Most objective observers and mainstream scholars believe that Ho was both a true patriot and a dedicated Communist, who did not see a contradiction in these positions. Clearly, he was a man of great charm, and yet, also someone who sought his goals with ruthless determination. Whatever else, he was a talented leader who was a gifted administrator, strategist, negotiator, conciliator, and motivator who led Viet Nam to national independence.

CECIL B. CURREY AND WILLIAM P. HEAD

See also Vietnam; Vietnam War

References and Further Reading

Duiker, William J. *Ho Chi Minh: A Life*. New York: Hyperion Press, 2000.
Fall, Bernard B., ed. *Ho Chi Minh on Revolution: Selected Writings, 1920–1966*. New York: Praegar, 1967.
Halberstam, David. *Ho*. New York: Random House, 1971.
Ho Chi Minh. *Selected Works*. 4 Volumes. Ha Noi, Foreign Language House, 1960–1962.
———. *Ho Chi Minh: Selected Writings*. Ha Noi: Foreign Language House, 1973.
La Courture, Jean. *Ho Chi Minh: A Political Biography*. Translated by Peter Wiles. New York: Vintage Books, 1968.

HONDURAS

The Republic of Honduras lies in the northwestern part of the Central American isthmus and borders Guatemala (256 kilometers) to the northwest, El Salvador (342 kilometers) to the west, and Nicaragua (922 kilometers) to the south. This mountainous country has an extensive Caribbean coast and a very small Pacific coast on the Gulf of Fonseca nestled between El Salvador and Nicaragua. Its total landmass is 112,090 square kilometers., more than twice the size of Costa Rica (a similar area to Louisiana). Ninety percent of Honduras's 6.8 million people are *mestizo* (a mix of European and Indian heritage); the remaining 10% are comprised of Arabs, Africans, Asians, and indigenous people. As in the rest of Central America, the vast majority of the population is Catholic, but Protestant church membership has grown significantly in the last thirty years.

Honduras, along with the rest of Central America, became independent of Spanish colonial rule in September 1821. Honduras initially joined the short-lived Mexican empire, and then the war torn United Provinces of Central America, before finally becoming a sovereign state in 1840. Central American unity, though, has remained an elusive goal of successive Honduran governments.

Honduras entered its independence period with no significant export product and a lack of domestic investment capital that would have been necessary to develop one. In response, the Honduran political elite actively sought foreign investment to revitalize a moribund mining industry and to develop the country's infrastructure. As in Costa Rica, railroad building companies used their land-grants to plant and cultivate bananas as they built the railroads. By the start of the twentieth century, bananas had become Honduras's principal export product, but it was dominated by US-owned companies rather than domestic interests. The banana companies controlled over two-thirds of the country's territory and they tended to interfere in Honduran politics to advance their economic interests. By the late 1920s, the three dominant banana companies merged to form the United Fruit Company, which remained a powerful political and economic force in the country. Even with these high levels of foreign direct investment, the country remained one of the poorest countries in Latin America.

In the 1960s, following an Import Substitution Industrialization (ISI) strategy, Honduras joined with other Central American republics to create the Central American Common Market (CACM). The goal was to foster economic development and industrialization across the isthmus through a free trade area that would be protected from international competition by high tariff barriers. In practice, the benefits from the CACM were unevenly distributed and tensions between the member states increased. These tensions culminated in a short war, commonly and disparagingly referred to as the "Soccer War" between Honduras and El Salvador in 1969.

As a result of these tensions and the rising tide of violence across the region, the CACM effectively ceased to exist by the late 1970s. In May 2004, the idea of a free trade zone was given new life when Honduras signed the CAFTA agreement with the US and other Central American countries, which is still waiting to be ratified by the US Congress.

Currently, Honduras remains the poorest country in Central America and while the traditional agricultural exports (bananas and coffee) have been in decline, non-traditional exports (farm-raised shrimp and fruits), and a maquila sector (textiles and clothing finishing), along with tourism, have become much more significant. Another major and growing sector of the economy is remittances from Hondurans working abroad. According to the US State Department, remittances from abroad will soon become the largest single source of revenue for the country, which is a reflection of the continued weakness of the economy.

Since the 1980s, Honduran political development has become increasingly democratic. For more than one hundred years, two political parties—Liberals and Nationals—have dominated the political life of the country. The existence of these established political parties, though, did not foster the establishment of a consolidated democracy. Instead, dictatorship, civil wars, and foreign intervention were the pattern of political life that continued until the election of a civilian president in 1981. An indication of the extent of the political turmoil during this period is the promulgation of twelve different constitutions from independence through 1982.

Honduras's political development in the late 1970s and 1980s, though, began to diverge from that of its neighbors. While revolution swept much of the region during this period with civil wars and increasingly repressive regimes in Guatemala, El Salvador, and Nicaragua, Honduran political and military elites moved to deepen the country's nascent democratization process.

For much of the 1980s, Honduras permitted the presence of US troops and counter-revolutionaries (Contras) from Nicaragua. The Contras used southern Honduras as a staging ground for attacks on Sandinista-controlled Nicaragua. The *quid pro quo* for supporting US regional foreign policy was extensive US sponsorship of major social and economic reform projects including the largest contingent of US Peace Corps workers in the world.

The ruling Liberal Party's questionable reading of the country's electoral law marked a second presidential election in 1985. Because the Liberal party was unable to agree on a single presidential candidate, the party decided to run two candidates and ruled the two Liberal party candidates' votes would be summed. Together the liberal candidates out-polled the National Party candidate. The more popular of the two Liberal candidates, José Azcona Hoyo, took office in 1986. This election marked the first peaceful transfer of political power since the 1950s.

Another scheduled presidential election in 1988 further deepened the adherence to democratic norms. The new President, Carlos Roberto Flores, introduced sweeping reforms including the creation of an independent Supreme Court, putting the military under civilian control, and promulgating a series of anti-corruption measures. These measures were tested when Hurricane Mitch pummeled Honduras in 1998 killing more than 5,600 people, leaving over 1.5 million homeless, and $2 billion in property damage. The government responded efficiently and without the high levels of corruption that had been expected.

The 1990s witnessed an increasing reliance on the ballot box to determine the political control of the country. There have now been six general elections and three peaceful transfers of power between the two major parties. Also, extra-parliamentary agencies have been created such as the Commissioner for the Protection of Human Rights (1992) to hold government officials accountable for their actions and the Constitution was also amended to place the military under civilian control to which the military acquiesced.

BRUCE M. WILSON

See also Central America: History and Economic Development; Central America: International Relations

References and Further Reading

Hall, Carolyn, and Héctor Pérez Brignoli. John V. Cotter, Cartographer. *Historical Atlas of Central America*. University of Oklahoma Press, 2003.

Mahoney, James. *The Legacies of Liberalism: Path Dependence and Political Regimes in Central America*. Baltimore, MD: Johns Hopkins University Press, 2001.

Medea, Benjamin. *Don't Be Afraid, Gringo: A Honduran Woman Speaks From The Heart: The Story of Elvia Alvarado*. 1987.

Perez-Brignoli, Hector. *A Brief History of Central America*. Berkeley, CA: California Univerity Press, 1989.

Striffler, Steve, and Mark Moberg (ed). *Banana Wars: Power, Production, and History in the Americas*. Durham, NC: Duke University Press, 2003.

United Nations Development Programme. *Human Development Report 2004* http://hdr.undp.org/.

HONG KONG

Hong Kong (officially Hong Kong Special Administrative Region) is located in South East Asia. It is spread over the Lantau and Hong Kong Islands and about 200 other very small islands, and a small portion of mainland. It is bordered on the north by the territory of Guangdong Province of People's Republic of China (PRC) and bounded on the east, south, and west by the South China Sea. The country has a land area of 1,092 square kilometers (422 square miles), comparatively its territory about 1.5 times larger than the territory of New York City in the United States. The climate in Hong Kong is subtropical. The average July temperatures range between 26°C and 31°C (78°F and 87°F); and February temperatures range between 13°C and 17°C (55°F and 63°F). Heavy rains are quite common in summer and autumn and annual rainfall is about 2,159 millimeters (85 inches). Hot and humid summers last from May to September. The winters are cool and usually dry and they last from December to March.

The population of Hong Kong was 6,855,125 in 2004 (Central Intelligence Agency [CIA] estimate). This figure does not include a number of illegal migrants from the PRC who moved into Hong Kong in search of jobs and business opportunities. Hong Kong has a population growth rate of 0.65% and migration rate of 5.24 migrant(s) per 1,000 people (2004 CIA estimate). About 95% of the Hong Kong population is Chinese, who mostly speak Cantonese dialect. Others include people from Southeast Asia, Great Britain, and some other countries.

The British established their control over Hong Kong in 1842. They forced the Chinese government to cede Hong Kong Island to Britain after winning the First Opium War. During the next few decades Hong Kong became an important trading port and military outpost for the British Navy. The colony provided financial and trading services to many large and small enterprises in the region and it served as a trade and economic window to mainland China. The Chinese government viewed the colonial control of British over Hong Kong as temporary and demanded the British government to return the territory under the control of the PRC. After a series of intensive consultations, Britain and China signed the Sino-British Joint Declaration in 1984. It stipulated that Hong Kong would come under Chinese rule in 1997. The Communist government of China agreed to grant Hong Kong a special status of the Special Administrative Region (SAR) of China under "one country, two systems" arrangement. The Declaration and a Chinese legal act—called the Basic Law—regulated the governance of the SAR, and they will be providing a high degree of economic autonomy for Hong Kong for next fifty years.

Hong Kong grew to its prominence during the twentieth century becoming one of the most important financial and trading centers in the world. Its economic development was facilitated by several factors. First, its economy was built around servicing commerce, trade, and shipping and therefore its government built most a favorable environment for free entrepreneurship, business, and trade. Second, it is located on the main shipping route in the western Pacific just in the midway between Japan and the Strait of Malacca, so Hong Kong established one of the most efficient seaport facilities in the world. For many decades its container terminals were among the largest in the world (by annual volumes). Third, it built the world's most efficient and sophisticated financial banking facilities that serviced trading needs of many countries in and outside of the region. Fourth, having a highly skilled and flexible workforce Hong Kong established a very competitive industrial sector that is specialized in skill-intensive manufacturing. It also became known as a tourist and shopping destination for wealthy Chinese and international tourists, businessmen, and travelers.

Hong Kong's services sector began its rapid development in the early twentieth century. The banking and trading services were established first, becoming cornerstones of the service sector in Hong Kong. They largely focus on services the international trade and commerce. For decades Hong Kong successfully re-exported products that were manufactured in other parts of China, in Japan, South Korea, Taiwan, and some other countries. That included clothing, textiles, telecommunications and recording equipment, electrical machinery and appliances, and footwear. The Heritage Foundation/*Wall Street Journal*'s Index of Economic Freedom ranked Hong Kong among most open economies in the world in 2004. In the post-World War II period tourism became another important sector as a modern airport, international class hotels, conference and other facilities were built here. About 18 million tourists arrive in Hong Kong every year, making tourism one of the major sectors of the national economy, though the severe acute respiratory syndrome (SARS) negatively affected it in 2003–2004.

The manufacturing sector has developed rapidly since the 1950s, although it slowed down in the late 1990s. For decades Hong Kong was known as a producer of various consumer goods, including clothing, textiles, toys, plastics, electronics, watches, etc. However, since the mid-1990s the manufacturing sector has been switching to production of more sophisticated goods, such as computer peripherals, high-end electronics and some categories of luxury goods. Meanwhile, a significant number of manufacturing facilities have been shifted to neighboring Guangdong Province of the PRC, where labor costs were much lower.

Hong Kong has a small but vibrant agricultural sector that supplies fresh vegetables, flowers, and meat to its population. Its fishermen have notable fishing fleet that supplies about two-thirds of the fresh fish to the city. Meat producers were hit hard in 2003–2004 by SARS, and had difficulties to recover their production to pre-SARS level.

China, the United States, Japan, Taiwan, and East Asian countries are Hong Kong's main trading partners, and the chief markets for its products. According to official statistics, Hong Kong's international trade grew rapidly throughout the post-World War II era. The consumer goods (electrical machinery and appliances, textiles, precious stones, etc.) and services remained the principal export products, while foodstuff, fuel, machinery and manufactured goods, transport equipment, raw materials and others remained the key import products. The primary trading partner is China, which accounts for about 42% of the total trade turnover (2004 estimate).

Hong Kong was affected by the Asian financial crisis of 1997 and by the global slowdown of 2001–2003, but recession was relatively mild. According to the World Bank's estimates the average annual growth stood at 6.4% between 1983 and 1993, but declined to 3.1% between 1993 and 2003 (2004 World Bank estimate). During last decade, the Hong Kong government maintained fiscal prudence and kept inflation under control. The Hong Kong dollar exchange rate has been fixed to the US dollar and remained stable for many years. In 2003–2004 the exchange rate of the US dollar against all major currencies was in decline boosting compositeness of the Hong Kong economy in the international market.

The population of Hong Kong enjoys relatively high living standards. However, during the last decade the inflow of illegal migrants and economic recession put significant pressures onto the labor market and there was growing social discontent among the people. Unemployment rate stood at about 6.8% in 2004. Nevertheless, Hong Kong managed to maintain high living standards among the population and remained one of the richest countries in South East Asia in terms of per capita income at the level of $25,430 US dollars. However, the wealth was distributed unevenly and was concentrated in few hands. The educational system is very strong in Hong Kong and literacy rate stood at about 93.5% (2004 estimate). Life expectancy is 78.7 years for males and 84.3 for females. In 2004, the United Nations Development Program (UNDP) Human Development Index (HDI) put Hong Kong in 23rd place out of 177, ahead of Greece, Singapore, and Portugal.

RAFIS ABAZOV

See also East Asia: History and Economic Development; East Asia: International Relations; Ethnic Conflicts: East Asia

References and Further Reading

Beatty, Bob. *Democracy, Asian Values, and Hong Kong: Evaluating Political Elite Beliefs*. Praeger Publishers, 2003.

Faure, David, and Pui-Tak Lee. *Economy: A Documentary History of Hong Kong*. Hong Kong: Hong Kong University Press, 2004.

Jayasuriya, Kanishka. *Asian Regional Governance: Crisis and Change* (RoutledgeCurzon/City University of Hong Kong South East Asia S.). London: Routledge/Curzon, 2004.

Li, Kui Wai, and Kui-Wai Li. *Capitalist Development and Economism in East Asia: The Rise of Hong Kong, Singapore, Taiwan and South Korea* (Routledge Studies in Growth Economies of Asia). New York and London: Routledge, 2002.

Patten, Christopher. *East and West: The Last Governor of Hong Kong on Power, Freedom and the Future*. London: Macmillan, 1998.

Roberts, Elfed Vaughan, *et al. Historical Dictionary of Hong Kong and Macau*. Lanham, MD, and London, Scarecrow Press, 1994.

Sung, Yun-Wing. *The Emergence of Greater China: The Economic Integration of Mainland China, Taiwan and Hong Kong* (Studies on the Chinese Economy). New York and London: Palgrave Macmillan, 2005.

HOUPHOUËT BOIGNY, FÉLIX

Born October 18, 1905, in Yamoussoukro, Ivory Coast, to a family of wealthy Baoule chiefs, Houphouët-Boigny grew up on his family's coffee-plantations and became a plantation owner himself. He thereby encountered the problems created by French colonial government for African planters. Determined to change French policies, he founded the African Agricultural Syndicate and devoted the rest of his long life to politics. In the 1940s and 1950s, he became prominent in the struggle for independence. At first he allied himself with the French Communist Party, which alone at the time opposed colonialism. However, when the left lost power in Paris and his Ivoirian supporters expressed distress at his militancy, he broke with the Communists and thereafter promoted General De Gaulle's policies.

Houphouët-Boigny attended the Ecole Normale William Ponty and Ecole de Médecine et de Pharmacie at Dakar, Senegal, and graduated in 1925, working afterwards as a bush doctor and as a coffee planter. He served as deputy to the French National Assembly from 1945–1959, founded the Rasssemblement Democratique Africain and its Ivoirian branch, the Parti Démocratique de la Côte d'Ivoire; and was elected to the French Constituent Assemblies in 1945 and 1946. He served as president of the Grand Council of French West Africa from 1957–1959 as well as serving as a French cabinet minister during this time. He served as president of the Constituent Assembly of the Ivory Coast from 1958–1959 and then as the head of Ivoirian government in 1959–1960.

He was elected the first president of the independent Ivory Coast (1960), while remaining secretary general of the ruling Democratic Party of the Ivory Coast. Though the Ivoirian constitution established a democratic republic and technically Houphouët-Boigny was re-elected president six times, in reality he imposed one-party government and controlled all developments. He maintained close ties with France. The number of French citizens working in the Ivory Coast doubled. Ivoirian exports and imports were centered on France. The French trained the Ivoirian military. Sons of the Ivoirian elite studied in France.

Houphouët-Boigny staked the country's economic future on the growth of agriculture for export. As the production of cash crops, mainly coffee and cocoa, increased he spent the additional revenues on improving infrastructure and education to promote further growth of exports. He also encouraged immigration from neighboring nations to enlarge the workforce. For years he was successful. Growth and political stability attracted foreign investments, and the annual gross national product rose steadily.

However, uneven distribution of incomes, droughts, and fluctuation of world prices for agricultural products endangered the economy and social problems mushroomed. Ethnic rivalries awakened as northern Ivoirian Muslims resented the ruling southern Christian elite which reaped most of the benefits from development. Internal mobility weakened family ties. Urban overcrowding increased misery, conflicts, and crime. Ivoirians objected to one-party rule and to the foreign presence, be it French or African. Protests against governmental action multiplied. There was also loud criticism of Houphouët-Boigny's enormous expenditures for personal glorification, which turned his native village into a modern national capital.

To maintain loyalty, Houphouët-Boigny gradually authorized political changes. He alternated repression with clemency; he exploited ethnic discord and political animosities and co-opted many by patronage. He made ethnically balanced cabinet appointments, and replaced older trusted personnel with younger Ivoirian technocrats. He showed awareness of the yearnings of the middle and lower classes by holding public dialogues, reminiscent of traditional palavers, where people could air their grievances to their leader. He appointed study committees to recommend reforms. In the 1980s, he accepted multi-party elections. But in practice his tactics and charisma preserved his autocratic rule and governmental stability, though the economy continued to falter.

He died on December 7, 1993, in Yamoussoukro. Since his death the Ivory Coast has been victimized by unprecedented xenophobia and government overthrows. Houphouët-Boigny remains controversial. Some remember him nostalgically as *"le vieux,"* the father of their country; others accuse him of having been a dictator, a lackey to the French, and blame him for the country's current difficulties.

L. NATALIE SANDOMIRSKY

See also Cote d'Ivoire; West Africa: History and Economic Development; West Africa: International Relations

References and Further Reading

Bailly, Diegou. *La restauration du multipartisme en Côte d'Ivoire, ou la double mort d'Houphouët-Boigny*. Paris: L'Harmattan, 2000.

Baulin, Jacques. *La politique intérieure d'Houphouët-Boigny*., Paris: Eurafor-Press, 1982.

Hommage à Félix Houphouët-Boigny. Dakar: Présence Africaine, 2000.

Nandjui, Pierre. *Houphouët-Boigny: l'homme de la France en Afrique*. Paris: L'Harmattan, 1995.

Siriex, Paul-Henri. *Houphouët-Boigny, an African Statesman*. Abidjan: Nouvelles Editions Africaines, 1988.

Woronoff, Jon. *West African Wager: Houphouët vs. Nkrumah*. Metuchen, NJ: Scarecrow Press, 1972.

HOXHA, ENVER

Enver Hoxha (1908–1985) was the chief architect of the Albanian Communist Party, and subsequently of the postwar Albanian government, which he directed for forty-one years.

Born in Gjirokaster, southern Albania, in 1908, Hoxha graduated from French Lyceum in Korce in 1930. He pursued higher education in France at the Universities of Montpelier and Paris. He worked in the Albanian Consulate in Brussels before returning to Albania in 1936 to teach at the Lyceum. He lost his job during the Italian occupation of Albania in 1939 and moved to Tirana the next year to organize an anti-Fascist underground. In 1941, he helped found the Communist Party of Albania, and was elected general secretary in 1943. After the war, in 1946,

Hoxha was appointed president of the Council of Ministers.

Foreign Policy

A subtle politician, Hoxha maneuvered to forge a succession of alliances with larger communist states, to obtain aid for development and buttress Albania's defense posture. The most important of these alliances was with the Soviet Union. For a dozen years, from 1948 to 1960, Moscow was the primary source of aid, credit, and technical assistance to Albania, without which it could not have made any meaningful progress toward development.

After the break of relations with the Soviet Union in 1961, ostensibly for ideological reasons, Hoxha allied Albania with China. In the 1960s and 1970s, China's economic and military aid not only furthered Albania's development, but very likely thwarted Moscow's political and economic blockade of the country, designed to overthrow Hoxha. When China severed its ties to Albania in 1978, Hoxha adopted an isolationist developmental policy.

Domestic Politics

Hoxha sought to build a modern Albania, with a strong economy and an egalitarian society. But projects for development, called Five-Year Plans, generally fell short of expectations. Despite Hoxha's strong-handed rule, Albania did make significant progress in many directions: agriculture, industry, health care, education, science and technology, the arts, and culture. One area of progress related to women.

Hoxha was a strong advocate of equal rights for women. He deplored women's inferior status in Albanian society, and created conditions that enabled them to free themselves from economic dependence. By the 1990s, women had made significant progress in all areas of society. They obtained jobs in the professions, management, politics, manufacturing, engineering, and other fields.

Support for Cultural Development

Hoxha also gave vigorous support to programs for the development of the arts and culture. Despite his limitations on free expression within the nation, he encouraged the cultivation of new art forms, and the creation of a vast network of cultural institutions.

On the other hand, he had a wavering or uncertain relationship with the intelligentsia, such as intellectuals, professional people, educators, writers, and artists. Hoxha realized that he needed the special talents of the intelligentsia, if plans for the development of the Albanian nation were to succeed. However, he believed intellectuals to be politically unstable, and a potential threat to his regime. Consequently, from time to time, he authorized campaigns to intimidate or punish various members of the intelligentsia, for alleged violations of Party norms and guidelines.

A peculiar feature of Hoxha's reign was the so-called Cultural Revolution, which unfolded over a period of four years (1966–1969). The chief goal of the revolution was to stimulate development by removing obstacles to production and social emancipation, posed by incompetent administrators and backward customs. The radical measures that were implemented at this time included the complete collectivization of agriculture and the abolition of religion.

Abolition of Religion

Enver Hoxha began to restrict the activities of religious bodies as early as the 1940s. In 1967, at the apex of the Cultural Revolution, he sanctioned the abolition of the religious establishment, on the grounds that religion was a medieval institution, rife with superstition, and a serious obstacle to development. Freedom of worship was restored in 1990.

As a matter of policy, Hoxha resorted periodically to the mechanism of the purge to achieve his ends. He regarded the purge as a necessary device for development, and for maintaining political power. His four-decades-long rule in Albania was marked by a series of purges of persons viewed as enemies of the regime. The latest and most sweeping of the purges, occurred in the 1970s and practically decimated the leaderships of the League of Writers and Artists, the army, and the top-ranking directors of the economy. The purges created a climate of terror in the country, and slowed down development.

Hoxha died in Tirana on April 11, 1985. He was a strong but flawed leader, bent on modernizing Albania.

PETER R. PRIFTI

See also Albania

References and Further Reading

Burke, John. "Museum of Marxism," *National Review*, 34, Nov. 12, 1982.

Fegley, Randall. "Land of Uncle Enver: Keeping Albania Backward," *Commonwealth*, 107, Aug. 29, 1980.

Halliday, Jon, editor. *The Artful Albanian*. London: Chatto & Windus, 1986.

Laber, Jeri. "Slouching toward democracy," *The New York Review of Books*, 40, Nos. 1–2, 1993.

O'Donnell, James. *A Coming of Age*. New York: Columbia University Press, 1998.

HUMAN RESOURCE DEVELOPMENT

The Human Resource Development Concept

Society can function properly when it has the basic resources: *natural resources* (land, rivers, oil, coal, etc.), *capital resources* (buildings, tools, goods etc.), *technology* (information, knowledge and techniques employed in producing goods and services), and, of course, *human resources*. The latter include the number and composition of the population, its level of education, health status and the specific skills and habits the people have developed. In a society, all the resources are interrelated, but the human resources have a great influence on the development of all others. The production of coal, the functioning of plants, the production of goods, etc. all depend on the number of the population, its health status, and educational level. Thus, the proper management of human resources is of paramount importance for the effective functioning of a given society. When we are interested in the effective management of the human part of the social systems, we talk about *human resources management* (HRM). HRM is an integral part of management and has all the aspects of management related to the reproduction of the population within a given country.

Since the general theme of human resources management is related to their development, it has been established as a separate subject known as *human resources development* (HRD). HRD is also known among scientists as *strategic human resources development* (SHRD). It emphasises on the strategic development of human resources in a long run.

The Content of Human Resources Development

Two meanings are implied when describing the developing approach toward human recourses. The *first* meaning is related to the development of society as a whole. It includes all the aspects related to the development of people living in a given country. General aspects of HRD are: *education, training, manpower planing, health care, unemployment, urban/rural settlements, mental health care, family planing, migration, birthright, mortality, women involvement,* and so on.

The individuals within a social system are functioning in various private and state organisations—production plants, schools, universities, hospitals, banks, etc. In order for a given organisation to be effective, the leaders and managers are highly interested in the development of the human resources it employs. In other words, small or big organisations also have a human development purpose. This is the *second* meaning used for HRD. It relates to the professional development of individuals working in a given organisation. In this respect, HRD includes: *training and development programs, employees' learning style, career development, recruitment process, selection process, performance evaluation, performance practices and models, strategic human resources planning, leadership styles, effectiveness,* etc. *Personnel development* is another term used when we talk about human resources development in organisations.

The development of human resources is a specific scientific area examining the previously mentioned statements. Besides, HRD includes a set of specific practices being used by managers, political, and state leaders. There are different institutions involved with the development of human resources in every country: research institutes, assessment centres, departments, governmental agencies, and ministries. They do expert assessments of the population and empirical examinations, assess employed staff, publish professional magazines and provide university master degrees in human resources development. International organisations provide different programs related to human resources, some of which are: United Nations Development Programme (UNDP), World Health Organization (WHO) human resources development programs, ASIA–Pacific Economic Cupertino (APEC) programs, and so forth.

HRD Present Condition

Despite certain differences, HRD is characterised by stable tendencies and specifics in the developed Western countries. This is due to their high economic growth, technological development, high living standard, and the establishment of some new approaches, related to society management, new organisational concepts, and new theoretical models of the individual human being. Until the end of the nineteenth century the stress was laid on economic and capital resources and technologies; not much attention was paid to the HRD. In the beginning of the twentieth century the so-called *scientific approach to the management* of industrial enterprises, taking into account production, the means of production, and the manufacturing instruments was introduced. It also put stress on the effectiveness of the human labour behaviour. During the 1930s, the so-called *humanitarian approach* was imposed. It accounted not only for the economic factors within the industrial sector, but also for the human factor—the human personality, its motivations, needs, interests, and so on. During the 1970s the concept of the organisation as a closed rational unit was put behind. The organisation was seen as *an open, dynamic social system*, which was constantly changing and developing. That would require a permanent change and development of its human resources. The *organic human model* was imposed, according to which the human being was considered to be a living, organised, growing, and developing organism. The result of all this is a stable social practice with respect to this phenomenon.

Change and Development of Human Resources

The resources within a society represent a dynamic combination, which is constantly changing. For the natural resources, that means *depletion and deterioration*: arable land is decreased and polluted; forests, drinking water, oil, and other natural resources decrease. For the human resources, that means *increase and improvement*: increase in population, health care improvement, educational funds. For example, with the increase of population and technological development, the percentages of educated people increases, as well as the educational methods improve. With the increase of the population in the future, the so-called distance learning will be imposed via the Internet. In the future this form of education will dominate over the classical form.

The HR development is triggered by the following changes. *First*, there are global changes in *international relations*, leading to the withering away of states, creation of new states, change in geopolitical strategies of the great powers, and so on, which of course reflects on HRD. There are three peak moments for these changes in the twentieth century: the end of World War I, the end of World War II, and the end of the Cold War, marked with the Eastern European revolutions in 1989. *Second*, there are *market changes*

in national, regional, and world aspects, having a significant influence over HRD. *Third, internal political changes* in the countries (the imposition of communism in Russia with its concentration camps, the Cultural Revolution in China, the Pol Pot regime in Cambodia, etc.) also play their role on HRD. *Fourth, demographic changes* and the migration waves, urbanisation, etc. related to them are one more significant reason leading to change in HR. *Fifth, management changes* and specifically management styles of economic organisations, of small and big social entities and of whole societies have a significant impact on HRD. *Technological changes and outbreaks* (as the AIDS outbreak) may be classified in a different category of factors influencing HRD. W*orld terrorism* may be another factor impacting HRD in the future.

HRD Specifics in the Developing World

Tendencies of change are typical of HR as a whole, but the dynamics of this change are different for different countries and regions. For example, in North America and Europe there is a tendency of decreasing birth rate and population ageing given the permanent increase in living standard, improvement in health care and education. On the other hand, in most developing countries there is the opposite tendency. Moreover, not only are there differences in HRD from region to region of states, but there are differences among states from the same region. Globally there is an extremely complicated picture of the condition and dynamics of HRD change. The HRD complexity arises from the world's differentiation in the political, economic, demographic, informational, and cultural aspects. As a result HRD has a different status in the western democracies, in the developing world, in the former socialist countries, in the countries of the rich North and the poor South. For example, one of the HR problems in the developing world is education and the lack of experts in the different social spheres. The situation in the former socialist countries is exactly the opposite—experts with university education create the major part of unemployment. Moreover, after the 1989 revolutions it was mostly people with university degrees that emigrated from those countries to Western democracies. Differences can be observed while comparing countries from the Asian region to Eastern-European countries. For example, during the 1990s there was a lack of experts with university degrees in South Korea. At the same time in Bulgaria, a country with extremely developed educational system, the situation was the opposite: due to the lack of employment during this period, 10% of the Bulgarian population moved abroad—primarily people with university education, doctors of science, university professors. Further on during that decade, big differences in the educational system may be observed even in countries formerly belonging to the Eastern Bloc. For example, two of the tendencies describing the Hungarian educational system are related to fast legislative changes and the slow changes in educational curriculums and programs. In Bulgaria the situation was the opposite—slow legislative changes in the educational system and fast changes in the educational programs and curriculums. The differentiation in HRD is obvious when related to population growth: the Third World countries are facing a high birth rate problem, while in the Eastern European countries the problem is low birth rate and population ageing. There are big differences even in countries from the same region: for example Albania is described as the country with the highest population growth, that is, as the youngest nation in Europe. The negative population growth characterises Bulgaria as one of the ageing European nations. It is impossible to draw conclusions about HRD based on ideological and political criteria, because very often the condition of this phenomenon varies greatly in countries with the same political system. The countries from the former Eastern Bloc that shared the same ideology may provide an example for this. In countries like Poland, Hungary, the Czech Republic, and Bulgaria, some of the basic aspects of HRD as centralised planning, educational liberalisation, and economic freedom tend to change. The same cannot be claimed for some of the former Soviet republics. Therefore, it is not correct to analyse HRD on the basis of some geographical, economic, or political features. Complex factors affecting change must be used. The situation becomes much more complicated when we discuss HRD in economic organisations, and specifically personnel development. The analyses and conclusions must be drawn on the basis of specific economic, political, cultural, and social conditions, existing in each given country.

KRUM KRUMOV

See also United Nations Development Program (UNDP); United Nations Economic and Social Council

References and Further Reading

Borman, W.C., Hanson, M.A., Hedge, J. W. *Personnel selection*. In: *Annual Review of Psychology*, 48, 299–337, 1997.

Dowling, P.J., Schuler, R.S., Welch, D. *International Dimensions of Human Resource Management (2nd ed.)*. Boston: PWS-Kent, 1994.

Ferris, G.R., Hochwater, W.A., Buckley, M.R., Harrell-Cook, G., Frink, D.D. *Human Resources Management: Some New Directions*. In: *Journal of Management*, Vol. 25 Issue 3, p.385, 31p, 1999.

Ferris, G.R., Rosen, S.D., Barnum, D.T. (Eds.), *Handbook of Human Resource Management*. Oxford, UK: Blackwell Publishers, 1995.

Graham, H.T. *Human Resources Management, 8th ed.*, London: Pitman, 1995.

Harrison, R. *Employee Development London*. Institute of Personnel and Development, 1997.

Massey, O.T. *Evaluating Human Resource Development Programs: A Practical Guide for Public Agencies*. Needham Heights, MA: Allyn & Bacon, 1996.

Mulder, M., Romiszowski, A.J., P.C. van der Sijde (Eds.). *Strategic Human Resource Development*. Amsterdam: Swets & Zeitlinger, 1990.

Robbins, S.P. *Organizational Behavior: Concepts, Controversies, Applications*. (8th ed.). Prentice Hall Upper Saddle River, New Jersey, 1998.

Rothwell, W., Kazanas, H. *Strategic Human Resource Planning and Management*. Englewood Cliffs, NJ: Prentice-Hall, 1991.

Schultz, D. P., Schultz, S.E. *Psychology and Work Today: An Introduction to Industrial and Organizational Psychology* (7th ed.). Prentice Hall Upper Saddle River, NJ, 1998.

Wright, P.M., Dyer, L.D., Boudreau, J.M., Milkovich, G.T. (Eds) *Strategic Human Resources Management in the Twenty-First Century*. Stamford, CT: JAI Press, 1999.

HUMAN RIGHTS AS A FOREIGN POLICY ISSUE

Human rights and foreign policy are intimately connected. Human rights are those rights that all human beings should have just by being human. In international law, human rights are those rights agreed upon by nation-states in international fora applicable to all human beings. An important part of the conventions and treaties signed is the obligation to protect and promote human rights. Foreign policy therefore clearly involves working towards better protection of human rights in the world as a whole. However, in practice states who sign international human rights agreements and follow their dictums domestically are often reluctant to do the same in the realm of foreign policy. The reasons are mainly that sometimes the support of human rights abroad goes against its political and economic interests. For example, neither the United States nor the European Community wants to risk their trade relations with the Chinese government despite its record of human rights violations. And the big weapon manufacturing states do not want human rights considerations to get in the way of selling arms. Despite the proviso that no arms are sold to countries that use them against their own people, weapons as well as instruments of torture are on the export lists of western European states.

Still, human rights are put firmly on the foreign policy agenda in the case of humanitarian intervention, sanctions, and conditional aid programmes. The dilemmas raised by supporting human rights while aiming to avoid harm (to another country's sovereignty, to foreign populations, or to economic self-interest) have been widely debated. Despite human rights being recognised by governments worldwide in conventions and declarations, the implications of those commitments are not always taken seriously. Although hardly anyone would argue that human rights are not part of a foreign policy agenda at all now, there are still many examples of where they take second place to other considerations in theory and in practice.

Here we want to give an overview of the development of the human rights agenda and argue that human rights are and should be an important part of foreign policy; not only in everyday diplomacy, but also in trade policy, aid policy and contributions to multilateral fora.

Human Rights

Human rights are those rights to which all individuals are inherently entitled. They have been increasingly codified in international law. Their history can be traced back to the notion of citizenship in the Ancient Greek city-states and has been developed further in the works of John Locke and the debates surrounding the American Declaration of Independence (1776) and the French Revolution (1789) (Freeman in Smith and van den Anker 2005). The development of the current human rights documents developed further through the Geneva Conventions on humanitarian rules of war and warfare and the League of Nations convention on slavery amongst others.

After the Second World War, the victorious allies established the United Nations with the aim of preventing world war and advancing peace. The Charter of the United Nations included human rights as part of its goals. Since the Second World War, international human rights law have developed into a detailed and complex field (Baehr in Smith and van den Anker 2005).

In 1966, the two twin Covenants were agreed upon, although the Cold War made it necessary to split them into separate documents: one on civil and political rights and one on economic, social, and cultural rights. The principle of non-intervention was gradually interpreted as allowing involvement of the international community with the human rights record of states. Dedicated conventions were established, a duty to report was developed and Special Rapporteurs were sent to assess the situation in specific countries. Recently, the International Criminal Court has been inaugurated which means that there is no longer impunity for crimes against humanity and other gross violations of human rights (Williams *et al.* in Smith and van den Anker 2005). Alongside the United Nations, other institutions have defended and codified international human rights law, like the International Labor Organization (ILO) and the regional human rights systems. The most effective is the European system which has a court and individual complaints procedures.

This development has not proceeded effortlessly; social movements and human rights lawyers fought hard for it (Gready 2004). Possibly the oldest human rights movement is the anti-slavery campaign. Generally trade unions, the anti-colonial nationalist movements and the women's rights movement resulted in further codification. Special campaigns on behalf of children's rights, minority, and indigenous peoples' rights led to the drafting of conventions. The Child Rights Convention is the most widely ratified convention in the world. Unfortunately the Draft Declaration on Indigenous Peoples of the United Nations has not yet been ratified.

Despite this enormous progress since 1945 and the renewed impetus after the end of the Cold War, nation-states still fight against outside interference with their human rights record. For a long time, states argued that how a government treated its citizens was a matter of domestic affairs. When gradually the idea of human rights as an international concern was accepted, states started to use arguments of cultural relativism instead. Especially with reference to Asian values, some states argue that although they do not reject human rights concerns, they claim the right to interpret international human rights according to their own culture (Svensson 2002). African leaders, too, have criticised the western conception of human rights. And Islamic states argue in favour of Islamic law governing Islamic states. Yet, in Vienna at the World Conference on Human Rights in 1993, human rights were accepted as universal. Although there is a way of tracing human rights back to Western concepts, there were several people from non-Western countries involved in the drawing up of the Universal Declaration; the values of human dignity and respect for all living beings can be found in many of the world's main religions and philosophies. Moreover, there are good philosophical arguments against relativism which leave respect for cultures in place (Caney and Jones 2000; Caney 2001).

Human rights have also been criticised from many other angles. Marxism holds that human rights are a bourgeois concept, protecting the interests of the property holding classes. However, Marx conceded that the rights of the citizen were a possible step forward, as they emphasised people's belonging in a political community and did not separate people from one another as property rights do (Waldron 1987). Utilitarians have famously called human rights "nonsense upon stilts" and argued that the overall happiness of a political community is more important than a set of rights (Bentham in Waldron 1987). Conservatives have argued against rights since the French Revolution; Edmund Burke, for example, thought that adopting a Declaration on the Rights of Man would lead to oppression due to revolutions always turning into oppressive forces once successful. In terms of the French Revolution he may have been accurately predicting, yet the question remains whether that is a reason to reject a basic set of human rights in favour of an organically developing society. Feminism, finally, has criticised human rights discourse for using a male perspective on what it means to be human and leaving out the concerns of women by focusing almost exclusively on the public realm. However, feminism has also supported women's rights as human rights and the Convention on the Elimination of All forms of Discrimination Against Women (CEDAW) has been instrumental in getting concerns like rape (in or outside marriage and as an instrument of ethnic cleansing in war time) and domestic violence on the international human rights agenda.

Mostly, human rights are a weapon for the struggle of oppressed people and campaigns against (former) dictators. However, human rights discourse is also used to justify wars, and many nations change their definitions of human rights when a threat to national security is perceived.

The History of Human Rights and Foreign Policy

Human rights as a foreign policy issue has had a bumpy ride in history, too. From the early documented struggle between the Spartans and the Athenians in Thucydides' *Peloponnesian wars* we already know the division between those who hold that all human action and therefore the treatment of other societies should be based on justice and those who base their actions on power. This division can be found again in modern International Relations theory between Realism which holds that the self-interest of the state

should guide foreign policy and Liberal institutionalism which holds that human values like justice, peace and freedom should guide external affairs of states. Historically, the liberal institutionalists are supported by theories developed by Kant in the eighteenth century and earlier on by Grotius in the sixteenth century. Kant argued that all moral action should be based on the principle of universalizability and Grotius argued that the principle of sociability was the basis for international law (van den Anker 2000). World system theories of international relations are skeptical of normative accounts of international relations as their structuralist analysis fears human rights will be used as a mask for underlying interests at least in cases where the social struggle for human rights is left out of the account. In some ways this leaves world systems approaches in the Realist camp on the divide between empirically based theories and normative theories of international relations. However, world systems theory does share a critical approach to power in international relations and does therefore have a basis to support at least some role for human rights in foreign policy. This would be subject to conditions of the actors being free from corrupting concerns for their state's interests.

The contrast between these different theories of international relations plays out in political debates on human rights as an issue of foreign policy. Explicitly ethical foreign policies were designed by Robin Cook in the United Kingdom and Jan Kavan in the Czech Republic. One of the prominently pro–human rights foreign policies was also the former United States president Carter's; although with hindsight his record was mixed. Former United States secretary of state Albright claims in her autobiography that human rights was one of her main concerns; however, the United States did not intervene in the Rwandan genocide that took place during her term in office.

The role of human rights in foreign policy is thus a hotly contested issue and after contextualising it in the wider discussion of ethics and international relations we will now look in more detail in which areas of foreign policy human rights play a role, how this role has been viewed both in contemporary and historical debates and what its role should be.

Basic Diplomatic Relations

The most well-known part of foreign policy is that of basic diplomatic relations. This area of foreign policy is directly related to human rights. For example should the United Kingdom cricket team play in Zimbabwe, where Robert Mugabe has been accused of dictatorship and human rights violations? The answers to this type of question rely on the judgment of what, if any, actions can assist in supporting human rights protection abroad. In addition, human rights play and should play a role in policies on the recognition of new nation-states. Should the right to self-determination, which is well protected in international human rights law, be given priority in cases where the recognition of a newly established nation-state is offensive to the former territorial power?

Humanitarian Intervention

The doctrine of humanitarian intervention holds that when fundamental human rights are persistently violated on a large scale, despite the Westphalian notion of self-determination as a basic value in international law, military intervention is a right of the international community. Moreover, in such cases there is not only a right to intervene, there is a duty on behalf of the affected population. This doctrine is a specific form of Just War which has been recognised in historical debates on international law. Humanitarian intervention can be defined as a military intervention to stop excessive human rights abuses in another sovereign state. The European Parliament defines humanitarian intervention as "the protection, including the threat or use of force, by a state or group of states of the basic human rights of persons who are subjects and/or residents of another state." This definition is wider than strictly military intervention; it includes the threat of force.

Historically, intervention was seen as linked to self-determination not only by a government but by the citizens of that state. Both Kant and J.S. Mill viewed non-intervention as based on the principle of self-determination of citizens to determine their own way of life. In addition to this principled stance against intervention, Mill viewed the bad consequences of intervention as good reasons against it. According to him, people can't hold onto freedom given by intervention and after intervention either a foreign power would rule or it would provide heavy support for the "free" government or civil war would ensue. Mill's list of practical difficulties would also include the lack of transparency to establish who are authentic "freedom fighters" and the fear that "dirty hands" of violent means might turn into "dangerous hands." In other words, lofty goals of intervention based on the right to self-determine the political power would mask imperialism by the intervening state (Doyle in Pogge 2001).

Historical arguments in favour of humanitarian intervention have included cosmopolitan arguments

holding that the right to freedom is valuable everywhere for all people and this should override the principle of non-intervention. Mill saw three other good reasons to override the non-intervention principle: (1) when non-intervention can neglect vital international sources of national security; (2) following a just war to remove "menace to peace"; and (3) when protracted civil war causes suffering for the non-combatant population. Walzer argues in favour of humanitarian intervention if national self-determination is undermined by domestic oppression. He recognises three cases: (1) when too many nations contest same territory; (2) when another power has intervened in a civil war; and (3) for humanitarian purposes in case of genocide, slavery, and so forth. These types of argument are also supported in the so-called doctrine of new interventionism. Doyle argues that this is due to both the revival of multilateralism in the early 1990s and the development of innovative forms of intervention like peacemaking, peacekeeping, peace-building, and peace-enforcing.

Generally, it is recognised that humanitarian intervention, just like other forms of just war, needs to be based on a set of criteria. Most lists have the following elements in common: proportionality of violence; last resort after negotiations; right reasons: impartiality; guided by international law and multilateral support. The questions that need to be answered in order to establish the limits of new interventionism are:

- When is it legitimate to intervene in another state?
- When, if at all, have humanitarian interventions ever produced good results and how, if at all, can they be safeguarded?
- Are there circumstances when the international community is required to intervene?

Simon Caney (2005) argues that humanitarian intervention can be justified on the basis of cosmopolitan principles, yet others argue for peaceful means of human rights protection, such as support for internal opposition. Humanitarian intervention remains a central part of the discussion on human rights and foreign policy and currently the consensus seems to be on some form of interventionism while the main threat seems to lie in the abuse of the human rights argument for wars based on geopolitical interests.

Economic and Trade Policy

Another pressing question to establish the link between human rights and foreign policy is the following: does the need for employment in Western countries outweigh the interests of people in East Timor suffering from weapons exported to Indonesia and people in Turkey from torture instruments imported from the West?

In contrast, should economic sanctions be implemented on states that have committed gross violations of human rights? It has been argued that when human rights are violated routinely, massively and seriously, sanctions are justified. In the case of South Africa, sanctions are thought to have had a positive impact on the time it took to dismantle apartheid. However, in the case of Iraq, sanctions were seen as harming the population, especially the Iraqi children. And Colombia has not been sanctioned, despite the civil wars and the disappearances and killings of trade unionists.

One of the main dilemmas in determining the balance between human rights and self-interested foreign policy lies in trade policy. The example of China shows this very accurately. United States president Clinton decided in 1994 to grant China Most Favoured Nation (MFN) status despite its human rights record; this was a move away from earlier policy which raised the issue of human rights in diplomatic and trade missions (Morris 2002). Some argue that economic development and integration in the world market will take care of China's human rights record. So where is China now that it has been partly integrated for some time? The scope for individual expression has widened. The living standard has gone up for most of the citizenry. Government transparency has increased. The press is less controllable. The harshest restrictions on freedom of movement have been weakened. Criminal, administrative, and civil law reforms have taken place. Experiments in local democracy have been extended and there is human rights education for law students. However, criminal sanctions are still being used against political dissidents. The death penalty is widely applied. The police still detain people without due process. The state exercises control over information. The government maintains a strict family planning policy. Discrimination on the basis of health status, especially for people who are infected with HIV/AIDS, still exists. There are still restrictions on freedoms of assembly, association, and religion. The most famous example is the suppression of the Falungong movement (Stearns in Smith and van den Anker 2005). And the occupation of Tibet remains severe.

What can be learned from the case of China is that foreign policy is one factor among others in promoting human rights; despite receiving MFN status without further discussion of the wide range of human rights violated in China, the country did move forward in terms of human rights. This may mean that a hybrid model of different forms of pressure may be more useful than strict adherence only to an ethical foreign policy which includes the heaviest pressure from diplomats and trade missions (Fleay 2004).

Development Aid: Conditionality

Historically, conditionality of development aid has been part of the agenda of good governance. It can be defined as the tying of aid by donors to conditions that must be fulfilled by recipients. Economic conditionality was a core element of the Structural Adjustment Programmes (SAPs) of the 1980s and 1990s. Some countries already included human rights and democracy in their aid policies in the 1970s although these policies were often more to strengthen local efforts than to make aid conditional. What donors demand varies, but despite the differences there are some common components: democracy and respect for human rights; some form of social justice and some emphasis on sustainable development to preserve the local environment.

Justifications for conditionality are usually based on either principles or predicted outcomes. Examples of justificatory principles are that democracy and human rights need to be protected around the globe and they are valid in their own terms, even if they do not bring about economic development directly. Justification in terms of results emphasises that political conditionality will bring about economic development, peace, stability, less migration to the West, more trading partners in the world economy and similar type of reasoning. Generally speaking the results are often supposed to be good for the receiving country as well as the donor country.

Conditionality has been criticised and in some cases has been withdrawn as a policy as a result. Widespread criticisms raise the question of whether political conditionality is successful in bringing about respect for human rights and democracy, whether or not democracy and human rights really aid economic development, and whether economic development is the real aim of political conditionality.

Here we would argue in addition that human rights and democracy are often mentioned as if they were basically the same thing in arguments for conditionality of aid. It makes sense to carefully distinguish between measures towards democratisation and measures to protect human rights. Although certain human rights violations are not compatible with democracies, others are not excluded from either the liberal democratic or the popular participation model of democracy.

Let us now assess whether the different parts of the argument for political conditionality work.

Human Rights and Development

Human Rights are often interpreted as meaning civil and political rights only, with an emphasis on freedom of the press and the rule of law. Any social and economic rights are seen as of lower priority which is rather strange if the aim is development.

In the political conditionality discourse, respect for human rights leads to economic development. But often in the debate on human rights and development, human rights were thought to be a barrier to development. Economic development was thought to be a priority and respect for human rights would come second. This trade-off theory is not very plausible. There is no guarantee that the postponed needs, equalities and freedoms are going to be restored once development takes off. The trickle-down theory of wealth has not been proven at all in practice nor in theory and to rely on the expectation that with democratisation there will be an automatic restoration of human rights is both naive and dangerous.

Although the theory of trade offs has been shown to be highly problematic, it is not clear at all that there is an automatic link between respect for human rights and economic development. It depends on which human rights are going to be prioritised whether or not their implementation is helpful to economic development. And it depends on what kind of economic development one envisages. For example, if social and economic rights are prioritised some argue that development will be harmed, because they aim at economic growth as an indicator of development. However, someone else may see the improved access to health care and education as an indicator of development. The main point here is that without a proper definition of the type of rights to be prioritised and the kind of development aimed for, the assumptions of the political conditionality discourse are no more than empty rhetoric.

A second line of argument holds that political conditionality is based on a Western concept of human rights. The universal applicability of human rights is contested and it is claimed that different cultures have different underlying values they adhere to. The West has therefore no right to impose its own values on the rest of the world. This argument from the position of cultural relativism is often complemented by an argument against the hypocrisy of the West in its implementation of penalties for human rights abuse. The general claim that rights should be different according to cultural values is plausible if what is meant is that the interpretation of the implementation of rights needs to be sensitive to cultural practices (Donnelly 1989). However, the list of rights that should be respected and enforced by any government cannot be open to cultural interpretation, since it would be unfair if a human being could be treated differently in terms of basic respect and dignity according to which place it was born.

Overwhelming evidence supports the argument about hypocrisy from the West. Strong and strategic countries like China, for example, can get away with literally murder, whereas small poor countries like Malawi will be criticised much more easily.

Democracy and Development

Democracy can be seen as one of two major models: the popular participation and the liberal democratic model. Depending on which model one adheres to, different priorities in policy will be emphasised. Some actors in the international aid arena see liberal democracy as strongly linked to principles of free markets with minimal government intervention. The requirements of such a democracy are mainly free and fair multi-party elections and adherence of the government to the rule of law. Others argue for stronger participation from citizens and more government intervention into economic matters. Investment of the government in a welfare system is seen as supportive of a well-functioning democracy. These differences in conception of democracy are important omissions in the debate on political conditionality.

Second, there is no overwhelming evidence that democratic regimes bring about economic development. This is partly due to a weak definition of democracy. Some countries have formal systems of multi-party elections, but in fact the old clientelism still exists.

Does Political Conditionality Bring About Economic Development?

There is no proper evaluation, but the conclusions are divided. Sometimes political conditionality is seen as having results, but these results are too superficial according to others. In terms of democracy it is said that only with a strong movement within the country itself the democratic regime is strong enough to make an impact on economic development.

Is Economic Development the Real Aim of Political Conditionality?

Some forceful critics argue that political conditionality has nothing to do with the aim of promoting economic development. This analysis is in line with the arguments put forward that human rights are hijacked in order to win support for self-interested policies. However, it is more likely that there is at least some concern for human rights involved in the policy of conditionality.

In summary, political conditionality must be defined more clearly. It must define its aims and objectives more clearly in order to be properly evaluated. Political conditionality must be clear on its justifications: principled or based on results; it must show those results are actually linked to political conditionality. Political conditionality must overcome objections based on its interpretation of the links between human rights and development and democracy and development; it must address the critique from cultural relativism that it is nothing more than imperialism of Western ideas. It must show that there is a higher moral aim to overcome the principle of non-intervention. It must look into the possibilities of non-governmental organizations (NGOs) in assisting the development of human rights practices and democracy from the bottom up. Examples: Amnesty co-operating with development NGOs. However, it is clearly an area of foreign policy where human rights are and should be relevant.

Conclusion

Historically, the theoretical division between ethical foreign policy and self-interest as the basis for external relations of states has made international politics a complex arena to assess for its morality. Although, with the development of international human rights law, human rights have taken up a place of growing importance in the actions of the international community, exactly how and to what extent they should be issues of foreign policy is still a matter of much political debate. Governments are still trying to balance their obligations under international law to protect and promote human rights everywhere in the world, with policies based on their economic and geo-strategical self-interest. These will not always clash but they may do sometimes.

In a time of globalisation, it is especially important to make the world's riches work for all and to confront the extreme poverty and deprivation for 47%

of the population living on less than two dollars a day. However, with human rights implementation instruments still prioritising civil and political rights, democracy and the rule of law over the provision for social economic and cultural rights the international community still has a long way to go. And despite regionalisation making clear that national interest can be overcome as the single motivating factor in external relations, cosmopolitan convictions to govern the world on humanitarian motives are not a reality yet.

Still, human rights are firmly believed to be a matter for the international community and with help from non-governmental organisations violations are legitimately raised at the highest levels in the United Nations.

We can't get away from the fact that HR are part of our dealings with other states and therefore of foreign policy in the widest sense. What foreign policy works best to implement human rights: economic sanctions, economic development, partnership and dialogue, support for dissidents, will depend on each specific case. With the current agendas of international terrorism and neo-liberal economic polices gaining ground, it remains (and increasingly so) true that human rights need to be fought for.

CHRISTIEN VAN DEN ANKER

See also Amnesty International; Balkan Wars of the 1990s; China, People's Republic of; Helsinki Final Act on Human Rights (1975); Human Rights: Definition and Violations; Military and Human Rights; Rwanda; Universal Declaration of Human Rights

References and Further Reading

Anker, van den, C. 'The Role of Globalisation in Arguments for Cosmopolitanism' *Acta Politica* 35(1): 5–36, 2000.
Baehr, P., in R.K. Smith and C. van den Anker (eds.) *The Essentials of Human rights.* Hodder: 345–347, 2005.
Baehr, P., and Castermans-Holleman, M. *The role of human rights in foreign policy.* Palgrave, 2004 (3d ed.).
Caney, S. *Justice beyond borders: a global political theory.* Oxford University Press, 2005.
Caney, S. in C. van den Anker (guest editor) Cosmopolitanism, Distributive Justice and Violence, Special Issue *Global Society* 14(4): 525–552, 2000.
Caney, S., and Jones, P. *Human rights and global diversity.* Frank Cass, 2000.
Doyle, M.W. 'The New Interventionism' in Th. W. Pogge *Global Justice* Oxford, Blackwell: 219–241, 2001.
Dunne, T. 'Foreign policy and human rights' in R.K. Smith and C. van den Anker (eds.) *The Essentials of Human rights.* Hodder: 110–112, 2005.
Fleay, C. *The impact of internal and external responses on human rights practices in China: the Chinese Government and the spiral model,* conference paper presented at BISA, Warwick, 2004.

Freeman, M., in R.K. Smith and C. van den Anker (eds.) *The Essentials of Human rights*. Hodder: 151–153, 2005.

Gready, P. (ed.) *Fighting for human rights*. Routledge, 2004.

Morris, S.C. *Trade and human rights. The ethical dimension in US-China relations*. Ashgate, 2002.

Smith, K., and Light, M. (eds) *Ethics and foreign policy*. Cambridge University Press, 2001.

Stearns, L. 'Human rights in China' in: R.K. Smith and C. van den Anker (eds.) *The Essentials of Human rights*. Hodder: 44–47, 2005.

Svensson, M. *Debating human rights in China. A conceptual and political history*. Rowman and Littlefield, 2002.

Waldron, J. *Non-sense upon stilts*. Methuen, 1987.

Williams, A., *et al.* in R.K. Smith and C. van den Anker (eds.) *The Essentials of Human rights*. Hodder: 198–200, 2005.

HUMAN RIGHTS: DEFINITION AND VIOLATIONS

Defining Human Rights

The concept of human rights as it is defined today did not exist in the past and is still denied by some political leaders in the present. Human rights advocates define human rights as legitimate claims that people can make on their societies or against their governments. The first modern, comprehensive statement on human rights was the Universal Declaration of Human Rights (UDHR) adopted by the United Nations (UN) General Assembly in 1948. According to the Declaration, the human rights to which all people are entitled because of their inherent human dignity include (but are not limited to): the rights to life, liberty, and security of person; freedom from torture and discrimination based on race, religion, ethnicity, or gender; freedom of thought, conscience, religion, opinion, speech, and press; the right to participate in the political system, to own property, to marry and have a family, to associate with others; freedom from arbitrary arrest and searches; the right to a fair trial, to confront prosecution witnesses, to put on witnesses and evidence in one's own defense; the right to work, to an education; and the right to maintain one's culture and native language.

The Declaration, however, is a legally non-binding, aspirational document that states may sign, but do not ratify. Subsequently, the UN General Assembly adopted numerous human rights conventions that states may ratify and thereby legally obligate themselves to protect the rights contained in the conventions.

Although the UDHR was not designed to be a legally binding document, more than 185 states have incorporated its principles into their constitutions. Therefore, some legal scholars now maintain that the UDHR has achieved the status of customary international law, meaning that it legally binds all governments, because it is a common standard of achievement for all people and all nations.

The Natural Law Justification for Human Rights

The various UN human rights documents proclaim that the justification or source for university human rights is the universal dignity of humankind. This justification derives from the natural law philosophies that Greek, Latin, Christian, Enlightenment, and other thinkers developed over the ages. The common ingredients of these philosophies consist in the beliefs that law is not humanly made in the first instance. It is inherent in nature or, according to theologians, created by god. Humans discover natural law through the application of their natural intellects and natural moral sense, and then fashion it into more particular rules of conduct.

This natural law justification for universal human rights was asserted eloquently in the American Declaration of Independence of July 4, 1776:

> We hold these truths to be self-evident, that all men are created equal, that they are endowed by their creator with certain inalienable rights, that among these are Life, Liberty and the pursuit of Happiness. That to secure these rights, governments are instituted among men, deriving just powers from the consent of the governed. That whenever any form of government becomes destructive of these ends, it is the right of the people to alter or abolish it, . . .

This writing was inspired by the seventeenth and eighteenth century English political philosopher, John Locke, who is often recognized as the father of human rights. Locke maintained that in nature people were equal and free, and that the ideal society was based on a social contract between the people and those who governed. Those who follow Locke's reasoning, argue that all humans are entitled to human rights because all people possess human dignity.

Locke's thinking also influenced the preamble to the 1948 Universal Declaration of Human Rights, which begins with these words: "Whereas recognition of the inherent dignity and of the equal and inalienable rights of all members of the human family is the foundation of freedom, justice and peace in the world . . . "

The Positivist Justification for Human Rights

Those jurisprudential scholars, known as legal positivists, reject natural law philosophies. They maintain that if human rights are to be conceived of as legal rights, that is, as something more than moral aspirations, then their source is in legal authority, not in god or nature. Legal positivists argue that unless and until the sovereign authority of a state grants human rights, they do not exist.

This idea of national sovereign authority originated in sixteenth and seventeenth century Europe as a counter to the theological basis of authority relied on by the Popes. It found support among the Machiavellian princes who wanted to carve up Europe into independent domains within which they could claim supreme authority unhindered in the treatment of their subjects by outside forces.

These princes located the ultimate source of sovereignty in their own persons. Hence, they called themselves sovereigns, and, according to such legal positivists as John Austin (1832), they were the ultimate source of law. Law, Austin wrote, is nothing more than the command of a sovereign person or group to subjects. Hence, human rights as legal rights were nothing more than the sovereign's law.

In the international arena, executive sovereignty meant that international law applied to relations between states exclusively. International law did not apply to human rights violations by sovereigns against their own subjects. That subject matter fell exclusively within the domestic jurisdiction of each state.

In order to counteract universalistic notions of brotherhood and sisterhood that might infringe on their prerogatives, sovereigns have promoted the ideology of ethnonationalism. This ideology claims that some population of humans is distinct from and superior to all others on the basis of some arbitrarily selected or artificially created set of biological and cultural criteria. This kind of thinking led to genocide in Europe during World War II, ethnic cleansing in Bosnia and Kosovo in the 1990s, and other grave human rights violations.

The counters to executive sovereignty and ethnocentric ethnonationalism are democracy and humanistic universalism. Democracy is the political philosophy that maintains that government is legitimate to the extent that its authority to rule is derived from the consent of the people. Humanistic universalism stands for the equal dignity of all persons regardless of their race, creed, class, sex, class, or political nationality.

Religion's Contribution to Human Rights

Religions historically did not grant individuals inalienable rights; instead they imposed duties on people to god or the gods, who threaten to punish violators in this world or the next. As Elaine Pagels, professor of history and religion at Columbia University, writes, "the notion of human rights was absent from the legal conceptions of the Romans and Greeks; this seems to hold equally true of the Jewish, Chinese, and all other ancient civilizations that have since come to light" (Pagels 1979: 2).

The universal religions did, however, help lay the foundation for human rights by holding that all peoples were created by the same god and by promoting the golden rule: "Thou shall love thy neighbor as thy self" or "Do unto other as you would like others to do unto you." These ideas help promote the belief in the equal dignity of all people.

Human Rights and Human Nature

The ultimate source of universal human rights may lay in the universal psycho-biological nature of humans, rather than in the abstract and idealized concept of natural law. Humans universally have magnificent brains that give them the ability to think, create, invent, imagine, manipulate abstract symbols, anticipate the future, and learn from the past. They have a complex vocal apparatus that enables the brain to express itself orally in the complex, highly developed communication systems we call language. Human bodies are, in part, self-regulating survival machines. Our nervous system tells us when we need nourishment, water, heat or cooling, rest or exercise. Our bodies naturally recoil from pain. We are naturally social beings who love others, bond with others, and develop mentally and emotionally through interaction with others.

Because of these natural endowments, humans naturally want and value the freedom to think, to express their thoughts, to bond with others, to be free from torture, to have an adequate diet, shelter, and clothing. They value and want to be free to learn and develop their mental abilities. Because of their shared psycho-biological nature, people universally do not want to be killed, tortured, enslaved, robbed of their vital possessions, starved, prevented from learning, thinking, communicating with others, or associating with their loved ones and friends, etc. These universal human wants and values have existed throughout human history. Consequently, whenever people were in a position to do so, they endeavored to secure these wants and values for themselves from their rulers. It is only recently that these protections have become, for some people, legal human rights.

The process whereby human wants and values were transformed into legalized human rights was a slow one that involved demands made by subjugated peoples against their contemporary and future rulers. The process involved social and political revolutions. The three documents commonly named as historic stepping stones to contemporary human rights conventions are: Magna Carta (1215), the American Declaration of Independence (1776), and the French Declaration of the Rights of Man and of the Citizen (1789). All three of these documents were associated with political revolutions. In all three cases, a proper-tied class of men demanded rights for themselves and imposed corresponding duties on their sovereigns. In the case of the American colonies, these propertied men also established the seeds for a political democracy—a political system in which even common people can effectively strive to translate their universal human wants and values into rights for themselves and corresponding governmental duties. Democracy locates the source of sovereignty in the people themselves, not in their rulers. Hence, democracy replaces executive sovereignty with popular sovereignty.

Unfortunately, the early American promoters of democracy were not as universal as they should have been. Slavery existed legally in the United States until 1865 (Thirteenth Amendment) and the voting rights amendment for women was not passed until 1920 (Nineteenth Amendment). It took a civil war and volatile civil rights movements to address racial and gender inequities.

The United Nations and Human Rights

Owing to the atrocities of World War II, governments committed themselves to creating the United Nations with the goal of securing peace by developing friendly relations among states and "respect for human rights and for fundamental freedoms for all without distinction as to race, sex, language, or religion" (UN Charter Art. 1.3). Within the UN, the responsibility for promoting human rights falls mainly on the General Assembly, the Economic and Social Council (ECOSOC), Commission on Human Rights, and High Commissioner for Human Rights (UNHCHR).

The UN Commission on Human Rights, an intergovernmental subsidiary body of ECOSOC, serves as the UN's central policy organ in the human rights field. It, along with other UN bodies such as the International Labor Organization, the United Nations Educational, Scientific and Cultural Organization (UNESCO), and the UN Commission on the Status of Women, has drafted a number of international human rights declarations and conventions, which it presented to the General Assembly for its adoption and, in the case of conventions, subsequent ratification by member countries. Among the most important of these have been the Universal Declaration of Human Rights, The Convention on the Prevention and Punishment of the Crime of Genocide (1948), the International Covenant on Civil and Political Rights together with its Optional Protocols (1966; 1989), the International Covenant on Economic, Social and Cultural Rights (1966), International Convention on the Elimination of All Forms of Racial Discrimination (1965), the Convention on the Elimination of All Forms of Discrimination against Women (1979), the Convention against Torture and Other Cruel, Inhuman or Degrading Treatment or Punishment (1984), and the Convention on the Rights of the Child (1989).

The International Bill of Human Rights

Because of their fundamental character, the 1948 Universal Declaration of Human Rights (UDHR), the International Covenant on Civil and Political Rights (ICCPR), and the International Covenant on Economic, Social and Cultural Rights (ICESCR) have together become known as "International Bill of Human Rights." These three instruments provide the basis for interpreting the somewhat abstract human rights provisions of the UN Charter, and most of the subsequent human rights conventions elaborate on their articles.

The UN General Assembly unanimously adopted the UDHR on December 10, 1948, by forty-eight positive votes and eight abstentions. Owing to disagreements between capitalist countries that favored civil rights over economic ones, and the communist countries that favored the opposite, the UN Commission on Human Rights decided to divide the rights contained in the UDHR between two separate instruments. The result was two covenants. The UN General Assembly adopted both in 1966 and, after achieving the requisite number of ratifications, they came into force in 1976. As of January 1, 2002, 144 countries (including the United States) had ratified ICCPR and 142 countries (excluding the United States) had ratified ICESCR.

The ICCPR incorporates almost all of the civic and political rights contained in the UDHR. It adds, as well, the right of peoples to self-determination and the right of ethnic, religious, and linguistic minorities to enjoy their own cultures, to practice their own religions, and to use their own languages. The covenant also calls for the establishment of a Human Rights Committee to study reports submitted by ratifying state parties on measures they have taken to give effect to the rights contained in the covenant.

Countries that become party to the covenant's First Optional Protocol also recognize the authority of the Human Rights Committee to consider and act upon communications from individuals claiming a state has violated one or more of their covenant rights. Countries ratifying the covenant's Second Optional Protocol agree to abolish the death penalty within their jurisdictions. This protocol, which came into force in 1991, has been favorably received by most western European and Latin American countries, but not by the United States.

The International Covenant on Economic, Social and Cultural Rights requires ratifying states to take steps toward progressively achieving the full realization of the rights recognized in the Covenant subject to the maximum of their available resources. Among its economic rights are the right to work, the right to just working conditions, trade union rights, the right to an adequate standard of living, and the right to social security. Its social and cultural rights include rights relating to the protection of the family, to health, to education, and to the preservation of one's culture. The covenant prohibits discrimination in the enjoyment of these rights on the basis of race, sex, language, religion, opinion, national or social origin, wealth, and birth or other status. State parties are required to report periodically to the UN Economic and Social Council on the steps they have taken and the progress they have made toward realizing these rights for peoples within their jurisdictions.

UN High Commissioner for Human Rights

The UN High Commissioner for Human Rights is appointed by the Secretary General to serve for a term of four years with the possibility of one additional term. The General Assembly charges the high commissioner with promoting all civil, political, economic, social, and cultural rights; coordinating human rights promotion and protection activities throughout the UN system; providing human rights advisory services and financial assistance to requesting states; and supervising the UN's Center for Human Rights in Geneva, Switzerland.

Generational and Positive Versus Negative Rights

The content and range of claimed human rights have progressively expanded through time, such that commentators often speak of three generations of rights, the first being civil and political rights (*liberté*); the second being of economic, social, and cultural rights (*égalité*); and the third being solidarity rights (*fraternité*).

The UN Covenant on Civil and Political Rights contains many of the first generation rights, while the Covenant on Economic, Social and Cultural Rights contains many of the second generation rights. Some commentators refer to first generation rights as negative rights, because, they claim, these require government non-interference in order for individuals to be able to freely exercise them. Typical first generation rights include the rights of free speech, press, religion, and thought. By contrast, some commentators have characterized second generation rights as positive, because they usually require government to act in order for individuals to enjoy them. For example, government action may be required in order for individuals to enjoy the right to social security, protection against unemployment, the worker's right to rest and leisure, including periodic holidays with pay; and the right to a standard of living adequate for health and well-being.

Third generation rights are often referred to as collective rights, in contrast to the mainly individual rights of generations one and two. Among the third generation rights are a people's right to political, economic, social, and cultural self-determination; the right of people to share the common heritage of humankind, including the mineral resources of the earth, the seas, and outer space; the right to benefit from science and other forms of human progress; the right to peace; and the right to a healthy and sustainable environment.

The conceptualization of three generations of rights, further divided into positive and negative ones, is more rhetorical than accurate. The rights associated with these three generations did not appear in neat chronological order. And many first generation rights do require governments to act positively to enable individuals to enjoy them. At a minimum, for example, government must act to prevent people from infringing on the rights of others to free speech, press, and religious practice. Finally, third generation rights are largely aspirational. By contrast to first and second generation rights, third generation rights are without widely accepted conventions supporting them.

Hierarchy of Human Rights

The International Covenant on Civil and Political Rights and some other human rights conventions contain a clause which allows ratifying countries to derogate from (i.e., suspend their obligation to honor) some of the rights contained therein in times of public emergency which threaten the life of the nation. However, such derogation clauses do not allow ratifying states to derogate from the following rights even in times of national emergency: the right to life, the right to be free from torture and other cruel punishment, the right not to be held in slavery or involuntary servitude, the right not to be imprisoned for inability to fulfill a contractual obligation, the right not to be held guilty of an act that did not constitute a criminal offense when committed, the right to be recognized as a person before the law, and the right to freedom of thought, conscience, and religion.

Given the derogation clauses with their specific exceptions and given the disagreement between capitalist and communist countries over the relative importance of civic/political rights versus economic/social rights, some commentators have argued that there exists a hierarchy of human rights, i.e., that some rights are more important than others.

Human rights advocates regard this position as reactionary and dangerous to the progressive development of international human rights. Consequently, they were responsible for the following portion of the declaration that resulted from the 1993 United Nations Conference on Human Rights in Vienna.

> All human rights are universal, indivisible and interdependent and interrelated. The international community must treat human rights globally in a fair and equal manner, on the same footing, and with the same emphasis. While the significance of national and regional particularities and various historical, cultural and religious backgrounds must be borne in mind, it is the duty of States, regardless of their political, economic and cultural systems, to promote and protect all human rights and fundamental freedoms.

Universalism Versus Relativism

Proponents of universalism claim that international human rights, as delineated in the International Bill of Human Rights, are and must be the same for all peoples regardless of their cultures or political systems. By contrast, cultural relativists argue that morality, and therefore human rights, is culturally contingent and variable.

Some leaders of non-Western countries maintain, like cultural relativists, that some of alleged universal human rights really are Western ideals that do not fit well with the cultural traditions of their own countries. These leaders are often critical of those rights affecting women, children, and family relationships, which they claim are based on Western Christian values and contrary to some non-Western cultures. Other spokespersons from countries with authoritarian political systems reject some of the democratic political rights, claiming that they would hinder needed economic development and political stability in their countries.

Rarely, however, are these criticisms made by oppressed people who want to benefit from universal human rights standards. In all countries there are groups that struggle for women's rights and democratic political rights.

The dichotomy of opposing views is most probably exaggerated. The vast majority of rights contained in the various human rights conventions are stated in relatively abstract and general terms, thereby allowing for a fair amount of variation in their actual application. For example, the European Court of Human Rights has developed the principle known as the "margin of appreciation" which permits European countries a degree of variation in the application of the European Human Rights Convention so as to accommodate local cultural differences.

If human rights derive from those universal human values that ultimately result from the universal psychobiological nature of humankind (as previously described), then there exists a solid basis for developing human rights that are truly universal.

Regional Developments

To greater or lesser degrees, the states of some of the world's regions have developed systems to promote and protect human rights in accordance with their own expansive or limited aspirations. Of these, the European human rights system, developed by the Council of Europe, is the most advanced.

In 1950, the West European countries that formed the Council of Europe adopted the European Convention for the Protection of Human Rights and Fundamental Freedoms. This convention, which entered into force in 1953, contains most of the human rights found in the UN International Covenant on Civil and Political Rights. For purposes of enforcement, the Convention originally created a European Commission of Human Rights and a European Court of Human Rights, both of which could hear human rights complaints brought by individuals against Convention member states. In 1998, the Commission and Court were merged to create a single court. Through the years European citizens and non-citizen residents have brought thousands of petitions or complains to the Court. State parties to the convention have generally honored the court's decisions, which are final and cannot be appealed.

In 1961, the Council of Europe also adopted the European Social Charter which resembles the UN Covenant on Economic, Social and Cultural Rights. The Council of Europe promotes the charter's provisions through the various committees and organs of the Council of Europe which accept and review periodic progress reports made to them by member states.

The Inter-American human rights system began in 1948, when the Ninth Pan-American Conference adopted the non-binding American Declaration on the Rights and Duties of Man, which sets out both the duties and rights of individual citizens. In 1959, the Ministers for Foreign Affairs of countries making up the Organization of American States (OAS) created the Inter-American Commission on Human Rights, which has undertaken the function of investigating human rights activities in the Americas. The OAS adopted the American Convention on Human Rights in 1969. This convention, which entered into force in 1978, established the Inter-American Court of Human Rights, which sits in San José, Costa Rica. In 1988, the OAS adopted the Additional Protocol to the American Convention on Human Rights in the Area of Economic, Social and Cultural Rights. The United States has neither recognized the jurisdiction of the Inter-American Court of Human Rights nor has it ratified the 1988 Additional Protocol.

The Organization of African Unity (OAU) adopted the African Charter on Human and Peoples' Rights in 1981. The great majority of African states subsequently ratified the Charter, which entered into force in 1986. The African Charter provides for civil and political rights as well as economic, social, and cultural rights. It recognizes the rights of groups, the family, women, and children, and grants special protections for the elderly and the infirm. Somewhat rhetorically, it also proclaims rights to national and international peace.

The African Charter provides for a human rights commission, which has both human rights promotional and protective functions. There is no restriction on who may file a complaint with it. The African Charter does not, however, call for a human rights court. Some African leaders claim that African tradition prefers mediation, conciliation, and consensus rather than the kind of adversarial court procedures that typify the West. But other leaders and many

African human rights advocates want a court, and they began planning for it in the 1990s.

The Council of the League of Arab States created the Permanent Arab Commission on Human Rights in September 1968. To date, this commission has focused primarily on Israel's human rights abuses against Palestinians living under Israeli occupation in the West Bank and Gaza. Arab intergovernmental and nongovernmental bodies have been responsible for the Universal Islamic Declaration of Human Rights (1981) and the Cairo Declaration on Human Rights in Islam (1990)—two non-binding documents.

The League of Arab States approved an Arab Charter on Human Rights in September 1994, but by 2002 not one Arab state had ratified it. The charter requires state parties to submit periodic reports to the league's Human Rights Committee. It also provides for an independent Committee of Experts to study reports and submit its own findings to the Human Rights Committee. However, the charter creates no court and contains no provisions for petitions by individuals.

Asia has no regional human rights regime. The governments of many Asian countries have been opposed to following the lead of the West in establishing regional human rights conventions, commissions, and courts. Many government leaders complain that human rights as commonly conceptualized are culture-bound Western creations with limited applicability to Asian cultures and societies. Many Asian people, however, have campaigned for more legal human rights protections. A group of Asia-Pacific NGOs (non-governmental organizations) adopted the Asia-Pacific Declaration of Human Rights in 1993 and the Asian Human Rights Charter in 1997. Both of these documents incorporated many universal human rights principles. But, Asian governments have not adopted either the declaration or the charter. However, governmental representatives of thirty Asian countries participating in a 1996 UN-sponsored workshop agreed to at least explore the possibility of establishing a regional human rights regime.

Violations

Most cases of human rights violations are adjudicated in the domestic courts of countries. The vast majority of states have human rights protections written into their constitutions. In addition, states that ratify human rights treaties are obligated to create the domestic legislation necessary to implement them. Consequently, in those countries that respect the rule of law, persons who violate the human rights of others can be prosecuted in domestic courts. This, of course, rarely happens in countries ruled by military juntas or dictators.

Despite the progress made in the ratification of human rights conventions by countries around the world, human rights abuses that violate those conventions are widespread. For example, in its 2001 annual report, Amnesty International (a non-governmental human rights advocacy organization) maintains that of the 149 countries covered in its survey, sixty-one of them had carried out extrajudicial executions (i.e., executions without trial) in 2000. Security forces, police, or other state authorities reportedly tortured or ill-treated persons in 125 countries. Confirmed or possible prisoners of conscience were held in sixty-three countries. People were arbitrarily arrested and detained, or held in detention without charge or trial in seventy-two countries. Armed opposition groups committed serious human rights abuses, such as deliberate and arbitrary killings of civilians, torture and hostage-taking in forty-two countries. Most of the countries with serious and widespread human rights violations were developing states located in Latin America, Africa, and Asia.

Widespread and systematic human rights violations are common during times of civil and international war. Historically, persons committing these violations have not faced trial and punishment, unless they were war losers. For example, at the end of World War II the victorious powers tried defeated German and Japanese military officers and officials for a variety of serious human rights violations. The post–World War II International Military Tribunal (IMT) at Nuremberg, for instance, prosecuted and punished German leaders for war crimes and crimes against humanity. War crimes consisted of: the murder and enslavement of civilians, the murder or ill treatment of prisoners of war, the killing of hostages, the plunder of public or private property, and the wanton destruction of cities. Crimes against humanity included murdering, enslaving, or committing other inhumane acts against a civilian population because of its political views, race, or religion.

In essence, the IMT stood for people's rights to life, freedom from torture and other cruel punishment, freedom of political thought and freedom of religion. Furthermore, it stood for the principle of universal jurisdiction—the claim that any state or combination of states has the legal authority to try persons allegedly responsible for grave violations of human rights (such as war crimes and crimes against humanity) regardless of the location of the crimes or the citizenship of the suspects or victims.

In 1993 and 1994, the UN Security Council invoked the principle of universal jurisdiction by creating international tribunals to prosecute persons allegedly responsible for war crimes, crimes against humanity and genocide in the conflicts of the former Yugoslavia and Rwanda. In the former Yugoslavia, Serbs, Croats, and Muslims fought each other for control of territory following the breakup of Yugoslavia's multi-ethnic federated republic. Military as well as paramilitary forces targeted civilians and engaged in rape, torture, and murder. From 1991 to 1994, an estimated 250,000 people were killed and many thousands more were wounded, tortured, or raped. In Rwanda, the Hutu military, paramilitary, and many ordinary citizens engaged in a widespread massacre of Tutsi citizens. Within a three month period in 1994, they mutilated and raped thousands and murdered an estimated 750,000 people. By creating the international tribunals, the UN Security Council asserted that the international community need not tolerate such massive human rights violations. Under international law, the international community can intervene in the sovereign affairs of states for humanitarian purposes.

In July of 1998, 160 UN member states authorized the adoption of a statute to create a permanent International Criminal Court (ICC) to prosecute persons suspected of committing crimes against humanity, war crimes, crimes of genocide, and crimes of international aggression. The ICC will become a reality after sixty countries ratify its statute. Once it comes into existence, the ICC will most probably replace the international tribunals for Rwanda and the former Yugoslavia. It will be capable of exercising jurisdiction in those countries that have ratified its statute as well as in other countries that the UN Security Council may determine need the court's services.

PAUL J. MAGNARELLA

See also Military and Human Rights; Self-Determination; Universal Declaration of Human Rights

References and Further Reading

Austin, John. *The Province of Jurisprudence Determined.* London: Weidenfeld and Nicolson, 1954 (orig. 1832).

Forsythe, David P. (Ed.) *Human Rights and Comparative Foreign Policy.* Tokyo; New York: United Nations University Press, 2000.

Garling, Marguerite, and Chidi Anselm Odinkalu (Compilers). *Building Bridges for Rights: Inter-African Initiatives in the Field of Human Rights.* London: Interights, 2001.

Henkin, Louis, Gerald L. Neuman, Diane F. Orentlicher, and David W. Leebron. *Human Rights.* New York: Foundation Press, 1999.

Jacobsen, Michael. *Human Rights and Asian Values: Contesting National Identities and Cultural Representations in Asia.* Richmond, Surrey: Curzon Press, 2000.

Janis, Mark W., Richard S. Kay, Anthony W. Bradley. *European Human Rights Law*. Oxford: Oxford University Press, 2000.

Lauren, Paul Gordon. *The Evolution of International Human Rights*. Philadelphia: University of Pennsylvania Press, 1998.

Locke, John. *Two Treaties of Government*. Cambridge: Cambridge University Press, 1690.

Martin, Francisco Forrest. *Challenging Human Rights Violations: Using International Law in U.S. Courts*. Ardsley, NY: Transnational Publishers, 2001.

Mower, A. Glenn. *Regional Human Rights: A Comparative Study of the West European and Inter-American Systems*. New York: Greenwood Press, 1991.

Pagels, Elaine. "The Roots and Origins of Human Rights," In *Human Dignity: the Internationalization of Human Rights*, Alice Henkin (Ed.) New York: Aspen Institute for Humanistic Studies, 1979, pp. 1–8.

Steiner, Henry J., and Philip Alston. *International Human Rights in Context*. Oxford: Oxford University Press, 2000.

United Nations. *Vienna Declaration on Human Rights*. UN Doc. A/CONF.157/23, 12 July 1993.

HUMANITARIAN RELIEF PROJECTS

Humanitarian relief projects are undertaken by governments, intergovernmental organizations (IGOs), and nongovernmental organizations (NGOs) in order to prevent starvation, disease, and other hardships among people who have experienced various kinds of disaster and displacement from their homes. Often humanitarian aid is provided in an emergency mode, where assistance agencies must act swiftly in order to prevent staggering losses of life. Although local or domestic aid providers may be the first to offer assistance, when humanitarian emergencies strike in developing countries, international humanitarian aid is often necessary to cope with the needs. Humanitarian emergencies are more likely to occur in developing nations than in developed ones because poorer countries are more vulnerable to disasters and less able to cope by themselves with their effects. Humanitarian relief projects in such cases can have a significant negative or positive affects on the economy and social infrastructure of beneficiary nations. Thus, while saving lives of distressed populations is the foremost objective in humanitarian relief projects, implementing agencies must also be sensitive to the long-term development impact of their emergency programs.

Principles of Humanitarian Relief

Although political factors and national interests affect when, where, and how humanitarian relief is undertaken, most of the players in the humanitarian assistance field, including IGOs and NGOs, as well as governments, understand that humanitarian aid should be fundamentally non-partisan. Wherever people are in distress owing to disasters, the international community should assist them. The primary motivation in provision of such assistance should be to alleviate human suffering. While the humanitarian principle should be kept foremost in mind, it is nonetheless true that no particular country is obliged to assist the disaster-stricken population of any other country. Financing of humanitarian aid is voluntary in nature. Countries friendly to a stricken nation are much more likely to act swiftly and generously to assist its afflicted population, whereas hostile governments are much less inclined to help if they help at all. IGOs and NGOs, on the other hand are more likely to behave in an impartial matter, although even these bodies may be driven by ideological or political motivations. Still most agencies active in the provision of humanitarian aid understand that such aid should be disbursed on the basis of need and not on partisan or political grounds.

In addition to the humanitarian principle, NGOs acknowledge several other principles in humanitarian aid projects, including nondiscrimination as regards race, religion, or nationality, and impartiality as regards assistance to contending political groups, and neutrality as regards belligerent groups. The International Red Cross and Red Crescent Movement and many other NGOs in a Code of Conduct have acknowledged several other principles of conduct. NGOs are especially concerned that they not be coerced into acting as instruments of government foreign policy. NGOs pledge in the Code of Conduct that they will respect local cultures and customs and build disaster responses cooperatively with local NGOs and institutions by incorporating program beneficiaries in the planning and implementation of projects. Relief aid and related projects should anticipate the reduction of vulnerabilities to disaster as they meet basic needs. NGOs recognize that they must be accountable both to charitable donors and to the recipient population, and that the latter should, even in the midst of terrible suffering be treated not as objects of pity but as persons deserving of dignity and respect.

While NGOs express high ideals in these principles, the political reality of humanitarian assistance is that governments dictate the pace and the provide most of the capacity for humanitarian assistance in times of disaster and conflict. Governments of disaster-affected countries determine when to seek assistance and from whom to seek assistance. They may turn to donor governments for the bulk of their needs. They may also turn to IGOs within the UN system for humanitarian assistance. Such agencies might include, depending on the nature of the disaster, the United Nations High Commissioner for Refugees (UNHCR), the UN Children's Fund (UNICEF), the World Health Organization (WHO), or the World Food Program (WFP). In requesting the assistance of other governments or of various IGOs, the host country must grant the agencies sufficient autonomy to do their work. In most instances the donor governments and IGOs will seek to work with appropriate ministries within the disaster-stricken country. They also routinely rely on a number of NGOs as implementing partners. The receiving country has the sovereign right to approve or to deny entry to NGOs, as it does any other form of outside aid.

Forms of Humanitarian Assistance

Meeting basic needs of disaster victims is the primary focus of humanitarian relief programs. Food aid is critical. When food needs can be met by local resources it is best to exhaust them first before relying on substantial imports so that local food prices do not artificially plummet, thus putting local producers at risk. However, when severe shortages occur, it may be necessary to rely of foreign sources of food aid. The United States, Australia, Canada, and numerous countries of Europe are the major food producing countries and the biggest donors. The WFP monitors food availability and coordinates international responses to humanitarian emergencies.

Access to potable water is another critical need for victims of disaster. Polluted water becomes a source of disease and, in all forms of disaster, access to clean water is often inhibited, thus putting disaster victims at risk. Sometimes clean water must be trucked into disaster areas, but in the long run assistance aimed at improving sanitation in disaster-stricken areas is essential for the establishment of adequate renewable sources of clean water. Among the UN bodies most frequently addressing clean water and sanitation issues is UNICEF.

Provision of health assistance is also a basic need of disaster victims. In cataclysmic disasters such as floods and earthquakes, emergency medical attention is often necessary, and in developing countries the scope of the need may quickly outpace the health infrastructure. In famines and refugee situations, treatment and prevention of infectious disease is critical, especially when inadequate housing, sanitation, and nutrition are available. Numerous agencies are involved in provision of such assistance, including

UNHCR, UNICEF, WHO, and numerous NGOs. Shelter is another basic need for refugees and displaced persons who have been forced to flee from their homes, or whose homes may have been destroyed by floods or earthquakes.

Special attention is paid to vulnerable groups in the provision of humanitarian assistance. Children, elderly persons, and pregnant and lactating mothers are in need of special nutritional requirements and medical assistance. Such groups are usually underrepresented among the politically active and in the traditional decision-making structures in many countries.

A major emphasis of humanitarian aid in recent decades has been to encourage self-reliance among the beneficiary populations. Self-reliance implies that the victims of disaster, the internally displaced and refugees, are employed in the task of their own recovery. WFP encourages this through implementation of food-for-work projects, such as rural road-building, reforestation, water development, and construction programs involving refugee housing, medical facilities, and schools. In this, WFP cooperates with the UN Development Program (UNDP) and with UNHCR where refugees are involved. These agencies also initiate vocational training programs and cottage industries in refugee and displaced persons camps.

Humanitarian Relief During Complex Emergencies

During the 1990s, as the Cold War waned, the United Nations began fielding peace-keeping and peace-making forces in many regions of long-standing conflict and civil war. Coupled with political settlements and military intervention were sizable humanitarian operations in such countries as Cambodia, Mozambique, Somalia, and the former Yugoslavia and in such regions as Central America and the Great Lakes region of Africa. In Cambodia and Mozambique, peace agreements were agreed upon prior to deployment of substantial international peace-keeping forces. In these cases repatriation of refugees and reintegration of internally displaced persons were facilitated by humanitarian aid organizations, while opposing armies were demobilized and reconstituted. Assistance for repair and reconstruction of economic infrastructure was provided as preparations were made for elections. De-mining operations were commenced to provide greater safety and security to refugees and returnees so that they might resume agricultural pursuits. In both of these cases, the recreation of civil society under the watchful eye of the international community produced relatively stable governments. Cambodia experienced later political upheavals, but eventually political stability was restored.

By contrast, in Somalia and the former Yugoslavia, the international community intervened with humanitarian assistance prior to the negotiation of peace agreements. UN forces were fielded to ensure the safety of humanitarian aid workers and the effective delivery of aid to those in need. In Somalia, where no effective central government existed, international forces which were deployed to provide security for the delivery of humanitarian aid prevented a massive famine, but when the UN forces attempted to disarm the local forces of Somali warlords, the situation deteriorated. The withdrawal of American forces and later those of other nations involved in the UN operation, signified the failure of the UN to establish a civil society in a country where general lawlessness prevailed. In the former Yugoslavia, the UNHCR provided humanitarian aid to besieged cities in Bosnia, but the UN forces sent to guard aid shipments, found themselves trapped in the cross-fire of an ongoing civil war.

The existence of peace plans enhanced international efforts to provide aid and to promote security and the emergence of civil society in Cambodia and Mozambique. In Bosnia and Somalia, the lack of such agreements hampered aid activities. Not until the Dayton Accords were promulgated did the situation in Bosnia improve, permitting repatriation and resettlement of displaced persons, and eventually the promotion of rehabilitation and reconstruction of the national economy.

A similar pattern can be discerned in contexts of complicated regional conflicts. In Central America, after years of negotiation, a peace agreement among contending parties was achieved. This was rapidly followed by deployment of UN observer forces, the repatriation and return of refugees and displaced persons, the demobilization of forces in Nicaragua, the preparation for and holding of national elections, and the application of development aid to enhance rural development through quick impact projects and longer term development assistance. This successful sequence of activities never materialized in the Great Lakes Region of Africa, where hundreds of thousands of Rwandan refugees adversely affected the economic situation in neighboring countries such as Zaire and Tanzania. In Rwanda, itself, genocide had taken a terrible toll among the Tutsi population and Hutus, fearful of retaliation, spilled into neighboring countries, where many died. The international community, slow to respond to the genocide, reacted fairly quickly in providing humanitarian aid to the Hutu refugees, but owing to the fact that the same

ruthless killers who had unleashed genocide dominated the Hutu refugee camps, provision of humanitarian aid was very difficult. The presence of such destabilizing elements led eventually to civil war and the overthrow of the government of Zaire. Instability and civil war in Zaire frustrated humanitarian relief efforts and left no room for consideration of longer term development aid.

Complex emergencies continue to offer the international community very difficult humanitarian assistance challenges, not the least of which, is how military forces are to be integrated with humanitarian agencies. The military may provide security for delivery of aid, but in the midst of a civil war, its primary task must be to bring force to bear against combatant elements, and this leaves humanitarian agencies in a very precarious and dangerous situation. Sometimes the military becomes the primary agent for delivery of humanitarian aid, as was demonstrated in Kosovo in 1998, and again in Afghanistan in 2001 when food packets were dropped by air in zones experiencing famine.

Ideally, international humanitarian aid gives way to longer term development, rehabilitation and reconstruction once peace has been reestablished in areas of conflict. That task requires the existence of governments committed to the maintenance of civil society. With the return of political stability and peace, resources can be shifted toward the goal of economic prosperity, and as such a transition unfolds, the humanitarian aid agencies and projects give way to projects aimed at fostering long-term economic development.

ROBERT F. GORMAN

See also Disaster Relief; International Committee of the Red Cross; Natural Disasters; Non-Governmental Organizations (NGOs); Refugees; United Nations Children's Fund (UNICEF); United Nations High Commissioner for Refugees (UNHCR); World Food Program; World Health Organization (WHO)

References and Further Reading

Belgrad, Eric A., and Nitza Nachmias, editors. *The Politics of International Humanitarian Aid Operations*. Westport, CT: Praeger, 1997.
Clarke, Walter, and Jeffrey Herbst. *Learning from Somalia: The Lessons of Armed Humanitarian Intervention*. Boulder, CO: Westview Press, 1997.
Gorman, Robert F. *Historical Dictionary of Refugee and Disaster Relief Organizations*. Lanham, MD: Scarecrow Press, 2000.
Minear, Larry and Thomas G. Weiss. *Mercy Under Fire: War and the Global Humanitarian Community*. Boulder, CO: Westview Press, 1995.

Natsios, Andrew S. *U.S. Foreign Policy and the Four Horsemen of the Apocalypse: Humanitarian Relief in Complex Emergencies*. Westport, CT: Praeger, 1997.

Weiss, Thomas G. *Military-Civilian Interactions: Intervening in Humanitarian Crises*. Lanham, MD: Rowman & Littlefield, 1999.

Weiss, Thomas G., and Cindy Collins. *Humanitarian Challenges and Intervention: World Politics and the Dilemmas of Help*. Boulder, CO: Westview Press, 1996.

HUN SEN

Born in Kampong Cham province, Cambodia, on August 5, 1952, Hun Sen was educated at Lycee Indra Devi, Phnom Penh. He graduated in 1969 and joined the Khmer Rouge in 1970. In 1977, however, he defected to Vietnam and joined troops fighting against the Khmer Rouge. He was a founding member of the United Front for the National Salvation of Kampuchea (UFNSK) in 1978 and returned to Cambodia to become minister of foreign affairs in the Vietnamese regime in 1979. He served as deputy Prime Minister and Foreign Minister from 1981–1985 and then as Prime Minister, 1985–1991. He participated in brokering the 1991 United Nations (UN) Paris Peace Agreement and was part of the coalition government for the next two years. Despite working with Prince Ranariddh of the National United Front for an Independent, Neutral, Peaceful and Cooperative Cambodia (FUNCINPEC) as First Prime Minister following UN supervised elections, he ousted Ranariddh in a violent 1997 coup. He became Prime Minister two more times following elections in 1998 and 2003.

Hun Sen seems to be a combination of contradictions: idealist and pragmatist, ruthless authoritarian and skilled negotiator. He initially joined the Khmer Rouge to free Cambodia from a government he felt was corrupt, but then defected when he experienced the excesses of Pol Pot's genocidal regime. When he achieved a position of political power with the help of the Vietnamese, he ruthlessly clung to his position. Supported by the army, he staged a violent coup in July 1997 during which Rannariddh fled Cambodia, calling Hun Sen a gangster. This action delayed Cambodia's acceptance into ASEAN until 1999, following elections in July 1998. The elections did not bring a clear victory for either major party and another brief period of violent unrest ensued. Eventually agreement was reached and Hun Sen became Prime Minister again in November although the inauguration ceremony was marred by a rocket attack outside the National Assembly. The CPP won the July 2003 elections, but a year passed before the National Assembly ratified the CPP-FUNCINPEC coalition government for a third term, with Hun Sen as Prime Minister.

Regardless of how one views Hun Sen's tactics, it cannot be denied that Cambodia has enjoyed relative political stability in recent years. This has enabled the country, under Hun Sen's undeniably strong leadership, to begin to make small but significant development gains in many areas.

Hun Sen recognises Cambodia's need for outside assistance in order to develop. He also accepts that Cambodia's legal, financial, and governance systems need reform, not only to benefit the Cambodian people, but also to gain international acceptance. His government has instigated economic, taxation, and legal reforms; and is demobilizing the military and fighting corruption, especially in the forestry industry. These, and other, ongoing reforms have inspired cautious but increased investor and donor confidence.

Hun Sen is wary of foreign control of Cambodia's affairs, particularly from the United Nations. He walks a fine line, inviting outside assistance and advice, and accepting aid, but pragmatically only compromising as absolutely necessary to ensure Cambodia gets the help it requires, while maintaining the country's sovereignty and his own powerful position. A good example being the ongoing negotiations to construct a tribunal and legal system to try the remaining members of the Pol Pot regime for war crimes. While accepting input from the UN and various countries, including the US, Hun Sen still insists on a hybrid Cambodian justice system that allows foreign participation, but not dominance.

Statistics show many sectors of Cambodia's economy are developing and the standard of living is slowly improving. How much is due to political stability and how much to Hun Sen's strong leadership is unsure. Providing Hun Sen's government can sustain the momentum of reforms, Cambodia's growth and development should continue.

JILLIAN BRADY

See also Cambodia; Southeast Asia: History and Economic Development; Southeast Asia: International Relations

References and Further Reading

Chandler, David P. *A History of Cambodia*, Boulder: Westview Press, 2000.

Ledgerwood, Judy (Ed.). *Cambodia Emerges from the Past: Eight Essays*. Dekalb, IL: Southeast Asia Publications, 2002.

Lizee, Pierre P. *Peace, Power and Resistance in Cambodia: Global Governance and the Failure of International Conflict Resolution*, Basingstoke: Macmillan, 2000.

Mehta, Harish C., and Mehta, Julie B. *Hun Sen: Strong man of Cambodia*. Singapore: Graham Brash, 1999.

"Respect our sovereignty", Interview with Cambodia's Hun Sen, *Asia Week*, November 26, 1999, Vol. 25 No. 47.

Roberts, David W. *Political Transition in Cambodia, 1991–99: Power, Elitism and Democracy*, New York: St. Martins Press, 2000.

HUNGARIAN CRISIS OF 1956

On October 23, 1956, Hungarian university students demonstrated in Budapest in solidarity with the Polish workers' revolt in the city of Gdansk a few weeks before. After the demonstration, they marched to the national broadcasting studio of Hungarian radio, demanding that their twelve-point program be broadcast to the nation. Secret policemen, stationed inside, fired on the unarmed crowd. Regular policemen and soldiers then gave their weapons to the students who attacked and conquered the building. In another part of the city, at Heros' Square, worker-demonstrators dismantled the giant statue of Stalin, leaving only his boots on the pedestal.

Erno Gero, the Communist Party chief, recently returned from Yugoslavia where he mended fences with Tito, ordered martial law and asked for Soviet troops stationed in Hungary. This turned the revolt into a national uprising against Soviet colonialism. In the next few days the fighting, mainly against the secret police, turned ferocious. The Soviet troops were withdrawn from Budapest after five days, but remained in the country. On October 28, a new government was formed, headed by Imre Nagy, a moderate national communist. Independent workers' councils were established in factories and municipalities. The secret police was disbanded. A new multiparty government was established. General Péter Maléter was appointed minister of defense and he was invited to negotiate with Russian officials for the withdrawal of the Soviet troops from Hungary. General Béla Király became commander of the newly formed volunteer national guard.

By November 3, the government was in complete control of the country. However, the prominent communist, János Kádár, a member of the government, fled with Soviet help from Budapest. He declared that the "events" represented an uprising against socialism. He formed a new counter-revolutionary government under Soviet control. On November 4, the Hungarian delegation negotiating with Soviet representatives was treacherously arrested and huge Soviet forces attacked Budapest and other revolutionary centers. Fighting continued until December. By January 1957, two hundred thousand Hungarians fled the country.

Kádár's counter-revolutionary government reestablished the Stalinist system in Hungary. In addition to those who died in battle, hundreds of revolutionaries were executed with or without trial and tens of thousands were jailed. The new government organized a party-army, made up of die-hard communists, who became an instrument of terror. The secret police was also reassembled. Hungary became an international pariah and the "Hungarian case" remained on the agenda of the United Nations for years. Although the United States–sponsored Radio Free Europe encouraged the revolution, the US government did nothing to help the Hungarians. It used the revolution as a propaganda tool in the Cold War. Only in 1963 did Kádár's regime felt secure enough to relax the terror, and gradually restore a semblance of normalcy in Hungary.

JOSEPH HELD

See also Central and Eastern Europe: History and Economic Development; Central and Eastern Europe: International Relations; Hungary

References and Further Reading

Aczél, Tamás. *Ten Years After. The Hungarian Revolution in the Perspective of History*. New York: Holt Reinhart, 1966.

Fehér, Ferenc, and Ágnes Heller. *Hungary 1956 Revisited. The Message of a Revolution a Quarter Century After*. London, Boston: Allen & Unwin, 1983.

Kecskeméti, Paul. *The Unexpected Revolution. Social Forces in the Hungarian Uprising*. Stanford, CA: Stanford University Press, 1961.

Lomax, Bill. *Hungary, 1956*. New York: St. Martin Press, 1976.

HUNGARY

Hungary's territory comprises 35,919 square miles. The country is in the Danubian River Basin in East-Central Europe. The population numbers about 10 million. Ethnicity: 89.9% Magyars, 4% Roma (Gypsies), 2.6% Germans, 2% Serbians, and even tinier minorities of Romanians and Slovaks. The capital city is Budapest. The center of the country consists of flatlands. The northeast and north are mountainous, the west and southwest are hilly. Hungary borders on Austria in the West, Slovakia and Carpatho-Ukraine in the north and northeast, Romania in the southeast and Croatia and Slovenia in the south. The climate is moderate.

During the last three hundred years, Hungary was part of the Habsburg Empire. When the empire collapsed after World War I, Hungary became an independent state. It was deprived of two-thirds of its former territory and one-third of its ethnically Hungarian population. Hungary had few economic resources left; its roads and railroads were cut at the new borders. During the first third of the twentieth century, Hungary struggled economically. With Hitler in power, Hungary came under German influence, especially after she regained some territory from Romania and Czechoslovakia with Hitler's help. Hungary participated in the war against the Soviet Union and suffered large numbers of casualties. In 1944–1945, Hungary became a battleground between Soviet and German armed forces.

In March 1944, the Germans occupied the country. A radical right-wing "Arrow Cross" movement established a reign of terror under German auspices, shooting its enemies, especially Jews, into the Danube River. The war completely ruined the economy. Factory buildings were damaged; stocks and machinery had been stolen. The housing stock did not fare any better. Most bridges were destroyed. Animal stocks were carried away or killed. Public transport disappeared. Railroad tracks were uprooted and road surfaces were destroyed.

In December 1944, a new government was formed under Soviet auspices. Parties entered a so-called "national independence front," including several communists returning to Hungary from Soviet exile.

In 1944 and thereafter, the Soviet Army and the Soviet secret police were arbiters of life and death in Hungary. There were hundreds of thousands of Hungarian "prisoners of war" in Soviet camps (some civilians "captured" by the Soviet army to serve as slave labor in the Soviet Union). Their return depended upon the behavior of the Hungarians at home. The amount of reparations demanded from Hungary also depended upon the good will of the Soviet dictator. Stalin forced the new Hungarian government to conclude trade agreements and establish joint Soviet-Hungarian companies. They were means for future exploitation of Hungary's resources.

The communist repatriates, including Mátyás Rákosi, Ern Ger, Mihály Farkas, and Zoltán Vas (the "Muscovites"), wanted to grab and hold power by any means.

Almost immediately after the war—in 1945—a new political (secret) police was established. It was under the control of the communist leaders who used it to suppress the opposition. Yet the first municipal elections, in October 1945, brought victory for the Smallholders Party, representing the opposition. In November, national elections were held with a similar outcome. The Communists and their allied Social Democratic Party received less than 30% of the vote. Nevertheless, Marshal Voroshilov, the Soviet representative of the Allied Control Commission, ordered the victors to form a coalition government with the communists. Soon the pressure of the Soviet government resulted in the destruction of the victorious party and the establishment, in 1947, of a communist dictatorship.

By 1946, the entire police apparatus—including the secret police—was under the direction of a radical communist, László Rajk. The police openly participated in the campaign against opponents of the Communist Party. A series of show trials started against the opposition but, in time, prominent Hungarian communist were also persecuted. The charge in most cases was the "culprit's" and his/her associates' alleged conspiracy to overthrow the government.

In 1947, Hungary was included in a new Soviet empire. The Hungarian government, dominated by the Rákosi-led Communist Party, signed the peace treaty that confirmed the separation of Hungarian minorities in the former Successor states and Romania. Hungary was obliged to pay a huge reparation to the Soviet Union, Czechoslovakia, and Yugoslavia. In addition, Soviet troops were stationed in Hungary on a permanent basis. In 1955, Hungary became a member of the Warsaw Pact Alliance.

After the non-communist political parties were eliminated, the Roman Catholic church came next. Its cardinal, Joseph Mindszenty and several leading bishops were incarcerated on trumped-up charges. Religious orders were dissolved. Literature now consisted mainly of political propaganda. The arts were streamlined along lines of "socialist realism." Newspapers and radio stations were mouthpieces of Soviet propaganda. Newspapers were copies of Soviet journals. All this was accomplished in an atmosphere of terror.

The Hungarian population, including some members of the Communist party, was demoralized. Education was augmented by large doses of Marxism-Leninism, and the study of the Russian language was required. Listening to foreign radio broadcasts was considered a crime. In 1949–1950, the peasantry was forced into Soviet-style collective farms, private landholding was abolished and compulsory delivery of foodstuff to the state was introduced. Factories, banks, and shops were nationalized.

The communist leaders introduced a process of forced industrialization. Hungary did not have natural resources to develop heavy industry. Yet industrialization was pursued with emphasis on heavy industry, serving Soviet military interests. Industrial production increased in a haphazard way and consumer industry and housing were neglected. Productivity stagnated; the chemical and electrical industrial capacity remained negligible.

By 1952, 210,000 Hungarian men were serving in the armed forces. In addition, the secret police had 140,000 officers. Thus, about 3.5% of the total population was under arms. The share of the military from the state budget was enormous. Hungarians were overburdened and became impoverished. Only by maintaining a constant level of terror could such a system survive.

However, the Communist party was unable to earn respect from the population. Respect for laws in general also deteriorated. Cynicism, crime, and petty pilfering from factories and shops were common. There was an ever widening gap between reality and Marxist-Leninist ideology. Living standards plummeted, except for the party elite. But society was changing; forced industrialization and general education created a more complex social structure. To govern such a society, a minimal consensus was necessary. But even within the Communist Party there was no consensus. The ordinary members lost faith in Marxism-Leninism and realized that the party served Soviet interests.

After Stalin's death, his successors had not released control over Hungary. Some of the top echelons of the Hungarian Communist Party turned against the ruling Rákosiclique. They were headed by Imre Nagy. He wanted to halt forced industrialization, ease pressure on the peasants, and increase the production of consumer goods. The resistance of the Rákosiclique to reform resulted in revolution in October 1956. People wanted to remove the Soviet army from Hungary and the establishment of humane Socialism.

The Soviet leadership could not accept Hungary's independence. On November 4, 1956, they ordered the arrest of the Hungarian leadership. Two hundred thousand troops and two thousand tanks suppressed the revolution. The attack was indirectly helped by the preoccupation of the Western powers with the war over the Suez canal. Nikita Khrushchev named János Kádár Prime Minister of Hungary and he took terrible revenge. Imre Nagy, who fled to the Yugoslav embassy in Budapest, was enticed to leave and, despite promises to the contrary, was arrested and deported to Romania. In June 1958, he was executed. Kádár instituted a new wave of terror, taking thousands of victims. Approximately two hundred thousand Hungarians fled to the West.

The Communist Party, dissolved during the revolution, was reorganized. Its new name was Hungarian Socialist Workers Party. It attracted mostly cynical opportunists. Even party members no longer believed in its Marxist-Leninist ideology. By 1968, the regime was desperate for legitimacy. It introduced a set of economic reforms, originally proposed by Imre Nagy. The peasants could now own a private plot. They were permitted to sell their produce on the open market. However, the prices of essential consumer goods were still regulated. State monopolies over foreign trade were retained.

After the reforms, unprecedented economic activities began, as the peasants were given a certain measure of controlling their lives. Commerce with the Soviet Union and its satellites began to increase. Consumer goods, such as refrigerators and automobiles appeared, providing incentives for the population. Hungarians were permitted some travel abroad. The press was encouraged to criticize lower party officials. Kádár co-opted some intellectuals and permitted a little more freedom of speech. Yet the old taboos remained; no one could criticize the Soviet Union or the Hungarian communist leadership. In spite of the reforms, Kádár's Hungary was not even a semi-democratic state. The communist chief was an old-fashioned dictator whose word was final in all matters. Yet, Hungary began slowly to emerge from the terrible days of terror. Kádár was gradually accepted as "better than most" dictators. As long as life improved, the system was acceptable for most of the population.

However, instability continued. There was a conflict within the communist leadership over the application of Marxist-Leninist ideology. There were also reversals in economic reform. In the 1970s, the radicals in the leadership succeeded in reversing policies favoring the peasantry. Consequently, food production declined and supplies for the cities shrank. The course was, therefore, hastily reversed. The oil crisis of 1973, however, provided heavy blows to the Hungarian economy. Production coasts increased, exports declined and Hungary had to borrow heavily abroad. Hungary's national debt reached the astronomical figure of $20 billion. The leadership did not use the loans for the modernization of industry. Instead, products that could not be sold at competitive prices were subsidized. By the mid-1980s, the deterioration of economic conditions was obvious and the shaky legitimacy of the Kádár-regime came to an end.

The ascendance of Mikhail Gorbachev to power sent a signal that the old ways of politics were over. Intellectuals were emboldened to demand greater freedoms. Political dissidents appeared and underground publications multiplied. Marxist-Leninist interpretation of history lost all credibility.

The younger members of the communist leadership realized that Kádár became a liability. In March 1988, he was removed as prime minister. The party which he created could not survive without him. The murdered Imre Nagy and his followers were rehabilitated in May 1989. On the same day, János Kádár died.

A new government was formed under the premiership of Miklós Németh, a young, dynamic leader. His Minister of Education and Culture, Ferenc Glatz, abolished the compulsory teaching of the Russian language and Marxism in the schools and universities.

In October 1989, the Hungarian Socialist Workers Party was dissolved. Two successors emerged, one the party of the reformers now called the Hungarian Socialist party, and the other retained the old name.

In the following free elections, a new party, the Hungarian Democratic Forum, emerged victorious; its closest rival, the Association of Free Democrats, and the revived Smallholders' party joined in a new coalition government. The Németh government decided to open the western borders to East German refugees, indirectly contributing to the collapse of the Honecker regime in East Germany. The East European Soviet empire disappeared. By July 1991, the last Russian troops left Hungary.

In May 1991, the Warsaw Pact was dissolved. A parliamentary democracy led by József Antall was formed in Hungary. It privatized most state-owned factories and the land. The media was freed of state-control. Unfortunately, problems of nationalism, anti-Semitism, and impatience with dissenters reemerged.

Ferenc Madl was elected president in June 2000; the next presidential election, which is held in the National Assembly, will be in June 2005. The National Assembly elected Ferenc Gyurcsany Prime Minster in September 2004.

Hungary's economy has become steadily stronger since the dissolution of the Soviet Bloc. Its growth rate is estimated at 2.9%, though its debt is estimated at 57% of its gross domestic product (GDP) (2003). Hungary joined NATO in 1999 and the European Union in 2004, and is a member of the World Bank and the IMF. Inflation has declined from 14% (1999) to 4.7% (2003). Unemployment remains steady at about 6%. Foreign investment is strong, with Germany as the country's largest economic partner.

JOSEPH HELD

References and Further Reading

Balogh, Sándor. *Magyarország a Huszadik Században* (Hungary in the Twentieth Century). Budapest: Kossuth, 1985.

Bibó, István. *Democracy, Revolution, Self-Determination (Ed. By Károly Nagy)*. Boulder, CO: East Eur. Monographs, Columbia University Press, 1991.

Berend, Iván T. *The Hungarian Economy in the Twentieth Century*. London: Crown and Helm, 1989.

Fejt, Francois. *History of the Peoples' Democracies*. Paris, 1979.

Gati, Charles. *Hungary and the Soviet Block*. Durham, NC: Duke University Press, 1986.

Hann, C.N. *Market Economy and Civil Society in Hungary*. London, 1990.

Held, Joseph. *The Columbia History of Eastern Europe in the Twentieth Century*. New York, London: Columbia University Press, Mansell Imprint, 1992.

Horváth, Ágnes, and Szakolczai, Árpád. *The Dissolution of Communist Power. The Case of Hungary*. London: Ruttledge, 1992.

Kornai, János. *The Economy of Shortage*. Amsterdam, 1980.

Macartney, Carlise A. *Hungary and Her Successors. The Treaty of Trianon and Its Consequences, 1919–1937*. Edinburgh: Edinburgh University Press, 1961.

Molnár, Miklós. *A Short History of the Hungarian Communist Party*. Boulder, CO: East European Monographs, Columbia University Press, 1978.

Sakmister, Tomas. *Hungary, The Great Powers and the Danubian Crisis 1936–1939*. Athens, GA: Georgia University Press, 1980.

Swain, Nigel. *Hungary. The Rise and Fall of Feasible Socialism*. London: Verso, 1992.

HUSSEIN, KING OF JORDAN

Hussein bin Talal, known to his people as "the humane king," is considered the father of modern Jordan. He was born in Amman on November 14, 1935, into the Hashemite dynasty, and could trace his roots exactly forty-two generations directly back to the Prophet Mohammed. The Hashemites were natives of what became Saudi Arabia, but were rewarded by the British for their fight against the Ottoman Turks with control of the League of Nations Mandates over Iraq and Transjordan. Hussein's grandfather, King Abdallah, consolidated the synthetic monarchy by bringing Jordan's Bedouin tribes into the government and the army.

Hussein attended elementary school in Amman, and went on to a thoroughly British education at Victoria College in Egypt, the Harrow School in London, and the Royal Military Academy at Sandhurst. Hussein's entire life was shaped by the turbulent nature of Middle East politics in the 20th century. The boy was ten years old when Transjordan gained independence from Britain, twelve when the first Arab-Israeli war sent tens of thousands of Palestinian refugees into the kingdom, and sixteen when, on July 20, 1951, he witnessed his grandfather's assassination, at the hand of a Palestinian nationalist on the steps of the Al-Aqsa Mosque in Jerusalem. Hussein's father, Talal, assumed the throne, but as he was mentally ill, was soon declared unfit to rule. Hussein was proclaimed King on August 11, 1952. A regency council ruled on his behalf until he reached age eighteen (under the Islamic lunar calendar) on May 2, 1953.

The young king may not have realized at first how treacherous his political environment was, but after a 1957 coup attempt led by pro-Egyptian military officers he decisively asserted royal primacy, imposed martial law, and banned political parties for the next thirty-five years. King Hussein had the last word on all important domestic and foreign policy decisions, yet brought elements of all political factions into his consultative process. He was often compared to a tightrope walker. He succeeded in creating the only moderate, relatively humane state in the Arab Middle East.

Never a warrior at heart, Hussein nevertheless joined Egypt and Syria in the Six Day War of June 1967. Israel quickly took control of the holy sites in Jerusalem and expelled the Jordanian Army from the West Bank. King Hussein endorsed United Nations Resolution 242 offering Israel peace in exchange for return of all land conquered in the war. Israel never accepted that offer, and Jordan was burdened with a massive new influx of Palestinian refugees whose loyalty to the kingdom was often secondary to their enthusiasm for the Palestine Liberation Organization (PLO). Events came to a head in September 1970 after two attempts by Palestinians on the king's life: Hussein's Bedouin army launched an all-out war against the PLO and drove them from the kingdom forever. He was thereafter judged by many Arabs to be an appeaser of the Israelis. According to some reports, Hussein gave Israeli Prime Minister Golda Meir advance warning of Egyptian and Syrian war plans in 1973.

In 1988, Hussein ceded authority over the West Bank to the PLO, demonstrating once again his skillful tactic of accommodating his most murderous enemies. When the Iraqi dictator Saddam Hussein (no relation) invaded Kuwait in 1990, King Hussein refused to join other states in the region in condemning that action. He probably did so with one eye on the restive Palestinians, who comprised more than 50% of the population of his kingdom. Saudi Arabia and other Gulf states suspended financial aid in retaliation, severely damaging the Jordanian economy.

In the 1990s, after being diagnosed with cancer, Hussein carefully steered Jordan toward he the legacy he wished to leave—cautious democratization—while retaining his royal prerogatives. He lifted the ban on political parties and abolished martial law in 1992. Multi-party elections were held in 1993. In that same year, Hussein helped Israel and the PLO to negotiate a peace agreement, which unfortunately came undone five years later. On October 26, 1994, Jordan and Israel signed a treaty formally ending their forty-six–year state of war. Israeli leaders had come to trust him; indeed, many secretly slipped across the border to consult with Hussein in his palace in Amman. In 1995, Hussein attended the funeral of assassinated Israeli Prime Minister Yitzhak Rabin, whom he called his "partner in peace" and his "brother." Other Arab leaders denounced Hussein, but he promised his people that peace with Israel would bring economic growth and foreign investment. The actual results were disappointing, but the king adroitly maintained his balance by inviting into his cabinet critics of his own foreign policy.

Hussein publicly confirmed that he had lymphatic cancer in July 1998. In October of that year he checked himself out of the American hospital where he was being treated to appeal to the Israelis and the PLO to revive their sputtering peace process. But his time was running out. On January 24, 1999, he stunned his countrymen by designating his son Abdallah as heir to throne. His bypassed brother, Crown Prince Hasan, accepted the decision without public rancor. On February 5, Hussein flew home to Jordan from the US and two days later he passed away. He was the longest-serving head of state in the world. Mourners at his funeral included President Clinton, former presidents Bush, Carter, and Ford, Israeli Prime Minister Benyamin Netanyahu, PLO leader Yasser Arafat, Russian President Boris Yeltsin, and Syrian dictator Hafez Assad. His son took the throne as Abdallah II and promised to continue his father's legacy.

Hussein's private life was colorful. He married four times; one wife was an Englishwoman and one an American. He enjoyed auto racing, motorcycling, and flying his own jet plane. He loved tennis and water skiing. He wrote three books including one entitled *Uneasy Lies the Head*. His long reign is remembered for a relatively good human rights record and huge improvements in his country's living standards.

ROSS MARLAY

See also Jordan; Middle East: History and Economic Development; Middle East: International Relations; Palestinian Diaspora

References and Further Reading

Dallas, Roland. *King Hussein: A Life on the Edge*. Fromm Intl., 1999.
Lunt, James. *Hussein of Jordan*. William Morrow, 1989.
Matusky, Gregory, et al. *King Hussein*. Chelsea House, 1987.

HUSSEIN, SADDAM

Saddam Hussein reined Iraq for twenty-four years of absolute power (1979–2003). Often dismissed in the West as deranged, Saddam possessed a keen instinct for human weakness and shrewdly mastered the calculus of power. His personalized, secular dictatorship was not truly totalitarian for it lacked a coherent ideology, but all Iraqis were kept in a state of terror.

Saddam Hussein al-Tikriti was born on April 28, 1937, into a landless peasant family in Tikrit District, about one hundred miles north of Baghdad. His father died either before or shortly after Saddam was born and his mother quickly re-married. Saddam ran away from his abusive stepfather to live with his maternal uncle, an anti-British nationalist and bigot who published a pamphlet the title of which foreshadowed Saddam's own views: "Three Whom God Should Not Have Created: Persians, Jews, and Flies."

Saddam's middle school education equipped him with little understanding of the West. He applied to Baghdad Military Academy but was rejected for poor grades. Revolutionary politics suited him better. Captivated by the pan-Arab rhetoric of Egyptian President Gamal Abdel Nasser, Saddam joined the Ba'ath (Renaissance) Party in 1956. Two years later Gen. Abdul Karim Kassem overthrew the Hashemite monarchy and Iraq became a republic. Saddam was part of a Ba'athist squad that tried to assassinate Kassem in 1959. Hussein was wounded in the shoot-out, but escaped to Syria and then to Egypt, where he remained until 1963. While ostensibly studying law, he collaborated with other Iraqi exiles. In February 1963, the Ba'athists finally succeeded in killing Kassem and Saddam returned home. He enrolled in Baghdad Law College and married his cousin Sajida. Saddam was arrested and imprisoned in 1964 for plotting to overthrow President Abdul Salem Aref, but he escaped in 1966.

Saddam's faction seized power in a coup (later termed a "revolution") on July 17, 1968. Saddam organized a secret police force whose first assignment was to purge Iraqi Jews. He was named Vice-President of the Revolutionary Command Council in November 1969 by his cousin, President Hassan al-Bakr, and for the next ten years gradually gathered power to himself. On July 16, 1979, al-Bakr resigned "for reasons of health," and Saddam became President. All potential rivals were swiftly eliminated in a wave of executions. To harden his teenage sons, Saddam made them witness these killings. Saddam trusted no one, and relied so heavily on his own clan that he outlawed the use of surnames to hide the fact that so many of his ministers were named "al-Tikriti" (indicating their origin in Saddam's home town).

Saddam modernized Iraq. Money flowed in after the Ba'athists nationalized the Iraq Petroleum Company (1972) and the Organization of Petroleum Exporting Countries (OPEC) quadrupled the price of crude oil. Saddam's government built roads and extended irrigation canals. Factories sprang up. Primary education was made compulsory and the university system was expanded. The position of women was greatly improved.

These social and economic advances came at an appalling price in human rights. East Germans trained Saddam's secret police force, which eventually grew to one hundred thousand men. Saddam Hussein sought security by making the Iraqi people, especially those close to him, desperately insecure. He personally shot a general for urging military caution and is rumored to have dropped a dissident into a vat of acid with his own hands. He killed his own brother-in-law and forced officials to execute other officials. Sometimes executions were televised.

All Iraqi newspapers echoed the government line, as did radio and television stations. Photographs of Saddam adorned public buildings and even private homes. Bronze statues of the autocrat on horseback appeared in the cities. Saddam apparently considered himself a reincarnation of King Nebuchadnezzar (who destroyed Jerusalem in 587 BC). He dreamed of overrunning the entire Middle East, permanently eliminating Israel, and asserting Iraqi primacy over Syria and Egypt.

Saddam's grandiose ambitions led to strategic blunders. The first was his disastrous war against Iran. It was not unprovoked, for the Ayatollah Khomeini had tried to use Arab Shi'ites (63% of the Iraqi population) to overthrow Saddam's Sunni-dominated regime. In September 1980, the Iraqi army invaded Iran and captured the Shatt al-Arab waterway, where the Tigris and Euphrates rivers merge to flow into the Persian Gulf. Saddam expected a quick victory, and when it did not materialize he executed three hundred high-ranking officers. The eight-year Iran-Iraq war featured the first use of poison gas since World War I and missile attacks against cities. When a cease-fire was finally signed in 1988, Iraq found itself $80 billion in debt, mostly to Kuwait and Saudi Arabia. This led to an even greater blunder—the Iraqi invasion of Kuwait.

Saddam's surprise attack of August 2, 1990, routed the Kuwaitis. He declared Kuwait the 19th province of Iraq and asserted that he had thereby redressed colonial injustice, but his main objective was to gain control of Kuwait's enormous oil reserves. Saddam evidently calculated that President George H.W. Bush would not react, for the American ambassador had told him that Washington had no position on territorial disputes "between Arabs and Arabs." Ignoring United Nations ultimatums, Saddam, who had never served in the army, promoted himself to the rank of field marshal and prepared his people for "the mother of all battles." The war began on January 16, 1991. After five weeks of aerial bombardment, Iraqi forces were so weakened that the ground war lasted only four days. Before a cease-fire was signed (February 27, 1991) Iraqi troops set fire to Kuwait's oil wells and dumped thousands of gallons of crude oil into the Persian Gulf. Then he proclaimed his defeat to be a victory. Saddam tried to have the first President Bush assassinated, which may have been a factor in his own undoing at the hands of the second President Bush.

In the wake of the war, Saddam faced twin uprisings, one by the Kurdish people of northern Iraq and the other by Arab Shi'ites in the south. The Kurds achieved *de facto* independence under the umbrella of a northern "no-fly zone" enforced by British and American jet fighter-bombers. A similar "no-fly zone" in the south could not protect the Shi'ites from Saddam's wrath. He drained the southern marshes, burned villages, and randomly shelled Basra with heavy artillery. Some captured rebels were made to drink gasoline and then set on fire.

Saddam attempted to arrange a political succession under which power would be inherited by his younger son, Qusay (born 1967). Saddam evidently had concluded that his older son Uday (born 1964), who personally tortured Iraqi Olympic athletes, had become unbalanced after a 1996 assassination attempt. His son-in-law, Hussein Kamil, had at one time been in line to inherit power, but he defected to Jordan, was lured home with promises of forgiveness, and murdered.

Saddam clung tenaciously to power until 2003. United Nations weapons inspectors crippled his nuclear, biological, and chemical weapons programs, but were unable to certify the total elimination of such weapons. The inspectors were expelled in 1998, and comprehensive economic sanctions remained in place. Saddam blamed the West for the misery the trade embargo brought to his people. He used revenue from oil exports permitted under the "oil-for-food" program to build more palaces, a total of twenty-six by one count. Saddam Hussein applauded the terror attacks of September 11, 2001. Influential members of the George W. Bush administration were already planning his overthrow. Saddam's final blunder was to refuse a Saudi offer of safe exile just before the American invasion of Iraq in 2003.

United States and coalition forces invaded Iraq in March 2003 and swiftly took Baghdad. Uday and Qusay were killed in a shootout in July. American infantrymen found Saddam on December 13, 2003, hiding in an underground vault near his home village. His captors faced a dilemma—how to try him for his crimes without allowing the cunning ex-dictator to portray himself to the world as a nationalist martyr. Saddam Hussein won a certain grudging respect from some Arabs who admired him for defying Israel and the West. In June 2004, Saddam and eleven other major defendants were handed into Iraqi custody with the return of sovereignty to the country.

Ross Marlay

See also Iran–Iraq War, 1980-1988; Iraq; Middle East: History and Economic Development; Middle East: International Relations

References and Further Reading

Al-Khalil, Samir. *Republic of Fear: The Politics of Modern Iraq.* Berkeley, CA: University of California Press, 1989.
Bengio, Ofra. *Saddam's Word: Political Discourse in Iraq.* New York: Oxford University Press, 1998.
Cockburn, Andrew and Patrick Cockburn. *Out of the Ashes: The Resurrection of Saddam Hussein.* New York: HarperCollins, 1999.
Coughlin, Con. *Saddam: King of Terror.* New York: HarperCollins, 2002.
Henderson, Simon. *Instant Empire: Saddam Hussein's Ambition for Iraq.* San Francisco: Mercury House, 1991.
Karsh, Efraim and Inari Rautsi. *Saddam Hussein: A Political Biography.* New York: Free Press, 1991.
Mackey, Sandra. *The Reckoning: Iraq and the Legacy of Saddam Hussein.* New York: Norton, 2002.

I

IMPORT SUBSTITUTION INDUSTRIALIZATION

Import substitution has been the dominant vehicle by which industrialization in large developing countries has proceeded. Many countries in Latin America, such as Argentina, Brazil, Chile, Colombia, and Mexico, have since the 1940s most vigorously pursued this strategy as their main growth-generating force. Other countries followed in the 1950s and 1960s. In the 1970s increasing disenchantment with this strategy emerged and an alternative approach, identified as outward (or export) oriented and associated with East Asian development, became more popular (Edwards 1993). However, remnants of the import substitution approach still persist in some Latin American countries and in Africa.

Import substitution is a process whereby a greater proportion of a country's total demand for goods is satisfied through its own domestic production. As the term implies, it involves substituting domestically made products for previously imported goods. By its nature, import substitution involves import restrictions such as tariffs, which are a tax on imports. These tariffs allow domestic producers to supply the product locally, and capture some or the entire market share, depending on how prohibitively high the tariff rate is set. Commonly, the protection package provided to fledgling local suppliers involved tariffs, quotas that restrict the quantity of imports of a product allowed into the country, and a favourable exchange rate.

All countries go through a process of "natural" import substitution. As average income rises, the domestic manufacture of processed foods, beverages, textiles, clothing, and other simple commodities is undertaken in response to growing local demand. Import substitution industrialization, however, occurs as a matter of deliberate development policy consciously guided by governments.

Why Was Import Substitution Industrialization Promoted?

Albert Hirschman (1971, p. 89) noted that

> Wars and Depressions have historically no doubt been most important in bringing industries to countries of the 'periphery' which up to then had remained firmly remained in the nonindustrial category. The crucial role of the two world wars and the Great Depression in undermining acceptance of traditional ideas about the international division of labor between advanced and backward countries is well known.

During the war years, with the sudden deprivation of imports and foreign exchange, developing countries had no option but to become self-reliant and set up domestic import-replacing industries. Persistent balance of payments deficits in peacetime were a further inducement to restrict imports. However, what started out as a response to circumstances was soon rationalized as a strategy to transform the structure of the economy to achieve higher levels of economic prosperity. Many of these poor countries were agricultural and natural resource-based producers.

Richer countries were primarily industrial nations. Efforts to promote industrialization were seen as an essential prerequisite to achieving comparable living standards.

By creating a domestic industrial base, import substitution would accelerate the movement of resources out of the low-productivity rural sector and into higher-skilled manufacturing. Initially, local suppliers would have to be nurtured and protected from the competitive pressures applied by long-established foreign producers. Over time, domestic inefficiencies would decline as these "infants" learned from experience and were able to reduce costs of production. The end result would be a far more diversified and self-reliant economic structure that is less dependent on the vagaries of the international market price for a small number of primary products like sugar, rubber, or tin. Developing countries had long been suspicious that, in their trade of primary products for imported manufactured goods, the terms of trade had been steadily moving against them. They then had to export more and more of their resource-based products to pay for the same amount of the imported manufactured goods (Meier and Seers 1984).

Import Substitution in Practice

The import substitution strategy has played a key role in the transformation of the economic structure of many developing countries. The process begins at the final stages of production where industries assemble parts and components and turn out finished consumer goods. By limiting the import of the final consumer good, but not the required inputs, an opportunity is created for producers to assemble the product locally. This phase appears to be very successful and tariff protection is provided for a wide range of final consumer goods production. Eventually, expansion of finished consumer goods capacity reaches the limit of the domestic market. There are then two options: expand the market through exports or deepen the process of import substitution through domestic production of the parts and components. The Latin American countries have mostly followed the latter path. A small number of East Asian countries began manufacturing for export and are pursuing an alternative development strategy.

Those countries that deepened their import substitution have done so by requiring their manufacturers to buy a certain percentage of their inputs locally and increasing the percentage progressively. The earlier consumption goods phase of import substitution was now being replaced with a capital and intermediate

goods phase, which requires more specialized and technically complex production processes. Domestic content regulations now placed increasing strains on local skills and capabilities.

Many of the problems associated with import substitution stem from this deepening process. Local producers need higher rates of protection to remain viable. The effective rate of protection is a concept economists use to measure the assistance that domestic producers receive. During the 1960s the average effective rate of protection on manufactured products in Brazil was 118% and Chile 182%. In India and Pakistan the rates were even higher (Little, Scitovsky, and Scott 1970). Often the infant industries remained as inefficient, high-cost producers selling their goods to the local population at grossly inflated prices. The increasing industrial complexity placed even more demands on overstretched government bureaucrats. In the quest for industrial planning there was a proliferation of administrative regulations and controls—differential taxation, import and investment licensing, tariffs, and quotas.

As the production processes became more capital-centred and technology driven, employment growth diminished. There was a shift away from labour-intensive industries such as textiles toward industries such as chemicals and metalworking that were more sophisticated and automated. A strong "urban bias" was another characteristic of this process. Resources were deliberately allocated to urban areas and the rural sectors were often neglected. Rural–urban migration and regional inequality were often consequences of this.

A Reconsideration

Import substitution has been an essential component of industrialization in large developing countries. The experiences of Latin America are instructive here. Before the Great Depression, development in Latin American countries was stimulated by export-propelled growth. This phase ended by roughly 1949. The next phase of Latin American growth came via growth of the domestic market through import substitution and flourished particularly in the 1950s. During the 1960s the enthusiasm for this approach was waning not only in this developing region, but also in India and Pakistan (Hirschman 1971).

The problems that have arisen relate to the lack of selectivity in the industries supported and the faulty incentive mechanisms used. Governments need to find the right activities to promote, to support them in ways that minimize distortions and inefficiencies, and provide appropriate incentives for firms to assimilate and improve technological capacity to achieve international best practice (Bruton 1998). Moreover, import substitution may be a transitional phase that eventually leads to an expansion of manufactured exports. Once the industrial base expands, as reflected in the scale and diversification of production and the availability of skilled personnel, industries initially producing for the home market move into export markets (Chenery, Robinson, and Syrquin 1986). This has happened in a number of countries and is one indicator of successful import substitution industrialization.

JOHN LODEWIJKS

See also Central Asia: History and Economic Development; Development History and Theory; East Asia: History and Economic Development; Export-Oriented Economies; Industrialization; Mexico: History and Economic Development; Northern South America: History and Economic Development; Southern Cone (Latin America): History and Economic Development; Technology: Impact on Development

References and Further Reading

Amsden, Alice H. *Asia's Next Giant: South Korea and Late Industrialization*. New York: Oxford University Press, 1989.
Bruton, Henry J. "A Reconsideration of Import Substitution." *Journal of Economic Literature*, Vol. 36, June 1998.
Chenery, Hollis, Sherman Robinson, and Moshe Syrquin. *Industrialization and Growth: A Comparative Study*. New York: Oxford University Press, 1986.
Edwards, Sebastian. "Openness, Trade Liberalization and Growth in Developing Countries." *Journal of Economic Literature*, Vol. 31, September 1993.
Hirschman, Albert O. *A Bias for Hope: Essays on Development and Latin America*. New Haven, CT: Yale University Press, 1971.
Krause, Lawrence B., and Kim Kihwan, eds. *Liberalization in the Process of Economic Development*. Berkeley, CA: University of California Press, 1991.
Little, Ian, Tibor Scitovsky, and Maurice Scott. *Industry and Trade in some Developing Countries*. London: Oxford University Press, 1970.
Meier, Gerald M., and Dudley Seers, eds. *Pioneers in Development*. New York: Oxford University Press, 1984.
World Bank, World Development Report 1987. *Industrialization and Foreign Trade*. New York: Oxford University Press, 1987.

INCOME DISTRIBUTION

Recent discussions on income distribution can be divided into three main debates, according to their focus. Initially, income distribution was a topic discussed in the context of social or distributive justice within one society, mainly although not exclusively in Western societies. Secondly, the theories developed in this debate were then used as a basis for evaluating if we took the notion of global justice seriously, what model of income distribution should be used to establish global distributive justice. Recently, the first set of considerations on models of welfare systems and principles of justice has been used to look into social policy in developing countries, where additional models to the existing set are acknowledged to exist, in addition to a normative debate on which, if any, of the existing models should be emphasised in the international effort to establish good governance in the global south. Of course, these categories are not impermeable: work done on the capabilities approach fits partly into the categories of domestic and of global justice when it proposes capabilities as the currency of justice instead of welfare, rights, or duties (Nussbaum 2001; Sen 1991, 1997, and 1999). A second line of work on this approach is the measurement of development via indicators that would describe people's capabilities. This line would fit into the category of social policy in developing countries.

Some people would also make a distinction between work on models of welfare provision and theories of social justice; this is a refinement of the categories above that would lead us into too much detail for the present purposes. Here, we will therefore use the distinction among the three areas of debate as a guideline for discussion of the issue of income distribution. This allows us to separate out theories with a domestic focus on justice and welfare, theories with a focus on global principles of justice, and work on applying theories to developing countries, without complicating matters too much.

Distributive Justice in One Society

The idea of redistribution through progressive taxation forms part of most liberal Western societies' social policy makeup. The design of welfare states started as early as the end of the nineteenth century with the call from newly formed labour unions for social security and especially sick pay and pensions. However, the main work on developing systems of social security and collective insurance against unemployment took place in the twentieth century. Arguments for social justice were initially made mainly in the context of political struggle, and the late US professor John Rawls is widely recognised as the instigator of contemporary theoretical debates on social justice. In 1971, after a long silence in political philosophy on anything to do with ethics and morality, he started up the debate again with his book *A Theory of Justice*. Rawls tried to systematise the thinking about justice after a period in which the utilitarian approach of cost-benefit analysis and the intuitive approach to justice were most popular. He proposed to use a thought experiment to derive principles of justice that could be accepted by all under certain just circumstances and should therefore be accepted in real life as fair. Principles of justice in Rawlsian theories are developed by asking, "What would free and equal people choose under circumstances of impartiality?" In order to arrive at those principles, Rawls introduced what he called an "Original Position" where people deliberate on principles of justice without knowledge of their position in society, talents, or earning potential. This is called the "veil of ignorance." Some additional criteria are that there is no envy, no risk taking, and generally a mutual disinterest: there are no special feelings toward anyone in the group. The principles that would be agreed to under those circumstances are, according to Rawls:

1. Equal liberty
2. a) Inequalities to the benefit of the worst off (Difference Principle)
   b) Positions open to all

These principles apply to the basic institutions of society that distribute the benefits and burdens of society. What is to be distributed fairly are the primary goods, i.e., goods that everyone needs in order to realise their conception of the good life: income, wealth, power, liberty, rights, and opportunities.

Criticism of Rawls

Rawls received two types of criticism: internal criticism that proposed modifications and external criticism that proposed alternatives to his theory. It was felt that the "no envy restriction" was not realistic and if people were allowed to include envy, then this would lead to a more equal outcome. The same could be said for the mutual disinterest: if people were allowed to include their altruism, the outcome would also be more equal. The mixture of self-interest with impartiality was regarded by some as incoherent. Impartiality should be the only basis for deliberation and the outcome would then again be more equal. Also, it was thought to be unclear what would count as benefiting the worst off. If capitalist investment is always seen to benefit the worst off, then what is the difference between Rawls and a libertarian? All these

criticisms can be seen as respecting Rawls' starting point but aiming for a more equal outcome by changing the circumstances under which the principles are chosen. This is why they are called internal criticisms.

External criticisms of Rawls were put forward by people who proposed alternatives to his theory. Robert Nozick, for example, developed a libertarian theory of justice in his *Anarchy State and Utopia* (1974). His main objection is that Rawlsian justice requires redistribution from the rich to the poor. Nozick holds that taxation of the rich infringes upon their property rights and he calls taxation "on a par with forced labour." However, this objection can be countered by noticing that if you do not work, you do not pay tax and therefore taxation does not force you to work. Property rights do not necessarily have to be absolute and the entitlements to the property could be unfair in the first place.

A later external criticism of Rawls, and liberalism more generally, came from a group of theorists sometimes called communitarians. The main proponents are Michael Sandel, Alasdair MacIntyre, and Charles Taylor. Their objection is that Rawls' contractarian approach assumes the individual to exist prior to society, whereas instead individuals are born into a society. This means that principles of justice should be found in the traditions of the community and not by abstract reasoning. Since individuals' goals and ethical judgements are bound up with community life, justice requires respect for communities and the values associated with it. Rawls' theory, according to communitarians, supports the divisive and over-individualistic tendencies in Western democracies.

However, a response to communitarian criticism of Rawls could argue that by taking the values of communities as given, their theory of justice cannot criticise existing practices. Moreover, it is not clear which community is most important: local, national, global? It is not clear who defines what the values of the community are. How are critics of the dominant group treated?

However, both libertarianism and communitarianism represent strongly held intuitions by large groups of people, and Rawlsian liberalism has responded by at least refining and making more explicit its position on the relevance of community and freedom. Rawls himself adopted a modified position in his *Political Liberalism* (1993) where he sets out that justice is not metaphysical but political, and there are no ultimate justifications but dialogue. Others have further pursued the original Rawlsian contractarian line, especially in the debate on Global justice, as we will see below.

Before we move on to the issue of global justice, we pay attention to two more external criticisms of

Rawlsian principles of social justice: feminism and Marxism.

Feminism is especially interesting because it has put forward both an internal and an external critique of Rawls' work. The main exponent of the internal criticism is the liberal feminist Susan Moller Okin (1989). Her main objections are that the Original Position only includes heads of households and they are assumed to be male; the family is not part of the basic structure to which principles of justice apply; sex is not included under the veil of ignorance; and finally, self-interest leads to a lack of benevolence. Okin, however, still finds Rawls' approach helpful: if these three aspects are changed, she argues, it would have radical consequences from a feminist point of view. In response Rawls could argue that heads of households could be women. Rawls has in fact argued that the family is in the basic structure of society, although he could also argue that gender is not relevant in the Original Position, since we all have knowledge of who are the worst off in society. Rawls could also argue that mutual disinterest is not egoism.

External critiques of Rawls by feminists have been put forward by Gilligan (1982), Nodding (1986), and Benhabib (1987), amongst others. Their main thesis is that liberalism leaves out women's voices. Gilligan claims that her research of moral judgments shows that women have a different perception of morality than men. The "different voice" is referred to as a perspective of care rather than a perspective of justice. A perspective of care differs from a perspective of justice in that it emphasises social relationships rather than rules and it is geared toward conflict resolution, and this means that justice is too abstract; it views individuals as separate and isolated; it focuses on the public domain; it advocates an impartial point of view, which ignores special ties; and it advocates one moral principle for all situations. The proposed alternative of feminist ethics holds that actual experience should inform moral theory; theory should be directly applicable in real life; real persons, related to others, should be the focus; the private should be included, with friendship as the model; and, finally, different ethics for different domains should be developed. Nodding, too, proposes the ethics of care as an alternative to justice. Benhabib views feminism as a critique that would lead to a different perspective on the world and therefore on justice based on gender inequality.

The external criticism of Rawlsian justice as put forward by Marxism is often also labelled as an egalitarian approach to justice, although not all egalitarians have a Marxist analysis. Here we give three prior warnings: (1) Marx's work is not the same as Marxism; (2) Marx's view of justice (and even whether he had one) is contested; and (3) Marx wrote before Rawls, so to say he criticised Rawls is an anachronism. Having put these warnings in place, we can safely say that Marx himself was critical of human rights, as he viewed them as divisive—especially the right to private property, but also the right to individual freedom as it was primarily based on keeping others out of one's sphere of autonomy. As an alternative, Marx proposed his famous principle, "from each according to capacity, to each according to needs."

Later expressions of egalitarianism criticised the Rawlsian approach for allowing the assessment of whether or not the worst off are better off with more inequality to include the idea of compensation for less income by employment opportunities, and they question what is used as the baseline of comparison. Less inequality can be more attractive than the status quo, yet proper equality can be even better. This type of critique leads into the discussion of what needs to be distributed fairly. Since we are discussing income distribution, it needs to be clear that egalitarians may not argue for complete inequality without attention to the overall level of income; yet, egalitarians would argue that Rawls' argument on incentives for the "talented" making some inequality more attractive for the worst off should be curbed, for example, by a maximum ratio of inequality between the highest and the lowest incomes.

Now we will look at how this debate on just principles of income distribution has affected thinking about global justice and about social policy models in developing countries.

Global Distributive Justice

The end of the Cold War and the process of globalisation could be seen as factors contributing to the growth in literature on global justice. The growing gap between rich and poor and the persistence of dramatic poverty, as well as deaths from preventable diseases, increasingly raise questions of responsibility beyond national borders. The changing economic order has instigated a discussion on fair rules of the game in world trade and duties of redistribution to guarantee the welfare rights of poor people wherever they are in the world. In other words, income distribution worldwide has become a major subject of discussion. Current debates range from proposals for a global progressive tax system to arguments for the satisfaction of basic needs through international institutions.

Cosmopolitanism's early roots lie in the works of the ancient Greeks and the philosophers of the

Enlightenment, especially Kant. The main source for Kant's cosmopolitanism is his Categorical Imperative: "Act only in such a way that I can also will that my maxim should become a universal law" (Kant 1991, p. 67). Contemporary cosmopolitanism can be seen as a continuation of the Rawlsian debate on justice. In 1993 Rawls argued for the basic rules of international law in his Amnesty Lecture, "The Law of Peoples" (Rawls 1993), but he did not argue for the globalisation of the Difference Principle. The Difference Principle was not applicable to international justice, according to Rawls, since persons' adverse fate is more often to be born into a distorted and corrupt political culture than into a country lacking resources. The only principle that does away with that misfortune "is to make the political traditions and culture of all peoples reasonable and able to sustain just political and social institutions that secure political and social institutions that secure human rights... distributive justice for this purpose" (Rawls 1993, footnote 52).

Others took up the theme of international justice and extended Rawls' original theory of justice as fairness (Beitz 1979; Pogge 1987). This tradition in political philosophy is now well established. In recent years, this tradition has also been seen as a valuable contribution to new approaches within international relations theory (Brown 1997; Beitz 1999).

Moral Duties Based on Global Interdependence: The Role of Globalisation

An important question for cosmopolitans is whether rich nations have duties to redistribute wealth to poor nations based on the interdependence created by economic and cultural globalisation, or whether they have these duties simply because they are rich. Or is it a duty based on historic injustice such as slavery and colonialism?

The main proponent of a moral theory based explicitly on growing interdependence is Beitz (1979). Although he altered his argument (Beitz 1983), many people share the intuition that globalisation causes a shift in the moral duties toward people across boundaries. In a historical period where we know of the existence of others and have intensive interaction with them, morality and obligations are denied only by outright moral sceptics. The form global interaction has taken, according to Beitz (1979), leads to a strong argument for global duties of redistribution. Since nation-states are no longer self-contained, justice becomes a global matter and cannot be coherently theorised within models of one society.

However, this position can be criticised for relying on empirical facts which can be disputed and moreover it can be rejected on the basis that normative positions should not be derived from them. A recently suggested alternative takes globalisation seriously as an element in the increasing demand for moral reasoning while not relying on it. O'Neill avoids the question "What are the obligations from one person to others in the world?" and asks instead, "What are our obligations in the present time?" (O'Neill 1996). In her argument for global justice she acknowledges that in today's world, theories of justice for a wider scope than national societies are unavoidable: "Today questions of global distributive justice will arise whether or not we can find the theoretical possibilities to handle them. Modern technical and institutional possibilities make far wider intervention not only possible but unavoidable" (O'Neill 1991, p. 277). This means that income distribution can no longer be an issue for single nation-states only. Her approach holds that when we interact with others across borders, we make quite complicated assumptions about the agents and subjects we deal with. It would be incoherent to deny those agents or subjects moral standing while clearly assuming their complexities when we interact.

Since in our world action, which is globally institutionalised, is a reality, O'Neill's approach shows that a more or less cosmopolitan view of moral standing is contingently appropriate. O'Neill concludes therefore that "[i]f we owe justice to those whose moral standing we acknowledge [by our actions] we will owe it to strangers as well as to neighbours and to distant strangers as well as to those who are relatively near at hand" (O'Neill 1995).

Some have argued that O'Neill's approach lacks a list of precise duties, for example, on global income redistribution. O'Neill can also be criticised for relying on a notion of human agency that, although it is a minimal one, is grounded in metaphysics. And if this is the case, then one may as well be explicit about one's metaphysical assumptions and bring them into the debate (Flikschuh 2000).

An alternative approach is to argue that rich countries are responsible for poverty as they are benefiting from the unequal trading rules (Pogge 2001). Whichever argument one opts for, it is clear that there are strong calls for global redistribution that would result in a more equal income distribution between rich and poor countries. Even global institutions like the United Nations Development Program (UNDP) and International Labor Organization (ILO) have called for global justice and fair globalisation (van den Anker 2005).

CHRISTIEN VAN DEN ANKER

See also Poverty: Impact on Development; Women: Role in Development

References and Further Reading

Anker, C. van den. "Global Governance and Global Justice: An Assessment of Recent Proposals" *Globalizations* 2(3), 2005.

Beitz, C. R. *Political Theory and International Relations.* Princeton, NJ: Princeton University Press, 1979.

———. "Cosmopolitan Ideals and National Sentiment." *Journal of Philosophy* 80, pp. 591–600, 1983.

———. "International Liberalism and Distributive Justice: A Survey of Recent Thought." *World Politics* 51, pp. 269–296, 1999.

Benhabib, S., and D. Cornell eds. *Feminism as Critique.* Cambridge, UK: Polity, 1987.

Brown, C. "Review Article: Theories of International Justice." *British Journal of Political Science* 27, pp. 273–297, 1997.

Flikschuh, K. "Metaphysics and the Boundaries of Justice." In C. van den Anker, ed., *Cosmopolitanis Distributive Justice and Violence. Special Issue of Global Society* 14(4), 2000.

Gilligan, C. *In a Different Voice: Psychological Theory* and *Women's Development.* Cambridge, MA: Harvard University Press, 1982.

Nodding, N. *Caring: A Feminine Approach to Ethics and Moral Education.* Berkeley, CA: University of California Press, 1986.

Nozick, Robert. *Anarchy State and Utopia.* New York: Basic Books, 1974.

Nussbaum, M. *Women and Human Development: The Capabilities Approach.* Cambridge, UK: Cambridge University Press, 2001.

Okin, S. Moller. *Justice, Gender, and the Family.* New York: Basic Books, 1991.

O'Neill, O. "Transnational Justice." In D. Held, ed., *Political Theory Today.* Cambridge, UK: Polity, 1991.

———. "Moral Standing and State Boundaries." *Christopher Thorne Memorial Lecture.* University of Sussex, December 5, 1995.

———. *Towards Justice and Virtue. A Constructive Account of Practical Reasoning.* Cambridge, UK: Cambridge University Press, 1996.

Pogge, Th. W. *Realizing Rawls.* Ithaca and London: Cornell University Press, 1987.

———, ed. *Global Justice.* Oxford, UK: Blackwell, 2001.

Rawls, J. *A Theory of Justice.* Oxford, UK: Oxford University Press, 1972.

———. "The Law of Peoples." In: S. Shute and S. Hurley, eds., *On Human Rights. The Oxford Amnesty Lectures 1993.* New York: Basic Books, 1993.

———. *The Law of Peoples.* Cambridge, MA: Harvard University Press, 2000.

Sen, A. "Equality of What?" In S. M. McMurrin, ed., *Liberty, Equality and Law. Selected Tanner Lectures on Moral Philosophy.* Cambridge, UK: Cambridge University Press, 1987.

———. "Development as Capability Expansion." In K. Griffin et al., eds., *Human Development and the International Strategy for the 1990s.* London: Macmillan, 1990.

———. *Development as Freedom.* Oxford, UK: Oxford University Press, 1999.

INDIA

The Republic of India is situated in southern Asia and occupies approximately 1.27 million square miles, which makes it roughly one-third the size of the United States. Geographically, India is split into three regions: the Indo-Gangetic Plain and the Himalayas, known together as North India, and South India. India is bordered by Pakistan in the Northwest and by China, Nepal, Bhutan, Burma, and Bangladesh in the Northeast and has approximately 4,400 miles of seacoast. The terrain varies from mountainous to flat and the climate varies from subtropical monsoon in the South to the more temperate in the North. The population is estimated at 1.05 billion with an estimated annual growth rate of 1.6%. The capital, New Delhi, is located in Northern India and has a population of 12.8 million.

India's present geographical boundaries were the result of British partitioning in 1947. Fueled by increasing hostility between Hindus and Muslims, the British decided to partition India. Consequently, this created an East and West Pakistan, whose populations were predominantly Muslim. East Pakistan would later become Bangladesh. Prior to British colonial rule, India was governed by a vast array of kingdoms, dating as far back as the Mauryan Empire (326–184 BC). While the Mauryan Empire was the first imperial kingdom, Indian civilization itself dates as far back as 2500 BC. Known as Harrapan culture (2500–1600 BC), remnants found at the two ancient cities of Mohenjo-daro and Harappa reveal a civilization with an advanced writing system, art, commerce, and sophisticated engineering. Harrapan culture was eventually displaced by invaders from the Northwest, the Indo-Aryans. The Aryans brought with them their own pantheistic religion, language system, familial structures, and social order.

The first Europeans to arrive in India were the Portuguese. In 1498, the voyager Vasco da Gama arrived in Calicut and claimed sovereignty of the Indian seas. He immediately came into conflict with the ruler of Calicut and was forced to withdraw, eventually making an establishment at Cochin. While the Portuguese never established an Indian empire, they were instrumental in establishing a thriving commercial trade as part of India's economic structure. After the Europeans defeated the Spanish Armada, it become increasingly clear that Portuguese domination of the Indian Ocean was subject to challenge.

British government interests in India were primarily economic. The British government initially did not run or control India, nor did they intend to, but rather organizations such as the British East India

Company (1603) did. Over time, commercial activities became increasingly involved in the political landscape of India. This entailed, among other things, being involved with local political rivalries between various rulers that often interfered with commerce. As the size of the Company grew, it found itself an Indian power in its own right. Often the Company found itself collecting taxes and running the affairs of other local rulers. The British government did not want commercial concerns to interfere in the affairs of foreign lands without its supervision and subsequently took steps to bring the activities of the Company under its control. The first step it took was the passage of the Regulating Act of 1773. Eventually, the British government realized that India could not be effectively run as a commercial enterprise. In 1858, India became the possession of the British Crown. India was a British colony until its independence in 1947.

Mohandas Karamchand Gandhi (1869–1948) was instrumental in securing popular support for an independent India. Armed with a law degree from England, his civil activist career started out unassuming enough. But his gentle nature, positive attitude, and persevering character would soon enthrall the whole of India. He was assassinated on January 30, 1948 on his way to an evening prayer.

When the British relinquished their claim to sovereignty over India, there were approximately 562 princely states. Each of the states was given the option of joining one of two countries, India or Pakistan. The subsequent partitioning had disastrous effects on India. Untold numbers of people lost their lives and property. There were numerous conflicts over the demarcation of boundaries, assets, and the equitable sharing of water. The control of Kashmir has been a particularly troublesome aspect of partitioning. Kashmir was predominantly Muslim and during partitioning it remained uncommitted to joining India. On October 27, 1947, however, after forceful induction by armed tribesmen and some regular troops from Pakistan, Kashmir was forced to sign an Instrument of Succession to India. The Pakistani government did not recognize the legality of the Instrument of Succession and war ensued. Kashmir remains a violently disputed territory to this day.

On August 15, 1947, India became independent. The British left India in very poor condition. India emerged from World War II with a deteriorating scientific and industrial base and a rapidly expanding population. Most people lived in small villages and were divided by severe inequalities in the distribution of wealth and basic services. Food production was disastrously low, which was exacerbated by a steady population growth rate of 5 million a year. It was the task of India's first prime minister, Jawaharlal Nehru, to rectify these problems of inequality.

Jawaharlal Nehru was prime minister of India from 1947 to 1964. He was from a wealthy Kashmiri Brahman family and was educated at Oxford. Nehru's first order of business as prime minister was to initiate land tenure reform, modernization of the agricultural system, and the development of irrigation facilities. Nehru abolished uneconomic land ownership, which historically consisted of intermediary parties controlling government-owned land that was cultivated by peasants. The abolishment of these policies created an impetus to the peasant in the cultivation of land. Modernization of the irrigation system brought millions of acres of previously uncultivated land into use. During this period the production of food grains increased by approximately 80%. Secondly, Nehru was also keenly aware that massive improvement in the nation's industrial base would be essential to improve the lives of the citizenry. To that end, he initiated broad-based programs designed to create a highly industrialized India. Initially, the government managed and organized the base industries (steel, heavy chemicals, machinery) that were made possible by financial assistance from the United States, Britain, and the Soviet Union. Industrialization brought with it the need for scientifically and technically trained personnel. Nehru was instrumental in restructuring the Indian educational system from the humanities-based system established by the British to one in which science and technology would take the fore. The third achievement of the Nehru administration was the transformation of Indian rural life. Historically, the rural populations that were concentrated in villages still retained the customs, social mores, craft-based economy, and primitive agricultural practices of the past. Nehru was able to initiate their modernization by consolidating any given eighty or ninety villages into one sizable community. Through consolidation it was easier to provide better sanitation, education, and housing. The objective was to create an environment wherein local leadership would develop, embrace the program of modernization, and thereby increase the quality of lives of rural Indians. The more far-reaching aspect of this program was the creation of self-governing democratic communities, known as *panchayati raj.* Community-elected officials, known as *panchas,* are entrusted with a large degree of self-government. Nehru's policies were effective. At independence, more than 80% of the population was illiterate and university admissions were only at three hundred thousand. After implementation of his modernization programs, the government sent nearly 80% of India's children to schools, with compulsory education for all children between six and eleven. Moreover, the number of universities doubled and enrollment exceeded 1 million. Nehru also removed barriers that held back Indian women. Through a series of legislative enactments, women were given the right to vote, to sue for divorce, to inherit property on equal terms with males, and to adopt children. In 1961 dowry was made illegal.

While Nehru enjoyed overall success with his domestic policies, the close of the 1950s beset his administration with a variety of problems, domestic and foreign. Domestically, food production began to stagnate and eventually declined. Nehru's foreign policy with respect to the Cold War was one of non-alignment. He sought to project India as a mediator between the superpowers in much the same manner as did Mao's China and Sukarno's Indonesia. However, the Sino-Indian friendship deteriorated when the Chinese invaded Tibet in 1959. The relationship of mutual respect embodied by the five principles of peace (*Panch Shila*) collapsed altogether when the Chinese invaded Ladakh and Assam in 1962. China's objective was the acquisition of territory necessary to control a road from Sinkiang through the Karakoram Pass to Tibet. The invasion in Assam was merely a diversion. Nonetheless, Nehru's policy of non-alignment was dealt a severe blow and revealed India's military vulnerability in the North. Nehru suffered a stroke and died in office in May of 1964.

Nehru's successor was Lal Bahadur Shastri (1964–1966). During his short tenure in office he was beset with a number of problems: widespread food shortages, violent anti-Hindi demonstrations in Madras, and the second war with Pakistan over Kashmir. The center of anti-Hindi violence was the Tamilnadu who were recalcitrant to subordinate their mother tongue to Hindi. Their fighting tactics were at times desperate and in some cases involved self-immolation. In the end, a compromise was struck that established English as the associate language for interregional communication. The war over Kashmir was short-lived as India and Pakistan received their arms and munitions from foreign manufacturers, which in an attempt to quell the violence withheld their sale. Finally, a cease-fire was achieved under the auspices of the United Nations. In January 1966, both parties met at Tashkent, the capital of the Soviet Republic of Uzbekistan, where Soviet leader Leonid Brezhnev brokered a settlement. Shastri died of a heart attack in Tashkent in 1966.

Indira Priyadarshani Gandhi (1966–1977), Nehru's daughter and no relation to Mohandas Gandhi, succeeded Lal Bahadur Shastri in 1966. Gandhi's administration was beset with many of the same problems as Shastri's. A drought in 1966 brought about a 19%

decline in food production. Fearing famine, India sought assistance from the United States, which provided enough grain to avert the disaster. From that point forward, Gandhi made increased agricultural modernization a key part of her administration. Part of this modernization process involved devaluing the rupee to increase aid from the United States. It also involved the dissemination of new seed varieties from Mexico and the Philippines that when combined with chemical fertilizers and enhanced irrigation would increase crop yields. The resulting "green revolution" was tremendously successful. In 1967–1968 agricultural production increased by 26% and national incomes rose by 9%, despite a burgeoning population growth of 2% a year. By 1970, agricultural production reached a peak of 100 million tons. That figure, however, was not reached in the five subsequent years, as production began to decline. Moreover, while production did increase, it was unevenly distributed. The new varieties of grain were often harvested on large farms with assured irrigation systems. These new varieties were therefore more likely than rice, planted on smaller, more scattered plots of land, to produce higher yields. Gandhi's agricultural policy also left wide social disparities. The new inputs were well suited to large-scale farming operations that required strong entrepreneurial skills and access to credit to which only the elite had access. Farming revenues were not taxed nor redistributed in any fashion. The small villager, while being marginally better off, remained comparatively worse off. Alleviating the sense of deprivation felt by the underprivileged would be the cornerstone of Gandhi's political activity in the1970s.

Gandhi won the 1971 election. Her party, the Congress Party, gained 352 seats in Parliament, which allowed her to push through legislation that might otherwise have been denied. She was successful at passing a constitutional amendment that restricted the fundamental right to ownership of private property. Insurance companies and coalmines were nationalized. She brokered an alliance with the Soviet Union that had a deleterious affect on India's relationship with the United States. Gandhi's greatest achievement, however, was in the manner in which she handled the war with Pakistan. By 1971, Bengalis were increasingly and openly rebellious toward the Punjabis that dominated the state. Yahya Khan, Pakistan's president, sought to curb the rebellion by military force. India sided with the Bengalis originally by offering covert aid but later with a full-scale invasion. The result was a total collapse of Pakistani authority in the East, which in combination with the emergence of the independent country of Bangladesh confined Pakistan to the West and decisively confirmed India's pre-eminence on the subcontinent. On June 12, 1975, the high court found Gandhi's election in 1971 wrought with corruption. In response, Gandhi claimed a state of emergency. The emergency regulations suspended civil liberties, applied press censorship, and banned opposition political parties. In March of 1977, Gandhi called for elections in which she sought approval and legitimacy for her emergency regime. She was promptly swept from office.

Morarji Desai (1977–1979) succeeded Gandhi as prime minister. Desai's focus was on increasing investment away from industrial centers and into the agricultural system. While food grain production did reach a record of 126 million tons in 1977–1978 and 131 million in 1978–1979, political squabbling amongst his party elite could not be ameliorated. He was forced to resign in 1979.

Charan Singh (1979) was India's first non-Brahman prime minister. However, his tenure in office was cut short by his failure to muster a majority in parliament. He left office after only one month.

Indira Priyadarshani Gandhi (1980–1984) was again elected as prime minister. Most critical in her second tenure was use of force against Sikhs at the Golden Temple in Amritsar. The Sikhs, with support from the Sikh diasporas in Canada and the United States, were calling for the creation of their own state, Khalistan. To that end, the prominent Sikh preacher, Sant Jarnail Singh Bhindranwale, and his followers blockaded themselves at the temple and would not leave until the creation of an independent Sikh state. Gandhi sent troops (Operation Bluestar) and killed Bhindranwale and thousands of Sikhs congregated on the temple grounds. Sikhs throughout India were enraged. On October 31, 1984, two of Gandhi's Sikh bodyguards killed her. The public was outraged and violence soon followed. Sikhs were the target of their anger. Over a thousand Sikhs were killed in New Delhi alone.

Rajiv Gandhi (1984–1991) succeeded his mother as prime minister. With a reputation for honesty and integrity, he had many friends in India and abroad. His task was to reduce violence in the Punjab and restore vitality to a sagging Indian economy. Rajiv achieved the first by accommodating demands for more regional contracts in the Punjab. He revitalized the economy by opening India's doors to capitalism. This included private investment incentives and a reduction in tax rates and licensing requirements.

Rajiv's honest image was tarnished by two poorly handled affairs. First, his handling of the 1983 Sinhalese-Tamil conflict in Sri Lanka was disastrous. The Sinhalese sought the forcible removal of the Tamil population. The Tamils (Tamil Tigers) responded with a guerilla-styled war. Originally, Rajiv covertly supported the Tamils. The Sri Lankan president, however, requested that India send troops to disarm the guerillas so elections could be held. India complied, intense fighting ensued, and many lives were lost. India soon lost the respect of both sides and extricated itself from the conflict. Second, the Bofors affair, in which Rajiv allegedly took kickbacks from a Swedish munitions firm in exchange for defense contracts. In response to the allegations, Rajiv terminated his finance minister, V. P. Singh, who then joined an opposition party. In May of 1991, while campaigning in Tamil, Rajiv was approached by a woman who detonated a bomb attached to her person, killing herself, Rajiv, and twelve others. She was believed to be a member of the Tamil Tigers terrorist group.

The 1990s were dominated by many short-term leaders. The first, Vishwanath Pratap Singh (1989–1990), succeeded Rajiv Gandhi. His decision to reserve civil service jobs for lower Hindu castes cost him the support of middle- and upper-class Hindus. He was replaced by Chandra Shekhar (1990–1991) who ruled only briefly. P. V. Narasimha Rao (1991–1996) succeeded Shekhar. Rao continued programs of modernization and economic liberalization. However, several political corruption scandals ended his career in 1996. Atal Bihari Vajpayee (1996) replaced Rao but was in office for only thirteen days. H. D. Deve Gowda (1996) replaced Vajpayee but his tenure was less than one year. Kumar Gujral (1997) replaced Gowda but his tenure was less than one year as well. Atal Bihari Vajpayee (1998–2004) was again prime minister. It was under his tenure that India detonated its first atomic bomb. Dr. Manmohan Singh became prime minister in 2004.

The Indian economy has progressed tremendously since its independence in 1947. In 1950, agriculture, forestry, and fishing accounted for 58.9% of the GDP while manufacturing accounted for 10%. Employment was primarily concentrated in the agricultural, forestry, and fishing industries. However, Indian leaders have continually sought to advance the Indian economy. By the 1970s, the economy had transitioned to heavy industry, telecommunications, and transportation. During the 1980s, the economy grew at an annual rate of 5.5%. Since the 1990s it has had an annual growth rate of 6%. By 2003, agriculture employed 60% of the labor force, industry 17%, and services 23%. As a percentage of GDP (2002 est.), these numbers translate to agriculture, 23.6%; industry, 28.4%; and services, 48%. Per capita GDP was $2,900 (2003 est.) and 25%of the population lives at or below the poverty line. India has a literacy rate of 59.5%. The infant mortality rate is 57.92 per 1,000. The life expectancy for males is 63.25 years and for females is 64.77 years.

W. John Hansen

References and Further Reading

Ludden, David. *India and South Asia: A Short History*. Oxford, UK: Oneworld Publications, 2002.
Mabbett, Ian W. *A Short History of India*. North Melbourne, Australia: Praeger, 1970.
Mayor, John. *India: Issues, Historical Background and Bibliography*. New York: Nova Science, 2003.
Metcalf, Thomas, and Barbara Metcalf. *A Concise History of India*. Cambridge, UK: Cambridge University Press, 2002.
Panikar, K. M. *A Survey of Indian History*. New York: Asia Publishing House, 1963.
Watson, Francis. *India, a Concise History*. New York: Thames & Hudson, 2002.

INDIAN–PAKISTANI WARS

The partitioning of India in 1947 to provide a homeland for the Indian Muslims left several unresolved issues. One of them has caused two wars, while the unusual geographical configuration of Pakistan has caused a third war. Minor clashes also have resulted from the same issues.

The partition plan drawn up by the British granted to Pakistan the Muslim-majority areas of the North–West Frontier Province, Balochistan, Sindh, and the contiguous Muslim-majority districts of the Punjab, along with Muslim-majority East Bengal, making a bifurcated country whose two parts were separated by 1,500 miles (2,400 kilometers) of what soon became hostile territory. Delineated with much urgency because of spreading ethnic strife throughout the subcontinent, the plan left undecided the fate of the 562 semi-autonomous princely states. Most of these quickly acceded either to India or to Pakistan. Leaders of three of them hesitated because of the geographical anomaly of their states. Located entirely within India's own territory, both Junagadh and Hyderabad had Hindu majorities but Muslim rulers. Believed to be the birthplace of Lord Krishna, Junagadh was prized by India's Hindus. The Nizam of Hyderabad, Mir Osman Ali Khan, would have preferred independence for his largest of the princely states. Hyderabad's court had long been a seat of Urdu culture that was precious to many of Pakistan's Muslims. But both Hyderabad and Junagadh were forcibly incorporated into India by military action.

Jammu and Kashmir (the princely state commonly referred to as Kashmir) had the unique problem of bordering both India and Pakistan and having a Muslim majority ruled by a Hindu, Maharaja Hari Singh. The maharaja, also hoping to remain independent, procrastinated in making a decision, but a decision was forced upon him when some two thousand armed Pathan tribesmen from Pakistan crossed into Kashmir and on the morning of October 22, 1947, seized the border town of Muzaffarbad. To prevent their advancing on Srinagar, the state capital, the maharaja hastily agreed to accede to India. The legality of the instrument of accession he signed has never been acknowledged by Pakistan, yet Pakistan has always insisted that its provision for a plebiscite be carried out—which India has refused to permit.

It appears that the government of Pakistan neither opposed nor assisted the marauding tribesmen, but when India airlifted troops into Srinagar, Pakistan became committed to the "liberation" of Kashmir. Although neither side made a formal declaration of war, an Indian infantry brigade quickly drove back the tribesmen; then, because of logistic problems of supply, the Indians were forced to retreat from border areas in November. Pakistan's troops had been guarding strategic locations only within Pakistan to prevent an attack, but when the Indian side mounted an offensive in the spring of 1948 to retake lost ground, the Pakistani army became directly engaged, bringing into Kashmir its mountain guns, two regiments of field artillery, a medium artillery battery, and a parachute brigade to assault the long Indian communications line. Since neither side wished to invade the other's territory, they accepted UN mediation. This brought the war to an end on January 1, 1949, and teams of UN observers were put in place to monitor the cease-fire line that now divided Kashmir into two unequal parts. Azad (free) Kashmir, as Pakistan called the portion under its control, was a narrow strip opposite its own border and the mountainous area to the northwest. All the rest ("Occupied Kashmir," in Pakistan's view) remained with India and contained three-fourths of the population and most of the arable land.

This longest of the three conflicts, the First Kashmir War (1947–1949) was least costly in human and material losses. It has been estimated that there were about 1,500 battle deaths, and India lost approximately five thousand square miles of territory. It was almost entirely a ground war; air power was minimal and there were no naval engagements; the terrain was not favorable for tank combat. The lasting effect of the war was the bitter animosity between India and Pakistan that has soured their relationships in most respects ever since.

Because of this animosity and the continuing effort of each country to probe weak spots of the other, a conflict occurred in the Rann of Kutch in January 1965 when each country claimed that patrols from the other side had intruded into its territory. The Rann of

Kutch adjoins the Indus delta, and when not under water is a salt desert where searing winds make human life insufferable. It has neither strategic nor economic value (unless, as some believe, there might be oil beneath its surface); but what mattered in this squabble was the lack of clear demarcation of the region when India was partitioned. After several inconclusive skirmishes, a cease-fire was put into effect on June 30, 1965.

Hostility, however, continued to smolder. Again, there was no formal declaration of war, but it is generally believed (though not acknowledged by Pakistan) that early in August 1965 guerrillas under Pakistan's control entered India's Kashmir to harass its troops stationed there. The first direct engagement between the armed forces of the two countries took place on August 14, 1965. The next day, after an artillery barrage, India captured important positions in the northern mountains. When Pakistan counterattacked later in the month, Indian forces thrust into Azad Kashmir and did not stop until they had penetrated several miles into Pakistan itself. In September, Pakistan turned hostilities southward and took a village inside Indian territory. Now, for the first time, war had come to the soil of both countries.

India's response was a powerful two-prong attack through the Punjab, aimed to take the city of Lahore, with a diversionary thrust toward Sialkot. Lahore was saved when the Pakistani army created a moat on its eastern flank by blowing up seventy bridges that crossed an irrigation canal. The defense of Sialkot resulted in the greatest tank battle on the plains of the Punjab since those of World War II in North Africa. During these engagements, both sides used air cover for their ground operations but each refrained from bombing the other's cities. There was naval action as well, on Pakistan's part the successful endeavor to prevent the shelling of its southern coast.

The war ended in stalemate with the acceptance of the UN's September 20 cease-fire resolution and was far more costly than the first Kashmir War. Pakistan lost 3,800 men, more than 700 square miles of territory, 200 tanks, and 20 aircraft. India lost 3,000 men, 300 square miles of territory, at least 175 tanks, and 60 to 75 aircraft.

The third armed conflict began as a civil war when the Awami League of East Pakistan won an overwhelming majority in the 1970 election that the government in West Pakistan was unwilling to accept. Negotiations dragged on for months until a Bengali liberation force (the Mukti Bahini) clashed with the army in East Pakistan. India sided with the Mukti Bahini and began amassing troops on its border with East Pakistan. In return, on December 3, 1971, the Pakistan air force made a preemptive attack against military targets in north India. India retaliated by mounting a coordinated ground, air, and navel assault on East Pakistan, by attacking the Pakistan Air Force headquarters in Peshawar in West Pakistan, and by bombarding the port facilities at Karachi. Pakistan tried to divert Indian attention away from East Pakistan by opening a series of engagements on India's western border; these ran from Kashmir to the Rann of Kutch. Once again a tank battle raged east of Sialkot. Farther south, the penetration of Rajasthan by a Pakistani armored regiment was countered by an Indian thrust into Sindh. But the Pakistan army's thirty-five infantry battalions along with support units and thirty-five thousand armed *razakars* recruited from the Urdu-speaking Biharis were no match for the six divisions India had thrown into East Pakistan when they converged on Dacca, along with their Mukti Bahini allies. After fourteen days the war ended in a cease-fire on December 17, and the sovereign state of Bangladesh became a reality.

Pakistan suffered about 9,000 deaths, India only 2,500. Pakistan lost two hundred tanks and seventy-five aircraft; India's losses were eighty and forty-five, respectively. India destroyed a Pakistani submarine in the Bay of Bengal; Pakistan sank an Indian frigate in the Arabian Sea. Ninety thousand Pakistani prisoners of war were left stranded in Bangladesh for months, and what remained of Pakistan was wracked by violent demonstrations when news of the defeat reached there.

Despite—or perhaps because of—these inconclusive wars, military adventurism has continued from both sides, and every perceived aggressive action is met tit for tat. In 1984, India moved troops into the region of the Saichen glacier to dispute the possession of land at an elevation of twenty thousand feet (six thousand meters), where it is almost impossible to exist, much less fight. In 1999, Pakistani troops occupied an area in the Kargil region of Kashmir claimed by India. In both cases skirmishing continued for months, with the loss of untold hundreds of lives.

Since the wars have escalated in violence, most unnerving were the five nuclear tests carried out by India at Pokhram in 1998, only 90 miles (150 kilometers) from Pakistan's border. Within two weeks, Pakistan responded with five nuclear tests of its own—thus removing any doubt about the nuclear capability of the two quarrelsome powers in the Indian subcontinent that, over fifty years, have found no means of peaceful coexistence.

CHARLES BOEWE

See also Awami League; Bangladesh; Central Asia: History and Economic Development; Central Asia: International Relations; Guerrilla Warfare; India; Kashmir Dispute; Pakistan

References and Further Reading

Brines, Russell. *The Indo-Pakistani Conflict*. London: Pall Mall Press, 1968.

Burke, S. M., and Lawrence Ziring. *Pakistan's Foreign Policy: An Historical Analysis*, 2nd ed. Karachi and New York: Oxford University Press, 1990.

Choudhury, G. W. *The Last Days of United Pakistan*. Bloomington: Indiana University Press, 1974; Karachi and New York: Oxford University Press, 1993.

Ganguly, Sumit. *The Origins of War in South Asia: Indo-Pakistani Conflicts since 1947*, 2nd ed. Boulder, CO, and London: Westview Press, 1994.

Gupta, Sisir. *Kashmir: A Study in India-Pakistan Relations*. Bombay and New York: Asia Publishing House, 1966.

Jackson, Robert Victor. *South Asian Crisis: India, Pakistan and Bangla Desh*, New York: Praeger, 1975.

Khan, Mohammed Matainur Rahman. *The United Nations and Kashmir*. Groningen: J. B. Wolters, 1954.

Lamb, Alistair. *The Kashmir Problem: A Historical Survey*. New York: Praeger, 1966.

Schofield, Victoria. *Kashmir in Conflict: India, Pakistan and the Unfinished War*. London and New York: I. B. Tauris, 2000

Stoessinger, John George. "Four Battles Over God: India and Pakistan in 1947, 1965, 1971, and 1998." In *Why Nations Go to War*, 8th ed. Boston: Bedford/St. Martin's, 2001.

INDIGENOUS MEDICAL PRACTICES

Indigenous or native medical systems and practices refer to those found throughout the world among premodern, or so-called traditional, societies. Many of these systems are found in small-scale societies and are based on oral tradition, others are heirs to medical knowledge that originated within major civilisations, such as China, South Asia, Mesoamerica, and the Andean region in South America.

The distinction between native medicine and Western or scientific medicine is far from unproblematic. From the rationalist standpoint of modern medicine, a recognized disease retains its identity wherever it occurs, regardless of the cultural context. However, as people actually experience disease indirectly and as culturally constructed illnesses, in practice this is often a matter of compromise and adjustment to local conditions. In native medical systems, concepts of disease are often inextricably linked to cultural classifications of adversity, natural or otherwise (Lieban 1974). Thus, the specialist considers the nature of illness the self-evident point of departure and the determinant factor as to how to proceed in the subsequent empirical treatment.

It is futile to attempt a delimitation of what is properly "medical" in native systems, where almost any performed ritual, communal or individual, is in some sense "medicinal." "Ritual" here means the manipulation of the inherent vital power, the soul, believed to be possessed by any person, place, thing, or event. The purpose of ritual is then to maintain the balance or restore the presence of this vital power (Herrick 1983). Embedded as it is in a cultural matrix, the discourse of native medicine has an essential mythic dimension. An example are the medical practices found among the Maya Indians in Guatemala, who retain to this day elements from pre-Columbian times, when medicine, myth, and advanced astronomical science formed an integrated whole.

Causes of Illness

Even if there is a great variation in medical systems throughout the world, when it comes to establishing the causes of illness and disease, an important distinction is between those illnesses with natural causes or those caused by witchcraft or supernatural agents. Many minor and sporadic ailments can be deemed as natural to begin with and be treated at home or routinely by an herbalist. However, the diagnosis can change if certain symptoms, such as the slow healing of a wound, are observed. In that case, the disease is usually attributed to human agency, the effect of witchcraft or sorcery. In those cases, a so-called witch-doctor or a shaman must be consulted. This is related to the ambivalent nature of spiritual power, which means that the same agent or material, human or spiritual, can either cause or cure disease. Such was for instance the ambivalent role of certain sacred objects called *minkisi* by the Kongo (a Bantu people in Congo Kinshasa), also found in many other African traditions and known generically as *fetiches* (Westerlund 1989).

Nature spirits and ancestor spirits are also agents of disease, for instance as a result of the breaking of taboos or norms. Whatever the cause established according to the local model of etiology, native systems employ disease terminologies of considerable precision. The sophistication sometimes achieved can be illustrated with the Hausa-Fulani in northern Nigeria, who distinguish 808 diseases and employ 637 plants to cure them, among them 32 different plants used to treat malaria (Etkin and Ross 1983)

Even deities may, through the inducement of illness, indicate demands on an individual or a group (Westerlund 1989). Among the Mapuche in South America, anguished dreams called *perimontun* may be an indication to someone that she or he is being called to become a shaman.

Specialists

Native medicine specialists differ in the methods and illnesses they treat. Often, the most important is the herbal practitioner who employs a variety of plants and drugs obtained from them throughout the world, many of proven efficacy such as quinine, sage, opium, coca, cinchona, curare, chalmoogra oil, ephedrine, and rauwolfia. Methods employed include infusions, plasters, enemas, suppositories, massages, sweating, thermal baths, and diets.

Among the reputed herbalists of the Andean Kallawalla, the use of a certain medicine chosen from a vast repertoire refers specifically to a certain part or function of the body. It is vital for the body to maintain a balanced flow of air, blood, feces, milk, phlegm, semen, sweat, and urine. As elsewhere, the intrinsic power of drugs must be enhanced by the proper ritual. For the Kallawalla herbalist, this means that it is indispensable to establish the proper relation between the patient and what can be called the cosmographic context. The view is that bodily processes are analogous to the flow of rain and wind observed in surrounding mountains and valleys (Bastien 1987). This can be seen as a special case of a principle of general validity in native South American medicinal thinking, the complementary concepts of intrusion and extraction.

The spiritual dimension of illness is treated by the shaman, who employs ecstatic trance as a means to achieve communication with spiritual forces and thus act as an efficient diviner and healer. Among the Waiká in Venezuela, the shaman inhales the powder of ebena (from the species Virola), that in a matter of minutes induces powerful hallucinations.

In many places, the prevalence of indigenous medical practices and beliefs has not prevented the utilization of modern Western medicine. In such intercultural settings, people tend to place illnesses in two broad categories: those more likely to respond to the treatment of a healer and those more likely to be cured by a physician. This creates a series of intercultural situations in which native and modern medicine both compete and cooperate with each other. Most illnesses eventually end in spontaneous recovery. When this occurs and the patients have been treated by local healers, confidence in indigenous medicine may be enhanced. When therapy for an illness is sought from both a physician and a healer, the combined efforts of both may cure the patient but only one of them may get the credit. In these cases, intercultural competence and familiarity is an integral part of effective health programs.

JUAN-CARLOS GUMUCIO CASTELLON

See also Health Care; Infant Mortality; Infectious Diseases; Mental Health; World Health Organization (WHO)

References and Further Reading

Balick, Michael, and Paul A. Cox. *Plants, People, and Culture. The Science of Ethnobotany*, chapters 2 and 5. New York: Scientific American Library, 1996.

Bastien, Joseph W. *Healers of the Andes. Kallawalla Herbalists and Their Medicinal Plants*. Salt Lake City, UT: University of Utah Press, 1987.

Gelfand, Michael, et al. *The Traditional Medical Practitioner in Zimbabwe*. Gweru, Zimbabwe: Mambo Press, 1985.

Landy, David, ed. *Culture, Disease and Healing. Studies in Medical Anthropology*. New York: Macmillan, 1977.

Lieban, Richard W. "Medical Anthropology." "In John Honigmann, ed., *Handbook of Social and Cultural Anthropology*. Chicago: Rand McNally, pp. 1031–1072, 1974.

Willis, Roy. *Some Spirits Heal, Others Only Dance: A Journey into Human Selfhood in an African Village*. Oxford, UK: Berg, 1999.

Westerlund, David. "Pluralism and Change. A Comparative and Historical Approach to African Disease Etiologies." In Anita Jacobson-Widding and David Westerlund, eds., *Culture, Experience and Pluralism. Essays on African Ideas of Illness and Healing. Uppsala Studies in Cultural Anthropology*, 13. Uppsala, Sweden: Acta Universitatis Upsaliensis, 1989.

Winkelman, Michael. *Shamans, Priests and Witches: A Cross-Cultural Study of Magico-religious Practitioners*. Tucson, AZ: Arizona State University, 1992.

INDONESIA

Indonesia, the world's fourth-largest nation, with a population of 210 million, straddles the equator between mainland Southeast Asia and Australia extending 3,198 miles (5,150 km) with a total land area of over 767,000 square miles (1,986,500 sq. km). It consists of over 13,000 islands (6,000 inhabited) with five main islands (Sumatra, Java, Kalimantan [Borneo], Sulawesi, and Irian Jaya) and two major archipelagos (Nusa Tenggara and the Maluku Islands). Many of the islands are mountainous, with peaks reaching 3,800 meters above sea level in western islands and as high as 5,000 meters in Irian Jaya. Because of the region's tectonic instability, there are 400 volcanoes, of which 100 are active.

The climate is tropical with a rainy season from November to March and a dry season from June to October. In coastal areas mean temperatures vary only slightly throughout the year 78°F–82°F (25°C–28°C). The temperatures in upland communities can be considerably cooler.

The official language is Bahasa Indonesia, which is based on Malay. There are over five hundred other mutually unintelligible languages and dialects. The major languages (those with 1 million or more speakers) include: Javanese, Sundanese, Malay, Madurese, Minangkabau, Balinese, Bugisnese, Acehnese, Toba Batak, Makassarese, Banjarese, Sasak, Lampung, and Rejang.

The capital of Indonesia is Jakarta, on the northwest end of Java. Java is also the home of over 60% of Indonesia's population. Hence, the Javanese are the most dominant ethnic group in Indonesia. Other major ethnic groups include the Sundanese (Java), the Madurese (Java/Madura), the Balinese, the Achenese (Sumatra), the Minangkabau (Sumatra), and various Dayak groups (Kalimantan).

History

The archipelago has long had state-level societies. A long succession of first Hindu, then Islamic states, which sometimes competed with each other, preceded European contact with the islands. The Dutch presence began when the first Dutch ships landed in Java in 1596. Except for a brief period of British rule (1811–1815), the Dutch ruled what became Indonesia for nearly 350 years.

As a backdrop for modern Indonesia, it is useful to briefly review major colonial policies, namely the Landrent System, the Cultivation System, and the Liberal Phase. The Landrent System operated on the assumption that the government was owner of all lands and the peasants, therefore, were renters who then paid a percentage of the estimated productivity of each crop as rent. Formally this system was in force from 1811 until 1830, however, government collection of rent for agricultural land was part of the revenue system until the end of Dutch colonialism. The Cultivation System, which was in full operation by 1840, was designed to encourage the cultivation of cash crops by requiring Javanese peasants to devote up to one-fifth of their arable land and one-fifth of their labor (sixty-six days per year) to the cultivation of coffee, indigo, and sugar. With the cash payments the peasants were supposed to receive, they were expected to settle their landrent debts (Boomgaard 1989).

The end of the nineteenth century and the beginning of the twentieth century were marked by increasingly liberal economic and social policies, which restored most pre-1800 landrights. The Liberal Period saw the slow transition from compulsory labor to a "free" labor market. Another feature of this period was an increasing amount of education available for the native population.

The Dutch lost control of the Indies for a second time when the Japanese army landed in Batavia (Jakarta) on March 1, 1942. Initially, many Indonesians welcomed the Japanese Occupation. However, in time the Japanese presence was resented by many. Unlike the Dutch, the Japanese were interested in exporting rice. The Japanese also conscripted over 4 million people for economic development and defense construction. These practice and the confiscation of other foods and necessities made the Japanese exceedingly unpopular. The Japanese period ended when the British military arrived in Jakarta in September of 1945. Shortly afterwards, the Netherlands reclaimed control of Indonesia.

Under Japanese Occupation, the nascent nationalist movement solidified. At the very least, the Japanese occupation disproved the myth of Dutch superiority. Under the Japanese, Malay started to become a national language. There were committees formed to standardize what became Bahasa Indonesia. The Japanese also encouraged the further development of modern Indonesian literature. Indonesians were allowed to participate in politics, administration, and the military. Although some Japanese collaborators were latter killed in retaliation for the harshness of Japanese policies in the closing years of the war, other collaborators, like Soekarno and Hatta, later the first president and vice president, worked to set the ground work for Indonesian independence.

Indonesia declared its independence on August 17, 1945. The Indonesian forces were a combination of national forces and Islamic militias. Independence was not easily gained. Toward the end, the Republican Army controlled only the palace of Yogyakarta. Shifting international opinion about colonialism forced the Dutch to abandon their claim and recognize Indonesian independence on December 27, 1949 (Kahin 1952)

Following independence, Indonesia was governed by Sukarno, the primary signatory to the Declaration of Independence. The first years of the post-independence Sukarno regime have been called the "Liberal Democracy" period or the "Democratic Experiment." 1957 marked the beginning of the "Guided Democracy" period, which was dominated by the personality of Sukarno, although army leadership played an important role.

In 1965, Guided Democracy ended abruptly. In the early morning of October 1, 1965, a number of generals in the Indonesian army were murdered. These murders were blamed on the PKI (*Partai Komunis Indonesia*; Indonesian Communist Party), which was at the time the largest communist party in the world (McVey 1965). What followed was a bloodbath of epic proportions, in which up to a half million people were killed or disappeared. In the aftermath of these events, Suharto emerged as the president of Indonesia.

Suharto served as president until May 1998, when he stepped down following student protests in the wake of a severe economic crisis, that as of 2004 still wracks the nation. Suharto was succeeded by his recently named vice president, Bachruddin Jusuf Habbibie. Submitting to popular demand, Habbibie held general elections on an accelerated schedule. With the Suharto-era limitations on political parties lifted, forty-eight parties competed in the 1999 parliamentary elections. Out of this process Abdurrahman Wahid was elected president. Megawatti Sukarnoputri, the daughter of Sukarno, who had been widely favored to become president, was named vice president. President Abdurrahman was also a Muslim cleric. His presidency was as controversial as it was short and it ended in July 2001. Megawatti finally followed in her father's footsteps. Whether Indonesia will complete its transformation into a democratic state remains to be seen. One positive sign was the emergence of direct presidential elections in 2004, which elected Susilo Bambang Yudhoyono as Indonesia's sixth president. However, his background in the military has concerned some observers.

World's Largest Islamic Country

Today, Indonesia is the world's largest Islamic country, although it is not an Islamic state. Throughout the Indonesian Republic's existence, the ongoing question for the Islamic community has been how to create a strong, pious, and faithful Islamic society in the context of a modernizing, globalizing, and secular state. There are two major variants of Sunni Islam in Indonesia, which are generally referred to as the Traditionalists and the Reformists.

The Traditionalists, who are affiliated with pesantren (Islamic boarding schools) and the organization Nahdlatul Ulama (NU; trans., "Renaissance of Islamic Scholars"), practice and maintain Traditional Islam, which is strongly associated with the theologies, considered opinions, legal theories and findings, and mystical theories of Medieval Islam found in texts called *kitab kuning* (classical texts; literally, yellow books) (Dhofier 1999). The pesantren community holds them to be of high importance in determining how to live as good Muslims in a globalizing and modernizing world.

Reformists, who are affiliated with the organization Muhammadiya, seek to reform Indonesian Islam so that it draws primarily on scriptural sources. Muhammadiya takes a position that the basis of

Islamic Law (*shariah*) is the Qur'an, *Hadith* (the sayings and actions attributed to the Prophet), and personal interpretation. Traditionalists are slightly more numerous than the Reformists (Peacock 1978).

Both NU and Muhammudiya sponsor schools, hospitals, and universities in keeping with their primary charter as social-religious organizations. However, prior to 1977, both functioned as political parties and after 1998, both sponsored new political parties.

Despite being considered by many observers to be an example of Liberal Islam, Indonesia has seen the emergence of terrorist groups and terrorist activities in recent years. Radical Islamist groups like Laskar Jihad and Jemaah Islamiyah comprise a small percentage of Indonesian Muslims; however, they have been responsible for a number of significant acts of violence.

Other Religions and Ideologies

Prior to 2000, the Indonesian government required all citizens to declare one of five religions: Islam (87% of the total population), Protestantism (6%), Catholicism (3%), Hinduism (3%), or Buddhism (1%). Followers of indigenous animist traditions either nominally converted to one of the major religions (often one of the forms of Christianity because they allow the consumption of pork) (George 1996) or redefined their traditional religion as a form of Hinduism and have worked long and hard to have it recognized as such (Schiller 1997).

Until the end of the Suharto regime in May 1998, all organizations had to claim as their basic ideology the *Pancasila,* or five principles: belief in one supreme God; humanitarianism; nationalism expressed in the unity of Indonesia; consultative democracy; and social justice.

Form of Government

Indonesia is a unitary republic with a high degree of centralization. There are thirty-two regional provinces that have their government appointed from Jakarta. Sometimes governors are not from the region they govern, which can lead to strife. As late as 1999, the police were a branch of the military and organized along these lines with a central command in Jakarta. There is a slow effort to put police powers in increasingly local hands.

The 1945 constitution establishes three branches of government: executive, judicial, and legislative, but has until recently favored the president. The president is elected every five years. Up through the 1999 election, the president was elected through a parliamentary-type system. Starting with the 2004 election, Indonesians elect their president directly.

Indonesia is a member of United Nations (UN), Association of Southeast Asian Nations (ASEAN), Nonaligned Movement (chair 1992–1995), and numerous other international organizations. It bases its relations with all major nations on principles of nonalignment.

Education

Indonesia has an adult literacy rate of 83.7%, which is defined in terms of the Roman alphabet. This rate does not reflect an older population that is literate only in the Arabic alphabet. Indonesia has a twelve-year primary and secondary education system. Prior to 1995, only six years of school were required for all citizens, but now nine years are required. Today, there are two basic government-recognized curricula: the National System, which is mostly secular, and the *Madrasah* System. The Madrasah System was originally established because many Muslim parents were leery of the mostly secular national schools and would not send their children to them. Private schools that wish to have government recognition must follow one of these two curricula.

In addition to these schools are the pesantren, Islamic boarding schools. Prior to the twentieth century, pesantren were the only formal education institutions found in Java and in most of what is now Indonesia. They taught an almost exclusively religious curriculum to a mix of students including future religious leaders, court poets, and members of the ruling class. First the Dutch, then the Nationalists, and later the Republic of Indonesia promoted an educational system focused on science, math, and other "secular" subjects (Anderson 1990, pp. 132, 243). In response to the demand for this type of education, as early as the 1930s many pesantren added government-recognized curricula. Starting in the 1970s, these new curricula became an important part of the pesantren community's strategy for negotiating modernity (Dhofier 1999; Lukens-Bull 2005).

Outlook

As of 2004, the future of Indonesia is uncertain because of a number of key issues. Despite the inauguration

of the first directly elected president in 2004, some observers are concerned that the reformation movement may have stalled out. An important component of democratization will be reducing widespread corruption in all levels of government and bringing to trial corrupters from previous administrations. Another issue concerns regional autonomy and separatist movements in North Sumatra and Papua. Key issues for the next decade will be whether Indonesia will be able to continue as a united republic and how efforts to keep the nation unified will impact democratization.

The recovery of the Indonesian economy seems to be dependent on a number of factors including the restructuring of banking systems, the reduction of corruption, the restoration of political stability, the control of terrorism, and the return of international investors.

The December 26, 2004, earthquake and tsunami off the coast of Sumatra may have some impact on these processes. However, the long-term effects of this event remain unpredictable. That said, a few things seem clear. The area hardest hit was Banda Aceh, which was the center of the separatist movement in North Sumatra. The Indonesian government could use this tragedy as an opportunity to either sway public opinion or crush the rebellion. Likewise, the Free Aceh Movement may use these events as an opportunity to garner support. In terms of Indonesia–United States relationships, the images of US troops cradling scared and injured Indonesian children has gone a long way to counter the impact of the images coming out of the Abu Ghraib prison scandal. There is also a possibility of the end of the military embargo by the United States.

RONALD LUKENS-BULL

See also East Timor; Southeast Asia: History and Economic Development; Southeast Asia: International Relations

References and Further Reading

Anderson, Benedict. *Language and Power: Exploring Political Cultures in Indonesia*. Ithaca, NY: Cornell University Press, 1990.
Benda, Harry J. *The Crescent and the Rising Sun: Indonesian Islam Under the Japanese Occupation*. The Hague: W. van Hoeve, 1958.
Boomgaard, Peter. *Children of the Colonial State: Population Growth and Economic Development in Java, 1795–1880*. Amsterdam: Free University Press, 1989.
Dhofier, Zamakhsyari. *The Pesantren Tradition: A Study of the Role of the Kyai in the Maintenance of the Traditional Ideology of Islam in Java*. Tempe, AZ: Arizona State University, Program for Southeast Asian Studies, 1999.
Geertz, Clifford. *Religion of Java*. Chicago: University of Chicago Press, 1960.

George, Kenneth. *Showing Signs of Violence: The Cultural Politics of a Twentieth-Century Headhunting Ritual.* Berkeley, CA: University of California Press, 1996.

Kahin, George McT. *Nationalism and Revolution in Indonesia.* Ithaca, NY: Cornell University Press, 1952.

Lukens-Bull, Ronald. *A Peaceful Jihad: Negotiating Modernity and Identity in Muslim Java.* New York: Palgrave McMillan, 2005.

McVey, Ruth. *The Rise of Indonesian Communism.* Ithaca, NY: Cornell University Press, 1965.

Peacock, James. *Purifying the Faith: The Muhammadijah Movement in Indonesian Islam.* Tempe: Arizona State University, Program for Southeast Asian Studies, 1992 [1978].

Schiller, Anne. *Small Sacrifices: Religious Change and Cultural Identity Among the Ngaju of Indonesia.* New York: Oxford University Press, 1997.

Schwartz, Adam. *A Nation in Waiting: Indonesia's Search for Stability.* Boulder, CO: Westview Press, 1999.

Woodward, Mark. *Islam in Java: Normative Piety and Mysticism in the Sultanate of Yogyakarta.* Tucson: University of Arizona Press, 1989.

INDUSTRIALIZATION

Defining Industrialization

Generally, industrialization represents a process of intense development of industrial activity. If at the beginning industrialization was just an effect of economic development, it became more and more a process of conscious orientation of forces and resources toward the develop of industrial activity, seen as the base of the general development of the society.

Industrialization is a process of social and economic change whereby a human society is transformed from a pre-industrial stage to an industrial one. Pre-industrial economies often rely on sustenance standards of living, in which large portions of the population focus their collective resources on producing only what can be consumed by them, though there have also been quite a few pre-industrial economies with trade and commerce as a significant factor, enjoying wealth far beyond a sustenance standard of living.

Sometimes industrialization might also be termed an "industrial revolution," but only two or three times in history, when the industrial landscape radically changed due to the scientific and technological leaps. There is still an ongoing debate whether the Industrial Revolution was a revolution or just an evolution, whether industrialization was a radical change or an inevitable development in the context of the continuing social and political changes, agricultural innovations, accumulation of capital, and expansion of trade that had taken place in the seventeenth century and earlier.

Industrialization as social and economic change is closely intertwined with technological innovation, particularly the development of large-scale energy production and metallurgy. Industrialization is also related to some form of philosophical change, or to a different attitude in the perception of nature, though whether these philosophical changes are caused by industrialization or vice versa is subject to debate.

Industry and Industrialization

In its broadest sense, industry is any work that is undertaken for economic gain and that promotes employment. An industry refers to an area of economic production and involves large amounts of capital investment before any profit can be realized. The word may be applied to a wide range of activities, from farming to nuclear activity. It encompasses production at any scale, from the local, sometimes known as cottage industry, to the multinational or transnational.

In a more restricted sense, industry refers to the production of goods, especially when that production is accomplished with machines. It is this limited definition of industry that is embodied by the notion of industrialization: the transition to an economy based on the large-scale, machine-assisted production of goods by a concentrated, usually urban, population of workers. Manufacturing, which literally means "making by hand," has come to describe mechanical production in factories, mills, and other industrial plants.

Industry became a key sector of production in European and North American countries during the Industrial Revolution, which upset previous mercantile and feudal economies through many successive rapid advances in technology, such as the development of steam engines, power looms, and advances in a large-scale steel and coal production. Industrial countries then assumed a capitalist economic policy. Following the Industrial Revolution, perhaps a third of the world's economic output was derived from industry—more than agriculture's share, but subsequently less than that of the service sector.

An industry is usually classified as belonging to one of the following four groups: primarily, secondary, tertiary, and quaternary. Primary industries, which collect or extract raw materials, are located where the resources are found. Secondary industries are those that process or convert the raw materials into finished products. Some of these manufacturing industries must be situated close to the raw materials they use, others are tied to their largest markets, and still others—independent of both resources and markets—are often located wherever it is cheapest at the time.

Tertiary industries are the service industries. These include retailing, wholesaling, transport, public administration, and the professions, such as law. Finally, quaternary industries comprise activities that provide expertise and information. Consultancy services and research organizations belong to this category. These are generally market oriented, but since today's electronic communication permits swift contact and the easy transmission of data, they may be located almost anywhere.

Science, Technological Innovation, and Industrialization

From the beginning, the industrialization and the industrial revolutions were intimately linked to the scientific and technological progress. In 18th-century England, the individual inventors increased the efficiency of the individual steps of spinning so that the supply of yarn fed a weaving industry that itself was advancing with improvements to shuttles and the loom or frame.

In 1733, John Kay patented the first of the great machines, the flying shuttle, and, in 1764, James Hargreaves, a weaver and carpenter, created the spinning jenny, a mechanical spinning wheel that allowed the spinners to keep up with the weavers. Four years later, Richard Arkwright built the water frame, a cotton-spinning roller that made it possible to spin many threads into yarn at the same time.

Edmund Cartwright invented the power loom in 1785 and it mechanized the weaving process. Mechanization was associated with the development of the factory system, and strict discipline of the workers and what had once been a home-based craft became an industry. American inventor Eli Whitney (1765–1825), among others, devised the cotton gin, a machine that enabled a worker to clean more than fifty times as much cotton a day. Unfortunately, it is considered that this device played a major role in the perpetuation of slavery in the United States.

Finally, the textile industry became so large that it outgrew the possibilities of its power source: water power. In the first part of the eighteenth century, Thomas Newcomen made an "atmospheric engine" in which a piston was raised by injected steam. Newcomen's device was used to pump water out of mines and, later, it was improved by James Watt. His steam engine of 1769, and particularly its adaptation to produce rotary motion, allowed the rapid and wholesale use of steam power in industry.

By 1720 the English iron industry was in trouble, owing to lack of wood to make charcoal; half the country's iron at this time was imported. In 1784 Henry Cort's puddling process allowed ironmasters to produce wrought iron from pig iron using coal. Further developments were enabled by James Watt's steam engine, which was used to create blast; by the hot blast inventions developed in 1828 by James Neilson; and by James Nasmyth, who developed a steam hammer to work wrought iron and steel in 1839. The iron industry grew rapidly and became a key element in industrialization.

In steel casting, Henry Bessemer invented, in 1856, the process that bears his name and, in 1861, William Siemens invented the open-hearth process. These new methods allowed the production of large amounts of mild steel from non-phosphoric ores, and in 1879 Sidney Gilchrist-Thomas learned how to use phosphoric ores by lining the converter with dolomite limestone. Steel was stronger and more malleable than cast iron, and rapidly replaced it as the main metal of the Industrial Revolution.

By the end of the nineteenth century, the United States had surpassed Great Britain in the production of iron and steel. The abundance of raw materials, a rapidly growing population, and the adoption of innovations such as the telegraph, the telephone, the electric light, and the refrigerator, along with petroleum products, provided the basis for a boom in American manufacturing.

The main contribution to world manufacturing made by the US in the late nineteenth and early twentieth centuries was the increase in the scale of production. Beginning in 1913, Henry Ford pioneered mass-production methods in his vehicle plants. From this time until the 1960s, the US excelled in the techniques of mass production and led the world in productivity. In recent years, however, the Ford approach has become discredited for its lack of flexibility and for diminishing the skills of the labor force. It has been replaced by more flexible and responsive systems of production, especially within Japanese companies.

Nowadays, the introduction of mass-production techniques and robotics has resulted in the growth of component industries. These supply parts to other industries that are devoted to assembling the finished product. The motor-vehicle industry, which has been greatly refined by the Japanese, employs "just-in-time" production methods to ensure that components arrive at car factories as they are needed, rather than accumulating in large, wasteful, and expensive stockpiles. This approach makes vehicle production more responsive to the market, and therefore more competitive.

The global industrialization view emerging to dominate information science research, envisages continued industrialization, national and global information infrastructures, and the transformation of less-developed countries (LDCs) to industrialized economies. Some research has already begun to explore the dimensions of sustainable information technologies within the global industrialization paradigm. Current information science research has been primarily concerned with facilitating all aspects of global industrialization.

Industrialization has brought increasing specialization, complexity, and individualization. Computer technology and information services have evolved to support industrialization. Libraries and information services have developed with industrialization to satisfy human information needs and continue to assume greater importance with LDCs' industrialization.

De-industrialization

De-industrialization describes the decline in the contribution made by manufacturing industry to a nation's overall economic prosperity. The process might be also named re-industrialization, because the shift is not away from industry altogether, but from secondary to tertiary and quaternary industry. In other words, a de-industrializing economy moves away from the manufacture of goods and toward the provision of services.

Those countries that industrialized first—the UK, France, the United States—are now undergoing de-industrialization. The ascendancy of the service economy in the context of the post-industrial society is characterized by a number of apparently negative features, such as a decline in manufacturing employment and a dependence on imports across a wide range of sectors. Although the loss of the manufacturing base is likely to create unemployment at first, it may not be an adverse development in the long term. Paradoxically, de-industrialization in the three countries mentioned above has been accompanied by a growth in the high-tech industries in different well-known areas. The long-term impact of de-industrialization has yet to be felt. It may be the speed of the process, rather than the process itself, that needs careful management.

Within the global industrialization view, permanent or temporary de-industrialization occurs in local and regional communities, and is regarded as a normal consequence of shifts in global industrialization and adjustments of a marketplace economy. De-industrialization is studied as the process of

decline and eventual closure of industries supporting local, regional, and national communities within a marketplace economy. Cases of de-industrialization have been documented in specific towns, cities, and regions in many parts of the world, within different countries.

De-industrialization often results from periods of economic restructuring by transnational corporations; changing labor markets; political and economic change; or relocating industries due to global, national, or regional competition. De-industrialization has been found to permanently or temporarily affect many aspects of a community and engender many specific social and economic problems.

Soviet-Inspired and State-Sponsored Industrialization

The countries from the former communist camp, starting with the former USSR, introduced a special theory and experience of industrialization. The communist power needed a strong and rapid industrialization due to two main reasons. First, the industry was seen as the most efficient method of development of the country and secondly, to make the absolute communist power stronger and everlasting. Communist power is based on the proletariat, at least from the ideological point of view, but in USSR and all the countries who followed Soviet leadership, the working class was less developed due to the reduced level of the industrial sector. One of the struggles of the communist powers was to restrain the number of people working in agriculture and to increase the proletariat.

The communist state owns all the means of production and only a few private possessions are allowed. The major economic decisions are made by command from above in accordance with planners and plan's demands. The prices are set by the state as is the direction of economic activities because there is a command, centralized, and plan-oriented economy.

Because for almost four decades, the USSR was the only communist state, excepting Mongolia, the communist precepts were experienced here before being implemented in the countries where the regime was imposed after the Second World War. In the USSR, Joseph Stalin forced a rapid industrialization with an emphasis on heavy industry in the years before World War II with the famous Five-Year Plans.

Stalin's aims were to erase all traces of capitalism and to transform the Soviet Union into an industrialized and completely socialist state. The first Five-Year Plan also called for transforming Soviet agriculture from predominantly individual farms into a system of large state collective farms. The Communist regime believed that collectivization would improve agricultural productivity and would produce grain reserves sufficiently large to feed the growing urban labor force. Collectivization was further expected to free many peasants for industrial work in the cities and to enable the party to extend its political dominance over the remaining peasantry. The main goal of Soviet policy makers, however, was to promote industrial, not agricultural, growth. Collectivization gave an initial impulse to industrialization, orienting the agricultural surplus income and manpower out of the countryside and towards the city. Finally, the anticipated surplus was to pay for industrialization.

The Soviet economic model and the emphasis on industrialization at any price was followed or rather imposed in the Central and Eastern European countries that entered the communist camp, after 1945. The centralization and state-controlled economy were copied also in parts of Asia, Africa, and Latin American that experienced socialist development. The European former Communist Party renounced this model at the beginning of 1990 and jumped into the transition from communism to capitalism—a totally new and sometime traumatic social, economic, and political experience for those nations. One of the most difficult situations these countries have to cope with is the problem of the socialist industry that they built, the enormous productive capacity they put into action, huge and not-so-modern plants that they have to privatize, to make them efficient, or just close them down.

The shift in focus on industrial development in the former communist countries is also seen as a manifestation of the phenomenon of de-industrialization. In the 1980s and early 1990s, more and more economies underwent market-oriented reforms.

Industrialization and Development

Many analysts have made the case that industrialization brings "development." The implicit assumption is that industrialization improves a nation's well-being along a number of dimensions, including education quality and attainment. At the same time, people have warned of the potential downside of industrialization, including increased pollution, growing inequality, and lower social cohesion.

It is no longer necessary for the newly industrialized countries to repeat the steps followed by the first industrialized countries in world history. With the technology and know-how available today, it has been only a question of national will and money to industrialize a country since the end of the 20th century. Most countries regard industrialization as a positive evolution fit to generate rapid economic growth, revitalize run-down areas, and confer influence in world affairs. Most also now recognize the need for a diversified industrial base to safeguard their economies from fluctuations in the market price for their own specialized product. The negative consequences of industrialization are sometimes more apparent in developing countries than in countries with established industrial structures, where the social dislocation and environmental problems that often accompany development began long ago.

In 1960 the economic historian W. W. Rostow hypothesized a model of the "stages of economic growth." Starting from a traditional agricultural society, Rostow suggested a long period in which the preconditions for takeoff were created—notably the creation of an agricultural surplus that could finance industrial development, and the development of suitable trading and governmental institutions. The takeoff is impelled by "leading sectors." Once these leading sectors begin to grow, a process of self-sustaining growth occurs and the economic development is underway. In eighteenth-century England the growth was based on certain staple industries, particularly textiles, coal, and iron. Once takeoff had begun, growth in one industry provoked growth in others by way of a complex set of interdependencies and led to associated developments in organization, power, and engineering. The countries had their takeoff moments in different periods—England in the eighteenth century, the US around 1850, and the Asian Tigers in the twentieth century.

Since the end of World War II, the relative significance of manufacturing in the economies of Europe and the US has declined, and its importance in the economies of East Asia has risen. Japanese manufacturing, in particular, has had a worldwide impact in a very short time, and other Asian economies have followed Japan's lead. The renewal of its industrial plants after World War II gave Japan the advantage of modern production facilities. Since the mid-1950s, Japanese industrial output has grown at an annual rate of at least 6%. Japan's manufactured goods are noted for their high quality, which is due to the use of advanced technology in the production process.

Theories of accumulation are closely allied to those of industrialization. For many development economists, particularly those in the developing world, industrialization is almost synonymous with economic development. Looking across the developing world at the beginning of the twenty-first century, there is a huge range of national experiences. The most prosperous newly industrialized countries are the successful economies of East Asia, such as China and South Korea; Southeast Asia, such as Thailand and Singapore; some oil-rich countries of the Middle East; and some Latin American countries. In the mid-1990s it appeared that much of Asia and Latin America was set on a more effective development path than before. But the failure of development in much of sub-Saharan Africa gave economists cause for concern.

The success of the East Asian and Southeast Asian economies has been a powerful influence on thinking since the 1970s and 1980s. These countries did not accept the pessimism about exports that most of the developing world did. Despite the protective barriers erected by industrial countries, these countries managed to generate rapid expansion of manufacturing exports by skillfully selecting products and markets. With this came fast economic growth, first for the "four tigers"—Hong Kong, South Korea, Singapore, and Taiwan—and followed by others such as Indonesia, Malaysia, and Thailand.

Far from developing rapidly, economies with large-scale government intervention, trade protection, and inward-looking development were looking very sick by the end of the 1980s. Recession in the world economy exposed their weakness. An unsustainable balance of payments, domestic deficits, rapid inflation, international debt, and low growth or even economic decline reached the point where it was widely acknowledged that things had to change. The fact that socialist economies too were beginning to throw off the rigidities of the command economy and move into varying degrees of reliance on free-market economy was influential.

A worldwide consensus began to arise that greater reliance on market forces was essential for speeding up development where it was lagging, although how far governments should be involved in the development process remained, and remains, controversial. The East Asian and Southeast Asian experience for some was a triumph of the marketplace; but for others it demonstrated the power of combining market forces with skillful government intervention.

The Tigers of Industrialization

The East Asian Tigers, sometimes also referred to as Asia's Four Little Dragons, refers to the economies of Taiwan, Hong Kong, South Korea, and Singapore. These nations were noted for maintaining high growth rates and rapid industrialization between the early 1960s and the 1990s.

The East Asian Tigers pursued an export-driven model of economic development. These nations focused on developing goods for export to highly industrialized nations. Domestic consumption was discouraged through government policies such as high tariffs. The common characteristics of the East Asian Tigers were: focus on exports to rich industrialized nations, sustained rate of double-digit growth for decades, non-democratic and relatively authoritarian political systems during the early years, high tariffs on imports, undervalued national currencies, trade surplus, and a high savings rate. The current criticism of the East Asian Tigers is that these economies focus exclusively on export-demand, at the cost of import-demand. Thus, these economies are heavily reliant on the economic health of their targeted export nations.

Many economists have pointed out that the governments of the tigers were quite active in their economies. East Asian Tigers all practiced aggressive land reform and made large investments in public health and elementary education. In addition, while the tigers relied on export markets to develop their economies, they also put in place high trade barriers, which protected local industries from foreign competition.

The East Asian Tigers were able to move from third-world status to first-world status in a few decades and were able to progress past other developing areas, particularly Latin America and sub-Saharan Africa. Until the mid-1970s it was not clear that the East Asian Tigers were a particular area of fast growth and that the Tiger development model produced superior results to either neoliberal, US-backed policies; the Soviet model; or import substitution development models. Because of the success of the initial Tigers, many nations have followed similar development models. In part, this led to the Asian Economic Crisis in the 1990s.

Over time, the economic term Tiger has become synonymous with nations that achieve high growth by pursuing an export-driven trade strategy. More recently, Indonesia, The Philippines, and Thailand have often been considered Tigers but the term is not limited to Asian nations. In Europe, Ireland has been called the Celtic Tiger for its rapid growth in the 1990s, while Estonia is known as the Baltic Tiger for its high growth rates.

MARIUS TITA

References and Further Reading

Blumer, Herbert, David R. Maines, and Thomas J. Morrione, *Industrialization as an Agent of Social Changes. A Critical Analysis.* New York: Aldine de Gruyter, 1990.

Bryce, Murray D. *Industrial development. A Guide for Accelerating Economic Growth.* New York: McGraw-Hill, 1960.

Byrne, D. 1995. "De-industrialization and Dispossession: An Examination of Social Division in the Industrial City." *Sociology*, 29(1), pp. 95–115.

Ferguson, Paul R., and Glenys J. Ferguson, *Industrial Economics Issues and Perspectives.* New York: Macmillan, 1994.

Hudson, Pat. *The Industrial Revolution* London: Edward Arnold, 1992.

Kim, L., and R. R. Nelson. *Technology, Learning, and Innovation: Experiences of Newly Industrializing Economies.* Cambridge, UK: Cambridge University Press, 2000.

Landes, David S. *The Unbound Prometheus: Technical Change and Industrial Development in Western Europe from 1750 to the Present,* 2nd ed. New York: Cambridge University Press, 2003.

O'Hearn, D. *Inside the Celtic Tiger.* London: Pluto, 1998.

Pack, H., and L. Westphal. "Industrial Strategy and Technological Change: Theory versus Reality." *Journal of Development Economics*, June 22, 1986, pp. 87–128.

Pollard, Sidney. Peaceful Conquest: The Industrialization of Europe, 1760–1970. New York: Oxford University Press, 1981.

Roberts, Mark, and James Tybout. *Industrial Evolution in Developing Countries: Micro Patterns of Turnover, Productivity and Market Structure.* New York: Oxford University Press, 1996.

Smith Alan H. *The Planned Economies of Eastern Europe.* New York: Holmes and Meier, 1983.

Stearns, Peter N. *The Industrial Revolution in World History.* Boulder, CO: Westview Press, 1998.

INFANT MORTALITY

Infant mortality is measured as deaths in the first year of life per thousand population, called the infant mortality rate (IMR). Its reduction requires clean water, nutrition, sanitation, education, and health care. It is highest in Afghanistan, Angola, Niger, and Sierra Leone, countries without surplus wealth, where the wealth is unevenly distributed, where there is little social capital and/or where there are cultural obstacles to equity. It is lowest in Finland, Japan, Singapore, and Sweden, democracies that value social capital. (Reliable IMR statistics can be hard to collect. Unless otherwise indicated, all statistical data is from the UNICEF Report for 1998.)

Wealth in terms of gross national product per capita (GNP) is a strong indicator of IMR, but allocation of resources is also significant. Improving the internal transfer of wealth and providing resources to the poor significantly lowered the IMRs in the latter half of the twentieth century in such countries as Peru, Indonesia, Sri Lanka, Costa Rica, and Zimbabwe. In Latin America, the Caribbean, and Tanzania, transfer of resources to the poor has resulted in much better IMRs than suggested by their GNPs. By contrast, in the USA, inequitable distribution of resources and consequently high IMRs for the Black non-Hispanic community, Native Americans, and Puerto Ricans result in a worse IMR ranking than would be suggested by its GNP. Unequal distribution of wealth also helps to account for relatively high IMRs in the oil-rich states of the Middle East.

Combating infant mortality requires giving priority to domestic humanitarian needs. For example, in a world where more than 1.1 billion people lack safe water (UNDP 1997), it requires placing domestic access to clean drinking water and basic sanitation above the demands of industry and power generation (Jackson 1990). It requires placing human life above economic rationalism. UNICEF has calculated that half a million children per year die as a result of the developing countries' burdens of debt, because governments cut their health and education budgets in order to meet escalating associated interest payments. Acute international economic crises also raise IMRs in many developing countries (Jackson 1990).

In some countries, gender discrimination is a major contributor to the IMR. In China, the preference for male offspring and the one child policy makes it the only country where the IMR for girls is actually higher than that for boys (by about 20%). In many other countries, however, gender discrimination raises the IMR by denying female access to education. Studies suggest that female literacy is second only to household income as an indicator of IMR (Caldwell 1993). By propagating knowledge about contraception, breastfeeding, and nutrition, female education reduces malnutrition in pregnant women and infants, which is a cause of over half of all child deaths in developing countries. Traditional restrictions on the education of Muslim women contribute to relatively high IMRs in Afghanistan, Algeria, Iran, Iraq, Libya, Oman, Pakistan, Saudi Arabia, and Yemen. By contrast, in Thailand, where women have very high literacy, high participation in the labour force, and a strong decision-making role, infant mortality has improved remarkably (103 in 1960 to thirty-one in 1996).

Level of health care is also a factor affecting the IMR, although this is less significant than GNP or maternal literacy because these are factors that contribute to maintaining the health of the child, whereas level of health care only becomes relevant once the child is already sick or malnourished (Caldwell 1993). In as many as thirty-five of the poorest countries, 30%–50% of the population have no access to health services (UNDP 1997).

Efforts to Correct the Problems

Survival is the most fundamental human right. The 1989 United Nations' Convention on the Rights of the Child has been ratified by every country in the world except two (USA and Somalia, both of which have signalled an intention to ratify by formally signing it). Article 24 of the Convention requires governments to take "appropriate measures" to reduce infant mortality. This has involved developing research-based national policies and programs that are supported by advances in medical science, technology, and disease control, although more research is needed to improve programs and determine their effectiveness. Immunisation programs have been particularly effective; by 1996 over 90% immunisation coverage had been achieved in eighty-nine countries and over 80% in another forty countries (D'Souza 1989). Other significant programs have contributed to improved nutrition through increased food production, fortification of staple foods, and improved household access to food.

National initiatives are enhanced by both international action and local operations. International action has included global aid programs and initiatives designed to help nations to help themselves. The 1996 Heavily Indebted Poor Countries Debt Initiative assists countries that implement reforms and channel resources to basic services. UNICEF's 20-20 Initiative involves donating matching funding when governments allocate at least 20% of spending to basic social services. Breastfeeding, which plays a particular role in reducing infant mortality, has been supported since 1981 by the World Health Organization's International Code to regulate marketing practices and the labelling of breast milk substitutes.

Breastfeeding has also been targeted by community-based programs. In this, as in many other areas, local involvement ensures community ownership of changes, that programs build upon existing good practice, and that innovations are accepted and adopted. The International Baby Food Action Network (IBFAN) was formed in 1979 to promote breastfeeding and now involves more than 150 citizen groups in ninety-four countries. In 1991 USAID and Wellstart International established the Expanded Promotion of Breastfeeding (EPB) Program; it has supported community programs promoting breastfeeding in Bolivia, Dominican Republic, Guatemala, Honduras, Mexico, and Nicaragua. In 1992 the World Health Organization (WHO) and UNICEF launched a Baby-Friendly Hospital Initiative to promote breast feeding. It has been implemented in over 170 countries.

Community initiatives have also been effective in promoting other aspects of infant health. In Africa, the Bamako Initiative of 1987 moved the management of health services into local communities. Similar measures are now operating in other regions. They ensure access to basic medical services and promote preventive activities. In Guinea, for example, prenatal care coverage went from less than 5% before the initiative to almost 80% in the mid-1990s.

A combination of strategies is often the most effective. Thus simultaneous attention to one or more of the key factors of maternal health care, women's education, promotion of breast feeding, provision of clean water, promotion of sanitation, and hygiene, can be enhanced by programs that target particular nutritional needs. Salt iodisation has been enhanced by consumer advocacy and legislative change at the local and national levels. By 2000, twenty-nine countries were using adequately iodized salt and salt iodization was protecting 70% of the world's population from iodine deficiency and the accompanying problems of poor growth and developmental delay, which in turn affect the economic health of nations (UNICEF 2000). Another specific measure, vitamin A supplementation, was endorsed globally as a strategy to reduce IMRs, but its application has depended greatly on existing health measures and community involvement.

From 1950 to 1996 the global IMR dropped from 139 (Horiuch, 1989) to 60 (UNICEF 1998), a trend that was reflected in all developing regions, but it has not been uniform. Political stability affects all the factors that govern infant mortality. Wars and displacement of people will always cause spikes in the IMR statistics. To continue to reduce infant mortality, the developed countries must promote world peace and must both assist and empower the developing countries; and every nation must both assist and empower its most disadvantaged people.

LEONORA RITTER

See also Basic Human Needs; Children and Development

References and Further Reading

Caldwell, John, and Pat Caldwell. "Women's Position and Child Mortality and Morbidity in Less Developed Countries." In *Women's Position and Demographic Change*, edited by Nora Federici, Karen Oppenheim Mason, and Solvi Songer. Oxford, UK: Clarendon Press, 1993.

Jackson, Ben. *Poverty and the Planet*. London: Penguin Books, 1990.

Mason, Karen Oppenheim. "The Impact of Women's Position on Demographic Change During the Course of Development." In *Women's Position and Demographic Change*, edited by Nora Federici, Karen Oppenheim

Mason, and Solvi Songer. Oxford, UK: Clarendon Press, 1993.

Ruzicka, Ladio, Guillaume Wunsch, and Penny Kane, eds. *Differential Mortality*. Oxford, UK: Clarendon Press, 1989.

United Nations Development Programme (UNDP). *Human Development Report 1997*, New York: Author, 1997.

UNICEF, *The Progress of Nations 2000*, http://www.unicef.org/pon00/

UNICEF, *The State of the World's Children 1998*, http://www.unicef.org/sowc98/mainmenu.htm

INFANTICIDE

Infanticide has a long global record as a pragmatic practice. It has been hypothesised that in Europe the motivation for female infanticide was the need to space the time between bearing children, with the theory that removing female infants as potential child bearers was more effective than eliminating males. In some eras and societies laws have required that deformed infants be put to death, in others infanticide has been promoted as a regular institution of an ideal state. Minimal attempts in Europe to limit the extensive killing of infants were made until the latter half of the nineteenth century. Although infanticide was a crime, few perpetrators were brought to trial.

In contrast to European practices, it has been argued that female infanticide was part of a population strategy in traditional China and it formed part of the economy of kinship. It had a necessary connection with the kinship system through the status of women and the nature of dowry. The Taiping Jing, a second-century Chinese text, rails against female infanticide. It notes the real scarcity of women and fears the cosmological implications of a weakening of female yin. Despite complex repercussions, infanticide has been practiced on every continent and in most cultures because it has satisfied significant family, economic, and social requirements.

In some societies the scarcity of women has been explained by denigrating attitudes towards female children and their consequent socioeconomic disadvantage. Direct infanticide is compounded by comparative neglect where male children are better nourished and enjoy access to family resources. Where children are viewed as being important to social reproduction, in terms of transmitting social values from one generation to the next and the means by which families perpetuate themselves, female children can be placed under threat. If daughters are not heirs, but serve mainly as brides in another family or clan lineage, their social role is less straightforward than that of sons, for boys are seen to reproduce their father's patriline.

Girls can be characterised as dangerous to the stability of an impoverished family and the stability of society. In many poorer countries an infant girl represents not just an economic, but a spiritual problem to a family with limited resources. If she is killed, the repercussions of the act of violence can be felt in the familial, public, and cosmic spheres. If she survives and marries above her station, she carries the potential to disrupt social order. The birth of an infant girl is therefore perceived as having the potential to precipitate crises that may end in her death.

A range of texts debate what acts constitute infanticide. Defined as the deliberate killing of a child in its infancy, the majority of cases are up to two years of age. Yet a blurred line also exists between deliberate killing and neglect that causes an infant's death.

Because abortion techniques in non-industrial societies are either relatively ineffective or dangerous, infanticide is sometimes the most dependable method to control family size. Infanticide is safer than abortion for a woman, who is a more valuable member of society than a newborn infant. Deliberate killing also allows a family or society to preselect infants of the preferred sex. Indeed, in societies with an ideology that supports fertility, there may be concomitant discussions that condone or sanction the eradication of infants. Authors suggest that taking the life of a newborn is explained within many societies as a caring act. It may be done to save the life of an older sibling not yet weaned but already cherished as a community member. Within some societies a child is not believed to be fully human until several years after birth, when they are named, or initiated as a member of the broader social group. Given that the most common methods are suffocation, abandonment, or exposure, and are enacted by the mother or a female kin or clan member, the emotional anguish of the killing is eased by not acknowledging their fully human status until later in the life cycle.

Yet children should not be constructed as a universal nuisance, to be kept in the world only when conditions suggest they will survive. In Africa, for example, society and population are shaped by pastoral life. Numerous children in a family become economic assets as pastoral work includes tasks that small children can perform, such as herding and field work. Consequently, small children's labour has social and economic value. Observers also poignantly propose that offspring are considered desirable due to the historical losses of people to the slave trade in Africa. The recent decimation of populations due to sexually transmitted disease also validates children's social presence and labour. In regions where infant mortality is extreme, large numbers of children help to ensure that some will reach adulthood.

Although few texts examine in detail the ways that targeted killing of infants by an enemy during war is a horrifying yet real aspect of infanticide, it is an important consideration, as the events in Rwanda in the late twentieth century exemplify. Few also consider the ways that increasing capitalism is shaping perceptions of the family, of children's economic worth, and which sex is preferable and profitable in economies that are driven by profit. Nonetheless, infanticide as an extensive practice throughout human history and within so many different cultures attests to its acceptance as an effective method of population control. Most infanticides continue to be performed to limit family and society size within the changing constraints of environmental and economic circumstances.

HELEN JOHNSON

See also Infant Mortality

References and Further Reading

Kuhse, Helga. *The Sanctity of Life Doctrine in Medicine: A Critique.*, Oxford, UK: Clarendon Press, 1997.
Rao, Aparna. *Autonomy: Life Cycle, Gender and Status among Himalayan Pastoralists.* New York, Oxford: Berghahn Books, 1998.
Waltner, Anne. "Infanticide and Dowry in Ming and Early Qing China." In *Chinese Views of Childhood*, edited by Anne Behnke Kinney. Honolulu: University of Hawaii Press, 1995.
Williamson, Laila. "Infanticide: An Anthropological Analysis." In *Infanticide and the Value of Life*, edited by Marvin Kohl. Buffalo, NY: Prometheus Books, 1978.

INFECTIOUS DISEASES

As the 1960s came to a close, the medical establishment was riding a wave of optimism. Vaccines were being employed to eradicate some of humanity's worst scourges. Antibiotics were saving millions from bacterial infections. The scope of the impending victory seemed so complete that the US Surgeon General, William H. Stewart, declared victory over infectious diseases in testimony before Congress.

Success Stories

Smallpox

Smallpox, a highly infectious disease caused by the *Variola* virus that killed as many as 30% of its victims and scarred most of its survivors, is the only major infectious agent that has been eradicated in the wild. Smallpox was eliminated by a sustained, global vaccination campaign.

Polio

Another highly infectious viral disease, polio can cause irreversible paralysis. The disease was targeted for eradication by the 41st World Health Assembly in 1988. According to World Health Organization (WHO) statistics, the number of cases has dropped from 350,000 the year the eradication campaign was launched to fewer than 800 in 2003. Those cases were concentrated in sub-Saharan Africa and the Indian subcontinent.

Leprosy

Leprosy, also known as Hansen's disease, is a chronic disease caused by the bacteria *Mycobacteria leprae*—a close relative of the bacteria that causes tuberculosis. Leprosy attacks the skin and nerves and severely disfigured its victims. The WHO proposed treatment of leprosy with three drugs at once over a period of six months to a year. The strategy has reduced the incidence worldwide from about 12 million cases in the 1980s to about 1 million cases in 2003. Most of the new cases are in a handful of countries in Southeast Asia, Africa, and the Americas.

Guinea Worm Disease

A parasitic worm, *Dracunculus medinensis*, causes Guinea worm disease. The disease is found in areas of sub-Saharan Africa where supplies of clean water are limited. The worm migrates in the tissue just below the skin, causing severe pain and swelling in its patients. While it does not kill its victims, it debilitates them and limits their efforts to feed themselves or otherwise maintain a decent quality of life. While there is no known treatment, the disease can be eliminated by providing clean drinking water. Guinea worm afflicted millions in the 1970s. The number of victims has dropped to fewer than one hundred thousand in 2000.

Chagas Disease

Chagas disease is caused by a single-celled animal parasite, *Trypanosoma cruzi*. The disease is typically transmitted by bloodsucking insects known as assassin bugs. While the initial course of the infection may be fatal—especially in young children—if the victim survives, the parasites remain in the body, invading many organs and debilitating the victims as systemic damage accumulates. Eradication efforts have focused on controlling the insect host by improving living standards in Latin America where the disease is endemic. Fewer than 20 million people have the disease, but, since the eradication campaign began, incidence rates have decreased by about 70% in the "Southern Cone" of South America—Argentina, Brazil, Chile, Paraguay, and Uruguay.

Tetanus

Neonatal tetanus, the disease commonly called "lockjaw," is caused by a toxin produced by the bacteria *Clostridium tetani*. The bacteria grow in wounds, or in the case of neonatal tetanus, in the umbilical cord following delivery. More than 95% of infants die without treatment. Tetanus can be prevented by vaccinating women of childbearing age and by clean delivery practices and neonatal care. According to United Nations Children's Fund (UNICEF) figures, the number of deaths has dropped from eight hundred thousand in the 1980s to 180,000 in 2002. The disease is still widespread throughout Africa and Asia.

Unending Challenges

High population densities, poverty, environmental degradation, and limited resources—especially clean water—have helped the spread of new diseases, and some old diseases are resurging after adapting to the weapons used against them.

In 2004, infectious and parasitic diseases and respiratory infections killed nearly 15 million people worldwide. The top ten infectious disease killers (as of 2002) were: (1) lower respiratory infections (3.9 million deaths); (2) HIV/AIDS (2.8 million deaths); (3) diarrheal diseases (1.8 million deaths); (4) tuberculosis (1.6 million deaths); (5) malaria (1.3 million deaths); (6) measles (610,000 deaths); (7) pertussis (whooping cough; 290,000 deaths); (8) tetanus (210,000 deaths); (9) meningitis (170,000 deaths); and (10) syphilis (160,000 deaths).

Disease Outlook

Lower Respiratory Infections

Lower respiratory infections primarily affect the lungs, bronchi, and trachea (or windpipe). They take an especially heavy toll on children. The main agents responsible for acute respiratory infections in children include *Streptococcus pneumoniae*, *Haemophilus influenzae*, respiratory syncytial virus, and parainfluenza virus type 3. *Streptococcus* and *Haemophilus* are bacteria—*Streptococcus* is a major cause of pneumonia, meningitis, and middle-ear infections, while *Haemophilus* causes Hib disease, which presents symptoms similar to meningitis. Respiratory syncytial virus is the largest cause of respiratory infections in infants and children, infecting 64 million and killing 160,000 each year.

Diarrheal Diseases

Diarrheal diseases include bacterial diseases such as shigellosis, typhoid and paratyphoid fevers, cholera, and salmonellosis; and viral diseases such as rotavirus. They may also be caused by toxins in food. Diarrheal diseases—especially if they cause dysentery, or bloody diarrhea—may cause massive fluid loss leading to severe dehydration and death if left untreated. Children under five years of age are most susceptible to severe illness and death from diarrheal diseases. Many can be relatively easily prevented by clean drinking water supplies, improved sanitation and wastewater treatment, and sanitary food handling and preparation. Vaccines may provide protection against some of these diseases as well.

Shigellosis, caused by several species of *Shigella*, a group of closely related bacteria, infects about 163 million people in developing countries and another 1 million in developed countries each year. Of those infected, about 1 million die. Shigellosis is spread by person-to-person contact. Outbreaks often follow in the wake of war and natural disasters.

Typhoid and paratyphoid fevers are caused by related bacteria, *Salmonella typhi* and *S. parathyphi*, respectively. Both are primarily water-borne—most infection occurs after consumption of contaminated water—but contaminated food is also a source of infection. About 16 million cases of typhoid are reported each year, and six hundred thousand deaths per year are attributed to it.

Cholera, one of the oldest epidemic-prone diseases known, is caused by the bacteria *Vibrio cholerae*. The source of infection is typically contaminated water or food. The seventh pandemic, or worldwide outbreak, of cholera began in 1961 in Indonesia and spread rapidly through Asia and Africa. It reached South America in 1991 and spread throughout that continent and into Central America. Cholera epidemics can arise suddenly and kill many of its victims in a short time. Cholera outbreaks killed nearly 40 million in India alone between 1817 and 1917.

Under International Health Regulations, cholera is one of three diseases (along with plague and yellow fever) that WHO member states are obligated to report. The organization estimates that only 5% to 10% of actual cholera cases are reported, however, because many WHO member states fear economic and other consequences, such as lost tourism.

Food-borne bacterial illnesses affect millions around the world, as well. In addition to some of the bacterial species already discussed, the major culprits include *Salmonella* (cousins of the typhoid and paratyphoid bacteria), *Listeria monocytogenes*, *Escherichia coli* serotype O157:H7, and *Campylobacter*.

Rotavirus is the leading cause of severe diarrhea and dehydration in infants worldwide. A 2003 study in the journal *Emerging Infectious Diseases* estimated that rotavirus infects nearly 140 million children annually, with 2 million hospitalizations and more than four hundred thousand deaths. Eighty-two percent of the deaths occur in the poorest countries. A vaccine, Rotashield, was introduced in 1998, but it was pulled from the market and production halted the following year because of complications.

Tuberculosis

One-third of the Earth's population is infected with the bacteria that causes tuberculosis, *Mycobacterium tuberculosis*, making tuberculosis the most widespread major infectious disease. It is airborne, but people infected with *M. tuberculosis* are not always infectious. The immune system can wall the bacteria up in nodules—tubercles—in tissues such as the lungs, thus giving the disease its name. The disease can be cured by a regimen of antibiotic treatment, but misuse of antibiotics and a lack of diligence in following treatment guidelines have helped spur the evolution of drug-resistant strains. The WHO estimated nearly 9 million active cases of tuberculosis in 2002.

Malaria

Malaria, or "bad air," is one of the most widespread and devastating parasitic diseases in the world. It is spread by infected *Anopheles* mosquitoes. Malaria causes flu-like systems—fever, headache, and vomiting—and destroys red blood cells, thus clogging blood vessels that supply the brain and other vital organs. Left untreated, symptoms can recur over time. It causes 300 million acute illnesses and kills 1 million annually.

Measles

Measles, a viral disease characterized by a rash, high fever, and flu-like symptoms, is a highly contagious but preventable disease that is the leading cause of blindness throughout the world. Measles, caused by *Morbillivirus*, is listed by the WHO as the direct cause of more than 610,000 deaths in 2002, but the disease, through complications from pneumonia, diarrhea, and malnutrition, may be the leading cause of death among children worldwide. Vaccination can prevent the disease, and the WHO has targeted measles for eradication.

Pertussis

The childhood disease whooping cough, or pertussis, is caused by a bacteria, *Bordetella pertussis*. It is characterized by intense coughing that culminates in a prolonged intake of breath—the "whoop." Pertussis can strike any age, but the effects are worse for the very young. The disease affects 20 million to 40 million each year and kills two hundred thousand to four hundred thousand. Ninety percent of cases are in the developing world. The disease is preventable via vaccination.

Meningitis

Bacterial meningitis is a contagious bacterial airborne disease caused by *Neisseria meningitide*. Infection manifests itself as pneumonia, septicemia (blood poisoning), or meningitis. Septicemia occurs when the bacteria spread through the bloodstream. It is very deadly and is characterized by circulatory failure and hemorrhagic rash. Meningitis is indicated by intense headache, fever, nausea, vomiting, light sensitivity, and a stiff neck, among other symptoms. Even with prompt treatment, the disease is fatal in up to 10% of cases, which averages about 170,000 deaths per year. Permanent neurological symptoms—including hearing and speech disorders, mental impairment, and paralysis—afflict as many as 20% of survivors. Overcrowding contributes to the spread of the bacteria, as do arid conditions in the tropical and subtropical regions and cold conditions in temperate regions.

Syphilis

While primarily thought of as a sexually transmitted disease, syphilis, caused by bacteria called *Treponema pallidum*, can also be transmitted person-to-person under unhygienic conditions. It can also be transmitted from mother to child. Initial symptoms are ulcers at the site of original infection. After a few weeks, the bacteria hide in other organs and the infected person may remain asymptomatic for years. In late stages of the disease, the nervous system, cardiovascular system, skin, or skeleton may be affected. Syphilis in the mother is a major cause of stillbirth as well as death of infants in their first year.

Regional Patterns

In 2002, lower respiratory infections took an especially heavy toll in Southeast Asia (1.5 million deaths) and Saharan and sub-Saharan Africa (1.1 million deaths), followed by the Western Pacific and East Asia (500,000 deaths), and the Mediterranean and West Asia (350,000 deaths). The highest death toll from diarrheal diseases was in Saharan and sub-Saharan Africa (710,000 deaths), Southeast Asia (600,000 deaths), the Mediterranean and West Asia (260,000 deaths), and the Western Pacific and East Asia (150,000 deaths).

Tuberculosis claimed 600,000 victims in Southeast Asia in 2002. In Saharan and sub-Saharan Africa, 350,000 patients died from the disease, followed by 370,000 in the Western Pacific and East Asia, and 140,000 in the Mediterranean and West Asia. Africa bears the brunt of the death toll from malaria. In 2002, more than 1.1 million died from the disease in Saharan and sub-Saharan Africa alone.

A New Threat

In 1978 something new appeared in gay men from Sweden and the United States and heterosexual men in Haiti and Tanzania. Four years later, in 1981, the US Centers for Disease Control and Prevention reported on an unusual suite of symptoms in gay and bisexual men. The suite of symptoms was named *acquired immune deficiency syndrome* (AIDS) in 1982, and in 1983 the virus that caused it, human immunodeficiency virus (HIV), was identified.

In AIDS, the virus attacks and destroys the body's immune system. Over time, AIDS patients succumb to a number of other diseases, such as Kaposi's sarcoma—a type of cancer—and pneumonia caused by *Pneumocystis carinii.*

HIV is primarily spread by sexual contact, although it can also be spread via blood transfusions and by sharing of needles used for injecting intravenous

drugs. The virus first appeared among homosexuals in developed nations such as the United States. The early association with "taboo" sexual practices has, to some extent, hindered adoption of measures to stem the spread of the virus. Also, rumors that HIV does not cause AIDS have likewise hindered efforts to slow the pandemic.

Nearly 40 million people are living with the virus, and the number is growing. Twenty million have died since the first diagnosis of what came to be known as AIDS in 1981. According to the Joint United Nations Programme on HIV/AIDS (UNAIDS), 5 million new HIV infections occurred in 2003 and 3 million died of AIDS that year.

HIV is having serious effects on social stability in areas where infection is widespread. A high proportion of adults aged fifteen to forty-nine is affected—this is the age group that drives the economy, raises children, and takes care of older adults. (Nearly all new infections are in the fifteen to twenty-four age group.) Sub-Saharan Africa has 12 million AIDS orphans—children who have lost parents because of AIDS—and the emotional scars of those children may have long-lasting effects on societies in the future.

Africa has the greatest number of HIV infections—25 million people, or nearly two-thirds of HIV patients worldwide—live in sub-Saharan Africa. Asia is next hardest hit, with 7.4 million infections, or about 20% of the world's total. The HIV infection rates are on the rise in Asia, too, with rapid rises in the number of cases in China, Indonesia, and Vietnam.

DAVID M. LAWRENCE

See also CARE; Disaster Relief; Doctors Without Borders/Médecins sans Frontières; Health Care; HIV/AIDS; Indigenous Medical Practices; OxFAM; Sex Trade/Trafficking; United Nations Children's Fund (UNICEF); Urbanization: Impact on Environment; Water Resources and Distribution; World Health Organization (WHO)

References and Further Reading

Aron, Joan L., and Jonathan A. Patz, eds. *Ecosystem Change and Public Health: A Global Perspective.* Baltimore, MD: Johns Hopkins University Press, 2001.
Brookmeyer, Ron, and Donna F. Stroup, eds. *Monitoring the Health of Populations: Statistical Principles and Methods for Public Health Surveillance.* New York: Oxford University Press, 2004.
Davis, Jonathan R., and Joshua Lederberg, eds. *Emerging Infectious Diseases from the Global to the Local Perspective: A Summary of a Workshop of the Forum on Emerging Infections.* Washington, DC: National Academy Press, 2001. http://www.nap.edu/books/0309071844/html/
DeSalle, Rob, ed. *Epidemic! The World of Infectious Disease.* New York: The New Press, 1999.

Drexler, Madeline. *Secret Agents: The Menace of Emerging Infections*. Washington, DC: Joseph Henry Press, 2002.

Fan, Hung Y., Ross F. Coner, and Luis P. Villarreal. *AIDS: Science and Society*. Boston: Jones and Bartlett, 2004.

Garrett, Laurie. *The Coming Plague: Newly Emerging Diseases in a World Out of Balance*. New York: Penguin, 1995.

Institute of Medicine. *Informing the Future: Critical Issues in Health*, 2nd ed. Washington, DC: Institute of Medicine of the National Academies, 2003. http://books.nap.edu/books/NI000517/html/index.html

Joint United Nations Programme on HIV/AIDS. *2004 Report on the Global AIDS Epidemic*. Geneva, Switzerland: Author, 2004. http://www.unaids.org/bangkok2004/report.html

McNeill, William H. *Plagues and Peoples*. New York: Anchor Books, 1998.

Price-Smith, Andrew T. *Health of Nations: Infectious Disease, Environmental Change, and Their Effects on National Security and Development*. Cambridge, MA: MIT Press, 2002.

World Health Organization. *Communicable Diseases 2002: Global Defence and the Infectious Disease Threat*. Geneva, Switzerland: Author, 2003. http://www.who.int/infectious-disease-news/cds2002/

World Health Organization. *The World Health Report 2004: Changing History*. Geneva, Switzerland: Author, 2004. http://www.who.int/whr/2004/en/

INTELLECTUAL PROPERTY RIGHTS

Intellectual property can be defined as creations of the labors of the human mind, which maybe incorporated in creative and inventive works. These may include literary works, paintings, inventions, designs, musical works, and trademarks. The legal entitlement conferred on such intellectual property creates a number of rights, which could vary in scope and duration in each case. With the conferment of such rights (which follow registration), the rights holder is in a position to control and regulate unauthorized use of his or her property and also to grant permission (known as licensing) for its use, including setting the terms for its use.

The various forms of protection of intellectual property rights may be classified as copyrights, trademarks, geographical indications, industrial designs, product patents, process patents, layout designs of integrated circuits, undisclosed information, and trade secrets. All of them are included in the Agreement on Trade-Related Aspects of Intellectual Property Rights (TRIPS). Even before this agreement the criteria of novelty, non-obviousness, and industrial utility applied before a patent would be granted. According to Article 30 of the TRIPS Agreement, the duration for grant of a patent is twenty years, after which it comes into the public domain. In the case of intellectual property rights such as trademarks and trade secrets, the rights generally extend to an indefinite period. Patents are the most sought-after category of individual property rights (IPRs).

While rights relating to intellectual property have been in existence since the period prior to the Industrial Revolution, the term has become universally familiar only in recent years, and particularly since the Uruguay Round of the General Agreement on Trade and Tariffs (GATT) brought forth the TRIPS Agreement in 1995.

Before the TRIPS Agreement the most important instruments that dealt with the protection of intellectual property rights were the Paris Convention (1967), the Berne Convention (1971), the Rome Convention (1961), the International Union for the Protection of New Varieties of Plants (UPOV), the Teaching, Learning and Technology Group (TLT), and the Budapest Treaty. The TRIPS Agreement, however, is the most comprehensive treaty dealing with the subject. It is also the most far reaching in so far as its implementation is likely to impinge on the time-honored sovereignty of nations, in particular impacting their domestic laws, as well as their economic systems and development priorities. It is the first time that IPR has been made a part of a trade regime. Additionally, since life forms may also be patented now, a radical departure has been made.

The countries that signed the TRIPS Agreement were given a time frame to make their domestic laws compliant with TRIPS provisions. All members were given one year—until January 1996. The developing countries were given four more years—until January 2000—and the least-developed countries ten years (i.e., until 2006). There is a reviewing procedure (a ministerial review to be held every two years) and a dispute settlement mechanism provided for in the TRIPS Agreement.

Examined from an historical perspective, the issue of intellectual property rights should probably not be a matter of great controversy between nations. The history of humankind shows that successive generations have built upon the inventiveness and the technological achievements of previous generations of humankind as a whole. It is as hard to imagine the invention of the motor car in the West without the invention of the wheel by some intelligent mechanical mind in Asia, as it is to visualize the granting of copyright for a book had paper not been invented in China. To extend the thesis further, inventions and technological progress must serve society's purpose, and in an increasingly globalized society with many common problems including infectious diseases and environmental emergencies like global warming, thought must be collectively given to the ways and means of tackling these problems rather than a strictly proprietary interest in the means to do so.

The proponents of legal protection for intellectual property rights state that a person has a natural right to the product of his or her brain. In addition, to the extent that he or she has produced something it finds useful, society must reward the person for it. The economic argument for protection of these rights is that it stimulates innovative and technological creativity and thus adds to society's resource of ideas. This in turn leads to economic growth.

Others challenge this view and point out that while the first patent was granted in 1449 by the king of England, the spate of inventive activity, which led to the Industrial Revolution, took place much later. They deny that instruments like patents contribute to encouraging creativity and inventiveness and point out that this view is based on an artificial and unrealistic construction of knowledge and innovation.

Before the TRIPS Agreement, the protection of intellectual property rights had existed at various levels and had been of several kinds. There had also existed, on the whole, a tacit understanding among countries that as incentive and reward for innovation, payment for particular patents was in order. But public interest was also given consideration, and toward this end, an attempt was made to have patented products, in particular medicines, be available to the public at affordable prices. Many countries passed laws relating to patents that provided for compulsory licensing for working of patents—in other words, for the local manufacture of the patented product. Patents were also used as a means for transfer as well as local development of technology.

By the early 1980s the US government and industry as well had begun to be increasingly vocal about greater intellectual property protection. The 1984 amendment to Section 301 of the US Trade Act authorized the US president to take corrective action in a situation where there was inadequate protection of intellectual property rights of US citizens in other countries. Soon after, in 1985, the US took action against the Republic of Korea under this amendment, resulting in Korea strengthening its copyright law and enforcement and also introducing patenting for medicines and chemicals.

The reason for the US wanting a strict protection system was that it perceived that the developing countries were demonstrating high efficiency in absorbing and replicating new technologies and thereby providing competition for US goods. The US trade deficit in the 1980s was $150 billion. The US felt that by enforcing US-type patent laws in the rest of the world, it could reduce its trade deficit. This, however, was one among the many reasons why the US and other developed countries wanted a stricter intellectual property regime.

At the time the US was pressing for inclusion of several areas of intellectual property in the proposed round of trade negotiations, several developing countries had put up a strong opposition. Among them Brazil and India took the view that the World Intellectual Property Organization, rather than any other forum, was competent to discuss the subject of intellectual property rights. The developing countries, despite their strong reservations on the matter, did not present a united opposition. Korea and the ASEAN countries had not been vocal regarding their opposition to the proposals of the developing countries. A review of the Uruguay Round of negotiations would certainly be of great help in getting information about the complex motivations, intentions, and apprehensions of the various participating countries regarding protection of intellectual property rights.

The developed countries—the US, the countries of Europe, and Japan—presented on the whole a consistent and united stand, insisting on higher levels of intellectual property protection from developing countries. It remains true, however, that there were differences among them, which the developing countries could have exploited. They did not do so, and also were not able at that crucial stage to provide alternate proposals to that of the US, with the result that the TRIPS Agreement went through.

It was clear by the end of the Uruguay Round of negotiations that even though a number of countries agreed to sign the TRIPS Agreement, its implementation would be a difficult and contentious process.

In 1967, the World Intellectual Property Organization (WIPO), under the United Nations, was the primary organization for protection of intellectual property rights in relations between nations. Since the WTO came into existence as a result of the Uruguay Round, it has been at the center of discussions and meetings relating to implementation of intellectual property rights. But different opinions on the matter do exist. While the mandate given to the WTO in the context of world trade is a strong one, certainly stronger than its predecessor GATT, the developing countries have frequently pressed for a greater role for WIPO. They perceive that the WTO is more a forum of the developed countries and they are able to push forward their own agenda in that organization.

It is clear from the Preamble to the TRIPS Agreement as well as the WTO Agreement that the protection of intellectual property rights has to be considered in the larger context of reducing barriers to trade and so ensure that enforcement of intellectual property rights does not result in "distortions and impediments to international trade."

The Preamble to the WTO Agreement also states that in view of the fact that the nations of the world are at different stages of development, there is need to support the "underdeveloped countries" to promote their technological and economic development by providing differential treatment, certain concessions, and special measures.

Therefore the TRIPS Agreement itself, while providing greater protection to intellectual property rights, also appears to set some limits to them. It will now depend upon the developing countries as to how they utilize these provisions to best achieve their interests, though the matter is not as simple as this in the case of all categories of rights.

Among the developing countries there does exist a perception that the protection of intellectual property rights as provided for in the TRIPS Agreement is an attempt by the developed countries, whose governments invariably support their transnational corporations, to coerce the developing countries, who are often not in a position to drive a hard bargain themselves, into accepting rules that do not really benefit them. At the same time they try through propaganda to make them believe that giving protection to intellectual property rights would encourage investment in particular foreign direct investment, as well as research and innovation. The WTO rules—which apply equally in the context of intellectual property rights, such as the supremacy of the principle of free trade, the "most favored nation" principle, and the principle that foreign nationals must have the same rights and privileges as the host country's citizens—are seen as institutionalizing the current system of global economic inequality.

It has been argued in the recent past, particularly by transnational corporations, that intellectual property rights confer exclusive rights. But if this were so, such rights would act to inhibit trade, which the WTO seeks above all to avoid.

While Article 28 of the TRIPS Agreement does confer "exclusive rights" on rights holders during the term of patent to prevent "third parties" from "making, using, offering for sale, selling, or importing" for these purposes that product, the TRIPS Agreement also provides, in Article 30, for "legitimate interests of third parties" and "use" by them; and in Article 31, for "other uses" by the government or authorized third parties "without authorization of the right holder." The "third parties" may include—in the case of pharmaceuticals, for instance—the generic pharmaceutical companies who may be interested in making the product in the period after the expiration date of the patent, consumers of patented medicines in a given country, and WTO member governments themselves. The affirmation of a third

party's rights to use the patented invention during the patent term is provided in Article 31. Similarly, Article 40 gives to the patentee the right to license and also protects the licensee against anti-competitive practices or exploitation by patent holders. Thus public interest has been addressed by the TRIPS Agreement.

An important aspect of IPRs relates to their effective domestic enforcement in various countries. Part III of the TRIPS Agreement includes, unlike previous treaties, a comprehensive list of procedures for enforcement of IPRs by domestic authorities. These will apply both at the border and inside the country. The implications for many countries will be to change their existing procedures, which could mean changes in the way their judicial and administrative systems operate. Article 41.5 states that there is no obligation on the part of member countries to put in place a judicial system for the enforcement of IPRs distinct from the enforcement of law in general, which does imply that remedies provided for the infringement of IPRs would be in accordance with the legal context and system of each separate country. Article 41.2 has provided that procedures for enforcement should not be unduly complicated or costly.

Diverse new issues will most likely come up as the debate on intellectual property rights proceeds in the developed world and between the developed and developing countries. Technological developments such as the increased use of the Internet have already given rise to questions relating to expanding the definition of copyright.

Biodiversity and the uses it has been put to in the area of genetic engineering is an emerging controversial field. Patents on life forms, for instance, have far-reaching economic and ecological implications, apart from ethical problems. In this sort of genetic engineering, the scientist merely moves the genes around—he or she does not create life. Such genetic engineering finds a fertile field in the biological diversity of the Third World, which multinational corporations are already laying claims to. This biological diversity has traditionally provided the base of much of the food, medicine, and even clothing in the developing countries. From an ecological standpoint, patents related to biological resources will have huge repercussions for the conservation of biodiversity and the way it is utilized. The patent holders in this case will virtually oversee and collect rent for the seeds sown by farmers and the medicines made with nature's bounty. This would inevitably throw already marginalized peoples of the Third World into an ever-more-desperate situation. India and several other developing countries recognize that the farmers who constitute the majority of their populations will in particular be adversely affected. Until recently, the biodiversity in Third World countries had been utilized by the community as a whole and in accordance with communal norms. To apply the principle of private property to a community resource and enable, through an intellectual property rights system, only corporations to have a legal personality and rights in relation to it, would be to jeopardize a way of life that has existed for centuries.

Those speaking for indigenous cultures, like the scientist and environmentalist Vandana Shiva, point out that indigenous knowledge often provides the leads for the useful traits in biological organisms. These are then transferred to Western knowledge systems and treated as an innovation. Legal rights (in the form of patents) are then claimed by corporate capital while introducing into the market what has already been there as indigenous wisdom in traditional cultures. This process has been referred to as *biopiracy*. There are numerous examples of this phenomenon. The *neem* tree of India has been known for centuries to have exceptional medicinal and purifying qualities and poor villagers have been able to access it for curing many ailments. The situation is set to change now as Western manufacturers in the past few years have "discovered" these properties of the tree and have taken out patents for various products made from it. In this process they have imported huge quantities of seed of *neem* leading to a scarcity in its land of origin and unavailability to the common person in India.

The TRIPS Agreement has moved in the opposite direction from the draft code of conduct on Transfer of Technology negotiated in the United Nations Conference on Trade and Development (UNCTAD) and the draft code of conduct for Transnational Corporations negotiated at the United Nations. Both of these had aimed at the transfer of technology from transnational companies to developing countries and also required them to act in accordance with the developmental requirements and goals of the host countries.

Despite a great deal of difference in the vantage points from which the developed countries and the underdeveloped countries view IPRs, the latter more readily accepts certain categories. Trademarks, requiring protection, are a subject that has been the least controversial, and trademarks had been recognized by the national laws of both developed and developing countries prior to TRIPS. Protection of trademarks had been fairly detailed in the Paris Convention, though the means of such protection had been left to individual countries.

The developing countries had used this freedom in implementation to restrict foreign trademarks so that prices for certain commodities including pharmaceuticals remained reasonably priced. This, however, has had to change under the principle of equal treatment to foreigners and nationals under TRIPS.

TRIPS has also provided a clear definition of trademark for the first time. It is defined as "any sign or any combination of signs capable of distinguishing the goods and services of one undertaking from those of other undertakings." These trademarks must then be registered. In the case of trademarks, unlike patents, local business has an interest in making sure of protection.

In addition to trademarks, certain products are closely connected with a geographical area—such as Darjeeling for tea from that area in India and Champagne from that district in France—and these indicators or signs represent the fund of goodwill and reputation built up over a period of time by a brand that connects it to the consumers. If a particular group has nurtured such a category of product through investment and other means, it would not like another group to use it to increase its sales.

Since the area of IPRs is one of fluid developments, one cannot conclude that these rights are fixed and unchanging. On the contrary, recent discussions and developments in particular at the Seattle and Cancun Ministerial would give rise to the understanding that there are several ways of implementing the provision of this Agreement, indeed that there are several ways of interpreting these provisions.

A noteworthy development is the emergence of what some observers have called the global civil society. Large sections of society in developed countries and NGOs have expressed skepticism regarding many provisions of the TRIPS Agreement. They have also offered active support to the developing countries to interpret TRIPS more flexibly so that they may continue to retain their developmental priorities, in particular those relating to public health and social security.

AMRITA SINGH

References and Further Reading

Bhagwati, J., and M. Hirsch, eds. *The Uruguay Round and Beyond: Essays in Honor of Arthur Dunkel.* Heidelberg and New York: Springer, 1998.

Correa, Carlos M. *Intellectual Property Rights, the WTO and Developing Countries: The TRIPS Agreement and Policy Options.* Penang, Malaysia: Zed Books, 2000.

Shiva, Vandana. *Protect or Plunder.* London: Zed Books, 2001.

Watal, Jayashree. *Intellectual Property Rights in the WTO and Developing Countries.* New Delhi: Oxford University Press, 2001.

INTER-AMERICAN DEVELOPMENT BANK (IDB)

Nineteen Latin American and Caribbean countries and the United States founded the Inter-American Development Bank in December of 1959. The Bank's historical origins can be traced back to a resolution calling for the creation of a development institution at the First Inter-American Conference, held in Washington, DC, in 1890. For more than half a century prior to its official inception, the countries of Latin America and the Caribbean worked to establish an official financial institution to address the economic, social, cultural, and political realities of the region. In 1958, Brazilian president Juscelino Kubitschek proposed that the heads of state initiate formal cooperation to promote economic and social development in the Western Hemisphere. A special committee of the Organization of American States, founded in 1948, drafted the Articles of Agreement that were then passed unanimously in a resolution before the General Assembly. With its headquarters in Washington, DC, the IDB was the first regional development bank to complement the Bretton Woods institutions made up of the International Bank of Reconstruction and Development (World Bank), the International Monetary Fund (IMF), and the General Agreement on Tariffs and Trade (GATT).

The Charter of the Inter-American Development Bank states that its principal functions are to utilize its own capital to finance the development of borrowing countries; to supplement private investment when private capital is not available on reasonable terms and conditions; and to provide technical assistance for the implementation of development plans and projects. The Bank's financial resources are in the form of ordinary capital raised in financial markets and the Funds in Administration that come from member contributions. The primary objectives are to foster the welfare of and maintain the solidarity among its forty-six member states that consist of twenty-six borrowing countries in Latin America and the Caribbean; twenty non-borrowing countries, including the United States, Canada, and Japan; sixteen European countries; and Israel. Each country's voting power is based on its subscription to the Bank's capital stock. Latin America and the Caribbean represent 50% of the voting power; the United States has 30%; Japan has 5%; Canada has 4%; and other non-borrowing countries have 11%.

The organization of the IDB reflects an identity closely tied to the cultural and managerial style of the Latin American and Caribbean countries. This regional character gives the Bank a key comparative advantage over other international financial institutions in understanding national and regional priorities, and in adjusting to new regional challenges of development. The longstanding political commitment to regional integration enables the Bank to tailor effectively policies and lending programs in response to local conditions. Early efforts toward integration entailed the financing of infrastructure projects such as ports, transportation, and power grids, and the collection and the broad dissemination of data on regional uses and flows of intellectual, commercial, financial, technological, and human resources. The Charter emphasizes the financing of specific projects, but also promotes an understanding of development that requires a balanced approach across multiple sectors. In the 1960s and 1970s, lending was channeled into social issues, particularly education and health, income generation, and job creation through micro-enterprise and small-scale farming projects, and basic infrastructure, such as roads, water, and sanitation. Technical cooperation complemented these lending programs by conveying knowledge to borrowing countries and strengthening institutional capacity. Technical assistance was made available to public institutions, regional and sub-regional organizations, and non-governmental organizations.

The rapid expansion of the Bank's bureaucratic apparatus resulted in a propensity toward formal approval procedures, multiple and overlapping oversight on expenditures, and extensive ex-post auditing. Although sometimes decried as overly rigid, this procedural focus emphasized fairness and transparency as essential components of project finance in the public sector. But, the political interplay between borrowers, non-borrowers, and private capital markets encouraged a proclivity for rules and procedures, a need for consensus and compromise, and a culture of public service and pragmatism among its staff and employees. The incorporation of additional non-borrowing members broadened the capital base and introduced alternative perspectives on the meaning of development over time. These institutional attributes were intended to maintain a neutral approach to individual countries.

As Latin America and the Caribbean confronted the polarizing effects of the Cold War and the difficulties of social and environmental decay during the 1980s, the excessive concentration on project approvals neglected the urgency for a new approach to multilateral regional governance. The debt crisis and inflation spiral of the 1980s caused a dramatic change in the philosophy of the IDB with regard to the limits of project finance. This change inspired a debate within the institution about the need to combine financial assistance with the adoption of policy changes driven by the so-called "Washington Consensus" that advocated fiscal austerity and monetary stability. The Bank sought an appropriate mix of "policy-based" and "investment" lending that moved the attention of both the Bank and its borrowers away from the internal technical details of projects and onto the transfer of resources in a more efficient and flexible manner. The Bank made serious efforts to reconcile the goals of policy reform with investments intended to enhance productivity.

The global economic recession of the early 1990s altered the conditions under which the Bank pursued its mission and policy priorities. Economic decline inspired a more consensual approach to governance in which member countries and executive and administrative bodies reassessed problems associated with periodic capital replenishments and sustainable levels of lending, the impact of increased volatility of private capital markets on sources of external finance to the region, the acceleration of the pace of technological change, and the rising demands for expertise and technical assistance. Out of this self-reexamination emerged a greater emphasis on social-sector reform and state modernization and the use of bilateral and non-governmental resources in partnership with the Bank's own funds. The capital replenishment of 1994 was the largest increase in resources in the history of the IDB. At the annual meeting in Guadalajara, Mexico, member countries approved a $40 billion replenishment aimed primarily at reducing poverty and promoting social equity in the region. The Eighth General Increase reflected the common desire of the IDB president, Enrique Iglesias (1988–), the Board Governors, and the Board of Executive Directors to reach a political compromise in which all shareholders would make financial commitments to new lending priorities and development objectives.

The gathering of officials from a variety of multi-lateral institutions; government delegations from Latin America, North America, and Europe; representatives of non-governmental and non-profit organizations; policy observers; and academics at the Conference on Strengthening Civil Society in September 1994 introduced an ambitious agenda for the coordination of state reform and economic adjustment with effective programs to alleviate poverty and to build democratic institutions. The conference generated intellectual and financial contributions from the Organization of American States, the United Nations Development Program, and the United States Agency for International Development. The distribution of IDB loans shifted accordingly over the next five years. By 1999, 29.1% of all lending went to social sectors in health and sanitation, urban

development, education, social investment funds, the environment, and micro-enterprise; 28.1% went to infrastructure in energy, transportation, and communications; 22.2% went to productive sectors in agriculture and fisheries, industry, mining and tourism, and science and technology; 15.6% went to the modernization of the state; and 5.1% went to export financing (IDB 2000, p. 9).

As most Latin American and Caribbean governments pursued the consolidation of democracy and the privatization of state assets in the 1990s, the Bank's lending for public-sector efficiency, decentralization of administrative responsibilities, and training programs to improve accountability and transparency increased dramatically. Such programs built on the economic stabilization and restructuring efforts associated with the Washington Consensus. For example, Brazil received a $300 million loan in 1999 to modernize tax collection, upgrade human resources, and improve information technology at the municipal level. In the same year, El Salvador used an $8.8 million loan to implement an ethics code in the Legislative Assembly and reduce procurement irregularities.

Furthermore, the IDB aimed to equip "the citizenry, the sum total of individuals and organizations that exist apart from government-groups of micro-entrepreneurs or environmentalists, civic and trade associations, political parties, philanthropic organizations, churches, indigenous communities, organized labor and women's and youth groups" (IDB 1995, p. 12). Most projects devoted to strengthening and broadening the participation of civil society in decision-making processes deliver financial and technical support to non-governmental organizations that advocate the demands of the urban laborers and rural workers, disabled veterans, illiterate women, underprivileged students, and indigenous groups. These projects are carried out through a host of collaborative activities and entities. The Inter-American Institute for Social Development conducts research on poverty alleviation; the Micro-Enterprise and Small Projects division finances lending to small and medium-size businesses; Women in Development addresses health and employment problems faced especially by single mothers; the Indigenous Populations and Human Resettlement section treats refugee, migrant, and land issues; and the Multilateral Investment Fund provides "start-up" capital and the integration of displaced workers, students, and single mothers into the formal private economy. These endeavors appeal to philanthropy, good will, and entrepreneurial initiative as key ingredients to eliminate poverty and achieve popular democratic participation and borrow significantly from the development strategy advanced by the

Kennedy administration's Alliance for Progress in the 1960s.

The ratification of the General Agreement on Tariffs and Trade (GATT) by Latin American and Caribbean countries in 1994 and 1995 elevated the IDB to new heights as an advocate of economic integration and free trade in the Western Hemisphere. At the First Summit of the Americas, held in Miami, Florida, in December 1994, the thirty-four heads of states agreed to establish the Free Trade Area of the Americas (FTAA) by the year 2005. The FTAA would be the world's largest integrated market, with approximately 850 million people with a combined gross national product of over $13 trillion. The Summit Implementation Review Group assigned the IDB the task of coordinating sub-regional trade and integration arrangements with the objectives of the FTAA. The Integration, Trade, and Hemispheric Issues Division offers technical assistance toward the policy harmonization of the North American Free Trade Agreement (NAFTA) between the United States, Canada, and Mexico, and the South American Common Market (MERCOSUR), the Caribbean Community (CARICOM), the Central American Common Market (CACM), and Andean Group trade groups.

The IDB recognizes that the complexities of regional integration and the challenges of development in the twenty-first century require political will, innovative projects, and strategic planning based on its distinct relationship with borrowing countries. Latin America and the Caribbean continue to be affected adversely by financial crises, severe inequality, rising crime and violence, volatile commodity prices, and rapidly rising expectations. These pressures call for what are referred to as "second-generation reforms" that go beyond the mandates of private markets and minimalist states to generate broad-based equitable growth. Consequently, the ability of the Bank to represent the region's diverse states and peoples depends heavily on the adoption of new initiatives arising from neighborhoods, communities, municipalities, and provinces across the Western Hemisphere.

MARK EVERINGHAM

References and Further Reading

Atkins, G. Pope. *Latin America in the International Political System*, 3rd ed. Boulder, CO: Westview Press, 1995.

Bulmer-Thomas, Victor, and James Dunkerley, eds. *The United States and Latin America: The New Agenda*. London: The Institute of Latin American Studies, 1999.

Inter-American Development Bank, *Basic Facts About the IDB*. Washington, DC: Department of External Relations, 2000.

Inter-American Development Bank. *Annual Report, 1994*. Washington, DC: Board of Governors, 1995.

Robinson, William. "Latin America in the Age of Inequality: Confronting the New 'Utopia.'" *International Studies Review*, 1, no. 3 (1999).

Sánchez, Manuel, and Rossana Corona, eds. *Privatization in Latin America*. Washington, DC: Inter-American Development Bank and the Johns Hopkins University Press, 1993.

Summit of the Americas Information Network. *Plans of Action 1994, 1996, 1998, 2001*. Washington, DC: Office of Summit Follow-Up, Organization of American States http://www.summit-americas.org/

Tulchin, Joseph, and Ralph Epach, eds. *Latin America in the New International System*. Boulder, CO: Lynne Rienner Publishers, 2001.

INTERNATIONAL AIR TRANSPORT ASSOCIATION (IATA)

In the post–World War II world, international air transport has been one of the most dynamic and fast-changing industries in the world. The International Air Transport Association (IATA), headquartered in Montreal, Canada, is an association of airlines founded in 1945 by airline corporations seeking to promote safe, regular, and economical air transport. IATA's objectives are to enable people, freight, and mail to move more efficiently throughout the world and to ensure that IATA member aircraft can operate safely and efficiently under clearly defined and understood rules. To facilitate this process, IATA assigns three-letter IATA airport codes and two-letter IATA airline designators. IATA also regulates the shipping of dangerous goods and publishes the *Dangerous Goods Regulations* manual, a reference source for airlines shipping hazardous materials. Many low-cost carriers who are not IATA members, however, have accused the association of being a cartel.

In early 2005, IATA had 262 members. More than half of the member airlines are based in the developing world. Sixty-nine member airlines are based in Asia. Members include Air China Limited, Air Macao, Asiana Airlines, Bangkok Airways, Cathay Pacific Airways, China Southern Airlines, Indian Airlines, Philippine Airlines, Royal Brunei Airlines, and Xiamen Airlines. Forty member airlines are based in Africa. Members include Aero Zambia, Air Botswana, Air Malawi, Air Namibia, Air Zimbabwe, Egypt Air, Ethiopian Airlines, Ghana Airways, Kenya Airways, and Royal Air Maroc. Thirty member airlines are based in Latin America. Members include Aerolineas Argentinas, Aeromexico, Air Jamaica, Avianca, Cubana de Aviacion, Lan Chile, Lan Ecuador, Lan Peru, Grupo Taca, and Varig. Twenty-six member airlines are based in the Middle East, the fastest-growing region in airline travel. Members include Ariana Afghan Airlines, El Al Israeli Airlines, Emirates,

Gulf Air Company, Iran Air, Kish Airlines, Kuwait Airlines, Qatar Airways, Royal Jordanian Airlines, and Saudi Arabian Airlines.

Flights by member airlines comprise more than 95% of all international scheduled air traffic. For air passengers and shipping customers, IATA simplifies the travel and shipping process. By helping to regulate airline costs, IATA facilitates cheaper tickets and shipping costs. Individual passengers can make one telephone call or one Internet visit to reserve a ticket, pay in one currency, and then use the ticket on several airlines to travel to several countries on different airlines. Despite differences in language, currency, law, and national customs, international airlines are able to coordinate individual networks into a single worldwide system.

MICHAEL R. HALL

References and Further Reading

Chuang, Richard Y. *The International Air Transport Association: A Case Study of a Quasi-Governmental Organization*. Groningen, Netherlands: Sijthoff Publishers, 1972.

Dogains, Rigas. *The Airline Business in the Twenty-First Century*. London: Routledge, 2001.

Morrison, Steven A. and Clifford Winston. *The Evolution of the Airline Industry*. Washington, DC: Brookings Institution Press, 1995.

INTERNATIONAL ATOMIC ENERGY AGENCY (IAEA)

The International Atomic Energy Agency (IAEA) is the world center of decision making and implementation on international cooperation on peaceful use of nuclear energy. The Agency engages mainly in three areas: Nuclear Safety and Security, Nuclear Science and Technology, and Safeguards and Verification.

The Agency was established as a result of the US nuclear policy transformation occurring in the mid-1950s. The United States abandoned a policy of strict denial of nuclear technology transfer and intended to seek a liberal regimen for a worldwide cooperation on peaceful use of nuclear energy. However, this policy transformation was not without condition: peaceful nuclear technology should not be diverted to military ends. This idea, promulgated by US president Eisenhower in his "Atoms for Peace" address to the General Assembly of the United Nations on December 8, 1953, gained endorsement from the United States' nuclear rival, the Soviet Union. The two nuclear giants initiated the negotiation of the IAEA Statute immediately and took the leadership in it. In September 1956, the Conference on the Statute convened at the headquarters of the United Nations.

(The United Nations only hosted the negotiation; it was not a sponsor.) On October 26, 1956, through the efforts of the "Twelve Nations Group," including members from Western and Eastern blocs who were led by the United States and the USSR, respectively, the Statute was drafted and open for signature. Eighty nations signed the treaty within ninety days and the IAEA Statute took effect on July 20, 1957. The IAEA Secretariat is now headquartered in Vienna, Austria, and has 137 member states.

The IAEA is an independent intergovernmental organization in the United Nations family. However, it is not a Specialized Agency under Article 57 of the Charter of the United Nations. The relation of the IAEA to the United Nations is unique: it is independent from the United Nations but may submit reports and questions to the United Nations Security Council directly (IAEA Statute Article III.B.4).

The IAEA consists of three statutory organs: the General Conference, the Board of Governors, and the Secretariat. The IAEA secretariat is the agency's headquarters in Vienna, Austria. It has a staff of 2,200 multi-disciplinary professional and support staff from more than ninety countries. The General Conference includes each member state; the Board of Governors is composed only of member states with advanced nuclear technology. The Board of Governors is vested a near plenary power in carrying out the Agency's function. In contrast, the power of the General Conference is limited to requesting reports and making proposals on any matter relating to the functions of the Agency (IAEA Statute Article V.F.2). The Director General and staff of the IAEA are under the authority of and subject to the control of the Board of Governors (IAEA Statute Article VII.B).

Through its various programs, the Agency promotes the use of peaceful nuclear technology for global welfare while working to prevent the use of nuclear technology for military purposes. Developing countries are primarily interested in the assistance programs that aid them in building nuclear technology and facilities; developed countries, especially under the leadership of the United States and the USSR in the aftermath of the 1962 Cuban missile crisis, have begun seeking to enhance measures in safeguarding peaceful nuclear activities. These two major programs interact at the political level and sometimes at more concrete financial and operational levels.

The founders of the Agency intended that the Agency's main function should be assisting in the research and application of nuclear energy. In the 1956 Statute, the founders proposed a modest nuclear safeguarding program: the Agency is only authorized to apply the safeguards to the extent of the Agency's supplies or at the request of the member states (IAEA

Statute Article III.A.5). However, the Treaty of Tlatelolco of 1967 and the Non-Proliferation Treaty of 1968 both vested the Agency with the power of safeguarding nuclear activities of Party States. Safeguards and Verification became the most important activities of the Agency. The history of the Agency's budget distribution evidenced such an evolution: while it was only 3.4% of the regular budget in 1962, the budget for Safeguards and Verification rose to 24.1% in 1981 and reached US$102,278,000 in the year 2004, exceeding the combined budgets for programs in Nuclear Safety and Security as well as Nuclear Science and Technology (US$76,085,000).

Some have accused the Board of Governors of using the strict membership requirements to shift the focus of the Agency tasks from assistance to safeguarding. Though the article overseeing the Board of Governors (Article VI of the Statute) restricts the size of the Board, its membership criteria are more favorable to developed nations. As a result, developed countries have prevailed in the Board of Governors. However, the subsequent amendments to Article VI of the Statute enlarged the Board of Governors (from twenty-three in 1957 to thirty-five in 2005) and consequently more and more developing countries participate in the IAEA decision-making process.

Despite the increasing number of developing nations with seats in the Board of Governors, the IAEA continues to strengthen its safeguards system, particularly with regard to improving the Agency's ability to detect undeclared nuclear activities. For instance, in May 1997, a strengthened safeguards system, known as the Model Protocol Additional to IAEA Safeguards agreements (INFCIRC/540), was approved by the IAEA Board of Governors. It shows that the Agency's efforts in enhancing the safeguards program have gained widespread support from its members, including the developing member states.

In the field of Nuclear Safety and Security, the Agency codifies and publishes standards, guides, and recommendations. Though not binding on member states, these international standards have substantial influence on national nuclear legislation governing radiation protection and nuclear reactor safety.

In addition to these activities, the Agency has initiated and sponsored an impressive list of treaties to resolve the international problems arising from the peaceful use of nuclear energy. The treaties cover issues such as the liability of nuclear operations, early notification of and assistance in nuclear accidents, and so forth.

Today the IAEA is an important organization in international relations. While it has shifted away from its primary objective of "accelerat[ing] and enlarg[ing] the contribution of atomic energy to peace, health and prosperity throughout the world" (Article II), it continues to work to prevent the destructive use of nuclear technology and to improve nuclear safety.

XINJUN ZHANG

References and Further Reading

El Baradei, Mohamed. *The Peaceful Use of Nuclear Energy: The Contribution of the IAEA.* Abu Dhabi: The Emirates Center for Strategic Studies and Research, 2003.

Fischer, David. *History of the International Atomic Energy Agency: The First Forty Years.* Vienna: International Atomic Energy Agency, 1997.

Fischer, David, Eric Chauvistré, and Harald Müller. *Extending the Non-Proliferation Regime: More Scope for the IAEA?* Heidelberg, Germany: Forschungsstätte der Evangelischen Studiengemeinschaft, 1994.

Rhyne, Charles S. *International Atomic Energy Agency: Personal Reflections.* Vienna: International Atomic Energy Agency, 1997.

Rhyne, Charles S., Amelito R. Mutuc, and Richard J. Chidester. *Law-Making Activities of the International Atomic Energy Agency.* Washington, DC: World Association of Lawyers, 1976.

Scheinman, Lawrence. *The International Atomic Energy Agency and World Nuclear Order.* Washington, DC: Resources for the Future, 1987.

———. *Nuclear Safeguards, the Peaceful Atom, and the IAEA.* New York: Carnegie Endowment and International Peace, 1969.

Schiff, Benjamin N. *International Nuclear Technology Transfer: Dilemmas of Dissemination and Control.* Totowa, N.J.: Rowman & Allanheld; London: Croom Helm, 1984.

Szasz, Paul C. *The Law and Practices of the International Atomic Energy Agency.* Vienna: International Atomic Energy Agency, 1970.

INTERNATIONAL BANK FOR RECONSTRUCTION AND DEVELOPMENT (IBRD) (WORLD BANK)

Founding

During the closing days of World War II, Allied governments planned for the post-war economy, determined to prevent the interwar era's trade dislocations and monetary disasters. A major part of this was the July 1944 conference held in Bretton Woods, New Hampshire. Delegates from forty-four states gathered to create an institutional structure for the international economy. One piece of the Bretton Woods system was the International Monetary Fund (IMF), developed to manage the monetary system, especially a fixed exchange-rate regime. Its sister institution, the

International Bank of Reconstruction and Development (IBRD), initially focused on rebuilding war-ravaged European states, and, later, turned to development. Founders envisioned the IBRD, or World Bank, complementing the IMF's work. While the IMF supported economy-wide programmatic changes, the Bank focused on smaller, more specific projects. The Bank often lent for infrastructure activities deemed necessary for economic development—building roads and ports for export, or hydroelectric ventures to provide energy for industrial production, for example.

The United States and Britain had competing visions for the Bank. Britain's representative to Bretton Woods, John Maynard Keynes, called for stronger states to help weaker ones. Further, he proposed a Bank with substantial resources. Its funds, he argued, should come from states with balance-of-payments surpluses. The IBRD could use its capital for "soft" or "concessional" terms, i.e., loans at below market rates. Harry Dexter White, who led the US delegation, represented the sole surplus state at the talks. Moreover, it was the only state likely to enjoy that position in the near term. Thus, under Keynes' plan the United States would have primary responsibility for Bank funding. Washington refused to take on that obligation, arguing that states in surplus had no duty to change their own economic policies. This greatly affected the Bank's capacities.

Thus, the Bank created at Bretton Woods had limited resources. Rather than using its own inadequate funds for loans, the Bank raised money on commercial markets, which it then lent. It used repayments to cover its own financial obligations. This meant that the Bank had a conservative bias, as its reputation depended on debtors honoring their commitments. As a result, the IBRD's lending was limited in scale and scope, as it could offer loans to only the most creditworthy states.

Institutions

The World Bank is a specialized agency of the United Nations (UN). Its nearly two hundred member states make decisions about loans, including financing, terms, and conditions. Members hold "shares," based on the size of their economies. Unlike the UN's General Assembly in which every member has an equal vote, the Bank uses weighted voting, with the United States having the largest vote and thus, the loudest voice. By tradition, the Bank's president is from the United States.

The Bank employs about ten thousand professional staff, including economists, social scientists, specialists on particular economic sectors, and policy analysts. Many staffers work from the Washington, DC, headquarters, but the Bank also maintains more than one hundred international offices. Despite this, many criticize the Bank, charging that employees spend inadequate time in borrowing states and thus, have incomplete knowledge of countries' particular conditions. They charge that Bank personnel have limited in-country contacts, often only high officials in economic- and finance-related ministries, which restricts the views they consider in making recommendations.

Since its inception, the Bank has evolved so that now it is common to refer to the "World Bank Group," made up of five institutions, described below. The original IBRD and the International Development Association (IDA) make up the "World Bank." Created in 1945, the IBRD has a twenty-four member Executive Board that handles day-to-day operations for the Board of Governors, on which all member states sit. The IBRD provides loan guarantees as well as loans to the Bank's wealthier members. In 2004, the IBRD made about $11 billion worth of new loans.

These loans are not concessional, as the IBRD itself borrows the funds on the commercial market through its AAA-rated bonds and notes, which obliges it to make payments to buyers on a set schedule. Essentially, the Bank, with its outstanding credit record, borrows at a cost far lower than the state that ultimately receives the money could secure. A borrower's default could jeopardize the Bank meeting its financial obligations. If the Bank lost its excellent credit rating, it could not obtain relatively cheap loans for its members. These loans do have longer repayment periods than commercial banks would offer. Generally, they have terms of fifteen to twenty years, with a grace period requiring no repayment for the loan's first three to five years. In response to criticism about its limited lending, in 1960, the Bank founded the IDA.

In contrast to the IBRD, the IDA makes highly concessional loans to the poorest member states, those that could not qualify for an IBRD loan. The IDA also grants some project support for undertakings considered vital for economic development. Along with funds, the IDA provides technical economic advice. Altogether, it seeks to help to implement poverty-reduction strategies. These include improving governance, providing for basic needs, opening recipients' markets, and increasing economic productivity.

IDA lending accounts for about one-quarter of Bank operations. Loans typically have a ten-year grace period, and borrowers have thirty-five to forty years for repayment. It could not use commercial funds for these loans. Instead, the Bank's richer members donate money every four years. In 2002, forty states contributed about $9 billion and the Bank itself donated more than $6 billion. Donor states agreed that a major lending focus should be the HIV/AIDS crisis and other issues that so severely affect numerous, extremely poor states. To focus on the neediest states, once a country reaches a certain economic level, it no longer qualifies for the IDA.

Together with the IBRD and IDA, three other bodies complete the World Bank Group. These agencies extend the Bank's resources in different ways. In each case, however, they encourage and facilitate using private capital for economic development.

In 1956, members created the International Finance Corporation (IFC) to encourage private investment in undercapitalized markets. The Corporation, together with private investors, makes equity investments (buys stakes) in businesses in less developed states. The IFC puts money into projects it considers economically viable, that investors have passed over because of location, lack of awareness, or the small size of the state's domestic capital pool. Neo-liberals have pushed vigorously for IFC growth as a means of increasing private-sector involvement in development.

Following World War II, foreign investment opportunities grew as states rebuilt and modernized, and former colonial states in Asia, Africa, and the Middle East developed sovereign economies. To facilitate investment, which it saw as enhancing economic development, the Bank created the International Centre for Settlement of Investment Disputes (ICSID). Beginning operations in 1966, it replaced the somewhat ad hoc practice of the Bank's president, or members of the president's staff, of personally intervening in disputes between investors and foreign governments. The Bank meant for the ICSID to encourage foreign investment by developing resolution mechanisms. The ICSID offers conciliation and arbitration facilities. Many investment agreements reference use of the ICSID in the event of disagreement. All states ratifying the Convention on the ICSID agree to recognize and enforce its arbitration decisions.

Finally, the Multilateral Investment Guarantee Agency (MIGA) dates to 1988. The MIGA "stretches" Bank resources by guaranteeing private direct investment in developing states, rather than providing such funds itself. It insures investors against "noncommercial" or "political" risks, that is, hazards beyond ordinary market operations. These include host states' expropriation of resources, war, or currency inconvertibility. Also, MIGA mediates disagreements between investors and borrowers. Finally, it provides technical assistance to countries seeking foreign investment and alerts international investors about unfamiliar business opportunities.

Operations

Initially, the Bank focused on European states' recovery from World War II, and on helping them to modernize and industrialize. Thus, the Bank's first loan was to France, which received $250 million for rebuilding. Given the IBRD's limited resources (initial US contribution about $570 million), however, the $12 billion in Marshall Funds that the United States gave to European states swamped the Bank's offerings. Thus, in its initial years of operation, the Bank was not particularly active.

The colonies of these European states began to gain independence after the war. Thus, in the 1950s and 1960s the international economy in which the Bank operated came to include a number of newly sovereign, but often economically weak, states. During this period, the Bank was famous (some argue "infamous") for lending for large, often dramatic infrastructure expansion in less developed states. Loans were not concessional, however, and went only to the most creditworthy (usually not the neediest) countries. Unhappy both with the low level of lending and with the loans' "hard" terms, members pushed for the 1960 creation of the IDA.

As the Bank involved itself fully in development, it sought to change the composition of borrowing states' economies. It recommended expanding production that took advantage of existing comparative advantages, often-abundant cheap but unskilled labor useful in agriculture, or usable quantities of some scarce mineral or metal with international demand. Production based on comparative advantage, classically trained economists at the Bank reasoned, meant lower prices and thus, a competitive export position. This would allow states to sell internationally, strengthening their economies, correcting economic imbalances—including balance-of-payments deficits—and enabling them to repay their debts. The Bank committed to long-term loans for infrastructure projects meant to fix structural problems. The Bank envisioned market-based solutions to economic underdevelopment.

Many borrowers traced underdevelopment to a different cause. They blamed the uneven terms of trade that favored (few) industrial producers relative to (many) agricultural producers. Many less developed states had comparative advantages in production of the same or similar goods. They chased the same buyers and had few tools, other than lower prices, with which to compete. The greater bargaining power of industrial producers meant they always benefited more from trade.

Rather than accept this status quo, many borrowers sought to create comparative advantages where they did not exist, especially developing industrial capacity in primarily agricultural states. Only in this way, they reasoned, could they "even" the terms of trade and gain equal benefits. Thus, many less developed states implemented Import Substitution Industrialization to develop national industrial bases. This usually required significant international borrowing.

In 1964, the first meeting of the UN's Conference on Trade and Development gave less developed states a forum for working together to develop and promote a common agenda for international economic change. They formed the Group of 77, which conceptualized and pressed for a New International Economic Order (NIEO). The NIEO called for redistribution of resources and power in the international system to make it more equitable, including technology transfer for industrial development in less developed states, debt relief, and restructured voting rights in the Bank to give borrowers a greater voice. While power did not shift, the Bank did give greater emphasis to basic social needs funding, for education, health care, and other development needs.

In response to world political events, the Organization of the Petroleum Exporting Countries (OPEC) raised oil prices sharply in 1973 and 1979. Enormous price hikes, for a vital industrial component, meant a huge inflow of US dollars for oil-producing states (regardless of nationality, parties generally bought and sold oil in dollars). The extreme price increases forced oil-importing states either to reduce oil consumption or to find money to cover now-quadrupled oil bills. The first option meant reduced economic production and the political problem of dropping living standards. The second option generally meant loans from banks holding OPEC dollar deposits. States had few choices that did not threaten economic development, either then, or in the future when loans came due. Exacerbating the situation, a global economic slowdown meant falling commodity prices for many exports, making loan repayment problematic.

The system collapsed abruptly in 1982, when Mexico, an oil producer that had borrowed assuming continued high energy prices, defaulted on its foreign debt when oil prices fell. The international banking community virtually stopped new lending as it sought to reduce exposure to default. The lending boycott by private banks, together with domestic conditions, put many borrowers in an impossible economic position. Both states that produced to existing comparative advantage and those that sought to create new industrial sectors experienced decreasing revenues as international prices fell and competition increased. In neither case could states generate enough foreign currency for debt repayment. Additionally, many infrastructure projects for which states borrowed were profitable —generating funds for debt repayment— only with growing exports. Finally, some loans went to corrupt authoritarian regimes that diverted at least a portion of funds for private use, which generated no means of repayment.

States and international financial institutions, such as the World Bank, stepped in to restructure loan packages, extending repayment to give debtors a better chance at full payment. The crisis meant that World Bank and IMF loans were many states' only option besides default (which bore reputational penalties and ended access to new money). The Bank's Structural Adjustment Loans (SALs) came with specific conditions that it argued included vital reforms of states' economic structures for future success. The SALs' conditions reflected the neo-liberal "Washington Consensus," so-called because it mirrored the preferences of the United States and its allies. The Consensus included macroeconomic policies leading to a return to production based on existing comparative advantage, reduction of the role of the state in the economy, opening of internal markets to international trade and investment, and curtailment of state regulations. The Bank argued that these conditions allowed more efficient market allocation of states' scarce resources. As well, it noted that reducing states' involvement both allowed in market forces and reduced opportunities for corruption. Finally, by opening economies to international forces, states gain access to goods, technologies, and capital far beyond national resources. This reasoning colored Bank lending, so SAL conditionality was fairly standard and predictable.

States had few options that did not include these conditions. Often, prior agreement with the Bank was a precondition to negotiating an IMF package, so-called "cross-conditionality." As well, the World Bank served as a major source of information (see annual *World Bank Development Reports*, for example) about states and their economies. Its involvement in an economy gave its "seal of approval," which went far to convincing others, including national aid agencies, to make additional loans or grants.

However, these conditions had significant economic and political implications that were extremely difficult for debtor states. While the Bank hewed to the notion that states (and citizens) had to accept short-term pain for long-term economic gains, many charged that its policies often were inappropriate and had devastating repercussions—degrading the environment, increasing poverty, and worsening conditions of life for the most vulnerable in societies—without solving underlying economic problems. In the 1990s, growing criticism, both internal and external, caused the Bank to reexamine its practices and led to some policy changes.

Answering Its Critics

In the 1990s, the Bank committed to poverty alleviation and enhancing good governance. The UN's Millennium Development Goals, which set specific targets and deadlines, have informed new Bank programs. For example, the Bank's poverty alleviation program goes beyond aggregate economic development to focus on social development, including equitable development of resources with regard to gender, vulnerable social groups, and environmental protection.

In 1996, to help the poorest debtor states, those that cannot possibly meet their foreign obligations based on debt-to-export or debt-to-government-revenue ratios, the World Bank and the IMF jointly developed the Heavily Indebted Poor Countries Initiative (HPIC). Participating states must meet a number of conditions, and must be eligible for IDA assistance. Also, they must have an ongoing commitment to, and record of, reform, as outlined in a Poverty Reduction Strategy Paper (PRSP). Debtor states wanting to participate go through various stages before qualifying for permanent debt cancellation. Not all eligible states have been able to complete the process and gain permanent debt reduction.

The Bretton Woods agencies conceived of HIPC as a way of bringing together public and private lenders, to work out agreements to cancel a significant portion of sovereign debt. The Bank committed to debt relief mainly through cancellation of IDA debt. While several states have agreed to cancel bilateral debt, few commercial lenders are participating in the HPIC process, limiting its effect. Further, many critics call for full and unconditional debt cancellation for all, not a small subset, of less developed states.

To address critics of the prescriptions attached to SALs, in 1999, the Bank moved to Poverty Reduction Strategy Papers, which borrowing states develop. These outline macroeconomic, structural, and social policies and programs to which borrowers commit, in return for international help. PRSPs are an enhancement, the Bank noted, as they are country-driven, comprehensive, long-term, and they force states to think through and to develop measurable goals.

Critics charge that PRSP development moves too quickly. This, they argue, leads to significant Bank influence on the final product, meaning that, as with SALs, PRSPs reflect elite, neo-liberal assumptions. Further, many agree that the PRSP process excludes the voices of the political opposition, women, vulnerable groups, and the poor. Critics point out that governments often commit to actions these groups directly oppose: ending food subsidies or closing state-subsidized medical clinics, for example. In 2004, the Bank began Development Policy Lending to give borrowers greater "ownership" of their programs and to enhance civil society participation in the drafting of national plans.

Addressing assessments that lenders, too, bear responsibility for their loans, in 2004, the Bank and the IMF introduced the Debt Sustainability Framework in Low-Income Countries. It seeks to link more closely borrowing and ability to repay. The Bank promotes the program as "proactive," and notes that it shifts some responsibility for sustainable debt levels to lenders. This could begin to address such issues as responsibility for "odious" debt, that is, loans incurred by dictators, which citizens must repay, and "moral hazard," the notion that banks make risky loans, knowing the Bank and IMF will secure repayment. Further, the Bank has begun to work more closely with non-state borrowers. It has involved itself with micro-credit lending, and has brought Non-Governmental Organizations into the lending process.

Still, many remain dissatisfied, seeing the neo-liberal, market-reliant philosophy that underpins the Bank's work as fundamentally inequitable. At the heart of this criticism, the questions of its founding remain: Who bears responsible for easing underdevelopment and encouraging development?

JANET ADAMSKI

See also African Development Bank (ADB); Alliance for Progress; Asian Development Bank; Debt: Impact on Development; Debt: Relief Efforts; Development History and Theory; Import Substitution Industrialization; Inter-American Development Bank (IDB); International Monetary Fund (IMF); Neoliberalism; Structural Adjustment Programs (SAPs); United Nations Development Program (UNDP)

References and Further Reading

Bretton Woods Agreements. http://www.yale.edu/lawweb/avalon/decade/decad047.htm
Broad, Robin, ed. *Global Backlash.* Lanham, MD: Rowman & Littlefield, 2002.
Danaher, Kevin, ed. *50 Years Is Enough: The Case Against the World Bank and the International Monetary Fund.* Boston: South End Press, 1994.

Chenery, Hollis, John Duloy, and Richard Jolly. *Redistribution with Growth*. Oxford, UK: Oxford University Press, 1985.

Le Prestre, Phillipe. *The World Bank and the Environmental Challenge*. Cranbury, NJ: Associated University Presses, 1989.

Mason, Edward S. and Robert Asher. *The World Bank Since Bretton Woods*. Washington, DC: The Brookings Institution, 1973.

Pincus, Jonathan R. and Jeffrey A. Winters, ed. *Reinventing the World Bank*. Ithaca, NY: Cornell University Press, 2002.

Ranis, Gustav. "The World Bank near the Turn of the Century." In *Global Development Fifty Years After Bretton Woods*. Roy Culpeper, Albert Berry, and Frances Stewart, eds. New York: St. Martin's Press, 1997.

Stiglitz, Joseph. *Globalization and Its Discontents*. New York: W.W. Norton, 2002.

The World Bank Web site: www.worldbank.org

The World Bank Group. *Learning from the Past: Embracing the Future*. Washington, DC: July 19, 1994.

INTERNATIONAL CENTER FOR THE SETTLEMENT OF INVESTMENT DISPUTES (ICSID)

In the 1960s and during the era of decolonisation, there was mass nationalization of foreign direct investment in their territories as a means of reasserting sovereignty over national wealth and resources. This caused conflicts between the investors and national governments. The International Bank for Reconstruction and Development (IBRD), the World Bank, thus set up an international institution to protect foreign investors against the risk of nationalization and to ensure that disputes were settled in an objective an apolitical manner. The Convention on the Settlement of International Investment Disputes Between States and Nationals of Other States—the *ICSID Convention 1966*—established an international forum that offers a legal framework for the settlement of investment disputes independent of any political considerations.

The ICSID is administered by the World Bank. It is an international legal entity authorized to enter into agreements and be party to legal proceedings. There are some special privileges and immunities granted to its staff to enable them to perform their tasks satisfactorily. The headquarters are in the World Bank in Washington, DC.

ICSID Jurisdiction

Both private investors and host countries that are parties to an investment agreement can lodge a dispute with the ICSID. The jurisdiction of the ICSID is governed by three conditions: that the dispute is a legal one arising from the investment agreement; that the dispute is between a member state and a national of another member state; and that the parties have consented in writing to submit the dispute to ICSID for a settlement.

The various articles of the Convention spell out the scope of the legal investment dispute, the requirements for membership of the Convention, consent of the parties to submit to the jurisdiction of the ICSID, and the effect of consent. There are also conciliation processes and provision for arbitration in terms of the conduct of the proceedings, its awards, and grounds for an annulment of awards.

Dispute Resolution Systems

Understanding a dispute resolution system helps to define more clearly the respective rights and obligations of the parties engaged in international trade. In *mediation* and *conciliation* there may simply be negotiations between the parties themselves. A neutral third party, the mediator assists the parties to a dispute to negotiate their own resolution of the problem. The term mediation is often used interchangeably with the term conciliation. An even more complex process is to go to *arbitration*. The arbitrator is a neutral third party, who may be authorized to resolve the dispute by issuing a binding determination or "award" and who assists the parties in settling the disputes themselves. In the United States there is a form of dispute resolution known as the *mini-trial*, in which there is a panel of people representing both parties together with a neutral facilitator who collectively have authority to settle the dispute. No third party has authority to issue a binding determination; the parties settle the dispute themselves.

Arbitration and *litigation* involve a binding determination by a third party—the arbitrator or judge. The arbitrator obtains his or her jurisdiction through the original agreement of the parties where they refer disputes to arbitration. Arbitrators do not exercise judicial authority and the composition of the arbitral tribunal is determined by agreement of the parties. This is an adversarial system made up of a judge who presides over the proceedings. The parties are generally represented by legal counsel who present their client's case. The outcome of the litigation process is a judgment in which one party is found to have a better claim than the other.

Facilitation is where a neutral third party meets with the parties in order to assist in finding a common course of action to resolve their dispute. The facilitator is an impartial third party with no pecuniary or other interest in the case. The facilitator also is there to bring into perspective an objective view of the situation to enable the parties to determine the best course of action in terms of resolving the dispute. In *expert appraisal,* the facts and questions in the dispute are put through an objective and independent determination by an expert. Similar to mediation, the parties themselves determine what the outcome will be and whether it is binding and final.

Private investors have often lacked *locus standi* before international fora. The term *locus standi* means a place of standing, the right to be heard in court or other proceedings. It is a legal term that is used by courts and other dispute settlement systems to identify those that have a right to come before that body to be heard. In the ICSID Convention the issue of non-standing is resolved by according international legal status to private investors. Thus, private investors, as opposed to those of governments and quasi-government bodies such as state-owned enterprises (SOEs), are able to bypass problematic national dispute settlement and protection of host states and gain direct access to an impartial third party for resolution of an investment dispute.

To date, however, ICSID services have been largely underutilized. As convention in international law dictates, signatories to any international convention have to return to their home parliaments and pass the necessary legislation in order to implement these as domestic law. Thus, for example, Australia enacted the *ICSID Implementation Act* 1990 (Commonwealth) to give effect to the Convention. This Act is embodied in Schedule Three of the *International Arbitration Act* 1974 (Commonwealth). Australia became the ninety-third party to the Convention in 1991. Australia has shown a preference to use ICSID mechanisms where possible. One example is the bilateral Investment Protection Agreement (IPA) in which both parties consent that a dispute be submitted to the ICSID for resolution in accordance with the terms on which the states are party to the Convention.

GEORGE CHO

See also International Bank for Reconstruction and Development (IBRD) (World Bank)

References and Further Reading

Broches, A. 1996 "Arbitration Under the ICSID Convention." Reprinted in M. Pryles, J. Waincymer, and M. Davies, *International Trade Law. Commentary and Materials.* Sydney: LBC Information Services, pp. 664–672, 1996.
Islam, M. R. 1999. *International Trade Law.* Sydney: LBC Information Services, Ch. 8 "Dispute Resolution," pp. 367–395.
———. 1993. "GATT With Emphasis on Its Dispute Resolution System." In K. C. D. M. Wilde and M. R. Islam, *International Transactions. Trade and Investment, Law and Finance.* Sydney: The Law Book Coy Ltd., pp. 225–239.
Pryles, M., Waincymer, J., and Davies, M. 1996. *International Trade Law. Commentary and Materials.* Sydney: LBC Information Services, Part Four Dispute Resolution, Ch. 12 "Negotiation, Mediation and Litigation," pp. 501–648; Ch. 13 "Arbitration," pp. 649–708; Ch. 15 "GATT/WTO and Dispute Settlement," pp. 764–828.
Schlemmer-Schulte, S. and Ko-Yung Tung, eds.. *ICSID Review—Foreign Investment Law Journal.* Baltimore, MD: Johns Hopkins University Press and Kluwer Law International, 2000.
Schreuer, C. H. *The ICSID Convention: A Commentary.* Port Chester, N.Y.: Cambridge University Press, 2001.
World Bank. *History of the ICSID,* 4 volumes. Washington, DC: 2000.

INTERNATIONAL COCOA ORGANIZATION (ICCO)

The International Cocoa Organization (ICCO) was created in London in 1973 with the implementation of the first International Cocoa Agreement (ICCA) signed in 1972, after sixteen years of negotiations. Cocoa is a key export commodity for a small number of countries in tropical Africa, Asia, and Latin America. Production of the beans is quite variable, based on yield and weather, whereas consumption remains quite stable over time. Production overall has increased from 1 million tons in 1960 to 3 million tons in 2004. Approximately 70% of cocoa is produced by small farmers on less than ten hectares of land.

The goals of the first International Cocoa Agreement and thus of the ICCO were to: prevent significant fluctuations in cocoa prices; stabilize or increase the export earnings from cocoa-producing countries; and consider the interests of consuming countries. The main economic features of this first agreement were annual export quotas, buffer stocks of 250,000 metric tons of cocoa, and a minimum price range of twenty-three to thirty-two cents per pound.

The decision-making body for the organization is the Cocoa Council, representing all members of the organization. It is responsible for carrying out the goals and spirit of the agreements but is limited in its powers. The exporting members together have one thousand votes and the importing members together have one thousand votes. The number of votes given to each individual member depends on that member's significance in the cocoa economy. However, no one member shall have more than four hundred votes.

In the second ICCA, dated 1976, the desirable price range for cocoa beans was increased to thirty-nine to fifty-five cents per pound. Throughout the years of this agreement, cocoa prices continued to rise and were close to $1.72 per pound. During the first and second agreements (1973–1980), the economic clauses of the agreements never went into effect because of high world cocoa prices.

During the negotiations and tenure of the third ICCA (1980), cocoa prices were on a downward slope and leveled off at seventy-five cents. The Cocoa Council was given authority to expand the buffer stocks if necessary from 250,000 tons to 350,000 tons. The mention of a price-stabilization scheme and an acceptable price range were absent from the 1980 agreement. Producing and consuming countries were unhappy with the ICCA and looked for ways to better the situation. To that end, the producing countries created the Abidjan Group to advocate for their interests.

During the negotiations for the 1986 ICCA, the International Cocoa Organization and the European Community suggested a scheme in which producing countries were required to withhold cocoa from the world market at their own expense when prices were low. Producers accepted this idea because they preferred this agreement over no agreement. This replaced the price-stabilization scheme and buffer stocks. By the end of the 1980s, there were 1.4 million tons in cocoa stocks and prices stayed low.

The 1993 International Cocoa Agreement tried to deal with this oversupply of cocoa and contribute to the stability of the commodity by creating a production-management plan. It would provide target production figures per country and would make the countries responsible for the national implementation of the plan. The details of this plan, however, were not worked out until 1998. At that time, the cited goal was to reduce production by 257,000 tons but the plan never went into effect. In the meantime, with the elimination of the economic clauses in the agreement, the buffer stocks were liquidated starting in 1993 and ending in 1998.

In 2000, the International Cocoa Organization stated its disagreement with the European Union's new "chocolate directive," which would allow up to 5% of vegetable fats (instead of cocoa butter) in European chocolate. The ICCO believed that this would result in a decrease in cocoa demand. It is not clear yet what the impact has been.

Not surprisingly, the Sixth International Coffee Agreement of 2001 does not include any economic clauses and focuses instead on a sustainable cocoa economy. It created a consultative board on the cocoa economy and encourages greater private-sector participation in the reaching of its goals. It encourages international cooperation in the world cocoa economy and serves as the repository for statistics and studies on cocoa.

The United States was never particularly interested in the International Cocoa Organization and the agreements, even though it is the most significant consumer of chocolate in the world. It participated in some of the negotiations but did not sign the agreements. It viewed cocoa as a primarily African commodity, which would be of greater interest to European countries. The United States is not currently a member of the International Cocoa Organization.

As of this writing, the International Cocoa Organization has thirty members. The exporting members are: Brazil, Cameroon, Cote d'Ivoire, Dominican Republic, Ecuador, Gabon, Ghana, Malaysia, Nigeria, Papua New Guinea, Togo, and Trinidad and Tobago. The importing members are: Austria, Belgium, Denmark, Finland, France, Germany, Greece, Ireland, Italy, Luxembourg, the Netherlands, Portugal, the Russian Federation, the Slovak Republic, Spain, Sweden, Switzerland, the United Kingdom. These countries represent 80% of production and 60% of consumption, respectively.

In 2002, a decision was made at the twenty-fifth Special Session of the Council to relocate the headquarters of the organization to Abidjan, Cote d'Ivoire. This was expected to strengthen the financial situation of the organization. Cote d'Ivoire alone currently produces just above 40% of the world's cocoa. As a result, economic and political events in Cote d'Ivoire have a significant impact on the world cocoa economy as a whole. The current unrest in the country has not helped the world cocoa economy and has delayed the move.

LAURA E. BOUDON

References and Further Reading

Clay, Jason. *World Agriculture and the Environment: A Commodity-by-Commodity Guide to Impacts and Practices*. Washington, DC: Island Press, 2004.

Dand, Robin. *The International Cocoa Trade*. New York: John Wiley and Sons, 1997.

Finlayson, Jock A. and Mark W. Zacher. *Managing International Markets: Developing Countries and the Commodity Trade Regime*. New York: Columbia Press, 1988.

Varangis, Panos and Gotz Schreiber. Cocoa Market Reforms in West Africa. In *Commodity Market Reforms: Lessons of Two Decades*, edited by Takamasa Akiyama, John Baffes, Donald Larson, and Panos Varangis. Washington, DC: The World Bank, 2001.

Weymar, F. Helmut. *The Dynamics of the World Cocoa Market*. Cambridge, MA: MIT Press, 1968.

INTERNATIONAL COFFEE ORGANIZATION (ICO)

The International Coffee Organization (ICO) was created in London in 1963 following the signature of the first International Coffee Agreement (ICA) in 1962 to assist with the production, pricing, and distribution of coffee. Coffee is a key export commodity for at least sixty countries throughout Africa, Asia, and Latin America and it provides a livelihood for approximately 100 million people. As with many export crops, coffee prices fluctuate with weather conditions, quality concerns, and annual production totals, thus making it difficult for producing countries to plan their economic development primarily around coffee exports.

The first ICA was the result of several related trends in the international community. During World War II, the United States engineered an international coffee agreement because of shipping shortages and the need to provide monies to developing nations. Later, following the end of World War II, there was significant interest among Western countries to increase international trade overall and specifically of agricultural products. In this spirit, the International Tin Agreement and the International Sugar Agreement were both signed in the early 1950s. The coffee-producing countries themselves had been working since the early 1930s to control the prices and availability of the caffeinated bean. Brazil in particular, as the world's largest coffee-producing country, was known for limiting its exports in order to raise coffee prices. Third, there was growing genuine interest on the part of large coffee-consuming nations in North America and Europe to assist Latin American and African coffee-producing countries in their economic development. The United States clearly changed its position on coffee in 1958, because of a growing fear that poor economic conditions in Latin America would give the Soviets an opportunity to get involved there. The US then provided much impetus for the negotiation of the first ICA.

The general goals of the first four International Coffee Agreements (1962, 1968, 1976, 1983) and therefore of the ICO during that time were thus: to achieve reasonable balance between the supply and demand of the various types of coffee (Arabica and Robusta), to contribute to the economic development of producer countries, to maintain reasonable coffee prices, to encourage coffee consumption throughout the world, and to foster cooperation on issues related to coffee production. The ICO was set up by Article Seven of the first ICA to administer the clauses of the agreement and supervise the mechanisms put in place.

The decision-making body of the ICO is the Coffee Council, which is made up of all the members of the organization. It approves the budget and annual program of activities for the organization; it admits and suspends members; it settles disputes; and it hosts agreement negotiations. Until 1986, it approved export quotas for the producing members. To pass a resolution, two-thirds of the members must be in favor of it. The votes of the exporting and importing members are weighed, so that each side has a total of one thousand votes, with no one country holding more than four hundred. The Council generally meets twice a year, in May and September.

Four significant issues that would regularly burden the ICO and its members came to the forefront during the tenure of the first International Coffee Agreement: the determination of acceptable price ranges for all parties and Arabica and Robusta coffee, the rules governing the quotas, rising national production levels, and the enforcement mechanisms put in place. At the beginning of the first ICA, it was clear that acceptable prices for coffee had not been agreed upon by the members. There would be more agreement on this after several years. Members argued regularly about how export quotas were set and changed throughout the year. The enforcement of the quota system lay in the hands of the consuming countries. They were responsible for a log of all coffee imports to be provided to the ICO.

Despite the best efforts of the organization and the agreements, coffee prices were still very dependent on weather and specifically frost in the largest coffee-producing country, Brazil. Prices rose significantly because of this in the late 1960s and mid-1970s as less coffee was available on the world market. The second agreement, which had begun to address some of the key issues facing the ICO, collapsed one year before its conclusion due to the high prices of the bean. Despite meetings in London in 1973 and 1974, it was not until 1975 that the simpler, third agreement was negotiated. In this 1976 agreement, quotas would only become effective when coffee prices were at 77 cents per pound or less. Also, national quota calculations became more standard; they were to be determined at 70% by the country's exports over the previous four years and at 30% by the country's coffee stocks. Coffee prices reached their all-time high in the spring of 1977, with the beans selling at $3.40 per pound, benefitting large coffee producers such as Colombia and Côte d'Ivoire. Brazil returned to pre-frost production levels in 1979 and the clauses of the third agreement finally went into effect. However, another Brazilian frost in late 1985 interrupted the economic clauses of the 1983 International Coffee

Agreement and was the beginning of difficult times for the International Coffee Organization, coffee-producing countries, and the ICAs.

Coffee markets had changed substantially since the creation of the International Coffee Organization in 1963. This change was exemplified in the membership of the International Coffee Organization. In 1985, European and North American members represented 95% of annual coffee consumption and producer countries not members of the ICO produced less than one hundred thousand bags of coffee each year (Bates and Lien 1985). The majority of the producing countries' members of the ICO in the mid-1980s were African and Asian countries, while in 1962, the majority had been Latin American countries with only a few African states. However, the membership of the ICO would continue to change over the next several years, with the key withdrawal of the United States from the International Coffee Organization in 1993. Following the end of the Cold War and the impetus for globalization, the US, which represents 40% of world coffee consumption, no longer saw the need for International Coffee Agreements.

Since 1993, the International Coffee Organization has survived, but with a significant change in its direction. Instead of monitoring the economic clauses of the ICAs, it is now primarily an intergovernmental organization, collecting and disseminating information about coffee and fostering cooperation among coffee-producing and coffee-consuming nations. It is a repository for statistics, studies, and information relating to coffee. It continues to host coffee-related conferences and has produced two additional International Coffee Agreements, simply stating its new mission and goals.

LAURA E. BOUDON

See also Agriculture: Impact of Globalization; Cartels

References and Further Reading

Bates, Robert. *Open-Economy Politics: The Political Economy of World Coffee Trade.* Princeton, NJ: Princeton University Press, 1997.
Bates, Robert, and Da-Hsiang Donald Lien. "On the Operations of the International Coffee Agreement." *International Organization* 39, 3 (1985).
Dicum, Gregory, and Nina Luttinger. *The Coffee Book: Anatomy of an Industry from Crop to the Last Drop.* New York: The New Press, 1999.
Fisher, Bart. *The International Coffee Agreement: A Study in Coffee Diplomacy.* New York: Praeger, 1972.
Gilbert, Christopher. 1987. "International Commodity Agreements: Design and Performance." *World Development*, 15, 5.
———. 1996. "International Commodity Agreements: An Obituary Notice." *World Development*, 24, 1.
Lucier, Richard. *The International Political Economy of Coffee: From Juan Valdez to Yank's Diner.* New York: Praeger, 1988.
Talbot, John. 1995. "Regulating the Coffee Commodity Chain: Internationalization and the Coffee Cartel. *Berkeley Journal of Sociology*, 40.

INTERNATIONAL COMMITTEE OF THE RED CROSS (ICRC)

The International Committee of the Red Cross (ICRC) is the world's oldest non-governmental organization devoted to the promotion of humanitarian principles during times of international war and domestic civil conflict. Adopting principles of neutrality and impartiality, it has become one of the premier emergency humanitarian aid agencies, focussing on the needs of the wounded and others in desperate need of basic food and medical assistance to assure survival in the midst of war and natural disaster.

Origins of the ICRC

The ICRC came into being in 1862, being the brainchild of the Swiss businessman Henri Dunant and of a committee of philanthropists who sought to ensure greater attention to the needs of the wounded and dying in time of war. Gustave Moynier was the organization genius who fostered the development of the ICRC, and who guided its growth as a humanitarian body dedicated to promoting the development of national Red Cross organizations, which in turn addressed the needs of the wounded and prisoners of war in times of armed conflict. Growing out of the ICRC was the League of Red Cross Societies, now known as the International Federation of Red Cross and Red Crescent Societies (IFRC), which coordinated the work of national Red Cross and Red Crescent chapters in responding not only to war but also domestic natural disasters. The ICRC oversees the implementation of various Geneva Red Cross Conventions aimed at ameliorating the condition of the wounded, prisoners of war, and civilian populations caught in civil conflict. It also promotes the dissemination of international humanitarian law, traces and fosters communication with political prisoners, and provides humanitarian aid to populations experiencing civil discord. It is in this latter capacity that the work of the ICRC most closely touches on the development situation in countries of assistance.

Development-Related Activities of the ICRC

The ICRC seeks and receives from numerous donor countries contributions towards its programs of assistance in dozens of countries throughout the world that are experiencing various levels of civil discord. Because of its strict reputation for neutrality and impartiality, the ICRC is able to negotiate a presence in many of the most intractable and fierce civil war situations throughout the globe. Specializing in the provision of medical and food aid to peoples caught in the cross-fires of civil war, the ICRC is usually able to negotiate access into war zones so that it can offer humanitarian aid to both sides engaged in conflict. Although the aid provided by the ICRC aims at meeting immediate emergency needs, it works closely with other aid-giving agencies to promote a humanitarian climate and eventually a situation admissible of peaceful resolution after which rehabilitation and reconstruction become feasible. The ICRC sits on the Interagency Standing Committee of the UN Office for the Coordination of Humanitarian Affairs, along with development agencies of the UN system. In this capacity it can make fruitful recommendations on the application of both emergency aid and on the longer-term development potential of a region.

ROBERT F. GORMAN

See also Non-Governmental Organizations (NGOs)

References and Further Reading

Forsythe, David. *Humanitarian Politics: The International Committee of the Red Cross*, Baltimore, MD: Johns Hopkins University Press, 1977.
Hutchinson, John F. *Champions of Charity: War and the Rise of the Red Cross*. Boulder, CO: Westview Press, 1996.
Moorehead Caroline. *Dunant's Dream: War, Switzerland and the History of the Red Cross*. New York: Carroll & Graf, 1998.

INTERNATIONAL CRIMINAL POLICE ORGANIZATION (INTERPOL)

Interpol is a global police organization. The second largest international organization behind the United Nations, it addresses transnational and organized crime by connecting the police forces of its 182 member countries. Interpol's efforts to identify the best police practices and raise awareness of crime helps developing nations create a secure environment necessary for social and economic advancement.

Criminals do not necessarily limit their activities to one country or one region. In the belief that human rights, public safety, and the fight against ordinary crimes are the concerns of both the developed and the developing world, countries at all stages of advancement have joined Interpol. Upon gaining independence, many developing countries joined Interpol as one of their first actions as sovereign nations.

Begun in 1923, Interpol seeks to halt crime that has occurred or is projected to occur in multiple countries. Each member state maintains and staffs a National Central Bureau (NCB) to direct Interpol intelligence while local authorities investigate and prosecute criminals according to national laws. Interpol's actions are limited to receiving requests for assistance, analyzing criminal activities that are not of a political, military, religious, or racial character, and disseminating notices published in four languages (English, French, Spanish, and Arabic) to its members. Despite popular belief, Interpol maintains no police force of its own.

Although headquartered in France, no country dominates the group and its funding is provided by a sliding scale membership fee that is based upon each country's gross national product (GNP). The organization's policies are set by a vote of its member countries while the governors on its Executive Committee are required to be drawn from different continents. The Secretary General, elected every five years by two-thirds of the members attending the annual General Assembly, is Interpol's chief executive and senior full-time official. Daily activities are conducted at the General Secretariat in Lyons with a staff of 384 who represent 54 different countries. National Central Bureaus (NCB) in member countries ferry Interpol information to appropriate local authorities who bear responsibility for apprehending and extraditing suspected criminals. Five NCBs also act as Regional Stations with Lyon covering Europe, North America, and the Middle East; Nairobi, Kenya responsible for Central Africa; Abidjan, Ivory Coast focusing on West Africa; Buenos Aires, Argentina addressing South America; and Bangkok, Thailand transmitting to Asia.

Interpol's interests change according to crime patterns. It currently focuses upon public safety and terrorism, including bio-terrorism; organized crime; illegal drug production and smuggling; weapons dealing; trafficking in human beings; sexual abuse of children; money laundering; cyber-crime; theft of intellectual property; and financial and high technology wrongdoing.

No nation is required to respond to an Interpol request. Some countries, notably the United States in the years leading up to World War II, have declined to fully cooperate with Interpol for fear that its files may be misused for the prosecution of political criminals. In 1956, the organization agreed to forbid any activities of a political, military, religious, or racial character but concerns remain that countries may ignore these guidelines. The chief fear of many member countries is that classified information may fall into the hands of terrorists since the distribution of intelligence cannot be restricted once it enters the Interpol system. Although this worry has reduced the amount of classified information flowing through Interpol, the organization has experienced a steady increase in information traffic. In 2000, Interpol transmitted 2.5 million messages, placed 15,116 notices of criminal activity in circulation, and projected that 1,400 people would be arrested or located as the result of Interpol intelligence.

Interpol notices are coded into ten different colors that represent different purposes. The red wanted notices are the most common and this type of communication requests the arrest of subjects for whom an arrest warrant has been issued and extradition will be sought. The other notices are: seeking the identity and location of subjects who have committed or witnessed criminal offenses (blue); providing warning about career criminals who have committed offenses in several countries (green); seeking missing or lost people, especially children abducted by parents (yellow); seeking the identification of corpses (black); warning of unusual modus operandi (purple); sharing knowledge of organized crime groups (gray); and advising of criminal activity with international ramifications that does not involve a specific person or group (orange). Stolen property notices are also distributed but are not coded.

Crime undermines the stability of governments and makes international investors hesitant to sponsor development projects. Since crime affects all aspects of life, effective policing is a chief concern of developing countries. Interpol offers the knowledge and expertise to fight crime. It addresses both the external and internal policing factors that permit criminal activities.

CARYN E. NEUMANN

References and Further Reading

Anderson, Malcolm. *Policing the World: Interpol and the Politics of International Police Co-operation.* Oxford: Clarendon Press, 1989.
Bresler, Fenton. *Interpol.* London: Sinclair-Stevenson, 1992.
Interpol. http://www.interpol.int
United States Department of Justice and United States Department of the Treasury. *Interpol: The International Criminal Police Organization.* Washington, DC: Government Printing Office, 2002.

INTERNATIONAL DEVELOPMENT ASSOCIATION (IDA)

The International Development Association (IDA) is the soft loan division of the World Bank, or the International Bank for Reconstruction and Development (IBRD). The IDA was set up in 1960 to provide loans on much easier terms than regular World Bank loans to the world's poorest and least developed countries for which private financing is not available on reasonable terms. IDA loans go to the eighty-one poorest World Bank member countries whose per capita income is less than $895 (2004 figure). About 2.5 billion people live in these countries, which is about half the developing world and approximately 1.5 billion of these live on less that two dollars a day. IDA loans are long-term loans, from twenty to thirty-five or even forty years for repayment with a ten-year grace period before any repayment is required, and IDA loans are interest free, although there is a small 0.75% service charge. Since 2002 at the suggestion of United States President George W. Bush in 2001, the IDA now provides a proportion of its aid in the form of grants. In 2004 grants were 19% of IDA aid; this is set to increase to 30% over the next three years. Unlike loans, which do have to be repaid, grants do not need to be repaid.

Since 1960, IDA has lent over $142 billion to 108 countries. Currently, the IDA lends about $7.4 billion a year. Most loans address basic needs, such as primary education, basic health services, and clean water and sanitation. IDA also funds projects to preserve the environment, encourage private business, build infrastructure, support liberal economic reforms, and strengthen state institutions. HIV/AIDS prevention, post-conflict (post-war) stabilization, gender equality, and debt relief are also high-priority projects. IDA projects are intended to pave the way toward economic growth, job creation, higher incomes, and better living conditions. Funds are allocated to the borrowing countries in relation to their income levels and record of success in managing their economies and their ongoing IDA projects. New commitments for IDA loans and grants in FY03 consisted of 141 new operations in fifty-six countries. Fifty-one percent of new commitments went to sub-Saharan Africa, 28% to South Asia, 8% to East Asia and the Pacific, 8% to Eastern Europe and Central Asia (ECA), and the remainder to North Africa and Latin America. The top IDA borrowers in FY03 are listed in Table 1.

The IDA is funded by contributions from the wealthier member countries every three years. They have donated over $118.9 billion since the inception of the association. The largest donations are made

Table 1: Top ten IDA borrowers

Top ten IDA borrowers, FY 2003	$ Millions
India	686
Bangladesh	554
Congo Democratic Republic	454
Uganda	407
Ethiopia	404
Vietnam	368
Pakistan	297
Tanzania	251
Sri Lanka	233
Nigeria	230

by the United States, Japan, Germany, the United Kingdom, France, Canada, and Italy. Combined, these countries account for about 70% of donor contributions. Nevertheless, there are thirty-nine donors, including some less well-off countries such as Argentina, Brazil, Mexico, Russia, and Turkey. The donors and borrowers meet every three years to negotiate their contributions. Each of these series of negotiations is know as a replenishment. In 2005, the members were concluding the negotiations for Replenishment 14. Replenishment 13 resulted in pledges to donate $23 billion to the IDA. Other funds, nearly 40%, for the IDA came from the repayments of earlier IDA loans. However, the World Bank has also forgiven $9 billion of IDA debt, which will affect future IDA income from repayments.

Since the 1980s, the United States has occasionally balked at paying its allocated share. Initially the United States provided 42% of IDA funds, far more than any other country. This percentage was equal to the relative share of the US economy in the world. With the third replenishment, the United States' share declined somewhat to 39% but still remained slightly higher than the relative size of the US economy to the world economy. The US allocation has shrunk to about 20% with the 13th replenishment. During the early 1980s the US Congress pushed to lower the US contribution and added conditions on US contributions. The United States insisted that no IDA credits go to Vietnam and threatened to withhold its payments until the United States won its concession. Again in the mid-1990s the US Congress withheld payments, which forced the World Bank to empanel an independent inspection team. US leverage over the IDA is strengthened by the fact that other members often prorate their own contributions to those of the United States. The United Kingdom's share has also been reduced, from 17% in

1960 to 10% in 2001–2004. Other wealthy countries whose economies boomed in the 1970s onward have increased their shares. For example, Japan's share was only 4% in 1960 and increased to 16% in 2001–2004, and Germany's share in 1960 was 7% and is now 10%.

The IDA counts among its successes some thirty-two countries that have graduated from the IDA. Their per capita incomes have increased beyond those allowed by the IDA, largely due to IDA loans and grants. The first graduate was Chile in 1961, and the latest graduate is Macedonia (FYR). The following are contemporary examples of IDA projects. In India, the National AIDS Control Project supported training of 52,500 physicians and 60% of nursing staff in HIV/AIDS management topics. In Yemen, the Taiz Flood Disaster Prevention and Municipal Development Project prevented serious damage from the 1996 floods, benefiting twenty-one thousand households directly and over half a million people indirectly. In Africa, more than 5 million textbooks (mostly locally developed and produced) were supplied to primary schools. In Asia, over 6,700 health care facilities were constructed or upgraded, then equipped and staffed to provide basic health care to rural populations. And in Latin America, projects under the social investment fund reach some 9.5 million beneficiaries. Activities supported by these projects generate almost a million person-months of employment.

JAMES A. NORRIS

See also Development History and Theory; Development, Measures of; International Bank for Reconstruction and Development (IBRD) (World Bank); United Nations Development Program (UNDP)

References and Further Reading

Burki, Shahid Javid, and Norman Hicks. 1982. "International Development Association in Retrospect." *Finance & Development*, 19, No. 4.

Culpeper, Roy. *The Multilateral Development Banks, Volume 5: Titans or Behemoths?* Boulder, CO and London: Lynne Rienner Publishers, 1997.

Hicks, Norman, Robert Ayers, Barbara Hertz, Jeffrey Katz, Danny Leipziger, and Josefina Valeriano. *IDA in Retrospect: The First Two Decades of the International Development Association.* New York and Oxford: Oxford University Press, 1982.

International Development Association (www.worldbank.org). Washington, DC: The World Bank Group, 2005.

Katz, Jeffrey A. 1989. "The Evolving Role of the IDA." *Finance & Development*, 26, No. 2.

Sanford, Jonathan E. *World Bank: Funding IDA's Assistance Program.* Washington, DC: Congressional Research Service, 2002.

INTERNATIONAL FINANCE CORPORATION (IFC)

(*See International Bank for Reconstruction and Development [IBRD] [World Bank]*)

INTERNATIONAL MARITIME ORGANIZATION (IMO)

The International Maritime Organization (IMO) is the agency of the United Nations (UN) responsible for improving the safety and security of international shipping and the prevention of marine pollution from ships. One of the smallest UN agencies, with less than three hundred employees, the IMO was established at a UN-sponsored international convention held in Geneva, Switzerland, on March 17, 1948. The IMO Convention went into effect in 1958 and the new organization met for the first time in 1959. As of 2004, there were 164 member states in the organization.

The IMO, which has its headquarters in London, does not implement legislation. The IMO was established to adopt legislation. Member nations are responsible for implementing the more than forty conventions sponsored by the IMO. The IMO, therefore, seeks to ensure that its conventions are ratified by as many countries as possible. Currently, IMO conventions cover more than 98% of the world's merchant shipping. The IMO also attempts to ensure that these conventions are properly implemented by the countries that have accepted them. The IMO has had considerable success in achieving its aim of safer shipping and cleaner seas.

When the IMO first began operations, its chief concern was to develop international treaties and other legislation concerning marine safety and pollution prevention. In 1960, the IMO's first action was to adopt a new version of the International Convention for the Safety of Life at Sea (SOLAS), an important treaty concerning maritime safety. Although safety was the IMO's most important responsibility, the amount of oil being transported by oil tankers was also of great concern. The IMO introduced a series of measures designed to prevent tanker accidents and to minimize their consequences. It also investigated the environmental threat caused by the cleaning of the cargo tanks. In 1973, the IMO introduced the International Convention for the Prevention of Pollution from Ships, which regulated accidental and operational oil pollution as well as pollution by chemicals, sewage, and garbage. In 1992, the Global Maritime Distress and Safety System (GMDSS) was launched. By 1999, the GMDSS was completely operational, so that any ship that is in distress anywhere in the world

can be virtually guaranteed assistance, even if the ship's crew does not have time to radio for help.

When the IMO began operations in 1959, international shipping was dominated by a few developed nations. During the last decades of the twentieth century, however, nations in the developing world have acquired a greater share of international shipping. Operation costs are shared among the member states in proportion to the size of each nation's fleet of merchant ships. The biggest fleets in the world are operated by Panama, Liberia, the Bahamas, Greece, the United Kingdom, Japan, Malta, the United States, Cyprus, and Norway.

MICHAEL R. HALL

References and Further Reading

International Maritime Organization. *Convention of the International Maritime Organization.* London: Author, 1982.
Mankabady, Samir. *The International Maritime Organization: International Shipping Rules.* London: Croom Helm, 1986.

INTERNATIONAL MONETARY FUND (IMF)

Founding

Allied leaders, planning for the post–World War II era, wanted to ensure that the economic crises of the 1920s and 1930s, which contributed to subsequent hostilities, did not recur. They worried that the end of hostilities and subsequent decline in demand would cause another depression. They also considered the dismal outcome of economic policies in the interwar period. For example, the international economy degenerated into exclusionary trading blocs and insurmountable tariff barriers, with significant contractions in trade volume. Additionally, the monetary system collapsed as states abandoned the gold standard and practiced competitive currency devaluations—beggar-thy-neighbor policies—as each sought to export more than it imported.

Further, they acknowledged the gold standard's flaws. It limited creation of money to an amount equal to gold mined, instead of linking it to an economy's efficiency and total production. Thus, if any state imported more goods than it exported, the gold standard required that it export gold to its creditors to bring accounts into balance. Since states printed money in proportion to their gold supply, reducing gold stock required withdrawal of an equal proportion of its currency from the economy. Gold transfers limited credit and investments, and it slowed growth. Artificially low money stocks created by slow growth in the world's gold supply often meant that maintaining the gold standard forced states to deflate their economies for reasons unrelated to strength or productivity. Creation of additional liquidity, from non-gold-backed money, depended on perceptions of the creditworthiness of the issuer. Many, for example, accepted British pounds sterling even once Britain printed paper bills exceeding its precious metal stocks, due to belief in its economy's soundness.

The failure of states' unilateral policies encouraged multilateral management of the international economy. In July 1944, at a meeting in New Hampshire, representatives of forty-four countries agreed to the Bretton Woods System of economic management, creating organizations to supervise international monetary relations (the International Monetary Fund, IMF) and reconstruction and development (International Bank of Reconstruction and Development, IBRD; also known as the World Bank).

To restart trade, states had to agree on relative values of their currencies, known as parities, or par values. Essentially, these gave the price of one currency in terms of another one. Thus, in 1946, sterling's par was about £1 = $4.03. This parity overvalued the pound, making it difficult to sell (overpriced) British exports abroad. Further, it forced the government to spend too much shoring up the value of the currency. This reduced funds for domestic programs. Therefore, in 1949, the government dropped parity to about £1 = $2.80.

The Fund helped states maintain their par values in order to create a stable currency system. The example of British sterling highlights another important lesson from the interwar period: when states had to choose between competing international and domestic commitments, inevitably they sacrificed external for internal concerns. Therefore, planners sought to help states to reconcile rival demands, through provision of temporary loans to ease short-term currency shortfalls, which ensured some policy flexibility.

Those meeting at Bretton Woods disagreed about how to accomplish this. They debated two institutional "blueprints." The first, presented by British representative, John Maynard Keynes, reflected a significantly different architecture than that proposed by US representative, Henry Dexter White. It is noteworthy that discussion centered on plans offered by these two hegemonic states. Today, many less developed states argue that the Bretton Woods System is inappropriate for their needs, given their different relative positions in the world economy.

Keynes called for an International Clearing Union (ICU), which gave priority to states' domestic preferences. It guarded states' economic sovereignty zealously, so they could enact policies appropriate to their domestic needs (in the case of Britain, full employment). States could change parity values up to 5% without Union approval. Also, Keynes called for creation of an international currency, the bancor, which states could use to settle their outstanding balances. The bancor would create additional liquidity, beyond gold and the British pound. Further, members would pay a quota, based on share of international trade. Keynes envisioned ICU resources equal to about $30 billion. States that bought more than they sold, and thus had shortfalls, could borrow up to one-half their quotas, without conditions. For additional funds, the ICU's governing board could recommend policies to borrowers, could insist they limit capital flows across their borders, could call for currency devaluations, or could require additional collateral. Finally, if two currencies moved out of parity, under Keynes' plan, both governments bore an obligation to fix the imbalance.

Responsibility for currency values accounted for only one of the major differences between the British and US plans. White put the full burden of currency imbalance on the deficit state. Moreover, he was less protective of sovereignty, calling for direct intervention in states' economic policies. This greater (and earlier) intercession authority meant the organization required fewer resources, as it addressed less acute problems. Thus, White called for resources of only about $5 billion. His plan further limited sovereignty by requiring permission for changes of more than 1% of par value. Of course, with the world's most powerful economy, US negotiators had little fear for national autonomy. Many in Congress, however, bridled at the possible loss of control.

The IMF, ultimately, reflected a compromise, one grounded in a commitment to liberalism and domestic responsibility for maintenance of the international system. By giving the body no immediate right of interventions, it preserved autonomy. However, the low funding, about $8.8 billion, meant members could draw on only limited resources. Further, the Fund placed full responsibility on deficit states, so-called asymmetrical adjustment.

As well, the IMF rejected the gold standard and created a "fixed but adjustable" system, pegged to the US dollar. Washington valued its currency at an undeviating $35 per ounce of gold. Internationally, it was convertible—dollars were exchangeable for gold. (However, to preserve gold reserves, the

United States restricted citizens' ownership.) As the country then possessed about 70% of the world's gold and created about 40% of its industrial output, this rate seemed solid and sustainable. Other IMF currencies then set a par value relative to the dollar.

Given this fixed relationship, if any currency were out of alignment with the dollar, it had to devalue (decrease) or revalue (increase) to return to par. States maintained parity within narrow margins, no more than 1% of par, and they could adjust values only minimally without IMF approval. This ensured orderly and non-predatory realignments. Unlike the gold standard, here members with balance-of-payment deficits did not have to devalue to bring external balances into alignment. Through the IMF, they could obtain short-term loans to cover deficits while preserving parity, as well as domestic spending and growth.

Institutions

The IMF is responsible to its members, but, as reflected in its institutions, states enjoy different degrees of influence. The main bodies are the Board of Governors, the Executive Board, and the International Monetary and Financial Committee. A bureaucracy of nearly 3,000 employees, from more than 140 countries, supports them. The majority of staff serves at Fund headquarters in Washington, DC, with additional offices in New York, Paris, Tokyo, and Geneva.

Officials from 180-plus member states comprise the Board of Governors. The Board meets annually to decide broadly on policy. Generally, states send finance ministers or central bank governors. An appointed managing director, traditionally a European, chairs meetings, assisted by three deputy managing directors. The IMF runs similarly to a public corporation: Governors hold voting rights proportional to their investment or shareholdings, called "quotas." The United States has the largest quota, about 17.5%, while Palau pays the smallest, about 0.001% of the total. The ten states with the highest quotas are the United States, Japan, Germany, France, the United Kingdom, Italy, Saudi Arabia, Canada, China, and the Russian Federation. Every five years, the Fund recalculates quotas to reflect states' relative share of the world economy. In addition to policy and quotas, the Board admits new members and allocates funds.

While the Board of Governors sets general policies, the Executive Board implements that agenda, carries out daily operations, approves specific programs, and conducts surveillance on borrowers. The twenty-four-member Board includes representatives of the five largest shareholders, as well as Saudi Arabia, China, and the Russian Federation. The remaining executive directorships go to those elected by the remaining members, geographically divided into "constituencies." Winners hold office for two years.

Finally, the twenty-four-member International Monetary and Financial Committee (IMFC) advises the Board of Governors. It convenes twice yearly, generally in fall before the Board's Annual Meeting and again in spring. It reports to and counsels governors on matters related to management of the international system. States with Executive Board appointment power each have a representative on the IMFC, as does each constituency that elects a member to the Executive Board. The Committee allows different international institutions, including the World Bank, to observe its meetings.

Weighted voting and unequal appointment prerogatives show that members wield different levels of influence. Many less developed states argue the Fund should equalize voting rights, giving them greater voice and representation, to democratize the organization, and to make it more responsive. States holding greater power note that they represent a larger share of the world's economy and that decision making should reflect that. In addition, as the largest contributors, they argue they have the right to direct use of their resources. Institutional (re)form and (re)distribution of power, with their concomitant implications for policy change, provide some of the Fund's most contentious debates.

Operations

As noted above, the IMF provides loans to members. Most funds come from state quotas. Members must provide a quarter of their quota in a widely accepted currency, such as the dollar or euro, or Special Drawing Rights (explained below). This is the gold tranche, so called because members originally had to provide gold. Generally, they pay remaining tranches in national currencies. Depending on the loan type, states may borrow some multiple of their quota, in any currency, with increasing restrictions the more they borrow. Given the limited size of many states' quotas, this represents a very small credit facility.

Initially, most international transactions were in US dollars or gold, so members borrowed dollars from the Fund. Given the US economy's size, it could generate enough currency for domestic spending and still provide sufficient liquidity externally. Over time, however, the United States printed so many dollars that some feared a loss in value and sought another reserve currency. To remove artificial limits set by gold, and to reduce pressure on the dollar, in 1969, the Fund developed Special Drawing Rights (SDRs).

These international reserve assets have no physical form; they simply represent a bookkeeping entry in members' accounts in proportion to their quotas. States may use SDRs to settle accounts bilaterally and with some international institutions. SDRs are a "basket currency"—a mix of the European Union's euro, the British pound, the Japanese yen, and the US dollar. Because it is not traded, the IMF determines its value based on daily market prices for constituent currencies. Every five years, the IMF reviews its composition to ensure it represents international currency usage.

Over time, the Fund developed several types of loans, or "facilities." These include Stand-By Arrangements, tied to the Fund's original mission—supporting states through short-term, balance-of-payment deficits. They usually last one to one-and-a-half years. In 1963, the IMF established a Compensatory Financing Facility to help cushion producers and consumers of cereals against price fluctuations. Its terms are similar to those of Stand-By Arrangements. The Fund created a new facility, the Extended Fund Facility, in 1974, to help members with problems beyond short-term balance-of-payment challenges. These loans extend up to three years. Finally, in 1997, the IMF created the Supplemental Reserve Facility to make large-scale, short-term loans to restore market confidence. None of these are concessional, that is, borrowers pay market interest rates, and in some cases, a surcharge, or lending fee. The IMF also provides loans on an emergency basis to members that have suffered natural disaster or armed conflict. These may have subsidized interest rates, and borrowers have five years, at the most, to repay them.

The above differ from loans made under the Poverty Reduction and Growth Facility (PRGF), available to nearly eighty low-per-capita-income members. These have interest rates of 0.5%, and generally extend to between five and ten years. Borrowers must prepare Poverty Reduction Strategy Papers that outline concrete steps and reforms to which they commit, to achieve the goals agreed upon with the IMF. According to the Fund, this process ensures country "ownership" of the plan and facilitates broad public participation, which privileges the state's own priorities. Finally, the IMF notes that these Papers strengthen governance, transparency, accountability, and management of public resources. As well, they

consider the plan's impact on society and poverty, generally. As discussed below, conditions attached to IMF loans are extremely controversial.

In addition to the loans based on quotas, the IMF may borrow, if it finds its own resources inadequate. In 1962, it founded the General Arrangements to Borrow (GAB), with eleven participants, including Switzerland, a non-IMF member (Saudi Arabia also has an associated arrangement). The IMF borrows from GAB members at market rates. Originally, only GAB states could borrow GAB funds, but that no longer holds. Still, GAB states must approve these loans. Additionally, in 1997, the IMF set up the New Arrangements to Borrow (NAB) with twenty-six participants. NAB funds are for alleviation of extraordinary threats to the international system, beyond what IMF resources alone can handle. While quotas provide a lending base of about $311 billion, these arrangements give the IMF access to another $50 billion.

Evolution

As states gained independence in the post-war period, Fund membership came to reflect vastly different levels of economic development. Rather than temporary deficits, many members suffered long-term shortfalls. Thus, the IMF shifted focus from short-term liquidity to structural changes that address chronic balance-of-payments problems.

In the late 1960s, the exchange rate system came under pressure. Some states, especially France, doubting the dollar's future value, began demanding gold. The "dollar overhang," more dollars than gold to back them, led Washington unilaterally to end convertibility and devalue the dollar, in 1971. This disrupted the fixed value of many currencies.

This, together with oil price shocks in 1973 and 1979, strained the international system. Price hikes meant a dramatic increase in dollar flows, as usually oil was dollar-denominated. It also meant non-oil-producing states scrambled to purchase this vital resource. Often, producers' dollars ended up in US banks, which then lent them to non-producing states to buy oil. Even some producer states borrowed heavily, anticipating continued high oil prices and thus, easy repayment.

Prices of oil, as well as other commodities, fell in the early 1980s, leaving debtors in an untenable situation. In 1982, Mexico informed Washington it could not service its foreign debt; technically, it defaulted. Mexico was the first of many less developed states caught in the "debt trap."

Commercial banks sought to reduce their exposure. They rushed to minimize exposure by ending new loans, which plummeted in the 1980s. The withdrawal of private capital forced debtors to turn to public lenders, including the IMF and the World Bank. The Fund responded with loans and restructuring programs that often mandated conditions including economic reform. These Structural Adjustment Programs (SAPs) usually required that borrowers enact neo-liberal economic policies, including reduction of state involvement and regulation of the economy, especially removal of obstacles to foreign trade and investment.

As noted above, the IMF defends these conditions as necessary for economic health, and as safeguards to ensure loan repayment. While the Fund praises "country ownership," of the Letters of Intent that precede loans, others criticize the commitments required as formulaic. They argue requirements reflect the Washington Consensus (i.e., preferences of the United States and its allies) rather than the particular needs of borrowers. Further, they condemn the agreements as IMF-crafted, with limited input from citizens of borrowing states, which denies voice to the population affected by conditionality. They also point to significant social costs from governmental spending reductions. Critics argue that cuts affect health, education, and nutrition programs, which limits future development. As well, public protests against the social, political, and economic costs of SAPs often make them difficult to implement.

The debt crisis prompts other concerns. The IMF now acknowledges that some indebted states never will be able to make repayments. Rather than a process of debt rescheduling and failure, the World Bank, together with the IMF, launched the Heavily Indebted Poor Countries Initiative (HIPC). This brings together public and private lenders with governments of the poorest states, to work out agreements to cancel a portion of debt, in exchange for state fulfillment of certain conditions. These include the usual neo-liberal requirements of reducing the size of the state sector, opening the state's economy to foreign goods and capital, and reducing regulations. As well, states in the program must reform economies and governments to make them more transparent, less open to corruption. An additional provision, meant to address ingrained poverty, is that funds that would have gone to debt servicing and repayment go to social spending instead. HIPC has a number of pre-conditions before debtors may begin negotiations for debt cancellation. These requirements have been difficult for many potentially eligible states to meet. As a result, not all candidate states have been able to complete the process of qualifying.

Debtor states with greater resources may work through the Sovereign Debt Restructuring Mechanism (SDRM), created in 2002. This gathers a debtor's multiple creditors and organizes "orderly" restructuring encompassing all foreign liabilities. The SDRM eases negotiations, preventing a single minority creditor from stopping a deal acceptable to the majority. Borrowing states want to see debt cancellation, as well as restructuring, included in these negotiations. Many argue that the citizens of debtor states, who ultimately repay the loans, deserve representation in the SDRM.

A coalition of religious groups, development Non-Governmental Organizations, and labor groups—organized as Jubilee 2000—took up the borrowing states' cause. They pushed for international debt forgiveness. Citing Leviticus 25, they reiterated the Biblical call for remission of all obligations, every fifty years. People from more than one hundred countries have signed petitions supporting debt cancellation. Jubilee 2000 argues that debt rescheduling, reduction, and conditionality cannot guarantee social justice, especially the disproportionate burden repayment places on the poor. Its "Breaking the Chains of Debt" campaign has helped publicize this issue.

Jubilee 2000 and others also have raised the matter of "odious" debt, that is, loans to dictators (e.g., Saddam Hussein), used for their private benefit. Many ask, why hold the citizenry, who neither borrowed the money, nor benefited from it, responsible for repayment? Many argue for the, at least, shared responsibility of lenders, maintaining they have a moral and ethical obligation to lend only to legitimate governments.

Such issues, together with the IMF's failures in addressing the Asian currency crisis of 1997, the Russian Federation's 1998 default, and Argentina's 2001 economic crisis, ensure continuation of this debate. Moreover, larger globalization discussions integrate these concerns. Sharp divides over the IMF among states, leaders, international institutions, and activists remain, with little resolution in sight.

JANET ADAMSKI

See also Debt: Impact on Development; Debt: Relief Efforts; Development History and Theory; International Bank for Reconstruction and Development (IBRD) (World Bank); Neoliberalism; Structural Adjustment Programs (SAPs)

References and Further Reading

Bordo, Michael D., Forrest Capie, and Angela Redish, eds. *The Gold Standard and Related Regimes.* Cambridge, UK: Cambridge University Press, 1999.
Bretton Woods Agreements. http://www.yale.edu/lawweb/avalon/decade/decad047.htm

Culpeper, Roy, Albert Berry, and Frances Stewart, eds. *Global Development Fifty Years after Bretton Woods*. New York: St. Martin's Press, 1997.

Gowa, Joan. *Closing the Gold Window*. Ithaca, NY: Cornell University Press, 1983.

International Monetary Fund. www.imf.org/external/index.htm

Jubilee 2000. www.jubilee2000uk.org

Kahler, Miles, ed. *Capital Flows and Financial Crisis*. Ithaca, NY: Cornell University Press, 1998

Payer, Cheryl. *The Debt Trap*. New York: Monthly Review Press, 1974.

Sachs, Jeffrey D., ed. *Developing Country Debt and the World Economy. A National Bureau of Economic Research Report*. Chicago: Chicago University Press, 1989.

Strange, Susan. *Mad Money*. Ann Arbor, MI: University of Michigan Press, 1998.

INTERNATIONAL ORGANIZATION FOR MIGRATION (IOM)

The International Organization for Migration (IOM) was initially founded in 1951 as an outgrowth of the International Migration Conference sponsored by the United States and Belgium at Brussels. This conference initially focused on the study of migration movements in Europe, and the permanent organization established to study and to address these movements was known as the Intergovernmental Committee for European Migration (ICEM). ICEM's work gradually began to include study of migration issues and program activities beyond the scope of Europe. Accordingly, in 1980 ICEM changed its name to the Intergovernmental Committee for Migration (ICM) to more accurately reflect the increasingly global nature of its operations. In 1989 its name was changed once again to its current designation, the International Organization for Migration. The work of the IOM includes response to migration and refugee emergencies as well as the relationship between development and migration.

Refugee Resettlement to Development

In its first decade ICEM focused primarily on the processing of refugees, displaced persons, and economic migrants from Europe to other countries. In the aftermath of World War II, Europe was inundated by displaced persons owing to the devastation and disruption of the war. The emergence of the Cold War led to further refugee and migration flows from Eastern into Western Europe, notably during the 1956 Hungarian Revolution. ICEM worked to find countries of resettlement for such refugees, provided medical attention, processed international documents, and arranged for transportation of hundreds of thousands of refugees and displaced persons so that they might find permanent settlement in other countries. In its first decade of existence it assisted more than a million migrants. In this work, ICEM closely cooperated with the UN High Commissioner for Refugees (UNHCR), other UN agencies, and non-governmental organizations (NGOs).

Although the focus of ICEM's work continued to be Europe, its involvement with refugee resettlement programs brought it into contact with governments throughout the world, and the impact of migration on development arose as a matter of concern. In 1964, ICEM initiated a program in Latin America designed to recruit and place highly qualified European migrants in Latin American countries needing their specialized expertise. As a matter of policy, ICEM saw the importance of matching migrants with professional skills with developing countries in need of such skills to enhance their economic development. As many more developing countries gained their independence in the 1960s and 1970s, ICEM expanded its Migration for Development Program, adding a special Return of Talent Program for Latin America, which encouraged talented Latin American citizens to return to the region, thereby strengthening to pool of talent so desperately needed in several Latin American countries. These Migration for Development Programs, including the Return of Talent Program, were subsequently extended to Africa in 1983 and Asia in 1985. In the early 1980s, ICEM, now known as ICM, participated in the first and second International Conference on Assistance to Refugees in Africa (ICARA I and II), at which the impact of refugee and returnee movements on the development of receiving countries was discussed. In 1990, when ICM became the IOM, it operated programs in Europe, Latin America, Africa, South Asia, and Indochina with assistance reaching 5 million people.

Contemporary Activities

In keeping with its traditional two-pronged focus on emergency assistance to migrants in special need, IOM continues to offer essential services to migrants fleeing from civil conflict, disasters, and general economic hardship. In 1990–1991, for instance, it returned migrants displaced by Iraq's invasion of Kuwait, and in the aftermath of the Persian Gulf War, it assisted about eight hundred thousand displaced Kurds. With the political disruptions in Yugoslavia and former states of the Soviet Union, IOM participated in special emergency programs to reunify families separated by the events in Yugoslavia, and it offered assistance to former Soviet Republics that faced widespread and large migration movements owing to the changes of government and to complicated demographic realities related to minority populations. In Africa, IOM successfully repatriated half a million refugees in Mozambique in 1993 and it assisted a quarter of a million Rwandan refugees in 1994. In subsequent years, its programs assisted Chechnyans, victims of Hurricane Mitch in Honduras, refugees from Kosovo, and displaced persons in East Timor. Its work extended to victims of earthquakes in India, internally displaced persons in Afghanistan, and refugees returning to Sierra Leone. By 2000, IOM assistance to migrants exceeded 11 million people.

While emergency situations continue to draw the attention of IOM, the organization continues to be mindful of how economic development issues stimulate migration, and how migration affects development. This work includes promotion of the study of migration. To this end, IOM publishes numerous journals and reports. Its journal *International Migration* is a leading publication in the academic study of migration and it also publishes a quarterly journal, *Migration*, on its work, as well as *IOM News,* in an effort to promote wider understanding of migration issues. It also issues reports and publishes books on a wide variety of migration issues. IOM works with governments to train officials responsible for dealing with migrants and refugees. It promotes the study and facilitation of labor migration programs, including the ongoing operation of its Return of Talent Program. It promotes the effective reintegration of refugees and returnees to their countries of origin in post-emergency settings. It helps governments to develop appropriate border control, including counter-trafficking and counter-smuggling policies. IOM programs, then, are aimed first and foremost at the welfare of migrants themselves, but the organization works with governments to explore ways in which migration can be channeled to enhance the prosperity and development of the countries of migration.

Although not formally part of the UN system, IOM is headquartered in Geneva, where it works closely with UN agencies dedicated to humanitarian, human rights, and development-related programs. Migration in all of its forms has become a major issue in international relations, and IOM serves as an important venue where governments, international agencies, NGOs, and academics can share knowledge and information for the benefit of migrants and of nations.

ROBERT F. GORMAN

See also Migration; Refugees

References and Further Reading

Carlin, James. *The Refugee Connection: A Lifetime of Running a Lifeline.* New York: MacMillan, 1989.
Marrus, Michael. *The Unwanted: European Refugees in the Twentieth Century.* New York: Oxford, 1985.
Perruchoud, Richard. "From the Intergovernmental Committee for European Migration to the International Organization for Migration." *International Journal of Refugee Law* 1:4 (October 1989).

INTERNATIONAL PLANNED PARENTHOOD FEDERATION (IPPF)

The International Planned Parenthood Federation (IPPF) was established at the Third International Conference on Planned Parenthood in Bombay, India, in 1952. National family planning associations from India, Hong Kong, the Netherlands, Singapore, Sweden, the United Kingdom, the United States, and West Germany were determined to create a global federation that would have the strength to combat cultures, traditions, laws, and religious attitudes that inhibited a woman's right to control her own fertility. The result is a non-governmental agency that seeks to increase access to quality reproductive health services for under-served populations worldwide.

Starting with just eight member organizations, by 2005 the IPPF included 149 member associations in every region of the world. The IPPF also works in sixteen countries—Equatorial Guinea, Malawi, Seychelles, Sao Tome and Principe, Zimbabwe, Oman, Somalia, Cook Islands, Kiribati, Myanmar, Papua New Guinea, Tuvalu, Serbia and Montenegro, Tajikistan, Macedonia, and Afghanistan—where there is no local planned parenthood organization. Millions of IPPF volunteers, particularly in the developing world, have assisted IPPF employees in five priority areas: adolescents, HIV/AIDS, abortion, access, and advocacy. IPPF activists attempt to enable people to make informed choices about their sexual lives and to receive care, counseling, diagnosis, and treatment. IPPF maintains forty thousand service outlets that provide counseling, gynecological care, HIV/AIDS-related services, diagnosis and treatment of sexually transmitted infections, mother and child health, and abortion-related services.

Planned Parenthood health centers offer a wide range of services that include family planning counseling and birth control; pregnancy testing and counseling; gynecological care, Pap tests, and breast exams; emergency contraception; HIV testing and counseling; medically accurate sexuality education; screening and treatment for sexually transmitted infections; infertility screening and counseling voluntary sterilization for women and men; reproductive medical exams for men; safer sex counseling; abortions or abortion referrals; adoption referrals; and referrals for specialized care. Planned Parenthood health centers also offer a wide range of programs that include programs for parents and teens designed to enhance learning about sexuality within the family; presentations on sexual and reproductive health issues at schools, places of worship, and community centers; and workshops and training seminars for teachers, physicians, nurse practitioners, social workers, and other health care professionals. In addition, Planned Parenthood health centers offer a wide range of information resources such as pamphlets, books, newsletters, and videotapes on a variety of topics.

Rapid population growth and highly populated communities contribute to the destruction of forests, misuse of agricultural land, expanding deserts, pollution, and the depletion of non-renewable resources. According to IPPF officials, providing people with access to the information and services they need to regulate their own fertility can help reduce population growth and thus help ease the pressure on the environment.

The IPPF, which is based in London, England, is divided into six geographical associations: the Western Hemisphere; Europe; the Arab World; Africa; South Asia; and Oceania, Southeast Asia, and East Asia. The International Planned Parenthood Federation's Western Hemisphere Region (IPPF/WHR), which was established in 1954, is the only region of the IPPF that is a separately incorporated entity. IPPF/WHR works primarily through a network of forty-six member associations in North America, Latin America, and the Caribbean. Each member association is a private organization established to supply family planning and other related health services according to local needs, customs, traditions, and laws. The Planned Parenthood Federation of America (PPFA), founded by birth control advocate Margaret Sanger in 1916, is the IPPF/WHR member association in the United States. The PPFA is the largest member association and is a separately incorporated entity. The PPFA does not receive funds from IPPF/WHR and is the only member of the IPPF/WHR that has its own international program for family planning.

The Planned Parenthood Federation of America—International (PPFA International) provides family planning education and services in the developing world. PPFA International's Global Partners program brings US-based Planned Parenthood associations together with family planning associations in the developing world in professional partnerships to share expertise, experience, and ideas. As of 2005,

PPFA International had projects in the following countries: Albania, Barbados, Belize, Benin, Bolivia, Botswana, Cameroon, Costa Rica, Dominican Republic, Ecuador, El Salvador, Ethiopia, Guatemala, Guyana, India, Ireland, Jamaica, Kenya, Latvia, Malawi, Mexico, Myanmar, Namibia, Nepal, Nicaragua, Nigeria, Peru, the Philippines, Puerto Rico, Russia, Senegal, Somalia, Sudan, Thailand, Trinidad and Tobago, Turkey, Uganda, Vietnam, and Zambia.

MICHAEL R. HALL

See also Children and Development; HIV/AIDS; Population Growth: Impact on Development; Public Health; Women: Role in Development

References and Further Reading

Chesler, Ellen. *Woman of Valor: Margaret Sanger and the Birth Control Movement in America.* New York: Simon & Schuster, 1992.

Grant, George. *Grand Illusions: The Legacy of Planned Parenthood.* Nashville, Tenn.: Cumberland House, 2000.

Marshall, Robert G., and Charles A. Donovan. *Blessed Are the Barren: The Social Policy of Planned Parenthood.* Ft. Collins, Colo.: Ignatius Press, 1991.

Planned Parenthood Federation of America. *A Tradition of Choice: Planned Parenthood at Seventy-Five.* New York: Author, 1991.

Suitters, Beryl. *Be Brave and Angry: Chronicles of the International Planned Parenthood Federation.* London: International Planned Parenthood Federation, 1973.

INTERNATIONAL RICE RESEARCH INSTITUTE (IRRI)

The International Rice Research Institute (IRRI) (http://www.irri.org) at Los Baños, Philippines, is a nonprofit research and training institution dedicated to the sustainable development of rice cultivation. The IRRI's research aims at increasing rice yields per acre while protecting the environment and preserving natural resources. The centre was established in 1960 by the Ford and Rockefeller Foundations in cooperation with the government of the Philippines and took up its research work in 1962 under founding director, Robert F. Chandler. The institute's headquarters, including its laboratories and training facilities on a 250-hectare experimental farm, are situated on the main campus of the University of the Philippines Los Baños about sixty km south of Manila. Additionally, the IRRI maintains regional offices in more than ten countries around the globe. The IRRI is one of sixteen nonprofit research institutes making up the Consultative Group on International Agricultural Research (CGIAR). The centre receives funding from twenty-one different countries and organisations such as the World Bank, the Asian Development Bank, the Food and Agricultural Organization (FAO), and the European Commission.

According to recent studies conducted by the FAO for the International Year of Rice 2004, rice is the staple crop for more than 3 billion people. Today, China, India, and Indonesia are the largest producers of rice, harvesting 166, 134, and 52 million metric tons of rice, respectively, in the year 2003. Rice is the predominant staple food for seventeen countries in Asia, nine countries in the Americas, and eight countries in Africa, providing about 20% of the world's dietary energy supply (compared to 19% provided by wheat and 5% by maize) (source: FAO). Following the centre's mission statement, it is the IRRI's prime goal to "improve the well-being of present and future generations of rice farmers and consumers, particularly those with low incomes." The institute seeks to achieve this primarily by breeding improved rice varieties with higher yields per acre. Furthermore, the IRRI is dedicated to the collection and preservation of information related to rice and rice cultivation. The centre has composed the comprehensive and frequently amended International *Bibliography of Rice Research;* maintains the Rice Knowledge Bank (http://www.knowledgebank.irri.org) and RiceWeb (http://www.riceweb.org); and publishes major research results, news, and its annual report in its biannual journal, *Rice Today.*

During the 1950s, the world community started to become aware of the ongoing "population explosion" and the food supply problem connected to the demographic development. The Rockefeller Foundation had already invested in agricultural research in Mexico during the 1940s and had succeeded in considerably increasing the local wheat and maize yield. Inspired by the Mexican success story, Warren Weaver and J. George Harrar submitted a paper to the Rockefeller Foundation in 1954 suggesting the establishment of an international rice research institute in Asia. Delayed due to the lack of additional investors, the IRRI was established in 1960 by the Rockefeller Foundation together with the Ford Foundation and the government of the Philippines. Three years later, the Ford and Rockefeller Foundations established the *Centro Internacional de Mejoramiento de Maíz y Trigo* (CIMMYT) in Mexico based on the earlier research in the region. Together, the IRRI and the CIMMYT became the most important carriers of the Green Revolution of the 1960s and 1970s. When research commenced at the IRRI in 1961–1962, the first goal was the breeding of a new variety of rice with a higher yield per acre that is more resistant against pests and more susceptible to artificial fertilizers. IRRI scientists developed an efficient method of rice cross-breeding

and presented the high-yielding rice variety IR8 in 1965. The improved varieties IR5 and IR20 were released in 1967 and 1969, respectively. In cooperation with national agricultural programs, the IRRI managed to spread the first high-yielding varieties (HYV) among Asian rice cultivators and thus brought the Green Revolution to Asia. Together with an expansion of the cultivated area, the introduction of the HYVs led to an increase of Asian rice production from 240 million tons in 1966 to 530 million tons in 1999. Since the mid-1980s the IRRI has been actively involved in genetic engineering and tries to improve the yield and pest resistance of rice by genetically modifying the plant.

In the 1980s the IRRI began its research on rice cultivation and sustainable development. IRRI started to invest in research on organic fertilisers and natural pest control with the help of insects and spiders. Today, integrated pest control (without the use of insecticides), organic fertilising, and the general sustainable development of rice cultivation rank high on IRRI's agenda. However, Green Revolution critics frequently accuse the IRRI of having worsened the situation of rice farmers and the ecosystem with the promotion of high-yielding varieties. The early HYVs in particular demanded a large supply of water and a constant input of chemical fertilisers and pesticides. Thus critics identify the agrochemical industry, large petrochemical companies, and large landowners as the main beneficiaries of the Green Revolution. The IRRI's involvement in genetic engineering since the mid-1980s is similarly criticised. The centre is accused of reducing the genetic diversity of rice and advocating the monoculture of hybrid rice varieties. Since the centre's inauguration, multinational chemical corporations have been among the chief donors to the IRRI. Critics accuse the institute of supporting the genetic patent policy of these major agrochemical companies.

ROLAND J. WENZLHUEMER

References and Further Reading

Barker, Randolph, and Robert Herdt. *The Rice Economy of Asia.* Washington, DC: Resources for the Future, 1985.

Bray, Francesca. *The Rice Economies: Technology and Development in Asian Societies.* Oxford, New York: Blackwell, 1986.

Chandler, Robert F. *An Adventure in Applied Science: A History of the International Rice Research Institute.* Los Baños, Philippines: IRRI, 1982.

Evenson, R. E., R. Herdt, and M. Hossain, eds. *Rice Research in Asia: Progress and Priorities.* Oxon, UK: CAB International, 1996.

Huke, Robert E., and Eleanor H. Huke. Rice Then and Now. Manila, Philippines: IRRI, 1990.

IRRI and the World of Rice: Questions and Answers about the International Rice Research Institute. Los Baños, Philippines: IRRI, 1996.

Khush, G. S., W. R. Coffman, and H. M. Beachell. "The History of Rice Breeding: IRRI's Contribution." In W. G. Rockwood, ed., *Rice Research and Production in the Twenty-First Century: Symposium Honoring Robert F. Chandler, Jr.* Los Baños, Philippines: IRRI, 2001, pp. 117–135.

Zeigler, R. S., ed. *Rice Research and Development Policy: A First Encounter.* Los Baños, Philippines: IRRI, 1996.

INTERNATIONAL TELECOMMUNICATION UNION (ITU)

The International Telecommunication Union (ITU), the world's oldest international organization, has been a specialized agency of the United Nations (UN) since 1947. It is a forum within which governments and the private sector can work together to coordinate the operation of telecommunication networks and services and advance the development of communications technology. Membership in the ITU is open to governments, that may join as member states, and private organizations, such as carriers, equipment manufacturers, and regional and international telecommunication organizations, that can join as sector members. The ITU's membership includes virtually all the world's nations and over 650 sector members.

The telecommunication age began in 1844 when Samuel Morse sent his first message over a telegraph line between Baltimore and Washington, DC. Within a decade, telegraphy was available to the general public, but since each country used a different system, telegraph lines did not cross national borders. Messages had to be transcribed and translated at frontiers and then re-sent over the telegraph network of the neighboring country. In 1865, to simplify the process, twenty European nations signed the first International Telegraph Convention in Paris, which resulted in the International Telegraph Union (ITU). Following the invention of wireless telegraphy in 1896, the first International Radiotelegraph Conference was held in 1906 in Berlin, which resulted in the first International Radiotelegraph Convention (IRC). By 1927, the IRC was monitoring the allocation of frequency bands to the radio services in existence at the time. In 1932, the ITU and the IRC merged to form the International Telecommunication Union (ITU), which was responsible for monitoring all forms of wire and wireless communication. In 1947, after the Second World War, the ITU, with the aim of modernizing the organization, became a specialized agency of the UN. In 1948, the ITU's headquarters were moved from Bern to Geneva, Switzerland.

In 1989, at the ITU conference held in Nice, ITU officials vocalized the importance of providing technical assistance to the developing world. To achieve this goal, the ITU established the Telecommunication Development Bureau to improve communications in the developing regions of the world. To meet the challenges of the rapidly expanding world of information exchange on the World Wide Web, the ITU insisted on the need for Internet domain names that reflect the geographical and functional nature of the Internet. The ITU has sought to make the Internet available to all people on a nondiscriminatory basis, especially in the Third World. The role of the ITU in the standardization of emerging technologies becomes more important as the world becomes more reliant on telecommunication technologies for communication, commerce, and access to information.

MICHAEL R. HALL

References and Further Reading

Codding, George A., and Anthony M. Rutkowski. *The International Telecommunication Union in a Changing World.* Norwood, MA: Artech House, 1988.

International Telecommunication Union. *Minutes of the Plenipotentiary Conference of the International Telecommunication Union, Nice, 1989.* Geneva: Author, 1990.

INTER-RELIGIOUS RELATIONS

The period of the eighteenth century Enlightenment saw faith in God challenged by faith in reason and rationality. The rise of urban civilisation and the development of science was linked with the collapse of traditional religious ideas. In Europe, secularism became the dominant world view, marginalising religion, increasingly rendering it a private affair. In the rest of the world, colonialism took with it missionaries who declared other faiths as superstition and placed Christianity as the apotheosis of civilised society. Post–World War II development policies saw religious practice as something to be removed if it hindered progress. Now, in the age of globalisation, there is a rise of religious nationalism and a public seeking of spiritual fulfillment. New religious communities have grown as international communication and migration create culturally diverse centres in which sacred space and practice need to be negotiated. Modernity's associated doctrine of plurality has introduced a new phase of inter-religious relations.

Defining Religion

Human history is in part a record of the quest for religious truth and certainty. Religions and religious rites have emerged in all cultures in history. This is no surprise, for the religious, spiritual dimension is part of our makeup as human beings (Cook 1994, p. 408).

There is an inherent difficulty in defining religion: it has an aspect of revelation and an aspect of interpretation within every culture. But generally it can be argued that its function is to provide a sense of meaning and order; to provide boundaries to what is ultimately "good" and "true" as points of reference for human action. Religion provides answers for questions about our origins and the reasons for universal dilemmas such as suffering, death, and love. Most religions provide a means for people to deal with their mortality through notions of a non-physical continuity or renewal. Religion provides both limits and plausibility structures, that is, the social reinforcement of particular boundaries, and the knowledge and practices that are possible within them (Berger 1969). Religion has a sacred element, which Madan (1992) defines as particular phenomena, a kind of knowledge, everyday practices, and a typology of social roles, and it can also be linked to the political sphere around questions of legitimacy and authority.

Religion exists in a social milieu. It is a tacit marker of community and consensus about the right way to act. From the point of view of western philosophy, religion has been identified as a projection of needs (Feuerbach); Marx called it the opium of the people, that is, a sign of oppression; Kierkegaard argued that it is passionate, an individual discovering his or her real existential platform from which to make a leap of faith. Two of the most influential writers in European thought on the role of religion in social life were Emile Durkheim and Max Weber.

Durkheim (1965) believed that inevitably social organisation results in the expression of its underlying aspirations or ideal elements in religious symbols. A society's notion of itself necessitates a particular idea or form of God, and religion therefore is a social manifestation of the sacred. He felt that religion is a set of practices rather than a set of beliefs—the belief only makes sense through ritual, which reinforces collective sentiment and social integration. Society is the source for such common practices and therefore is the source of religion. Durkheim takes a very functionalist view, that is, only looking at religion's function in society and not substantively examining some of the associated effects of religiosity such as faith. His prediction that science would eventually overtake religion has never really come to pass despite a much-heralded faith in science in the modern world, perhaps because humanity has never fulfilled his requirement of providing science with a moral base.

Weber also emphasised the essential relationship of religion to society—there was no society without religion. His famous thesis, *The Protestant Ethic and the Spirit of Capitalism* (1958), drew the conclusion that Protestant doctrine underpinned the development of capitalist economics by sanctioning new behaviour, including investment, money lending, and the deferral of gratification.

The key to the link between Protestant ethics and the development of capitalism was in rationalising existing (Catholic) religious practice, that is, removing some of what were considered superstitious elements, and developing what was considered a rational theology, system of ideas, and practices. Weber suggested that the Reformation began this process of the rationalisation of ethical life, which then spread out into the economic sphere. The motivating force acting on the Protestant community was religious in nature but the offshoot was economic activity. The Protestant (Calvinist) would plan the activities of the day to ensure his or her life was a model of good actions.

Weber's ideas have been critiqued over time. There were other transformations occurring in Europe such as the establishment of accounting systems that supported economic development. He is also widely regarded as being too Euro-centric. Amin (1989) argues that the idea that capitalism could only have developed out of a Christian movement is a myth designed to support colonialism. According to Amin, some of the Arabic states were beginning to develop sophisticated economies but their development was hindered by European intervention.

In the case of China, the belief that Confucianism permeated every aspect of Chinese life and obstructed its capitalist development has been questioned by researchers such as Lufrano (1997). He suggested that merchants, retailers, and small business owners from the sixteenth century began to shrug off the hegemony of a Confucian elite and reappropriate Confucian values in their own way, while still accepting the role of loyal, stable citizens. This argument is the basis for recent analysis of the rapid economic development of the industrial Tigers in East Asia, and the thesis that there are in fact Asian values that can underpin economic activity in this region.

The contradiction associated with Weber's trajectory of economic development today is that once capitalism had become established it no longer needed religion as a motivating force. Once the spirit of capitalism had permeated other areas of life and had in turn rationalised and established practical structures and institutions, then religion was no longer needed. This is the heart of Bell's (1976) cultural contradiction of capitalism. The early European capitalists were not interested in wealth per se but in leading a good life.

They became rich as a consequence of abstinence, discipline, control, and good investment. In contemporary society, capitalism encourages debt, consumption, and loss of control. Weber himself was very pessimistic about the impact of rationality in European society. He spoke of an "iron cage" of bureaucracy and a feeling of "disenchantment."

Later twentieth-century writers speak of religion becoming invisible, emigrating from churches, which are now only relics, to new social forms. Personal identification diverges more and more from institutionalised religion, to become something more private and personal. Bellah (1965) speaks of the development of a civil religion, that is, great traditions remain but the religion that plays a public role in society is a diluted, generalised set of tenets without any particular consequences.

This removal of religion from the public to the private sphere is also described as secularisation. This process, linked with rationalisation, was a major foundation stone of development policies that were translocated to the Majority World, including countries with vastly different religious systems.

Religion and Development

The effect of the spread of development and global religions such as Christianity on small-scale societies ranges from the denigration and virtual replacement of local religions, to their syncretic hybridisation, to a resurgence, as shall be seen later in this essay, to combat the ill-effects of development and globalisation. The contact between European traders and military forces from the nineteenth century even led to the creation of new religions such as the Cargo Cults found in Melanesia. Adherents believed that in the new millennium the spirits of their ancestors would return to distribute cargoes of modern goods.

In many cultures, and subsets of cultures, prior to the introduction of systematic modernisation, systems of religious order were integral to everyday life. For example, research into the peasant economy in a Malay village showed a link between economic and social units within structurally defined groups of kin and community affiliations or through other institutions such as religion. These units were in other ways autonomous, ad hoc, informal, and invisible, often forgotten in the development debate. Generally, single-purpose, small-scale, and confined to rural areas to deal with the uncertainties of peasant life, they could include informal lending institutions sometimes based in temples or other religious institutions (Scott 1977).

The impact of first colonialism and later development on processes of rationalisation and denigration

of local religions, and subsequently the dislocation of social organisation, is highlighted if the links between social practice and religion are emphasised. Ways of communication, perceptions of the individual and his or her relationship to the collective, economic and political relationships, time and space, defining boundaries of morality and permissible and non-permissible behaviours, limits and regulations on consumption and production, concepts of justice and punishment, and the use of technology and knowledge can be determined, influenced and reinforced by religious practice and edict.

The process of modernisation saw the reorientation of these boundaries, including boundaries of the sacred, and what is and isn't market inalienable with regard to religious iconography. Development founded on rationality and the renunciation of the metaphysical placed religion outside the field of legitimation of the social order. It proposed an ending that was based entirely on material progression and excluded the spiritual dimension. This linear, monochronic concept of time opposed the polychronic circular understandings of Buddhist and Hindu philosophy, for example.

Development involved a rationalisation of goal setting and goal attainment, and the reexamination of cultural symbols, which in traditional societies tended to have strong religious affiliations (Bellah 1965). In particular, modernism shifted the centre of authority to the individual. The increase in control over the environment included the inner environment of the self, which was also at odds with the communal nature of many religious practices and beliefs. Buddhism is posed with a serious dilemma when faced with a modernity that is based on the "I" as the centre of the social world. Buddhist philosophy suggests that there is no self, no soul. A separate individual is only an intellectual idea.

Secularisation saw the increased removal of religion from the public to the private sphere. In Western society, foundational systems such as politics, economics, and justice do not have overtly religious underpinnings, although it can be argued that justice in particular is founded on Christian moral codes. This is a contentious issue for jurisprudence in contemporary multicultural societies where religious law comes into conflict with civil law, or for human rights activists in countries where religious law opposes the universal declaration of human rights. When codes governing state authority have been secularised, religion no longer functions as a supporter of state decisions, but it still functions as a supporter of the existing identity of an individual claiming exemption from a civil law. Truth, once associated with religion, now became associated with the state and its machinery, and with the idea of development.

Industrialisation, urbanisation, and social plurality have increased the process of secularisation. Highly differentiated compartments for work, social, and religious practices have developed. Some writers declare that time, and even capitalism itself, have become the new gods, and work the new basis for authority and identity. The individual becomes responsible for moral decision making, increasing the regard for the worth and the rights of the individual, and increasing the importance given to concepts such as civil justice to replace communal faith.

As Durkheim predicted to some degree, faith has shifted to science and reason. Development was regarded as a *soteriology*—a doctrine of salvation. According to Bellah (1965), for historic religion to maximise its contribution to modernisation there was a need to:

- Rephrase religious symbols to give meaning to worldly pursuits;
- Channel motivation from religious discipline into worldly pursuits;
- Contribute to national integration but not dominate or sanction as an ultimate;
- Give positive meaning and highly value, that is, sanction, long-term social development as a goal;
- Contribute to the idea of the responsible and disciplined person; and
- Adopt a new role to balance secularism—but in a private, voluntaristic form.

If modernisation was to be successful, religion had to make this transition, or withdraw and allow secular ideologies to take over.

Berger (1969) argues that the decline in religious belief comes about not so much because of scientific rationality and secularism but because of rising plurality, that is, rising challenges and subsequent doubts about existing structures. Modernisation brought with it a plethora of ideas, institutions, and of gods even. The church or temple became just one ideology among others and as an institution it had to justify its existence even in Western countries. Globalisation has heightened this sense of diversity.

A major theoretical response to plurality has been post-modernity; the argument that there is no meta-narrative, no universal or overarching truth. This can engender extreme cultural relativism, that is, what is true and valued is only relevant in a particular cultural context. It can also engender extreme fundamentalism as a search for meaning turns people back to (neo) traditions. Other responses to modernity, none of which are mutually exclusive, include the construction of a reformist vision of traditional religion, compatible with modernity, or the use of modern methods to

defend traditional values, on the grounds of rationalising of means not goals (Bellah 1965). For example, the rise of the Hindu political party, the Bharatiya Janata Parishad (the Indian People's Party, BJP), to power in India meant that they had to reversion some of the language of their rhetoric when faced with the realities of global economics.

There is a tension between spiritual values and economic development even in the West. It is what Bell (1976) describes as a crisis of the self as religious beliefs and values are eroded. Bell claims that a post-industrial society cannot provide a transcendent ethic, therefore there is a need for the resurrection of traditional faith and the restoration of continuity, humility, and compassion for others. This is perhaps a utopian view, although the numbers of Westerners seeking solace in Eastern religion and new sects is probably an indication of the human need for a spiritual dimension (there will be an estimated 67% growth in new religions between 1993 and 2006). Bell has been accused of being a neo-conservative and nostalgic, however his ideas that traditional religious symbols be resurrected is apparent in Majority World countries as a means to reclaim control over the development process.

Inter-Religious Relations in the Global Era

Globalisation (in particular the elements of international communication and migration) has brought religions increasingly in contact with each other. On one hand, there is a movement to use religion as a means to revitalise societies that have been decimated by rationality. This includes western societies. Berger (2001) argues there is a process of "Easternisation" occurring, a movement from East to West. The spread of Buddhism, the growth of communities based on Hindu teachings, the adoption of Islam by marginalised communities particularly in urban centres in the West, pose a challenge to the established Christian church. These cross-cultural challenges also feed into a hardening of boundaries. In the melange of globalisation, identity politics has gained an ascendancy, and religion and religious symbols have played a part in defining nationalist, at times extreme, opposition to the West and the processes of globalisation.

Religious Nationalism

The theorist Samuel Huntington predicted increasing clashes between civilisations, which he delineated by using, among other elements, their major belief systems. Oppositional movements against westernisation have taken the form of religious nationalism or oppositional movements against central bureaucratic forms such as the state or targets associated with globalisation such as transnational corporations. Examples of such movements include the Khalistani (Sikh) movement in India in the 1980s, the rise of Islamic fundamentalism in the Middle East and South Asia, Jewish fundamentalism in Israel, the rise to power of the BJP in India (the political wing of the Hindu right), and the rise of Christian fundamentalists in the United States. There is an increased importance of links with the global diasporic community in many of these examples. Religious nationalism does not know boundaries in the same way as the state, and new communication technology means that a global community based on religio-cultural affiliations is possible.

Juergensmeyer (1993) documents the rise of religious nationalism in response to what is perceived as a degradation of values and beliefs by the imposition of the westernised state. The modern state is the ultimate secular body and all other markers of identity were expected to be subsumed by it. Nationalism, like religion, is an expression of faith, identity, and loyalty to a larger community, exuding moral legitimacy, that is, a source of values, beliefs, and behaviours (Juergensmeyer 1993). But the state and religion are in fact competing ideologies of order. They both define a "right way" of being in the world and orientate individuals to social organisation that is not always synonymous. It is a dilemma for the state that it must find a way to reappropriate or accommodate religion while still being secular. In many cases, the rhetoric of religious nationalism is of waging a struggle against neocolonialism, with the aim of reinstating a religious order.

With its often confrontational approach to the United States, fundamentalism in the Islamic community is the focus of much debate in terms of poor relations and misunderstanding between religious ideologies and practices. Fundamentalism itself is a loaded term, a western concept, whereas according to Juergensmeyer's research, for some Islamic religious nationalists there is no clear distinction between religion and politics. Islam is regarded by its proponents in this scenario as a "culturally liberating force."

The characteristics of religious nationalism include: rejection of secular nationalism and perceptions of Western neocolonialism; the use of religious ideology; and the offering of a religious alternative. The relevance of religion to everyday life and the moral and communal identity of a nation is usually stressed. The underlying reasons for conflict often involves changes in economic and social order brought about in many cases by modernisation policies, leading to frustrated expectations. The Iranian revolution in the late 1970s that overthrew the more westernised Shah and brought Ayatollah Khomeini to power, is a prime example of this trend.

This opposition is a form of defensiveness, restraining the secularisation of the West, and revitalising local culture by reappropriating religious symbols in new contexts. This reappropriation of culture has also become a mark of localisation in the marketing of global goods, which are now packaged in local frames to be more palatable for consumers. While localisation is critiqued as an extension of the market, the use of religious symbols is to some extent still market inalienable, and therefore these are still powerful when used by religious-based movements.

The Revitalisation of Religion

Bell suggested in the 1970s a return to the unity of the sacred and the secular, in which spirituality will play an integral part in defining "the existential predicaments, the awareness in men [sic] of their finiteness and the inexorable limits to their power . . . and the consequent effort to find a coherent answer to reconcile them to the human condition" (Bell 1976, p. xxix). This again is an idealistic view as it is difficult to assert that even in "traditional" societies the sacred and secular were so united. However, there are religious-based movements currently attempting to at least redress the imbalance between the secular and the spiritual.

While a form of Christianity is said to have played a role in the establishment of capitalism, as noted earlier, its role as a motivating force has become marginalised. Now a full circle appears to have been turned, with Christianity taking on a more radical and syncretic role, again becoming a motivating force this time to undo the damage of maldevelopment. Founded by Gustavo Gutierrez, who rejected the term "development," the ideas of Liberation Theology have been used throughout Latin America in particular in the 1970s, but also in Africa, Asia, and in the Black community in the US. Gutierrez advocated communities undertake socioeconomic analysis before embarking on critical reflection; liberating the tradition of the Bible that Gutierrez saw as a subversive book; and taking a preferential option for the poor.

The basic idea is that theology can become a corrective. Rather than just a theology of the political order or a new version of a Christian social ethic, it is conceived in the public sphere and becomes a social medium. It is necessarily political and is an ethic of change rather than order. Liberation theory should rise out of practice, that is, theory should only be verified by its social functions.

Buddhist writers have also used their system of religion to counter what they feel are the ill effects of development. Sulak Sivaraksa has lobbied for the revitalisation of religious institutions such as the temple in Thailand. He argues that larger cultural groupings, such as the religious community, can become a focus for political life. Sivaraksa's translation of development cites four aspects that need to be integrated if it is to be authentic: the culture, spirituality, and the social and economic dimensions of a nation (Sivaraksa 1990). These elements are not mutually exclusive but must be ordered according to a country's particular priorities.

India provides a rich tradition of thought with regard to inter-religious relations and the utilisation of religious resources. It is the birthplace of two of the largest faith systems (Buddhism and Hinduism). It is home to ancient and more recent religions (Jains, Zoroastrians, and Sikhs). It has a Muslim minority that remained after the Islamic Moghal rulers of the Middle Ages departed. And it also has minority populations of Jewish and Christian communities.

With the passing of time there has been evidence of syncreticism—the sight of Shiva lingams in Catholic churches, for example. But there is also a growing voice of dissent from religious extremists opposed to the secular state since its inception in 1947, and to the more recent influx of transnational corporations and western cultural products following economic liberalisation in 1991. The rhetoric of Hindu nationalists increasingly has been one of superiority over what is considered an amoral if not immoral West, particularly represented by the United States, using spiritual and religious behaviour as the yard stick.

The 1990s and early twenty-first century in India have been marred by communal violence and some argue that secularism has failed to make any headway at all (Madan 1992). The rise to power of a Hindu nationalist political party would appear to be linked with people's need for certainty in a period of rapid change, which the state was unable to provide in its secular rhetoric. Much of the rhetoric of Hindu nationalism is in opposition to westernisation or globalisation, again centred on the notion of Hindu values that focus on the family and regulating consumption, as opposed to what is perceived as the materialism and subsequent dysfunction of the West.

As a counterbalance to these more militant voices there are those that wish to rejuvenate India using the cultural resources available to them. The work of Indian writer S. Kappen (1995) outlined his solution

to what he regards as the cultural decay and undermining of identity that has come with modern development. His writings portrayed the position of the divine in contemporary society as an "ungod" because of the role of religion in recolonisation and the monotheism of capital. As a remedy he examined the narratives of dissent in Indian religious traditions, including Buddhism and the medieval Bhakti movement. Kappen stated that there was a need for redefining a sense of the divine more in tune with a true collective vision in which existence could be anchored.

However, like many of the advocates of neo-traditionalism, the vision is idealistic, often relying on ideas of tradition that no longer exist, and not fully encompassing the differences between the philosophy of religion and its practices. Hinduism, for example, is practiced diversely throughout India, with a fundamental impulse to worship, not theorise (Berger 1969). The caste system is problematic as it maintains a social order that ensures a particular sector of society is considered lowly simply by fate. In using cultural resources such as religious symbols in a contemporary context, the distance of time can easily blur the past.

Conclusion

From the one extreme of cultural imposition has emerged a polarisation: the absolute truth of western modernisation now faces challenges from the absolutism of differently focused religio-cultural claims. The rise of identity politics and a new bout of religious nationalism has seen increased impetus in the twentieth and twenty-first centuries for a genuine ecumenical movement to improve inter-religious understanding. The ecumenical movement is emphasising an interdependence between all things and is often linked with new ideas in the environmental movement that emphasise a kind of eco-spiritualism.

Eck (1993) believes there are three social and political responses to religious diversity: exclusivism (there is no authentic religion but mine), inclusivism (there are other religions but mine is the authoritative one), and pluralism. The first two are implicated in the formation of religious nationalism, and the latter in the formation of real engagement between religions. In each scenario, interpretations will have social and political ramifications.

The search for new terms for a modernity that is not westernisation but is imbued with local religious values as part of the cultural sphere is also part of the task of nationalists and neo-traditionalists. Juergensmeyer (1993) suggests that new forms of the nation-state are emerging as the state and religion reassess their relationship. His examples include Sri Lanka, India, Iran, Egypt, Algeria, Central Asia, and Eastern Europe. Although vague on how these case studies are different from the modern nation-state, he believes they are creating something new in a synthesis between religion and the secular state, merging cultural identity and the legitimacy of former religiously sanctioned monarchies, and the democratic and organisational structures of contemporary industrial society.

Writers and academics from the Majority World are increasing the available knowledge within development discourse by questioning the motives, methods, and purpose of globalisation. Self-reliance and empowerment programs rooted in religious institutions are representative of the new thoughts and alternatives being devised. New knowledge articulated outside the confines of a monocultural interpretation, using other systems of religious representation and myth, will reinforce the detachment of the power of truth from current global standards.

MELISSA BUTCHER

See also Buddhism; Cultural Perceptions; Globalization: Impact on Development; Hinduism; India; Islam; Liberation Theology

References and Further Reading

Amin, Samir. *Eurocentrism*. New York: Monthly Review Press, 1989.
Bell, Daniel. *The Cultural Contradictions of Capitalism*. London: Heinemann, 1976.
Bellah, R. N. *Religion and Progress in Modern Asia*. New York: Free Press, 1965.
Berger, Peter. *Religion and Globalisation, the 2001 lecture in Culture and Social Theory*. Institute for Advanced Studies in Culture, University of Virginia, 2001.
———. *A Rumour of Angels: Modern Society and the Rediscovery of the Supernatural*. New York: Pelican, 1969.
Cook, David. "'A Plural Society." In *The World's Religions*, 2nd ed. UK: Lion Press, 1994 [1982].
Durkheim, Emile. *The Elementary Forms of Religious Life*. Translated by Joseph Swain. New York: Free Press, 1965.
Eck, Diana. *Encountering God*. New York: Penguin, 1993.
Gutierrez, Gustavo. *A Theology of Liberation*. New York: Orbis, 1971.
Huntington, Samuel. *The Clash of Civilisations and the Remaking of World Order*. New York: Simon & Schuster, 1996.
Juergensmeyer, Mark. *Religious Nationalism Confronts the Secular State*. India: Oxford University Press, 1993.
Kappen, S. *Spirituality in the Age of Recolonisation*. India: Visthar, 1995.
Lufrano, John. *Honorable Merchants: Commerce and Self-Cultivation in Late Imperial China*. Honolulu: University of Hawaii Press, 1997.
Madan, T. N., ed. *Religion in India*, 2nd ed. Oxford, UK: Oxford University Press, 1992 [1991].
Scott, J. *The Moral Economy of the Peasant*. New Haven, CT: Yale University Press, 1977.
Sivaraksa, Sulak. *Siam in Crisis*, 2nd ed. Bangkok: Thai Inter-Religious Commission for Development, 1990.
Smart, N., and B. Srinivasa Murthy, eds. *East-West Encounters in Philosophy and Religion*. London: Sangam Books, 1997.
Stackhouse, Max, ed. *God and Globalisation*. Harrisburg, PA: Trinity Press International, 2000.
Weber, Max. *The Protestant Ethic and the Spirit of Capitalism*. New York: Scribner's, 1958.

INTIFADA

The Arabic term *intifada* is typically translated into English as "uprising." The word refers specifically to the Palestinian uprising against Israeli military occupation of the regions known as the West Bank and the Gaza Strip, an occupation that began following the 1967 Six-Day War. The actual translation of the term comes closer to the idea of the "shaking off" or removing of the occupation from these regions.

The First Intifada (1987–1993) and the Israeli Response

The first *intifada* began in early December 1987 as a spontaneous, grass-roots movement by the Palestinian residents of the West Bank and Gaza Strip against the twenty-year-old Israeli military occupation. Until this point, the occupation had rendered the Palestinian community economically and politically powerless. A lack of citizens' rights, domination by the Israeli political apparatus, and general social malaise well describe the living conditions of the Palestinians during this time.

During the occupation, the political branch of the Palestinian liberation movement was centered outside of western Palestine, first in Jordan, and later Lebanon, and then Tunisia. Thus, while in time, the Palestine Liberation Organization began to play a significant role in the coordination and development of the uprising, most would argue that what made the *intifada* unique was that it represented, for the very first time, a complete and full Palestinian rejection of the Israeli military occupation from *inside* the territories that Israel had conquered and occupied during the 1967 Six-Day War.

Other aspects of the uprising were also unique. The most active Palestinian participants in the *intifada* were young, that is, the *shebab* or Palestinian youth. Moreover, the tactics of the participants were limited primarily to rock throwing, tire burning, and other acts of protest. Civil disobedience was also employed. While the *intifada* cannot be construed as totally non-violent, the acts by and large were of a non-threatening nature to the Israeli state. Rather, the protesters saw themselves as freedom-fighters fighting against the occupation of their land by outside forces. Their use of rocks, sticks, bottles, and other non-lethal weapons was a result of expedience, and was also symbolic of the "David vs. Goliath" nature of their struggle against the massive strength of the Israeli military forces.

In addition to the use of street protests and repeated confrontations with Israeli soldiers, the *intifada* was also carried out through economic means. The refusal to pay taxes to the Israeli authorities, the holding of general strikes during which Palestinian shops remained closed and shuttered, and the boycotting of Israeli goods (such as *Time* cigarettes, for example) were all used in an attempt to draw attention to the concerns of the Palestinian people living under Israeli military control and economic domination.

The Israeli military response to the Palestinian *intifada* was severe, and disproportionate to the Palestinians' activities. For example, then Minister of Defense Yitzhak Rabin suggested during the early days of the uprising that one way of bringing a halt to rock throwing by the Palestinian youth would be to "break their bones." Such an extreme policy, it was believed, would serve to eventually snuff out any hints of Palestinian resistance; the more severe the punishments meted out, the sooner the *intifada* could be nullified and ultimately extinguished.

Such policies were largely ineffective, however. World public opinion increasingly viewed the Palestinians as underdogs in a conflict in which, historically, Israel had been seen in such a light. Media coverage played a key role in revealing the harsh and at times inhumane treatment of Palestinian youth at the hands of Israeli soldiers. As public opinion began to shift, so too were the Palestinians emboldened to continue their struggle despite the personal risks involved.

The Palestinian *intifada* was not able to sustain itself at the same high level of intensity for long. By the early 1990s, the regularity of the "cat-and-mouse" game played out by young Palestinian rock-throwers and similarly young Israeli soldiers had run its course. At the same time, however, the image of Israel and of the ongoing occupation of the Palestinian territories was severely damaged. It was in this context that a conference was held in Madrid in October 1991 in an effort to bring the Arab and Israeli sides together and, under US auspices, develop a genuine peace process to finally resolve the conflict.

The Madrid meeting led to still further meetings between the two sides, which were arranged secretly in Oslo, Norway. These meetings resulted in the signing of the Oslo Accords by Israeli Prime Minister Yitzhak Rabin and Palestinian leader Yasser Arafat, witnessed by US President Bill Clinton, on September 13, 1993, effectively bringing the *intifada* to an end.

It is these Accords that were to have provided a foundation for the eventual end to the Israeli occupation of the West Bank and Gaza Strip. From the outset, however, the Oslo Accords were viewed as flawed. While the creation of a Palestinian Authority and the staged withdrawal of Israeli forces from the primary population centers of the West Bank and Gaza did provide the Palestinians with limited autonomy and suggested the eventual creation of a permanent solution to the Palestinian problem—namely the creation of a Palestinian state—the Accords provided only a limited structure within which Palestinian independence might be achieved. In truth, Oslo offered a starting point for independence, but failed to explicitly map out how to move from Israeli occupation to complete Palestinian sovereignty and statehood.

Chief among the obstacles that Oslo failed to resolve were the final status of the disputed city of Jerusalem, the right of Palestinian refugees to return to what is today Israel, the future status of Jewish settlements in the occupied territories following Palestinian independence, and so on. It was these issues that were discussed at length by President Clinton, Israeli Prime Minister Ehud Barak, and Arafat in the summer of 2000. Camp David II, as this set of meetings came to be known, again failed to resolve any of these issues in a manner that satisfied both sides. This opened the door to yet another uprising, the *al-Aqsa intifada*.

The al-Aqsa Intifada (2000–)

The *al-Aqsa intifada* derived its name from what was seen as a provocative action by then Minister of Defense Ariel Sharon who, on September 28, 2000, took a well-guarded political contingent to the Temple Mount/al-Haram ash-Sharif where the al-Aqsa mosque is located in a show of Israeli dominance and power. Palestinian riots erupted in Jerusalem in response to this act, and soon spilled over throughout the West Bank and Gaza in a manner similar to the outbreak of the 1987 uprising.

However, the *al-Aqsa intifada* differed from its predecessor in a number of ways. First, this uprising used terror—especially suicide bombings—as its primary tactic. Moreover, most (though certainly not all) such attacks were carried out within Israel itself, not within the occupied Palestinian territories. Perhaps the most notorious of such actions took place March 27, 2002, with an attack at a Passover *seder* holiday meal in Netanya. Some twenty-two were killed and 140 injured in the attack. Although later attacks at clubs, on buses, and in other public places killed as many or more, this particular attack received a great deal of media attention due to its gruesome nature and timing.

Second, the *al-Aqsa intifada* often took on religious, rather than nationalistic, undertones. Whereas the first *intifada* was fought with the expressed goal of seeking national sovereignty and Palestinian independence, the *al-Aqsa intifada* was often seen to be fought on religious grounds, where the elimination of the foreign, non-Muslim Israeli state from the heart of the Muslim realm (*Dar al-Islam*) was at the center of the new Palestinian struggle. Those who died as a result of suicide bombings during the *al-Aqsa intifada* were seen as *shaheeds*, Muslim martyrs who are to be honored and praised for the sacrifice they have made in striving to cleanse the land of Zionist forces.

As was the case during the first *intifada*, the Israeli response to the second uprising was again severe. Houses throughout the West Bank and Gaza were razed, mass arrests were frequent, and communal punishment was implemented with regularity. And yet, unlike the first *intifada*, world sympathies again shifted to the Israeli side. Suicide attacks again Israel were increasingly viewed as but part and parcel of Arab Muslim terror globally; the September 11, 2001, attacks, and the deposition of Iraqi President Saddam Hussein—a strong supporter of suicide bombings in Israel—served to largely mitigate any hopes or expectations that the *al-Aqsa intifada* would produce any substantive results in the long term.

Looking to the Future

Today, the *al-Aqsa intifada* appears to have run its course. This is not to say that resistance to the Israeli occupation of some parts of the West Bank and Gaza, and the failure to resolve key disputes regarding Jerusalem, the refugees, and similar issues, do not remain central to the Palestinian–Israeli conflict. But the uprising is no longer seen as providing any hope of moving the situation forward—if indeed it ever had been viewed in such a light.

This is also not to suggest that future Palestinian uprisings, civil disobedience, and terror on the order of the first and second *intifadas* may not continue to occur. So long as the Palestinian people lack a fully sovereign and independent state, frustration, anger, and resentment will continue to plague the cities and towns of the West Bank and Gaza—the very

ingredients that helped spark the first and second Palestinian *intifadas*.

STEVEN C. DINERO

See also Israel; Middle East: International Relations; Palestine; Palestine Liberation Organization (PLO); Terrorism

References and Further Reading

Abed-Rabbo, Samir, and Doris Safie. *The Palestinian Uprising*. Northampton, MA: Interlink, 1990.
Beitler, Ruth M. *The Path to Mass Rebellion: An Analysis of Two Intifadas*. Lanham, MD: Lexington Books, 2004.
Carey, Roane, ed. *The New Intifada: Resisting Israel's Apartheid*. London and New York: Verso, 2001.
Freedman, Robert O. *The Intifada: Its Impact on Israel, the Arab World, and the Superpowers*. Gainesville, FL: University Press of Florida, 1991.
Lockman, Zachary, and Joel Benin. *Intifada: The Palestinian Uprising Against Israel Occupation*. Cambridge, MA: South End Press, 1989.
Mishal, Shaul, and Reuben Aharoni. *Speaking Stones: Communiques from the Intifada Underground* (Contemporary Issues in the Middle East). Syracuse, NY: Syracuse University Press, 1994.
Peretz, Don. *Intifada: The Palestinian Uprising*. Reading, MA: Perseus, 1990.
Schiff, Ze'ev, and Ehud Ya'Ari. *Intifada: The Palestinian Uprising—Israel's Third Front*. New York: Simon & Schuster, 1990.
Wingate, Katherine. *The Intifadas (War and Conflict in the Middle East)*. New York: Rosen Publishing Group, 2003.

IRAN

Iran is a country of 1.65 million square kilometers and a population of 69,018,924 (July 2004 est.), in Southwest Asia, bordering Iraq, Turkey, Russia, Afghanistan, Pakistan, the Indian Ocean, and the Persian Gulf, with rugged terrain, marked by mountains and deserts, less than 10% of which is arable. With a GDP in 2003 of roughly $480 billion, Iran produces about 4 million barrels of oil per day, of which slightly more than 2 million are exported, comprising 80% of its exports.

Iran has a long imperial tradition and national history, carried into the modern era by the Safavid (1501–1722), Qajar (1793–1925), and Pahlavi (1925–1979) dynasties, and the Islamic Republic, declared in 1979. Shah Ismail (1494–1524) and Shah Abbas I (1587–1629), the two most powerful rulers of the Safavid period, built a centralized state on the pillars of Shi'i Islam and a gunpowder-based standing army of converted Christian slaves, or *ghulam*. At its height, Safavid rule extended across Iran into Iraq and Afghanistan, also increasing trade in porcelain, silk and wool textiles, and other products designed for the growing European market.

Following the overthrow of the Safavids in 1722, and an extended period of internal conflict between competing tribal alliances, Fath Ali Shah (1794–1834) established the Qajar dynasty in 1794. Qajar rule was less centralized and more dependent on tribal leaders than Safavid rule had been, and during the 19th century, *mujtahids*, scholars of Muslim doctrine, emerged as powerful arbiters of political legitimacy, asserted control over the educational and judicial systems, and established strong ties to Iran's urban merchant class, the *bazaaris*. Growing Russian and British competition in Asia increased external political and economic influence in Iran. In 1857, Nasir al-Din Shah (1848–1896) signed a commercial agreement giving British traders advantages similar to those already enjoyed by Russians in Iranian markets, insuring that Iran remained an exporter of raw materials like cotton, silk, and wheat. As indigenous industries declined, carpet weaving was one industry that did grow in the nineteenth century, to meet Western demand for high-quality hand-woven rugs.

Nasir al-Din Shah also launched administrative reforms, expanded state-run education, and created the Cossack Brigade, trained and led by Russian officers, to expand his power over tribal leaders, landowners, and the *ulama*, which in Islam means Council of Learned Men. The reforms had their greatest impact in the cities, while agricultural techniques and productivity remained largely unchanged outside regions cultivating cash crops. Lacking funds for industrial development, Nasir al-Din Shah turned to Europeans for investment and expertise, as with the 1872 Reuters Concession, granting a monopoly to build and operate railroads, along with mineral rights to pay for expenses. Russian pressure, along with popular protest, forced cancellation of the Reuters Concession, and Iran had virtually no railroads until the Trans-Iranian rail was built after World War I.

Opposition to the Reuters Concession came from a coalition of urban groups—ulama, *bazaaris,* and an emerging urban professional class. In 1890 another concession gave a British company a fifty-year monopoly over Iranian tobacco. A popular boycott of tobacco, led by the coalition, forced Nasir al-Din Shah both to quit smoking and to cancel the tobacco concession. During the Constitutional Revolution of 1906–1911, the coalition of religious, commercial, and intellectual elites mobilized the people to demand a constitution and an elected parliament. Muzaffer al-Din Shah (1896–1907) eventually agreed to a new parliament, or *Majlis,* and a constitution, but Muhammad Ali Shah (1907–1909) was openly hostile to the constitution and interfered with the Majlis.

After he was deposed in 1909, the Majlis split between conservatives tied to the ulama and landowners, and reformers favoring secularization, expansion of state-run education, and land reform.

In 1911, a financial advisor from the United States, W. Morgan Schuster, was hired to organize the state's finances, increase tax collection, control spending by the royal family, and increase the effectiveness of revenues from oil royalties. Fearing a strong Iranian state, the Russians sent an ultimatum to force Schuster's dismissal. Chief among British concerns was Iran's petroleum, controlled by the Anglo-Persian Oil Company, formed in 1908, and taken over by the British government in 1914. Through World War I, Iran faced an increasingly chaotic situation, with an ineffective Majlis and a weak ruler, Ahmad Shah (1909–1924), and Russian and British domination of the economy and large amounts of territory.

After World War I ended, Iran was independent and free of foreign occupation, but with virtually no central authority, no trade, and in total financial ruin. Into this situation rode Reza Khan, commander of the Cossack Brigade, who declared himself Reza Shah Pahlavi (1925–1941), and implemented another series of political, economic, institutional, and cultural reforms to strengthen the power of the Shah, and Iran's military and central state, against the ulama, landowners, tribal leaders, ethnic minorities, and the Russians and British. Another US advisor, Arthur Millspaugh, was appointed in 1922. In 1935, Tehran University opened, and women were admitted in 1937. Reza Shah also outlawed the veil in urban areas in 1936, and squads patrolled city streets, harassing those not in compliance. Unveiling went along with new styles of clothing, music, and social interaction. The major economic force in Iran continued to be the Anglo-Persian (Anglo-Iranian after 1935) Oil Company, which controlled all of Iran's exports, paying a minor share of profits directly into the Shah's treasury, a practice that made the Shah wealthy, but promoted more corruption than economic development.

During the 1930s Reza Shah sought better relations with Germany, but after the German invasion of Russia in 1941, the British and Soviets jointly occupied Iran, deposed Reza Shah, and with the United States took over the Trans-Iranian Railway to carry supplies, which caused shortages, inflation, and famine in the countryside. The replacement of Reza Shah with his young son Muhammad Reza Shah (1941–1979) allowed the tribal leaders, ulama, and the Majlis to reassert some autonomy, and following the war, Muhammad Mosaddeq (1882–1967) united a coalition of ulama, urban professionals, nationalists, and parties in the Majlis, which nationalized Iranian oil in 1951. Fearing a communist takeover, and Soviet control of the oil, the US CIA and British MI6 sponsored a coup in August 1953 to remove Mosaddeq, and restore Muhammad Reza Shah's power.

Oil revenues, which rose from less than $300 million in 1960 to $12 billion in 1974, to $49 billion in 1978, fueled the Shah's autocratic rule and grand development projects like his "White Revolution." The White Revolution promised land reform and agricultural development, literacy and education, modernization of institutions and economic development, and changes in the status of women. Ayatollah Ruhollah Khomeini (1902–1989) denounced official corruption and oppression, portraying the Shah as an enemy of religion and a puppet of foreign interests. Khomeini's arrest and exile set off a wave of strikes and protests in Tehran and other cities, which the police and military suppressed with force.

Over the period 1963–1978, Iran's GDP increased an average of 12% per year, fueled by increasing oil revenues and state-sponsored economic programs. The Shah also increased military spending, and US advisors helped train the military and SAVAK, the secret police. Most development during this period came in urban areas, especially Tehran, which more than doubled its population between 1963 and 1978. Expenditure of oil revenues on the military, on large-scale industrial complexes, and on the royal family, meant the people suffered the burdens but saw little direct benefit.

By the mid-1970s, increasingly dependent on his military and secret police, and US support, to maintain his legitimacy, the Shah had alienated a wide spectrum of the Iranian population, including ulama, *bazaaris*, ethnic and religious minorities, and the urban middle class. Since moderate reforms were blocked by the Shah, more radical solutions gained rapid support, in particular communism and Islamism. Jalal Al-e Ahmad wrote of "Westoxication," the poisoning of Iran by Western culture and materialism, while Ali Shariati, who had been educated in France, proposed combining Marxist and Shi'i principles in a revolution for equality and social justice. Shariati advocated emulating Husayn, the martyred grandson of Muhammad, to devote one's life to replacing the corrupt, oppressive regime with one based on authentic Iranian Shi'i civilization.

From exile in Iraq, Ayatollah Khomeini reemerged as the spokesperson of a wide spectrum of opponents of the regime, calling for the overthrow of the Shah in favor of *vilayet-i faqih*, "governance of the jurist," in which parliament and popular sovereignty would be overseen by *mujtahids*, acting in the name of the vanished twelfth Imam. When Khomeini supporters protested in January 1978, security forces opened fire. The deaths set off more protests that grew throughout the

year, and the Shah responded ambivalently, knowing that he was dying of cancer, but uncertain of US support, due to President Jimmy Carter's calls to display greater respect for human rights. The protests of 1978 brought together religious opponents, the Westernized urban middle class, ethnic minorities, and merchants in a coalition similar to that of the 1906–1911 Constitutional Revolution. With the economy crippled, and unsure of the loyalty of his own military, the Shah left Iran on January 16, 1979.

Ayatollah Khomeini returned on February 1 to create an Islamic Republic, a hybrid form of parliamentary government with a Council of Guardians, made up of *mujtahids,* whose duty was to ensure that all legislation passed by the Majlis complied with Islamic doctrine and practices. As Supreme Islamic Jurist for life, Ayatollah Khomeini controlled the Council of Guardians. Khomeini supporters faced violent opposition to their control over Iran. The Revolutionary Guards—the military wing of the Islamic revolution—revolutionary courts, and vigilante groups imprisoned, tortured, and executed opponents, suppressing internal opposition. Women were pushed out of the workforce, while new laws enforced dress codes and segregation of the sexes.

The United States recognized the new government and continued diplomatic relations until November 1979, when students took US citizens hostage following the Shah's admission into the United States for medical care. Fifty-three hostages spent 444 days in captivity, being released only on the day the new US president, Ronald Reagan, was inaugurated.

In September 1980 Iraq invaded Iran, setting off a devastating eight-year-long war that caused about five hundred thousand Iranian casualties and billions of dollars in damage. The end of the war in 1988, and the death of Khomeini in 1989, led to some moderation of revolutionary zeal, and more concentration on economic development during the presidency of Ali Akbar Hashemi Rafsanjani.

Under the Islamic Republic, Iran's economy has remained dependent on oil revenues, but more effort has been devoted to priorities largely ignored by the Shah, including support for the poor and war widows and orphans, investment in agriculture, rural development, and construction of housing. The demand for labor, and loss of men in the war, also allowed women to rejoin the workforce, and female students now comprise about half of Iran's university students.

Still, inflation, shortages, unemployment and underemployment, embargoes, mass emigration of Iran's technical elite, military spending, and the war have all impeded the development of the Islamic Republic. In the presidential elections of 1997 and 2001, Muhammad Khatami, a reformist candidate, won nearly 70% of the vote, especially from women and young voters who had grown up in the Islamic Republic on a platform of reform and opening to the West, although religious conservatives have shown their own continuing power.

At the beginning of the twenty-first century, it appears that two major forces will shape Iran's development in the coming decades: an authoritarian political system, confronting challenges from reform-minded groups seeking restrictions on the power of the supreme leader; and Iran's dependence on the export of petroleum. Thus, the same issues that dominated Iran's development in the twentieth century will continue to shape internal political dynamics and economic development, and Iran's regional and international relations.

JOHN M. VANDERLIPPE

See also Anglo-Iranian Oil Company (AIOC); Iran–Iraq War, 1980-1988; Islam; Islamic Fundamentalism; Khomeini, Ayatollah Ruhollah; Middle East: History and Economic Development; Middle East: International Relations; Mossaddeq, Muhammed; Pahlavi, Shah Muhammed Reza

References and Further Reading

Abrahamian, Ervand. *Iran Between Two Revolutions*. Princeton, NJ: Princeton University Press, 1982.
Beck, Lois, and Guity Nashat, eds. *Women in Iran from 1800 to the Islamic Republic*. Urbana, IL: University of Illinois Press, 2004.
Cordesman, Anthony. *Iran's Military Forces in Transition: Conventional Threats and Weapons of Mass Destruction*. Westport, CT: Praeger, 1999.
Hooglund, Eric, ed. *Twenty Years of Islamic Revolution: Political and Social Transition in Iran since 1979*. Syracuse, NY: Syracuse University Press, 2002.
Katouzian, Homa. *State and Society in Iran: The Eclipse of the Qajars and the Emergence of the Pahlavis*. London: I.B. Tauris, 2000.
Keddie, Nikki. *Roots of Revolution: An Interpretive History of Modern Iran*. New Haven, CT: Yale University Press, 1981.
Mathee, Rudoph. *The Politics of Trade in Safavid Iran: Silk for Silver, 1600–1730*. Cambridge, UK: Cambridge University Press, 1999.
Moghadam, Fatemeh. *From Land Reform to Revolution: The Political Economy of Agricultural Development in Iran, 1962–1979*. London: I.B. Tauris, 1996.
Mottahedeh, Roy. *The Mantle of the Prophet: Religion and Politics in Iran*. New York: Simon & Schuster, 1985.
Nafisi, Azar. *Reading Lolita in Tehran: A Memoir in Books*. New York: Random House, 2003.

IRAN–IRAQ WAR, 1980–1988

The Iran–Iraq War was the most destructive conflict between two neighboring Third World countries in the twentieth century. The cost of the war for Iran amounted to $75–90 billion and for Iraq, $95–112 billion. These figures do not include the cost of military imports, which ranged from $10–12 billion for Iran and $40–50 billion for Iraq. The total casualties of the war (dead and injured) reached 8 million people. The war began on September 22, 1980, when Saddam Hussein's army invaded Iran, and ended, inconclusively, on August 20, 1988. Neither country lost much territory after the termination of the war. In effect, the *status quo ante* was established after eight years of fighting.

The Iranian Revolution of 1978–1979 brought about profound transformations in Iran's domestic and international politics. The new Islamic government in Iran was perceived by Iraq as a threat to its secularist regime. Ayatollah Ruhollah Khomeini's triumphant return to Iran in February 1979 coincided with an upsurge of Shia political activism in Iraq. Numerous anti–Saddam Hussein demonstrations in Iraq's holy cities of Najaf and Karbala were reported in early 1979. Anti-regime demonstrations had even spread to Saddam City (now called Sadr City), the poor Shia neighborhood in Baghdad. The genesis of these demonstrations was purely local as they were organized under the aegis of the Iraqi opposition party al-Da'wa (The Call). However, many demonstrators carried pictures of Khomeini, along with banners containing slogans such as "Yes to Islam, no to Saddam." Moreover, an eminent Shia scholar and the spiritual guide of *al-Da'wa*, Ayatollah Mohammad Baqir al-Sadr, began to publicly support the goals of the Iranian Revolution and expressed hope that similar ideas would take root in Iraq.

In the months preceding the Iraqi invasion of Iran, both countries routinely charged each other with border violations. Such incidents had been common along the Iran–Iraq border regions even before the advent of the Islamic Republic in Iran, and had never been viewed by either side as a *casus belli*. On September 17, 1980, Iraqi leader Saddam Hussein gave a clear signal of what was to follow by denouncing the Algiers Agreement and tearing up a copy of it on television. Ironically, it was Saddam Hussein who had signed that Algiers Agreement in 1975 with the Shah of Iran agreeing to accept the *thalweg* (mid-channel) as the maritime boundary with Iran along the Shatt al-Arab waterway. After unilaterally abrogating the Algiers Agreement, Saddam Hussein proceeded to invade Iran in order to, *inter alia*, conquer Iranian territory, and bring the Shatt al-Arab under total Iraqi control and sovereignty.

During the initial phase of the war, Iraq was able to advance on several fronts into Iranian territory and bomb Iranian military and economic targets. On

September 28, 1980, the UN Security Council passed Resolution 479 urging both sides to declare a cease-fire. Iraq immediately offered to comply if Iran accepted Iraq's complete sovereignty over Shatt al-Arab. Iran, on the other hand, rejected the terms of this resolution so long as the Iraqi forces were in control of Iranian territory. By mid-November, Iraq had captured several major cities, such as Khorram-shahr, in the oil-rich Iranian province of Khuzestan. Beginning in April 1981, the newly reinvigorated Iranian army and irregular forces succeeded in preventing the Iraqi forces from any further advancement into Iran, but they failed to evict the occupying forces. Iraq's successful siege of the city of Abadan, which contained the world's largest refinery, deprived Iran of much-needed revenue from its petroleum resources.

Between March and June 1982, Iran recovered its lost territory as the Iranian forces pushed back the Iraqis across the border. For the first time since the war started, the Iranians were able to inflict heavy casualties on the retreating Iraqi forces. On June 9, 1982, Iraq announced its readiness to accept a cease-fire, but Iran refused to accept the offer unless Saddam Hussein was removed from office. Iran then sought to conquer the southern Iraqi city of Basra in July of that year. The battle for Basra required the deployment of nine full divisions and involved the largest infantry combat since World War II. Throughout the course of the war, Iran tried to reach the strategic Basra–Baghdad highway, but it failed to accomplish this important task. By late February, Iran's most significant military victory came in the battles in the Haur al-Hawizeh marshes and the seizure of Iraq's oil-rich Majnoon Islands.

As the Iranians began to achieve some military victories, the United States decided to support Iraq in order to prevent an Iranian victory that, according to Washington's thinking, would have frightened the United States' client states in the region. The first sign of US tilt toward Iraq came in 1982 when the State Department removed Iraq from the list of countries supporting "international terrorism." This allowed the US to extend some $2 billion in credits to Saddam Hussein's regime, thereby alleviating financial pressures that were pushing Iraq to the edge of bankruptcy. The Reagan administration further extended over $500 million in loans (through the Export- Import Bank and private corporations) to assist Iraq in the construction of an oil pipeline through Jordan.

In 1983, the Reagan administration dispatched Donald Rumsfeld to Baghdad as its personal emissary to meet with Saddam Hussein and cement the burgeoning US–Iraqi ties and to reassure Saddam Hussein of America's continuing support of his war efforts against Iran. The US–Iraqi military ties were strengthened after the November 1984 resumption of diplomatic relations between Washington and Baghdad, which had been severed since the 1967 Arab-Israeli war. From the Iranian perspective, the most disturbing aspect of the US tilt toward Iraq was Washington's indirect encouragement of Iraqi attacks on Iran-bound oil tankers in the Persian Gulf. The Reagan administration also offered naval escorts to tankers in the southern part of the Gulf but not to ships approaching Iran's main oil terminal at Kharg Island.

As the Iran–Iraq War continued to escalate, Kuwait became increasingly aligned with Iraq and Iraqi war efforts. Despite Kuwait's declared neutrality in the Iran–Iraq War, it became evident that Kuwait was not only involved in direct financing of the Iraqi war efforts, but it was also a major transshipment point for Iraqi-bound materials. Furthermore, Kuwaiti, as well as Saudi oil refineries, were providing Iraq's energy needs in its war with Iran. Consequently, the Iranian leadership began to view Kuwait as an active ally of Iraq. Iran's warning to Kuwait to desist from aiding the Iraqi war efforts went unheeded. As Iraq initiated and later escalated the so-called "tanker war" in 1984 by attacking Iran-bound commercial ships, Iran's Supreme Defense Council adopted a policy of responding in kind to every Iraqi attack on Iranian ships. Unable, or unwilling, to dissociate itself from the Iraqi war efforts, Kuwait instead sought protection for its ships from outside powers, especially the United States.

The American decision to reflag (re-register) Kuwaiti ships followed the May 17, 1987, incident in the Persian Gulf when the American frigate USS *Stark* was hit by Iraqi Exocet missiles, killing thirty-seven American sailors. In a memorial service for the dead sailors, President Reagan publicly accepted Iraq's apology for this "inadvertent" attack while blaming Iran as the real villain. In his press conference of May 27, 1987, President Reagan called upon the "barbaric country" of Iran to not interfere with Gulf shipping. The Reagan administration's gratuitous verbal attacks on Iran for Iraq's missile attack on USS *Stark* puzzled the Iranian leadership.

The tension between Iran and Iraq reached new heights in the spring of 1988 in a series of simultaneous Iraqi and US attacks on Iranian targets. By that time, the United States was heavily involved in providing intelligence and logistical support to the Iraqi forces and had become an active belligerent in the war against Iran. On April 18, 1988, American naval forces in the Persian Gulf mounted an air and sea attack on Iranian frigates and oil platforms in response to damage inflicted a few days earlier on a US ship by a mine allegedly laid by Iran. Direct US–Iranian military confrontations in the Gulf boosted Iran's political and diplomatic position by portraying Washington as a direct participant in the Iran–Iraq War, thus damaging US claims of neutrality in the Gulf. Moreover, since the aforementioned US–Iranian clashes coincided with a major Iraqi attack to recapture the Faw peninsula, Iran was convinced that the United States had coordinated its actions with Iraqi forces in order to distract Iran. The Iranian government further accused the United States of providing air support to the Iraqis in their drive toward Faw.

The event that had a profound impact on the course of the Iran–Iraq War was the shooting down of Iran Air flight 655 by the cruiser USS *Vincennes* on July 3, 1988, killing 290 passengers. The United States claimed that the USS *Vincennes* mistook the Airbus jetliner for an F-14 fighter. Furthermore, Washington contended that since hostilities had broken out earlier in the day between US and Iranian forces in the Gulf, the USS *Vincennes* was still in combat mode, and its captain thought that the Iranian passenger airliner was an attacking plane when it failed to respond to warnings issued by the US cruiser. Although the United States expressed regrets about the loss of innocent civilian lives, it began to issue self-serving statements praising the "heroic" US forces in the Gulf. President Reagan called the shooting down of the Iranian passenger jetliner an "understandable accident" because the ship's crew thought they were under attack.

For many Iranians, the shooting down of the unarmed passenger plane was tantamount to "premeditated murder" and demonstrated the immense difficulty of prosecuting the war against Iraq under excruciatingly adverse conditions. The Iranian government contended that Iran Air flight 655 was a regular flight from the Iranian port city of Bandar Abbas to Dubai. The plane was in the usual air corridor, the same route it traversed five times every week in its regularly scheduled flight path. Its schedule was published and available to all parties, including the US forces and USS *Vincennes*.

Furthermore, Iran rejected the US claim that the jetliner should not have been in a war zone. The only declared war zone in the Persian Gulf was the northeast corner of the Gulf. As a self-proclaimed neutral and non-belligerent party in the Iran–Iraq War, the US had no legal right to unilaterally designate war zones in the Persian Gulf. Besides, the air traffic was normally heavy in the Strait of Hormuz, some seven hundred flights having passed over the area in the ten-day period preceding the destruction of the Iranian jetliner.

Given Iran's predicament, it became clear that Tehran was finally going to accept the UN Security Council Resolution 598, which had been passed on July 20, 1987. This resolution called for an immediate cease-fire between Iran and Iraq, a return to internationally recognized boundaries, exchange of prisoners of war, and the establishment of a commission to investigate responsibility for the initiation of the war. Except for the last item, the other provisions of the resolution were identical to the demands of the Iraqi regime. At the time of the passage of Resolution 598, Iraq was on the defensive, its military situation was deteriorating, and Iran was in possession of Iraqi territories along the border areas. But by 1988, conditions had changed, and the tragedy of Iran Air flight 655 had left a profound mark on the Iranian psyche.

Ensuing events, such as Iranian tactical military setbacks, the loss of Iraqi territories held by Iran, worsening economic conditions in Iran, the struggle between the regular armed forces and the Revolutionary Guards over the conduct of the war, and jockeying for power among various factions of the clerical leadership in view of Khomeini's deteriorating health, all led to a major reassessment of Iran's tactics and international posture. On July 18, 1988, Iran formally accepted UN Resolution 598 and a month later the Iran-Iraq War came to an end.

NADER ENTESSAR

See also Hussein, Saddam; Iran; Iraq; Kuwait; Middle East: International Relations

References and Further Reading

Bill, James A. *The Eagle and the Lion: The Tragedy of American–Iranian Relations.* New Haven, CT: Yale University Press, 1988.
Daniel, Elton L. *The History of Iran.* Westport, CT: Greenwood Press, 2001.
Hiro, Dilip. The Longest War: The Iran–Iraq Military Conflict. London: Paladin/Grafton Books, 1989, 1990.
Krosney, Herbert. *Deadly Business: Legal Deals and Outlaw Weapons: The Arming of Iran and Iraq, 1975 to the Present.* New York: Four Walls Eight Windows, 1993.
Mottale, Morris Mehrdad. *The Origins of the Gulf Wars.* Lanham, MD: University Press of America, 2001.
Schaffer, David. *The Iran–Iraq War.* San Diego, CA: Lucent Books/Thomson Gale, 2003.

IRAQ

Iraq, a country of 437,072 square kilometers in Southwest Asia, borders Turkey, Iran, the Persian Gulf, Kuwait, Saudi Arabia, Jordan, and Syria. Its population of 25,374,691 (July 2004 est.) is 75%–80% Arab, 15%–20% Kurdish, and about 5% Turkmen, Assyrian, and other ethnic minorities. About 60%–65% of Iraqis are Shi'i Muslims, and 32%–37% are Sunni.

Before World War I, most of current-day Iraq was ruled by the Ottoman Empire as three separate provinces, Mosul, Baghdad, and Basra. Through the wartime Sykes-Picot Agreement, the British and French agreed to divide the Arab lands between them, and by 1918 the British occupied all of Iraq. To extend control over the northern provinces, the RAF asked Winston Churchill, Lord of the Admiralty, for permission to experiment with chemical weapons against "recalcitrant" Arabs, to which he replied, "I am strongly in favor of using poisonous gas against uncivilized tribes." With a mandate granted by the League of Nations, the British suppressed a 1920 popular uprising demanding independence, resulting in about ten thousand Iraqi casualties. Convinced that direct rule would be too costly, the British installed Faysal, son of the Hashemite Sherif Hussain of Mecca, and leader of the Arab revolt during the war, as king of Iraq, founding a Hashemite dynasty that lasted until the revolution in 1958.

Under the terms of a 1922 treaty, the British continued to rule Iraq indirectly, controlling finances and the military. The British-controlled Iraq Petroleum Company, which had discovered oil before the war, paid royalties of about 15%, but retained all control. In 1932 Iraq gained independence, and a seat at the League of Nations, but British influence remained predominant. Iraqi politics was dominated by the British, the Hashemite kings, and advisors who had risen from modest backgrounds through careers in the Ottoman military before and during the war. The most prominent was Nuri al-Said (1943–1958), who served several terms as prime minister. Sunni Muslims, less than half of the population, held the vast majority of cabinet offices, while Shi'i Muslims and Kurds were underrepresented in political office. In 1923, Shi'i *mujtahids* led protests, while Kurds revolted against central authority periodically throughout the 1920s and 1930s. The military also played an increasingly important role in Iraqi politics. In 1936, General Bakr Sidqi, famous for the 1933 massacre of Assyrian Christians in northern Iraq, led the first of a series of military coups that shaped the Iraqi state in the twentieth century.

Pro-German officers staged a coup on April 1, 1941, but a British force invaded to depose the government of Rashid Ali al-Gaylani, and bring the solidly pro-British Nuri al-Said back to power. From 1941 to 1958, pro-British regimes remained in power, and in 1955, Iraq joined Turkey, Pakistan, and Iran in a western-sponsored, anti-Soviet, joint defense scheme known as the Baghdad Pact. But memories of British interference in "sovereign" Iraq's affairs, combined with the Arab states' poor performance in the 1948–1949 Arab–Israeli War, shaped Iraqi politics in the post-war period.

By the 1950s military officers were secretly organizing to bring about radical change. These officers, generally born after 1918, were inspired by the Egyptian Free Officers' Movement, and saw the Hashemite monarchy as illegitimate. Moreover, in 1958, some 80% of population was landless sharecropping peasants. About 1% of the landowners owned 55% of all private land, while Iraq's tremendous oil wealth remained in the hands of foreign companies until nationalization in 1972.

In July 1958, a coup ended the Hashemite monarchy, with the execution of Faysal II (1939–1958) and Nuri al-Said. The Revolutionary Command Council (RCC) became the center of power as General Abd al-Karim Qasim (1958–1963), son of a small farmer, emerged as the dominant figure in the new government. Qasim began a program of land reform, withdrew from the Baghdad Pact, and established ties with the Soviet Union. Qasim used Iraqi communist support to balance the influence of pan-Arabists, who sought union with Egypt under the leadership of Gamal Abdul Nasser.

Qasim was killed in a coup in 1963, and another coup in 1968 firmly established the power of the Ba'ath (Resurgence) Party. The Ba'ath Party called for Arab unity, the end of western domination, secularism, land reform, expansion of education, women's rights, and state-led economic development, fueled by oil revenues, which reached $476 million in 1968 and $26 billion in 1979.

With the 1968 coup, Ahmad Hasan al-Bakr (1968–1979), chair of the Ba'ath Party, became president, prime minister, and chair of the RCC. His relative and protégé, Saddam Hussein (1979–2001), became vice-chair of the RCC. Saddam Hussein, born in 1937 to landless peasants in the village of Tikirit, had joined the Ba'ath Party in 1957. In 1966, al-Bakr appointed Saddam Hussein secretary general of the party, and from 1968 to 1979 al-Bakr and Hussein established ever-tighter control of the party and state apparatus, purging non-Ba'thists, executing scores of opponents, and promoting relatives and fellow Tikritis to positions of power. Al-Bakr's retirement in 1979 made Hussein president of Iraq, secretary general of the Ba'ath Party, chair of the RCC, and commander-in-chief of the armed forces.

Saddam Hussein's rise to absolute power coincided with the Iranian Revolution, which coincided with revolts by Kurds in the north and Shi'i Muslims in the south. Since World War I, Kurds had revolted periodically against British and Hashemite rule. Mustafa al-Barzani led revolts in the 1960s, and in 1974–1975 with Iranian support. After the revolt ended in 1975, Hussein combined policies of granting the Kurds limited autonomy in northern provinces, while also forcibly resettling about 250,000 Kurds in the Arab south, and manipulating conflicts between Barzani and Jalal Talabani, another Kurdish leader. By the late 1970s Kurds had risen up again, with support from the Islamic Republic of Iran. In 1977 a revolt of Shi'a in the south began, and was one factor in Hussein's decision to invade Iran on September 22, 1980.

Iranian resistance proved stronger than anticipated, and Iranians rallied to stop the Iraqi advance, then pushed the war back into Iraq, before their offensive also bogged down. A war of attrition dragged on until 1988, resulting in about five hundred thousand Iraqi casualties, and about $100 billion in damages. During a final offensive in 1988, the Iraqi air force dropped chemical weapons on the town of Halabja in the northeast, killing about five thousand Kurdish civilians. In 1984, the Iraqis had begun attacking Iranian oil tankers, and Iran retaliated against Kuwaiti and Saudi tankers carrying Iraqi oil. Kuwait and Saudi Arabia loaned Iraq $50–60 billion during the war, and the United States openly sided with Iraq, by reflagging tankers in the final year of the conflict, but also by selling Iraq weapons and supplies of anthrax and other materials needed to build chemical weapons.

Deeply in debt at the end of the war, the Iraqis faced the immediate problem of rebuilding infrastructure and the military, a problem exacerbated by a global oil crash in 1986. Kuwait, which had loaned Iraq money during the war, had also increased its oil production beyond its OPEC quota, thus keeping prices down. Saddam Hussein also accused the Kuwaitis of illegally extracting oil from an oilfield straddling the Iraq–Kuwait border, which added to the fact that Iraq had never recognized the sovereignty of Kuwait. On August 2, 1990, Iraqi forces invaded and occupied Kuwait.

The United States reacted immediately, and strongly, to the invasion and the possibility of an Iraqi invasion of Saudi Arabia, which would mean Iraqi control of about half the planet's petroleum. The United Nations imposed sanctions and a boycott, while the George H. W. Bush administration constructed an international coalition, including nearly all of the Arab states, and more than five hundred thousand US troops, for Operation Desert Shield (the protection of Saudi oilfields), and Desert Storm (the liberation of Kuwaiti oilfields). Saddam Hussein tried to tie the liberation of Kuwait to the liberation of the West Bank and Gaza Strip from Israeli occupation, and during the war, Iraq launched missiles at Israeli cities, in hopes of pulling Arab states away from the coalition.

Less than a day after the UN deadline for withdrawal, the US began the largest aerial assault in history, with six weeks of around-the-clock bombing of military as well as civilian infrastructure targets in Kuwait and Iraq. By the time the ground assault began on February 24, Iraq had virtually no defenses, and the Iraqi military retreated piecemeal up the "highway of death." After one hundred hours, Bush declared Kuwait liberated and the war over, choosing not to continue with an invasion of Iraq.

As the war ended, Shi'a in south and central Iraq and Kurds in the north revolted against the Ba'athist regime. The Iraqi military moved to crush the rebellions, and as troops moved northward, nearly 1.5 million Kurds fled into the mountains, hoping to cross the Iranian or Turkish borders, which remained closed. The US and British governments then imposed "no-fly zones" in the north and south, to protect the rebels and curtail Iraqi sovereignty.

UN sanctions remained in place as inspectors searched Iraq for weapons of mass destruction, and the Ba'athist government tried to obstruct the inspectors and protect its secrets. Under the sanctions, importation of a long list of military and "dual-use" materials, including chlorine, was prohibited. As Saddam Hussein continued to refuse to cooperate with weapons inspectors, the sanctions regime took a huge toll on the Iraqi population. The UN estimated that between 1990 and 2000, more than six hundred thousand people, mostly elderly and children, died as a result of poor hygienic conditions or lack of medicine due to the sanctions. In 1996 the UN agreed to the "oil-for-food" program, which allowed Iraq to begin selling oil in exchange for food and medicine. The oil-for-food program did little to help the Iraqi people, but it did allow the United States to purchase most of the Iraqi oil at below-market prices, and it strengthened Saddam Hussein's position, allowing him to use scarce resources as rewards for loyalty to the regime.

In January 2002, George W. Bush declared Iraq a member of an "Axis of Evil," and claimed the Iraqis could soon deploy nuclear weapons. When the UN and US allies failed to act with sufficient alacrity, the United States and Britain went ahead and invaded Iraq in March 2003, along with a token number of troops and advisors from countries like Japan and Bulgaria. Within weeks of the invasion, the Iraqi government had fallen and Saddam Hussein had fled into hiding. The Coalition Provisional Authority was set up, and on May 1, George Bush landed on an aircraft carrier to announce, famously, "mission accomplished," although "insurgents" opposed to the US-led invasion continued to harass and kill occupation troops, civilian contractors, and Iraqis working with the occupation forces, sometimes kidnapping and beheading their captives.

In June 2004 a new interim government came into being, led by acting Prime Minister Iyad Allawi. In

January 2005 Iraqis went to the polls to elect slates of candidates to form a constitutional assembly, charged with writing a new constitution and overseeing elections to form a new elected government. A slate backed by Ayatollah Ali al-Sistani garnered 48% of the popular vote, not enough for a majority in the assembly, while Kurdish voters in the north overwhelmingly supported the concept of autonomy, and Sunni Arab voters stayed away in large numbers.

Throughout much of the twentieth century, three major challenges confronted Iraq: establishing a viable state, a national identity, and popular loyalty; building political institutions and developing the economy; and ending foreign domination and establishing a sovereign position in the region. With the demise of the Ba'athist government and foreign occupation, Iraq has entered the twenty-first century in much the same situation.

JOHN M. VANDERLIPPE

See also Ba'ath Party; Baghdad Pact; Ethnic Conflicts: Middle East; Hussein, Saddam; Iran–Iraq War, 1980–1988; Kurdistan; Kurds; Middle East: History and Economic Development; Middle East: International Relations; Persian Gulf War, 1991; Persian Gulf War, 2003

Resources and Further Reading

Batatu, Hanna. *The Old Social Classes and the Revolutionary Movements of Iraq.* Princeton, NJ: Princeton University Press, 1978.

Cordesman, Anthony. *Iraq and the War of Sanctions: Conventional Threats and Weapons of Mass Destruction.* Westport, CT: Praeger, 1999.

Farouk-Sluglett, Marion and Peter Sluglett. *Iraq since 1958: From Revolution to Dictatorship,* 3rd ed. London: I.B. Tauris, 2001.

Gunter, Michael. *The Kurdish Predicament in Iraq: A Political Analysis.* New York: St. Martin's, 1999.

Hiro, Dilip. *The Longest War: The Iran–Iraq Military Conflict.* New York: Routledge, 1991.

Lichtmann, Richard. "The Gulf War: Participation in Modernity." In Antonio Callari, et al., eds., *Marxism in the Postmodern Age: Confronting the New World Order.* New York: Guilford Press, 1995, pp. 518–25.

Makiya, Kanan. *Republic of Fear: The Inside Story of Saddam's Iraq.* New York: Pantheon, 1989.

Marr, Phebe. *The Modern History of Iraq.* Boulder, CO: Westview Press, 2004.

Ritter, Scott. *Endgame: Solving the Iraq Crisis,* 2nd ed. New York: Simon & Schuster, 2002.

IRRIGATION

Irrigation is the application of water to the field by any artificial method enabling it to meet the water requirement of a crop at a given time of its vegetative cycle so as to ensure that the crop/plant grows even when there is little or no rainfall. The irrigation water can be supplied from surface water resources such as lakes, rivers, or streams, or from groundwater abstracted from open wells or tubewells.

Water requirement for irrigation is dependent on the type of crops and climatic conditions under which the crops are grown. The latest technology ensures scientific determination of the crop water requirements factoring agronomic and meteorological parameters. Traditionally, China, Egypt, and India (including Sri Lanka) have been practicing irrigated agriculture for several thousands of years.

The methods of irrigation can be broadly classified as:

- Surface irrigation, in which the entire or most crop area is flooded;
- Sprinkler irrigation, which simulates rainfall;
- Drip irrigation, in which water is dripped on to the soil above the root zone only;
- Underground irrigation of the root zone by means of porous pots or pipes placed in the soil; and
- Sub-irrigation, in which the groundwater level is raised sufficiently to dampen the root zone.

Rainfed agriculture refers to the practice of cultivation on land with water input only from the available rainfall (having its vagaries of variation in space and time in certain cases, especially in arid and semi-arid areas). Area suitable for cultivation (whether rainfed or irrigated) is termed as "arable" or "culturable" area. Presently, total cultivated area on Earth is about 1,500 million hectares (Mha), that is, about 12% of total land area. Globally, rainfed agriculture is practised on about 83% of cultivated land, and supplies about 60% of the world's food. In other words, from only about 17% of the area that is irrigated, over 40% of the food is produced. In water-scarce tropical regions such as the Sahelian countries, rainfed agriculture is practised on more than 95% of cropland. The risks of crop reduction from rainfed agriculture, however, are more on account of droughts and dry spells. To reduce such risk, the option of supplementary irrigation has proved better.

Globally, while an annual increase of 4 to 5 million hectares of irrigated area was recorded between 1950 and 1980, this fell to just around 2 million hectares per year in the 1990s and later. Reasons for this include rising capital cost to reclaim lands that are relatively more difficult for irrigation, impacts of commodity prices resulting in low returns on investment, problems of operation and maintenance, low efficiency of water use, low level of water charges and hence revenues, increase in soil salinity levels, siltation, and so forth. To a sizeable extent, donor funding for works launched in developing countries was curtailed after 1990. However, it is being realized that food security would be feasible only with interventions in and support to appropriate irrigated agriculture.

Irrigated agriculture produces 4 to 8 times higher yields than rainfed, besides playing a major role in providing food sufficiency and security as well as in poverty alleviation. It also helps to protect the rainfed crops of the rural people from natural disasters such as droughts and famines. The poor landless people find employment opportunities in construction and maintenance works of irrigation schemes, while the increased agricultural yields mostly from irrigated areas and overall infrastructural improvements help to attract investments in rural agro-based industries. The World Food Summit, 1996, estimated that 60% of additional food required to sustain the world population in the future must come from irrigated agriculture, which needs more investments and sustained efforts at expansion and improvement. For arid and semi-arid areas, irrigation is an essential input for farming, even during the rainy season. Provision of irrigation facilities and watershed development in rainfed areas together can make the agriculture in a river basin sustainable and more productive.

About 70% of freshwater resources are being used globally by the agriculture sector, which nevertheless generates food for the ever-increasing population, especially in the developing countries in the African and Asian continents. However a competition is growing from the "people" and "environment" sectors for more water allocations. Techniques for increasing the efficiency of water use in irrigation to generate "more crop per drop" are therefore currently being devised. Projections, however, indicate that even with optimistic views about productivity growth, efficiency, and the expansion of irrigated area, 14% more water will be needed for irrigated agriculture in the developing countries by 2030 to cope up with the needs of increasing population by that time. This will require some 220 billion cubic meters of extra storage.

Presently, a total of about 272 million hectares of land are being irrigated throughout the world. The growth of irrigation in India and China has been exceptional. These two countries are the world leaders in irrigated agriculture and together form over 40% of the world's total irrigated area. The table below presents some salient irrigation- and drainage-related figures for prominent agricultural countries.

Drainage of irrigated lands is an important activity that should receive more attention in the coming decades in order to ensure consolidation of the gains of productivity both from irrigated and rainfed cultivable areas. Not all the irrigated areas are presently covered by adequate drainage, affecting the sustainability of agriculture by way of loss of land due to waterlogging, salinity, and so forth. The International Commission on Irrigation and Drainage (ICID) has focussed particular attention on promoting the best practices regarding irrigation and drainage by water management and water savings, besides measures to improve drainage (including bio-drainage), in recent times.

Table 2: Agricultural statistics for ten countries with largest irrigated and drained area

Country	Population (millions)	% of population economically active in agriculture	Total area (million ha)	Arable land (million ha)	Irrigated area (million ha)	Drained area (million ha)
India	1,050	59	329	170	55	5.8
China	1,288	66	960	136	54	20
USA	287	2	963	179	22	48
Pakistan	144	47	80	22	18	6
Iran	66	26	165	16	8	0.04
Mexico	102	21	196	27	7	5.2
Thailand	63	56	51	18	5	0.15
Indonesia	217	48	190	34	5	0.27
Russia	144	10	1,708	127	5	7.4
Turkey	67	46	78	27	5	3.14
Total	3,426		4,718	755	184	96
World	6,215		13,425	1,497	272	190

From International Commission on Irrigation and Drainage, 2004.

The status of water management systems (supply infrastructure, drainage, irrigation) in agricultural cultivation in different continents is seen in the table below.

While water is an essential input for agriculture, it also needs other inputs like fertilisers, pesticides, seeds, cold-storage facilities, animal/mechanical power, animal husbandry services, market, transportation, electric power, credit, agricultural implements, and services for maintenance.

The establishment of Water Users Associations (WUAs) and transferring responsibility for operation and maintenance of irrigation systems to the associations has been considered a desirable intervention to promote local management of irrigation systems with a strong emphasis on farmers' participation. The participatory irrigation management (PIM) refers to the involvement of irrigation users in all aspects and at all levels of irrigation management. This includes planning, design, construction, maintenance, and financing for the main irrigation system and all subsystems.

Though India has a large irrigated area, the contribution from the irrigated area to the food basket is placed at 52%; the remaining 48% is attributable to rainfed area. Effective water management in irrigated agriculture has assumed significance for the last two decades as water is becoming a scarce commodity and has divergent claimants from various other sectors. The requirements of environment (nature sector) can be aptly addressed if the irrigation water requirement for food security could be reduced with better management practices, thereby sparing water for other purposes like the Nature and People sectors. This is all the more important for the developing world where the present level of managerial efficiencies is low and water management must have a broader scope. Every country needs to set up its own policies and institutional structures to deal with water in the wider context of national welfare.

The Earth Summit Declaration adopted by 178 participating countries at Rio de Janeiro in June 1992 had addressed the need for ensuring adequate food and water for all people on this globe. Among other requirements, crop production must increase by 3%–4% per annum, mainly by increasing the productivity of irrigated lands. Demands for available freshwater have increased due to growth of population and improved lifestyle. Irrigation requirements for the food sector are largely consumptive. Larger increases are projected in the developing countries in order to meet food security as most of the food produced in these countries is consumed locally. Countries like India and China pursue a policy of self-sufficiency in food.

The water diversions for irrigated agriculture and their significant use for irrigation have been viewed in some quarters to be in conflict with the requirements of environmental protection. In fact, in the hydrological cycle, water unused by plants returns back to surface water runoff or infiltrates to augment groundwater. The water used by the plant also returns mostly to the atmosphere by the process of evapotranspiration or remains as a part of the biomass. ICID endeavours to promote the best practices in irrigation and drainage as well as activities for water saving to ensure more crop per drop of water used in irrigation.

Table 3: Status of water management in agricultural cultivation practices in different continents and categories of countries

Continent	Total area in 10^6 ha	Arable land in 10^6 ha	Total population in millions	Water management practice in % of the arable land		
				No system	Drainage [1]	Irrigation [2]
Asia	3,339	547	3,765	56	10	35
Africa	3,031	201	840	92	2	6
Europe	2,299	307	732	77	15	8
Americas	4,016	384	850	72	17	11
Oceania	856	55	31	91	4	5
World	13,425	1,497	6,215	69	13	18
Developed countries	3,877	445	1,137	67	22	11
Developing countries	7,231	903	4,332	69	8	23
Least developed countries	2,433	145	750	87	2	12

From International Commission on Irrigation and Drainage, 2004

[1] In total about 130 million hectares of rainfed areas and 60 million hectares of irrigated areas have drainage.

[2] Irrigation may include drainage as well.

Country-Specific Issues of Development and Management in Irrigation

India

India is a large country in South Asia that ranks second in the world in population, next to China, and ranks seventh in the world in land area. The total geographical area of the country is 328.73 million hectares. Agriculture provides about a third of India's national income. Compared with the total geographical area of 328.73 million hectares, the net sown area is 142.5 million hectares (about 77% of the cultivable area in the country). The rainfall in India is confined to three to four months in a year in the form of a monsoon season and varies from ten centimeters in the western parts of Rajasthan to over one thousand centimeters in Cherrapunji in Meghalaya. The principal water resources used in India come from surface waters through rivers and streams, and groundwater. It has been estimated that out of the total precipitation of about 400 million hectare meters (Mham), the water availability is about 186.9 Mham. The average yearly utilisable water resource is estimated at 690 billion cubic meters (BCM). Ninety percent of the groundwater assessed at 432 BCM. is considered for exploitation for irrigation, drinking, and other uses.

Since 1947 when India became independent from British colonial rule, rapid strides in irrigation have taken place with the planned development adopted by India. The initial successive plans assigned a major investment for this purpose until the 1990s. Irrigation development in India has a judicious mix of major, medium, and minor irrigation schemes depending on project location, economic viability, and environmental consideration for equitable and sustainable development. This classification is based on size of projects with major, medium, and minor projects covering irrigated areas of over ten thousand hectares (ha), between two thousand and ten thousand ha, or less than two thousand ha, respectively. As a result of this development, irrigation potential has been planned to go up to about 101 million hectare (Mha) as compared with 22.6 Mha at the time of independence. Food grain production, which was a meager 51 million tonnes (MT) at that time, has increased four fold to about 212 MT at this writing. This has made the country not only self-sufficient, but also an exporter of the food grains. It has been estimated that as much as 52% of the rise in food grain production has been solely on account of an increase in irrigated area.

India has created a total live storage capacity of about 177 BCM. Dams to create additional live storage of 75 BCM are under various stages of construction.

The dams under formulation/consideration will provide an additional live storage of 132 BCM. The present and projected pattern of water utilisation is shown below:

Table 4: Water Utilisation Patterns

Purpose	Present Utilisation (1997)	Future Utilisation (2025)
Irrigation	501	611
Domestic	30	62
Industry	20	67
Energy	20	33
Others	34	70
Total	605	843

All values in the table are in billion cubic meters.

The ultimate irrigation potential in the country is estimated to be 139.9 Mha of which 58.48 Mha. have been developed. The gross irrigated area is 120 Mha and the gross irrigated area under food and non-food crops is 90 Mha. The rainfed area in the country is 110 Mha of which the gross area under food crops is 72 Mha. During the period 2003–2004, the food grain production was 216 million tonnes. The demand for food in the future (year 2025) is estimated to be on an average 345 million tonnes. The country has a comprehensive National Water Policy, April 2002, which among other things addresses all aspects pertaining to irrigation, while the National Agriculture Policy and National Environmental Policy address areas of pertinent interest that affect them.

China

The People's Republic of China is a country in Eastern Asia with the world's largest population. The rainfall in China varies greatly. The deserts of Xinjian and inner Mongolia receive less than 100 mm of rainfall. Southern China receives 1,000 mm of annual rainfall, while the rainfall is 630 mm in Beijing. Agriculture production is the backbone of China's economy. China can be divided into three zones (not counting Qingzang cold plateau, which has no agricultural production)—the perennial irrigation zone where the average precipitation is less than 400 mm, the unsteady irrigation zone where the average annual precipitation is between 400 mm and 1,000 mm, and the supplementary irrigation zone where the average annual precipitation is more than 1,000 mm. The total internal water resources of China are estimated to be about 2800 BCM, out of which 460 BCM are withdrawn. The irrigated area of the country stands at 54 Mha. Of this area, 51.16 Mha are farmland, 2.31 Mha are forest and orchard irrigation area, 0.81 Mha are grazing land irrigation area, and 0.467 Mha are for other purposes. The number of reservoirs in the country is 84,905, with a total capacity of 457.1 BCM. Out of these reservoirs, 394 are large reservoirs with storage of 72.4 BCM and 81,893 are small reservoirs with storage of 58.6 BCM. There are more than five thousand large and medium-sized irrigation districts in China, which are the main production areas for commodity food and cash crops. In China, irrigation is managed according to the "Regulations for Irrigation Area Management" stipulated by the Ministry of Water Resources.

The Fourth Session of the Eighth National People's Congress of China approved the Ninth Five-Year Plan for National Economic and Social Development and the long-range objectives up to the year 2010. The reform in the water sector in China is focussed on the establishment of five management systems, namely:

- Multi-channel, multi-level investment system;
- Scientific and complete water assets operation and management system;
- Rational and complete pricing system;
- Complete and effective legal and regulation system; and
- High-quality and efficient service system.

Pakistan

Pakistan is a nation in southern Asia that has India, China, Afghanistan, and Iran as its neighbours. The present population of Pakistan is 145 million (2001 est.). The total geographical area of Pakistan is 79.61 Mha. Punjab and Sind are the two provinces in which the real agricultural wealth of Pakistan lies. These areas fall in the Indus Basin. Pakistan has agricultural land potential of about 28.39 Mha. Rainfalls in the country vary spatially—less than ten cm in some parts and more than 50 cm in the other parts. Most of the rainfall occurs during the monsoon period (July to September). The contribution of rain to crops in the irrigated areas of the Indus Basin has been estimated at about 7.4 BCM. The flows of the Indus rivers system constitute the major surface water resources of Pakistan. The average runoff of these rivers is about 199 BCM. The estimated usable groundwater potential in the country is 66.6 BCM. About 95% of the country's water resources are used for agriculture. The total cropped area in the country is 23.04 million hectares. The present irrigation system comprises three storage reservoirs, twenty-one barrages or headworks, twelve inter-river long canals, two major siphons, and forty-five main canals. The annual water withdrawn from canals for irrigation is presently about 140 BCM. To stagger the peak flows, three surface reservoirs have been constructed in the past. These are the Mangla reservoir constructed in 1967 on River Jhelum with a live storage capacity of 6.6 BCM, Chashma reservoir on the Indus constructed in 1971 with a capacity of 0.6 BCM, and Tarbela on the Indus constructed in 1975 with a capacity of 11.5 BCM.

The chemical quality of water from the rivers is excellent for irrigation. The quality of groundwater is highly variable in various parts of the country, ranging from completely fresh to extremely saline. In total, 60% of the Indus plain is underlain by useable groundwater. In order to achieve the envisaged growth target in agriculture, irrigation water requirements as estimated for the year 2000 and 2013 would be 176.5 and 254.6 BCM (143.1 and 206.4 Ministry of Agriculture and Forestry [MAF]), respectively. With the three major dams completed, the water availability for the future has been estimated to be 156.2 BCM (126.6 MAF) in the year 2025.

Iran

The Islamic Republic of Iran is situated in the middle-east region of southwestern Asia. The population of Iran is about 71 million (2001). The estimated population for the years 2008, 2021, and 2050 is likely to be 83.5 million, 100 million, and 129.5 million, respectively. About 52% of the country consists of mountains and deserts. Out of the total land area of 165 Mha, 51 Mha are cultivable. The Caspian Sea Coast is Iran's only region of abundant rainfall at 1600 mm per year. The average rainfall in the country is 250 mm. Agriculture accounts for about 12% of the country's GNP and deploys about 36% of the workers. Only about 12% of the land can be farmed. Wheat and barley are grown on about 75% of the cultivated land. Internal renewable water resources of Iran are estimated at 128.5 km^3 per year. Surface runoff represents a total of 97.3 km^3 per year and groundwater recharge is estimated at about 49.3 km^3 per year. The water withdrawal from surface area is in the order of 38.3 km^3 per year, while that from groundwater is 43.3 km^3 per year.

Based on a comprehensive water study for Iran (Jamab 1996), with proven sources of water that can be extracted using the country's present technology in the main water basins, it is estimated that an amount of 121 km^3/year of water can be supplied by the year 2021. Of this, 46.5 km^3/year will consist of groundwater and the remaining 74.5 km^3/year of surface water.

This forms 88% of the total renewable water resources of the country, which can be considered as the ultimate development of these resources. Presently, an area of 8.84 Mha in Iran is irrigated while 9.66 Mha is rainfed. The agricultural land availability is not a constraint in the development of irrigated agriculture. The irrigable land is estimated at more than 12 Mha. The policy of the Islamic Republic of Iran is that agriculture should become the center and pivot of all development activities. The main qualitative objectives of the water sector in the five-year plans are:

- Securing the water requirements of the various sectoral users of water;
- Increased efficiency in water resource use; and
- Strengthening decision making and management capability in the water sector.

(Source: International Commission on Irrigation and Drainage [ICID])

See also Pollution, Agricultural; Pollution, Industrial; Water Resources and Distribution

References and Further Reading

Abrams, Len. "Water for Basic Needs." *1st World Water Development Report*. Water Policy International,: 2000, 2001.
Conley, A. H. "To Be or Not to Be? South African Irrigation at the Crossroads." In M. Kay, T. Franks, and L. Smith, eds., *Water: Economics, Management and Demand*. London: E & FN Spon, 1997.
Dhawan, B. D. *Irrigation in India's Agricultural Development*. New Delhi: Sage, 1988.
———. *Trends and New Tendencies in Irrigated Agriculture*. New Delhi: Sage, 2003.
Food and Agricultural Organization of the United Nations. *Crops and Drops: Making the Best Use of Water for Agriculture*. Rome: Author, 2002. http://www.fao.org/documents/show_cdr.asp?url_file=/DOCREP/005/Y3918E/Y3918E00.HTM
Jackson,-C. 1998. "Gender, Irrigation, and Environment: Arguing for Agency." *Agric. Human Values*, 15 (4) pp. 313–324.
Loker, William M., ed. *Globalization and the Rural Poor in Latin America*. Boulder, CO: Lynne Rienner Publishers, 1999.
Mabry, Jonathan B., ed. *Canals and Communities: Small-Scale Irrigation Systems*. Tucson, AZ: University of Arizona Press, 1997.
Merrey, Douglas, J. and P. G. Somaratne. *Institutions Under Stress and People in Distress: Institution-Building and Drought in a New Settlement Scheme*. Colombo, Sri Lanka: International Irrigation Management Institute, 1988.
Postel, S. *Pillar of Sand: Can the Irrigation Miracle Last?* London: W.W. Norton, 1999.
Rosegrant, Mark W. and Mark Svendsen. "Asian Food Production in the 1990s: Irrigation Investment and Management Policy." *Food Policy*, Vol. 18, No. 1, pp. 13–32.
Van Koppen, B. *More Jobs per Drop: Targeting Irrigation to Poor Women and Men*. Amsterdam: Royal Tropical Institute, 1998.
Wade, Robert. "Irrigation Reform in Conditions of Populist Anarchy: An Indian Case." *Journal of Development Economics* 14 (3), pp. 285–303.
Zwarteveen, M. Z. "Water: From Basic Need to Commodity: A Discussion on Gender and Water Rights in the Context of Irrigation." *World Development*, Vol. 25. No. 8, pp. 1335–1349.

ISLAM

Basic Facts

With a 2004 estimate of 1.48 billion followers, Islam is the religion of roughly 23% of the world's population (based on CIA Fact Sheet 2004). Most Muslims live in the region that extends from North Africa to Southeast Asia, but Muslim minorities across Europe and the Americas are the second- or third-largest religious communities (Esposito 1999, p. 690). Islam comprises people from almost every ethnicity, including Arabs (19%), Turks (4%), Indians/Pakistanis (24%), Africans (17%), and Southeast Asians (15%). The largest Muslim population is in Indonesia (194 million), and the largest number of Muslim minorities live in India (150 million), China (38 million), Russia (28 million), France (6 million), and the United States (6 million). Most Muslims in non-western countries are indigenous nationals who belong to the local ethnicity and culture. However, the majority of Muslims living in the West are educated immigrants who migrated for various reasons related to the phenomenon of "brain drain" from their original countries.

Muslims believe in the absolute oneness of God, the prophethood of Muhammad (570–632 CE), and the Qur'an as the final message from God to humankind as revealed to Muhammad (The Holy Qur'an, Chapter 33: Verse 40). Muslims grew from a small and oppressed group in Mecca, now in western Saudi Arabia, at the beginning of the seventh century to an established "Islamic State" that overpowered both the Roman and Persian empires by the end of the same century. Islam, then, became the religion of a variety of cultures and a flourishing civilization that spanned over the medieval centuries. The early postprophetic era, however, witnessed violent tribal disputes in Arabia, which eventually led to the formation of a few politico-religious sects within Islam in addition to the Sunni mainstream (92% of Muslims), namely, Shia or Twelvers (now 5.8% of Muslims, mainly in Iran, Iraq, and Lebanon), Ibaddis or Kharijites (now 1% of Muslims, mainly in Oman), Zaidis (now 1% of Muslims, mainly in Yemen), and Alawites (now 0.1% of Muslims, mainly in Syria). Eventually, the Islamic State's internal problems, especially political dictatorship, patriarchy, and racial disputes, led to severe deterioration, colonization from outside powers, and ultimate disintegration by the late nineteenth century. The second half of the twentieth century witnessed widespread political liberalization and initiation of modern processes of development across the Muslim world (Esposito 1999, p. 643).

Islam and Development

According to the 2004 United Nations Development Program (UNDP) report, most Islamic countries (i.e., countries with a Muslim majority) rank within the "medium" range of the comprehensive Human Development Index (HDI), which is calculated using indexes of life expectancy, enrollment in education, and standard of living. However, some Islamic countries, specifically the oil-rich Arab states, rank comparatively much higher in terms of income per capita and much lower in terms of female literacy and Gender Empowerment Measure (GEM), which includes women's political participation, economic participation, and power over resources (UNDP 2004, p. 221). In addition to Muslim minorities who live in developed countries, countries with Muslim majorities that were ranked under "high human development" are Brunei, Bahrain, Kuwait, Qatar, and United Arab Emirates (which collectively represent less than 1% of Muslims). The bottom of the HDI list includes Yemen, Nigeria, Mauritania, Djibouti, Gambia, Senegal, Guinea, Ivory Cost, Mali, and Niger (which collectively represent around 10% of Muslims).

Islam is both a belief system and a comprehensive way of life that governs Muslims as individuals, families, and societies. Islamic principles in the form of prescribed "good deeds" and forbidden immoralities play a constructive role, from a development perspective. However, historical interpretations of Islamic scripts that evolved into established traditions in some predominantly Muslim countries do impede development, especially in the areas of politics and women's rights. Nevertheless, modern Islamic scholarship seeks reform through novel reinterpretation theories. Numerous Islamic organizations embrace these theories and work on the ground to materialize reform. However, there is a need for more theoretical investigation of the concept of development itself in non-western Islamic contexts. The following paragraphs will elaborate on these topics.

Principles Conducive to Human Development

The Qur'an views humankind as vicegerents on Earth, whose mission is "betterment and reform" (for example, Qur'an 11:88, 26:152). The Qur'an also states, "let there be no compulsion in religion," "the noblest of humankind is the best in conduct," "no bearer of burdens can bear the burden of another," "stand out firmly for justice, even as against yourselves, or your parents, or your kin, and whether it be against rich or poor," "male or female: you are members, one of another," "if the enemy inclines toward peace, do you also incline toward peace, and trust in God," and that dialogue is "the means that is best" (Qur'an 2:256, 49:13, 17:15, 4:135, 3:195, 8:61, 29:46, respectively). Based on these verses and others, a Universal Islamic Declaration of Human Rights was announced in 1981 by a large number of scholars who represented various Islamic entities at the United Nations Educational, Scientific, and Cultural Organization (UNESCO). Supported by a number of Islamic scripts mentioned in its references section, the declaration contains all basic rights declared in the Universal Declaration of Human Rights (UDHR), such as rights to life, freedom, equality, justice, fair trial, protection against torture, asylum, freedom of belief and speech, free association, education, and freedom of movement (Bora Laskin Law Library 2004). However, since 1981, a debate is still alive, especially in the United Nations High Commission for Human Rights (UNHCHR), on whether this Islamic declaration "gravely threatens the inter-cultural consensus on which the international human rights instruments were based" or whether Islam "adds new positive dimensions to human rights, since, unlike international instruments, it attributes them to a divine source thereby adding a new moral motivation for complying with them" (UNHCHR 2003).

On the practical level, there are specific "acts of worship" that Islam prescribes that could contribute to human development. These are, for example, seeking and teaching knowledge, spending and consuming moderately, sponsoring orphans, forgiving debts, assisting the disabled, ensuring hygiene, helping one's relatives and neighbors, treating prisoners of wars kindly, avoiding transgression, being "kind and just" to those of a different religion, and annual donating up to 10% of every Muslim's wealth, which is given to the needy in society and other social causes (for example, Qur'an 2:177–179, 17:23–38).

Additionally, all forms of corruption are considered "major sins" in Islam, such as bribery, conflict of interest, fraud, and the use of one's political power for personal gains. The prophet Muhammad was reported to have judged whether an employee has a right to accept a certain gift by asking whether that employee would still have been offered the gift if he or she had never been employed.

Historical Interpretations Impeding Development

Despite the strong moral ideals of the Qur'an listed above, some verses of the Qur'an had been interpreted in ways that serve certain agendas of dictatorship, patriarchy, or violence. For example, the Qur'an states: "To those against whom war is made, permission is given to fight, because they are wronged; and verily, God is most powerful for their aid. They are those who have been expelled from their homes unjustly" (Qur'an 22:39–40). These verses and similar ones had been interpreted a millennium ago to mean that the entire world is divided into two exclusive zones, the "land of Islam" and the "land of war," which are expressions mentioned nowhere in the scripts themselves. Other verses that encouraged Muslims to fight "for the sake of the oppressed" (Qur'an 4:75) are claimed to have abrogated (i.e., legally annulled) all other verses that advocated mercy, cooperation, and dialogue with any non-Muslim. These binary classifications of the world are still endorsed by some violent political groups.

Certain verses of the Qur'an that encourage Muslims to respect and cooperate with their leaders in addition to verses that mention "security" as a blessing from God are repeatedly interpreted to mean that loyalty to de facto rulers is an Islamic obligation, regardless of their conduct. Therefore, seeking to change unjust leaders, even through peaceful means, is considered an act of deviance that "jeopardizes the blessing of security." Similar interpretations, historically popularized by the Abbasid dynasty (758–1258 CE), sanction tribal monarchies as the only form of acceptable Islamic regimes and go further to claim that a Muslim ruler should be only from "noble Arab lineages." Based on these interpretations, resources in some Muslim countries are distributed over citizens based on their lineages, and "noble" rulers have the right to make dictatorial decisions. "Mutual consultation" (Qur'an 42:38), which is a clear Islamic instruction, is interpreted to mean that the ruler should consult the ruled, but without being under any obligation to follow what they choose.

Other verses, which specifically advised Prophet Muhammad's female followers to take certain precautions during Medina's revolts, around 624 CE, to protect themselves from assaults (Qur'an 33:59), are often taken out of their historic context to entail that all women are to be "protected" by isolating them from places of work and even mosques. Such interpretations further render women incapable of making political, legal, financial, or personal choices, or even driving cars. Examples of Muslim groups that have subscribed to such opinions are the Taliban, former rulers of Afghanistan, and the Wahhabis, an extreme Sunni trend influential in Saudi Arabia.

Modern Interpretations and Reform

An Islamic reform movement has been initiated that rejects extreme traditional interpretations, redefining many basic Islamic concepts, and modernizing the Islamic law itself. Fazlur-Rahman, for example, criticized medieval Islamic thought for not producing "a single work of ethics squarely based upon the Qur'an, although there are numerous works based on Greek philosophy" (Fazlur-Rahman 1979:257). He called for a contemporary interpretation of the Qur'an based on ethics and reform of the Islamic law to emphasize "purposes" rather than "quantified actions." Abdul-Karim Soroush supported new interpretations of the Qur'an that differentiated between verses that are "functions of a cultural, social and historical environment" and other verses that are universal (Kurzman 1998:248). Contemporary Islamic reform started across the Islamic world one century ago with "modernist" Islamic scholars, as will be explained next.

In the first half of the twentieth century, a number of Islamic reformists "sought to reconcile Islamic faith and modern values, such as constitutionalism, as well as cultural revival, nationalism, freedom of religious interpretation, scientific investigation, modern-style education, women's rights, and a bundle of other themes" (Kurzman 2002, p. 4). Two key pioneers of modern Islamic reform are Mohammad Abduh (1849–1905), the Chief Egyptian Mufti at his time, educated in both Al-Azhar and France, and Mohammad Iqbal (1877–1938), an Indian poet-lawyer-philosopher educated in England and Germany. Both scholars, from both geographical sides of the Islamic world, integrated their Islamic and western education into proposals for Islamic reform. A common theme in both proposals was the reinterpretation and reconstruction of

Islamic thought. Iqbal distinguished between universal principles of Islam, on one hand, and their relative interpretation in practical life, on the other. Abduh wrote a Qur'anic exegesis based on a direct understanding of the Qur'an's Arabic language and without quoting any previous exegete for the first time in Islamic scholarship history.

Through new interpretations of the Qur'an, Abduh and his student, Qassim Amin (1863–1908), promoted education of girls and women, restriction of polygamy, and granting Muslim women divorce rights (Kurzman 2002, p. 61). Their writings eventually influenced Egyptian laws and many other Muslim legal systems. Qasim Amin's book, Liberation of Women, published in 1899, initiated women's liberation literature in the Arab world as well as Iran, after its translation into Persian in 1900. Interestingly, women's rights movements in Iran also started due to the works of modernist Islamic (male) scholars. For example, Ahmad Kasravi Tabrizi (1880–1946), originally from Azerbaijan, called for academic and political freedoms and the equality of women and men in education. At present, women's rights activists in the Muslim world are typically women in both Islamic and secular establishments, who promote more advanced forms of social and political equality and development (Krause 2005).

Whether Islam is a "religion that has a political character" is a question posed in 1925 by Ali Abdel-Raziq (1888–1966), an Azhari judge and Oxford graduate, and the topic has sparked heated debates since. In a strong reinterpretation style, Abdel-Raziq quoted numerous Quranic verses and prophetic traditions to prove that Prophet Muhammad had only had "authority as a prophet and not dominion as king, caliph or sultan" (Kurzman 2002, p. 32). Abdel-Raziq's view was that the Islamic law is neutral about political systems; hence, Muslim societies are free to choose any political system they deem suitable, without making any political system an "Islamic obligation." These new interpretations opened up possibilities for Islamic scholars after Abdel-Raziq to call for changing dominant monarchical systems throughout the Islamic world, which have been supported by traditional Islamic interpretations.

Present-day popular Muslim politicians, such as Mohammad Khatami, Iran's fifth president; Benazir Bhutto, former president of Pakistan and the first Muslim female president in modern history; Rachid Ghannouchi, founder of the Tunisian Renaissance Islamic Party; and several others, all have supported democracy and democratic practices based on new interpretations of the Islamic scripts (Khatami 1998; Kurzman 1998). Abdulaziz Sachedina, an Islamic scholar from the University of Virginia, recently explored the "Islamic roots of democratic pluralism" in the Qur'an and evidences of "civil society" in the early Muslim community that Prophet Muhammad formed in order to "legitimize modern secular ideas of citizenship in the Muslim political culture" (Sachedina 2001, p. 132)

Islamic Organizations that Contribute to Development

The above Islamic principles of justice and charity and modern interpretations of social equality and political reform inspire numerous Islamic organizations across the Muslim world. These organizations, in effect, contribute to the process of human development in the Muslim world even though they might not have specific agendas for development per se. Organizations are thereby categorized as Islamic if they are attached to mosques or announce mission statements or projects that signify religious Islamic goals. Examples of such organizations are given below.

A large number of organizations across the developing world operate through local mosques in order to offer literacy programs, basic health care, orphan-sponsoring projects, and charity collection and distribution programs. Besides contributing to human well-being, these organizations are indirectly contributing to the process of political liberalization, civil society expansion, and "democratization from below" (Krause 2005). Moreover, several organizations directly promote democracy, minority rights, and cross-cultural dialogue in the Muslim world on an Islamic basis, through academic publications, public lectures, activist awards, and research workshops. Specifically active is the Washington-based think-tank, Centre for the Study of Islam and Democracy (CSID), the National Endowment for Democracy (NED), and the Ibn Khaldun Center for Development Studies.

Muslim women's organizations also contribute to the process of social reform. An important example is Women Living Under Muslim Laws (WLUML), an international solidarity organization that rejects unjust laws and customs resulting from different interpretations of Islamic religious texts and the political use of Islam. Another example is the Sisterhood Is Global Institute (SGI), in Jordon, which led a campaign to outlaw honor killing as un-Islamic. Its founder, Jordanian lawyer Asma Khader, was acknowledged by an award from the United Nations Development Program in 2003.

Theoretical Considerations for Development

The concept of development is a product of western modernism and has been shaped over the past five centuries by the European and American models. Muslim scholars and politicians have dealt with this concept in a spectrum of ways, although two extreme and rather popular positions can be identified. Traditional Islamic scholars and extreme Islamic political groups reject the concept of development altogether based on its western origin and "centricity" (i.e., self-projection), a critique interestingly similar to the western postmodernist critique. On the other hand, several modern reformers and politicians in the Islamic world, in addition to some western politicians, invite Muslims to give up their heritage and follow the modern western development model as the only way to achieve prosperity and solve their problems. As popular as they are, neither of the two positions has been able to achieve a balance between development values, which has attained an undisputed success in the West, and the Islamic heritage, which represents the core religious and cultural identity of Muslims. Muslim countries cannot prosper if they continue to view the world through medieval eyes and ignore the valuable experience of western development. On the other hand, asking Muslims to dissolve into another's cultural paradigm is ethnocentric, unsympathetic, and unrealistic. There is a need for Muslim thinkers and politicians to absorb the western experience and integrate its lessons of development into their Islamic heritage and identity. The concept of "human development," as proposed by the United Nations, could be a basis for this much-needed middle ground. Human development, the 2004 UNDP report states, is about "rejecting claims that cultural differences necessarily lead to social, economic and political conflict" (UNDP 2004, p. v). Human development is about realizing basic human rights, for which Islam called fourteen centuries ago.

GASSER AUDA

See also Brain Drain; Islamic Fundamentalism; Taliban; United Nations Development Program (UNDP); Universal Declaration of Human Rights; Women Living Under Muslim Laws (WLUML)

References and Further Reading

Bora Laskin Law Library, University of Toronto. "International Protection of Human Rights." http://www.law-lib.utoronto.ca/resguide/humrtsgu.htm (2004).
Centre for the Study of Islam and Democracy (CSID). http://www.islam-democracy.org
Esposito, John L., ed. *The Oxford History of Islam*. Oxford, UK: University Press, 1999.
Fazlur-Rahman. *Islam*, 2nd ed. Chicago: University of Chicago Press, 1979.
Khatami, Seyyed Mohammed. *Islam, Liberty and Development*. New York: Institute of Global Cultural Studies, Binghamton University, 1998.
Krause, Wanda. "Civil Society in the Democratization Process: A Case Study on Cairo Islamic Women's and Secular Feminist Organizations." *Global Development Studies* 3, no. 4 (2005).
ed. *Liberal Islam: A Sourcebook*. Oxford, UK: Oxford University Press, 1998.
Kurzman, Charles, ed. *Modernist Islam, 1840–1940: A Sourcebook*. Oxford, UK: Oxford University Press, 2002.
Sachedina, Abdulaziz. *Islamic Roots of Democratic Pluralism*. Oxford, UK: Oxford University Press, 2001.
The Holy Qur'an, Text, Translation and Commentary. (1st ed., 1934) 1983 ed. Translated by A. Y. Ali. Beltsville, Md.: Amana.
United Nation Development Programme (UNDP). "Annual Report 2004" http://www.undp.org/annualreports/2004/english/
United Nations High Commission for Human Rights (UNHCHR). "Specific Human Rights Issues." http://www.unhchr.ch/Huridocda/Huridoca.nsf/(Symbol)/E.CN.4.Sub.2.2003.NGO.15.En

ISLAMIC FUNDAMENTALISM

Islamic fundamentalism is a vague term that describes in modern vocabulary the militant ideology of contemporary Islamic movements in the various parts of the Muslim world. However, the term Islamic fundamentalism refers to a group of those Muslims who adhere to the traditional Islamic way of life, accept the traditional Islamic values, and maintain the traditional Islamic worldview. They include reformists (*salafīyya*), conservatives (*usūlīyya*), and the so-called militant Islamists. One important characteristic that is common among them is their rejection of secularism and modernity in all their manifestations, which is a hallmark of the West. This serves to highlight their fundamentalist construct of going back to the basic teachings of the religion of Islam and the *sharī'a* law (Islamic law).

Thus, in order to view correctly the phenomenon of Islamic fundamentalism and place it in its proper perspective, we need to analyze it by examining how it came to appear in the Muslim world in parallel to what took place in the Western world. It forms a pattern of interaction between the Muslim world and the Western world as it is a reaction against the secularism, which is the outcome of Western modernity, and a resistance to colonial powers at the turn of the twentieth century. As a result, the phenomenon of Islamic fundamentalism in the Muslim world can be explained by analyzing the two tendencies that are its characteristic features. The first tendency is featured among the reformists (*salafīyya*) who initially began the movement to achieve independence from the colonial powers and at the same time reform the Muslim society by advocating the return to the Islamic model of society that existed in the glorious past of Islam. Hence, they tended to conceive of the *sharī'a* law as a universal framework in which the Muslim conduct of life must be incorporated and adapted to the consideration of the needs and necessities of modern times. They favored acquiring knowledge of Western sciences and technology and also tried to implement them. Failing to see any success, the conservatives (*usūlīyya*) advocated going back to the roots and basic principles of the *sharī'a* law, rejecting modernity, secularism, and any kind of Westernization. But finding the penetration of the Western mode of secularization in the Muslim world and thwarted by the intrusion of the Western powers therein, some conservatives from among these fundamentalists, whom we have called militant Islamists, may sometimes react radically and take extreme measures of violence.

Both of these tendencies are manifest in today's Muslim world, and, obviously, these Islamic fundamentalists are not successful in realizing their goal. This raises the question of what is the cause of their failure. To find an explanation, one needs to look at the paradigm of modernity and secularism that reigns in every aspect of Western society and operates on all levels of modern life in the Western world. The basic mistake of Muslim reformists was to think that it was possible to borrow scientific knowledge and technology from the West without adapting to the secularization of Western modernity. The Muslim reformists thought that they would restrict modernity by utilizing the achievements of modern Western sciences and knowledge of technology, not realizing that modernity is a Western project that began in the period of Enlightenment. And it claims, as Kant says, to release humankind from past tutelage and makes it rely on reason, knowledge, and autonomy of man. It is true that Islam encourages the pursuit of knowledge and research, but it should be subservient to and in accordance with the Qur'ānic values and ethics. From this one can discern the basic fallacy of thinking of Muslim reformists and the reason for the failure of their movements. Thus, the militant Islamists from among the fundamentalists find themselves at odds when they are unable to keep pace with Western modernity; its rapid progress and developments in science, technology, industry; and its organizational skills in political, social, ethical, cultural, and economic institutions. They feel their failure is due to the Western

intrusion in the affairs of the Muslim world and not knowing better what to do, they resort to violence. It is in this sense that Islamic fundamentalism is a reaction against the West. One can say that there is a sense of urgency on the part of the Western world to be alarmed in the face of this perceived threat from militant Islam, which directs its attacks on the values of secularism as embodied in the West and its path of development. The danger to the Western world is that this trend of violence, due to the religious movement of militant Islam, may spill into it and become a fertile territory for terrorist activities and a constant source of disturbance.

However, even after such a shocking event that the entire world witnessed on September 11, 2001, the extreme form of fundamentalism that manifests itself in militant Islam cannot be characterized as terrorism. Such activities are simply the outcome of desperation on the part of militant Islam. They certainly do not translate into religious revival or reformation, or bring any changes into the society that Islamic fundamentalism intend to achieve.

In short, there has not yet been an emergence of any spontaneity of thought in these Islamic movements after the colonial period that synthesizes various elements of modernity, transforms them from the perspectives of Islamic religious orientation, and constructs them according to the Muslim legacy, traditions, and worldview.

HUSAIN KASSIM

See also Islam; Taliban

References and Further Reading

Choueiri, Youssef M. *Islamic Fundamentalism*. London: Pinter, 1990.
Davidson, Lawrence. *Islamic Fundamentalism*. Westport, CT and London: Greenwood Press, 1998.
Esposito, John L. *The Islamic Threat: Myth or Reality?* New York and Oxford: Oxford University Press, 1992.
Huntington, Samuel P. "The Clash of Civilizations." *Foreign Affairs*, Summer 1993.
Kepel, Gilles. *Jihad: The Trail of Political Islam*. Translated by Anthony F. Roberts. London and New York: IB Taris, 2002.
Lewis, Bernard. "The Roots of Muslim Rage." *Atlantic Monthly* 226:3, September 1990.
Tibi, Bassam. *The Challenge of Fundamentalism*. Berkeley, Los Angeles, and London: University of California Press, 1998.

ISRAEL

The State of Israel is located on the eastern Mediterranean Sea, on a land bridge that connects Asia with the

African continent. In general, the country experiences long, hot summers, and brief, wet winters. Climate varies, however; in the mountainous Galilee region in the north, summers are considerably cooler than in the Negev Desert of the south, a desert that comprises roughly 60% of Israel's land mass. Tel Aviv, on the Mediterranean, is known for a hot, humid climate, while Jerusalem, only sixty kilometers inland, is located in the Judaean Mountains, and often experiences light snow in the winter. Thus, despite the country's small size, a variety of topographies and climates may be found.

Some observers see the creation of the modern State of Israel in 1948 as nothing short of miraculous, while for others, it was the beginning of a long hard struggle against a new form of colonialism that seems to have no imminent ending. What is certain is that the country was born in conflict, and has experienced political strife from that moment onward. For while it is true that the birth of the State of Israel was the ultimate realization of the Zionist dream, Israeli independence is seen from the Palestinian perspective as *al-Nakba*, that is, the catastrophic destruction of Arab Palestine. Israel's entire society, culture, political structure, and economy are, in many ways, directly impacted by the country's ongoing efforts to resolve this inherent contradiction.

Israel's Raison d'être

The foundation of Israel's creation in the Middle East following the British decolonization of Palestine was premised upon the ideology of Zionism, that is, Jewish nationalism. Developed in western Europe, the early Zionist movement sought to (re)create a Jewish presence in Palestine, and to reconstitute the Jewish commonwealth, destroyed two millennia earlier (68–70 CE). This was to be achieved primarily through *aliyah*, that is, mass Jewish immigration to the land of Palestine. The Zionist motto, "a land without a people for a people without a land," well explains this ideology. What most early Zionists failed to recognize, however, was that the land of Palestine was not empty at all, but was home to a long-established Palestinian Arab community.

Thus, the founding of the State of Israel on May 14, 1948, following the end of the British Mandatory period (1917–1947), was viewed by the Jewish Zionists as the fulfillment of a dream. The subsequent attack by five Arab states on the following day, and the bloody war that ensued, were ultimately overcome by the young Jewish army, and the State was preserved. That said, the war well established the fact that the Arab world could not and would not accept the existence of what they saw as a colonialist, imperialist State in its midst, and would do everything in its power to, in time, eliminate it and restore Palestine to rightful Arab rule. The outflow of Palestinian refugees from Palestine and into many of the neighboring Arab states only further emphasized to these countries the injustice that the creation of Israel had brought upon the Arab people.

Therefore, the early goals of the State of Israel were twofold. The first priority was the effective absorption of Jewish refugees, primarily from Holocaust-torn Europe and later, in the 1950s and 1960s, from the Arab/Muslim Middle East and North Africa. The second priority was security, insofar as the 1949 armistice with the Arab combatant states did not at all protect the fledgling State of Israel from future military incursions.

Absorption of Jewish immigrants, many coming to the new state with only the shirts on their backs, demanded a huge economic investment. Communal farms, known as *kibbutzim* and *moshavim*, played one key role in the new state. Initiated in the early part of the twentieth century during the Ottoman period (the first *kibbutz* was created in 1910), the movement exemplified the Zionist spirit and mythos of "draining the swamps," "sowing the fields," and ultimately, "making the desert bloom." Moreover, it was typical that these farms be strategically placed, serving not only as agrarian communities, but also as a first line of defense against the Arabs' ability to threaten the young Jewish community, known prior to statehood as the *Yishuv*.

Given the European roots of Israel's founding fathers and mothers, a strong, centralized economy evolved throughout the 1950s as well. Based upon socialist principles, the Israeli political and economic systems relied directly upon planning as the centerpiece of its ideology. Thus, a system of absorption centers was developed very early on (*mercaze klitah*) through which thousands of immigrants, especially those from the Middle East and North Africa, passed prior to taking up permanent residence in the country. Planned new communities, known as "development towns," were also created throughout the country, designed both to serve as centers of immigrant absorption, as well as to create a de-centralized urban system of "facts on the ground." Thus, these towns performed multiple functions by establishing a permanent Jewish presence in the country outside of the Tel Aviv conurbation, which helped the Israelis to further lay claim to, as well as to defend, the new state.

Clearly then, the goals of security and absorption often overlapped. The political environment of the

1950s also demanded the development of a strong and prepared military, composed in part of newcomers who typically spoke no Modern Hebrew (*Ivrit*), and who had limited military experience. *Zahal*, the Israeli Defense Force, thus served both to protect the new state from threat, as well as to help absorb new immigrants socially and culturally.

The role of the military was not limited to external defense, however. Internally, the Israeli government also sought to control and pacify the Palestinian Arab community that, as a result of the Independence War, now lived under Israeli sovereignty. While Israeli citizenship was conferred upon these Arabs in 1951, the community remained under military administration until the mid-1960s, largely viewed by the Israeli establishment as the enemy within.

The Role of the Arab–Israeli Conflict in Israel's Development

The history of the State of Israel from its establishment in 1948 to the present day has been punctuated regularly by war, guerrilla terror, and communal uprisings. This conflict has played a key role in the State's economic, political, and social development, and is central to an understanding of Israel's positioning in regional affairs. It is significant to point out, however, that though the "Arab–Israeli" conflict and the "Palestinian–Israeli" conflict share much in common, the two should not be conflated into a single issue.

On the Arab–Israeli front, Israel was at war with her Arab state neighbors from the inception of the creation of the state. The primary combatant was Egypt, which, under Gamal Abdul Nasser, sought throughout the 1950s to disrupt the Zionist presence in Palestine by allowing *fedayeen* raids to be conducted from Egyptian territory. Israel's response to these incursions, as well as to the growing sense that an Egyptian-led pan-Arab coalition against Israel's security had grown to a viable threat against the state, led to the Sinai Campaign of 1956. Sharing the desire to topple Nasser, the British and French assisted Israel in its move against Egypt. Ultimately though, the Eisenhower Administration stepped in, and Israel was forced to withdrawal to the 1949 armistice lines.

The Six-Day War of 1967 may be seen as the most significant war ever fought between Israel and her Arab neighbors. The war was a watershed in Israel–Arab relations, ultimately fostering a split in the Arab–Israeli and Palestinian–Israeli conflicts. Conquering the Sinai peninsula and Gaza Strip from Egypt, the Golan Heights from Syria, and the West Bank and East Jerusalem from Jordan, Israel was able in six days to effectively annihilate any threat against her future survival. The Arab states were understandably devastated; Nasser offered to resign from the Egyptian presidency as a result and, though the Egyptian people refused his offer, he died a clearly weakened leader only three years later.

As for Israel, these conquests in many ways were considerable, yet potentially damaging to her future development. Having moved on the world stage from the role of "David" to that of "Goliath," Israel now had the unenviable responsibility of governing over 1 million additional Palestinian Arabs who, unlike the Arabs of Israel, were not offered citizenship, and who would remain under military occupation for decades.

Elated and euphoric with a newly found sense of power, the Israeli government began the process anew of settling the conquered lands through the use of "facts on the ground." Settlements were built, mostly in the West Bank, some in Gaza, and a handful in the Sinai and the Golan. While the ideology behind building settlements in Gaza, the Sinai, and Golan was largely military and defensive, settlement of the West Bank had an altogether different meaning. Known by Jews as "Judaea and Samaria," this territory comprised much of the Jewish heartland of the Hebrew bible, lands with far greater historic and religious significance than, ironically, those lands upon which the State itself had been established.

Seeking to redress the travesty of the 1967 War as well as to establish himself as a legitimate heir to Nasser, Egyptian President Anwar as-Sadat led an attack against Israel on October 6, 1973, the beginning of the Yom Kippur/Ramadan War. Though no land was acquired through this war and the Palestinian plight remained unresolved, the war succeeded insofar as it helped to establish el-Sadat as a strong Arab leader willing to stand up to the by-now formidable Israeli Defense Forces. Having proven himself in war, as-Sadat then offered peace. In November 1977, he traveled to Jerusalem where, in front of the Israeli *Knesset* (Parliament), he offered to make peace with the Israeli State.

The subsequent peace treaty, the Camp David Accords, was signed in 1979 by as-Sadat, Israeli Prime Minister Menachem Begin, and US President Jimmy Carter. In return for Israeli withdrawal from its occupation of the Sinai Peninsula, Egypt offered Israel a permanent peace. The treaty effectively ended the Arab–Israeli conflict though not, despite some minor verbiage in the Accords to the contrary, Israel's ever-festering conflict with the Palestinian people.

The Role of the Palestinian Occupation in Israel's Political and Social Development

As refugees or people under occupation, the Palestinian community refused to accept Israel's existence. The creation of the State was known as *al-Nakba*, the catastrophe, which effectively destroyed Arab Palestine as it had been known before the end of the British Mandate.

Thus the Palestinian refusal to accept Israel as a reality was translated primarily into acts of what Israel saw as unacceptable violence and terror. Much of this terror was formalized in the late 1960s, following the creation of the Palestine Liberation Organization in 1964. Often directed at non-combatants, this reign of terror came to a head when, at the Olympic Games held in Munich, West Germany, in the summer of 1972, Palestinian guerrillas took Israeli athletes and trainers hostage. A rescue attempt was foiled, and eleven Israelis died in the aftermath.

The constant fear of terror, both inside Israel as well as wherever Israelis might travel, took its toll on Israeli society. A "siege mentality" began to develop whereby Israelis felt that, though not actively at war, the terror that the Palestinians carried out against them made security increasingly paramount. This was most clearly seen following the conquest of the West Bank and Gaza Strip, where civil liberties expected in a democratic state such as Israel suffered under the strain of the need to maintain security. The end result was a military occupation of these Palestinian territories that was heavy-handed and at times, quite brutal. Thus, the occupation of these lands served to damage the development of civil society within the Palestinian community, while at the same time, jeopardized the very nature of the State of Israel as the "only true democracy" in the Middle East region.

The Palestinian uprising (*intifada*) against the military occupation of the West Bank and Gaza (1987–1993) was a turning point in Palestinian–Israeli relations and indeed, as a result, in Israel's political and economic development as a whole. Armed primarily with stones, the Palestinian protesters (typically young boys) squared off against Israeli tanks in a demonstration of unprecedented defiance. Israel's response was a policy of harsh military actions (shootings with live ammunition, tear gassings, and the like). The nature of the Palestinian *intifada* movement as a grassroots protest against the injustices of the occupation found sympathy worldwide, and brought about pressure upon the Israeli State to finally help resolve the Palestinian problem.

The Oslo Peace Accords, secretly negotiated at Oslo, Norway, and signed by Palestinian leader Yasser Arafat, Israeli Prime Minister Yitzhak Rabin, and US President Bill Clinton in 1993, appeared to clear the way for the resolution of Israel's conflict with the Palestinians. Following the "land for peace" formula, Israel committed to a staged withdrawal from the West Bank and Gaza similar to its withdrawal from the Sinai. In return, the Palestinians offered peace, and the renunciation of future claims to the part of historic Palestine that was now Israel.

At the same time, the resolution of the Palestinian problem allowed Jordan to sign a peace treaty with the Israelis in 1994, and other Arab states to similarly move toward formally recognizing Israel and accepting her into the Arab neighborhood. An Arab boycott against corporations dealing with Israel was lifted, allowing for an unprecedented influx of new direct foreign investment into the Israeli economy. The likes of Intel and other large high-technology firms came to Israel to establish bases in southwest Asia.

Israeli Prime Minister Benjamin Netanyahu was one of a number of Israeli architects of this new economy. Throughout the 1990s, he and others helped foster an era of privatization and movement away from Israel's historic roots as a socialist state. *Kibbutzim* and *moshavim* abandoned their communally oriented ideologies for a more individually based capitalistic economic orientation. With ceasing hostilities with her Arab neighbors and with a newly found emphasis on free enterprise, the Israeli economy boomed.

Significantly, this boom coincided with a major influx of Jewish refugees now free to relocate from the former Soviet Union. Over 1 million new immigrants relocated from the region during the 1990s. Two significant though smaller waves of immigrants from Ethiopia relocated to Israel during the late 1980s and 1990s as well. Socially, politically, and economically, the decade proved to be a particularly successful period of development for the Israeli state.

Israel in the Twenty-First Century

The outbreak of the *al-Aqsa intifada* (uprising) in September of 2000 once again altered the Israeli political landscape. Now armed with machine guns instead of stones, the Palestinian combatants of the new uprising bore little resemblance to their predecessors of nearly a decade earlier. The Israeli response to this uprising was similar, however, in that once again, Israel followed a policy of disproportionality. Simply put, for every action (roadside attack, killing, assassination) on the Palestinian side, Israel responded with an even greater action—"two eyes for an eye," one could say. Such a policy was intended to serve as a deterrent to Palestinian activism; in actuality, it did not appear to work, but did apparently serve to further escalate the conflict. The process toward Palestinian statehood and Israeli "normalcy" begun under Oslo in 1993 thus proved to be an excruciatingly slow one.

The death of Yasser Arafat, president of the Palestinian Authority, in late 2004 signaled a possible improvement in Palestinian–Israeli and Arab–Israeli relations. Labeled by the Israeli Government as an "irrelevant" obstacle to peace during the height of the al-Aqsa intifada, Arafat remained a symbol of tenacious Palestinian resistance to Israeli interests and demands throughout his seventy-five years. His passing ushered in a new period of reconciliation between Israel and her Arab neighbors that offered new opportunities for the country to finally find a recognized place within a neighborhood that had for so long denied her very existence or legitimacy.

And yet, while the conflict with the Palestinians showed some signs of subsiding in the early part of the twenty-first century, a number of economic and social concerns in Israel not connected directly to the conflict are equally relevant. As Israel has developed economically, the land available for growth has been rapidly shrinking. Resource limitation, most especially fresh water and arable land, continue to plague the country. As Israel urbanizes, these limitations are even more acute. Over 90% of the Israeli population lives on 40% of the land; excluding the desert, Israel is one of the most densely populated countries in the world. Though the desert remains largely ignored, the future development of the state will likely rely in part upon its more effective use.

Socially, the future role of two minority populations in Israel is also likely to be significant. First among these is the religious Jewish community, whose population is rapidly growing. This community has placed demands and expectations on the State which, throughout the 1980s and 1990s, put it at odds with secular Israel. The imposition of certain halachic (Jewish legal) regulations has created considerable conflict between and among the majority of Israelis, who do not embrace these rules. The prohibition against the national air carrier El Al flying on Saturdays, the ability of drivers to use certain roads during the Sabbath, the sale of pork and other non-kosher products in the country (increasingly relevant since the arrival of the immigrants from the former USSR), and so on have all proven to be potentially explosive areas of national debate.

Lastly, the role of Israel's Palestinian citizen minority cannot be ignored. The community has consistently comprised nearly 20% of the population throughout the 1990s and early 2000s. Were it not for the Soviet Jewish immigration, this percentage would by now be far higher. And yet, this community continually argues that it is largely neglected by the State, and is often ignored altogether. It is apparent in all sectors—education, health care, and public services of all kinds—that the Arab community is underserved. Recent politicization of the community and a marked movement toward an association with the Islamic political parties suggest that ignoring this community and treating Arab Israelis unequally may, in the long run, backfire if policies are not altered significantly.

Thus, resolution of the Palestinian–Israeli conflict, though central to Israel's political and economic interests, is but one of many concerns that the State of Israel will continue to contend with in coming years. Born in conflict, the State remains a land of contradictions and uncertainties. That said, it is likely that the early Zionists, were they able to see the modern, high-tech society that has been developed in Israel over the past several decades, might marvel at how their fantastic dream is now an existing, albeit constantly evolving, reality.

STEVEN C. DINERO

See also Arab–Israeli Wars (1948, 1956, 1967, 1973); Camp David Accords (1979); Ethnic Conflicts: Middle East; Middle East: History and Economic Development; Middle East: International Relations; Palestine; Palestine Liberation Organization (PLO); Palestinian Diaspora; Zionism

References and Further Reading

Arian, Asher. The Second Republic: Politics in Israel. New York: Chatham House Publishing, 1997.

Ben-Porath, Yoram, ed. The Israeli Economy: Maturing Through Crises. Cambridge, MA: Harvard University Press, 1986.

Feiler, Gil. From Boycott to Economic Cooperation: The Political Economy of the Arab Boycott of Israel. London and Portland, OR: Frank Cass & Co., 1998.

Garfinkle, Adam. Politics and Society in Modern Israel: Myths and Realities, 2nd ed. Armonk, NY: M.E. Sharpe, 2001.

Gerner, Deborah J. One Land, Two Peoples: The Conflict over Palestine (Dilemmas in World Politics), 3rd ed. Boulder, CO: Westview Press, 2001.

Karsh, Efraim, ed. Israeli Politics and Society Since 1948 (Israel: The First Hundred Years). Portland, OR: International Specialized Book Service, 2002.

Lustick, Ian S., and Barry Rubin, eds. Critical Essays on Israeli Society, Politics, and Culture (Books on Israel, Vol 2). Albany, NY: State University of New York Press, 1991.

Netanyahu, Benjamin. A Durable Peace: Israel and Its Place Among the Nations. New York: Warner Books, 2000.

Peleg, Ilan. The Middle East Peace Process: Interdisciplinary Perspectives (Suny Series in Israeli Studies). Albany, NY: State University of New York Press, 1998.

Peretz, Don and Gideon Doron. *The Government and Politics of Israel*, 3rd ed. Boulder, CO: Westview Press, 1997.

Plessner, Yakir. *The Political Economy of Israel: From Ideology to Stagnation (Suny Series in Israeli Studies)*. Albany: State University of New York Press, 1994.

Rabin, Yitzhak. *The Rabin Memoirs*. Berkeley and Los Angeles: University of California Press, 1996.

ITAIPÚ DAM

Itaipú Dam, located on the upper Paraná River that forms the border between Paraguay and Brazil, is the world's largest-capacity hydroelectric plant, although it will lose the honor to China's Three Gorges Dam when that project is completed. Construction on Itaipú began in 1975, and electricity production began in May 1984. Installed capacity reached 12,600 MW when the last of the planned eighteen generators came online in 1991. Two additional generators brought installed capacity to 14,000 MW in 2004. In 2000, actual production peaked at 93.4 billion kWh, providing 95% of Paraguay's electricity consumption and 24% of Brazilian demand. Itaipú Binacional, the binational state corporation that owns the project, estimates that annual production could exceed 100 billion kWh in favorable years.

Brazil began pre-feasibility studies of the hydroelectric potential of the upper Paraná River in 1956. A territorial dispute with Paraguay in the area of the Guairá Falls was resolved with the Act of Yguazú in 1966, in which Paraguay and Brazil agreed to joint and equal ownership of the hydroelectric energy of the river and to study the utilization of the resource. Importantly, the Act also opened up the Paraguayan side of the border to Brazilian colonists, some three hundred thousand of whom entered the region by 1980.

Argentina was also interested in exploiting the potential electric production of the upper Paraná River. In 1973, Paraguay signed the Itaipú Treaty with Brazil and an agreement with Argentina to construct a major dam at Yacyretá. However, construction at Yacyretá would not begin until 1985, after Itaipú was already producing electricity. Rivalry between Brazil and Argentina had long been reflected in their policies towards Paraguay, and Brazil's greater capacity to sustain financing of the Itaipú project gave it the advantage. However, critics have argued that this "pseudo-rivalry," to use Osny Duarte Pereira's term, masked what was actually collusion between the two powers to gain control of Paraguay's share of this resource.

Construction of Itaipú had significant environmental, economic, and political implications, especially for Paraguay. Creation of the reservoir behind the dam submerged Guairá Falls, the world's largest waterfalls. Peasant farmers, large agribusiness enterprises, and a growing number of towns moved into the isolated region of the reservoir, home to threatened wildlife and indigenous peoples. The Brazilian "economic miracle" of the 1960s and 1970s helped finance the project. The massive investments in Itaipú helped to generate the Paraguayan "economic miracle," a period of high rates of economic growth fueled by construction and agricultural exports. Paraguay's GDP per capita grew at an average annual rate of 5.07% between 1971 and 1981. Many authors attribute the poor economic performance over the rest of the 1980s (average annual GDP per capita growth at –0.66%) to the conclusion of major civil works at Itaipú. The decline of resources for patronage undoubtedly contributed to the collapse of the regime of Alfredo Stroessner in 1989.

Contracts for civil works, and the associated corruption in the bidding process, created new wealth for well-connected Paraguayan businessmen, who came to be known as the "Barons of Itaipú." Foremost of these was Juan Carlos Wasmosy, President of the National Consortium of Paraguayan Firms, a major contractor. Wasmosy, a member of the long-ruling Colorado Party, won a controversial election to become President of the Republic for the term 1993–1998.

By 1991, when Itaipú was at full production, Paraguay consumed just 1.9% of the total output, but depended on Itaipú-generated royalties and compensations for 35% of the central government's revenue. Royalties paid to both Brazil and Paraguay attracted the attention of local governments on both sides of the river. Brazil passed a royalties law in 1991, calling for distribution of royalties from Itaipú directly to the affected states (Paraná and Mato Grosso do Sul) and municipalities. Departmental and municipal governments in Paraguay successfully pushed a bill through Congress in 1998 for the distribution of royalties to all local governments, but favoring those districts most affected by Itaipú and Yacyretá. These payments are distributed by the Paraguayan central government, not Itaipú.

Nationalists in Paraguay, such as Domingo Laíno, three-time opposition candidate for president, have long called for the renegotiation of the Itaipú Treaty, a proposal Brazil has firmly resisted. The terms of the treaty do not permit renegotiation for fifty years, or until 2023. The treaty requires the parties to sell excess shares of electricity only to the other party, and only at production costs rather than the opportunity cost for alternative sources of energy. Payments for the sale of excess shares are called compensations. In practice, of course, only Paraguay has excess energy to sell. Brazil has been able to use energy from other sources, made available by the enormous capacity of Itaipú, to sell to Argentina during periods when Argentina suffers energy shortages. Argentina, with a similar arrangement with Paraguay regarding Yacyretá, has been able to return the favor to Brazil thanks to Paraguay's inability to consume its share of the Paraná's hydroelectric production. The prominent critic Ricardo Canese points to this arrangement, and the opposition from Brazil and Argentina to proposals that would allow transfer of energy between the two dams on Paraguayan territory, as evidence of collusion on the part of the regional powers.

The Itaipú Binacional is a state corporation with twelve councilors, two general directors, and a twelve-person Executive Directorate. The posts are evenly divided between Brazilians and Paraguayans. The Binacional is charged with the administration of the dam and with Itaipú's related projects. Not only is Itaipú expected to transfer royalties to the two governments, but it is also expected to generate its own development projects in its zone of influence. Again, it is on the Paraguayan side that the impact is the greatest. In 2004, Itaipú Binacional reported spending US$15 million in Paraguay to help alleviate problems in the rural sector, spending on education, health, police, road construction, potable water, and even assisting peasant cooperatives and micro-industries. This is in addition to the monthly payments of over US$20 million in royalties and compensations.

BRIAN TURNER

See also Argentina; Brazil; Corruption, Governmental; Paraguay; Southern Cone (Latin America): History and Economic Development; Stroessner, Alfredo; Three Gorges Dam

References and Further Reading

Borda, Dionisio. *Auge y Crisis de un Modelo Económico: El Caso Paraguayo*. Asunción, Paraguay: Universidad Católica, 1994.

Canese, Ricardo. *Itaipú y la Cuestión Energetica en el Paraguay*. Asunción, Paraguay: Universidad Católica, 1983.

Duarte Pereira, Osny. La Seudo-Rivaldad Argentino-Brasileña: Pro y Contra de Itaipú. Buenos Aires, Argentina: Ediciones Corregidor, 1975.

Ferradas, Carmen Alicia. *Power in the Southern Cone Borderlands: An Anthropology of Development Practice*. Westport, CT: Bergin & Garvey, 1998.

Nickson, R. Andrew. *Historical Dictionary of Paraguay*, 2nd ed. Metuchen, NJ and London: The Scarecrow Press, 1993.

———. "The Itaipú Hydro-electric Project: The Paraguayan Perspective." *Bulletin of Latin American Research* 2, no. 1 (1982): 1–20.

Rosa, J. Eliseo da. "Economics, Politics and Hydroelectric Power: The Paraná River Basin." *Latin American Research Review* 18, no. 3 (1983): 77–107.

J

JAGAN, CHEDDI

Since 1945, politics in Guyana, characterized by ethnic and racial divisions between the Indo-Guyanese and the Afro-Guyanese, have been dominated by two politicians: Cheddi Jagan (1918–1997) and Linden Forbes Burnham. An integral part in Guyana's struggle for independence from the British, in 1950 Jagan formed the People's Progressive Party (PPP). To broaden support for the PPP, Jagan invited Burnham, who came from an upper middle class Afro-Guyanese family, to join the party. Burnham became the party chairman, while Jagan led the PPP's parliamentary group. Jagan was the prime minister of British Guiana from 1961 to 1964 and the president of Guyana from 1992 until his death in 1997.

Jagan, the son of ethnic Indian plantation workers, was born in British Guiana on March 22, 1918. In 1943, after earning a degree in dentistry from Northwestern University and marrying Janet Rosenberg, a Jewish woman from Chicago, Jagan returned to Guyana and immersed himself in politics. In 1946, Jagan was elected to the colony's legislative body. By establishing the PPP, Jagan hoped to increase the pace of the decolonization process in Guyana. Guyana's ethnic conflict, a result of British Guiana's colonial past when European planters imported vast numbers of African slaves and indentured servants from India to work on the sugar plantations, however, threatened to slow the process of decolonization. The PPP, therefore, was initially a coalition of lower-class Afro-Guyanese and rural Indo-Guyanese. During the 1953 elections, campaigning on a center-left platform, the PPP won eighteen of twenty-four seats in the Legislative Assembly, a new institution created by the Waddington Constitution that granted a limited degree of local autonomy to the Guyanese people. The PPP's introduction of the Labour Relations Act, however, sparked a confrontation with the British, who saw the legislation as a threat to order and stability. On October 9, 1953, the day after the act was passed, the British government suspended the colony's constitution. The PPP had only been in office for 133 days.

By the time the British scheduled new elections in 1957, an open split had developed between Jagan and Burnham. Regardless, Jagan's faction of the PPP won the 1957 elections. Jagan and his supporters in the new government pushed for more rice land, improved union representation in the sugar industry, and more government posts for Indo-Guyanese. Jagan's veto of British Guyana's participation in the West Indies Federation resulted in the total loss of Afro-Guyanese support. In the 1961 elections, under the new Internal Self-Government Constitution, the PPP won twenty of the thirty-five seats in the Legislative Assembly and Jagan was named prime minister. Jagan's government, however, was quite friendly with Fidel Castro's government, refused to observe the US economic embargo on Cuba, and signed trade agreements with Hungary and East Germany. In 1962, Jagan admitted that he was a communist. Concerned about his Marxist ideology, the United States and the United Kingdom conspired to remove Jagan from office. In 1964, new electoral policies facilitated Jagan's removal from power. A constant presence in the Guyanese political arena, Jagan won the 1992 presidential elections. By this time, however, he had abandoned his socialist philosophy and began to move Guyana toward a free-market capitalist system. He was dedicated to neo-liberal economic policies and privatization of the state-run industries. Within four years of taking power, Jagan reduced the nation's inflation rate from over 100% to less than 5% a year. He lured foreign investors to Guyana's agricultural, mining, and timber sectors. Before his term was finished, however, Jagan died in the Walter Reed Army Medical Center in Washington, DC.

MICHAEL R. HALL

See also Guyana; Northern South America: History and Economic Development; Northern South America: International Relations

References and Further Reading

Huntley, Eric L. *Cheddi Jagan: His Life and Times.* London: Bogle L'Ouverture Press, 1998.

Jagan, Cheddi. *The West on Trial: My Fight for Guyana's Independence.* London: Hansib Publications, 1997.

Mars, Perry, and Alma H. Young. *Caribbean Labor and Politics: Legacies of Cheddi Jagan and Michael Manley.* Detroit, MI: Wayne State University Press, 2004.

Rabe, Stephen G. *The Most Dangerous Area in the World: John F. Kennedy Confronts Communist Revolution in Latin America.* Chapel Hill, NC: University of North Carolina Press, 1999.

JAMAICA

Jamaica, the third largest of the four islands known as the Greater Antilles, forms the northern boundary of the Caribbean Sea. It is located between Cayman Trench and Jamaica Channel, the main sea-lanes for the Panama Canal. Known by the Arawak Indians as "Xaymaca" or land of wood and water, Jamaica has long been noted for its natural beauty. The island, with its capital at Kingston, is 146 miles (235 kilometers) long, varying in width from 22 miles (35 kilometers) to 51 miles (82 kilometers). It is actually the tip of a submerged mountain with its topography marked by valleys and mountains. Two-thirds of Jamaica is covered with sedimentary rock, primarily white limestone. The hot and humid climate is tropical, with temperate patches found inland. The population is estimated at 2,713,130 with 91% descended from African slaves and 1.3% descended from Indian indentured servants. Nearly 20% of Jamaicans live below the poverty line with this percentage expected to grow in future years. The Jamaican economy is heavily dependent on services, which now account for 70% of the gross domestic product (GDP). The country continues to derive most of its foreign exchange from tourism, remittances, and bauxite/alumina.

Jamaica became a Spanish colony when Christopher Columbus stopped at Discovery Bay in 1494 in search of gold. The Spanish never found much in the way of mineral wealth and almost abandoned the colony in 1513 before focusing on agriculture. Agricultural goods would become the mainstay of the Jamaican economy until the twentieth century. The Spanish focused on cattle raising. When the British invaded in 1655, they began using African slaves to produce sugar. Jamaica soon became the most productive of the British sugar colonies and the one most notorious for extreme brutality against slaves. The island is famed as the world's first commercial producer of rum, a derivative of sugar, and this Jamaican national drink remains a major export. Sugarcane remains a major agricultural product in the twenty-first century along with bananas, coffee, citrus, yams, vegetables, poultry, goats, milk, crustaceans, and mollusks.

Gradual dissatisfaction with direct rule from London in the 1930s prompted Jamaicans to protest against being a British Crown Colony. Labor leaders pushed for increased wages as well as political reform, linking the labor movement closely with politics from its inception. In 1944, Jamaica received a new constitution that provided for the full adult suffrage that labor leaders had demanded and gave more power to local elected officials. Two political parties, the Jamaica Labor Party and the People's National Party, formed to vie for control of the government. On August 6, 1962, Jamaica became independent from Great Britain.

The boom in consumer goods and tourism that followed World War II proved to be a bonanza for Jamaica. The Jamaican government, with the support of Great Britain, made a concerted effort to move the economy from its historical focus on agricultural products and heavy reliance on imported goods. The manufacture of cement, utilizing the large limestone deposits in the hills east of Kingston, began in 1952. Jamaica's abundance of sea and sunshine attracted tourists to Montego Bay, Port Antonio, Kingston, and Ocho Rios. The rise of postwar spending on consumer goods, automobiles, and aircraft led to an increase in the demand for aluminum. Jamaica's limestone contains huge bauxite deposits, especially in St. Ann, Manchester, St. Elizabeth, and Clarendon. Bauxite, composed chiefly of hydrous aluminum oxides and aluminum hydroxides, is the principal ore of aluminum. North American companies invested millions of dollars to establish Jamaican bauxite mining and to refine the ore to the intermediate stage of alumina. By the early 1960s, Jamaica had become the world's largest producer and exporter of bauxite and alumina. The mining, processing, and export of the mineral have remained mainstays of the Jamaican government with Jamaicans holding jobs at all levels of the bauxite industry. Other major industries included textiles, wearing apparel, light manufactures, paper, chemical products, and telecommunications.

The Jamaican economy began to sour in the late 1960s because of structural faults and a deterioration of living standards as well as political missteps. This decline has continued. The expansion in light manufacturing, food processing, and chemicals had slowed by the end of the 1960s. The Jamaican sugar industry collapsed in the 1970s from slow production and low prices. Kingston, a metropolis of over a million residents with thousands commuting from nearby towns to city jobs, experienced infrastructure problems because of sudden massive growth. Jamaica's population grew faster than available resources. As unemployment rose, economically disadvantaged Jamaicans used an increasing number of illegal guns to commit violent crimes. Depressed economic conditions also led to gang violence fueled by the drug trade. The violence badly damaged the tourism industry and prompted rising numbers of Jamaicans to flee the island. Environmental woes also contributed to Jamaica's tourism decline with heavy rates of deforestation, coastal waters polluted by industrial waste and sewage, and damage to coral reefs.

Jamaica had always been closely aligned with Western countries. During the Cold War, the People's National Party government of Michael Manley sought to better Jamaica's ties to communist Cuba. Manley's actions, in the 1970s, scared both wealthy Jamaicans and investors from the United States who feared a communist takeover of Jamaica. The Manley government also began nationalizing financial institutions and tourism properties to protect jobs. Prosperous Jamaicans emigrated and disinvested. The illegal export of capital, estimated to amount to several hundred million dollars, forced the government to seek other sources of capital.

Jamaica is now heavily in debt. In the 1980s, the government engaged in massive borrowing from multilateral lending agencies, primarily the World Bank, Inter-American Development Bank, and the International Monetary Fund. Jamaica's national debt doubled in less than a decade, with little money now available for government projects. The lending agencies now dictate Jamaican economic policy. Inflation is expected to remain in the double digits.

The Jamaican economy faces serious long-term problems. Unemployment is large-scale and crime continues to hamper economic growth. Interest rates are high. While foreign competition is increasing, the trade deficit grows. The Jamaican government has to maintain its debt payments and resolve these challenging problems.

CARYN E. NEUMANN

See also Caribbean: History and Economic Development; Caribbean: International Relations; Ethnic Conflicts: Caribbean

References and Further Reading

Black, Clinton V. *History of Jamaica*. London: Collins Clear-Type Press, 1958.
Henke, Holger. *Between Self-Determination and Dependency: Jamaica's Foreign Relations 1972–1989*. Barbados: The University of the West Indies Press, 2000.
Mordecai, Martin, and Pamela Mordecai. *Culture and Customs of Jamaica*. Westport, CT: Greenwood Press, 2001.
Roberts, W. Adolphe. *Jamaica: The Portrait of an Island*. New York: Coward-McCann, 1955.
Sherlock, Philip, and Hazel Bennett. *The Story of the Jamaican People*. Kingston: Ian Randle Publishers, 1998.

JARUZELSKI, WOJCIECH

Wojciech Witold Jaruzelski (born July 6, 1923 in Kurow, Poland) was a Polish army general and politician, premier of Poland from 1981 to 1985 and first secretary of the Polish United Workers (Communist) Party from 1981 to 1990; council of state from 1985 to 1989, and president of Poland from July 1989 to December 1990.

The German-Soviet invasion of 1939 trapped Jaruzelski and his family. Jaruzelski, captured by the Soviets, was transferred to work in a coal mine in Kazakhstan. In 1943, he joined the Polish army led by the Soviet Union and trained in the Soviet cadet school, Ryazan. After his training, he fought in the battle that liberated Warsaw from the Germans. After the war (1947), he formally joined the Polish Communist Party and reached the rank of brigadier general at the age of thirty-three (1956).

In 1960, he became deputy minister of defense. In 1964, he became a member of the Central Committee and was elected the deputy minister of defense. In 1968, he became the minister of defense. Jaruzelski rose to political leadership due to the troubles experienced by the Solidarity movement in the 1970s. The Soviet Union placed pressure on the Polish communist party to contain the striking workers in Gdansk and other key industrial cities. Jaruzelski was widely respected in the Kremlin and in Warsaw. Many viewed him as the only leader who could best represent Polish interests but also still maintain a strong relationship with Moscow.

In 1981, facing a national crisis and believing that he had no choice to avoid a Soviet invasion, Jaruzelski authorized martial law. The effort was designed to crush the Solidarity movement and to restore political and economic stability. As a result of his action, he became unpopular with many workers and was viewed as a Soviet puppet who was more interested in Moscow's interests than the Polish people. In 1985, he changed his position to Council of State, which still did not bring much success. Jaruzelski defended his actions as necessary and ones that favored Poland. Years later, he wrote in his defense that he felt that he had no choice but to declare martial law or else fall under direct Soviet control. For example, Kremlin documents indicate that Soviet authorities deployed many divisions of combat-ready troops around Poland's borders and in the western USSR. The Soviet Union also conducted a long series of Warsaw Pact military exercises within Poland.

Jaruzelski's administration ultimately failed to suppress the Solidarity movement and the Polish people who sought a more democratic, multi-party form of government. In April 1989, in the first open election allowed, Solidarity won every open seat in the upper house. Due to the limited number of seats available, the communist party managed to keep control by one seat. The new elections resulted in Jaruzelski becoming president in July 1989. However, by September, Jaruzelski's shaky Communist coalition was forced to agree to a Solidarity prime minister. In December 1990, Lech Walesa succeeded Jaruzelski as the first president of post-communist Poland.

Jaruzelski's views were conservative communism, essentially maintaining the status quo. In 1993, Jaruzelski was charged with criminal conduct for allegedly ordering soldiers to fire on striking workers in 1970, but the motions were dropped in 1996 due to jurisdictional issues. After the collapse of communism in Poland, Jaruzelski, like other former communist leaders, became more moderate in his ideology. For example, in 1998, he stated that the 1968 Soviet invasion of Czechoslovakia (which Poland had a minor role in) was a political and moral mistake.

JOSIAH R. BAKER

See also Central and Eastern Europe: History and Economic Development; Central and Eastern Europe: International Relations; Poland

References and Further Reading

Flam, Helena. *Mosaic of Fear: Poland and East Germany before 1989*. Published: [Boulder]: East European Monographs; New York: Distributed by Columbia University Press, 1998.
Pelinka, Anton. *Politics of the Lesser Evil: Leadership, Democracy, & Jaruzelski's Poland*. Published: New Brunswick, NJ: Transaction Publishers, 1999.
Swidlicki, Andrzej. *Political Trials in Poland, 1981–1986*. Published: London; New York: Croom Helm, 1988.
Westlake, Martin. *Leaders of Transition*. Published: New York: St. Martin's Press, 2000.

JIANG ZEMIN

Jiang Zemin served as general secretary of the Communist Party of China (CPC) from 1989 through 2003. Although semi-retired, he still holds the most powerful position of Chairman of the CPC's Central Military Commission. During his thirteen-year tenure as CPC's top leader, he managed to maintain the momentum of China's economic reform engineered by Deng Xiaoping in later 1970s, and brought about one of the most remarkable period of economic growth in China's recent history.

Born in Jiangsu Province in 1926 to an intellectual family, Jiang joined the Communist Party of China (CPC) in 1946 and participated in the communist underground movement in Shanghai while a college student. He received his college degree in electrical engineering and received some technical training in the former Soviet Union in mid-1950s. Before the Cultural Revolution (1966–1976), Jiang worked for many years as a low-ranking factory manager, served several times as a party leader, and acted as chief of a number of research institutes. Little is known about his role in the Cultural Revolution. His rapid ascendance within the party started in 1980 when he was given a position as vice-chairman of the State Commission on Imports and Exports. He later worked for the State Commission on Foreign Investment, and was believed to play certain roles in the creation of the special economic zones (SEZ) in China's coastal provinces. One of the SEZs, Shenzhen, later became a showcase for China success in market-oriented reform. He was appointed as mayor of Shanghai, China's largest industrial city, and later as secretary of the Shanghai Municipal Party Committee.

Jiang's political career took a dramatic turn in 1989 when a major political turmoil erupted in Beijing over the death of the former party general secretary Hu Yaobang. Hu was believed to be unfairly removed by the party's conservative old guards in 1987. Jiang, because of his peaceful handling of the similar turmoil in Shanghai, was hand-picked by Deng Xiaoping to become the party's new general secretary, replacing the more liberal Zhao Ziyang. Lacking political charisma and experience, Jiang was overshadowed by the still powerful Deng Xiaoping until Deng's death in 1993, when Jiang was appointed president of the PRC.

Under Jiang's leadership, Mainland China has gone through a process of depoliticalization where economic development took precedent over anything else. His era has been characterized as a period of relative political stability and sustained economic growth. China maintained an average gross domestic product (GDP) growth at 8% annually and fulfilled its goal of quadrupling the nation's total GDP. Jiang's other achievement included the peaceful return of Hong Kong and Macao, China's acceptance into the World Trade Organization (WTO), and China's selection as host city for the 2008 Summer Olympics. Jiang also attempted to leave behind a theoretical legacy which has been codified as the Theory of the Three Represents. The theory emphasizes the need for the CPC to adapt to the changing economic and political environment. The new theory laid someground work for future party and political reform.

However, Jiang was also known for his poor handling of the Falungong, a popular semi-religious group that emerged in the 1990s, and his conservative attitude towards political reform. At the sixteenth Party Congress in 2003, he helped to engineer the first formal, peaceful power transfer within the CPC, and relinquished most of his power to the younger leader Hu Jintao.

BAOGANG GUO

See also China, People's Republic of; Chinese Communist Party

References and Further Reading

Fewsmith, Joseph. *China since Tiananmen: The Politics of Transition, Cambridge Modern China Series.* New York: Cambridge University Press, 2001.
——. *Tiger on the Brink : Jiang Zemin and China's New Elite.* Berkeley, CA: University of California Press, 1998.
Kuhn, Robert Lawrence. *The Man Who Changed China: The Life and Legacy of Jiang Zemin.* New York: Crown Publishers, 2004.
Lam, Willy Wo-Lap. *The Era of Jiang Zemin.* Singapore; New York: Prentice Hall, 1999.
Tien, Hung-mao, and Yun-han Chu. *China under Jiang Zemin.* Boulder, CO: Lynne Rienner Publishers, 2000.
Wang, Gungwu, Yongnian Zheng, and National University of Singapore. East Asian Institute. *Damage Control: The Chinese Communist Party in the Jiang Zemin Era, Politics & International Relations.* Singapore: Eastern Universities Press, 2003.

JIHĀD

The subject of *jihād* is widely misunderstood in the West in the past as well as in the present. Equally, it has been misused in the Muslim world in the past for political power by Muslim rulers in the name of the religion of Islam. At other times, it was used by Muslims against the Christian world in the past and came to be called "holy war," the phrase being coined during the times of the Crusades. Therefore, it should not be confused with the real meaning of the word *jihād*.

Jihād is an Arabic word. It comes from the verb *jahada* and means to strive, struggle, and exert efforts. In the Qur'ān, the word *jihād* is frequently followed by the phrase *fī sabīl allah* (in the path or cause of God). One can strive by serving God in several ways and one of the ways is fighting against the enemy and thereby the association of the word *jihād* with the military connotation. It is true that in the Qur'ān, one finds verses that call for *jihād* and there are also verses which ask for peace. Therefore, one needs to examine the context in which the specific issue is addressed and also how and in what context the idea of *jihād* as just war and war for the cause of religion developed in the formation of *sharī'a* law (Islamic law).

It should be made clear from the very outset that the word *jihād,* which is usually translated as a holy war, is not correct. There is no adjective attached to the word *jihād*. It simply means war. *Jihād* is considered holy because God commanded it and when it is fought in the cause of God. When the Qur'ān provides a direct command to Muslims to fight when they are done wrong, it uses the word fighting (*qitāl*) and not striving (*jihād*). Thus *jihād* in defense of one's life, religion, property and land is a defensive war and is considered a just war. In such a case, Islam does allow the use of force and military action, when all possibilities of reconcilliation (*sulha*) are exhausted. Hence, the term fighting (*qitāl*) and its derivatives are employed for the practice of war. Outside the Qur'ān itself, the concepts of *jihād* and *qitāl* came to be associated with one another in the Islamic tradition, but we must keep in mind the implication of the distinction that is ascribed to the prophet Muhammad between the "lesser *jihād*." namely, fighting (*qitāl*) and the "greater *jihād*." namely, striving in the cause of God and not just for the military expansion of the territory of Islam (*dār al-Islām*) or any other such motives.

The classical notion of *jihād*, though it entails the idea of warfare (*qitāl*), has an overwhelming emphasis on the spiritual striving to spread faith and establish peace and order by means of self-discipline and example. Thus the core meaning of *jihād* is inner spiritual striving and purification. It refers to the inner and spiritual striving an individual goes through in fighting against his inclinations, selfishness, and pride. It is an inner and major battle while the fighting and military expeditions are an outward and minor battle.

This becomes evident from the narration of the prophet Muhammad when he returned from a military expedition and said to his companions (ashāb, sing., sahābī): "This day we have returned from a minor jihād (military expedition) to the major jihād (self control).

In the sharī'a law, jihād is considered a collective responsibility (fard kifāya) as against an individual responsibility (fard 'ayn) unless of course the enemy attacks the territory of Islam or threatens the Muslim community (umma). In such a case, it becomes an individual responsibility of a Muslim. It is considered a just war and in that case every Muslim is obligated to participate in it. This war is limited to defensive warfare. For offensive warfare, that is, war for the expansion of the territory of Islam (dār al-Islām) and the conquest of non-Muslim territory (dār al-harb), the individual members are not obligated to take part in it. Thus the distinction between defensive and offensive jihād, namely, just war and war in the cause of religion revolves around the religious obligations of a Muslim in his individual capacity and as a member of the Muslim community (umma). This means that jihād as just war is the primary and essential obligation incumbent upon every Muslim as an individual and, therefore, sometimes it is called the sixth pillar of Islam. Jihād as a offensive combat upon an enemy territory carries not a great priority and, as a matter of fact, is of secondary importance and, as such, depends upon the context in which it is carried out and also in consideration of war ethics as it came to be formulated later in the sharī'a law during the time of 'Abbasids.

The notion of jihād as war in the cause of religion developed in the sharī'a law in a context and in circumstances wherein different factors came into play. The Muslim jurists in the formation of the sharī'a law and its regulations had to take into account these factors and accommodate them in construing the sharī'a law. The context in which the term jihād as a war came into use was in connection with the expansion of the territory of Islam (dār al-islām) by the conquest of the non-Muslims (dār al-harb) during the time of 'Abbasids. The terms dār al-Islām and dār al-harb do not occur in the Qur'ān. They were coined later during the 'Abbasid time when there occurred a vast expansion of the territory of Islam. Thus the notion of jihād as a war to increase the territory of Islam originated only later. Only the Sunnite jurists considered jihād in the sense of offensive war as a collective duty of Muslims in consideration of maintaining mutual relations of the Muslim community with other nations. But the Shi'īte scholars differed in their view because of the context and other political reasons.

Thus the notion of jihād as a just war understood as war in defense of religion as it emerges from the Qur'ān does not become an issue for Western modernity, since every nation-state has the right to defend itself and safeguard the rights of its citizens. The problem lies with the jihād as an offensive war. But as already explained, it was the political context during the period of 'Abbasids that the sharī'a law was formally developing thus forcing Muslim jurists to accommodate the changing conditions that occurred due to the expansion of the territory of Islam so that the Muslim community (umma) could maintain its mutual relations (mu'āmalāt) and regulate the sanctions concerning worldly affairs (ahkām al-dunya) with different religious communities and people.

On the whole, it can be said that jihād, as an offensive war, is no more relevant to the Muslim world in the modern context due to the changing conditions that have occurred due to modernity.

HUSAIN KASSIM

See also Islamic Fundamentalism

References and Further Reading

Abedi, Mehdi and Legenhausen, Gary. Jihād and Shahādat: Struggle and Martyrdom in Islam. Houston, TX: The Institute for Research and Islamic Studies, 1986.
Boisard, Marcel A. Jihad: A Commitment to Universal Peace. Indianapolis, IN: American Trust Publications, 1988.
Firestone, Reuven. The Origins of Holy War in Islam. Edinburgh: Edinburgh University Press. 1960.
Johnson, James Turner. The Holy War Idea in Western and Islamic Traditions. University Park, PA: Pennsylvania State University Press, 1997.
Kassim, Husain. Modernity in Islam: Muslim modus vivendi and Western Modernity. Lewiston, NY: Edwin Mellen Press, 2005.
Kelsay, John. Islam and War. Louisville, KY: John Knox Press, 1993.
Lewis, Bernard. Cultures in Conflict: Christians, Muslims and Jews in the Age of Discovery. Oxford: Oxford University Press, 1996.
Sachadina, Abdulaziz A. "Revelation and History" in Cross, Crescent and Sword, edited by James Turner Johnson. New York: Greenwood Press, 1990.

JORDAN

The most important aspect of the Hashemite Kingdom of Jordan is its location. It is a small country (about the size of the state of Indiana) strategically positioned along what have been the major trade routes in the Middle East during most of the first two millennia of the Common Era. Early on, this area served as a buffer zone between regional tribes, countries, and empires. The British made a deal with Emir Abdullah I of the powerful Hashemite family that if he successfully led the Arabs to revolt against the Ottoman Empire during World War II (known as the "Arab Revolt"), that the British would reward him. With the demise of the Ottoman Empire at the end of World War I, Britain acquired protectorate status over what is today Palestine, Jordan, and Iraq. With the Treaty of London in March 1946, Jordan became a kingdom sharing a common border with Iraq as both countries were to be ruled by brothers of the Hashemite family. So that Jordan would not be landlocked, its border was extended to the Gulf of Aqaba where it created the port city of Aqaba along its twenty-six–kilometer coast. Today, Jordan is surrounded by Israel to the west, Syria to the north, Iraq to the east, and Saudi Arabia to the east and south.

Its location has been both a burden and a blessing. The land has few natural resources except for some phosphates and potash located in the Dead Sea region. It has no oil, no natural gas, and inadequate water resources. It receives almost all of its oil from Iraq at reduced rates. It shares a long border with Israel, which has caused Jordan to be drawn into three Arab wars. Although the Jordanian armed forces performed admirably against the Israeli military, they were still defeated, resulting in lost land and hundreds of thousands of fleeing Palestinian refugees. Jordan also borders Iraq, which, during the reign of Saddam Hussein, forced Jordan to make strategic choices about whether to side with the United States-led coalition against Iraq in 1991 (Operation Desert Storm) and again in 2003 (Operation Iraqi Freedom). King Hussein decided to remain neutral in 1991 due to his concern about unrest among Jordan's majority Palestinian population if he sided with the West against an Arab nation. As a result of Jordan's lack of support, the Gulf countries expelled most immigrant workers back to Jordan, causing a significant strain on its economy. King Abdullah II decided to side with the West in 2003, and was rewarded with a significant increase in the annual economic and military foreign aid provided by the United States.

On the other hand, because of its location along the historic regional trade routes, the area was developed by successive empires from the Assyrian, to the Roman, and ending with the Ottoman. It also witnessed some of the historic Crusader campaigns during the turn of the first millennium. As such, there are numerous historic forts, castles, and cities within Jordan that are world-class tourist sites, including the famous Nabatean red-rock city of Petra. The natural beauty of the Dead Sea, residing on the lowest point on the Earth's surface at 1,224 feet below sea level, draws tourists from around the world.

Much of Jordan is located on a desert plateau. Its capital, Amman, sits at 3,500 feet above sea level, which minimizes humidity. The temperature is moderate year-round, with lots of sun and little rain. As a result, the only area where agriculture can be effectively cultivated is around the Jordan River (which serves as its border with Israel) to the west and northwest.

The population of Jordan is over 5.5 million, with around 3 million people living in and around the capital city of Amman. Over 60% of the population is Palestinian, most with ties to the West Bank and Israel. Over 35% of Jordan's population is under fifteen years of age. The median age of the population is only twenty-two years old. King Abdullah II, in his early 40s, is older than over 60% of the population. Most Jordanians are Sunni Muslims.

The education system is British-based and comprehensive. King Abdullah II decided to capitalize on his citizens, the country's most valuable resource, by focusing his country on information technology (Jordan holds the Guinness World Record for most internet cafes on a city block—in Irbid). The government employs more than 40% of the population; nevertheless, Jordan's unemployment rate hovers around 30%, which is a continuing source of instability. On the other hand, Jordanian expatriates working in other Arab countries send back remittances exceeding US$1 billion every year, constituting Jordan's leading source of income.

Although Jordan is a constitutional monarchy, the king maintains extensive legal powers, including the power to appoint the prime minister, other cabinet ministers, all of the military commanders, and all members of the Senate. He even has the power to dismiss the National Assembly, consisting of the Senate and House of Representatives, and rule by decree. The Prophet Mohammed was also a member of the Hashemite family. Hence, the King of Jordan is one of only two kings in the Arab world able to claim direct lineage to the Prophet (the other being Morocco).

Jordan's Armed Forces are among the best trained in the Arab world. The JAF consists of around 110,000 people serving mostly in the Army followed by the Air Force, Special Forces, and the Navy. King Abdullah II was the Commander of the Special Forces before he was selected to be king by his father, King Hussein. King Abdullah's full brother, Prince Feisal, became Commander of the Royal Jordanian Air Force in 2002.

Finally, Jordan prides itself on being the peacemakers of the Arab world. It concluded a formal peace treaty with Israel in 1994. King Hussein, although stricken with cancer, was instrumental in the successful conclusion of the Wye Plantation Arab-Israeli summit in 1998. King Abdullah II continues the effort leading Arab states in the global war against terrorism.

STEPHEN R. SCHWALBE

See also Hussein, King of Jordan; Middle East: History and Economic Development; Middle East: International Relations

References and Further Reading

Metz, Helen C. *Jordan: A Country Study*. Washington DC: Federal Research Division, Library of Congress, 1991.

Susser, Asher. *Jordan: A Case Study of a Pivotal State*. Policy Papers #53. Washington, DC: The Washington Institute for Near East Policy, 2000.

Wilson, Mary. *King Abdullah, Britain, and the Making of Jordan*. Cambridge: Cambridge University Press, 1987.

JUDAISM

Judaism is the religion of the Jewish people and one of the earliest recorded monotheistic faiths. The history and foundations of Judaism constitute the historical roots of other monotheistic religions, such as Christianity and Islam.

Jews understand Judaism in terms of its four thousand-year history. During this period Jews experienced slavery, self-government, conquest, occupation, and exile. Ancient Egyptian, Babylonian, Persian, and Hellenic cultures as well as more modern movements such as the Enlightenment and the rise of Nationalism have influenced them. Thus, it transcends recognized boundaries.

Historical View

Historians assert that Judaism can be distinguished from other religions that were prevalent when it developed by two characteristics. The first is monotheism. The significance of this belief lies in that Judaism holds that God created people and cares about them. In polytheistic religions, in contrast, humankind is oftentimes created by accident, and the Gods are primarily concerned with their relations with other Gods, not with people.

The second characteristic is the laws that the Torah instructed the Children of Israel to follow. Other religions at the time had temples in which priests would worship their Gods through sacrifice. The Children of Israel, in contrast, worshipped God through everyday actions.

By the Hellenic period, most Jews came to believe that their God was the only God, and so the God of everyone, and that the record of His revelation (the Torah) contained within it universal truths. Jews began to struggle with the tension between the particularism of their claim that only they were required to obey the Torah, and the universalism of their claim that the Torah contained universal truths.

The outcome of this tension is a set of beliefs and practices concerning identity, ethics, one's relation to nature, and one's relation to God. The subject of the Hebrew Bible is an account of the Israelites' relationship with God since the beginning of time until the building of the Second Temple (approximately 350 BCE).

Rabbinical View

According to religious Jews, Abraham was the first Jew. Rabbinic literature asserts that he was the first to take on the world and proclaim the folly of worship. As a result, God promised he would have children, starting with Isaac, who would inherit the Land of Israel (then called Canaan) after having been exiled and redeemed. According to the Bible, God gave Isaac's son Jacob the name Israel, meaning "he who struggles with God," and dedicated his descendents to be his nation.

God sent Jacob and his children to Egypt, after they eventually became enslaved, God sent Moses to redeem the Israelites from slavery. After the Exodus from Egypt, God led them to Mount Sinai and gave them the Torah, and eventually brought them to the Land of Israel.

The Torah given on Mount Sinai was summarized in the five books of Moses and together with the books of the prophets is called the Written Torah. The details which are called the Oral Torah were to remain unwritten. However, along the years, as Jews faced persecutions, some of these details were recorded in the Mishna, the Talmud, as well as other holy books.

According to Jewish Law, someone is considered to be a Jew if he or she was born to a Jewish mother or converted in accordance with Jewish Law. A Jew who ceases to practice Judaism is still considered a Jew, as is a Jew who does not accept Jewish principles of faith and becomes an agnostic or an atheist, so too with a Jew who converts to another religion. However, in the latter case, the person loses standing as a member of the (practicing) Jewish community and becomes known as an apostate in said community, though this might not affect his standing with non-practicing Jews.

The basis of Jewish Law and tradition (*Halakha*) is the *Torah* (the five books of Moses). According to rabbinic tradition there are 613 commandments in the Torah. Some of these laws are directed only to men or to women; some only to Kohanim or Leviyim (members of the tribe of Levi), and many laws were only applicable when the Temple in Jerusalem existed. Less than three hundred of these commandments are still applicable today.

Halakha, the rabbinic Jewish way of life, is based on a combined reading of the *Torah*, and the oral tradition—the *Mishnah*, the halakhic *Midrash*, the *Talmud* and its commentaries. The *Halakha* has developed slowly, through a precedent-based system. The literature of questions to rabbis, and their answers is referred to as a practice (in Hebrew, *Sheelot U-Teshuvot*). Over time, as practices develop, codes of Jewish Law are written, the most important one being the *Shulkhan Arukh*, which determines Jewish religious practice until today.

Jewish Denominations

Judaism today is commonly divided into the following denominations:

1. Orthodox Judaism (includes Hassidic Judaism, Haredi [or Ultra Orthodox] Judaism and Modern Orthodox Judaism)—this denomination holds that God and Moses wrote the Torah, and that the original laws within it are binding and unchanging. While Orthodox Judaism is in many senses what Judaism has been since the Middle Ages, its formation as a movement was a direct response to the formation of Reform Judaism.

2. Reform Judaism (outside of the United States also known as Progressive Judaism, and in the UK as Liberal Judaism) originally formed in Germany as a reaction to traditional Judaism, stresses integration with society and a personal interpretation of the Torah. The original intent was to keep Jews "in the fold" who might otherwise leave the religion and community.

3. Conservative Judaism—outside of the United States is it known as Masorti (Hebrew for "Traditional") Judaism. "Masorti" is its official title in the State of Israel as well, though most Israelis use the word in a more general sense. According to Conservative Jews, the Torah, while unchanging, is subject to interpretation.

4. Reconstructionist Judaism started as a stream of philosophy by a rabbi within Conservative Judaism, and later became an independent movement.

Jewish Identity in Modern Israel

Israelis tend to classify Jewish Identity in ways that are very different than diaspora Jewry. Most Jewish Israelis classify themselves as "secular" (*hiloni*) or as "traditional" (*masorti*). "Secular" is more popular among Israeli families of Western (European) origin, whose Jewish identity may be a very powerful force in their lives, but who see it as largely independent of traditional religious belief and practice.

The term *masorti* is most common among Israeli families of "Eastern" origin (Middle East, Central Asia, and North Africa). This term, as commonly used, has nothing to do with the official "Masorti" (Conservative) movement in the State of Israel. There is a great deal of overlap between the two and they cover an extremely wide range in terms of ideology and religious observance.

What would be called "Orthodox" in the diaspora includes what is commonly called *dati* (religious) or *haredi* (ultra-Orthodox) in Israel. The former term includes what is called "Religious Zionism" or the "National Religious" community, as well as what has become known over the past decade or so as *haredi-leumi* (nationalist *haredi*), which combines a largely haredi lifestyle with nationalist ideology. *Haredi* applies to a population that can be roughly divided into three separate groups along both ethnic and ideological lines: Lithuanian (non-Hassidic) *haredim* of Ashkenazi origin, Hassidic *haredim* of Ashkenazi origin, and Sephardic *haredim*.

CARMELA LUTMAR

See also: **Balfour Declaration; Begin, Menachem; Ben-Gurion, David; Christianity; Inter-Religious Relations; Islam; Israel; Meir, Golda; Palestine; Religion; Zionism**

References and Further Reading

Cohen, Asher. Israel and the politics of Jewish identity: the secular-religious impasse. Baltimore, MD: Johns Hopkins University Press, 2000.

Dosick, Wayne. *Living Judaism: The Complete Guide to Jewish Belief, Tradition, and Practice*. New York: Harper Collins Publishers, 1998.

Gillman, Neil. *Conservative Judaism: The New Century*. Behrman House, 1995.

Johnson, Paul M. *A History of the Jews*. New York: Harper Collins Publishers, 1988.

Ezra Mendelsohn, ed. *Essential papers on Jews and the Left*. New York: New York University Press, 1997.

Rubinstein, Amnon. *From Herzl to Rabin: the changing image of Zionism*. New York: Holmes & Meier, c2000.

Weber, Max. *Ancient Judaism*. New York: Free Press, 1967.

Wertheimer, Jack. *A People Divided: Judaism in Contemporary America*. Boston: Brandeis University Press, 1997.

K

KASHMIR DISPUTE

The Kashmir Dispute is a conflict between India and Pakistan over the possession of the state of Jammu and Kashmir in the northwest part of India. Kashmir has been part of India since October 26, 1947, when the state, according to India, acceded to India. No official Instrument of Accession, however, has ever been publicly shown by the Indian government. Pakistan claims the state properly belongs to Pakistan. It has been the source of innumerable incidents and three wars between the two sovereign nations. Under the rubric of "national security," the Pakistani military expends a great deal of time, money, and manpower in the attempt at controlling Jammu and Kashmir. The Indian government, which sees itself in competition with China rather than Pakistan, states that there is no Kashmir issue to discuss. Nonetheless, the Kashmir issue is the most serious threat to peace in South Asia.

The state of Jammu and Kashmir was created by the British on March 16, 1847, with the signing of the Treaty of Amritsar. It was a state with an overwhelming majority of Muslim citizens ruled by a Hindu maharaja. From 1925 until 1947 the state was ruled by Mahararaja Hari Singh (1895–1961), a Hindu Dogra Rajput. He acceded to India rather than Pakistan in spite of the fact that Kashmir was over 75% Muslim and in some areas over 90%.

Kashmir became part of India, rather than Pakistan, because of the role of the last Viceroy of British India, Louis Mountbatten (1900–1947). He became Viceroy in March 1947. On June 23, 1947, he announced that India would become independent and would be partitioned between India and Pakistan.

The formerly quasi-independent Indian states, some six hundred of them including Kashmir, would accede either to India or Pakistan. It was expected that Kashmir, because of its overwhelming Muslim population, would join Pakistan.

To delineate the border between India and Pakistan, Boundary Commissions for the Punjab and Bengal were appointed and chaired by British judge, Cyril Radcliffe (1899–1977). If Kashmir was to be connected with India the territory south of Kashmir, especially the districts of Gurdespur and Batala, would need to become part of Indian territory. Radcliffe initially awarded them to Pakistan but then Mountbatten intervened with Radcliffe who reversed himself and awarded them, as well as four other Muslim-majority districts, to India. This gave India access by land to Kashmir.

The Maharaja of Kashmir, however, delayed acceding to either India or Pakistan until Pakistani tribesmen from the northwest frontier spontaneously invaded Kashmir on October 22, 1947, to seize the territory for Pakistan, although Indian troops had been infiltrated into Kashmir long prior to this date. This unorganized foray into Kashmir by Pakistani tribesmen was supported by independent action by officers of the regular Pakistan Army. Accession to India on October 26 by the Maharaja, led to military intervention by India, organized by Mountbatten, who had been appointed the first Governor-General of India, and India was able to secure Kashmir for India with its capital at Srinagar. Pakistan, however, was able to keep the western part of Kashmir, Azad (Free) Kashmir, with its capital at Muzaffarabad.

This initial conflict between India and Pakistan led to the first war between India and Pakistan as Indian troops expelled the Pakistanis from Kashmir. On July 18, 1948, the Karachi Agreement established a Line of Control, which has been under observation ever since by nearly forty United Nations observers. A ceasefire took effect on January 1, 1949.

In 1957, Kashmir was incorporated into the Indian union under a new constitution. In 1962, China invaded India in the northeast and many in the Pakistan army believed Pakistan was ready to capture Kashmir. It was not until March 1965, however, when a skirmish developed between India and Pakistan in the Rann of Kutch on the Arabian Sea, that the Pakistan Army believed it was ready to defeat the Indian Army. Demonstrations in Kashmir against the Indian government led to unrest in Pakistani cities and a war atmosphere developed in Pakistan. This was led by Foreign Minister Zulfiqar Ali Bhutto (1927–1979) and his Kashmir Committee. On August 8, 1965, Pakistan launched the clandestine "Operation Gibraltar" against the Indian Army in Kashmir. Four Pakistani soldiers were captured and the operation failed almost immediately. To save Pakistani forces in the area the Pakistan Army then initiated "Operation Grand Slam," which was launched on August 30, 1965, met heavy Indian resistance, and collapsed in three days. In response, India, on September 6, attacked all along the Pakistani border with the city of Lahore as its main target. India could not break through but it was a debacle for Pakistan as the United States withheld provisions and by September 15, Pakistan had almost completely run out of military supplies. The United Nations Security Council became involved and a ceasefire was signed, the Tashkent Agreement, between Indian Prime Minister, Lal Bahadur Shastri (1904–1966) and Pakistan President Ayub Khan (1907–1974) on January 10, 1966, at Tashkent, USSR.

Five years later, when civil war broke out in East Pakistan over the issue of the independence of East Pakistan, India intervened and invaded East Pakistan on December 5, 1971. India easily defeated the Pakistani forces who were cut off from supplies in West Pakistan. India also saw this as an opportunity to destroy Pakistan's military might and attacked Pakistan all along the West Pakistani border. In a massive, carefully planned attack, military and communications centers and oil and industrial sites were destroyed by Indian naval and air forces. This attack also included Kashmir as India invaded Azad Kashmir and created a new line of control.

Totally defeated, Pakistan's only real battleground was the United Nation's Security Council. Debate began on December 8, 1971, when Pakistan was represented by Zulfiqar Ali Bhutto. On December 16, 1971, the Pakistani Army surrendered to the Indian Army in Dacca. This led to the creation of the state of Bangladesh and a new ceasefire agreement, the Simla Agreement, signed between Bhutto and Indian Prime Minister, Indira Gandhi (1917–1984) on July 2, 1972. The Simla Agreement committed India and Pakistan to respect the new line of control in Kashmir of December 1971.

At the end of 1989, Kashmiris began to arm themselves to resist what they called Indian occupation. The state government was dissolved and Kashmir was governed by the central government of India. India reinforced its forces in Kashmir accusing Islamabad of fomenting disorder. Declaring that it would not be cowed, Pakistan responded by massing its forces on the ceasefire line and by declaring a national state of emergency citing the infiltration of Indian forces into Azad Kashmir. In the 1990s, the insurgency in Kashmir, aided and abetted by Pakistan, led to the death of some fifty thousand people. Both Hindus and Muslims have either fled, or been forced to flee their homes, and refugee camps exist on both the Indian and Pakistani sides of the ceasfire line. Skirmishes between Indian and Pakistani forces in Kashmir continue.

The Kashmir dispute took on new dimensions with the development of India and Pakistan's nuclear weapons program. India detonated its first nuclear test at Pokharon in 1987; Pakistan responded very quickly with its own nuclear tests and the development of nuclear weapons and rockets to deliver those weapons. By the beginning of the new millennium, both countries were believed to have numerous nuclear bombs and the means to deliver them.

In 1999, a "glacier" war developed over the Kargil glacier, Point 5353, a 17,397 foot peak in Indian territory, 127 miles north of Kashmir. The Pakistanis captured the glacier but the battle continued for eleven weeks and cost some 1,200 lives. Pakistan eventually withdrew. In October 1999, General Pervez Musharraf came to power in Pakistan in a military coup. The glacier war led to a two-year freeze in official contacts between the two countries. Both sides exchanged artillery fire in Kargil on July 20, 2001, and the area remained a site of conflict as local people exited the area en masse and the state government built hundreds of underground shelters.

Tensions between the two countries continued to remain high and a full-scale war seemed a distinct possibility following the terrorist attack on the Indian parliament in New Delhi on December 13, 2001. Six gunmen stormed into the parliament house with grenades, automatic rifles, and a suicide bomb initiating a ninety-minute battle with security forces. All six terrorists were killed, seven Indians were also killed, and nearly twenty people hospitalized. The attack bore similarities to a raid on the Kashmir state assembly on October 1, 2001, when thirty-eight people were killed. India blamed Pakistan for the attack on the parliament. Pakistani President Pervez Musharraf immediately condemned the attack as did the All Parties Hurriyat Conference, an umbrella group of two dozen groups in Kashmir demanding self-determination for Kashmir. Nonetheless, the Indian Army went on high alert all along the Pakistani border and the Pakistani Army responded in a similar manner.

The Indian government blamed the Lashkar-e-Taiba (Army of the Pure), one of the most extremist Muslim separatist groups, for the attack of December 13 and demanded that Pakistani arrest members of the group along with leaders of Jaish-e-Mohammad (Army of Mohammad), another militant group, and seize their financial assets. Pakistan refused to be dictated to by India and relations reached a critical stage as India recalled its High Commissioner to Islamabad on December 21, cut travel links between India and Pakistan, and both armies mobilized for war. Missiles were moved to the Kashmir border with India stating that the missiles were "in position" and Pakistan responding that their missiles were "on alert." Indian planes flew near the Pakistani border every few minutes and frontier forces exchanged gunfire.

At the end of December 2001, Pakistan gave signs that it was willing to crack down on Islamic militants and thus brake the stalemate between the two countries. On December 24, Pakistani President Pervez Musharraf froze the bank assets of the Lashka-e-Taiba and the Jaish-e-Mohammad. In addition, in a speech given on December 25, Musharraf stated that Pakistan had become a "nightmare" because, in part, of the militants. This was a profound change in Pakistani politics, as Islamic militants had almost never been criticized in Pakistan before. It was in line, however, with the September 11, 2001, attacks by Islamic fundamentalists and the American-led war against Osama bin Laden and the Taliban in Afghanistan. Musharraf had aided and abetted the American response and Musharraf's attack on Pakistani militants was viewed within the worldwide war on extremists. Indian Prime Minister Atal Behari Vajpayee, however, stated that the two countries were moving closer to war.

A turning point in the crisis occurred on January 12, 2002, when President Musharraf gave a sixty-two–minute televised address to the nation with the rest of the world listening eagerly. He announced that a number of Islamic extremist organizations had been banned and that strict action would be taken against anyone engaging in terrorism, even in behalf of the freedom of Kashmir. He promised to end the use of Pakistan as a base for terrorism in Kashmir. In future all madrassas (religious schools) and mosques would be registered and controlled by the government. While he reiterated Pakistan's position that negotiations should be held with India over Kashmir, and refused to hand over the twenty or more Pakistani citizens wanted by India, the speech was a highly conciliatory one for a Pakistani president and was viewed as nothing less than a breakthrough in the stalemate.

It was hailed as the most important speech given in three decades by a Pakistani leader as it reversed thirty years of state-supported militancy among religious groups. The Pakistani press hailed Musharraf as the savior of the nation. Over five hundred extremists were arrested and five religious groups banned. By the end of January 2002, the threat of war seemed to have passed although tensions remained high and no one believed that the Kashmir issue would cease to bedevil India-Pakistan relations and be the cause of tension, skirmishes, and perhaps even war in the future.

ROGER D. LONG

See also Central Asia: History and Economic Development; Central Asia: International Relations; India; Pakistan

References and Further Reading

Akbar, M. J. *Kashmir: Beyond the Vale.* New Delhi: Viking, 1991.

Birdwood, C. B. *Two Nations and Kashmir.* London: Robert Hale, 1956.

Brecher, Michael. *The Struggle for Kashmir.* Toronto: The Ryerson Press, 1953.

Government of Pakistan. *White Paper on the Jammu and Kashmir Dispute.* Islamabad: Ministry of Foreign Affairs, Government of Pakistan, 1977.

Jha, Prem Shankar *Kashmir, 1947: Rival Versions of History.* Delhi: Oxford University Press, 1996.

Korbel, Josef. *Danger in Kashmir.* Princeton, N.J.: Princeton University Press, 1966 (orig. 1954).

Lamb, Alastair. *Birth of a Tragedy: Kashmir 1947.* Karachi: Oxford University Press, 1994.

———. *Kashmir: A Disputed Legacy, 1846–1990.* Karachi: Oxford University Press, 1992.

Suharwardy, A. H. *Tragedy in Kashmir.* Lahore: Wajidalis, 1983.

Wirsing, Robert G. *India, Pakistan, and the Kashmir Dispute: On Regional Conflict and its Resolution.* New York: St. Martin's Press, 1994.

Zutshi, U. K. *Emergence of Political Awakening in Kashmir.* New Delhi: Manohar, 1986.

KAUNDA, KENNETH

Kenneth Kaunda is one of Africa's pre-eminent statesmen. He led Zambia (formerly Northern Rhodesia) to independence in 1964 and served as that country's first president until 1991. In 1953, Kaunda's fierce resistance to the British imposition of the Federation of Central Africa—what became the Federation of Rhodesia (now Zimbabwe) and Nyasaland (now Malawi)—culminated in the formation of the African National Congress (ANC). In 1958, he broke from the ANC to form the Zambia African National Congress, of which he was the president until his imprisonment, from May 1959 to January 1960, for inciting political agitation. Kuanda used his time in prison to develop his political philosophy, the Zambian Humanism, with which he sought to redefine the main values of Zambian society.

Upon his release, Kaunda became the president of the United National Independence Party (UNIP). Working with Dr. Banda's Malawi Congress Party in Nyasaland, Kaunda achieved the dissolution of the Federation of Rhodesia and Nyasaland in 1963. With the advent of Zambia's first black government in 1962, when the UNIP won fourteen seats in the Legislative Assembly, Kaunda became the Minister of Local Government and Social Welfare. He was elected the prime minister of Northern Rhodesia, from January until October 1964, when he assumed the presidency of independent Zambia. In addition to these internal accomplishments, Kaunda was at the forefront of Pan-Africanism, together with such notables as Kwame Nkrumah, Julius Nyerere, and Leopold Sénghor.

Kaunda's Political Philosophy: Zambian Humanism

In a number of speeches and books, Kaunda promoted his philosophy of humanism—a human-centered doctrine couched in a high valuation of egalitarianism, communalism, racial equality, and non-violence in political life. First promulgated in 1967, Kaunda's humanism is not much different from the African socialism popularized in the 1960s, and even beyond, by African leaders such as Ghana's Nkrumah and Tanzania's Nyerere with his notion of *Ujamaa* (or familyhood). What sets Kaunda's humanism apart from the others is the primacy it accords to human dignity, Christian ethics, and the principle of non-violence. Kaunda latter equivocated on his position on violence, at the zenith of the Rhodesian liberation struggle, with the realization that the issue of violence can hardly be conceptualized in "either/or" terms. As he puts it in *Kaunda on Violence*, "It does not always follow that the way of non-violence is the more perilous. There may be times when it is the only sane

course of action. Nor is armed struggle always the guarantor of national security" (p. 29). Like other versions of African socialism, Kaunda's humanism derives much of its insights from African traditions. At the same time, Kaunda was pragmatic enough to embrace ideas not only from modern Zambia, but also from the economic and political systems of the East and the West. We thus find Fola Soremeku, once likening Kaunda's humanism, in an article in the *Times of Zambia* (February 12, 1971) to Janus—the Roman god of gates, with one face looking back and another looking forward.

Contribution to National and International Development

With judicious reliance on both private and public sector enterprises, Kaunda made a remarkable contribution to Zambia's post-independence development, especially in the areas of education, health care, manufacturing, and electrification, and also helped alleviate the forms of institutional and individual racism that were so prevalent in Zambian society. Zambia had no more than one hundred university graduates and 1,200 people with secondary education when it became independent, and Kaunda saw education as the first major problem to be tackled if Zambians were to be truly independent. Within eighteen months of the nation's transitional Development-Plan, instituted after independence, the number of secondary school students was doubled; and by the time the first full Development-Plan was completed in 1970, there were more than five times many students in secondary schools as in 1964. Meanwhile, the nation's first university, University of Zambia, established in 1965–1966, had more than one thousand undergraduate students by 1970.

Aided by the high prices of copper (the leading export) throughout the 1960s, Kaunda developed infrastructure across the country: An oil pipeline was extended from Dar es Salaam, Tanzania, to Zambia in 1969; the Great North and Great East Roads were expanded and tarred; and electricity was extended to many parts of the country. Drawing on his humanist philosophy, Kaunda increased the size and role of the public sector and boosted local control of the Zambian economy, which was dominated by foreigners at the time of independence. To limit personal aggrandizement among politicians and senior civil servants, Kaunda instituted a code of leadership in 1970, a move that caused intense apprehension among the elites. Individual liberties were for the most part respected during the reign of Kaunda, notwithstanding occasional internal political and ethnic tensions, as well as threats from Zambia's white minority-ruled neighbors. In 1972, faced with increasing opposition, Kaunda made Zambia one party state, banning all parties except his UNIP—quite an ironic, if not unfortunate, move for a leader who advocated for human rights with his humanist philosophy.

In addition to these achievements within Zambia, Kaunda served as the President of the Pan-African Freedom Movement and as the Chairman of the Front Line States. At a great political and material cost, Kaunda offered his country as a base for liberation movements from countries such as Angola, Mozambique, and Rhodesia. Kaunda was instrumental, with the likes of Desmond Tutu and Julius Nyerere, in the release of Nelson Mandela in 1990. Also, Kaunda was actively involved in the Nonaligned Movement, having served as its Chairman in the early 1970s. In 1991, intense pressure compelled Kaunda to return Zambia to multi-party elections in which his UNIP lost to the Movement of Multiparty Democracy, led by Frederic Chiluba. Kaunda handed over power to Chiluba, who amended the Zambian constitution to prevent Kaunda from contesting in the nation's next election. Kaunda retired from politics in 2000, devoting much of his time to peace and conflict resolution in Africa, through the Kenneth Kaunda Peace Foundation.

JOSEPH MENSAH

See also Organization of African Unity

References and Further Reading

De Gaay Fortman, Bastiaen. *After Mulungushi* (forwarded by Kenneth Kaunda). Nairobi: East African Publishing, 1969.

Hatch, John. *Two African Statesmen: Kaunda of Zambia and Nyerere of Tanzania*. London: Secker & Warburg, 1976.

Kandeke, Timothy K. *Fundamentals of Zambian Humanism*. Lusaka: National Education Company of Zambia, 1977.

Meebelo, Henry E. *Main Currents of Zambian Humanist Thought*. Lusaka, Nairobi, Dar es Salaam, Addis Ababa: Oxford University Press, 1973.

Roberts, Andrew. *A History of Zambia*. London, Nairobi, Ibadan, Lusaka: Heinemann, 1976.

Tordoff, William, editor. *Politics in Zambia*. Manchester: Manchester University Press, 1974.

KAZAKHSTAN

Lying at the conjunction of Europe and Asia, land-locked Kazakhstan shares borders with Russia to the north, China to the east, and Turkmenistan, Uzbekistan, and Kyrgyzstan along its southern margin. The country is the ninth largest in the world in area, but contains a population of only about 17 million. Most of this massive state is either arid steppe land or true desert, although the eastern borderlands intersect the Tien Shan and Altai ranges, and Khan Tengri, a peak that lies on the Kazakh-Chinese border, approaches 23,000 feet in elevation. Three large lakes punctuate the dry landscape from west to east: the Caspian Sea, the Aral Sea, and Lake Balkash. Kazakh-stan is dominated by a dry variant of continental climate, with lengthy cold winters and relatively short warm summers. Winter temperatures in the northern section of the country average only around $0°F$, while summer highs in the south sometimes reach near $100°F$.

The foundation of Kazakh ethnicity dates from the Mongol invasions of the thirteenth century, when Mongol and Tatar elements intermingled with nomadic Turkic peoples occupying this section of the Eurasian steppe. An emergent identity was reinforced through the establishment of the Kazakh Khanate in the early 1500s, which eventually led to the formation of three divisions, or *hordes*: the Great Horde, whose territory lay in eastern Kazakhstan, the Middle Horde which occupied the central and northern steppe, and the Small Horde, living in the lands adjacent to the Caspian in the west. From the late 1600s to the early 1700s, the Kazakh state was nearly overrun by an invasion of the Kalmyks, an Asiatic people from Siberia. This threat forced the Kazakhs to seek assistance from Russia, a request that paved the way for eventual absorption of the Kazakh steppe lands into the Russian Empire. Under Soviet rule, in 1936 Kazakhstan was granted the status of an SSR (Soviet Socialist Republic) until declaring independence in 1991. During the period of collectivization under the Soviets (1929–1938), it is likely that at least 1 million Kazakhs starved to death, and the number of livestock in the republic declined dramatically.

Kazakhstan is well endowed with natural resources, and possesses abundant land for crop cultivation and animal husbandry. Wheat is a major crop in the northern reaches of the country, while irrigated cotton, rice, and specialty crops dominate in the south. Much acreage is devoted to pasture, particularly in the drier regions. Large coal deposits are found near the city of Qaraghandy (Karaganda), and significant quantities of valuable ores (gold, silver, chrome, tungsten, zinc, copper, iron) are present throughout the country. Most significantly for the country's future, large deposits of petroleum have been discovered in the west, along the littoral of the Caspian Sea. The industrial base of Kazakhstan is concentrated in the northern half of the country and in Almaty, the former capital and largest city. Industrial output emphasizes the production of steel, petrochemicals, machine tools, and agricultural equipment.

Significant petroleum deposits were discovered in western Kazakhstan in the late 1960s, and by the late 1980s some 6 billion barrels worth of proven reserves had been identified in the Tenghiz field, lying roughly between the Ural River and the Aral Sea. Foreign oil companies have shown considerable interest in these resources, particularly Chevron, which in the mid-1990s had committed to investing nearly $20 billion in the region.

A major obstacle to the development of Kazakhstan's oil resources has been the country's geographic isolation and distance from global markets. Several pipeline routes have been proposed that would allow Kazakh oil to reach ports in nearby countries, and when completed will allow for the exportation of possibly seven hundred thousand barrels per day. Kazakhstan's oil, industrial capacity, and relative stability have enabled it to attract a greater amount of foreign investment than any other Central Asian state. Some additional income is collected through a leasing agreement with Russia, which allows the Russian space agency to continue to use the Baikonur Cosmodrome, the main launch site for the Soviet space program.

Environmental damage from the Soviet period continues to plague independent Kazakhstan. Two regions in particular were devastated under the Soviets: the Aral Sea and its environs, and the city of Semey (Semipalatinsk), which is located near the main nuclear testing site used by the Soviet military. Hundreds of atmospheric and underground nuclear tests were conducted in Kazakhstan between the late 1940s and late 1980s, and near Semey high rates for birth defects, certain cancers, and infant mortality have been linked to testing during the Soviet regime. The Aral Sea has undergone an unprecedented decline in recent decades, as the rivers supplying it with fresh water were overused by cotton producers in Uzbekistan and Kazakhstan.

The ethnic geography of Kazakhstan compounds the challenge of constructing a civil society. At independence, Russians accounted for approximately 38% of the population, with Kazakhs holding almost the same percentage, at about 40%. Although the percentage of Russians may have dropped since the early 1990s, several of the northern regions contain either a Russian majority or plurality. The divide between Kazakh and Russian culture has made the effort to create the apparatus of a "Kazakh" state more problematical, as many in the Russian minority resent efforts to make Kazakh a national language and view any movement to reinvigorate Kazakh society's Muslim roots as an attempt to "Islamicize" the country.

The development of democratic institutions has been slow to materialize. Although certainly more democratic than most of its neighbors, even by late 2001 the Kazakh administration continued to operate in an authoritarian mode, limiting the activities of unofficial media and opposition parties, with the greater part of political power concentrated in the hands of President Nursultan Nazarbaev. On the other hand, Kazakhstan has avoided the instability that has troubled some other Central Asian states, and shown the capability to capture badly needed foreign investment. Given its great size, vital resources, and strategic position, Kazakhstan is poised to become a major regional and international player on the global stage.

REUEL R. HANKS

See also Commonwealth of Independent States: History and Economic Development; Commonwealth of Independent States: International Relations; Soviet Bloc

References and Further Reading

Beisenova, Aliya. "Environmental Problems in Kazakhstan," in *Sustainable Development in Central Asia*, edited by Shirin Akiner, Sander Tideman and John Hay. New York: St. Martin's Press, 1998.
Conquest, Robert. *The Harvest of Sorrow*, (see especially chapter nine, "Central Asia and the Kazakh Tragedy,"). New York and Oxford: Oxford University Press, 1986.
Gleason, Gregory. *The Central Asian States*. Boulder, CO: Westview Press, 1997.
Hanks, Reuel. "Directions in the Ethnic Politics of Kazakhstan: Concession, Compromise, or Catastrophe?" *Journal of Third World Studies*, Vol. XV, No. 1 (Spring 1998).
Olcott, Martha. *The Kazakhs*, 2nd edition. Stanford, CA: Hoover Institution Press, 1995.
Sagdeev, Roald Z. and Susan Eisenhower, editors. *Central Asia: Conflict, Resolution, and Change*. Chevy Chase, MD: CPSS Press, 1995.

KENYA

The Republic of Kenya is located in the eastern region of Africa. It borders the Republic of Uganda to the west; the Republic of Tanzania to the south; the Indian Ocean to the southeast; the Republic of Somalia to the east; the Republic of Ethiopia to the north; and the Republic of Sudan to the northwest. Bisected by the equator, it lies between approximately 4° N and 4° S and 34° E and 41° E. It has a total area of 580,370 square kilometers, including 13,369 square kilometers of permanent water surface. Kenya's topography is characterized by erosional plains that rise from the Indian Ocean towards the highlands in the central region, forming their base at about 1,500 meters above sea level. The highlands have isolated extinct volcanoes, including Mount Kenya (5,200 meters) in the central region and Mount Elgon (4,321 meters) on the western border of the country. The Great Rift Valley cuts across the country from north to south through the highlands, where it measurers 65 kilometers wide and bounded by escarpments of 600–900 meters high. The plains generally incline westwards to Lake Victoria on the southwestern border of the country.

About 84% of Kenya's area has arid and semi-arid climatic conditions. This vast area in the northern, northeastern, and parts of the eastern regions of the country receive unreliable rainfall of less than 760 millimeters annually. Only 16% of the country receives adequate rainfall for cultivation. This agriculturally high potential area is found in the highlands, the Lake Victoria basin and along the coastal strip of the Indian Ocean. The settlement pattern has seen 80% of Kenya's population of 29 million (as per the 1999 population census) concentrated in the agriculturally high potential regions while the rest is found in the marginal areas. Whereas the arid and semi-arid regions are the least populated with a density of three persons per square kilometer, the density in the high potential regions is over 230 persons per square kilometer.

The boundaries of Kenya were drawn up during the colonial period. When the British government took over its formal administrative responsibility in June 1895, the territory was named the East Africa Protectorate. To facilitate communication between the Indian Ocean and Uganda, where they had also established their "sphere of influence," the British started the construction of the Kenya–Uganda railway, which reached Kisumu (then known as Port Florence) on the shores of Lake Victoria in 1902.

Initially, the British did not have immediate plans on what to do with the territory other than securing a way to Uganda from the Indian Ocean. It happened that the Kenya–Uganda railway cut across some of the country's best agricultural land. It was on this land that the British started to experiment with the possibility of establishing commercial farming. A policy decision was subsequently made to embark on large-scale plantation agriculture by white farmers to produce coffee, tea, sisal, and pyrethrum for export. This required large tracts of land for exclusive white settlement. It was made available through the alienation of agriculturally high potential land in the highlands from the indigenous Africans, who were henceforth relocated to agriculturally marginal lands that were labeled "reserves."

This settlement arrangement was accompanied by a racial approach to the development process where European settled areas were developed at the expense of the "reserves." Africans were barred from growing lucrative cash crops like coffee and tea in order to ensure that they remained poor in order to supply cheap labor on European farms at a minimum wage. They were also restricted to their unproductive "reserves" by introducing identification cards (*Kipande* in *Kiswahili*) that were used to monitor their movement and labor provision. Medical, educational, and other social services were organized on strict racial lines, with Africans getting the worst or none at all, yet they were heavily taxed to fund the provision of the services. This lopsided development formed the basis of the rise of African nationalist movements to fight for independence. Besides the various political organizations that were formed after World War II, the *Mau Mau* rebellion of 1952 was the most effective in the struggle for independence. Though the rebellion was militarily defeated in 1953, the British responded to the uprising by initiating economic, social, and political reforms between 1953 and 1960, culminating in the granting of independence to Kenya in 1963. Jomo Kenyatta, who led the Kenya African National Union (KANU) to beat its archrival, the Kenya African Democratic Union (KADU), during the independence elections, became the first president of the country.

At independence, the KANU government inherited the colonial regime's capitalist approach to socio-economic development. In 1965, it moved to adopt African Socialism as its development ideology through Sessional Paper No. Ten on "African Socialism and its Application to Planning in Kenya." This ideology aimed at reviving traditional African society in the midst of a modern monetary economy. Social egalitarianism, mutual responsibility, social justice, equal opportunities for all, human dignity. and the elimination of the exploitation of man by man were some of the objectives of African socialism. They were to be realized through a mixed economy that would combine capitalist and traditional African society ideals. While foreign investment and private ownership of property were to be allowed, there would be control against excessive personal accumulation; provision of social welfare services by the state; and substantial participation of the state and the co-operative movement in the economy. Nevertheless, the structural means to realize these were not put in place, such that the private sector became a leading actor in the economy and provision of social services. Indeed, capitalism formed the basis for the transfer of land in the former "white highlands" to indigenous ownership in order to Africanize agriculture. Land was made available to anyone who had the ability and capacity to purchase without any limits on accumulation. Co-operative savings and credit schemes were started to enable groups and individuals to raise funds for the purpose. Further private land ownership reforms, including land adjudication, consolidation and registration, were initiated in the early period of independence. These efforts in land reform partly contributed to the predominance of agriculture in the Kenyan economy, despite attempts to industrialize and a flourishing tourist trade.

Kenyan's record of socio-economic development since independence has generally been on a downward trend. Between 1964 and 1973, the country achieved commendable economic growth that translated into improved living conditions of the people. gross domestic product (GDP) grew on average by 6.6%. With per capita income growth rate of 2.6% per year and a steady growth in the provision of social services by both the state and the private sector, the majority of Kenyans were able to satisfy most of their basic needs. During this period, Kenya was referred to as the "African miracle" due to the exemplary economic and general development performance. This good performance was, however, not sustained.

From 1974, the growth rate of GDP declined throughout the remainder of that decade. This was due to the poor linkage between agriculture and industry, especially the reliance on imported intermediate inputs and machinery in the manufacturing sector that could not fuel agricultural productivity; rising oil prices following the first international oil crisis of 1973; recurrent drought; global economic recession; and worsening terms of trade at the international market. By the early 1980s, the rate of economic growth could not keep pace with the rate of population growth, culminating in a tremendous decline in per capita income. This situation reversed the steady and continuous gains in the standard of living that most of the citizens had enjoyed. This downturn in economic performance and the general development process compelled the government to adopt the World Bank and the International Monetary Fund (IMF) prescribed Structural Adjustment Programs (SAPs) in the early 1980s. Nevertheless, the implementation of SAPs did not help much as the rate of economic growth continued to decline. People's living conditions deteriorated with the average growth rate of per capita income falling to 0.4% by 1989.

In 1991, Kenya was hit hard following the suspension of development aid by bilateral and multilateral donors due to bad governance and the violation of human rights by President Moi's regime. This saw the GDP growth rate decline to 2.3% while per capital

income fell to its lowest level of −2.0%. In 1992 and 1993, the GDP growth rate further declined to 0.5 and 0.2%, respectively. This decline in economic performance was reflected in the deterioration of people's livelihoods. The introduction of "cost-sharing" in the provision of social services as prescribed by SAPs, in the midst of increasing unemployment and rising inflation rate, worsened people's living conditions. Most Kenyans became unable to meet medical and educational expense. On its part, the government could not afford to maintain or develop the socio-economic infrastructure.

There were signs of economic recovery in the mid-1990s when economic performance picked up relative to the early years of the decade. The country recorded improved GDP growth rates of 4.8 and 4.6% in 1995 and 1996, respectively. However, this rate dropped once again to 2.3% in 1997 following the suspension of aid by donors, citing corruption and bad governance. Since then, the annual growth rate of GDP has been on the decline. Whereas this rate stood at only 1.8% in 1998, it had declined to 1.4 in 1999. Economic performance in the year 2000 even worsened following the long draught that culminated into the worst shortage of electricity and water in the country. These commodities had to be rationed for consumers, resulting into a sharp drop in the manufacturing sector. The GDP growth rate fell to its lowest ebb of −0.3%. The economy, however, started picking up in 2003 when the GDP growth rate rose to 1.3%.

As in the previous decades, the worsening economic performance from the mid-1990s was accompanied by an increase in the level of poverty. The national overall poverty level stood as 52.6% in 1997. Whereas 53.1% of the population in the rural areas was absolutely poor, 50.1% of the urban dwellers were living below the poverty line. It was estimated that 54% and 56% of Kenya's population were absolutely poor in 2000 and 2002, respectively. The implication is that the level of poverty in Kenya has been rising over the years, but more so in the 1990s decade.

There has been an interesting correlation between the trend of socio-economic development and the growth of civil liberty in Kenya. During the first decade of independence when the country recorded commendable achievements in socio-economic development, there was a relatively competitive political environment that afforded citizens the liberty to participate in the political process as a result of Kenyatta's "princely" style of personal rule. The "prince," unlike the autocrat, does not seek to destroy politicians who represent potential challenge to his power, but plays them off against each other while seeking to bring them into ever-closer dependence on him. He is a manipulator who avoids committing himself to any course of action, but rather moves with the consensus that he manipulates competing factions to achieve. Thus, Kenyatta created and manipulated various patronage factions to achieve his ends. The competition that ensued among these factions to get Kenyatta's favors, coupled with a semi-competitive parliamentary electoral system, contributed to the evolution of a relatively pluralist political environment that tolerated civic participation in the political system.

Nevertheless, the rising criticisms against the state from the mid-1970s saw Kenyatta change his governance style to autocratic personal rule in order to stamp out critics and assert his authority. It is during this era of increased authoritarianism, when civic liberties were curtailed, that the pace of socio-economic development started to slacken. This worsened during the Moi era following the death of Kenyatta in 1978. Former President Daniel arap Moi's regime was essentially an autocratic personal rule that extended authoritarianism beyond the level Kenyatta had left it. Moi curtailed civic liberty by establishing himself as the master of the political stage and went on to dominate as well as direct all centers of political power, including civil society organizations. Kenya's development record worsened in the meantime. Though increased authoritarianism contributed to the emergence of more civic organizations to demand for political pluralism, culminating into the adoption of a multi-party political system in 1991, democratic governance remained an illusion throughout the Moi era.

A united opposition coalition eventually brought to an end four decades of KANU rule in the December 2002 general elections. In the run-up to the elections, fourteen of the hitherto weak and fragmented opposition political parties formed the National Rainbow Coalition (NARC) to challenge KANU and went on to win the election. The NARC government has adopted a laissez faire approach to administration where the president, unlike his predecessor who strode the entire political scene, has given his ministers room to run their ministries without interference. There is remarkable freedom of expression as evidenced by more liberal and critical electronic and print media. The government is also in the process of completing the review of the country's constitution that has been the source of authoritarianism. In the economic field, the government is putting in place structures to revive the economy and there are prospects for improved economic performance and socio-economic development relative to the previous regime.

FREDRICK O. WANYAMA

References and Further Reading

Barkan, Joel D. "The Rise and fall of a Governance Realm in Kenya", in Goran Hyden and Michael Bratton, editors, *Governance and politics in Africa*. Boulder and London: Lynne Rienner Publishers, 1992.

————, editor. *Beyond capitalism Vs socialism in Kenya and Tanzania*. Nairobi: East African Educational Publishers, 1994.

————, editor. *Politics and Public Policy in Kenya and Tanzania*. New York: Praeger Publishers, 1984; Nairobi: Heinemann, 1984.

Bienen, Henry. *Kenya: The politics of Participation and control*. Princeton, NJ: Princeton University Press, 1974.

Cheru, Fantu. "Kenya", in *The Oxford Companion to Politics of the World*, edited by Joel Krieger. Oxford: Oxford University Press, 1993.

Gertzel, Cherry. *The politics of Independent Kenya*. Evanston, IL: Northwestern University Press, 1970.

Gibbon, Peter, editor. *Markets, Civil society and Democracy in Kenya*. Uppsala: The Scandinavian Institute of African Studies, 1995.

Leys, Colin. *Underdevelopment in Kenya: The Political Economy of Neo-colonialism*. Berkeley, CA: University of California Press, 1974.

Morgan, W.T.W. "Kenya: Physical and Social Geography", in *Africa South of the Sahara 1997*, 26th Edition London: Europa Publications Ltd., 1997.

Ochieng, W.R. *A History of Kenya*. London: Macmillan Publishers, 1985.

Rake, Alan. "Kenya: Recent History", in *Africa South of the Sahara 1997*, 26th Edition. London: Europa Publications Limited, 1997.

Schatzberg, Michael, editor. *The Political Economy of Kenya*. New York: Praeger, 1997.

Van Buren, Linda. "Kenya: Economy", in *Africa South of the Sahara 1997*, 26th Edition. London: Europa Publications Limited, 1997.

Widner, Jennifer A. *The Rise of a Party State in Kenya: From Harambee to Nyayo*. Berkeley, CA: University of California Press, 1992.

KENYATTA, JOMO

The first president of Kenya, Jomo Kenyatta (1863–1918) was a member of Kenya's largest tribe, the *Kikuyu*. Respectfully referred to as *Mzee*, a deferential term meaning "wise elder," Kenyatta's life was intricately intertwined with the relatively short yet immensely influential era of British colonial rule in Kenya. His tenure as head of state from 1963 to 1978 reflected the incongruity between the initial optimism that enveloped liberation and the difficult realities of governing newly independent, multiethnic nation-states in the twentieth century.

Born Kamau wa Ngengi in Kiambu District, Kenya, in 1893 (date unconfirmed), Kenyatta attended the Church of Scotland Missionary School, where he received primary education and carpentry training. Later, he was employed by Nairobi City Council as water meter reader and stores clerk. He became active in the *Kikuyu Central Association* (KCA) and in 1929 was sent to London to present the Kikuyu case of grievance for land dispossession to the British Colonial Office. He ended up spending over fifteen years of his life in Europe, in the process taking both a Master's degree and a British wife. While there he adopted his name— *Jomo* means "burning spear"and *Kinyata* a type of beaded belt he favored—and used it to publish *Facing Mount Kenya*. Though ostensibly an ethnographic account of Kikuyu culture, written as his MA thesis under the tutelage of eminent anthropologist Bronislaw Malinowski, in reality this was a highly symbolic political statement. Here was a major scholarly work on the internal workings of an indigenous African society written by a member of that group. The cover featured Kenyatta dressed in a traditional animal skin cape while fingering the point of a spear.

After his return to Kenya in 1946, organized the World Trade Union Conference and co-founded *Pan-African Federation*. In 1947, he was elected President of the *Kenya African Union*, an incipient political organization thinly cloaked as a trade/labor union. Kenyatta spent the next few years urging his fellow Africans to work hard, shun idleness and alcohol while simultaneously lobbying the colonial government to return Kikuyu land that had been given to white settlers. For both settlers and the colonial administration Kenyatta became symbolic of *Mau Mau*—a guerilla movement based in the Mount Kenya forests. Paradoxically, Kenyatta was not involved in active resistance. Indeed he went to great lengths to disassociate himself from this movement, whose members referred to themselves as the *Land and Freedom Army* and were led by figures such as Dedan Kimathi. Nonetheless, Kenyatta, an articulate and charismatic public figure, was perceived as a threat. Consequently he and five colleagues were arrested, tried, and convicted of treason. They were imprisoned in a remote region of northwest Kenya from 1953 to 1961.

After release from prison, and just prior to Kenya's independence, in a masterfully crafted speech delivered in Nakuru, on August 12, 1963, Kenyatta convincingly reassured three hundred white settler farmers that they had little to fear from him and that their interests would be well represented in his government. To the chagrin of many freedom fighters, his prophesy turned out to be accurate.

He was appointed prime minister of Kenya on December 12, 1963, and elected president exactly a year later. He would be re-elected twice, in 1969 and 1974. Under his slogan *harambee*—"let's all pull together"—the first years of Kenyatta's leadership reflected the euphoria that pervaded post-independence

Africa. While Tanzania to the south took a more socialistic approach to development called *ujamaa* or "familyhood," based upon the vision of President Julius Nyerere, Kenya under Kenyatta took an unbridled capitalistic tack (Barkan 1984). National income doubled as coffee and tea exports did well on world markets. Schools based upon the *harambee* principle flourished, establishing a basis for universal primary education. Conversely, wealth disparities between rich and poor grew alongside nepotism and political patronage. Ultimately a new label— *wabenzi* (literally "people of the Mercedes Benz")— came to describe those who profited from Kenyatta's rule.

Kenyatta's first administration also witnessed the coming of one party rule, beginning with the merger of the *Kenya African National Union* (KANU) with the *Kenya African Democratic Union* (KADU) in 1964. This effectively ushered in a pattern of *single party politics* —first *de facto* then *de jure* after 1982— that continued until the end of 1991. Kenyatta's government quickly became highly intolerant of dissent. In 1966, the country's first vice president, Oginga Odinga, resigned and left KANU. He was later arrested and imprisoned over his attempt to found the opposition *Kenya People's Union* (KPU). In 1969, the Minister for Economic Planning, Tom Mboya—like Odinga, a Luo—was assassinated, arousing inter-ethnic tensions between Luo and Kikuyu. A lone Kikuyu youth was later executed for the murder. J.M. Kariuki, an outspoken member of parliament whose slogan was "Kenya has become a nation of ten millionaires and ten million beggars," was found dead under mysterious circumstances in 1975. No suspects were ever caught. Kariuki was a Kikuyu and a former Mau Mau detainee, but by this time class based politics had come to outweigh both ethnicity as well as sacrifices made during the independence struggle.

Kenyatta died in his sleep of natural causes on August 22, 1978. He was succeeded by Daniel arap Moi, a Kalenjin, who despite the slogan *nyayo*, "footsteps," has continued much of the class-related conflict that occurred under Kenyatta's rule.

BRUCE D. ROBERTS

See also Kenya; Mau Mau

References and Further Reading

Barkan, Joel D, editor. *Politics and Public Policy in Kenya and Tanzania*. New York: Praeger, 1984.
Edgerton, Robert B. *Mau Mau: An African Crucible*. New York: Ballantine, 1989.
Haugerud, Angelique. *The Culture of Politics in Modern Kenya*. Cambridge: Cambridge University Press, 1995.

Leys, Colin. *Underdevelopment in Kenya: The Political Economy of Neo-Colonialism*. Berkeley, CA: University of California Press, 1975.

Odinga, Oginga. *Not Yet Uhuru: The Autobiography of Oginga Odinga*. London: Heinemann, 1967.

KHAMA, SIR SERETSE

Seretse Khama was born in 1921 in the village of Serowe in the British protectorate of Bechuanaland. His father Sekgoma Khama was the son of Kgosi Khama III who ruled the central region of the protectorate. Young Seretse's father died when he was four and Seretse's uncle Tshekedi Khama was made his guardian. Tshekedi sent Seretse to boarding school in South Africa and to Fort Hare University College where he obtained a BA degree in 1944. In 1945, he was sent to England to study law and after a year at Balliol College at Oxford he began legal studies at the Inner Temple in London.

In 1947, he met and soon after married Ruth Williams, an act that infuriated Tshekedi who ordered Seretse to return to Botswana and divorce his wife. Seretse did return to his homeland, but his wife accompanied him and he began speaking to the local people. He won their political support and personal loyalty and when the people turned against his uncle, Tshekedi went into voluntary exile.

The prospect of having an African chief with a white wife enraged neighboring South Africans whose Afrikaner nationalist government successfully persuaded the British government to bar Seretse from his birthright, his chieftainship in Bechuanaland. Britain did so because it wanted South Africa's gold and uranium. The British government suppressed a 1951 report that declared Seretse able to rule, and instead declared him unfit. On the basis of this deception it forced both Seretse and Ruth Khama to return to England. In 1952, the new Conservative government made the exile permanent but its treatment of the Khamas received international press coverage and outrage over the racist behavior of the British in their treatment of Seretse Khama. In 1956, British leadership began to separate itself from South Africa's racist government and policies, and Seretse's official exile was lifted. He returned to Botswana in 1961, became the country's founding president, and eventually was knighted.

Upon his return to Botswama, Seretse became the head of the Bechuanaland Democratic Party, which he along with Dr. Quett Masire, who succeeded him as president, had created. The BDP won the emerging nation's inaugural election in 1965 and Seretse Khama became prime minister. In 1966, he became president of the Republic of Botswana and during his tenure Botswana became a successful economy. Though the country has suffered from a severe HIV/AIDS epidemic since the 1990s, Botswana has some of the continent's most advanced programs to contain and fight the disease. Politically Seretse Khama's legacy was efficient, honest, and open government. Externally he played a key regional role in the creation of the Southern African Development Community (SADC).

ROBERT L. CURRY, JR.

See also South Africa; Southern Africa: History and Economic Development

References and Further Reading

Carter, Gwendolyn, and E. Philip Morgan, editors. *From the Frontline: Policy Speeches of Sir Seretse Khama*. London: Rex Collins, 1980.

Colclough, Christopher, and Stephen McCarthy. *The Political Economy of Botwana*. Oxford: Oxford University Press, 1980.

Parsons, Neil, Thomas Tlou and Willie Henderson. *Seretse Khama, 1921–1980*. Gaborone and Braamfontein: Botswana Society and Macmillan, 1995.

Picard, Louis, editor. *The Evolution of Modern Botswana*. London: Rex Collins, 1985.

KHMER ROUGE

In the early 1960s, then "neutralist" ruler of Cambodia (Kampuchea), Prince Norodom Sihanouk, coined the term Khmer Rouge (KR) (literally Red Khmer) to describe the indigenous Communist Party of Kampuchea (CPK). The CPK had begun as a nationalist anti-French independence movement in the 1950s with ties to the Vietnamese communists. Its leaders were mostly Buddhist, traditionally educated, and rural moderates. By 1962, they had evolved into a more doctrinaire group as a younger group of urban, Paris-educated, anti-Vietnamese Marxist radicals, led by Pol Pot, gained control of the standing committee of the CPK Central Committee. They were known as the party "Center." Pot, born Saloth Sar in rural Kampuchea in 1925 (some say 1928), had gone, on scholarship, to Paris to study but became so involved in the Marxist movement he lost his scholarship and returned, in 1953, to join the communist revolutionary movement in his homeland.

In 1970, Sihanouk was overthrown by pro-American forces led by General Lon Nol. Sihanouk fled to the countryside and, in an effort to regain power, allied himself with the CPK/KR. He soon discovered that the Center was in ever increasing control. Pragmatic to the extreme, the Center officially allied the KR with the Democratic (Socialist) Republic of Viet

Nam (DRV) in the war against the United States and her allies, while covertly purging thousands of CPK members who were moderates and/or Vietnamese-trained. Among those purged in the 1970s were moderates or independents who supported Sihanouk or intellectuals like Hou Yuon. Throughout this period, Pot denounced dissidents for being corrupted by materialist desires and neglectful of ideological purity. In retrospect, it is also clear that these rivalries were fraught with regional overtones since most anti-Center members were concentrated in eastern Kampuchea.

In spring 1975, the KR defeated Lon Nol's forces occupying the capital of Phnom Penh shortly after the chaotic departure of US. personnel in April. What followed was a scene from Dante's Inferno. To a nation already devastated by years of war, the KR leaders added Draconian measures for implementation of their twisted vision of Marxist ideological purity. Literally overnight 2 million city dwellers were herded out of urban centers into rural forced labor camps.

At first the rural population supported the KR but soon even they were forced to perform unpaid collective labor. This "Stalinist" depravity included total abrogation of all civil rights and basic liberties. Religion was outlawed, as was land ownership. Rival members of all political parties were rounded up and summarily executed. Families were splintered with children encouraged to spy on their parents and teens drafted into unpaid military service or labor camps. Hundreds of thousands died. According to Ben Keirnan, foremost expert on the subject, of a total population of 7.89 million Kampucheans in 1975, 1.67 million died directly at the hands of the KR during their four-year rule of terror.

In the mid-1970s, the KR reserved a special hell for ethnic minorities undertaking a systematic campaign of genocide by massacring two hundred thousand Chinese, one hundred thousand Cham Muslims, twenty thousand Thais, and ten thousand Vietnamese. In May 1978, they announced a campaign to "exterminate 50 million Vietnamese" and "purify" the Kampuchean population of all Vietnamese culture and influence. This led moderate communists in the "Eastern Zone" to rebel against the KR. While the KR killed nearly 250,000 of the 1.5 million people in eastern Kampuchea, they could not completely crush the rebellion. At the most critical moment, forces of the DRV joined the rebels eventually defeating the KR and occupying Phnom Penh on January 7, 1979. Pol Pot and his KR forces fled to jungle sanctuaries along the eastern border of Thailand. In the 1980s, supported by the Vietnamese occupiers, Eastern Zone moderates like Hun Sen, who became prime minister in 1985, worked to rebuild Kampuchea's economy and bring peace to the war-torn nation.

In 1989, the Vietnamese withdrew their forces and, two years later, the KR, Phnom Penh faction, and two smaller rebel groups signed a pact designed to disarm all factions, bring peace, and lead to free elections. Indeed, the 1993 UN-sponsored elections did lead to a coalition government comprised of several leftist factions including Sen's government faction and (by then) King Sihanouk's party. However, at the last-minute Pol Pot and the KR, who never disarmed, refused to support the elections. Instead, he and his ten thousand-man army continued the bloody civil strife often supported by the People's Republic of China (PRC), mainly because of its conflicts with Viet Nam; powerful Thai elements; and even, at times, the United States who feared Vietnamese domination of the region.

In August 1996, Pol Pot's former brother-in-law and chief collaborator, Ieng Sary, along with four thousand guerillas, defected to the government side. In return for Sary's control of western portions of Kampuchea, King Sihanouk, now titular head of state, reluctantly granted him a royal amnesty. In early 1997, the government coalition began to splinter into a bitter and often violent conflict between the two co-prime ministers, Hun Sen and Prince Norodom Ranariddh. At the same time, new conflicts arose within the KR. Even so, negotiations began between dissident KR leader Khien Samphen and Ranariddh's National United Front to absorb the KR back into a government in opposition to Hun Sen's Cambodian People's Party if the KR would purge Pol Pot.

Pol Pot reacted violently by executing long time KR defense minister Sien Sen and fifteen of his family and friends. Pot's forces captured Samphen and the KR negotiating team. But, resupplied by Ranariddh's faction the dissidents finally defeated Pot's faction on June 19, 1997, near Anlong Venh. The sickly seventy-two-year-old Pol Pot surrendered lying on a stretcher. Brother Number One's bloody career was over. However, with peace within reach, on July 6, Hun Sen seized power forcing Ranariddh to flee the country and the KR to return to their jungle hideout. Early that fall, at KR headquarters in Anlong Venh the new KR leaders held a show trial in which Pol Pot, dazed and leaning on a cane, was summarily convicted, not of genocide, but plotting against fellow KR leaders. He was sentenced to life in prison.

Instead of peace, this left KR leaders (whose guilt was as great as Pol Pot's) allied with Ranariddh's military forces in a continuing struggle against Hun Sen's government forces. On April 15, 1998, Pol Pot died but the struggle, albeit sublimated, continued with more than 2 million Kampucheans having paid the ultimate price for Marxist ideological purity. Indeed, thirty years of war and revolutionary violence have devastated the population, the economy, the social fabric, the political process and the lives of millions of otherwise peaceful people. This once "peaceful kingdom" of rural prosperity is now one of the most underdeveloped nations on earth. Prospects for the future are grim and bloodshed seems to be the endless legacy of the Khmer Rouge.

WILLIAM P. HEAD

See also Cambodia; Southeast Asia: History and Economic Development; Southeast Asia: International Relations

References and Further Reading

Becker, Elizabeth. *When The War Was Over*. NY: Simon and Schuster, 1986.

Chandler, David P. *The Tragedy of Cambodian History: Politics, War, and Revolution, Since 1945*. New Haven, CT: Yale University Press, 1993.

——. *Brother Number One: A Political Biography of Pol Pot*. Revised Edition, Boulder, CO: Westview Press, 1999.

Chonda, Nayan. *Brother Enemy*. NY: Harcourt, Brace and Jovanovich, 1986.

Kiernan, Ben. *How Pol Pot Came to Power: A History of Communism in Kampuchea, 1930–1975*. New Haven, CT: Yale University Press, 1987.

——. *Genocide and Democracy in Cambodia: The Khmer Rouge, the United Nations and the International Community, 1993*. Monograph No. 41, Yale Southeast Asia Series. New Haven, CT: Yale University Press, 1993.

——. *The Pol Pot Regime: Race, Power and Genocide in Cambodia under the Khmer Rouge, 1975–1979*. New Haven, CT: Yale University Press, 1998.

KHOMEINI, AYATOLLAH RUHOLLAH

The Ayatollah Khomeini (1902–1989) inspired a religio-political revolution against Iranian monarch Shah Reza Pahlavi and founded the Islamic Republic of Iran. Khomeini brought down the Shah with an odd combination of religious mysticism and legalism, and for the last ten years of his life (1979–1989) ruled Iran with supreme self-confidence, even as the country plunged into a disastrous war with Iraq. Khomeini was uninterested in anything outside Persian culture and Shi'a Islam, yet shrewdly used mass media to mobilize religious revolutionaries.

Ruhollah Al-Musavi was born in Khomein, a small town south of Tehran, on September 24, 1902. ("Ayatollah" is an honorific title meaning "the sign of God." Al-Musavi began using his birthplace as a surname at age twenty-nine.) Khomeini's father Mustafa Musavi was murdered before the boy was a year old, so he was raised by his mother and an aunt.

Ruhollah received a religious education from his older brother. He studied Arabic and is said to have memorized the entire Koran. His mother and aunt both died when he was sixteen. In 1919, he began formal Islamic studies under a conservative teacher. The turbulent Persian politics of the 1920s left their mark on the young man. A military officer named Reza Khan seized power in 1921 and four years later changed the country's name from Persia to Iran. Reza Khan was a Westernizer and modernizer whose ideas echoed those of the Turkish revolutionary, Ataturk. In 1926, Reza Khan crowned himself *shahanshah* (king of kings) and Khomeini began his lifelong struggle against the monarchy. Soon he was under police surveillance.

In 1929, Khomeini married Batul Saqafi, the ten-year old daughter of an ayatollah. Their first son, Mustafa, was born in 1932, followed in time by three daughters and another son. Khomeini taught Islamic jurisprudence in Qom, where his lectures attracted a growing circle of students. In 1937 and 1938, he made religious pilgrimages to Mecca and to the Shi'ite holy city of An-Najaf in Iraq.

British and Russian forces invaded Iran in 1941 to prevent the pro-Fascist Reza Shah from allying with Nazi Germany. They deposed Reza Shah but allowed his son, Mohammad Reza Shah Pahlavi to succeed him. Khomeini declared that "all orders issued by the dictatorial regime . . . have no value at all." In 1944, with the war still on, he denounced the royal family and called on the nation to "rise up for God." His call was finally answered thirty-five years later.

By the early 1960s, the Shah's program of rapid economic development had generated a conservative backlash. Innovations such as voting rights for women and secular education for the masses offended the devout, and the Shah's land reform program threatened the financial base of the Shi'ite establishment. Khomeini mounted bold public attacks against the government. On March 22, 1963, the Shah sent paratroopers into the *madrasa* (Islamic school) in Qom. They killed eighteen people and arrested Khomeini. When released, the Ayatollah resumed his public denunciations of the Shah. On June 5, 1963, Khomeini was arrested again and sentenced to three months in jail.

In October 1964, Khomeini accused the Shah of treason. This time the Ayatollah was sent into exile, first to Turkey and then to Iraq, from where he smuggled tape-recorded sermons back into Iran. In 1970, Khomeini published a tract, *Islamic Government*, in which he railed against "the Jews and their foreign masters" who were "plotting against Islam and preparing the way for the Jews to rule over the entire planet."

The Shah, who once styled himself a reformer, was by the late 1970s bogged down in extravagance and nepotism. His secret police tortured opponents and they may have murdered Khomeini's son, Mustafa. In December 1977, students in Tehran demanded Khomeini's return. A cycle of popular protest and violent repression built up. By September 1978, Tehran was under martial law and protesters were being shot by the hundreds. The Shah prevailed on Saddam Hussein to expel Khomeini from Iraq. This proved to be a tactical blunder, for Khomeini simply moved to France, from where he deftly orchestrated the growing street demonstrations in Iran.

Khomeini's potent charisma derived not from any special oratorical ability but rather from messianic Shi'ite theology. Shi'ites believe in a "twelfth Imam," who vanished a thousand years ago but never died, and whose return will initiate a reign of divine justice on earth. In the minds of many, Khomeini was that Imam.

On January 16, 1979, the Shah departed Iran, leaving a temporary government unable to command popular obedience. One million people marched in Tehran calling for the Ayatollah to return. When Khomeini arrived on February 1, delirious crowds swamped his motorcade. The Ayatollah delivered his verdict on the Shah's designated prime minister, Shahpur Bakhtiar: "I shall slap this government in the mouth. I shall determine the government with the backing of this nation, because this nation accepts me." Khomeini appointed his own prime minister, Mehdi Bazargan, but undermined him by reserving all final decisions for himself.

The Islamic Republic of Iran was established by popular referendum in March 1979. Khomeini called it the "Government of God," and set about erasing "all the corrupt practices of the West." He banned independent newspapers and Western music (except for military marches). A special militia, the Army of the Guardians of the Islamic Revolution, carried out an estimated seven thousand executions of political enemies, petty criminals, homosexuals, and members of religious and ethnic minorities. On November 4, 1979, students entered the American embassy in Tehran, seized fifty-two hostages, and held them for 444 days.

The new Iranian constitution named the seventy-seven-year-old Khomeini *Velayat Faghi* (Spiritual Leader) for life. It was an unrestricted grant of power to a man who claimed that "during my long lifetime I have always been right about what I said." With no experience in running a country, Khomeini could only try to balance the interests of competing secular and religious interest groups. The economy descended into turmoil as the government nationalized banks and factories.

The uncompromising Ayatollah lacked a sense of caution. He denounced both the Soviet Union and the United States while waging war against Iraq. The war settled into a bloody stalemate because the military advantage lay with the defensive on both sides. Approximately nine hundred thousand Iranian youths lost their lives. Eventually, the Iraqis used poison gas on the battlefields and launched missiles at Iranian cities. Khomeini finally agreed to a cease-fire on August 20, 1988.

The Ayatollah Khomeini died on June 3, 1989. In his last will and testament he denounced the United States as "a terrorist state," King Hussein of Jordan as "a professional criminal," and the House of Saud as "traitors to the House of God." At Khomeini's funeral, eight mourners were crushed to death in a frenzied stampede to touch his body.

Ross Marlay

References and Further Reading

Bakhash, Shaul. *The Reign of the Ayatollahs: Iran and the Islamic Revolution.* New York: Basic Books, 1984, Rev. ed. 1990.

Fallaci, Oriana. "An Interview With Khomeini," *New York Times Magazine.* October 7, 1979, pp. 29–31.

Khomeini, Ayatollah Sayyed Ruhollah Mousavi. *A Clarification of Questions.* (Translated from the Persian by J. Borujerdi). Boulder and London: Westview, 1984.

———. *Islam and Revolution.* (Translated and Annotated by Hamid Algar). London: KPI Ltd., 1981.

Mackey, Sandra. *The Iranians: Persia, Islam and the Soul of a Nation.* New York: Plume, 1996.

Martin, Vanessa. *Creating an Islamic State: Khomeini and the Making of a New Iran.* London and New York: I.B. Tauris, 2000.

Mottadeh, Roy. *The Mantle of the Prophet: Religion and Politics in Iran.* New York: Simon & Schuster, 1985.

Taheri, Amir. *The Spirit of Allah: Khomeini and the Islamic Revolution.* (Bethesda, MD: Adler & Adler, 1986).

KHRUSHCHEV, NIKITA

Nikita Sergeevich Khrushchev (1894–1971) was born in Kalinovka, Kursk province, Russia, in 1894. He attended elementary school, then worked as farmhand, coal miner, and mechanic. He was active in promoting the 1917 agrarian revolutionand joined the Bolshevik (Communist) party the following year. He fought on Red side in Russian civil war and, as a party district committee secretary in Yuzovka region, backed Stalin's faction in intraparty struggle. In 1929, he enrolled in the Industrial Academy in Moscow, where he came to Stalin's notice and rose to become a Central Committee member in 1934.

Appointed the first secretary of Moscow city and regional party committttees in 1935, Khruschev helped to construct Moscow metro (subway) system and to purge party organizations of Stalin's critics, and became a full member of the Politburo in 1939. During World War II, he served as political commissar on various front councils and reached the rank of lieutenant-general. After the war, as the chairman of the Ukrainian Council of Ministers from 1944–1947, he was charged with responsibility for postwar reconstruction, but moved back to Moscow to take a post as the Central Committee secretary. In 1949, he became the head of the party organization in the capital, and soon after Stalin's death in March 1953 won control of the party apparatus.

He did much to dismantle the tyrant's heritage, win popular backing for the regime's policies, and promote socio-economic development. Yet he clung to the Leninist ideology of unremitting class struggle and maintained a belligerent stance towards Western "imperialism" that in 1962 brought the world to the brink of nuclear catastrophe. Millions of prisoners were released from forced-labor camps (Gulag) and the security police, renamed KGB, was brought under the party leadership's control. At the twentieth CPSU congress (February 1956) Khrushchev indicted Stalin for his arbitrary and terroristic methods, thereby irrevocably shattering the defunct leader's aura of infallibility and unleashing a process of critical thought that soon threatened to get out of hand. But the Hungarian revolution (October 1956) was violently suppressed and dissidents elsewhere silenced.

The crisis nearly cost Khrushchev his job. His Stalinist colleagues plotted to remove him but in June 1957 he outwitted them, thanks to the suport of pro-reform cadres, and went on to become the head of the Soviet government in 1958, meaning building up an apparatus of loyal officials, some of whom helped to foster a new "personality cult" centered on him. Continuing with his reformist inclinations, he introduced an ambitious new party program at the twenty-second Communist congress in 1961. Yet his position was less absolute than Stalin's had been and many groups, including the military, took exception to his impetuous, populist leadership style. In 1962, under US pressure, Khruschev withdrew nuclear-armed missiles from Cuba. In October 1964, his colleagues on the party Presidium, many of them his protégés, forced his resignation. Under his successor, Leonid Brezhnev, the USSR reverted to a more conservative course. Khrushchev was allowed to retire in Moscow and despite harassment wrote valuable, if self-serving, memoirs. He died in Moscow on September 11, 1971.

Khrushchev's peasant origins showed in his commitment to better the condition of hard-pressed Soviet farmers. Agricultural prices were raised, delivery quotas reduced, and farm managers' qualifications improved. Machinery and fertilizer output increased dramatically, as did the cultivation of corn as livestock fodder. A vast program was launched to grow grain on marginal land in Kazakhstan and other eastern territories. But Khrushchev shunned market-oriented reforms, holding fast to the principle of collectivized agriculture, with its bureaucratic interference and inadequate incentives for producers. Likewise in industry administrative devolution did not make for greater efficiency, since prices were still fixed centrally by the planners, and producer goods, especially for the military, continued to be given precedence over those catering to consumer needs. Even so, there was a better choice of foodstuffs in the shops and the provision of urban housing improved. Public opinion was generally supportive, the popular mood being boosted by propaganda hailing Soviet successes in space exploration (Sputnik I 1957; first manned cosmic flight 1961). Dissent among intellectuals was still mainly confined to cultural issues, in which Khrushchev often meddled crudely, as he did also in scientific decision-making. Under his rule, civil rights remained precarious, yet a generation grew up that proved capable of taking independent inititative after 1985, once the shackles of conformity were again loosened by Mikhail Gorbachev, whose policies Khrushchev up to a point anticipated.

JOHN KEEP

References and Further Reading

Breslauer, George W. *Khrushchev and Brezhnev as Leaders*. London and Boston: George Allen and Unwin, 1982.

Khrushchev, Sergei Nikitovich. *Nikita Khrushchev and the Creation of a Superpower*, translated by S. Benson. University Park, PA: Pennsylvania State University Press, 2000.

McCauley, Martin. *The Khrushchev Era, 1953–1964*. London: Longman; New York: Longman House, 1995.

———. *Nikita Khrushchev, 1894–1971*. London: Cardinal, 1991.

Taubman, William, Khrushchev, Sergei, and Gleason, Abbott (editors). *Nikita Khrushchev*, translated by David Gehrenbeck, Eileen Kane and Alla Bashenko. New Haven and London: Yale University Press, 2000.

Tompson, William J. *Khrushchev: A Political Life* Basingstoke: Macmillan; Oxford: St. Antony's College, 1995.

KIRIBATI

The Republic of Kiribati (pronounced *kee-ree-bas*) lies in the central Pacific (4° N–3° S latitude and 173°–177° E longitude). Its territory straddles the equator, lying to the west of the International Date Line. Thirty-three mainly coral atoll islands (land area: 810 square kilometers, 313 square miles) are scattered across 5.2 million square kilometers (2 million square miles) of the Pacific Ocean. Kiribati is part of Micronesia and bordering countries are Tuvalu to the south, the Marshall Islands to the northwest and Nauru to the west. Most of the islands are volcanically formed atolls with a central lagoon surrounded by islets or coral reefs. The nation comprises three administrative units: (1) eight of the eleven Line Islands, including Kiritimati (formerly Christmas Island), (2) seventeen Gilbert Islands including Banaba (formerly Ocean Island), and (3) eight Phoenix Islands. The capital, Bairiki, is on Tarawa atoll.

The population (ninety-nine thousand in 2003) is nearly all Micronesian, with about 30% concentrated on Tarawa. The population is growing at 2.3% per annum and approximately 40% of the population is zero to fourteen years old. Birth and death rates are 31.2 per 1,000 and 8.6 per 1,000 respectively and life expectancy for males and females is 58 and 64, respectively. The official language is English; the other main language is I-Kiribati. I-Kiribati, as the nationals are called, are mostly Christians; about half are Roman Catholic and 45% are Protestant.

Kiribati has few natural resources. Fishing and growing taro, bananas, and coconuts form the basis of the largely subsistence economy and livestock (mainly pigs and poultry) are raised for local consumption. Fish and copra became the chief exports after phosphate mining on Banaba ended in 1979. Development is constrained by the country's remote location, geographic fragmentation and poor infrastructure. Tourism is similarly constrained but nonetheless provides 20% of the gross domestic product (GDP). The country's economy depends on financial aid from Australia, the United Kingdom, Japan, New Zealand, Taiwan, and China. Remittances from I-Kiribati working overseas (mainly in the marine industry) are a significant source of foreign exchange. The GDP in 2003 was $54 million ($404 per capita).

A member of the British Commonwealth, Kiribati is a republic with an elected president, cabinet and a forty-two–member, unicameral legislature. The islands were administered (1892–1916) with the Ellice Islands as a British Protectorate that became, in 1916, the British colony of the Gilbert and Ellice Islands. The islands gained self-rule in 1971. The Ellice Islands became, with independence in 1978, Tuvalu, and the Gilbert Islands were granted independence in 1979 as Kiribati. US claims to several islands, including Kanton (formerly Canton) and Enderbury, were abandoned in 1979 and, in 1983, the United States Senate recognized Kiribati's sovereignty over the Line and Phoenix Islands.

The elected members of the House of Parliament choose presidential candidates from among their members and those selected compete in a general election to serve as president for a four-year term. In 1994, Teburovo Tito was elected president and reelected in 1998. Anote Tong replaced him as president in July 2003.

Austronesians from Southeast Asia first settled Kiribati between 200 and 500 AD. Samoans migrated to the islands in the eleventh and fourteenth centuries. Tongans and Fijians invaded in the fourteenth century, remaining as settlers on the islands. European explorers and whalers visited the islands, which were mapped by 1826. Islanders were kidnapped into slavery by Peruvian, British, Australian, and other slave ships to work in Fiji, Samoa, Tahiti, Hawaii, and Central America. Britain proclaimed the islands a British Protectorate in 1892 and annexed Banaba in 1900 after the discovery of rich phosphate deposits.

The Japanese bombed Banaba and landed on Tarawa and Butaritari Islands shortly after the attack on Pearl Harbor, but by November 1943, after fierce fighting, American forces took control of Tarawa and other islands occupied by the Japanese. In 1945, Banaba was liberated from the Japanese but all but one man of the labor force imported by the Japanese from other islands had been massacred. In 1957 and 1962, Britain used Kiritimati (Christmas) Island, to carry out atmospheric tests of three hydrogen bombs.

Islanders were given more control of their affairs in 1963 and became an independent nation on July 12, 1979. The Banabans sued in the British High Court in 1975 to be compensated for damage to their island from phosphate mining. They also sought independence from Kiribati. They were paid $9.04 million in compensation and, while the constitution ensures Banabans a seat in the Kiribati House of Assembly, they were not granted independence. In 1999, Kiribati became a member of the United Nations. In order to promote tourism the International Dateline was moved to its present delineation and one of the islands renamed Millennium Island as Kiribati competed with the Chatham Islands to become the first country welcoming the dawn of the twenty-first century.

The climate is equatorial maritime: hot throughout the year with the heat moderated by northwest and southeast trade winds. Temperatures range between 22°C–32°C and humidity is always high: 70%–90%. Strong, tropical storms (typhoons), while rare, can occur at any time of the year but are more common between November and March. Rainfall varies between islands, with those in the far north receiving up to 3,000 mm (118 inches) per year. Islands further south, such as Banaba are drier and can get droughts.

Twenty-one of the thirty-three islands are inhabited and overpopulation on many of the islands is a serious problem. In 1988, over 4,500 people living on more densely populated islands were resettled onto less populated islands. More recently, with a grant of $400,000 from the Asian Development Bank, five of the Phoenix Islands are being developed as settlements for people from the overpopulated Tarawa Islands. Pollution is not a major problem within the country as a whole but lagoons adjacent to densely populated areas, such as the Tarawa Islands, have sewage pollution as traditional use of tidal areas as latrines continues. The environment on Banaba Island was destroyed by phosphate mining, and Banabans were moved in the 1940s to Rabi Island in Fiji.

Most of the islands are low-lying (one to three meters above sea level; the highest point in the nation is on Banaba Island: eighty-seven meters above sea level). This nation is very susceptible to the sea level rise that will accompany global climate warming. Aside from coastal erosion and flooding, sea level rise will result in salinization of freshwater aquifers on which many inhabitants depend for drinking water. Communicable diseases (respiratory tract infections, diarrhea, and skin infections) are leading causes of morbidity and tuberculosis poses a serious public health problem. Lifestyle changes (smoking, alcohol consumption) and changes in diet (more processed foods) have led to an increase in diabetes, cardiovascular disease and cancers. In 2000, a United Nations Development Program report concluded that HIV/AIDS rates in the nation were as high as those in some African nations.

PATRICK L. OSBORNE

See also Oceania: History and Economic Development; Oceania: International Relations

References and Further Reading

Central Intelligence Agency (2003). Kiribati. The world fact book. http://www.cia.gov/cia/publications/factbook/geos/kr.html.

World Health Organization (1998). Country situation and trends: Kiribati. http://www.wpro.who.int/chip/kir.htm.

KOREA, NORTH

The Democratic People's Republic of Korea, or Choson to its inhabitants, is situated on the northern half of the Korean Peninsula. Its coasts border on Korea Bay and the Sea of Japan, and its land boundaries are with China, South Korea, and a tiny nineteen-kilometer border with Russia. The climate is continental. Winters tend to be very cold, due to winds blowing from the Siberian plain, with frequent snowfall. North Korea is also located within a monsoon region, making summers short, hot, and very rainy, with at least one typhoon every summer on the average. The population is estimated at 22,697,553, with a growth rate of 0.98% (CIA est. July 2004). The capital is Pyongyang, located in the southwest of the country near Korea Bay; the population of the capital city is estimated at 2.8 million.

Histography of North Korea

The collapse of the Soviet Union, the People's Republic of China's adoption of market-oriented economic policies and the implementation of *Juché*-based economy has left North Korea (the Democratic People's Republic of Korea, or DPRK) as one of the last bastions of communism as well as one of the most isolated regimes on the planet. Located on the northern half of the Korean Peninsula, North Korea has chosen a self-sufficient course of economic development and been in self-imposed economic and diplomatic isolation since the early 1990s. In contrast with the capitalist south, North Korea has pursued a hybrid model of Stalinist economic development, *Juché* or a self-reliant economic policy. The *Juché* ideology would serve as the central principle of North Korean social policy, politics, economics, international relations, and national defense.

The Democratic People's Republic of Korea emerged out of World War II as competing Cold War interests established rival regimes on the Korean Peninsula following Japan's surrender on August 15, 1945, that ended World War II. The geopolitical vacuum north of the thirty-eighth parallel, created by the expulsion of the Japanese colonial administration was quickly filled by Kim Il Sung (Kim Il-sŏng), a Soviet-Korean backed by the Kremlin. In the South, a government ruled by right-wing nationalists supported by the United States seized power. His personal rivalry with South Korean leader Syngman Rhee (Yi Sŭngman), would eventually lead the two fledgling countries into a bitter civil war that would later come to define the Cold War.

From a Cold War perspective, North Korea's importance lay from its geopolitical position as a buffer against the growth and expansion of the international capitalist system in Northeast Asia (e.g., South Korea, Japan, and the United States). While, the Korean War solidified the hitherto disputed borders and the permanent division of the Korean Peninsula, North Korea lay in ruin. What industrial that wasn't destroyed by the retreating Japanese Imperial Army at the end of World War II, was completely destroyed by American bombing during the Korean War. Thus, at the end of the Korean War, North Korea was faced with the daunting task of developing a viable economy from scratch. The manner in which North Korea pursued its economic self-reliance policy is unique in the history of economic development.

Developing a hybrid economic model of Marxist-Leninism called *Juché*, Kim Il Sung attempted to build an independent, self-reliant national economy through the establishment of a all-encompassing command economy, limiting economic relations with other countries while playing Cold War allies, the Soviet Union and China against each other in order to extract generous subsidies that helped sustain the anemic North Korean economy until the early 1990s when the collapse of the Soviet Union and China's economic reorientation meant the cessation of economic support to North Korea. This created widespread shortages throughout the entire economy, something North Korea has yet to recover from.

Economic Development—Past and Present

As late as the 1880s, Korea had been an agricultural society, aspiring to industrialization based on the much-hated Japanese model, but without the skills, raw materials or capital necessary to sustain their economic expansion. By the end of the Japanese colonial period (1910–1945) North Korea was primarily an agricultural economy, but inherited a varied industrial base, with considerable manufacturing capability, essential to build a modern economy. Most of the industrial centers were concentrated in and around Pyŏngyang, strategically located near ports to connect them with Japan. The Korean War saw the near total destruction of the North Korean economic infrastructure.

Following the war, North Korea pursued what is considered to be the most centralized and planned economic development strategy of any country in the world utilizing a hybrid of Marxism-Leninism called *Juché* (independent or self-reliance). North Korean economic policy and development strategies can be divided into several distinct phases: (1) the Socialist Nation–building period (1945–1960); (2) the Evolution of *Juché* Economy period (1961–1970); (3) the Implementation of the *Juché* Economy period (1971–1980); (4) opening of the *Juché* Economy period (1981–1990); and (5) the Economic Collapse period (from 1991).

Between 1953 and 1960 all agriculture was collectivized, followed by the nationalization of industries. All factories that were owned by the Japanese or their Korean cohorts were confiscated by the state. The introduction of the *Ch'ŏllima* movement, in 1956, was the embodiment of the *Juché* philosophy. The *Ch'ŏllima* movement was a mass-mobilization movement to develop light industry and agriculture in conjunction with heavy industry through the utilization of local resources to build local consumer goods industries, thus stimulating the entire industrialization process and the collectivization of agriculture to develop rural areas.

During the 1960s, North Korea achieved faster economic growth and greater economic equality and stability utilizing central economic planning. Agricultural output rose by over 12% annually. Industrial output grew by an estimated 23% during the 1960s. Self-sufficiency had apparently been attained. This belied the fact that economic aid from the Soviet Union and China had been significantly decreased as a consequence of Khrushchev's policy of de-Stalinization and the "Cultural Revolution," respectively. Thus, North Korea was forced to continue its industrialization process without the aid of its closest allies.

In the 1970s, the geopolitical events and faltering economic performance meant that North Korea faced the prospect of establishing economic relations with capitalist countries. As a consequence, Pyŏngyang began to emphasize exports, a conflicting plan from its *Juché* policy. Despite its attempts at importing advanced technology from the West, chronic trade deficits coupled with low level of exports meant that North Korea soon defaulted on its international debt obligations.

In the early 1980s, North Korea tried to re-establish economic relations with the outside world as it neared the limits of self-sustained economic growth. The North Korean leadership sought to import advanced technology from the West. Yet, at the end of the 1980s, three-quarters of North Korea's trade was still with China and the Soviet Union. This overdependence on foreign trade with its Communist brethren would come to haunt North Korea as geopolitical events dictated a change in the international environment. The world was moving toward a post–Cold War international order.

Soviet and Chinese assistance to North Korea had virtually disappeared by 1991. North Korea edged closer towards bankruptcy as the Soviet Union and China began to seek payment in hard currency and charge "market" prices. As Pyŏngyang became increasingly isolated, both economically and diplomatically, small markets began to appear throughout North Korea. The growth of these new markets did not seem to undermine the cohesive of North Korean society as the state maintained tight controls over daily life.

Juché

It is hard to pinpoint the origins Juché ideology. North Korean historians have attempted to place the origin of Juché in the early experiences of Kim Il-Sung. Nonetheless, in order to achieve economic self-sufficiency, Kim Il Sung needed to transform North Korea's war-ravaged agrarian economy through a far-reaching development strategy. Kim developed an alternate economic policy called Juché which was not fully articulated until December 1955 when Kim Il Sung introduced Juché ideology in response the political situation of North Korea vis-à-vis the Soviet Union. Juché would transform pre-war agrarian society into a modern industrial state through the utilization of domestic resources. Eventually the Juché ideology would become the foundation of the entire North Korean economic and political system.

Under the Juché economic model, North Korea would implement a self-sufficient inward-looking economic development strategy utilizing planning goals, guidelines, and targets while shunning economic relations with other countries. The major tenets of Juché development strategy were: (1) North Korea should seek balanced economic development; (2) Industrialization would be achieved primarily relying on domestic resources; and (3) In order to develop technologies domestically and increase productivity, the state would emphasize human capital formation. In short, North Korea would achieve economic self-sufficiency through the implementation of Juché model of autonomous industrialization utilizing indigenous resources and internal demand.

Juché slowly evolved from a development strategy to become the official guiding principle in all facets of North Korean life. Kim Il-Sung utilized Juché to force North Koreans into a total mobilization system as the North Korean economy began to slow and stagnate. Politics, foreign policy and national defense policy would also be guided by Juché's principle of self-reliance. Thus, Juché provided a theoretical basis for North Korea's closed-door policy. By 1965, Juché had become a comprehensive political theory. Eventually, Juché became a totalitarian political system that encompassed all aspects of daily life in North Korea.

North Korean Economic Decline

Since 1991, the North Korean economy failed as a result of dual (internal and external) economic conditions. Domestically, the economy stagnated as a result of ill-conceived Juché policies. Internationally, major changes in the international system, including the dissolution of the Soviet Union and China's rapid economic and political reorientation meant the end of generous subsidies that subsidized the North Korean economy and the severing of economic ties with Soviet Bloc countries meant a precipitous economic decline that has seen a shortage in food production followed by a decline in industrial output. The very structure of the North Korean economy compounded the economic downturn as the interdependence of the industrial sector binds the highly integrated economy. A setback in one industry triggers a domino effect in other sectors of the economy.

The unexpected death of Kim Il Sung on July 8, 1994, further strained the economy as his son and successor, Kim Jŏng-Il declared a three-year mourning period. It is unclear if North Korea will be able to reverse its economic decline. As long as North Korea remains committed to its Juché economic policies, the leadership will be unable to introduce the steps required to move away from an inward-looking economic development strategy to outward-looking economic development strategy necessary to resuscitate its deteriorating economy.

North Korea is currently on the brink of disaster. The country has suffered through five successive years of famine. Residents of Pyŏngyang reported survive on a combination of food rationing. Much of the population outside of Pyŏngyang suffers from an acute food shortage and survives on humanitarian aid.

KEITH A. LEITICH

See also Authoritarianism; Communist Economic Model; East Asia: History and Economic Development; East Asia: International Relations; Ethnic Conflicts: East Asia; Korea, South; Marxism; Rhee, Syngman; Totalitarianism

References and Further Reading

Breidenstein, Gerhard, and W. Rosenberg. "Economic Comparison of North and South Korea." *Journal of Contemporary Asia*, vol. 5, no. 2, pp. 165–204, 1975.

Brun, Ellen, and Jacques Hersh. *Socialist Korea: A Case Study in the Strategy of Economic Development*, New York: Monthly Review Press, 1976.

Buzo, Adrian. *The Making of Modern Korea*, London, New York: Routledge, 2002.

Byun, Hyung-yun. "A Comparative Study of Economic Systems in South and North Korea." *The Journal of Asiatic Studies*, vol. XIII, no. 3, 1970.

Chae, Hi-jun. "North Korea's Economic Management System." *Vantage Point*, vol. V, no. 6, June 1982.

Chun, Hong-Tack, and Jin Park. "North Korean Economy: A Historical Assessment." In Dong-se Cha, Kwang

Suk Kim, and Dwight H. Perkins, (eds.) *The Korean Economy 1945–1995: Performance and Vision for the 21st Century*. Seoul: Korean Development Institute, 1997.

Chung, Joseph Sang-hoon. *The North Korean Economy: Structure and Development*. Stanford, CA: Hoover Institution Press, 1974.

———. "Economic Planning in North Korea." *North Korea Today*, Robert A. Scalapino and Jun-yop Kim (eds.), Berkeley, CA: Center for Korean Studies, Institute of East Asian Studies, University of California, 1983.

Foster-Carter, Aidan. "North Korea: Development and Self-Reliance." In Gavan McCormack and John Gittings, (eds.), *Crisis in Korea*. Nottingham, UK: Bertrand Russell Peace Foundation for Spokesman Books, 1977.

Halliday, Jon. "The North Korean Model: Gaps and Questions." *World Development*, vol. IX, no. 9/10, 1981.

Hwang, Eui-Gak. *The Korean Economies: A Comparison of North and South*. Oxford: Oxford University Press, 1993.

Koo, Bok-hak. *Political Economy of Self-Reliance: Juche and Economic Development in North Korea, 1961–1990*. Seoul: Research Center for Peace and Unification of Korea, 1992.

Lee, Chong-Sik. "The Political Economy of North Korea," *NBR Analysis*, vol. 5, no. 2, Seattle, WA: The National Bureau of Asian Research, 1994.

Park, Han S. *North Korea: Ideology, Politics, and Economy*, Englewood Cliffs, NJ: Prentice Hall, 1996.

KOREA, SOUTH

The Republic of Korea, or Han'guk to its inhabitants, is situated on the southern half of the Korean Peninsula. Its coasts border on the Yellow Sea and the Sea of Japan. Its only land border is the demarcation line with South Korea, or the People's Republic of Korea. The climate is temperate, with a rainy season in the summer. The population is estimated at 48,598,175, with a growth rate of 0.62% (CIA estimate July 2004). The capital is Pyongyang, located in the northwest of the country near the Yellow Sea; its population was 10,276,968 at the end of 2003.

Histography of South Korea

Geography, culture, and history combined to give South Korea a unique place as the intersection of Northeast Asia. Located on the southern half of the Korean Peninsula, South Korea has been vulnerable to influence by its more powerful East Asian neighbors, China and Japan. Throughout much of recorded history, the Korean Peninsula has been a crossroads of culture, trade, and war because of its strategic geographic location. Japanese rulers considered Korea as a gateway to continental expansion while Chinese emperors' viewed Korea as a protective safeguard against foreign invasion of the Eastern border of the Middle Kingdom.

The Republic of Korea (South Korea) emerged out of World War II as competing Cold War interests established rival regimes on the Korean Peninsula following Japan's surrender on August 15, 1945, that ended World War II. The geopolitical vacuum south of the thirty-eighth parallel, created by the expulsion of the Japanese colonial administration was quickly filled by Syngman Rhee (Yi Sŭng-man), an American-backed Korean expatriate whose personal ambition outweighed the needs of nascent republic. His personal rivalry with North Korean leader Kim Il Sung (Kim Il-sŏng) would eventually lead the two fledgling countries into a bitter civil war that would later come to define the Cold War.

From a Cold War perspective, South Korea's importance lay from its geopolitical position at the intersection of conflicting great powers (e.g., the People's Republic of China, the Soviet Union and the United States). While, the Korean War solidified the hitherto disputed borders and the permanent division of the Korean Peninsula, much of South Korea lay in ruin. Seŏul was completely devastated and millions of people were left homeless. Deprived of pre-war industrial resources located in Pyŏngyang, the restoration of the economic base of South Korea would be seen as the pivotal in the struggle against Communism. As such, the integration of South Korea into the international capitalist system was of primary importance to the United States to buffer South Korea against Communist influence.

Economic Development—Past and Present

Following World War II, South Korea could hardly be thought of as a candidate for economic development that would shape the course of the latter half of the twentieth century. Prior to the colonization of the Korean Peninsula, Korea had been an isolated agrarian kingdom that had been forcibly opened through 'gunboat' diplomacy in the later half of the nineteenth century.

As late as the 1880s, Korea had been an agricultural society, aspiring to industrialization based on the much-hated Japanese model, but without the skills, raw materials, or capital necessary to sustain their economic expansion. As such, the Korean government found itself vulnerable to external economic and political pressure. During their colonial occupation, the Japanese built the beginnings of an economic infrastructure—a road and rail network—albeit to serve their needs; the export of raw materials needed to support military expansion and conquest throughout Asia. It has been argued that the Japanese laid the foundation for the latter development through the introduction of comprehensive educational system coupled with the spread of literacy. In addition, the Japanese oversaw the development a native bureaucracy, the emergence of an entrepreneurial class that would serve as a base to economic development.

The years between 1948 and 1960 saw a brutal civil war, the permanent division of the Korean Peninsula, and the emergence of an authoritarian government in South Korea that combined civil and military administration to govern the state with military-like discipline. The Korean War laid waste to much of the economic infrastructure as well as depriving South Korea of industrial resources. In the years following the civil war, South Korea had a crippled economy and was heavily dependent on foreign—primarily American—aid and assistance. It wasn't until the adoption of export-led development in the 1960s that economic development took off thereby reducing their dependence on American aid.

By the early 1960s, South Korea had many of the necessary ingredients for rapid economic growth: integration into the post-war international political and economic order, access to foreign capital and technology, an entrepreneurial class and cadre of low-cost, educated workers. The coup d'état that that led to installation of Park Chung Hee (Pak Chŏng-hŭi) as president of South Korea signaled a turning point in the economic development of South Korea. Park's primary focus was on attaining national wealth and power through economic development. As such, the government established the basic strategy for economic development to which it adhered to for the next forty years. The first part of the strategy was the introduction of the first Five-Year Economic Development Plan was in 1962 which established the basic guidelines for development: economic development was to be achieved through industrialization; economic development was to achieved under government direction and control; foreign capital inflow was to be reduced; and growth was given a higher priority than income distribution and uneven economic development. Nonetheless, during the 1960s the rate of growth of South Korea surpassed that of all developing countries.

During the late 1970s and early 1980s, the South Korean government export policy gradually shifted from export of labor-intensive manufactured goods to an export policy that emphasized gradual export substitution in capital skill-intensive industries. The shift in policy was a change from earlier policy in that emphasis went from maximizing export growth to strengthening competitiveness. The government introduced a variety of legislative measures designed to restructure competitive industries, introducing market mechanisms, stimulating private initiatives as well as enhancing price stability.

At the beginning of the 1980s, the second oil crisis and Korean domestic political turmoil gave rise to difficulties as the Korean government experienced the first negative growth since the implementation of the first development plan and a huge current account deficit. The government undertook a series of structural adjustment measures to enhance economic efficiency. The priority of the Korean economic policy shifted from growth to stability and actively encouraged the adjustment of duplicated investment and liquidation of troubled enterprises. At the same time, opening of the economy and deregulation were pursued on a case-by-case basis as part of the move to private initiative in economic management.

The Rise of the Korean "Tiger"

The success of South Korean economy is one of the unsurpassed stories of the post–World War II era. Beginning in the early 1960s, South Korea had one of the most dynamic economies in the world. Devoid of natural and physical resources, South Korea would enjoy a cumulative rate of growth that far exceeded that of most of the other Third World countries during the same period.

Different theories have been posited as to explain the successful pattern of development in South Korea. Much of the debate centers on the political basis of economic development. Did South Korea have culturally built in conditions that pre-disposed South Korea for the phenomenal growth that has fascinated policymakers and theorists alike? While it is agreed that economic growth in South Korea, and East Asia (e.g., Taiwan, Singapore, Hong Kong) for that matter, was based in large measure on government intervention in support of light export manufacturing. Others argue about the role of the state. Initially, observers posited that trade liberalization, private enterprise, and the restricted role of the state in economic affairs led to economic development. Later, scholars questioned the previously held assumption that the state played an indirect and minimal role in economic development as evidence suggested that centralization of power in the bureaucratic polity enhanced economic development.

Much of the development literature suggests historical and developmental conditions under which state economic development is possible: international relations with states and multi-national corporations, access to export markets as well as development resources, including large amounts of capital and technology. This is called the neo-classical model, which is based on free market economics forces. According to this model, South Korea benefited from privileged access to US and foreign markets. The economic benefits, in turn, were used to strengthen and sustain economic growth.

Despite continued US development assistance and increasing levels of foreign direct investment by multi-national corporations in South Korea, economic development did not stimulate general development of the South Korean economy; democracy did not take root, nor was their equitable distribution of income. This school of thought argued that economic links between the developing world and the capitalist system produced exploitation and economic stagnation. This is called the dependency school. Scholars asserted that economic integration of a developing country into the capitalist system encouraged import-substitution led growth that created a structural imbalance that created dependency on foreign capital and technology that would constrain development.

Neither of these models can fully explain the unique set of circumstances that led to the remarkable economic development achieved in South Korea. What is agreed is that state economic intervention is an essential component of growth. South Korea fit that model as it had a series of authoritarian governments that combined civil and military administration to govern the state with military-like discipline through the implementation of comprehensive state-managed economic programs through its control of extensive bureaucracy fostered close collaboration between the government and tightly-held commercial conglomerates (*chaebol*). Furthermore, what is known is that economic growth in South Korea was stimulated and conditioned by a number of international, social, political, and cultural factors.

International Factors

Following the Korean War, the Republic of Korea little or no economic infrastructure. What little industry that was left by the Japanese was destroyed during the Korean War. Following the Korean War, the United States wanted a capitalist democracy and opposed any leftist influence. As such, the integration of South Korea into the international capitalist system was of primary importance to the United States to buffer South Korea from Communist influence. The eventual adoption of export-oriented policies that stimulated the rapid economic development coupled with the protectionist policies of South Korea allowed the development of capital and technology-intensive industries with entrée to the capitalist system thereby allowing privileged access to US and other Western markets.

Domestic Political and Social Factors

Outside pressure(s) cannot entirely explain economic development and growth in South Korea. Certain domestic conditions and circumstances existed that laid the foundation for the rapid transformation from an agrarian society into an industrial society. In contrast with other developing nations, the absence of any organized class opposition to industrialization in South Korea allowed for the rise of an entrepreneurial class. This removed the political barriers to the transfer of landed wealth and into commerce and industry thereby strengthening economic growth. Social factors also played a key role in industrialization. South Korean workers were not only highly-skilled but comparatively inexpensive.

The Role of Culture

It is generally acknowledged that a unique set of cultural traits aided in the economic development of South Korea. In spite of centuries of foreign invasion and colonization, Korea remained relatively homogeneous. This gave people a sense of unity—*han minjok*—which the government was able to tap into and manipulate. The South Korean government was able to subordinate sub-state loyalties to clan or region and use cultural nationalism as an ideology to mobilize support for development planning. Furthermore, the government was able to tap into the immediate past memory of the Japanese colonial occupation to intensify nationalist feelings and the sense of national pride of Koreans to match or outdo the achievements of their former colonial masters.

KEITH A. LEITICH

See also East Asia: History and Economic Development; East Asia: International Relations; Ethnic Conflicts: East Asia; Korea, North; Neoliberalism; Rhee, Syngman

References and Further Reading

Amsden, Alice H. *Asia's Next Giant: South Korea and Late Industrialization*. New York: Oxford University Press, 1989.
Buzo, Adrian. *The Making of Modern Korea*. London, New York: Routledge, 1996.

Cotton, James (ed.). *Korea Under Roe Tae-Woo: Democratisation, Northern Policy and Inter-Korean Relations.* St. Leonard's, Australia: Allen & Unwin, 1993.

Eckert, Carter J., Ki-baik Lee, Young Ick Lew, Michael Robinson and Edward W. Wagner. *Korea Old and New: A History.* Seoul: Ilchokak Publishers, 1990.

Haggard, Stephan. *Pathways from the Periphery: The Politics of Growth in the Newly Industrializing Countries.* Ithaca, NY: Cornell University Press, 1990.

Hinton, Harold. *Korea Under New Leadership: The Fifth Republic.* New York: Praeger, 1983.

Jones, Leroy P., and Il Sakong. *Government, Business, and Entrepreneurship in Economic Development: The Korean Case.* Cambridge, MA: Harvard University Press, 1980.

Kendall, Laural, and Griffin Dix (eds.). *Religion and Ritual in Korean Society.* Berkeley: University of California Press, 1987.

MacDonald, Donald. *The Koreans: Contemporary Politics and Society.* Boulder: 1988, 2nd Ed, Boulder, CO: Westview Press, 1990.

Mason, Edward S., Mahn Je Kim, Dwight H. Perkins, Kwang Suk Jim and David C. Cole. *The Economic and Social Modernization of the Republic of Korea.* Cambridge, MA: Harvard University Press, 1980.

Soon, Cho. *The Dynamics of Korean Economic Development.* Washington, DC: Institute for International Economics, 1994.

Steinberg, David I. *The Republic of Korea: Economic Transformation and Social Change.* Boulder, CO: Westview Press, 1989.

KUBITSCHEK, JUSCELINO

Juscelino Kubitschek de Oliveira (1902–1976), president of Brazil and builder of Brasília, was born in a decayed diamond-mining district of Minas Gerais, a state once wealthy from colonial gold mining. His father, of Czech descent, died before he was born. His mother earned a meager income as a school teacher.

To rise out of poverty he studied to become a doctor, working as a telegraph operator. He married into a socially prominent family and established a thriving surgical practice in the state capital, Belo Horizonte.

Coming to the attention of the local political establishment, he was named mayor of Belo Horizonte in 1940. Having successfully raised himself out of poverty, he resolved to use public office to do the same for his society, emphasizing economic development through industrialization. Benefiting from increased world demand for minerals from Minas Gerais during the Second World War, Kubitschek used revenue from exports to enhance the physical infrastructure of his city by improving roads, electricity, and sewage. He even inaugurated a modernist architectural complex in the city, bringing together the leading Brazilian architects, landscape designers, and painters.

Elected governor of Minas Gerais in 1950, he again concentrated on improving infrastructure; he expanded the number of roads, bridges, hydroelectric plants, schools, and clinics. Improvements in transportation and energy were fundamental in order for the state to achieve economic development and modernization.

In 1955, he won election as president of Brazil, basing his appeal on an alliance with populist political forces and upon a program of national economic development that outlined a sequence of goals that his government would achieve. He promised that in his five-year presidential term there would be "fifty years of progress in five." He further promised that he would move the federal capital from Rio de Janeiro to a new city in the central highlands, to be named Brasília.

His plan for economic expansion concentrated on the development of industry and physical infrastructure. The Kubitschek government had as its goals specific increases in the production of iron, steel, cars, roads, electricity, etc. It achieved dramatic increases in production together with a wider distribution of national income. These accomplishments made of Kubitschek an enduring symbol of successful, democratic civilian government in Brazil.

Brasília was built in the central highlands of Brazil in order to transfer the center of power and population to the interior of the country. The futuristic city highlighted Kubitschek's effort to modernize the country and brought together the country's chief architects, planners, painters, sculptors, and landscape designers. It was a symbol of Kubitschek's goals for national economic development and modernization.

Although his presidency was successful in terms of achieving its industrialization goals, it spurred a cycle of inflation that burdened the Brazilian economy well into the end of the twentieth century. Moreover, conservative and military forces scorned him for his political alliance with populist and radical elements and for the alleged corruption of his administration.

Kubitschek had his political rights denied by a military regime that came into power in 1964. He died in 1976 in an automobile accident between São Paulo and Rio de Janeiro.

EDWARD A. RIEDINGER

See also Brazil

References and Further Reading

Alexander, Robert J. *Juscelino Kubitschek and the Development of Brazil.* Athens, OH: Ohio University Center for International Studies, 1991.

Bourne, Richard. *Political Leaders of Latin America: Che Guevara; Alfredo Stroessner; Eduardo Frei Montalva;*

Juscelino Kubitschek; Carlos Lacerda; Eva Peron. New York: Knopf, 1970.

Kubitschek, Juscelino. *Por que construí Brasília* [=*Why I Built Brasília*]. Rio de Janeiro: Bloch, 1975.

Medaglia, Francisco. *Juscelino Kubitschek, President of Brazil: The Life of a Self-Made Man.* New York: 1959.

KURDISTAN

Kurdistan constitutes the geographical area where Turkey, Iran, Iraq, and Syria converge. Before World War I, Kurdistan was divided between the Ottoman Empire (mostly) and the Persian Empire. Following World War I, Kurdistan was divided among five different states. Turkey has the largest portion (43%), followed by Iran (31%), Iraq (18%), Syria (6%), and the former Soviet Union (now Armenia and Azerbaijan—2%) (Izady 1992).

Kurdistan is landlocked and mountainous. Although the rugged terrain contributes to the lack of Kurdish unity, these mountains have protected the Kurds from being fully conquered or assimilated by their neighbors. The Zagros range constitutes the most important portion of these mountains, running northwest to southeast. Portions of the Taurus, Pontus, and Amanus Mountains also rise within Kurdistan.

The climate of these mountains is cool throughout the year. Central Kurdistan, however, enjoys a lower elevation and thus a warmer, even relatively balmy climate, though summers can be very hot and humid. Winters in most areas are bitterly cold and snowy. These climatic contrasts have been sharpened by deforestation due to overgrazing, logging for fuel or construction, and the effects of war. In contrast to most other parts of the Middle East, much of Kurdistan enjoys adequate and regular rainfall. Agriculture products include corn, barley, rice, cotton, tobacco, and sugar beets. Animal husbandry (goats, sheep, cows, and buffaloes) continues to be a mainstay.

Because of its water (in the Turkish and Iraqi parts) and oil (in the Iraqi section), Kurdistan has great economic and geostrategic importance. Despite being economically underdeveloped compared to the non-Kurdish areas of Turkey, Iran, Iraq, and Syria, Kurdistan witnessed a tremendous amount of economic, political, and social modernization during the twentieth century. Indeed, Iraqi Kurdistan's economy surpassed that of the rest of Iraq in the late 1990s due to the oil-for-food-program funds it received through the United Nations (UN). The Turkish, Iranian, and Syrian portions of Kurdistan still lag behind economically.

The Kurds are a largely Sunni Muslim, Indo-European-speaking people. They are distinct ethnically from the Turks and Arabs, but related to the Iranians.

No reliable estimates of the Kurdish population exist, as most estimates are politically biased. A significant number of Kurds have assimilated into the Arab, Turkish, or Iranian populations. In addition, Kurdish enclaves exist outside of Kurdistan, while communities of Turks, Turkomans, Arabs, Assyrians, among others, live within Kurdistan.

A reasonable estimate counts 12 to 15 million Kurds in Turkey (18% to 21% of the population), 6 million in Iran (11%), 4 million in Iraq (20% to 23%), and eight hundred thousand in Syria (7%). At least one hundred thousand Kurds also live in parts of the former Soviet Union, while recently a Kurdish diaspora of more than 1 million has risen in western Europe, with more than five hundred thousand Kurds in Germany. Some twenty thousand Kurds live in the United States.

The Kurds were Islamicized in the seventh century CE and today constitute a mixture of various groupings, the result of earlier invasions and migrations. The Kurdish language (which is related to Iranian) has two main variants, Kurmanji (or Bahdinani) spoken mainly in the northwest of Kurdistan, and Sorani spoken mainly in the southeast. In addition, Dimili (Zaza) is also spoken in parts of Turkish Kurdistan, while Gurani is spoken in sections of Iraqi and Iranian Kurdistan. These Kurdish dialects (or languages) are only partially mutually understandable.

Until recently, Kurdish tribes received more loyalty than any sense of Kurdish nationalism. In the various Kurdish revolts of the twentieth century, significant numbers of Kurds from other tribes have supported the government because of their antipathies for those rebelling. The aghas (feudal landlords or tribal chieftains) and sheikhs (religious leaders) continue to command strong allegiances.

Turkey

Ataturk's creation of a secular and purely Turkish state led to three great, but unsuccessful Kurdish revolts in the 1920s and 1930s. As a result, the Turkish authorities decided to eliminate anything that might suggest a separate Kurdish nation. A new Kurdish insurgency began in the 1980s and continued until the end of the twentieth century when Abdullah (Apo) Ocalan, the leader of the *Partiya Karkaren Kurdistan* (PKK) or Kurdistan Workers Party was captured by Turkish authorities and sentenced to death. Turkey's candidacy for European Union membership forced the government to suspend Ocalan's execution.

Iraq

The Kurds in Iraq have been in an almost constant state of revolt since World War I. Mulla Mustafa Barzani (1903–1979) eventually emerged as the leader and fought the Iraqi government with his *peshmerga* (literally, those who face death, or guerrillas) for more than half a century. Despite his conservatism and tribal mentality, he was the guiding spirit in the establishment of the Kurdistan Democratic Party (KDP) in 1946, and at the height of his power negotiated the March Manifesto of 1970 which provided for Kurdish autonomy under his rule. When Iran and the United States withdrew their support in return for Iraqi concessions in 1975, Barzani's uprising collapsed. His son Massoud Barzani eventually emerged as the new leader of the KDP, while Jalal Talabani established his Patriotic Union of Kurdistan (PUK) as a rival. The two Iraqi Kurdish parties have alternated between cooperation and conflict ever since. They also have suffered from such horrific repression as Saddam Hussein's chemical attack on Halabja in 1988 and genocidal *Anfal* campaigns of 1987–1988.

After the Gulf War and failure of the ensuing Kurdish uprising in March 1991, Kurdish refugees fled to the mountains. The United States reluctantly created a safe haven and no-fly zone in which a Kurdish state began to develop in northern Iraq. A 1991 UN Security Council Resolution condemned the treatment of Iraqi Kurds and demanded an end to the oppression. Never before had the Kurds received such official international mention and protection.

The KDP and PUK battled from 1994–1998. The resulting instability and power vacuum drew in neighboring Turkey, Iran, and Iraq since for reasons of state none of them wanted to see an independent Kurdistan. The United States finally brokered a successful cease-fire. There are now two separate rump governments in Iraqi Kurdistan.

By the late 1990s, the economic situation had begun to improve in Iraqi Kurdistan due to the oil-for-peace funds, the cessation of internal fighting, and border customs collected by the KDP on its frontier with Turkey. A relatively free, liberal, and prosperous civil society began to develop both in the KDP and PUK regions. The problems of Saddam Hussein and numerous internally displaced persons continued, however.

Iran

Until these developments in northern Iraq, the short-lived Mahabad Republic of Kurdistan (1946–1947) in northwestern Iran represented the only Kurdish state in the twentieth century. This was destroyed and its president Qazi Muhammad hanged. Iranian agents also assassinated Abdul Rahman Ghassemlou, the leader of the Kurdistan Democratic Party of Iran (KDPI) in 1989 and his successor Sadegh Sharafkandi in 1992.

The Kurdish movement in Iran has been less developed than in Iraq or Turkey. The Iranian province of Kordestan represents the only usage of the term in any state for even part of the historical territory of Kurdistan.

MICHAEL M. GUNTER

See also Kurds

References and Further Reading

Barkey, Henri J. and Graham E. Fuller. *Turkey's Kurdish Question*. New York: Rowman & Littlefield, 1998.
Bruinessen, Martin van. *Agha, Shaikh and State: On the Social and Political Organization of Kurdistan*. London: Zed, 1992.
Chaliand, Gerard, ed. *A People without a Country: The Kurds and Kurdistan*. New York: Olive Branch, 1993.
Gunter, Michael M. *The Kurds and the Future of Turkey*. New York: St. Martin's, 1997.
———. *The Kurdish Predicament in Iraq: A Political Analysis*. New York: St. Martin's, 1999.
Izady, Mehrdad. *The Kurds: A Concise Handbook*. Washington: Crane Russak, 1992.
Kreyenbroek, Philip G. and Stefan Sperl, eds. *The Kurds: A Contemporary Overview* London: Routledge, 1992.
McDowall, David. *A Modern History of the Kurds* London: I.B. Tauris, 1996.
Meho, Lokman I., com. *The Kurds and Kurdistan: A Selective and Annotated Bibliography*. Westport, CT: Greenwood, 1997.
Meiselas, Susan. *Kurdistan: In the Shadow of History*. New York: Random House, 1997.

KURDS

Until the middle of the nineteenth century, Kurds had enjoyed an effective or actual independence in the homeland of Kurdistan. Although at other times, the Kurds—or rather, their princes—had paid homage to various powers in the area, this had never mounted to a direct rule. The introduction of technological innovations in armament mustered by their neighboring imperial powers, however, gradually ended this independence. What has followed to the present day is a relentless state of rebellion and warfare by the Kurds.

Kurdistan consists basically of the mountainous areas of the central and northern Zagros, the eastern one-third of the Taurus and Pontus, and the northern half of the Amanus ranges. Despite its mountainous nature, Kurdistan has more arable land proportionately than most Middle Eastern countries.

Although presently an Indo-European-speaking groups with a strong European genetic admixture, Kurds, like most other large nations, are culturally and genetically an aggregate group. Genetically, Kurds are the descendants of all those who came to settle in Kurdistan, and not any one of them. Thus, ancient peoples such as the Kurti, Guti, Mede, Mard, Carduchi/Gordyene, Adianbene, Zela and Khaldi, each constitute only *one* ancestor and not *the* ancestor of the modern Kurd.

The earliest evidence so far of a unified and distinct culture (and possibly, ethnicity) by people inhabiting the Kurdish mountains dates back to the Halaf culture of 8,000–7,400 years ago. This was followed by the Hurrian cultural period, which lasted for nearly 4,000 years from circa 6,300 to 2,600 years ago. The Hurrians divided into many clans and subgroups, who set up city-states, kingdoms and empires. By about 4,000 years ago, the first vanguard of Indo-European-speaking peoples were trickling into Kurdistan. They formed the aristocracy of the Mitanni, Kassite, and Hittite kingdoms. Meanwhile, around 3,800 years ago, the name "Kurti" (Kurd) made its first debut into ancient records for a people and a kingdom located on the south shores of Lake Van and the Hakkari heights.

By about 3,000 years ago, the trickle had turned into a flood, and Hurrian Kurdistan was fast becoming Indo-European Kurdistan. By 300 BC, Kurds had established important dynasties in Anatolia. These had become Roman vassals by the end of the first century BC. In the east the Kurdish kingdoms of Adiabene, Sophene, Gordyene, Cortea, Media, and Kirm had, by the first century BC, become confederate members of Parthia. By the third century BC, the use of the name Kurd (Greek: Kurti; Latin: Cyrti) for the people inhabiting modern Kurdistan and other Kurdish colonies had become prevalent in the classical Graeco-Roman texts.

While all larger Kurdish kingdoms of the west gradually lost their existence to the Romans, in the east they survived into the third century AD and the advent of the Sasanian Persian empire. The last major Kurdish dynasty, the Kayosids, fell in AD 380. Smaller Kurdish principalities (called the *Kofyâr*, "mountain administrators") however, preserved their autonomy into the seventh century and the advent of Islam.

The eclipse of Sasanian and Byzantine power by the Muslim caliphate, and its own subsequent weakening, permitted the Kurdish principalities and "mountain administrators" to set up new, independent kingdoms. The Ayyubids stand out by the vastness of their domain. From their capital at Cairo they ruled territories of Libya, Egypt, Nubia, Yemen, western Arabia, Syria, the Holy Land, Armenia, and much of Kurdistan. As the custodians of Islam's holy cities of Mecca, Medina, and Jerusalem, the Ayyubids were instrumental in the defeat and expulsion of the Crusaders from the Holy Land.

By AD 1500, there were over a score of independent and autonomous Kurdish kingdoms and principalities. None, however, showed any serious inclination for a unification of Kurdistan. The advent of the Safavid and Ottoman empires in the area in the sixteenth century, their division of Kurdistan into two uneven imperial dependencies, and their introduction of heavy artillery and a scorched-earth policy into Kurdistan was a new, and devastating development.

Nonetheless, this is when for the first time, Kurdish authors begin calling for a unified Kurdish kingdom to guard the land and foster Kurdish culture and language. Thus the historian Bitlisi wrote in 1597 the first pan-Kurdish history, the *Sharafnâma*, as Ahmad Khani, the collector and versifier of the national epic of *Mem-o-Zin*, called in 1695 for a Kurdish state. Kurdish nationalism had been born.

It is noteworthy that, prompted by externally-induced national distress, a century earlier than Europeans the Kurds were writing of the need for a unitary Kurdish ethno-national state—a "nation-state."

The disintegration of the Ottoman authority highlighted by the virtual independence of Egypt and Arabia, meanwhile, persuaded the ancient, autonomous Kurdish princely dynasties to sue for full independence. The first of these was the principality of Soran (central Kurdistan). In the early 1830s, a scion of the Rewandid dynasty, Dostakid Prince Muhammad, embarked on establishing an independent kingdom of Kurdistan. At his capital of Rewanduz, he established foundries to forge artillery and firearms, enabling his army in 1834 to score a major victory against the Ottoman forces that included the Prussian officer Helmuth von Moltke (future general and conqueror of Paris in 1871). Prince Muhammad's realm spread to cover the entire central Kurdistan, including Arbil and Kirkuk, where justice and law reigned supreme. A contemporary visitor, J. Baillie Fraser, wrote:

> The great contrast which is observed between Turkish and Koordish territories. In the former, all villages were deserted, the inhabitants having taken flight to avoid the government imposts... On the other hand, no sooner did [one] reach Altoun Kupree [on the border], than all people flocked out, wearing flowers on their heads as on holidays, and shouted and cheered... They depend on no country but their own for the supply of all their

wants. Everything they require is produced at home, and while their mountains form impregnable defenses against foreign invaders, their rugged sides and valleys, with little effort, produce abundantly everything they desire to cultivate, and afford a never-failing supply of wood, water, and pasture.

Prince Muhammed's undertakings were aborted when a local grand mullah was bribed to issue a religious edict in 1836, forbidding Muslim Kurds from fighting the Ottoman Sultan/Caliph. Deserted, Prince Muhammed surrendered and was murdered in captivity at Trabzon the following year.

With the fall of Soran, the neighboring principality of Jezira (modern Cizre), under Bokthi Prince Badir (1802–1868) pursued the same goal by establishing links with other Kurdish princely houses at Muks, Bitlis, Kars, Hakkari and even the Ardalans in Persia, extending his dynasty's influence to most of Ottoman Kurdistan by 1840. To his diverse subjects, Badir attracted the allegiance of the Christian Armenian, Assyrian, and Chaldian inhabitants of Kurdistan. Awakened to the threat posed by Prince Badir and other Kurdish royalties, the Ottomans, now resuscitated by vast military support from Prussia/Germany, brought their full force against the fledgling Kurdish kingdoms. After three years of full-scale war, by 1848, the Ottomans had succeeded in shelling all Kurdish princely capitals into surrender. Jezira/Cizre, the ancient and charming capital of the Bokhti principality, was utterly leveled.

By 1867, the House of Ardalan—the last autonomous Kurdish principality in Persia—had been likewise extinguished. For the first time in history, the Ottomans and Persians now ruled all of Kurdistan directly, via governors.

The loss of independence and/or autonomy of Kurdish provinces created a political turmoil in the land which was to be further exacerbated after the end of WWI and the effective fragmentation of Kurdistan into five isolated sectors.

Modern Times

Following World War I, the territories of the Ottoman Empire which contained three-quarters of Kurdistan was divided between the European winning colonial empires. The Treaty of Sèvres (signed between Ottoman state and the European victors on August 10, 1921) anticipated an independent Kurdish state to cover a small portion of the former Ottoman Kurdistan. A larger portion—in fact the entire northern Kurdistan, from Van to Ardahan, from Bitlis to Bayezid—was scheduled at Sèvres for inclusion in a planned independent "Armenia." Luckily for Kurds, none of this came to pass.

Unconcerned with the natives' call for independence, France and Britain divided former Ottoman territories according to their own needs, with Kurdistan apportioned to the new states of Turkey, Syria, and Iraq. The Treaty of Lausanne (signed June 24, 1923) formalized this division. Kurds of Persia/Iran and Russia/USSR, meanwhile, were kept where they were before by Teheran and Moscow. Even though Lausanne dashed the Kurds' hope for independence for the rest of the twentieth century, it saved them from the ethnic cleansing that had been openly planned and partly implemented by the Armenians in large portions of the Kurdish territories scheduled by the Treaty of Sèvres for inclusion in an independent Armenia.

The drawing of well-guarded state boundaries dividing Kurdistan has, since 1921, afflicted Kurdish society with such a degree of fragmentation that its impact is tearing apart the Kurds' unity as a nation.

The 1920s saw the setting up of a Kurdish Autonomous Province ("Red Kurdistan") in Soviet Azerbaijan. It was dissolved in 1929. In 1945, Kurds set up a Kurdish republic at Mahabad in the Soviet occupied zone in Iran. It lasted one year, until the Iranian army reoccupied it.

After the fall of the monarch in Iraq in 1958 and the effective exit of Britain from that state, the successive juntas attempted at centralizing the power in Baghdad, thus running afoul of the Kurds who had enjoyed a benign autonomy under the British mandate and the monarchy. War broke out between the Kurds, led by the charismatic tribal leader and the head of the Kurdistan Democratic Party (KDP), Mustafa Barzani, and Baghdad, culminating in a Kurdish defeat in 1975. This lead to a political split among the Kurds, leading to the emergence of a rival, Patriotic Union of Kurdistan party (PUK), headed by Jalal Talabani.

A year earlier in 1974 and as a preventive measure, the Iraqi Kurds had been offered by Baghdad a limited autonomy in about half the Kurdish territories which went into effect in 1975. Ever since, they have enjoyed an official autonomous status with varying degrees of actual autonomy in a portion of that state's Kurdistan. By the end of 1991 and the conclusion of the Gulf War I, they had become all but independent with the help of the United States. By 1995, however, the Kurdish government in Arbil (the autonomous region's capital) was engaged in a factional fighting between various Kurdish warlords. In August 1996, the Barzani faction called the Iraqi army into Kurdistan to help it dislodge the rival Talabani faction. An American brokered cease-fire stopped the bloodshed by distributing the income from Iraqi oil, transit fees (and various other licit and illicit trades) equitably among the two primary Iraqi Kurdish factions: the Barzani and Talabani parties.

The Gulf War II in 2003 saw an unusual cooperation between the Iraqi Kurds on the one hand, and the Coalition Forces on the other. The fruits of this atypical Kurdish cooperation and wise choice of ally culminated in the enshrinement of Kurdish autonomy in three Iraqi Kurdish provinces (comprising about 60% of the Kurdish-inhabited regions of Iraq) in the provisional constitution of Iraq (March 2004)

Since 1987, the Kurds in Turkey—by themselves constituting a majority of all Kurds—have waged a war of national liberation against Ankara's seventy years of heavy-handed suppression of any vestige of Kurdish identity and its rich and ancient culture. The massive uprising had by 1995 propelled Turkey into a state of civil war. The burgeoning and youthful Kurdish population in Turkey is now demanding absolute equality with the Turkish component, and failing that, full independence.

In the Caucasus, the fledgling Armenian Republic in the course of 1992–1994 wiped out the entire Kurdish community of Red Kurdistan (Lachin, Kelbajar, Zangelan). Having ethnically cleansed its Kurdish inhabitants, Armenia has effectively annexed Red Kurdistan's territory that separates the Armenian exclave of Nagorno-Karabakh from Armenia. The fate of Red Kurdistan should serve as a model of what was in store for northern Kurdistan, had it been included into Armenia in 1920 by the provisions of the Treaty of Sèvres.

Following World War I and until 1991, Kurdistan was administered by five different sovereign states, with the largest portions of land respectively in Turkey (43%), Iran (31%), Iraq (18%), Syria (6%), and the Soviet Union (2%). Since the dissolution of the USSR in the year, Kurds find themselves natives of an additional five states which include Armenia, Azerbaijan, Georgia, Turkmenistan, and Uzbekistan. (Kurds of Kazakhstan and Kyrgyzstan are deportees.)

Iranian Kurds have lived in that state and the Battle of Chaldiran in 1514. Excepting occasional spells of independence, the other three-quarters of the Kurds lived in the Ottoman Empire from 1514 until its break-up in 1918. The French Mandate of Syria received pieces, and the British incorporated central Kurdistan or the "Mosul Vilayet" and its oil fields at Kirkuk into their Mandate of Iraq. The Kurds in Russia/USSR had passed into that sphere when territories were ceded by Persia in 1807–1828, and by the Ottomans in 1878.

Today the Kurds remain the only ethnic group in the world with indigenous representation in four world geopolitical blocs: the Arab World (in Iraq and Syria), NATO (in Turkey), the South Asian-Central Asian bloc (in Iran and Turkmenistan), and the Russian-dominated bloc (since 1991, Armenia, Azerbaijan, and Georgia). As such, the Kurdish nation as a whole lacks a natural ally, and each of her nine fragments must deal with different settings, alliances, countries, and political realities within different world power blocs. This has rendered a pan-Kurdish external (or even internal) policy impracticable if not self-defeating.

M. R. IZADY

See also Ethnic Conflicts: Middle East; Iran; Iraq; Kurdistan; Middle East: History and Economic Development; Middle East: International Relations; Minorities/Discrimination; Turkey

References and Further Reading

Arfa, Hasan. *The Kurds, An Historic and Political Study*. London: Oxford University Press, 1966.

Bruinessen, Martin van. *Agha, shaikh, and state: the Social and Political Structures of Kurdistan*. London; Atlantic Highlands, N.J.: Zed Books, 1992.

Ciment, James. *The Kurds: State and Minority in Turkey, Iraq, and Iran*. New York: Facts on File, 1996.

Driver, G.R. "Studies in Kurdish History," *Bulletin of the School of Oriental Studies*, II (1921–1923).

Ferhad Ibrahim, Gülistan Gürbey. *The Kurdish Conflict in Turkey: Obstacles and Chances for Peace and Democracy*. New York: St. Martin's Press, 2000.

Hay, W.R. *Two Years in Kurdistan: Experiences of a Political Officer, 1918–1920*. London, 1921.

Izady, M. *Kurds: A Concise Handbook*. London and Washington: Taylor and Francis, 1992.

———. *The Sharafnama or the History of the Kurdish Nation*. Costa Mesa: Mazda Publishers, 2005.

Kirişci, Kemal. *The Kurdish Question and Turkey: An Example of a Trans-state Ethnic Conflict*. London; Portland, Or: Frank Cass, 1997, 1998.

McDowall, David. *A Modern History of the Kurds: Third Edition*. London: I.B. Taurus, 2004.

Meiselas, Susan. *Kurdistan: In the Shadow of History*. New York: Random House, 1997.

Minorsky, V. "Les origines des Kurdes," *Actes du XXe Congrès International des Orientalistes* 1938 (1940).

Nikitine, Basil. *Les Kurdes. Etude Sociologique et Historique*. Paris, 1956.

Ninnane, Drek. *The Kurds and Kurdistan*. London: Oxford University Press, 1964.

KUWAIT

The state of Kuwait lies at the northwestern end of the Persian/Arabian Gulf. It encompasses 17,818 square kilometers (about 7,000 square miles) of land, including several islands, the most important of which are Failaka, a repository of ancient ruins off the coast of the Salmiya district, and Warba and

Bubiyan, low, marshy flats lying off the northern coast. Kuwait's topography slopes gently from west to east but is mostly level, except for one "mountain" in the south and a ridge in the north. It has a hot, desert climate. There is a short period of cold weather in the winter. Dust storms occur mostly during spring. Summer temperatures can rise very high, occasionally surpassing 50°C (122°F). The 2003 population of Kuwait was estimated as 2.4 million persons, 37% of whom are Kuwaiti citizens. The vast majority of citizens are Muslims, approximately 30% of whom are Shi'i and the rest Sunni.

Desert nomads roamed for centuries across what are now Iraq, Kuwait, and Saudi Arabia looking for water for their flocks; however, the political community grew from an urban nucleus on the seaside, settled early in the eighteenth century by refugees fleeing a prolonged drought in the central Arabian Peninsula. "Kuwait" is thought to be a diminutive of *kut*, or fort, but the community also was known as Qrain. In 1752, the Sabah family was chosen by community leaders to provide Kuwait's rulers but, until the late nineteenth century, Kuwaiti merchants and ship owners were richer and more powerful than the Sabahi amirs. Merchant wealth came from pearling and from buying and selling goods transported by dhow across south Asia, the Arabian Peninsula, and east Africa.

The balance of power between rulers and merchants changed with the reign of the amir Mubarak (r. 1896–1915), the only Kuwaiti ruler to come to power through a coup. Having killed his predecessor, Mubarak did not hesitate to bring other political forces to heel. He played the Ottomans off against the British in a mostly successful attempt to preserve his autonomy, ensure access to income independent of taxes paid by the merchants, and guarantee that the right of succession would be limited to his direct descendants. In return, Mubarak surrendered authority over Kuwait's foreign policy and as-yet undiscovered oil reserves to Britain.

Oil is the foundation of the modern Kuwaiti economy. Its exploitation rescued Kuwait from economic devastation resulting from tribal warfare, British competition in the transit trade, and the loss of markets for natural pearls caused by the advent of cheaper cultured pearls. The Kuwait Oil Company (KOC), a joint venture owned by a British and a US oil company, discovered oil in 1938. KOC began commercial exports of crude in 1946. Production capacity expanded rapidly, spurred by a British and US-led boycott of Iranian oil in the early 1950s. Kuwait is estimated to possess about 10% of global oil reserves. It was a founding member of the Organization of Petroleum Exporting Countries (OPEC) in 1960. In spite of extensive overseas investments, Kuwait continues to depend on oil sales for more than 90% of its GDP. It produced about 2.4 million barrels of crude per day in 2004.

By the mid-1950s, under the amir Abdullah al-Salim (r. 1950–1965), generous programs were inaugurated that distributed a large portion of the nation's oil income to the citizen population in the form of social services and cash payments. Health care and income support raised the quality of life for Kuwaitis along with their life expectancy, which rose from less than forty-five years in pre-oil Kuwait to nearly seventy-eight years in 2004. Education is compulsory for girls and boys between six and fourteen years of age. By 2003, 90% of Kuwait citizens ten years or older were literate. Most Kuwaitis are employed in the public sector but recent changes in employment policies such as the requirement that social allowances go to citizens working in the private sector as well as to government employees are making private-sector employment more attractive. Virtually all unskilled labor and workers employed in hazardous industries are foreigners whose wages are substantially lower than what Kuwaitis earn. The disparity in living standards between citizens and non-citizens is visible in nearly every aspect of life in Kuwait.

Kuwaiti citizenship was shaped by two experiences of invasion. Wahhabi raiders from Saudi Arabia invaded Kuwait from the south in 1920, reaching Jahra, an agricultural settlement to the west of the city, in October. Anticipating attack, the amir Salim (r. 1917–1920) called upon the residents to build a wall around the city. Toiling throughout the hot summer, the Kuwaitis completed the wall some weeks before Jahra, which Salim himself went out to defend, was attacked. The invaders were defeated at Jahra but the citizenship laws of the modern state defined as originally Kuwaiti only those families who had resided in the city in 1920, during the construction of the wall.

The second invasion occurred in August 1990 when Iraq seized Kuwait and claimed it as Iraq's "nineteenth province." The Iraqi occupation lasted until the end of February 1991 when an international coalition led by the United States expelled Iraqi forces and liberated Kuwait. The occupation was a defining event that united Kuwaitis as citizens but also divided them according to their experiences inside or outside the country during this period. Liberation marked a resumption of democratization. In 1992, responding to pressure from Kuwaiti citizens and governments that had spearheaded the liberation effort, the Kuwaiti government ended a six-year suspension of the constitution and parliament with parliamentary elections in October.

Despite this, Kuwait is not yet a democratic state. Women are not permitted to vote or run for political office, while the relationship between parliament and government leaves the lion's share of power with the latter, still firmly controlled by the Sabahi. Kuwaitis are not eager for revolutionary change in their country but across the political spectrum and hope for its gradual transformation into a constitutional monarchy. Civil society, buttressed by traditional institutions like family businesses and the *diwaniyya* (weekly home-based meetings), supports a highly diversified collection of religious and secular voluntary organizations and political movements. They contribute significantly to Kuwait's democratic potential even though some Islamist groups oppose democratization and seek to make religious law (*Shar'iah*) the basis of the legal and political system.

MARY ANN TÉTREAULT

See also Middle East: History and Economic Development; Middle East: International Relations; Organization of Petroleum Exporting Countries (OPEC); Persian Gulf War, 1991

References and Further Reading

Al-Mughni, Haya. *Women in Kuwait: The Politics of Gender*. London: Saqi Books, 1993/2001.
Anscombe, Frederick F. *The Ottoman Gulf: The Creation of Kuwait, Saudi Arabia, and Qatar*. New York: Columbia University Press, 1997.
Crystal, Jill. *Oil and Politics in the Gulf: Rulers and Merchants in Kuwait and Qatar*. Cambridge, UK: Cambridge University Press, 1990.
————. *Kuwait: The Transformation of an Oil State*. Boulder CO: Westview, 1992.
Herb, Michael. *All in the Family: Absolutism, Revolution, and Democracy in the Middle Eastern Monarchies*. Albany: State University of New York Press, 1999.
Longva, Anh Nga. *Walls Built on Sand: Migration, Exclusion, and Society in Kuwait*. Boulder, CO: Westview, 1992.
Tétreault, Mary Ann. *The Kuwait Petroleum Corporation and the Economics of the New World Order*. Westport, CT: Quorum Books, 1995.
————. *Stories of Democracy: Politics and Society in Contemporary Kuwait*. New York: Columbia University Press, 2000.

KUWAIT FUND FOR ARAB ECONOMIC DEVELOPMENT

The Kuwait Fund for Arab Economic Development ("the Fund") is a lending institution that finances development projects in Third World states. It operates as a public corporation managed by a board of directors with up to eight members appointed and formally chaired by the prime minister, who may delegate these powers to the minister of finance. The Fund's daily operations are overseen by the director general, who is appointed by decree of the Emir on the recommendation of the board of directors. Since 1986, the position of director general has been held by Bader Mishari al-Humaidhi. In 2003, the Fund's management was transferred from the ministry of finance to the ministry of foreign affairs.

The Fund was established on December 31, 1961, shortly after Kuwait gained its independence from the United Kingdom. It was the first aid agency in the developing world. Originally endowed with an operating capital of Kuwaiti dinar (KD) 50 million (KD 1 = $3.43, March 3, 2005) this was increased to KD 200 million in 1966, KD 1 billion in 1974, and KD 2 billion in 1981. Within a decade of its inception, the Fund had extended loans to all Arab states, with the exception of oil-producers Oman, Qatar, and Saudi Arabia. The Fund's mandate was originally limited to other Arab states. In July 1974, as high energy prices swelled the Kuwaiti treasury, its scope was extended to include all developing countries. Despite this broader mission, the Fund has been most heavily involved in Arab countries (53% of all loans), followed by South Asia and the Pacific (21%), and West Africa (9%).

While it has no formal restrictions on the type of projects it can sponsor, the Fund focuses mainly on transportation (32% of all loans), energy (22%), agriculture (16%), water and sewage (11%), and industry (11%). As of December 7, 2004, it had made 659 loans over its lifetime. Tunisia, Yemen, and China had the greatest number of loans, at twenty-nine each. Egypt had received the most credit, at KD 322 million. The Fund had also committed KD 328 million to fellow development institutions, the most important of which was the Arab Fund for Economic and Social Development, at KD 169 million. Its loan commitments totaled KD 3.4 million, disbursements reached KD 2.7 million, KD 1.5 million of which had been repaid.

The Fund is empowered to extend loans not only to sovereign states, but also sub-national governments, development institutions, and private non-profit corporations. Its assistance can take the form of direct loans, guarantees, joint financing with other agencies, advisory services, or capital subscription for development institutions or enterprises. The recipient must be a developing country, or, in the case of a non-state borrower, a national of a developing country. The Fund does not provide budgetary or balance of payment assistance. The criteria for evaluating project finance applications include: (1) economic justifications; (2) environmental impact; (3) total cost; (4) managerial capacity; and (5) technical viability. Interest rates are determined on a case-by-case basis, averaging 3.5% annually with a mean maturation period of twenty-two years. In general, the Fund funds a maximum of 50% of the total cost of a project and uses the Kuwaiti Dinar as its unit of account. The board of directors may grant exemptions from both these rules for reasons related to the nature of the project or the economic circumstances of the beneficiary country. The Fund does not require recipients to purchase any goods or services from Kuwait.

During the Fund's first two years of existence, the World Bank ("the Bank") provided it with an advisor to guide it in its operations. The legacy of this early tutelage remains visible, for example in the Fund's tendency to privilege large infrastructure projects. There are, however, significant differences between the two organizations. The Fund limits itself to providing loans, whereas the Bank openly seeks to influence recipient states's fiscal policy. The Bank funds not only individual projects, but sectors of the economy and government institutions as well. The Fund's smaller size allows it to have an average project cycle of six months, as opposed to eighteen for the Bank. As the first Arab aid agency, the Fund has served as an example to other oil-rich governments in the creation of similar entities. The most prominent of these are the Abu Dhabi Fund for Development, established in 1971, and the Saudi Fund for Development, founded in 1974. Moreover, the Fund has played a major role in building and financing a number of multilateral aid agencies. These include the Arab Fund for Economic and Social Development in 1968 (headquartered in Kuwait), the Arab Bank for Economic Development in Africa in 1974, and the Inter-Arab Investment Guarantee Corporation (also headquartered in Kuwait), the OPEC Fund for International Development, and the Islamic Development Bank, all in 1975.

Officially, the Fund's sole purpose is to foster development in the Third World. However, the government has also recognized it as one of Kuwait's foreign policy tools. Jordan's 1970 military action to expel the Palestine Liberation Organization resulted in a suspension of the Fund's most high-profile activities there. Tentative approval for a loan to Iraq was withdrawn under government pressure in 1973, following the latter's occupation of a Kuwaiti frontier post. Egypt's establishment of diplomatic ties with Israel led to a freeze on new loans, though the Fund honored its pre-existing commitments. Liberia suffered similar consequences when it restored diplomatic ties with Israel in 1983. Shortly after the 1990 Iraqi invasion, Kuwaiti Emir Sheikh Jaber al-Ahmad al-Sabah announced before the UN General Assembly the cancellation of all outstanding interest payments due to the Fund. This amounted to arrears of KD 12.4 million, shared by forty-three countries. Conversely, aid to Jordan, Sudan, and Yemen was suspended when they supported Baghdad.

ADAM ALLOUBA

See also Middle East: History and Economic Development

References and Further Reading

Demir, Soliman. *The Kuwait Fund and the Political Economy of Arab Regional Development.* Praeger Publishers: New York, 1976.

McKinnon, Michael. *Friends in Need: The Kuwait Fund in the Developing World.* St. Martin's Press: New York, 1997.

Moubarak, Walid E. "The Kuwait Fund in the Context of Arab and Third World Politics." *The Middle East Journal* 41, no. 4 (1987): 538–552.

KYRGYZSTAN

The Kyrgyz Republic (also known as Kyrgyzstan and by convention called Kirgizia until 1991) is located in Central Asia, bordering with China in the east, with Tajikistan in the south, Uzbekistan in the west, and Kazakhstan in the north. The country has a land area of 198,500 square kilometers (76,640 square miles) and is the second smallest in the Central Asian region.

The population of Kyrgyzstan is estimated at just over 5 million (2004). It is predominantly rural with only around 35% of the people living in cities and towns. The country's capital city, Bishkek (known as Frunze between 1926 and 1991), is home to seven hundred thousand people (2001) or 14% of the population. Kyrgyzstan has a population growth rate of 1.44% and it is estimated that its population could double by 2044. Kyrgyz and Russian share status as official languages; Uzbek is also spoken. The major religion is Islam, with 75% of the population; 20% are Russian Orthodox.

For centuries, the Kyrgyzstanis have been engaged in animal husbandry, raising horses, sheep, goats, and cattle. The mountainous land can support millions of sheep, but only 7% of the countryside is arable. Relations between Kyrgyzstanis and their neighbors have often been interrupted by devastating wars and military conflicts, which have had a negative effect on Kyrgyzstan's economic and social development. Consequently, Kyrgyzstan entered the nineteenth century as a feudal country with most of the population engaged in subsistence economy. Gradually, the Russian Empire established political control over the Kyrgyz land.

Major economic and social changes were brought to Kyrgyz society with the arrival of the Russians in the nineteenth century. The Russian Revolution of 1917, which was directed against the imperial regime and promised social justice, had profound effects on the Kyrgyz elite. In 1924, with Soviet assistance, Kyrgyzstan was established within its present borders, becoming a Soviet Autonomous Oblast (province), a constituent part of the Russian Federation. The Kyrgyz Communist Party came to power, to remain the single ruling party for the next sixty-six years.

The Soviet concept of development in Kyrgyzstan included radical political and economic changes, state control of all types of economic activities and central state planning. At the same time the government suppressed basic political freedoms; however, it eliminated mass illiteracy, developed extended free education and medical services to all sectors of the population, and installed a comprehensive welfare network. Between the 1930s and 1980s the government forced all farmers to join large-scale farming centered around *kolkhozy*, state-controlled collective farms (specializing in animal herding, cotton, silk, etc.). During and after World War II, it emphasized state-led industrialization which included defense, heavy industry such as agricultural machinery, light industries such as textile and garment, and mining in antimony, gold, uranium ore, and so on. As in most socialist countries, almost all economic activities in Kyrgyzstan were state-controlled, and private entrepreneurial initiatives were limited. Until the 1990s, the Soviet Union and the East European countries remained Kyrgyzstan's main trading partners, and the chief market for its products. According to official statistics, the Kyrgyzstan economy grew at an average annual rate of 6% to 9% between the 1930s and 1960s, but was stuck at 2% to 4% in the 1970s.

Major changes came in the middle of 1980s with the relinquishing of the centrally planned economy, and the introducing of limited democratization and economic experiments within the socialist system. These changes were largely peaceful, since they were initiated by the ruling elite under the influence of the Gorbachev's *perestroika* policy. In 1990, the Constitution of Kyrgyzstan was amended and the first multi-party election for the *Jogorku Kenesh* (Parliament) was held. The CPK was challenged by the newly formed Democratic Movement of Kyrgyzstan and some others. The CPK gained almost 80% of the seats in the new Parliament and formed the government, but its representative, Apsamat Masaliyev, lost the Presidential election to Dr. Askar Akayev, a candidate supported by the opposition.

Recent Development

Kyrgyzstan declared its independence from the USSR on August 31, 1991. President Akayev showed great toleration toward the opposition and promoted genuine reforms, liberalizing the political system and introducing a new Constitution (1993) and a new unicameral Parliament (1994). However, as Akayev won two consecutive presidential elections (in 1995 and 2000) there was evidence of increasing authoritarianism. It is important to note, however, that the transition in Kyrgyzstan was largely peaceful and, unlike many Third World countries, its military does not play any active role in its politics. After the parliamentary elections in 1995 and 2000 the *Jogorky Kenesh* emerged as a stronghold for opposition.

In the economic area, from the early 1990s the Kyrgyzstan government adopted an IMF-designed program of radical economic changes (the so-called shock therapy approach). This program is based on three main mechanisms: rapid mass-privatization, rapid price liberalization and currency reform with the assistance of international organizations such as the World Bank and the IMF. The government quickly abandoned the centrally planned economy and focused on mass-privatization, promotion of private entrepreneurship, liberalization of its trade, and opening up the national economy to international investment. It was able to privatize most of the enterprises in the industrial and agricultural sectors, establish a freely convertible currency system (Kyrgyzstan's *Som* was introduced in May 1993 and has remained relatively stable), and achieve macroeconomic stabilization. At the same time, the state downsized the social welfare system, and privatized medical services, educational institutions and the pension system. Due to its rapid and extensive economic liberalization, Kyrgyzstan became the first among the Commonwealth of Independent States to be accepted into the World Trade Organization (WTO) in 1998.

However, the state's sudden change of the economic policy and withdrawal of subsidies, combined with the disintegration of the Soviet market, led to a steep de-industrialization and transitional recession affecting almost all sectors of the economy. According to the IMF, Kyrgyzstan's economy declined at an average annual rate of 4.1% between 1989 and 1999 (between 1992 and 1995 the industrial sector alone declined at an average annual rate of 20%), while the United States was experiencing a decade of unprecedented growth. The country increasingly relies on the export of raw materials to the international market, and it is extremely vulnerable to fluctuations in world prices for its major export products—gold and agricultural products. Kyrgyzstan needs considerable foreign direct investments and international assistance to modernize existing technologies and to conduct major economic changes. However, both local and foreign investors are reluctant to invest in the economy due to the small size of the market, the weakness of the legal system and the inability of state institutions to implement property rights and contract law.

Agriculture, industries, and services are the three main pillars of post-Soviet Kyrgyzstan's economy, contributing 39.4, 26.4 and 34.2% respectively to the gross domestic product (GDP) (2000 World Bank estimate). Kyrgyzstan's exports are narrowly based on sales of raw materials in international markets. The country's main exports are nonferrous metals (accounting for almost 41% of total export earnings in 1998), garments and textiles, electricity, and agricultural products. The mining industry is largely concentrated around the single largest mining field, Kumtor. The country depends heavily on imports of machinery, fuel, industrial consumer goods, and food products. Due to the transitional recession and the disappearance of aid from the former USSR, Kyrgyzstan's economy increasingly relies on foreign aid and credits. Total external debt has reached almost $1.4 billion US dollars (2001), quite a large figure for a nation of only 5 million people.

Despite macroeconomic stability and success in structural changes, the economic changes led to a steady decline in living standards among pensioners, rural people, and women with children. The country remains one of the poorest countries of the former Soviet Union, with 52% of population living below the poverty line (2001 estimate) and a sizeable number of people are leaving for other countries in search for jobs and better standards of living. In 2001, the United Nations Development Program (UNDP) Human Development Index (HDI) put Kyrgyzstan in ninety-second place out of 162, behind all the former Soviet countries except only Moldova, Uzbekistan, and Tajikistan.

RAFIS ABAZOV

See also Commonwealth of Independent States: History and Economic Development; Commonwealth of Independent States: International Relations

References and Further Reading

Abazov, R. 'Policy of Economic Transition in Kyrgyzstan', *Central Asian Survey*, Vol. 18, no. 2, 1999, pp. 197–223.

Akayev, Askar. *Kyrgyzstan: an Economy in Transition.* Canberra: Asia Pacific Press, 2001.

Allworth, Edward. *Central Asia: 130 Years of Russian Dominance. A Historical Overview.* Durham, NC: Duke University Press, 1994.

IMF. *Kyrgyz Republic: Recent Economic Developments.* Washington, DC, International Monetary Fund, 1998.

Kirgizskaia Sovetskaia Sotsialisticheskaia Respublika: entsiklopediia (Kyrgyz Soviet Socialist Republic: Encyclopedia). Frunze: Glav. red. Kirgizskoi Sovetskoi Entsiklopedii, 1982.

Pomfret, R. *The Economies of Central Asia.* Princeton, NJ: Princeton University Press, 1995.

UNDP. *Kyrgyz Republic. National Human Development Report.* Bishkek, UNDP, 2000.

World Bank. *Kyrgyzstan: the Transition to Market.* Washington, DC: World Bank, 1993.

L

LAAR, MAART

Born in 1960, Maart Laar proved to be one of the most influential politicians to emerge during the intense period of economic, political, and social transition in post-independence Estonia. Laar was credited with Estonia's rapid advancement towards European integration during the 1990s.

Laar was born in Viljandi, Estonia in 1960. Laar received a BA in history and later an MA in philosophy from the University of Tartu. From 1990–1992, Laar served on the Estonian Congress and Estonian Committee, as well as the Supreme Council, positioning himself to become an active participant in Estonian politics. The thirty-one-year-old, self professed "grandson of Margaret Thatcher," was chosen by president Lennart Meri as prime minister in 1992. Laar would serve as Estonian Prime Minister from 1992–1994 and again from 1999–2002.

Expectations were enormously high for Laar's first government, led by the *Isamaa* (Fatherland) party. The young parliament members were perceived as being intrinsically honest in comparison to the former Soviet governments. The ambitious Laar set out upon a course of reforms and programs to realign Estonia with Western Europe. Laar established a radical neo-liberal economic regime; including the elimination of all tariff restrictions and replacing the existing tax code. The progressive income tax was replaced by a fixed, flat rate of 26% in the hope of allowing individuals greater economic choices. Unlike Laar's peers in other successor states of the Soviet Union, Laar was most concerned about leading Estonia toward a clearly Western orientation rather than the Commonwealth of Independent States (CIS). While this policy proved to stimulate economic growth, it led to great economic hardship for many Estonians.

The harsh reforms set in motion by *Isamaa* and Laar's personal arrogance ultimately led to the failure of his first government. *Isamaa* mandated strict new legislation concerning the Russian population in the country, demanding that the nation's five hundred thousand former Soviet citizens register for residency or risk expulsion from the country. The severe economic dislocation caused by the market reforms led to questions of major social implications, including a rising crime rate. Local elections in October 1993 only served to prove the public's growing discontent with the *Isamaa* government. Of sixty-four seats on the Tallinn City Council available, only five went to Laar's party. In response, Laar stated that Estonia could either move forward toward European integration or find itself as a full member of the CIS. This arrogance, and accusations of corruption proved to be Laar's first undoing. After the revelation that 2.3 billion Soviet rubles were withdrawn from circulation and sold to Chechnya without parliamentary consent, a vote of no-confidence was held, and Laar stepped down on September 26, 1994.

Laar reemerged as prime minister in 1999 after parliamentary elections, creating a coalition government consisting of *Isamaa*, the Estonian Reform Party, and the Moderates' Party. The government's main concern was preparing Estonia for formal European Union accession and the expansion of the high technology sector of the economy. Laar resigned from office in January 2002 amidst growing tensions within the coalition and was replaced by Siim Kallas.

JONATHAN H. L'HOMMEDIEU

See also Estonia; Vähi, Tiit

References and Further Reading

Lauristin, Marju and Peeter Vihalemm, ed. *Return to the Western World: Cultural and Political Perspectives on the Estonian Post-Communist Transition*. Tartu: Tartu-University Press, 1997.
Smith, David J., Artis Pabriks, Aldis Purs, and Thomas Lane. *The Baltic States: Estonia, Latvia, and Lithuania*, New York: Routledge Press, 2002.

LABOR

Labor encompasses primarily the physical activity of work, though following a Marxist view the idea of labor-power is often implied. Labor-power is the worker's need/ability/desire to sell his or her work to employers, in return for compensation, which can be in the form of wage, salary, or non-monetary means, as has been the case historically in many developing countries. For example, in the late nineteenth and even the early twentieth century, mining workers, who lived and worked in very remote areas, often received so-called company-tokens which they could–or had to–exchange for expensive food and other life-supporting commodities. In the process, workers frequently became indebted. In many developing countries, share-cropping is a familiar sight. In return for their work, peasants are entitled—more often by tradition than by legal contract—to a certain and perhaps negotiated share of land or of the harvest. Thus land, and more specifically land ownership, has been and continues to be of crucial importance for peasants all over the developing world.

Labor not only describes the physical activity of work or the laborer's need to sell his/her work to any given employers, but most importantly, labor connotes a social relationship—and thus also a relationship of power, including also (mutual) dependence—between two or more categories of social actors. History has seen an endless number of variations of that social relationship, including slave-labor, wage-labor, and more recently so-called full-time labor, part-time labor, sub-contracted labor, outsourced labor, stock-holding labor, informal labor, and more. Following both Marx and Weber, the relationship between labor and employers is a class relationship that has also a political dimension to the degree to which labor, that is, workers, are interested in (a) obtaining suffrage (more the historic case of European than developing

countries) and (b) improving wage and working conditions, in short, improving their social rights (as understood by TH Marshall). In their pursuit of social rights, workers most often appeal to the state and in so doing can choose between two political approaches: revolution or reform, although the latter may have its own variations, for example, the so-called "third way" (Europe), "corporatism" (Latin America) or, more recently and adopted worldwide, the "neo-liberal" phase. Historically, workers have not been very successful in bringing about major socio-political and economic changes via revolution. Reasons for this are complex and multiple. Following Marx, workers need to organize in the labor movement, which in turn helps workers obtain "true consciousness" which in turn prepares them for the revolution and the seizure of political power. The role of working-class parties has often contributed to the improvement of workers' social rights, but at the cost of accommodation and postponement of revolution. Despite unprecedented industrialization, no country has ever produced a pure working-class political majority; hence even revolution by suffrage alone (as compared to the violent overthrow of the so-called bourgeois state) has not occurred. The country that came closest to that was most likely Chile in 1970, in which a Socialist was elected President, with a program to gradually move from capitalism to socialism. But even there, working-class parties were not able to control Congress, and political divisions led the country to the brink of civil war in 1973. With the fall of the Soviet Union and the end of Communism, Cuba and North Korea notwithstanding, radical working-class parties where they still exist(ed), have become more accepting of capitalism and democracy. Hence the role of working-class parties—or of parties who claim to represent "the working people"—becomes crucial for workers' interest, and this is nowhere more evident than in the Social-Democratic types. And while this option puts the revolution forever on "hold," workers have obtained substantial gains over the last two centuries.

Yet, for many workers in developing countries, even this "second-best" scenario (Social Democracy) remains elusive, in part precisely because many countries have not been able to industrialize to the degree to which this has occurred in developed countries. In other words, they have not been able to "repeat" the development path taken by the developed world. Therefore, agriculture remains a crucial economic activity and peasants often labor in conditions similar to those a century ago. Thus, in part as a result of structural conditions related to economic development, working-class parties in most developing countries remain small and mostly bereft of any major political power. In developing countries, modernization of agriculture is relatively widespread, though the effects on labor are heterogeneous. In some cases, increased use of technology has had positive effects on wages and/or working conditions, but the trade-off to this economic policy is frequently unemployment or low job creation that usually cannot keep up with population growth. Hence, in many developing countries, the countryside has had an ambiguous view on modernization. Many workers and families welcome better jobs, but many realize that work in and of itself is not always an improvement to working and living conditions. Often, too, there is fear that modernization replaces or changes culture and customs.

With the end of Keynesian economic policies and Import-Substitution Industrialization (especially in Latin America), so-called neoliberalism has become the latest economic "model." Most if not all Latin American and Asian countries (see here especially the "NICs"—the newly industrialized countries of Southeast Asia) have over the past two to three decades adopted that neo-liberal model in one way or another. One important consequence of this has been the reduced role of the state in the economy. For many developing countries, this has not been an easy choice and favorable macroeconomic indicators do not always tell the whole story. Not surprising then, many workers in developing countries are beginning to resent Neo-liberal economics. Those workers who are organized in labor unions often resort to strikes and protests in order to defend what they believe to be their interests and rights. However, unionization has witnessed a major decline beginning in the late 1970s and early 1980s, and as rule, unions in developing countries do not enjoy the kind of "strength" witnessed in developed countries (especially Northern Europe). Therefore, workers often have to rely on their own luck in finding work that permits them a livable wage. Nevertheless, many democratic governments of the developing countries were eager to adopt neo-liberal policies, in part because of the conviction that state-led development had contributed to low productivity, inefficient enterprises, budget deficits, and more.

While the social division of labor frequently denotes workers' position in any given economic and political structure, the sexual division of labor calls attention to the way in which males and females experience work differently—as workers but also often as husbands and wives, fathers and sons, and daughters and mothers. In other words, the dual structures of work and household affect women differently from men. Domestic labor is still mostly a female place, underpaid, and not sufficiently appreciated by state, economy, and society of all countries.

To what degree developing countries "lag behind" in their cultural, economic, and political recognition of female labor is very much debated in academia. And even though Modernization and Dependency Theory of the 1960s and 1970s, respectively, each had their own insights to the "problem," it is clear that equality for female labor, at work and at home, is still a major challenge in the new millennium of developing and developed countries alike.

VOLKER FRANK

References and Further Reading

Cardoso, Fernando H and Enzo Faletto. *Dependency and Development in Latin America*. Berkeley, CA: University of California Press, 1979.
Giddens, Anthony. *Beyond Left and Right. The Future of Radical Politics*. Stanford, CA: Stanford University Press, 1994.
Marx, Karl. *Wage-Labour and Capital, Value, Price and Profit*. New York: International Publishers, 1976.
Offe, Claus, and Volker Runge. "Theses on the Theory of the State." *New German Critique*, 6:137–148.
Portes, Alejandro, Manuel Castells, and Lauren Benton. *The Informal Economy: Studies in Advanced and Less Developed Countries*. Baltimore, MD: Johns Hopkins University Press, 1989.
Przeworski, Adam. *Capitalism and Social Democracy*. Cambridge, UK: Cambridge University Press, 1985.
Rueschemeyer, Dietrich, Evelyne Huber Stephens, and John Stephens. *Capitalist Development and Democracy*. Chicago: University of Chicago Press, 1992.
Worsley, Peter. *The Three Worlds: Culture and World Development*. Chicago: University of Chicago Press, 1984.

LAKE CHAD BASIN COMMISSION

The Lake Chad Basin Commission (LCBC) was created by the Fort Lamy (N'Djamena) Convention signed on May 22, 1964, by the heads of state of four countries that share the Lake Chad, namely, Cameroon, Niger, Nigeria, and Chad. The Central African Republic was admitted as the fifth member state in 1994, which more than doubled the area of the new Lake Chad Conventional Basin, from 427,300 square kilometers to nearly 1 million square kilometers. Lake Chad was once the sixth-largest lake in the world, but since 1964, the lake level has continuously fallen with the surface area reducing from about 25,000 square kilometers in the 1960s to less than 2,000 square kilometers today, while its volume has decreased by close to 60%. There are several reasons for this shrinking of Lake Chad but perhaps the biggest reason was the severe droughts in the region in the 1970s and 1980s, combined with diversion for irrigation. Despites its low level readings, according to the Famine Early Warming Systems Network, hydrological station readings indicate that the levels are slowly rising.

The Lake Chad Basin is a source of life, socio-economic diversity, and biodiversity for this region of the world. The population of the conventional basin, according to its Executive Secretary Abubakar B. Jauro, is about 20 million distributed as 2,550,000 in Cameroon, 193,000 in Niger, 11,376,000 in Nigeria, 5,048,530 in Chad, and about 634,283 in Central African Republic, respectively. A majority of this population survives directly from the practice of agriculture, nomadic and semi-nomadic animal husbandry, and fisheries. There are more than 150,000 fishermen living on the lake's shores and its islands. According to the WWF International and its Living Waters Programme, the current estimate of annual fish production from the lake is sixty thousand to seventy thousand tonnes. The raising of cattle, sheep, and camels is also economically important, together with the cultivation of some traditional crops. The most common system is the lake-bottom cropping or receding moisture cultivation, which has been a response to the contraction of Lake Chad. In addition to direct support for livelihoods, according to the WWF International and its Living Waters Programme, the lake also plays an important socio-economic role in regulating annual water supply, recharging ground water, and helping to control flooding. WWF International also reports that over one hundred species of fish have been recorded from the upper Chari system, while over 120 species are know from the lake itself and the lower reaches of the Chari River. Furthermore, the region is also notable for the Kuri ox, a domesticated breed of *Bos Taurus longifrons* at risk of extinction.

The LCBC was established for the regulation and planning of the uses of the waters and other natural resources of the convention basin. Today, the LCBC is also mostly concerned with, but not limited to, collecting, evaluating and disseminating information on projects prepared by member states and to recommend plans for common projects and joint research programmes in the Lake Chad basin; drawing up common rules regarding navigation and transport; examining complaints and promoting the settlement of disputes and the resolution of conflicts; promoting regional cooperation, coordinating regional programmes; and planning, mobilization, and following up of national projects with regional implication.

JOSE DA CRUZ

See also Biodiversity Conservation; Cameroon; Central Africa: History and Economic Development; Central Africa: International Relations; Central African Republic; Chad; Environment: Government Policies; Niger; Nigeria; Sustainable Development; Water Resources and Distribution; Wildlife Preservation

References and Further Reading

Chrétien, Jean-Pierre. *The Great Lakes of Africa: Two Thousand Years of History.* New York; Cambridge, MA: Zone Books; Distributed by MIT Press, 2003.

Harmon, Daniel E. *Central and East Africa: 1880 to the Present: From Colonialism to Civil War.* Philadelphia: Chelsea House Publishers, 2002.

Jauro, Abubakar B. "Lake Chad Basin Commission: (LCBC) Perspectives." *International Conference: Water and Sustainable Development.* Paris: March 19–21, 1998. http://www.oieau.fr/ciedd/contributions/atriob/contribution/cblt.htm.

LAND DISTRIBUTION PATTERNS

Land distribution patterns reflect and underpin social power so that changes in patterns of land ownership necessarily involve changes in the structure of society itself. Land reform means the redistribution of land and other agricultural resources to reduce or eliminate the concentration of assets in the hands of a small number of powerful and wealthy elites. Land reform entails a comprehensive overhaul of the way in which agricultural land is held or owned, the methods of cultivation that are employed, or the relation of agriculture to the rest of the economy. The term *agrarian reform* is also used to refer to a fundamental change in access to and use of land in a broader sense to include agricultural institutions, such as credit, taxation, rents, and cooperatives. Sitting governments or political parties introduce such reforms to resolve or prevent economic and political crises. The main objectives are to abolish exploitive control of farms and related labor and to generate economic development on behalf of poor peasants and indigenous peoples who rely on land for livelihood and welfare. Governments often intervened to transfer land ownership from an established landed class to the state or key constituents in the countryside. Although land reform resulted in lower agricultural productivity in some cases when it included collectivization, it generally increased productivity when land was redistributed directly to the tiller.

Land reform has its origins in the classic eras of Greek and Roman empires, but land redistribution is more closely associated with the Enlightenment period and the major liberal democratic revolutions in Western Europe and the United States. The equitable distribution of land and the right to own land as a fundamental human right lie at the heart of democratic egalitarian societies as envisioned by the

US and French experiences. However, centuries of enclosure and eviction in much of Europe created a vast displaced population whose only recourse was to migrate to the industrial centers. Peasant uprisings were based on the demands of small freeholders, yet the modern state, the crown and the church resisted the restructuring of land ownership to protect the interests of aristocrats and oligarchs. In the wake of the abolition of slavery in the United States after 1865, freed people of African descent sought fundamental shifts in social relations in land tenancy and labor conditions in southern states. Many former slaves became family farmers, often working land they rented through various sharecropping arrangements, although many blacks continued to work in relationships reminiscent of slave-like dependence on white landlords.

Latin America

The creation of new nation-states in Latin America in the nineteenth century eliminated communal ownership of land among indigenous communities. A variety of liberal dictatorships designated vast land holdings in private individual or family titles causing many indigenous communities to lose their customary property rights to private estate owners. Farm land was often sold without consent or just seized outright. By the late nineteenth century, many indigenous villages disappeared and native peoples were forced into destitution as agricultural laborers and miners. The desperate need for land reform was a major force behind the Mexican revolution of 1910. Emiliano Zapata championed the resurrection of communal land access which was given official legal status in Article 27 of the 1917 Constitution. State-held *ejido* land was distributed to poor indigenous cultivators in perpetuity. However, amendments to Article 27 in 1992 weakened *ejido* restrictions on the sale and division of land into individual parcels.

The onset of the Cold War introduced an ideological dimension to struggles for access to land. From 1952 through the 1970s, a wave of nationalist revolutionary movements in Latin America led governments to implement agrarian reforms on behalf of constituents among the rural poor. The reforms failed to address marginalized indigenous peoples, notably Bolivia, Ecuador, and Peru. Military rule in Brazil in the 1970s and 1980s spawned intense pressure for land reform led by the Landless Peoples Movement. Land reform in Chile under the government of Salvador Allende (1970–1973) was reversed once the military dictatorship of Augusto Pinochet took power in 1973.

The communist regime in Cuba embarked on agrarian reform after 1959 through the nationalization of the sugar sector that was mainly responsible for lucrative agricultural exports and miserable rural living standards. The goals were to increase production and rationalize labor inputs, but state intervention led to inefficiency and resistance.

The modern history of Central America is replete with conflict over land. The repression of peasant uprisings in El Salvador in 1932, and the subversion of a genuine attempt at agrarian reform in Guatemala in the early 1950s, eventually led to the emergence of revolutionary guerrilla organizations that advocated land redistribution. In El Salvador, a military coup by junior officers in October 1979 installed a provisional government that proposed limited land redistribution. The Basic Agrarian Reform Law promulgated in March 1980 affected about 15% of farmland. Additional provisions allowed renters or sharecroppers to claim legal titles, and several commercial banks were nationalized to reallocate credit to the reformed sector. The Christian Democratic government attempted to utilize land reform as a disincentive for landless peasants to join the guerrilla insurgency. In Guatemala, the overthrow of the democratic government of Jacob Arbenz in 1954 catapulted the country into a ferocious civil war for the next four decades. The issues of land reform and indigenous rights to land were central features of the peace accord sponsored by the United Nations in 1996. Upon the fall of the Somoza dynasty in Nicaragua in 1979, the Sandinistas embarked on agrarian reform primarily with the property of the Somoza family and its closest allies. The revolutionary government collectivized some rural production in cooperatives and state farms, but did not intend to attack the non-Somoza landed elite. However, in July 1981, the regime announced broader legislation that permitted the confiscation of large tracts of abandoned, idle, or underutilized land. When the Sandinistas lost the presidential election in 1990, the new government privatized state land and dismantled agricultural cooperatives.

Sub-Saharan Africa

The African national liberation movements against colonial rule subsumed tribal and peasant demands for land under a broad agenda of political self-determination and popular will. The socialist experiment in Tanzania under Julius Nyerere aimed to persuade the peasantry to accept the moral rectitude of the control of land by the state. However, the policy of rural resettlement became coercive in the 1970s. The use of militia against farmers who rejected the village scheme poisoned relations between the regime and the countryside. Kenyan tribal and agricultural elites circumvented pressures for wholesale restructuring of land ownership in the 1970s, while the state attempted to resettle and title land to over a million progressive small farmers. The government's efforts to register titles, consolidate fragmented holdings, and adjudicate subsequent land disputes were hampered by intransigent relationships between local land patrons and clients that cut across ethnic, regional, and family lines.

In Zimbabwe, the Lancaster House agreement in 1979 protected the position of white farmers who were allocated twenty seats in parliament. Land reform, specifically the redistribution of white-owned land to landless black peasants, was promised but was delayed to smooth the transition to black majority rule. During the 1980s, the government of Robert Mugabe increasingly moved away from its Marxist rhetoric and toward support for political and economic liberalization in southern Africa. Yet, under pressure from the democratic opposition, Mugabe announced a controversial program of land redistribution in 1997. About 1,500 white-owned commercial farms, nearly half of the country's total commercial farmland, were designated to be seized without compensation and divided among landless blacks and blacks with only small landholdings. The ongoing process of land reform in South Africa is a direct response to the history of land dispossession during the colonial period in the eighteenth and nineteenth centuries, the Natives Land Act of 1913 and subsequent legislation in 1936 creating *native reserves* for African populations, and the forced resettlement of 3.5 million Africans into *homelands* by the apartheid government after 1948. The democratic government led by the African National Congress embarked on a multi-pronged approach to land reform in 1994. The program addressed restitution, redistribution, and tenure security. However, political, fiscal, and technical problems slowed progress during a decade of democratic rule.

Global Perspective

Other notable cases of land reform are connected historically to world war and revolution in the twentieth century. The Bolshevik revolution in Russia in 1917 led to a type of land reform known as collectivization in which all arable land became state property and peasant farmers cultivated and harvested under state control. Land reform was an essential part of the transition to democracy in Japan after World War II. United States occupation forces supervised land redistribution that transferred over 80% of Japan's cultivated land from absentee landlords to permanent tenants by 1949. Taiwan and South Korea adopted limited land reforms in response to the Maoist revolution in China in 1949 and the ideological split of the Korean peninsula in 1953, respectively. In China, dynastic rule and warlord competition, combined with Japanese occupation and a debilitating civil war in the 1920s and 1930s, contributed to the acute concentration of land in the hands of estate owners and foreign exporters with ties to the nationalist regime. The communist regime redistributed land among the peasant population in the form of massive communes. This policy had disastrous effects on food production and led to starvation in the countryside. The commune system was abolished in favor of market-oriented agriculture in the 1980s.

Indigenous peoples regard themselves as belonging to their lands. Land reform became an essential element of the movement for sovereignty among aboriginal peoples and indigenous communities in North America, Australia, and New Zealand. The movement for political independence from British rule in Scotland in the late 1990s also hinged on profound land reform. Scotland has one of the most concentrated patterns of land ownership in the world. Upon the promulgation of the independent Scottish parliament, an array of public officials and intellectuals advocated land reform as a means to achieve fairness in access to land and to secure the public good through land use policies.

MARK EVERINGHAM

See also Agriculture: Impact of Globalization

References and Further Reading

Abrahams, Richard, editor. *Villagers, Villages and the State in Modern Tanzania.* Cambridge, UK: Cambridge University Press, 1985.
Brockett, Charles. *Land, Power, and Poverty: Agrarian Transformation and Political Conflict in Central America.* Boston: Unwin Hyman, 1988.
Browning, David (1983). "Agrarian Reform in El Salvador," *Journal of Latin American Studies* 15(2): 269–294 (1983).
Coldham, Simon. "Land Tenure Reform in Tanzania: Legal Problems and Perspectives," *Journal of Modern African Studies* 33, no. 2, pp. 227–242 (1995).
———. "Land Tenure Reform in Kenya: the limits of law," *Journal of Modern African Studies* 17, no. 4, pp. 615–627 (1979).
Cousins, Ben, editor. *At the Crossroads: Land and Agrarian Reform in South Africa into the Twentieth Century.* Cape

Town, South Africa: Program for Land and Agrarian Studies, University of the Western Cape and the National Land Committee, 2000.

Deere, Carmen Diana, Peter Marchetti, and Nola Reinhardt. "The Peasantry and the Development of Sandinista Agrarian Reform Policy, 1979–1984," *Latin American Research Review* 20, no. 3, pp. 75–109 (1985).

Enriquez, Laura. *Harvesting Change: Labor and Agrarian Reform in Nicaragua, 1979–1990*, Chapel Hill: University of North Carolina Press, 1991.

Human Rights Watch. *Fast Track Land Reform in Zimbabwe*. Country Reports, 14, no. 1 (A), March 2002. http://www.hrw.org/reports/2002/zimbabwe.

Iglehart, Ed. *Territory, Property, Sovereignty, and Democracy in Scotland*. Edinburgh, Scotland: Caledonia Center for Social Development, 1999.

Levin, Richard and Daniel Weiner. "The Politics of Land Reform in South Africa after Apartheid," *Journal of Peasant Studies* 23, nos. 2/3, pp. 93–119 (1996).

Mamdani, Mahmood. *Citizen and Subject: Contemporary Africa and the Legacy of Late Colonialism*. Princeton, NJ: Princeton University Press, 1996.

Montgomery, John, editor. *International Dimensions of Land Reform*. Boulder, CO: Westview Press, 1984.

Prosterman, Roy and Jeffrey Riedinger, editors. *Land Reform and Democratic Development*. Baltimore, MD: Johns Hopkins University Press, 1987.

Strasma, John. "Unfinished Business: Consolidating Land Reform in El Salvador," *In Search of Agrarian Reform in Latin America*. William Thiesenhusen, editor, New York: Allen Unwin, 1989.

Thiesenhusen, William. *Broken Promises: Agrarian Reform and the Latin American Campesino*. Boulder, CO: Westview Press, 1995.

LANDSBERGIS, VYTAUTAS

Vytautas Landbergis, with Lech Walesa and Vaclav Havel, is one of the Central Europe's "velvet revolution" beacons: a musician who went on to liberate his country, Lithuania, from the Soviet/Russian domination.

Landsbergis was born on October 18, 1932, in Kaunas, Lithuania. He graduated the Lithuanian Conservatoire in Vilnius in 1955. He began his career as a tutor in 1952 at M.K. Čiurlionis Music School and remained in the teaching profession until entering politics in 1990. He authored ten books in musicology, arts and history of music, five books on political developments, and a volume of verses. His chief topic of research and writing is the life and work of Lithuanian artist and composer M.K. Čiurlionis, for which he was awarded the Lithuanian State Prize. He was also actively involved in musicians' community life, including as a head of M.K. Čiurlionis Society, Chairman of the Organizing Committee of the International M.K. Čiurlionis piano and organ competition, and M.K. Čiurlionis Competition Foundation.

On June 3, 1988, Landbergis was elected member of the initiative Group of the Lithuanian Reform Movement "Sąjūdis," during Sąjūdis Founding Congress on October 22–23 of the same year—to the Sąjūdis Seimas (Assembly) and Seimas' Council, and a month later, Chairman of the Sąjūdis Seimas' Council. Since December 15, 1991, he has been Sąjūdis' Honorary President. He has chaired the Lithuanian Conservative Party—Homeland Union—since its founding in 1993.

On March 26, 1989, the city of Panevėžys elected Landbergis to represent Lithuania in the USSR Congress' of People's Deputies. Following his election to the Supreme Council of Lithuania on February 24, 1990, he was elected on March 11, 1990, to lead the Council as its President and Head of State. In this capacity, he chaired parliamentary session, which declared the independent Republic of Lithuania's reestablishment, and was part of the Baltic States Council (1990–1992), chaired Commission for the New Constitution (1990–1991), and led the State Delegation to the negotiations with the USSR. Under his leadership Lithuania resisted the armed violence and Moscow-imposed blockade and achieved an agreement for withdrawing Russian troops from Lithuania.

Landbergis is a staunch anticommunist. He firmly opposes Russian Soviet domination over Baltic countries as well as over other territories, especially Caucasus. As a politician, he advocates individuals' freedom, civil society, and private market economy.

On June 13, 2004, Landbergis became a European Parliament Member. With money from the Norwegian People's Peace Prize he established the Vytautas Landbergis Foundation to support care and education of handicapped children and young performing artists.

STEPHAN E. NIKOLOV

See also Glasnost and Perestroika; Gorbachev, Mikhail; Lithuania; Soviet Bloc

References and Further Reading

Landsbergis, Vytautas. *Lithuania Independent Again: The Autobiography of Vytautas Landbergis*. Seattle: University of Washington Press, and Cardiff: University of Wales, 2000.

Lieven, Anatol. *The Baltic Revolution: Estonia, Latvia, Lithuania and the Path to Independence*. New Haven, CT: Yale University Press, 1993.

Misiunas, Romuald and Rein Taagepera. *The Baltic States: Years of Dependence 1940–1990*. Berkeley, CA: University of California Press, 1993.

Onken, Eva-Clarita. *Demokratisierung der Geschichte in Lettland. Staatsbürgerliches Bewusstsein und Geschichtspolitik im ersten Jahrzehnt der Unabhängigkeit*. Hamburg: Krämer, 2003.

LANGUAGE, INFLUENCE ON DEVELOPMENT

Development

The measure of human progress through most of the twentieth century was the country's economic performance computed on the basis of gross domestic product (GDP) and the annual income per capita. This approach to development ignored all non-economic factors as indicators of progress. Toward the end of the last century new indices were recognised as crucial components of development and now feature prominently in the World Bank and United Nations Development Program (UNDP) Development Reports. For example, a country's development rating takes into consideration the country's human rights record, the proportion of its population that has access to clean water and sanitation, basic education, health services, and so on.

Language, being a significant aspect of culture, merits consideration when human development and progress is being computed. For example, access to good education depends to a large extent on the medium of instruction, the selection of which is part of a people's educational language rights (ELRs). In a situation where children are introduced to school education in a strange language, they are disadvantaged and therefore denied one of their fundamental human rights.

In recognition of the importance of language as a right, the United Nations **(UN) Declaration on the Rights of Persons Belonging to National or Ethnic Religious, and Linguistic Minorities**, which was adopted by the UN General Assembly in December 1992, has the following clauses:

Article 1.1: States shall protect the essence of the national or ethnic, cultural or religious and linguistic identity of minorities within their respective territories, and shall encourage conditions for the promotion of that identity.

Article 4.3: States should take appropriate measures so that, whenever possible persons belonging to minorities have adequate opportunities to learn their mother tongue or to have instruction in their mother tongue.

Unfortunately for most of the developing countries, the national languages are minority languages since the countries have adopted ex-colonial languages as their official languages. This means that most of the crucial public functions such as court and parliamentary deliberations, education, mass communication, and public administration are carried out in foreign languages, mainly English, French, Portuguese, and Spanish in the case of Africa. The implication of this state of affairs is that the majority of the citizens in these countries are excluded from the management and control of the critical national institutions which are entrusted with the development matters in the country. The lack of participation by the majority in the development programmes can be seen as a language-related problem and unless this is redressed through a deliberate national language policy, its effects will continue to manifest themselves in the form of reduced productivity of individuals, limited national integration and slow national econo-industrial progress.

Language, Thought, and Culture

Culture is a shared way of life, which includes: shared social identity, shared attitudes, shared knowledge and skills, and a shared communication system. These shared attributes are those aspects of the group's life which by consensus the group members have agreed upon as valuable to the community. Language as a medium of expression is considered to be the embodiment of that culture and for many, language and culture have meant one and the same thing.

According to Ong (1982:74), since "the spoken word proceeds from the human interior and manifests human beings to another as conscious interiors as persons, the spoken word forms human beings into close-knit groups."

Language is, therefore, critical in shaping human consciousness and the definition of self and identification of dialectical relationships in the physical and nonphysical world.

The critical relationship between language and culture can be traced back to the Linguistic Relativity Hypothesis, which in its strong form proposes that language structure determines the manner in which one thinks and perceives the world around him. In Whorf's (1956) words:

> The linguistic system fashions the ideas, it is the programme and the guide of individual mental acivity, the cause of their analyses of impressions, the cause of their syntheses which operates his mental stock.

The deterministic view of the relationship between language and thought has been criticised by many sociolinguists. First, the hypothesis is preoccupied with people living in a monolingual and homogenous speech community and disregarding the many language-contact phenomena such as code-mixing and borrowing. The hypothesis also ignores the dynamic nature of language and the deliberate actions of speakers on their language. In other words, speakers are not helpless before the grammar of their language; they can willingly and consciously change their language.

Notwithstanding the sound criticisms of linguistic relativity, the hypothesis in its weak form has continued to influence the discussion on language and culture, especially in the area of language maintenance and the protection of minority languages for cultural advancement of their speakers. The influence of language on the way people identify themselves as a social group cannot be gainsaid and the loss of a language is still regarded as a devastating cultural loss.

Of all the modes of identification, the language system is the most salient and symbolic. In most developing countries, thus, the existence of many languages has been viewed as a source of political conflict and economic backwardness. This perspective has its roots in the eighteenth century when language and nationality were seen to be the source of cultural and political strength by European states. Language was also strongly regarded as representing the cultural origin of humankind. One of the best known thinkers of that era was Herder, who associated language with the national culture, the integrity of the nation and the way a country's citizens think. According to this view "culture derives from the people, language expresses the spirit of the people, the love of the nation" (Williams 1992).

The question that arises from this position is what happens to the developing nations that have had to adopt a foreign language as a national language and have to deal with many indigenous languages? Can a foreign language still express the 'spirit of the people'? Can the country's citizens think in a non-native language? Can the love of a nation be expressed in an imported language? Or can true development be achieved through a non-native language? In his discussion of multilingualism as a resource in the developing countries, Bamgbose (1994), however, gives the following arguments to disentangle language from ethnicity and nationality:

1. If the relationship between language and ethnicity was that strong, a member of an ethnic group would not speak more than one language. In fact, the reality in many African countries is that children grow up with more than one language, some of which they learn simultaneously at home and in the neighbourhood.

2. If the argument was valid, members of different ethnicities would not speak the same language. One linguistic universal according to Noam Chomsky is that all humans are born with a Language Acquisition Device (LAD) which enables us to acquire any natural language. Language is, therefore, not culture-specific; that is, acquiring language is an innate predisposition which has nothing to do with the cultural surrounding in which one is born.

3. The absence of a common language does not preclude ethnic identification since boundary-marking can occur through other means such as religion, literary tradition, types of food and eating habits, architecture, aesthetic values and customs. For example, the Abasuba of Kenya have virtually lost their language to the extent that the few that speak it are bilingual in Olusuba and Dholuo. However, the Abasuba still identify themselves as a distinct cultural group from the Luos. Similarly, the Irish, Scots, and Welsh have adopted English as the primary language but they still would insist on being identified as the Irish, Scottish, and Welsh people and not as the English people. The objection to the strong link between language and ethnicity is summed up by Eastman (1984) as follows:

> What we have changed is our 'language use aspect' of our ethnicity but 'the primordial sense of who we are and what group we think we belong to, for the remainder remain intact.

Cultural identification does not depend only on the material aspects of culture such as architecture or literary works; it has its very strong anchor in the way members of a community would like to be identified and the way they perceive themselves to be different from "Others." The non-material aspects like attitudes, sense of history, myths, and stereotypes might for some groups, play a more important role in boundary-marking than language, architecture or mode of dressing. We can, therefore, achieve development through a language other than our own provided some conditions are meant, as we see in the next section.

Language Planning for Development

The surest way to avoid the possibility of using language to achieve unfair socio-political advantage is to plan for all languages in the same way we plan how to exploit other national resources for development. The

Republic of South Africa, for example, recognised this and the 1996 Constitution Chapter One **Founding Provisions** Section Six (Two) reads:

> Recognising the historically diminished use and status of the indigenous languages of our people, the state must take political and positive measures to elevate the status and advance the use of these languages.

The fact that the state has a constitutional responsibility to protect, recognise, and develop minority languages, speakers of these languages will feel safe within the national borders of their country and would be in a state to think of development. The Organisation of African Unity also took up the language issue quite seriously and drew up the **OAU Language Plan of Action for Africa** to be used as a blueprint for national language planning projects, aimed at liberating Africa from linguistic imperialism. The following are three of the seven objectives outlined in the document:

(1) To encourage each and every member state to have a clearly defined language policy;

(2) To ensure that all the languages within the boundaries of member states are recognised and accepted as a source of mutual enrichment;

(3) To liberate the African peoples from undue reliance on the utilisation of non-indigenous languages as the dominant, official languages of the state in favour of the appropriate and carefully selected indigenous African languages in this domain.

The main issue with the use of non-indigenous languages is that they inhibit intellectual development of the African children and retard economic and industrial development. The use of European languages for education in the early years of primary school does not allow children to exploit their creativity and other cognitive abilities to the full. Although there is some merit in using European languages in education, research shows that there is greater benefit if children learn educational concepts in school through their mother tongues for at least six years before they change over to a non-indigenous medium. The argument is that children easily transfer literacy skills to a new language once they have mastered the skills well in their mother tongue. (Cummins 1984).

In government administration, it is increasingly being recognised that the use of an unfamiliar language in the provision of public service tends to alienate sections of the population and leads to disinterest and apathy. European languages as official languages in Africa are seen as languages of *exclusion* since they lock out the majority of the population from the management of the affairs of their country. This, according to Vic Webb and Kembo-Sure (2000), leads to:

- Restricted access to knowledge and skills;
- Low productivity and ineffective performance in the workplace;
- Inadequate political participation by the public, manipulation, discrimination, and exploitation by the ruling powers, national division, and conflict; and
- Linguistic and cultural alienation.

At the core of planning for minority languages is the **allocation of functions** for each language so that they acquire **social prestige**. When a language is assigned an important task, for example, medium of education, it acquires new importance. When there is deliberate state intervention to make sure a language has a function for its users we are talking of **status planning**. That is, the language is given enhanced status. Status planning bestows social prestige on the language and adds group pride to its speakers. Since the members of the community see their cultural and political worth in the new linguistic status of their language we also talk of **ethnolinguistic vitality**. The ultimate goal of language planning for minority languages is to **revitalise** them so that they enter active use in important domains of public life, such as education, the mass media, judicial administration, and parliamentary debates. Increased employment of these languages in important public domains assures them continued existence lest they go into disuse and begin to **decline** or become **obsolete**. Languages which are neglected gradually get displaced by *stronger* languages, what we call **language shift**, and eventually die.

In economic development discourse, the use of indigenous languages by the Asian *Tigers* and their phenomenal economic and industrial progress have been cited. There may not be a neat causative relationship between language and economic and/or industrial development, but it is instructive to note that the two Koreas, Malaysia, Indonesia, and earlier, Japan, have carried out their development programmes in the indigenous languages. In Africa, Tanzania may not have experienced an industrial takeoff as is the case with the South Asian countries cited here, but it has used Kiswahili effectively for mobilisation of its citizens; achieving over 90% literacy rate and becoming the most unified state in Africa. The political maturity of Tanzania is demonstrated by the regular national elections and the peaceful changeover of leadership since the retirement of the first head of state, Mwalimu Julius Nyerere, a feat that has been achieved by very few African countries. Although political integration is not a sufficient condition for a country's development, it is certainly a necessary one and it cannot be achieved without a well coordinated language policy.

KEMBO-SURE

See also Language, Influence on Politics

References and Further Reading

Bamgbose, Ayo. *Language and Exclusion: The Consequences of language Policies in Africa.* Hamburg: Lit Verlag Munster, 2000.
———. *Language and the Nation: The Language Question in Sub-Saharan Africa.* Edinburg: Edinburg University Press, 1994.
Cummins, Jim. *Bilingualism and Special Education.* Clavendon: Multilingual Matters, 1984.
Eastman, Carol. "Language, Ethnicity and Identity." In *Linguistic Minorities, Policies and Pluralism* edited by John Edwards. London: Academic Press, 1984.
Lo Bianco, Joseph. *Language as an Economic Resource.* Pretoria: Department of Culture, Art, Science and Technology, 1996.
Ong, W. *Orality and Literacy: The technologizing of the Word.* London: Methuen. 1982.
Phillipson, Robert. *Linguistic Imperialism.* Oxford, UK: Oxford University Press, 1992.
Roy-Campbell, Zaline. "Globalisation, Language and Education: A Comparative Study of the United States and Tanzania." In *International Review of Education* 47 (3–4) 267–282, 2001.
Ting-Toomey, Stella and Korzenny, Filipe editors. *Language, Communication and Culture.* Newbury Park: Sage, 1989.
Webb, Vic and Kembo-Sure, editors. *African Voices: Introduction to Languages and Linguistics of Africa.* Cape Town: OUP, 2000.
Whorf, Benjamin. *Language, Thought and Reality.* Cambridge, MA: MIT Press, 1956.
Williams, Glyn. *Sociolinguistics: A Sociological Critique.* London: Routledge, 1992.

LANGUAGE, INFLUENCE ON POLITICS

Language as a Tool

In the empirical and deductive tradition, the study of language was regarded as scientific and language as an autonomous object which could be studied in the same way that we do materials and substances in the physical sciences (Bloomfield 1935). The positivistic view was challenged later by Chomsky's Generative Grammar revolution of the 1960s, which emphasised the cognitive character of language (Chomsky 1965). The positivistic approach as well as the generative grammar, however, excluded the social and affective aspects of language from linguistic theory, arguing that those areas would not be objectively and empirically handled.

However, in recent years the study of language as a social reality has given rise to new disciplines in linguistics such as: Critical Linguistic Study (CLS), Sociolinguistics, Politics of language, Pragmatics, and Discourse Analysis. These disciplines differ only in the degree of emphasis of certain aspects of language, but they all agree on the centrality of the dialectical relationship between society. In this respect they all regard the primary data as coming from language in use and not some idealised texts and speakers. They all study language in context.

In a society or country where two or more languages/varieties are spoken, a language or variety reflects and reinforces the power-sharing patterns in the community. The language of power is often in short supply and the privileged group endeavours to limit access to it by the underprivileged groups. Language, in this sense, becomes a significant site of class struggle as it is regarded as a critical factor of production alongside human labour and land.

According to the Deficit Hypothesis, developed by a British sociologist, Bernstein (1972), working class children are exposed to the variety of language which does not promote critical and creative thinking and this he called the **restricted code**. On the other hand, middle class children are exposed to what he calls the **elaborated code**, which allows for divergent and rational thinking. According to Bernstein (1960), working class children were disadvantaged at school since the school demands the use of the elaborated code with the consequence that children from working class homes fail to develop their potential in the education system dominated by middle class speech forms and discourse styles.

If we agree with Bernstein's categorisation then language becomes a factor in deciding who fails and who succeeds in an education system and thus reflects and reproduces class categories. Middle class children succeed in school, come out and occupy civil service and important private sector jobs, and thus monopolize and control decision-making institutions in the country. Children from poor families content themselves with low-level jobs that require minimal manipulation of the officially declared respectable code.

Language and Power

The emergence of nation states in earnest in eighteenth century Europe saw the monopolisation of power by the political elite and language became a formidable tool in the exercise of power. For example, the state decided which language or variety to be used for what purposes in which institutions. The thinking then was that a single language was desirable for state administration; that is, one language used throughout the country would ensure effective collection of taxes, uniform application of law, and equitable delivery of education and health services.

In the developing world the same notion was inherited from ex-colonial administrations, which promoted the European languages in the administration of the colonies and marginalised all the local languages. The small elite group who were trained in the foreign languages replaced the European officials and entrenched in the administrations the use of European languages as official languages of their independent states.

Even for the few countries which adopted local languages as official such as Tanzania, India, Indonesia, and Algeria, the elite have often circumvented the spirit of the language policy by sending their children to private schools which provide education through European languages. The graduates of the private schools are often preferred by employers, especially by multinationals who find them suitable candidates for the promotion of corporate culture globally. In countries where the foreign language is official, critical jobs in both public and private sectors are reserved for those candidates with 'good' mastery of European languages. The result is that European languages are equated with political power and economic prosperity whereas the local languages are associated with servitude and poverty.

In most of these countries one of the qualifications demanded of those wishing to be members of the legislature is proficiency in the official language. Since proficiency in a foreign language is acquired only in school, the great majority of the population is excluded from the law-making process. Besides, the fact that only those who can speak a European language become candidates, the electorate are disfranchised in a sense that they cannot vote for the person they want if he cannot speak the official language to a level acceptable to the ruling elite. In Kenya, the Minister of Local Government has proposed a bill in parliament requiring mayors of all towns and cities to have university degrees whereas such requirement does not exist for members of parliament and the head of state. One of the complaints about the present mayors is that some of them can hardly speak English. English therefore becomes a justification to exclude a section of the population from running the affairs of their country.

The area where the choice of a foreign language is most controversial is education. The choice of a foreign language as medium of instruction is in a way interpreted as a strategy by the ruling elite to limit access to higher education. The fact that the majority of the underprivileged children have limited exposure to the official language, they often fail not only in the language as a subject but also the other subjects taught through the language. School drop-outs and educational failure can thus be explained partly by the choice of medium of instruction adopted by an education system.

In rural Africa, children go to school with proficiency in two or more languages, but at school none of those languages they speak is taught or used to teach school subjects. One of their first reactions is that their languages and the related cultures are useless and irrelevant to them if they have to succeed in the life. The fact that the local languages are so devalued, their speakers are disempowered and are persuaded by the artificially created circumstances to disrespect them.

A national language policy which marginalises the majority of the population on the basis of their linguistic background is consistent with a political plan which concentrates power in the hands of a small group and few institutions which control the state apparatus. The language of the elite and the relevant institutions is therefore the language of power and control.

Democratisation of Linguistic Ecology

Language can be used to promote greater political participation as it can be used for exclusion. The first step to ensure participation is for the state to ensure protection and recognition of all languages. That is, learning of and through one's mother tongue should be recognised as a human right. Secondly, every citizen must be guaranteed public service in the language of their choice, preferably their mother tongue.

By providing education and other social services through a familiar medium more people are brought into active participation in the affairs of their country and therefore enabling them to determine their political future. It is a step towards political inclusion of the critical population of the nation.

Another strategy is to ensure equitable and effective provision of foreign-language education. The intranational and international importance of a foreign language demands that all children receive quality language instruction to the level that no one is disadvantaged on the basis of speaking a non-standard variety or that they were not exposed sufficiently to the official variety. Access to adequate foreign-language teaching would then be considered a child's human right as is general education.

Democratisation of language policy entails the abandonment of the dichotomy between the official language and other languages. There should not be a situation of either the foreign language or the indigenous language(s). Languages in this sense are all regarded as cultural, social and economic resources whose utilisation must be deliberately and carefully planned for the benefit of all.

Whenever necessary, language policy decisions should be guided by a constitutional provision specifically guaranteeing protection and recognition of all languages. This is what the Republic of South Africa has done having experienced a historic tragedy of balkanisation along linguistic and racial lines. The South African new constitution recognises eleven official languages but also guarantees protection of all non-official languages. This is a recognition that language policy, to a large extent, determines who does what in which political institution.

Deliberate government moves to democratize the linguistic environment are motivated by the recognition of multilingualism as a resource and not a curse. The protection and recognition of all languages is an endorsement of the policy of pluralism.

KEMBO-SURE

References and Further Reading

Bernstein, Basil. Language and Social Class, *British Journal of Sociology*, 11, 271–276, 1960.

Bloomfield, Leonard. *Language*. London: Allen and Unwin, 1935.

Chomsky, Noam. *Aspects of the Theory of Syntax*. Cambridge, MA: MIT Press, 1965.

Crystal David. *English as a Global Language*. Cambridge, UK: Cambridge University Press, 1997.

Fairclough, Norman. *Language and Power*. London: Longman, 1987.

Mazrui, Alamin. The World Bank, the Language Question and the Future of African Education. *Race and Class* 38(3): 35–48, 1997.

Parakrama, Arjuna. *De-hegemonizing Language Standards: Learning from (Post) Colonial Englishes about 'English'*. Basingstoke and New York: Longman, 1991.

Pennycook, Alastair. *The Cultural Politics of English as an International Language*. Harlow: Longman, 1994.

Tollefson, James. *Planning Language, Planning Inequality*. London and New York: Longman, 1991.

Wa Thiong'o, Ngugi. *Moving the Centre. The Struggle for Cultural Freedoms*. London: James Currey; Nairobi: EAEP, 1993.

LAOS

Laos, officially the Lao People's Democratic Republic, is a landlocked country, covering approximately 91,400 square miles (236,800 square kilometres), surrounded by China, Vietnam, Cambodia, Thailand, and Myanmar.

The terrain is mostly forest-covered mountains, with deep river valleys and abundant wildlife. The Annamese Cordillera lies along the Vietnamese border with many secondary mountain ranges. The highest point is Mount Bia at 9,245 feet (2,818 metres). There are two significant plateaux: the Plain of Jars in the north, characterized by grassy, scrub-covered, limestone and sandstone hills; and the Bolovens Plateaux in the south, having fertile basaltic soil and a high rainfall, but mostly undeveloped, covered by brush and tall grass. Limestone karst landscapes are found in central areas, with fertile lowlands lying along the eastern banks of the Mekong River. All the major rivers in Laos flow into the Mekong, which forms the border with Myanmar and most of Thailand. The Mekong floods regularly along its southern reaches.

The climate is tropical monsoon with cooler temperatures in mountain regions. During the wet season, from May to October, the average rainfall is 1,778 millimetres (70 inches). Temperatures range from minimums of approximately 16°C (60°F) in the cool months of December to February to maximums of approximately 32°C (90°F) during March and April. The average temperature from May to November is 27°C (80°F).

Laos' ethnically and linguistically diverse population of 5,660,000 (2003), mostly living in rural lowland areas, makes it the most sparsely populated, least urbanized Asian country. The population is young, with a high birth rate offset by high infant mortality.

History

The Kingdom of Lan Xang formed from numerous small principalities in 1353, covering modern Laos and much of northern and eastern Thailand. In the 1700s, Lan Xang was dissolved into three kingdoms centred on Luang Prabang, Vientiane (the current capital), and Champassak. Siam (Thailand) captured these lands, but France entered in 1893. Following treaties with Siam in 1904 and 1907, France gained control over the area now known as Laos. In 1953, after Japanese WWII occupation, the French granted independence, but Lao nationalists began a protracted civil war. After a series of failed coalition governments, the Pathet Lao, supported by communist Vietnam, gained control in December 1975, immediately embarking on radical socialism. The fall of communism in the USSR forced Laos to liberalise economic and social reforms. The US trade embargo was lifted in May 1995. In July 1997, Laos was admitted to ASEAN. Kaysone Phomivihan lead Laos from 1975 until his death in 1992. Nouhak Phoumsavane became President, succeeded by Kham Thai Siphandone in 1998.

Economy

Laos remains one of the world's poorest countries. Gross national income (GNI) is $310 US dollars and gross domestic product (GDP) is $2 billion US dollars (World Bank 2002). The GDP growth rate has slowed from 7.3% in 1999 to 5% in 2003. Agriculture's share of the GDP is 57.5%, industry, 17.7% and services sector, 24.7%. Main exports are hydroelectricity and timber products. Large disparities exist between urban and rural areas where most of the population survives on subsistence agriculture. Poor roads and no railways hinder economic growth. Freedom from civil war and liberalization of government controls are beginning to bring economic growth, but much of the annual budget is still met by foreign aid.

Development Since 1954

Prior to 1953, apart from road construction, the French did little to develop Laos. The following two decades of civil war precluded any significant development in spite of massive amounts of US aid. Concerned that Laos would fall to communism, from 1955 to 1963, the USA contributed more assistance per capita to Laos than any other country including South Vietnam. Much of this funded the Royal Lao Army, built road and communication networks of military value, and disappeared into the pockets of Lao officials. Between 1953 and 1959, military spending equaled $184 million, but only $1.3 million went to over 90% of the population engaged in agriculture.

Small improvements in living standards were achieved, mostly in urban areas. Three years of primary school education was compulsory, but many villages had no school and only about 30% of children attended. Very few continued to secondary education.

Education and health systems suffered a lack of trained personnel. Three hospitals were established with foreign aid, but there was no medical school. Most Lao still survived on subsistence agriculture. Industry was rudimentary, the legal system outdated, and transport and communications inadequate.

Between 1964 and 1974 development in Laos was non-existent due to the Vietnam war, during which Laos suffered heavy bombing by the USA.

The next decade from 1975 to 1986 was characterized by the new communist government's attempts to create a centralized socialist economy including agricultural collectives, nationalized industry and commerce, and 're-education camps' for dissenters, resulting in 10% of the population fleeing to Thailand. US aid ceased, partially replaced by aid from Vietnam and the USSR. Thailand seriously restricted trade. Inflation and drought forced the government to request rice from the United Nations (UN).

In 1986, recognizing the failure of the reforms, the government pragmatically began to liberalize controls. Collectivization was abandoned and the New Economic Mechanism endorsed. Self sufficiency in rice was achieved, but problems were caused by high reliance on foreign aid, lack of trained personnel and corruption. More children enrolled in school but education standards fell. More health clinics existed, but trained personnel and medicines were severely lacking. Malaria and other endemic diseases increased. However, personal and religious freedoms improved. Buddhist festivals were permitted again, although monks were obliged to study Marxism-Leninism.

A difficult period of rising prices, poor investment decisions, drought and reducing hydroelectricity production (Laos' main export) in 1987 and the collapse of the USSR, forced Laos to reform the state sector and allow foreign investment, leading to liberal investment laws, improved relations with Thailand and increased international aid.

In 1991, the constitution was adopted. Legal, economic, and environmental reforms continued. Following Vietnam's example, Laos continues to pursue economic reforms while maintaining a one party socialist political system. In 1994, the first bridge (built with Australian aid), across the Mekong to Thailand was opened, symbolizing the opening of Laos to increased trade, tourism, and international influence. A road transport route between China and Thailand is being constructed through Laos. Massive hydroelectric projects have been constructed, with more planned. The impact of increased foreign trade, tourism, and HIV/Aids upon Laos' fragile traditional culture is a concern as are environmental pressures such as deforestation, pollution, soil erosion, and ecological damage caused by the illegal logging, slash-and-burn agriculture and hydroelectric dam construction.

The reforms have improved the economy, but Laos is still developmentally about thirty years behind its neighbours. Poverty and health indicators are extremely poor. Low education standards, weak legal system, inadequate infrastructure, and heavy reliance on foreign aid hinder Laos' development, but relative political stability, continuing reforms, and openness to foreign investment are encouraging.

JILLIAN BRADY

See also Southeast Asia: History and Economic Development; Southeast Asia: International Relations

References and Further Reading

Anderson, Kym. *Lao Economic Reform and WTO Accession: Implications for Agriculture and Rural Development.* Singapore: Institute of Southeast Asian Studies, 1999.

Castle, T.N. *At War in the Shadow of Vietnam: US Military Aid to the Royal Lao Government, 1955–1975,* New York: Columbia University Press, 1993.

Evans, Grant. *A Short History of Laos: the Land in Between, Crows Nest.* Australia: Allen and Unwin, 2002.

Hamilton-Merritt, J. *Tragic Mountains: the Hmong, the Americans, and the Secret Wars for Laos, 1942–1992.* Bloomington, IN: Indiana University Press, 1993.

Iereson-Doolittle, Carol, and Geraldine Moreno-Black. *The Lao: Gender, Power and Livelihood.* Boulder, CO: Westview Press, 2004.

Otani, Ichiro and Chi Do Pham (eds.). *The Lao People's Democratic Republic: Systemic Transformation and Adjustment.* Washington, DC: International Monetary Fund, 1996.

Stuart-Fox, Martin. *A History of Laos.* Cambridge, UK: Cambridge University Press, 1997.

Zasloff. J.J., and Unger, L. (eds.) *Laos: Beyond the Revolution.* London: Macmillan, 1991.

LATIN AMERICAN INTEGRATION ASSOCIATION (ALADI)

The Latin American Integration Association, more commonly known in Latin America as the Asociación Latinoamericana de Integración (ALADI), was established in 1980 by the governments of Argentina, Bolivia, Brazil, Chile, Colombia, Ecuador, Mexico, Paraguay, Peru, Uruguay, and Venezuela. ALADI replaced the defunct Latin American Free Trade Association (LAFTA), which had been formed in 1960 to create a common economic market for its members through progressive tariff reductions. Although regional trade in Latin America increased during the 1960s and 1970s, it did not approach the lofty goals expounded upon in the Montevideo Treaty of 1960. LAFTA's failure can be blamed on the lack of adequate transportation infrastructure between neighboring nations, the absence of strong trading links between neighboring countries, the incompatibility of goods being offered by member nations, and differing levels of national development. In addition, the larger nations in the association consistently valued their domestic markets over the potential of expanding into regional markets. The larger nations, which were engaged in aggressive import substitution industrialization, continued to protect their nascent industries behind tariff barriers. Although LAFTA's deadline to eliminate tariff barriers by 1973 was extended to 1980, the association was doomed to fail. On August 12, 1980, eleven Latin American foreign ministers, realizing that LAFTA's goals were untenable in the immediate future, disbanded the organization and signed the Montevideo Treaty of 1980, which resulted in the creation of ALADI. Unlike LAFTA, ALADI, which is headquartered in Montevideo, Uruguay, has no deadline for the implementation of a common economic market in Latin America. ALADI has the more limited goal of encouraging free trade in Latin America.

All Latin American nations are eligible to join ALADI. On August 26, 1999, Cuba became the twelfth full member of the association. Nations with observer status include Costa Rica, the Dominican Republic, El Salvador, Guatemala, Honduras, Italy, Japan, Nicaragua, Panama, People's Republic of China, Portugal, Romania, Russia, South Korea, Spain, and Switzerland. Observer organizations include the Andean Development Corporation, the European Community, the Inter-American Development Bank, Inter-American Institute for Cooperation on Agriculture, the Latin American Economic System, the Organization of American States, the United Nations (UN) Development Program, the UN Economic Commission for Latin America and the Caribbean, and the World Health Organization.

ALADI supports the creation of an area of economic preferences, with the ultimate goal being the creation of a common economic market in the region. ALADI encourages tariff preference for products originating in the member countries; regional economic agreements, such as the Southern Cone Common Market (MERCOSUR); and favorable conditions of economic engagement for the less developed members, such as Bolivia, Ecuador, and Paraguay, within the association. In addition, ALADI supports the promotion and regulation of trade, the development of complementary economies, and market expansion.

Recent economic difficulties in the economies of the larger member states, such as Argentina, Brazil, and Venezuela, has limited the ability of ALADI to implement its agenda. Nevertheless, although economic cooperation and development has not proceeded as quickly as originally envisioned, there has been progress toward lowering trade barriers in the Americas, especially since the creation of MERCOSUR in 1991 and the North American Free Trade Agreement (NAFTA) in 1994.

MICHAEL R. HALL

See also Central American Common Market (CACM); Free Trade Area of the Americas (FTAA); North American Free Trade Agreement (NAFTA); Southern Cone Common Market (MERCOSUR); United States–Dominican Republic–Central American Free Trade Agreement

References and Further Reading

Bour, Enrique, Daniel Heymannm, and Fernando Navajas. *Latin American Economic Crises: Trade and Labour.* Gordonville, VA: Palgrave MacMillan, 2004.

USA International Business Publications. *Latin American Integration Association Investment and Business Guide.* Washington, DC: USA International Business Publications, 2001.

Wiarda, Howard J. and Harvey F. Kline. *Latin American Politics and Development.* Boulder, CO: Westview Press, 2000.

LATVIA

The Republic of Latvia covers approximately 64,500 square kilometers of territory on the eastern shores of the Baltic Sea. Latvia shares borders with Estonia to the north; Belarus and Lithuania to the south; Russia to the east; and the Baltic Sea on the west. Latvia consists of low-lying plains with rolling hills in the eastern part of the country. Latvia has a maritime climate, consisting of cool, wet summers, and moderate winters. Latvia has few natural resources. The primary Latvian resource is peat. Peat bogs cover nearly 10% of the nation's total land. In addition, timber, gypsum, and amber consist of the remainder of Latvia's resources. In an attempt to lower the reliance on foreign sources of energy, major hydroelectric plants have been constructed along the Daugava River. The estimated population is approximately 2.3 million, with an estimated declining population at −.71%. Riga, the capital city, and its metropolitan area consist of 1 million inhabitants. Other important cities are Daugavpils, an industrial center in the north; and Leipaja, an ice free port.

Due to political instability caused by the 1917 Russian Revolution and Germany's defeat in World War I, Latvia first became an independent nation in November 1918. Prior to 1918, the territory of Latvia was subject to German, Polish, Swedish, and Russian hegemony, dating to the thirteenth century. Latvian independence, however, was threatened by the presence of Soviet and German troops still occupying Latvian territory between 1919 and 1920. National sovereignty was not secured until the signing of the 1920 Latvian-Russian peace treaty.

Janis Cakste was elected Latvia's first president in 1920. The 1922 constitution established a democratic system of government. Throughout the 1920s, the large number of political parties created a plethora of weak coalitions within the Saeima (parliament), resulting in widespread political instability. Based on a claim of a Communist conspiracy to overthrow the government, Prime Minister Karlis Ulmanis declared a state of emergency in 1934. Ulmanis abolished political parties and suspended parliament. Most Latvians, however, tacitly supported the Ulmanis dictatorship as a justification to preserve democracy in Latvia. Ulmanis maintained power throughout the 1930s. As a result of a secret protocol contained in the 1939 German-Soviet Nonaggression Pact, Latvia was incorporated into the Soviet Union in August 1940. World War II and the Soviet occupation created lasting consequences in Latvia's demographics. Due to Soviet exiles and murders; the Holocaust; wartime casualties; and emigration; nearly three hundred thousand Latvians were killed, deported, or fled the country. Sovietization policies increased the ethnic Russian presence to over 30%, while simultaneously decreasing the ethnic Latvian presence to 55%.

Gorbachev's liberalization of the USSR during the 1980s, led to a renewed spirit of Latvian nationalism. Following the failed August 1991 coup in Moscow, Latvia regained its independence from the Soviet Union. In September 1991, the Soviet government recognized the independence of Latvia, which was admitted to the United Nations later in the month. The first parliamentary elections were held in 1993, leading to Guntis Ulmanis's election as president. In the hope of undertaking a more western orientation, Latvia became an associate member of the European Union (EU) in 1995.

Latvia began the arduous task of implementing sweeping economic reforms in the hopes of creating a western style market economy. As a result of being fully incorporated into the Soviet command economy, the primary reform was the privatization of all Latvian industries. Economic policies restricted government spending; loosened restrictions on the banking system; eliminated price control; and lifted regulations on small businesses. Due to the disintegration of the USSR and Latvia's few natural resources, the industrial sector entered a period of crisis, resulting in low output and high unemployment. The economy did not start go grow until 1994. Growth was temporarily halted in 1995 due to a major banking crisis. The crisis led to the government establishing a stronger regulatory institution to control the banking system. The establishment of the Latvian currency, the *Lat*; and the economic growth during the late 1990s attracted large amounts of foreign investment and created one of the most stable economies among all former Soviet republics.

The estimated 2004 gross domestic product (GDP) was $23.9 billion. The service sector contributed 70.9% of the GDP, whereas industry consisted of 24.5% and agricultural production 4.5%. Despite non-membership in the Commonwealth of Independent States (CIS), Latvia's primary trading partner is Russia. Russia purchases nearly one-quarter of Latvia's exports, and in return contributes one-fifth of the nation's imports. Other major trading partners include Germany, the United Kingdom, Finland, Sweden, and Lithuania. Major exports include forestry materials, foodstuffs, machinery, and textiles. Imports consist primarily of energy sources, as well as industrial machinery and textiles. Latvia is a member of the International Monetary Fund (IMF), the International Bank for Reconstruction and Development (World Bank), the World Trade Organization, and the European Bank for Reconstruction and Development.

Domestic politics in the post-independence period have been marred by disputes over economic transformations, social policies, and fighting corruption. The severe economic dislocation caused by the faltering industrial sector in the early 1990s and the banking crisis of 1995 proved to be major catalysts in the collapse of many coalition governments in the Saeima. There were constant strains between political parties that promoted free trade and foreign investment and those that demanded higher tariffs to protect the agricultural sector. Due to fears of the large Russian minority, the Saeima passed legislation in 2002 requiring all elected officials to be fluent in the Latvian language. Later this legislation was repealed to assist in the EU accession process. Recent legislation, however, such as the February 2004 law mandating Latvian as the official language of instruction in schools has upset the large Russian-speaking population. Despite such problems, in comparison to other eastern European countries, Latvia has made great strides. In 1999, the Saeima elected Vaira Vike-Freiberga as president—the first female president in Eastern Europe. Vike-Freiberga was reelected in 2003. In May 2004, Latvia became a full member of both the European Union and NATO.

JONATHAN H. L'HOMMEDIEU

See also Ulmanis, Guntis

References and Further Reading

Dreifelds, Juris. *Latvia in Transition*. Cambridge, UK: Cambridge University Press, 1996.
Lieven, Anatol. *The Baltic Revolution: Estonia, Latvia, Lithuania, and the Path to Independence*. New Haven, CT: Yale University Press, 1994.
Plakens, Andrejs. *The Latvians: A Short History*. Stanford, CA: Hoover Institution Press, 1997.
Smith, David J., Artis Pabriks, Aldis Purs, and Thomas Lane. *The Baltic States: Estonia, Latvia, and Lithuania*. New York: Routledge Press, 2002.

LEBANON

The Lebanese Republic is situated at the eastern end of the Mediterranean Sea, bordered to the south by Israel and to the east and north by Syria. It has approximately 225 kilometres of coastline and is about 80 kilometres at its widest point. There is a narrow coastal strip that rises quickly to a mountainous interior, although the northeast of the country is dominated by the fertile Biqa' Valley. Lebanon has a Mediterranean climate with hot, dry summers and cool, wet winters with heavy snow falling in the mountainous regions. The population is estimated at 3.8 million, with an estimated annual growth rate of 1.3%. Its capital since independence is Beirut with a population estimated at over 1.6 million.

The mountainous nature of much of Lebanon had provided an effective sanctuary for religious minorities for hundreds of years, and it is the relationship between these groups, and with foreign powers, that has had the most profound effect on Lebanon's development. Due largely to the longstanding French links with one of these minorities, the Maronite Christians, the Sykes-Picot Agreement of 1916 promised France mandatory control over the Syrian territories of the Ottoman Empire after its defeat. In 1920, the State of Greater Lebanon was established, appending surrounding areas to the Christian-dominated Mount Lebanon in order to make it economically viable. The newly created entity was unpopular with many Sunni Muslims and, in order to reconcile the differences between the confessional groups' attitudes to the new state of Lebanon, an unwritten agreement known as the National Pact of 1943 was struck between the leading Christian politician Bishara al-Khoury, and the Sunni Riad al-Solh. The Pact established a *modus vivendi* between the different confessional groups in their relations with the new state, including the apportionment of political representation. Using the 1932 census figures as the basis, the number of parliamentary seats was set as a ratio of 6:5 favouring the Christians, and the positions of President, Prime Minister, and Speaker were to be filled by a Maronite Christian, Sunni Muslim, and Shi'a Muslim respectively. Independence from France was formally achieved in 1943, and the last French forces left Lebanon in 1946.

Throughout the 1950s and 1960s, the Lebanese state largely prospered owing to unwillingness by the political elite to invoke their confessional differences over fundamental domestic or regional political issues. Ultimately though, the inability of the informal political arrangement to reform in the face of demographic changes (particularly the increasing size of the Shi'a Muslim minority), and the impact of regional political issues such as the Palestinian situation, plunged the country into a ruinous civil war between 1975 and 1990 that killed more than one hundred thousand people. The civil war was ended with the signing of the Ta'if Accord, and since that time the country has been under the political influence of neighbouring Syria, given the permanent stationing of tens of thousands of its troops in Lebanon. The conventions of the National pact were largely retained, although parliamentary seats are now divided equally between Christians and Muslims, and the powers of the President have been reduced.

Lebanon's relatively weak central government has meant that the country has been hostage to the vagaries of regional politics, and has suffered from foreign military intervention for many years. The Cairo Agreement of 1969 gave Palestinian militias, resident since 1948, freedom of movement to launch operations against Israel from Lebanon's south, and their numbers were boosted following the expulsion of Palestinian guerillas from Jordan in 1970. Israel conducted a limited invasion of Lebanon in 1978 and a full-scale one in 1982 in an effort to destroy the Palestinian presence. The 1982 invasion resulted in an occupation of Southern Lebanon by the Israelis, and also led to the emergence of the Shi'a militia group Hezbollah, which was fostered by their co-religionists from Iran. The Israelis withdrew in May 2000 in the face of mounting casualties from Lebanese guerrilla groups including Hezbollah. Syria entered Lebanon as part of an Arab peacekeeping force in 1976, and has maintained a large military presence since that time.

Lebanon's liberal banking laws and cosmopolitan national makeup had made it the regional financial and tourism capital during the 1960s, but the civil war put an end to Lebanon's financial and recreational dominance. Since the end of the civil war, reconstruction of war-torn Beirut and national economic infrastructure became a priority. Impressive gains have been made in that time with much rebuilding completed, government revenue being received and inflation brought under control. Much of the reconstruction, however, was financed through heavy borrowing, and the burgeoning national debt has been serviced through cuts to government services and large contributions from donor countries. The economy has been heavily reliant on the services sector, particularly banking, since prior to the civil war, although it has some industrial capacity (oil refining) and agricultural exports such as citrus fruits, grapes and olives. The per capita gross domestic product (GDP) was estimated at $4,800 in 2003, and 28% of the population was living below the poverty line (1999 estimate).

The adult literacy rate is approximately 87%, and the country possesses several universities, the most famous of which, American University of Beirut, attracts regional and international students. The quality of Beirut's health system had made it a regional health care centre prior to the civil war, and it is slowly regaining this reputation to a degree, although the public health system is still recovering. Life expectancy for males is sixty-nine years and seventy-four years for females. The infant mortality rate is twenty-five out of one thousand live births. While Lebanon produces many well-educated graduates, employment opportunities are limited and many have to emigrate to find work. The unemployment rate is estimated to be 18%.

RODGER SHANAHAN

See also Christians in the Middle East; Middle East: History and Economic Development; Middle East: International Relations; Palestinian Diaspora

References and Further Reading

Ajami, Fouad. *The Vanished Imam*. Ithaca, NY: Cornell University Press, 1987.
Barakat, Halim (ed). *Toward a Viable Lebanon*. London: Croom Helm, 1988.
Hanf, Theodore. *Coexistence in Wartime Lebanon*. London: I.B. Tauris, 1993.
Hudson, Michael C. *The Precarious Republic: Political Modernisation in Lebanon*. New York: Random House, 1968.
Norton, Augustus Richard. *Amal and the Shi'a: Struggle for the Soul of Lebanon*. Austin, TX: University of Texas Press, 1987.
Saad-Ghorayab, Amal. *Hizbu'llah: Politics and Religion*. London: Pluto Press, 2002.
Salibi, Kamal. *A House of Many Mansions*. London: I.B. Tauris, 1988.

LEE KUAN YEW

As Prime Minister of Singapore from 1959 to 1990, Lee Kuan Yew (b. 1923) was the leading figure in its transformation into a flourishing and dynamic First World economy. The small population and size of the island enabled him to be involved in the minutiae of policy formulation and even implementation. At different times he took particular interest in defence and economic planning, industrial relations reform, and social welfare policy. Although he resigned the Prime Ministership in 1990, he continued as an influential cabinet member with the title Senior Minister.

Born in 1923, Lee's first job was as a transcriber in Japanese Propaganda Department. He went on to study law at Cambridge University, where he took first class honors and was admitted to the London bar in 1949. He returned to Singapore the following year and worked as an attorney for the next several years, representing many trade unions. The speed with which the Japanese military routed the British in Southeast Asia in early 1942 had shocked Singapore and shattered the idea of British superiority, and Lee led the struggle for independence through the formation of the People's Action Party (PAP) in 1954. As the PAP leader he became Singapore's first Prime Minister in 1959.

In the early 1960s, it seemed obvious that Singapore needed the Malay hinterland as a market and source of raw materials, food, and water. Singapore joined the Malaysian federation in 1963 to meet those needs, but it was soon clear that the Malay leadership on the peninsula wanted to control Singapore's Chinese majority. Lee broke away from Malaysia and created the independent Republic of Singapore in 1965.

Economic development, defence, and social harmony were the major challenges facing Lee in the mid 1960s. Pragmatism and realism rather than ideology guided his search for solutions. Lee's commitment to open markets and economic competition was combined with selective government intervention in the economy and society. Lee chose ministers who shared his thinking about development to fill key positions. These included the first three Finance Ministers Goh Keng Swee, Lim Kim San, and Hon Sui Sen. Lee followed their advice to switch from his initial emphasis on import replacement to export promotion as the central plank of trade policy.

Even though international trade continued to be essential it alone could not ensure sustained economic growth. Lee created a Tourist Promotion Board to boost tourism and this industry soon provided many jobs in services like transport, catering, and cleaning. The British military presence contributed 20% to the gross domestic product (GDP) so Lee was alarmed in 1968 to hear of their plans to withdraw. He tried to persuade them to delay the process but when this failed he appointed Hon Sui Sen to oversee the conversion of the military bases and equipment to profitable civilian uses. Lee also took a direct role in building the Singapore Armed Forces as well as cementing alliances with other Commonwealth countries in the Five Power Defence Agreement. Race riots involving Chinese and Malays during the 1960s were dealt with through the rigorous but non-discriminatory enforcement of the criminal law. Later Lee oversaw changes in housing laws to ensure that the Chinese, Malays, and Indians, who make up nearly the whole population, would live in mixed neighborhoods.

The Central Provident Fund (CPF) was set up by the colonial government as a pension scheme in order to create a social security without a welfare state. Lee gradually increased the amount that workers paid into their individual CPF accounts and extended its functions so that workers could draw on savings to purchase homes and pay for medical services. The Housing Development Board (HDB) was established in 1960. Its slum clearance project was completed in the 1960s. The HDB built homes that workers bought with their CPF funds. Home ownership also secured support for the government, contracts for the building industry and employment for building workers.

An important part of Singapore's economic transformation was the creation of industrial estates the most famous of which was Jurong. Lee was keen to attract multinational corporations (MNCs) for their capital, technology transfer and as providers of skill enhancement. Finding Singapore's tax breaks, stable economy, strong work force, and infrastructure assistance a hospitable environment, many MNCs set up factories, offices, and training facilities. Lee particularly admired leaders of US MNCs for their drive to succeed and innovate and willingness to transfer technologies and skills. Texas Instruments, National Semiconductors, and Hewlett-Packard were three of many US MNCs to make long-term commitments in Singapore.

In 1968, the Economic Development Board was created to co-ordinate various aspects of development. Lee encouraged a corporatist model of co-operation between government, business and labor. Industrial Relations Tribunals mediated disputes and from 1972 a National Wages Council set pay rates so that raises were not higher than either productivity growth or the capacity of business to pay. In the 1980s, Lee encouraged a shift from industry to company unions to promote worker-employer co-operation at the workplace level. He supported the formation of trade union co-operatives which provided cheap goods and services to their members. These included taxi and insurance services and retail stores.

In the 1980s, Lee encouraged a shift of emphasis from manufacturing to services in computing, information technology, business and banking. Although he continued to welcome foreign capital, new investments could increasingly be financed by Singaporeans' own savings. The Government Investment Corporation, established in 1981, was the conduit through which money flowed from the CPF to various businesses and investments.

Lee has been criticized for Orwellian social engineering, repressive laws, and interference with his citizens' privacy. For example, in the early 1980s Lee oversaw the creation of a Social Development Unit whose task was to encourage highly educated people to marry and have more children. Tax incentives and other measures reinforced this goal. Lee was concerned that the high birth-rates of the poorly educated and the low rates for the well-educated would gradually lower the quality of the people and adversely affect the country in the long-term. Laws proscribing chewing gum, an Internal Security Act that allowed lengthy detention without trial, and media laws that restrict freedom of the press have attracted criticism and ridicule.

Lee ruled Singapore for three decades before resigning as Prime Minister in 1990, though he was immediately appointed Senior Minister in his successor Goh Chok Tong's cabinet. Perspectives on Lee's achievements differ markedly. Some regard him as a visionary politician and statesman who within a generation turned Singapore from a poor country into a prosperous nation with a highly-educated population and few of the social problems that afflict the modern West. Critics of Lee emphasise his authoritarian streak, the structures and forces that undermine the democratic institutions, and the resulting usurpation of politics by administration.

CHRIS CONEY

See also Goh Chok Tong; Singapore

References and Further Reading

Barr, Michael. *Lee Kuan Yew: The Beliefs Behind the Man.* Richmond, Surrey: Curzon, 2000.

Chew, Ernest and Lee, Edwin, editors. *A History of Singapore.* Singapore and New York: Oxford University Press, 1991.

Haas, Michael, editor. *The Singapore Puzzle.* Westport, CT: Praeger Publishers, 1999.

Josey, Alex. *Lee Kuan Yew: The Struggle for Singapore.* Sydney: Angus & Robertson, 1974.

Minchin, James. *No Man Is an Island: A Portrait of Singapore's Lee Kuan Yew.* North Sydney: Allen & Unwin, 1990.

Turnbull, C. M. *A History of Singapore, 1819–1988.* Singapore and New York: Oxford University Press, 1977; second edition, 1989.

LEGAL SYSTEMS

More than 260 nation states ('states') exist around the world today. Each recognises a set of laws that regulates its relations with other states, as well as possessing a legal system that governs its own citizens. The laws that regulate a states' relations with other states are known as international laws, while those laws that govern the behaviour of a state's citizens within its own boundaries are known as municipal or domestic laws.

International law regulates three types of international relationships: between states, between states and persons, and between persons in different states. These relationships are often referred to as public and private international law. Public international law is a distinct body of law in its own right dealing with relations between states, and between states and persons. Private international law, also known as conflict of laws or laws of conflicts, deals with persons (natural or juridical) where there is a conflict between states. However, in recent years it has become difficult to differentiate between public and private international law as the lines between them has became increasingly blurred. Contemporary international law now regulates any conduct that falls outside state boundaries.

During the twentieth century, three dominant legal families could be identified: (Romano-Germanic) civil law, (Anglo-American) common law, and Sino-soviet (socialist) law. However, the failure of communism in the early 1990s resulted in the demise of Sino-soviet law and as a result it is no longer necessary to consider it as a dominant legal system. While Marxist-Leninist thought and socialist law still have a role to play in some states, for example, China, North Korea, Cuba, and Algeria, most of the former communist states have turned to the civil law.

Civil law is the dominant legal system in Europe, as well as forming the basis of most legal systems in Central and South America, parts of Asia and Africa. Its codificatory style of law-making made it a much more amenable system to adopt than common law with its origins embedded in case law and precedent. Common law can be found in most of the former colonies of the British Empire. In the Middle East and parts of Asia, Islamic law plays an important role in the legal system of the state. Islamists will argue that Islamic law (*Shar'iah*) is a complete set of laws, not just a religious law system, and that because it is God's will it is superior to man-made laws. It is also possible to identify elements of customary law influencing the legal systems of many states.

Cultural, economic, political and, perhaps today most importantly, religious factors shape not only political systems but also legal systems. While the legal systems of common law countries such as the US, Australia, and Malaysia are all based on common law principles, significant differences still exist between the laws of each state. A similar comparison can be made between civil law states such as France, Germany, and Brazil. These factors not only produce differences among states with common systems, but can also lead to more profound consequences. For example, the collapse of communism in the early 1990s resulted in the demise of Sino-Soviet law; the growth of the European Community has led to the development of a new legal system (European Community law); the weakening of the nation state because of globalisation has heightened the influence of various religious movements and their laws in parts of the developing world; rejection of western values in non-Western states resulting in a resurgence of customary law.

The Civil Law System

The Meaning of the Term "Civil Law"

The term *civil law* has several meanings. First, it can mean a reference to an entire system of law that has its origins in Europe and which establishes all basic principles of law in a Code through the adoption by a parliamentary body of an authoritative and exhaustive set of rules of law. Second, in a civil law system it can be a reference to private law, which governs the relations between citizens and corporations, as distinct from public law where the State is a party. The distinction is important because there are different hierarchies of courts dealing with public and private law. Third, it can be used to describe the substantive body of private law that is based on the French Civil Code of 1804, and can be contrasted with commercial law which is not regulated by the Civil Code. Finally, it can be a reference to the type of proceedings that might be commenced in a common law system to regulate disputes between private individuals and provide the injured party with a remedy, as distinct from the criminal law which involves offences against the State by a person and which involves punishment if the person is found guilty. It is in its first sense that civil law is most relevant here.

Origins

The origins of the civil law system, also known as the continental European system, can be found in Roman law, and in particular the four compilations (or codification) of Roman laws, known as the *Corpus Juris,* by the Roman Emperor Justinian (527–565 AD). However, it was not until the beginning of the 11th century AD when scholars began to study and interpret the *Corpus Juris Civilis* that Roman law began to form the basis of a common law of Europe. Even then it took a further five centuries to produce a common law of Europe (the *jus commune*), consisting of a mixture of local statutes and customs based on Roman law (or the *Corpus Juris*) and reinforced by canon law (or the law of the Church). Over the following three centuries civil law became codified as *droit coutumier* or customary law, that were local compilations of legal principles recognized as normative. From these sources developed perhaps the two most influential civil law systems as they formed models for most other contemporary civil codes and are the basis of modern civil law: the French Napoleonic Code and the German Civil Code. While both Codes are different in style and tone, they are both based on laissez-faire economics and autonomous rights for citizens.

The prototypical civil law country is France. In 1804, the French Napoleonic Civil Code was enacted. It set out flexible general rules in clear and concise language for use by its citizens, producing Europe's first single system of law. Structurally similar to the *Corpus Juris Civilis*, its authors relied heavily on the *jus commune,* as well as incorporating many of the principal ideas of the French Revolution including the right to own property, freedom to contract, and the autonomy of the patriarchal family.

The German Civil Code was enacted almost a century later. Like the French, the Germans relied on the *jus commune* and made extensive use of the *Corpus Juris Civilis*, but unlike the French they focused on the underlying principles and organisation of the *Corpus Juris Civilis*. The German Civil Code, the Burgerliches Gesetzbuch (the "BGB") was issued in 1896, and came into effect on January 1, 1900. The BGB unified private law in the German Empire, emphasising the individual and their need for freedom to achieve social justice. The language of the BGB is precise and technical and was meant for the use of civil lawyers rather than the layperson.

Features

The essence of a civil law Code is twofold: first, it is independent of government and secondly, it contains a comprehensive statement of rules, many of which are framed as broad, general principles so as to deal with any dispute that may arise.

Under the civil law, the judge's role is inquisitorial. It is limited to the application of the law to the facts of each case. If there was no law to cover the situation, the judge was expected to refer the case to the legislative body which would then pass a law to deal with the situation. However, the reality has proved to be rather different with the legislative bodies discovering that they could not make laws quickly enough to meet all the different circumstances coming before the courts. As a result an unwritten system of judicial precedent similar to, but not the same as, that found in common law systems where lower courts will generally follow the decisions of higher courts has developed over time. The difference between the two legal systems is that civil law judges are not *per se* bound to follow previous decisions of higher courts, as are their counterparts under common law, but the reality is that the previous decisions do have *de facto* authority, particularly under German law where some recourse to case law is necessary.

Under the civil law, unlike the common law, it is the judge who investigates the facts and when arriving at a decision, based on deductive reasoning rather than the inductive reasoning found in common law systems, s/he will not (publicly at least) state reasons for that decision to the parties. The judiciary in civil law countries does not play the central role in interpreting and 'making' the law as it does in common law jurisdictions. However, the reasons for the particular outcome of a case are kept, albeit confidentially, as part of the court file which other judges can then access. Outwardly at least, the common law application of the doctrine of precedent and the need to follow previous decisions in like cases cannot apply. However, the reality is somewhat different and civil law courts may choose to follow previous decisions if they feel them to be appropriate although the Code is still central in the decision-making process.

In civil law states there is a sharply drawn distinction between private law (the law of persons, family law, property law, the law of succession, the law of obligations, commercial law, and labour law) and public law (constitutional and administrative law), the latter having been treated in a variety of ways in the civil law states with some countries establishing special agencies to deal with public law matters while others have created Constitutional Courts. In the majority of civil law systems, criminal matters aside, the jurisdiction of the ordinary courts is limited to dealing with disputes governed by the private law. This can be contrasted with the common law system which does not provide a separate court to deal with public law matters, instead providing different remedies for the private citizen.

The Common Law System

The phrase 'common law' may be used in at least three different ways. First, it may refer to the basic principles of law originally found in the written decisions of judges, rather than relying on codification of the law. English law was never influenced by Roman law in the way that continental Europe was: English common law was already well established by the time that a common law of Europe was developed. Today, common law includes case law derived from the common law courts and courts of equity, as well as statute law and while the common law is increasingly turning to the use of comprehensive codes, their importance, application, and validity are still determined through case law. Second, it may be used to describe the decisions of judges in the common law courts as distinct from the decisions made in the courts of equity. Finally, it can be a reference to that body of legal rules that can be found in countries that have adopted or adapted the English system of law and which predominantly consist of law made by the judges. The term 'common law' is being used here to both describe a legal system and that part of English law which has been applied or accepted in other jurisdictions around the world.

Origins

The origins of the common law system can be traced back to William the Conqueror. In order to consolidate his position, he began to centralise the legal system. He appointed a number of judges and instructed them to begin administering a uniform system of law in the name of the King—the common law. To assist judges in their decision-making, the judges began keeping records (known as plea rolls) setting out not only the facts and judgement of each case, but often the reasoning behind the judgement. This enabled judges in later similar cases to follow the decisions of the judges in the earlier cases. It is the common law's reliance on court decisions or precedent that is the principal feature distinguishing it from Romano-Germanic civil codes.

By the fourteenth century, the common law was procedurally both complex and very strict. To overcome the deficiencies of the common law, litigants began to petition the King to hear their pleas. By the fifteenth century, Courts of Chancery had been established to administer this new body of law—known as equity law—but the growth of this jurisdiction led to clashes with the common law. In 1620,

James I decided that in the event of a conflict between equity and common law, equity would prevail.

The role of Parliament as a law making body began after the forced signing of the Magna Carta by King John in 1215. Legislation was made initially by the King after the meeting with Parliament was over. However, by the reign of Henry VI (1422–1461), laws were being framed and discussed by the two Houses of Parliament. By the middle of the nineteenth century, the majority of law came from Parliament in the form of statutes to consolidate or fill gaps in existing law. Where a conflict arose between statute law and case law, statute law prevailed.

Features

The common law system does not provide a separate court to deal with public law matters, instead providing different remedies for the private citizen. Under the civil law system, there is a sharply drawn distinction between private and public law with separate courts to deal with each.

The procedural basis of common law is adversarial or accusatorial. The parties are required to produce appropriate evidence and to be responsible for proving their case. The judge's role is to ensure that the parties observe the rules of procedure. The judge is not expected to take an active role in the proceedings to get to the truth of a matter, as would be the case in a civil law system.

Certainly one of the main distinguishing features of the common law system is its use of case law as precedent. A precedent is a judgement or decision of a court of law cited as an authority for the legal principle embodied in its decision. This is known as *stare decisis*, which literally means "to stand by a decision." The doctrine of precedence seeks to ensure that people will be treated equally and fairly over a long period. This gives everyone the opportunity to conduct their affairs in the knowledge that certain rules and procedures operate to make it possible to predict, with a fair degree of certainty, what the likely outcome will be in the event of a dispute.

In order for precedent to operate there has to be in existence a court hierarchy where the lower courts will be bound by the decisions of higher courts. Precedent may be binding or persuasive. In the case of a binding precedent, each court is bound by the decisions of courts of the same level or higher, whether or not the judge believes a decision is correct, unless the judge can 'distinguish' the case on its facts, or law, or both from the precedent. It is only the *ratio decidendi* (the reason for the decision) which can create a binding precedent. Anything else said in a judgment about the law is classified as *obiter dicta* (sayings by the way), and is at best only capable of being of persuasive value.

Common Law Countries

The application of English law to new colonies depended on whether it was a conquered or ceded colony, or a settled colony. In the case of the former, it was recognized that a legal system was already in existence and the laws of the conquered people continued to exist, thereby creating a form of legal pluralism where common law co-existed with customary and/or religious law, unless or until they were repealed by statute, for example, Malaysia, India.

Where the new territory was regarded as *terra nullius* or unoccupied land, that is there were no settled inhabitants or there was no recognised legal system, the settlers took with them the law of England, for example, North America, Australia, and New Zealand.

European Community Law

The development of the European Union (EU) or 'European Community' has led to the growth of a new regional legal system—European Community Law. While it has its roots in the Franco-German civil codes and has been influenced by common law traditions such as precedent, it also has its own distinctive legal characteristics. As a result, it falls somewhere between an international organisation and an association of states and can best be described as "supranational," a regional system but one created by law.

Origins

The driving force behind European unification was the desire for peace. The establishment of a unified Europe was seen as being one way to reduce the chances of war between the Community's Member States. Unity would only endure where equality could be established. To that end, not only are all Community citizens equal before the law, but no State is to have precedence over another.

Unlike the civil law and common law legal systems, the history of European Community Law is relatively recent with a history that can be traced back to the 1950s and post-World War II Europe. The Treaty of Paris in 1951 and the Treaty of Rome in 1957 laid the foundations for the establishment of the European Community (EC) when they created the European Coal and Steel Community (1951), the European Atomic Energy Community (1958), and the European Economic Community (1958).

The *Single European Act 1986* committed EC Members to establish a progressively free single market with four basic freedoms—free movement of goods, persons, services, and capital—and its rules on competition. The *Treaty of Maastricht* in 1993 which established the creation of the European Union (EU) and established the EU as an international organisation in its own right. The 'European Economic Community' was renamed the 'European Community' to give recognition to its change from that of a purely economic community to a political union but it did not otherwise affect its status. The legal acts of the respective bodies of the EC still constitute legal acts of the Community and have precedence over national law of the Member States.

The Treaty of Amsterdam in 1997 made substantial changes to the Treaty of Maastricht. Of particular legal significance was the greater emphasis on safeguarding of fundamental rights of EU citizens, and the adoption by the EU of a co-decision procedure (the legislative procedure involving the European Parliament and the Council), with the European Parliament now playing a much greater role in the legislative processes.

In 2001, the European Council met to consider establishing a Constitution for Europe. Among other issues, this included recommending a merger of the Treaties and the attribution of legal personality to the EU. The constitution, discussed for two years and passed at the European Convention of 2003, aims to streamline decision-making in an expanded EU of twenty-five members, with agreement expected to be reached among member States in mid-2004.

Features

Unlike the written Constitutions that establish the legitimacy of most States, the EU constitution is not contained in a comprehensive constitutional document (yet). The EU is dependent on law for its unification, and its existence.

Member States are not absorbed into the EU, nor do they lose their national identities when they become members. They are, however, expected to limit their legislative sovereignty in the interests of solidarity and unity, requiring them to not only observe the Community treaties and secondary legislation but to also implement it and bring it into existence. Where the direct rights and obligations of the Community

citizen conflict with a rule of national law, Community law will have supremacy as long as it has been made in accordance with the Treaties.

Fundamental rights and civil liberties are firmly established in the constitutions of EU Member States with the individual a main focus on the Community, although the Treaties establishing the European Communities do not spell out any details of fundamental rights. However the Court of Justice of the European Communities has established a body of case-law to serve as a basis for safeguarding fundamental rights through a number of provisions in the Treaties dealing with equality and equal treatment. The direct applicability of Community law principles confers rights and imposes obligations directly on Community institutions and the Member States, as well as the Community's citizens.

The European Court of Justice (ECJ) is the highest and only authority on matters of Community law, with each member State sending one judge, and together with the Court of First Instance, the only authority. The ECJ has sole responsibility for monitoring, interpreting and developing Community law and to achieve these ends, the Court's work involves legal advice in the form of opinions as well as adjudication. The Court of First Instance was established to relieve the pressure on the ECJ. It is a constituent component of the Court of Justice, but in organisational terms it is an autonomous body with its own Registry and rules of procedure.

European Community Law Countries

Currently there are twenty-five member countries of the Economic Community, placing it only behind the United States as a political and economic superpower. From the six founding States in 1951— Belgium, Germany, France, Italy, Luxembourg, and the Netherlands—it has grown to a membership of twenty-five States. The United Kingdom, Denmark and Ireland joined in 1973. In 1981, Greece became a member and was followed by Portugal and Spain in 1986. Austria, Finland, and Sweden joined in 1995 in what had by then become the European Union following the adopting of the Treaty of Maastricht in 1993. Of these fifteen Member States, only the United Kingdom and Ireland have common law systems.

In 2004, ten new States were admitted to membership, and the Greek side of Cyprus, Malta, and eight from the old Soviet bloc—the Czech Republic, Hungary, Estonia, Latvia, Lithuania, Poland, Slovakia, and Slovenia. Applications for membership have also been received from Turkey (1987), Switzerland (1992, though processing of the application subsequently stopped), and Bulgaria (1995). A referendum in Norway resulted in voters rejecting membership in 1993 and Greenland voted by referendum to leave the EU in 1982.

Islamic Law

Within Muslim society, there is no separation between church and state as in Western countries. Government, religion, and law are one and the same. It follows that Islamic law (*Shar'iah* or the path to follow God's law) will be an integral part of Islamic religion. *Shar'iah* contains the rules by which a Muslim society is organized and governed and may be viewed by westerners as a moral code more concerned with ethical behaviour than as being a legal system in its own right. This is because it controls, rules, and regulates all public and private behaviour as well as prescribing specific rules for religious matters.

Origins

Shar'iah is derived from a number of sources rather than relying on one source for its broad knowledge base. The first and primary source of guidance and rulings in *Shar'iah* is the *Qur'an*, which is authoritative in Arabic only. As it is considered to be the direct word of Allah, it is the final arbitrator.

The second source of Islamic law is the *Sunnah*. It consists of the teachings of the Prophet Mohammad and helps to explain the *Qur'an*, detailing concepts, laws, and practical matters stated in the *Qur'an*, as well as providing rulings on some matters not explicitly stated in the *Qur'an*. It is a complementary source to the *Qur'an*, but it cannot be interpreted or applied in any way that is inconsistent with the *Qur'an*. The content of the *Sunnah* is found in *hadith*, or traditions. *Hadith* are statements passed through a reliable chain of communication to present adherents directly from the Prophet and its importance is judged on its reliability.

The third source of Islamic law is known as the *Ijma* (or consensus). The *Ulama*, or Muslim religious scholars may be consulted on a range of issues that are not found explicitly in the *Qur'an* or the *Sunnah* and when the *Ulamas* reach a consensus on an issue, it is interpreted as *Ijma* and forms part of the *Shar'iah*. Islamic judges are then able to examine the *Ijma* for solutions to problems that come before them.

The fourth element of *Shar'iah* is that of *Qiyas*, or analogical reasoning. The *Qiyas* are not explicitly found in the *Qur'an*, *Sunnah*, or given in the *Ijma* and can be used by a *Shar'iah* judge (or *Qadi*) to decide new case law.

Features

The closing of the door of *ijithad* (deducing rules of law through juristic reasoning from original sources) in the tenth century AD, three centuries after the founding of Islam, by the Sunnite Muslim authorities declaring the principle legal issues of the *Shar'iah* to be complete. The effect has been to produce a legal system that is often at odds with the modern world. Attempts to reopen the door of *ijtihad* by Sunnites have been vehemently opposed by traditionalists. Shi'ite Muslims have always recognised *ijtihad*.

One of the important features of *Shar'iah* is its emphasis on the correlation between rights and obligations or duties.

Unlike Western thinking, under *Shar'iah*, law is perceived as constituting an integrated part of social organisation and is not seen a separate branch of human activity. Law is seen as an expression of God's will and as a consequence, from an Islamic perspective, it is difficult to imagine a secular state or secular legal system.

Islamic Influence

There are over 1.5 billion Muslims worldwide. They make up 25% of the world's population. There are thirty-five nations with population over 50% Muslim, and there are another twenty-one nations that have significant Muslim populations. There are nineteen nations which have declared Islam in their respective constitutions. Islamic law is the principal source of law in Iran and Saudi Arabia.

Sino-Soviet (Socialist) Law

A majority of comparative lawyers regard socialist law as a family of law separate to the civil law family. While it is possible to identify a number of similarities between the two systems, principally in the codificatory style of law-making, the use of civil law institutions and the role of legal scholars as a source of law, it is the influence of Marxist-Leninist ideology that differentiates the two systems, and distinguishes it from any other systems for that matter.

In socialist countries, the Communist party, as the dominant (and often the only) political party, viewed the legal system as a political tool to be used by the State and its agencies to promote its political aims and objectives. Law was considered to be subservient to the economy and the creation of a new economic order to safeguard worker's interest.

Certainly one of the most important distinguishing features of socialist law was its treatment of property. Under socialist law, property was classified as either socialist property or personal property. Socialist property involved collective ownership through the State of any property which contributed to the means of production, including farms, while personal property was the property owned by individuals for their own personal needs. Other distinguishing characteristics of socialist law included the lack of separation of powers; the role of the courts as advocates of government policy; and the inability to criticise either party policy or the legal system.

The triumph of capitalism over socialism by the early 1990s resulted in the collapse of communism in most countries around the world and led to the decline of the socialist legal system as a dominant legal system. Indeed, as a result of the collapse of communism, many of the former socialist States have returned, or turned, to civil law. While countries such as North Korea, Uzbekistan, and Cuba have retained large elements of socialist legal theory, most of the remaining communist countries, such as mainland China, have slowly lost many of the distinctive command economy features that highlighted their legal systems, as they move to adopt more free-market economies.

Customary Law

Customary law consists of rules that have developed in the community and become accepted by the community as establishing a pattern of behaviour that is binding on the members of that community. For customary practice to become accepted as customary law, it is generally accepted that it is necessary to first establish consistent and recurring action, and secondly that the citizens of the community recognize the custom as binding. The origins of both the modern codification of civil law and common law can be traced back to customary law. In addition, many Asian and African states still contain aspects of indigenous custom in their legal systems, for example, the use of *chotei* procedure (conciliation) under Japanese law and tribal law in the case of many West and East African states.

Hybrid Systems

To a layperson a hybrid system is usually taken to mean one where more than one legal system co-exists, but to a comparative lawyer this usually means where common law and civil law types of law can be found operating together as a result of colonisation, annexation, occupation, or adoption. The laypersons understanding of 'hybrid systems' is used here for convenience. It is being taken to mean any country which has two or three types of laws or legal traditions operating all at the same time, and is what many comparative lawyers would describe as legal pluralism.

ANDY GIBSON

References and Further Reading

Curran, Vivian G., ed. *Comparative Law: an Introduction.* Durham, NC: Carolina Academic Press, 2002.
Danner, Richard A. and Bernal, Mary-Louise H., eds. *Introduction to Foreign Legal Systems.* New York: Oceania Publications, 1994.
de Cruz, Peter. *Comparative Law in a Changing World.* London: Cavendish Press, 1999.
Edge, Ian, ed. *Comparative Law in Global Perspective.* Ardsley, NY: Transnational Publishers, 2000.
Glen, H. Patrick. *Legal Traditions of the World*, 2nd ed. Oxford, New York: Oxford University Press, 2004.
Glendon, Mary A., Gordon, Michael W., Carozza, Paolo G. *Comparative Legal Traditions in a Nutshell.* 2nd ed. St Paul, MN: West Group, 1999.
Katz, Alan N. *Legal Traditions and Systems: an International Handbook.* New York: Greenwood Press, 1986.
Legrand, Pierre and Munday Roderick. *Comparative Legal Studies: Traditions and Transitions.* Cambridge, UK: Cambridge University Press, 2003.
Markesinis, Basil S. *The Coming Together of the Common Law and the Civil Law.* Oxford, UK: Hart, 2000.
Tan, Poh-Ling, ed. *Asian Legal Systems.* Butterworths, 1997.
Zweigert, Konrad and Kotz, Hein. *An Introduction to Comparative Law*, 3rd rev ed. Oxford, UK: Clarendon Press, New York: Oxford University Press, 1998.

LESOTHO

The Kingdom of Lesotho is a small country surrounded by the Republic of South Africa. Formerly known as Basutoland, the kingdom gained independence from Great Britain and is now an independent, limited monarchy.

The Basuto tribe developed only recently in Africa's history. It resulted from the disruption of the "Wars of Calamity" brought about by Shaka, king of the Zulus, in the early nineteenth century. While many Bantu, Suto, and Nguni clans were disrupted by the Zulu raiders, a minor chief named Moshoeshoe gathered those he could on the plateau of Thaba Bosiu, near the Caledon River in what is now northwest Lesotho. Moshoeshoe was then able to avoid conflict with the Zulus.

Soon after Moshoeshoe's organization of the remnants of the original tribes in 1823, another conflict, this time with the European Dutch settlers known as the Boers, developed. In the early 1800s, the Boers began to move away from coastal south Africa as the British came in greater numbers, and by 1831 they had begun to move into the area inhabited by the Basuto. Reports of Boer mistreatment of Africans led Moshoeshoe to seek the protections of the British. In 1848, Moshoeshoe agreed to permit Great Britain to control the territories around the area he controlled.

Relations between Moshoeshoe and the British deteriorated soon, however, and in 1852 the Basuto and British fought one another. Moshoeshoe diplomatically brought the fighting to an end, and despite clashes with British settlers over the next few years, the Basuto remained free until the Great Basuto War, fought against the Boers, led Moshoeshoe to ask the British for formal protection again.

The Boers, who were Calvinists, had angered the British through their religious repression of Protestant missionaries in the region, and Great Britain agreed to annex Basutoland, placing it under local British control in the province of Natal.

Following Moshoeshoe's death in 1859, Basutoland was formally annexed into Britain's Cape Colony in 1871. The increase in British influence made the region more productive and profitable, but when British forces attempted to disarm the Basuto the tribal members resisted, fearing that without weapons they would be unable to protect themselves from the Boers. Following the "Gun War," which went badly for the British, the Basuto were eventually allowed to keep their weapons, and in 1883 Basutoland was disannexed. The next year, Moshoeshoe's son, King Letsie, agreed that the Basuto would become British subjects and British rule was established in Basutoland.

The British had learned to accept some tribal customs in their dealings with Africans, and in Basutoland this meant that Letsie, the Paramount Chief, was in fact still in control of the territory. This freed the British from having to deal with internal conflicts among the Basuto. Only the Basuto were permitted to own land, and eventually the Basuto (with British encouragement) developed a National Council to provide some degree of representative government. However, over several decades of this indirect rule Basutoland did not prosper and by the 1950s efforts to revise the power structure were made by the British.

A constitution was put in place in 1959 and elections were held in 1960 to form a new government, although Basutoland would still be one of Britain's High Commission Territories (along with Swaziland and Bechuanaland). This government, the Basutoland National Congress, took power on March 12, 1960.

Basutoland's geographic location, totally surrounded by the nation of South Africa, was the basis for a new concern. When Great Britain ruled South Africa as well as the High Commission Territories some degree of consistency could be established for the region. However, the Republic of South Africa was established and withdrew from the British Commonwealth. South Africa had developed its *apartheid* policy of racial segregation and exclusion, and with Great Britain's influence in southern Africa reduced, Basutoland's status as a colony was seen more as a liability than an asset. In 1963, a constitutional commission recommended rapid independence for Basutoland, and on October 4, 1966, the British territory of Basutoland formally became the independent nation of Lesotho, a constitutional monarchy.

Since independence Lesotho has been ruled sometimes by democratic institutions, but the government was overthrown by force by the military in 1998, resulting in widespread violence and destruction of property. Order was restored by intervention from forces from South Africa and Botswana in 1999, and Lesotho had orderly parliamentary elections in 2002.

The economy of Lesotho is largely dependent on employment in South Africa. While most of the adult workforce in Lesotho survives by subsistence farming, nearly one-third of the adult males work as migrant laborers in South Africa, which provides economic benefits for the families of the workers. While such use of migrant laborers is seen by some as exploitation, it does provide a means by which some wealth can be transferred from prosperous regions to others.

Lesotho's primary industrial export is electricity generated by the Lesotho Highlands Water Project, a joint venture between South Africa and Lesotho. This project began in 1984 and is expected to be complete by 2020.

The cooperation between Lesotho, Swaziland, South Africa, Namibia, and Botswana in the Southern African Customs Union (SACU) creates a regional trading bloc that has contributed to economic development in the region.

THOMAS P. DOLAN

See also Ethnic Conflicts: Southern Africa; Southern Africa: History and Economic Development; Southern Africa: International Relations; Southern African Customs Union (SACU)

References and Further Reading

Maane, Willem. *Lesotho: A Development Challenge.* Washington, DC: International Bank for Reconstruction and Development, 1975.

Pollock, N.C. *Studies in Emerging Africa.* Totowa: Rownam and Littlefield, 1971.

Robertson, A.F. *The Dynamics of Productive Relationships: African Share Contracts in Comparative Perspective.* Cambridge, UK: Cambridge University Press, 1987.

Robson, Peter. *Economic Integration in Africa.* Evanston, IL: Northwestern University Press, 1968.

Stevens, Richard P. *Lesotho, Botswana, & Swaziland: The Former High CommissionTerritories in Southern Africa.* New York: Frederick A. Praeger, Publishers, 1967.

LIBERATION THEOLOGY

Liberation theology arose within Roman Catholicism in Latin America as an effort to reinterpret the message of the Gospel while confronting political oppression and economical deprivation. It seeks to express religious faith by helping the poor and working for political and social change. The intellectual roots of this movement can be traced to certain European theologians, such as J. Moltmann and D. Bonhoeffer. Its ecclesiastical and social origins were made public in 1968, after the Latin American Bishops' Conference in Medellín, Colombia. That final declaration can be seen as a milestone, with its clear affirmation of the rights of the poor and denunciation of the industrialized nations, accused of enriching themselves at the expense of the exploited and deprived masses of the Third World.

Drawing inspiration from certain aspects of Marxist theory, emphasis was placed on the liberating potential of social action, at the level of the local community or of global revolution. Without denying eternal life, salvation is thus seen in terms of achieving the kingdom of God on earth, through the creation of a society based on justice and equality. In the words of one of the founders of the liberationist movement, the mission of the church is "at all times to protest against injustice, to challenge what is inhuman, to side with the poor and the oppressed" (1971). The ultimate justification for this position is to be found in the nature of God, conceived as being historically engaged against oppression and injustice. The fundamental act of divine liberating immersion is found in the Incarnation and the universal value of Jesus Christ resides in his total commitment of struggle for the poor and the outcast.

Opposing a conventional theology that legitimises the interests of the powerful, a truly liberating theological reflection was seen emerging out of an historical commitment, praxis of engagement in the interests of the poor. An important aspect of this focus on social action was the creation in various Latin American countries of hundreds of grassroots religious communities ("*comunidades de base*"). During the period of widespread social unrest and civil war in Latin America, in the decades of 1970–1980, many of these communities were targeted by repressive regimes as feared hotbeds of revolutionary subversion. Thus, tens of thousands of their members, leaders, nuns, and priests, became the victims of repression, particularly in Central America. The progressive Archbishop of El Salvador, Mons. Oscar Romero, was murdered in 1980, an outrage tragically repeated in 1989, with the murder of the liberation theologian Ignacio Ellacuría and several of his close associates.

From the beginning liberation theology was criticized by conservative church circles and the Vatican for a dependence on Marxist tenets and proclivity for revolutionary violence. Several of its representatives were sanctioned and silenced, as in the case of the Brasilian Leonardo Boff. Critical voices from within Protestantism pointed to the insistence by liberation theologians of salvation through social change and the neglect of the personal and emotional aspects of religiosity. They were also quick to remind that liberation has always been at the heart of Christianity and that Scripture rather than praxis should continue to be the fundamental theological guideline.

Liberation theology has undergone significant development over the years, partly as a result of changed political conditions—not the least the fall of Eastern European socialism—and above all, as in any intellectual movement, through the development of thinking expressed by its proponents. Although perhaps not in the sense anticipated by its early adherents, liberation theology has, by the beginning of the twenty-first century, diversified and expanded in several directions. It now includes the liberation of women from patriarchal structures, the liberation of ethnic groups and minorities within nation states, and an increased awareness of the need to address, in the face of global ecological degradation, the nature of the relation between man and nature; in other words, to liberate theology from the fetters of an older perspective of domination and move on to develop a perspective of stewardship and participation.

Most significantly, there has been growing interest in the specifically theological meaning of the concept of liberation. Without renouncing the essential commitment for a more just society, there is an increased inward focus on the importance of scripture as a basis for theological reflection and personal spiritual development, as can be seen in the work of, among others, Aloysius Pieris in Sri Lanka, and bishop Pedro Casaldáliga in Brasil.

There has been, in general, a shift away from an early idealisation of socialism without abandoning a critical stance against capitalism and the neo-liberalism of globalization.

At the same time, the expansion of liberation theology into other parts of the world, such as Africa, Asia and the Middle East, has resulted in the acceptance of the cultural implications of its basic tenets. Among other things, this means that the constructive realisation that the idea of an ultimate reality as a personal being that creates the cosmos out of nothing and summons human beings to a redeeming encounter with his divine Self, is almost nowhere to be found outside Semitic monotheism. This means, for instance, the beginning of a dialogue on equal terms with Aymara religion in the Andes of South America, with religious syncretism in Brasil or with Maya religion in Central America. It means also the emergence of a Black Theology in North America and a generous and open-minded attitude towards what can become a portentous long term cultural meeting with the vast tradition and rich symbolism of Asian religiosity.

Thus, there are today not one but several liberation theologies. There are various regional issues to assume, as when Christian Palestinians invoke a liberationist outlook in their struggle to attain nationhood, and there is also the challenge of formulating a viable alternative to the mechanisms within the current process of globalization that maintain and even aggravate poverty and inequality for millions of human beings.

JUAN-CARLOS GUMUCIO CASTELLON

References and Further Reading

Kidwell, Clara Sue, Homer Noley, and George E. Tinker. *A Native American Theology*. Maryknoll, NY: Orbis Books, 2001.
Cone, James H. *Risks of Faith: The Emergence of a Black Theology of Liberation, 1968–1998*. Boston: Beacon Press (distrib. by Houghton), 1999.
Ellacuría, Ignacio, and Jon Sobrino. *Mysterium Liberationis: Fundamental Concepts of Liberation Theology*. Maryknoll, NY 1993.
Gutierrez, Gustavo. *A Theology of Liberation*. Maryknoll, NY: Orbis Books, 1971.
Lorentzen, Lois, David Batstone, Eduardo Mendieta, and Dwight Hopkins, eds. *Liberation Theologies*. New York: Routledge, an imprint of Taylor & Francis Books Ltd, 1999.
Pieris, Aloysius. *An Asian Theology of Liberation*. Maryknoll, NY: Orbis Books, 1988.

LIBERIA

Liberia, like neighbouring British Sierra Leone, was born of mixed motivations to spread Christianity and Western civilisation to Africa, while ridding the United States of an undesired class of freed Blacks. In 1816, the American Colonisation Society, with the support of a US congressional grant, began to transport freed slaves back to Africa. Following the US abolition of the slave trade in 1819, the settlements proved a dumping ground for recaptive slaves seized by the American anti-slave trade squadron. Between 1822 and 1892, over sixteen thousand freed slaves were resettled in scattered settlements under the control of the Society's various state chapters.

In 1831, the Maryland chapter broke with the Society and established its own Maryland County colony. Such chapter rivalry was reflected in fragmentary administration, though not development assistance. Many of freed blacks had urban skills, not applicable to the frontier conditions, and found themselves in competition with indigenous peasants. Some became absentee planters, using recaptive labourers to grow sugarcane, coffee, rice, and so forth. Many turned to petty trading, some to illicit slave trade—the most viable economic venture available.

Britain refused to recognize the sovereignty of the American Colonisation Society and the United States was ambiguous; it refused to accept responsibility but tended to oppose British and French territorial ambitions. The Americo-Liberian seized the initiative, declaring Liberia a republic, on July 26, 1847. Maryland County was subsequently annexed in 1857.

Until the 1890s, Monrovia controlled only isolated coastal enclaves. The dominant Americo-Liberian elite, with their Christian faith, American colonial lifestyle, and racial prejudices, looked down upon the indigenous 'savages' and the recaptives as only slightly better.

In 1869, Edward Roye of the new True Whig Party became the first fully Black Liberian president. An educated and financially successful businessman, Roye sought to offset falling revenue with a series of British loans, commencing a downward debt spiral. Roye's death in 1871, under mysterious circumstances, led to a brief revival of Republican power, but triumph by the True Whig Party in 1877 ushered in over a century of one-party rule.

The economy was increasingly threatened by a glut of tropic produce and imperial shipping cartels undercut the older Americo-Liberian coastal cutter trade. Simultaneously, Liberia was forced to defend its territory against British and French imperialism by demonstrating its 'effective-control' of the interior, resulting in clashes with indigenous rulers.

President Arthur Barclay (1904–1912) introduced a system of 'native administration' based on British 'Indirect Rule' through native chiefs, who received a share of local revenue. He also increased ports of entry, thus legitimising a trade the state could not control, and initiated a new loan agreement, negotiated by the famous British explorer, Sir Harry Johnston. The new loan was to retire existing debts, some $800,000 in 1906, with the balance used for development by the British Liberian Rubber Corporation. In return, a British official was placed in control of Liberian Customs. Much of the money disappeared when Harry Johnston's Liberian Development Company collapsed. When Pres Barclay tried to renegotiate the loan, the British government insisted on greater controls over Customs and a Liberian Frontier Force under British Officers. Increased British hegemony aroused French demands and American intervention. US Afro-American officers replaced the British officers.

In 1912, the United States organised an international loan of $1.7 million, to pay off Liberia's debts, but Liberian Customs was placed under an American-chaired international receivership. Government retrenchments, continued corruption, and falling terms of trade, exacerbated by the sharp wartime decline in trade with Germany, Liberia's largest trading partner, led to native uprisings amongst the Kru and Kpelle. British hostility to Liberia's wartime neutrality and support for the Kru was thwarted by American intervention. The Kru were brutally crushed and Liberia subsequently followed the US into declaring war on Germany.

In response to an attempted Anglo-Dutch rubber cartel, in 1927, Harvey Firestone sought a ninety-nine–year lease on a million acres, in return for a 5 million dollar loan to Liberia and the replacement of the international receivership by US control of the budget. The world price of rubber collapsed shortly thereafter but not repayments on the loan.

The other scandal of the 1930s concerned exploitative contract labour from Liberia to Spanish Fernando Po. The League of Nations pilloried Liberia, though Spain and other colonial exploiters were largely ignored. Liberia's international reputation was resuscitated during World War II, when it became the principal source of Allied rubber with the expansion of Firestone's investments, and a base for air-strikes against North Africa from what became Roberts Field airport outside Monrovia.

President William Tubman, inaugurated in 1944, adopted a US "open door" policy to promote foreign investment and, unlike his predecessors, encouraged some local participation in government. He died in 1971 and was succeeded by William R. Tolbert, who continued the free-enterprise policies but sought a less conservative image and strengthened ties with West African nations. An attempt to promote domestic rice production through higher prices led to demonstrations in 1979.

In 1980, Master Sgt Samuel K. Doe assassinated Tolbert and overthrew the government. Doe abrogated the constitution and ruled in conjunction with a People's Redemption Council (PRC). He doubled army pay and publicly executed thirteen former ministers in a backlash against more than a century of Americo-Liberian political and economic exploitation of the indigenous population. Despite international protests, the United States recognised the regime and increased the level of assistance.

Doe won the 1985 presidential elections and his National Democratic Party of Liberia secured a majority, amid accusations of electoral malpractice. Many opposition figures died under suspicious circumstances. Then, in 1989, Charles Taylor of the National Patriotic Front of Liberia launched an invasion from Cote d'Ivoire, supported by Gio tribesmen. The ensuring civil war, with its complex tribal factions, was fueled by an illicit diamond and drug trade, in exchange for arms.

Despite intervention by Economic Community of West African States (ECOWAS) the brutal fighting continued. Doe was eventually captured and tortured to death by a rival warlord. The war created desperate food shortages and a total breakdown of civil society, with hundreds of thousands of refugees.

There were numerous peace conferences and discussion, leading to elections in 1997, won overwhelmingly by Charles Taylor on a platform of vote for continuing atrocities or me. Taylor murdered, imprisoned or drove out his rivals, holding onto power with the support of illicit diamond smuggling by his RUF allies in neighbouring Sierra Leone. In 2002, rebels of Liberians United for Reconciliation and Democracy (LURD) seized control of most of the north and advanced on Monrovia. By 2003, the rival rebel Movement for Democracy in Liberia (MODEL) controlled most of the west. Under pressure from rebels and facing an indictment by the United Nations (UN) Special Court in Sierra Leone, Taylor fled into exile in Nigeria.

A multi-party transitional government was established in 2003; and under President Gyude Bryant, a local businessman, a UN-sponsored disarmament program was initiated.

DAVID DORWARD

See also West Africa: History and Economic Development; West Africa: International Relations

References and Further Reading

Beyan, Amos Jones. *The American Colonization Society and the Creation of the Liberian State: a Historical*

Perspective, 1822–1900. Lanham, MD: University Press of America, 1991.

Ellis, Stephen. "Liberia's Warlord Insurgency," in *African guerrillas,* edited by Christopher Clapham. Oxford: James Currey, 1998.

Gifford, Paul. *Christianity and Politics in Doe's Liberia.* Cambridge, UK: Cambridge University Press, 1993.

Hlophe, Stephen S. *Class, Ethnicity and Politics in Liberia: A Class Analysis of Power Struggles in the Tubman and Tolbert Administrations from 1944–1975.* Washington, DC: University Press of America, 1979.

Liebenow, J. Gus. *Liberia: The Evolution of Privilege.* Ithaca, NY: Cornell University Press, 1969.

Saha, Santosh C. *A History of Agriculture in Liberia, 1822–1970: Transference of American Values.* Lewiston: E. Mellen Press, 1990.

Sisay, Hassan B. *Big Powers and Small Nations: A Case Study of United States-Liberian Relations.* Lanham, MD: University Press of America, 1985.

Weller, M., ed. *Regional Peace-keeping and International Enforcement: The Liberian Crisis.* Cambridge, UK: Cambridge University Press, 1994.

LIBYA

The country's conventional name is Great Socialist People's Libyan Arab Jamahiriya or most commonly known as the *Libyan Arab Jamahiriya* is situated in north Africa, next to Egypt and Algeria.

The northern part of Libya has a typical Mediterranean landscape and climate, with an average rainfall of about fifteen inches annually and temperatures ranging from 86°F to 46°F. Towards the middle and southern part of the country the average rainfall decreases gradually, it becomes very dry and the desert takes over most of the territory: more than 90% of the country is desert or semi-desert. Southern Libya has a desert climate with daytime winter temperatures ranging between 59°F and 68°F, falling below zero at night. During the summer months, there is virtually no rainfall and temperatures soar to over 122°F.

The present population is estimated at 5.6 million, with a growth rate of about 2.37% annually. Libya is between the countries with the lowest population density in the world. The urban population is 86%, a high value in the region. The port of Tripoli, the capital city, has a population estimated at 1.7 million. The official language is Arabic, with Italian and English also understood in major cities. Most people's religion is the Sunni Muslim, which accounts for approximately 97% of the population.

Libya was formerly occupied by the Roman Empire, inherited by the Byzantines until it was conquered by the Arabs. During the sixteenth century, the Turks invaded and imposed a series of dynasties until 1912 when the Italians, by Mussolini's order, conquered the native tribes. After World War II, the territory was assigned to France and Great Britain but soon Libya gained and declared its independence on December 24, 1951, before any other African country that had been formerly under European control. Libya was proclaimed a constitutional and hereditary monarchy and Sheikh Sidi Idris was proclaimed King Idris I. During Idris's mandate, Libya maintained a tendency favourable to the western countries until on September 1, 1969, a small group of military officers led by Muammar Qaddafi staged a *coup d'etat* against King Idris, a fact later known as *The Libyan Revolution.* The new regime abolished the monarchy and proclaimed the new Libyan Arab Republic. Qaddafi's political system was a combination of both Socialism and Islam (Muslims beliefs) which he called the *Third Universal Theory.*

During the 1980s, Libya incurred in some conflicts with the United States all of which resulted in a boycott by the United States to Libya. Later, in 1992, the United Nations (UN) Security Council condemned Libya to political and economical isolation during the 1990s. UN sanctions were suspended in 1999 and finally lifted in 2003 after Libya resolved the Lockerbie case. Libya then began establishing important reforms such as privatization of the country's oil sector and the incorporation of Libya to the World Trade Organization, giving up in some way to Qaddafi's socialist philosophy.

Since 1959, Libya's oil and petroleum export revenues have accounted for more than 90% of its earnings. Libya's economy depends primarily upon revenues from the oil sector, which contributes practically all export earnings and about one-quarter of the gross domestic product (GDP). In 2004, the GDP was estimated at $35 billion with per capita income of $6,400, quite high for the region. The non-oil manufacturing and construction sectors account for about 20% of the GDP and agriculture sector only contributes with 8% of the GDP. Because climatic conditions and poor soils limit agricultural activities, Libya imports about 75% of its food.

Despite Libya's relatively strong economic growth and high per capita income, unemployment remains high as the country's population grows rapidly and new jobs are not created rapidly enough. The unemployment rate was estimated at 30% in 2001. Libya has a relatively poor infrastructure (i.e., roads and logistics) having only a well-developed net of oil pipelines from the inner part to the sea.

However, the incomes generated by the petroleum exploitation have allowed the government to implement social welfare plans, which have improved the people's living conditions. All health international standards show that Libya's health conditions have improved in the last five decades. Between 1970 and 1985, the number of medical doctors and dentists increased seven times and the number of hospital beds tripled. A net of public hospitals and health centres provides free and medium quality health service accessible for all citizens. The infant mortality rate experienced significant improvement: it passed from being 105 infants (per 1,000 live births) in 1970 to only 16 in 2002. Also the under-five mortality rate passed from being 160 per 1,000 live births in 1970 to 19 in 2002. As a result of this the general life expectancy at birth has improved from being 58 years in 1970 to 72 years in 2002 (UNDP 2004). Consequently the country is qualified among those with medium human development by the United Nations Development Program (UNDP 2004), which situates it better than any other African country. Progress included eradication of malaria, malnutrition, and significant gains against trachoma, tuberculosis, and leprosy. However, diseases such as typhoid, infectious hepatitis, rabies, meningitis, and venereal diseases remain a problem.

Primary education between six and fifteen years in Libya is free and compulsory. The primary school enrolment ratio was 96% in 2000. Secondary school is attended until the age of eighteen and scholars have the chance to enter one of the twelve universities. The major universities are the University of Garyounis in Banghazi and the Al-Fateh University in Tripoli. The adult literacy rate has improved a lot in the last decades: it was 60% in 1985, then 75% in 1995 and finally it reached 81% in 2002.

A project called the Great Man Made River project, is being implemented to bring water from underground aquifers beneath the Sahara to the Mediterranean coast, which will reduce the country's water shortage and its dependence on food imports by encouraging the development of agriculture.

DIEGO I. MURGUÍA

See also Ethnic Conflicts: North Africa; Libyan Cultural Revolution; North Africa: History and Economic Development; North Africa: International Relations; Qaddafi, Muammar

References and Further Reading

Anderson, Lisa. *The State and Social Transformation in Tunisia and Libya, 1830–1980*. Princeton, NJ: Princeton University Press, 1986.
Blundy, David and Lycett, Andrew. *Qaddafi and the Libyan Revolution*. Boston: Little, Brown, 1987.
Deeb, Marius K., and Deeb, Mary Jane. *Libya Since the Revolution: Aspects of Social and Political Development*. New York: Praeger, 1982.
Harris, Lillian Craig. *Libya: Qadhafi's Revolution and the Modern State*. Boulder, CO: Westview Press, 1986.
Joffe, E. G. H., and McLachlan, K.S. (eds.). *Social and Economic Development of Libya*. Wisbech, UK: Middle East and North African Studies Press, 1982.
Simons, Geoff. *Libya and the West: from Independence to Lockerbie*. New York: Palgrave Macmillan, 2004.
Vandewalle, Dirk. *Libya since Independence: Oil-state Building*. Ithaca, NY: Cornell University Press, 1998.
Wright, John. *Libya: A Modern History*. Baltimore: Johns Hopkins University Press, 1982.

LIBYAN CULTURAL REVOLUTION

The Libyan Cultural revolution was launched in April 1973 on the Prophet Muhammed's birthday anniversary by Libya's charismatic leader Colonel Muammar Qaddafi. Libya's monarchy had been overthrown in a bloodless coup by Qaddafi and a troupe of fellow officers in 1969. With Qaddafi as the chair of the Free Unionist Officers, Libya was to embark on a path to full independence from foreign influence, to Arab unity, socialism, and freedom. By 1973, dissatisfied with the progress of the "revolution" Qaddafi had consolidated enough of a powerbase to lead the revolution in a new direction. Qaddafi announced that drastic measures were required to preserve the revolution. The Libyan state and society would be revolutionized along the guidance of Qaddafi's Third Universal Theory, which he elaborated in the three volumes of the *Green Book* published soon afterwards. The pillars of the new Libyan state were egalitarianism, socialism, pan-Arabism, and anti-imperialism. Qaddafi's Third Universal Theory was offered and recognized as a third and uniquely Arab alternative to capitalist and communist development.

The Libyan Cultural Revolution was apparently modeled after China's Cultural Revolution, but Qaddafi denies this. Its goals were (1) to replace all imperialist laws with revolutionary laws, (2) to weed out counter-revolutionaries, (3) to foster an administrative revolution that would sweep away bourgeois bureaucracy, (4) to replace the state bureaucracy with people's committees, and (5) to eliminate all imported and foreign ideas. Qaddafi hoped to combat bureaucratic inefficiency and resistance in the state while simultaneously instilling the people of Libya with revolutionary fervor and participation.

The most important innovation of the Cultural Revolution was the People's Committees. The People's Committees were to be the primary instrument of the revolution, and they were created at all levels to take over administration and governance. People's Committees were formed to administer universities, private business firms, schools, farms, public utilities, government bureaucracies, the broadcast media, and municipalities. Thousands of government bureaucrats were fired. Estimates vary, but by August 1973 from one thousand to two thousand People's Committees were created. The People's Committees replaced all alternative forms of representation in government. At the top of this new system was the General People's Congress (GPC). Later Qaddafi would add "Revolutionary Committees" to guide the People's Committees. Qaddafi's intention was to bring Libya "true democracy," instead of Western representative democracy. Qaddafi renounced his formal titles, but remained the head of the army and the Leader of the Revolution, hence, the de facto ruler of Libya.

The Cultural Revolution also brought forth other reforms; Libya was to be egalitarian, socialist, and Arab. Properties were seized from landlords and given to their occupants. Private property was abolished. Workers were encouraged to take over their places of employment and create a system of self-management. Retail trade was to be abolished. Libyan embassies were converted into people's bureaus. The Libyan army was demobilized and replaced by a People's Army, and military training was made mandatory from high school age onwards for both men and women. Private savings accounts were eliminated.

JAMES A. NORRIS

See also Libya; North Africa: History and Economic Development; Qaddafi, Muammar

References and Further Reading

Anderson, Lisa (2001). "Muammar al-Qaddafi: The King of Libya," *Journal of International Affairs*, 54, no. 2 (2001).

El-Kikhia, Mansour O. *Libya's Qaddafi: The Politics of Contradiction*. Gainesville, FL: University Press of Florida, 1997.

Harris, Lillian Craig. *Libya: Qadhafi's Revolution and the Modern State*. Boulder, CO: Westview Press, Beckenham: Croom Helm, 1986.

Vandewalle, Dirk. *Qadhafi's Libya, 1969–1994*, New York: St. Martin's Press, 1995.

LITHUANIA

Lithuania, situated on the east coast of the Baltic Sea, covers approximately sixty-five thousand square kilometers. Lithuania shares borders with Belarus, Latvia, Poland, and the Russian Oblast of Kaliningrad. Lithuania mainly consists of lowlands with rolling hills in the east. Lithuania has a maritime climate in the west and a continental climate in the east. Summers and winters are moderate although the climate in the east is more variable. Lithuania lacks an abundant supply of natural resources. What resources are available include peat, sulfates, limestone, chalk, sand, gravel, and amber. There are limited oil and gas holdings available offshore. Lithuania, however, is an exporter of electricity with its nuclear power industry. The population is estimated at 3,608,000 with a declining population of −.33% annually. Vilnius, Lithuania's capital, is the major urban center consisting of 16% of Lithuania's population with 518,000 inhabitants. Other important cities include Kaunas, Klaipeda, and Siauliai.

Unlike Estonia and Latvia, Lithuania acquired statehood prior to the twentieth century. Through a dynastic marriage in the fourteenth century and the threat of an expanding Muscovy, the kingdoms of Lithuania and Poland were united by the Union of Lublin in 1569. The union created a Polish-Lithuanian commonwealth (Rzeczpopolita) stretching from the Baltic Sea to the Black Sea. The Polish partitions of the late eighteenth century resulted in Lithuania's incorporation into the Russian Empire. As a result of World War I and the 1917 Russian Revolution, Lithuania declared its independence in February 1918. There were major issues that plagued Lithuania's claim to independence. Immediately following Lithuania's declaration, Bolshevik forces invaded Vilnius and established a pro-Bolshevik government. The provisional government, exiled to Kaunas, organized a national army to expel the Bolsheviks. Due to Polish ambitions, Lithuania lost the Vilnius region to Poland. Kaunas served as Lithuania's capital during the interwar period. A permanent constitution was drafted in August 1922 officially creating an independent, democratic Lithuania. The constitution called for a unicameral legislature, the Seimas, and an elected president. Due to the ineffectiveness of competing liberal and conservative politicians in the Seimas, President Antanas Smetona led a military coup d'état on December 17,1926. Smetona expelled liberal members of the Seimas and changed the constitution, granting him supreme authority until fleeing the country in 1940.

The secret protocol contained in the September 1939 German-Soviet Nonaggression Pact relegated Lithuania to a German sphere of influence. Later in September, however, Lithuania was shifted to the Soviet sphere. In exchange for the possession of Vilnius, Lithuania signed a mutual assistance pact with the USSR in October 1939, paving the way for Soviet annexation. In August 1940, Lithuania became a constituent member of the USSR. Nazi Germany occupied Lithuania from 1941–1944, resulting in 200,000 Lithuanian casualties including an estimated 160,000 Jews. Following the defeat of Germany, the USSR systematically exiled as many as 350,000 Lithuanians to prison camps. Although many

Russians immigrated to Lithuania, it was not of the same magnitude in comparison to Estonia and Latvia. Liberalization of the Soviet system and the *Sajudis* (Lithuanian Movement for Reconstruction) led to a renewed demand for independence. In March 1990, Lithuania became the first Soviet republic to declare independence. However, it was not until August 1991 that the USSR recognized Lithuania's independence claim. Lithuania undertook the path of a more western orientation by becoming an associate member of the European Union in 1995.

Lithuania's economic reorientation was initially very turbulent. High-energy costs and price deregulation gave way to sharp inflation, plunging Lithuania into depression during the early 1990s. Lithuania's gross domestic product (GDP) dropped significantly each year until 1994. The privatization of the agricultural sector established many small inefficient farms throughout the country. The introduction of a new currency, the *Lita*, in 1993, helped establish a more stable economy. The *Lita,* initially tied to the US dollar in 1994, however, was pegged to the Euro in 2002, reflecting Lithuania's ambition to join the European Union. Lithuanian goals for European Union (EU) accession were secured by becoming an associate member in 1995. Lithuania was rocked by a banking crisis in 1995. The government due to embezzlement charges closed Lithuania's two largest banks—the Innovation Bank and the Litimpeks Bank. The 1998 Russian economic crisis caused a recession in Lithuania in 1999. Despite this tumultuous period, Lithuania's economy emerged as one of the strongest of former Soviet republics.

The 2004 estimated GDP was $40.8 billion. The service sector contributes 63% of the GDP, whereas industry consisted of 31% and agricultural production 6%. Lithuania's major imports and exports include mineral products, textiles, machinery, transportation equipment, mineral fuels, metals, and consumer goods. Other important trade partners include Germany, Poland, Latvia, the United Kingdom, France, Denmark, Sweden, Estonia, and Switzerland. Lithuania is a member of the International Monetary Fund (IMF), the International Bank for Reconstruction and Development (World Bank), the World Trade Organization, and the European Bank for Reconstruction and Development.

Public discontent due to Lithuania's rapid economic transformation and corruption plagued Lithuanian politics in the 1990s. Lithuania's first post-Soviet government collapsed under pressure from a population suffering from a decline in living standards and growing unemployment. Since the mid-1990s, living standards have improved, but Lithuanian politics faced mounting pressure due to corruption in the public sector. Lithuania's first president, Algirdas Brazauskas, demanded the resignation of Prime Minister Adolfas Slezevicius in February 1996 after allegations that Slezevicius withdrew his personal savings from Innovation Bank two days prior to the bank's collapse. Brazauskas decided not to run for reelection in January 1998, paving the way for Lithuanian-American ecologist Valdas Adamkus's presidential election. Adamkus is widely credited for attempting to eradicate corruption in Lithuanian politics and leading Lithuania towards full EU and NATO membership. Lithuania became a full member of the EU and NATO in May 2004. Despite widespread popularity, Adamkus was defeated in the January 2003 runoff election to former Prime Minister Rolandas Paksas. Paksas, however, was impeached and removed from office in April 2004 due to implications of personal contacts with Russian organized crime and threats to national security. Adamkus was reelected president in July 2004.

JONATHAN H. L'HOMMEDIEU

See also Landsbergis, Vytautas

References and Further Reading

Ashbourne, Alexandria. *Lithuania: The Rebirth of a Nation: 1991–1994.* Lanham, MD: Rowman and Littlefield Publishers, 1999.
Lieven, Anatol. *The Baltic Revolution: Estonia, Latvia, Lithuania, and the Path to Independence.* New Haven, CT: Yale University Press, 1994.
Smith, David J., Artis Pabriks, Aldis Purs, and Thomas Lane. *The Baltic States: Estonia, Latvia, and Lithuania.* New York: Routledge Press, 2002.
Vardys, Vytas Stanley, and Judith B. Sedaitis. *Lithuania: The Rebel Nation,* Boulder, CO: Westview Press, 1996.

LOMÉ CONVENTION

The Lomé Regime, a political framework within which economic processes are carried out, comprises four conventions entered into between the European Union (EU) and a group of African, Caribbean, and Pacific countries (ACP) from 1975 to 1999. Each convention lasted for five years. Against the backdrop of the failed attempt by the developing countries at the United Nations (UN) to usher in a New International Economic Order (NIEO), Lomé I (1975) was touted as an example of an equitable world order. An increase in the number of ACP states adhering to this regime from forty-six in Lomé I, to fifty-eight in Lomé II, sixty-six in Lomé III, and to seventy-one in Lomé IV (bis) in 1999 begins to validate this contention. Seemingly, the regime's signature products—trade and aid and provisions and

Europe's commitment to promoting industrialization in the ACP states—were its principal baits. The preferential treatment granted ACP products under Lome was more attractive than the Generalized System of Preferences (GSP), privileges granted by most developed countries to imports from developing countries. However, a critical examination, shows that the regime's impact on the development of its ACP partners has been minimal. Changes in the international environment such as the end of the Cold War and the growth of neoliberalism as promoted by the Washington consensus, the advent of the World Trade Organization (WTO) rules as well as the increase in EU membership and the signing to the Maastricht Treaty have led to a change in the Lomé "spirit" which privileged partnership.

Under Lomé, about 97% of ACP products were allowed free entry into the EU market. Instability in earnings from primary commodity exports (groundnuts, cotton, and hides) were compensated, to a large extent, by the Stabilization of Export Earnings (STABEX) facility as well as SYSMIN which aids mineral producing countries (copper, cobalt, manganese, and phosphates) if their production is affected by circumstances such as a fall in world prices or a political crisis. Despite these, the ACP share of EU's overall imports continued to decline, from 20.5% in 1975 to 16.6% in 1985. Seen through another prism, imports from the ACP between 1975 and 1992 grew by 2.28% as compared to those from Latin America, the Mediterranean, and Asia which increased by 5.97%, 5.87%, and 11.7% respectively. Rules of origin stipulations and the imposition of non-tariff barriers (NTBs), to a large extent, helped to stymie its growth. Under the rules of origins provision, no less than 50% of the value added in ACP goods must originate from the ACP states and/or the EU. Studies have shown that Commonwealth Africa cannot benefit from this provision "because they have only between 20% and 48% of value added as a proportion of their gross value" (Cosgrove Twitchett 1978). Also contributing to trade distortion was the threat of the imposition of non tariff barriers, though outlawed by the Treaty. A threat by the United Kingdom, for example, to invoke the Safeguard Clause in the Treaty forced Mauritius to conclude a voluntary export restraint restricting its textile exports to the EU (Parfitt 1981). Other impediments include supply side factors such as the effects of natural disasters, drought desertification and the lack of capacity. The composition of ACP exports, however, changed as twenty-eight states developed a capacity to export some seventy new commodities to the EU.

The aid package increased from European Currency Unit (ECU) 4,362 in Lomé I to 5,409 million, 8,500 million, and 12,000 million for Lomé II, III, and IV respectively. Consisting of mostly grants and soft loans, they were administered by the European Development Fund (EDF). Under the first three conventions, about 70% of the funds were set aside for the projects under the National Indicative Programs (NIPs). Decisions over funding amounts were, however, the prerogative of the EU. The remainder of the non-programmed EDF aid was allocated to other mechanisms, notably STABEX and SYSMIN. Until 1990, STABEX funds had to be repaid. That these funds were inadequate is demonstrated by their failure to completely compensate for shortfalls. Payments were more than halved in 1980 and 1981 and in 1987 claims amounted to over ECU 803 million while the fund had only ECU 375 million. Financing for the fast disbursing Sectoral Import Programs (SIPs) for the import of necessary inputs in sectors such as agriculture and industry was introduced under Lomé III. Despite the increase in absolute terms of the aid package, it decreased considerably over time from the vantage point of its per capita value. It dropped by 30.9% between Lomé I and II and 12.5% between Lomé II and III (European Report, 1988).

Lomé was also committed to promoting industrialization among the ACP states. The Industrial Development (CID) was to serve as the lead structure in this process. But it was hobbled by several factors. Funding for the transformation of the ACP economies, despite the guarantees, were never put in place. Even when this finally occurred, the funding was grossly inadequate. The CIDs budget, for example, was increased from ECU 40 million in Lomé III to 60 million in Lomé IV. This paled in the face of demands which increased dramatically, jumping from 575 projects in 1994 to 1,248 in 1995. Of those approved in 1995, only 400 could be funded. Even the European Investment Bank could not fill this lacuna. For a five-year period in the 1980s, Edwin Carrington, the Secretary General of the ACP notes, it could only disburse one third of the ECU 600 million over a five-year period. Over this period, the African Development Bank had invested over 1 billion US dollars (Parfitt and Bullock 1990).

Lomé IV bis, concluded for a twenty-year period after a fifteen-month debate of the European Commission's Green Book focuses on the fight against poverty. ACP attempts to protect their *acquis* were to no avail. Given the tendency in the EU to align its policies with those of the WTO and the Washington consensus, STABEX, SYSMIN, non-reciprocity and trading preferences have disappeared. But to cushion the shock, the European Union conceded that the present trading regime be maintained during a preparatory period (2000–2008). The parties shall also use this period to negotiate a new trading accord that would be put in place between 2008 and 2020 (Crozet and Lopez-Caniego 2000). Aid has been streamlined as it now consists of three instruments only: long-term, regional, and investment assistance. Conditionalities similar to those in the World Bank's Structural Adjustment Programs have been introduced. An early sign of the rapprochement was the insistence of the EU that Malawi accept conditionalities, prior to their definition by the Bank, as a basis for financing its SIP.

NANTANG JUA

References and Further Reading

Asante, S.K.B. "The European Union- Africa-Caribbean-Pacific (ACP), Lomé Convention" *Africa Insight*, Vol. 26, NO.4, 1996.

Barbarine O. *The Lomé Conventions and Development: An Empirical Assessment*. Avebury: Aldershot, 1994.

Davenport, Michael, Adrian Hewitt, and Antonique Koning. *Europe's Preferred Partners: The Lomé Countries in World Trade*. London: Overseas Development Institute, 1995.

Grilli. E. *The European Community and Developing Countries*. New York: Cambridge University Press, 1993.

Kappel, R. *Post-colonial Cooperation Africa and Europe: Is There a future for the Lomé Convention*. Leipzig: Institute of African Studies, 1996.

Lister, M. *The European Community and the Developing World: The Role of the Lomé Convention.*, Avebury: Aldershot, 1988.

Parfitt, Trevor W. and Sandy Bullock, "The Prospects for a New Lomé Convention: Structural Adjustment or Transformation", *Review of African Political Economy*, No. 47, Spring 1990.

Ravenhill J. *Collective Clientelism: The Lome Conventions and North-South Relations*. New York: Columbia University Press, 1995.

LUMUMBA, PATRICE

When Belgium rushed to grant independence to the Congo on June 30, 1960, Patrice Lumumba rapidly emerged as a key political contender for national leadership of this enormous country.

In the colonial division of Africa at the 1885–1886 Berlin Conference, King Leopold of Belgium became the only head of state to acquire his personal colony, the Congo Free State. Intense international pressure brought to bear on the abusive imperial rule of the country resulted in the takeover of the colony by the Belgian Parliament in 1908. Between then and 1960, Belgian governmental paternalism and protected private mining enterprise utterly failed to prepare the colony for independence.

Belgium's grudging reluctance to allow any indigenous political participation in the colony ultimately led to civil riot in the capital in 1959 and worsening unrest, which brought a complete breakdown of civic order. Hastily granted independence, agreed to only in January 1960, allowed for the first national elections only a month before the end of Belgian rule. No single party showed sufficient strength to form a government. The two leading contenders agreed to share the two main offices. Joseph Kasavubu became president and Patrice Lumumba assumed the prime minister post.

Within days after independence, the army mutinied and two outlying provinces immediately seceded. In the midst of chaos, the mineral-rich state became a pawn in the Cold War, which prompted the dispatch of a large United Nations peacekeeping force, staying in place until June 1964. Among all political rivals, only Lumumba appeared to stand for a unitary, centralized government, in part perhaps because he came from a minor tribal group in the country's distant interior. He served only two months as prime minister before he was incarcerated by rivals and thereafter murdered in January 1961 by opposition elements.

A fiery orator and leader of the only political party to seek national representation, he lacked the skills of coalition building to secure a national government. Viewed as visionary and martyr by his supporters and mercurial and diabolical by his opponents, he collected enemies easily. Intense, high energy, and uncompromising, he became engulfed in internal factionalism, seized upon as a symbol by anti-imperial elements elsewhere on the continent, and supported by Moscow seeking ideological gain in the emergent Third World.

The importance of Patrice Lumumba lay in his brief leading role as an indigenous, Third World, anti-imperial spokesman, and early pursuer of a wider, non-tribal, political posture, which simulated a nationalist impulse. Africa's pre-colonial history, characterized by massive internal people migrations with no common sense of destiny, followed by colonial-drawn artificial borders and imperial rule, left Sub-Saharan Africa without a common legacy of organizing political sentiments on a macro scale. Factionalism, clientelism, and tribalism, as opposed to nationalism, for the most part have governed Africa's political relations. Lumumba tried to change that course for his country.

JAMES E. WINKATES

References and Further Reading

Lemarchand, Rene'. *Political Awakening in the Congo*. Berkeley, CA: University of California Press, 1964.

Merriam, Alan P. *Congo; Background of Conflict*. Evanston, IL: Northwestern University Press, 1961.

Witte, Ludo de. *The assassination of Lumumba*. New York: Verso, 2001.

Young, Crawford. *Politics in the Congo; Decolonization and Independence*. Princeton, NJ: Princeton University Press, 1965.

LUTHULI, ALBERT

Albert John Luthuli (1898–1967) (also spelled "Lutuli"), Africa's first winner of the Nobel Prize for Peace and the president-general of the African National Congress (ANC) from 1952 until his death, is recognized as the father of the non-violent campaign for civil rights in apartheid South Africa.

His exact birthday unknown, Luthuli was born Albert John Mvumbi (Zulu for "continuous rain") Luthuli around 1898 in Southern Rhodesia where his father served as a Seventh-Day Adventist missionary at the Solusia Mission Station (near Bulawayo) among the Matabele people. After his father passed away around 1906, Luthuli and his mother returned to their native Groutville in the Natal region of South Africa where his grandfather served as chief of a small Zulu community, an elective post that Luthuli, after many years of being a teacher, applied for in 1935 and won. This became the first occasion when Luthuli's Christian faith (instilled through his family and education) was tested by the everyday realities of the country's racial politics. In 1946, while chief, Luthuli also briefly served as a member of the Natives Representative Council, a board of black South Africans advising white senators who "represented" the black population at the parliament. The board was abolished after it protested the government's violent suppression of the black miners' 1946 strike at the gold mines of Witwatersrand.

Luthuli joined the African National Congress (ANC) in 1944, and became the president of the party's Natal province office in 1951. When on June 26, 1952, Luthuli led the party's non-violent "Defiance Campaign" against the discriminatory laws passed by the Afrikaner National Party, which ruled the country since 1948, the government deposed him from his Chieftainship, an act which only made Luthuli's political stature more prominent. In response, Luthuli wrote "The Road to Freedom is Via the Cross,"

a speech issued in public barely a month before the ANC elected Luthuli its President-General in December 1952.

Regardless of the repeated bans the government issued against the ANC under the "Suppression of Communism Act," Luthuli remained politically active and was arrested and brought to court along with 155 others for high treason in December of 1956 (a charge he was acquitted of a year later for lack of evidence). Luthuli continued to organize successful, peaceful strikes throughout the late 1950s, but after the Sharpeville Massacre in 1960, when state forces crushed a peaceful protest of black Africans protesting the pass-laws, and the government outlawed all African (black) political organizations, Luthuli began to experience his growing irrelevance as a tempered voice within his now banned party. On December 16, 1961, a day after Luthuli returned from Oslo as the first African to receive the Nobel Peace prize for his non-violent struggle against racial discrimination, Unkhonto we Sizwe ("The Spear of the Nation"), ANC's military wing dramatically announced its emergence by attacking government installations. Luthuli's non-violent campaign had been abandoned and a new era was dawning for resistance against apartheid.

Luthuli remained as ANC president-general until his death on July 21, 1967, when he was hit by a train while on his regular walk near his small farm where he had been living in government-enforced isolation.

YIANNA LIATSOS

See also African National Congress; Apartheid; South Africa

References and Further Reading

Benson, Mary. *Chief Albert Luthuli of South Africa*. London: Oxford University Press, 1963.

Callan, Edward, ed. *Albert John Luthuli and the South African Race Conflict*. Kalamazoo, MI: Western Michigan University Press, 1962.

Gordimer, Nadine (1959). "Chief Luthuli." *Atlantic Monthly*, 203: 34–39.

Legum, Colin and Margaret. *The Bitter Choice: Eight South Africans' Resistance to Tyranny*. Cleveland, OH: World Pub. Co., 1968.

M

MACAU/MACAO

Macau is located in East Asia approximately 60 kilometers (37 miles) southwest of Hong Kong, bordering China. It comprises Macau city and the islands of Taipa and Coloane. The country has a land area of 21 square kilometers (8.3 square miles). Comparatively, the territory of Macau is a quarter of the size of Manhattan. Macau is linked to the Chinese province of Guangdong by a narrow land corridor.

The population of Macau was estimated at 469,903 in July 2003, and it is virtually all urban. In 2003 the birth rate stood at 12.07 per 1,000 and this low level is mainly attributed to the effect of urbanization. The death rate in that year stood at 3.85 per 1,000. The estimated population growth rate is 1.72%, although unofficial estimates show higher figures due to high net migration rate, which, according to the *CIA World Factbook,* stands at the level of 8.93 migrants per 1,000. Macau has one of the highest population densities in the world, at around 22,370 people per square kilometer (or 58,100 per square mile).

Macau was established as a Portuguese colony on the small islands on the Pearl River in 1556. Gradually it became an important international trading port that remained under Portuguese control until the twentieth century. Its significance as a trading center rose over several centuries as the Chinese government maintained a policy of voluntary isolation from the world, allowing international trade only in few assigned ports. Portugal proclaimed Macau a free port in 1849. However, in the nineteenth century the importance of Macau declined with the rise of the British colony of Hong Kong. In 1951 Portugal officially made Macau an overseas province, and in 1974 the new democratic Portuguese government offered Macau back to China. On December 20, 1999, Macau was officially returned to Chinese jurisdiction. Macau became a Special Administrative Region (SAR) of the People's Republic of China (PRC) with a "high degree of autonomy" in domestic affairs and remained so for a period of fifty years, under the principle of "one country, two systems." In 1999 Edmund Ho became the first governor appointed by China's central government. He replaced General de Rocha Vieira, the last Portuguese governor of the territory. According to the Macau's Basic Law, the territory's legal code, the governor has a strong policy-making and executive power, which is limited only by the central government in Beijing and by the Macau legislature.

Traditionally, the Macau economy has relied on manufacturing and services. Macau, like Hong Kong and Singapore, has an export-oriented economy, which benefits from growing trade with Western Europe and the United States. Throughout the twentieth century it specialized in manufacturing various products for export and servicing international merchants and bankers. Throughout the twentieth century the Macau administration has maintained a free-market economy, which, in combination with local entrepreneurship and political stability, contributed to economic growth. Macau's main exports are textiles, clothing, and services, though it stays behind Hong Kong and Singapore in the proportion of value-added production. Tourism also plays a significant role in the national economy. However, it was the gambling industry that greatly contributed to the image of Macau as a major tourist destination among residents of Southeast Asia and China. Gambling is the main source of revenue in Macau, accounting for 44% of total revenue (1999). The pataca, the Macau currency, is linked to the Hong Kong dollar at the rate of 1.03 patacas per Hong Kong dollar. Unlike South Korea, Thailand, or Indonesia, the pataca has remained remarkably stable. The gambling industry also attracted highly organized criminal syndicates, the so-called "triads," which are involved in gambling, illegal trafficking of persons, prostitution, and pirated production of various goods, including music and computer CDs. During the 1990s the government made considerable efforts to restrain and eliminate the power of these criminal groups. This campaign contributed to a decrease in violent crime, although experts say that the "triads" still have considerable stakes in the various sectors of the local economy.

Recent Development

Since handover in 1999 Macau has continued to attract investments and technologies to its manufacturing industry (mainly textiles, clothing, toys, and electronics) due to its low cost and efficient range of production for export to Europe and the United States. However, the manufacturing sector share in the gross domestic product (GDP) has been steadily declining due to the strong competition from China's Special Economic Zone in Guangdong. The Macau administration has considered liberalizing and promoting further its gambling, tourism, and financial industries in order to attract new investments and obtain additional sources of revenue. Between 1997 and 1999 the Macau economy experienced three consecutive years of recession caused by the Asian financial crisis of 1997. However, the country experienced a remarkable recovery between 2000 and 2004. The travel and gambling industries were also hit by the region-wide fear of the Severe Acute Respiratory Syndrome (SARS) in 2003 and in 2004, although Macau itself managed to escape an outbreak of SARS.

Macroeconomic stability and success in structural changes brought prosperity and better living standards to Macau. The country's average incomes remain far above that in the neighboring People's Republic of China, and immigrants continue to travel to Macau searching for jobs and better standards of living.

RAFIS ABAZOV

See also East Asia: History and Economic Development

References and Further Reading

Joao De Pina-Cabral, et al. *Between China and Europe: Person, Culture, and Emotion in Macao (London School of Economics Monographs on Social Anthropology)*. New York: Continuum, 2002.
Macau: EIU Country Report. London: Economist Intelligent Unit, December 2003.
Macau: EIU Country Profile. London: Economist Intelligent Unit, 2003.
Porter, J. *Macau, the Imagining City: Culture and Society, 1557 to the Present*. Boulder, CO: Westview Press, 2000.
World Trade Center. *Trade Policy Review: Macao, China 2001 (Trade Policy Review)*. Washington, DC: World Trade Center, 2001.

MACEDONIA

Location

Macedonia, officially referred to as Former Yugoslav Republic of Macedonia (FYROM), is located in southeastern Europe. Macedonia occupies a strategic and central position in the Balkans as a communication axis between the cities of Belgrade in Serbia-Montenegro and Thessaloniki, Greece. With a land area of 25,713 square kilometers, Macedonia, a landlocked country, is surrounded by Albania to the west, Bulgaria to the east, Greece to the south, and Serbia-Montenegro to the north. The population of 2,046,209 (July 2001) is divided among Slavic-Macedonian (64.2%), Albanian (25.2%), Turks (3.8%), Gypsies (2.7%), and Serbs (1.8%).

Land and Climate

Macedonia is a mountainous country. The highest peak, Golem Korag, lies along the Albanian border (2,753 meters). The country is bisected by the Vardar River running from northwest to southeast. Three major lakes are divided by at least one frontier: Lake Ohrid, Lake Prespa (west), and Lake Doiran (southeast). The Macedonian climate is continental with warm and dry summers and relatively cold winters. Macedonia is located in an area of seismic risks. In 1963 an earthquake heavily damaged the capital city Skopje (six hundred thousand inhabitants).

Current Economic Situation

Macedonia is a poor country with limited resources (chromium, lead, zinc, manganese, tungsten, nickel, low-grade iron ore, sulfur, and timber). The industrial sector is dominated by light industry, though overall underdeveloped and outmoded (oil refining, mining, textile production, and manufacturing). Agricultural products include wheat, corn, other vegetables, rice, and tobacco. Tourism is also an important sector around the lakes of Ohrid and Prespa.

Macedonia faced an irregular transition after its independence from Yugoslavia in 1991. The UN sanctions against Yugoslavia, one of Macedonia's major markets, and two Greek embargoes (1992, 1994) damaged economic growth until 1995. Although the economy improved after 1995, these results were undermined with the bombing of Serbia (1999) and the Albanian insurgency (2001). The GDP was negative until 1995. It went from 2% in 1996 to 4% in 1998, 0.3% in 2002 then rose to 2.8% in 2003. Between 1992 and 2001 Macedonia benefited from about 570 million Euros, mostly in grants, from the European Union. Germany, Greece, Italy, and the US are the major trade partners. Like most of the ex-communist states, Macedonia suffers from corruption and a substantial "gray economy," which for 1998 was estimated to account for about 50% of the Republic's GDP. Unemployment is constantly rising: 32% in 2000 and estimated at 44% in 2003.

History Until 1945

The history of Macedonia is linked to a larger area, an historical region also named Macedonia. It included the northern part of modern Greece and the southwestern part of Bulgaria. At the end of the fourteenth century, like most of the Balkan Peninsula, the historic Macedonia was integrated into the Ottoman Empire. From the nineteenth century on, the destiny of Macedonia was marked by turbulence with the decline of the Ottoman Empire and the formation of new states as Greece, Serbia, and Bulgaria competed to integrate Macedonian territories within their borders. The Internal Macedonian Revolutionary Organization, created in 1893, fought to promote Macedonian national identity.

The Balkan Wars of 1912–1913 brought a radical solution: partition. The treaty of Bucharest, signed on August 10, 1913, established the departure of the Turks and the division of the Macedonian territories amongst four states: Greece (Aegean Macedonia, 51.3%), Serbia (Vardar Macedonia, 38.4%), and Bulgaria (Pirin Macedonia, 10.1%), while Albania was granted a small territory. Each of these states began to assimilate the population into their respective territories and the name Macedonia disappeared from the European map.

During 1945–1946 the part of Macedonia that had been integrated into Serbia became one of the six republics that constituted Yugoslavia under the name Yugoslav Socialist People's Republic of Macedonia.

Macedonia's Developments After 1945

After 1945, for the first time, the Yugoslav government provided a national Macedonian frame. National institutions were created, a president and a parliament were elected, a language had been agreed upon in 1947, the Macedonian Orthodox church was reestablished in 1958, and the Macedonian Academy of Sciences created in 1967 promoted Macedonian culture and strengthened national identity. Until Tito's death (1980) Macedonia remained under the control of Belgrade. The creation of Macedonia served the purpose of establishing a difference between the Slavs living in this country and those living in Bulgaria or in Serbia. Under Tito's regime, Macedonia benefited from substantial economical and financial aid that contributed to setting up a modern infrastructure. However, social progress remained slow and limited. Macedonia's people have undergone a major transition from a traditional patriarchal rural society to a mixed urban industrial-agricultural society with 40% still living in the countryside.

Macedonia's departure from Yugoslavia in 1991 is considered as a success story as the country remained at peace during the war of 1991–1995 when Yugoslavia collapsed. On September 8, 1991, following a referendum, independence was proclaimed.

The transition toward democracy was realized with the establishment of a parliamentary system: a new constitution was adopted (1991), a multiple political party society emerged, and elections have been held every four years. The president Kiro Gligorov (1991–1999), a major political figure since the 1960s, was succeeded by Boris Trajkovski, who died in a plane crash in February 2004. The ex-prime minister Branko Crvenkovki was elected president. However, corruption plagues the system as clientelism, as with the rest of the region, is endemic.

The development of Macedonia has been challenged by two major issues: First, the international recognition was delayed by Greece's opposition to the use of the name and flag, considered as Hellenic symbols. In

1993, the UN recognized the state under the temporary name FYROM, a move that was followed by most of the EU states. Greece lifted its embargo only in 1995. Bulgaria was the first Balkan state to recognize the independent Macedonia in 1991, but it denied the existence of the Macedonian nation. Albania established diplomatic relations with Skopje in 1993.

Second, the status of the Albanian minority has led to a continuing major crisis. They are concentrated in the western part of Macedonia around the city of Tetovo. Following independence, Skopje has had an uneasy cooperation with the Albanians: since the elections of 1994 Albanians participate in the political arena and hold legislative, ministerial, and administrative positions. However, Albanians ask to be recognized as "constituent people" and continue to feel treated as "second-class citizens." In 1999, during the war in Kosovo, around 350,000 Albanian refugees entered FYROM, threatening to disrupt the fragile political balance. Later many returned to Kosovo but tensions grew.

In 2001, the country narrowly escaped civil war when Albanian rebel members of the National Liberation Army took up arms and started major fights around Tetovo. The Albanians were divided between moderate and nationalist elements: some were asking for full equality with the Macedonians while others defended the creation of "greater Albania" or even "greater Kosovo." In June of that year, EU officials negotiated a cease-fire that was followed by the Ohrid Agreement, signed in August, in which NATO soldiers would disarm the guerrillas. In November, the parliament modified the constitution granting broader rights to the Albanian minority. Albanian became one of the country's two official languages. However, the situation remains volatile. The country still needs international security assistance. UN and NATO forces have maintained a presence since 1993 and 1997, respectively.

NADINE AKHUND

See also Central and Eastern Europe: History and Economic Development; Central and Eastern Europe: International Relations

References and Further Reading

Barker, Elisabeth. *Macedonia: Its Place in Balkan Power Politics.* Hertfordshire: Royal Institute of International Affairs, 1950.
Crampton, Richard, J. *The Balkans Since the Second World War.* New York: Longman, 2002.
Danforth, Loring M. *The Macedonian Conflict: Ethnic Nationalism in a Transnational World.* Princeton, NJ: Princeton University Press, 1995.
Hristo, Andonov-Poljanski, ed. *Documents on the Struggle of the Macedonian People for Independence and a Nation-State,* Vol. 2. Skopje, Macedonia: 1985.
Jelavich, Barbara. *History of the Balkans,* Vol. 2. Cambridge, UK: Cambridge University Press, 1983.
Kofos, Evangelos. *Nationalism and Communism in Macedonia.* Thessaloniki, Greece: Institute for Balkan studies, 1964.
Perry, Duncan. *The Politics of Terror: The Macedonian Liberation Movement 1893–1903.* Durham, NC: Duke University Press, 1988.
Pettifer, James, ed. *The New Macedonian Question.* New York: St. Martin's Press, 1999.
Poulton, Hugh. *Who Are the Macedonians?* Bloomington, IN: Indiana University Press, 2000.
Roudometoff, Victor. *Collective Memory, National Identity, and Ethnic Conflict: Greece, Bulgaria, and the Macedonian Question.* London: Praeger, 2002.

MACHEL, SAMORA

Samora Moises Machel, third of five sons in a family that was relatively well-off by local standards, was born on September 29, 1933, at Chilembene, now the Chókwè district, Gaza province, in southern Mozambique. His father, Mandande, retired from the gold mines of South Africa and invested in agriculture and cattle.

Declining an offer to enter a seminary, in 1952 Samora began a nursing course in the Miguel Bombarda Hospital in Lourenço Marques (now Maputo) to become a full-time nurse in 1954. When the Mozambique Liberation Front, FRELIMO, was formed in Dar es Salaam in June 1962 under the leadership of Eduardo Mondlane, Samora was ready to join it. In 1961–1963 Machel was chased and interrogated by the Portuguese political police PIDE, and he decided to leave the country.

Machel was among the second group of FRELIMO recruits sent to Algeria for military training in 1963. On his return he was put in charge of the Kongwa training camp in Dodoma, and entered the war zones of Mozambique in November 1965. A year later, Machel was appointed military commander of FRELIMO. In April 1969 after Mondlane was killed, Michel was elected to lead the movement, confirmed by the Central Committee in May 1970.

Machel was independent Mozambique's first president. He initiated a single-party Marxist state, nationalized all industry, and abolished private land ownership. He was a devoted Marxist, who firmly believed that centrally planned collective economy will bring prosperity to his country and all Africa. With Mozambican support, Zimbabwe, formerly Rhodesia, achieved independence in April 1980.

In September 1980 formal ranks were introduced into the armed forces, and Machel himself became

Marshal of the Republic. In 1982, to prevent South African attacks, he requested negotiations, which resulted in the Nkomati Accord on Non-Aggression and Good Neighborliness, signed on March 16, 1984, by Machel and P. W. Botha of South Africa. Samora Machel continued the search for peace in the region, which involved negotiations with Presidents Banda of Malawi, Kaunda of Zambia, and Mugabe of Zimbabwe. In the fall of 1986 Machel threatened to place missiles along the border with Malawi and close it to traffic. On October 19, Samora Machel flew to Zambia for a summit meeting to discuss a solution to destabilization with the presidents of Zambia, Angola, and Zaire. He never returned—the Tupolev 134A in which he flew crashed mysteriously into a hillside at Mbuzini in South Africa, killing Machel and all thirty-four members of his team.

STEPHAN E. NIKOLOV

See also FRELIMO (Front for the Liberation of Mozambique); Mozambique

References and Further Reading

Christie, Ian. *Samora Machel. A Biography.* London: Panaf.; New York: St. Martin's Press, 1989.
Munslow, Barry, ed. *Samora Machel: An African Revolutionary. Selected Speeches and Writings.* Translated by Michael Wolfers. London: Zed Books, 1985.

MADAGASCAR

Madagascar is an island country 250 miles off Africa's southeastern coast. At 224,500 square miles it is the world's fourth-largest island. The narrow shape, 995 miles long and 360 miles wide, is significant as it contributes to great climatic differences between regions. Madagascar's total Gross Domestic Product (GDP) is $5.5 billion (2003), making it one of the world's smallest economies. Madagascar has one of the world's lowest levels of development, and 72% of the population lives in abject poverty.

Madagascar has a population of approximately 17.5 million people, growing at 3% per year. While this makes for a relatively low population density, the scant 5% of arable land creates agricultural pressures for a vast portion of the island's inhabitants. A 30% urbanization rate, increasing rapidly, creates a further development challenge.

Madagascar is generally considered to have eighteen ethnic groups. People of the largest ethnic group, the *Merina* of the central highlands, tend to have stronger Indo-Malay features where coastal groups tend to have darker African features. This ethno-racial divide is also the most important socio-political divide in Madagascar's history.

Europeans first came to Madagascar in 1500. Feudalism began to grow with the fomentation of a caste system and monarchism which, as in Europe, grew out of feudal centralizing tendencies. A *Merina* Monarchy began to take seed in the eighteenth century. Small lordly kingdoms reacted to hostilities by supporting the rise of King Andrianampoinimerina in 1787. When his son Radama took the throne in 1810 he created an alliance with the British. By the time he died, eighteen years later, most of the island was under *Merina* control, and a class system began to rise with coastal peoples at the bottom.

In the 1880s and 1890s Madagascar felt the blows of both British and French expansionism. The French sought to overtake the island while certain *Merina* groups sought, in vain, British support to repel them. On August 6, 1896, France deposed Queen Ranavalona III and made General Joseph Gallieni governor. Madagascar was colonized by the French.

From 1896 to 1946 the French ruled directly but used the *Merina* Monarchy as an organizational mechanism. As a result, *Merina* benefited disproportionately in terms of trade, jobs, education, and quality of life. In 1947 rebels, seeing the relatively small numbers of French soldiers and hearing rumors of American support for their cause, attacked military garrisons and settlers. The response was epic. By the time rebels surrendered in March 1949 an estimated one hundred thousand people were killed by French soldiers, soldiers brought by the French from Senegal, and *Merina*. The *Merina* divide from coastal peoples, especially *Betsimisiraka* of the northeastern coast, was made all the greater.

At independence it was clear that a *Merina* president would lead to conflict. Philibert Tsiranana, an ethnic *Tsimihety*, was an original provincial assembly delegate who became prime minister in 1958. When Madagascar became independent in 1960 the French supported his rise to power. Adamantly pro-French, many accused him of fostering neo-colonialism. By 1969 political patronage, economic favoritism, and poor liberalization left the economy in tatters. Tsirinana was ousted by General Gabriel Ramanantsoa, a *Merina* from a high caste, in 1972 in what many Malagasy consider to be the country's "real" independence. Violence against *Merina* rose as the economy continued to slide. Ramanantsoa's power was gradually being undermined by General Richard Ratsimandrava in 1973. Also *Merina*, Ratsimandrava was more palatable to the population as he came from a slave caste. When Ratsimandrava ousted Ramanantsoa in February 1975, his intended reforms and inclusiveness threatened the bourgeois *Merina* establishment.

He was assassinated six days later. The military directorate appointed the Foreign Minister, Lieutenant-Commander Didier Ratsiraka, to head of state. A *Betsimisiraka* who spoke perfect *Merina* dialect and French, he was seen as someone who could win the hearts of the coast while enriching the *Merina* elite.

While nominally in the Chinese tradition, Ratsiraka's government was more anti-Western than it was pro-ideology. In December 1977 Ratsiraka introduced a new investment plan leading to the massive nationalization of private industry. The result was catastrophic. Within three years inflation was rampant, national debt was mounting, and the currency was kept afloat only by unrealistic political controls over exchange rates. In 1981 Madagascar requested the assistance of the International Monetary Fund (IMF).

The 1980s saw the rise of a small elite class in Madagascar through the opening of doors to the West. However, economic rationalization meant a significant devaluation of the currency and a 25% freefall in gross domestic product. Life for the majority poor became much more difficult. To maintain power, Ratsiraka became politically more autocratic. Elections were merely ratifications of leadership. The only candidates who could run were members of the socialist National Front for the Defense of the Revolution (FNDR). Opposition leaders fled to France where they formed their own alliances. Civil society groups formed, such as the Council of Christian Churches of Madagascar (FFKM). These both became political forces directly challenging the president's authority.

Heading into the 1989 elections, a strong and growing opposition fragmented and President Ratsiraka gained ground in the legislature, winning a sizable victory in the presidential elections. However, his successes were his undoing as it led to a groundswell of support for his ouster. With no Soviet Union to turn to, Ratsiraka had to turn back to France and the West. He instituted more economic reforms, but it was too little too late. On June 10, 1991, Zafy Albert, head of the *Hery Velona* (Living Forces) opposition coalition, led a one hundred thousand-person civil servants strike, bringing the country to a halt. Zafy set up a parallel government and forced Ratsiraka into a transitional government on October 31, 1991. A new constitution was written and adopted and new elections were held in November 1992. After a second round of elections Zafy became the head of Madagascar's first democratic republic.

Madagascar's third republic was a significant break from the past. A referendum in September 1995 changed the character of the Constitution, shifting power from the prime minister to the president. While a successful revolutionary, Zafy proved to be a less-than-impressive president. His efforts to centralize power brought accusations of political malfeasance. He also suffered from the persistent divide between *Merina* and the coastal population. He was accused of corruption and exceeding his constitutional power and was impeached in July 1996.

In the elections that followed, the only viable choices presented to voters were the former autocrat claiming he was reformed or the recently impeached Zafy. Ratsiraka became president again in 1997 and his AREMA party gained control of the legislature a year later. A 1998 referendum pulled power from the capital to Ratsiraka's base in the provinces. The country saw modest economic gains, but satisfaction with Ratsiraka both at home and abroad was low as he sought to re-establish his personalized network of rule.

Six months before the December 16, 2001, presidential elections it appeared there was none of the growing field of candidates who could challenge Ratsiraka. Then Marc Ravalomanana, the handsome, popular mayor of Antananarivo, declared his desire to run. Ravalomanana is a self-made man—founder of Tiko, the country's largest food products company. He campaigned on a slogan for national unity and change, promising to use his business acumen to move the country forward.

By election day it was clear Ravalomanana was the favored candidate. However, the National Electoral Council (CNE) of the sitting Ratsiraka government shut down the transparency of the vote-counting process. Both Ravalomanana and a committee of independent observers said that Ravalomanana had won better than 50% of the vote. But the CNE said he won only 46.6%, requiring a run-off election. Fearing electoral manipulation, Ravalomanana refused to stand in a run-off. The matter went to the High Constitutional Court (HCC), but Ratsiraka had stacked the court prior to the elections so it let the results stand. Ravalomanana took his cause to the streets. By the end of January 2002 more than half a million people took to the streets of the capital, Antananarivo, and the country was shut down. On February 22 Ravalomanana declared himself president. This set off a maelstrom and the country was Balkanized between Ratsiraka supporters in the provinces and Ravalomanana supporters in the capital. Heated military and diplomatic actions ensued until Ratsiraka was ultimately forced to flee from Madagascar on June 14, 2002.

Ravalomanana's presidency has been characterized by both a political and an economic sea change. Politically, he has worked to grow the business class while strengthening democratic institutions. Economically, he rapidly entered into a liberalization program, which drew significant support from the World Bank and the IMF. Both of these actions have deepened Madagascar's relationship with liberal democracies around the world, most notably the United States and Germany.

RICHARD R. MARCUS

References and Further Reading

Brown, Mervyn. *A History of Madagascar*. Princeton, NJ: Markus Wiener, 1995.

Campbell, Gwyn. *An Economic History of Imperial Madagascar 1750–1895, or, The Rise and Fall of an Island Empire*. New York: Cambridge University Press, 2004.

Cole, Jennifer. *Forget Colonialism? Sacrifice and the Art of Memory in Madagascar*. Berkeley, CA: University of California Press, 2001.

Feeley-Harnik, Gillian. *A Green Estate: Restoring Independence in Madagascar*. Washington, DC: Smithsonian Books, 1991.

Goodman, Steven M. and Bruce D. Patterson, eds. *Natural Change and Human Impact in Madagascar*. Washington, DC: Smithsonian Books, 1997.

Kull, Christian. *Isle of Fire: The Political Ecology of Landscape Burning in Madagascar*. Chicago: University of Chicago Press, 2004.

Larson, Pier M. *History and Memory in the Age of Enslavement*. Portsmouth, NH: Heinemann, 2000.

MAGHRIB PEOPLES

The region known as the *Maghrib* (pronounced and sometimes written as Maghreb) corresponds to the modern North African states of Morocco, Algeria, Tunisia, Libya, and the disputed region of the Western Sahara (currently under Moroccan sovereignty). Mauritania is often associated with the region in both social and political terms, but due to geography and a more heterogeneous population, it can best be termed an intermediate state between North and sub-Saharan Africa. The term Maghrib is itself an Arabic term meaning "west" and people throughout the Arab world sometimes refer to North Africans (minus Egypt) as *al-Maghribi*, or westerners. The region is dominated by the Sahara desert and Atlas Mountains, while the majority of the population (roughly 90%) lives along the more fertile Mediterranean and Atlantic coasts.

The inhabitants of the region are predominantly Caucasoid "Arab-Berbers," but this term implies a complete and even fusion of the two groups, which is not the case. Arab (in the Maghrib sense) can best be termed a linguistic classification that covers an expansive area, whereas the Berbers are the region's dominant group in both genetic and historical terms. In fact, most Arabs are believed to be *arabized* (those who adopted the Arabic language, culture, and Muslim faith) Berbers and other peoples as well as some

being of actual partial Arab ancestry. The Berbers (derived from a Greek term meaning *foreigner*) refer to themselves as the *Imazighen* or free men and are the region's earliest known inhabitants. They appear to have expanded from their North African base further south into the Sahara even before the arrival of Islam. Both displaced and mingled with black sub-Saharan peoples in what is today Mauritania (a term that was once used to denote a region overlapping Morocco and Algeria), as is often the case with many of the Tuareg, who are well-known in the west as the Blue Men due to their distinctive blue robes. Interaction with sub-Saharan Africa has had a significant impact throughout the Maghrib for centuries, with some groups showing partial sub-Saharan ancestry, and cultural aspects such as music have definitive black African roots. In contrast, numerous theories abound about the origins of the Berbers, who do not appear to be of sub-Saharan origin, with the latest identifying them with the Capsian culture that inhabited the region between 9000 and 7000 BCE. The Berbers appear to have migrated from their Red Sea homeland as part of a larger Afro-Asiatic group that dispersed many millennia ago and settled in North Africa, with some having reached as far west as the Canary Islands (a people there called the *Guanche* are believed to be of partial Berber descent). Modern self-identifying Berbers appear to be a majority only in Morocco, where estimates place the population at roughly 60%. There is also an active minority in Algeria (up to 33% of population), particularly in the Kabyle region, that is quite prominent and vocal about Berber cultural rights. Small numbers of Berbers are also found in Tunisia and Libya where the arabization process has significantly reduced any overt examples of Berber culture. By contrast, Mauritania has a more stratified society with Arab-Berbers acting as a single unit, but one that is outnumbered by the so-called black Maurs and sub-Saharan peoples. Unlike their Maghribi neighbours, the vast majority of people in both Tunisia and Libya simply identify themselves as Arabs.

The Maghrib peoples are a complex combination of groups who have settled in the region over time. Phoenicians, Greeks, Romans, Vandals, and Byzantines have been prominent invaders and immigrants to the region. Christianity took root in the region a few centuries after the death of Christ and prominent figures such as the half-Berber theologian St. Augustine of Hippo played a pivotal role in the early years of the faith. During the seventh century CE, Muslim Arabs conquered the region and named it the Maghrib, but it was not until the second millennium that the majority of the region's inhabitants became nominal Arabic speakers and Islam fully supplanted

Christianity. Adding to the cultural landscape were Iberian Muslims and Jews who were forced to flee to North Africa following the Spanish *Reconquista*. Ottoman Turks took control of most of the North African coast by the 1600s and during their reign, Barbary pirates and corsairs terrorized European and American vessels. Finally, European expansion resulted in French control of Algeria and Tunisia during the nineteenth century and Morocco by the early twentieth century. Spain also emerged as a dominant power in Morocco and the Western Sahara region, and later Italy would attempt to colonize Libya. During this period large numbers of *colons* (colonists) arrived from southern Europe and France, and they eventually made up 10% of the population in Algeria alone. During this tumultuous period, the colons dominated all aspects of sociopolitical life, and this persisted until their expulsion following the various independence movements that culminated with Algerian independence in 1962. Spain is the exception as they continue to hold two small city-states called Ceuta and Melilla along the Moroccan Mediterranean coast.

The modern states of North Africa reflect these nineteenth- and twentieth-century borders and do not correspond to any specific ethnic or linguistic cleavages. Currently, the countries of the region associate with each other through the Maghrib Union and are prominent in the Arab League as well. Sunni Islam, the Arabic language, and a rise in Berber nationalism as well as the use of French (except in Libya) in aspects of public life are some of the common traits found in various parts of the region. Mauritania has a different situation due to the ethnic and linguistic conflict between its "white" Arab-Berber minority and the largely sub-Saharan majority. In addition, millions of North Africans have moved to Western Europe for various reasons ranging from early movements of Francophiles who fled after various independence movements to those seeking better economic prospects. Their cultural impact has altered the landscape, particularly in France, with some signs of assimilation as well as cultural conflict. Remittances by guest workers have been important for the economies of Algeria, Tunisia, and Morocco.

The region remains largely undemocratic by Western European standards. Democracy has had a sporadic history in the region with Algeria having reversed elections when Islamists won preliminary elections in 1991, while Tunisia has moved towards some plurality recently by allowing opposition parties. Morocco has a monarchy that allows multiple political parties to take part in its government, while Libya continues to be dominated by the vague yet totalitarian regime of Colonel Muammar Qaddafi. Mauritania has had

elections since 1991, but accusations of fraud and single-party dominance have marred progress there as well. Islamic jurisprudence and tradition play a substantial role throughout the region, ranging from the more secular societies of Algeria and Tunisia to the so-called Green Law found in Libya. The impact upon women's rights has been fraught with difficulty, but some limited progress has been made in Algeria and Tunisia where women are increasingly entering the workplace, while Berber women, especially those in villages at the foothills of the Atlas Mountains, often go unveiled and share many responsibilities with men as they have since pre-Islamic times.

Economic development has transformed the region and globalisation has helped to integrate it into the world economy, with the EU emerging as an important trading partner. Oil and natural gas play prominent roles in terms of regional income for Libya and Algeria, while Morocco and Tunisia have more mixed economies. Tunisia is also engaged in significant manufacturing and has become an important tourist attraction due to its appealing Mediterranean climate, inexpensive environment, and stable sociopolitical landscape. Agriculture is quite important in Morocco and Mauritania, but remains limited due to unpredictable rainfall. Capitalism and free enterprise have expanded throughout the region in recent years with mixed results. Urbanization is a continuing trend as more and more people have moved to the cities seeking employment. Literacy and education have made inroads throughout much of the region with some Maghribis studying abroad as well. The Maghrib has emerged as the most economically vibrant region of Africa and is more on a par with the Middle East to which it is culturally, historically, and ethnically very closely linked.

ALI AHMED

See also Algeria; Berbers; Libya; Mauritania; Morocco; North Africa: History and Economic Development; Tunisia

References and Further Reading

Abu-Nasr, Jamil M. *A History of the Maghreb*. Cambridge, UK: Cambridge University Press, 1971.

Brett, Michael and Elizabeth Fentress. *The Berbers*. Oxford, UK: Blackwell, 1997.

Gellner, Ernest and Charles Micaud, eds. *Arabs and Berbers: From Tribe to Nation in North Africa*. Lexington, MA: Lexington Books, 1972.

Hourani, Albert. *A History of the Arab Peoples*. New York: Warner, 1992.

Lapidus, Ira M. *A History of Islamic Societies*. Cambridge, UK: Cambridge University Press, 1988.

Metz, Helen C. *Algeria, A Country Study (Area Handbook Series)*. Washington, DC: Federal Research Division, Library of Congress, 1995.

Nelson, Harry D. *Morocco, A Country Study (Area Handbook Series)*. Washington, DC: Federal Research Division, Library of Congress, 1986.

MAGSAYSAY, RAMON

Ramon Magsaysay (1907–1957) was born at Iba, the capital of Zambales Province, Philippines, on August 31, 1907. Son of an artisan, he graduated from Jose Rizal College in 1932. He worked as a mechanic at Try Transportation Bus Company in Manila where he became general manager.

Early in World War II, Magsaysay served with the Philippine 31st Infantry Division. During the Japanese occupation he fought as a guerrilla and became commander of the Zambales Military District composed of some ten thousand fighters located near Mount Pinatubo. The Japanese army put a never-collected reward of fifty thousand pesos on his head.

In February 1945, US General Douglas MacArthur appointed Magsaysay as military governor of Zambales. In 1946 he ran as a Liberal for his nation's House of Representatives and won with the biggest margin in Zambales history. He served as a member of the House Committee on National Defense. Reelected in 1949 he became the committee's chairman.

In April 1950 Ramon Magsaysay journeyed to Washington, DC, seeking grants-in-aid. There he met Colonel Edward Geary Lansdale, who would become his lifelong friend and mentor.

That same year, President Quirino asked him to become Secretary of National Defense and Magsaysay quickly accepted. He instituted many reforms to counter widespread corruption within the armed services: He raised the pay of his soldiers. He made constant and unannounced visits to military units. He ordered military lawyers to represent civilians who could not afford to hire one. His soldiers labored on public works projects. And he harshly punished military crimes.

Magsaysay instituted a system whereby anyone throughout the country who had a problem could send a free telegram to him, and he promised that it would be answered within a few days. The first year he received fifty thousand of them—and answered all of them.

He fought the *Hukbo ng Bayan Laban sa Hapon* (People's Anti-Japanese Army) commonly known as the Hukbalahaps, or Huks. Having fought as leftist guerrillas during the war, they were infuriated by the central government's treatment of their demands and began an insurrection. Official efforts to destroy them failed.

Sometime earlier Colonel Lansdale had been assigned to the Philippines. His instructions were to support Magsaysay in the struggle against the Huks, to encourage his social engineering, and to groom him for higher office. The two men planned and initiated ways to improve life in the Philippines and sought methods that would be successful in the war against the Huks. Magsaysay began by basing anti-Huk tactics on small—rather than large—unit attacks. Lansdale suggested to him dozens of ideas on conducting psychological warfare against them.

The anvil of peace held out to the Huks was the promise of "land for the landless." If they surrendered and turned in their weapons, the government would provide for them, on the island of Mindanao, an acreage of fifteen to twenty-five acres, farm tools and animals, seed, initial start-up food, a home with electricity—an unheard-of luxury among Asia's teeming multitudes. This program, known as the Economic Development Corporation (EDCOR), broke the back of the guerrilla movement. As early as 1955 over 1,500 Huks had quit their rebellion.

In 1953 Magsaysay agreed to run for the presidency against Elpidio Quirino. He won handily, his campaign supported by voters wearing pins emblazoned "My Guy, Magsaysay." His popularity remained immense.

On March 16, 1957, he made a political trip to Cebu along with twenty-five others, including members of his cabinet, aboard his presidential plane, *Mount Pinatubo*. After ten busy hours he and the others filed aboard his plane for the return flight to Manila. The aircraft took off just past 1 AM on March 17. A few minutes later and twelve miles out, the *Mount Pinatubo* crashed against the side of Mount Manunggal. All aboard died.

CECIL B. CURREY

See also Philippines

References and Further Reading

Abueva, Jose. *Ramon Magsaysay: A Political Biography*. Manila: Solidaridad, 1997.

Currey, Cecil B. *Edward Lansdale: The Unquiet American*. Boston: Houghton Mifflin, 1988.

Lansdale, Edward. *In the Midst of Wars: An American's Mission to Southeast Asia*. New York: Harper & Row, 1972.

Quirino, Carlos. *Magsaysay of the Philippines*. Manila: Ramon Magsaysay Memorial Society, 1958.

Starner, Francis L. *Magsaysay and the Philippine Peasantry: The Agrarian Impact on Philippine Politics, 1953–1956*. Berkeley, CA: University of California Press, 1961.

Taruc, Luis. *Born of the People*. New York: International Publishers, 1953.

———. *He Who Rides the Tiger: The Story of an Asian Guerrilla Leader*. London: Geoffrey Chapman, 1967.

MAHATHIR BIN MOHAMAD, DATO SERI

Considered the major architect of the so-called Malaysian economic miracle of the 1980s and 1990s, Dr. Dato Seri Mahathir bin Mohamad (b. 1925) (pronounced Mahat'hir) was the prime minister of Malaysia from 1981 to 2003. Throughout his career as the leader of the Malaysian government he continuously advocated and propagated active intervention of the government and state institutions in economic development and economic restructuring of the country. During his term in office Malaysia experienced one of the fastest rates of economic growth in the region.

Mr. Mahathir was born in Alor Setar, Kedah. He graduated from the University of Malaya in Singapore in 1953 and was working in the government medical services until 1957. He became actively involved in politics from 1945, when he joined the Kedah Malay Union and Kedah Malay Youth Organization. He joined the United Malays National Organization (UMNO), the leading political party in Malaysia, and won a parliamentary seat in 1946. Mahathir was highly vocal in his criticism of the UMNO leadership for not addressing the economic and social imbalances and growing disparity among the major ethnic groups in the country, i.e., Malays, Chinese, and Indians. In 1969 he was expelled from the UMNO and lost his parliamentary seat. In 1970 Mahathir published the highly controversial book *The Malay Dilemma,* in which he outlined his views on the problem of Malays and Malaysian development. The book was banned by the government, but it won the author substantial popularity among ordinary members of the UMNO and among the Malay community. With the change of leadership in the UMNO, Mahathir was readmitted to the organization. In 1974 he won a parliamentary seat and was appointed as the minister for education. In 1976 he became the deputy prime minister and in 1978 he acquired the portfolio of the minister for trade and industry. In 1981 Mahathir Mohamad became the president of the UMNO, the prime minister, and the minister for home affairs.

As the prime minister of Malaysia, Mahathir Mohamad launched the "Look East Policy," which envisioned rapid economic growth of the country through developing new work ethics, adaptation of new technologies, and developing quality education. He believed that to achieve these goals the Malaysians had to turn to the so-called "Asian values." He also promoted an economic strategy that was based on three pillars: state-led industrialization of the country; measured privatization, and a concept of "Malaysia Incorporated" (the latter meant positive relations between private and state sectors of the country). Mahathir-led government continued to use five-year indicative plans, which were introduced in the middle of the 1960s, as a basis for the official development strategy "Malaysia 2020." Malaysian five-year indicative plans target certain economic growth and social changes and allocate public resources for priority sectors of the economy and for infrastructure development. Malaysia had never instituted centralized control over the state's economy at the level seen in China or the former USSR. Among the priority projects controlled by the five-year indicative plans were the national car (Proton) scheme, construction of a large steel complex (Perjawa), and several other large industrial enterprises. Some of the projects, especially in heavy industry, proved to be controversial, as the international organizations, such as the IMF and World Bank, were highly critical of the Malaysian government subsidies to the loss-making enterprises and of protectionist tariffs, which Malaysia temporarily established in several sectors of the economy. Yet, the Malaysian government was successful in attracting electronic assembly plants to the country in the 1990s, which made Malaysia the world's third-largest producer of integrated circuits and one of the leading producers of domestic appliances. Some of the world's largest corporations, such as Dell and Microsoft of the USA, NEC and Mitsubishi of Japan, and others, opened their branches in Malaysia. In the mid-1990s Mahathir launched the Multimedia Super Corridor (MSC) project, aiming to attract leading multinational corporations to move their assembly and Research and Development (R&D) to Malaysia, thus transforming the country into the world's leading player in information technology. As part of the project, the Malaysian government decided to move federal political and administrative institutions into newly built Putrajaya City on the outskirts of Kuala Lumpur. However, the Asian financial crisis in 1997 and the US's new economy crash in 2000 severely undermined the MSN project and the Malaysian information technology sector.

However, it was the extraordinary reaction of the Mahathir-led government to the Asian financial crisis in 1997 that placed Mahathir and his government in the center of criticism by the international financial institutions. In 1997 Malaysia was heavily affected by the Asian financial crisis that started with the currency collapse in neighboring Thailand. Unlike Indonesia and Thailand, however, Malaysia became the only country in Southeast Asia to reject the IMF's package of conditions and financial assistance. Mahathir, blaming international speculators for creating the crisis, opted for direct state intervention in dealing with it. The government imposed temporary restrictions on the currency exchange market, instituted tough capital-control measures to contain capital outflow, and introduced some other measures, which were against the recommendations of the IMF. The Malaysian currency, the Ringgit, was pegged to the US dollar at a fixed rate of RM3.8 per US dollar (according to the IMF, out of 16 larger emerging market economies only China and Malaysia have pegged their currencies). As a result, the Malaysian economy experienced a much milder recession than neighboring Indonesia or Thailand, although the economic recovery and new direct foreign investments were slow to occur.

Mahathir also initiated several political and constitutional changes between 1983 and 1992. The power of the Malaysian king (constitutional head of the Malaysian Federation) and sultans (heads of the states) was considerably reduced and the royal immunity from legal prosecutions was removed. In 1997 and 1998 Mahathir was involved in a bitter conflict with Mr. Anwar Ibrahim, his deputy and official successor-to-be. The conflict started as a personal dispute over the economic policy in reaction to the Asian financial crisis, but grew into a battle of political personalities and political factions within the UMNO. Anwar Ibrahim was sacked from the government and unsuccessfully tried to relaunch his political career as a major opposition figure and the leader of the movement for democratic reforms. He was arrested and put on trial over sexual and corruption charges, which he vigorously denied. In 2000 Anwar was sentenced to nine years of imprisonment. This trial and sentencing provoked widespread national and international criticism of Mahathir Mohamad and his government for authoritarianism in dealing with political opposition and independent mass media. The prime minister dismissed the criticism, insisting that it was a purely criminal case.

In the international arena Mahathir regularly voiced his grievances against the western domination over the international economy and "unfair treatment" of the developing countries by western governments, international organizations, and multinational corporations. He played an active role in strengthening regional free trade and cooperation within the ASEAN and APEC, although he resisted opening the Malaysian economy for international or regional trade. In 2003 he voluntary resigned from all his official positions.

RAFIS ABAZOV AND ALFIA ABAZOVA

See also Malaysia

References and Further Reading

Mahathir, bin Mohamad. *The Malay Dilemma*. Singapore: Asia Pacific Press, 1970.
Milne, R. S. and Diane K. Mauzy. *Malaysian Politics Under Mahathir*. London, New York: Routledge, 1999.
Teik, Khoo Boo. *Beyond Mahathir: Malaysian Politics and Its Discontents*. London: Zed Book, 2004.
———. *Paradoxes of Mahathirism: An Intellectual Biography of Mahathir Mohamad*, 2nd ed. Kuala Lumpur, Malaysia: Oxford University Press, 2003.
World Bank. *The East Asian Miracle: Economic Growth and Public Policy*. New York: Oxford University Press, 1993.
———. *Malaysia: Matching Risks and Rewards in a Mixed Economy*. Washington, DC: 1989.

MALAN, D. F.

Daniel Francois Malan was an Afrikaner nationalist politician born in Riebeeck West in 1874. He began his career as a pastor in the Dutch Reformed Church. His political career was launched when he became the founding editor of *Die Burger* ("The Citizen") newspaper in 1915.

When J. B. Hertzog formed the National Party (NP) in 1914, Malan became the NP's Cape provincial leader. *Die Burger* became a leading advocate of Afrikaner nationalism under Malan. The NP (deploying the slogan "South Africa First") opposed South Africa being a British dependency and opposed English being the sole national language. In 1924 an NP/Labour Party coalition came to power under Prime Minister J. B. Hertzog. Malan became Minister of the Interior in Hertzog's government (1924–1934). Under this government Afrikaans was made a national language, given equal status to English (1926); South Africa achieved a measure of autonomy from Britain (the Balfour Declaration, 1926); and South Africa got a new flag (1928). In 1934 Hertzog and Jan Smuts formed the United Party (UP). The NP ceased to exist. Malan regarded Smuts as pro-British Empire and pro local (Anglo-run) capitalism. He saw Hertzog as having capitulated to British imperialism. Consequently, Malan refused to join the UP. Instead he founded the "Purified" NP. These "purified" Nationalists were opposed to British colonial domination; wished to create an Afrikaner-controlled republic, independent of Britain; and advocated state interventionism to overcome Afrikaner poverty. Malan's "Purified" NP advocated Christian Nationalism—an ideology arguing that all groups had a right to their own sovereign states. Malan's Christian Nationalists saw themselves as engaged in a struggle against three "foreign," "materialist," and "Godless" ideologies, namely capitalism, fascism, and communism. Capitalism's single-minded pursuit of profit was opposed as "Godless materialism". Fascism was rejected as "unChristian," and Communism was especially passionately opposed because it advocated materialist atheism. In the 1940s Malan's NP fought a struggle against both the local Nazis (*Ossewabrandwag*) and Smuts' capitalist "integrationism," advocating instead for "separation" of South Africa's ethnic groups under the slogan "apartheid" (separate-ness). Smuts' capitalist "integrationism" was seen as "unjust" because it was grounded in a white supremacist segregation logic, while Malan's NP argued their apartheid policy represented a "just" (and Christian) separation based upon "cultural autonomy" and "mutual respect" (for cultural differences). The local Nazis were opposed for their resistance to democratic-constitutional government and their radical, unchristian attitude toward "others."

In 1939 Malan and Hertzog's Nationalists came together to form a "Reunited" NP. This Reunited NP, led by Malan, defeated Smuts' UP in1948. Malan became Prime Minister. The 1948 elections ended Anglo political domination, initiated the Afrikanerization of South Africa; and launched the era of "separate-ness" (apartheid). Under Malan apartheid's early foundations were laid. Malan appointed both the Sauer and Tomlinson Commissions to examine South Africa's racial problems. The Sauer Report (1948) codified the basic apartheid program, advocating political-partition/"vertical separation," and the halting of black mass migration to the cities. The Tomlinson Report (1955) proposed the partition of South Africa into eight states. Seven of these "homelands" would be built from existing "black reserves" to which new land would be added. From the Sauer and Tomlinson Commissions grew the apartheid model. Following the Sauer report Malan advocated black tribes "develop along their own lines in their own fatherlands"; separate "black homelands" be created; and African detribalisation (and migration to the cities) be stopped. Racially mixed marriages were prohibited (1949) and racial segregation enforced by the Group Areas Act (1950); Communism was banned (1950); and "internal passports" were created for black people (1952). Malan tried to take coloureds off the voters roll (1951), but this legislation was overturned by the High Court. Malan retired as Prime Minister in 1954. Under Malan, ANC support dramatically increased due to the Defiance Campaign (1952). Malan's vision of development can be summed up in the term "*volkskapitalism*" (people's capitalism). This involved encouraging Afrikaner businesses to deliberately challenge Anglo capital and an "affirmative action" project to upgrade Afrikaners impoverished by capitalism following the Boer War (1899–1902). Malan's NP captured the state and used it to create opportunities for Afrikaner advancement. This generated an ethnic-patronage system (e.g., public service jobs). A separate Afrikaner education system (schools, colleges, and universities) was built to upgrade the NP's

constituency during the 1950s–1960s. Separate Afrikaner socioeconomic structures were created alongside and parallel to Anglo structures. The parallel infrastructure was paid for by taxing businesses (generally Anglo-owned). The trade-off was that the state facilitated the exploitation of black workers by the business sector. Under Malan, a racial-capitalist framework was consolidated, which meant businesses could—even after paying tax—generate substantive profits from exploiting black workers. This laid the foundations for significant capital accumulation and industrialization in the 1960s. Malan died in 1959.

P. Eric Louw

See also Apartheid; South Africa

References and Further Reading

Kruger, D. W. *The Making of a Nation*. Johannesburg and London: MacMillan, 1969.
Louw, P. E. *The Rise, Fall, and Legacy of Apartheid*. Westport, CT: Praeger, 2004.
O'Meara, Dan. *Volkskapitalism. Class, Capital and Ideology in the Development of Afrikaner Nationalism*. Johannesburg: Ravan, 1983.
Worden, Nigel. *The Making of Modern South Africa*. Oxford and Malden, MA: Blackwell, 2000.

MALAŴI

Malaŵi, formerly the British colony of Nyasaland, is an elongated, landlocked country in Southern Africa (land area: 94,080 square kilometers). Surrounded by Mozambique to the east, south, and southwest; Zambia to the west; and Tanzania to the north, Malaŵi is dominated by the southern end of the East African Rift Valley. Lake Malaŵi (area: 29,600 square kilometers) fills 580 kilometers of the rift valley along the eastern border. The lake is drained by Malaŵi's only large river, the Shire, which flows through much smaller Lake Malombe, and the low-lying Shire valley to its confluence with the Zambezi. The central plateau of Malaŵi is hilly with elevations between 750 and 1,250 meters. In the north, the rolling grasslands of the Nyika and Viphya plateaus rise to over 2,500 meters. The isolated massifs of the Mulanje and Zomba Mountains dominate the south of the country. Altitude varies from thirty-seven meters above sea level (Shire Valley) to the summit of Mount Mulanje (3,050 meters above sea level).

The climate is tropical and monsoonal with a wet season (November–May) and a dry season (May–November). The dry season is mostly cool but hot and humid prior to the first rain. Maritime influences ameliorate the dry season in the Shire Highlands with periods of light, misty drizzle, locally known as *chiperoni*. Mean temperatures in October range from 21°C in the highlands to 29°C at low altitudes. Corresponding figures for July are 15°C and 22°C, respectively. Areas above one thousand meters are cool with annual temperatures ranging from 14°C to 18°C. Temperatures in the lower Shire Valley may reach 37°C. Frosts occur at altitudes above 1,800 meters. Rainfall varies between six hundred and three thousand millimeters depending on altitude, but most of the country receives sufficient rain for at least seasonal, dry-land farming.

The predominant vegetation is savanna woodland (*miombo*), adapted to the monsoonal climate. Evergreen forests grow where soil water remains plentiful. Grasslands are found on high plateaus. Wildlife in Malaŵi is largely restricted to national parks and game reserves and includes elephants, giraffes, lions, leopards, zebras, monkeys, and several antelope species. Hippopotamuses and crocodiles inhabit large rivers and lakes. Fish diversity in Lake Malaŵi is very high with over four hundred species, most in the family Cichlidae.

Bantu speakers colonized Malaŵi between the first and third century AD. At the time of early European (mainly Portuguese) contact, Malaŵi was peopled by small, localized tribes each owing allegiance to a chief. Colonization by Yao and Swahili speakers from the coast saw the establishment of trade in ivory, skins, copper, and slaves with the Arabic commercial center in Zanzibar. The Yao established political control in southern Malaŵi and the slave trade peaked in the nineteenth century, controlled by Swahili speakers and Yao.

The arrival of missionaries, notably David Livingstone, inspired further exploration and strong anti-slavery sentiments in Europe. The Church of Scotland established a station in 1876 that developed into the present-day commercial capital, Blantyre. A British Consul was appointed in 1883 and the country became a British Protectorate in 1891. The slave trade ended, and the colonial period resulted in construction of railways and roads and the occupation of much land by foreign settlers who developed coffee, cotton, tea, and tobacco estates, particularly on the rich soils of the Shire Highlands. African smallholder farming initially focused on food crops but expansion into the cash crops of cotton and tobacco was promoted in the 1960s and now constitutes a significant component of the economy.

In 1944, the Nyasaland African Congress was formed as the first indigenous political party. A federation of the colonial entities of Southern Rhodesia, Northern Rhodesia, and Nyasaland was formed in 1953. The Federation was disliked by much of the African population in Nyasaland, and poor social conditions and land alienation fostered political dissent. The return of Dr. Hastings Banda after 40 years in exile provided leadership and united anti-colonial political factions into the Malaŵi Congress Party (MCP). The independence struggle culminated in the dissolution of the Federation in 1963 and independence for Malaŵi in 1964. In 1966 Malaŵi became a Republic, with President Hastings Banda as its first Head of State. Banda concentrated power in his own hands and established a one-party dictatorship. He declared himself life president in 1971. Through Banda's anti-socialist views and recognition of the apartheid regime in South Africa, aid and capital investment from the West and South Africa fostered a strong economy in the 1970s. The capital was moved from Zomba to Lilongwe to consolidate Banda's power in the region where his support was strongest. Those suspected of opposition to his rule were imprisoned, executed, or assassinated and potential rivals went into exile. Proponents of human rights criticized Banda's regime and in 1992 Roman Catholic bishops circulated a pastoral letter decrying the lack of political freedom, economic inequalities, and human rights abuses. This act precipitated civil unrest, reductions in foreign aid, and the development of political parties opposed to the MCP. A referendum held in 1993 indicated support for the creation of a multi-party state. Despite significant civil unrest instigated by the Young Pioneers, the military wing of the MCP, political change occurred with free elections held in 1994. Of the 193 seats in the National Assembly, the United Democratic Front (UDF) won eighty-four, the MCP won fifty-five, and the Alliance for Democracy won thirty-six. In the presidential elections, Bakili Muluzi defeated Banda. The UDF also won the election held in 1999 with ninety-four seats. Under President Muluzi, Malaŵi has regained some investor confidence but corruption scandals have plagued his two administrations. Economist Bingu wa Mutharika was elected president in May 2004. Muluzi and the United Democratic Front supported his candidacy.

The population of 11,651,000 (2003 estimate) is growing at 2.21% with 47% of the population in the zero to fourteen years age group. With a population density of 98 persons per square kilometer, Malaŵi is one of the most densely populated countries in Africa. Life expectancy at birth is 37.9 years (2003). Only 14% of the population lives in urban areas; the balance lives on smallholdings growing maize, cassava, millet, sorghum, groundnuts, rice, and fruit and vegetables to feed themselves, selling any surplus in local markets. Malaŵi's population is dominated by Chewa and Nyanja. Other ethnic groups include Tumbuka, Yao, Lomwe, Sena, Tonga, Asian (mainly Indian), and European. Religions include traditional animist,

MALAWI

Christianity, and Islam, the latter two of which spread into Malaŵi with the slave trade.

Malaŵi is one of the least developed countries in the world. Poor infrastructure, limited access to seaports, and few mineral resources have hindered economic development. The economy is largely agricultural and major exports are tobacco, tea, sugar, cotton, coffee, peanuts, and wood products. In 2001, agriculture provided 40% of GDP, 90% of export revenues, and 85% of the country's employment. Malaŵi's principal trading partners are South Africa, Germany, Japan, the United Kingdom, the United States, and Mozambique. Mineral resources include limestone and coal and unexploited deposits of uranium and bauxite. Industrial development is limited to food processing, tobacco products, soap, furniture, footwear, and textiles. Artisanal fisheries operate on Lakes Malaŵi, Malombe, and Chilwa. Labor was a major export in the 1970s, with some 250,000 Malaŵians employed outside the country, most in South Africa. Migrant labor is much reduced now. The government has recently introduced market-based interest rates, removed direct control on credit, and improved access to finance for both local and foreign investors.

The government faces major challenges in meeting the demands of the growing population for education and improved access to health services. In 1998, 59% of the population had attended primary school. A further 8% had attended secondary school and only 0.3% had a post-secondary school education. HIV/AIDS infection rates are rising and this disease is putting additional stress on health resources already stretched through the prevalence of endemic diseases such as malaria, schistosomiasis, leprosy, and tuberculosis. Recent surveys suggest that 20% of the sexually active population in urban areas is HIV positive. Health problems also include high levels of under-five mortality, high rates of maternal mortality, malnutrition, and contaminated drinking water. Malaŵi has traditionally been self-sufficient in food, but malnutrition among children became more common in the 1990s. In 2002, the World Bank approved a $50 million drought recovery package to provide famine relief. Pressure to increase agricultural production has led to increasing deforestation and soil erosion.

PATRICK L. OSBORNE

Further Reading

Harrigan, J. *From Dictatorship to Democracy: Economic Policy in Malaŵi, 1964–2000.* Aldershot, UK: Ashgate, 2001.
Kalinga, O. J. and C. A. Crosby. *Historical Dictionary of Malaŵi.* 3rd ed. Lanham, MD.: Scarecrow Press, 2001.

Kelly, R. C., N. D. Youngblood, and S. Doyle. *Country Review: Malaŵi 1999/2000.* Houston, TX: Country-Watch, 1999.

MALAYSIA

Malaysia is a federation of thirteen states that incorporates the southern tip of the Malay Peninsula, excluding the island/state of Singapore, and two territories in North Borneo, Sabah and Sarawak (but not the enclave of Brunei). Its capital is Kuala Lumpur, and its population is approximately 25 million, divided among three principal ethnic groups: Malays or *bumiputera* ("sons of the soil") are the majority, with approximately 52%; ethnic Chinese make up approximately 35% and Indians make up approximately 10%. There are other minorities as well, including hill tribes generically referred to as *orang asli* (literally, "original people"). Islam is practiced by approximately 55% of the population, Christianity is practice by approximately 35%, and Hinduism and Buddhism account for approximately 7% each (religion loosely follows ethnic lines). The climate is tropical, with rainy and dry seasons dictated by monsoons (seasons differ depending on location).

Malaysia was a British colony, and the British ruled through local sultans. The regions in Borneo were run privately by the North Borneo Trading Company (this region became Sabah) and by the descendants of James Brooke, a British adventurer who became known as the "White Raja" (this region became Sarawak). The British consolidated the territory following World War II, and began moving toward decolonization. Because the ethnic Chinese controlled a disproportionate amount of wealth, the majority Malays were concerned with the first system that the British proposed, the Malayan Union Plan. In response, the British created the Federation of Malaya Plan, which favored Malays in terms of representation, but in turn angered ethnic Chinese, triggering the Malayan Emergency and a Chinese-led communist scare. The conflict eventually lessened in intensity, and Malaya became independent in 1957, led by Tunku Abdul Rahman and his United Malays National Organization in alliance with the Malaysian Chinese Association and the Malaysian Indian Congress. In 1963, Singapore, Sabah, and Sarawak were incorporated into the Federation of Malaysia. Just two years later, Singapore peacefully left the Federation over ethnic and political differences (Singapore is predominantly ethnic Chinese). The alliance formed by Tunku became the *Barisan Nasional* (National Front) in 1973, and remains the predominant force in Malaysian politics. Malaysia's long-serving prime

982

minister, Mahathir Mohamad, stepped down in 2003 after twenty-two years in that post, and was replaced by Abdullah Ahmad Badawi.

The British introduced extractive industries and widespread cash cropping during their reign. Tin mines in the interior employed mostly imported Chinese labor, and rubber and palm oil plantations employed Chinese and Indian migrants. The colonial legacy of producing cash crops for export to provide raw materials for the British (and others) continued after independence until the early 1970s, when the Malaysian economy began to expand into other sectors including manufacture, and most recently, information technology. Malaysia's economy grew rapidly, with a significant drop in poverty and a rise in wages. Foreign investment poured in, spurred by Malaysia's stability, openness, and lower degree of corruption than some of its neighbors. Malaysia's stability during the Mahathir years was enforced through severe restrictions on the press and political opposition, backed by willing courts, and supported by Mahathir's insistence on the existence of a set of "Asian Values" that were appropriate to the region but distinct from Western ideals of human rights and democracy—an argument shared by the leaders of neighboring states, especially those of authoritarian regimes (although the "Asian Values" claim is debated among civil society in the region, and is seen as a way for leaders to consolidate their power without opposition).

In 1990, Mahathir instituted "Vision 2020," a plan to have Malaysia "fully developed" by the year 2020 through a series of five-year plans (similar to five-year plans that Malaysia had already been implementing). Vision 2020 calls for universal primary education, emphasizing human capital, eradicating poverty, increasing the role of *bumiputera* in the economy, increasing private sector investment, and other ideals (one physical manifestation of Vision 2020 is the Petronas Towers, currently the world's largest building). The plan was temporarily sidetracked during the 1997–1998 economic crisis, but Malaysia has emerged much better off than some of its neighbors. One significant casualty of the economic crisis was Anwar Ibrahim, Mahathir's Deputy Prime Minister. In the early phases of the economic crisis, activists took to the streets in support of *reformasi* (reform), as they did in Indonesia. Anwar became a figure in support of this reform movement, and criticized publicly Mahathir's economic policies, only to be sacked, leading him to turn to more open rivalry for political power. Unlike Indonesia, however, the reform movement did not oust the leadership, but rather lost much of its steam as Anwar was tried and found guilty of sodomy, charges largely perceived to be trumped up. The *reformasi* movement provided somewhat of a spark for traditionally weak civil society in Malaysia, including the founding of the opposition National Justice Party by Anwar's wife, Wan Azizah Wan Ismail. Civil society in general, however, remains weak and not deeply rooted. Anwar was released six years to the day after being imprisoned, under Malaysia's new Prime Minister, Badawi.

Racial tension between *bumiputera* and ethnic Chinese remains, although it seldom boils to the surface as in Indonesia. As part of Mahathir's development plan, *bumiputera* are favored through a sort of reverse affirmative action, in which the majority population benefits in order to lessen differences among ethnic groups. Under the plan, new businesses must include *bumiputera* as part owners, *bumiputera* are assigned quotas at universities and access to scholarships, and other incentives are offered as a means to offset the disproportionate wealth of the ethnic Chinese. Short- and long-term problems associated with Malaysian development include urbanization, the equitable distribution of wealth, the fate of *orang asli* (mostly in Sabah and Sarawak) in their attempts to modernize without losing their culture or being taken advantage of, and environmental problems associated with rapid industrialization. Unlike most of its neighbors, Malaysia does not have any serious separatist movement threatening the unity of the state.

CHRISTOPHER LUNDRY

See also Southeast Asia: History and Economic Development; Southeast Asia: International Relations

References and Further Reading

Embong, Abdul Rahman. *State-Led Modernization and the New Middle Class in Malaysia*. New York: Palgrave, 2002.

Jesudason, James V. *Statist Democracy and the Limits of Civil Society in Malaysia*. Singapore: Department of Sociology, National University of Singapore, 1993.

Steinberg, David Joel, ed. *In Search of Southeast Asia: A Modern History*. Honolulu: University of Hawaii Press, 1987 (1971).

Verma, Vidhu. *Malaysia: State and Civil Society in Transition*. Boulder, CO: Lynne Rienner, 2002.

MALDIVES

The Republic of Maldives is a country consisting of a group of atolls in the Indian Ocean, southwest of India. The numerous coral reef islands, 1,190 in total, form an archipelago of twenty-six natural atolls. The climate is tropical and hot all year. The humid and rainy season takes place between June and August and the dry season between November and March. The Maldives population is estimated at 298,000, with a growth rate of about 1.4% annually. The capital city, Male, unlike any other island in the country, is a city of high-rise buildings and paved roads. It houses about one-third of the country's population with seventy-five thousand inhabitants.

In olden times, the islands provided the main source of cowrie shells, then used as currency throughout Asia and parts of the East African coast. Historically, Maldives has had a strategic importance because of its location on the major marine routes of the Indian Ocean. Therefore, already in the year 1558 the Portuguese established themselves in the country. Later they were expelled by Maldivian rebels and the country came under the influence of the Dutch, and from 1887 on, of the British as a protectorate, but Maldives has always had a significant level of self-government and freedom. Maldives remained a British crown protectorate until 1953 when the sultanate was suspended and the First Republic was declared under the short-lived presidency of Muhammad Amin Didi. However, a year later the sultanate was restored. As in many other states, finally, on July 26, 1965, Maldives gained independence under an agreement signed with Britain. In a national referendum in March 1968, Maldivians abolished the sultanate and established a republic on November 11. The British continued to maintain an air base on the island of Gan in the southernmost atoll until 1976. The Second Republic was proclaimed in November 1968 under the presidency of Ibrahim Nasir who ruled until 1978. That year Maumoon Abdul Gayoom was elected president, a position that he acquired by winning all the intervening elections by a large amount of the votes.

The Maldivian's religion is Islam, which was introduced early, in 1153 CE, as the cornerstone of their history. From then on, the King adopted the Muslim title and name of Sultan Muhammad al Adil, initiating a series of six dynasties consisting of eighty-four sultans and sultanas that lasted until 1932 when the sultanate became elective.

Maldives' estimated gross domestic product (GDP) for 2002 was $1.25 billion, with a per capita income of about $3,900. The economy is based on tourism, its largest industry, and also on fishing, its second largest. Since the first establishment of a resort in 1972, the number of tourists has gradually increased. In the year 2000, tourist arrivals exceeded 466,000. This industry accounts for approximately 20% of the GDP and more than 60% of Maldives' foreign exchange receipts. In second place is the fishing sector, which employs about 20% of the labor force and contributes about 10% of the GDP. Fish is also the major export on the islands, along with cowrie shells, fish meal, and copra, sent to their main export partners: the United States, Thailand, and Sri Lanka. The imports are what the island can't produce: rice, sugar, wheat flour, petroleum products, and intermediate and capital goods.

Agriculture and manufacturing continue to play a lesser role in the economy, constrained by the limited availability of cultivable land and the shortage of domestic labour. Only subsistence crops such as coconuts, bananas, breadfruit, papayas, mangoes, taro, betel, chilies, sweet potatoes, and onions are grown. Industry consists mainly of garment production, boat building, and handicrafts, and accounts for about 18% of the GDP.

Maldives is situated among the countries with a Medium Human Development level, ranking eighty-four in the general list of the United Nations Development Program (UNDP, 2004). The life expectancy at birth for both males and females is sixty-seven years (2002), much better than it was thirty years ago (fifty-one years in 1975). The adult literacy rate is at about 97%, quite high for the region, due to the good educational system of the islands. The modern schools, run by both the government and private sector, provide primary and secondary education. Primary school enrolment is over 98% and secondary school enrolment over 44%.

The health expenditure in 2002 was 5.6% of the GDP, similar to the Netherlands or other developed countries. Also, almost 100% of the population is immunized against tuberculosis and measles. The infant mortality rate is 58 per 1,000 live births, much better than it was in 1975 (121 per 1,000). Notable achievements have also been made in the control of communicable diseases. There has been no indigenous case of malaria seen for the past ten years. The health services are organised under the Primary Health Care approach. These services are provided through a countrywide referral network of Family Health Workers, at least one in each inhabited island; twenty-seven Atoll Health Centres; four Regional Hospitals; and a central-level hospital in Male. In 2000 there were 226 doctors in the country, with a ratio of 8.4 per 10,000 population. There were also a total of 470 beds in the hospitals, giving a population-to-bed ratio of 577 to one.

So as to solve the scarcity of fresh water and to prevent water-borne diseases, through the help of Danish aid, desalination plants have been installed. Also, sewage systems have been installed to prevent the country from pollution- and water-borne epidemics, among other diseases.

More recently, the tsunami (a giant tidal wave generated by an earthquake in the ocean) generated in December 2004 in the Indian Ocean saw many parts of Maldives sink under sea water and many people end up homeless. This situation created severe social problems for the country's inhabitants.

Another potential problem for the country is the global warming effect as it is said that this could increase the mean sea level and make the atolls disappear under the ocean.

DIEGO I. MURGUÍA

See also Central Asia: History and Economic Development; Central Asia: International Relations; Ethnic Conflicts: Central Asia

References and Further Reading

Adeney, M. and W. K. Carr "The Maldives Republic." In *The Politics of the Western Indian Ocean Islands*, edited by John M. Ostheimer. New York: Praeger, 1975.

Armsler, Kurt. *Maldives*. New York: Smithmark Publishers, 1995.

Chawla, Subash. *The New Maldives*. Colombo, Sri Lanka: Diana, 1986.

United Nations Development Program. *Human Development Report 2004. Cultural Liberty in Today's Diverse World*. New York: Hoechstetter, 2004. (http://hdr.undp.org).

MALI

The West African landlocked Republic of Mali lies south of Algeria, surrounded east to west by Niger, Burkina Faso, Ivory Coast, Guinea, Senegal, and Mauritania. The northern half of Mali lies in the Saharan and Sahelian zones, where aridity is exacerbated by the harmattan. The area is home to only about 20% of the population; migration southward or abroad is frequent. The southern region, where rainfall is heavier, is covered by the savanna and thin forests. Population density is high only on the fertile lands around the Senegal and Niger Rivers. The latter crosses the country from west to east, deviating northward in a wide bend forming a large interior delta, which moderates the climate and irrigates the land. Poverty due to climate is exacerbated by high population growth. After 1973, recurrent droughts leaving in their wake famine, dead cattle, dry wells, and villages buried under sand, have made Mali one of the poorest nations on Earth. Since 1992 , due to better management and free market trade, the country, while remaining poor, is no longer subject to famine and remains eligible for international aid.

Agriculture employs 82.4% of the population and constitutes 45% of the Gross Domestic Product. The main crops are millet, sorgho, rice, peanuts, and cotton. The cotton crop, grown mainly for export, has become essential to economic development. Next in importance is cattle-raising, which represents 20% of the Gross National Product and is also exported.

Fishing, a traditional activity in interior waters, is an important source of food. Salted, some fish is also exported to neighboring countries. Mali has mineral resources, but exploitation is embryonic. The only mineral presently exported is gold, obtained by panning. The industrial and service sectors provide little employment to date.

Mali's past wealth did not come from the resources of its land, but rather from its location at the crossroads of trans-Saharan trade routes where caravans successively spawned the empires of Ghana, Mali, Songhai, and the Bambara kingdoms, between the eight and the eighteenth centuries. Economic and social conditions gave rise to major cities, which became centers of Islamic learning. However, by the end of the eighteenth century, Malian empires vanished, as European seafaring shifted trade centers to the Atlantic coasts. In the nineteenth century the area saw successive Islamic jihads and the spread of French colonialism.

In control of Mali, the French amalgamated it with their other West African holdings into the Federation of French West Africa (AOF) in 1895. They neglected Mali's development because the country lay far from the coasts. After World War II, Mali, like all AOF members, progressed toward independence. The 1950s saw the emergence of a Malian leader Modibo Keita, co-founder of a new political party, the Sudanese Union. After a brief unsuccessful attempt at federation with Senegal in 1959, Mali became the Republic of Mali in 1960, and Keita its president.

A Marxist, Keita adopted socialist policies and established close ties with communist nations. Eager to erase all traces of colonialism, he Africanized civil service, nationalized key sectors of the economy, instituted agricultural collectivism, and declared currency independence. Results were disastrous; food production plummeted, requiring major purchases abroad. Keita had to reverse course and request French support for the Malian currency.

Notwithstanding his international prestige as one of the major representatives of African nationalism, he was unable to stabilize Mali. He responded to protests and strikes with repression, purges, and a Maoist cultural revolution. In 1968 he ordered the National Assembly dissolved and the party's political bureau closed. He was overthrown in a bloodless coup in November of the same year, led by junior army officers, and spent the rest of his life under house arrest.

Lieutenant Moussa Traoré, who had led the coup, became head of state and promised democracy and economic liberalization, which never occurred. He did not cancel those socialist programs that were popular, but rather sought international aid to implement them. However, in order to receive the latter he had to restructure the economy and cut governmental spending. The changes caused widespread unemployment and economic hardship, which triggered unrest. To pacify the country, Traoré instituted several reforms. He dismissed some corrupt officials, gave civilians partial access to government, and made minor economic concessions. Foreign donors balked at these and suspended aid. As the government found itself unable to meet payrolls, rebellion spread. Discord even arose within the military junta.

Willing to undertake structural adjustment, Traoré, however, rejected any form of democracy and remained in total command as president and head of the military-sponsored political party, the Mali People's Democratic Union (UDPM). Corruption was rampant. Costly wars caused additional destabilizing expenditures. Rebellions by nomadic Tuareg in northern Mali generated upheavals; only after Traoré's fall from power did negotiations begin to bring fruit.

Traoré did endeavor to improve conditions by increasing the yield of subsistence farming and introducing new agricultural techniques for the cultivation of the main cash crops, peanuts and cotton. However, his attempts were overshadowed by his obsession with absolute power. Opponents took advantage of the small steps towards liberalization, forced upon him by foreign pressure, to organize. Matters came to a head when, in 1991, young people took to the streets and Traoré ordered soldiers to shoot into the crowd. There were close to one thousand victims. Shortly thereafter he was arrested by paratroopers prodded by lieutenant-colonel Amadou Toumany Touré, who took over the reins of government and appointed a provisional government to draft a new democratic constitution and hold free elections These resulted in Alpha Oumar Konaré of the Alliance for Democracy in Mali (ADEMA) becoming president in 1992.

Konaré reestablished democracy and tried to mend political enmities by commuting Traoré's death sentence to life imprisonment and sponsoring a national forum charged with revising the constitution and electoral laws to strengthen guarantees against a return of one-party rule.

Changes were numerous and positive and under Konaré's presidency progress was made with regard to resettlement of the Tuareg. However, the regime was burdened by inherited foreign debts, which required unpopular structural adjustments.

Presidential elections in 2002 were won by Amadou Toumany Touré, briefly interim president in 1991–1992. Although there were claims of electoral fraud, Touré's win was ultimately validated by the country's Constitutional Court, but Touré, widely popular prior to his election win, faces significant problems.

Instability within his government and perpetual economic difficulties keep Mali among the world's poorest nations, despite France's 2002 promise to write off 40% of the country's debt.

L. NATALIE SANDOMIRSKY AND IAIN WALKER

See also West Africa: History and Economic Development; West Africa: International Relations

References and Further Reading

Ajayi J.F. Ade and Michael Crowder, eds. *History of West Africa*, 2nd ed. New York: Columbia University Press, 1974.

Boilley, Pierre. *Les Touaregs Kel Adagh, Dépendance er Révolte: du Soudan Français au Mali Contemporain.* Paris: Karthala, 1999.

Brenner, Louis. *Controlling Knowledge, Religion, Power and Schooling in a West African Society.* Bloomington, IN: University of Indiana Press, 2001.

Cissoko, Diango. *La Fonction Publique en Afrique Noire, le Cas du Mali.* Rouen: Université de Rouen, 1995.

Diarrah, Oumar. *Le Défi Démocratique au Mali.* Paris: L'Harmattan, 2000.

Gérard, Etienne. *La Tentation du Savoir en Afrique: Politiques, Muyhes et Stratégies d'Éducation au Mali.* Paris: Karthala, 2000.

Gifford, Prosser and William Roger Lewis, eds. *The Transfer of Power in Africa: Decolonization 1940–60.* New Haven, CT: Yale University Press, 1988.

Lucke, Lewis. *Waiting for Rain: Life and Development in Mali, West Africa.* London: Christopher Publishing House, 1998.

Manning, Patrick. *Francophone Sub-Saharan Africa, 1880–1995*, 2nd ed. New York: Cambridge University Press, 1998.

MALVINAS/FALKLANDS

Nearly three hundred miles east of the southern coast of Argentina lie two main islands and about two hundred smaller islands, occupying an area of 4,618 square miles. Under British control since 1833, and claimed by Argentina, these islands are referred to by the British as the Falkland Islands, while the Argentines called them Islas Malvinas.

With approximately three thousand English-speaking inhabitants, the islands' economy was largely dependent on wool exports until 1990. Since then, the selling of fishing licenses to foreign fleets to fish within the islands' fisheries accounts for their principal source of revenues. Additionally, there are indications of possible oil deposits on the ocean floor.

Originally settled by the French in 1766, the islands were ceded to Spain in 1769. Argentina, after gaining its independence from Spain, claimed the islands and settled them in 1823. In 1833, Great Britain invaded the islands and expelled the Argentines.

In the 1900s, Argentina undertook diplomatic efforts to recover the islands. Great Britain responded by extending its sovereignty over the South Georgia and South Sandwich Islands, also claimed by Argentina. After World War II, the slogan of "Malvinas Argentinas" became an important component of General Juan Domingo Perón's nationalistic rhetoric, but there were no attempts to recover the islands either by diplomacy or by force.

Argentina's quest to recover the islands was strengthened in 1960 when the United Nations General Assembly approved Resolution 1514 calling for self-determination for colonial possessions. In 1965, the General Assembly passed Resolution 2065, urging Argentina and Great Britain to proceed with negotiations concerning the islands' sovereignty and taking into consideration the interests of its inhabitants.

For seventeen years, both countries engaged in negotiations. Argentina's position was clear: it wanted sovereignty over the islands. Great Britain, on the other hand, interpreted the interests of the inhabitants as their wishes to remain British.

Frustrated by British delaying tactics, the military junta led by General Leopoldo Galtieri decided to put into effect a plan to recover the islands by force. Judging a British military response to be minimal and believing that Argentina's covert military aid to the Contras in Nicaragua would convince the United States to press the British into a diplomatic solution favorable to Argentina, the junta continued its recovery preparations. Furthermore, the junta believed that Third World nations would support the takeover as a just war against colonialism.

The recovery attempt was scheduled for July 1982. However, the junta was forced to implement the plan ahead of schedule when a series of protests against its economic policies spread throughout Argentina in March. In an effort to neutralize public discontent, the junta launched "Operation Rosario." On April 2, 1982, Argentine commandos landed on Port Stanley (Puerto Argentina) and quickly occupied the islands and South Georgia. By late April, twelve thousand Argentine troops were on the islands.

Reaction in Argentina was ecstatic as demonstrations in support for the junta's action occurred throughout the country. Stunned by "Operation Rosario," British Prime Minister Margaret Thatcher, who had been experiencing a wave of unpopularity, ordered a twenty-eight thousand-man task force to set sail for the islands on April 6 and declared a two hundred-mile exclusion zone around the islands.

At the United Nations Security Council, Argentina suffered a diplomatic setback when the Council passed Resolution 502, calling for the immediate withdrawal of Argentine forces and urging a diplomatic solution. On the other hand, member nations of the Organization of American States—with the exception of Chile, Colombia, and the United States, which abstained—sided with Argentina.

United States Secretary of State Alexander Haig shuttled between Buenos Aires and London, offering possible diplomatic solutions, only to be met with intransigence on both sides. By April 25, the British had regained South Georgia and on April 30, the United States joined the European Common Market in imposing economic sanctions against Argentina. Moreover, the United States began giving the British logistic and intelligence support.

On May 1, the British began bombarding Puerto Argentina. The following day, Peruvian President Fernando Belaúnde Terry offered a mediation plan calling for an Argentine and British withdrawal, resumption of diplomatic negotiations, recognition of the islanders' interests, and an interim international administration. Both sides appeared favorably inclined to accept the plan and a jubilant Belaúnde announced that an accord would be signed that evening. However, at 4:00 PM, the Argentine cruiser *Belgrano*, which was sailing toward the mainland, outside the exclusion zone, was torpedoed by the HMS *Conqueror*, leaving 360 sailors dead. President Belaunde's plan dissipated with the *Belgrano*'s sinking and the war intensified as Argentine planes sank the British destroyer *Sheffield* two days later.

On May 27, British forces launched an offensive at Goose Green, which was defended by Argentine conscripts. While the conscripts were no match for the British, the Argentine air force proved to be extremely effective. Although it lost fifty-seven planes during the campaign, the air force sank nine British vessels and damaged thirty-two others. By June 11, however, the British had surrounded Puerto Argentino and on June 14, the Argentines surrendered.

The Argentine defeat not only resulted in the junta's downfall, but with the exception of the air force, it discredited the military. Ironically, the defeat opened the way for democratic rule, as elections were held in 1983. Although Argentina has remained politically stable, its civilian leaders have been unable to effectively deal with a perennial economic crisis caused by industrial stagnation, hyperinflation, and a gargantuan foreign debt. In Great Britain, the victory resurrected Thatcher's popularity, but for many years, the government had to devote a large share of its budget to the defense of "Fortress Falklands."

Diplomatic relations between Great Britain and Argentina have been reestablished. Although Argentina still maintains its sovereignty claims over the islands, it has declared that it will no longer use force. Great Britain, on the other hand, has rejected proposed Argentine negotiations concerning the islands, and the possibility of a solution for their future appears bleak.

JOSÉ FERNÁNDEZ

See also Argentina; Malvinas/Falklands War, 1982

References and Further Reading

Coll, Alberto T. and Anthony C. Arend, eds. *The Falklands War: Lessons for Strategy, Diplomacy and International Law*. Boston: G. Allen and Union, 1985.
Hastings, Max and Simon Jenkins. *The Battle for the Falklands*. New York: Norton, 1984.
Moro, Rubién O. *The History of the South Atlantic Conflict: The War for the Malvinas*. New York: Praeger, 1989.
Rock, David. *Argentina 1516–1987: From Spanish Colonization to Alfonsín*. Berkeley, CA: University of California Press, 1985.
Scheina, Robert L. *Latin America: A Naval History, 1810–1987*. Annapolis, MD: US Naval Institute, 1987.
The Sunday Times. "The Falklands War." London: Times Newspaper, 1982.

MALVINAS/FALKLANDS WAR, 1982

The Malvinas/Falklands War in 1982 was a conflict between Great Britain and Argentina for possession of a group of two large (East and West Falkland) and two hundred small islands in the South Atlantic, three hundred miles east of Argentina. The origins of the dispute date to eighteenth-century claims by Spain and Great Britain. Argentina gained independence from Spain in 1822 and claimed the islands as national territory and established settlements. In 1833 Great Britain took the islands and expelled the Argentinean settlers and named the islands the Falklands. The islands proved useful for raising sheep and by the twentieth century were home to some two thousand British subjects. Argentina never relinquished claim and referred to the archipelago as the Malvinas. Argentina renewed interest in the Malvinas during the first presidency of Juan Perón (1946–1955). Perón used the issue to raise nationalistic fervor as part of his vision for a "greater Argentina." The United Nations encouraged the two parties to resolve the issue in a 1965 resolution. While the islands were thought to be of little economic value to Great Britain or Argentina, negotiations were stalled by the islanders who desired to remain under Great Britain. A later complicating factor was the possibility that the waters surrounding the islands had vast deposits of oil.

Juan Perón returned to power via election in 1973 but died on July 1, 1974. His third wife, Isabel, who had served as his vice president, assumed the presidential sash. Argentina, largely due to Peron's policies during his seventeen-year exile, had suffered political instability. His death and Isabel Perón's ineffectiveness as a leader led to even more chaos. Isabel Perón was overthrown by the Argentine military in 1976, which established a military junta to run the country.

By 1982 the military regime had proved ineffective in dealing with Argentina's economic malaise and was increasingly repressive in dealing with dissidents. In an attempt to regain a measure of popular support, the army commander and head of the junta, General Leopoldo F. Galiteri, ordered preparations for the invasion of the islands. Galiteri surmised that the nearing 150th anniversary of the British takeover of the islands would rally the average Argentine citizen to the cause. In addition, the British had reduced their military forces on the islands and seemed not to be as committed as they once were to retaining possession.

On April 2, 1982, Argentine troops landed on East Falkland near the capital of Stanley. A small contingent of Royal Marines briefly resisted but was soon captured. Argentina proclaimed possession and placed the two thousand islanders under a military governor. Initially, the bold attack had the effect that Galiteri desired and there was an outpouring of patriotic support for his regime. However, the international community was shocked and the United Nations Security Council passed a resolution supporting the British position. The United States attempted to mediate a withdrawal of Argentine forces to be followed by negotiations, but this attempt failed. Great Britain, led by Prime Minister Margaret Thatcher, assembled a naval task force and vowed to retake the islands.

As the British task force steamed the eight thousand miles to the islands, the British nuclear-powered submarine *H.M.S. Conqueror* sunk the Argentine cruiser, *General Belgrano*. On April 18, crack troops of the British Special Air Service began infiltrating the islands to prepare for the main task force. Successful raids were conducted on Pebble Island on May 15, resulting in the destruction of a radar station, eleven aircraft, and supply dumps. These raids were followed by an amphibious assault on Port San Carlos, which provided an adequate harbor and bridgehead for the campaign to take the capital of Port Stanley.

After securing the bridgehead, British forces crossed the island and engaged the Argentine army at Goose Green on May 27. The battle at Goose Green was a significant British victory and opened the way for the siege of Port Stanley beginning on June 11. For three days and nights there was fierce fighting in the hills on the outskirts of the capital. However, Argentine forces had been effectively cut off from supply from the mainland by superior British air and naval power. On June 14 all Argentine forces on East Falkland surrendered.

On June 20 the British declared an end to the war. Argentine casualties included 746 men killed, 1,336 wounded, and 11,400 soldiers who became temporary prisoners of war. British losses included 256 killed and 777 wounded. Only three civilian residents of the islands lost their lives in the brief conflict.

The outcome of the war boosted the prestige of Margaret Thatcher and her Conservative Party, which soon won reelection. The hard-fought victory also made Britain determined to hold the islands and to commit additional force to deter any future Argentine aggression.

For the Argentine military government, the war was an unmitigated disaster and led to the resignation of General Galiteri and the return to civilian rule in 1983. In addition to losing political power, the Argentine military lost its credibility with the public. Soon there were calls for investigations of human rights abuses. The war was also a setback for Argentina's economic and social development. The war was costly and Argentina entered a period of hyper-inflation. In addition, any immediate prospects of obtaining the Falklands and exploiting petroleum deposits were lost. On the other hand, Argentina needed to focus on its domestic problems and could no longer use the Malvinas issue as a reason not to do so.

GEORGE M. LAUDERBAUGH

See also Argentina; Malvinas/Falklands

References and Further Reading

Coll, Alberto R. and Anthony C. Arend, eds. *The Falklands War: Lessons for Strategy, Diplomacy and International Law*. Boston: G. Allen & Unwin, 1985.
Hastings, Max and Simon Jenkins. *The Battle for the Falklands*. New York: Norton, 1984.
Laffin, John. *Fight for the Falklands*. New York: St. Martin's Press, 1982.
Moro, Rubén O. *The History of the South Atlantic Conflict: The War for the Malvinas*. New York: Praeger, 1989.

MANDELA, NELSON

Nelson Mandela was born into the Thembu royal house in the tribal lands of the Xhosa people in Transkei, South Africa. Growing up in the royal residence after the death of his father, Mandela was exposed to the ideals of democracy within the context of the tribal council, parliament, and judiciary.

Enrolled in the University College of Fort Hare, Mandela studied English, anthropology, politics, native administration, and Dutch Roman law. Mandela became active in student government, advocating

change through greater representation for the underclassmen and the residents. At the end of his second year, in 1940, he was expelled for refusing to accept his elected position on the Student Representative Council (SRC). A majority of the students boycotted the elections in an effort to air their grievances. Mandela believed his refusal to accept the election results was morally right and, that the SRC did not have the confidence of the majority of the student body. His decision set the stage for his future activism.

Arriving in Johannesburg in 1941, Mandela found work as an articled clerk (a lawyer's apprentice) in one of the largest firms in town. He began attending meetings of the African National Congress (ANC). As he became increasingly interested in the liberation movement, he enrolled in the law program as the only African student at the University of Witwatersrand (Wits). While at Wits, Mandela became friends and political allies with a variety of people from all racial groups who would later become leaders in the anti-apartheid movement.

As Mandela's political acumen grew, he began to devote his life to the liberation struggle. In 1943, Mandela, along with a number of his contemporaries, approached the president of the ANC with their intention to form a Youth League and initiate a campaign to mobilize mass nationwide support for the liberation movement. The ANC president supported this new commitment and the Youth League was officially formed in 1944 with Mandela serving on the Executive Committee. The ideology animating Mandela was African nationalism—the idea that African liberation would only come at the hands of Africans themselves and not from the blind adoption of foreign ideologies such as communism or Western democracy.

In 1948, the ANC adopted Mandela's Youth League-inspired Programme of Action only after the Afrikaner National Party came to power in an all-white election and the government began to enact increasingly repressive apartheid (racial segregation) laws. The new policies of the Youth League advocated the use of boycotts, strikes, civil disobedience, non-cooperation, and mass demonstrations as a means to fight against the National Party regime. Furthermore, the Programme called for the attainment of full citizenship rights for all races, direct parliamentary representation, and free and compulsory education for all children. This new agenda would set the social, political, and economic course of interactions with the South African government for the next forty years. The development of South Africa was intricately entwined with the anti-apartheid liberation struggle; the government's effort to maintain its power; and the political, economic, and cultural status of its white population. The liberation movement would ultimately set up a power dynamic between white and black, rich and poor, developed and undeveloped that would adversely effect and destabilize not only South Africa but also the entire region.

A number of Mandela-led ANC initiatives during the 1950s brought the wrath of the apartheid state. The 1952 Campaign of Defiance was a nationwide civil disobedience campaign designed to resist the burgeoning apartheid system. The 1955 Congress of the People's adoption of the Freedom Charter called for the end of racial discrimination, equal rights for all, and a participatory democracy. The Charter was a rallying cry for the liberation struggle and a blueprint for the future South Africa. Shortly after, Mandela and others were arrested on charges of high treason and conspiracy to overthrow the state. The Treason Trial lasted more than four years, at the end of which Mandela and his co-defendants were found not guilty.

With all channels of peaceful protest exhausted, in 1961 the ANC made the decision to put aside their nonviolent principles in order to combat the growing repression and violence of the state. With Mandela as the commander-in-chief, the ANC formed *Umkhonto we Sizwe* (Spear of the Nation) as its military wing. Mandela left the country in 1962 to gain international support for the anti-apartheid liberation struggle. Upon his return he was again arrested and charged with illegal exit from the country and incitement to strike. He was convicted and sentenced to a five-year prison term. While serving this sentence he, along with a number of his colleagues, were charged with sabotage. The subsequent trial, known as the Rivonia Trial, drew the attention of the world to South Africa's liberation struggle and condemned Mandela to a life sentence.

During the 1980s South Africa came under increasing international pressure to end apartheid. Finally, the National Party government was forced to capitulate and begin negotiations with the liberation movement. After refusing on a number of occasions to be conditionally released, Mandela began meeting with government officials in 1988 to discuss the future of South Africa. In mid 1989, he met with state president P. W. Botha shortly before Botha's resignation due to health problems. Late in 1989 many of Mandela's political prison-mates were released. In December 1989, Mandela then met for the first time with Botha's successor, F. W. de Klerk. In February 1990 the ban on the ANC and other political organizations was lifted after thirty years. On February 11, 1990, Nelson Mandela was unconditionally released from prison.

The difficult work of forming a government of national unity, which included the dismantling of the apartheid system, was to begin. Mandela became

president of the ANC in 1991, was awarded the Nobel Peace Prize along with F. W. de Klerk in 1993, and was inaugurated the first democratically elected president of South Africa on May 10, 1994. During his five-year term as president, the ANC government enacted the Reconstruction and Development Programme, which was a socioeconomic program to reconstruct South Africa and reconcile it with its past. Furthermore, the government, led by Mandela, enacted the Truth and Reconciliation Commission as a means to shine the light on the hidden truths of the apartheid era and heal the wounds it had caused.

Mandela retired to private life in 1999, near the village of his birth in the Transkei. He continues to be a prominent statesman and advocate for social justice and travels the world as the struggle of his life continues.

DEE F. MATREYEK

See also Apartheid; De Klerk, Frederik W.; South Africa; Southern Africa: History and Economic Development; Southern Africa: International Relations

References and Further Reading

Clark, Steve, ed. *Nelson Mandela Speaks: Forging a Democratic, Nonracial South Africa.* New York, London: Pathfinder Press, 1993.

Crwys-Williams, Jennifer, ed. *In the Words of Nelson Mandela.* Seacaucus, NJ: Carol Publishing Group, 1998.

Johns, Sheridan and Hunt R. Davis, eds. *Mandela, Tambo, and the African National Congress: The Struggle Against Apartheid, 1948–1990: A documentary survey.* New York, Oxford: Oxford University Press, 1991.

Meer, Fatima. *Higher than Hope: The Authorized Biography of Nelson Mandela.* London: H. Hamilton, 1988; New York: Harper & Row, 1990.

Meredith, Martin. *Nelson Mandela: A biography.* Great Britain: Penguin Group; New York: St. Martin's Press, 1998.

Ottaway, David. *Chained Together: Mandela, De Klerk and the Struggle to Remake South Africa.* New York: Times Books, 1993.

Sampson, Anthony. *Mandela: The authorized biography.* New York: Knopf, 1999.

MAO ZEDONG

Mao Zedong (1893–1976), elected leader of the Communist Party of China from 1945 to 1976, is said to have developed Marxism-Leninism by adapting it to the special situation in China and merging it with elements of traditional Chinese thought. The Chinese Communist Party (CCP) adopted Mao Zedong Thought as its leading ideology and still clings to it, although after Mao's death most of his theoretical contributions made after the CCP's rise to power were criticized as being left deviationism.

Mao was born December 23, 1893, in Shaoshan, Hunan, China, to a peasant family. He was educated in China and became a librarian at Beijing University, where he encountered Marxist debates and became a Marxist under the influence of the Russian Revolution of 1917. He was one of the founders of the CCP in 1921, but not acknowledged as one of its leaders until the Long March (1934–1935).

He was elected leader of the CCP in 1945 at the Seventh Congress of the CCP, and Mao Zedong Thought was declared the guiding principle of the Party. He proclaimed the founding of the People's Republic of China (PRC) on October 1, 1949.

Mao Zedong's thinking on questions of development was mainly aimed at formulating a strategy of the Chinese revolution in which China's peasantry was mobilized to fight with military means for political aims. With the end of internal and external wars, Mao had to shift focus from military concerns to political and economic strategies in overcoming poverty in China. Instead he led the country into the Korean War and mobilized the population against class enemies both outside and inside the party. Mass mobilization was for him the main tool to avoid the kind of fossilization and degeneration he observed in the Soviet Union under Khrushchev and Breshnev.

Mao started developing his ideas on a post-colonial future in China in the early 1940s. He blamed imperialism for having hindered the evolution of capitalism in China and therefore asked for a transitional period of "new democracy" to be inserted between the semi-colonial and semi-feudal present and the socialist future. During the "new democratic" period, the Communist Party was supposed to take over a leading role in society, guaranteeing that China could make up for its underdevelopment without having social inequality arise. Different forms of property rights would coexist, and different parties were allowed to articulate the political interests of their respective memberships. This kind of rationally planned and restricted capitalism was supposed to give enough room to accelerated economic growth while at the same time paving the way for a socialist future under proletarian dictatorship.

After the Communist takeover in 1949, however, Mao grew suspicious about his own theories and stressed that class struggle would have to go on even after the rise to power of the Communist Party. Much in contrast to the mainstream in the then-international Communist movement and to most leading members of the CCP, he did not believe that the main contradiction in socialist societies was the contradiction between underdeveloped means of production and the highly developed organization of production. For him the contradiction between bourgeoisie and the working classes was still of major importance, which is why he heralded the continuation of class struggle as the top priority for guaranteeing development in the political, social, and economic sense of the term. Whoever propagated to shift the focus of the Party from political revolution to economic development would meet with Mao's suspicion if not be criticized for right opportunism and empiricism.

According to this theory, the problem of the shortage of capital was to be solved by making use of the enormous manpower China was endowed with; the low productivity of China's industry was to be overcome by the growing motivation and consciousness of the workers. That is why these workers were to be trained politically and not technically, and their motivation was not to be fostered by economic incentives but rather by convincing them politically of the bright future of socialism in China.

As this strategy of overcoming underdevelopment by mass mobilization met with criticism inside and outside the Party, Mao Zedong saw his suspicion proven and replied to his critics by using his position as the charismatic leader of the Party to directly mobilize the masses against them and accelerate the speed of reform. That is how he changed his ideas of slowly expropriating the so-called "national bourgeoisie," depriving her of the opportunity to contribute to economic development in China; he also turned away from earlier thoughts of land reform as "giving land to the tillers" and instead introduced the system of "People's Communes," hoping for private and collective ownership to disappear from the countryside as soon as possible. Intellectuals having been attracted by the CCP in great numbers in the hope of a privileged position as consultants for the new regime, were selected as targets of vigorous attacks beginning in the early 1950s, instead of being mobilized as political supporters and experts. With inner party struggle as a direct reflection of conflicts between social classes, Mao hoped for the nation to reach the classless society of communism as soon as possible. Even when he saw that his plans could not be realized, he still envisaged China as, by moral and political standards, the most advanced socialist country of the world. As a consequence, he was suspicious of international contacts and wanted the country to be self-reliant and self-contented.

Every time Mao Zedong succeeded in putting his theories into practice, the country was hit by a major economic crisis. During the Great Leap Forward (1957–1958), the mobilization of the peasant population was supposed to quickly raise China's steel production, but instead left the country with a severe shortage of grain. In 1966, with the launching of the

Cultural Revolution, the industrial sector was severely disturbed so that after ten years of political turmoil, the economy was at the fringe of collapse and several parts of the country again were hit by severe famine. Under the conditions of crisis, Mao realized that the legitimacy of the Communist regime was subverted by its lack of economic success. He was therefore willing to divert from his theories and agreed to the policy of readjustment introduced by Zhou Enlai in the aftermath of the Great Leap.

He continued to serve as the chair of the CCP until his death on September 9, 1976.

SUSANNE WEIGELIN-SCHWIEDRZIK

See also China, People's Republic of; Chinese Communist Party; Chinese Revolution; Communist Economic Model; Deng Xiaoping; Marxism; Nationalism, Definition; Zhou Enlai

References and Further Reading

Knight, Nick, guest ed. "The Philosophical Thought of Mao Zedong: Studies from China (1981–1989)." *Chinese Studies in Philosophy* No. 23. Armonk, NY, London: Sharpe, 1992.

McFarquhar, Roderick, Timothy Cheek, and Eugene Wu, eds. *The Secret Speeches of Chairman Mao. From the Hundred Flowers to the Great Leap Forward.* Cambridge, MA: Harvard University Press, 1989.

Martin, Helmut, editor, *Mao Zedong Texte, Schriften, Dokumente, Reden, Gespräche*, Vols. 1–6. Münich, Vienna: Hanser, 1979–1982.

Schram, Stuart R. *The Thought of Mao Tse-tung.* Cambridge, UK: Cambridge University Press, 1989.

Spence, Jonathan. *Mao Zedong.* New York: Viking, 1999.

Teiwes, Frederick C. *Leadership, Legitimacy and Conflict in China: From a Charismatic Mao to the Politics of Succession.* Armonk, NY: ME Sharpe, 1984.

MAQUILADORA PROGRAM

The Maquiladora Program is a set of international trade policies and regulations that permit a business firm of the United States, or another "originating" nation, to temporarily transfer goods to Mexico, where they receive added value with minimal or no tariffs being applied to the goods so long as they are shipped back to the originating nation. Almost all instances of the Maquiladora Program involve the United States as the originating nation. The intended benefits of this program are low labor costs for the firm, lower prices for consumer goods, economic development for Mexico, and political good will. Critics point out that these benefits come at the expense of job loss for the originating country, creation of "sweatshop" working conditions in Mexico, and greater international dependence for the originating country.

The term "maquiladora" is derived from the Spanish verb "*maquilar*," which historically referred to the milling of wheat into flour, the "*maquila*" being a portion of the product given as payment to the miller and to other workers instead of cash wages. The modern meaning of "maquilar" is "to assemble" and "maquiladora" is generally translated into English as either "bonded assembly plant" or "twin plant." A bonded assembly plant is a factory that is authorized by the Mexican government to temporarily import goods duty free. Once the goods have been combined through an assembly process, or in other ways have received additional value, they are then re-exported to the originating country or, less frequently, to another country. While in Mexico, the goods are under the supervision of Mexican customs officials who insure that the goods are delivered directly to the factory, are kept separate from other goods, and that they do not leave the factory until they have been modified. In certain circumstances, a bond must be posted by the firm as a guarantee that the goods will leave Mexico in a timely fashion and not be sold on the local market, thereby avoiding normal duties. The advantages of the Maquiladora Program to the firm are convenience and financial in that they do not pay tariff duties unless the goods are sold in Mexico, and the wage rates are lower than in the originating country.

A twin plant, sometimes referred to as a "production sharing plant," is a common arrangement for taking advantage of the Maquiladora Program whereby a US firm locates two factories in close proximity but on opposite sides of the US–Mexican border. The plant on the US side of the border prepares materials for assembly and the plant on the Mexican side of the border does the assembly work. This twin plant arrangement minimizes transportation time and costs and it allows for centralized management control. Several paired US–Mexican border towns have experienced economic growth because of twin plant activity and have developed extensive cross-border relationships. Examples include Los dos Laredos (Nuevo Laredo, Mexico and Laredo, Texas) and Los dos Nogales (Nogales, Mexico and Nogales, Arizona). The Maquiladora Program is, essentially, a program of the Mexican government, created in the mid-1960s to replace the earlier "Bracero" program.

As discussed by Kelly (2001) there are three ways to establish a Maquiladora Program in Mexico. The most common method is to establish a wholly-owned subsidiary in Mexico that would own and operate the maquiladora. The second method is to use a shelter operation that invests in facilities, hires employees, and manufactures products for a fee based on labor costs and profit. The shelter operator generally relies upon the manufacturer to provide the equipment required for the plant. The third method is to use a subcontractor whose charges are based on unit cost rather than labor cost, and who is usually responsible for obtaining equipment.

Background of the Maquiladora Program

Because of the drain on factory, railroad, and agricultural labor caused by the Second World War effort, the United States faced labor shortages in the early 1940s. Mexican immigrants, legal and illegal, helped to fill the need, especially in the agricultural sector. In order to provide for the regulation of working conditions of this international work force, the United States and Mexico entered into an agreement known variously as "The Mexican Farm Labor Supply Program," "The Mexican Labor Agreement," and "The Labor Importation Program of 1942–1964." Perhaps the most widely recognized name given to the program is, simply, the "Bracero Program"—from the Spanish noun *brazo* (arm) indicating physical labor. From the US perspective, the program was created to obtain badly needed temporary workers for US farmers, but it was also intended to insure that Mexican workers were provided with basic necessities as required by Mexican statutes governing the treatment of workers in Mexico. US support for the program was made available through Public Law 45 of 1943. Specifically, the US statute made funds available for the following: the recruiting and transportation of workers, their families, and necessary property; furnishing of health, medical, and burial services, training, subsistence, protection, and shelter for workers and their families; advancing sums due from US employers; personnel, and expenses to carry out these purposes.

The Bracero program was modified several times until it was discontinued in 1964. In 1948, the contractor role was moved from the US government to the individual farm employer. Through Public Law 78, enacted in 1951, the US Congress modified the program substantially to allow the Secretary of Labor to arrange for recruitment of Mexicans for temporary agriculture work only when there were not enough US workers available. Major criticisms of the program were that enforcement methods were intimidating and insufficiently staffed, that it was creating an artificial labor market and reducing employment opportunities for US citizens, and that it was keeping a cap on US wage levels.

From 1949–1959, the number of Braceros increased from 8,500 to 84,000 and then dramatically decreased due to agricultural mechanization. In 1962, Bracero wage rates were raised sharply to a level determined to protect the wages of US workers. In addition, because so many Mexicans were attempting to enter the United States, Mexico was experiencing a labor shortage crisis. Opposition from workers' unions and the Kennedy administration tipped the balance, and when Public Law 78 was presented for renewal in 1963, the US congress extended it for only one year and it finally came to a formal end on December 31, 1964.

Immediately after the termination of the Bracero program, illegal immigration increased dramatically, although many workers were not successful in finding work in the border region. A number of studies were conducted to determine how to fill the needs of Mexican workers for employment and US manufacturing firms for low-wage workers. These studies led to several initiatives, one of which was the Border Industrialization Program (BIP), which made it possible for foreign-owned firms to build assembly plants in Mexico; these assembly plants became known as maquiladoras.

The BIP was enacted by the Mexican government in 1965. The major objectives of the BIP were to continue developing the economies of the country through attracting foreign investment and to provide employment opportunities for workers that had lost jobs due to the termination of the Bracero Program. The underlying strategy of the BIP was to take advantage of US Tariff Schedule 807, which allowed certain goods to be exported from the United States to another country where they would be modified and then re-exported to the United States with no tariff duties attached. "Tariff Schedule 807" is a classification found in the Tariff Schedule of the United States (TSUS), which was implemented in 1963 and replaced in January of 1989 by classification "9802" of the Harmonized Tariff Schedule of the United States (HTS). The HTS is administered by the United States International Trade Commission (formerly United States Tariff Commission). The founding legislation for this provision is the Tariff Act of 1930 (Hawley-Smoot), which is currently included as Chapter Four of Title 19 (Customs Duties) of the Code of the United States of America. The major mechanism used to achieve the goals of the BIP was the establishment of maquiladoras as described above.

Development of the Maquiladora Program

Although the BIP provided the opportunity for maquiladoras to be established and to operate, several modifications since 1965 have resulted in a more formalized, more highly regulated and controlled program. In order to provide for more standardization, the Mexican Government issued the Maquila Decree on December 22, 1989. This decree, as amended several times, is the basis for the Maquiladora Program as it operates today. Specifically, the Maquila Decree (*Decreto para el Fomento y Operación de la Industria Maquiladora de Exportación*) established the Mexican Secretariat of Commerce and Development (SECOFI, later renamed Ministry of Economy) as the governmental agency responsible for the regulation of maquiladoras and the agency that issues permits for operation of a maquiladora. Further, it specified that while the maquiladora is a registered Mexican corporation, 100% of the capital investment, ownership, and management of the firm may be foreign. Similarly, it specified that the firm is entitled to import, duty free, on a temporary basis, all equipment and materials necessary for operation of the business. Also, it allowed that land may be completely owned by the foreign investors except for two narrow strips along the US border and the coasts. Maquiladoras may be located anywhere in Mexico except Mexico City, Guadalajara, and Monterrey because of congestion already present in those cities.

A major element of the decree relates to the application of Mexican labor laws, which are the most restrictive aspect of the program. Among the labor requirements are: (1) every salaried and hourly employee must have a written employment contract; (2) maximum work week of six 8-hour shifts; (3) calculation of wages on a daily rate with a seventh nonworking day included; (4) payments to social security and national housing funds; (5) paid pregnancy leave, profit-sharing, national holidays, vacations, and severance benefits; and (6) payment of normal corporate income and asset taxes.

On December 24, 1993, the Maquila Decree was amended and, essentially, the effect was to relax several regulations. It was no longer required that 100% of the firm's product be exported; time limits for temporary storage of tools, materials, trailers, and containers were extended; a restriction on the manufacturing of textile products was removed; and the time limit on the application of sanctions by SECOFI was extended. With the implementation of the North American Free Trade Agreement (NAFTA) in 1994, trade between the United States and Mexico grew rapidly, yet direct influences on the operation of maquiladoras and on the trends in overall maquiladora output were minor. Analysis conducted by Gruben and Kiser (2001) indicated that certain aspects of NAFTA may have encouraged maquiladora growth, some had little impact, and others may actually have discouraged maquiladora growth. They determined that US industrial production in general, and international currency and wage variability specifically, had the greatest influence on maquiladora employment.

One major difficulty that NAFTA initially posed for the maquiladora program, however, was Article 303 of the NAFTA agreement, which required that tariff duties be applied to all materials used in manufacturing that had originated outside of NAFTA countries. This was particularly problematic in the electronics industry, which had traditionally imported electronic products from Asia as components for products that were assembled in maquiladoras and then exported to the United States. An ingenious solution to this problem was developed by the Mexican government with the establishment of Industrial Sector Promotion Programs (PROSEC) through a decree issued on December 31, 2000. PROSEC stipulated that a firm would be in literal compliance with Article 303 if the items brought in from a non-NAFTA country, to be assembled with other components for re-export to a NAFTA country, had not traditionally been available in Mexico. So long as this opportunity to import such items was available to all Mexican firms, and no Mexican firm would supply the items, then Article 303 would not have an effect on the maquiladora.

On May 12, 2003, the Maquila Decree was amended once again. These modifications resulted in clarifying five distinct forms of maquiladoras: maquila operation (excludes services); industrial maquila (manufacture and transformation of goods); holding maquila (manages two or more operations under one firm); services maquila; submaquila. In addition, the 2003 amendments require more detailed proposals by firms desiring to establish a maquiladora, expand NAFTA regulation exceptions to the European Union and the European Free Trade Association, and, in general, provide greater regulatory specifications.

STEVEN PAULSON

See also 807 Industries; Caribbean Basin Initiative; North American Free Trade Agreement (NAFTA); Mexico: History and Economic Development

References and Further Reading

Bacon, David. *The Children of NAFTA: Labor Wars on the US/Mexico Border.* Berkeley, CA: University of California Press, 2004.

Baz, Aureliano Gonzalez. "Manufacturing in Mexico: The Mexican In-Bond Maquila Program." www.udel.edu/leipzig/texts2/vox128.htm. (Accessed October 4, 2004).

Feenstra, Robert C., Gordon H. Hanson, and Deborah L. Swenson. "Offshore Assembly from the United States:

Production Characteristics of the 9802 Program," pp. 85–122. In Robert C. Feenstra, ed., *The Impact of International Trade on Wages.* Chicago: University of Chicago Press, 2002.

Foreign Trade Practice Group Mexico. *Amendments to the Maquiladora Decree.* Zurich, Switzerland: Baker and McKenzie, August 2003.

Gruben, William C. and Sherry L. Kiser, "NAFTA and Maquiladoras: Is the Growth Connected?" pp. 22–24. In Federal Reserve Bank of Dallas, *The Border Economy,* June 2001.

Kelly, Patrick J. "Mexico, Maquiladoras and NAFTA." *Fredrikson and Byron's International Focus Newsletter,* (March 2001) http://www.fredlaw.com/articles/international/intl_0103_ pjk.html.

MARCOS, FERDINAND

As the sixth president of the Republic of the Philippines, Ferdinand E. Marcos (1917–1989) took office in 1965 amid heightened expectations and with the good will of most Filipinos. He won the election running on an anti-corruption platform, and vowed in his inauguration speech "to make this country great again with the help of the masses." Even when he declared martial law in 1972 and effectively ended twenty-six years of democracy, many Filipinos welcomed the event and expected some good to come from it. After all, Marcos had been raised by parents who passed on to their son a notion of excellence in everything he would attempt. Born in Sarrat, Ilocos Norte, in 1917, Marcos was valedictorian in his grammar school and high school and only narrowly missed being valedictorian of his graduating 1935 class at the University of the Philippines Law School. In 1939 he made the highest score in history in the national bar examination. During World War II, he carried out guerilla activities against the Japanese occupation and served in the US Army's 14th Infantry Division, then returned to Ilocos Norte in 1946 and began a criminal law practice.

He was elected to the House of Representatives in 1950 and married Imelda Romualdez, a former Miss Manila, in 1954. Five years later, he won a Senate seat and worked his way up the political ladder to election as President of the Senate in 1963. Two years later, he was elected President.

Despite the veneer of reputability, Marcos' corruption had begun while he was a congressman and head of the import control board, where he took huge bribes for approving import licenses. As only a representative in congress on a small salary, Marcos had already become a millionaire. As president, his lust for personal aggrandizement acquired epic proportions. While corruption seemed a characteristic of many politicians in the Philippines, the scale of the plunder carried out by Marcos and his cronies defied the imagination of his cohorts. A conservative estimate would be that Marcos looted, diverted, and laundered around $5 billion in public assets in extraordinarily complicated legal and semi-legal schemes.

Marcos did not end corruption and smuggling (as he promised many times) but, instead, brought it into Malacañang (the presidential palace). He did not create new, productive jobs (as he promised many times) but, instead, created a swollen bureaucracy loyal only to him. By the late 1960s discontent grew as the economy faltered. In 1968 a dozen former university students reorganized the banned Philippine Communist Party, formed the New People's Army, and prepared for a long rural guerrilla war.

The following year, in an allegedly fraudulent election, Marcos won a second presidential term, the first time in Philippine history that a president had been elected to a second term. Major disturbances rocked the Philippines, and more than two thousand demonstrators marched on Malacañang.

The economy spiraled downward, the gap between the rich and the poor widened, and protestors filled the streets of Manila. On September 23, 1972, Marcos imposed martial law. Supposedly aimed at the multiple rebellions of Manila students, communists, and the Muslims in the southern Philippines, the declaration of martial law was itself a prime example of the corrupt Marcos. Marcos knew that he needed a specific incident to make martial law acceptable to the public, and that incident was the alleged machine gun attack on Secretary of National Defense Juan Ponce Enrile's car by communists. After the fall of Marcos, Enrile himself confessed that the attack had been faked. Citing the threat of communism, Marcos sent his troops throughout the country to arrest scores of opposition politicians, journalists, students, and others critical of Marcos' rule as well as to shut down newspapers and broadcast stations. (Marcos had already put his relatives and ethnic mates in charge of the armed forces.)

He rewrote the Constitution to empower himself even more, and over the next five years his security forces imprisoned more than seventy thousand people. Many, however, at first welcomed martial law, accepting Marcos' explanation, enjoying the decline in street violence, and expecting improvements in the economy, which did, indeed, show some initial signs of strength.

Meanwhile Marcos and his cronies encouraged export-oriented growth, with exports such as sugar and coconuts, and created a small number of huge enterprises that were controlled either privately by Marcos intimates or by the government, which itself came to control more than three hundred corporations in a Mussolini-style collusion between industry and government. First Lady Imelda Marcos squandered public funds on public-relations projects such as a multi-million-dollar center for the arts.

In August 1983 opposition leader Benigno Aquino returned from exile in the United States and was assassinated upon his arrival at Manila International Airport. General Fabian Ver, military chief of staff and a cousin of Marcos, was charged with Aquino's slaying, along with twenty-five other army officers. In November, bowing to US pressure, rioting in the streets of Manila, and calls from the Philippine business community and the Roman Catholic church, whose priests proclaimed a pastoral critique of Marcos in churches throughout the Philippines, Marcos set presidential elections. When Ver and the others were acquitted, Aquino's widow, Corazon, announced as candidate for president. The election was held in February 1986, and the consensus was that Aquino won despite widespread fraud by Marcos supporters. Nevertheless, the Marcos-controlled National Assembly proclaimed Marcos the winner. Aquino called for a nonviolent campaign of strikes and boycotts.

Later in February both Marcos and Aquino took the oath of office in separate ceremonies. Marcos' ceremony, however, was attended by only a handful in Malacañang, while Aquino's ceremony was attended by half a million or so in the great central park of Manila, Rizal Park. Later that day, Marcos took a helicopter to the US air base in central Luzon and then flew on to exile in Hawaii.

After twenty years of rule, Marcos left the country with a historically greater gap between rich and poor, a starved economy that was way behind neighboring countries, and an even stronger Muslim and communist insurgency.

In 1988 Marcos and his wife were indicted by the US government, mainly on charges that they used embezzled money to buy real estate in the United States. Marcos was, however, too ill to stand trial, and the charges were dropped. He died in exile in Honolulu in September 1989, and was finally laid to rest in the Philippines three years later.

ROBERT LAWLESS

See also Aquino, Benigno and Corazón; Philippines; Southeast Asia: History and Economic Development; Southeast Asia: International Relations

References and Further Reading

Bonner, Raymond. *Waltzing with a Dictator: The Marcoses and the Making of American Policy*. New York: Times, 1987.
Bresnan, John. *Crisis in the Philippines: The Marcos Era and Beyond*. Princeton, NJ: Princeton University Press, 1986.
Burton, Sandra. *Impossible Dream: The Marcoses, the Aquinos, the Unfinished Revolution*. New York: Warner, 1989.
Celoza, Albert F. *Ferdinand Marcos and the Philippines: The Political Economy of Authoritarianism*. Westport, CT: Praeger, 1997.
Reid, Robert H. and Eileen Guerrero. *Corazon Aquino and the Brushfire Revolution*, Baton Rouge, LA: Louisiana State University Press, 1995.
Rempel, William C. *Delusions of a Dictator: The Mind of Marcos as Revealed in His Secret Diaries*. Boston: Little, Brown, 1993.
Rosenberg, David A. *Marcos and Martial Law in the Philippines*. Ithaca, NY: Cornell University Press.
Seagrave, Sterling. *The Marcos Dynasty*. New York: Harper and Row, 1988.

MARSHALL ISLANDS, REPUBLIC OF

The Marshall Islands people have had development thrust upon them, as well as pursued their own development concerns. Commitment to a cash economy has increased as the population has grown from less than twenty thousand after World War II to fifty-six thousand in 2005. Local resources are not adequate to provide for today's needs such as food, housing, medical care, and education. The current push towards privatization is dependent on further outside assistance.

Political Developments

The Marshall Islands gained independence in 1983 after almost forty years of administrative rule by the United States as part of a United Nations Trust Territory of the Pacific Islands (TTPI). Previous colonisation by Spain, then Germany, Japan, and the United States, as well as the aftermath of World War II, fought on their territory, has left a number of alternative foreign ideologies which Marshallese have made their own. The desire to control their own affairs has been mitigated by the need to finance administrative programmes.

The new Republic of the Marshall Islands (RMI) elected to continue its relations with the United States under a Compact of Free Association, signed in 1987, for a period of fifteen years, and a second Compact was signed in 2004 for a further fifteen-year period. In return for allowing the United States to continue to use Kwajalein atoll as a Missile-Testing Range, the RMI receives an annual injection of funds from Washington, decreasing over the next fifteen years; a community fidelity fund for the future; and access to certain US federal programmes. It has control of its own internal affairs.

The Constitution of 1983 provided for a parliamentary-style government headed by a president and

Cabinet with a Legislature and a Council of Chiefs charged with monitoring traditional affairs. The first commoner president, elected in 1999, followed a president who had held dual authority as senior *iroij* (chief) and elected president, and thus commanded much respect. The commoner President Kessai Hese Note marks a new era in RMI politics as he strikes a path toward improved solvency, greater accountability, and the people's concerns (Pollock 2004). The matter of land rights as the basis for collateral for loans looms large as outside demands for financial sustainability come face to face with the foundation of Marshallese identity—land.

RMI maintains its position in the Pacific by its close collaboration with its neighbours and former TT members, Palau and the Federated States of Micronesia. The nation is also an active member of the Pacific Forum, and other Pacific-wide agencies such as the Secretariat for the Pacific Community, Forum Fisheries Agency, and Pacific Arts Association.

Economic Development

Marshall Islands' resources remain underdeveloped. As a nation of twenty-six atolls and low coralline islands, surrounded by a large section of the Pacific Ocean, land resources are minimal compared to the potential of their marine resources. During Trust Territory times, little was done by the United States as trustee to further economic development other than to triple the TT administrative budget after 1963 (Hanlon 2001).

RMI relies on external inputs in the form of aid and grants. The United States provides 70% of government income, with Japan, ROC/Taiwan, and Australia contributing small additional amounts. The Asia Development Bank provides advice and funding in line with US policies. Concessional loans amounted to 18% of all external assistance in 1999–2000, but the amount varies from year to year (Hughes 2001).

The financial situation of the government remains precarious, heavily dependent on these outside sources. For households, the four Section 177 communities—Bikini, Enewetak, Rongelap, and Utrik—have assured quarterly income from their nuclear compensation claims, but the rest of the population must rely on income from a few government jobs, and expectations from the growth of private business. The subsistence sector on the outer islands has diminishing income from copra (dried coconut meat), together with use of local foodstuffs from breadfruit, pandanus, taro, and fish. Transportation to these twenty-four scattered atolls is a vital link.

Copra has been the main source of earned revenue since German times, but its export value is diminishing. The activities of fisheries have increased since independence, with Taiwanese fishing boats having a notable presence in Majuro lagoon. For many Marshallese, fishing is a recreational activity, but attempts by Marshall Islands Marine Resources Association to develop it as an economic resource are thwarted by difficulties of transportation, fresh water, and marketing. Pearl fishing, the shrimp industry, and marine conservation are growing.

Tourism struggles. High costs of transportation to the mid-Pacific, and limited hotel facilities hamper further development. Dive Bikini offers opportunities for underwater exploration of the WWII battleships that the United States sank in Bikini lagoon as part of their nuclear tests.

Urbanisation by outer islanders seeking jobs and social services in either of the two urban centres, Majuro or Ebeye (Kwajalein atoll), now accounts for 60% of the resident population. Polarisation of urban and outer island lifestyles is a development trend being addressed by loans and grants supported by agencies such as ROC/Taiwan (Marshall Islands Journal 2005). Downsizing the public service in 2001–2002 has placed greater pressures on households seeking cash to feed and support their members. Some 10% of Marshallese have established communities in US states.

Social Developments

Under the UN Trust Territory administration, social development was largely unplanned and unmonitored. The Marshall Islands administration drew on its funds to provide education, health, and transport facilities, but these met only minimal needs.

Advanced health and education facilities have been centred in the two urban areas. While clinics and primary schools provide basic services on outer atolls, the hospitals and secondary schools contribute to increased urbanisation. Youth assistance programmes are offered both through government- and church-funded agencies. The churches play an important role in social support. Women's affairs are coordinated through a Non-Governmental Organization (NGO), Women United Together Marshall Islands, which links outer islanders with urban women, as well as with church and secular groups. With fewer than ten women in elected or appointed government positions, gender relations appear unbalanced. Yet women provide the strength for all communities.

The media in the form of a newspaper *(Marshall Islands Journal)*, radio, and television provide for social commentary. These media have become more vocal over issues associated with settlement of the second Compact, and thus their future.

Conclusions

The major issue facing Marshall Islands development is the degree of control they can exercise over their own future. RMI government relies on financial support derived from US need for continued use of Kwjalein Missile Range. The degree to which that dependence will reduce over the next fifty years will stem from marine projects, fishing, possibly mining, and other global developments. The country's strategic location in the mid-Pacific may become a casualty of global warming and sea level rise, or it may prove vital in future world developments.

NANCY J. POLLOCK

See also Asian Development Bank; Ethnic Conflicts: Oceania; Oceania: History and Economic Development; Oceania: International Relations; United Nations Trusteeship Council

References and Further Reading

Half Life—Critical Review of US Nuclear Testing Programme in the Pacific [Video recording]. Canberra, Australia: ABC Four Corners programme, 1985.
Hughes, Tony. *Marshall Islands—Meto 2000.* Manila, the Philippines: Asian Development Bank, 2001.
Johnson, Giff. *Collision Course at Kwajalein.* Honolulu: Pacific Concerns Research Centre, 1985.
Pollock, Nancy J. *These Roots Remain.* Hawaii: Institute for Polynesian Studies and University of Hawaii Press, 1992.
———. "The Marshall Islanders." In *Endangered Peoples of Oceania,* J. Fitzpatrick (ed.), Ch. 5. Westport, CT: The Green Press, 2001.
———. "Three Pathways to Compensation for Nuclear Testing in the Marshall Islands." *Journal of Social Justice* 3:191–206.
———. *Republic of the Marshall Islands.* Country Study for National Integrity Systems Pacific Study. Canberra, Australia: 2004.
Sen, Amartya. *Development as Freedom.* Oxford, UK: Oxford University Press, 1999.
Van der Velde, Nancy (coordinator). *The Marshall Islands—Living Atolls Amidst the Living Sea.* Majuro: National Biodiversity Team of RMI, 2000.

MARTINIQUE

Martinique is a French *département d'outre-mer* (overseas department) in the Caribbean. The northernmost of the Windward Islands, Martinique occupies 1,060 square kilometers of territory. The island, which is sixty-five kilometers long and twenty kilometers wide, is located between Dominica to the north and St. Lucia to the south. Fort de France, the capital, is located on the western side of the island. Mt. Pelée, the highest point at 1,397 meters, is in the north. The northern half of the island is much more mountainous than the southern half. Beaches on the northern half of the island have black sand, while beaches on the southern half have white sand. Most of Martinique's 430,000 people are French-speaking Roman Catholics of African descent. The most famous person born in Martinique was the Empress Josephine (ne. Beauharnais), the daughter of wealthy sugar plantation owners and the wife of Napoleon Bonaparte.

When Christopher Columbus discovered Martinique in 1502, it was occupied by hostile Carib Indians. Spain's attempts to settle the island during the sixteenth century were frustrated by fierce resistance from the Indians. In 1635, a group of French settlers established the first permanent settlement on Martinique at St. Pierre. In 1640, the French built a large fort above the harbor at Fort de France. By 1660, the French successfully removed the Indians from the island and established a successful sugar-producing colony based on African slave labor. The British intermittently occupied Martinique from 1794 to 1802. French planters, frightened by the excessive violence that accompanied the French and Haitian Revolutions, willingly accepted the British occupation. The French planters, who were able to sell their sugar in British markets, prospered during the British occupation. Although Martinique was eventually restored to French control, the importance of the sugar industry declined after slavery was abolished in 1848.

On May 8, 1902, Mt. Pelée erupted, destroying the colonial capital of St. Pierre and killing the town's twenty-nine thousand inhabitants. The only survivor was a prisoner—Louis Auguste Cyparis, who eventually joined the Barnum and Bailey Circus—locked in a solitary confinement dungeon in the jail. Before the eruption, St. Pierre had been known as the Paris of the West Indies. French Governor Louis Mouttet, eager to keep the population in the city for the upcoming May 11 elections, ignored the minor explosions that began at the end of April and prohibited people from leaving the city. Although St. Pierre was eventually rebuilt, the capital was moved to Fort de France.

Repeated attempts by the inhabitants of Martinique during the twentieth century to gain greater autonomy often resulted in violence. The enhanced racism and authoritarianism exhibited by the Vichy government after it came to power in 1941 shattered the illusions that the people of Martinique had about color-blind French brotherhood. A significant number of people on the island began to embrace the philosophy of negritude, which urged black people to reject cultural assimilation and emphasize their African heritage. Author Aimé Césaire (b. 1913), the mayor of Fort de France from 1945 to 2001, consistently sought greater autonomy for the island. Basing his ideas on a blend of negritude, anti-colonialism, and communism, Césaire believed that the political assimilation of the French colonies into the French Republic would guarantee the human rights of the people of Martinique.

In 1946, Guadeloupe, Martinique, and French Guiana officially became French overseas departments. Although Martinique was offered independence in 1958, the inhabitants, motivated by economic factors, voted to continue their relationship with France. As an overseas department of France, Martinique is entitled to elect two representatives to the French Senate and four representatives to the French National Assembly. The French president, on the advice of the French Minister of Interior, appoints a governor, known as a prefect, to represent the interests of the French government in Martinique. The power of the prefect—Yves Dassonville since 2004—is largely ceremonial. Local power is vested in a General Council consisting of forty-five members and a Regional Council consisting of forty-one members. The presidents of the General and Regional Councils are elected by their respective members. Claude Lise was elected president of the General Council in 1992. Alfred Marie-Jeanne, president of the Martinique Independence Movement (MIM), was elected president of the Regional Council in 1998.

By 2004, agriculture, once the mainstay of the island's economy, only generated 5% of the island's revenue. Banana exports have surpassed sugar exports as the primary agricultural commodity. Although limited attempts at light industry have been implemented, tourism has become the most important source of foreign exchange. Revenue from tourism, which was enhanced by a large increase in the number of US cruise ships visiting Martinique, was hurt by the tragic events of September 11, 2001. Hurricanes have had a negative impact on both agriculture and tourism. France continues to provide huge subsidies.

MICHAEL R. HALL

See also Caribbean: History and Economic Development; Caribbean: International Relations; French Guiana; Guadeloupe

References and Further Reading

Burton, Richard D. E. and Fred Reno, eds. *French and West Indian: Martinique, Guadeloupe, and French Guiana Today*. Charlottesville, VA: University Press of Virginia, 1995.

Dessalles, Pierre, Elborg Forster, and Robert Forster. *Sugar and Slavery, Family and Race: The Letters and Diary of Pierre Dessalles, Planter in Martinique, 1808–1856*. Baltimore, MD: Johns Hopkins University Press, 1996.

Scarth, Alwyn. *La Catastrophe: The Eruption of Mount Pelée, the Worst Volcano Disaster of the Twentieth Century*. Oxford, UK: Oxford University Press, 2002.

Sutton, Paul. *Dual Legacies in the Contemporary Caribbean: Continuing Aspects of British and French Dominion*. London: Frank Cass Publishers, 1986.

Wideman, John Edgar. *The Island: Martinique*. Washington, DC: National Geographic, 2003.

MARXISM

Marxism is the name given to a critical theory of society first elaborated by Karl Marx, a German philosopher of the nineteenth century who lived most of his adult life in England, that became one of the principal currents of socialist thinking, first in Europe and then worldwide. Endorsed by the Bolshevik wing of the Russian Social Democratic party led by V. I. Lenin, it became the official ideology of the Communist Party of the Soviet Union, and hence of the government of that one-party state, after the "October Revolution" of 1917; it retained this position, often under the more accurate label "Marxism-Leninism," until the dissolution of Communist political dominance there in the early 1990s. Meanwhile, within the institutional framework of the Third Communist International, Communist parties in many nations submitted, in varying degrees, to centralized political and ideological control exercised by the Soviet leadership in the name of Marxist theory. In the aftermath of World War II, a number of the nations of Eastern Europe as well as China, North Korea, and later North Vietnam acquired Communist governments, and Communist parties played important roles—often in hostile opposition, sometimes in temporary collaboration—in the political life of many developing nations as well as in some developed ones, notably France and Italy. By the end of the twentieth century, Marxism or Marxism-Leninism remained the official ideology of North Korea, China, Vietnam, and Cuba, and it continued to claim many intellectual adherents, although far fewer than in previous decades.

The Marxism of Marx

As Marx's friend, collaborator, and popularizer, Friedrich Engels, recounted it, Marx drew on three main intellectual traditions—those of "utopian socialism" (a label they attached above all to the theories of the Count de Saint-Simon, Charles Fourier, and Robert Owen), of early capitalist economic theory beginning with Adam Smith, and of G. W. F. Hegel's philosophy, with its dialectical view (that is, development as taking place through successive internal oppositions) of history and reality in general. On this account, socialism moved from mere utopian wishful thinking to being a scientific worldview when Marx derived "the secret of surplus value" from his analysis and internal critique of bourgeois political economy and used Hegel's method, purged of its idealistic conception of history as the self-unfolding of "Spirit" or God in the world and understood instead in a purely materialist way, to demonstrate that capitalism would eventually have to collapse through its own internal contradictions.

By the "secret of surplus value" Marx meant the perception that human labor power is treated as a commodity like any other within a capitalist economic system, inasmuch as it, too, is bought and sold on the market, but that it has the unique capacity of being able to produce more than it costs—that is, more than the subsistence wage paid to the worker for his or her upkeep, plus reproduction of the next generation of workers. Agreeing with Smith's premise that labor is the ultimate producer of value within this exchange system, Marx contended that the difference between the amount of time needed for the worker to add enough value to the product on which he or she is working in order to earn subsistence, on the one hand, and the total amount of time (per day, week, or year) that the worker has agreed to work in order to be hired, on the other, constitutes "surplus value" extracted by the owners of capital. Marx's early, more ethically-oriented work, notably his *Economic and Philosophical Manuscripts of 1844* (which were not widely known until the mid-twentieth century), emphasized the *alienation* of workers—from their own life-activity, from its products, and from one another— in this competitive system wherein they are ostensibly free but in fact must work, under conditions not of their choosing, just in order to live. In the great classic of his later years, *Capital (Das Kapital),* Marx combined these insights with a more complicated and mathematically oriented analysis of the workings of the system to demonstrate that it tends in the direction of a polarization between a relatively few owners of large concentrations of capital and the vast majority of workers, the proletariat, who will eventually be in a position to wrest the means of production away from the owners with comparative ease.

Although nothing in Marx's complex analysis of the variable factors in the system (which includes, e.g., the possibility of achieving vast and rapid increases in productivity through automated machinery, and the great expansion of capitalist trade and exploitation to other parts of the world that were not yet fully capitalist in the mid-nineteenth century) led deductively to the conclusion that it would reach its final crisis anytime soon, Marx himself expected that this crisis was imminent. This is clear in his *Manifesto of the Communist Party* (1848) and in numerous personal letters. Engels, who outlived Marx by twelve years, had more doubts, especially as industrial workers, especially the more skilled ones, though on the whole still living in miserable circumstances, began here and there to enjoy some small prosperity. Disputes that were at once both theoretical and practical broke out within the large German Social Democratic Party and similar parties elsewhere over whether, *inter alia*, to treat Marx's analyses as scientific predictions of an inevitable future and hence in no need of active implementation, or as implying the necessity of violent revolutionary action in order to be realized.

Imperialism and the Marxism of Lenin and His Successors

Lenin, who treated the first of these views as an anti-Marxist heresy that he labelled "Economism," strongly supported the latter view. He argued that, particularly in light of the extremely repressive political conditions of Tsarist Russia, the formation of a group of professional revolutionaries who would serve as the "vanguard" of the proletariat was required. Moreover, he believed that it was unnecessary for Russia, with its relatively underdeveloped industry, to wait to "catch up" with Western capitalist countries before undergoing a Marxist revolution. He saw World War I, which to him was essentially a struggle between the principal European imperialist powers for control over colonies in the rest of the world, as providing the occasion for just such a revolution in backward Russia, which could then spark similar upheavals worldwide. The collapse of the Tsarist army and weaknesses in the provisional government headed by A. F. Kerensky enabled Lenin's Bolsheviks to take power from the latter within a few months of the revolution's formation. After a brief period of comparative openness, the new regime, menaced by both armed domestic opposition and the dispatch of expeditionary forces to portions of the Russian territory by several Western governments, and disappointed by its lack of success in encouraging revolutionary uprisings elsewhere, became authoritarian and repressive, insisting on an ideological conformity that enthroned a rigid interpretation of Marxism as official dogma.

The civil war ended and the expeditionary forces left, but Joseph Stalin, Lenin's successor as General Secretary of the Soviet Communist Party and hence supreme director of the international Communist movement as well as ruler of the federation that took as its name the Union of Soviet Socialist Republics, intensified these tendencies. He drove his former comrade Leon Trotsky into exile—thus incidentally spawning a rival version of Marxism, Trotskyism, which insisted on the need for a worldwide revolution and regarded the Soviet regime as a bureaucratic betrayal of Marxist principles—and conducted bloody purges of other former rivals, of dissidents, and of rural small landholders. He also promoted rapid, forced industrialization and created a chain of "*gulags*," or slave labor camps, for political prisoners. His substitution, in effect, of a new form of Russocentrism for the Marxism of Marx may, however, have helped him to rally citizens behind him in repulsing Hitler's invasion during World War II, at the end of which Stalin was accorded control over the group of Central and East European countries that (with the slightly later addition of Czechoslovakia) became known as the Soviet Bloc or the Warsaw Pact. By the time of Stalin's death in 1953, the superpower rivalry and struggle called the Cold War, thought to oppose the Communist "East" (a geographical designation given greater apparent legitimacy as a result of the success of the Marxist revolution in China under the leadership of Mao Tse-Tung) to the democratic "West," was conducted to a considerable degree in ideological terms, with "Marxism" being identified by both "camps" as the ideology of Communism.

Western Marxism and Other Marxisms

While there had always been adherents of Marxism, besides Trotskyites, who treated it more as an insightful philosophical method to be employed in social criticism than as the rigid, deterministic, scientific worldview that Soviet Marxist "orthodoxy" claimed it to be, the development of schools of thought known collectively as "Western Marxism" was strongly abetted by a widespread post-World War II revulsion against the many remaining vestiges of European colonialism, to which Marxism's revolutionary spirit seemed clearly opposed, as well as, on an intellectual plane, by the new dissemination of Marx's early, "humanistic" writings. Among the best-known Western Marxists were members of the German "Frankfurt School" of critical theory, notably Herbert Marcuse and, from a later generation, Jürgen Habermas. Future postcolonial leaders in Africa and Asia had often come into contact with, and been inspired by, Marxist thinking during their studies in France, the United Kingdom, and other Western countries, and the existence of growing numbers of self-described Marxists who did not accept Communist Party discipline was a further encouragement to many of them to advocate and pursue socialist policies when they attained positions of influence. One example, among many, of such intellectual fertilization that was also political in nature was the endorsement given by the prominent French philosopher, Jean-Paul Sartre, during the long Marxist phase of his career, to the writings and work of Franz Fanon, the Martiniquan-born psychiatrist who threw in his lot with the Algerian revolution against French domination. A center of Marxist-inspired resistance to the intellectual hegemony of the Soviet version of Marxism, one that provided special encouragement to East European Marxist dissidents, was the "*Praxis* Group" of independent-minded but still avowedly Marxist philosophers in Yugoslavia, a country posed as a more or less neutral buffer between East and West, and of which the long-time President, Marshal Tito, contributed significantly to the creation of the movement of developing "Third World" countries during the 1950s. In Latin America, too, Marxism inspired many revolutionary and reform movements (including an important hybrid Marxist-Christian movement known as "liberation theology"), particularly in the wake of Fidel Castro's ascendancy to power in Cuba and subsequent self-avowal as a Marxist and Communist.

Dénouement

The "Thaw," a loosening of political and ideological constraints that was initiated by Stalin's successor, Nikita Khrushchev, who also made public some previously-concealed facts about Stalin's enormous excesses, for a time rendered more thinkable a climate of genuine debate and criticism within the officially Marxist countries similar to that promoted by Western, Yugoslavian, and some Third World Marxists. It was soon nullified, at least in large measure, by Soviet suppression of a popular worker-supported government in Hungary that had briefly replaced the Soviet-sponsored one. This 1956 event already occasioned widespread loss of hope for serious reform of Soviet socialism and, given the common though not entirely justified identification of the two, a concomitant decline in Marxism's attractiveness to many and an increasing cynicism concerning it. Equally or perhaps even more damaging along the same lines was the 1968 Soviet invasion of Czechoslovakia, another Warsaw

Pact member state, where Prime Minister Dubcek had been attempting to carry out internal reforms known as the "Prague Spring." Twenty-one years later, the "Velvet Revolution" in that same country met with little or no military resistance and heralded the break-up of the Warsaw Pact, the end of Communist Party dominance, and the eventual dissolution, into separate, smaller entities with often highly nationalistic orientations, of the Soviet Union, Yugoslavia, and even Czechoslovakia itself. Marxism had always been touted as a unique combination of theory with political practice; so it is not surprising that the disappearance of so many actual regimes that had claimed to be Marxist, combined with the aggressive advocacy, on the parts of Margaret Thatcher, Ronald Reagan, and other Western leaders, of such capitalist practices and institutions as privatization and global free markets that are the objects of Marxism's severest criticism, has led to a palpable decline in its influence. Nevertheless, there are those who continue to find elements of classical Marxism to be of use in generating new critical social theories, particularly with respect to the current course of global development.

WILLIAM McBRIDE

See also Communist Economic Model

References and Further Reading

Anderson, Kevin. *Lenin, Hegel, and Western Marxism: A Critical Study*. Urbana, IL: University of Illinois Press, 1995.
Aronson, Ronald. *After Marxism*. New York and London: The Guilford Press, 1995.
Avineri, Shlomo, ed. *Karl Marx on Colonialism and Modernization: His Despatches* [sic] *and Other Writings on China, India, Mexico, the Middle East and North Africa*. Garden City, NY: Doubleday, 1969.
Fanon, Frantz. *The Wretched of the Earth*. Preface by Jean-Paul Sartre, translated by Constance Farringto. New York: Grove Press, 1966.
Kolakowski, Leszek. *Main Currents of Marxism: Its Rise, Growth, and Dissolution*. Translated by P. S. Falla. Oxford, UK: Clarendon Press, 1978.
Lenin, V. I. *What Is to Be Done?* New York: International Publishers, 1943.
Marcuse, Herbert. *Soviet Marxism: A Critical Analysis*. New York: Random House, 1961.
Marx, Karl. *Capital: A Critique of Political Economy*. Translated by Samuel Moore and Edward Aveling. New York: International Publishers, 1967.
———. *The Communist Manifesto*. Translated by Samuel Moore, edited by Frederic L. Bender. New York and London: Norton, 1988.
———. *Karl Marx: Early Writings*. Edited and translated by T. B. Bottomore. New York: McGraw-Hill, 1964.
Petrovic, Gajo. Marx in the Mid-Twentieth Century: A Yugoslav Philosopher Reconsiders Karl Marx's Writings. Garden City, NY: Doubleday, 1967.
Schweickart, David. *After Capitalism*. Lanham, MD: Rowman & Littlefield, 2002.

MAU MAU

Mau Mau was an armed anti-colonial rebellion that broke out in 1952 and took to the use of violence to compel the colonial government in Kenya to address African grievances. Its activities were concentrated in central Kenya, particularly among the Kikuyu ethnic group; but the uprising was not simply a Kikuyu affair. It recruited fighters from various ethnic groups in Kenya, like the Luo, Samia, and Banyala of Western Kenya; the Maasai of Southern Kenya; the Kamba of Eastern Kenya; and the Meru of Central Kenya. That the rebellion started in central Kenya, with the Kikuyu as the majority of its fighters, was due to the fact that British colonialism started there and the Kikuyu were the most exposed to the colonial pinch.

The colonial administration in Kenya created the economic, social, and political conditions that contributed to the outbreak of the rebellion, for it was essentially a reaction to the sustained underdevelopment of the Africans throughout the colonial period. The inception of colonialism in Kenya saw many Africans, especially the Kikuyu, loose their fertile land to the European settlers in the highlands. Whereas this disrupted African agriculture, pastrolism, particularly among the Maasai, was also disrupted as Africans were henceforth confined to specific geographical localities known as "reserves," where grazing land was inadequate. In addition, smallholder agricultural production in the "reserves" was confined to subsistence farming, for Africans were barred from growing cash crops. In the midst of this economic downturn, the colonial administration imposed heavy taxation on Africans to compel them to provide cheap labor on European plantations. The colonial administration also introduced the carrying of identification cards (known as *kipande* in Kiswahili) in order to restrict the movement of Africans into other areas that would have satisfied their economic interests. This arrangement cemented an economic squeeze for Africans.

There was also the color bar in the social realm. Besides racial segregation in the residential areas, social services were provided along racial lines. Africans attended separate medical and educational institutions, which were often poor compared to those of the Europeans and Asians. Moreover, it is the missionaries who attempted to provide such services to the Africans and not the government, yet Africans paid taxes. Whereas missionaries were making great effort in this regard, their rejection of African culture drew yet another bone of contention between the Europeans and the Africans, especially among the Kikuyu who insisted on practicing female circumcision to the chagrin of the missionaries. The resultant tensions and quarrels with the missions led, among other things, to the establishment of independent schools by the Kikuyu. Other communities in the country complained of the generally poor conditions regarding health, education, employment, taxation without representation, police brutality in the urban areas, and so forth.

Landlessness was, however, the immediate cause of the uprising. The demobilization of soldiers who had fought in the Second World War increased the demand for land among the Africans. Whereas white soldiers were settled on fertile land to engage in lucrative cash-crop farming, African soldiers were not given land but only a small amount of money to start a business. The frustrated soldiers concurred with an emerging radical African mass in the conclusion that only force would compel the colonial government to address African grievances, particularly the land question. To this end, a mass political movement emerged under the leadership of the Kenya Land Freedom Army (KLFA), an underground force that targeted the colonial administration and its African sympathizers. The assassination of Chief Waruhiu, who was reputed for serving the interests of the colonial administration, in Kiambu on October 7, 1952, was linked to the activities of this movement.

The declaration of a state of emergency by the governor, Sir Evelyn Baring, on October 20, 1952, in order to track down the activities of KLFA, exploded into an open violent rebellion against British authority in the name of *Mau Mau*. In response to the guerrilla war in the forests, the British put up a fierce military campaign that saw thousands of Africans lose their lives while many others were arrested and detained. By 1953, the rebellion had been militarily defeated, but occasional skirmishes continued into 1956.

Despite the military defeat, *Mau Mau* paved the way for economic, social, and political reforms in the remainder of the 1950s, which contributed to development among the African population. In the economic sphere, the colonial government set up a commission under R. T. M. Swynnerton to make recommendations on how to avoid a similar rebellion in future. This commission came up with "a plan to intensify the Development of African Agriculture in Kenya" in 1954, which was christened The Swynnerton Plan. Among other things, it recommended land reform for the development of African agriculture as the first step in the then-expected agrarian revolution in Kenya. Land was to be consolidated and registered under individual title deeds. This marked the onset of private land ownership among Africans in Kenya.

The Swynnerton Plan also recommended that Africans be allowed to grow cash crops. This enabled Africans to participate in the cultivation of profitable export crops like tea, coffee, and pyrethrum as well as dairy production. With the privatization of land tenure, African farmers could obtain credit against land titles for the improvement of agricultural production. Agricultural extension services were also extended to African farmers for the first time, partly for the purpose of ensuring that agricultural credit was utilized properly. This transformation of African agriculture laid the foundation for economic development.

Mau Mau also forced the colonial regime to embark on political reforms that saw greater African participation in the colonial state from the mid-1950s. Political activities and organizations that had been proscribed were allowed. Various constitutional reforms were also made specifically to improve on the representation of Africans in the Legislative Council and Local Authorities. These political reforms paved the way for Kenya's independence in 1963. It is against this background that *Mau Mau* has been credited with facilitating the granting of independence to the country.

FREDRICK O. WANYAMA

See also Kenya

References and Further Reading

Barnett, D. L. and K. Njama. *Mau Mau from Within.* London: McGibbon and Kee, 1966.
Clough, Marshall S. *Mau Mau Memoirs: History, Memory and Politics.* Boulder, CO, and London: Lynne Rienner Publishers, 1998.
Furedi, F. *The Mau Mau War in Perspective.* London: James Currey, 1989.
Kanogo, Tabitha. *Squatters and the Roots of Mau Mau, 1905–63.* Athens, OH: Ohio University Press, 1987.
Ochieng', W. R. *A History of Kenya.* London: Macmillan, 1985.
Rosberg, Carl G. and John Nottingham. *The Myth of Mau Mau.* New York: Praeger, 1966.
Throup, David W. *Economic and Social Origins of Mau Mau, 1945–53.* London: James Currey, 1987.

MAURITANIA

The Islamic Republic of Mauritania is located in Northwestern Africa. It is bounded on the west by the North Atlantic Ocean, with a 754-kilometer coastline. It is bordered on the north by Western Sahara, the northeast by Algeria, the southeast by Mali, and the south by Senegal. Around 40% of the nation is composed of the Sahara Desert and about 30% is semi-desert. There is a narrow band of fertile land along the Senegal River, the only permanent stream.

Climate is constantly hot, dry, and dusty; average temperature in January is 16°C–20°C, in July 30°C–32°C; precipitation is about fifty to four hundred millimeters annually. Terrain is mostly barren, flat plains of the Sahara, with some central hills, and a narrow band of fertile land along the Senegal River. Most of the population—estimated at 2,998,563 (July 2004)—is concentrated in the capital city of Nouakchott (population 612,000), Nouadhibou (population 113,000), and along the Senegal River in the southern part of the country.

Territory of present Mauritania has been settled since the end of the Neolithic Era. About the beginning of the first millennium it was colonized by nomadic Berbers, and during the eighth to ninth centuries most of the population converted to Islam. In the eleventh to twelfth centuries Mauritania was the cradle of the Almoravid movement, which spread Islam throughout the region and for a while controlled the Islamic part of Spain. European traders began to show interest in Mauritania in the fifteenth century. First the Portuguese established a coastal observing station to facilitate naval travel, and this was followed by the Dutch, English, and French.

In 1814, direct French rule was instituted, and in 1920 Mauritania was made part of French West Africa. In 1946 Mauritania was given the status of an overseas territory under France, and in 1958 it became an Islamic republic within the French community. Two years later, on November 28, 1960, it obtained independence under President Moktar Ould Daddah. Morocco for a time tried to absorb it. In 1978, Daddah was ousted by a military coup d'état instigated by a military committee. The committee was dismissed in 1981 by Col. Maaouya Ould Sid Ahmed Taya, who was elected head of state in December 1984, and reelected in 1992 and 2003.

In 1989 ethnic tension with Senegal mounted, but it improved by 1992. Mauritania annexed the southern third of the former Spanish Sahara (now Western Sahara) in 1976, but had to retreat three years later because of raids by the Polisario guerrilla front seeking independence for the territory. Opposition parties were legalized and a new constitution adopted in 1991. Two consequent multi-party presidential elections were widely perceived as being flawed. In reality, Mauritania remains a one-party state, with the Democratic and Social Republican Party (PRDS) ruling almost unopposed. Politics continue to be tribally based. In 2003–2004, three failed coup attempts were staged by dissident army officers, and there has been suppression of Islamic radicals who form the backbone of the civilian opposition. In the end of 2004, about 180 military personnel and civilian opposition figures went on trial at a remote military barracks in the desert, charged with plotting to overthrow the president.

This country still experiences ethnic tensions between the dominant Maur (Arab-Berber) population and its 30% black minority. Nearly 100% of the population are Muslims. Mauritanian claims to the Western Sahara have been dormant in recent years.

Half the Mauritanian population still depends on agriculture and livestock for a livelihood, even though repetitive droughts in the 1970s and 1980s forced many of the nomads and subsistence farmers to the urban areas. Mauritania has extensive deposits of iron ore, which account for nearly 40% of total exports. Because of the decline in world demand, production has dwindled. The coastal waters are among the richest fishing areas in the world, but over-exploitation by foreign vessels endangers this key source of revenue.

In the past, drought and economic mismanagement resulted in a buildup of foreign debt. In February 2000, Mauritania qualified for debt relief under the Heavily Indebted Poor Countries (HIPC) initiative and in December 2001 received strong support from donor and lending countries. In 2001, exploratory oil wells in tracts eighty kilometers offshore indicated potential extraction at current world oil prices. The Chinguetti offshore field was to be the first to start production in the first half of 2005, producing around 75,000 barrels per day for export. The even bigger neighboring Tiof field was scheduled to follow.

An investment code adopted in December 2001 enhanced the opportunities for direct foreign investments. Negotiations with the IMF involve issues of economic reforms and fiscal discipline. In the meantime, the government underscores reduction of poverty, improvement of health and education, and promoting privatization of the economy. Per capita GDP was estimated in 2003 at $1,800.

There are 717 kilometers of railways, 7,720 kilometers of highways of which only 830 kilometers are paved, and some ferry traffic on the Senegal River. Of the country's five maritime ports, only the one near Nouakchott is deepwater (opened in 1986). There are eight airports with paved runways, out of a total of twenty-four, of which only three are able to receive large aircrafts. The literacy rate among the adult population is less than 42% (among males, almost 52%; among females, 32% [2003 estimate]). Reforms provide for unification of the education system, promotion of vocational and technological training, strengthening of education in sciences and foreign languages, and both civic and confessional teaching. The main academic institution in Mauritania is Nouakchott University, founded in 1981, and there is also the National Institute of Pedagogy. Mauritania officially banned slavery only in 1981, but despite official denials, it still exists. According to the World Health Organization (WHO) data from 1995, there are approximately fourteen physicians and sixty-two nurses for every one hundred thousand people. Life expectancy for males is fifty years and 54.5 years for females (2004 estimate). The population growth rate is 2.91% annually (2004 estimate) and the infant mortality rate is 72.35 deaths for every one thousand live births.

STEPHAN E. NIKOLOV

See also Ethnic Conflicts: West Africa; Morocco; Senegal; West Africa: History and Economic Development; West Africa: International Relations

References and Further Reading

Abun-Nasr, Jamil M. *A History of the Maghrib*, 2nd ed. Cambridge, UK: Cambridge University Press, 1975.
Damis, John. *Conflict in Northwest Africa: The Western Sahara Dispute*. Stanford, CA: Hoover Institution Press, 1983.
Diallo, Garba. "Military Rule, Racism and Democratisation in Mauritania: Comparison with Sudan." *Policy Studies and Developing Nations*, vol. 2, pp. 257–258. JAI Press, 1995.
Parker, Richard B. *North Africa: Regional Tensions and Strategic Concerns*. New York: Praeger, 1984.
Pazzaita, Anthony G. *Historical Dictionary of Mauritania*, 2nd ed. London: Scarecrow Press, 1994.
Seddon, David. "The Political Economy of Mauritania: An Introduction." *Review of Political Economy*, no. 68, pp. 197–214. ROAPE Publications, 1996.
Segal, Ronald. *Islam's Black Slaves: The Other Black Diaspora*. New York: Farrar, Straus & Giroux, 2002.

MAURITIUS

Mauritius, a 1,860-square kilometre island of volcanic origin, lies in the Indian Ocean east of Madagascar. The topography is varied: from the central highlands the land slopes to the coastal plains, most extensive in the north and east where sugar is the dominant crop. The climate is tropical and the island lies within the cyclone belt. The economy is healthy: per capita Gross National Income (GNI) in 2003 was $4,090 and growth rates during the period 1983–2003 averaged over 5%. The country includes the island of Rodrigues, five hundred kilometres to the east, which is significantly less prosperous and culturally quite distinct.

Uninhabited when discovered by Europeans, Mauritius was first permanently settled by France in 1722 and transferred to British administration in 1814. Economic development in the British period was synonymous with sugar- and slave labour-fuelled growth; following the abolition of slavery in 1835, indentured labourers from India were imported to work in the cane fields. Today the island's largely French-speaking population of 1.2 million may be subdivided into Hindu (approximately 50%) and Muslim (20%) Indians, Creoles of mixed African and European ancestry (30%), and small but economically significant Chinese and Franco-Mauritian ("white") minorities.

Towards the middle of the twentieth century, stagnant sugar output levels and rapid population growth raised concerns about the island's future. The colonial administration, recognising that independence was inevitable, commissioned an economic survey of the island that would provide a framework for future policy. The ensuing report, published in 1961 and known as the Meade report, was a thorough, influential, and somewhat pessimistic analysis of the island's economy. It made it clear that economic diversification and industrialisation were essential if the island were to have any hope of achieving real and sustained growth.

Policies established in the 1960s were initially aimed at encouraging import substitution industrialisation (ISI). Although not without results, ISI failed to have the desired impact, both for want of a sufficiently skilled workforce and due to a reluctance on the part of the sugar estate owners to invest their capital. Consequently, when Mauritius acceded to independence in 1968, sugar still accounted for 95% of export earnings and the first post-independence government shifted emphasis to manufacturing for export. It established an Export Processing Zone (EPZ), aimed at attracting both foreign and domestic capital into an industrialization program through an attractive package of incentives including tax relief; subsidies, and credit facilities; assurances of good infrastructure; and a competent, cheap, and reliable labour force. At the same time, quotas and preferential tariffs guaranteed sugar sales in Britain and the EEC, providing a reliable source of revenue for economic growth.

Based principally on textiles, the EPZ was a success but it was dependent upon the health of the sugar sector. In the early 1970s, while world sugar prices were extremely buoyant, Mauritius produced several bumper crops and the resultant profits fuelled growth. Sugar profits also funded investment in the tourism sector and in services, as well as providing increased government revenue, thus permitting improvements to social services and general infrastructure development.

The worldwide recession in the mid-1970s, competition from other developing nations, and two devastating cyclones led to an economic downturn and rising external debt. In 1979 the government was obliged to implement an IMF-imposed program of structural adjustment that included state disengagement from the economy and a greater emphasis on free market forces. Nevertheless, the government maintained its commitment to social programs, including free education and health care; these policies were costly, and there was little improvement in the economy until the mid-1980s, when a healthier international climate finally allowed renewed growth in the increasingly important tourism sector and accompanied a similar increase in industrial output, again largely in textiles.

Since the 1980s the government's emphasis on continued diversification has led to growth in the financial services sector, particularly in offshore banking, as well as in transport (flag-of-convenience shipping) and other offshore operations. Annual growth rates have regularly been on the order of 6%–7% and unemployment remains low. The public health and education systems are both free and of high quality; literacy rates and life expectancy are high, while infant mortality and population growth rates are low. Nevertheless, some 10% of the population, excluded from the benefits of economic growth, continues to live below the poverty line.

The success of Mauritius may be attributed to several factors, and some are clearly more important than others. A stable democratic system, based on the Westminster model, is a reflection of a more fundamental feature of Mauritius, that of its identity as a European colonial construct. Descriptions of Mauritius as an "enigma" and a "miracle" among developing African states are misleading: Mauritius is not an African country except in a geographical sense, and that only tenuously. Economically and politically, Mauritius is a creation of the colonial world and as such has always been firmly inscribed within the Western economic system.

If Mauritius was formerly underdeveloped, then this was a result of the island's place in this system and not, as was the case in most African countries, its absence therefrom. Social, economic, and political constraints on capitalist development are noticeably absent in Mauritius; the educational system is resolutely Western, and the country has also benefited from a predilection for a strong, socially committed state, inherited from post–Second World War Britain. An emphasis on social policies, including social security and equality of income, has been a feature of all Mauritian governments regardless of their political orientation, and it is of note that there have only been three prime ministers in the thirty-five years since independence. The role of domestic capital in local investment has also been important: unlike many other developing nations, Mauritius is less subject to the whims of foreign investors.

Other advantages, such as the lack of a standing army (removing the risk of military intervention in the political process), the small size of the island (facilitating infrastructure development), and the country's ethnically diverse population, have also contributed to Mauritius' success. This last feature has hitherto been far more of a help than a hindrance: inter-ethnic tension is rare; no group is dominant socially, economically, or politically, and as a result of its cultural diversity Mauritius maintains a range of links with various parts of the Indian Ocean and beyond.

Despite the successes, the government is aware that there is no cause for complacency. Diversification notwithstanding, the economy remains dependent upon external markets and the economic base remains narrow: textiles, tourism, banking, and sugar. Furthermore, the country's success has depended upon privileged access to European markets under the terms of the Lomé Convention and not upon free market forces. Continued diversification and increased competitiveness are thus seen as priorities as growth rates start to slow and unemployment increases.

IAIN WALKER

References and Further Reading

Bowman, Larry W. *Mauritius: Democracy and Development in the Indian Ocean.* Boulder, CO: Westview Press, and London: Dartmouth, 1991.

Carroll, B. W. and T. Carroll. "Accommodating Ethnic Diversity in a Modernizing Democratic State: Theory and Practice in the Case of Mauritius." *Ethnic & Racial Studies*, 23, no. 1:120–142 (2000).

Dabee, Rajen and David Greenaway, eds. *The Mauritian Economy. A Reader.* Basingstoke, UK: Houndmills, and New York: Palgrave, 2001.

Dommen, Edward and Bridget Dommen. *Mauritius: An Island of Success. A Retrospective Study 1960–1993.* Wellington, New Zealand: Pacific Press, and Oxford, UK: James Currey, 1999.

Meade, J. E., et al. *The Economic and Social Structure of Mauritius.* London: Methuen, 1961.

Meisenhelder, Thomas. "The Developmental State in Mauritius." *Journal of Modern African Studies*, 35, no. 2: 279–297 (1997).

Miles, William. "The Mauritius Enigma." *Journal of Democracy*, 10, no. 2: 91–104 (1999).

Selwyn, Percy. "Mauritius, the Meade Report Twenty Years After." In *African Islands and Enclaves*, edited by Robin Cohen. Beverly Hills, CA: Sage, 1983.

Simmons, Adele. *Modern Mauritius: The Politics of Decolonization.* Bloomington: Indiana University Press, 1982.

Wellisz, Stanislaw and Philippe Lam Shin Saw. "Mauritius." In *Five Small Open Economies*, edited by Ronald Findlay and Stanislaw Wellisz. New York: Oxford University Press, 1993.

MBEKI, THABO

Thabo Mbeki (b. 1942) became president of the Republic of South Africa in 1999. He was born in Idutywa, Transkei, on June 18, 1942. His father, Govan, joined the ANC as a student (1935), later was elected chairman (1956), and spent twenty-three years in prison alongside Nelson Mandela, who was later to become the first majority-elected president of the Republic of South Africa (1994).

Mbeki attended high school at Lovedale and joined the African National Congress (ANC) Youth League at age fourteen. He was expelled from high school following student strikes, and continued in home study, ultimately earning a master's degree in economics from the University of Sussex as a correspondence student. Two years after the government banned the ANC, in 1960, Mbeki was sent overseas for his higher education. He served in a number of ANC positions abroad, including posts in London, Zambia, Swaziland, Nigeria, and Botswana, and received military training in the USSR. He did not return to South Africa until 1990.

While abroad, Mbeki rose in prominence in the ANC. He became a member of the ANC National Executive Committee in 1975 and was appointed political secretary to the ANC president in 1978. As the director of the ANC's Department of Information and Publicity (1984–1989), Mbeki acted as the organization's chief international spokesman. Meanwhile, he led ANC delegations in secret talks with the South African government and the private business sector, which resulted in the unbanning of the ANC and release of political prisoners, including Nelson Mandela in 1990. Mbeki was elected chairman of the ANC in 1993 and president of the organization in 1997. Two years later, he was elected president of South Africa.

Polished and charming, easygoing, and politically pragmatic, Mbeki proved to be an excellent choice to advance the ANC from a political liberation movement and guerrilla army to success at the ballot box. However, compared to Mandela, Mbeki appears more detached and less a man of the people.

The largely peaceful evolution of South Africa from a nondemocratic, national security state with deep racial, political, and economic distortions to the continent's largest democracy, most successful economy, and regional leader has both domestic and international implications. Its 43 million people, 75% of whom are black, share understandably higher expectations with the end of apartheid rule. Its white minority citizens (13%), tracing their African origins to the establishment of a naval refreshment station by the Dutch East India Company at the Cape of Good Hope in 1652, also stand as claimants to South African heritage.

The decade of the 1990s saw more than forty African governments hold national elections, marked dramatically by Mandela's election in 1994. The South African national economy accounts for 40% of Sub-Saharan Africa's gross domestic product. Nevertheless, Africa on the whole has more wars, the most poverty, the highest number of displaced peoples due to civil war, climatic catastrophes, and pandemic disease, including the most AIDS casualties of any world region. South Africa shows the most capabilities and potential of any state in its region and on the continent. The state carries a heavy burden of high expectations among the G-7 advanced, industrial nations. A common perception is that as goes South Africa, so goes the continent.

Mbeki's opposition quickly points to the nation's standstill economic growth, a 40% adult unemployment rate; the free fall of the national currency in the world market; the worst per capita murder rate in the world; and inability to provide clean water, adequate housing, medical care, public education, and jobs. Mbeki's repeated denials of the link between HIV and AIDS have detracted from his image in South Africa and globally. On another front, his refusal to criticize Zimbabwe president Mugabe for sponsoring violent attacks on his political opposition and the forcible takeover of white-owned farms generates moral and political outrage.

President Mbeki has tried to build upon Mandela's success at reconciliation of bitter ethnic hostilities and to pursue transformation that ensures political, economic, and humanitarian advancement.

JAMES E. WINKATES

See also Apartheid; Mandela, Nelson; South Africa; Southern Africa: History and Economic Development; Southern Africa: International Relations

References and Further Reading

Grundy, Kenneth W. "South Africa: Transition to Majority Rule, Transformation to Stable Democracy." In *The Uncertain Promise of Southern Africa*, edited by York Bradshaw and Stephen N. Ndegwa. Bloomington, IN: Indiana University Press, 2000.

Harvey, Robert. *The Fall of Apartheid: The Inside Story from Smuts to Mbeki*. Basingstroke, UK: Palgrave, 2001.

Parsons, Raymond. *The Mbeki Inheritance: South Africa's Economy, 1990–2004*. London: Hodder & Stoughton, 2000.

Thompson, Leonard. "Mbeki's Uphill Challenge." *Foreign Affairs*, 78, No. 6 (1999).

MEIR, GOLDA

Golda Meir (1898–1978) was instrumental in the creation, development, and survival of the State of Israel. As an early pioneer, she was familiar with every aspect of the Jewish occupation of Palestine. She was one of Israel's biggest promoters abroad, personally raising the millions of dollars to assure its survival. Although the primary focus of her activities was labor, she held many political posts throughout her career, eventually becoming prime minister. Her primary goal was to help establish a homeland in which Jews from anywhere in the world could find refuge.

She was born Golda Mabovitch in Kiev, Russia. She immigrated to the United States as a child in 1906 and lived in Milwaukee, Wisconsin, the child of a carpenter father and grocer mother. As a young woman, she worked with her father for the People's Relief Committee. She taught Yiddish to children at a Labor Zionist Party school, joining the Party herself at seventeen and engaging in both speechmaking and fundraising. After marrying Morris Meyerson, she emigrated with him in 1921 as part of the Third *Aliyah,* or wave of Jewish immigration, to Palestine.

Meir's contribution to the development of Israel can be divided into three phases: the work she did during the Jewish occupation in Palestine under British Mandate Rule; her World War II and pre-independence activities; and her political involvement after the formation of the State of Israel in 1948.

The Jewish Occupation of Palestine (1921–1939)

Golda Meir's contribution during her early years in Palestine consisted primarily of working on behalf of the *Histadrut* (General Federation of Jewish Labor). Shortly after arriving in Palestine, the Meyersons applied for permission to join Merhavia, a kibbutz, where they lived for two years before her husband's health required them to return to Tel Aviv and then Jerusalem, where, over the next four years, she bore and raised two children. She eventually returned to Tel Aviv to work for the Histadrut.

Her first job with the Histadrut was that of secretary of the Women's Labor Council in 1928. This council ran the workingwomen's farms that trained immigrant girls in agricultural skills. Meir served as a labor representative during that time to a number of international conferences abroad, but much of her work involved talking about the conditions of Jews in Palestine and raising funds in the United States, working on loan as national secretary of the Pioneer Women in the United States.

Eventually, she was appointed to the Executive Committee of the Histadrut and remained there for fourteen years, working on setting up an unemployment fund and resolving the myriad problems associated with immigration, which increased considerably after Jews from Germany began to

enter Palestine. It was during this time that she got to know people such as David Ben-Gurion and Levi Eshkol, who would play important roles in the establishment of the State of Israel, as well as in Meir's own career. As chair of the Board of Directors of the Workers' Sick Fund, Meir continued to raise funds for the Histadrut and was instrumental in establishing its shipping business through her US fundraising efforts. The purchase of ships would be the means by which European Jews found their way to Palestine.

In 1939, when the British issued a White Paper reversing their position on the establishment of a Jewish state and limiting Jewish immigration to a maximum of seventy-five thousand Jews for five years, while also restricting the purchase of land by Jews in Palestine, Meir shifted her focus away from labor problems to helping as many Jews as possible find their way to Palestine.

World War II and Pre-Independence Activities (1939–1948)

Following Ben-Gurion's position, "We shall fight Hitler as if there were no White Paper and fight the White Paper as if there were no Hitler," Meir served on the War Economic Advisory Council during World War II, assisting the British with the war effort and negotiating fair wages for Jewish civilian workers, but also working to get as many Jews into Palestine as possible in spite of the illegality of the process. The so-called Committee of the Illegal Immigration met in her apartment, and she personally wrote some of their leaflets.

In 1946, Meir organized a hunger strike to protest the British exclusion of two ships of Jewish refugees headed for Palestine. The ships were eventually released and refugees allowed to enter. Later, Meir became acting head of the political department of the Jewish Agency, becoming its leader when Moshe Shertok was imprisoned and Ben-Gurion was kept out of Palestine under threat of arrest.

In 1947, the United Nations Commission of Inquiry recommended an end to the British Mandate and the partition of Palestine into equal parts, an act that the Jews accepted but the Arabs did not. Meir was part of the Zionist negotiations with the British and worked actively to raise $50 million in the United States to arm the State of Israel in anticipation of the war of independence it would have to fight once the British withdrew. On May 14, 1948, the day of that withdrawal, Golda Meyerson was one of thirty-eight signers of the Proclamation of Independence that created the State of Israel.

The State of Israel (1948–1978)

After the formation of the State of Israel, Meir held diplomatic and cabinet posts, but for the most part continued to raise money, to work to solve the problems of the new state, and to assure its survival. She was Ambassador to the Soviet Union, appointed in 1948. In January 1949, Israel won its war of independence and an armistice was declared. The first elections were held and Meir became a member of the Israeli cabinet, working as the first Minister of Labor, a job that involved responsibility for housing, job training, buildings, and roads for what she called "my seven good years." During this time, there was an ever increasing migration to Israel and increased unemployment and inflation. Meir oversaw the building of permanent public housing, a network of roads, and other projects for which she continued to raise money on trips to the United States and Europe. In this post, Meir was instrumental in the passage of labor laws limiting the maximum number of work hours, providing national insurance, and guaranteeing paid maternity leave.

In June 1956, Meir became Foreign Minister of Israel, and it was at this time that she officially changed her name from Meyerson to the Hebrew *Meir,* which means "to illuminate." In this post, she represented Israel at the United Nations, which was especially important following the Sinai War in 1956. Meir also played a key role in extending knowledge and assistance to many developing African and Asian countries, sending experts to assist and inviting foreign students to come to Israel, and providing fellowships for that purpose as part of her International Cooperation Program.

After serving as Secretary General of the Labor Party, Meir retired in 1968, only to be called upon six months later in 1969 to become Prime Minister of Israel after the death of Levi Eshkol and to avert a potential Labor Party split. She held the office until 1974, when disillusionment with her party's handling of the October War (also known as the Yom Kippur War) and its high death toll led to a general loss of confidence in the Israeli military leadership. She resigned the office on April 11, 1974.

When she died of cancer on December 7, 1978, she was given a state funeral without eulogies, according to her wishes. It was attended by dignitaries from all over the world.

SUSAN LOVE BROWN

See also Arab Nationalism; Arab–Israeli Wars (1948, 1956, 1967, 1973); Balfour Declaration; Begin, Menachem; Ben-Gurion, David; Egypt; Ethnic Conflicts: Middle East; Israel; Judaism; Middle East: History and Economic Development; Middle East: International Relations; Palestine; Palestine Liberation Organization (PLO); Palestinian Diaspora; Sadat, Anwar; Zionism.

References and Further Reading

Davidson, Margaret. *The Golda Meir Story.* New York: Charles Scribner's Sons, 1981.
Gilbert, Martin. *Israel: A History.* New York: William Morrow, 1998.
Mann, Peggy. *Golda: The Life of Israel's Prime Minister.* New York, Putnam, 2001.
Martin, Ralph G. *Golda: Golda Meir: The Romantic Years.* New York: Charles Scribner's Sons, 1988.
McAuley, Karen. *Golda Meir.* New York: Chelsea House, 1985.
Meir, Menachem. *My Mother Golda Meir: A Son's Evocation of Life with Golda Meir.* New York: Arbor House, 1983.
Syrkin, Marie. *Golda Meir: Israel's Leader.* New York: G. P. Putnam's Sons, 1969.

MENCHÚ TÚM, RIGOBERTA

Rigoberta Menchú Túm, a Quiché-Maya Indian woman, was born to a relatively poor family on January 9, 1959, in Chimel, a village in the province of El Quiché, Guatemala. It is Central America's poorest and most populous country with approximately 14.3 million people, half of whom are direct descendents of the Maya Indians. Although Maya are the majority population in Guatemala, historically they have been an oppressed group. Menchú Túm's family are *Quiché,* the largest of the country's twenty-two Indian groups.

Rigoberta Menchú Túm is perhaps the most famous indigenous person in the world and certainly the most famous Guatemalan. She first rose to international prominence in the early 1980s when her *testimonio,* told to Venezuelan anthropologist Elizabeth Burgos-Debray, was published in Spanish. The *Testimonio, I, Rigoberta: An Indian Woman in Guatemala,* told the story of the condition of Guatemala's indigenous population from the 1954 military coup that ended Guatemala's nascent democratic regime through the impact of Latin America's longest-running civil war and the subsequent series of military governments. While the book was banned in Guatemala, it won the prestigious "Casa de las Americas" prize for best testimonial, which helped provide Menchú with an international forum for her message. This authority to talk on behalf of indigenous people in Guatemala was further enhanced when she was awarded the UNESCO Prize for Education for Peace in 1990.

The country's military regimes governed without respect for individual rights or traditional Indian rights. The military regimes' stated motivation was to fight communism in the country. The regimes' counter-insurgency operations had a profound impact on the majority Indian population. As the military strengthened its position in Guatemala, its leadership became increasingly repressive toward the indigenous population. In particular in the early 1980s, General José Efraín Ríos Montt let loose a wave of repression against the indigenous population in the countryside, forcing them to join self-defense militias or to be killed. Indeed, in a 1982 *New York Times* article, the General articulated his policy toward the indigenous people stating, "If you are with us, we'll feed you; if not, we'll kill you." Government repression was aided by right-wing death squads, most notably the *Mano Blanca* (White Hand), that were given free reign to act against the indigenous peoples.

It was this military repression that drew the Menchú family into the country's political life and eventually many of them were killed as a consequence. Rigoberta's father, Vincente Menchú, a peasant activist and smalltime landowner, was killed during the occupation of the Spanish Embassy in Guatemala City in January 1980. The occupation ended in an inferno that reduced the embassy to rubble and killed thirty-nine people including the Spanish Ambassador, many of his staff, and the protestors who had taken over the embassy to protest government human rights violations. The cause of the fire is still inconclusive; the military accused the occupiers of torching the building, but the occupiers' sympathizers have consistently blamed the military.

Later in the same year, Rigoberta's mother, Juana Túm Kótojá, was kidnapped by the military and was never seen again. As the violence worsened, Menchú Túm left Guatemala and sought refuge in Mexico.

By the mid-1980s the country began a gradual return to democratic rule. A new constitution and new government institutions, including a more independent Supreme Court and a Human Rights Ombudsman's office, were created. But this process remains incomplete even with the most recent elections of January 2004. Violence against human rights workers remain a persistent problem.

Menchú Túm's work toward a resolution to the 36-year civil war in Guatemala was recognized on the anniversary of the five hundredth anniversary of the European colonization of Latin America in 1992 when she was awarded the 1992 Nobel Peace Prize. Rigoberta Menchú used the money from the prize to establish the Rigoberta Menchú Túm Foundation (RMTF) in Guatemala, Mexico, and the United States. The Foundation fights for Human Rights and the rights of Indigenous Peoples, and facilitates peace processes both in Guatemala and abroad.

According to Arturo Arias, a noted Guatemalan academic and novelist, prior to her return to Guatemala in 1988, Rigoberta Menchú Túm was a virtually unknown figure in her native country, even among the Mayan people. This was changed in a flash by the Guatemalan military through their handling of her return. Menchú Túm was asked to return by the administration of President Vinicio Cerezo (1986–1991) to show to the world that Guatemala was now a full-fledged democracy governed by the Rule of Law. Menchú Túm returned to her country with three other exiled leaders of various banned opposition groups. When Menchú Túm's plane touched down in Guatemala City, she was immediately arrested, but the increasingly independent Supreme Court demanded her release. The military's heavy-handed treatment of Menchú's return was on the front pages of newspapers around the world, including in Guatemala.

Menchú was involuntarily thrust into the middle of an ongoing "culture war" in the United States during the 1980s and 1990s when some leading universities required that her book, *I Rigoberta*, be taught in place of some European classics. Moreover, US anthropologist David Stoll's fieldwork investigations into the veracity of Menchú Túm's *testimonio* of Guatemala's civil war revealed some inconsistencies between Menchú's own account of the fate of her family and reports of other Guatemalans on her family's life. The media picked up on the debate and the story appeared on the front page of the *New York Times* in 1998. The newspaper article sparked an international debate concerning the accuracy of Menchú's version of events in Guatemala's civil war and added a new chapter to the culture war, reigniting the shrill debate between the left and right of the political spectrum both in Guatemala and in universities across the United States. Menchú's book and the resulting debate about factual accuracy also raised a discussion about the role of *testimonio* as a form of literature.

Despite the debate surrounding Rigoberta Menchú's account of the fate of her family, there is little doubt that she has had a profound impact on alerting the world to the repression and violence in Guatemala and the needs of indigenous people around the world.

BRUCE M. WILSON

See also Ethnic Conflicts: Mexico and Central America; Guatemala

References and Further Reading

Arias Arturo, ed. *The Rigoberta Menchú Controversy*. Minneapolis: Minnesota University Press, 2001.

Burgos-Debray, Elisabeth ed. *I, Rigoberta Menchú: An Indian Woman in Guatemala*. New York: Verso, 1984.

Menchú Túm, Rigoberta. *Crossing Borders*. New York: Verso, 1998.

Rohter, Larry. "Tarnished Laureate." *The New York Times*, December 15, 1998, A1–A8.

Sommers, Doris. "Not Just a Personal Story: Women's Testimonios and the Plural Self." In *Life-Lines: Theorizing Women's Autobiography*. Ithaca, NY, and London: Cornell University Press, 1988.

Wilkinson, Daniel. *Silence on the Mountain: Stories of Terror, Betrayal, and Forgetting in Guatemala*. New York: Houghton Mifflin 2002.

MENEM, CARLOS

Carlos Saul Menem was the flamboyant president of Argentina from 1989–1999. Menem was born in 1930, the son of Syrian immigrants. Raised as a Sunni Muslim, Menem converted to Catholicism in his youth. Menem was trained as a lawyer. He has had a contradictory but interesting role in Argentine history as a president with populist appeal who carried through conservative economic reforms, who was indicted on corruption charges, and who has re-emerged as a political force. Menem also seemed to provide strong leadership to Argentina after a long period of economic decline.

Menem is a member of the Peronist Party, with long-standing ties to the CGT (*Confederación General de Trabajo*) labor union and the Peronist leadership. The Peronist Party was geared around the charismatic Juan Peron, who had developed a strong and deep popular appeal as well as ties to Argentina's labor unions. Following a military coup, Peron had been in exile in Spain through much of the 1960s. Peron made a brief return to Argentina in 1973, before he died. The Peronist movement, now led by Peron's second wife, stuttered amidst a growing economic crisis, which precipitated a military coup in 1976. Menem served as governor of the province La Rioja from 1973–1976 and from 1983–1989. As a prominent member of the Peronist Party, Menem was imprisoned by the military government in 1976. Amidst continuing hyper-inflation, and the disgrace of the loss of the war with the United Kingdom over the Falklands/Malvinas Islands, the military finally gave up power.

Democracy was restored to Argentina in 1983 and Raul Alfonsin of the Unión Cívica Radical was elected president. Although Alfonsin was successful in stabilizing democracy in Argentina, the economy continued to suffer from both high inflation and unemployment. Menem surprised many in winning the 1989 presidential election, garnering 49% of the vote. He was an old-style Peronist candidate, promising a return to government intervention and spending and a reduction in unemployment. Menem took the party by surprise, when, after taking office, he adopted the opposite set of policies. Menem traveled to the United States and Great Britain soon after taking office. In 1990 he gave pardons to military officers for human rights abuses. Menem also passed major economic reforms by decree in early 1990. He engaged in tight fiscal and monetary policies and moved toward privatization of key industries, including ENTEL (telecommunications); Aerolineas Argentinas (the national Airline); YPF (the national oil company); and the electricity system (dominated by SEGBA). He liberalized the economy, opening up Argentina for investment through the elimination of restrictions; eliminating export taxes and most quota restrictions on imports; and reducing other import duties. Menem completed his full-scale transformation from former labor leader to neoliberal with new labor regulations. Menem's erstwhile minister of the economy, Domingo Cavallo, tied the Argentine currency to the dollar in 1992, which seemed at the time to pay big dividends in terms of increasing investment in the country and stabilizing national accounts, particularly in controlling inflation. Menem made important steps forward in the MERCOSUR (see Southern Cone Common Market [MERCOSUR]) integration process. Menem was hailed as a hero and economic statesman at that point, and used his popularity to push through a Constitutional amendment permitting him re-election. He was easily re-elected in 1995, with 50% of the vote but no close contender. Menem seemed to have created a new, more moderate wing of the Peronist Party around his "revolución productiva," called "Menemismo," though dissidents formed the FREPASO alternative.

By the late 1990s, however, unemployment remained in the double digits in the country. Wage data do not reveal any significant increases during the 1990s. The exact reasons for the Argentine meltdown remain controversial, but many analysts suggest the maintenance of the fixed exchange rate was unnecessary after inflationary expectations had declined. As well, there is some evidence that the privatizations had little lasting effect on overall levels of external debt or the fiscal deficit, and much of the investment in the country remained in quickly withdrawn portfolio capital accounts. Brazil's devaluation in 1999 hastened the end of the Argentine "boom," with an accentuation of a balance-of-trade deficit adding to these long-term problems. By 2001, confidence in Argentina began to quickly erode, setting up the financial crisis that began in that year. Menem's political career took a nosedive with the economic downturn and came to a seeming end. His attempt to change the Constitution again to allow for a third term failed. He was tied to a corruption scandal involving arms sales to Croatia and Ecuador in 2001. Though the Supreme Court ruled that there was insufficient evidence, Menem's political career seemed over.

Based on public exasperation of the seemingly feeble state responses to the economic crisis and a search for stability, Menem attempted a comeback in the 2003 special presidential elections, which had been called on account of the collapse of the government due to the economic crisis that began in 1999. Menem appeared a strong candidate at first, winning the first round of the primary with 24% of the vote. However, as rival Nestor Kirchner pulled away, Menem withdrew from the race. Nonetheless, Menem has continued to work behind the scenes as a political leader. Amidst the depression Argentina entered into starting in 2002, Menem somehow became a renewed symbol of nationalism with the appeal of former elements of the Peronist Party.

ANIL HIRA

See also Argentina; Southern Cone Common Market (MERCOSUR); Southern Cone (Latin America): History and Economic Development

References and Further Reading

Corrales, Javier. "Do Economic Crises Contribute to Economic Reform? Argentina and Venezuela in the 1990s." *Political Science Quarterly*, v. 112, n. 4 (Winter): 617–44.
Escude, Carlos. *Foreign Policy Theory in Menem's Argentina*. Gainesville, FL: University Press of Florida, 1997.
Huser, Herbert C. *Argentine Civil–Military Relations: From Alfonsin to Menem*. Washington, DC: National Defence University Press, 2002.
Lewis, Colin M. and Nissa Torrents. *Argentina in the Crisis Years, 1983–1990: From Alfonsin to Menem*. London: Institute of Latin American Studies, 1993.
McSherry, J. Patrice. 1997. *Incomplete Transition: Military Power and Democracy in Argentina*. New York: St. Martin's Press.
Romero, Luis Alberto. *A History of Argentina in the Twentieth Century*. University Park, PA: Pennsylvania State University Press, 2002.
Tulchin, Joseph S. with Allison M. Garland, ed. *Argentina: The Challenges of Modernization*. Wilmington, DE: SR Books, 1998.

MENTAL HEALTH

While almost all aspects of health are low priorities on global and national agendas, mental health has always been among the lowest. Countries with inadequate or struggling economies pay little attention to health in general, putting what few resources they have into creating political, economic, and military security. The resources that are committed to health go to urgent and visible public health issues and the provision of basic human needs. Mental health is no less urgent and no less of a threat to development, but it is far less visible—and thus often overlooked.

Common definitions of mental health encompass psychological well-being and reasonable adjustment to one's life. Mental illness includes an extensive range of disorders and disabilities that vary from mild to severe, including Alzheimer's disease, autism, depression, epilepsy, learning disabilities, schizophrenia, and substance abuse. In 2000, mental and behavioral disorders accounted for 12.3% of the global burden of disease, with an estimated 450 million people affected worldwide (World Health Organization 2001). Populations in both industrialized and developing countries experience mental illness; such illnesses place an even heavier burden on those in developing or transitioning countries, who lack services, treatment, and support due to the problematic political, economic, social, and health care environments. Availability, access, and quality of mental health services in developing countries vary considerably, and are usually seriously deficient.

Many of the barriers to access for physical health care are magnified for mental health care. These barriers include travel and housing expenses to often very distant health care clinics, prohibitive official or unofficial costs (bribes) of health care, poor quality of treatment, lack of medicines, and stigma or psychological costs. For example, patients in India may have to spend the equivalent of several months' salary for transportation to a clinic (Narayan 2001). In areas of Africa, nearly 90% of epilepsy patients do not have access to anti-convulsant medications (Weissman, Ustun, and Eisenberg 1999).

Additionally, mental health care diagnosis and treatment is seriously lacking in many developing countries. Doctors and other health care workers lack training in mental health, and thus fail to diagnose distress and disorders. This is understandable, perhaps, given the immediate physical health problems they must treat under comparatively difficult circumstances, but health care workers in developing countries thus fail to address the overlap between physical and mental health. There is also the common misperception that mental health disorders remain untreatable. Along with a lack of resources, the lack of attention to mental health explains these deficits and misperceptions.

In the mid-1990s, the Global Burden of Disease study utilized the Disability Adjusted Life Years (DALYs) method for measuring disability as well as mortality indicators. (Each DALY is equivalent to one healthy year of life lost.) Though mental health diagnosis by health care practitioners is limited, surveys of clinic patients and other tools do enable researchers to estimate incidence of mental illness. Once disability was added to the equation, five of the top ten causes for lost disability-adjusted life years in the world were related to mental health. The burden of mental and behavioral disorders exceeded DALYs lost to HIV/AIDS, cancer, and tuberculosis. Depression, alcohol abuse, bipolar disorder, and schizophrenia topped the list (Murray and Lopez 1996).

Mental health's historic "Cinderella" status means there have been far fewer comprehensive studies of its impact in developing countries than one might expect. It may be one item included in larger public health studies, but until recently, few development studies focused solely on mental health or its overlap with physical health or development issues. Despite continued debate over specific causal effects and cross-cultural applications, there is growing recognition that mental health is integrally related to not only physical health but also development issues such as poverty, economic productivity, political instability, conflict, provision of basic human needs, social cohesion, and human rights. These relationships are complex and inseparable, particularly for the most common mental and behavioral disorders.

The World Health Organization (WHO) updated the Global Burden of Disease study in 2000; three mental health disorders rank in the top twenty causes of lost DALYs: depressive disorders, alcohol abuse, and self-inflicted injuries. Additionally, among ages 15–44, the top two causes of years of life lived with disability (YLDs) are depressive disorders and alcohol abuse (WHO 2001). While most people in developing countries remain mentally healthy, they face increased risks due to the political and economic environments. Depression, substance abuse, and suicide thus have a significant impact in developing countries. Cultural differences, dislocations, and violent conflict further complicate the impact of these three disorders. The process of development itself creates both benefits and challenges to progress toward mental health in developing countries.

world, and caused the fourth-highest burden of disease in 2000. For all age groups, among both men and women, depression caused 4.4% of DALYs lost. The situation is even bleaker for ages fifteen to forty-four, where depression ranks number two at 8.6% of DALYs. It is also the second leading cause for women in that age group. Estimates suggest that, by 2020, depression will account for 5.7% of DALYs, making it the second leading cause of burden of disease for all age groups of both sexes (WHO 2001).

Depression presents both psychological and physical symptoms. Feelings such as worthlessness, inadequacy, sadness, hopelessness, and diminished pleasure in life combine with sleep disturbances, weight changes, fatigue, headaches, and chronic pain. A diagnosis of depression comes when these symptoms are present over a period of time. Both biologic and social in origin, depression can be episodic or chronic, mild or severe. Chronic depression is most common, and disrupts an individual's ability to function at home, at work, and in society. Treatment, at least in the Western world, includes medication and psychotherapy.

Studies show a high incidence of depression in developing countries, with up to 30% of women and up to 40% of all health care patients exhibiting symptoms of depression. In Africa and Latin America, surveys suggest that depression is the main reason that one-fifth to one-third of all patients seeks care. Lack of mental health training, cultural differences, and stigma, however, often prevent the diagnosis. Patients present their physical rather than psychological symptoms. This not only inhibits diagnosis and treatment of depression, but also can lead to unnecessary health care costs as doctors seek to address the physical condition only (Desjarlais *et al.* 1995; Patel 2001).

Links between socioeconomic conditions and depression remain ill-defined, though studies generally conclude that uncertain political and economic conditions in developing and transitioning countries place populations at higher risk for depression. Unfortunately, citizens of these countries, if diagnosed, have less access to treatment for depression. Medications may be expensive or unavailable. There is considerable question as to whether Western psychotherapy would be effective treatment in other cultures. Most authors call for further research to determine best practices for treating depression in developing countries.

Depression

Depressive disorders, specifically unipolar depressive disorders, seriously impact societies throughout the

Substance Abuse and Dependence

Substance abuse and dependence are increasingly common in developing countries, with alcohol the most common addiction. Substances used vary across regions and include alcohol, tobacco, opium and heroin, cocaine, sedatives, stimulants, and solvents. As a cause of burden of disease, alcohol dependence ranks in the top twenty, accounting for 1.3% of DALYs lost. For men ages fifteen to forty-four, alcohol dependence is the fourth leading cause of burden of disease, at 5.1% of DALYs lost (WHO 2001).

Health care professionals distinguish abuse from dependence. Abuse, or harmful use, occurs when substance use prevents individuals from functioning economically and socially, leads to physical or mental damage, drives individuals to seek more despite harmful consequences, and results in withdrawal symptoms when usage stops. Dependence goes beyond abuse and entails a compulsive need to take the substance, inability to control use, withdrawal symptoms when usage is reduced or stopped, neglect of personal and other needs, and continued use regardless of consequences to self or others (Desjarlais *et al.* 1995; WHO 2001).

Desjarlais *et al.* (1995) point out that "drug abuse is often a consequence of rapid social change (even social turmoil) brought on by factors such as rapid modernization and urbanization, civil strife, disease epidemics, and extreme economic hardships." These conditions are all too common in developing countries and create vulnerable populations. Alcohol, for example, can create feelings of relaxation and freedom that are desirable to individuals facing social and economic difficulties. However, it also depresses the nervous system and can lead to depression, violence, and impaired functioning. Excessive, long-term drinking leads to physical complications such as cirrhosis and mental health complications such as psychotic episodes and hallucinations. Alcohol abuse is directly linked to accidents, interpersonal violence, and suicide.

Treatment for alcoholism is very limited in developing countries. Alcoholics receive treatment only for disorders and wounds resulting from substance abuse, not for the addiction (Patel 2001). Studies encourage policy makers and health care workers in developing and transitioning countries to alter policies and perceptions to focus on treatment of dependency. Addressing alcohol dependence is important because alcohol abuse has consequences for communities and societies as well as individuals: increased crime, violence, traffic accidents, unemployment, and reduced productivity. It is difficult to quantify the cost of alcohol dependence to developing societies, but estimates suggest it costs at least 1% of a developing country's gross domestic product (GDP).

The vulnerability of developing and transitioning country populations to alcohol, tobacco, and other substance dependence is exacerbated by the economic benefits associated with substance sales. Governments tax sales of alcohol and other legal substances and thus gain substantial revenues. Health professionals insist that the human cost outweighs any economic gain and indirect costs of alcoholism, such as health care, lost productivity, and law enforcement exceed revenues collected. They seek changes in government policies related to alcohol sales and consumption. Governments remain unconvinced, and the tension between the economic gains and human costs of alcohol dependence remains. A mid-1980s campaign against alcohol in the Soviet Union illustrates this point. For nearly three years, the government limited hours for alcohol sales, jailed those selling alcohol illegally, increased vodka prices, and had police arrest those drinking in public. Estimates suggest the campaign saved over half a million lives and reduced mortality rates in Russia. However, the campaign also reduced government revenue, perhaps by as much as 10% of indirect taxation, and is blamed in part for the Soviet Union's subsequent financial collapse.

Though many cultures accept usage of traditional drugs, substance abuse and dependence place an increasing burden on developing and transitioning societies. Without mental health and policy intervention, substance dependence will likely continue to limit opportunities for development.

Suicide

Depression and alcohol abuse are related to each other and to self-inflicted injuries and suicide. In 1995, for countries that reported such statistics, suicide was one of the top ten causes of death (Desjarlais *et al.* 1995). The World Health Organization considers suicide a serious public health problem. The Global Burden of Disease 2000 study ranks self-inflicted injuries, including intentionally killing oneself, eighteenth among causes of burden of disease at 1.3% of disability-adjusted life years lost. Suicide rates are consistently higher among men worldwide; suicide is the seventh leading cause of death for men ages fifteen to forty-four, accounting for 3.0% of DALYs.

Suicide rates vary considerably, geographically and culturally. As well, statistics on the subject are unreliable and sometimes unavailable. The general perception that suicide occurs primarily in industrialized countries is, however, a myth. As of 1995, the country with the highest rate of suicide was Sri Lanka (Desjarlais *et al.* 1995). Between the 1980s and 1990s, suicide increased nearly 62% in Mexico and 54% in

India, but decreased by 5% in the United States and 14% in Japan. These overall figures may disguise increases in regions within countries or in particular age groups (WHO 2001). The human cost of suicide is clear for both victims and their survivors. The economic cost is less clear.

Desjarlais *et al.* (1995) assess determinants of suicide, considering severe stressors as well as psychiatric disorders. The relationships between severe stressors and suicide are often indirect or inconsistent across countries. They find no direct link between suicide and modernization or urbanization, though social forces related to modernization do affect suicide rates. These forces—all of which can be present in developing countries—include economic insecurity and unemployment, social instability, political repression and protests, and both collective and domestic violence. The authors conclude that "simply put, personal troubles might be less important than social problems," particularly in developing or transitioning countries. Other studies reinforce this conclusion as they document increases in suicide during civil war, ethnic conflict, and their aftermath. Preventing such severe stressors is key to reducing suicide, but remains a challenge in most developing and transitioning societies.

These four examples demonstrate the presence, complexity, and severity of mental health disorders in developing countries. And, of course, many more are present. The Global Burden of Disease 2000 study documents years lived with disability (YLDs) as well as DALYs. Conditions affecting years lived with disability also include Alzheimer's, schizophrenia, panic disorders, obsessive-compulsive disorders, and post–traumatic stress disorders. In fact, for men ages fifteen to forty-four, the top four causes of YLDs are all mental health disorders (WHO 2001).

Many factors complicate mental health in developing countries. Political, economic, and social conditions are as important as biological predispositions for depression, substance dependence, suicide, and other mental health disorders. Developing countries experience conditions that are more extensive than or not present in industrialized countries. Cultural differences complicate mental health. Treatments for many mental health disorders are determined in industrialized countries and there is a question of effectiveness in other cultural contexts, as noted above with regard to depression. The status of women provides another example of cultural complications. Worldwide, men have higher rates of suicide. In China in 1998, however, suicide was the leading cause of death in rural areas among women but ranked third among causes of death for men (WHO 2001). Explanations include the low status of women in China, the reproductive repression they face, more general constraints on life choices, and a culturally based tradition of suicide and the threat of suicide as a "lever of domestic power and form of protest" among Chinese women (Desjarlais *et al.* 1995).

Disasters and dislocations also seriously complicate mental health in developing and transitioning countries. Industrialized countries have stronger support systems and economic reserves to deal with both natural and man-made disasters. International organizations suggest up to 50 million people are displaced, either within their own countries or as refugees. The situations that prompted flight are also likely to prompt mental distress or severe stressors that contribute to mental disorders. Refugee and internally displaced populations have little access to health care of any kind. Relief planning gives increasing attention to mental health services but obstacles to their effective provision are numerous, including funding, safety, and overwhelming numbers of people needing assistance. Again, cultural differences also serve as a challenge; many argue the diagnosis and treatment of post–traumatic stress disorders are specific to Western culture. Nonetheless, there is general recognition of the significant impact of disasters and dislocation on mental health.

Conflict and state or structural violence are usually treated as a category separate from disaster, as they involve longer-term stressors. War, ethnic conflict, state terror, and political repression all create serious political, social, economic, and psychological threats to mental health. These threats can be direct, such as immediate psychological trauma, and indirect, such as disruptions of communities, cultures, and traditions. Estimates suggest up to one-half of all populations affected by conflict suffer mental distress or disorders. Post-traumatic stress disorder is common in these situations. As most social services break down during conflict, what little mental health care was available is likely to disappear. Thus, while difficult, preventing such conflict and violence is deemed the most effective means of preventing the resulting mental distress. With regard to treatment in or after conflict situations, Desjarlais *et al.* (1995) argue that the impact of conflict and violence is mitigated in resilient, unified communities and therefore suggest community-level mental health interventions would be more effective than individual-level therapy.

A successful process of development may itself diminish these complications to mental health by reducing conflict and dislocations and through cultural changes that accompany modernization. More generally, development may improve the political and economic environments and thus reduce some stressors, increase resources for mental health, and lead to better support systems. But development does not automatically increase mental health. The preconception that industrialized countries suffer from more suicides may be false, but it grew out of the fact that psychosocial disorders (and attention to them) did increase in many countries when their economies were growing rapidly. Even positive developments like increased life expectancy complicate mental health, as individuals will live long enough to experience Alzheimer's disease or other age-related mental disorders.

When the 1996 Global Burden of Disease (GBD) report was issued, a stunned public health community realized just how neglected mental health had been throughout the world. The World Health Organization's World Health Report 2001 focuses on "Mental Health: New Understanding, New Hope." It bluntly acknowledges that the public health community has long neglected the importance of mental health to overall well being. Current attention to mental health will give it priority on global health agendas and, perhaps, national agendas. However, the significant political, economic, and social challenges in developing and transitioning countries remain unchanged, making it difficult for them to immediately address mental health or, indeed, health in general. As Desjarlais *et al.* (1995) point out, "To think about mental health, then, we must consider a range of interrelated forces that, at first glance, might not appear to be 'mental health' problems." Until these interrelated forces are successfully addressed, mental health may well remain a low priority in developing and transitioning countries.

PAMELA A. ZEISER

See also Public health; World Health Organization (WHO)

References and Further Reading

Desjarlais, Robert, Leon Eisenberg, Byron Good, and Arthur Kleinman. *World Mental Health: Problems and Priorities in Low-Income Countries.* New York and Oxford: Oxford University Press, 1995.

Dunbar, Scott. *Women and Mental Health.* London: Zed Books, 1995.

Harpham, Trudy and Ilona Blue, eds. *Urbanization and Mental Health in Developing Countries.* Aldershot, UK: Avebury, 1995.

Murray, Christopher and Alan D. Lopez, eds. *The Global Burden of Disease.* Geneva: World Health Organization, 1996.

Narayan, Deepa. *Voices of the Poor: Can Anyone Hear Us?* Oxford and New York: Oxford University Press, 2001.

Patel, Vikram. "Poverty, Inequality, and Mental Health in Developing Countries." In *Poverty, Inequality, and Health: An International Perspective*, edited by David

Leon and Gill Walt. New York and Oxford: Oxford University Press, 2001.

Ustun, T. Bedirhan. "The Global Burden of Mental Disorders." *American Journal of Public Health*, 89, no. 9 (1999).

Weissman, Myrna, T. B. Ustun, and Leon Eisenberg. "Epidemiologic Strategies to Address World Mental Health Problems in Underserved Populations: Task Force Report." *International Journal of Mental Health*, 28, no. 2 (1999).

World Health Organization. *The World Health Report 2001—Mental Health: New Understanding, New Hope.* Geneva: World Health Organization, 2001.

MEXICO: HISTORY AND ECONOMIC DEVELOPMENT

Mexico forms the southern part of North America and stretches into Central America. Its borders are with the United States to the north and with Belize and Guatemala to the east. Mexico's long coastline borders three bodies of water: the Gulf of Mexico, the Caribbean, and the Pacific. Mexico is the third-largest country in Latin America: at 761,600 square miles, it is approximately three times the size of Texas. It is home to an estimated 105 million people; in addition, more than 20 million Mexicans and their descendants live in the United States. Approximately 20% of the population, or 21 million, live in metropolitan Mexico City.

Mexico is a country of great geographical diversity. Two major mountain ranges, the Sierra Madre Occidental and the Sierra Madre Oriental, run parallel to the Pacific and Gulf Coasts before meeting in the Sierra Volcánica Transversal and tapering off in the Isthmus of Tehuantepec. The peaks of the Sierra Volcánica include Mexico's highest mountains: the Citlaltépetl (also known as Pico de Orizaba), the Popocatépetl, and the Ixtaccíhuatl. These mountain ranges contribute to a great variety of climate and terrain ranging from the deserts of the north to the tropical rainforests of Chiapas. As a result, Mexico numbers among the most diverse developing nations in terms of mineral and agricultural resources. Mexican mineral exports have had a significant impact on global markets. In the late eighteenth century, what was then the Spanish colony of New Spain was the world's largest silver producer, and by the 1890s, silver pesos provided cash flow in South and East Asia. By then, copper mining had transformed the border state of Sonora, and shortly thereafter, an oil boom began in the Gulf states. Today, Mexico is one of the world's leading oil producers not affiliated with OPEC (Organization of Petroleum-Exporting Countries). Agricultural products include coffee, flowers, fruit, and sugar, along with basic foodstuffs such as corn, which is thought to have originated in Mexico. However, only 13% of the country's territory is arable, and Mexico depends on imports for feeding its growing population.

This population is as diverse as the country it inhabits. Prior to the age of European exploration, what is now central Mexico was the most densely populated area of the Americas. The Aztec empire alone was home to an estimated 16 million to 25 million people, and millions more lived in the east, where the great Mayan civilization had once flourished. The conquest by Spain beginning in 1519 not only brought colonial rule, but also exploitative labor systems and epidemics unknown to the indigenous people—diseases that wiped out approximately 90% of the native population during the century that followed. During the seventeenth and eighteenth century, a miscegenated society emerged in Mexico that combined indigenous, European, and African elements, while the indigenous population slowly began to recover. Despite this ethnic mixture, Mexico is still home to more than 16 million indigenous people, and the country features sixty-two living indigenous languages in addition to Spanish, the official language.

The Mexican economy forms a bridge from the highly developed North American economies of Canada and the United States to the less developed economies of Central and South America. In the last fifty years, Mexico has emerged as one of the more highly industrialized countries of the developing world. Service and industrial occupations amount to 82% of all employment, and remittances from migrant workers in the United States constitute an important source of national income. In 2003, per capita Gross Domestic Product (GDP) was estimated at $9,000, after Argentina the second highest among the independent nations of Latin America but less than one-fourth that of the United States. Even before the 1992 signing of the North American Free Trade Agreement (NAFTA), a treaty that will create a single North American market by 2009, the economic linkages between Mexico and the United States overwhelmed ties to other regions of the world. In 2003, the United States absorbed 87.6% of Mexican exports, and 61.8% of Mexican imports were of US origin.

Wealth has always been unevenly distributed in Mexico. In 2002, the poorest 10% of the population enjoyed just 1.6% of household income, while the top 10% accounted for 35.6%. The Gini index—a key measure of social justice that increases with inequality—reads 53.6 for Mexico, compared to forty-four for the United States and twenty-five for Sweden. By way of comparison, this figure resembles that of Chile and Peru, whereas the Gini index for Brazil, the country with which Mexico is most frequently compared in terms of economic performance, is 60.8. In general terms, the distribution of wealth follows ethnic lines, with the more European elements of the population enjoying greater access to economic opportunity as well as political power.

While the Spanish conquest and colonial period sowed the seeds of this inequality, the two centuries since independence have featured several attempts to redress the imbalance. The independence movement began in 1810 with the Hidalgo Revolt, a movement rooted in the peasantry of central Mexico. In the 1850s, the Liberal Reform swept an indigenous leader—Benito Juárez—to power even as the Liberals disentailed the Catholic Church and handed its land over to private investors. Landless peasants, including the indigenous army of Emiliano Zapata, played a key role in the Mexican Revolution of 1910, along with workers, the middle classes, and disaffected members of the elite, and the Constitution of 1917 enshrined land reform and the rights of workers as important and inalienable rights. During the 1920s and 1930s, a succession of governments put some of these promises into practice. At each juncture, however, popular demands for social change confronted powerful advocates for the status quo that included landowners, political bosses, entrepreneurs, and foreign investors. Hidalgo was captured and shot by colonial authorities; Juárez's liberalism eventually gave way to the authoritarian dictatorship of Porfirio Díaz; and the Mexican Revolution finally fell under the control of a single party that controlled the presidency from 1929 to 2000. Renamed the PRI (*Partido Revolucionario Institucional,* or Party of the Institutional Revolution) by President Miguel Alemán Valdés in 1946, this ruling party epitomized both popular demands for change and the efforts of a new elite to co-opt and even to thwart those demands. This became obvious as recently as 1994, when a rebel army that called itself the EZLN (*Ejército Zapatista de Liberación Nacional,* or Zapatista Army of National Liberation) rose up in protest against NAFTA, an agreement the rebels believed to be prejudicial to indigenous peasants in the southern state of Chiapas and in Mexico in general. Mexican history since 1945 has therefore followed three basic trends: rapid industrialization and urbanization; a deepening crisis of legitimacy of the PRI that finally cost the party its hold on power; and increasing integration into the North American (and hence, global) economy. These trends occurred over the course of three phases: the so-called Mexican miracle (1948–1968), a populist era (1968–1982), and the neoliberal era (beginning in 1982).

A time of rapid economic growth and industrialization, the Mexican miracle was rooted in growing US demand for Mexican export products. The immediate postwar period had been a time of economic crisis. As Mexico had helped the Allied war effort in large part by furnishing strategic raw materials, the postwar drop in demand for such products hurt the Mexican economy severely. At a time when the end of the war removed a major stimulus for the US economy, US businesses also turned away tens of thousands of Mexican workers hired under the Bracero Program in the early 1940s, adding pressure to a labor market already straining under the weight of a growing population. At the same time, mounting inflation, particularly in foodstuffs and other items of necessity, confounded the expectations of many Mexicans that the Allied victory in the war would benefit them.

Faced with this slump, the Mexican government joined other large Latin American nations in embracing the advice of the Argentine economist Raúl Prebisch, the president of the United Nations' Economic Commission for Latin America. Prebisch had diagnosed the reliance on externally driven development—the export of raw materials to pay for imported industrial goods—as the cause for the economic underdevelopment of Latin America. According to Prebisch's analysis, trading raw materials for manufactured products constituted an "unequal exchange," as the prices of most raw materials tended to decline in the long run in comparison to those of manufactured goods. To solve this problem, Prebisch proposed government-assisted import-substitution industrialization (ISI) programs accompanied by a protectionist trade policy. Picking up on an industrialization project that had brought many light industries to Mexico over the course of the preceding sixty years, the Mexican government joined those of Argentina and Brazil in making a strong push toward state-assisted modernization. This effort did not imply a move toward autarky so much as it changed the type of dependence on the United States and, to a lesser extent, Western Europe. Instead of buying hardware from the United States, for example, Mexican companies purchased the machinery needed to produce such hardware. Another phenomenon was the opening of foreign-owned assembly plants in Mexico during the 1950s and 1960s.

With the help of strong US demand for Mexican products and a growing interest in Mexico as a tourist destination, ISI produced results that looked impressive: an average growth rate of 8% in the 1948–1968 period, accompanied by great strides in literacy and health care. Aside from Mexican companies, many multinational corporations began production in Mexico. For example, in 1966, Volkswagen began to produce its signature Beetle automobile in its new plant in the city of Puebla. Likewise, *maquiladoras,* or partial assembly plants, dotted the northern states close to the US border, from where the maquiladoras shipped their products to be fully assembled in the United States. The result was a more urban society: Mexico City grew from 650,000 inhabitants in 1945 to 20 million fifty years later, and other metropolitan centers such as Guadalajara, León, Monterrey, and Puebla also experienced exponential growth. Much of this growth attested to the fact that poverty was on the rise even as national income improved, as a ring of *ciudades perdidas,* or shantytowns, came to surround Mexico City and other metropolitan areas.

This effort relied on a ruling party that centralized power in the presidency with a corporatist model developed in the 1920s and 1930s, and particularly following the influence of Presidents Alvaro Obregón, Plutarco Elías Calles, and Lázaro Cárdenas del Río. The PRI not only worked to take power from the military *caciques* who had continually defied central authority in the two decades following the Revolution of 1910, but it also claimed to represent the revolution itself. By incorporating several mass-based organizations, including the CNC (*Consejo Nacional Campesino,* or National Peasant Council) and the CTM (*Confederación de Trabajadores Mexicanos,* or Confederation of Mexican Workers), the PRI mediated social conflict at the same time that it supported the president in carrying out the ambitious industrialization program and engineered a string of electoral victories. The resulting balancing act provided a friendly environment for investors even while a succession of presidents decreed higher wages and new benefits for workers.

If this system worked fairly well during times of economic growth and political stability, the late 1960s put it to a severe test. After 1966, the global economy slowed down at the same time that an opposition student movement emerged in Mexico—a movement heavily influenced by similar trends in countries such as France, the United States, and West Germany. These students decried the PRI state as a one-party dictatorship that did not allow dissenting voices to be heard. For the student movement, the 1968 Olympics in Mexico City became a prime opportunity to showcase its concerns, as the Mexico City Olympics were the first ones to be held in a developing nation. On October 2, 1968—only two weeks before the opening of the Olympic Games—Mexican security forces massacred hundreds of student protesters in the Plaza de las Tres Culturas in Tlatelolco, Mexico City, and the PRI had shed its mask as the defender of the revolution. At the same time, the student movement had shown the degree to which Mexican society and culture reflected global trends. Not only was this movement just as politicized as those in the United States and Western Europe, but it also represented a counterculture: in 1970, Mexico featured its own version of the famed Woodstock music festival near the small town of Avándaro.

By then, Mexico had entered a populist era in which the PRI government again invoked the social and political promises of the Revolution of 1910. Presidents Luis Echeverría Alvarez (1970–1976) and José López Portillo (1976–1982) represented themselves as latter-day versions of former president Cárdenas, a beloved icon of the Mexican left wing who had died shortly before Echeverría's inauguration. Across Mexico, former adherents of the student movement decapitated at Tlatelolco went underground: some joined urban guerrillas, and others— like the rebel Lucio Cabañas—organized a rural uprising in the state of Guerrero near the resort town of Acapulco. Between 1970 and 1976, abductions and political assassinations rocked Mexico: the guerrillas killed a wealthy Monterrey industrialist, Eugenio Garza Sada; Cabañas' forces kidnapped a federal senator; and a revolutionary group held for ransom Echeverría's father-in-law, Guadalupe Zuno Hernández.

Echeverría responded to this popular challenge with a mixture of coercion and co-optation. He sent over ten thousand federal troops into Guerrero to carry out a scorched-earth policy that killed hundreds of innocent bystanders along with Cabañas and twenty-seven of his closest collaborators. He also knew, however, that he needed to make concessions to the proponents of reform, many of whom desired more radical change in Mexican society than he was prepared to offer. Thus, Echeverría revived the long-dormant land distribution program, parceling out more land to peasants than his four predecessors combined; he lowered the voting age to eighteen, and he inaugurated an ambitious profit-sharing scheme designed to increase the gross pay of workers. To detract from his own "dirty war" against guerrilla insurgents and other opponents of his regime, he also offered asylum to South Americans fleeing the recently established military dictatorships of Chile (1973) and Argentina (1976). While the Mexican government thus muzzled its own opposition, Mexico City became the cultural capital of Latin America as the new home of hundreds of dissident intellectuals from the Southern Cone.

For his part, López Portillo built on Echeverría's populist style. The discovery of new oil deposits fueled optimism in government circles about Mexico's future as an economic power at a time of high oil prices. And yet, the crisis that had begun in 1968 continued to fester. Corruption was rampant, and criticism of the PRI's stranglehold on the political process even resonated in the government-sponsored newspapers. Like Echeverría, López Portillo attempted to use an active foreign policy to cover up the domestic shortcomings of his regime (see Mexico: International Relations). Convinced that the gushing oil wells constituted a sort of cornucopia, the president attempted to translate newfound economic riches and diplomatic successes into political capital. He also borrowed heavily from foreign banks to finance ambitious social programs and government subsidies for housing and food.

This effort to revive the populist rhetoric of the 1920s and 1930s to cover up the shortcomings of the PRI state failed in the aftermath of the debt crisis of 1982. In a climate of high interest rates and falling oil prices, the Mexican government defaulted on its mounting foreign debt. In a panicked effort to prevent massive capital flight, López Portillo nationalized the country's banks, but it was already too late. By June 1983, the peso had fallen 85% against the dollar, and over the course of the administration of López Portillo's successor, Miguel de la Madrid, real incomes fell almost 40%. To reestablish creditworthiness with foreign banks, de la Madrid accepted a severe austerity program prescribed by the International Monetary Fund. This program not only mandated a balancing of the government's books, but also enjoined de la Madrid to sell off state-owned assets and end the fifty-year experiment in making the state a major player in the economy.

The de la Madrid administration ushered in the most recent period in Mexican history: the neoliberal era. De la Madrid and his successor, President Carlos Salinas de Gortari (1988–1994), officially dismantled the image of the PRI as a revolutionary party, and Salinas even led a successful effort to strike many of the nationalist and social reformist provisions of the Constitution of 1917. In doing so, de la Madrid and Salinas publicly likened the restructuring and privatization to Mikhail Gorbachev's *perestroika* in the Soviet Union, even though Mexico, unlike the Soviet Union, had never left the path of state-sponsored capitalism. Salinas also spearheaded the effort to win approval of NAFTA in Canada, Mexico, and the United States, and he considered the passage of NAFTA his signature achievement. In the late 1980s and early 1990s, the sale of state-owned assets and a global economic recovery marked a brief return to the growth rates of the 1950s and 1960s. Not even the Zapatista rebellion of 1994, which plagued the last year of Salinas' government and that of his successor,

Ernesto Zedillo—a last-minute replacement for Luis Donaldo Colosio, Salinas' hand-picked successor who was assassinated under mysterious circumstances in April 1994—could dispel the optimism that reigned in government circles. The following year, however, Mexico once again entered a downward cycle with the peso crisis of 1995, and ordinary Mexicans were again hit hard as their currency lost almost two-thirds of its value. Although the crisis passed fairly quickly, thanks in part to swift intervention by the US government, Mexicans dubbed the time they lived in the "*décadas perdidas*," or lost decades—a far cry from the upbeat rhetoric from the national government.

As his own term neared a close, Zedillo realized that the PRI had finally reached the twilight of its undisputed rule. Already in 1988, Salinas had won a highly questionable victory over the left-wing opposition candidate Cuauhtémoc Cárdenas amidst allegations of fraud. Since that time, the PRI had steadily lost influence in northern Mexico to a conservative opposition party, the PAN (*Partido de Acción Nacional,* or National Action Party). Zedillo understood well that his own legacy could either consist of prolonging the rule of the PRI by illegal means, or serving as the president who at long last brought democracy to Mexico. As a result, he consented to a wide-ranging electoral reform that gave greater opportunities to opposition parties at the precise moment when the PAN offered a charismatic leader, the former Coca-Cola executive Vicente Fox Quesada. In July 2000, Fox's triumph in the national elections ushered in a new era in Mexico—one in which the PRI is only one of three major parties. Although Fox's rule has been overshadowed by yet another economic crisis and inefficient government, Mexico is today more truly democratic than at any other point in its history. It remains to be seen whether political democracy can translate into greater social justice or sustainable economic development that benefits the majority of the population.

JÜRGEN BUCHENAU

See also Fox, Vicente; North American Free Trade Agreement (NAFTA); Party of the Institutionalized Revolution (PRI); Salinas de Gortari, Carlos; Zapatista National Revolutionary Army (EZLN)

References and Further Reading

Aguilar Camín, Héctor and Lorenzo Meyer. *A la Sombra de la Revolución Mexicana: Un Ensayo de Historia Contemporánea de México*. Mexico City: Cal y Arena, 1990.
Bortz, Jeffrey. *Industrial Wages in Mexico City, 1939–1975*. New York: Garland Publishing, 1987.
Brachet-Marquez, Viviane. *The Dynamics of Domination: State, Class, and Social Reform in Mexico, 1910–1990*. Pittsburgh, PA: Pittsburgh University Press, 1994.
Camp, Roderic A. *Entrepreneurs and Politics in Twentieth-Century Mexico*. New York: Oxford University Press, 1989.
Davis, Diane E. *Urban Leviathan: Mexico City in the Twentieth Century*. Philadelphia: Temple University Press, 1994.
Harvey, Neil. *Rebellion in Chiapas: Rural Reforms, Campesino Radicalism, and the Limits to Salinismo*. La Jolla, CA: Center for US–Mexican Studies, University of California, San Diego, 1994.
Lustig, Nora. *Mexico: The Remaking of an Economy*, 2nd rev. ed. Washington, DC: Brookings Institution, 1998.
Miller, Michael N. *Red, White, and Green: The Maturing of Mexicanidad*. El Paso, TX: Texas Western Press, 1998.
Niblo, Stephen R. *Mexico in the 1940s: Modernity, Politics, and Corruption*. Wilmington, DE: Scholarly Resources, 1999.
Schmidt, Arthur. "Making It Real Compared to What: Reconceptualizing Mexican History Since 1940." In *Fragments of a Golden Age: The Politics of Culture in Mexico Since 1940*, edited by Gilbert Joseph, Anne Rubenstein, and Eric Zolov. Durham, NC: Duke University Press, 2001, 23–68.
Zolov, Eric. *Refried Elvis: The Rise of the Mexican Counterculture*. Berkeley, CA: University of California Press, 1999.

MEXICO: INTERNATIONAL RELATIONS

Mexico is the only developing nation that shares a land border with a highly industrialized society. As a result, since independence in 1821, Mexican international relations have centered first and foremost on the country's relationship with the United States. For Mexicans today, the secession of Texas (1836) and the US–Mexican War (1846–1848) hold far more traumatic memories than the French Intervention (1862–1867) because these military engagements with US forces resulted in the annexation of half of the nation's territory. Among more recent instances of US intervention, Mexicans remember the occupation of Veracruz (1914) and the Punitive Expedition against Mexican revolutionary Pancho Villa (1916–1917). Distant in time, these events burned themselves into the national consciousness and made national icons out of Villa and others who resisted the United States. And yet, Mexicans have long recognized that the relationship with the United States is vital for the economic development of their country.

As a result, Mexican foreign policy has sought to take advantage of US capital and technological know-how while attempting to limit direct attacks on the country's sovereignty. In this scheme, relations with countries other than the United States have sought to mitigate the powerful influence of Mexico's northern neighbor, either by seeking European investments and immigration to balance US economic influence, or by encouraging nationalist and anti-imperialist movements in Latin America. Therefore, President Porfirio Díaz (1876–1880 and 1884–1911) courted British, French, and German investments even as he oversaw what came to be known as the "Pacific Conquest" of Mexico by US investors, and he supported Central American leaders critical of US influence such as Nicaragua's José Santos Zelaya. Similarly, the governments of the Mexican Revolution (1910–1940) sought to force foreign investors to obey Mexican laws, and in 1938, President Lázaro Cárdenas even expropriated the foreign-owned oil industry—all at a time when US investments in Mexico had reached a new high. Finally, President Manuel Avila Camacho supported the United States and its allies in World War II but turned a deaf ear to US demands to extradite ethnic Germans and Japanese and to nationalize property held by Axis nationals and Mexicans of German and Japanese descent. Instead of confiscating this property and closing down German and Japanese mercantile establishments, as many Central and South American governments did, Avila Camacho placed them under the supervision of a government agency.

Since 1945, this effort to enjoy the benefits of the vicinity of the United States without its attendant risks has become even more complicated. As the Cold War began to polarize world politics, migration and the maturation of transnational business networks integrated Mexico into an even closer relationship with the United States. To add to this trend, World War II had left the United States as the only regional power in the Caribbean era. These incentives to support the US side, however, were at least partially offset by the enduring legacy of an anti-imperialist foreign policy dating back to the nineteenth century. This legacy, and the social forces that sustained it, prodded the Mexican government to support social revolution and criticize US intervention. Furthermore, the very strengthening of US power dictated a policy that showcased Mexico as an independent nation rather than an ally of the United States.

At the end of the war, Avila Camacho's first foreign-policy priority was to assist the project of import-substitution industrialization (see Mexico: History and Economic Development). Avila Camacho and his successor, Miguel Alemán Valdés, maintained close ties to the Monterrey Group, the country's most important network of industrialists. With the help of the Mexican state, the Monterrey Group participated in joint ventures with US multinational corporations that accelerated the industrialization project. As US exporters could not meet the burgeoning Mexican demand for manufactured items,

and since industrialization provided opportunities for the export of capital goods, the US government supported Mexican import-substitution industrialization. As a result, postwar US–Mexican relations were harmonious. In 1947, Alemán and US President Harry S. Truman exchanged state visits in an unprecedented show of goodwill. During his visit, which coincided with the centennial of the US–Mexican War, Truman honored the *niños héroes* (boy heroes), the young cadets from elite Mexican families who had died defending Chapultepec Castle against the advancing US forces.

Alemán also moved to improve relations with Mexico's former enemies during World War II. Even before the resumption of diplomatic relations with Germany and Japan in 1952, the president took steps toward normalization by returning government-administered German property to its owners. However, the appropriately named president, whose last name translates to "German" in the Spanish language, disappointed many Japanese-Mexicans whose property had been sold during or immediately following the war.

Alemán began a diplomacy that distinguished itself for its support of the United States in the Cold War and by its anticommunism. Mexico backed the United States on a variety of matters ranging from the Korean War to Eastern Europe, and it maintained cool relations with the Soviet Union. The anticommunism of Alemán and his successor, Adolfo Ruiz Cortines, resulted in part from personal conviction, in part from ceaseless US mass media propaganda in Mexico, in part from the Mexican government's desire to discourage radical protest movements, and in part from a keen sense of political opportunity. In the fall of 1949, the communist triumph in China had heightened the US fear of a world revolution. By the summer of the next year, the US involvement in the Korean War had led to a complete military mobilization. As mobilization entailed lucrative contracts for Latin American mineral exporters, an anticommunist stance could help procure these contracts for Mexico. The victory of World War II hero Dwight D. Eisenhower in the 1952 US presidential elections made an anticommunist diplomacy even more important. As the CIA-assisted coup d'état in revolutionary Guatemala (1954) demonstrated, Eisenhower intended to quash economic nationalism and socialism in Latin America. In this context, anticommunism was a strategy of political survival.

As the case of Guatemala revealed, however, this anticommunist stance found its limits in the matter of US aggression in Latin America. To avoid US hostility, Mexican diplomats presented their objections at an international diplomatic forum. On the occasion of the Tenth Inter-American Conference held in Caracas in March 1954, US Secretary of State John F. Dulles presented a resolution against communist subversion in the western hemisphere. Seeing the resolution as a thinly veiled cloak to justify US intervention in Guatemala, Mexican diplomats introduced a number of motions designed to weaken it. When a majority of the delegates defeated most of these motions, Mexico joined Costa Rica and Argentina as the only countries to abstain from the final vote. Although the Ruiz Cortines administration remained silent throughout the coup d'état, it also allowed supporters of the ousted Guatemalan government free entry into Mexico. This stance constituted a compromise between the demands of geopolitics and the business elite on the one side and the nationalist left led by ex-President Cárdenas.

By the late 1950s, new President Adolfo López Mateos found conditions ripe for a more assertive and independent foreign policy. Throughout a decade of rapid economic growth, Mexico's international prestige had grown immensely, and the recovering European and Japanese economies took notice of its potential as a trading and investment partner. Furthermore, international issues played an increasing role in political discourse. Labor and peasant unrest prompted by the unequal distribution of the fruits of economic growth prompted López Mateos to display a nationalist foreign policy. In particular, the triumph of Fidel Castro and Che Guevara in Cuba left a great impact on Mexican public opinion, and López Mateos found himself between an anti-Castro business community and largely pro-Castro popular organizations. In addition, the beginning of decolonization in Africa and the emergence of champions of the so-called "Third World" such as Egypt's Gamal Nasser weakened the dominance of NATO and the Warsaw Pact in the United Nations General Assembly and provided new openings for criticism of US policy.

López Mateos' foreign policy was remarkably balanced between friendship with the United States and these new opportunities. López Mateos maintained cordial relations with US President John F. Kennedy. In 1961, Mexico embraced the Alliance for Progress, a program designed to forestall Castro-type revolutions in Latin America with US-sponsored economic and social reform. A year later, Kennedy proclaimed during a visit to Mexico City that the goals of the Alliance for Progress were identical to those of the Mexican Revolution. Nonetheless, López Mateos also sought to open up new economic and political partnerships around the globe. His government gravitated toward the nascent Non-Aligned Movement, and Mexico became one of the founding members of the Latin American Free Trade Association (LAFTA). The president was particularly proud when Mexico City was selected as the host city for the 1968 Summer Olympics as the first (and so far only) Latin American city to host the event.

The Cuban Revolution revealed both the possibilities and the limits of this new foreign policy. Initially, López Mateos welcomed Castro's victory. When Castro proclaimed himself a socialist, however, the Mexican government ceased to praise the Cuban leader. Instead, López Mateos defended Cuba's right to self-determination and maintained that posture in the face of enormous US pressure after the unsuccessful Bay of Pigs invasion of April 1961 sponsored by the CIA. Not even the Cuban Missile Crisis of October 1962 could make a dent in this opposition to US intervention. While López Mateos joined Kennedy in condemning Castro for requesting Soviet nuclear missiles, he cautioned that his action did not imply acquiescence to a US invasion of Cuba.

This policy of reserved toleration of the Cuban Revolution continued into the succeeding decade, albeit accompanied by an increasing distance between the Mexican and Cuban governments. Under President Gustavo Díaz Ordaz (1964–1970), Mexican politics moved to the right at the same time when Castro made sporadic efforts to encourage Latin Americans to emulate his revolution. Invoking the same arguments that it had used in the defense of the Cuban Revolution, the Mexican government opposed what it viewed as interference in the internal affairs of other nations. Far from being an issue of international principles, this stance sought to discourage the Mexican left from seeking Cuban assistance. In fact, however, Díaz Ordaz need not have worried, as Castro never aided subversive movements in Mexico. The Cuban leader either spared Mexico because of its principled diplomatic efforts, or he feared US reprisals if he were to stir up trouble in a country that bordered the United States. In any case, however, Díaz Ordaz did not share his predecessor's tolerance for Castro's revolutionary experiment. Mexican–Cuban relations deteriorated during his administration, and the Cuban hijacking of Mexican commercial airliners in May and June 1970 led to a low point in relations. Nonetheless, he never publicly condemned the Castro regime, and the appearance of tolerating the Cuban Revolution and defying US policy therefore remained.

From 1970 to 1976, the presidency of former Secretary of Gobernación Luis Echeverría Alvarez, the man whom many Mexicans considered responsible for the massacre of hundreds of student protesters at Tlatelolco, witnessed a turn toward an even more independent foreign policy. Echeverría sought to recover the ground his party had lost at Tlatelolco by shifting official rhetoric dramatically to the left. As part of this effort, Echeverría proclaimed himself a champion of the "Third World" and asserted that Mexico would assume a position of leadership in what is now known as the Global South. Continued by his successor, José López Portillo, this self-proclaimed leadership role increasingly clashed with US policy, particularly as regarded Mexican positions in the United Nations and toward social revolution in Cuba and Central America. Taking advantage of a number of international trends that allowed a degree of independence from US objectives, this assertive Mexican foreign policy was designed above all to make people forget Tlatelolco.

The international panorama offered an opportunity for a more independent foreign policy. At the time, the United States was bogged down in Vietnam and engaged in a process of détente with the Soviet Union. In Latin America, Mexico increasingly appeared to represent a "middle way" between two opposing tendencies: the rise of military regimes in Brazil, Paraguay, and Uruguay, and revolutionary nationalism in Cuba and Salvador Allende's Chile. In the early 1970s, it appeared unlikely that the United States would launch a military intervention against either the Chilean or the Cuban Revolution, and Echeverría believed that Mexico enjoyed an unprecedented margin for an assertive foreign policy.

Thus encouraged, Echeverría launched a diplomatic offensive on several fronts. Pointing to the unfavorable terms of trade of most developing nations, he called for global economic justice with vaguely defined references to a new commodity price structure. He also nationalized the tobacco and telephone industries, pointing to these sectors as examples of foreign exploitation. The Mexican president also invented himself as a critic of the Cold War. He became one of the leaders of the "nonaligned movement" within the United Nations and maintained a dialogue with Castro. To make his point even clearer, he posed for photo ops with Palestinian leader Yasser Arafat, a symbol of anti-Zionist and anti-"American" sentiment in the Middle East, and he openly befriended Chilean leader Salvador Allende. When a CIA-assisted coup overthrew Allende, Echeverría granted asylum to thousands of Chileans fleeing the ensuing repression. After another coup overthrew Argentine president Isabel Perón three years later, Echeverría opened Mexico's doors to Argentine refugees as well. Mexico's status as a safe haven for South American refugees detracted attention from Echeverría's own "dirty war" against Lucio Cabañas and other insurgents operating in the Mexican countryside after the Tlatelolco massacre.

If Echeverría had primarily asserted Mexican objectives in the United Nations and in exile policy, López Portillo returned to Mexico's traditional role as a middle power in Central America. In May 1979, the López Portillo administration broke relations with the Somoza dictatorship in Nicaragua. Two months later, the Sandinista leadership of a movement that had fought Somoza since 1963 arrived in Managua aboard a Mexican jet to begin eleven years of revolutionary rule in Nicaragua. In the first years of the revolution, López Portillo generously lavished favors on the "new Nicaragua." Awash in petrodollars, the Mexican government awarded $39 million in cash and goods to the Sandinistas. When US President Ronald Reagan began to undermine the Sandinistas, whom he regarded as the work of Cuban-Soviet subversion, López Portillo helped Nicaragua on the diplomatic front. He sponsored a US–Nicaraguan dialogue in the Mexican port town of Manzanillo, and he also unsuccessfully took up the subject of Nicaragua in the course of two meetings with Reagan in the first half of 1981. That same year, López Portillo also participated in an attempt to end a protracted civil war in El Salvador between a government controlled by right-wing death squads and left-wing opposition groups. In August, he and French President François Mitterrand issued a joint communiqué that recognized both opposition groups, the Democratic Revolutionary Front (FDR) and the Farabundo Martí National Liberation Front (FMLN), as "political forces representative of the Salvadoran people."

If the year 1981 was the high watermark of Mexican foreign policy in the postwar period, the following year forced López Portillo into retreat. Citing Soviet influence in the Sandinista junta and alleging Nicaraguan aid to the rebels in El Salvador, the Reagan government trained and armed thousands of Nicaraguan exiles, also known as Contras, in bases in Florida and Honduras, from where they launched forays into Nicaragua as part of an undeclared US war on the Sandinistas. At the same time, Mexico entered a severe economic crisis due to the collapse in oil prices and mounting foreign debt. As a result, Mexico soon returned to the cautious policy that had marked the 1950s and 1960s. New President Miguel de la Madrid shifted from lending direct assistance to the Sandinistas to seeking a mediated solution to the multiple crises in Central America. De la Madrid undertook this effort through the Contadora group made up of Colombia, Panama, and Venezuela.

De la Madrid's course proved prudent, as relations with the United States demanded his full attention. In particular, undocumented immigration complicated relations. During the 1970s, the number of undocumented Mexicans in the United States had grown rapidly; after 1982, the effects of the economic crisis added significantly to these numbers. Even while the US Congress debated measures to crack down on further immigration, the increasing trafficking in illicit drugs came to the fore as another explosive issue.

In the face of these difficulties, de la Madrid and his successor, Carlos Salinas de Gortari, decided to cast Mexico's lot with the United States and embrace neoliberal policies (see also Mexico: History and Economic Development). The culmination of these policies was the passage of the North American Free Trade Agreement (NAFTA), which not only set Canada, Mexico, and the United States on the path toward a common market, but also committed Mexico to relinquishing its postrevolutionary tradition of economic nationalism. If Echeverría had been a trendsetter for developing nations in the 1970s, the Harvard-trained Salinas became a poster child for the wave of globalizing policies that swept the developing world in the late 1980s and 1990s. Other moves toward free trade made Mexico a member of the General Agreement on Tariffs and Trade (GATT) and ultimately resulted in the signing of free trade agreements with Chile and the European Union. NAFTA set off acrimonious debate in Mexico, where Salinas had faced a stiff electoral challenge from Lázaro Cárdenas' son, Cuauhtémoc Cárdenas, who had broken ranks with the ruling PRI. The younger Cárdenas decried NAFTA as an attack on national sovereignty and a move to make Mexico an economic appendage of the United States. In particular, he worried that the treaty would reverse seventy years of land reform in Mexico, a process that had turned more than 80 million acres of land over to peasant cooperatives. This critique, however, paled in comparison to the response of a guerrilla group in Chiapas. On January 1, 1994, the day that NAFTA took effect, the *Ejército Zapatista de Liberación Nacional* (EZLN, or Zapatista Army of National Liberation) began its uprising, in large part to protest the adverse effects of the treaty on land tenure and social justice in Mexico. The EZLN successfully distributed its message by means of radio, television, and the Internet, however, it could not reverse the neoliberal trend.

Within a year after the beginning of the Zapatista uprising, new Mexican President Ernesto Zedillo confronted a turbulent landscape. In March, the assassination of Luis Donaldo Colosio, Salinas' handpicked successor, had rocked Mexico. Investors responded immediately by taking money out of Mexico, pulling down the country's foreign currency reserves by more than $10 billion within one month. The ensuing capital flight undermined the Mexican currency. On December 19, Zedillo allowed the peso to fall 15% against the dollar. The devaluation turned

into a free fall, and the currency continued to decline for a few years until it leveled off at ten new pesos to the dollar (ten thousand old pesos): one-third of its 1994 value. Just as in 1982, the Mexican government stood at the brink of default, and it was only after US President Bill Clinton put together an emergency loan package that it averted even more serious consequences. Resulting in the second precipitous drop of living standards since 1982, this crisis shook the faith of many Mexicans in neoliberalism and spelled the end of the PRI's hold on power. Ironically, however, the end result was the triumph of a movement even more committed to neoliberalism than Zedillo's PRI. In July 2000, the victory of former Coca-Cola operative Vicente Fox, the candidate of the opposition *Partido de Acción Nacional* (PAN, or National Action Party), in the presidential elections spelled the end of seventy-one years of PRI rule and also ushered in the rule of a man who vowed to further improve relations with the United States.

As Fox has discovered, however, the Mexican government is still caught in an uneasy balancing act between the United States and nationalist demands at home. In early 2003, during Mexico's most recent term as a member of the UN Security Council, the Mexican delegate confronted the efforts of US President George W. Bush to win United Nations support for the impending war against Saddam Hussein's Iraq. Aware that the vast majority of Mexicans opposed the Bush administration on this matter, Fox instructed the delegate to vote against the United States. Even in an age when transnational networks have weakened the nation state, it still behooves the Mexican government to pay attention to dissenting voices that desire a greater distance from the interests of Mexico's powerful northern neighbor.

JÜRGEN BUCHENAU

See also Mexico: History and Economic Development; North American Free Trade Agreement (NAFTA)

References and Further Reading

Buchenau, Jürgen (2000). "México y las Cruzadas Anticomunistas Estadunidenses, 1924–1964." *Secuencia* 48: 225–253.
———. "México como Potencia Mediana: Una Perspectiva Histórica." *Secuencia* 41: 75–94.
Herrera Zúñiga, René, Manuel Chavarría, and Mario Ojeda. "La Política de México en la Región de Centroamérica." *Foro Internacional* 23.4: 423–440.
Mares, David. "Mexico's Foreign Policy as a Middle Power: The Nicaragua Connection, 1884–1986." *LARR* 18.1: 81–107.
Niblo, Stephen. *War, Diplomacy, and Development: The United States and Mexico, 1938–1954.* Wilmington, DE: Scholarly Resources, 1995.

———. *Mexico in the 1940s: Modernity, Politics, and Corruption*. Wilmington, DE: Scholarly Resources, 1999.

Ojeda, Mario. *Alcances y Límites de la Política Exterior de México*. Mexico City: El Colegio de México, 1976.

———, ed. *Las Relaciones de México con Los Países de América Central*. Mexico City: El Colegio de México, 1985.

Paz, María Elena. *Strategy, Security, and Spies: Mexico and the Allies in World War II*. University Park, PA: Pennsylvania State University Press, 1997.

Pellicer de Brody, Olga. *México y la Revolución Cubana*. Mexico City: El Colegio de México, 1972.

———, and Esteban L. Mancilla. *Historia de la Revolución Mexicana, 1952–1960: El Entendimiento con los Estados Unidos y la Gestación del Desarrollo Estabilizador*. Mexico City: El Colegio de México, 1978.

———, and José Luis Reyna. *Historia de la Revolución Mexicana, 1952–1960: El Afianzamiento de la Estabilidad Política*. Mexico City: El Colegio de México, 1978.

Schuler, Friedrich. *Mexico Between Hitler and Roosevelt: Mexican Foreign Relations in the Age of Lázaro Cárdenas, 1934–1940*. Albuquerque, NM: University of New Mexico Press, 1998.

Torres Ramírez, Blanca. *Historia de la Revolución Mexicana, 1940–1952: México en la Segunda Guerra Mundial*. Mexico City: El Colegio de México, 1979.

Zorrilla, Luis G. *Relaciones de México con la República de Centro América y con Guatemala*. Mexico: Editorial Porrúa, 1984.

MICRONESIA, FEDERATED STATES OF

The Micronesian archipelago in the western Pacific Ocean includes four island groups located south of the Marianas and west of the Marshall Islands, including the high volcanic islands around Pohnpei, Kosrae, and Chuuk (Truk), and the low-lying group around Yap. The 607 islands and islets of Micronesia are scattered across an expanse of ocean larger than Western Europe, but in total land area these chains comprise only 607 square miles. Archaeological evidence of advanced human occupation dates from at least 500 BCE, and Spanish explorers in the sixteenth century named the islands the New Philippines. In 1899 Germany acquired most of the islands from Spain, but lost them to Japan in World War I. Japan established garrisons on the main islands, and in World War II these outposts were used to launch attacks on other Pacific islands, including Guam. The harbor at Truk served as Japan's main naval base in the region. After World War II, the United States assumed administrative authority over the islands.

Japan's early administration in Micronesia was managed by its "South Seas Bureau," a governmental entity headed by a civilian governor. The Bureau worked through the village chiefs on the main islands, using them to collect taxes from and communicate official pronouncements to the local population. There were isolated instances of native resistance, including the burning of a Japanese school and social restrictions enforced against those who collaborated with the Japanese; the Japanese made occasional arrests of the resistance leaders.

Micronesia's commercial development accelerated in the 1880s, when Japan's ships carried the islands' copra, coconut, and coconut oil exports. In 1906 Japanese companies controlled 80% of the total trade with German Micronesia, and by the start of World War I, much of the agricultural production, fishing, and freight and passenger services to the islands were Japanese-controlled. Once in power, Japan provided capital to develop phosphate mines, sugar plantations, and fishing. While Japanese were barred from owning land, they did lease land from local owners. The colonial government, meanwhile, seized commonly held acreage on the larger islands and allocated it to support the influx of Japanese colonists in the 1930s. Later, the Japanese military seized additional land for military facilities.

The United States' wartime "island-hopping" strategy in the Pacific largely bypassed Micronesia, and in 1944 Japan abandoned the base at Truk. The United States seized the islands, which came under US Navy administration. The United Nations later placed the islands under US authority in a unique "strategic trust" arrangement that obligated the United States to promote the political, economic, social, and educational advancement of local inhabitants, including aiding their preparation for self-government.

In actuality, US defense concerns took precedence and the welfare of the population was generally neglected. US interests in the region centered upon nuclear testing in the Marshall Islands to the east. In 1962 the Kennedy administration launched an investigation of living conditions in the islands, and subsequently ordered that US federal welfare programs be extended to all the US trust territories in the Pacific. Income support, housing assistance, and medical programs were introduced, and Peace Corps volunteers were dispatched to teach and build housing and local facilities. By the late 1960s these initiatives began attracting people to the principal islands, away from traditional homesteads on outer islands. Higher unemployment soon emerged, as agricultural and traditional pursuits were abandoned in favor of widespread dependence upon federal welfare programs.

Other US-funded assistance initiatives expanded after 1979 when a constitutional government, known as the "Federated States of Micronesia" (FSM), was formed and entered into a "Compact of Free Association" with the US government. Envisioned as the final stage of local political evolution preceding full independence, the arrangement saw Washington provide the islands with access to federal aviation regulation, weather prediction, and postal services, as well as several programs aimed at attracting capital investment and creating jobs. Such subsidies were estimated at more than $2.5 billion over a fifteen-year period beginning in 1986, when President Ronald Reagan signed the legislation that put the "compact" into effect. Micronesia's transition to full independence was completed in 1991, and the FSM joined the United Nations that year. Even so, the FSM still retains many elements of its "compact" relationship with the United States, including continuing receipt of economic development assistance.

In 2000 the FSM's population was estimated at 118,000, with an annual growth rate of around 2%. Universal education and the rights to reside and work in the United States have produced a trained yet mobile work force. The lack of domestic employment opportunities has caused substantial levels of emigration by young workers to Guam and the mainland United States. Remittances from these migrant workers to family members in the FSM constitute an important source of household income throughout the country.

Domestic economic activity is concentrated in the subsistence agriculture and fishing industries and in the modern government services sector, including education, utilities, and the administration of government programs. Bilateral economic aid from the United States, Japan, and Australia supports numerous official FSM initiatives. In 2003 US and FSM negotiators reached agreement on renewal of the "compact" subsidies made available to the islands. The United States pledged to provide at least $1.8 billion in economic assistance to the FSM over twenty years, while also continuing its annual contributions to a trust fund designed to finance future economic development requirements in the FSM. Despite post-September 11 security concerns, Washington agreed to permit FSM citizens' continued immigration to the United States.

As a member of the Asian Development Bank (ADB), the FSM receives loans that stimulate private sector growth, including expansion and modernization of FSM's deep-water fishing industry. The ADB, aware that waterborne diseases affect at least 5% of the FSM population annually, has also granted loans to modernize water supply facilities. With electricity transmission to private homes limited and supplies to businesses unreliable, priority has been assigned to upgrading the islands' electricity grid. New sewers, pumping stations, wastewater treatment plants, underground electricity transmission lines, and a power generation station are being built, with most improvements concentrated on the principal islands. Environmental remediation efforts have also been made where aging facilities have created contamination hazards.

LAURA M. CALKINS

See also Asian Development Bank; Oceania: History and Economic Development; Oceania: International Relations

References and Further Reading

Brower, Kenneth. *Micronesia: The Land, the People, and the Sea.* Baton Rouge, LA: Louisiana State University Press, 1981.
Brown, Christopher. *Federated States of Micronesia: Recent Economic Developments.* Washington, DC: International Monetary Fund, 1996.
Grieco, Elizabeth M. *The Remittance Behavior of Immigrant Households: Micronesians in Hawaii and Guam.* New York: LFB Scholarly Publishing, 2003.
Heine, Carl. *Micronesia at the Crossroads: A Reappraisal of the Micronesian Political Dilemma.* Honolulu: University of Hawaii Press, 1974.
Hezel, Francis X. *The New Shape of Old Island Cultures: A Half Century of Social Change in Micronesia.* Honolulu: University of Hawaii Press, 2001.
Peattie, Mark R. *Nanyo: The Rise and Fall of the Japanese in Micronesia 1885–1945.* Honolulu: University of Hawaii Press, 1983.
Nevin, David. *The American Touch in Micronesia.* New York: Norton, 1977.
Ranney, Austin and Howard R. Penniman. *Democracy in the Islands: The Micronesian Plebiscites of 1983.* Washington, DC: American Enterprise Institute for Public Policy Research, 1985.

MIDDLE EAST: HISTORY AND ECONOMIC DEVELOPMENT

The Middle East occupies a strategic geographical location at the crossroads of three major continents, Europe, Asia, and Africa. The area defined as the Middle East for the purposes of this work stretches from Turkey in the north, to Iran in the east, Israel in the west, and the Arabian Peninsula in the south. These countries are Israel, Lebanon, Jordan, Syria, Turkey, Iraq, Iran, Saudi Arabia, Bahrain, Qatar, United Arab Emirates, Oman, and Yemen.

The size of these countries varies from the smallest being the tiny island of Bahrain, which has an area of only 665 square kilometers, to the neighboring kingdom of Saudi Arabia, which has an area of 1.960 million square kilometers. Iran is the next-largest country, with a total area of 1.648 million square kilometers.

The value of the Middle East has long been measured in terms of its oil, despite the fact that only a small number of countries have significant oil reserves. In the 1930s and 1940s, exploration for oil rights by US and British companies in the Gulf countries made the region important for Western interests. However, it is only since World War II that oil has been produced and exported in commercial quantities. Continuing Western dependence on oil as an energy source heightens the importance of oil-exporting Middle Eastern countries today.

Society

Most of the countries in the Middle East share similarities in ethnicity, language, and religion. However, given the vastness of the region, there are also exceptions.

The majority of the population in the Middle East is ethnically Arab and shares Arabic as a common language. But though most countries are Arabic-speaking, there are differences in regional dialects. The spoken Arabic of a Jordanian Arab does not sound the same as that of an Arab from the Gulf states, though the two may still be able to understand each other. The written, classical form of Arabic is standard throughout the Middle East, however. All Arabs therefore share a linguistic and ethnic bond.

Turkey and Iran are exceptions to the predominantly Arab Middle East. The Turks and the Persians are the two largest non-Arab ethnic groups in the region. Linguistically, they also differ. Turkish is the dominant language of Turkey, while Farsi is used in Iran. The Kurds are the fourth-largest ethnic group, and they are spread out in Turkey, Iran, Iraq, and Syria. They have their own Kurdish language, though as citizens of Arab countries, their linguistic rights are not officially recognized.

Religion is another issue on which, superficially, the Middle East appears to be homogeneous. The majority of people in the Middle East are Sunni Muslims. Iran and Iraq are unique because they have predominantly Shi'a Muslim populations. Iraq has an approximately 60% Shi'a population, while Iran is 89% Shi'a. Two smaller countries, Bahrain and Yemen, have Shi'a majorities.

The significance of Sunni-Shi'a differences in the Middle East is based on politics. Since the Iranian Revolution brought an Islamic theocracy to power in Shi'a-dominated Iran in 1980, the country's neighbors have experienced fears of similar Shi'a uprisings. In Iraq, Saddam Hussein's ruling regime was predominantly Sunni and therefore feared a revolt from the

majority Shi'a population. In the case of Saudi Arabia, the monarchy feared a challenge to its strict political control and puritan Wahhabi religious ideology from the Shi'a minority in the Eastern Province.

Religious identity drives politics in Lebanon. The Lebanese political system stands out in the Middle East because it is based on confessional politics. However, the system failed under pressure from rising tensions between the four religious minorities. Conflict between Maronite Christian and Muslim groups erupted into a fifteen-year-long civil war beginning in 1975.

Israel is an exception in the Middle East as a non-Muslim country, one with a predominantly Jewish population. Though there were small Jewish communities in other countries in the region, there was generally a migration to Israel after 1948. Israel has a mixture of secular Jews, Ashkenazi, and Sephardic Jews, in addition to a small minority of Arab-Israeli citizens. The Palestinians in the Israeli-occupied West Bank and Gaza are not counted as part of the official Israeli population.

Geography

Much of the Middle East is arid land and does not receive much precipitation. The topography varies considerably, from valleys to desert to mountain ranges. There are limited fertile, agricultural areas, and these are dependent on access to water and irrigation systems.

The coastal regions of Yemen, eastern Turkey, the Tigris and Euphrates valleys in Syria and Iraq, and the coast of the Mediterranean in Lebanon are all examples of agricultural areas. Mountainous areas are found in the Taurus mountains in Turkey, the Elburz and Zagros in Iran, and the highlands of Yemen. Major river systems include the Tigris and Euphrates in Iraq and Iran; the Kizil Irmak, or the Red River in Turkey; and the Litani, Orontes, and Jordan Rivers that pass through Lebanon, Israel, Jordan, and Syria.

Water is a valuable natural resource in the Middle East. Access to water resources is the basis of territorial or border disputes along the Shatt al Arab (between Iran and Iraq) and the Jordan River.

Lack of uniform rainfall in the region is the reason why agricultural output is concentrated in certain countries. The Middle East is a net importer of grain. Turkey and, interestingly enough, Saudi Arabia, both produce wheat, and sometimes have a wheat surplus. In terms of tree crops, the Mediterranean countries produce olives, citrus fruits, and dates.

Political Systems

Political systems vary across the Middle East, ranging from monarchies to authoritarian military rule to parliamentary republics. Jordan and the Gulf countries of Saudi Arabia, UAE, Bahrain, and Qatar are all ruled by kings or shaikhs. The Shah of Iran was overthrown in 1980 by the Iranian Revolution. The Revolution replaced the monarchy with a theocratic republic, an Islamic regime of rule by jurists, led by Ayatollah Khomeini.

The military has played a dominant role in politics in the region, whether overtly or covertly. In Syria and Iraq, military coups in the late 1960s resulted in the consolidation of authoritarian dictatorships under Ba'ath Party leaders Hafez al Asad and Saddam Hussein, respectively. The Iraqi regime was overthrown by US military intervention in 2003, while Syria maintains the same political system under the leadership of Bashar al Asad, the son of Hafez al Asad. In contrast to Syria and Iraq, which experienced an uninterrupted stretch of thirty years of authoritarian rule, the Turkish military has stepped in only intermittently, in 1960, 1971, 1980, and 1997, in Turkish politics. The rest of the time, elected civilian governments have been in power.

Impact of Colonialism

The impact of colonialism has been uneven in the Middle East. The strategic location of the region made it important to both the British and French, as they divided up the region amongst themselves after WWI. In some cases, these colonial powers shaped the map of the region. Jordan (initially known as Transjordan) and Iraq were both created as artificial states in the early 1900s, with Arab kings who would be willing to protect British interests in the region set on the throne. In Jordan, the Hashemite family continues to rule up to the present day, with the current ruler, King Abdullah. In Iraq, the monarchy was overthrown by military officers in 1958. The third country affected by British colonial rule is what is known today as the State of Israel. Israel was created in 1948, after the British Mandate in Palestine ended and the British withdrew from the region.

The French had control over Syria and Lebanon, which lasted until the mid 1940s when the two countries became independent. The French policy of divide and rule kept the various ethnic and religious minorities living in the area under separate administrative units. This instigated political instability, which continued after independence, as well. For example, the French favored the Christian Maronites of Mount Lebanon under the guise of the French imperial, religious, and moral duty to protect Christian communities of the region. This preference alienated the Muslim communities, which made up the majority of the population. In Syria, French colonial policies marginalized the Alawi and Druze religious minorities from the majority Sunni Muslim population. When Syria became independent in 1946, the new political state had to contend with the distrust between these groups.

In contrast to these four countries, others in the region had limited interaction with colonial powers. The Arabian Peninsula remained uncolonized, although the British had negotiated treaties with the ruling sheikhs of Kuwait, Qatar, Bahrain, and Oman, in order to maintain the stability of its empire. The British were particularly concerned about their trade routes and established a port at Aden, at the southern tip of the Peninsula.

Economy

Development

The contrast between oil-exporting countries and non–oil-rich countries in the Middle East is responsible for different paths toward industrialization and economic development in the region. While oil-rich Gulf states such as Saudi Arabia and the United Arab Emirates have experienced high gross domestic product (GDP) per capita income growth, other countries such as Jordan and Yemen have lagged behind. According to the UN Human Development Report, Yemen had a GDP per capita (in purchasing power parity terms) in 2002 of $870, while the UAE had the highest for the region, at $22,420. The gap between these two countries is emblematic of the uneven distribution of per capita income in the region.

Human development has lagged significantly in the Middle East as a whole, despite rapid levels of industrialization and urbanization in the last few decades. There is a vast gap between the highest- and lowest-ranking countries in the region, according to the 2004 Human Development Index (HDI). Israel has the highest rank of twenty-two, while Yemen has the lowest at 149. The HDI ranking looks at indicators such as life expectancy, school enrollment, literacy, and income, in order to determine the overall state of human development in a country.

A comparison of GDP per capita income and HDI rankings illustrates the fact that even though some countries may be doing well based on GDP per capita, such as the UAE and Qatar, their populations are lagging in overall human development. These countries had an HDI rank of forty-nine and forty-seven respectively, behind Israel's twenty-two. However, Israel's GDP per capita value was lower than theirs. Israel's GDP per capita in 2002 was $19,530, while the UAE had $22,420 and Qatar $19,844 (United Nations Development Program [UNDP] 2004).

When looking at the difference between the HDI rank and the GDP per capita rank, most countries received a negative value, meaning that their per capita income was higher than the overall well-being of the population. The only countries that had positive values were Israel, Lebanon, Jordan, Syria, and Yemen, indicating a balanced growth pattern in economic and human development. It is noteworthy that with the exception of Israel, the other countries are on the lower end of the GDP per capita scale (UNDP 2004).

Oil

Oil plays a critical role in shaping political and economic development in the Middle East. Oil was first discovered in the region in the early 1900s, but commercial exploration and production did not occur until the middle of the century. The British were the first to claim concession rights to oil exploration and production in Iran at the end of the nineteenth century. The Anglo-Iranian Oil Company and the Iraqi Petroleum Company were the first foreign oil companies in the region. Saudi oil was not discovered until the 1930s, when a US oil company, Standard Oil of California (SoCal), gained concession rights from the Saudi king, King Abdul Aziz ibn Saud.

The importance of oil was such that the Middle East became a strategically important region to Western countries, especially to the United States. By 1948, seven Western oil companies controlled oil concessions in the region. Four were US—Standard Oil of New Jersey (later Exxon), Mobil, SoCal, and Texaco; one was British, British Petroleum; and the last was a joint British–Dutch company called Royal Dutch-Shell.

Today, the state controls oil output and export in each of the oil-rich countries. This has resulted in a unique type of rentier state, a state in which the government relies on oil revenues to drive economic growth and sustain the material well-being of its population. The government becomes the primary distributor of oil profits in the form of subsidies and loans to its people. In particular, it does not tax its people in return for their acceptance of the state's distribution

of benefits (Beblawi 1987). Saudi Arabia is a classic example of a rentier state. The challenges for rentier economies will be discussed in more detail below.

Today, there is a gap between oil-producing and non-oil countries in the Middle East. Though the general image of the Middle East is often that of an expanse of sand with oil rigs dotting the desert, in fact, there are only a few major oil-exporting countries: Saudi Arabia, Iraq, Iran, and the United Arab Emirates. Saudi Arabia is the leader, with approximately 25% of the world's petroleum deposits located in the country. It also accounts for the majority of the region's oil exports, at 6.652 million barrels of crude oil a day. According to OPEC statistics, the UAE and Iran are the next-highest oil producers and exporters, after Saudi Arabia. Iran exports 2.396 million barrels of crude oil a day, while the UAE exports 2.048 million barrels a day. Iraq was also a major exporter until the first Gulf War in 1991. Since the second Gulf War, its oil production and export remain uncertain since its infrastructure was destroyed during the war.

Global oil prices have fluctuated drastically in the last fifty years. They are affected by events in the region in addition to general market supply–demand conditions regulated by OPEC. Price fluctuations are marked by several notable highs and lows. For example, in 1973–1974, the OPEC oil boycott almost quadrupled the price of oil per barrel. Later, at the outbreak of the Iran–Iraq war in 1980, disruption in oil production in these two countries resulted in another price hike. However, the second half of the 1980s and early 1990s saw a worldwide decline in oil prices, resulting in lower revenues for petroleum-exporting countries.

The regional implications of fluctuations in oil prices include changes in the amount of Arab aid from Gulf countries to non–oil-producing countries. For example, Saudi Arabia gave aid to Iraq during the Iraq–Iran war in the form of grants and loans. Syria was a recipient of aid from its wealthier Arab neighbors, as well. When oil revenues declined, it meant that the non-oil, aid-recipient countries received less Arab assistance as well. In the Syria case, this was partially responsible for an economic crisis in the early 1980s.

Oil-exporting countries also attract many workers from non-oil countries, since they have a high demand for labor needed to maintain the petroleum industry. There is a significant amount of labor migration in the region to the Persian Gulf countries, mainly from Jordan, Syria, and Yemen. When oil revenues declined, labor remittances from these workers back to their home countries also declined, affecting those economies in a ripple effect that permeated the entire region.

The domestic implications for oil-rich countries are also important to note. Oil is a non-renewable resource. Its supply is limited, and therefore countries that are heavily dependent on oil revenues to maintain their political and economic systems face an eventual cessation. This requires not only a diversification of the economy to include non–petroleum-based sectors of production, but also a move away from rentier economic systems.

In conclusion, oil is both a boon and a blessing for the Middle East. For the countries that have been lucky enough to have significant petroleum reserves, it has spurred rapid industrialization and modernization processes, which have allowed a dramatic increase in growth. However, these same countries also face the instability of being dependent on the fluctuations of oil prices and therefore a certain degree of political and economic instability in the long term, as well. At some point, when the oil reserves run out, they will face a rude awakening. For example, Saudi Arabia has already had to face tighter spending controls as a result of low oil revenues in the 1990s and it continues to struggle with the challenge of economic diversification.

Foreign Aid

Foreign aid has played an important role in the economies of some Middle Eastern countries. Israel is one of the largest recipients of foreign aid in the Middle East, primarily from the United States. A 2003 estimate placed external aid from the United States to be at $662 million. This aid is directed toward economic and military expenditures.

The Soviet Union and Gulf Arab countries have also been aid donors in the Middle East. Syria was dependent on Soviet aid during the 1970s and 1980s, until the collapse of the Soviet Union in 1990. Syria also received aid from richer Gulf Arab countries. After 1979, when oil prices declined, Arab aid to Syria decreased drastically over the course of several years, from $1.6 billion in 1980 to $500 million in the early 1980s (Heydemann 1993).

In general, there has been a steady decline in aid flows to the Middle East in the past two decades. In 1980, the aid-to-GDP ratio was 7%. In 2000, it was a little above 2%. However, in periods of strategic importance in the aftermath of conflict, there have been temporary spikes in aid levels. For example, after the Israeli–Egyptian peace agreement in 1979, after the first Gulf War in 1991, and after the Oslo Agreement in 1995, there were momentary increases in aid to the region (World Bank 2003).

Labor Force

The oil-rich countries in the Persian Gulf have traditionally had small populations, and have needed to import labor from outside in order to meet their needs. In the mid-1970s, there was a wave of labor migration to these Gulf countries, in particular from Jordan and Yemen. From 1975 onward, about 40% of the Jordanian workforce, including Palestinians, worked abroad. By 1981, remittances from these workers were valued at 27.8% of the Gross National Product (GNP). With the fall of oil prices in the 1980s, the Jordanian economy also suffered from a decrease in remittances.

Expatriate workers in the Gulf also come from the Indian subcontinent and Southeast Asia. The numbers of Asian workers in the Gulf countries increased dramatically in the 1970s and 1980s. There are several reasons why there was a demand for nationals from these countries. First, the need for skilled and semi-skilled labor was not being met by workers from Arab countries. Second, the labor supply in Asian countries was cheaper and the labor market was more organized. Lastly, these non-Arab workers were less likely to stay permanently in the Gulf countries, and therefore were less likely to be politically troublesome as members of society in the long term. Three decades later, these expatriate workers are still considered "temporary workers," even though many of them have spent their entire working lives in the Gulf countries.

The political ease with which governments can expel expatriate workers was demonstrated by the Iraqi invasion of Kuwait in 1990. Yemeni workers in Saudi Arabia were roundly expelled because the Yemeni government professed support for Iraq. Palestinians working in Kuwait and Saudi Arabia were also "punished" for Arafat's support for Iraq by expulsion from these two countries. These actions demonstrated the fact that expatriate workers are politically expedient pawns, which the government can manipulate when it is under pressure.

The current outcome of this labor migration is that there is a significant expatriate population with the skills and human capital to run the country's businesses and industries in most of the Gulf countries. In Saudi Arabia, there are roughly 7 million expatriate workers. In the UAE, the foreign population outstrips the local population.

This dependence on foreign human capital has handicapped economic development in these countries, creating a lack of qualified workers from within the national population. There has been political pressure in the past decade to substitute expatriate workers with nationals in Saudi Arabia, as the country has faced increasing unemployment rates, high population growth, and economic slowdown because of low oil prices. The relative success of this policy of "Saudization" remains to be seen.

The Need for Change

Economic activity in the Middle East has relied up to now on several factors: oil revenues, a state-dominated public sector, foreign aid, and workers' remittances. The economic model based on these factors is no longer sustainable in the long term. Factors such as high unemployment rates, inefficient state-dominated economies, declining foreign aid levels, and lower oil prices are spurring a move toward economic reforms in the region.

First, as noted earlier, dependence on oil revenues has made the economic patterns of oil-exporting countries dependent on global oil price fluctuations. A decline in average (real) oil prices over the last twenty years has put an end to the rapid burst of economic growth that characterized the Gulf countries in the 1970s. In addition, the fact that oil is a non-renewable energy resource means that these countries also have to look at other ways to sustain GDP growth in the long term. Thus, rentier states such as Saudi Arabia have had to focus on diversifying their economy to focus more on non-oil sectors in the 1990s. Currently, oil revenues make up about 75% of the Saudi budget, and account for 45% of the GDP. The Kingdom has encouraged some private-sector growth in order to balance GDP growth from the oil sector, but change has been incremental.

The United Arab Emirates is an example of a Gulf country that has been more successful in making this transition to an emphasis on non-oil sectors. Despite the fact that it has the world's third-largest recoverable oil reserves and significant natural gas reserves, it has focused on growth in non-oil sectors of its economy, as well. It spent the 1990s diversifying to include petrochemicals, fertilizers, cement, aluminum, tourism, trade, and manufacturing sectors. By 2000, these non-oil sectors of the economy accounted for 70% of the GDP, and 43% of exports. Overall GDP growth has averaged 7% a year since 1993.

Among its policies for encouraging private-sector growth and trade has been the creation of twelve free trade zones, of which Dubai's Jebel Ali free trade zone is the largest. Companies established in the free trade zone are allowed to have 100% foreign ownership, which is in contrast to other Gulf countries where there are significant government restrictions on foreign investment and ownership in companies. In addition, the UAE has a strong telecommunications and trade infrastructure, which has also fostered foreign investment. However, despite the economic success of the UAE, the country remains dependent on foreign labor for its human capital. About 90% of the labor force is composed of expatriate workers, mostly from the Indian subcontinent, other parts of the Middle East, and the Philippines (World Bank 2003).

Another factor that characterizes economic development models in the Middle East is a strong state dominance in the economy and especially in the public sector. In the 1970s and 1980s, under the leader Hafez al-Asad, the Syrian economy was dominated by state-run industrialization efforts. The combination of a socialist-oriented economy and an authoritarian political system created a closed and ultimately inefficient development process. Ultimately, economic crisis propelled the Syrian government into instituting a series of limited economic reforms. Since the 1990s, Syria has had to move away from the state-dominated model and toward allowing the private sector greater flexibility for economic participation, though it is debatable as to the real extent of this private-sector participation (Anderson 2001).

Socialist economies are not the only ones that have strong government control. As a rentier state dependent on oil revenues, the Saudi government also exercises far-reaching domestic economic control. Oil revenues have allowed the government to institute a system of heavy subsidization of basic resources, in addition to provision of healthcare, education, and other social services. Royal patronage of industrialists and indirect royal ownership of private-sector ventures is also common in Saudi Arabia (Anderson 2001).

One of the realities causing a shift away from heavy state dominance in the public sector is the shortage of jobs. A lack of jobs has created high rates of unemployment in many countries. For example, Syria has a 2002 estimate of 20% unemployment. The 2004 estimate of the unemployment rate in Saudi Arabia is 25%. Iran has a 15.7% unemployment rate, based on 2004 estimates (*CIA World Factbook* 2004). In addition, these countries also have a high percentage of young people who will be entering the workforce shortly, only to find that the government-subsidized jobs that their parents had are no longer available to them. Encouraging private-sector growth as a source of potential employment for the growing population is an imperative for countries that have traditionally relied on a highly government-subsidized economic system.

Political and Economic Reforms

For the past two decades, there has been pressure for political and economic reforms in the Middle East that will open up the countries to foreign trade and investment as well as allow greater political freedoms to the populations. The underlying assumption in this line of argument is that the current state is temporary, and that these countries are in the process of developing in the direction of greater economic and political openings. To some degree, this assumption is valid, since most countries have state-dominated economies and limited political rights and freedoms. With the exceptions of Turkey and Israel, which have elected leadership, ruling regimes in most other countries remain entrenched in power on the basis of dynastic rule or military/authoritarian power.

Popular political representation, political accountability of the leadership, and greater economic and political participation for women are all key political reform issues. Some countries, such as Bahrain and Qatar, have taken steps in this direction by allowing reasonably free elections. In October 2002, Bahrainis elected members of the lower house of Bahrain's reconstituted bicameral legislature, the National Assembly. Women candidates were allowed to vote and to run for office for the first time in these elections. But unfortunately, no female candidates won a seat. The same outcome took place in Qatar's municipal elections in 1999, where, again, none of the six women candidates won any seats. However, it is important to note that these were the first democratic elections in these countries, in a region where if there are any elections, their results are usually predetermined by the state.

Jordan and Oman are other examples of countries with limited female political participation. The Jordanian assembly has reserved seats for women in the House of Representatives, and in 2003, three women were also appointed to cabinet positions. Oman has two female members on its consultative council, but they are not elected positions.

The role of civil society in creating democratic governance is also important to note. Debate on this issue centers around what constitutes civil society in the Middle East, whether it exists, and its prospects for future development, given the authoritarian nature of the state in most countries. State responses range from repression to limited openings for civil society. Thus, the response to these questions is not clear-cut. In Iran, the post-Revolution Islamic regime has cracked down on all forms of opposition that do not conform to the state's ideological position, and continues to restrict political freedoms of the population. The government routinely arrests journalists, activists, and other members of civil society organizations who voice any critique or opposition to the regime.

In contrast, Qatar has permitted limited political reforms, most recently embodied in changes to the country's constitution in 2003, which allow for the right to assembly and the right to establish associations. The most far-reaching policy, though, was the removal of all domestic restrictions on freedom of the press by Emir Hamad bin Khalifa al-Thani in 1995. This paved the way for the 1997 launch of Arab TV satellite channel al-Jazeera. The channel has shaped the development of civil society in the region through fostering debate and discussion on sensitive issues that governments have traditionally not been willing to tackle on state-controlled media.

One line of argument on the issue of political and economic reforms in the Middle East is that market-oriented economic reforms need to take place in conjunction with political reforms that allow for greater power-sharing between the state and its people. However, the competing line of argument states that economic reform can and does occur without recourse to political liberalization. In other words, the two do not necessarily have to go together. Syria is an example of an authoritarian state that instituted economic liberalization reforms from 1982 to 1992 without engaging in significant changes to its political system.

The debate on how far-reaching and how meaningful democratic political reforms can be, or how much they can change the distribution of power in the political system, continues. While there may have been political reforms that are democratic in nature in the Middle East, few of these reforms have led to a definitive establishment of a full-fledged democracy. In contrast to political liberalization, moves toward economic liberalization have been relatively more extensive in the region. The extent to which this economic and political development process will result in meaningful change in the Middle East remains to be seen, however.

UZMA JAMIL

See also Arabian American Oil Company (ARAMCO); Ethnic Conflicts: Middle East; Iran; Iraq; Israel; Jordan; Middle East: International Relations; Organization of Arab Petroleum Exporting Countries (OAPEC); Organization of Petroleum Exporting Countries (OPEC); Syria; Turkey

References and Further Reading

Anderson, Roy, Robert F. Seibert, and Jon G. Wagner. *Politics and Change in the Middle East: Sources of Conflict and Accommodation.* Upper Saddle River, NJ: Prentice Hall, 2001.
Arab Human Development Report 2003. New York: UNDP, Arab Fund for Economic and Social Development, 2003.
Beblawi, Hazem and Giacomo Luciani, eds. *The Rentier State.* London: Croom Helm, 1987.
Heydemann, Steven. "Taxation Without Representation: Authoritarianism and Economic Liberalization in

Syria." In *Rules and Rights in the Middle East*, edited by Ellis Goldberg, Resat Kasaba, and Joel Migdal, 69–101, Seattle: University of Washington Press, 1993.

Norton, Augustus Richard. *Civil Society in the Middle East.* Leiden, the Netherlands: Brill Publishers, 1995.

OPEC Annual Statistical Bulletin 2003. Vienna, Austria: Organization of the Petroleum Exporting Countries, 2004.

Trade, Investment and Development in the Middle East and North Africa, MENA Development Report 2003. Washington, DC: World Bank, 2003.

MIDDLE EAST: INTERNATIONAL RELATIONS

Cultures have crossed and contended in the Middle East since the beginning of recorded history. In ancient times the region witnessed the rise of empires and the wars between the Persians and the Greeks leading to conquests of Alexander the Great and the Roman Empire. In general, three types of struggles have occurred there—geo-political, ethnic, and religious. In the Middle Ages, after the Arab conquests of the seventh century, religious wars erupted between the Moslems and the Byzantine Christians on their border in Anatolia. The conquest of Anatolia by the Seljuk Turks in 1070 led to the Crusades from the eleventh to the thirteenth centuries when Western Christians were temporarily able to control certain portions of the areas.

The basic ethnic conflicts among Moslems centered on Persians, Arabs, and Turks. The geo-political conflicts revolved around Persia, Egypt, and Syria. By the end of the fifteenth century, the Moslem Ottoman Turks came to rule the entire region excepting Persia but including even the European Balkans. After reaching their height in the sixteenth century, the Ottomans began to retreat as European powers took over their lands in Europe and various Moslem war lords and independent pashas carved out their territories around the Empire.

Beginning in the eighteenth century, the Great European powers began to wrest concessions from the Ottoman Empire, known as "the sick man of Europe," and gain control over its economy. In World War I the Ottomans sided with the Central Powers, and France and England secretly planned to carve up its territory with the Sykes-Picot agreement. Russia, which also had hoped for spoils, was eliminated after the Bolshevik Revolution. At the same time, the British sponsored a revolt by the Arabs against Istanbul and, with the Balfour Declaration, promised the Jews a homeland in Palestine.

After World War I the Turkish Republic under Mustafa Kemal Atatürk managed to retain its independence through war and agreements with the victorious Allies. Atatürk renounced claims to the other Ottoman territories, which the Allies, particularly Great Britain and France, took over directly or indirectly through League of Nations mandates or prewar agreements. The interwar period, however, witnessed much unrest as various leaders fought each other for control, national movements attempted to overthrow foreign rule, and radical and secular movements fought traditional leadership. During the Second World War there was more disruption, especially after the fall of France in 1940. The Allies were for the most part able to keep the Axis out of the Middle East (excluding North Africa where Italy had colonies), but the idealism of national liberation grew even stronger.

After the war British imperialism around the world began to disintegrate and the countries of the Middle East took shape based on traditional and colonial formations. In the postwar world several major issues and factors determined the course Middle East politics. First was the question of liberation and the establishment of modern nation-states; second, the relations of the great powers with the countries of the region; third, the role of oil in the world economy and the politics of the region; fourth, the attempts by strong persons to dominate the region; fifth, the clash of various political groupings in the region, e.g., radicals as opposed to traditional monarchists, secularists vis-à-vis various religious parties, and rival ethnicities; and last but certainly not least, the question of Israel and Palestine.

The issue of national liberation concerned the attempts by the Middle Eastern countries to wrest control from European occupation. During World War II the Free French allied to the United Nations stated it would not continue French rule over Syria and Lebanon (their League of Nations mandates). However, when victory was won, Paris was reluctant to relinquish control. After several months of negotiations in April 1946, the French left and Syria and Lebanon gained independence. London's position in the region was stronger since unlike the French, England did not lose to Germany and had continued occupation of its mandates and territories during the war. However, in 1923 London had already recognized partial independence of Jordan and in March 1946 granted it full independence under Emir Abdullah who became king. In 1949 the country officially became the Hashimite Kingdom of Jordan. Palestine was divided into a Jewish and Arab state by United Nations resolutions in 1947, and the British left. In the subsequent war between the Jews and the neighboring Arab States in 1948, the Jews won and established Israel, occupying more territories than the

UN had allotted. The remaining areas were taken over chiefly by Jordan, but an independent Arab Palestine state was not formed.

Saudi Arabia was granted full independence in 1932 but it still depended on British and US subsidies. Egypt, too, was formally recognized as an independent monarchy in 1923, but the British continued to exert control over the government and British troops remained in the country. Anti-British sentiment was prevalent in the country and after the fall of the monarchy in 1952, conflict between London and Cairo reached the level of hostilities culminating in the Suez Crisis of 1956. In the small states of the Arabian Peninsula, Britain retained its protectorates until 1968 when it withdrew its troops. Kuwait remained under British protection until 1961 when London recognized its independence, but it still relied on Britain, the United States, and other states to protect it from Iraq, which had coveted its oil-rich territory since 1938. Bahrain declared its independence in 1971, and signed a treaty of friendship with Great Britain. Oman and Qatar received full independence about the same time. Bahrain followed Saudi foreign policy and had difficulty with Iran over its pro-Western policies. In 1990 Bahrain supported with air bases and ports the coalition against Iraq. Abu Dhabi led the move for the creation of the United Arab Emirates (UAE) out of the seven small trucial states after the British left in 1973. The UAE, threatened by Iran and Moslem fundamentalism, helped found the Gulf Cooperation Council (GCC), an alliance of the small Gulf states, in 1981 and joined the Arab League and the UN in 1991. It quarreled with Iran over disputed Persian Gulf islands and also supported the Desert Storm coalition. On the southern end of the Arabian Peninsula the two states of Yemen and North Yemen gained independence in 1977, and in 1990 they united.

Iran, which was technically independent, in fact really lay under the domination of Russia and Britain in the nineteenth century. With the Bolshevik Revolution and the Soviet renunciation of concessions in Iran, the British were left in control. In the 1920s Reza Khan rose to power and in 1925 had himself crowned as Reza Shah Pahlevi. Reza Shah promoted the ethnic difference of the Iranians from the Arabs and in fact changed the traditional name of the country, Persia, to Iran (Aryan), to emphasize their links with the Indo-Europeans, the linguistic group to which the Farsi language belongs. In the 1930s, to counteract British influence, Reza Shah made commercial concessions to Nazi Germany. During World War II the Soviets and British invaded his country and forced him to abdicate in favor of his son Mohammed Reza Shah.

After the war the nationalist Mohammad Mossadeq came to power, ousting the Shah, but his anti-Western policies, including nationalizing the oil industry, led to a Western-backed coup, bringing back Mohammad Reza Shah. The shah now was dependent on the West and maintained power through dictatorial instruments, especially the secret police he created— SAVAK.

Neighboring Iraq had been part of the Ottoman Empire and Britain obtained a League of Nations mandate over the country after the war. In 1932 London granted the country independence under King Faysal. The military, however, gained control of the country, and during World War II, the British occupied the country. Between 1945 and 1958, riots, upheavals, martial law, and coup d'etats punctuated Iraqi life. The country was divided religiously between Moslems and Christians and the Moslems between Shiites and Sunnis. There was also a significant Kurdish minority. There was contention between the younger and older political leaders, dissent in the army, and disputes between the young King Faysal II and his regents. There was popular unrest over the Palestine crisis, and anti-Western feeling because of British and US concessions over the country's oil resources and the monarchy's pro-Western policies. Finally in 1958, a group of army officers ousted the king.

In the years after World War II, the Middle East was also a battleground in the Cold War. The lead in Western interests in the region was assumed by the United States. Their opponent was the Soviet Union. The two major issues were oil and the Israeli–Palestine conflict. In addition, Britain and France joined Israel in 1956 to prevent Gamal Abdul Nasser of Egypt from seizing the Suez Canal. The Western oil companies pushed their governments to maintain treaties with the Middle East countries that gave them favorable concessions, but the oil-rich nations looked to their own advantage. However, since the Soviet Union backed radical governments, the traditional monarchies tended to favor the West. These included Saudi Arabia, Jordan, Iran under the shah, and most of the small states of the Persian Gulf—Kuwait, the United Arab Emirates, Oman, and Bahrain. On the Israeli–Palestine question, even the conservative governments sided with the Palestinian Arabs. The West took a more ambivalent stance—supporting Israel's right to exist, but at first reluctant to appear too pro-Israeli. The Soviet Union initially supported the creation of Israel, in part on the hope it would become a socialist ally in the immediate postwar years. Furthermore, the horror of the Holocaust coupled with the need to resettle survivors and rebuild Europe made the existence of a Jewish homeland important to both the Soviets and the West. However, in the 1950s Moscow turned away from Tel Aviv, giving complete support to the Palestinians. After the Six-Day War of 1967, Moscow and most of its allies broke off relations with the Jewish state. Furthermore, the Western states, chiefly the United States, supplied Israel with arms. Washington was also giving arms to its allies in the Middle East—Saudi Arabia, Iran, Turkey. Domestic politics in the United States made support of Israel important for Washington's position.

Although communist parties existed in the Middle East, they never made much headway in domestic politics. The Soviet Union then supported anti-Western nationalist states in Syria, Iraq, and Egypt whom Moscow supplied with arms. They also maintained friendly diplomatic relations with the shah, even though the latter was clearly in the pro-Western camp. Turkey, which had a long history of hostility with Tsarist Russia, joined the Western camp. Ankara joined the United Nations coalition in Korea and even became a member of the North Atlantic Treaty Organization (NATO). Furthermore, Iran and Turkey, two Moslem but not Arab countries, recognized Israel. Washington and London formed the Middle East Treaty Organization (also known as the Baghdad Pact, where its headquarters were located) in 1955. Turkey, Iraq, Iran, Pakistan, and Great Britain were founding members. Like NATO, it was directed against the Soviet Union and especially interested in protecting the oil resources of the region. In 1959, after the fall of the king, Iraq left and the headquarters moved to Ankara, and the United States became an associate member. The organization was renamed the Central Treaty Organization or CENTO. In 1979 the Shah fell and the organization was dissolved.

Ankara invaded Cyprus in 1974 and established the Turkish Republic of Northern Cyprus, which received no other recognition. Then Turkey moved closer to the Soviet Union in the 1970s, mistrusting the Western position on Cyprus. However, it still leaned more toward the West, seeking trade relations with the European Union. It supported the coalition against Iraq in 1991, but the strength of the Islamic party in the country caused problems with this pro-Western stance.

A number of Middle East states joined the Non-aligned Movement (NAM) starting with Egypt in 1964, three years after the start of the organization. Others that have joined over the years include Bahrain, Iran, Iraq, Jordan, Kuwait, Lebanon, Oman, Qatar, Saudi Arabia, Syria, the UAE, and Yemen. The NAM tried to develop policies for those countries not associated with either the West or the Soviet bloc.

Oil resources have played a major role in the politics and international affairs of the region. It has brought great wealth to a number of the states, especially those of the Arabian Peninsula. Oil is also found in Iran and Iraq, but only in limited amounts in Turkey. It is not found in Israel, Jordan, or Lebanon. In 1961 the oil-rich countries joined a number of others from around the world to form the Organization of Petroleum Exporting Countries (OPEC) to regulate the production of oil. This cartel, along with increasing world demand, helped to drive the price of oil to increasingly high levels. However, in general, except for some isolated cases, OPEC based its policies on economic rather than political issues. Saudi Arabia did carry out a short oil boycott in 1973 over Washington's support of Israel. By 1984 the Saudis had gained complete control of ARAMCO, the Arabian-American Oil Company.

Another factor determining the domestic and international politics of the Middle East has been the rise of strong personalities who have attempted to play a dominant role in the region. The first of these in the postwar world was Colonel Gamul Abdul Nasser of Egypt. In 1952, on a strong anti-Western nationalistic policy, he led a coup d'etat against the dissolute king of Egypt, Farouk. In 1958 he convinced Syria to unite with Egypt in the short-lived United Arab Republic, which ended in 1961 after a coup in Damascus brought new leadership that wished for independence. In 1964 he became the first Arab leader to join the NAM, disassociating Egypt from either bloc in the Cold War, although he signed treaties with both sides and in fact stood close to Moscow, inviting Soviet military advisors into the country along with Soviet arms. However, the main issue that Nasser as well other Arab leaders used to promote themselves was the Palestinian cause. Nasser, like many others in the Arab world, called for the elimination of the Jewish state, and he participated in two wars with Israel. In 1956 he announced his plans to nationalize the Suez Canal, which Egypt operated under international regulations. He planned to use the tolls to finance his project to build the Aswan dam for irrigation. This provoked Britain and France, who had interests in the Suez Canal Company, to join Israel in the seizure of the canal. Israel, aroused by Nasser's bellicose pronouncements, support for Arab raids, their ban from using the canal, and his blockade of the Straits of Tiran at the mouth of the Gulf of Aqaba, readily agreed. The three countries easily occupied the canal but they were not backed by Washington, and the United Nations forced them to leave. Nasser reached a compromise settlement, paying off the shareholders of the canal company and ending the blockade of the Straits of Tiran. For the Egyptians he emerged a hero.

In June 1967 the tension between Israel and its neighbors once more was raised to fever pitch as a new Syrian government began making raids into Israel and amassing troops on its borders. The Syrians egged Nasser to join in and he sent his troops into the Sinai Desert, which was being guarded by UN peacekeepers. He also renewed his blockade of the straits of Tiran, closing Israeli access to the Red Sea. When Jordan also joined the coalition, Israel struck first and in six days completely defeated all its adversaries, seizing their land including the Sinai, the West bank of the Jordan, as well as all of Jerusalem and the Syrian Golan Heights. Nasser's plans for Arab leadership were over, although he remained a hero to the Egyptians who rejected his offer to resign. The Soviet Union replaced the planes and armaments he lost in the war, but he turned to Washington to seek some peace overtures with Israel. Three years after the 1967 war, Nassar died suddenly of a heart attack.

Although from North Africa rather than the Middle East, the Libyan leader Muammar Qaddafi played a major role in the politics of the region. Qaddafi seized control of Libya in 1969 when he overthrew King Iris I. The Arabs of North Africa had not shown much interest in the Palestinian question before 1967, but Qaddafi used the issue to try to unite Arabs from the Middle East with those of North Africa. However, he was never able to make much headway in his goal to get other leaders to follow him. He sought a union with Egypt, Tunisia, and the Sudan, but geopolitical and ideological conflicts prevented these alliances. In fact, in 1977, as a result of the more conservative policies of Nasser's successor Anwar Sadat, an inconclusive war between Libya and Egypt erupted. Qaddafi also supported guerilla movements around the world, culminating with his support of the terrorists responsible for the bombing of Pan American Airlines Flight 103 over Lockerbie, Scotland, in 1988. In 1986 the United States air force conducted air raids over the country, injuring one of Qaddafi's daughters. The UN placed sanctions on Libya because of its terrorist activity. Qaddafi ultimately gave up his support of terror and in 2004 promised to dismantle efforts to create weapons of mass destruction, as a result of which relations with the West improved.

Another figure who must be counted as one of the strong leaders of the Middle East is Yasir Arafat. Although he never had a state to rule and therefore lacked the base to be a dominant political leader like Nasser, his position as leader of the Palestine Liberation Organization (PLO) gave him the authority to mobilize large number of sympathetic Arabs and Moslems and direct Middle Eastern politics. Arafat

took over direction of the PLO in 1969, replacing the infective Ahmed Shuquari as a consequence of the Arab defeat in the 1967 Six-Day War. In the beginning of his leadership, he was committed to the total destruction of Israel and its replacement with a Palestinian state where Jews, Christians, and Moslems may live, but where Jewish immigration would not be permitted. He used terror and attacks on Israel as the method of achieving this. He was behind the hijacking of airlines and assassinations in order to achieve his goals, but in the end this was unsuccessful. His use of raids into Israel and a policy of guerilla warfare earned him the title of terrorist by his enemies and freedom fighter and revolutionary by his friends. In 1972 he made a speech before the United Nations General Assembly, which saluted him as a hero. Although he was able to build a cohesive following of Palestinians living in refugee camps in Jordan, Egypt, and elsewhere around the world, he was never fully accepted by other Arab leaders, and they did not push hard to achieve an independent state or resettle the Palestinian refugees. Nevertheless, his popularity forced them to pay heed to his leadership, and international Arab organizations permitted the PLO to join as a recognized entity.

After the Gulf War of 1991, in which the United States led a coalition of both Western and Middle Eastern States to expel Sadam Hussein of Iraq from Kuwait, there was a renewed effort to settle the Palestinian–Israeli issue. This was continued by President William (Bill) Clinton after he replaced George Bush who had led the Gulf War. The talks led to agreements in the Oslo Accords and an historic meeting between Arafat and Israeli Prime Minister Yitzhak Rabin in the United States, including a handshake between the two. However, the agreements did not last. An Israeli extremist assassinated Rabin, and a new wave of terror by Palestinians hit Israel. Arafat did not follow up on the peace proposals and lost real control of the Palestinians, unable to stop the terror. The Israelis blockaded him in his citadel on the West Bank, not allowing him to leave until his death in 2004.

Saddam Hussein, the ruler of Iraq, was a charismatic leader, the head of the Ba'ath Party. He had been one of a group of officers who overthrew President 'Abd al-Salam 'Arif in 1968. Gradually Hussein assumed absolute control of the country by ousting his colleagues. A member of the minority Sunni sect, he kept strict control over the majority Shiites and another minority, the Kurds of the north. He brutally suppressed the Kurdish revolt of 1988 using poison gas. He also joined other Arab states in the wars against Israel. Like Nasser he aspired to be a leader of all Arabs, but he ran into difficulties with other leaders in the area. In 1981 the Israelis bombed his Osirak nuclear research laboratory out of fear that he was planning to build bombs. He also had a border war with the Iranians after the Shiite religious revolution in that country in 1979 that brought down the shah. The war lasted eight years (1980–1988) without much change. During that period he was supported by the United States, as Tehran was an avowed enemy of Washington.

Hussein now felt emboldened to add oil-rich Kuwait to his realm, believing Washington and the West would not intervene. However, the move caused a coalition of Western and Middle Eastern states led by the United States to declare war and utterly destroy his forces, driving him from Kuwait, but leaving him in Iraq. The United Nations imposed a series of sanctions on Baghdad to force him to allow inspections of his armaments. His refusal to comply over the next decade led to numerous air raids and bombings of his country. Hussein in the meantime looked for new support in the Arab World. As religious fundamentalism became a popular movement among Moslems, he turned from his previous secularism and attempted to put on a religious front. In 2002 President George W. Bush, the son of the president who had ordered the Gulf War, invaded Iraq to topple Hussein, whom he believed was in contact with the al-Qaeda terrorists who had bombed New York's World Trade Center the year before and was building weapons of mass destruction. Although both beliefs were erroneous, the US-led coalition toppled and arrested Hussein, but found itself in a difficult war in Iraq fighting anti-US insurgents.

Another factor in Middle Eastern politics has been the rivalry of various movements and governments in the regions. After the war, most of the countries were controlled by monarchies, the majority of which claimed descent from the prophet Muhammad. In Iran the monarch was the shah, the son of the ruler who had declared himself to be a king. These monarchies tended to be authoritarian and conservative. Some, like in Saudi Arabia, ruled by Islamic law. Some shared the largess they achieved through oil wealth with their citizens. Most monarchs also tended to be pro-Western. However, in the 1950s and 1960s secular radical movements attempted to seize power. The most successful was the Ba'th movement, a form of Islamic socialism. Ba'th parties were successful in Syria and Iraq.

Another form of conflict involved ethnic confrontations. Most prominent were the struggles between the Kurds and the various countries they inhabited—Turkey, Syria, Iraq, and Iran. Their attempts to establish an independent Kurdistan failed, and they suffered various forms of harassment for their efforts.

In Turkey, Kurdish leaders were censored and imprisoned. In Iraq, Saddam Hussein attacked Kurdish villages with poison gas. Some conflicts were geopolitical. Saudi Arabia and Oman fought over their border in the 1950s and confronted Nasser who supported North Yemen and railed against the Saudi monarchy. Qatar and Bahrain, who were allied in the GCC, still argued over the ownership of the Hawar islands. There were also religious conflicts. In Lebanon, Moslems and Christians fought a civil war (1975–1976), causing neighboring Israel and Syria to invade and occupy the country. The country was virtually destroyed, and finally found itself under the domination of Syria. The Iraq–Iran War was a war between Sunni-led Iraq and Shiite Iran, but it also involved an Arab country, Iraq, against non-Arab, Persian Iran.

Perhaps the most important issue of post–World War II Middle Eastern foreign policy is the Palestinian–Israeli issue. During World War I, the Arabs hoped to regain the lands of their medieval caliphate from the Ottoman Empire and were allied to the British who supported their revolt. Furthermore, Jewish Zionists, who had been purchasing land from the Sultan since the 1990s, also hoped for a restored Jewish homeland there as London had promised in the Balfour declaration. However, after the war, Palestine was controlled by the British under a League of Nations mandate. The term "Palestinians" then designated Jewish immigrants who continued to work for the Zionist goal of resettlement. Jewish–Arab battles occurred throughout the interwar period, and Britain limited the number of Jews allowed to immigrate into the area. This became a critical issue during the rise of Nazism in the 1930s and especially during the years of the Holocaust in World War II when only limited immigration was possible and even then difficult. In the immediate postwar years, the British still barred many of the survivors, although a number were able to enter the region both legally and illegally. Strife between the Arabs and Jews continued and the Jews began a war of terror against the British. In 1947 the United Nations voted to divide the region into Jewish and Arab portions, and in May 1948 when the British left, the Jews declared their new country called Israel. Arab armies from Jordan, Lebanon, Syria, Egypt, and Iraq invaded the Jewish portion to eliminate the state, but not only did the Israelis drive them out, they also occupied more than their allotted portion and encouraged the Arabs to leave the area although many still remained. With the armistice, fighting ended, but the Arab states refused to recognize the legitimacy of Israel. The Palestinian Arabs who left settled in refugee camps where they remained for the rest of the century.

While Israel continued to develop as a modern state, welcoming more Jews, Arabs from refugee camps from time to time entered into the country to commit acts of terror. Meanwhile, the Arabs still living in Israel were better off in many ways than those in the refugee camps, but lived as second-class citizens. After the initial influx of Holocaust survivors, it was difficult for Tel Aviv to persuade Jews from Europe and the Americas to immigrate, so the Israelis looked for immigrants from the Arab countries and from the Soviet Union and Eastern Europe. It was hard, however, for the 5 million Soviet Jews to get permission to leave the country. Eastern Europe was a different story and at various times from the 1940s to the 1960s, large numbers entered from Bulgaria, Romania, and Poland.

As mentioned above, in 1956 Israel joined Great Britain and France against Egypt, after Nasser nationalized the Suez Canal. Nasser in his attempts to become the leader of all Arabs had consistently supported anti-Israeli propaganda and even the raids from the Sinai into Israel. During the war, Israel drove the Egyptians back to the canal and occupied the Sinai, but Washington did not support the alliance and the United Nations restored control of the canal to Egypt. Nasser continued to promote anti-Israeli propaganda, but the Jewish state became less of an issue in his policies and in Arab politics in general, although Arab states refused to recognize the country. However, in the mid-1960s the Ba'ath party, which had seized power in Syria, stepped up guerrilla attacks on Israel. In May 1967 the relations between Israel and her neighbors reached a crisis when Jordan and Egypt blockaded the port of Elat, cutting off Israel's access to the Red Sea. After a stalemated debate in the United Nations Security Council where the Soviet Union backed the Arab action and the United States supported Israel, the Israelis struck against all its neighbors on June 5, quickly defeating their armies in the "Six-Day War."

Israel was now in control of the entire Sinai, the West Bank of the Jordan, the whole city of Jerusalem where they had moved their capital, and the Golan Heights of Syria. Furthermore, Israel was now seen to be the dominant military power of the Middle East. When Anwar Sadat took over in Egypt after the death of Nasser, he planned another war against Israel. In 1973 this broke out on the holiest day of the Jewish calendar, Yom Kippur. Despite some initial successes and significant Israeli casualties, the Arab forces were unable to regain territory.

Although it had shown that Egypt could stand with Israel in battle, the Yom Kippur War profoundly affected Sadat as he lost his brother, an Egyptian pilot, in the war. The Egyptian leader now was prepared to make peace with Israel. He traveled to Jerusalem, and Israeli Prime Minister Menachem Begin went to Cairo. The two leaders, under the auspices of President James Carter, then went to Washington and worked out a negotiated peace. The two countries changed ambassadors, and Israel returned the Sinai to Egypt. The other Arab countries condemned Sadat as a traitor, but Sadat and Begin shared the Nobel Peace Prize for 1978. Three years later, a Moslem extremist assassinated Sadat while observing a military parade commemorating the Yom Kippur War, just as in 1995 a Jewish extremist had assassinated Yitzhak Rabin for negotiating with Arafat.

In 1985 Israel left Southern Lebanon but still maintained control of the West Bank, the Golan Heights, and Gaza. Thus Jerusalem had a large number of Palestinian Arabs under its control. In 1987 the Palestinians, especially the youth, reacted with stone-throwing attacks on Israeli forces, the *intifadah*. Israeli forces retaliated with water cannons and rubber bullets, causing a number of injuries. Against terrorist invaders they responded with harsher actions. During the Gulf War of 1991, Washington persuaded Israel not to retaliate against Iraq, which had sent Scud missiles against the country trying to break up the coalition against it, which included a number of Arab countries. Jordan recognized Israel in 1993 and King Hussein became the custodian of the Moslem Holy Places. In 2000 Palestinian organizations like Hamas and Islamic Jihad began a systematic use of suicide attacks (the second *intifadah*) with individuals who were mostly teenagers—men and women, moving into crowded areas in Israel with bombs strapped to their bodies. Once again Israel responded with force, invading Palestinian areas trying to destroy terrorist bases. The most serious invasion took place in February 2002 when they invaded the headquarters of Arafat, although they had promised Washington that they would not kill the Palestinian leader. Jerusalem also built a wall separating Israeli land from Palestinian territory, causing a great deal of controversy and condemnation from the United Nations and the World Court. Jewish settlements on Palestinian land have been condemned by both friends and foes of Israel alike. However, attempts by the government to remove them have aroused dissent inside the country, causing domestic political difficulties.

FREDERICK B. CHARY

See also Arab–Israeli Wars (1948, 1956, 1967, 1973); Bahrain; Ethnic Conflicts: Middle East; Hussain, Saddam; Iran; Iran–Iraq War, 1980–1988; Iraq; Israel; Jordan; Khomeini, Ayatollah Ruhollah; Kurdistan;

Kurds; Kuwait; Lebanon; Middle East: History and Economic Development; Mossaddeq, Muhammed; Nasser, Gamal Abdel; Oman; Qatar; Sadat, Anwar; Saudi Arabia; Syria; Turkey; United Arab Emirates; United Arab Republic (UAR); Yemen

References and Further Reading

Binder, Leonard. *Ethnic Conflict and International Politics in the Middle East.* Gainsville, FL: University of Florida, 1999.

Bozdaglioglu, Yucel. *Turkish Foreign Policy and Turkish Identity: A Constructivist Approach.* New York: Routledge, 2003.

Breger, Marshall J. *The Vatican–Israel Accords : Political, Legal, and Theological Contexts.* Notre Dame, IN: University of Notre Dame Press, 2004.

Brown, L. Carl, ed. *Diplomacy in the Middle East: The International Relations of Regional and Outside Powers.* London, New York: I.B. Tauris, 2001.

Dumper, Michael. *The Politics of Sacred Space: The Old City of Jerusalem in the Middle East Conflict.* Boulder, CO: Lynne Rienner Publishers, 2002.

Esposito, John L. *The Iranian Revolution: Its Global Impact.* Gainesville, FL: Florida International University Press, 1990.

Gerner, Deborah J. *Understanding the Contemporary Middle East.* Boulder, CO: Lynne Rienner Publishers, 2000.

Halliday, Fred. *The Middle East in International Relations : Power, Politics and Ideology.* Cambridge, UK: Cambridge University Press, 2005.

Ismael, Jacqueline S. *The Gulf War and the New World Order: International Relations of the Middle East.* Gainesville, FL: University Press of Florida, 1994.

Ismael, Tareq Y. *The Iraqi Predicament: People in the Quagmire of Power Politics.* London: Pluto Press, 2004.

———. *Middle East Politics Today: Government and Civil Society.* Gainesville, FL: University Press of Florida, 2001.

Kandiyoti, Deniz. *Gendering the Middle East: Emerging Perspectives.* New York: Syracuse University Press, 1996.

Rubin, Barry M. *Turkey in World Politics: An Emerging Multiregional Power.* Boulder, CO: Lynne Rienner Publishers, 2001.

Waterbury, John. *The Egypt of Nasser and Sadat: The Political Economy of Two Regimes.* Princeton, NJ: Princeton University Press, 1983.

Weiss, Thomas George. *Wars on Terrorism and Iraq: Human Rights, Unilateralism, and U.S. Foreign Policy.* New York: Routledge, 2004.

MIGRATION

Differences in living standards and opportunities explain why an increasing pressure for migration exists between countries of the Southern and Northern Hemispheres, as well as among countries of the Southern Hemisphere. As economies expand, as communications, transportation, and education offer people access to modernity, people move within their countries and abroad. Powerful social, cultural, economic, political, and psychological factors facilitate migration from the South to the North or from the South to more developed countries in the South.

In the 1980s, the report of the Brandt Commission (*Common Crisis: North, South: Co-operation for World Recovery*), which received its name from its president, the former German Chancellor Willy Brandt, favoured a global project to promote Third World development that would, among other things, bring work to the labour force rather than the labour force to the work. However, a global redistribution of employment has not proved possible, and in the 1990s the emphasis was on development of the countries of the South to allow these countries to become more competitive internationally.

Historical Overview

Why is industrial transformation generally followed by rural-to-urban migration, which contributes to urbanization? Some theorists suggest that internal and international migrations are induced by the same processes of social and economic development. The volume of emigration is determined by the degree of economic integration between the sending region and the region of destination.

In pre-industrial societies, economies are characterized by an agricultural sector organized around village-based peasant agriculture. When elites outside the peasantry, such as landed aristocrats, political leaders, capitalists, foreign companies, or international agencies try to substitute capital for labour, and to create markets, peasant agricultural production is destabilized; peasant farm workers begin to be underemployed, and redundant to agricultural production. The economic development of the peasant agricultural production contributes thus to the creation of markets, and the selling of labour. Peasant farmers may work as sharecroppers or as daily wage workers. Markets created for the purpose of economic exchange emerge: markets for land, capital, labour, food, consumer goods, and so forth. These processes weaken individuals' social and economic ties to rural groups and let appear large-scale migration.

In Britain, these processes took place in the late eighteenth and early nineteenth centuries (Massey 1988); a similar process occurred in Mexico at the end of the nineteenth century (Cardoso 1980). One of the most important reasons for migration is the uneven economic development of different regions or countries (Hoffmann-Nowotny 1973). Rural–urban migration thus brings about a progressive urbanization of societies. In European countries, during the nineteenth and early twentieth centuries, urban areas did not absorb all of these rural–urban migrants. Large groups immigrated instead to countries overseas. This immigration is generally regarded as an outcome of economic development under a market economy.

The cyclical nature of industrialization in urban areas, linked to a constant pressure for out-migration from rural areas, creates large groups of possible migrants who respond to development processes. When no political-administrative barriers exist, a demand for immigrant workers in a foreign country, and a wage differential that covers the cost of relocation are sufficient to let appear international migration. The uneven geographic distribution of economic growth within countries and between countries leads to a structure of emigration: as an economy enters a difficult economic cycle, there are other overseas destinations with economic development, and a demand for labour. Furthermore, in more recent years, the declining real costs of transportation and communication let increase the net returns to international movements. The construction of railroads and roads, and the establishing of phone, radio, and television communications led to an integration of developing countries into international markets. People's personal networks became increasingly connected to communication systems of developed economies overseas. Consequently, development rendered international movements easier, and cheaper.

The immigration to developing countries can be explained by the creation of a pool of migrants through capital formation, market creation, and by disparities in economic development across time and space. This structural condition for international movements is accentuated by improvements in transportation and communication systems. It becomes clear that every country and region that has developed its economy has experienced migration. However, there are differences among countries in the amount of emigration: nineteenth-century France experienced rather low levels; during the same period, Britain experienced a mass exodus. Differences between countries depend on the state of the world economy, colonial relationships, technologies, and political factors. The economic links between the developing country and the country of destination are, nevertheless, important factors of explanation. In general, an increasing integration and interdependence let increase the volume of migration.

B. Thomas demonstrated this fact for the developing Atlantic economy of the nineteenth century. The link between the Mexican oil boom and the US economic boom of 1982–1987 has been clearly

established, too (Massey 1988). Recruitment of workers from less developed countries by agents from more developed economies was widely used in history: European workers came to the United States in the late nineteenth and early twentieth centuries; in the 1960s, Western Europe recruited workers from major trading partners, especially former colonies (Castles and Kosack 1973; Massey 1988).

Emigration was thus a common response to economic development not only in Europe, but in developing societies, too. Internal migrations are linked to the same economic and social development as international migrations. Workers respond to differences in wages, urbanization, and education. With the growth of economic integration, large-scale movements of labour between countries occur. Massey indicated a close relation between the onset of industrial development and the migration flows (the beginning correlation is 0.59) and later peak of emigration (correlation is 0.49) (Massey 1988). B. Thomas studied figures on emigration from Britain, Ireland, and Germany with economic development in the United States, and Britain from 1830 to 1913. D. Thomas (1941) studied population movements in Sweden between 1750 and 1933. She found that US business cycles were positively correlated with emigration; and rural–urban migration was positively correlated with the Swedish economic cycle. The work of these scholars shows that emigration is closely linked to economic development. The transformation of peasant economies created a constant rural out-migration directed to internal or international centres. Emigration fluctuated with the changes in the European economy.

Theories: Migration and Development

This subsection addresses the question of whether migration triggers development or does development trigger migration. The large international and internal income differences have been considered by sociological theory (Hoffmann-Nowotny 1973) as one of the most important factors bringing about internal or international migration. Hoffmann-Nowotny showed that migrants from poorer European countries move to richer countries. He studied this phenomenon in Switzerland and Canada in the 1970s. Schuerkens' study of the Congo (Brazzaville) and Sudan (1981) was influenced by this approach. In this study it was found that regional economic, urban, and educational differences influenced the direction and the level of migration. However, poorer regions contributed only on a small scale to internal migrations, whereas regions which were situated on a higher level of development contributed to a much higher degree to internal migrations.

In many parts of the developing world, migration processes led to high rates of urbanization during the 1980s and 1990s, processes that demonstrate these mutual links. Today, it is no longer obvious that an increase in per capita income reduces migration, as Hoffmann-Nowotny and I suggested in our studies. The statement that the best migration policy is development policy, which means that an increase in income would reduce out-migration, is challenged. According to Fischer, Martin, and Straubhaar (1997), the relation between migration and development is actually considered with the concept of a "modified inverted U-curve." They wrote: "Development often first enhances and thereafter reduces the scope and incentives for migration, but the sequencing of enhancement and reduction is usually different for different types of migration."

Classic economic theory considers that sending regions obtain benefits from out-migration for their development processes. Another economic school argues that out-migration may be an obstacle for the development of the sending areas. The "brain-drain" discussion is linked to this second approach: high-level migrants drain poor countries of valuable resources that are needed for development. Migration may further development in the core countries at the expense of the poor periphery. Whether so-called *convergence* or *divergence* processes (countries either get closer to each other or still increase their differences) predominate depends on the particular economic development of a region. Empirical studies indicate that migration seems to have positive short-term effects for regions of out-migration and in-migration. In the long term, empirical studies suggest that migration does not strongly influence the development process. There seem to be "turning points" in development when migration becomes more important.

One of the simplest economic explanations of migration is that people move with the aim to improve their situation. On an international level, this would mean that large groups of migrants move from poor to rich regions. However, the total number of migrants is rather small: it is estimated by international organizations, such as the International Labour Organization, the International Organization of Migration, and the United Nations High Commissioner for Refugees, as about 1.5% of the world population. Furthermore, most migrations are internal rather than international in spite of large international income differences. South-to-North migrations are small compared to South-to-South migrations, for instance, from West Africa to Nigeria, or from Southern Africa to South Africa. The direction of migration flows reveals the predominance of cultural and historical links as well as geographical distance. As mentioned above, the largest migration flows come from countries that are not the poorest ones. Moreover, the position of countries in international migrations changes over time. Changing income levels induce a rise or a fall as an emigration area; for instance, sending countries are becoming receiving countries: Italian migrants went to Germany in the 1960s; in the 1990s, Italy had already become an immigration country for African immigrants.

Fischer et al. emphasize that "international migration is *partly* dependent on differences in income and development between macro-level areas." Lack of comparable data and measurement problems render international comparisons of migration groups rather difficult. Nevertheless, Fischer et al. "calculated correlation coefficients between the net number of people born abroad in percent of total population and relative average real per capita GDP." They found the following correlations:

These scholars concluded their study by writing: "Despite plenty of reservations to be made as far as the data used are concerned, the calculations derive a relation between the net stock of foreign-born people and GDP per capita which is overall positive, with a correlation value of +0.46." In fact, the correlation of Europe is quite strong with +0.81. The correlation coefficients for the Middle East (+0.89) and the United States (+0.73) are high, too. The low coefficients for Africa and the former Soviet Union let us presume that in these regions, political reasons for migration are more important than economic reasons.

In order to differentiate still more the relation between development and migration, Fischer et al. restricted their migration typology to three migration subgroups:

Table 1: Correlation coefficients

Region	Note	Correlation value
World	Ex-Soviet Union excluded	0.46
Europe	Maghreb and Turkey included	0.81
Africa	Maghreb excluded	0.43
United States		0.73
Middle East	Turkey excluded	0.89
Far East and Australia		0.73
Ex-Soviet Union		−0.19

a. Internal (short-distance) migration
b. International (long-distance) migration of low-skilled workers
c. International (long-distance) migration of high-skilled workers.

They understand by high-skilled workers those migrants who are "qualified for employment above, say, the level of simple manufacturing jobs."

Regions with low per capita income levels usually do not participate in international migration flows because of lack of financial possibilities. In these regions, people exploit natural resources or work in agriculture. Countries that are more developed are frequently known for having large spatial (rural–urban) inequalities that lead to internal migration movements. In these countries, international migration can be attractive for high-skilled migrants who possess the necessary financial means and information about other life-possibilities abroad. Yet, the majority of the population has at their disposal no financial means to realize a migration. Countries with still higher per-capita income try to reduce internal regional differences. Thus, they slow down incentives for internal migration. Nevertheless, financial possibilities to engage in international migration increase, and more low- and high-skilled people will decide to move because of higher possible benefits of out-migration. But most of the people will not leave their place of residence.

The *convergence* effect of migration can be shown when differentiating the impact of migration on development in both the short- and the long run. Migration influences wages in emigration and immigration regions in the short term to medium terms. Migrants who sent parts of their income to the country of origin *(remittances effect)* influence the economy of their home countries. Migrants' contribution to the financing of public services in the country of immigration causes effects on public transfers. The availability of labour may furthermore lead to changes in the production structure and may influence the terms of trade of both countries. What about the quantity effect of labour in the South (abundant) and in the North (scarce)? Migration from the South to the North decreases wages in the North and increases them in the South.

Neo-classical growth models have often been tested empirically. These tests reveal that convergence takes place, but at a slow rate of about 2%–3% per annum. However, most of the growth can be explained by changes in technology and not by neo-classical convergence processes. It is a matter of fact that one finds convergence within Northern countries and Southern countries as two different groups, but rather little convergence between the South and the North.

Marx, Myrdal, Hirschmann, and Wallerstein argued that migration increases rather than decreases development differences in the world. These scholars think that technological progress does not spread from the Northern core to the Southern periphery. For them, as Fischer *et al.* wrote:

Wages and/or returns on investment will therefore remain lower in the disadvantaged region. The latter can only catch up by improving its technology and efficiency, which becomes more difficult once factors of production begin to leave. If in the extreme case all input factors were mobile, the disadvantaged location would in the long run face a total outflow of production factors, until 'the last turns off the light.'

Immigration into economically more important areas strengthens their position as core economies, while smaller economies lose their competition effects. Structural changes or the integration of markets, which induce migration flows and their direction, may determine which economy becomes core and which periphery. "The mobility of people is therefore one of the potential determinants of core-periphery structures" (Fischer *et al.* 1997).

In conclusion to this issue, we can say that empirical case studies let appear the co-existence of the convergence and divergence theses related to migration. Periods of economic development of regions and countries exist when migration causes divergence effects. They may be followed by periods when migration induces convergence effects. The actual link between migration and development thus remains an empirical question studied in concrete situations.

Fischer *et al.* concludes in the following manner:

For most countries, the impact of international migration on development tends to be positive but essentially short-term. Especially labour-market and balance-of-payments problems are frequently eased, sometimes some growth effects due to increased consumption are noticeable. Convergence, rather than divergence effects of migration on development are usually detected. But migration rarely seems to be able to induce the far-reaching social and economic changes that are required to advance the development process in most countries of the South.

Remittances

Central to the links between migration and development are remittances, a part of migrant workers' earnings sent back from the country of employment to the country of origin. These remittances depend on the rules and characteristics of workers abroad; levels and types of economic activity in sending and host countries; and the difference in wage, exchange, and interest rates. These factors influence the decisions of the migrants and their families on remittances: whether they spend funds in their country of origin or spend them abroad; whether they remit through official or informal channels; how they use their earnings, for consumption or for investment.

Remittances are private transfers and only a part of them flows through official channels. Estimates about official remittances can be derived from the International Monetary Fund's *Balance of Payments Statistics Yearbook*. Nevertheless, data are not reported for all countries and some countries report them in different categories of the balance-of-payments statistics. Three categories are of relevance: workers' remittances, migrants' transfers, and labour incomes. World Bank studies include all three categories when analysing remittance flows. But not all scholars follow this definition, a fact that results in an extreme disparity of research results. A recent study found that nominal remittance credits increased from US$43.3 billion in 1980 to US$65.6 billion in 1989 (Russell 1992).

For many international emigration countries, remittances constitute sizeable proportions of exports, imports, and GDP. In some countries, remittances can be 25%–50% of the value of merchandise exports and 10%–30% of merchandise imports. Yet, remittances are volatile, and countries may experience economic shocks following the disrupting of flows. There is evidence that remittances constitute an important mechanism of money transfer between developed and developing countries. The nominal net transfers (that is, credits minus debits) from developed to developing countries rose from US$21.1 billion in 1980 to nearly US$31 billion in 1989. In 1988, official development assistance was US$51 billion, a fact that revealed the minor influence of development aid as a means to reduce migration pressures (Russell 1992).

What about the use of remittances? There is some contradiction in the empirical evidence on this point, which results from the fact that, for instance, expenditures of migrants are not separated from those of non-migrants. In general, migrants have to choose between consumption and investment expenditures. But analysts do not agree on the effects in the wider economy. Some scholars argue that remittances are used for the purchase of land and housing, jewelry, and general household consumption, rather than *productive investments*. They conclude that remittances do not stimulate regional or national development.

Another group of scholars argues that migrants save and invest, and that expenditures for land, housing, and jewelry have positive multiplier effects in the wider economy, and reduce government spending on infrastructure, subsidies, and services.

There is empirical evidence to support both points of view. For instance, Sahelian migrants in France often hold low- or unskilled jobs in France. A significant portion of their savings is utilized by migrant associations to finance the social infrastructure of their home villages: schools and dispensaries. Yet, the households of these migrants use remittances primarily for consumption (food, clothing) (Condé *et al.* 1986).

Evidence on the consequences of remittances for development is mixed, too. Scholars found no *automatic mechanism* by which international migration and remittances resulted in development. The effects of migration on poverty depend on the extent to which poor people migrate. In Pakistan, scholars found that remittances raised the average income of migrant households by nearly 31%. However, migrants come often from above-average income households. Remittances may increase income inequality, as scholars found in Egypt, where upper-income households produce a greater part of migrants. Direct economic aid from overseas relatives often raises income levels, the material quality of life, and the social position of those left behind. For Pakistan, scholars argued that remittances were equally distributed over the national population. One of the major migration dilemmas of the sending countries is whether they should subsidize the development of emigration areas or try to maximize the development impact of remittances at the macro level (Russell 1992).

High-Level Skills Migration and Return Migration

It is rather difficult to identify professional categories who migrate. The notion of *brain drain* was coined in the United Kingdom to stigmatize the migration of British physicians or biologists who left for the US in the decades following the Second World War. Despite theoretical and ideological controversies, the notion was implanted and began later on to include migrations from the countries of the South to those of the North, if these migrants possessed qualifications that were likely to be absent in their country of origin.

The central question about this topic is: which experiences losses and/or gains, the country of origin or the country of settlement. It is difficult to measure the contribution of international highly qualified migrants in both contexts. Do they contribute to the scientific progress in their country of origin? Would they produce the same output in their own country? Do they try to establish links from their country of settlement with elites in their country of origin? In fact, this problem is confronted with two viewpoints. *Internationalists* analyse this sort of migration to the countries of the North as a normal phenomenon of an international market, by arguing that qualified manpower goes to places where optimum salaries and productivity exist. In contrast, *nationalists* argue: (1) the international economy does not permit an equal distribution of expert knowledge, which tends to go to the North and is missing in the South; and (2) highly qualified migration movements are artificial, because they are induced by select migration policies of the countries of settlement with the aim to raise their own gains. This second argument was retained by the United Nations for international policy measures. Politics that favoured return migrations could be integrated into national development policies.

The idea of returning to the country of origin is linked to international migration, even if this idea remains mythical or virtual. It contributes to the identity formation of the migrant during his or her residence in an alien country. The migrant's decision to return is associated with taking stock of his or her life: the outcome of costs and benefits of a return migration influenced by professional, economic, familial, cultural, or emotional factors. Several countries, such as Taiwan and South Korea, implanted national policies to invite their elites to return to their countries of origin. Financial measures and a strengthening of the exchange of ideas between the expatriated elites and the national scientific community should contribute to these endeavours. Return migration is thus potentially a real development factor. In this sense, the International Organization of Migration created a programme to favour the return of highly qualified manpower to South America, Asia, and Africa. The TOKTEN (Transfer of knowledge through expatriate nationals) programme of the United Nations Development Programme (UNDP) tried to gather the expert knowledge of expatriates in numerous agricultural, scientific, and technical programmes. Yet, this programme does not plan a definite return, but rather the utilization of the expert knowledge of expatriates in the countries of the South. Furthermore, the creation of specialized research institutes, in India and South Korea, for instance, offers conditions that are able to attract expatriates who are looking for international co-operations and worldwide collaborations.

Policy Measures

Theories developed to understand processes of international migration focus on very different causal mechanisms. Policy measures are thus influenced by various models and policy makers might attempt to regulate international migration by changing wages and employment conditions in destination countries; by promoting economic development in origin countries; by establishing programmes of social insurance in sending societies; by reducing income inequality in places of origin; by improving futures or capital markets in developing regions; or by some combination of these actions. Or one might advise that all of these programmes are fruitless given the structural imperatives for international movement growing out of global market relations (Massey *et al.* 1998).

Given the importance of contemporary international migration flows, policy measures on international migration will be most important in the following decades. *Durable solutions* have to be found to emigration pressures through improved international relations. In an increasingly international economy with open borders for movements of information, commodities, and capital, it is difficult to close borders for people. A long-term solution for the reduction of international migration seems to be sustainable development in poor countries, which enables economic growth and integrates the growing labour force. Measures may include national strategies, trade policy, development aid, and international relations.

A labour-sending country needs to assess its domestic development strategy in order to find the sources of migratory pressure. This would reveal the possible breaks between the macro-economic development strategy and trade and labour policies on one side, and the migration objectives of the country on the other side. In the past, many countries adhered to the import-substitution approach with neglect of the export sector, and a low use of the abundant labour force. This policy meant less employment in the organized sector, and low earnings in the agricultural and informal sectors, which, in turn, encouraged emigration. These policy inconsistencies can obviously be corrected. An employment-oriented policy will therefore focus on the dynamic use of low-cost labour and a systematic focus on a growing technological level, an upgrading of existing products, and a production of higher-value goods. Labour with more skills may be employed gradually; foreign direct investment and aid may contribute to the industrialization and economic growth of the country. This strategy has been followed by Asian NICs, which were able to control their emigration pressure. Even if this strategy has to be adapted to the particular historical situation of a country and the world economy, its different elements continue to be essential for migrant-producing countries.

Since 1986, many countries with an abundant labour force have announced unilateral trade liberalization in order to benefit from an open trade policy. An absence of trade barriers in Organization for Economic Cooperation and Development (OECD) countries, for instance, would mean growth and employment in migrant-producing countries of the Southern Hemisphere. On the other hand, a rising level of trade protectionism would weaken trade reforms in countries with an abundant labour force. Often, it is important to diversify the export sector, with special attention to the development of trade in services, which creates employment. This way has been successfully adopted by some Asian countries in the computer industry. Nevertheless, changes will only come gradually, because of the fact that politicians are not willing to confront their own labour force in times of recession.

Development aid is another strategy to reduce international migration over the long term. Several decades of development policies have resulted in a still-growing gap between poor and rich countries. Inequality within the countries of the South has also grown between the wealthy elites and the impoverished masses. Credit policies controlled by the International Monetary Fund and the World Bank led to increased debt services in many countries, and meant an increased dependency from the North.

Development aid can be used at three levels. At the macro level, it can support programmes that tackle the generation of employment and income, demographic change, human capital development, promotion of trade, and foreign investment. At a micro level, it can focus on particular regions that produce migrants. At an intermediate level, development aid can target sectors such as the services sector, and small enterprises in the informal sector, which are important to migration flows. Results of these methods may be mutually reinforcing.

Aid can act as a facilitator to increased foreign direct investment and improved technologies. The newly industrializing countries in East Asia were able to increase their development by widening their links with foreign companies. The availability of low-cost labour in these countries was one of their assets. Nevertheless, in the contemporary world economy, a certain development of the human capital and infrastructural facilities is needed to attract foreign direct investments. Technical and financial aid programmes may be helpful to prepare countries of the South for the inflow of foreign direct investments. As conditions for investments improve, governments may be in a better position to deal with foreign companies.

Another course of action concerns micro-enterprises in the informal sector, where millions of people in the developing world earn their living. Development aid can improve the productivity and labour-absorption capacity of these enterprises through training, supply of credit, the development of co-operatives, and so forth. The growing interest of international donor countries in this sector can be linked to the policies to reduce emigration. Aid-financed projects can target small-scale industries and agro-based industries linked to rural and regional development.

The World Employment Programme of the International Labour Office has developed a programme of study to examine the prospects for relieving migration pressures through official development assistance, with possibilities appropriate to the particular problems of source regions: regional development in Mexico; urban job creation in Sri Lanka and the Philippines; rural development in India, Bangladesh and Pakistan; population programmes in Algeria and Tunisia, and so forth.

Case Studies

What about the present magnitude of migration? According to Appleyard (1992), a large proportion of the estimated 1 million permanent migrants each year to the so-called traditional receivers (United States, Canada, Australia) are from developing countries and as many as 70 million persons, mostly from developing countries, work either legally or illegally in other countries.

The potential for emigration is much more important: the majority of the world's present and projected future population lives in developing countries. According to Golini et al. (1991), developing countries have the capability of employing in only twenty years an additional number of workers (733 million) much greater than the 1990 stock of the entire developed world (586 million). The central issue here is whether enough jobs are available for these large groups of people. The prognosis is not favourable, with high rates of unemployment or underemployment in the countries of the South. Therefore, emigration pressures from developing countries will be one of the most acute development problems of the coming decades. The Human Development Report stated that unless trade barriers are reduced, South–North migration (and South–South migration) will increase. Aid, similar to the Marshall Plan, has been suggested as an appropriate measure in light of the differences between the North and the South. This aid could help to reduce inequalities and, in turn, emigration pressures, even if, in the short term, emigration resulting from development would increase.

Conclusion

"[T]he almost inevitable global population of 11 billion within a century will create increasing emigration pressures in developing countries" (Appleyard 1992).

The question of how long the inequality gap between rich and poor countries can continue widening, and the policy of the developed countries to manage flows of economic resources, including labour, from the South to the North according to their own interests, are certain to remain major topics of the political debate for the following decades. In our increasingly integrated world system, it is important to examine population movements that seem to be an important element in the changing world order. A broader knowledge of international migration flows, and of the impact of decisions of governments and individual migrants on patterns, causes, and impacts of migration will contribute to insights on the new world order of the twenty-first century.

In order to understand more deeply the actual migration and development patterns, case studies based on country- or region-specific macro-conditions are needed. A uniform South does not exist and the effects of migration on development will not be the same for all countries of the South. A dynamic theory of migration and development has to consider the mutual links of migration and development, the influence of a beginning development on migration, and the effects of migration on development. Such a theory should connect theoretical approaches originating from different disciplines.

The analysis of the development–migration link leads us to expect growing international migration flows between the South and the North. More and more people of the South are included in the world economy. Their level of per capita income increases. These processes induce migration as an option for increasing parts of populations in the South. However, development processes are subject to very complex determinants and not just to the mobility of people. In most cases, migration is a minor factor of development, although this may be due to the rather limited scale of migrants. In the short run, empirical evidence suggests that migration has had positive effects for countries of emigration and immigration. However, long-term impacts of migration are rather difficult to identify, because of the complexity of real situations.

ULRIKE SCHUERKENS

See also Labor; Population Growth: Impact on Development; Refugees

References and Further Reading

Appleyard, Reginald T. "Migration and Development: A Global Agenda for the Future." *International Migration*, 30, no. 2 (1992).
Cardoso, Lawrence. *Mexican Emigration to the United States 1897–1931.* Tucson, AZ: University of Arizona Press, 1980.
Castles, Stephen and Godula Kosack. *Immigrant Workers and Class Structure in Western Europe.* Oxford, UK: Oxford University Press, 1973.
Condé, Julien et al. *Les Migrations Internationales Sud-Nord: Une Étude de Cas: Les Migrants Maliens, Mauritaniens et Sénégalais de la Vallée du Fleuve Sénégal en France.* Paris: Development Centre of the OECD, 1986.
Fischer, Peter A., Reiner Martin, and Thomas Straubhaar. "Interdependencies Between Development and Migration." In *International Migration—Immobility and Development: Multidisciplinary Perspectives*, edited by Tomas Hammar et al. Oxford, New York: Berg, 1997.
Gaillard, Anne Marie and Jacques Gaillard. *Les Enjeux des Migrations Scientifiques Internationales: De la Quête du Savoir à la Circulation des Compétences.* Paris: L'Harmattan, 1999.
Golini, Antonio et al. "South–North Migration with Special Reference to Europe." *International Migration*, XXIX, no. 2 (1991).
Ghosh, Bimal. "Migration-Development Linkages: Some Specific Issues and Practical Policy Measures." *International Migration*, 30, no. 3–4 (1992)
Hoffmann-Nowotny, Hans-Joachim. *Soziologie des Fremdarbeiterproblems: Eine Theoretische und Empirische Analyse am Beispiel der Schweiz.* Stuttgart: Enke, 1973.
Massey, Douglas S. "Economic Development and International Migration in Comparative Perspective." *Population and Development Review*, 14, no. 3 (1988).
———. et al. *Worlds in Motion: Understanding International Migration at the End of the Millenium.* Oxford, UK: Clarendon Press, 1998.
Russell, Sharon Stanton. "Migrant Remittances and Development." *International Migration*, 30, no. 3–4 (1992).
Schuerkens, Ulrike, ed. *Transnational Migrations and Social Transformations.* Special Issue of *Current Sociology*, 53, Monograph 2 (2005).
Thomas, Brinley. *Migration and Economic Growth.* London: Cambridge University Press, 1954.

MILITARY AND CIVILIAN CONTROL

Civil–Military Relations in Theory and Practice

The issue of civilian control of the military involves the proper role that the national armed forces occupy in relation to a country's political institutions and centers of decision-making power. While government by civil authorities has prevailed in both the industrialized and Communist countries, the intervention of the military in politics has been a standard occurrence in the majority of developing nations since the Second World War. The extent to which armies are involved in political activity is therefore a critical aspect of development, as it can affect the prospects for establishing democratic governance or maintaining the stability necessary for achieving economic prosperity.

In traditional theories of civil–military relations, the officer corps is instilled with the doctrine of "professionalism," or conservative values that create an ethic of political neutrality and subservience to national leaders. In the former Soviet Union and the socialist republics of Eastern Europe, its equivalent was referred to as the commissar system, in which the agenda of the military was directly controlled by the ruling party through a political officer who presided over the command unit at every level of its organization. This "civilian control model" also asserts that a clear division between the army and civil institutions is best maintained when military doctrine is oriented toward the traditional task of defending national sovereignty against external threats.

However, in reality military command structures do not always adhere to these restrictions. In a nation that won its independence from a colonial power through armed struggle, the military may be regarded as the founding stone of the republic. Thus, it can be repeatedly called upon to reinforce the status quo in periods of crisis or change. In other settings, the government may integrate the functions of the military bureaucracy and party ministries, giving them a direct stake in political decisions. Further, it is apparent that military officers also possess their own political interests and goals. The policies of an incumbent government regarding salaries, status, and general privileges afforded to the national army can motivate officers to react to or even challenge the present regime. The delicate balance between abstention and direct involvement in politics is especially pronounced in countries that are still undergoing a transition between types of political and economic systems. Such issues are particularly pertinent to the structural characteristics of developing countries, and have a considerable impact upon whether efforts at democratization and market reform will be successful.

The Nature of Civil–Military Relations in the Developing World

The role of the military in the structure and function of the modern state has traditionally been separated

into three areas: (1) *military security*, or the defense of national sovereignty from foreign powers; (2) *internal security*, or the protection of the state from subversion from within its territorial boundaries; and (3) *situational security*, or the preservation of state power against unforeseen social or environmental changes. In many nations of the Third World, the second category has been the primary concern of the armed forces. This preoccupation with maintaining internal stability is often linked to the inability of some governments to effectively manage the shocks created by such conditions as economic crisis, ethnic tensions, or increased demands for participation. In the Western European experience, the formation of state bureaucracies involved the recruitment of both civil and military elites for the essential tasks of governance, among them the provision of an adequate national defense, the preservation of public order, and tax collection. In circumstances in which the process of state construction is incomplete or being redefined—in effect, the developing and transitional societies—the orientation of the military toward these concerns gives it an inherently political purpose. The absence of broad popular legitimacy, combined with the weakness of post-colonial institutions, have caused many leaders in the Third World to resort to military force to suppress dissent and consolidate their political power. In this situation, national military organizations were most often arrayed not in the defense of civil society, but against the populace for the purposes of preserving the existing government. It is this fundamental distinction that calls the professional ethic into question, and further contributes to conditions for a politicized military.

Models of Civil–Military Relations in the Developing World

An examination of civil–military arrangements across developing countries reveals that the nature of the polity and the balance of political forces in the process of state-building are often related to the government's policies on deployment and defense posture. The function and purpose of national armies are therefore strongly conditioned by the characteristics of the institutional order in which they are situated. In more than a few post-colonial nations, the military has played a predominant role in the founding and consolidation of the state. Revolutions or wars of national liberation often place former commanders at the helm of the new regime whose experience with the practice of governance is limited. Therefore, when subsequent leaders are faced with the necessities of political or institutional reform, the army is frequently referred to as a source of authority. Conversely, some militaries are said to act as a "moderating power," which intervenes only in the event that the effectiveness of the incumbent government is threatened by internal polarization or institutional failure. The various models of civilian control employed by developing country governments reflect such distinctions. For example: in Turkey, the army serves as guarantor of the secular state; in China, it has representatives within the Communist party apparatus; in several South American countries, it has ruled in direct collaboration with the dominant civilian party. Conflicts of interest between conservatives and reformers within ruling parties, or opposing factions in coalition governments, may also involve military leaders who support one policy position or another. In this manner, the political agendas of military elites are expressed even where there is no motivation to interfere directly in the decision-making process.

Prospects for Civil–Military Relations in the Developing World

In the contemporary world climate, there has been a major shift away from the prevalence of authoritarian and socialist regimes in many countries toward democratic governments and market-based economies. This change of conditions also stands to have a significant impact on the issue of civilian control of the military in the developing nations. In particular, it calls into question the purpose that militaries will serve in these new systems, as well as their ability to adapt to the decentralized environment of deliberative governance. If a regime transition coincides with the resolution of internal conflict such as a guerilla insurgency, the armed forces must convert their strategic doctrine from counter-offensive to peacetime operations. If economic reforms increase the number of actors in society that are involved in production and distribution, then the military may become a participant in the management of industries and facilitating foreign investments as well as national defense.

However, the global trend toward participatory government in Third World states does not entirely eliminate the threat of military intervention in politics. Attempts at restoring or introducing competitive electoral processes have sometimes been unsuccessful. The holding of elections without substantial restructuring of institutions might allow a reversal to authoritarianism. This could invite the military to play a more prominent role in managing an uncertain

political environment. The problem of maintaining civilian oversight in the course of democratic transitions is especially pronounced in circumstances where pacts or constitutional arrangements may allow militaries to retain their previous positions of influence. Additionally, traditional national security doctrines directed at controlling subversion by organized dissident groups may take considerable time and effort to reform. If the army maintains a doctrine in which mass protest is identified as a threat to public order rather than a popular expression of grievances, serious violations of civil liberties could result. Thus, the issue of maintaining politically neutral and effective national armed forces will continue to impact the politics of developing countries in the years to come.

JASON E. STRAKES

See also Military and Development; Military and Human Rights

References and Further Reading

Desch, Michael C. *Civilian Control of the Military: The Changing Security Environment*. Baltimore, MD: The Johns Hopkins University Press, 1999, pp. 8–17.

Handelman, Howard. *The Challenge of Third World Development*, 3rd ed. Upper Saddle River, NJ: Prentice Hall, 2003, pp. 227–253.

Huntington, Samuel P. *The Soldier and The State: The Theory and Practice of Civil–Military Relations*. New York: Vintage Books, 1957.

Kennedy, Charles H. and David J. Louscher. "Civil Military Interaction: Data in Search of a Theory." In *Civil–Military Interaction in Africa and Asia*, edited by Charles H. Kennedy and David J. Louscher. E. J. Brill, 1991, pp. 1–10.

Koonings, Kees and Dirk Kruijt, eds. *Political Armies: The Military and Nation Building in the Age of Democracy*. London: Zed Books, 2002.

Stepan, Alfred. *The Military in Politics: Changing Patterns in Brazil*. Princeton, NJ: Princeton University Press, 1971.

MILITARY AND DEVELOPMENT

The role played by the armed forces in the economic and political development in developing countries has varied enormously from situation to situation. In some cases the military has been a primary agent of change, while in all too many others, it has hindered development.

The concept of "development" is a decidedly Western one. It has been generally assumed that economic development and political development are interdependent processes that lead countries to adopt systems that approximate the forms enjoyed by the advanced industrial democracies. Economic development generally entails the adoption of new technologies, industrialization, and diversification of production away from a purely agriculturally based economy. While elites in developing countries have for the most part desired economic development, the commitment to the Western view of political development goals has varied considerably. This view of political development ideally includes the establishment of a democratic republic, with civilian control of government and guarantees of basic political freedoms. Civilian control over the armed forces is the sine qua non of proper civil–military relations in this model of political development.

Several national military institutions have played pivotal roles in economic modernization, industrialization, and technology acquisition through the influencing, or even the imposition of, specific policies. It has been less common to find military institutions in developing countries that have been as adept or as enthusiastic in fostering political development, in the sense of establishing democratic institutions and protecting basic civil rights, though some armies have supported democratic civilian rule.

Military Attitudes

One common stereotype of the military institution sees it as essentially conservative. There are many good reasons for this view. However, the military has often shown itself to be the motor for social, political, and economic change in the appropriate circumstances. The military has often been the elite group most outspoken in its call for modernization, political development, or industrialization. Especially in those regions where conflict between the rapidly advancing Western European states and non-Europeans was most constant, the internal struggles within the non-Western powers pitted the military and other elites against traditionalists. The military officers often literally bore the brunt of these conflicts against Western forces, and were most anxious to adopt the means that Westerners were using to defeat them in battle.

A striking example of the military playing this sort of revolutionary role may be found in the late Ottoman Empire and in the Turkish Republic that replaced it. Within the declining Ottoman Empire of the nineteenth century, it was mainly the officer corps, along with the more cosmopolitan segments of the middle classes (physicians, students, and merchants), that struggled against the traditionalist rulers in order to adopt not only military tactics and weaponry from the West, but also technological know-how,

industrialization, and political practices. Officers were among the most forceful backers of the Constitutional (Tanzimat) Movement in the mid-nineteenth century, which sought to limit the power of the sultan. They were among the leaders of the various quasi-nationalist movements, the Young Ottomans, and later the Young Turks, which advocated the adoption of European political arrangements and concepts in the Empire. The military tended to support modernizing policies as the only means for stopping the encroachment of European powers, and of resisting the breakaway nationalist movements in the Balkans. They opposed an extremely conservative sultanate and religious establishment, which were reluctant to adopt any Western innovations, on the premise that the non-Muslim powers could not possibly have superior methods and institutions. In the view of these traditionalists the answer to this apparent decline was not to adopt Western ways, but to redouble efforts to reassert the traditional ways of Islamic civilization.

The Ottoman Empire was broken up after World War I. A shadow of the former Empire tenuously ruled the Anatolian Peninsula, but under British, French, and Italian spheres of influence. Mustafa Kemal, one of the few recognized military heroes of the Ottoman army during the war, was infuriated that the sultan had signed a humiliating treaty with the European powers, and was doing nothing to stop Greek penetration into Anatolia. He and his followers revolted against the Empire, drove back the Greeks, and established the Republic of Turkey. Mustafa Kemal, taking the surname Atatürk, then instituted a series of sweeping reforms meant to reorient Turkey toward Europe, to modernize its institutions and mores, and to bring the new republic into the "modern" world. Among these innovations were the promulgation of a new European-influenced constitution and a civil code borrowed from the Swiss, the expansion of education, and the granting of women's suffrage. Policies were also introduced and enforced that were intended to Westernize Turkish culture, such as the adoption of a new Latinized alphabet, the standardization of surnames, and the banning of the fez. Policies were also introduced to modernize and expand industry and trade. The army became the repository for and defender of the philosophy culled from the program of Atatürk, known as Kemalism. Since the 1920s, the military has remained the bastion of Kemalist republican modernization and secularism, defending it against challenges by Marxists no less than by Islamist movements.

Similar modernizing aspirations could be discerned in Latin American officer corps in the mid-nineteenth century. Middle-level officers were often frustrated by the inability or unwillingness of the civilian elites to effectively pursue economic modernization. As the Latin American republics fell further behind Europe and North America, they were more easily exploited by outside powers, particularly Britain. Though these officers were educated in the new professional manner of the European officer corps, this training made them all the more painfully aware of just how far their countries lagged behind, especially in the areas of industry and technology. Many soon came under the sway of the philosophy of Positivism, which derived from the works of the French philosopher Auguste Comte. Distilled into its Latin American version, Positivist ideas emphasized a dynamic program of modernization and education, especially in the sciences, which would create the conditions that would lead these weak republics out of the doldrums. Positivist clubs and parties were formed throughout the hemisphere. The new doctrine was particularly popular among army officers. In many states the military as an institution began to pressure their governments to adopt more forward-looking policies. The movement was perhaps strongest in Brazil, where, after a military-led coup ousted Emperor Pedro II and established a republic in 1889, the motto of the Positivists, "Order and Progress" (*Ordem e Progresso*), was prominently displayed on the new national flag. Some modernization did occur in limited regions of certain Latin American countries, but overall, what progress there was came in fits and starts. In countries like Brazil and Mexico, where Positivist officers had taken power or held influential positions, it was not long before their progressive policies were abandoned for baser political practices.

Civic Action and the Military in Newly Emerging Nations

Until World War II, most of Africa, Asia, and the Caribbean were still under the direct control of the great European empires. But very soon after the end of the War, the imperial systems began to weaken and break apart, beginning with Britain's withdrawal from India and Palestine in 1947. Some colonies were supposedly being "guided" toward independence, while in many others local independence movements began to grow. Some of the guerrilla groups fighting for liberation would become the nuclei of national militaries once independence was won.

Most of the former colonies were woefully underdeveloped upon achieving independence. Infrastructure was minimal, and usually nonexistent outside of the region of the capital city or major ocean ports.

There was generally very little industry. Education in the Western sense barely existed outside the largest cities. In many cases, political elites were inexperienced at ruling, and economic elites were often unprepared to compete in a worldwide industrial and trading system dominated by the advanced European and North American countries.

Policy makers and political scientists in the West began to recommend models of government and economic systems for the so-called "Newly Emerging Nations." Western theories of "developmentalism" advocated a series of steps that would lead emerging states to expand their middle classes, achieve "take-off" in economic modernization, and establish democratic republics.

The conditions in these new independent states varied so widely that the notion that one meta-model could fit all cases was soon revealed to have been surprisingly naive (though competing models advocated by the Soviet Union, and later by China and Cuba, proved no less so). These new states were confronted with so many pressures and handicaps that it was hard to know where to begin the process of development. Many of the Asian and African states were made up of dozens, sometimes hundreds, of tribal, ethnic, linguistic, "national," and religious groups. The international boundaries of these artificial states divided identifiable groups more often than they united them. With such natural disunity and inter-group rivalry present in so many of these new states, "nation building" became a top priority for the new political elites.

In the late 1950s and early 1960s, Western scholars and policy makers began to tout the idea that the armed forces in developing countries were ideally suited to act as the main institution for fostering national unity and political development in the newly emerging nations. This nation-building and nation-serving function was known as "civic action." In such new and weak states, national government agencies were struggling to professionalize, and to expand their authority and legitimacy from the capital cities out to the more remote regions. The military was assumed to be the most organized and efficient institution with a national scope. It was poised, according to advocates of this model, to undertake a variety of activities that could help to push the country forward. Its engineering units could be employed to build roads, bridges, irrigation systems, and other elements of infrastructure. Its national scope would allow it to draw people from the disparate ethnic, religious, and linguistic groups, and socialize them into a new national identity. The structure of the army could also be used to teach useful new skills to recruits, and improve the health of recruits from impoverished areas. The army would also be in a position to represent the new national government in extending essential services to the populations in remote areas.

Another assumption of this policy derived from the less naive notion that an army was essentially a fighting force. In a situation where the government was weak, where few other national authorities existed, and where local loyalties were a constant threat to national unity, it might be necessary to make sure that the army was gainfully employed in productive projects, so that they would not readily revert to using force against the government, or against national minorities.

However, the very attributes that recommended the armed forces for civic action programs also made it the strongest single entity within the government. By virtue of its monopoly of arms, many military institutions would pit themselves against other government agencies or political parties, sometimes from frustration at the inefficiency of the bureaucracy, or at its corruption, and sometimes at the behest of officers who were little more than warlords and political bosses. Despite the promise of civic action in theory, the military often became a major obstacle to political development rather than its sponsor.

While many of the newly independent countries struggled with the perplexing problem of nation building, there were some that managed to achieve a certain satisfactory level of political development, at least according to the idealized model. India is a particularly striking case of a newly independent state with multiple and competing linguistic, religious, and national groups, which nevertheless managed to create a reasonably stable democratic republic. Most notably for this discussion, the military very closely followed the model of an institution that serves elected civilian political leaders. The military is a very influential organization in Indian society, due in no small part to India's international security environment, as well as its pretensions to regional power status. Its military industries have been the focus of significant investment, and there were hopes here, as in many other third-world countries anxious to modernize, that such investment would yield industrial and technological spin-offs for civilian industry. Scholars still differ as to whether government investment in military industrialization contributed to civilian industrialization, or whether these funds might have been better invested in the civilian economy or spent on the provision of social services. Nevertheless, India does offer an important example of the viability of the Western model of civil–military relations in developing countries.

Economic Development Precedes Political Development

The dependent position of almost all newly independent nations, as well as those few that had achieved independence in the nineteenth century (mainly in Latin America), persisted, and was a constant source of frustration for the political and economic elites. A variety of strategies were tried, and alliances were made with one or the other of the rival Cold War powers to achieve advantage. But development remained elusive.

By the 1960s, a very small and varied group of states, most controlled by the military, embarked on rigorous courses of economic development. These regimes pursued the establishment of heavy industry, often centered on arms production, and the acquisition of cutting-edge technologies. In those states ruled by the military, most notably South Korea and Brazil, military control allowed for the suppression of dissent from opposition politicians and intellectuals, and especially from those social groups that suffered most from the imposition of these policies. Military governments were also able to co-opt those elites who benefited directly from the new growth, and who therefore went along with government control over investment, credit, and financing, and establishing production priorities (usually oriented toward exports). Among those states that successfully modernized, there was no one pattern that was followed. In countries like Israel (with a Western-style parliamentary regime) and Brazil, industrialization was led in large part by the arms industries, which received special attention from the government. In South Korea, Taiwan, and Chile, arms industrialization was eventually pursued, but this was not the primary focus of industrial policy. The salient common denominator among these successfully industrializing states was that in none of these cases was the developmentalist model prescribed by Western policy makers and academics followed, even if there was some element of civic action thrown into the mix. In all the successful cases, there was extensive government involvement and direction of economic policy, usually accompanied by strong protectionist measures.

Of course, neither military control, nor influence over the government, nor centralized government control over the implementation of economic policy was a guarantee of successful industrialization. For example, the People's Republic of China was characterized by extensive inter-penetration between the leadership of the ruling Communist Party and the upper echelons of the armed forces. Government and Party exercised extensive control over economic policy, and the military was politically influential and received preferential treatment from the regime. However, industrial policy was erratic, and was for several decades determined more by ideological imperatives than by pragmatic concerns. Defense industries were established, but were isolated from other sectors of the economy. With the extensive economic reforms initiated in the late 1970s, the segregation of defense industries from the rest of the economy was ended. At the same time, the presence of high-ranking military officers in the Communist Party leadership was diminishing. Insofar as recent Chinese economic modernization can be judged successful, it has been achieved in part because of the relative de-politicization of the military. Seen in this light, the case of China provides an important alternative scenario to that of Brazil, Chile, Israel, South Korea, and Taiwan as discussed above.

Success in industrialization and technology acquisition on the part of military regimes or states with strong defense needs, and therefore an extremely influential military institution, are not the norm. Most developing countries ruled by military regimes that undertook such policies ultimately failed to achieve positive results. Other military or one-party regimes with centralized control over economic policies simply transformed into kleptocracies or autarchic authoritarian states.

Neoliberal Globalization and Military Concerns

In the 1980s and 1990s, many authoritarian regimes collapsed and were replaced by democratic systems (some became authentically democratic, others only nominally so), most notably in Latin America, Eastern Europe, and the former Soviet Union. This also meant that the armed forces in these countries took on a new role, now serving elected civilian leaders (or, at least, civilian ruling elites), following the Western model of civil–military relations.

With the end of the Cold War and the subsequent emergence of the era of globalization, most developing countries still remained woefully behind in terms of both economic and political development. Neoliberal ideology has become the dominant paradigm for development and the policy model that international institutions such as the International Monetary Fund, the World Bank, and the World Trade Organization impose upon economically struggling countries. While there is still a great deal of variation in the response of the people in developing countries to neoliberal globalization, from enthusiastic embracing

of its prescriptions, to resignation, to outright resistance, these policies present a unique problem for military officers.

The neoliberal paradigm calls for a reduction in the role of the state, fewer regulations, less government involvement in economic affairs, the privatization of government enterprises, reduced subsidies, and the scaling back of protectionist policies. Barriers to international investment and the flow of capital and profits were to be gradually eliminated. Advocates of these policies promise economic growth and modernization to those who faithfully follow the new rules. Professional officers, as noted above, have often been at the forefront of movements for economic modernization and industrialization. Therefore, the promise of these new policies holds a certain attraction for the military. On the other hand, critics of neoliberalism claim that wholesale adoption of these policies could lead to the erosion of national sovereignty and the surrender of decision making to foreign actors and international capital markets.

As an essentially nationalistic institution, dedicated to the defense of the nation and to its independence and sovereignty, some officers are inclined to fear neoliberalism as a very real threat to national independence. Indeed, the most extreme neoliberal visionaries speak of an end to the traditional nation-state, an idea that constitutes a major challenge to the worldview of professional officers, which sees the state as the essential expression of the nation. Many officers therefore find themselves in a painfully ambiguous situation as a result. By embracing neoliberalism, their countries may take advantage of massive foreign investment and have access to cutting-edge technologies, but at the cost of compromising their national sovereignty. By resisting global neoliberal institutions such as the World Trade Organization, their countries may preserve national autonomy but cut themselves off from the most dynamic international markets.

There is no single pattern that developing countries have followed since achieving independence. Likewise, there is no single pattern of civil–military relations in developing countries, or of military influence or involvement in economic and political development. With the current trend toward democratization in many developing countries, there is an expectation that their armed forces will become increasingly professionalized. Professionalization should then reinforce military support for the Western civil–military paradigm.

DAVID SCHWAM-BAIRD

See also Military and Civilian Control; Military and Human Rights

References and Further Reading

Ball, Nicole, *The Military in the Development Process: A Guide to Issues.* Claremont, Calif.: Regina Books, 1981.

Bienen, Henry. *The Military and Modernization.* Chicago: Aldine-Atherton, 1971.

Bowman, Kirk S. *Militarization, Democracy and Development: The Perils of Praetorianism in Latin America.* University Park, PA: Pennsylvania State University Press, 2002.

Diamond, Larry and Marc F. Plattner. *Civil–Military Relations and Democracy.* Baltimore, MD: Johns Hopkins University Press, 1996.

Hanning, Hugh. *The Peaceful Uses of Military Forces.* New York: Praeger, 1967.

Huer, Jon. *Marching Orders: The Role of the Military in South Korea's "Economic Miracle," 1961–1971.* New York: Greenwood Press, 1989.

Janowitz, Morris. *The Military in the Development of New Nations: An Essay in Comparative Analysis.* Chicago: University of Chicago Press, 1964.

Millett, Richard L. and Michael Gold-Bliss, eds. *Beyond Praetorianism: The Latin American Military in Transition.* Miami: North-South Center Press, 1996.

Pion-Berlin, David, ed. *Civil–Military Relations in Latin America: New Analytical Perspectives.* Chapel Hill, NC: University of North Carolina Press, 2001.

Shambaugh, David. *Modernizing China's Military: Progress, Problems, and Prospects.* Berkeley, CA: University of California Press, 2002.

Trimberger, Ellen Kay. *Revolution from Above: Military Bureaucrats and Development in Japan, Turkey, Egypt and Peru.* New Brunswick, NJ: Transaction Books, 1978.

Van Doorn, Jacques. *The Soldier and Social Change.* Beverly Hills, CA: Sage, 1975.

Wolpin, Miles D. *Militarization, Internal Repression and Social Welfare in the Third World.* New York: St. Martin's Press, 1986.

MILITARY AND HUMAN RIGHTS

Historical Background

Rules of armed conflict have existed for centuries, if not millennia. Medieval European knights along with warrior castes such as the Samurai of Japan had their rules of chivalry and codes of honor that applied to battle situations. Generals and kings saw the practical benefits of rules limiting unnecessary killing and property destruction, since the victors benefited from those who remained alive to work the land and businesses that survived the war intact. The modern rules of human rights in the context of armed conflict are called "international humanitarian law" (IHL). They developed primarily in Europe and have spread to the rest of the world. Contemporary international law divides IHL into two sets of rules: those justifying the initiation of war, known in Latin as *jus ad bellum,* and those governing the conduct of war, *jus in bello.*

Jus ad Bellum

Christian theologians maintained that countries should engage in just wars only. The seventeenth-century Dutch philosopher Hugo Grotius wrote that for a war to be just, it must be initiated by a legitimate sovereign for a just cause after more peaceful alternatives have failed. The amount of force employed should not exceed that which is needed for the justified objective, and the war should be undertaken with peace as its ultimate goal. In the twentieth century, various theorists maintained that the war against fascism, national liberation struggles against colonial powers, and humanitarian interventions to protect subjugated people against tyrannical rulers constituted just wars.

The United Nations Charter confines just wars to self-defense and humanitarian interventions, initiated by the Security Council. The Charter prohibits the acquisition of foreign territory by force. Charter Article Two states that, "All members shall refrain in their international relations from the threat or the use of force against the territorial integrity or political independence of any state, or in any other manner inconsistent with the purposes of the United Nations." Article 51 holds that, "Nothing in the present Charter shall impair the inherent right of individual or collective self-defense if an armed attack occurs against a Member of the United Nations." In 1991, an American-led armed force with a UN Security Council mandate employed military might to oust Iraqi forces from their illegal occupation of Kuwait, and in 1999 North Atlantic Treaty Organization forces, without a UN mandate, bombed Serbia to force the Belgrade regime to stop ethnic cleansing of Albanians from Kosovo. Both of these operations were justified by the principle of humanitarian intervention, since they were engaged in to protect the human rights of subjugated peoples.

Customary Jus in Bello

Once war has been initiated, its conduct is subject to the rules of armed conflict or *jus in bello.* This branch of IHL relies on treaty law as well as customary law. The latter consists of those customary principles of war that the leaders of most states regard as legally obligatory, even though they may violate them in practice.

The customary international law principle of proportionality concerns the interrelationship between weapons, targets, and resulting damage. In general, a warring party should attack military targets with weapons whose destructive power does not significantly exceed that which is necessary for the legitimate objective. Attacks violate the principle of proportionality and human rights if they kill or injure civilians or damage civilian property to a degree that is excessive in relation to the anticipated military advantage of the attack. Under most conditions, the use of nuclear weapons would violate IHL because such weapons would cause civilian casualties and environmental damage disproportionate to the value of the military targets they destroy.

The principle of discrimination obligates warring parties to carefully discriminate military from nonmilitary targets, both in their selection and aiming of weapons. Area bombardments that by their nature do not distinguish between military and civilian targets are prohibited. The use of biological or chemical weapons, whose lethal power can be carried away in the atmosphere to unintended areas and victims, are also illegal. Germany's World War II rocket attacks on London and the United States' atomic bombing of Nagasaki and Hiroshima all involved indiscriminate weapons and excessive civilian deaths, thereby violating the principle of discrimination as well as other IHL principles.

The principle of military necessity requires that attacks be confined to those non-civilian targets that contribute directly to the enemy's military strength. Combatants are justified in attacking targets whose nature, location, purpose, or use makes an effective contribution to military action and whose total or partial destruction, capture, or neutralization, in the circumstances of the time, offers a definite military advantage. Legitimate military targets include: an enemy's armed forces, barracks and installations, war ministries, munitions and fuel dumps, vehicles, airfields, rocket launch ramps, and naval bases. Legitimate infrastructural targets include those communication facilities, railway lines, roads, bridges, tunnels, and canals that are of fundamental military importance. Legitimate military-industrial targets include factories producing weapons, transportation vehicles, communications equipment, or other products for military purposes. Generally, libraries, museums, concert halls, hospitals, civilian homes, schools, and cultural monuments are not targets justified by military necessity. Attacks on them violate IHL.

Related to the principle of military necessity is the principle prohibiting the use of weapons that cause unnecessary suffering or superfluous injury. In 1869 a number of European powers issued the St. Petersburg Declaration, which established the principle prohibiting the employment of weapons that cause unnecessary suffering. The European leaders reasoned that the only legitimate object during war is to weaken the enemy's military forces by disabling the greatest possible number of its military. Therefore, weapons that unnecessarily aggravate the sufferings of disabled soldiers are contrary to the laws of humanity. Poisoned bullets, barbed bayonets, and dumdum bullets designed to flatten on impact are generally regarded as prohibited because they cause unnecessary suffering and superfluous injury. This principle also prohibits the use of explosive projectiles filled with undetectable, clear glass fragments that make soldiers' wounds more difficult to treat.

Twentieth-Century Tribunals and Humanitarian Law Codes

While World War II was still raging, the Allies began a series of meetings to plan the creation of a post–World War II tribunal to try major war criminals of the European Axis powers. Meeting in London in August 1945, US, British, French, and Soviet representatives reached an agreement establishing the International Military Tribunal (IMT) at Nuremberg. Article 6 of the IMT Charter listed the following acts as IHL crimes falling within the jurisdiction of the Tribunal and for which there would be individual responsibility:

1. Crimes against peace: namely, planning, preparation, initiation, or waging of a war of aggression, or a war in violation of international treaties, agreements, or assurances;

2. War crimes: namely, violations of the laws and customs of war … [including] murder, ill-treatment or deportation to slave labor or for any other purpose of civilian population of or in occupied territory, murder or ill treatment of prisoners of war or persons on the seas, killing of hostages, plunder of public or private property, wanton destruction of cities, towns, or villages, or devastation not justified by military necessity; and

3. Crimes against humanity: namely, murder, extermination, enslavement, deportation, and other inhumane acts committed against any civilian population, before or during the war, or persecutions on political, racial, or religious grounds in execution of or in connection with

any crime within the jurisdiction of the Tribunal, whether or not in violation of the domestic law of the country where perpetrated.

The first two categories of violations concerned international relations, specifically war between states. The second category was based on the Hague Convention of 1907, signed by a number of European states.

The third category—crimes against humanity—attacked the very heart of state sovereignty by defining gross human rights violations against citizens by their own governing powers as international crimes subject to universal jurisdiction. Crimes against humanity covered atrocities committed by Germans against German citizens as well as against others. This, of course, included the Nazis' treatment of Jews, Gypsies, homosexuals, and other "undesirables" in concentration camps, factories, and so forth. Prior to the IMT, a government's violations of its own citizens' human rights, with few exceptions, was considered internal affairs not covered by international humanitarian law.

The IMT also firmly established the principle of individual responsibility for gross human rights violations. In its 1946 "Opinion and Judgment" the Court wrote: "Crimes against international law are committed by men, not by abstract entities, and only by punishing individuals who commit such crimes can the provisions of international law be enforced." The IMT had no provisions for securing indemnity for victims.

In the first and most famous of the IMT trials, twenty-two notorious Nazi figures—including Herman Wilhelm Göring—were prosecuted. Hundreds of other Germans were prosecuted by the Allied occupying powers under Control Council Law Ten. US General Douglas MacArthur, the Supreme Allied Commander in Japan following the war, created the Tokyo Tribunal, modeled after the IMT, to prosecute senior Japanese officials.

The Interim Years

After World War II, the International Committee of the Red Cross, a private organization headquartered in Switzerland, codified much of then-existing IHL in the four Geneva Conventions of 1949 and their Additional Protocols of 1977. Together, the 1949 Geneva Conventions list the human rights duties that warring parties have toward the wounded and sick on land or at sea, prisoners of war, and civilians. The Conventions contain a list of grave breaches of IHL that

includes: willful killing; torture or inhuman treatment (including medical experiments); willfully causing great suffering or serious injury to body or health; extensive destruction and appropriation of property not justified by military necessity and carried out unlawfully and wantonly; compelling a prisoner of war or civilian to serve in the forces of the hostile power; willfully depriving a prisoner of war or protected civilian of the rights of a fair and regular trial; unlawful deportation or transfer of a protected civilian; unlawful confinement of a protected civilian; and taking of hostages.

Additional Protocol I of 1977 expanded the list of grave breaches to also include: making civilians and non-defended localities the object or inevitable victims of attack; the perfidious use of the Red Cross or Red Crescent emblem; transfer of an occupying power of parts of its population to occupied territory; unjustifiable delays in repatriation of POWs; apartheid; attack on historic monuments; and depriving protected persons of a fair trial. Under the Geneva Conventions and Additional Protocol I, states must prosecute persons accused of grave breaches or hand them over to a state willing to do so. Protocol II of 1977 addresses human rights duties and violations in the context of internal war.

Countries that have ratified the Geneva Conventions are required to instruct their military personnel about the Conventions' contents. For this purpose, the US Army uses Field Manual 27-10: The Law of Land Warfare.

UN War Crimes Tribunals

During the fifty years after Nuremberg, an estimated 250 armed conflicts occurred, causing approximately 170 million human casualties. Due to the Cold War division within the UN Security Council between the Western and Communist camps, it failed to address IHL violations in a unified way. Consequently, until the 1990s, political and military leaders responsible for war crimes, genocide, and crimes against humanity generally enjoyed impunity. Eventually, with the collapse of the Soviet Union and the specter of atrocities on the doorstep of Western Europe, the Security Council acted creatively and in unison.

There were many astonished by the brutality of the conflicts in the former Yugoslavia that erupted in June 1991 and intensified thereafter. As part of the UN response to the conflicts, the Security Council created the International Criminal Tribunal for the Former Yugoslavia (ICTY) under Chapter VII of the UN Charter. By utilizing Chapter VII, the Security

Council obliged all UN member states to cooperate with the Tribunal and to honor any lawful requests it makes for assistance under its statute.

The ICTY differs from the post–World War II Nuremberg and Tokyo tribunals. Unlike its predecessors, the ICTY does not have the competence to adjudicate crimes against peace. Its jurisdiction covers war crimes, genocide, and crimes against humanity. Secondly, whereas its predecessors dealt only with IHL violations associated with an international armed conflict, the ICTY is empowered to adjudicate IHL violations committed in the course of conflicts within or between the states of the former Yugoslavia. Thirdly, the ICTY is not the organ of a particular group of victor states, but an organ of the international community and consists of judges from many different countries, regionally disbursed and representing different legal traditions.

The ICTY was authorized to apply the established rules of international humanitarian law, which bind all states. These include the laws applicable in situations of armed conflict as embodied in: the four Geneva Conventions of 1949; the Hague Convention of 1907; the Convention on the Prevention and Punishment of the Crime of Genocide of 1948; and the Charter of the International Military Tribunal of 1945.

Articles Two to Five of the ICTY Statute empower the Tribunal to prosecute civilian persons accused of ordering or committing grave breaches of the four Geneva Conventions, violating the laws or customs of war, committing genocide, or being responsible for crimes against humanity.

Statute Article Three, "Violations of the Laws and Customs of War," is based on the Annex to the 1907 Hague Convention, which was subsequently reaffirmed by Article 6(b) of the Nuremberg Charter. Its list of violations includes: the employment of poisonous or other weapons calculated to cause unnecessary suffering; wanton destruction or devastation of cities, towns, and villages not justified by military necessity; attack on or bombardment of undefended towns, villages, dwellings, or buildings; seizure, destruction, or willful damage of religious, charitable, scientific, art, or educational institutions or of historic monuments; and plunder of public or private property.

Article Four of the ICTY Statute replicates Articles Two and Three of the Convention on the Prevention and Punishment of the Crime of Genocide (1948) and defines genocide as any of the following acts committed with intent to destroy, in whole or in part, a national, ethnic, racial, or religious group: killing group members; causing serious bodily or mental harm to group members; deliberately inflicting on the group conditions calculated to bring about its complete or partial physical destruction; imposing measures intended to prevent birth within the group; and forcibly transferring children to another group. Persons who commit genocide or who attempt, conspire, or incite others to commit genocide are punishable.

Statute Article Five, "Crimes against Humanity," follows the Nuremberg Charter. It empowers the Tribunal to prosecute persons responsible for the following crimes against any civilian population committed during an international or internal armed conflict: murder; extermination; enslavement; deportation; imprisonment; torture; rape; persecutions on political, racial and religious grounds; and other inhumane acts. The crimes constituting "ethnic cleansing," a term closely associated with the conflicts in the former Yugoslavia, are covered by Articles 2–5.

The ICTY, located in The Hague, the Netherlands, has been actively prosecuting Serbs, Croats, and Bosnian Muslims suspected of IHL violations.

In 1994 Rwanda erupted into one of the most appalling cases of genocide that the world had witnessed since World War II as radical Hutu attempted to eliminate moderate Hutu and Rwanda's entire Tutsi population. The UN Security Council, having just created an international criminal tribunal for humanitarian law violators in the European states of the former Yugoslavia, decided it could do no less for African Rwanda. Consequently, it created the UN Criminal Tribunal for Rwanda, modeled after the earlier one for the former Yugoslavia. The Security Council authorized the ICTR to apply existing international humanitarian law applicable to non-international armed conflict. The humanitarian law included in the Tribunal's statute consists of crimes against humanity (as defined by the Nuremberg Charter), genocide, Article Three Common to the 1949 Geneva Conventions, and Additional Protocol II.

ICTR Statute Article Three, "Crimes against Humanity," is based on Article 6(c) of the Nuremberg Charter, but it eliminates the requirement that such crimes must have been committed "before or during the war." Consequently, crimes against humanity do not need a war nexus.

Article Four of the statute empowers the ICTR to prosecute persons committing or ordering to be committed serious violations of Article Three common to the four Geneva Conventions of 1949 and of the Additional Protocol II thereto of 1977. These violations include: (a) violence to life, health, and physical or mental well-being of persons, in particular murder, torture, or mutilation; (b) collective punishments; (c) taking of hostages; (d) acts of terrorism; (e) outrages upon personal dignity, in particular humiliating and degrading treatment, rape, enforced prostitution, and any form of indecent assault; (f) pillage; g) sentences or executions rendered extra-judicially or without due process; and (h) threats to commit any of the foregoing acts.

The ICTR, located in Arusha, Tanzania, has successfully prosecuted a number of high-ranking Hutu officials responsible for the mass murder of fellow Rwandan citizens. Neither the ICTY nor the ICTR can compensate victims for injuries, medical expenses, pain and suffering, destroyed property, rehabilitation, and so forth. However, both can order the return of any property and proceeds acquired by criminal conduct to their rightful owners.

The International Criminal Court

On July 16, 1998, after fifty years of effort, the international community endorsed the creation of a permanent International Criminal Court (ICC) by a vote of 120 to 7 with 21 abstentions. This historic step took place in Rome at a United Nations diplomatic conference. Only Libya, Iraq, Qatar, Israel, Yemen, China, and the United States voted no.

The Court is designed to bring to justice those who commit the most serious IHL violations, including genocide, war crimes, crimes against humanity, and aggression (to be defined later by a special law commission). It also criminalizes the recruitment of children under sixteen years into militias. In order for the ICC to become a reality, its statute, officially entitled the "Rome Statute of the International Criminal Court," must be ratified by sixty states.

The ICC's jurisdiction will extend to IHL violations committed in both international and internal armed conflicts. Because the ICC will have jurisdiction over the citizens of many more states than any of its predecessors, its potential for contributing to the cessation of IHL violations, achieving justice, contributing to the reconciliation of the parties, and deterring future humanitarian law violations is greater.

The Rome Statute is also designed to secure indemnity/compensation for victims. Article 79 directs the Assembly of States Parties to the Statute to create a trust fund for victims and their families. It also authorizes the ICC to order money and property collected through fines and forfeitures to be transferred to this fund. Article 75 directs the ICC to establish principles for determining the amount of restitution, compensation, and rehabilitation it may award victims and their families. The ICC may assess convicted persons the cost of the above or it may authorize awards from the Trust Fund.

Like its predecessors, the ICTY and ICTR, the ICC is designed to guarantee the due process and other rights of victims and defendants as recommended in the most recent human rights conventions. Hence, it should be a model court for the protection of human rights of victims and defendants.

Conclusion

Some IHL violations most probably have been committed in most wars. Modern democratic states appear to regard IHL more seriously than others. IHL violations are quite common during military conflicts within or between undemocratic countries that are afflicted with severe economic problems and intense competition for resources. During such conflicts, certain unscrupulous political or military leaders convince at least some of their followers that the enemy's inhumanity justifies the worst kind of treatment.

Advocates of IHL within the militaries of technologically advanced states claim that modern weapons that can be more precisely aimed at legitimate military targets, markedly diminish the number of civilian casualties and IHL violations. As recent military conflicts have shown, however, even so-called "smart bombs" can kill civilians, in violation of IHL, when they are negligently deployed or deployed with inaccurate intelligence.

PAUL J. MAGNARELLA

See also Military and Civilian Control; Military and Development

References and Further Reading

Bell, Christine. *Peace Agreements and Human Rights.* Oxford, UK: Oxford University Press, 2000.
Best, Geoffrey. *War and Law Since 1945.* Oxford, UK: Clarendon Press, 1994.
Cassese, Antonio, et al. *The Rome Statute of the International Criminal Court.* Oxford, UK: Oxford University Press, 2002.
Detter, Ingrid. *The Law of War.* Cambridge, UK: Cambridge University Press, 2000.
Magnarella, Paul J. *Justice in Africa: Rwanda's Genocide, Its Courts, and the UN Criminal Tribunal.* Aldershot, UK: Ashgate, 2000.
Robertson, Geoffrey. *Crimes against Humanity: The Struggle for Global Justice.* New York: New Press, 1999.
Steiner, Henry J. and Philip Alston. *International Human/ Rights in Context.* Oxford, UK: Oxford University Press, 2000.

MILOŠEVIĆ, SLOBODAN

One of the most influential and notorious politicians of the 1990s, the Serbian Communist Party leader, president of Serbia and of the Federal Republic of Yugoslavia for a decade, Slobodan Milošević is a controversial figure. To many Serbs he embodies the modern vision of Greater Serbia; to others he is simply "the butcher of the Balkans." Milošević presents himself as a moderate nationalist technocrat. His personality is marked by stubbornness and conservativism.

Milošević was born August 20, 1941, in Pozarevac, Serbia, to a father who was a teacher of religion and a mother who was an ardent communist. Milošević's father left the family when he was in elementary school; he committed suicide in 1962. Milošević's mother also killed herself, in 1974.

Milošević graduated with a law degree in 1964 and started his career in the Socialist Party of Yugoslavia. He achieved Belgrade party leadership between 1984 and 1986, but remained an obscure technocrat until 1987 when, on the six hundredth anniversary of the battle of Kosovo, at which the medieval Serbian statehood was crushed by the Turks, he gave a seminal speech in front of a 1-million-strong crowd and became the symbol of historical Serbian resistance.

His rise to power as chief secretary of the Serbian Communist Party was supported by his mentor and godfather, Ivan Stambolić, who became president of Serbia in September 1987, on the fermentation ground of suppressed but growing nationalism in the fragile country. However, in December of that year, Milošević forced his former mentor's resignation from office. In 2000 Stambolic was kidnapped and murdered.

By the end of the 1980s, Milošević became the speaker of the dominant Serbian stratum of the Yugoslav society, who were angered by the marginalisation of Serbians under Tito and who opposed the federal autonomy granted in 1974 for the provinces Voivodina and Kosovo, which contained large ethnic Hungarian and Albanian minority populations. Milošević pursued a policy of ethnic homogenization as well as conservation of the territorial integrity and unity of Yugoslavia. His first action of Serbian ethnic dominance in 1989 after being elected president of Serbia was the abolition of the autonomy of Voivodina and Kosovo.

Acting against the tide of economic and political changes, he clung adamantly to the socialist economic model. Despite proclaiming political pluralism, he maintained the state-directed economy. Milošević managed to maintain a low profile in the media, yet preserve the nationalist and populist bases of his power.

The Creator of Greater Serbia

After the collapse of the Soviet bloc, each new nation tried to redefine itself and its borders. The Serbians were frustrated not to have achieved a Greater Serbia. They considered themselves the core element of the Federal Republic of Yugoslavia, fostered by their relative majority status in population, and the Slavic resistance against Turks and Germans in the Balkans. They felt it was time to convert Serbian ethnic dominance, under the guise of Pan-Slavism, into the presence of Greater Serbia.

In January 1990, Milošević worked to reduce the powers of the republics, which would empower the relative majority population, the Serbs, causing the final rift in the Yugoslav Communist Party, the Croatian and Slovenian delegations leaving the congress. Soon afterward he founded the Socialist Party of Serbia and orchestrated the transformation of Serbia into a republic, whose first president he became after the elections of 1990.

In response to Serbian threats of hegemony led by Milošević, Slovenia and Croatia seceded from the federation in June 1991, followed in September by Macedonia and in March 1992 by Bosnia and Herzegovina. The secession was unrecognized by the Serbian-dominated federal leadership and the Yugoslav army went to war to crush it.

The Serb minorities in Croatia and Bosnia demanded that their sections of the territories remain in Yugoslavia. On the incitement of Milošević, the Serbs of Croatia (580,000 or 11% of the population) started organizing their own secessionist state, called the Serbian Republic of Krajina. It encompassed the Serbian majority enclaves and one-third of the Croatian territory. The Yugoslav army fought to secure the Serbian majority enclaves of Croatia and Bosnia, the latter with a 1.6 million or 32% Serbian population, demanding independence if their annexation to Serbia would not be possible.

The disintegration of Yugoslavia led to the collapse of the internal markets and to hyper-inflation aggravated by the arms embargo, which turned into a general embargo against Serbia. In 1992 the inflation rate reached 8,700% and the war efforts led to an 11% decline of the gross domestic product (GDP). At the height of the war, financed through hyper-inflation, the inflation rate reached to a staggering 300,000% in 1993, leading to currency reform in 1994. In spite of a new convertible dinar linked to the strongest European currency, the German mark, an even greater recession of −19% followed, during the Kosovo war.

Increasing international outrage about ethnic cleansing as well as economic recession led Milošević to the conviction that the creation of Greater Serbia had to be postponed, but that an advantageous peace could be negotiated in Bosnia and win also the sympathy of the West. In 1995, Milošević began presenting himself as the moderate, pro-western leader, and therefore a suitable treaty counterpart to Bosnian Serb leaders. He shifted to a cautious approach toward Serbian unification. On behalf of the Bosnian Serbs he had negotiated an advantageous peace treaty with Franjo Tudjman on behalf of the Croats and with Alija Izetbegovic, the Islamist leader of Bosnia, under US pressure. Under the Dayton Agreement, Milošević secured 49% of the territory for the 32% Serbian community. By bringing an end to the war, he was credited in the West as a pillar of stability, while hard-line Serbians considered him a traitor to the Greater Serbia ideal.

The West had supported Milošević's regime following the overturned local elections of 1996, despite democratic opposition. Later, in 1997, Milošević recognized the opposition victory, but he retained his power in the form of federal presidency of Serbia and Montenegro. In 1998, his regime fell from the West's good graces following the start of a hard-line Serbian crackdown on Kosovo Albanians.

The Savior of Kosovo

After "losing" the Croatian war due to international pressure and obtaining only a moderate victory in Bosnia, the Serbian nationalist anger turned inward against the loudest minority voice, that of ethnic Albanians looking for self-determination and eventual unification with Albania. In 1998 the so-far peaceful resistance of the Albanian majority turned into an armed uprising, which led to brutal Serbian army offensives and police reprisals.

The Albanians called for international intervention as the campaign caused their mass exodus—840,000 Albanians fleeing to neighboring countries. The West, fed up with aggressive nationalism and intent on avoiding a new Balkan war, called in NATO forces, which engaged in air strikes against the Federal Republic of Yugoslavia from March to June of 1999. This resulted in Serbia's subsequent military withdrawal from Kosovo in spite of a desperate attempt of the Serbian parliament to drive Russia into the conflict by declaring union with it. Milošević's popularity initially increased during the bombings, but then began to fall.

The Downfall

Yugoslavia held presidential elections in September 2000. Despite Milošević's confidence that he would

win, the opposition received a majority of the votes. Milošević refused to acknowledge the election results, leading to mass demonstrations and, consequently, his regime's downfall. Vojislav Kostunica became president and Zoran Djindic, a pro-western liberal reformer, became prime minister. Djindic had Milošević arrested in 2001 on charges of abuse of power and regime-linked corruption. On June 28, 2001, as a result of an ultimatum by the US Congress that made Milošević's prosecution a condition of economic aid to Serbia, Milošević was extradited to the War Tribunal in The Hague, where he was charged with genocide and war crimes.

Laszlo Kocsis

See also Balkan Wars of the 1990s; Ethnic Conflicts: Central and Eastern Europe; Ethnicity: Impact on Politics and Society; Serbia; Socialist Economic Model; State-Directed Economy; Territorial Disputes; Tudjman, Franjo; Yugoslavia

References and Further Reading

Bujosevic, D. and I. Radovanovic. *The Fall of Milosevic*. New York: Palgrave Macmillan, 2003.

Cohen, L. *The Serpent in the Bosom—The Rise and Fall of Slobodan Milosevic*. Boulder, CO: Westview Press, 2001.

LeBor, A. *Milosevic: A Biography*. London: Bloomsbury, 2002.

Nikolic, M. *The Tragedy of Yugoslavia: The Rise, the Reign, and the Fall of Slobodan Milosevic*. Baben-Baden, Germany: Nomos, 2002.

Ramet, S. *Balkan Babel: The Disintegration of Yugoslavia from the Death of Tito to the Fall of Milosevic*. Boulder, CO: Westview Press, 2002.

Sell, L. *Slobodan Milosevic and the Destruction of Yugoslavia*. Durham, NC: Duke University Press, 2002.

MINORITIES/DISCRIMINATION

Where discrimination and intra-state conflicts are being discussed, there is often talk of minorities. Underneath the global structure of currently 193 states there are probably some ten thousand ethnic, national, religious, linguistic, and other minorities. In addition to these "old minorities," thousands of migrant communities constitute "new minorities" in a very large number of states. To place the content of ethnic, national, or religious conflicts on a par with that of minority conflicts is, in many cases, mistaken. The terms minorities and discrimination seem in need of elucidation; the main frameworks for them are the nation state and the international community at large. Unfortunately there are only a few studies that compare various regional and local attempts at dispute resolution within the framework of state policies on minorities and nationalities. The states' interaction with the minorities in their territory range, in ascending order, from racial segregation; through unilateral assimilation and ideas about melting pots (social and racial amalgamation); to purely formally equal integration; to the replacement of unitary-cum-homogenist ideas with the notion of "diversity in unity"; and, ultimately, to inclusion, respect, protection, and encouragement for otherness on an equal basis—for example, within the framework of multicultural tolerance and affirmative action, and for ethnic and national minorities in the form of autonomy arrangements, free association, or federalism. More far-reaching demands by the latter minorities, which claim the status of nations or nationalities, point to structural differences between minority and nationality policy. Generally, the term "minorities" is applicable in most countries of Asia-Pacific, the Americas, and Europe. In most of Africa the term doesn't make sense since there is no national or ethnic majority; this reflects the fact that Africa is culturally and ethnically the most heterogeneous continent.

The concept of minority, and the reality, in which minorities are created and obliged to live, point up a variety of facets that are often ignored in the debate about minority, religious, or ethno-national conflicts. The most important seems to be that the concept of minority is essentially ascriptive in nature: as a rule, it is the state that decides what makes a minority and to which circle of people the term will apply. The state itself is often dominated by, or in the ownership of, a particular ethnic group that defines itself as a majority but often is not one in demographic terms. National censuses and demographic statistics are hot issues and often just one more battlefield for all actors concerned. Statistics are usually presented according to predetermined political conditions. In extreme cases, an ethnic group apostrophized as a minority is only a political minority, measured in terms of power, while demographically it constitutes the majority (as in the case with the Oromo in Ethiopia or the Mayan peoples in Guatemala). The case of large transnational minority peoples (such as Berbers in a dozen northern African counties or Kurds in five West Asian countries) seems similar.

In the international discourse about the minority question, the dual concept of national minorities has come into increasing use in recent years. This is a consequence of the increased attention that has been paid to the contentious minorities issue in post–Cold War Europe and the Former Soviet Union; but it also means that a compromise formula has been found, ostensibly bridging or unifying the varying usages in Eastern and Western Europe.

The concept of minorities requires elucidation for a variety of other reasons as well. Many nationalities that find their rights curtailed by states, or are harassed, discriminated against, threatened, or persecuted by them, do not regard themselves as minorities; they do not share the socio-psychological characteristics of classic minorities—on the contrary, some even cultivate a robust nationalism.

Forms and Definition of Discrimination

Discrimination means that the dominant ethnic or national majority mostly regards national minorities as subordinate segments of the state's society, whereby it may deny them basic rights and freedoms; impede their social, cultural, and economic development; and obstruct political representation and participation. Minorities have special phenotypic and cultural peculiarities ascribed to them. These kinds of ascribed markers are looked down on by those segments of the state society that are dominant (either in terms of power or numerically). Some traditional societies, among them most indigenous peoples, derive their distinctiveness and reproduce themselves on the basis of their non-integration into market economies; in a few cases they have developed a whole series of autonomous, self-supporting modes of production. But many more minorities are vulnerable and find no way of escaping discrimination.

There is a vast scope of different forms of discrimination against minorities. The victims are usually members of a multitude of non-dominant groups. Minorities exist in almost every state, only their composition between indigenous minorities (national or language minorities), religious communities of belief and origin, diverse migrant communities, asylum-seekers and refugee populations, and so forth, and their proportion of the resident population may change from country to country. Specifically targeted are undocumented migrant workers, Muslim communities in Islam-phobic environments, (semi)nomadic peoples, and women of minority groups. Gender, ethnicity, belief, and illegality are factors that profoundly contribute to appalling situations of multiple discriminatory practices.

Discrimination against minorities has structural features that are generated by the way economic, political, and social institutions operate. Structural racism categorizes and marks people, makes minority members visible, and denies such people equal access to jobs, education, medical facilities, social welfare, leisure, and habitation. Governments, local and state administrations, the education system, domestic companies and transnational corporations, and (not least) the media are part of the apparatuses that form a *dispositif* against different categories of minorities; these are the forces producing "others" and "aliens" and shaping public attitudes toward others, such as national minorities, and aliens, such as the new minorities of migrants, refugees, asylum seekers, and trafficked people.

The worst form of discrimination is the one based on what is perceived as race or colour. As a rule, racist discrimination in the developed world is not perceived as the splitting up of a population but as hostility toward an alien group of others (as opposed to its own breed of us-self); the terms of racialization and scapegoating, coined in a decade-old debate by social scientists, is essential to understand the nature of new domestic racism that replaced the old colonial racism. With the increase of new minorities in the past decades, racists found it easier to construct scapegoats and to blame aliens and minorities for socioeconomic losses. In the Americas the legacies of racial discrimination against Native Americans, Blacks, and Hispanics are still powerful and destructive; compared with that, the new Asian minorities suffer less discrimination due to above-average income and education. There is an increasing tendency in the developing world for post-colonial states to claim as citizens or to reject a number of nationalities, such as ethnic minorities and/or indigenous peoples.

Globalization does not exclude fragmentation, as exhibited by the global trend toward an increase in intra-state conflicts. While discrimination toward ethnic minorities was, in empirical-cum-historical terms, one of the most dangerous sources of conflicts and wars both in the post-colonial wars of Africa (since the period of decolonization) and, since 1989–1990, in the former socialist states—with two-thirds of current wars being susceptible to "ethnic" interpretation—violence against minority groups again became a reality in Europe, in its eastern and southeastern parts, in Yugoslavia and the Caucasus. If we take the examples of Bosnia (Serbs versus Croats) or Rwanda (Hutu versus Tutsi) and compare these with objective attributes (see next section), we will find very little or no ethnic distinction at all. Often ethnicization and racialisation occur on the basis of minor differences. The decisive factors are not the perceived differences but the interest of political elites to use them as resources for their power struggle and as a source for mobilizing the mobs. Those conflict types suitable to ethnic and racial interpretation—with ethnicization or racialisation as mobilizing forces—seemed to grow fastest in the South (underdeveloped), although they have been prominent for quite some time, and appear again in the North (developed), as organized violence against minorities, racial and ethnic discrimination, or "ethnic cleansing."

In fall 2001 Rwanda's parliament passed a law imposing prison terms and a fine on any person practicing discrimination and segregation. This is one of the lessons drawn from the devastating 1994 genocide. The new law aims at enforcing positive discrimination in favour of vulnerable groups like the Batwa minority (1% of the populations of both Rwanda and Burundi). The law gives a comprehensive legal definition of discrimination as "any act, utterance or writing aimed at depriving a person or group of persons, their rights, by reason of sex, ethnicity, age, race, color, opinion, religion, nationality or origin."

Minorities and Ethnic Communities

The term "ethnic groups" is used as a technical term; according to linguists there are some 6,500 ethnic core groups worldwide. The general supposition is that religions, like nationalities, generate a transcendent identity-forming link, whereas ethnicity, though identity forming, has a divisive effect. This supposition does not seem to fit all cases. Connections (or rather conflicts) between religion, nationality, and ethnicity ought not to be denied. One of several possible approaches to the subject focuses on attributes based on clusters of special features or social specializations, which are both seen as constituting "ethnic markers."

Ethnic markers are only relevant within the framework of inter-ethnic relations. Often they only become a major focus of perception when situations of conflict arise. The attributes of an ethnic community include, as a minimum, a self-reproducing community with a name, a culture, a distinct language, a memory, and solidarity between its members. These attributes by no means constitute a definitive checklist; they are, rather, an attempt to get closer to the problem of ethnicity, the individual elements of which need to be examined more closely and be defined in detail for each concrete instance. An ethnic community in the position of a non-dominant group may be regarded as a national minority or nationality—a nation without its own state—if, despite the claims to dominance and sovereignty from outside, it constitutes a distinct space of communication and interaction, i.e., it is able to form or maintain a public sphere of its own; it has a particular mode of production and life identifiable with it, and is able to reproduce it; it maintains some form of political organization; it has settled an identifiable area of land (more than a neighbourhood) or a demarcated territory; it is distinctive, i.e., its members identify themselves or are identified by others as members of this particular community.

In the case of migrant communities, several of these attributes do apply while others are obviously obsolete due to changed life conditions. Ethnicized or racialised characteristics are only relevant within the framework of inter-ethnic relations and it is primarily in conflict situations that they become a major focus of perception. The same characteristics—particular sociocultural practices, for example—may be totally unimportant in various situations of interaction, but in a different context they may suddenly acquire huge significance. For example, skin colour and other phenotypic features are of secondary importance in most societies of the Southern hemisphere; but in Western societies, physical characteristics are one of the main distinguishing features.

Ways to Combat Discrimination

Combating discrimination, racism, and destructive ethnicization and the prevention of violence are political imperatives for the twenty-first century. The task to explore policy strategies and measures to address these problems starts with rethinking definitions and core concepts. Efforts to accommodate ethnocultural difference are an essential part of anti-racist strategies; they have conflict-preventive force and contribute to the long-term transformation of intrastate conflicts. The main topics are laws against discrimination, cultural and other autonomies, collective rights, self-governance, and nationality policies. The political-cum-humanitarian concern is to ensure that all possible means of avoiding violent forms of multi-ethnic interaction are exploited, strengthened, and made more attractive to the majority populations.

An important approach in improving mutual relations between majorities and minorities is the policy option that discrimination toward non-dominant groups should be outlawed and that some measure of temporary and targeted affirmative action should be institutionalized. However, it comes as no small surprise to realize that only a third of the respondents in Eurobarometer polls (regularly made by the EU) agree with outlawing discrimination, though 60% were classified as more or less tolerant. Nevertheless, in 2000, an EU Council directive incorporated the principle of racial equality and a second directive established a general framework for equal treatment in employment and occupation.

As a rule, the victims of discrimination and xenophobia are members from among a multitude of "minorities-at-risk" (Gurr 2000). When talking about discrimination, most West Europeans first think of migrant communities (especially Muslim communities) as victims, while people in the Americas, Eastern Europe, Asia, and Africa think of indigenous, religious, and ethnic minorities; historic nationalities; and other non-dominant groups. But even in the enlarging European Union, the population of indigenous non-dominant groups is numerically exceeding that of migrant communities by far. Many minorities are either permanently confronted with everyday discrimination and racism (for example, the sad examples of 15 million Roma all over Europe, 30 million Afro-Americans, and 180 million Dalit of India), or they are discriminated upon in different ways by the respective demographic majorities or otherwise dominant groups. Anti-discrimination policies ought to address the rejection of non-dominant groups by large national-chauvinists groups among the majority populations in many states.

The focus should be on activities that are essential to combat discrimination of manifold minorities. Among others, a list of essentials to such policies has to include combating and outlawing militant chauvinism and racism. The conception of new policies for preventing and combating discrimination follows strategies that are targeting its structural, institutionalized, and organized forms. The political-cum-humanitarian concern to find ways of avoiding structural and direct, personal forms of discrimination leads on to the questions of how ethnic and cultural difference can be acknowledged and recognized; how destructive forms of interaction between states and communities and between majorities and minorities can be prevented; how violent, militant forms of racism and xenophobia can be effectively combated; and which institutions, legal measures, and policies are most appropriate for these purposes.

Structural Prevention of Conflicts Between Majorities and Minorities

Regarding forms of structural prevention of troubles, the word "structural" implies that new frameworks and institutions are created to avert discrimination and possible direct violence and reduce structural violence, manly all forms of discrimination against non-dominant groups. Johan Galtung developed the concept of structural violence in the 1970s, based on his path-breaking distinction between direct personal violence and structural violence; Galtung also reflected on cultural violence, e.g., values that promote/justify violence and superiority complexes that result in aggressive attitudes. Structural prevention aims at ending discrimination, repression, injustice, and racism, which are ingrained in many state policies and which are also inherent part of the cultural attitudes held by many dominant groups.

However, there are practical problems politicians face in promoting preventive measures and policies—beyond rhetoric. When it comes to implementing declared policies, the difficulties are threefold: the unspectacular and long-term character of many such measures makes them not really attractive if quick results are required, the difficulty in measuring their effectiveness, and a number of rather diverse institutions—measures and policies have preventive character but they often remain unrelated or only partially implemented.

In preventing discrimination against minority groups there are no easy solutions. The great diversity of cultural and political characteristics exhibited by different types of minorities demand different regulatory mechanisms. Steps to mitigate and pre-empt destructive forms of interaction between majorities and minorities should be prioritised. The classic solutions for indigenous minorities range from cultural autonomy, special rights, and territorial self-governance, to forms of de facto sovereignty. Protection of ethnic and national minorities by means of a variety of autonomy arrangements did not begin until the twentieth century, triggered by a worsening of the so-called "minorities problem" in Europe, as a result of revolutions and the regroupings in the wake of two World Wars.

Account should be taken of positive policies of a number of multinational states when it comes to looking for methods of preventing and dealing with latent or open ethno-national conflicts. Many states have been able to pursue active and successful policies of prevention of troubles by making concessions and negotiating offers involving elements of reactive minority protection and proactive nationality policy, in Europe most prominently by granting home rule for the Faeroese and the Inuit in the Kingdom of Denmark from 1948 onward. Others have—often with limited success—used similar offers to try and resolve armed conflicts that have already escalated (for example, the regionalization and granting of autonomy to Basques, Catalonians, Andalusians, and Galicians in post-Franco Spain).

Nationality policies are generally conceived of as solutions to discrimination but not to conflicts that are smoldering or have already erupted. Some procedures aim more at containment, or pose the nationality question in a purely sociopolitical context. But such policies are part of the problem that they claim to be solving. A detailed comparison ought to be made of the different approaches to nationality policy pursued by selected states such as Denmark, Italy, Spain, and the former USSR (maintained in the Russian Federation). This might include comparison with lessons learned from affirmative action in the United States as well as autonomy and constitutional arrangements realized in the past fifty years in China, India, and Panama, and more recently, in Colombia, Australia, Nicaragua, and Ethiopia.

One factor of major importance in preventing discrimination toward minorities is not only the focus on basic rights of these groups (and the granting of citizenship and autonomy/self-governance) but also the extension of international norms and standards of protection for non-dominant minorities. The role of multilateral regimes in preventing discrimination of minorities and resolving latent and violent conflicts should be discussed more systematically in order to draw the "lessons learned" from it. Critical reviews should focus on the activities undertaken by NGOs in protecting minorities, the efforts of the Council of Europe in regard to national minorities, similarly the efforts of the Organization for Security and Cooperation in Europe (OSCE), as well as the efforts of the UN Human Rights Commission to work out minimum standards for the rights of minorities and indigenous peoples. New paths in this direction have been embarked on with the Framework Convention for the Protection of National Minorities issued by the Council of Europe, which laid great emphasis on the protection of national minorities, and the creation of the institution of a High Commissioner for National Minorities within the OSCE. Legal instruments are not sufficient in themselves in promoting good relations between majorities and minorities. In addition to such standard-setting activities, more confidence-building and practical measures at the grass-roots level aimed at increasing tolerance and understanding between citizens belonging to different ethnic communities are required.

CHRISTIAN P. SCHERRER

References and Further Reading

Anderson, Benedict R. *Imagined Communities. Reflection on the Origin and Spread of Nationalism.* London: Verso, 1983; rev. ed., New York: Verso, 1991.
Chrétien, Jean Pierre and Gerard Prunier. *Les Ethnies ont une Histoire.* Paris: Karthala, 1994.
Ethnic Conflicts Research Project, Compilers and Studies. Moers: IFEK–IRECOR, various.
Galtung, Johan. *Peace by Peaceful Means: Peace and Conflict, Development and Civilization.* London: Sage, 1996.

Gurr, Ted Robert. *Peoples Versus States*. Washington, DC: US Institute of Peace Press, 2000.

Horowitz, Donald L. *Ethnic Groups in Conflict*. Berkeley, CA: University of California Press, 1985.

Kemp, Walter, ed. *Quiet Diplomacy in Action: The OSCE High Commissioner on National Minorities*. Dordrecht, The Hague, Boston, New York, and London: Kluwer Academic Publishers.

Kymlicka, Will. *Multicultural Citizenship. A Liberal Theory of Minority Rights*. Oxford, UK: Oxford University Press, 1996.

Scherrer, Christian P. *Ethnicity, Nationalism and Conflict*. Aldershot, UK: Ashgate, 2002.

———. *Structural Prevention of Ethnic Violence*. London/New York: Palgrave, 2001.

Smith, Anthony D. *National Identity*. London: Penguin Books, 1991.

Trifunovska, Snena and Fernand de Varennes, eds. *Minority Rights in Europe. European Minorities and Languages*. The Hague: TMC Asser Press, 2001.

United Nations. *Seeds of a New Partnership: Indigenous Peoples and the United Nations*. New York: Author, 1994.

Yamskov, Anatoly N. "The 'New Minorities' in Post-Soviet States." *Cultural Survival Quarterly*, 18, nos. 2–3 (1994): 58–61.

MIXED ECONOMY

Different countries engage different economic systems to allocate scarce resources. In the *command (planned)* economy, the government decides what, how, and for whom to produce. The government sets the economic objectives and the course of action. There is no private ownership and no market incentives. In the *free market (capitalist or laissez faire) economy,* households and firms (private sector) have freedom to make their own economic decisions. Price mechanism is the main force in the market. Prices of products are determined by the demand for and the supply of such products.

A *mixed economy* has the features of both command and market economies. It functions in the framework of a capitalist market with the intervention of the government. A mixed economy embraces the mixture of private and public decision making and ownership. The government and the private sector work closely with each other to determine what, how, how much, and for whom to produce. The private sector is encouraged to create jobs, income, and wealth within the legal framework. However, the main objective of the private sector is profit maximization, not serving the public. Thus, the government has to intervene when there is market inefficiency. Certain industries considered essential to national sovereignty and security may be nationalized. Yet, there are exceptions in some countries. McTaggart (2003) observed that some economies are based on custom or religion such as the caste system in India or the Islamic banking systems in Middle Eastern countries. The secular government may be less powerful and have to compromise with religious leaders in making decisions.

Overall, the level of government intervention varies from country to country.

Private and Public Sectors

In a mixed economy, the economic activities are performed by both the public and private sectors. Private enterprises usually engage only in business that can maximize profits and the interests of stakeholders. However, some industries in the economy are not attractive enough for the private sector, so the public sector will take the lead in industries that are vital for national security or cannot generate enough profit to attract the private sector. Recently, *privatization* has been introduced to release the burden of public sector inefficiency. The most common form of privatization is to sell public sector enterprises to private owners. Because they must turn a profit, private owners have more incentive to better manage the business. In addition, *deregulation* has been implemented in some industries that were previously controlled tightly by the government, such as airlines, banking, telecommunication, energy, and water supply. On the other hand, the government may continue regulating industrial and business standards to improve job opportunities, workplace safety, occupational health, consumer protection, free and fair competition, and so forth.

Forms of Government Intervention

In a mixed economy, the government provides the legal framework and ensures the enforcement of law. The most popular forms of government intervention are economic regulations (price control, setting quotas, promoting free and fair competition), social regulations (workplace safety, occupational health), and fixed business standards. Trade legislation contributes to the stabilisation of the economy. Anti-discrimination acts prevent some groups of people (minorities, the disabled, women, indigenous people, etc.) from being marginalised from the mainstream of society.

Allocation of scarce resources to meet public need is also a type of government intervention. The government directs some amount of resources to provide goods and services (roads, defense, policing, currency, programs that care for the elderly and those that promote health) that are essential to the public and the country and that cannot be effectively and efficiently produced by the private sector.

Lastly, the government has to competently manage government revenue and expenditures by redistribution of income through taxation and subsidies.

When, Why, and How Can the Government Intervene?

The government often intervenes when there is market inefficiency. Market failure has many indicators.

The first indicator is *public goods* possessing two characteristics, non-exclusion and non-rivalry. Non-exclusion means nobody will be excluded in the usage of public goods whether or not they pay for them. Non-rivalry means everybody can enjoy the same level of satisfaction when consuming the same product. A good example of public goods is the street light. The private sector will not provide this type of goods due to the "free-rider" problem in which people want to use but do not want to pay for such goods. The government will have to provide such vital goods and services in order to promote economic stability and maintain a minimum standard of living for citizens.

The second indicator of market imperfection is externality. *Externality* refers to the external costs or benefits generated from economic transactions that are incurred by third parties who are not involved in such transactions. In *negative externality*, external cost is incurred during the production process when Marginal Social Cost (MSC) is bigger than Marginal Individual Cost (MIC). For instance, a chemical factory can generate external costs by polluting the air and the water with its chemical waste, which affects the environment. External cost is incurred during the consumption process when the Marginal Social Benefit (MSB) is smaller than the Marginal Individual Benefit (MIB). For example, many people drive cars, which may cause congestion and noise. Individuals can enjoy some benefit by driving their own cars, while the benefit to the society is minimal. In this case, the external costs are environmental problems. Thus, the government has to reduce the amount of negative externalities by levying taxes that may increase the prices of cars (if the sellers do not absorb the taxes), impose charges, or tighten the issue of permits/licenses. *Positive externality* can be incurred during the production process when the MSC is smaller than the MIC. Research and development is a good example since the total cost incurred by the

society is smaller than the cost paid by a firm. External benefit is generated during the consumption of a product when MSB is more than MIB. When individuals travel by public transport, the social benefit of getting less noise and congestion is much higher than the individual benefit. Therefore, the government encourages the consumption of such products by providing goods and services at lower prices or subsidizing the needy. More incentives to preserve the environment are also implemented to improve market performance.

Third, *asymmetric* information is another indicator of market failure. Some consumers may not have sufficient knowledge of or receive distorted information about products they want to buy or consume. Their ignorance may harm them physically, emotionally, or financially. The government may intercede by providing accurate information and setting policies, regulations, standards, or codes of conduct to prevent businesses from misleading the consumers. The government encourages the establishment of business and consumer associations or watchdogs and works closely with them to address these problems.

Fourth, *monopoly* occurs when there is only one supplier of products that have no close substitutes in the market. Other competitors can hardly enter the market because of high overhead costs, economies of scale, a franchise with exclusive rights, and legal barriers (government license and patents). In this case, one monopolist firm is the price setter and dominates the market. Customers will suffer because of higher price and lower quality. Thus, a mixed-economy government will discourage monopoly by promoting free and fair competition. Antitrust law has been introduced in the United States, the United Kingdom, and other countries to eliminate sole market power. However, in some industries, natural monopoly is acceptable. *Natural monopoly* happens when the cost of producing a product will increase when there is more than one supplier in the market. Nevertheless, the government also regulates natural monopoly.

Fifth, the government needs to intervene when there is *economic inequality*. Inequality may arise because of the provision and usage of merit goods. *Merit goods* possess two main characteristics: (i) the private sectors can provide merit goods but at a very expensive price, and (ii) the more consumers consume merit goods, the more the society can enjoy their benefits. To address the inequality, the government will transfer some payments from the higher-income class to the lower-income groups in terms of social security, price subsidy, or manipulation of income tax. People with higher income have to pay more taxes, while the unemployed, the needy, or the disadvantaged will receive social security. In some countries, the farmers receive price subsidies that go against the international agreements on free and fair trade.

A mixed-economy government not only protects consumers but also supports businesses. Fiscal and monetary policies are utilised to stabilise the economy. Other macroeconomic policies are taken into account in order to solve the problems of high unemployment and inflation rates.

Advantages of a Mixed Economy

Since a mixed economy is the combination of command and market economies, it has all the strengths and weaknesses of these two systems.

In a mixed economy, individuals and firms have the freedom to decide what they want to do as long as their activities are within the legal framework. Both public and private sectors can operate in the market and can substitute for or complement each other. Competition gives more incentive to the market and allows customers the choice of more varieties of products with better quality and at cheaper prices. Both consumers and firms are protected by rules and regulations.

A government may help allocate scarce resources more efficiently. Some countries have economic committees that help all sectors in the economy make better economic choices and decisions.

Property ownership rights encourage people to protect their own possessions and thus can address the problem of "common property" and waste of public resources.

Disadvantages of a Mixed Economy

Similar to the free market, there is little protection for individuals in the mixed economy. In some countries, the government can provide financial assistance to the needy (social security to the unemployed, the disabled, or the aged; or grants to new parents or first-time home buyers). In other countries, there is no such assistance or only very limited, short-term assistance.

Redistribution of income may inadvertently create inequality. It is not easy to measure externalities and their consequences, to apply different levels of assistance to different groups or levy different levels of taxes to firms. There is no incentive for the firms to implement "good practices" if, for example, the cost incurred by using advanced technology, which can

reduce negative externalities, is higher than the amount of taxes they have to pay.

Lack of knowledge and information about the market and the inefficient performance of public servants may cause inconvenience to the public and create opportunities for bureaucracy, red tape, and corruption.

Ineffective regulations may immobilise factors of production. Input factor immobility and the time lags between the policy making and implementation processes can cause economic disequilibrium. Poor management of price controls may cause shortages and surpluses of some products and the economy may fall into a recession.

Too many restrictions will create disincentives in the market. Too frequent changes in policies related to taxation, subsidies, ISO standards, and so forth also make it difficult for firms to comply.

In short, each system has its own advantages and disadvantages. However, political stability, good leadership with clean government, and proper economic policies, which can encourage both private and public sectors as well as civil societies to share the burden of allocation of scarce resources, will help countries achieve their goals and objectives.

HA THI THU HUONG

See also Capitalist Economic Model; Communist Economic Model; Development History and Theory; Free Market Economy; Marxism; State-Directed Economy

References and Further Reading

Besanko, D., Dranove, D., Shanley, M., and Schaefer, S. *Economics of Strategy*. New York: Wiley, 2004.
Jackson, John, McIver, Ron, McConnell, Campbell, and Brue, Stanley. *Economics*. Sydney: McGraw-Hill, 1994.
McTaggart, Douglas, Findlay, Christopher, and Parkin, Michael. *Microeconomics*. Sydney: Addison-Wesley, 2003.
Schnitzer, Martin C. *Comparative Economic Systems*. Madison, OH: South-Western College Publishing/Thomson Learning, 2000.
Sloman, John and Mark Sutcliffe. *Economics for Business*. Harlow, Essex, UK: Financial Times/Prentice Hall, 2001.
Stiglitz, Joseph E. and Carol E. Walsh. *Economics*. New York: Norton, 2002.

MODERNIZATION

Bridging the disparity between economically rich and poor nations—whether referred to as developed and developing countries, First World and Third World, the North and the South, or industrialized and non-industrialized economies—has been a major impetus for interest in modernization. Thus modernization may be understood as the planning and management of economic development and concurrent social change, which together would facilitate, in principle at least, the emulation of developed countries by the less-developed. The issue was particularly topical in the immediate post–World War II era as many former colonies gained their independence as nations from European powers. Colonialization was a subtle form of modernization as the colonists' society was promoted as an example of progress, advancement, and superiority. In the immediate post-colonial era, especially, developing countries were keen on economic progress but wary of the accompanying cultural imperialism or "Westernization," as it was commonly called. The term modernization is closely linked with the terms social change and economic development, though the latter terms tend to be the more contemporary and commonly used, while the former is now largely associated with a particular school of thought. Before discussing explanatory theories of the twentieth century, the roots of modernization thought in the previous century are worth exploring briefly.

Theoretical Origins

The social, cultural, political, and economic changes in Europe brought about by the Renaissance in the seventeenth century and the Enlightenment in the eighteenth century were the catalyst for differentiating between previously medieval and presently modern societies. Thus, modern societies were defined as being composed of autonomous and enquiring individuals who by their reliance on reason and experience in turn stimulated the growth of scientific and technological innovation. The Industrial Revolution in Europe brought about widespread socioeconomic change and prompted much interest by scholars in how societies could, should, or did indeed develop. The ideas of Charles Darwin about evolution in the natural sciences also influenced thinking in the social sciences, particularly the notion that societies might evolve through incremental stages toward a utopian ideal of economic, social, and technological advancement. The industrialized society that developed consequently would be increasingly characterized by democratic participation, social mobility, education, bureaucratic organizations, rational planning, market economics, and secular institutions. These constitute much of the ideals of modernity and thus the process of modernization to the present day.

The ideas of three European thinkers of the nineteenth century on industrialization, social change, and economic development have stood the test of time, though their approaches are somewhat divergent. Emile Durkheim was concerned with how societies are organized, and saw a contrast between what he saw as traditional and modern types of societies. The former was characterized as undifferentiated, while the latter was characterized by the division of labor and consequent interdependency of its members. While Durkheim did not explain exactly how modernization takes place, apart from it being a natural outcome of population growth, his ideas influenced modernization thinkers of the twentieth century. Max Weber held the view that Calvinist Protestantism motivated people to seek this-worldly success to demonstrate to others, as well as to themselves, that they had been predestined for eternal salvation. Not without controversy did he conclude that the requisite willingness to accumulate for longer-term success was prior to, and provided the ideological change instrumental in, the rise of modern capitalism, and thus industrialization and modernization. Karl Marx, on the other hand, believed that the ideological structure of society was based upon the modes of production. Changes in the economic infrastructure were for him the prime agents of social change and modernization, and thus were not value-free. While all three thinkers examined the rapid social change of their times, they differed on its antecedents and consequences, thus influencing different schools of thought on modernization.

Underdevelopment to Industrialization

Modernization is concerned with the process of transforming an underdeveloped country into a developed one. Development is defined as social and economic progress by countries considered developing, less developed, or Third World. Its achievement is measured primarily by economic growth, as well as statistics such as food self-sufficiency, nutrition, health care, life expectancy, shelter, communications, employment, literacy, and education. More recently, other indices have been gradually introduced such as human rights, environmentalism, quality of life, and so on. Countries are then classified into developed versus developing countries, the latter term growing in preference to the value-ridden "less-developed" and "underdeveloped." But the much larger category and quite diverse nature of developing countries has precipitated the creation of sub-categorization schemes by various intergovernmental agencies or non-governmental organizations (NGOs). These have resulted in such classifications as newly industrialized countries (NICs), least-developed countries (LDCs), big emerging markets (BEMs), middle-income economies (MIEs), and the like.

Generally speaking, economic, social, and political development is considered to be achieved through modernization, namely by following the model of the developed countries, through their aid and investment, training, and transfer of technology to developing countries. In the name of "nation-building" in the newly post-colonial country, the state often takes a significant role in the planning and management of development, with the help of Western agencies. As a consequence there is disenfranchisement of civil society out of fear that any dissent expressed might undermine progress. The expectation is for the country as a whole to achieve economic growth and thus all its citizens will experience a significant increase in financial income and material well-being. But economic reversion rather than development is possible and indeed has happened, to the impoverishment of its people. Many in developing countries that have embarked on the road to modernization have experienced uneven development, inequitable structures, even discrimination and oppression. Blame has then been placed inappropriately on colonialists up to 50 years after independence, though some blame may be justifiably assigned to foreign multinational corporations (MNCs), in collusion usually with corrupt and incompetent leadership in the developing country.

Modernization is closely linked to industrialization or the mechanization of production processes through the use of electricity, steam, oil, and other forms of energy. This technological change is characterized by shifts from personal labor to machine process, individual workshop to factory, crafted to standardized products, agricultural to mineral inputs, and from small-scale to large-scale production. Industrialization results in the declining emphasis on primary production or agriculture amidst growth in size and importance of secondary production or industry and tertiary production or services. The need for raw materials as well as markets for finished products prompted much of the colonialization imperative of previous centuries. One legacy has been the interdependence of nations and economic imperialism or neo-colonialism by multinational corporations. While industralization developed in Western Europe in the nineteenth century, it took thinkers like Eisenstadt to argue that by no means need it be a phenomenon confined to the West but rather one replicable through the world, and thus the means of modernization for the developing world.

Modernization Theories

Although development and social change are recognized as complex multi-causal processes, there was still a tendency among modernization theorists to see economic factors as the pre-eminent determining ones. Walt Whitman Rostow, for instance, claimed that with adequate preparation an economy would take off into a period of self-sustained growth through mass consumption, which is taken as a litmus test of a modernized society. The newly independent third-world countries in the postwar era were most interested in this viewpoint but soon came to realize that the influx of capital was not a sufficient factor in and of itself. The rapid modernization of some countries but not others, despite similar levels of capital investment, was put down to the lack of appropriate social institutions, human resource development, and appropriate cultural values. David McClelland, in particular, pointed out the critical importance of people having an "achievement motivation" if a society was to develop or modernize through innovation and risk-taking. Such an argument belies the continuing influence of Weber on modernization thought.

While this initial paradigm espoused certain socio-demographic and structural prerequisites for modernization globally, research in developing countries actually undermined these notions and demonstrated the ahistoricity, paternalism, and ethnocentricity of such functionalism and thus modernization theories. For one thing, capitalism grew out of the peculiar European feudal system of the sixteenth to nineteenth centuries that has few equivalents elsewhere. For another, the path of modernization in the so-called West subsequently has not been without social and economic crises as it is made out to be when upheld as a model for the developing world. Each national society is composed of multiple sub-systems of social, cultural, and economic organization that differentiate one society from another. It is such differences that extend or limit the choices that a society has in relation to the process of modernization. Whether politically, economically, socially, or culturally, the developing world is simply not composed of homogeneous developing nation-states as modernization theorists presuppose, let alone clones of the developed world prior to industrialization. Thus the wholesale transfer of institutions, practices, and policies from the developed to the developing worlds, particularly through financial and technological aid, is no guarantee of modernization.

Functionalist Interventions

Structural-functionalists analyze how functions adapt to maintain a stable social structure composed of mutually dependent sub-systems, or fail to adapt resulting in dysfunctions. Influential on sociologists of this century, the structural-functionalist Talcott Parsons believed in the inevitability of modernization resulting in economic growth, universal education, and political democratization worldwide. Modernization theorists advocated precipitating dissatisfaction with traditional life as a means of stimulating aspirations for the material benefits of modern society. The role of media in modernization, as the functionalists theorized, was to democratize access to and choice in cultural products, and facilitate gradual cultural change without threatening the social system. In fact, modernization was seen as a process by which empathy with the idea of social mobility was fostered through the media. Notably, Daniel Lerner claimed that the media was a key accelerator of the transition into modernization along with urbanization, literacy, and political participation. Consequently, specific media policies were prescribed for developing countries as a means of achieving modernization and its benefits. The media were believed to aid in widening horizons, promoting empathy with different lifestyles, focusing attention on social mobility, raising material expectations, and changing attitudes and values, among other helpful effects for modernization.

Many governments in the developing world introduced television as a means of promoting modernization, either directly through development programming or indirectly through Westernized entertainment programming. But influential as structural-functionalism was in media development, research on its effects in the developing world bore equivocal results. Indeed, when Everett Rogers investigated diffusion of innovations, he found that the media were important to the earliest stage of awareness of innovations but it was interpersonal communication that was critical to the final stage of their adoption. Marketing and advertising have also been considered as benefiting modernization through encouraging competition, production efficiency, product innovations, and lower prices, as well as subsidizing the mass media. However this appears an argument for the dominance of commercial broadcasting emphasizing entertainment over public broadcasting focusing on education. Investigating the effect of modern institutions in developing countries, sociologists found that schools, the factory workplace, and the media were equally powerful in influencing modernization.

Dependency Theories

Taking a more radical or critical approach, dependency theorists argue that underdevelopment is caused not by sociocultural factors but by politico-economic ones, namely the exploitation of developing countries by capitalist developed ones. This view originates with Marx who explained historical transformation of societies through the growth of capitalism, which in turn was due to the exploitation of the working class. Lenin expanded this model to incorporate the relationship between imperial powers and their colonies. The need to update this Marxist perspective led to the dependency model, which asserted that persistent underdevelopment of a society was a symptom of its place within an exploitative world capitalist system. Even though many developing countries may be politically independent from their previous colonizers and seem to have national sovereignty, they are still subject to neo-colonialism. A form of economic and political dependency, this is achieved through developed-country investments in developing countries, infrastructural distortion of the latter's economies, and suppression of any independent policies by the developing world. As such, any effort to achieve economic development such as import substitution is fraught with difficulty, and even aid from the developed world can serve to perpetuate the exploitation.

The only alternatives left open to each developing country were to isolate itself from the capitalist world system, or seek to have the terms of international trade radically revised. The former alternative was tested by some countries such as those of the former Second World, which sought to set up a socialist-communist world system and found it wanting. The latter solution is currently being pursued via the General Agreement on Tariffs and Trade (GATT) and resultant World Trade Organization (WTO) with greater impetus since the end of the Cold War in the 1990s. But dependency theorists are skeptical of the value of GATT and WTO for developing countries, especially those in financial strife and coming increasingly under the control of the World Bank and International Monetary Fund (IMF), which are themselves driven by US foreign policy. After all, the Third World's lobbying over the 1970s and early 1980s for a New International Economic Order (NIEO) through the United Nations was impeded by the United States and other first-world countries, which preferred GATT as their platform since in it the developing countries were not a collectivity. Thus some thinkers from or sympathetic to the Third World consider the WTO to be a thinly-veiled attempt by the developed countries to control world trade and provide opportunities for their multinational corporations to dominate third-world markets. In what is sometimes described as recolonization, developing countries seem to be forfeiting their already limited economic sovereignty in their desire for integration into the capitalist global economy controlled by the industrialized First World, without any guarantees of affluence. But as critics of structural-functionalism, dependency theorists tend to err in the opposite direction by propounding theories emphasizing the forces of conflict and disruption, and often failing to acknowledge the forces for social order and stability.

World-Systems Theories

Through his study of modernization in Africa, Wallerstein became convinced that the state was not the valid unit of analysis when the economic system, of which it was a part, spanned the world. Thus he formulated "world-system" theory, a variation of dependency theories which states that a global economic system exists through which capitalist-developed or core countries and their multinational corporations exploit developing or "periphery" countries through low prices for raw material and high prices for finished goods. As part of the system, semi-peripheral countries were both dependent on the core countries and exploitative of the periphery ones. In his later prognosis, global integration of this system in favour of the inequitable status quo between nation-states would result in resistance, fragmentation, and its ultimate collapse, but for the buffer of semi-peripheral states.

Thus world-systems theory might be seen as merely a reaction to the inadequacy of modernization theory, which had used developed nations as the basis of comparison for developing countries, but which failed to demonstrate political and economic relations between the two systematically. Criticisms of world-systems theory revolve around its simplistic one-dimension analysis of causality, namely economic exploitation. The assumption that the world system is formed by developed and developing nation-states in an unequal relationship is questionable when it can be argued that the world system preceded the existence of these nation-states and was even instrumental in the latter's formation. Some critics have put forward alternative models of geopolitical factors, primarily citing political power rivalry between nation-states. Those from the classical economics school would argue instead for the theory of comparative advantage, which holds that all countries involved are better off through unrestricted trade than if they did not trade at all. Therefore peripheral countries choose to trade with the core because they find it to their advantage, core countries need not coerce them to do so, and peripheral countries are not necessarily exploited when core countries progress.

Third-World Applications

Many First World thinkers have defended the value of capitalism in bringing about economic development in the Third World. Like others before and since, Berger is persuaded that the efficient productive power and high standard of living of the masses generated in advanced industrial nations of the First World are being replicated in those Third World nations which are well incorporated into the global capitalist system. Of particular interest are Asia's newly industrializing countries, such as South Korea, Hong Kong, Taiwan, and Singapore, which seem to demonstrate that genuine economic growth can occur despite state intervention in the economy and their relative dependency on the global capitalist system. But as in the First World, capitalism promotes a class system that permits social mobility, individual autonomy, and democratic processes, though these are slow processes given the traditional culture and society of the Third World. This contrasts with the failure of industrial socialism of the Second World, but it need not necessarily imply that there is an intrinsic link between it and inefficient economic systems and authoritarian political culture. The commitment to capitalism in many Asian, African, and Latin American countries has not resulted in sustained economic development, and in some cases has resulted in dire economic strife, requiring rescue by the IMF and World Bank. Others have questioned whether the authoritarian control by governments in some of these capitalist countries in pursuit of such economic progress is a cost worthy of the ideals of modernization to which societies are to aspire. For this reason, Herman Daly and John Cobb devise an alternative measure of economic activity, which incorporates the negative costs that traditional economists have long ignored. They point out that not only are developed nations depleting natural capital and actually achieving negative growth, but developing countries involved in modernization are also being drawn into the same self-defeating process instead of aiming at sustainable development. Recent decades have seen adverse reactions in some countries to cultural consequences of rapid modernization. Most notable among these are probably Iran, where the religious leaders succeeded in bring about a revolution against the modernizing impetus of the last Shah, and Cambodia, which under the Khmer Rouge attempted to turn back to a pre-industrial era. While there have not been recent reversals, the turn of the twenty-first century sees creeping influence of cultural and religious fundamentalist movements in developing countries opposed to Western neo-colonialism and imperialism, both cultural and economic. There has also been an astounding growth of networks of informal social movements and non-governmental organizations, which question the purported benefits of modernization and point out the obvious disadvantages for various sectors of society in both the developed and developing countries.

Role of Culture

Modernization involves changes in individual attitudes, values, and behaviors, as well as in social organization. Cultures conducive to modernization are said to have their roots in that of nineteenth-century Western and Northern Europe where industrialization first began, and then spread to parts of the world that were settled, rather than simply colonized, by its migrants—namely North America, Australasia, and to a lesser extent South Africa. In much of the developing world, the impetus to modernization has come from socially marginal groups and entrepreneurial subcultures, many of which predate colonialization but were co-opted or at least tolerated by European colonialists. Widely acknowledged examples of these are the Overseas Chinese in Southeast Asia, the Gujerati Indians in East Africa, and the Lebanese in Latin America. Among the indigenous peoples of developing countries, it was often the traditional elites, such as landowners and royalty, who collaborated with colonial authorities and postcolonial leaders in their agenda of modernization and industrialization, though sometimes it was a new educated or merchant class that was at the forefront. The crony capitalism or corrupt links between business and government that have bedeviled many developing countries, even some of the successful models are symptomatic of this phenomenon.

There has been a tendency since Durkheim and Weber to contrast tradition and modernity, and to imply that traditional culture with its orientation to the past, emphasis on kinship, and fatalistic worldview is an impediment to modernization. Harrison, Huntington, and other contributors to their recent edited volume argue that culture matters immensely in economic development and political democratization, and by implication that there are modernization-prone and modernization-averse cultures. Not only are cultural attitudes and values explanatory variables of the wide variation of modernization among developing countries, but these can also comprise a dependent variable in that economic development changes cultures in turn. But any survey of societies in the developing world would soon reveal the inadequacy of any typology of traditional, pre-industrial versus modern, industrialized societies. Even in the most modern of societies, traditional elements such as kinship and religion persist, while some groups in so-called traditional societies have capitalized on opportunities to adopt modern economic practices. The conservatism and passivity that are said to permeate traditional societies may have more to do with their historical experience of exploitation from inside or outside the country such as via colonialization and imperialism. Hence, the allegations of idleness and non-ambition may be revealing of the failure of authorities, colonial or national, to understand the complex social and economic structures that pre-existed in local communities. These have often proven to be more sustainable and functional than the large-scale or national projects being imposed in the name of modernization based on a Western industrialized model.

Counting the Costs

Modernization is often proffered by its proponents as a panacea for the economic and social ills of countries in the developing world. Although academics have long expressed reservations over the claimed benefits of modernization, only in recent decades, even years, has there been much popular dissent in both the developing and developed world. Life-expectancy and infant survival rates are higher in modernizing societies, but these lead to rapid population growth with which developing countries are not ready to cope in terms of infrastructure. There might be a decline in infectious and parasitic diseases, but a rise in unhealthy lifestyle and the stress-related and degenerative illnesses associated with modernized societies. Migration to cities in search of jobs and a more materialistic lifestyle often results in unfettered urbanization, shantytowns, inadequate services, high unemployment, crime, and other forms of urban blight. Rising expectations by the masses about consumption, fueled by advertising and the media, cannot realistically be fulfilled in many developing countries in Asia, Latin America, and Africa.

Currently the much less populated developed world utilizes the lion's share of the world's energy and natural resources. If the developing world were to catch up with the developed world in terms of standard of living, the depletion of resources would be at an alarming and unsustainable rate. Yet the de-industrialization of the developed world and adoption of a lower standard of living by its citizens seems an unrealistic hope. At the same time, many developing countries are determined to emulate the social and economic practices of the developed West, and even those that are succeeding seem to have acquired massive debts. E. F. Schumacher's seminal idea of intermediate development is less about the why and how of development than it is about what is appropriate for developing countries wishing to modernize. His proposal of appropriate technology or incremental, small-scale innovation may be a valuable solution but there has been little interest in it by governments in developing countries, except for some rural communities. It is certainly not supported by aid agencies and multinational corporations from the developed world who have vested interests in promoting their large-scale technologies to developing countries.

Late Capitalism and Globalization

Perhaps in response to the criticisms of Immanuel Wallerstein's view of monolithic global capitalism, other theorists adopt a more multi-causal perspective on modernization. With the onset of the postmodern age, nation-states are seen as co-players along with multinational corporations (MNCs), non-governmental organizations (NGOs), and other inter-governmental bodies (IGOs) on the world stage. In lieu of Marxist and non-Marxist periodizations, Scott Lash and John Urry offer a three-stage model of the development of capitalist economies: liberal, organized, and disorganized. The present "disorganization" of capitalism in the industrialized nations they attribute to four trends: the rise of multinational corporations and international financial markets, the decline of mass industries, devolution of government and dispersion of population, and the growth of a "service class" of white-collar professionals. Through their analysis of the major developed economies of the late twentieth century, Lash and Urry demonstrate that they are collectively well on the road from being modern to the next stage of being globalized, postmodern societies.

Worldwide changes in technology, education, and mass communications have led in turn to new consequences in social issues, conflict, and political institutions in the capitalist West, liberalizing the communist world and developing countries alike. One widely acknowledged outcome is the declining political interest in nationalism and increasing popular support for supra-national entities and ethnic identities. Increasing regionalization and globalization seem also to make a mockery of domestic economic policy in the West because Western countries generally fail to consider developments in other countries, particularly in the Third World. This is quite evident in the intransigence of the economies in the developed world at the turn of the twenty-first century to domestic policies designed to create growth and employment. These policies fail simply because they do not recognize the changed global political and economic environment of which the nation-state is a part.

Globalization is conceived of in contemporary academic literature as a process of linking individuals and organizations that transcends the boundaries of the system of nation-states that comprise the manifest world political-economic system. Thus events and decisions in one part of the world come to have significant consequences for communities in other, often quite distant parts. Hence, Giddens conceives of globalization as influenced by four factors: capitalism, the inter-state system, militarism, and industrialism. Globalization is seen as a natural outgrowth of modernization when traditional social institutions in any country are superseded by global ones. Achieved through better communications, this phenomenon results in a greater sense of world citizenry or of interdependence on a global basis among individuals. The lynch-pins of economic and political globalization today are said to be the worldwide growth of capitalism with its accompanying processes of commodification and marketization. In recent years, globalization seems to have superceded modernization as the primary focus of social change, and this might be thought of as an inevitable outcome of the modernizing process.

Modernity Versus Postmodernity

Down through the ages modernity has been a term used to contrast a present era with a previous one regarded as outmoded. Enlightenment thinkers of the eighteenth century considered themselves modern in relation to the ancient and medieval societies. In our era, modernity has been the badge of modern industrialized society and is characterized by a disdain for the past and a love of novelty. Modernity defines people as autonomous individuals within a free society rather than primarily as members of an ascribed collective. It favours reason and rationality, which undergirds scientific discovery, technological advancement, and material progress considered vital to modernization. Modern society and culture is based on industrialization, bureaucracy, the nation-state, and economic growth. As such the fragmentation of post-colonial nation-states, the globalization and marketization of the economy, hybridization of cultures, the resurgence of religion, subjectivism in morality, among other symptoms that have occurred in recent decades have suggested to some thinkers that the world has entered into a postmodern age. Whether this applies equally to the developing world as to the developed one in which such views are formulated, remains an unresolved issue.

Postmodernism may be thought of as the skeptical aftermath of the optimistic humanism and technological utopianism of the modern industrialized era. Like globalization, postmodernity is a phenomenon over which there is little consensus of definition. Some thinkers portray postmodern society primarily as a consumer society characterized by fragmentation and chaos, pastiche and schizophrenia. Thus distinctions between reality and imagination are eroded, making impossible a comprehensive grasp of postmodernism. Others consider postmodernism to be in continuity with modernism and simply the cultural logic of late capitalism. Societies seem to be converging in economic and technological aspects but diverging especially in social aspects, while staying the same in yet other aspects. Cultural hybridity, for instance, takes a range of forms from mimicry, syncretism, and creolization, to global mélange and counter-hegemony, a phenomenon evident in the Third World across the arenas of television, music, theatre, sport, food, movies, and a range of popular culture. Perhaps globalization ought to be seen as an openness to cultural eclecticism that characterizes postmodern societies as a late consequence of modernization.

AMOS OWEN THOMAS

See also Capitalist Economic Model; Communist Economic Model; Development History and Theory; Industrialization; Mixed Economy; Newly Industrialized Economies (NIEs); Socialist Economic Model; State-Directed Economy; Technology: Impact on Development; Third World; Underdevelopment

References and Further Reading

Berger, Peter. *The Capitalist Revolution*. New York: Basic Books/Harper Collins, 1991.
Daly, Herman E. and John B. Cobb. *For the Common Good: Redirecting the Economy Towards Community, the Environment and a Sustainable Future*. Boston: Beacon Press, 1989.
Durkheim, Emile. *The Division of Labour in Society* [trans. W. D. Halls]. London: Macmillan; New York: The Free Press, 1984.
Eisenstadt, Shmuel Noah. *Modernization: Protest and Change*. Englewood Cliffs, NJ: Prentice Hall, 1966.
Etzioni-Halevy, Eva and Amitai Etzioni, eds. *Social Change: Sources, Patterns, and Consequences* 2nd ed. New York: Basic Books, 1973.
Giddens, Anthony. *The Consequences of Modernity*. Cambridge, UK: Polity Press, 1990.
Harrison, Lawrence E. and Samuel P. Huntington. *Culture Matters: How Values Shape Human Progress*. New York: Basic Books, 2000.
Haverkamp, Hans and Neil J. Smelser, eds. *Social Change and Modernity*. Berkeley, CA: University of California Press, 1992.
Lash, Scott and John Urry. *The End of Organized Capitalism*. Cambridge, UK: Polity, 1987.
Lerner, David. *The Passing of Traditional Society: Modernizing the Middle East*. Glencoe, IL: Free Press, 1958.
Robertson, Roland. *Globalization: Social Theory and Global Culture*. London: Sage, 1992.
Rogers, Everritt. *The Diffusion of Innovations*. New York: Free Press, 1962.
Rostow, Walt W. *The Stages of Economic Growth: A Non-Communist Manifesto*. Cambridge, UK: Cambridge University Press, 1960.
Todaro, M. *Economics for a Developing World*. 3rd ed. London and New York: Longman/Pearson Education, 1992.
Wallerstein, Immanuel. *The Capitalist World Economy*. New York: Cambridge University Press, 1979.

MOLDOVA

The Republic of Moldova lies in the southeast part of Central Europe. Its neighbours are Ukraine in the north, south, and east, and Romania in the west. Its surface area is 33,700 square kilometers and its population is about 4,446,455 inhabitants (CIA estimate July 2004). The capital city of Moldova is Chişinău. Beginning in the nineteenth century the present Republic of Moldova was known as Basarabia. The population is divided as follows: Romanians 64.5%, Ukrainians 14%, Russians 13.5%, Găgăuzi 3.5%, Bulgarians 2%, Jews 1.5%. On the whole over sixty nationalities are represented here. Regarding religions practiced here, 98% of the population are Eastern Orthodox; 1.5% are Jewish; and the remaining 0.5% are of varying religions, including Baptist. The landscape of Moldova is composed of plains and low hills and the climate is temperate. The forests, which used to cover a quarter of the country, represent less than 10% nowadays.

In the fourteenth century the Principate of Moldova was established, which included the territories east of the Nistru and the Black Sea. In 1792, Transnistria was annexed to tsarist Russia and transformed in a "gubernia" (county), with the capital at Tiraspol. After the Russian–Turkish war of 1806–1812, won by the Russians, the Tsarist Empire took the territory between the Prut and the Nistru (that belonged to the feudal state of Moldova) and gave it the official name of Basarabia. In 1917 the Communist Revolution led by Lenin took place and the tsarist regime was abolished. On December 2, 1917, the Country's Council (Parliament) proclaimed the Democratic Federative

Moldavian Republic, which voted in the independence of the new republic in January 1918. On March 27, 1918, the Country's Council proclaimed the union with Romania. In 1924, Moscow approved the forming of the Autonomous Soviet Socialist Republic of Moldova, on the territory of Transnistria, then a part of the Ukrainian Socialist Federative Republic.

Beginning in June 1940, the Soviet Army initiated its piecemeal occupation of Moldavia and, when completed on August 2, 1940, changed the territory's name to Socialist Soviet Moldavian Republic. The occupation of Basarabia and North Bucovina meant a real tragedy for the population. A terror regime was set up, much persecution took place, many people were deported, and there were even massacres among the Romanians. On June 22, 1941, the marshal Ion Antonescu, the leader of the Romanian State supported by the people and the political power, started the war against the Soviets and reintegrated Basarabia into the Romanian frontiers. After three years of Romanian administration between 1941 and 1944, Basarabia was occupied again by the Red Army as a result of the front evolution during the Second World War.

The Paris Peace Treaties (1947) established the Soviet–Romanian frontier according to the borders in existence on June 22, 1941. Between 1944 and 1953, hundreds of thousands of Moldavians were killed, locked in labour camps, or deported to Siberia by the Soviet government. Through a political diversion the Romanian language (a Romance language) in Basarabia was called the "Moldavian language" and adopted the Russian characters.

After Mihail Gorbaciov took power in the USSR, he introduced the "glasnost" and "perestroika" policies. The Democratic Movement in Moldova was founded in 1986. It organised a great meeting on August 27, 1989, which imposed the Romanian language as an official language and restored the Latin alphabet. After the Communist regime had fallen in Europe, the Chişinău Parliament adopted the Declaration of the Sovereignty of the Socialist Soviet Moldavian Republic on June 23, 1990 (which had Transnistria as one of its territorial components). On May 23, 1991, a new name of the country was adopted—the Republic of Moldova. According to the Constitution, Moldova became a presidential republic. The legislative powers belong to the president and to the Parliament and the executive powers belong to the Council of Ministers, named after legislative elections. In December 1991, Moldova joined the Commonwealth of Independent States.

The economy of the Republic of Moldova is mainly agricultural, and consists of cereal, tobacco, sugar beets, sunflowers, and vineyards. The main industrial branches are food processing, textiles, and heavy machinery or home improvement construction (tractors, television sets, washing machines, etc.). The most important natural resources are imported from Russia, which creates an economic dependence. After 1990, the Republic of Moldova took important steps toward democracy and a free market economy but the transition has been difficult. Most of the population lives in poverty, and corruption increased. The new liberal prices started the process of privatization but foreign investments remained scarce, because of the political instability and the complicated bureaucracy. In 1992, Transnistria (with the tactical support of Russia, which has established an important military arsenal in the area) proclaimed itself an autonomous republic, starting a civil war. The Transnistrian crisis remains unresolved, and the breakaway region has yet to be recognized by any country or international body. Moldova is a member of the Commonwealth of Independent States (CIS) and is the first of the CIS countries to be fully admitted into the European Council. Furthermore, Moldova signed the Cooperation Treaty with the European Union, in which it is stated as the final goal that Moldova integrate into the European Union. While the liberal and democratic parties desire this orientation toward the West, the conservatives look more toward Moscow, especially after the Communist victory in the 2000 elections.

Moscow declared (in 2004) that, to resolve the Transnistrian crisis, Moldova and Romania should reunite their borders, giving the example of the unification of the two German states. Transnistria would then be part of the Russian Federation. But such a reunification would slow Romania's integration process considerably; therefore the Romanian political class rejected the project, although it still remains a possibility for the future.

ILIE RAD

See also Commonwealth of Independent States: History and Economic Development; Commonwealth of Independent States: International Relations; Ethnic Conflicts: Commonwealth of Independent States; Romania; Soviet Bloc

References and Further Reading

Bârlea, Octavian. *Romania and the Romanians.* Los Angeles: American Romanian Academy of Arts and Sciences, 1977.

Castellan, Georges. *A History of the Romanians.* New York: Columbia University Press, 1989.

Durandin, Catherine. Histoire de la Nation Roumaine. Bruxelles: Editions Complexe, 1994.

Fischer-Galaţi, Stephen and Dinu C. Giurescu, eds. *Romania. A Historic Perspective*. New York: Columbia University Press, 1998.

Pop, Ioan-Aurel. *Romania and the Romanians. A Brief History*. New York: Columbia University Press, 1999.

Seton-Watson, R. W. *A History of the Romanians, from Roman Times to the Completion of Unity*. Cambridge, UK: Cambridge University Press, 1934; Hamdon, CT: Archon Books, 1963.

Treptow, Kurt W. *A History of Romania*. Iaşi, Romania: The Center for Romanian Studies, 1997.

MONARCHIC GOVERNMENT

Monarchy, possibly the oldest form of government, is rule by one. A monarch stands alone above his or her subjects rather than as one among them: his or her role and demeanor are parental rather than partisan. In Benedict Anderson's words, the monarch occupies the "high center" in a "dynastic realm," one from which tiers of subjects cascade downward. The monarch's sovereignty radiates outward, gradually attenuating into porous frontiers where boundaries marking one realm from another mix imperceptibly together. Monarchical authority partakes of the divine, modeled in scriptures and demanded by priests. The "Mandate of Heaven" legitimizing the Emperor of China was inferred from its absence. Calamities like earthquakes, hurricanes, plagues, crop failures, and military defeats signified the withdrawal of heavenly approval of a ruling house and conferred permission on subjects to overthrow it.

Aristotle thought that monarchy was the best government, disinterested and free from internal conflict. But every ideal has its evil opposite. For monarchy, it is tyranny, a self-interested rather than a disinterested high center. To the tyrant, the subject is a means to satisfy his or her desires, whims, and perversities. While religious strictures might reduce or regulate the propensity of populations to rise up against tyrants, they offered no protection against them. The horrors of tyranny encouraged philosophers and revolutionaries to think of ways to curb monarchical power.

Philosophers like Thomas Hobbes, John Locke, and Jean Jacques Rousseau sought to restrain the power of rulers through contracts and laws. Constitutional government evolved as customary practice and in discrete formal documents, creating permanent institutions independent of monarchs and rules of engagement circumscribing their interaction. Revolutionaries overthrew monarchies, replacing them with new forms of rule by the few and, gradually, by the many. The popular image of the nation slowly shifted from a hierarchy cascading from a high center to a horizontal arrangement of equal citizens. Yet these changes were neither uniform nor worldwide. The career of Belgium's King Leopold II is an extreme example of how European imperialism kept tyranny alive abroad despite democratization at home. His rule over the Belgian Congo was ruthless and brutal. It suppressed all native opposition and was intolerant of freedoms for native residents.

After World War II, imperialism became untenable and former colonial possessions gradually became independent. Conventional wisdom also predicted the end of monarchy despite lingering remnants in such places as Britain, Japan, and Scandinavia: other monarchical survivals would be like them, merely ceremonial. In the words of Walter Bagehot, they would be "dignified" rather than "efficient." While a vestigial monarch might reign, he or she no longer would rule.

Yet several years into the twenty-first century, efficient or ruling monarchs remain, most of them in the Middle East and North Africa. This can't be explained simply as the result of tradition; some of these regimes are relatively new. The end of imperialism did not automatically lead to the end of monarchy. Some former dependencies did overthrow emperors and monarchs. Others still have theirs, the result perhaps of a combination of crafty adjustments by rulers and second thoughts by citizens that their neighbors' efforts to end monarchy in places like Egypt, Iraq, Iran, and Syria had merely produced another, more efficient form of tyranny. Observing that monarchies appear to be more resilient than expected, scholars have tried to explain why.

Lisa Anderson suggests that monarchies persist for psychological reasons. Monarchs are uniquely able to act as nation-builders because their authority depends on their personal qualities, especially military valor, and because they evoke primordial loyalty. Loyalty comes from religious authority and is ceremonially reinforced in rituals like the annual ram sacrifice in which the King of Morocco plays a dominant role. The monarchies of the Persian Gulf present themselves as epitomes of Arabian tribal values and call upon primordial loyalties to the "family" of the nation. The monarch is thus a *pater familias*, the legitimate representative of his (or her) family/subjects who wields life-and-death power over them.

Explaining the persistence of monarchy in oil-exporting countries, Hazem Beblawi combines a tacit image of the monarch as father-provider to an elaborate picture of the state as the owner of oil revenues. Monarchs of such "rentier states" stay in power as long as they can earn enough money from foreign oil sales to buy off likely revolutionaries and provide high levels of welfare to their populations. Yet the rentier state thesis does not explain the overthrow of the monarchy in Iran or the persistence of the monarchy of Jordan.

Michael Herb argues that the persistence of monarchy results from well-crafted institutions able to adjust to the pressures of modernity. He says that "dynastic monarchies," which include Morocco and the Persian Gulf kingdoms and emirates, are resilient because of the structure of interests within the ruling class. In dynastic monarchies, kingship is not passed from father to son but rather by consensus among powerful ruling family members. Errors in judgment that produce an obviously incompetent ruler can be rectified by the same procedure. Other family members control key positions in government, thereby eliminating power bases that could be occupied by potential revolutionaries. Yet dynastic monarchies in Kuwait and Saudi Arabia have failed to remove moribund rulers while the late King Hussein of Jordan decided suddenly on his own to substitute his son Abdullah for his brother Hassan as Crown Prince. While these situations demonstrate the stability of dynastic monarchies, they also illustrate their fragility.

The continuation of monarchical rule in the twenty-first century is undoubtedly the result of effective statecraft, but it also reflects good luck and a hospitable international environment. Most of today's ruling monarchies were able to find protectors during the Cold War and, until recently, could expect outside support to counteract some effects of internal opposition. Any explanation for the persistence of monarchy thus must include a role for external actors and conditions as well as psychological and structural supports for this ancient form of rule.

MARY ANN TÉTREAULT

References and Further Reading

Anderson, Benedict. *Imagined Communities: Reflections on the Origin and Spread of Nationalism*, rev. ed. London: Verso, 1991.

Anderson, Lisa. "Dynasts and Nationalists: Why Monarchies Survive." In *Middle East Monarchies: The Challenge of Modernity*. Edited by Joseph Kostiner. Boulder, CO: Lynne Rienner, 2000.

Beblawi, Hazem. "The Rentier State in the Arab World." In *The Arab State*, edited by Giacomo Luciani. Austin, TX: University of Texas Press, 1990.

Herb, Michael. *All in the Family: Absolutism, Revolution, and Democracy in the Middle Eastern Monarchies*. Albany: State University of New York Press, 1999.

Hochschild, Adam. *King Leopold's Ghost*. New York: Mariner Books, 1999.

MONEY LAUNDERING

Money laundering is the process through which criminal and illegal money is "laundered," creating the illusion that it is legally earned. Laundered money refers only to money that goes against anti money-laundering legislation and is not necessarily synonymous with dirty money. Dirty money is money that violates any laws in its origin, movement, or use. Therefore, defining money laundering as the handling of any sort of criminal or tax-evading proceeds is inaccurate. The United States, for example, still maintains dozens of categories of criminal money that remain outside the anti money-laundering legislation.

Anti money-laundering legislation varies from country to country. In some countries, for example, it is an offence to launder the proceeds of another person's criminal conduct. In others, laundering is regarded as an ongoing offence; hence, the actual timing of the criminal activity is not seen as relevant. Therefore, what in one country may be considered as laundered money may not be so regarded in another.

It is estimated that every year the equivalent of one trillion US dollars is laundered worldwide. According to Raymond Baker, a leading money-laundering expert at the Brookings Institution, approximately half of this sum is generated by violent criminal activities, such as organized trafficking in drugs, weapons, or people. The other half is illegal capital flight—tax-evading money derived from kickbacks, bribes, falsified invoices, and sham transactions by overseas nationals who place that money into outside secure accounts, mostly in US institutions.

Money Laundering and Terrorism

Terror organizations also use money-laundering techniques to move money around the globe. Terrorists finance their operations through criminal activity, or they may also use funding from legal sources. In either case, terrorist groups utilise financial networks in the same way that other criminal groups do. Consequently, after the events of September 11, several countries have changed their anti-money laundering legislation. Special measures have been taken also by the Financial Action Task Force on Money Laundering (FATF). Established by the G-7 Summit in Paris in 1989, the FATF initially developed forty recommendations. Members of the FATF comprise twenty-nine countries and jurisdictions—including European, North and South American, and Asian major financial centres—as well as the European Commission and the Gulf Cooperation Council.

After September 11, the FAFT expanded its mission in order to focus on eliminating terrorist financing. It issued new international standards to combat terrorist financing, and is involved in identifying the systemic weaknesses in the anti-money laundering programmes of certain jurisdictions. The FAFT also attempts to identify emerging new methods and trends used for laundering money.

Laundering Drug Money

To counteract the anti-money laundering policies, Latin American drug traffickers have developed the Black Market Peso Exchange. This system is elusive to traditional monetary controls because it does not involve the physical movement of cash from one country to another.

In the early days of the Medellin drug cartel, cash was flown back to Colombia by the same planes that took the drugs to the United States. Once in Colombia, the process of converting dollars into pesos was very slow and required the help of local bankers. Drug traffickers had to store huge amounts of cash. One Colombian drug trafficker buried so much cash on his property that when it rained heavily, the floods washed US dollars downstream, clogging the sewage system. US dollars are of no use to the Colombian drug cartel or to the Revolutionary Armed Forces of Colombia (FARC), the terror group acting as its militia, or to the Shining Path/Sendero Luminoso in Peru. Members of these organizations need domestic money to pay local growers, to buy protection, to bribe politicians, to recruit, and to purchase arms and explosives.

In the 1990s, drug traffickers and terror groups infiltrated the Colombian currency black market and transformed it into the Black Market Peso Exchange. The drug traffickers ship to and sell the narcotics in the United States; in exchange they receive US dollars in cash, which they hand over to a money broker inside the United States. The broker agrees to exchange it at a discount to the official rate, generally around 40%, and to deliver the corresponding pesos in Colombia within a few weeks. The broker then distributes the cash to a vast staff of runners, who deposit it in small amounts into thousands of US bank accounts under their names. Once the money is in the bank, it is "clean." To avoid being monitored by the US monetary authorities, bank deposits and purchases are always below the $10,000 limit imposed by the IRS. Breaking down large sums of deposits into several transactions of less than $10,000 is illegal in the United States.

At the same time the broker has an office in Colombia where locals go to buy foreign products, ranging from US cigarettes to TV sets, which they acquire using pesos. The purchases are done with an exchange rate that generally is 20% above the official exchange rate. The US money broker buys the goods in the United States using the drug money deposited by its runners, often from companies that know the origins of the funds; the broker then ships the products to his or her office in Colombia where they are sold for pesos. These pesos are then used to pay back the drug traffickers.

The Black Market Peso Exchange is also used by South American professionals to send dollars to their children studying in the United States. According to the IRS, from 1999 to 2003, the volume of money laundered via the Black Market Peso Exchange increased from US$1 billion to $6 billion.

Origins of Money Laundering

The history of money laundering is that of hiding money or assets from the state to protect it from confiscation or taxation. People have used money laundering to move money resulting from crime, but also to hide it from governments, including oppressive regimes. Two thousand years before Christ, merchants in China hid their wealth from rulers. Often, they invested it in businesses in remote provinces or even outside China. Thus, the birth of the offshore industry and tax evasion coincides with the advent of money-laundering activities.

Through the ages, the principles of money laundering have not changed. What has changed are the mechanisms. When gold coins were worth their weight in gold, it was immaterial what country had issued them. The value of the coins was determined by the quality and quantity of the gold. Melting the coin was an easy and efficient money-laundering technique. Today, gold remains one of the main non-currency means of holding money, including laundered money.

The use of the term "money laundering" is a modern phenomenon. It is linked to the rise of the famous US gangsterism, which originated from the Prohibition of the 1920s—the banning of the sale of alcohol in the United States. Organized crime utilized several mechanisms to disguise the illegal origins of profits generated by the import and sale of alcohol and other "rackets" such as gambling. The money was in cash, often in small-denomination coins, and could not be deposited into banks unnoticed. So they used businesses, such as laundries that generated profits in coins, to filter through their profits. This is how the term "money laundry" was born.

LORETTA NAPOLEONI

See also Banking; Black Market/Shadow Economy; Terrorism

References and Further Reading

Baker, Raymond. *Capitalism's Achilles Heel*. New York: Wiley, 2005.

Financial Action Task Force on Money Laundering. http://www.fatf-gafi.org.

Giacomo, Carol. "World Bank Corruption May Top $100 Billion." *Reuters*, May 13, 2004.

Global Policy Forum, Selection of Articles on Money Laundering. http://www.globalpolicy.org/nations/launder/general.htm.

Lilley, Peter. *Dirty Dealing: The Untold Truth About Global Money Laundering, International Crime, and Terrorism*. Sterling, VA: Kogan Page, 2003.

Money Laundering. http://www.moneylaundering.com.

Napoleoni, Loretta. *Terror Inc*. London: Penguin, 2004.

Robinson, Jeffrey. *The Laundrymen: Money Laundering the World's Third Largest Business*, new ed. New York: Arcade, 2004.

"That Infernal Washing Machine." *The Economist*, July 24 1997.

Woods, F. Brett. *Art and Science of Money Laundering*. Boulder, CO: Paladin Press, 1998.

MONGOLIA

Mongolia (also known as Mongolian People's Republic [MPR] until 1992) is located in Inner Asia, bordering with China in the south and Russia in the north; a small strip of the Chinese territory in the west separates Mongolia from Kazakhstan. The country has a land area of 1,565,000 square kilometers (604,250 sqare miles); comparatively, the territory of Mongolia is slightly smaller than the state of Alaska, the largest state in the United States.

The population of Mongolia was 2,712,315 (July 2003, CIA estimate), up from 1,564,000 in 1979. It is predominantly urban with about 58% of the people living in cities and towns. The country's capital city, Ulaanbaator (Ulan Bator), is home to about 780,000 people or almost one-third of the population. Mongolia has a population growth rate of 1.42% (CIA estimate 2003) and it is estimated that its population could double by 2050. Major languages include Khalkha Mongol (90%), Kazakh (4%), Russian, and Chinese. The major religion is Tibetan Buddhist Lamaism, 96%, with the remaining 4% practicing Shamanism and Christianity.

For centuries, the Mongols have been engaged in animal husbandry, raising horses, sheep, goats, and cattle. The vast dry prairie land can support millions of sheep, but only about 8% of the countryside is arable. Until the twentieth century, relations between Mongolia and its neighbors have often been characterized by devastating wars and military conflicts, which have had a negative effect on Mongolian economic and social development. Consequently, Mongolia entered the twentieth century as a feudal country with most of the population engaged in subsistence economy. In the nineteenth and early twentieth centuries the Chinese and Russian Empires competed with each other to establish political control over this strategically important area.

The major economic and social changes were brought to Mongolia after the national revolution of 1920–1921. The Mongolian People's Party, with Soviet assistance, successfully fought its opponents, and in 1924 the Mongolian People's Republic was declared. However, it took many decades before the international community recognized the MPR, and only in 1961 did the country become a member of the United Nations. The Mongolian People's Party (renamed the Mongolian People's Revolutionary Party in 1924) remained the single ruling party for the nearly seventy years.

Under Soviet influence, the Mongolian government introduced radical economic changes, including state control of all types of economic activities and central state planning. It eliminated mass illiteracy and developed extended free education and medical services for all sectors of the population, but at the same time the government suppressed basic political freedoms, banned opposition, and did not allow private entrepreneurship. In the 1930s, the government forced all farmers to join large-scale farming centered around *negdels*, state-controlled collective farms. The *negdels* traditionally specialized in animal herding, grain, and so forth. During and after World War II, the government developed the industrial sector of the country with major investments from the Soviet Union. The state-controlled industrial enterprises included agricultural machinery, mining, and light industries such as shoes, garments, and food processing. During the Socialist era, all economic activities in Mongolia were state-controlled, and private entrepreneurial initiatives were limited. Until the 1990s, the Soviet Union and the East European countries remained Mongolia's main trading partners and the chief market for its products. According to the International Monetary Fund (IMF), the Mongolian economy grew at an average annual rate of 6.0% between 1979 and 1989, which was one of the highest growth rates in communist countries.

Under domestic and external pressures, the Mongolian government introduced major changes in the late 1980s, abandoning the socialist economic model in favor of a centrally planned economy and total political and economic control. These changes were largely peaceful since they were initiated by the ruling elite under the influence of the neighboring Soviet Union and China. In the early 1990s, the international organizations such as the International Monetary Fund and the World Bank together with the Mongolian government formulated a program of radical economic changes (the so-called shock therapy approach). This program was based on three main mechanisms: rapid mass privatization, rapid price liberalization, and currency reform. Under this program, the state privatized major sectors of its economy including housing, catering, retail, and agricultural enterprises; allowed private ownership of the land; liberalized its domestic and international trade; and opened the national economy for international investors.

Initially, the country experienced an economic slow down and a "transitional recession." According to the IMF, Mongolia's economy declined at an average annual rate of 0.1% between 1989 and 1999, while the United States experienced a decade of unprecedented growth. However, after the completion of the first stage of the reform, the national economy experienced moderate annual economic growth of about 3%–4%. Due to its rapid and extensive economic liberalization, Mongolia was accepted into the World Trade Organization (WTO) in 1997.

Mining, agriculture, and agricultural product processing are the three main pillars of the Mongolian economy. The modern Mongolian economy largely relies on export of raw materials to international markets. The country's main exports are copper concentrate (which accounted for almost 47% of its total export earnings in 1998), cashmere (the country produces almost 30% of world's cashmere), textiles, and meat products. The mining industry is largely concentrated around the second- and third-largest Mongolian cities, Erdenet and Darhan. The country depends heavily on imports of machinery, fuels, industrial consumer goods, and food products since it has very limited industrial capacities. Due to the transitional recession and disappearance of aid from the former USSR, Mongolia's economy increasingly relies on foreign aid and credits. Total external debt has reached almost US$1.037 billion (World Bank estimate 2002).

Recent Development

Transitional reforms in Mongolia conducted throughout the 1990s with World Bank and IMF assistance brought mixed results. On the one hand, they disassembled the state control over the economy, allowed private entrepreneurship, and diversified international trade partners. On the other hand, they brought widespread poverty; a diminishing social welfare system, especially health care and education; a rise in organized crime; and extreme income polarization. The country increasingly relies on the export of raw

materials to the international market, and it is extremely vulnerable to fluctuations in world prices for its major export products—copper and agricultural products. Mongolia needs considerable foreign direct investments and international assistance to modernize existing technologies and to conduct major economic changes. However, both local and foreign investors are reluctant to invest in the economy due to the small size of the market, the weakness of the legal system, and the inability of state institutions to implement property rights and contract law. In addition, small private farmers, without state support, have become highly vulnerable to environmental changes and extreme weather conditions.

Despite macroeconomic stability and success in structural changes, the economic changes led to a steady decline in living standards among pensioners, rural people, and women with children. In 2004 the World Bank classified Mongolia as a low-income economy with a Gross National Income (GNI) per capita of $430, with about 52% of its population living below the poverty line (2002 est.). In 2003 the UNDP's Human Development Index (HDI) put Mongolia in 117th place out of 175, behind Bolivia, Honduras and Equatorial Guinea, but ahead of Gabon and Guatemala.

RAFIS ABAZOV

References and Further Reading

Akiner, S., ed. *Mongolia Today*. London, 1992.
Human Development Report Mongolia 2003: Balancing Rural and Urban Disparity. Ulaanbaatar, UNDP, and Government of Mongolia, 2004.
International Monetary Fund. *Growth and Recovery in Mongolia During Transition*. Working Paper No. 03/217. Washington, DC: Author, 2003.
Mongolia: EIU Country Report. (quarterly)
Mongolia: Toward a Market Economy (A World Bank Country Study). Washington, DC: World Bank, December 1992.
Mongolia. Statistical Annex. Prepared by Kevin Fletcher, Sanjay Kalra, Catriona Purfield, and Sergei Dodzin. Washington, DC: World Bank, January 2000.
The Mongolian Economy: A Manual of Applied Economics of an Economy in Transition. Edited by F. I. Nixson, Bernard Walters, B. Suvd, and P. Luvsandorj. Aldershot, UK: Edward Elgar, 2000.

MONTENEGRO

Montenegro is a small democratic republic located on the west Adriatic coast of the Balkan Peninsula between Bosnia, Serbia, and Albania. A mountainous country with 120 miles of coastline, it covers slightly over forty-nine thousand square miles. Its sandy beaches are suitable for tourism, and its climate ranging from continental to sub-tropical along the coast allows for general as well as specialized farming. The mountains, however, rise sharply, causing obstacles for communication into the interior. The rivers of Montenegro have cut deep gorges in the area creating spectacular scenery, and the low level of development has left much of the country's mountains, rivers, and forests in a pristine condition.

Many Montenegrins consider themselves to be Serbs. Yet a separate Montenegrin national consciousness has persisted, encouraged by a post–World War II Yugoslav governmental philosophy emphasizing the federal character of the country. Montenegrins speak a dialect similar to Serbo-Croatian and the majority belong to the autocephalous Montenegrin Orthodox church, but their pre-1919 history is separate from that of Serbia except for a short period in the Middle Ages when they were part of the Serbian empire. According to the 1991 census, 62% of the population identified themselves as Montenegrin and only 9% as Serbian. The country's 620,000 population also has a large Albanian and Muslim minority.

Formally part of the Ottoman Empire in the early modern period, the country was in fact an independent monarchy led by its Eastern Orthodox bishop, a member of the Njegoš dynasty. In 1852 Prince Danilo secularized the dynasty, whose independence the European powers recognized in 1878. In 1919 his son Nikola (proclaimed king in 1910) reluctantly left the throne as the Kingdom of Serbs, Croats, and Slovenes (renamed Yugoslavia in 1929), which the victorious World War I Allies created under the rule of the Karadjorjević family, absorbed the tiny mountain monarchy. During World War II the Axis powers broke up Yugoslavia, recreating the Montenegrin kingdom, but linking it to the Italian monarchy. After World War II when the victors once more restored Yugoslavia, Montenegro returned to the state.

In 1945 Josip Broz-Tito established Communist rule in the country and changed it into the Yugoslav Federation of Republics. Montenegro became one of six autonomous republics. In 1948 Tito broke with Josef Stalin and successfully established a separate Communist course from the Soviet Union emphasizing decentralization in the economy.

During the period between the world wars, Belgrade paid little attention to the economic development of Montenegro. Many Montenegrins left the country for better opportunities elsewhere. Because of the area's poverty and its pan-Slav traditional friendship with Russia, many Montenegrins supported the Communist Party, and thus the postwar republic gave Yugoslavia a disproportionate number of officials, police, and army officers. Montenegro had the greatest proportion of members on the ruling Federal Executive Council and Central Committee of the League of Yugoslav Communists than its population (3% of the total) warranted, usually 20% or more. However, one of the most famous Montenegrins, the one-time Communist Milovan Djilas, was a critic of both Stalin and Tito, and the latter imprisoned him many times.

Montenegro received much federal aid and incentives such as tax breaks, and industrialization began, but its development never reached expected goals. Belgrade attempted to develop the steel industry in the republic and exploit the region's bauxite mines. The difficulty of integrating Montenegro into the main industrial and economic areas of the country and the republic's remoteness hampered this development. The government did not begin the development of the coast as a tourist region until the 1980s.

Yugoslav policy in the postwar years siphoned resources and money from the richer republics, especially Slovenia and Croatia, to develop the poorer ones (Montenegro, Macedonia, and Bosnia), creating a great deal of hostility and tension. Croats especially accused Belgrade of robbing their republic to develop South Serbia and Montenegro—an example of the Greater Serbian politics of domination that characterized Yugoslavia in the monarchal period.

The 1947 plan to industrialize Yugoslavia emphasized fantastically high increases in development à la the Soviet five-year plans, especially in basic industries. New factories were destined for underdeveloped areas like Montenegro. The ambitious, naive plan was doomed to fail and the rupture of relations with Moscow insured it. The 1957 five-year plan gave Montenegro, as an underdeveloped area, federal grants and budget and tax incentives for industrial development. However, in 1961 a recession forced changes, and a special development fund was established for underdeveloped regions. Statistically, Montenegro profited more than other countries.

The 1964 index for net national product ranged from 190 (Slovenes) to thirty-five (Kosovo). Montenegro was sixty-eight. Social backwardness and technical lagging hampered development. The ambitious and primitive plans as well as annual changes in those plans furthered inefficiency. Montenegro's steel mill was a disaster. Construction began in 1953 at Nikšić, but a rail connection to the Adriatic did not appear for eight years, a road for over ten, and a standard-gauge railroad not until 1975.

In 1988–1989 a pro-Milosević (who has Montenegrin relatives) political faction controlled the republic, and Podgorica joined Belgrade in its wars in Bosnia and Croatia. After 1991 Montenegro was forced to face the dilemma of its relation to Serbia. On the one hand, the federation provided it with resource opportunities, but the isolation of Serbia because of its involvement in ethnic cleansing in Bosnia and Kosovo hurt its reputation and harmed the tourist industry. In 1992 with the breakup of Yugoslavia, Montenegro and Serbia formed a new federation, and ten years later, in March 2002, the two states created an even looser federation called "Serbia and Montenegro."

The Liberal Alliance, the major opposition party, has promoted the independence of Montenegro from Serbia, especially as Serbia's international reputation has declined under the rule of Slobodan Milošević, but the ruling Democratic of Party of Socialists led by president Milo Djukanović (2002) favored the continued alliance with Belgrade. In the 1990s many associations in the West such as the Montenegro Association of America and Montenet UK promoted relations between Montenegro and the West, its separation from Serbia, a retelling of its separate history and culture, and the economic development of the country.

FREDERICK B. CHARY

See also Balkan Wars of the 1990s; Central and Eastern Europe: History and Economic Development; Central and Eastern Europe: International Relations

References and Further Reading

Adamovic, Svetlana and Vukasin Pavlovic. "Environmental Issues and Policies, with Special Attention to Montenegro." In *Beyond Yugoslavia: Politics, Economics, and Culture in a Shattered Community*, edited by Sabrina P. Ramet and Ljubiša S. Adamovic. Boulder, CO: Westview Press, 1995.

Andrejevich, Milan. "Politics in Montenegro." In *Beyond Yugoslavia: Politics, Economics, and Culture in a Shattered Community*, edited by Sabrina P. Ramet and Ljubiša S. Adamovic. Boulder, CO: Westview Press, 1995.

Boehm, Christopher. *Montenegrin Social Organization and Values: Political Ethnography of a Refuge Area Tribal Adaptation*. New York: AMS Press, 1983.

Rusinow, Dennison. *The Yugoslav Experiment: 1948–1974*. Berkeley, CA: University of California Press, 1977.

The Economist Intelligence Unit. *Country Profile: Macedonia, Serbia-Montenegro*. London: The Unit, 1996.

Stevenson, Francis Seymour. *A History of Montenegro*. New York: Arno Press, 1971.

Warren, Whitney. *Montenegro: The Crime of the Peace Conference*. New York: Brentano's, 1922.

MONTONEROS

The *Movimiento Peronista Montonero*, more commonly known as *Montoneros*, was one of three Peronist guerrilla movements active in Argentina during the 1970s. They sprang from the multifaceted left-wing faction of the Justicialist Movement, which was inspired and led by Juan Domingo Perón, and had the ultimate objective of instituting a socialist system in Argentina through armed revolutionary struggle. In order to further their cause, the *Montoneros* relied on an eclectic support base that included trade unions, student organizations, radical members within the Catholic Church, and the dispossessed urban classes. The *Montoneros* were the first revolutionary group in Latin America to successfully carry out urban guerrilla operations with far-reaching political implications, including violent attacks against Argentinean authorities and elites as well as foreign capital interests. At the height of their activities in the 1970s, the *Montoneros* had up to seven thousand guerrilla fighters.

The origins of the *Montoneros* can be traced back to Perón's first presidency (1946–1955). In order to rally support for his political leadership, Perón introduced sweeping labor reforms that significantly improved the working conditions of the urban proletariat, including increased wages, pensions, a reduced working week, and housing and health benefits. However, far from being an anti-capitalist, Perón favored a corporatist path whereby the interests of both capital and labor would be balanced out in the administration of the economy. In this context, Perón resorted to a message of social justice that translated into tangible gains for the working class, earning him a loyal following that sustained him in power for almost ten years. The end of his regime was orchestrated by the local capital elites, who saw their fortunes slide as the clout of labor increased under Perón, and by foreign interests, mainly the United States, who saw Perón as a potential threatening figure too closely attached to socialist ideals.

After Perón left office, a large segment of his supporters acknowledged the need to perfect Perón's sketchy vision of social justice by fundamentally changing the course of political action. This leftist *Peronista* segment, increasingly influenced by revolutionary socialist ideas, proposed that the national capitalist elites and their foreign counterparts should not be included in the equation for a progressive society precisely because they themselves were the source of the problem. From this perspective, a diverse coalition of Perón's supporters set out to organize a national party that would fuse urban guerrilla warfare with the popular struggles of the *Peronista* movement as the means to bring about a socialist revolution in Argentina. It is important to note that the initial common ground for the *Montonero* membership, which included members of the Catholic Church, socialists, and at first even right-of-center middle class *Peronistas*, revolved around a rather broad nationalistic sentiment that sought the return to national self-determination and economic prosperity. However, as the direction of Argentinean politics tilted in favor of capital and national elites, the *Montoneros* also shifted their ideological platform by favoring the ways of socialism and armed struggle, to the exclusion of all other methods, as the paths to vindicate their interpretation of *Peronista* social justice.

The *Montoneros* began their violent political actions against the Argentinean state and foreign multinational corporations in the late 1950s, concentrating on the assassinations of high-ranking public officials and perpetrating kidnappings of rich businessmen to finance their activities. Their activities continued in the 1960s, but these were sporadic and registered little political repercussions. In 1973, a frail Perón returned to Argentina and won the presidential election that year, but instead of uniting the different currents of *Peronismo*, his victory managed to pull them further away. As violence erupted between the *Montoneros* and right-wing *Peronistas*, and as demands from each side put pressure on the decision making of the new government, Perón sided with the conservative faction. In May 1974, the *Montoneros* were officially expelled from the Justicialist Movement by Perón. However, the *Montoneros* vowed to continue fighting for what they believed were the revolutionary ideals of authentic *Peronismo*.

A fundamental turning point that fueled the armed activities of the *Montoneros* came in March 1976, when a military junta, led by General Jorge Rafael Videla, ousted the government that Perón's wife had taken over after his death in 1974. Now operating under an openly repressive political atmosphere, the *Montoneros* raised their activities to new heights. During this turbulent period, their most significant operations had to do with the kidnappings and ransoming of members of the business elites, the assassinations of executives from General Motors and Chrysler, and the massive bombing of the Federal Intelligence Department in Buenos Aires in July 1976. The upholding of the armed struggle as the only means to face the military junta radicalized the activities and ideology of the *Montoneros'* rank and file, losing the support of more moderate members and at times engaging in internal ideological feuds that curtailed the success of their political and military activities by turning members against each other.

The military junta answered the *Montoneros'* offensive with a systematic campaign of terror. Between 1976 and 1983, *La Guerra Sucia* (dirty war) was conducted by fostering and protecting groups of vigilante death squads, such as the Argentine Anti-Communist Alliance (Triple A), that engaged in activities that targeted perceived enemies of the junta and supporters of revolutionary groups. These death squads engaged in mass arrests, torture, extra-judicial executions, and disappearances of up to thirty thousand people during those years, instituting a regime of generalized state terror that managed to neutralize the activities of opposition groups, including the *Montoneros*. Close to one-quarter of the *Montoneros'* active membership had been killed by 1978, their operations had been disrupted, and the surviving members were forced to either disperse or go into exile.

The last remnants of the *Montoneros* were effectively defeated by the early 1980s, and it was not until 1984 that civilian rule returned to Argentina. Although unsuccessful in bringing about the "authentic Peronist vision" through armed struggle and radical politics, the legacy of the *Montoneros* remains in the relevance of the core goals they fought for: the need for social justice and national self-determination.

CARLOS VELÁSQUEZ CARRILLO

See also Argentina; Perón, Juan Domingo

References and Further Reading

Gillespie, Richard. *Soldiers of Peron: Argentina's Montoneros*. Oxford, UK: Clarendon Press, 1982.
Hodges, Donald C. *Argentina, 1943–1987: The National Revolution and Resistance*. Albuquerque, NM: University of New Mexico Press, 1988.
Kohl, James and John Litt, eds. *Urban Guerrilla Warfare in Latin America*. Cambridge, MA: MIT Press, 1974.
Lewis, Paul. *Guerrillas and Generals: The "Dirty War" in Argentina*. Westport, CT: Praeger, 2002.
Moyano, Maria Jose. *Argentina's Lost Patrol: Armed Struggle, 1969–1979*. New Haven, CT: Yale University Press, 1995.

MONTSERRAT

Montserrat, a pear-shaped island in the Leeward Islands, is forty-three kilometers southwest of Antigua and seventy kilometers northwest of Guadeloupe. The 102-square kilometer island is an overseas territory of the United Kingdom. Montserrat, which means jagged mountain, is named after a mountain of the same name in Barcelona, Spain. Of volcanic origin, Montserrat has active sulfur vents in the mountainous south-central region. Because of its lush tropical rain forest, travel brochures repeatedly refer to the island as the Emerald Isle. Over 90% of Montserrat's people are of African descent. Owing to uncertainty about the island's economic future, most of Montserrat's people do not favor independence. Montserrat is a member of the British Commonwealth of Nations and the Organization of Eastern Caribbean States.

Although British officials are responsible for defense and foreign relations, local elected officials are responsible for all internal affairs, except security.

Queen Elizabeth II, the head of state, is represented locally by a governor—Deborah Barnes Jones (b. 1956) since 2004—who oversees the Legislative Council. The governor is appointed by the British government. Nine of the eleven Legislative Council members are directly elected by the people of Montserrat. The attorney general and the financial minister serve as ex-officio members of the Legislative Council. Although appointed by the governor, the chief minister—John Osborne (b. 1936) since 2001—is normally the leader of the majority political party in the Legislative Council.

Arawak and Carib Indians were the first inhabitants of the island. Christopher Columbus, who discovered the island in 1493, named the island Santa Maria de Montserrat. The British were the first Europeans to colonize the island, in 1632. The first settlers were Irish Roman Catholics. The cultural footprint of the Irish is evident in the predominance of Irish surnames today. During the colonial period, the British landowners implemented an agricultural system based on large estates. In 1958, like the rest of the British Caribbean, Montserrat joined the ill-fated West Indies Federation, which lasted until 1962 when Jamaica and Trinidad and Tobago withdrew from the association. Beginning in the 1960s, hundreds of North Americans and British subjects began to arrive on the island and build luxury homes. Real estate development and construction became a key component of Montserrat's economy.

The dominant figure in Montserrat's political system since the 1970s has been Chief Minister John Osborne, whose People's Liberation Movement (PLM) was the largest political presence in the Legislative Council from 1978 to 1991. In 1984, Osborne startled the people of Montserrat by suddenly calling for independence. His pronouncement was based on the British government's veto of Montserrat's decision to send a police force to participate in the police action in Grenada after the 1983 US-organized invasion following the overthrow of Maurice Bishop. Although most of Montserrat's people supported the US invasion of Grenada, they were against independence. Osborne subsequently promised that no decision on independence would be made until a referendum was held. In 1991, Osborne's main rival, Reuben Meade, leader of the National Progressive Party (NPP), became chief minister. A reinvigorated PLM returned to power in 2001.

In 1995, the Souffriere Hills volcano began to show signs of volcanic activity. In 1996, minor eruptions led to the evacuation of the southern third of Montserrat, where Plymouth, the capital, was located. Fortunately, all 3,500 people in Plymouth were evacuated. Subsequent eruptions in August 1997 covered the capital with lava and ash. The island's only airport was destroyed and the capital city was reminiscent of Pompeii. Of the island's eleven thousand inhabitants, over eight thousand fled to neighboring islands and the United Kingdom. A large portion of the island's annual income, therefore, comes from remittances by overseas citizens. The tourist industry, which only lured twenty-five thousand visitors per year to the colony during the early 1990s, came to a virtual stop in the aftermath of the volcanic eruptions. In 1998, the British government moved the capital of Montserrat to Brades in the Carr's Bay vicinity in the northern part of the island.

People who live in the northern part of the island are protected from the Souffriere Hills volcano by a mountain range in the center of the island. Thus, there is no danger to citizens and tourists in the northern region of the island. Therefore, since 1998, thousands of Montserrat's refugees began to return to their homeland. The government's tourist bureau has also made energetic attempts to lure tourists back to Montserrat. The dome of the volcano collapsed in 2003, which has greatly reduced volcanic activity in the region. Nevertheless, the volcano is still active and entry into the southern region of the island is restricted. Trespassers in the restricted zone are subject to fines and imprisonment. The British have implemented a multi-million-dollar recovery program to help reconstruct the economy. Included in the redevelopment program are plans for a new airport in the northern part of the island. The southern half of the island, however, will remain uninhabitable until 2010.

MICHAEL R. HALL

See also Bishop, Maurice; Caribbean: History and Economic Development; Caribbean: International Relations; Grenada; Organization of Eastern Caribbean States (OECS)

References and Further Reading

Fergus, Howard. *Montserrat: History of a Caribbean Colony*. London: Macmillan, 1994.
Ramos, Aaron Gamaliel and Angel Israel Rivera. *Islands at the Crossroads: Politics in the Non-Independent Caribbean*. Kingston, Jamaica: Ian Randle Publishers, 2001.
Taylor, Jeremy, ed. *The Caribbean Handbook*. St. John's, Antigua and Barbuda: FT Caribbean, 1986.
Wheeler, Marion M. *Montserrat West Indies: A Chronological History*. Plymouth, Montserrat: Montserrat National Trust, 1988.

MOROCCO

The Moroccan Kingdom, "*Al Mamlaka Al Maghriby*" in Arabic, is a North African constitutional monarchy with a bicameral legislature. Its capital is Rabat and the largest city is Casablanca (over 3.5 million inhabitants in 2001), located on the Atlantic coast. Morocco's total population is 30,645,305 (July 2001 estimate) and the rate of population growth is about 1.7%. The country's official religion is Islam, with Christian (1.1%) and Jewish (0.2%) minorities. Arabic is the official language, although French is widely spoken and is the language of business, government, and diplomacy. Spanish is commonly used in the northern provinces. There are tensions between Morocco and Spain concerning the alleged violations by Spain of Moroccan waters and illegal immigration. Tensions between Morocco and Algeria over Morocco's Western Sahara cloud the relationships between the two neighbors.

Morocco is strategically located along the Strait of Gibraltar. The country's total area (including the Western Sahara) is 710,850 square kilometers. The climate is Mediterranean on the coastal regions and hot, dry, and continental in the interior. The northern coast and interior are mountainous with large areas of bordering plateaus and rich coastal plains. The main natural resources are phosphates, iron ore, manganese, lead, zinc, fish, and salt. The national currency is the Moroccan dirham (8.4 units to the US dollar as of February 28, 2005).

Morocco became independent from the French authority on March 2, 1956, under Mohammed ben Youssef, also known as King Mohammed V. He died on February 26, 1961, and Hassan II was crowned king of Morocco the same day. It is under the reign of Hassan that Morocco started its movement toward modernization.

Between 1945 and 1956, Morocco was under French authority. During this period most projects were set up by colonial authority. In the agricultural sectors, modern farms were created in the most productive areas of the Gharb, Doukkala, Saiss, and Haouz. The French administration continued to build roads and railroads to facilitate transportation of phosphates and other natural resources to Europe. French and Spanish banks and industrial firms set up subsidiaries or mergers, mainly in Casablanca. However, there was no genuine interest in developing the Moroccan economy in the long run and for Moroccans. The investments (aside from railroads) had a short-term vision and monopoly profits for non-Moroccan investors.

Between 1956, the year of independence, and 1972, there was an effort to increase literacy rates and reduce unemployment. There were efforts aimed at strengthening the economy, but these were hampered by several political issues that ultimately led to severe human rights abuses, including the assassination of the political leader and militant Mehdi Benbarka in France, allegedly by conspiracy between Moroccan and French authorities.

In 1973, Morocco instituted the *Moroccanization* law according to which foreigners cannot own more that 49% of a Moroccan business. While by today's standards this would be viewed as detrimental to the economy, it did help stop the financial hemorrhage practiced by foreign (mostly French) firms. Throughout the 1970s, the central government emphasized the public sector's role in the economy. It increased food subsidies to offset the effects of agricultural protection. The sharp increase in world prices for phosphates helped secure significant revenues. However, in 1977–1978, phosphate prices fell sharply and the military spending increased as a result of the war in the Western Sahara. Consequently, financial imbalances increased. In 1980, the World Bank proposed a structural adjustment plan but due to the severity of the reforms involved, the Moroccan government could not pursue it. In the following year, an International Monetary Fund stabilization program that required increases in prices and reduction of subsidies caused riots in major cities and forced the government to postpone price reforms. In 1980–1983 the current account deficit approached 10% of gross domestic product (GDP) and the government budget deficit exceeded 12% of GDP.

The year 1983 marked a turning point in the relations between Morocco, and the World Bank and the IMF. Loans became linked directly to reform programs, for example, an agricultural-sector adjustment loan in 1985 and an education-sector loan in 1986. Structural reforms proceeded gradually between 1983 and 1989 and during most of the 1990s. A substantial amount of the required funds was disbursed by the World Bank. During 1983–1990 Morocco began implementing liberalization programs. Several favorable factors helped these programs. The dirham was depreciating, which helped to strengthen manufacturing exports. External factors included a sharp decline in oil prices (Morocco imports most of its oil) and favorable weather. Consequently, in the early 1990s, Morocco was viewed by world financial institutions as a potential success story.

In September 1993 Morocco repealed the *Moroccanization* law (only agricultural land and some mining industries remain subject to restricted foreign ownership). In addition, tax reforms, including changes in the corporate profit tax in 1984 and the introduction of the value-added-tax (VAT) in 1986, have led to simplification, neutrality, and more transparency of the tax system. Trade liberalization was enhanced by the introduction of current account convertibility in 1993. Morocco also privatized the

Casablanca stock exchange (CSE) in 1993. Between 1993 and 2001, Morocco privatized many public enterprises in different sectors of the economy. In addition, Morocco has achieved a high degree (perhaps one of the highest in the Arab world) of decentralization and localization of authority.

Over half of Morocco's trade is with EU nations. Morocco signed the Euro-Mediterranean Association Agreement on March 1, 2000. The Agreement includes clauses on the gradual liberalization of trade over a period of twelve years, by the end of which a free-trade area will be in effect. A timetable for abolishing customs tariffs for industrial products entering Morocco is set in the agreement. Morocco also started negotiations in September 2001 concerning the gradual liberalization of trade in agricultural products.

While Morocco has achieved significant progress in macroeconomic stabilization, many social developments in education, poverty alleviation, and gender issues have yet to be implemented. The literacy rate among Moroccans age fifteen and over is only 51% (World Bank 2000). In 1997, the World Bank found that although Morocco had stabilized the economy through budget deficit reduction, it failed to foster employment and achieve higher economic growth, and improve social development.

Under the reign of the current monarch, Mohammed IV, Morocco has undertaken several steps to enhance democracy and social welfare. Several dissidents, including Abraham Serfaty, a Moroccan Jew, have returned to the country.

MINA BALIAMOUNE

See also North Africa: History and Economic Development; North Africa: International Relations

References and Further Reading

Denoeux, G. P. and A. Maghraoui. "The Political Economy of Structural Adjustment in Morocco." in Azzedine Layachi, ed., *Economic Crisis and Political Change in North Africa*. Westport, CT: Praeger, 1998.

Hamdouch, B. "Adjustment, Strategic Planning and the Moroccan Economy." In N. Chafik, ed., *Economic Challenges facing Middle eastern and North African countries*. London: Macmillan Press, 1998.

———. "the Free Trade Area between Morocco and the European Union." In R. Safadi, ed., *Opening Doors to the World, A New Trade Agenda for the Middle East*. Cairo: The American University in Cairo Press and Ottawa: IDRC, 1998.

Henry, Clement M. *The Mediterranean Debt Crescent: Money and Power in Algeria, Egypt, Morocco, Tunisia, and Turkey*. Gainesville, FL: University of Florida, 1996.

Jbili, A., K. Enders, and V. Treichel. "Financial Sector Reforms in Algeria, Morocco, and Tunisia: A Preliminary Assessment." *International Monetary Fund Working Paper* WP/97/81 (1997).

Nsouli, S. M., S. Eken, K. Enders, V-C Thai, J. Decressin, and F. Cartigila, "Resilience and Growth Through Sustained Adjustment: The Moroccan Experience." *IMF Occasional Paper*, no. 117 (1995).

Zriouli, M. *La Région Economique au Maroc, Quel Avenir?* Editions Okad, 1990.

MOSSADDEQ, MUHAMMED

Dr. Muhammed Mossaddeq (1882–1967) was born in Tehran on May 19, 1882, into arguably the most prominent Iranian political family of the past century. Mossaddeq traveled to Europe, where he studied in France and Switzerland and acquired a doctorate in law. Beginning in 1921, he served in numerous political positions including finance minister, deputy in Iranian parliament (Majlis), and finally as prime minister from 1951 to 1953.

On October 1949, at the age of sixty-seven, Muhammad Mossaddeq was the moving force behind the establishment of the National Front. This loose coalition of political groups professed liberal democratic goals and strongly opposed all forms of foreign influence in Iran, particularly that of the Anglo-Iranian Oil Company (AIOC). The Anglo-Iranian Oil Company was a symbol of British influence in Iran's post–World War II affairs, and one that served to bolster Iranian nationalism. The AIOC was believed to be a host company for British political officers who indirectly had been controlling the political destiny of Iran.

Dr. Mossaddeq, who was the chair of the oil committee in the Majlis, and several members of the Majlis who belonged to the National Front under his leadership, pushed for the nationalization of the AIOC. The news in 1951 of the new arrangement between Aramco (The Arabian-American Oil Company) and Saudi Arabia and their agreement to a fifty-fifty profit-sharing plan advanced the cause of nationalization in Iran. On April 30, the Majlis passed a nine-point enabling law that included a provision for compensating the AIOC. The British government protested the nationalization and insisted that under the 1933 agreement Iran should submit to arbitration. The Iranian government replied that the British government had no right to interfere in a matter between Iran and an oil company. On April 28, Mossaddeq was appointed prime minister and on the same day the Majlis voted unanimously to seize the company's properties in Iran. On May 2, 1951, the young Shah signed the Nationalization Bill, completing the process.

Events occurred swiftly and surprised practically everyone concerned with the crisis. The British were surprised to see that Iran was not intimidated by threats, the freezing of Iranian assets, or even the sending of gunboats to the Persian Gulf. In the course of the crisis, which lasted two years, half a dozen alternative proposals were made, most of them accepting the principle of nationalization, but they all failed to bring about a solution. The British complained to the United Nations. In September 1952 Mossaddeq went to New York to defend Iran's case, contending that nationalization was an internal matter and subject to no international jurisdiction. The Security Council referred the question of jurisdiction to the World Court and the Court decided in favor of Iran, stating that the problem was an internal question and outside of the competency of the World Court or of the United Nations.

The British government, refusing to accept a reduced role in Iran, persuaded President Eisenhower's administration to intervene directly to overthrow the Mossaddeq government. The British government used the threat of a possible communist takeover as its major tactic in attracting American involvement. On August 19, Iranian conservatives, Britain, and the United States cooperated fully to oust Mossaddeq. The coup was successful and an era of intense US involvement in the support of the dictatorship of the Shah of Iran began. Muhammed Mossaddeq was arrested, tried by a military tribunal, and found guilty of treason. He spent three years in prison and the rest of his life under house arrest. He died in 1967.

The 1953 coup changed Iran's history in fundamental ways. It was clearly a setback for Iran's political development. The coup alienated Iranian intellectuals and weakened the moderate, liberal nationalists represented by such organizations as the National Front, and it paved the way to extremism.

NASSER MOMAYEZI

See also Iran

References and Further Reading

Cleveland, William L. *A History of the Modern Middle East*. Boulder, CO: Westview Press, 2004.
Goldschmidt, Arthur. *A Concise History of the Middle East*, 7th ed. Boulder, CO: Westview Press, 2001.
Goode, James. *The United States and Iran: In the Shadow of Musaddiq*. New York: Palgrave Macmillan, 1997.
Jelen, Ted G. and Clyde Wilcox, eds. *Religion and Politics in Comparative Perspective: The One, the Few, and the Many*. New York: Cambridge University Press, 2002.
Kinzer, Stephen. *All the Shah's Men: An American Coup and the Roots of Middle East Terror*. Hoboken, NJ: Wiley, 2003.
Moaddel, Mansoor. *Jordanian Exceptionalism: A Comparative Analysis of State-Religion Relationships in Egypt, Iran, Jordan, and Syria*. New York: Palgrave Macmillan, 2002.

MOZAMBIQUE

Mozambique has considerable human and natural resources. However, the violent cross currents of its recent history and complexity of its social fabric have considerably complicated its development. The past of this region is immeasurably ancient since it is where the human species itself developed.

To the north Mozambique is bordered by the country of Tanzania; along the east by the Mozambique Channel, which separates it from the island of Madagascar in the Indian Ocean; along the south lie Swaziland and South Africa; to the west, Zimbabwe; and the northwest, Zambia and Malawi. Mozambique is approximately the size of Alaska. It is dominated by mountains and plateaus in the north. These descend to highlands in the central region. Curving through the central portion of the country is the Zambezi River, the fourth largest in Africa. The southern part of the country consists of rolling lowlands. The native minorities of Mozambique divide into numerous subgroups. They differ extensively in their historic economic pursuits, social structures, and sizes and roles relative to each other.

Mozambique's population of almost 20 million people is very diverse, and contains many different tribes. In addition, foreign trade and invasions have produced minorities of Western Europeans, mainly Portuguese; southern Asians, mainly Indians; and *mestiços* or mixed bloods of Africans and Europeans. Although Portuguese has long been the language of official business, only 27% of the population speaks it. Several dozen native languages are used; Makhuwa, Tsonga, Lomwe, and Sena are four of the major ones. Religious diversity accompanies this cultural complexity. Religions include native-spiritism (about 50% of the population), Christianity (30%, mainly Catholicism but also small Protestant sects), Islam (20%), and syncretisms of native-spiritism and Christianity.

The Portuguese were the colonial overlords of the region from the sixteenth century onward. They developed trade in slaves, minerals, and foodstuffs along the coastal region and up the Zambezi valley. The south has been the traditional economic and administrative center of the country. Trade with South Africa increased with the late-nineteenth-century development there of gold and diamond mining. White southerners and their allies controlled commerce. Early in the twentieth century, hundreds of miles of rail lines were laid into the interior.

Until independence in 1975, the dominant elite in Mozambique was a tiny minority of white Portuguese. Supporting the Portuguese were further small minorities of mixed-race *mestiços* and natives who had been assimilated (*assimilados*) into European ways. Portuguese influence decreased, however, as one advanced into the interior. Portugal attempted systematic settlement there toward the end of the nineteenth century and as other European nations enlarged their interests in Africa.

Mozambicans have tended to divide between northerners and southerners. A complex of antagonisms has grown around differences between colonized and colonizer, debtor and creditor, governed and governor, rural and urban, black and white, victim and combatant, non-Christian and Christian, upland and lowland, and native and foreign.

Various degrees of poverty are common to all the country, but what sparse wealth does exist concentrates in the south and mostly in Maputo, the capital, and a few other cities. The poverty of Mozambicans results from the very unbalanced development that occurred under Portugal.

Independence occurred on July 25, 1975. Most Portuguese administrators, businessmen, and professionals fled the country. Civil war broke out between two rival groups trying to dominate the new national government.

In 1964 the Marxist-Leninist *Frente de Libertação de Moçambique* (FRELIMO—Mozambique Liberation Front) began armed struggle for independence. It assumed the national government in 1975. However, Mozambique's powerful capitalist, white-dominated neighbors, Rhodesia and South Africa, formed and financially backed an anti-Communist movement, the *Resistênica Nacional Moçambicana* (RENAMO—Mozambican National Resistance). It was strongly backed by US President Gerald Ford and Secretary of State Henry Kissinger. FRELIMO received support from the Soviet Union. Events unraveled in a manner similar to those occurring at the same time in Portugal's other major African colony, Angola.

RENAMO maneuvered against FRELIMO throughout the country, attacking in the south and occupying strongholds in the highlands. FRELIMO held the capital in the south, and RENAMO raided around there and in the north. The conflict assumed a north–south character, and everywhere it left hundreds of thousands dead, wounded, or displaced. Only the end of apartheid in South Africa and of the Cold War between East and West brought a tentative reconciliation between FRELIMO and RENAMO, a peace of exhaustion.

Mozambique reconstituted itself in 1990 as a multiparty state, established regular elections, and allowed private investment. In the latter part of the 1990s, Mozambique began to offer some possibility of fulfilling its economic promise. In 1999 it achieved an annual rate of economic growth of 10%, reaching a per capita income with purchasing power of US$1,000.

However, in 2000 epic floods ravaged the land and people, who mostly reside in the rural interior. A cholera epidemic broke out in the wake of the floods. Public health issues are widespread in Mozambique, which has one of the highest rates in Africa of people infected with the HIV virus or suffering from AIDS. Parents who have died from this disease have left many orphans. War produced a sizable minority of handicapped soldiers and civilians, refugees, displaced persons, and further orphans.

While the country has an exceptional birth rate of nearly 3.8%, its rate of population growth is just under 1.5%. Only 3% of the population is over 65, and nearly two-thirds of this group is female. Life expectancy is less than forty years for both sexes. Two-thirds of the population is under twenty-one. Both adults and, even more so, older people are minorities. There are 1.5% fewer males than females, a surprising balance given the years of warfare. However, the number also reflects how war along with disease has equally devastated soldiers and civilians.

Mozambique has used education, particularly emphasis on literacy, as a basis for attempting to lift itself up. Such an effort may offer some long-term opportunity for a common, beneficial development among the country's varied peoples.

EDWARD A. RIEDINGER

See also FRELIMO (Front for the Liberation of Mozambique); Southern Africa: History and Economic Development; Southern Africa: International Relations

References and Further Reading

Alden, Chris. *Mozambique and the Construction of the New African State: From Negotiations to Nation Building.* New York: Palgrave, 2001.

Azevedo, Mário Joaquim, Emmanuel U. Nnadozie, and Tombe Nhamitambo Mbuia-João. *Historical Dictionary of Mozambique* 2nd ed. Lanham, MD: Scarecrow Press, 2003.

Cabrita, João M. *Mozambique: The Tortuous Road to Democracy.* New York: Palgrave, 2000.

Christie, Frances and Joseph Hanlon. *Mozambique and the Great Flood of 2000.* Bloomington, IN: Indiana University Press, 2001.

Darch, Colin. "Mozambique." *World Bibliographical Series*, vol. 78. Oxford, UK: ABC-Clio Press, 1987.

Ferraz, Bernardo and Barry Munslow. *Sustainable Development in Mozambique.* Trenton, NJ: Africa Free Press, 2000.

Hall, Margaret. *Confronting Leviathan: Mozambique Since Independence.* Athens, OH: Ohio University Press, 1997.

Hanlon, Joseph. *Peace Without Profit: How the IMF Blocks Rebuilding in Mozambique.* Oxford, UK: James Currey, Heinemann, 1996.

Newitt, M. D. D. *A History of Mozambique*. Bloomington, IN: Indiana University Press, 1995.

Pitcher, M. Anne. *Transforming Mozambique: The Politics of Privatization, 1975–2000*. Cambridge, UK: Cambridge University Press, 2002.

MUBARAK, HOSNI

Hosni Muhammad Mubarak became Egypt's president in 1981. Born in Minufiyya province to a middle class family, Mubarak graduated from the Military Academy in 1949 and from the Air Force Academy the following year. He did not take part in the military coup that has come to be called the Egyptian Revolution of July 1952. After a brief stint as a fighter pilot, he served as an instructor at the Air Force Academy from 1954 to 1961. He spent the following academic year at the Soviet General Staff Academy and in 1964 took charge of training Egyptian pilots at the Frunze Military Training Center in Moscow. He was the commandant of Egypt's Air Force Academy from 1967 to 1969, air force chief of staff from 1969 to 1971, and commander-in-chief from 1971 to 1974. He took charge of Egypt's aerial preparations for the October (1973) War and was promoted to the rank of air marshal for his outstanding wartime performance. Egyptian President Anwar al-Sadat appointed him vice president in 1975, and Mubarak served him loyally for the next six years. He played no conspicuous role in the Camp David peace talks with Israel or in any of Sadat's other spectacular initiatives during that time.

After Sadat was assassinated on October 6, 1981, Mubarak assumed the presidency, was soon officially nominated by the National Democratic Party (NDP), and was confirmed by a nationwide referendum. Upon taking office, he promised to address Egypt's economic and social problems, publicly curbed the favoritism and corruption that had marred Sadat's final days, and released many of the political and religious leaders whom Sadat had imprisoned. Although the Egyptian people knew little about him, his earliest policies as president won widespread approval.

While restoring diplomatic relations with the USSR, Mubarak maintained Egypt's ties with the US government, on whose military and economic aid it had come to depend under Sadat. He did not break diplomatic relations with Israel (although he did recall Egypt's ambassador from Tel Aviv during Israel's invasion of Lebanon) and he gradually resumed good relations with the other Arab governments and the Palestine Liberation Organization, which had withdrawn their ambassadors from Cairo soon after Sadat signed the 1979 Egyptian–Israeli Peace Treaty. Although his government still encouraged Western and Arab investment in Egypt's economy, he curbed the operation of foreign multinational corporations within the country. He also increased the state's role in economic planning and protecting the welfare of the workers.

The failure of his efforts to mediate the 1990 dispute between Iraq and Kuwait became a precipitating factor in Saddam Hussein's decision to invade and occupy Kuwait. Although Mubarak initially hoped that the Arab leaders would resolve the crisis, his government soon rallied behind the US-led Operation Desert Shield, sending forty thousand troops to join the allied coalition in Saudi Arabia (but refusing to invade Iraq). Egypt was later rewarded by the cancellation of some $14 billion worth of accumulated foreign debt to various Arab and Western countries. The plan for Egypt and Syria to provide a long-term peacekeeping force to stabilize the Gulf States foundered on Kuwait's opposition.

During the first decade of Mubarak's presidency, Egypt made some progress toward democracy. Political parties created under Sadat were allowed to grow, publish newspapers, and run growing numbers of candidates in the legislative elections. Since 1992, however, the government has tried to limit the proliferation of parties, restricted freedom of the press, and curbed movements that it deems subversive. Mubarak has been reelected to the presidency—without opposition—in 1987, 1993, and 2000. He has never appointed a vice president, and many Egyptians believe that he is grooming his son, Gamal, a rising star within the ruling NDP, to succeed him. The Emergency Laws, under which Egypt has been governed almost continuously since World War II, have remained in effect throughout his presidency.

The Mubarak government initially countenanced the resurgence of Islamist movements in Egypt, most notably *al-Jihad* and *al-Jam'a al-Islamiyya*. The former was responsible for the plot to assassinate Sadat and has formed ties with *al-Qa'ida*. The latter was implicated in numerous attacks on cabinet ministers, Copts, and foreign tourists. In recent years, however, the government has tried to stop terrorist activities, especially after an attempt was made on Mubarak's life in Addis Ababa in June 1995 and an attack on tourists at Luxor in November 1997 took sixty-two lives. Because of Egypt's heavy dependence on revenues from tourism, Mubarak's policies opposing Islamic-inspired terrorism have so far enjoyed public support, but the ability of the Supreme Council for Islamic Affairs to censor books and films and of the legislature to Islamize some of the nation's laws have also increased during Mubarak's presidency. The long-established Muslim Brotherhood retains its influence, especially in the professional associations, but it has renounced terrorism. Egyptians believe that the Islamists' influence has blighted their country's literary, artistic, and journalistic creativity and harmed its cultural preeminence in the Arab world.

Mubarak's government has continued the process of privatizing state-owned firms begun under Sadat; has reduced government subsidies on consumer goods used by the poor; and has inaugurated the Toshka Project, a massive public works scheme to divert Nile waters backed up behind the Aswan High Dam to irrigate portions of the Western Desert. Despite numerous government efforts to improve Egypt's economy, population growth continues to offset economic gains. As of July 2004, Egypt's population was estimated to be 76 million; it was 19 million in 1947. The gap between rich and poor Egyptians remains wide—a potential threat to the stability and survival of his regime, which has lasted longer than any since the reign of Muhammad Ali (1805–1849). Egypt's close relationship with the US government, which furnishes about $2 billion in economic and military aid each year, has lost public support because of the Iraq War and the perception that George W. Bush's administration favors Israel over the Arabs. Some say that the Egyptian people, if they were empowered to elect their own leader, would choose Amr Moussa (the Arab League's current secretary general) over Mubarak.

ARTHUR GOLDSCHMIDT, JR.

See also Egypt; Jihād; Middle East: International Relations

References and Further Reading

Baker, Raymond William. *Islam Without Fear: Egypt and the New Islamists.* Cambridge, MA: Harvard University Press, 2003.
Cantori, Louis J. "Egyptian Policy Under Mubarak: The Politics of Continuity and Change." In Robert O. Freedman, ed., *The Middle East After the Israeli Invasion of Lebanon.* Syracuse, NY: Syracuse University Press, 1986, pp. 323–344.
Kienle, Eberhard. *A Grand Delusion: Democracy and Economic Reform in Egypt.* London: I.B. Tauris, 2001.
MacFarquhar, Neil. "Looking for Political Reform? See the Grim Reaper." *The New York Times* (August 11, 2004): A4.
Remnick, David. "In Mubarak's Egypt, Democracy is an Idea Whose Time Has Not Yet Come." *The New Yorker* (July 12, 2004): 74–83.
Sela, Avraham, ed. *Continuum Political Encyclopedia of the Middle East.* New York: Continuum Press, 2002, s.v. Mubarak, Husni.
Springborg, Robert. *Mubarak's Egypt: Fragmentation of the Political Order.* Boulder, CO: Westview Press, 1989.
Sullivan, Denis J. "The Struggle for Egypt's Future." *Current History* 102 (January 2003): 27–31.

MUGABE, ROBERT

As one of the leaders of the revolutionary uprising known in Zimbabwe as the second Chimurenga (rising) of the 1960s and 1970s, Robert Gabriel Mugabe (b. 1934) led the Zimbabwe African National Union of the Patriotic Front to victory over the undemocratic regime of the Rhodesia Front's white Prime Minister Ian Smith. After the liberation war ended in 1979, the new African state of Zimbabwe elected Mugabe as its first prime minister in March 1980. Mugabe formed a multi-party Government of National Unity of black and white Africans. When Zimbabwe's government took a presidential form, Mugabe became the first executive president—replacing the nominal head of state—as leader of the government, the principal political party, and the state. He has won reelection every five years including in 2000.

In the late 1990s and the early twenty-first century, Mugabe has become increasingly autocratic. Unlike other aging liberators such as Nelson Mandela, he has refused to step aside and permit a new generation to assume leadership.

Mugabe was born on February 21, 1924, at Kutama in Zvimba, near the Rhodesian capital of Salisbury (renamed Harare after independence in 1980). He attended Kutama's Jesuit Mission elementary school and teacher training college. He developed a dual passion for education and later for the socialism of Kwame Nkrumah, Ghana's liberator from British colonialism in 1957.

In 1934 Robert's father, Gamaliel Mugabe, left his family to work in Bulawayo and then South Africa. That same year, Robert's older brother Miteri (Michael) died. Robert had a younger brother, Dhonandho (Donald), and a sister, Sabina. The family engaged in subsistence farming, as the vast majority of Zimbabwe's black African population still do.

In the 1890s the British South Africa Company (BSAC) expropriated the best land for European "pioneers," including Christian missions. The BSAC's Cecil John Rhodes induced the British crown to recognize his company as the government of its colony until a settler government took over in the 1920s. The Africans' lot was subsistence farming by which they produced their staple food of maize. The BSAC forced them to assume a dependency on the company and missions for education, work, and religion. In turn the Europeans denounced African culture, including African religion, food, dress, and language, as "heathen."

At the Roman Catholic mission school Mugabe became a voracious reader and highly disciplined student of the Jesuit fathers. When he was 14 he announced his ambition to become a teacher. He followed that vocation from 1942–1960 in his pre-revolutionary days in Rhodesia and Ghana up to the time of his marriage to his first wife, Sally, in 1961. During his imprisonment by the Ian Smith regime in the 1960s and 1970s Mugabe set up a school for his fellow prison inmates. At the same time he pursued external degrees in education, law, and economics from the University of London to add to his B.A. from Fort Hare University in South Africa through correspondence programs while he was in prison.

His rise to leadership in the socialist liberation movement in Rhodesia was gradual, but persistent. He was a persuasive speaker and had clear ideas of the interests of Africans in their fight for one-person, one-vote democracy and their desire to reclaim the land they had lost in the 1890s, a desire that continues to the present. Without external assistance, however, the revolution could not be sustained, and Mugabe was a primary force in seeking diplomatic recognition for his party and its struggle in the capital cities of the capitalist West and the communist East.

Because most of the support for the African liberation movement came from the communist bloc nations led by the Soviet Union and China, Mugabe's political sympathies became increasingly Marxist and Maoist. Since the Soviets favored the Zimbabwean African People's Union (ZAPU) leader Joshua Nkomo, a member of the Ndebele ethnicity, Mugabe found his source of arms and training for his soldiers in Eastern Europe and Asia. Thus his forces used the general title of Patriotic Front, although they were bifurcated in their sources of military arms and foreign political support.

But humanitarian aid came from both the communist East and the capitalist and socialist West. Sweden, Switzerland, Norway, and individual donors in other European states and the United States, offered funds for education, medicine, and government organization, as did non-governmental agencies such as the World Council of Churches' Program to Combat Racism. Ultimately the Frontline States of Africa and the United Nations supported majority rule, despite the support of the British and US governments for UN sanctions against what they argued was Rhodesia's illegal claim to an independent republic in 1965. Zimbabwe's diplomatic success was largely the result of Robert and Sally Mugabe's persuasive entreaties. Sally lived in exile in Ghana and London for over a decade while Robert was in prison, during which time two of their young children died.

The story of Robert Mugabe's later years is more difficult to explain than his rise to eminence. During the liberation phase from 1961 to 1979, Mugabe established himself as the triumphant leader in a military and political struggle to topple European control of Rhodesia/Zimbabwe. In the second phase of his leadership, from 1979 to the mid-1990s, he devoted himself to fulfilling his prewar aims to build an educational system to promote literacy in Zimbabwe; to construct a socialist system of cooperative farms and state-run businesses; and to restructure the government into a one-person, one-vote democracy of equal justice under the law. For his work in both of these phases he received international acclaim as a significant voice for African independence and Africa's capacity for self-rule.

However, from the mid-1990s into the twenty-first century, Mugabe's behavior changed considerably. Veterans of his liberation army have been employed to inflict harm on his African political enemies and the shrinking white minority. He has ceased to use his capacity for diplomacy that won the peace in 1979, and has instead intimidated the press, the courts, the military, and police.

Robert G. Mugabe has lived with accusations that he committed atrocities against whites and Africans, even comrades in the 1970s liberation leadership. Sorting out such claims has not been easy for objective historians. Records of Ian Smith's police and Selous Scouts were destroyed at the end of the war, and those of the Mugabe government and its armed militias are not readily available. In addition, the anecdotes of oral witnesses of Smith's and Mugabe's enemies and friends remain to be sorted out. In fact, there is a great shortage of academic interest in Zimbabwe at the present time.

The most adequate record of the years since the 2000 election, which Mugabe won in spite of a solid effort by the opposition Movement for Democratic Change led by Morgan Tsvangirai, must be sought in press reports and op-ed evaluations, mainly in the British media. Brutality and tampering have accompanied elections since 1980, and land grabs have tarnished Mugabe's record in recent years.

NORMAN H. MURDOCH

See also Zimbabwe

References and Further Reading

Editorial Collective of Seven Authors. *Sally Mugabe: A Woman with a Mission.* Harare, Zimbabwe: ZANU PF Central Committee, 1994.

Mugabe, Robert G. "Struggle for Southern Africa." *Foreign Affairs*, Winter 1987/88.

Smith, David, Colin Simpson, and Ian Davies. *Mugabe.* Salisbury, Rhodesia: Pioneer Head, 1981.

MUJAHEDIN

Mujahedin, literally "those who struggle," but also interpreted as "holy warriors," is a word used widely to describe many Islamic military groups, but usually refers to the Muslim fighters that fought against the Soviet forces in Afghanistan during the Soviet Union's incursion into that country from 1979 to 1989. The Mujahedin was not only composed of native Afghan fighters, but also Muslim fighters from throughout the Islamic world transcending tribal, racial, and ethnic groups. Many of the fighters answered the call to come to the aide of their Muslim compatriots in Afghanistan.

The Soviet Invasion of Afghanistan

The emergence of the Mujahedin began in the turmoil that was Afghanistan in the late 1970s. A coup in 1978 deposed and killed military dictator General Muhammad Daud, who had seized power from his cousin, King Zahir Shah, in 1973. The immediate power vacuum was not filled, and an intense struggle for control ensued. The struggle between the two leftist leaders, Hafizullah Amin and Nur Muhammad Taraki, was won by Amin. Outside of Kabul, the countryside was in revolt. Making the most of Afghanistan's unstable situation in 1979, the Soviet Union began its invasion of that country to remove Amin from power and install its pro-communist dictator of choice. Amin was executed in the process. Moscow settled on Babrak Karmol, a communist leader in Afghanistan's People's Democratic Party, to fill the leadership void.

Many former adversaries united against their Soviet occupiers. International condemnation of the Soviet intervention yielded no change of agenda for Moscow. The Mujahedin was at first composed of native tribesmen such as the Pashtun, Hazara, and Tajik. The composition of the Mujahedin was as complex as Afghan society itself in terms of ethnicity, tribe, Islamic interpretation, and region. Prior to the invasion by the Soviets, the Pashtuns had dominated Afghan society. In fact, the term Afghan is used to refer to the Pashtuns. The rallying of the various peoples of Afghanistan, whether Tajik, Uzbek, Sunni, Sufi, Shi'a, or otherwise, involved the recruitment of community elders. These measures of recruitment reached fruition in the form of a loose collection of allies stable enough to hold the Soviets at bay. The Pakistani leader, Zia ul-Haq, and Pakistan's Inter-Services Intelligence (ISI) favored Islamist leaders over more moderate and nationalist ones. However, the plight of Afghanistan was an important struggle

for the entire Islamic world, as well as for the anti-communist West. Recruits for the Mujahedin came from Arab countries, neighboring Pakistan, Central Asia, and elsewhere. With the secret backing of the United States and its Central Intelligence Agency (CIA), Pakistan's ISI, the government of Saudi Arabia, and others, the Mujahedin became a force to be reckoned with for the Soviet invaders. Monetary and human reinforcements streamed in from Saudi Arabia and other Gulf states concerned with the plight of their Afghan brethren. One individual involved was the eventual founder of *al-Qa'ida*, Usama Bin Ladin. Muslims from other countries ranging from Saudi Arabia to the United States eventually joined the Mujahedin. The effort would not have stood a chance against the superior Soviet force otherwise. The Mujahedin exercised guerrilla warfare against the Soviets. Eventually, the Soviet army's advantage in its Hinds helicopter gunships was checked by the introduction of US stinger missiles into the battlefield in 1986. During the war, the Mujahedin operated out of thousands of bases in both Afghanistan and Pakistan. Some of the Mujahedin would continue to fight for the freedom of Afghanistan even after the evacuation of the Soviets and the ousting of their chosen leader. The new threat was from Islamic extremists, known as the Taliban, many of whom had fought the Soviets as Mujahedin during the 1980s.

Across the border into Pakistan in 1985, the various Mujahedin groups formed for a united cause against the Soviets. By this time, much of Afghanistan's population had left the country, mostly for refugee camps in neighboring Pakistan and Iran. Also at this time, the new leader of the Soviet Union, Mikhail Gorbachev, promised an eventual withdrawal of the Red Army. In 1986, Babrak Karmal was replaced by Najibullah as the Soviet-backed leader of Afghanistan. In 1988, Afghanistan, Pakistan, the Soviet Union, and the United States signed peace accords, and the Soviet pullout began. Afghan casualties from the war are estimated at over a million, while Soviet casualty estimates range from the official Soviet number of thirteen thousand to other estimates of around twenty-eight thousand.

Post-Soviet Afghanistan

The last Soviet troops left Kabul International Airport on February 15, 1989, but the Afghan civil war continued. The Mujahedin sought to eradicate any Soviet-influenced presence, including Najibullah. After Washington and Moscow agreed to stop all financial support of the warring parties, the Mujahedin succeeded in capturing Kabul and ousting Najibullah in 1992. A Tajik, Burhannuddin Rabbani, was appointed president by the Mujahedin groups in 1993. Conflict emerged between Rabbani and the Pakistani-favored Gulbuddin Hekmatyar, a radical Islamist known for throwing acid in the faces of women not wearing a *burqa* (veil). A shaky alliance between the two was established to the detriment of the loyalty of Rabanni's supporters. The little success that this alliance achieved was short-lived.

One of the most successful, respected, and enduring commanders of the Mujahedin is the figure of Ahmed Shah Massoud. Near the end of the war with the Soviets, Massoud is reputed to have commanded a force of over ten thousand. His fighters, along with those under former Soviet-backed General Abdul Rashid Dostum, were the two forces able to close in and capture Kabul in 1992. Massoud, a Tajik from the Panjshir Valley, held the area even after the Pashtun-dominated Taliban's rise to power. Areas under his control remained the only parts of free Afghanistan. Massoud's Northern Alliance held some regions in the north of the country and continued to resist Taliban control. The Mujahedin were eventually beaten back by the Taliban, and in 1996, the Taliban were successful in taking over Afghanistan. Massoud was assassinated by two *al-Qa'ida* operatives posing as a film crew on September 9, 2001, just two days before the September 11 attacks in the United States. Despite his death, Massoud's legendary status has reserved him a place as an icon in both the East and the West. Massoud's Northern Alliance joined with other Mujahedin and US forces to oust the Taliban from power and destroy the *al-Qa'ida* presence within Afghanistan beginning in late 2001. Those Mujahedin forces included that of Afghanistan's first democratically elected president, Hamid Karzai. The Mujahedin forces have largely disbanded, and many of the fighters now serve in the Afghan army.

WHITNEY D. DURHAM

See also Afghanistan; Central Asia: History and Economic Development; Central Asia: International Relations

References and Further Reading

Bradsher, Henry. *Afghan Communism and Soviet Intervention.* New York: Oxford University Press, 1999.
Crile, George. *Charlie Wilson's War.* New York: Atlantic/Grove Press, 2002.
Edwards, David. *Before Taliban.* Berkeley, CA: University of California Press, 2002.
Ewans, Martin. *Afghanistan.* New York: HarperCollins, 2002.
Kaplan, Robert. *Soldiers of God.* New York: Vintage Departures, 2001.
Roy, Oliver. *Afghanistan: From Holy War to Civil War.* Princeton, NJ: The Darwin Press, 1995.
Rubin, Barnett. *The Fragmentation of Afghanistan.* New Haven, CT: Yale University Press, 2002.
Tamarov, Vladislav. *Afghanistan: Soviet Vietnam.* San Francisco: Mercury House, 1992.
Yousaf, Mohammad and Mark Adkin. *Afghanistan—the Bear Trap.* Havertown, PA: Casemate, 2001.

MUJIBAR RAHMAN, SHEIKH

Born near Dacca, Bangladesh, on March 17, 1920, to middle-class landowners, Sheikh Mujibar Rahman (1920–1975) attended Islamia College, Calcutta, and studied law at Dacca where he began his political career with the Muslim Students' Federation in 1940. A Bengali nationalist, he organized student demonstrations against the imposition of Urdu as the national language at the cost of Bengali. He spent six days in prison as a result and was expelled from university. He then organized a strike of university workers, was arrested, and spent two and a half years in prison. While in prison he was elected secretary of a new party, the Awami League, founded by H. S. Suhrawardy in 1949. He became the principal organizer of the party in East Pakistan.

In 1956 he led demands for provincial autonomy in the East Pakistan assembly and advocated separation of East Pakistan from West Pakistan. Between 1956 and 1957 he served as the minister of commerce in the government of East Pakistan. When the Pakistan Army staged a military coup in 1958 he was jailed under the Public Safety Ordinance and held without charge for 18 months. In 1962 he refused to abstain from politics for five years and was imprisoned for a further six months. With the death of Suhrawardy in 1963, Mujib became the leader of the Awami League. In 1966 he proclaimed the Six-Point Program, the *Mukti Sanad* (Charter of Freedom), which called for a federal government with control only of foreign affairs and defense, a separate currency or separate fiscal accounts, taxation at the provincial level only, control of all provincial foreign exchange earnings by each provincial government, and a militia for each province. He was imprisoned in 1967 and again in 1968 and brought before a military court along with thirty-five others in the Argatala Conspiracy Case.

When rioting brought down the government of Ayub Khan in 1969 he returned to East Pakistan a hero. In December 1970 he led the Awami League to an overwhelming victory in the general elections in East Pakistan, winning 167 of 169 seats. On March 26, 1971, he proclaimed the independence of East

Pakistan as Bangladesh. He was imprisoned and served most of his imprisonment under sentence of death. Civil war followed in East Pakistan, which India ended on December 16, 1971, when the Indian Army occupied Dacca. On January 10, 1972, Mujib returned to East Pakistan a national hero and the prime minister of an Awami League ministry. On December 16, 1972, the new constitution set up a cabinet form of government based on the four principles of Mujibbad (Mujibism): nationalism, secularism, democracy, and socialism. On February 25, 1975, however, he amended that constitution to create a presidential system with himself as president. On June 7, 1975, he made Bangladesh a one-party state and banned all existing parties. His Awami League formed the nucleus of a new party, the Krishak Sramik Awami League (BAKSAL). However, he lost support of the urban and military elite after he identified with the state, ignored charges of corruption, and installed his relatives in high government positions. He was killed, along with over twenty members of his family and political allies, in a military coup on August 15, 1975.

ROGER D. LONG

See also Awami League; Pakistan

References and Further Reading

Baxter, Craig. *Bangladesh: A New Nation in an Old Setting.* Boulder, CO: Westview Press, 1984.
Khan, Zillur Rahman. *Leadership Crisis in Bangladesh.* Dhaka, Bangladesh: Dhaka University Press, 1984.
Mascarenhas, Anthony. *Bangladesh: A Legacy of Blood.* London: Hodder and Stoughton, 1986.
Ziring, Lawrence. *Bangladesh: From Mujib to Ershad: An Interpretive Study.* Karachi, Pakistan: Oxford University Press, 1992.

MULTINATIONAL CORPORATIONS AND DEVELOPMENT

Multinational Corporations (MNCs) can be defined as large for-profit businesses that operate in multiple nations. MNCs usually maintain their headquarters in one larger company (the parent company) located in their country of origin, generally an industrialized Western nation, and keep smaller companies (subsidiaries) in foreign countries as part of their overall operations. Despite MNCs' global geographical presences, evidence shows that the crux of their research and development programs and their profit repatriation patterns are concentrated in their parent companies and home countries.

The impacts that MNCs have had when dealing with developing countries have been mixed. On the one hand, MNCs are acknowledged as key contributors to development due to the flows of investment they inject into national economies, which create jobs, transfer needed technology, and generate taxes for public treasuries. On the other hand, MNCs are often the cause of concern given their mobile nature, allegations of their disregard for labor and environmental standards as a way to maximize profits, and the large repatriation of profits to parent companies rather than local economies. This debate has acquired a new character in the era of globalization as the economic power and influence of MNCs have increased substantially. This has allowed the most powerful MNCs to become more important players in the configurations of global exchange and production than many national-states.

MNCs: Origins, Operational Patterns, and Their Relevance to Development

MNCs have existed for several centuries. The origins of the modern MNC can be found in the East and West Indies traders of the European mercantilist period (sixteenth–eighteenth centuries). With the emergence of the Industrial Revolution, the first MNCs, as conceived in their modern form, were established as they expanded their activities to multiple markets and took advantage of abundant raw material sources. Yet, the management and capital of these early MNCs were still confined to the boundaries of the country of origin. By the latter part of the twentieth century, and with many state-dominated telecommunications facilities, power generation systems, and financial monopolies moving into the functioning of international markets, the MNC had become a key dominating player in the global trade of goods and services.

As strategies of penetration, MNCs usually utilize the purchase of shares in existing national firms, create new subsidiaries using fresh capital, or they participate in the takeover of national firms as part of privatization programs. More precisely, MNCs follow a strategy of internalization to take advantage of their competitive strengths by operating under a bargaining strategy so as to gain the most when dealing with competitors and regulators. Essentially, this bargaining strategy considers MNCs as part of a multi-player game in which national governments set rules to accommodate MNC activities in their domestic plans, while MNCs attempt to out-compete their rivals and to minimize the regulatory burdens imposed by governments. Hence, the impact of MNCs on national economies and the success of their penetration strategies can only be entirely understood by analyzing their relationship vis-à-vis the capacity of state regulation.

Within this context, MNCs count on two primary strategies for expansion: A North–South or "outsourcing strategy" strategy and a North–North "market consolidation" strategy. In the first instance, the North–South strategy is promoted by MNCs in an effort to minimize production costs as they invest abroad in countries with cheaper labor, energy, and real estate, often complemented with low transportation costs and trade barriers. Secondly, the North–North strategy is sought when MNCs attempt to have access to large consumer markets, and as such, investment is directed to gain that market access. The success of these strategies depends on several factors, especially the capacity of MNCs to use state regulation to their advantage; the localization of foreign direct investment (FDI) in places and quantities that best suit the particular goals of the company; and the favorable conditions, or not, presented by international business cycle patterns.

Developing countries are important elements within the framework of these MNC expansionary strategies. This growing relationship between the developing world and MNCs has yielded both positive and negative results (see below for more information), and although it would be hard to generalize a common trend among poorer countries to assess their associations with MNCs, the former have been active in attracting FDI as a potential booster of national development. As the relevance of MNCs in the pursuit of developmental programs grows, developing countries have to transform or consolidate their economic, legal, and political systems so as to make them more accommodating to the profit-seeking interests of FDI. With globalization, competition to attract FDI is increasingly among host countries, as opposed to MNCs competing against each other to gain access to local markets. This trend has allegedly forced developing countries to lower regulatory standards in order to attract FDI. Others argue that it is high but fair standards which constitute the determinants that guide the allocation of FDI.

The factors that determine the injection of FDI are several and multifaceted: political and macroeconomic stability; transparent and non-discriminatory legal and regulatory configurations; and minimal bureaucratic and procedural rigidity. Beyond this institutional background, MNCs generally favor countries committed to liberal market-oriented policies, favorable taxing schemes, fiscal incentives, and free trade. Furthermore, MNCs take into account the growing market patterns of the host country's domestic and regional economic contexts, the existence of efficient communication and transportation systems, and the conditions of the domestic labor pools as they relate to the specific business strategy of the MNC. These are just several of many factors that influence MNC decision making; however, it can be asserted that the attraction of FDI by developing countries requires the establishment of specific rules that pose a central question: Does the accommodation of FDI demands necessarily imply the achievement of national development in the long-run?

MNCs and Development: The Positive Contributions

The advocates of MNC expansion into developing countries provide several arguments to substantiate their claims. In essence, they argue that the capital and technology transfers supplied by MNCs constitute an imperative element in order for developing countries to boost their chances of success in an increasingly globalized economy. Without access to foreign capital and technology, they argue, economic development in poor countries would be very difficult and even impossible. One key aspect of MNC contributions to development is job creation in the host country. By and large, MNCs are very likely to create more jobs, pay higher wages, and have higher labor standards than domestic firms. Moreover, a transfer of expertise and knowledge from parent countries as well as a tendency for MNC investment to shift toward capital-intensive production may result in high-skill, high-paying jobs for local workers. This also helps in the diversification of the domestic marketplace, allowing previously marginalized groups, such as women, to integrate themselves as active economic players in society. The impressive growth experienced by the Southeast Asian region, and current positive experiments in India, Chile, and Turkey, have partially been achieved through the helpful impact that MNCs have had by investing capital and creating jobs.

Another important contribution of MNCs is the transfer of technology and managerial know-how. For most developing countries it is extremely expensive to develop a domestically grown technological base, and thus MNCs represent a crucial source of technology that enables poor countries to access innovative methods and practices to promote long-term national development. Moreover, by translating into practical results the theoretical knowledge related to the technological and managerial aspects of FDI, key sectors of the domestic economy, such as agriculture, industry, and pharmaceuticals, could experience significant improvements in productivity and diversification. Without the access to MNC technology and knowledge, the economies of many developing countries could face stagnation and poor competitiveness in international markets.

Finally, the supporters of MNC operations in the developing world argue that FDI can be of great help in helping nation-states deal with economic and financial reform. MNCs provide a tax base that enhances public coffers, and their largely positive role in the manufacturing and agricultural sectors allow for more high-quality and competitive products to be exported. Both these elements help national governments deal with budget deficits. Furthermore, FDI can participate in the privatization of public firms by purchasing them, not only turning them into potentially more productive and efficient entities, but also providing another source of income for governments that can be allocated toward pressing national needs. In the end, MNC penetration into the economies of developing countries, combined with the proper state regulation and policies, could prove to be extremely beneficial for long-run growth and productivity.

MNCs and Development: The Negative Side

The critics of MNCs point out that their business operations fundamentally lack ethical and human rights standards in terms of labor and the environment. In order to reduce costs and maximize profits, many MNCs invest in developing countries that must reduce labor and environmental standards in order to receive the investment in the first place. Therefore, there is a general perception that MNCs sacrifice the human rights of their employees and their working conditions in the name of more profits. Companies such as Reebok, Nike, and Levi Strauss have been accused of systematic labor exploitation in Southeast Asian countries where the wages received by workers are significantly lower than the retail value of most of the commodities they produce. Even if the economies of some of these countries are booming due to MNC investment, this is being done at the expense of perpetuating inhumane living conditions and illegal wages for the millions of workers.

Secondly, there is a great deal of concern over the profit-repatriation practices of many MNCs. In other words, MNCs tend to send back to the parent company most of the profits they have reaped in their operations in the developing world. This is problematic because this practice discourages the reinvestment of capital in the local economies/communities, and also represents a regrettable drain of limited foreign

exchange resources and a burden on the developing country's balance of payments (that is, trade deficits or surpluses). Thus, the repatriation of profits reinforces the accusations of exploitation by MNCs as resources and wealth produced using the labor and resources of developing countries are drained out, leaving very little or nothing for domestic use. Moreover, poorer developing countries in need of capital often offer very favorable tax exemptions and fiscal incentives to MNCs in order to receive investment, foregoing a potentially important source of revenue for the national treasury.

Finally, the critics of MNCs argue that the highly mobile nature of MNCs represents a key concern that often affects the interests of developing countries. As a logical step, MNCs tend to establish subsidiaries in places where conditions are most favorable, but if these conditions change to their disadvantage or an economic downturn takes place, they also tend to relocate their operations. As a result, MNCs are accused of not possessing a sense of loyalty to, and responsibility for, the countries where they invest. In addition, their ability to close down their business whenever they see it fit gives them tremendous leverage and clout when negotiating with national governments that often depend on the jobs provided by MNCs. In this context, MNCs are seen as opportunistic and exploitative entities that place their own interests ahead of those of the countries where they operate and the people they employ.

By the end of the twentieth century, and with the intensification of market globalization, the role of MNCs in the world economy had grown exponentially. Currently, they account for 70% of the total global trade of $7 trillion, and the revenues of the top five MNCs are more that double the total gross domestic product of the world's one hundred poorest countries combined. The relationship between MNCs and developing countries is bound to grow in the future, but the challenges for the latter will revolve around their ability to channel the potential benefits of FDI to benefit their societies while trying to minimize the disadvantages that this relationship is likely to recreate.

CARLOS VELÁSQUEZ CARRILLO

See also Capital Flight; Foreign Direct Investment (FDI); Globalization: Impact on Development; Industrialization; Modernization

References and Further Reading

Alschuler, Lawrence. *Multinationals and Maldevelopment: Alternative Development Strategies in Argentina, the Ivory Coast, and South Korea.* London: Macmillan Press, 1998.

Birkinshaw, Julian and Neil Hood, eds. *Multinational Corporate Evolution and Subsidiary Development*. New York: St. Martin's Press, 1998.

Dunning, John H. and Jean-Louis Mucchielli. *Multinational Firms: The Global-Local Dilemma*. London: Routledge, 2001.

Grosse, Robert. *Multinationals in Latin America*. London: Routledge, 1989.

Hood, Neil and Stephen Young, eds. *The Globalization of Multinational Enterprise Activity and Economic Development*. New York: St. Martin's Press, 2000.

Klein, Naomi. *No Logo: Taking Aim at the Brand Bullies*. Toronto: Vintage Canada, 2000.

Lipsey, Robert E. *Foreign Direct Investment and the Operations of Multinational Firms: Concepts, History, and Data*. Cambridge: National Bureau of Economic Research, 2001.

Madeley, John. *Big Business, Poor Peoples: The Impact of Transnational Corporations on the World's Poor*. London: Zed Books, 1999.

Markusen, James R. *Contracts, Intellectual Property Rights, and Multinational Investment in Developing Countries*. Cambridge: National Bureau of Economic Research, 1998.

Moran, Theodore. *Multinational Corporations: The Political Economy of Foreign Direct Investment*. Toronto: Lexington Books, 1985.

Oman, Charles. *Globalization and Regionalization: The Challenge for Developing Countries*. Paris: Development Centre of the OECD, 1994.

Tolentino, Estrella. *Multinational Corporations: Emergence and Evolution*. New York: Routledge, 2000.

United Nations Conference on Trade and Development. *The Competitiveness Challenge: Transnational Corporations and Industrial Restructuring in Developing Countries*. New York: United Nations, 2000.

MUSLIM BROTHERHOOD

The Muslim Brotherhood is an Islamic organization founded in 1928, after the collapse of the Ottoman Empire, by its first Egyptian leader Hassan al Banna. Its aim was to restore the principles of the Koran and to unite Muslims in a caliphate. It expanded through most parts of the Arab world, with cells in Syria, Palestine, Jordan, Lebanon, Sudan, Israel, Saudi Arabia, and other countries. Nowadays it has branches in over seventy countries all over the world.

The Brotherhood's ideology claims that Islam is a way of life and that it is not possible to live in an Islamic society unless the whole of the society, including the government, is adapted to strict Islamic principles. This idea led the Brotherhood to conflicts with several governments, especially when those were under the influence of Western countries who the Brothers considered as the enemy. It has also been a fundamental principle that Muslims should establish a pan-Islamic state, going beyond all current political and geographic boundaries.

The organization has proven to be extraordinary powerful, and has often been described as a "state within the state." This power was an encouragement for the development of the countries, as long as they supported the current government, but otherwise the Brotherhood proved to be a drawback. For instance, in 1948 the organization blamed the Egyptian government for being passive against "Zionists" and joined the Palestinian side in the Egyptian war against Israel. That same year a Muslim Brother assassinated the prime minister of Egypt and in response to that, Al-Banna himself was killed by government agents in Cairo in 1949.

However, the Brotherhood on other occasions contributed to the reinforcement of democracy by participating in free elections, as it did in 1961 in Syria, winning ten seats in the Parliament, or when in the 1950s Jordanian members supported King Hussein of Jordan against political opposition. Another valuable contribution was the cooperation with the Socialist Labour Party and the Liberal Socialist Party to form the Labour Islamic Alliance in 1987 in Egypt, obtaining seats and fostering democracy.

Nevertheless, the Brotherhood has in the past engaged in acts of terrorism: an attempt to assassinate President Nasser in 1954, the assassination of Egyptian President Anwar Sadat in 1981, and more recently the accusation on behalf of the Egyptian government of offering tacit support for the military groups that launched a campaign in the 1990s to bring down Hosni Mubarak's government.

The Muslim Brotherhood has been more influential in some countries than in others, taking prominent roles in countries like Jordan and Sudan and less of a role in others such as Syria. After Hassan al Banna, other leaders have included Seid Kutub Ibrahim and Mohammed Abed Alsalam Faraj, the founder of the Egyptian Jihad organization.

Currently, the Egyptian Islamic Brotherhood exists as a clandestine group. The Brotherhood is also internationally connected with military and resistance organizations such as Hamas (the Arab acronym for Islamic Resistance Movement), Gama'a al-Islamiya, and Islamic Jihad.

DIEGO I. MURGUÍA

See also Egypt; Islam; Jihād; Nasser, Gamal Abdel; Sadat, Anwar

References and Further Reading

Abu-Amr, Ziyad. *Islamic Fundamentalism in the West Bank and Gaza: Muslim Brotherhood and Islamic Jihad*. Bloomington: Indiana University Press, 1994.

Ahmed, Akbar. *Islam Today: A Short Introduction to the Muslim World*. London: I.B. Tauris, 1999.

Boulby, Marion. *The Muslim Brotherhood and the Kings of Jordan, 1945–1993*. Atlanta, GA: Scholars Press, 1999.

Muslim Brotherhood Movement. http://www.ummah.org.uk/ikhwan/.

Sackur, Zina. *Egypt, Islamic Fundamentalist Organizations: The Muslim Brotherhood and the Gama'a al Islamiya*. United Nations High Committee for the Refugees (UNCHR), 1994.

Timmerman, Kenneth R. *In Their Own Words: Interviews with Leaders of Hamas, Islamic Jihad and the Muslim Brotherhood: Damascus, Amman and Gaza*. Los Angeles: Simon Wiesenthal Center, 1994.

Wiktorowicz, Quintan. *The Management of Islamic Activism: Salafis, the Muslim Brotherhood and State Power in Jordan*. Albany: State University of New York Press, 2001.

MUSLIM LEAGUE

The Muslim League is a political organization in Pakistan. It was founded in 1906 by Agha Khan III in order to protect the interests of Muslims in British India and later became instrumental in the creation of Pakistan. The role it played in the creation of Pakistan can be best described by the slogans that Muslims of India used during the time of their struggle for freedom from the British and even after Pakistan became an independent country in 1947:

- *Pakistan Zindabad* (Long Live Pakistan)
- *Muslim League Zindabad* (Long Live Muslim League)
- *Quaid-i-Azam Zindabad* (Long Live Quaid-i-Azam)

It was Quaid-i-Azam Mohammad Ali Jinnah who propounded the two-nations theory and the idea that the Muslims of India are a separate nation from Hindus culturally, religiously, and socially. However, it was Muhammad Iqbal, the philosopher-poet of Indian Muslims, who first advocated the idea of establishing a separate Muslim nation in his presidential address at the Annual Muslim League Session held at Allahbad in 1930. Three years later, Chaudari Rahmat Ali, a law student at Cambridge, came up with a name for an independent Muslim nation-state to be called Pakistan, "the Land of the Pure," to consist of the Sindh, Punjab, Baluchistan, North West Frontier Province, and Kashmir where the majority of Muslims resided. However, it was Jinnah who played a role of great importance in restructuring the Muslim League. He gave it a new life by organizing various activities and by entering into alliances with the political leaders of various provinces. He made speeches in public appealing directly to the people on the issue of the two-nations theory.

By 1940, under the leadership of Mohammad Ali Jinnah, the Muslim League gained strength and was then in a position to demand a separate Muslim state. In March of 1940, Muslims from all over India gathered in Minto Park at Lahore. Jinnah put forward the two-nations theory in this gathering and argued for the creation of a separate Muslim state. It was passed as the Lahore Resolution. This stirred the emotions of Muslims throughout India and they joined the Muslim League in its struggle for the creation of Pakistan. As a result, the Muslim League in the 1946 Indian elections captured all the Central Assembly seats in the areas where Muslims were a majority, except in the North West Frontier. This provided strong evidence for the creation of a separate state for the Muslims of India.

Thus, the following year partition of India took place and Pakistan came into being on August 14, 1947, and the Muslim League became its major political party. But, after the creation of Pakistan, the Muslim League could not hold together its forces, nor was it able to visualize the future of the newly born country in terms of its ideology or articulate its agenda or planning by which one could foresee how and where it would go further. This could be attributed to the fact that there were many factions in the organization itself with conflicting interests. This led to formation of several different political parties within the Muslim League itself. By 1958, the Muslim League became impotent as a political power and General Ayub Khan imposed marshal law in the country. In the meanwhile, the Muslim League was reformed into the Convention Muslim League (under Ayub Khan) and the Council Muslim League; the former ceased when Ayub Khan resigned in 1969 and the latter saw its death blow in the elections of 1970. Thereafter, Pakistan became subject to military rule and marshal law. After a long interval, the Islamic Democratic Alliance, a coalition of political parties, won the majority of seats in the Parliament when the elections were held in December 1990, and Nawaz Sharif of the Pakistan Muslim League became prime minister. In July 1993, Sharif, under the pressure of military power, resigned the office. In the February 1997 elections, the Pakistan Muslim League again won the majority of seats and Sharif became the prime minister only to be ousted in October 1999 by General Pervez Musharraf. The future prospects of the Pakistan Muslim League remain to be seen.

HUSAIN KASSIM

See also Ayub Khan, Mohammed; Pakistan

References and Further Reading

Jalal, A. *The Sole Spokesman: Jinnah, The Muslim League and the Demand for Pakistan*. Cambridge, UK: Cambridge University Press, 1974.

Muhammad Ali, C. *The Emergence of Pakistan.* New York: Columbia University Press, 1967.

Talbot, Ian. *Freedom's Cry.* Karachi, Pakistan: Oxford University Press, 1996.

Wolpert, S. *Jinnah of Pakistan.* New York: Oxford University Press, 1984.

MYANMAR

Myanmar (formerly known as Burma) is located in Southeast Asia, bordering the Andaman Sea and the Bay of Bengal, between Bangladesh and Thailand. It also shares borders with China, India, and Laos. With an area of just under 262,000 square miles, Myanmar is slightly smaller than the state of Texas; with a population of close to 42 million, it falls between Spain and France in size. Myanmar has a tropical monsoon climate, with cloudy, rainy, hot, humid summers but with mild temperatures, lower humidity, and little rainfall during the winter.

Natural hazards include earthquakes and cyclones, while flooding and landslides are common during the rainy season (June to September). Two distinct geographic characteristics divide the country physically and ethnically: the central lowlands and the surrounding high mountainous regions along the country's borders with India and China. The lowlands of the Irrawaddy delta are populated by significant numbers of ethnic hill tribes, including the Shan, Karen, Arakan, Kachin, Chin, and Mon. While Myanmar is 90% Buddhist and ethnic Burmese constitute 68% of the population, the major hill tribes and other ethnic minority groups are large enough to have been waging war with Myanmar's central governments since the end of World War II.

Politically, Burma is run by a military dictatorship called the State Peace and Development Council (SPDC), which took over from the previous military council, SLORC, in 1997. The SPDC allows no opposition political parties, holds no competitive elections, and keeps the Burmese tightly controlled and watched. The people enjoy no civil liberties, with the SPDC controlling the press, all travel, and all civil society. This situation has prompted several countries, including the United States, to impose economic sanctions on Myanmar, strictly limiting US economic investment and aid.

The SPDC has had limited success in opening up Myanmar to foreign economic investment and encouraging private economic activity, which is mostly centered in agriculture, light industry, and transport. The state controls most other sectors, including energy, heavy industry, and the rice trade. Government policy in the 1990s aimed at revitalizing the economy after three decades of tight central planning, and private activity did increase in the mid-1990s, but began to decline shortly thereafter due to frustrations by investors with the unfriendly business environment and political pressure from Western nations. Much of Myanmar's foreign trade is thus understated because it occurs on the black market or involves illicit border trade with Malaysia and Thailand. And, while the current government has made strides in forging peace agreements with several tribal groups, the problems inherent in these conflicts are still present: In the state of Shan alone, estimates of the number of refuges who have fled to Thailand to avoid conflict and economic displacement range from five hundred thousand to 1 million.

Ethnic conflict is, however, but one problem for a country that has been dubbed "a rich country gone wrong" (Sesser 1993). Myanmar is seen by many as a negative and contradictory model of economic development. Once the world's leading rice exporter when it was under British colonial rule, in the last decade of the twentieth century it has had trouble feeding itself. It is a nation with abundant natural resources, including arable land, oil, coal, gas, timber, fish, teakwood, and fertile soil, yet is now one of the poorest countries in Southeast Asia. And, since 1988, when a popular democracy movement was crushed by the military government, Myanmar has been at war not only with minority ethnic tribes, but with large elements of its own population, leaving an economy largely dependent upon the selling of its natural resources, from drugs to timber to precious gems. Ironically, to the outside world, Myanmar's most famous export is one of its jailed citizens, Aung San Suu Kyi, the woman who led the 1988 democracy movement and received the Nobel Peace Prize in 1991 for her non-violent approach to dissent. Suu Kyi has been in and out of jail since 1988 and was put under house arrest again in September of 2000 for organizing her party, the National League for Democracy.

Myanmar secured its independence from Great Britain in 1948 and until 1962 struggled under parliamentary democracy. These fourteen years of democratic government were marred by ethnic conflict, a communist insurrection, and political corruption. Still, Myanmar's current stagnant economic development and dismal international and domestic political situation can largely be attributed to xenophobic policies and the abysmal economic plans of its military governments, starting with General Ne Win and his "Burmese Path to Socialism" in 1962.

The military virtually sealed Myanmar off from the outside world after Ne Win came to power, with the aim of "liberating" the country from any reliance on foreign goods, capital, and outside markets. Under a single-party dictatorship, military officers took control of the economy, and in the process expelled most ethnic Chinese and Indians, who were the country's skilled merchants and technicians. The result for Myanmar was unfortunate: In the mid-1950s the country's per-capita income of $200 was roughly comparable to that of Thailand and South Korea, but by the mid-1980s, while Myanmar's per-capita income remained at $200, Thailand's was $1,200 and South Korea's was 20 times higher. And, while Myanmar's external debt was $100 million in 1970, by 2000 it had reached $6 billion.

There have been some encouraging signs regarding prospects for future foreign investment and economic development in Myanmar, with the most important being its acceptance into the Association of Southeast Asian Nations (ASEAN) in 1997 and increased economic contacts with China and ASEAN member nations Singapore and Indonesia. Nevertheless, Myanmar's problems are many: international condemnation and sanctions (which sharply limit foreign aid, especially World Bank funds); opium addiction and smuggling; continued ethnic strife and refugee flows; internal barriers to foreign investment; harsh military rule and the subsequent suppression of political groups and Aung San Suu Kyi; and high inflation rates and increasing governmental corruption. Thus, the prospects for significant economic development in the near future are negligible.

BOB BEATTY

See also Aung San Suu Kyi; Southeast Asia: History and Economic Development; Southeast Asia: International Relations

References and Further Reading

Beck, Jan. *Historical Dictionary of Myanmar*. Lanham, MD: Scarecrow Press, 1995.

Carey, Peter, ed. *Burma: The Challenge of Change in a Divided Society*. New York: St. Martin's Press, 1997.

Fink, Christine. *Living Silence: Burma Under Military Rule*. London: Zed Books, 2001.

Krann, Khan Mon. *Economic Development of Burma: A Vision and Strategy*. Singapore: SUP, 2000.

Sesser, Stan. *The Lands of Charm and Cruelty*. New York: Knopf, 1993.

Smith, Martin. *Burma: Insurgency and the Politics of Ethnicity*. London: Zed Books, 1999.

Suu Kyi, Aung San. *Freedom from Fear and Other Writings*. New York: Penguin, 1991.

N

NAMIBIA

The Republic of Namibia was formerly South West Africa, a territory of the Republic of South Africa. However, in 1966, the United Nations passed Resolution 2145, which revoked South Africa's mandate and changed the country's name to Namibia. Namibia is bounded on the north by Angola and Zambia, on the east by Botswana and South Africa, on the South by South Africa, and on the west by the Atlantic Ocean. The total area of Namibia is 824,269 square kilometers. Windhoek is the capital and the main city.

Population in 2004 (est.) was 1,954,033 with an estimated 1.25% growth rate. Racially, Black Africans make up 87.5% of the population, white Africans 6%, and people of mixed race 6.5%.

About 50% of the population is Ovambo and 9% Kavango. Other ethnic groups include Herero 7%, Damara 7%, Nama 5%, Caprivian 4%, San or Khoikhoi 3%, Baster 2%, and Tswana 0.5%.

English is the official language of the country, but only about 7% of the population speaks it. Afrikaans is commonly spoken, and is the primary language of about 60% of the white population. About 32% of the population speaks German; indigenous languages such as Oshivambo, Herero, and Nama are also spoken.

Christianity is the major religion in the country, practiced by between 80% and 90% of the population. At least 50% of these are Lutherans. Approximately 10% to 20% of the population follows indigenous religions.

Prior to being a territory of South Africa, Namibia (then South West Africa) was a German colony. South Africa occupied the colony during World War I and took charge of its administration before annexing South West Africa after World War II.

The South West Africa People's Organization (SWAPO), a Marxist guerrilla group founded in 1960, began fighting for the country's independence in 1966. The United Nations achieved a breakthrough in 1977 when South Africa accepted the so-called Western Contact Group consisting of the United States, United Kingdom, France, West Germany, and Canada. This granted the United Nations jurisdiction over the territory of South West Africa. Only in 1988, however, did South Africa agree to withdraw from Namibia. Namibia held United Nations-supervised elections in November 1989. A total of 90% of eligible voters voted, and SWAPO won decisively, with Sam Nujoma, one of the leaders of the independence movement, elected president. Namibia became officially independent on March 21, 1990. This was not a random date; rather, it was symbolically chosen to commemorate the thirtieth anniversary of the Sharpeville massacre of black protesters in South Africa.

After independence, SWAPO pursued a course of compromise with opposition groups and of gradualism in addressing racial inequalities within the country. In the November 2004 elections, Hifikepunye Pohamba was elected president, replacing Nujoma.

The currency is the Namibian dollar; the South African rand is also used. Mining accounts for 20% of the gross domestic product (GDP). The main exports of Namibia are diamonds, copper, uranium, gold, lead, tin, lithium, cadmium, zinc, salt, vanadium, natural gas, hydropower, fish, silver, and tungsten. The mining sector employs about 3% of the population; about half of Namibia's population is dependent on subsistence agriculture. Namibia imports a number of products and goods such as foodstuffs, including cereals and other staples; petroleum products and fuel; machinery and equipment; and chemicals.

Agriculture constitutes 11% of the Namibian GDP, industry 28%, and services 61%. However, the agriculture sector employs 47% of the labor force, industry 20%, and services 33%.

Namibia faces many problems, politically, economically, and socially. It has limited water resources. Desertification, land degradation, and wildlife poaching have also been serious problems. The unemployment rate is more than 30%. The spread of the human immunodeficiency virus (HIV) has been increasing; 20% of adults in Namibia are currently infected. The continued presence of Angolan rebels and refugees in Namibia has also caused problems.

On the positive side, Namibia was the first country in the world to include laws regarding environmental protection in its constitution. This has ensured that around 14% of the land is protected, including almost all of the Namib Desert. The government has ratified international environmental agreements pertaining to biodiversity, climate change, desertification, endangered species, hazardous wastes, law of the sea, ozone layer protection, and wetlands. It has also joined many international organizations such as Interpol and the World Trade Organization (WTO).

NILLY KAMAL EL-AMIR

See also Southern Africa: History and Economic Development; Southern Africa: International Relations

References and Further Reading

Amoah, G. Y. *Ground Work for Government for West Africa* Nigeria: Obenle Press, 1988.

Arnold, Guy. *A Guide to African Political and Economic Development*. London: Fitzory Dearborn, 2001.

Bohonnan, Paul. *Africa and Africans*. New York: The Natural History Press, 1964.

Chazan, Naome et al. *Politics and Society in Contemporary Africa*. London: Macmillan, 1988.

Crabal, Patrick. *Power in Africa: An Essay in Political interpretation*. New York: St. Martin's Press, 1992.

Deng, F. and W. Zartman, eds. *Conflict Resolution in Africa*. Washington DC: Brookings Institution, 1991.

Egyptian International Trade Point. *Group of Common Market for Eastern and Southern African Countries (COMESA)*. Cairo: Ministry of Economy and Foreign Trade, 2001.

NASSER, GAMAL ABDEL

July 23, 1952, the date on which a group of Free Officers carried out the Egyptian Revolution, is widely accepted as a key day in contemporary Egyptian history. General Mohammed Naguib and Colonel Gamal Abdel Nasser (1918–1970) led the army coup that overthrew King Farouk I and that finished the Ali dynasty installed in Egypt since 1805. Democracy was from then on to be Egypt's political regime.

Naguib was in charge of the Revolutionary Committee until 1954 when, accused of participating in an attempt on Nasser's life carried out by the Muslim Brotherhood, he was arrested. In October 1954, Nasser became the sole leader of the revolutionary process and two years later he ran unopposed and was elected president of Egypt. He then promoted a new constitution and established a political regime known as "Arab Socialism." He was one of the most influential leaders in Egyptian history.

Among his first important measures were an agrarian reform, through which the government expropriated large amounts of fields that belonged to a small group of landowners; the nationalization of several banks and of an important part of the industries; the establishment of extensive educational programmes for both boys and girls; and the development of the country's medical infrastructure.

Within an international context of a Cold War between the Western and the socialist Eastern Bloc, the sudden introduction of such nationalistic and socialist measures was not well seen by the occidental developed countries, who quickly withdrew their economic and political support for the Egyptian Revolution.

In order to resolve his economic issues, Nasser decided to raise funds by implementing another radical measure. Hence, on July 26, 1956, President Nasser announced through the national papers the nationalization of the Suez Canal Company and accordingly of the Suez Canal, so as to collect funds to build the Aswan High Dam with the income from tolls on the traffic on the canal. Until then, the Suez Canal had been occupied by Anglo-French forces. Consequently, the English and French invaded the Canal zone, especially the Port Said area. At the same time Egypt entered into a military conflict with Israel, which quickly turned in favour of the latter when they occupied the Sinai Peninsula. However, the 1956 war didn't finish until the United Nations (UN), mainly supported by the United States and the Soviet Union, took action. In the end, the Anglo-French and Israeli troops withdrew from the zone and Egypt kept the management of the Canal.

This was Nasser's first and probably most important achievement. He gained renown throughout the

Arab and the Third World as well as immense popularity among his own people. Beyond the economic value, the nationalization of the Canal and the withdrawal of British troops had a stunning symbolic value for the Egyptians as it meant the end of colonialism for them.

Perhaps Nasser's second great contribution was the construction of the Aswan High Dam, begun in 1960 and inaugurated in January 1971. The execution of this pharaonic work had begun with North American and British support years before, but the refusal of those countries to continue the project in 1956 forced Nasser to look elsewhere for aid. Therefore the fulfillment of the dam project was done with technical and financial support of the Soviet government. The opening of the dam in 1971 was beneficial to Egypt's development, as it provided hydroelectric power to the industrial sector and to the general population. In addition to that, the Aswan High Dam benefited irrigation projects and the fishing industry in Egypt, although it also caused contamination, land erosion, and agricultural conflicts.

Prior to the dam's inauguration, Nasser had decided in 1958 to look for allies and therefore signed a self-defense and political union pact with Syria, setting up the United Arab Republic (UAR). This treaty only lasted three years and was broken in 1961 when a rebel group seized power in Syria and it became again an independent country. However, Egypt kept the name UAR until 1971 as a symbol of Nasser's hope and dream to construct the Pan-Arab Union.

Despite having had so much success in building the dam and keeping the Suez Canal under Egyptian control, Nasser's external politics weren't so successful and during 1967 led the country to a third war with Israel. This time not only Egypt (at that time the UAR) was involved, but also the whole Arab League (UAR, Iraq, Saudi Arabia, Lebanon, Jordan, Syria, Yemen, Libya, Sudan, Morocco, Kuwait, and Algeria), equipped with Soviet weapons, against Israel. This war, due to its short time frame, was called the Six-Days War, and its consequence was an outstanding defeat of the Arab countries.

This was a bitter result for the whole League, but especially for Nasser and the Egyptians who had been quickly beaten again by the same enemy. Nasser felt guilty and presented his resignation letter to the National Assembly on June 9, 1967. However, he was widely supported by a large crowd that took over the streets of Cairo (Egypt's capital city) to support him.

On June 10, 1967, the National Assembly accepted the withdrawal of his letter and Nasser became president again. He served until his sudden death of a heart attack September 28, 1970. He will always be remembered as a pioneer and as the most prominent socialist leader of Egypt.

Diego I. Murguía

See also Arab–Israeli Wars (1948, 1956, 1967, 1973); Arab Nationalism; Egypt; Middle East: History and Economic Development; Middle East: International Relations; Muslim Brotherhood; United Arab Republic (UAR)

References and Further Reading

Aburish, Said K. *Nasser. The Last Arab, a Biography*. New York: Thomas Dunne Books, 2004.
Baker, Raymond. *Egypt's Uncertain Revolution under Nasser and Sadat*. Cambridge, MA: Harvard University Press, 1978.
Cremeans, Charles D. *The Arabs and the World: Nasser's Arab Nationalist Policy*. New York: Praeger, 1963.
Gordon, Joel. *Nasser's Blessed Movement: Egypt's Free Officers and the July Revolution*. New York: Oxford University Press, 1992.
McDermott, Anthony. *Egypt from Nasser to Mubarak: A Flawed Revolution*. London: Croom Helm, 1988.
Stephens, Robert Henry. *Nasser: A Political Biography*. London: Allen Lane, 1971.
Waterbury, John. *The Egypt of Nasser and Sadat: The Political Economy of Two Regimes*. Princeton, NJ: Princeton University Press, 1983.

NATION BUILDING

The idea and practice of nation building is most closely associated with US foreign policy and the influential theories of modernization and development that emerged in the Cold War era. In general terms, nation building can be defined as an externally driven attempt to form or consolidate a stable, and sometimes democratic, government. Post-1945 US efforts in West Germany and Japan were directed at building stable democratic polities, while the emphasis in the case of South Korea and South Vietnam, for example, was on stable anti-communist governments. In the early years of the post–Cold War era, there has again been greater emphasis on democracy as part of wider nation-building efforts. Nation building in the Cold War era was usually a US- or Soviet-sponsored effort, with important relative exceptions such as United Nations (UN) involvement in the Congo from July 1960 to June 1964. The *Operation des Nations Unies au Congo* (ONUC) was the biggest UN action since the Korean War (1950–1953), which was formally a UN initiative despite the fact that it was an overwhelming US operation in practice. Furthermore, it was not until the post–Cold War era, when the United Nations again began to play a somewhat more significant role in nation-building efforts, that it intervened on the scale of its operation in the Congo in the early 1960s.

While democracy emerged as central to UN- and US-sponsored nation-building initiatives in the 1990s, the scope and scale of post–Cold War nation-building efforts (even in Iraq since 2003, which will be discussed below) is far more limited than it was in the immediate post-1945 era, such as in West Germany and Japan. These were two of the most intense and substantial nation-building efforts of the entire post-1945 era. In both cases the United States initially expected formal occupation would be relatively brief, but it ended up assuming the responsibilities of an occupying power for a number of years. In the context of the Marshall Plan (1947) the United States, along with Britain and France, presided over the establishment of a federal government in West Germany by 1949, but military occupation continued until 1955. Of course, significant numbers of US troops remained after 1955, but their deployment by this stage was as a front-line force in the Cold War rather than as an occupation force. In Japan, nation building was supervised directly by General Douglas MacArthur, with the majority of US troops remaining until 1952. In Germany and Japan, nation building included the reconstruction and reform of the education system, the press, industry, and the legal system, as well as the retraining of the police, and major disarmament, demobilization, and demilitarization initiatives.

Nation-building efforts in West Germany and Japan encouraged subsequent attempts in the emerging Third World; however, the level of US commitment to nation building decreased in the wake of the failed effort at nation building in South Vietnam (Washington spent over US$120 billion on the Vietnam War between 1965 and 1973). At the start of the 1960s there had been an increased emphasis in US foreign policy circles (symbolized by the election to the US presidency of John F. Kennedy, 1961–1963) on the need for a more ambitious nation-building and counterinsurgency strategy in the so-called Third World. This involved taking the initiative in Asia and Latin America, as well as the Middle East and Africa, to counter the communist threat via the infusion of increased levels of military and economic aid, advice, and support. Nation building also emerged as an important concern of North American political science in the 1950s in the context of the Cold War and the rise of modernization theory. Some observers define modernization theory in a way that includes development economics, a sub-discipline of economics that emerged in the 1940s to address the problem of "underdevelopment" in what would come to be called the Third World. However, it is probably more precise to view development economics as having provided the earliest systematic formulations of development theory generally, while modernization theory can be said to have appeared in the late 1950s as a particularly North American response by political scientists to the perceived failure of development economics to come up with a political framework for nation building. In this situation, the late 1950s and early 1960s can be characterized as an era in which modernization theory rose to prominence in US academic and foreign policy circles. In the context of the Cold War, modernization theorists sought to articulate a non-Marxian alternative for the developing nations. They systematized an evolutionary and elite-oriented conception of political change and nation building grounded in a romanticized conception of the history of the United States of America. Furthermore, although early modernization theorists were rhetorically committed to "democracy," their vision of democracy was elitist and technocratic and stability was generally regarded as more important than democracy.

These themes are apparent in the work of Lucian Pye, an influential advocate of nation building in the 1950s and 1960s. Pye's work combined an explicitly psychological approach to political behavior with the examination of political change in the emerging nation-states of Asia and Africa. His first book, published in 1956, was on the communist insurgency in British Malaya. He argued that the fundamental basis of the appeal of communism in Malaya and other "underdeveloped" countries was the insecurity experienced by people who had lost their "traditional way of life" and were undergoing psychological stress as part of their effort to achieve a "modern" existence. Pye's analysis meshed with the thinking that increasingly underpinned the US nation-building and counterinsurgency efforts in South Vietnam by the early 1960s. According to Pye, if peasants in "transitional societies" joined guerrilla movements to acquire a modern identity, then the way to defeat the guerrillas was to establish governing institutions that were more effective, more appealing, and more modern than those provided by the Communists. In a 1962 study by Pye, *Politics, Personality and Nation-Building: Burma's Search for Identity,* he argued that, as colonies in Africa increasingly moved toward decolonization, they, like the new nations of Asia, would be "crucially affected by deep psychological conflicts." In this context he lamented the apparent lack of "nation building" doctrines, the formulation of which had been constrained by an "unreasoned expectation" that democracy was "inevitable" and by the assumption that political development was a "natural" process that could not be "rationally planned or directed." Pye emphasized that there was a "need to create more effective, more adaptive, more complex, and more rationalized organizations" to facilitate nation building.

South Vietnam, more than any other country, encapsulated US nation-building efforts by the early 1960s. For President Dwight D. Eisenhower (1953–1960), and more particularly his successor, John F. Kennedy, the regime of Ngo Dinh Diem (1955–1963) was to be a "showcase" for nation building that would make clear the pre-eminence of North American institutions and values in the global Cold War. With the election of Kennedy, US efforts in South Vietnam entered a new phase. In 1961 the fighting between the South Vietnamese regime and the National Liberation Front of South Vietnam (NLF), a popular front organization that had been established in December 1960, was steadily increasing. In 1962 and 1963 the Strategic Hamlet Program emerged as central to Washington's nation-building policy in South Vietnam. The Kennedy administration encouraged and facilitated the removal of peasants from widely dispersed villages, placing them in concentrated settlements that could be controlled more directly by the Saigon government. The State Department scheduled almost US$90 million to be spent on strategic hamlet programs for fiscal year 1963. Using this strategy, the US Military Assistance Command (MACV) and the Agency for International Development (USAID) sought to prevent, or at least seriously weaken, the NLF's ability to get intelligence, food and other supplies, as well as recruits. They also sought to inculcate new ideas about national citizenship that were centered on loyalty to the government of South Vietnam. In 1962 it initially appeared as if the strategic hamlets were undermining the influence of the NLF; however, the guerrillas acted rapidly to counter this trend. The NLF promised the peasants (many of whom were profoundly alienated from the government that had forced them from their villages) that following the revolution they would be allowed to return to their old villages. The NLF also intensified its military attacks on, and recruitment activities in, the strategic hamlets, undermining the effectiveness of the nation-building effort.

By the time of the military overthrow of the Diem regime, and the assassination of Diem and his brother Nhu Dinh Diem in late 1963, the term "strategic hamlet" was being dropped from the counterinsurgency lexicon. However, subsequent efforts to resettle and control the rural population reworked the basic nation-building framework that underpinned the efforts of the early 1960s. The United States had hoped that the overthrow of the unpopular Diem regime would improve the stability of South Vietnam;

however, the deterioration in the military situation following the coup paved the way for the escalation of US involvement and direct military intervention by 1965 (at its peak, in January of 1969, the number of US personnel stationed in South Vietnam was 542,400). The pervasive reliance on the United States, economically, militarily, and politically, generated growing possibilities for government and private corruption that completely undermined the South Vietnamese government's nationalist credentials. While a significant number of people in the south were hostile to the Communists, they also lost interest in fighting for the corrupt and despotic US-backed regime in Saigon. Furthermore, in their effort to build a modern nation-state in the southern half of Vietnam, US policy makers overlooked the fact that many southerners identified with the culturally and historically delineated nation of Vietnam that was larger than the post-1954 polity presided over by Diem and his successors.

In the context of the escalation of the war in Vietnam, the creation of institutions and organizations that could provide order became even more important for proponents of nation building. The assumptions and concerns of the officials who carried the United States into full-scale war in Vietnam were closely connected to the revised theories of modernization and nation building that emerged during the 1960s. For example, the major concern of Samuel Huntington's influential 1968 book, *Political Order in Changing Societies,* was to determine what might or might not be necessary to ensure continued social order and political stability. He held up political order as the ultimate goal of any society. He argued that, contrary to earlier expectations, the instability in Asia and the rest of the Third World since World War II was primarily the result of "rapid social change and the rapid mobilization of new groups into politics coupled with the slow development of political institutions." Furthermore, US foreign policy since 1945 had, in his view, missed this point, because Washington had placed too great an emphasis on the "economic gap," while overlooking the "political gap." He emphasized that the political gap had been ignored because of the assumption in North America that political stability flowed from "social reform" stimulated by economic development. However, in his view it was actually the process of modernization that led to political instability. For Huntington, organization was the "road to political power" as well as the "foundation of political stability." In a famous article, also published in 1968, Huntington argued that the key to combating wars of national liberation in South Vietnam and elsewhere was to adopt a policy of "forced-draft urbanization" and "modernization," which would quickly shift the nation-state in question beyond the stage where a rural-based revolution has any chance of building up enough support to capture national political power. Huntington's prescriptions held out the possibility that successful nation building in South Vietnam and elsewhere remained within Washington's power. However, with the Tet Offensive in early 1968, the elite consensus in North America that US power could turn South Vietnam into a stable capitalist nation-state and achieve military victory against the North had been completely undermined. With the elevation of Richard Nixon to the presidency (1969–1974), the United States began to look for ways to withdraw "with honor."

US nation-building efforts in the early 1960s also focused on Latin America. Under the auspices of the Alliance for Progress, the Kennedy administration sought to contain the "communist threat" to Latin America in the wake of the Cuban Revolution of 1959. The Alliance for Progress started as a ten-year program of land and economic reform. The United States made an initial contribution of US$1 billion and a commitment to raise another US$20 billion overall from both public and private sources. As part of an effort to encourage the consolidation of stable capitalist and democratic polities, it set the achievement of an annual economic growth rate for the region of at least 2.5% as one of its main goals. It also sought to achieve greater productivity in the agricultural sector, stimulate trade diversification, generate improvements in housing, eradicate illiteracy, and ensure better distribution of incomes. But an important, albeit implicit, goal was the protection of US investments in Latin America, an objective that many of the Alliance's proposed reforms endangered. Trade diversification would undermine the monopoly of primary agricultural products and mineral extraction enjoyed by a number of US-based corporations. At the same time, land reform threatened the power of the still largely land-based ruling elites in Latin America. This meant that the reformism of the Alliance for Progress was increasingly sidelined by Washington's deepening commitment to military and police aid, along with support for authoritarian governments and counterinsurgency programs. By the late 1960s, high rates of economic growth in many Latin American countries had been achieved. However, high growth rates exacerbated social inequality, while politics, instead of becoming more democratic, moved increasingly toward authoritarianism. This was reflected in the fact that there were sixteen military coups in the region in the 1960s.

The waning of the Alliance for Progress and the US defeat in Vietnam provided the context for a shift in US nation-building efforts. While the United States still sought to stabilize and consolidate anti-communist states, the quantity and character of economic support shifted, while direct US military involvement decreased dramatically. Furthermore, while the United States continued to support authoritarian military regimes in the Middle East, Africa, and Central America in the 1970s and 1980s, there was limited emphasis on democracy and Washington's military commitment virtually always remained indirect. Then, with the end of the Cold War, there was another reorientation of the US role. While the focus of US foreign aid by the 1980s had been changed to reflect the ascendancy of "free market" ideas, with the end of the Cold War, President Bill Clinton (1993–2000) presided over a range of reforms that ostensibly sought to reduce the significance of security concerns in the disbursement of foreign aid. USAID was still expected to promote economic development by encouraging trade, investment, and market-oriented reform, but it also established new programs aimed at building democratic political institutions. A greater emphasis was also placed on humanitarian assistance and sustainable development. However, this reorientation, symbolized by the passage of a new foreign aid bill by Congress in 1994, still involved a major commitment to US geo-strategic and security concerns. For example, Israel and Egypt continued to receive over one-third of all US foreign aid. In 1994 Israel received US$3 billion and Egypt received US$2.1 billion, while Sub-Saharan Africa was allotted a total of US$800 million. Foreign aid was also directed increasingly at the former Soviet bloc, again for security reasons. The long shadow of the Vietnam era also continues to shape nation building in the post–Cold War era. For example, despite increased emphasis on humanitarian intervention, the death of eighteen US soldiers in Somalia in 1993 reconfirmed for US policy makers that there was a need to avoid making significant commitments in those parts of the world where there is no obvious "national interest" at stake. Meanwhile, the idea of nation building more specifically still carries with it connotations of the US defeat in Vietnam. In the post–Cold War and particularly the post-9/11 era, the term has been reinstated albeit reluctantly. For example, on September 25, 2001, President George W. Bush reassured the US public that the new "war on terrorism" would not involve nation building in Afghanistan. However, by early 2002, Washington was not only engaged in nation building in Afghanistan, but the Pentagon had also begun planning the military invasion of Iraq and the State Department had begun developing plans for post-war nation building in Iraq (plans, however, that the Pentagon ignored after the fall of Baghdad).

Meanwhile, as noted above, the 1990s saw the expansion of UN-sponsored peacekeeping and nation building, but the ouster of Saddam Hussein (1979–2003) and the subsequent occupation of Iraq were initially notable for the complete absence of the United Nations, while subsequently its role has remained relatively marginal. The initial US intervention in Iraq was organized around a "coalition of the willing" and had no formal UN involvement. This flowed from the fact that while the UN played a long-standing role in weapons inspection in, and the maintenance of sanctions on, Iraq, the US-led overthrow of the regime in Baghdad had been preceded by increasingly antagonistic relations between the United States and the UN, particularly with key members of the Security Council, over how to deal with Baghdad, with the United States eventually deciding to embark on nation building in Iraq without the authorization of the UN Security Council. As the US occupation of Iraq progresses, the UN has once again become involved, although it remains primarily a US operation, which appears set to be at the center of US foreign policy and the ongoing debate about successful and unsuccessful nation building for the foreseeable future.

MARK T. BERGER

See also Afghanistan; Alliance for Progress; Congo, Democratic Republic of the; Congo, Democratic Republic of the; Iraq; United States Agency for International Development (USAID); Vietnam War

References and Further Reading

Dacy, Douglas C. *Foreign Aid, War, and Economic Development: South Vietnam, 1953–1975.* Cambridge, UK: Cambridge University Press, 1986.

Gendzier, Irene L. *Managing Political Change: Social Scientists and the Third World* Boulder, CO: Westview Press, 1985.

Hunt, Richard A. Pacification: *The American Struggle for Vietnam's Hearts and Minds.* Boulder, CO: Westview Press, 1995.

Huntington, Samuel P. *Political Order in Changing Societies* New Haven, CT: Yale University Press, 1968.

———. "The Bases of Accommodation." *Foreign Affairs,* vol. 46, no. 3, 1968.

Latham, Michael E. *Modernization as Ideology: American Social Science and "Nation Building" in the Kennedy Era.* Chapel Hill, NC: The University of North Carolina Press, 2000.

Leys, Colin *The Rise and Fall of Development Theory.* Bloomington: Indiana University Press, 1996.

McMahon, Robert J. *The Limits of Empire: The United States and Southeast Asia Since World War II.* New York: Columbia University Press, 1999.

Pearce, Kimber Charles. *Rostow, Kennedy, and the Rhetoric of Foreign Aid.* East Lansing, MI: Michigan State University Press, 2001.

Pye, Lucian W. *Guerrilla Communism in Malaya: Its Social and Political Meaning.* Princeton, NJ: Princeton University Press, 1956.

———. *Politics, Personality, and Nation Building: Burma's Search for Identity.* New Haven, CT: Yale University Press, 1962.

Shafer, D. Michael. *Deadly Paradigms: The Failure of U.S. Counterinsurgency Policy.* Princeton, NJ: Princeton University Press, 1988.

Stubbs, Richard. *Hearts and Minds in Guerrilla Warfare: The Malayan Emergency 1948–1960.* Singapore: Oxford University Press, 1989.

Von Hippel, Karin. *Democracy by Force: US Military Intervention in the Post-Cold War World.* Cambridge, UK: Cambridge University Press, 2000.

NATIONAL ACTION PARTY

Mexico's National Action Party (generally referred to by its Spanish acronym, PAN) was founded in 1939. The PAN emerged in response to the semi-authoritarian form of government and the state-driven reformist economic model espoused by the Institutional Revolutionary Party (PRI), the political party that monopolized political power in Mexico between 1929 and 2000. Originally, leaders of the PAN proposed a twofold ideology. The party advocated liberal democratic principles, which emphasized free and fair elections, sociopolitical pluralism, transparent and accountable government, as well as responsible management of public finances. The PAN also furthered a set of moral principles dubbed "catholic humanism," which provided guidelines for the civic education and spiritual improvement of Mexicans, and demanded greater economic welfare as well as social justice.

These two ideological currents have cohabited uneasily throughout the PAN's history. By the mid-1970s, the catholic humanist wing of the PAN had drifted to the left, denouncing capitalism for the socioeconomic abuses it generated, and promoting abstention from Mexico's electoral process as an act of dissent against the PRI's authoritarian rule. This stance alienated the more socially and economically conservative PAN supporters. In reaction, the party's liberal democratic wing set forth a platform proposing a reorientation of the PAN away from left-leaning ideological concerns and toward greater voter mobilization and electoral participation. This faction ultimately sought to further the democratization of Mexico's political regime, reduce the power of the government, and promote market-based economics. The liberal democratic wing hoped that such a strategy would enhance the PAN's electoral base by channeling the growing popular dissatisfaction with the PRI's repressive tendencies and inability to deal with the country's pressing economic difficulties. After significant infighting, the liberal democratic faction's platform prevailed. Nevertheless, ideology continues to represent a significant source of internal tension, and normative Catholic prescriptions still permeate the PAN's policy orientation.

From the 1940s to the 1960s, the PAN constituted a party of notables, whose leadership was centralized in Mexico City and held strong ties to Catholic organizations. As a result of its aforementioned mid-1970s ideological reorientation, the PAN increasingly attracted the support of Mexico's middle classes and businesspersons, enticed by the PAN's liberal political and economic orientation. This new breed of members—referred to as "neopanistas"—generally lived outside of Mexico's capital city. In fact, since the early 1980s, the PAN's electoral strength has been mostly concentrated in the northern and some central states, as well as in the Yucatan peninsula. Furthermore, the PAN typically draws its electoral support from urban-based and educated citizens, who enjoy medium to high levels of income.

During the 1980s and 1990s, neopanistas gradually captured the PAN's leadership, bringing to the party important technical skills, powerful business connections, as well as sizeable financial resources. At the same time, the PRI progressively liberalized the electoral process, in the hope of re-legitimizing its rule, and hence grew more tolerant of PAN victories—although it still restricted gains from the leftist opposition. In order to take advantage of this opening, the PAN chose to enter into limited strategic alliances with the PRI. The PAN also privileged capacity building at the sub-national level. The PAN's flexible ideological platform, its dynamic organization, as well as its efficient campaigning style attracted the support of an increasingly large segment of the population, frustrated with the PRI-led authoritarian regime. As a result, the PAN significantly improved its representation in the local and state parliaments, and secured seven state governorships between 1989 and 2000. This produced a coattails effect, as the PAN's share of seats in the national legislature steadily increased through the 1990s.

The transitional elections of 2000 represent a high point in the PAN's electoral popularity. The party's candidate—businessman Vicente Fox—claimed the presidency, thus ending the PRI's authoritarian rule. The PAN also obtained two-fifths of the seats in the Chamber of Deputies. Nonetheless, this success was followed by less impressive showings in subsequent regional and national elections. This is largely attributable to the citizenry's disappointment with President Fox's inability to fulfill the majority of his ambitious electoral promises. Indeed, the resistance of opposition parties—which controlled Mexico's parliament between 2000 and 2006—and poor communications between the federal administration and the PAN's congressional fraction have hindered the adoption of President Fox's comprehensive reformist policy program. The PAN has also been plagued by serious factional power struggles since 2000.

JEAN F. MAYER

See also Fox, Vicente; Mexico: History and Economic Development

References and Further Reading

Arriola, Carlos. *¿Como Gobierna el Pan?* Mexico City: Noriega Editores, 1998.
Chand, Vikram. *Mexico's Political Awakening.* Notre Dame, IN: University of Notre Dame Press, 2001.
Middlebrook, Kevin. *Party Politics and the Struggle for Democracy in Mexico: National and State-Level Analyses of the Partido Acción Nacional.* La Jolla, CA: Center for US–Mexican Studies, University of California, 2001.
Mizrahi, Yemile. *From Martyrdom to Power: The Partido Acción Nacional in Mexico.* Notre Dame, IN: University of Notre Dame Press, 2003.
Rodríguez, Victoria and Peter Ward. *Opposition Government in Mexico.* Albuquerque, NM: University of New Mexico Press, 1995.
Shirk, David. *Mexico's New Politics: The PAN and Democratic Change.* Boulder, CO: Lynne Rienner Publishers, 2005.

NATIONAL FRONT FOR THE LIBERATION OF SOUTH VIETNAM (NFLSV)/NATIONAL LIBERATION FRONT (NLF)

The *Mat Tran Dan Toc Giai Phong Mien Nam,* literally the National Front for the Liberation of South Vietnam (NFLSV), best known as the National Liberation Front (NLF), was formed on December 20, 1960, in Tay Ninh Province in South Vietnam as a result of decisions reached at the Third National Congress of the Vietnamese Workers' Party (VWP) in Hanoi in September 1960. Congress members decided that after six years of trying to unify the country through political means, they should accept the recommendations of Central Committee member Le Duan and approve the use of armed violence through the NFLSV's military arm, the People's Armed Liberation Forces (PLAF), or as the Allies called them, the "Viet Cong." In an effort to gain wide national support, NFLSV leaders, concealing the Front's Communist leanings, publically declared that the NFLSV was a broad-based "front" opposing the US-backed regime of Ngo Dinh Diem in Saigon.

While the NFLSV directly replaced the Fatherland Front *(Mat Tran To Quoc)*, created in Hanoi in 1955, its ideological antecedent was the League for the Independence of Vietnam, commonly known as the Viet Minh, established in May 1941 as an anti-Japanese and later anti-French nationalist movement. The NFLSV, like the Viet Minh, sought reunification through any means based on widely shared objectives such as national independence and social justice. While the NFLSV had major southern components, it was dominated by northern Communists.

The NFLSV's organizational structure was similar to the Viet Minh. At the top was an elected central committee and a presidium. The chairman of the presidium was Nguyen Huu Tho, a lawyer who had been involved in resistance activities since the late 1940s, but who publicly downplayed his Communist ties. Similar committees existed at the provincial and district levels. At the heart of the NFLSV were grassroots organizations that appealed to specific constituencies such as peasants, workers, women, students, writers, and artists, as well as oppressed ethnic and religious groups.

Local associations served as the initial contact points between the Front hierarchy and the common people and provided a means for channeling local aspirations into support for the programs of the movement. Talented and dedicated members of such organizations were then enlisted into upper levels of the NFLSV, PLAF and/or the People's Revolutionary Party, a southern branch of the VWP. During the 1960s, the NFLSV became the focus for the revolutionary movement in South Vietnam, with membership reportedly in the millions.

The reality was that the NFLSV was a classic Communist front organization comprised of Communists and non-Communists. Its primary purpose was to mobilize the anti-Diem forces in South Vietnam. Like the Viet Minh before them, NFLSV leaders made temporary alliances with any southern group who opposed US intervention and the Saigon regime.

The NFLSV's attacks on the Diem government concerned Saigon and Washington. From the birth of NFLSV, Washington policy makers claimed that Hanoi alone directed the armed struggle in South Vietnam. Key members of both President John F. Kennedy's (1961–1963) and Lyndon Baines Johnson's (1963–1969) administrations argued that the flow of troops and supplies from the north to the PLAF kept the revolution alive. This became the official basis for US involvement in the conflict and provided its justification. Even under the administration of Richard M. Nixon (1969–1974), US foreign policy focused on efforts to stop this "externally supported insurgency" by interdicting the flow of men and materials.

Especially in the 1960s, US officials believed South Vietnam could be stabilized if they could prevent the North from re-supplying their NFLSV and PLAF "puppets." Those who opposed US intervention argued on the other hand that the insurgency was essentially a civil war. They suggested that the NFLSV was a southern organization that had risen out of southern initiatives responding to southern demands. The complicated part of the NFLSV is that this was partly true. Indeed, most southern members of the NFLSV and PLAF believed this to be true.

PLAF attacks against US Army installations at Pleiku and Quy Nhdn in February 1965 convinced the Johnson administration that they had to stop the infiltration of soldiers and supplies. It was impossible, they concluded, to build a stable government in Saigon while the Democratic Republic of Vietnam (DRV) and its Communist supporters waged a war of aggression. Johnson therefore ordered retaliatory air attacks on North Vietnamese targets, thus leading to *Operation Rolling Thunder*, the sustained bombing campaign of 1965–1968. US ground operations also changed when Military Assistance Command, Vietnam (MACV), General William C. Westmoreland requested two US Marine battalions to protect Da Nang Air Base. Johnson approved the General's request, sending the first major contingency of US ground troops to Vietnam in March 1965.

Soon, US troops began "search and destroy" operations designed to interdict supplies and destroy PLAF and PAVN forces. Westmoreland hoped he could inflict higher casualties on enemy forces than they could replace. Theoretically, this would diminish Communist will and lead to a negotiated settlement.

The NFLSV reached its pinnacle of power during the Tet Offensive of 1968 when Communist forces launched coordinated attacks against nearly every major urban center in South Vietnam. Although they suffered heavy military loses, according to most experts the NFLSV gained a great psychological victory. The Front had demonstrated its ability to attack heavily guarded cities, long thought to be safe havens. The PLAF attack on the US Embassy in Saigon had a great impact on policy makers in Washington. Many longtime supporters began to question the optimistic predictions of Johnson's administration. This led to Johnson's decision not to run for re-election. As Tet died down, talks opened in Paris and the NFLSV sent its own representatives, Nguyen Thi Binh and Tran Buu Kiem, to the conference.

In 1969, the NFLSV oversaw the creation of the Provisional Revolutionary Government (PRG), which hoped to come to full power in the South after the war ended. It was designed to be a legal counterpart to the government in Saigon. As the war dragged on, regular northern forces played a growing role in the Communists' southern strategy. Eventually, this created tensions between the NFLSV and leaders in Hanoi. The NFLSV suffered heavy losses during the final years of war. In December 1976, over a year and a half after the fall of Saigon, to the dismay of many NFLSV members, it was merged into the Fatherland Front, while only a handful of its officials were incorporated into the new national government.

CECIL B. CURREY AND WILLIAM P. HEAD

References and Further Reading

Duiker, William J. *The Communist Road to Power in Vietnam*. Boulder, CO: Westview Press, 1981.

Long, Ngo Vinh. *The Tet Offensive and Its Aftermath*. Ithaca, NY: Cornell University Press, 1991.

Pike, Douglas. *Viet Cong: The Organization and Techniques of the National Liberation Front of South Vietnam*. Cambridge, MA: MIT University Press, 1966.

Thayer, Caryle A. *War by Other Means: National Liberation and Revolution in Viet Nam, 1954–1960*. Sydney, Australia: Allen & Unwin, 1989.

NATIONAL LIBERATION ARMY (ELN) (COLOMBIA)

The National Liberation Army (*Ejército de Liberación Nacional,* ELN) is one of three irregular forces in Colombia listed by the US State Department as terrorist organizations, primarily for its frequent use of kidnapping and extortion. It has an estimated strength of some five thousand fighters, concentrated mostly in central and northern Colombia. Its ideology is nominally Marxist-Leninist.

The ELN, like most of Colombia's guerrilla groups, can trace its origins to the period known as *La Violencia*, which began in 1948 and formally ended with the restoration of democracy in 1958. And like the country's other groups, the ELN was founded, in part, by Liberals and other guerrillas who refused to lay down their arms at the close of hostilities. It also incorporated disaffected members of the Liberal Revolutionary Movement (MRL), which was disbanded in 1964, and radical students who had traveled to Cuba in 1962 for training in Ché Guevara's *foquismo* tactics. The latter held that guerrilla groups would serve as the seeds of insurrection in Latin America, rallying peasants to their cause and waging war from the countryside.

The ELN burst upon the scene with an attack on the town of Simocota in the northern department of Santander in July 1964. While the attack failed, its audacity attracted the attention of radical Roman Catholic priest Camilo Torres and his group, United Front. Torres joined forces with the ELN but was killed in an armed action in 1967. The ELN's early base of support was among the petroleum workers of the Middle Magdalena region and one of its historic causes has been to protect Colombian oil from foreign exploitation. But the ELN—and other guerrilla groups—assumed incorrectly that Colombia was in a pre-revolutionary state and its actions were designed with a fairly rapid victory in mind. This belief led to disastrous results and the group was nearly annihilated by the Colombian military in 1973.

But the group survived under the leadership of Spanish-born priest Manuel Pérez, weathering the authoritarian presidency of Julio César Turbay (1978–1982), resisting efforts to sign a cease-fire in 1984, and becoming known as a single-issue movement due to its persistent calls for the nationalization of the country's petroleum industry, all the while blowing up sections of the main pipeline and kidnapping prominent oil company officials. In the late 1980s, it joined forces with the *Fuerzas Armadas Revolucionarias de Colombia* (Revolutionary Armed Forces of Colombia, FARC) to form the National Guerrilla Coordinator (CNG). The latter negotiated with the government of President César Gaviria in 1991 and 1992 but failed to reach another cease-fire. While the CNG continues to exist nominally, the ELN is largely independent of the larger FARC. Tensions arose when the FARC signed a cease-fire with President Andrés Pastrana that included the concession of a sizeable tract of land in the Colombian Llanos, to the southeast of Bogotá. At the time, the ELN insisted on receiving its own "zone" in the Middle Magdalena region, which Pastrana refused. Negotiations, which have become few and far between, are now carried out on a one-to-one basis between the ELN and the government.

Over the course of the 1990s, the ELN became known for a number of daring mass kidnappings, the most infamous of which took place in a suburb of Cali in 1999. A total of 143 people were abducted from a church in an affluent neighborhood but all but thirty-six were soon released. Another hijacking involved a Venezuelan commercial airliner. In recent years, though, the kidnappings and other activities have decreased and the ELN has stated a willingness to negotiate concerning three major issues: national sovereignty, drug trafficking, and petroleum. Informal talks have occurred outside of Colombia so far but no real progress has been achieved.

LAWRENCE BOUDON

See also Colombia; Guerrilla Warfare; Revolutionary Armed Forces of Colombia (FARC); Terrorism

References and Further Reading

Bergquist, Charles, Peñaranda, Ricardo, and Sánchez, Gonzalo, eds. *Violence in Colombia 1990–2000*. Wilmington, DE: SR Books, 2001.

Braun, Herbert. *Our Guerrillas, Our Sidewalks: A Journey into the Violence of Colombia*, 2nd ed. Lanham, MD: Rowman & Littlefield, 2003.

Kline, Harvey. *State Building and Conflict Resolution in Colombia, 1986–1994*. Tuscaloosa, AL: University of Alabama Press, 1999.

Stafford, Frank and Marco Palacios. *Colombia: Fragmented Land, Divided Society*. New York: Oxford University Press, 2002.

NATURAL DISASTERS

On December 26, 2004, a massive earthquake shook the Indian Ocean floor off the coast of the Indonesian island of Sumatra. Thousands of residents of Aceh Province, on the northern tip of the island, died in the initial temblor. Within minutes, a series of massive tsunamis struck the coastline, killing thousands more.

The waves raced across the Indian Ocean basin, transmitting death and destruction to destinations as disparate as Thailand, Sri Lanka, India, and Somalia. More than 250,000 perished. The Sumatran earthquake tragedy illustrated many factors, both natural and man-made, that make developing nations especially vulnerable to natural disasters.

The developed world is not immune to natural disasters. The Atlantic and Gulf coasts of the United States are especially vulnerable to hurricanes. Tornadoes may rip through the cities of the Great Plains. Fires are a bane to the residents of California. Active volcanoes, earthquakes, and tsunamis are threats all along the Pacific Rim, even to the thriving metropolises along the West Coast of the United States and in Japan.

Even though the developed world is not immune to natural disasters, a number of factors combine to make developing nations especially vulnerable. Among them are factors that cannot be controlled—that is, geography—coupled with human factors such as a lack of monitoring and forecasting resources, communications networks, transportation networks, emergency preparedness (and training), public health infrastructure, or basic civil services (such as adequate food and water supplies).

Natural disasters can inflict a heavy toll on populations in the areas affected, even in developed nations with adequate resources and planning. But the magnitude of suffering in the aftermath of a disaster can be magnified in regions caught unprepared.

Natural Hazard Versus Natural Disaster

A natural hazard is some natural phenomenon that may harm humans. A natural disaster is some destructive event—caused by a natural hazard—that affects many people over a widespread area.

Natural hazards come in basically two types: climatic hazards and geologic hazards. Climatic hazards include hurricanes, winter storms, droughts, floods, thunderstorms, and tornadoes. The rate and intensity of climatic hazards may be influenced by normal climatic cycles, such as the El Niño/Southern Oscillation (ENSO), or by global climate change. Geologic hazards include earthquakes, volcanoes, tsunamis, and mass movements (landslides and avalanches). Climate, geology, and human activities often interact to enhance or mitigate an impending natural disaster.

Climatic Hazards

Tropical Cyclones

Tropical cyclones have a variety of names including hurricanes and typhoons, and are massive storms with maximum sustained surface winds of at least 74 mph (120 km/hr) that bring thunderstorms with heavy rain, intense winds—including tornadoes—and storm surges and other flooding to affected areas. The storms cover wide swaths of the Earth's surface, averaging 350 miles (600 kilometers) in diameter, and are characterized by spiral circulation—counterclockwise in the Northern Hemisphere, clockwise in the Southern Hemisphere—with low central atmospheric pressures.

The center of a tropical cyclone is likewise characterized by an eye, an area of clear skies and calm conditions surrounded by a bank of clouds—the eye wall—beyond which the storm rages. The storms, fueled by high temperatures and massive amounts of water, typically originate over tropical waters in the Atlantic, Indian, and Pacific oceans. Tropical cyclones are also powerful—one storm can expend as much energy as the average amount of electricity consumed each year in the United States and Canada.

The largest tropical cyclones have sustained winds as high as 190 mph (305 km/h). As the winds blow, they drive the water at the surface of the ocean ahead of them to produce a wall of water called the storm surge—the height of which can be increased depending on whether the storm makes landfall at high tide as opposed to low tide. Tropical cyclones thus pack a lethal wallop of wind and water that can weave a path of destruction over large regions.

The most active ocean is the Pacific. By virtue of its size—it is the largest of the ocean basins—the storms have wide expanses of warm tropical waters to fuel their development and plenty of room to roam to increase in size. Pacific storms lash the Asian mainland, including Japan, Taiwan, and the Philippines; Australia and Oceania; and the West Coast of the Americas.

The Atlantic Ocean is the second largest of the world's oceans. Hurricanes that form in the Atlantic (including the Gulf of Mexico and Caribbean Sea) affect North and Central America, the Bahamas, the Caribbean Islands, and northern South America.

While the Indian Ocean is the third-largest ocean, it has the unfortunate distinction of having the deadliest tropical cyclones. Indian Ocean cyclones can strike anywhere from Africa eastward to Indonesia and Australia. The Bay of Bengal is most vulnerable to cyclones. Bangladesh, most of which lies within the Ganges Delta, is very low lying and prone to severe flooding—even without a massive storm surge and accompanying rainfall.

The deadliest hurricane in recent memory was the Bhola Cyclone, which slammed into Bangladesh (at the time known as East Pakistan) with 120-mph (190 km/h) winds and a storm surge on top of an exceptionally high tide on the night of November 12–13, 1970. The official death toll was put at 150,000—with 100,000 missing. Some estimates, however, put the number of deaths at half a million. Approximately 139,000 died in another cyclone in Bangladesh on April 29, 1991.

Two of the deadliest typhoons in the Pacific Basin struck China early in the twentieth century. An August 1922 typhoon killed sixty thousand. Ten years earlier, in August 1912, a storm killed fifty thousand. In the Atlantic, the Great Hurricane of 1780 killed more than twenty thousand in the Antilles. Hurricane Mitch stalked the Caribbean and Central America between October 22, 1998, and November 5, 1998, killing about eleven thousand.

Droughts

Arid climates occupy a large portion of the Earth's surface—especially in the subtropics as well as in continental areas far away from large bodies of water. A prolonged dry spell in an area that receives a small amount of rain every few months or years thus is not a drought—it is normal.

Droughts occur instead when a region gets less precipitation than it normally receives in a given season. This typically happens in areas under the periodic influence of subtropical or continental highs. High-pressure cells are characterized by subsiding air, which warms and essentially dries out as it descends toward the Earth's surface.

Below-average precipitation in a region may have a host of adverse effects on the local population, from disrupting water supplies, to crop failures, to an increase in fire frequency. Droughts typically have the greatest effect on human societies in semiarid grasslands and savannas where some of the range has been converted to cropland and pastureland. Prolonged droughts can accelerate deforestation, which in turn can lead to increased soil erosion—thus ironically increasing the potential for crop failure—when the rains return.

Possibly the worst drought-related famine in history occurred in China in 1907 where 24 million are believed to have died. China has had three other droughts in the twentieth century that claimed 3 million or more victims. The Sahel region of Africa, along the southern border of the Sahara, has been through periodic waves of drought and famine in which hundreds of thousands have died. The last big Sahel drought was in 1984–1985.

Fires

Fire is often associated with drought, as natural vegetation dries out from lack of rain, thus becoming tinder awaiting a suitable spark. Fire is a common natural disturbance in tropical savannas and other grassland environments, and is often necessary for maintenance of the health of those environments, thus it rarely rises to the level of a natural disaster in the more arid portions of the developing world. But fires can be devastating in tropical forests.

Borneo—the island shared among Indonesia, Malaysia, and the Sultanate of Brunei—was hard hit by destructive fire outbreaks in the 1980s and 1990s. While few human lives were lost, large swaths of tropical rainforest were destroyed on the island. Forests that survive the flames are often left more vulnerable to human exploitation. The cumulative effects have rendered much of Borneo's spectacular animal life—including a number of threatened and endangered species—homeless.

Floods

Floods are caused by a number of factors. Coastal flooding is usually related to weather systems (such as tropical cyclones, above) or to tsunamis (see below). Flooding is often seasonal, triggered by monsoon rains or spring snowmelt. Since the earliest human settlements were typically along bodies of water—water being essential for life—floods are one of the oldest and most frequent natural disasters referred to in the historical record.

Flooding is an especially significant problem in monsoon climates, such as that of South and East Asia. In these types of climates, the prevailing winds originate from the interior of a continent—and thus are relatively dry—during part of the year. The winds originate from the oceans—and thus have high water content—the remainder of the year. In extreme cases, an area with a monsoon climate can have no rain for several months, then receive several feet (more than a meter) of rain during the monsoon months. Mountain ranges, such as the Himalayas, can enhance the effect of monsoons, forcing wet air masses to rise, cool, and unload more moisture than they would otherwise do over flat terrain.

Some of the worst non-tropical cyclone-related floods in history have occurred in China and Southeast Asia. For example, the Yangtze River escaped its banks in July and August of 1931, leaving 3.7 million dead from drowning, starvation, and disease. More than 51 million people were affected.

In nearby Vietnam, flooding in the Red River Delta killed more than one hundred thousand in August 1931. One of the heaviest monsoons in the twentieth century flooded three-fourths of Bangladesh. Only about 1,300 died, but about 30 million were left homeless.

Flooding can be a problem even in arid climates. A storm system over Iran in 1954 produced heavy rains and flooding that claimed one thousand casualties.

Other Climatic Hazards

Winter storms and tornadoes mainly affect the developed world, with winter storms primarily affecting the temperature latitudes of the Northern Hemisphere—Asia, Europe, and North America. The United States has more tornadoes by far than any other nation in the world. Nevertheless, both types of storms can be problematic in developed nations.

Winter weather can strike alpine areas anywhere—even in the tropics. A blizzard that struck Iran in 1972 killed more than four thousand people. Tornadoes and waterspouts may appear anywhere that large thunderstorms are generated, such as the thunderstorms spun off of tropical cyclones. Bangladesh has been hit by several killer tornadoes. On the night of February 19–20, 2005, a tornado capsized a ferry boat near Dhaka—the capital of Bangladesh—and killed more than one hundred passengers and crew.

El Niño/Southern Oscillation (ENSO)

The Southern Oscillation is a cyclical reversal of the distribution of warm and cold waters in the equatorial Pacific Ocean. Normally, cold surface waters prevail in the Eastern Pacific off the coast of South America, while warm surface waters prevail in the Western Pacific in the neighborhood of the Malay Archipelago. ENSO events can disrupt oceanic currents in the Pacific Ocean as well as atmospheric circulation patterns globally.

During an El Niño, warm surface waters are located in the Eastern Pacific and cold surface waters in the west, causing significant climate disruptions: Below-average precipitation in the Malay Archipelago and Southeast Asia may cause devastating droughts and fires, as described above. In the Americas, unusually high rainfall and storm activity in the areas along the Pacific Coast can lead to coastal erosion, landslides, and other natural disasters.

Geologic Hazards

Earthquakes

Earthquakes typically occur along boundaries between large segments of the Earth's crust known as tectonic plates. The plates move apart from one another along divergent margins or rift valleys, collide into one another along convergent margins, or slide past one another along transform faults. The vast majority of earthquakes are associated with these three types of plate boundaries.

The most devastating earthquakes occur along convergent margins, but large earthquakes can occur along transform faults as well. The December 26, 2004, earthquake and tsunami in the Indian Ocean occurred along a convergent margin where the dense oceanic crust of the Indian plate is forced under the less dense continental crust of the Burma plate. The largest earthquake on record, a magnitude 9.5 (Richter Scale) temblor in Chile on May 22, 1960, also occurred at a convergent margin where the Pacific plate is forced under the South American plate.

The Pacific Ocean's "Ring of Fire" is in fact lined with convergent margins. Ten of the largest eleven earthquakes since 1900—including the two earthquakes mentioned above—have occurred along the Ring of Fire. Most have occurred in the North Pacific region—three in Alaska and the Aleutian Islands, two in Siberia's Kamchatka Peninsula, and one in the Kuril Islands north of Japan; two in or near South America (Chile, above, and off the coast of Ecuador);

and two in Indonesia (the December 26, 2004, earthquake off Sumatra and another in the Banda Sea).

The deadliest earthquakes in history have occurred along convergent margins where two continental plates collide. The mountain belt stretching from Western Asia to Eastern Asia—which includes the Himalayas—is raised by the collision of the Indian plate with the Eurasian plate. The situation is further complicated to the east with the collision of the Eurasian and Pacific plates. The collisions also generate faults where the crust is fractured and blocks slide past one another, even further clouding matters.

The other member of the top eleven earthquakes list struck Tibet and India's Assam Province on August 15, 1950. Between twenty thousand and thirty thousand were killed. But magnitude isn't always correlated with death toll. Less powerful quakes may produce far higher death tolls. For example, the deadliest earthquake in history, a January 23, 1556, temblor that struck Shansi Province in China, is estimated to have killed more than eight hundred thousand.

China has had at least four other earthquakes that have killed more than one hundred thousand: a July 27, 1976, quake in Tangshan that killed 255,000 (officially; but other estimates place the death toll as high as 655,000); one on December 16, 1920, in Gansu that killed two hundred thousand; another on May 22, 1927, in Xining that killed two hundred thousand; and a September 1290 earthquake in Chihli that killed one hundred thousand. Iran, where the Arabian and Eurasian plates collide, has had its share of deadly quakes: one on December 22, 856, in Damghan in which 230,000 died; and another on March 23, 893, in Ardabil in which 150,000 died. In what is now Turkmenistan, 110,000 died in a temblor on October 5, 1948.

One of the deadliest earthquakes in history, however, occurred on August 9, 1138, along a transform fault—the Dead Sea Transform, which marks the boundary between the Arabian and African plates. More than 230,000 were killed. One of the most active and deadly earthquakes zones in recent history is along another transform fault—the North Anatolian Fault—that runs from northern Turkey across the Aegean Sea into Greece. The North Anatolian Fault marks the boundary between the Anatolian and Eurasian plates. An earthquake near Izmit, Turkey, on August 17, 1999, killed more than seventeen thousand.

Volcanoes

Volcanic activity is also driven by tectonic processes. The most violent volcanoes are located near convergent margins, where plate collisions generate heat and where slabs of crust are forced deep into a molten layer called the mantle. As the affected rocks melt, the magma formed from the melting rises, fueling eruptions at the surface.

Extensive volcanic activity along the Pacific Rim led to the name commonly given to the region—the Ring of Fire. Most deaths from volcanic eruptions arise from famine, tsunamis, ash flows or falls, or mudflows. Because volcanic soils are often very fertile, human populations encroach upon the slopes of volcanoes, and thus are at significant risk.

The two deadliest volcanic eruptions in history occurred in what is now Indonesia. Tambora, on the island of Sumbawa, erupted on April 10, 1815, in one of the largest explosions in history. Tambora blasted fifty cubic kilometers (about eleven cubic miles) of material as high as forty-three kilometers (twenty-six miles) above the Earth's surface. The eruption had global effects, as ash blocked incoming sunlight and dropped global temperatures an average of 1°C (1.8°F).

More than ninety thousand residents of Sumbawa and nearby islands died—about ten thousand directly from the eruption, the rest as a result of famine and disease. Because of the climatic effects—the following year, 1816, was known as the "year without a summer" in the Northern Hemisphere as well as some parts of the Southern Hemisphere—the eruption may have triggered disease outbreaks and famines that killed tens of thousands as far away as the British Isles. (The weather was so gloomy in Europe that it may have helped inspire Mary Shelley to write "Frankenstein.") Tambora's eruption may even have contributed to the biggest cholera pandemic of the nineteenth century.

On August 26–27, 1883, Krakatau (or Krakatoa), a volcano in the Sunda Strait just west of Java in what is now Indonesia, began a series of cataclysmic eruptions that climaxed in the obliteration of two-thirds of the island. The eruption is arguably the most famous in history—save for possibly Vesuvius in 79 CE. It was the loudest blast in recorded history, heard 4,600 kilometers (2,900 miles) away—as far west as Rodriguez Island and Sri Lanka, and as far east as Australia. The volcano collapsed into the sea and generated a tsunami with waves as high as 40 meters (130 feet). The waves swept the Sunda Strait, killing thirty-six thousand in Java, neighboring Sumatra, and surrounding islands. The tsunami waves—measured as far away as the English Channel—swept around the world's oceans several times.

The third-deadliest eruption occurred in the Caribbean, on the island of Martinique. The main volcano on the island, Mount Pelée, erupted on May 8, 1902, and destroyed the city of St. Pierre with a *nuée ardent* (glowing cloud)—a glowing mass of ash and other particles that speeds downslope with the force of a hurricane. Destruction of St. Pierre was total—twenty-nine thousand died. There were only two survivors of the blast: a shoemaker named Léon Compere-Léandre and a man named Louis-Auguste Cyparis, who was a prisoner incarcerated in the city's dungeon. Cyparis was badly burned, but the building—with only one small opening above the door—protected him from the worst. He was rescued four days later.

In addition to explosions and clouds of hot gas, volcanoes can be just as deadly with mud and water. Nevada del Ruiz, a glacier-capped volcano in the Andes Mountains near Bogota, Colombia, erupted on the night of November 13, 1985. The onrush of hot ash and debris rapidly melted the ice and snow at the summit, triggering lahars—debris flows—that tore down canyons lining the mountain and picked up more debris as they went. A town at the base of the mountain, Armero, lay in an area that had twice been destroyed by similar debris flows in the previous four hundred years. Despite the fact that town officials knew the town lay on a particularly hazardous site, preparations for prompt evacuation in the event of another eruption were inadequate. More than twenty-three thousand died when a lahar destroyed the town.

Volcanoes loom over many cities in the developing world—Bogota, Colombia; Goma, Democratic Republic of the Congo; Jakarta, Indonesia; Manila, Philippines; Mexico City, Mexico; and San Salvador, El Salvador, for example. Some of the largest, such as Manila and Mexico City, because of rapid growth coupled with underdeveloped infrastructure, may be unable to adequately respond to volcano hazards.

Other Hazards

Tsunamis are devastating waves generated by earthquakes or volcanic eruptions, and thus have been discussed above. Mass movements are smaller-scale events that, as part of a larger event, may cause large numbers of casualties—such as in the lahar that destroyed Armero, Colombia, following the eruption of Nevada del Ruiz, or in the landslides and mudslides that caused most of the casualties in Central America during Hurricane Mitch.

Disaster Preparedness

As illustrated in the disaster that swept the Indian Ocean basin following the earthquake and tsunami on December 26, 2004, developing nations face a number of challenges in adequately preparing for natural disasters.

First, many lack the resources to devote to monitoring and forecasting natural hazards. For example, observatories monitor earthquake activity in the Pacific basin. When an earthquake occurs, warnings are issued to nations lining the Pacific Rim if the tsunami risk is judged to be high enough. The warnings have been effective in reducing the number of casualties from tsunamis in the Pacific. However, the nations lining the Indian Ocean, facing a number of other pressing problems, had not judged the risk of deadly tsunamis high enough to warrant the implementation of a tsunami warning system in that basin—the last significant tsunami had followed the 1883 eruption of Krakatau, more than 120 years before the 2004 disaster. Several nations are now preparing to implement a warning system.

Second, officials in many developing nations lack the personnel and training needed to respond quickly to an emergency. In the case of the Sumatra earthquake, scientists elsewhere noted the risk of a tsunami, but had no officials to call in the affected nations to warn of the impending disaster. Even as the tsunami swept away from Sumatra, officials within the affected region failed to notify their colleagues to begin evacuating people at risk along the coast. Even if officials had notified one another, there is no guarantee that they could have reached enough of the at-risk populations with warnings, as communication networks are sketchy in parts of the affected region.

Third, many developing nations lack adequate transportation networks to mount effective evacuations from at-risk areas (this problem is not restricted to developing nations, however). Many people fled on foot in the face of the tsunami waves crashing onto the shore throughout the area affected by the December 26, 2004, disaster. Even boat traffic was disrupted in some areas close to shore. But some nations have improved emergency procedures substantially following devastating events. Bangladesh, where hundreds of thousands have died in the past century following floods and tropical cyclones, has improved evacuation procedures and shelter facilities. Death tolls from more recent floods and tropical cyclones have been considerably reduced as a result.

Fourth, in developing nations where basic civil services are underdeveloped, a disaster such as the Indian Ocean earthquake and tsunami can have long-lasting effects on the survivors. Contaminated water supplies can trigger outbreaks of diseases like cholera. Interrupted food supplies can trigger famines. Public health facilities can be overwhelmed by the initial casualties of the disaster. As people fall ill due to inadequate food or fresh water, and as interrupted transportation and communication networks prevent re-supply and/or reconstruction of health facilities, public health networks may collapse, adding to the casualty figures following a disaster. Improved medical care in many of the nations affected by the December 26, 2004 disaster, coupled with a swift international response, appears (at press time) to have staved off the type of epidemic that many experts initially feared would follow.

DAVID M. LAWRENCE

See also Deforestation; Desertification; Disaster Relief; Environment: Government Policies; Environmentalism; Erosion, Land; Global Climate Change; Infectious Diseases; Irrigation; Rain Forest, Destruction of; Urbanization: Impact on Environment; Water Resources and Distribution; Wildlife Preservation; World Health Organization (WHO)

References and Further Reading:

Abbott, Patrick Leon. *Natural Disasters*. New York: McGraw-Hill, 2001.
Bryant, Edward. *Natural Hazards*, 2nd ed. New York: Cambridge University Press, 2004.
Lawrence, David M. *Upheaval from the Abyss: Ocean Floor Mapping and the Earth Science Revolution*. New Brunswick, NJ: Rutgers University Press, 2004.
McGuire, Bill, Ian Mason, and Christopher Kilburn. *Natural Hazards and Environmental Change*. New York: Oxford University Press, 2002.
Pelling, Mark. *Natural Disaster and Development in a Globalizing World*. New York: Routledge, 2003.
Prager, Ellen J. *Furious Earth: The Science and Nature of Earthquakes, Volcanoes, and Tsunamis*. New York: McGraw-Hill, 1999.
Winchester, Simon. *Krakatoa: The Day the World Exploded: August 27, 1883*. New York: HarperCollins, 2003.
Wisner, Benjamin. *At Risk: Natural Hazards, People's Vulnerability, and Disasters*, 2nd ed. New York: Routledge, 2004.
Zebrowski, Ernest. *The Last Days of St. Pierre: The Volcanic Disaster that Claimed 30,000 Lives*. New Brunswick, NJ: Rutgers University Press, 2002.
———. *Perils of a Restless Planet: Scientific Perspectives on Natural Disasters*. New York: Cambridge University Press, 1999.

NDI, NI JOHN FRU

Ni John Fru Ndi (b. 1941), the chairman of Cameroon's Social Democratic Front (SDF), was born in Baba II in the North-West Province. He attended the Basel Mission and Native Authority primary schools before proceeding to the Lagos City College in Nigeria. Entering the labor market early, he worked with the West Coast Fisheries and as a traffic officer at Ikeja Airport (Nigeria) between 1957 and 1960. Thereafter he served as the assistant manager of Eastwood and Chaples Company in Lagos and as director of Sameday Cleaners in Ibadan (Nigeria). He returned to Cameroon in 1966 and became a hawker of fresh vegetables and eventually started the Bahemo Vegetable Society. Following a six-month training course in bookselling with the British Council in Britain, he opened the EBIBI Book Center in Bamenda. He has been the chairman of the Social Democratic Front (SDF), the main opposition party in Cameroon since its formation in 1990. His social ascendancy was fostered when he served as president of an elite division football club, the PWD, between 1979 and 1988, and president of the Lions International Club (Bamenda branch) between 1987 and 1988.

Endowed with this capital, he ran for Parliament for Mezam Central on the "khaki" list for the Cameroon People's Democratic Movement (CPDM) in 1988 and lost. That these elections were rigged in favor of the "white" list is evidence of the reticence of the ruling oligarchy. A commitment to promoting transparency and the rule of law caused Ndi and others to form the SDF, which was launched in May 1990 at a historical juncture when fear was the only mode of consciousness. Because of the police rule of law, six people were killed at the launch of this party. This thrust Ndi into national prominence and his popularity grew in the face of his defiance of the authoritarian regime and an unflinching decision to "live with the truth." Fondly referred to as "Pa" or "the Chairman," he contributed enormously to enriching Cameroon's protest repertoire with obtrusive modes of protest. Prominent among these was the ghost town operation (*villes mortes*), a form of civil disobedience that brought the country to a complete halt in an attempt to force the government to introduce democratic reforms. That the opposition in most other African countries adopted these modes of protest shows that it is constituted of people who believe themselves to be mobile. Staying the course, unlike most Cameroonian opposition leaders who joined the government with a view to practicing the "politics of the belly," further helped to enhance his stature. He is seen as having paranormal powers because he has survived several government attempts to kill him.

As candidate of the Union for Change, a group of opposition parties, he supposedly won the March 1992 presidential elections that were flawed. And since the Supreme Court, while acknowledging this, still declared Paul Biya the winner, Ndi was for a long time considered the legitimate president. It is with a view to ending this apparent bicephalism and curbing post-electoral violence that the government declared a state of emergency in the North-West Province and placed him under house arrest. This decision brought the women back into the public sphere as it resuscitated the *takembeng:* Consisting mostly of old women, dubbed the "Amazons of the SDF," they successfully built a defense perimeter around Ndi's house, thereby preventing him from being arrested by the police force. This signaled an engendering of the struggle for democratic change and the fact that old modes of protest can be used successfully to confront new modes of violence.

Unlike most other Cameroonian politicians, Ndi has remained connected to the people and has resorted to the use of unobtrusive modes of protest. He led cleanup campaigns in towns where the SDF had won the 1997 municipal elections, defended the interests of hawkers who abound in the informal sector, and has been in the forefront in the fight against HIV/AIDS in Cameroon. In short, he has been involved in confidence-building measures needed to revalorize a population whose productive capacities have witnessed a free fall, and is not willing to consign its future to a government that suffers from a legitimacy deficit. Believing in a politics of inclusion, he has been involved in Gandhi-like treks to inaccessible places, which have not known the state except for its extractive capabilities, around the country. This overwhelming presence in the public sphere has caused his house to be dubbed as the "Ntarikon palace."

To foster the probability of alterations in the October 2004 elections, he joined other opposition parties to form the National Council for Reconciliation and Reconstruction (NCRR). He was not chosen as its standard bearer and decided to go it alone. Criticism of this decision by some voices in the opposition and civil society showed that his popularity, though not depleted, had waned. In the elections that the SDF and some independent observers considered rigged, Ndi came in second to Paul Biya with 17%. To a large extent, he is still considered an emblematic figure to the powerless whom he has helped to empower.

NANTANG JUA

See also Cameroon

References and Further Reading

Anu, Christopher Fobeneh. *The Man: Ni John Fru Ndi*. Nigeria: Morningstar Communications, 1993.
Gwellem, Jerome. *Fru Ndi and the SDF Revolution*. Bamenda, Cameroon: Unique Printers, 1996.
Krieger, Milton. "Cameroon's Democratic Crossroads." *The Journal of Modern African Studies*, 32(4): 604–628, 1994.
Takougang, Joseph and Milton Krieger. *African State and Society in the 1990s: Cameroon's Political Crossroads*. Boulder, CO: Westview Press, 1998.

NEHRU, JAWAHARLAL

Jawaharlal Nehru (1889–1964), also addressed later on as *Pandit* (a learned person), was raised in an affluent upper-caste family in India. His father was a lawyer, a leader of the Indian liberation movement, and a major influence on Nehru. Nehru got his degree at Cambridge and studied law in London. He returned to India in 1912 and started his law career. In 1916, he met Gandhi, whose name had already become famous in India because of his successful political victories in South Africa. Gandhi became an ally, a political mentor, and a father figure.

In 1929, while Nehru was the president of the Congress Party (Indian National Congress), the resolution for full independence of India was passed. He was elected president of the party six times and became the most important figure in the Indian liberation movement, next only to Gandhi. He was imprisoned nine times in all, for a total of more than nine years, and wrote extensively while in prison.

Elections were held in 1937 all over India and the Congress Party swept the legislative seats. The Congress Party passed the "Quit India" resolution in August 1942. The British agreed to give independence to India, provided the Congress Party work out a solution with the Muslim League party representing the Muslim minority in India and resolve their differences. From 1946 Nehru served as prime minister in the interim government with Lord Mountbatten as the governor general.

India gained freedom in 1947. Nehru had assumed the office of India's first prime minister in the interim government in 1946 and continued to serve in that position. Nehru resumed his positions as prime minister and minister of external affairs after the Congress Party won the elections in 1950. He continued with his platform of industrialization and socialization of industry and commerce.

The policy of the British government, often described as "divide and rule," succeeded in developing animosity among the different religious groups and castes in India. Though he was against the partitioning of India, the riots in India in the months prior to independence convinced Nehru that it was necessary in order to avert a possible civil war. The partition resulted in mass migration of more than 10 million people and a loss of more than two hundred thousand lives in India and Pakistan.

Nehru's vision was the attainment of national independence first and foremost. In addition, it also included a secular democratic government, economic and social development, social reforms, nonalignment of the third-world countries, and international peace. After Gandhi's assassination in 1948, Nehru carried on as leader of the country. He wanted to modernize India through government-owned, large-scale projects such as the construction of steel mills and the building of dams for irrigation and electricity. He had to seek capital for these developments from outside the country, especially from the Soviet Union. More than six hundred independent princely states were brought under the rule of the Indian government during his administration. Nehru also strongly encouraged the development of science and technology, and the establishment of the atomic energy commission and now-famous technological institutes. Throughout his career he tried to improve the social and economic situation of minorities, including women, untouchables, Muslims, and the agrarian rural poor, but only succeeded partially. He was also a believer in a secular parliamentary form of democracy. He also believed in socialism, though he was aware of the drawbacks of the system.

Nehru straddled both the Indian and Western worlds and was an internationalist at heart. Nehru, the best-known politician to emerge from any colonial country, exerted an influence on the world scene far beyond India. He participated in the Bandung conference in 1955 as one of the major leaders of the Third World nonalignment movement along with Nasser of Egypt and Tito of Yugoslavia. His doctrine of *Panchsheel* or *Panchshila* (five principles) of peaceful co-existence and non-aggression was endorsed by China and adopted with modifications at the Bandung conference. He set an example for many developing countries by agreeing to join the British Commonwealth, with India participating as an independent nation.

On the other hand, Nehru has also been described as indecisive and vacillating. He was not always firm or practical in his policies and actions, and was not keenly interested in day-to-day administration. In spite of his knowledge of the international scene, he was quite naive in his implicit trust of other countries. For example, in 1962, India was caught unprepared when the Chinese attacked occupied parts of the country. This was perhaps the most severe blow to his foreign policy and personal reputation as a leader, as Nehru had championed the entry of China into the United Nations. Many leaders in the Western countries thought that the Indian policy of nonviolence and nonalignment was hypocritical in view of the police action India initiated against Goa, a Portuguese territory in India.

Nehru's tenure as a prime minister has been criticized by many Indians because of the resultant slack in economic growth. He has also been blamed for the unresolved Kashmir problem. The country is still riddled with communalism and casteism in spite of the official policy of secularism. India has developed atomic weapons though it is in favor of world peace.

Nehru died after his last stroke in 1964, but many of his visions for India's future still live. India, for example, is still the largest functioning democracy in the world. A political dynasty was another unintended legacy of Nehru. His daughter, Indira Gandhi, and his grandson Rajiv Gandhi have both served as prime ministers of India.

SUBHASH R. SONNAD

See also Gandhi, Indira; Gandhi, Mohandas; Gandhi, Rajiv; India; Indian–Pakistani Wars; Kashmir Dispute; Nonaligned Movement; Pakistan

References and Further Reading

Brown, Judith M. *Nehru*. London: Longman, 1999.
Gopal, Sarvepalli. *Jawaharlal Nehru: A Biography*, 2 vols. Cambridge, MA: Harvard University Press, 1976.
Judd, Denis. *Jawaharlal Nehru*. Cardiff, Wales: GPC, 1993.
Lengyel, Emil. *Jawaharlal Nehru: The Brahman from Kashmir*. New York: F. Watts, 1968.
Mende, Tibor. *Nehru: Conversations on India and World Affairs*. New York: G. Braziller, 1956.
Tharoor, Shashi. *Nehru: The Invention of India*. New York: Arcade Publishers, 2003.

NEOCOLONIALISM

As a term, colonialism has been explained as the policy of a nation seeking to extend or retain its authority over other peoples or territories of another nation. In this regard and on the basis of its core meaning, neocolonialism—or "new" colonialism—is the desire to continue the same policies of the colonial powers by a new set of administrators trained and educated by the colonialists, long after they have quit the region.

In other words, neocolonialism is the continuation and retention of the same policies and permanent interests of the colonialists along with the method of control that originated and was implemented during colonial rule. In addition, this is continued with the same zest and dedication by the subalterns. Simply put, neocolonialism has been defined by the *Webster's Encyclopedic Unabridged Dictionary* as "the policy of a strong nation in seeking political and economic hegemony over an independent nation or extended geographical area without necessarily reducing the subordinate nation or area to the legal status of a colony."

With this in mind, the agents of "neocolonialism" provide a justification for the marginalization of the natives' heritage in their educational system and replace it with colonial norms and method of control.

Neocolonialism continues to oppress the native people. It distorts, disfigures, and destroys the country's connection with its past and its history along with its language and its ties to the native soil. Thus, neocolonialism is a process by which old colonial policies are culturally constructed and ideologically loaded by recreated historical information that is shaped to benefit the sociopolitical and socioeconomic mold designed to allow the colonial philosophy and mission to flourish that were laid down at the time of colonization. Interestingly enough, this newly constructed mission statement is hammered down and implemented by the so-called cadre in the civil servants established and encouraged from among the native population to promote the grand design and methods of the colonialists.

Neocolonialism in its initial task makes sure to sustain and keep the focus on the destruction of the people, the land, their history, and national heritage, prior to colonial times, and rewrites the glories of precolonial days by replacing them with its so-called "achievements" in the colonial era. Therefore, the past and its heritage is labeled as a hindrance to progress and for its basic nature is weeded out as an age of ignorance. In such an environment the seeds of Macaulayism championed by Thomas Babington Macaulay (1800–1859) were sowed in earnest during English India. Macaulay was a British essayist and historian who worked in India from 1834–1838 laying the foundation of English rule in South Asia. With this vision, he looked forward to leaving a permanent impact and a set of teeth in the manner that colonialism will continue to thrive and function as machinery long after the mother country has left the landscape. Thus, in order to understand the true nature of the idea behind the creation of "neocolonialism," we need to study the philosophy and the vision of Macaulayism in its details.

Lord Macaulay's "Minute on Indian Education" and its total political support by Lord William Bentinck, the then-Governor General of Bengal, was stated in these words: "I give my entire concurrence to the sentiments expressed in this Minute." In fact, "Macaulayism" became the official policy of British rule in India and it contained the recipe of what came to be known as "neocolonialism."

As the president of the Committee of Public Instruction in Bengal in 1834, Macaulay declared that "a single shelf of a good European library is worth the whole native literature of India and Arabia" (Anderson 1991). Furthermore, John Clive reported that Macaulay proposed that an immediate halt be put upon the printing of Arabic and Sanskrit books. Macaulay sought to curb native civilization and culture at its very roots. He also recommended that both

Sanskrit College in Calcutta and the Madrassa should be closed down. Thus, instead of engrafting English to an already existing Arabic/Persian/Sanskrit foundation, Macaulay advocated total Anglicization by demanding complete substitution of native languages by English as a medium of instruction. Macaulay as an imperial agent was scheming to destroy native history and creating a space for neocolonialism as a matter of governance beyond the age of imperial rule in English India.

Macaulay believed, and wanted others to believe with him, that the West or the colonial Masters were not only superior to the natives in language and heritage, but will produce and enhance their lives more than their backward life styles and ways of thinking. In 1836, Macaulay outlined his plans for colonizing Bengal, wherein he intended "to turn idolaters 'not so much into Christians, as into people culturally English'" (Anderson 1991, p. 91). This is to say that Macaulayism is the mouthpiece of colonialism, and in this case, English colonialism. However, it must be noted that Macaulay did not recommend or envision neocolonialism for Ireland as he did for India. Needless to mention, the nineteenth-century Anglicists had already implemented in Ireland what he was trying to implement for English India. Interestingly enough, the "backwardness" of Ireland Macaulay blamed upon the Catholic Church and not the oppressive laws of colonialism. For him the natives in Ireland were responsible for their woes and hardships, not colonial England. Macaulay must have felt that it was the failure to implant "an English education" and the permission to allow a native administrative system that had kept the Irish people attached to their religion. Nevertheless, it must be pointed out that unfortunately for the English policy, English education failed to transform both the Indians and the Irish people into nations that were "culturally English."

This is not to deny the creation and the existence of cultural elites in both these countries. Elites who have been transformed into what are called *Bhodro Lok* (gentlefolk) in South Asia and the ruling elites in Ireland; however, their influence was not strong enough to alter the lifestyle and overall condition of the natives in their respective nations. The formation of these people as the ruling bastion and the promotion of their idea of civil administration is what can be termed as "neocolonialism."

In India, "Macaulayism" or "neocolonialism" merely succeeded in creating a dent because of two reasons: (1) between the Indian War of Independence in 1857 and India's ultimate freedom in 1947, the British ruled for only ninety years; and (2) "Macaulayism" created such a siege mentality among Indian nationalist writers that they mostly wrote in their native languages.

Neocolonialism is an extended arm of the colonial powers, serving the interests of the colonies: be it England, France, or Germany (to name just a few). In the post-colonial era, other steps to carry the ball of colonialism were seen first in the formation of a federation of former colonies as was seen in Australia and New Zealand in 1931. Another form was seen in the construction and the promotion of camaraderie in the British Commonwealth of Nations after the demise of the British Empire as a sociopolitical power and economic entity because of the ultimate effects of the Second World War in 1945. Today, there are fifty-four former nations of the British Empire who have agreed to form the British Commonwealth. This is a group of nations and dependent territories that are united by a common allegiance to the British Crown. Only Ireland, it must be pointed out, refused to join the Commonwealth. Obviously, these nations are associated by their own choice of common social, political, and economic interests with the former power of colonial England. In all candor it can be acknowledged that the ruling forces in almost all these nations have been trained and educated by the colonial machine, and as stated earlier, formed the fabric of colonialism.

This entire notion of "neocolonialism" as a dominant force can be better understood by the speech of Frantz Fanon at the Congress of Black African Writers, in 1959, in which he said: "Colonial domination ... very soon manages to disrupt in spectacular fashion the cultural life of a conquered people. This cultural obliteration is made possible by ... expropriation, and by the systematic enslaving of men and women" (Fanon 1959).

This "systematic enslaving" of individuals that Fanon articulates refers to the continuation of mental slavery of the people of the so-called free and independent nations that were granted political freedom in the late 1940s.

In this regard it becomes crystal clear that Thomas Babington Macaulay's firm belief in colonial "Eurocentric education" and its power of metamorphosis in eternally changing the mindset of the native peoples is finally proven true. The dream and desire of neocolonialism as to eradicate and replace that mindset with colonial doctrines become a harsh reality.

Neocolonialism is therefore, as Fanon concludes in his speech with reference to the colonial experience in Africa, the product of a national culture under colonial domination. According to Fanon, "a national culture under colonial domination is a contested culture whose destruction is sought in systematic fashion.... There is no taking of the offensive and no

redefining of relationships" (Fanon 1959). Colonial policies are continued by the natives as administrators because in this post-colonial phase even the indigenous people feel that the colonial policies are not only superior but they are the only road to progress.

SYED HASSAN

See also Colonialism: History; Colonialism: Legacies

References and Further Reading

Anderson, Benedict. *Imagined Communities*. New York: Routledge/Verso, 1991.
Fanon, Frantz. Speech at the Congress of Black African Writers, 1959. Available: www.marxists.org/reference/subject/philosophy/works/ot/fanon.htm.
Hassan, Syed K. M. "William Butler Yeats, Resistance in Ireland." Doctoral dissertation. West Lafayette, IN, May 1994.
Macaulay, Thomas Babington. "Minute on Indian Education," 1835. Available: http://www.geocities.com/bororissa/mac.html.
Sartre, Jean-Paul. *Colonialism and Neocolonialism*. New York: Routledge, 2001.
Smith, Donald Eugene. *India as a Secular State*. Princeton, NJ: Princeton University Press, 1963.
Webster's Encyclopedic Unabridged Dictionary. Gramerbooks: New York: Avenel, 1983.

NEOLIBERALISM

Neoliberalism is one of the most polarizing terms in development. There are very strong feelings both for and against neoliberalism that cut across the spectrum of economic, political, and social issues by groups both in the developed and the developing world. Neoliberalism evokes such strong concerns because it most generally describes the controversial economic policies that countries have adopted across the globe. This set of policies is seen by some as the only possible avenue of economic development, and by others as a most exploitative and repressive set of policies.

Although neoliberalism is sometimes conflated with US foreign policy and fragile democracies in the developing world, neoliberalism is more accurately defined as a set of economic liberalization policies that are expected to lead to both economic efficiency and growth. Neoliberal reforms have often occurred in two stages. In the first stage, designed to control inflationary pressures and create accurate prices, government spending is cut and the money supply is reduced. In addition, the economy is opened up to foreign trade and investment. Tariffs and quotas on imports and taxes on exports are lowered or eliminated. Restrictions on the flow of investment are reduced or eliminated. In the second stage, state-owned enterprises are privatized, and regulations and institutions regarding the market are developed, such as strengthening contract laws. Financial and fiscal reforms also are pursued, including the attempt to raise taxes and create stability within the banking system. In addition, the country starts to enter into international trade agreements to expand reciprocal access to free markets. Not surprisingly, this second stage of neoliberalism, which includes creating clear results such as unemployment from privatized companies and attempting to pass new tax legislation, have met with fierce resistance, both on a domestic and international level.

The origins of neoliberalism can be traced in large part to the writings of Friedrich Von Hayek and the group of University of Chicago economists, particularly Milton Friedman. The basic orientation of these economists is to point out the optimality of allowing markets to determine economic outcomes. In tandem with this aspect, they have a generally profound skepticism of any government intervention into national economies. However, unlike the classic "liberal" thought of Adam Smith and David Ricardo, neoliberal economists see that limited government intervention in order to ensure the smooth functioning of markets and to provide for "externalities" is necessary. Neoliberal thought thus generally sees the government's role in economic terms as regulating markets, such as providing transparent price information, and ensuring the smooth functioning of commodities markets. Neoliberals concede that there are some areas, such as providing for national defense, in which the government must take the lead.

In the developing world, the neoliberal revolution really began in Chile in 1975, when "the Chicago Boys" became the primary government advisors. They shaped a new economic program in line with the education they received at the University of Chicago in the 1950s and 1960s on an exchange program. One of the main contributions of Chicago thinking was a new approach to fighting inflation, which had previously followed a more Keynesian type of analysis. When, in 1973, the Organization of Petroleum Exporting Countries (OPEC) successfully raised world oil prices to four times what they had been, the international economy experienced a new situation of both economic recession and inflation (rising prices), called at the time "stagflation." The Chicago line of thinking focused on inflation as the central obstacle to creating sustainable economic growth. In Chile, the policy prescriptions were carried out in the guise of a wide-ranging monetary policy-based "shock treatment" in 1975. While the program was successful in cutting inflation, it was accompanied by a severe recession and unemployment, a combination that continues to haunt neoliberal policies today.

By 1977, with inflation under control, the Chilean economy began to rebound. The Chicago Boys then introduced a broad-ranging program called the "Seven Modernizations." The new modernizations moved beyond controlling government spending and tightening the money supply to embracing wide-scale privatizations and liberalization of trade and investment in Chile. These initiatives reduced tariffs and subsidies and taxes on investments so that foreign investors and exporters could have relatively open access to the Chilean economy. The new policies also weakened the labor code, and the government began a series of experiments in targeting social welfare spending to those most needy. The move toward reform of the pension system in the early 1980s in Chile, as well as the boom in new exports, made Chile a great "success story" of neoliberal policies that helped them spread throughout the developing world.

When oil prices rose again in 1979, the United States and the United Kingdom were hit especially hard by a new round of stagflation. The elections of Ronald Reagan and Margaret Thatcher in 1980 to leadership of their respective countries brought the neoliberal "revolution" to the international arena. When the US Federal Reserve severely raised interest rates in 1982 to control inflation, the resulting liquidity shock was felt throughout the already reeling developing world. The US program to "whip" inflation fed directly into a very severe external debt crisis that continues to plague developing countries today. Some countries owe up to a third of their national annual production (GNP) in debt.

In the 1980s, with the United States and the United Kingdom at the forefront, the wider version of neoliberalism, including not just control of inflation, but also privatization, deregulation, and liberalization of investment and trade, became the dominant paradigm, or way of thinking, across the globe. With the debt crisis looming over them, developing countries had little choice but to cut back severely on government spending, open the economy to new investment, increase exports, and attempt to control runaway inflation. As a result, neoliberalism swept across the globe in the 1980s, leading Francis Fukuyama to coin the 1990s as "the end of history," in the sense that free markets and democracies were seen as the best ways to run politics and economics. Country after country, from socialist strongholds Ghana and Tanzania in Africa to India in Asia, adopted neoliberalism as their dominant perspective. For a brief while, it did appear to be the last wave of history, as the Soviet Union and the possibility and promise of creating Communist societies seemed to disintegrate. With the conversion of former Communist countries such as China and Vietnam to the market-based fold, the phrase TINA (there is no alternative) seemed apt for describing the revolution in ideas. Populist leaders such as Fujimori in Peru, Menem in Argentina, and Rawlings in Ghana as well as the rise to prominence of finance ministers such as Cavallo in Argentina and Singh in India signaled the widespread support of neoliberal reforms in the early 1990s.

Neoliberalism is attractive to developing country policy makers as it gives them a more positive view of these wholesale changes in their economies. Neoliberal thinking has it that the construction of competitive private markets yields up new efficiencies. Thus, the productivity rate of newly privatized economies should be on the rise. Moreover, neoliberal thought on the optimality of markets extends to the efforts toward international integration. So, the move toward the European Union, the North American Free Trade Agreement, and the MERCOSUR pact in the Southern Cone are seen as very positive developments that create larger, more competitive markets. The ultimate beneficiary is the consumer who experiences lower prices everywhere.

To be sure, there seem to be a number of improvements in the developing world as a result of the neoliberal revolution. First, there is much more accountability on the part of governments. Governments are now keenly aware of their need to balance their budgets. Second, as governments have stepped back from interference with markets, there is arguably a considerable dropoff in corruption and disincentives for new types of production. Developing countries' government-run companies in the post–World War II period often became behemoths of political patronage and corruption, with huge payrolls. Third, in a large number of developing countries, inflation has been brought under control for the first time in thirty years. Inflation made long-term investment decisions extremely difficult, and led rich classes in developing countries to put their savings in foreign countries and currencies. This phenomenon, known as "capital flight," meant that a developing country had a very small pool of its own domestic capital available for investment. Since the middle and particularly the upper classes were able to "hedge" in this and other ways against inflation, the poorer classes really paid the heaviest price. Fourth, by the end of the 1970s, with industrialization experiments running out of steam, developing countries found themselves in many cases with inefficient and uncompetitive domestic industries. Moreover, neither these highly protected industries, which often relied upon imports of foreign inputs, expertise, and parts, nor the often regressive and highly taxed agriculture sector, were able to create the new export productivity to pay off the debt and to grow. By contrast, the export sector in many developing countries has become dynamic and more diversified, reaping the benefits of new foreign investment attracted by the more inviting neoliberal policies.

While there have been some important benefits from the turn to neoliberal policies in the developing world, there remain a number of important, purely economic issues as well. Foremost, the renewed growth that has occurred in the developing world has been notoriously uneven. There has been a growing *relative* inequality gap between the rich and the poor, both internationally and in the developing economies. The growth has also benefited certain sectors, namely those associated with exports. Neoliberalism does not seem to have made a dent into the problems of either unemployment or access to education and health for most developing countries' citizens. As privatized state-owned companies lay off thousands of workers, there has been no sign that export growth can absorb any significant proportion of these idled employees. In several cases, such as that of Menem in Argentina, the privatization process was tainted with scandal. Privatization and investment liberalization have not made a dent into the huge external debt burdens of many developing countries. Moreover, as we saw in the 1980s and 1990s in a series of financial crises, the developing world finds itself subject to highly volatile international financial flows. Thus, neoliberalism has not yet delivered on the sustained and stable growth that it promises.

In most developing countries, there has been a strong backlash against some aspects of the neoliberal program in the form of street protests and political mobilization. This resistance has held up some key aspects of the neoliberal reform, such as lifting price controls on basic food items, in a number of countries. Some countries have been able, furthermore, to grow faster and attract more investment than others. For example, while the World Bank and the International Monetary Fund (IMF) have anointed Ghana as a great example of the success of neoliberal policies, there has been little indication of long-term investment in the country. Indeed, we might say that the results of neoliberal policies have largely been to move Ghana and other developing countries back toward neocolonial reliance on primary product exports, such as cocoa, which they sought to change with their state-led industrialization over the last thirty years. As a new stagnation of growth and the weight of adjustment from the state-led system hits developing economies, we are seeing signs of increasing mobilization against neoliberal policies, such as in Argentina.

While there is strong criticism of neoliberalism, there is as yet no real alternative that has been forwarded to replace it. The alternative of socialism seems to have died with the Cold War. Moreover, the developing world remains racked with massive external debts and the need and desire to obtain trade access and investment from the First World. International organizations that regulate access, such as the World Bank, the IMF, and the World Trade Organization, are thus seen as the enforcement agencies for the neoliberal order. To be sure, the First World has much greater leverage on the developing world because of the economic context of trade and investment. However, there are a number of interesting contrasts in both the level and type of response to neoliberalism across the developing world. For example, Malaysia recently instituted capital controls to slow capital flight in the wake of the financial crisis in Asia. The development of the MERCOSUR treaty marked a South–South integration scheme among South American countries that is in sharp contrast to the NAFTA treaty between Mexico, the United States, and Canada. There are a number of countries who have not fully privatized their state-owned sector, or who have found other ways to intervene in their markets. These countries are really not that different from First World countries who, despite a general neoliberal orientation, continue to heavily protect and subsidize strategic sectors of their economies, such as agriculture, high technology, and health care.

In both the developing and the developed world, the retreat of the state from economic issues under neoliberalism has left societies reeling. With uneven and volatile growth in much of the world, and a new feeling of vulnerability, there is a strong and growing countercurrent to the widespread acceptance of neoliberalism. The international countercurrent stems in part from the dismantling of the social safety nets that have accompanied neoliberal policies. Moreover, the development of new private markets has not always led to lower prices and higher levels of competition. Indeed, there is strong evidence that key markets in several developing markets are inefficient and uncompetitive, putting consumers at the mercy of a dominant foreign or domestic private monopoly or oligopoly. As a result, a spate of new moderately anti-neoliberal candidates began to be elected in the developing world by the late 1990s, particularly in Latin America. These include Gutierrez in Ecuador, Lula in Brazil, Chavez in Venezuela, and Kirchner in Argentina. In India, the party associated with the neoliberal reforms of the 1990s, the BJP, lost to the Congress Party in elections in 2004. An international social movement leading to protests of international trade summits and international organizations such as the WTO and World Bank became an organizing force for anti-neoliberalism across the North

and South. These groups organized a World Social Forum as an alternative to the business-oriented World Economic Forum. However, the movements seems to lack a clear alternative strategy that could unite the diverse groups and lead to new policies.

The most recent neoliberal response to some of these accusations has been, in part, to recognize their merits. International organizations that back neoliberal policies began in the last decade to place greater emphasis and resources on social funds during adjustment and to encourage local participation at the grassroots level, generally through non-governmental organizations (NGOs). Moreover, means tests and "workfare" programs seek to create new incentives for those who need temporary social help to become active again in the labor market. Fiscal reform to create more effective and progressive tax systems is high on the agenda of almost every developing country. Last but not least, there are a number of new initiatives to develop "civil society" and "governance." These initiatives recognize the importance of developing strong, independent, and fair markets and institutions that are responsive to, and include input from, the public. The outcome of these experiments at modifying the neoliberal model for broader sustainability will be fascinating, to say the least.

ANIL HIRA

References and Further Reading

Aryeetey, Ernest, Jane Harrigan, and Machiko Nissanke. *Economic Reforms in Ghana: The Miracle and the Mirage.* Trenton, NJ: Africa World Press, 2000.
Bates, Robert. *Toward a Political Economy of Development: A Rational Choice Perspective.* Berkeley, CA: University of California Press, 1988.
Friedman, Milton. *Capitalism and Freedom.* Chicago: University of Chicago Press, 1962.
Hira, Anil. *Ideas and Economic Policy in Latin America: Regional, National, and Organizational Case Studies.* Westport, CT: Praeger, 1998.
Veltmeyer, Henry, James Petras, and Steve Vieux. *Neoliberalism and Class Conflict in Latin America: A Comparative Perspective on the Political Economy of Structural Adjustment.* New York: St. Martin's Press, 1997.
Von Hayek, Friedrich. *The Road to Serfdom.* Chicago: University of Chicago Press, 1994.
Williamson, John. *The Political Economy of Policy Reform.* Washington, DC: Institute for International Economics, 1994.

NEPAL

The Kingdom of Nepal, situated in the centre of Asia, is a small country between the world's most populated countries: China and India. Nepal is a landlocked country, surrounded by India on three sides and by China's Xizang Autonomous Region (Tibet) on the north. Nepal covers an area of 56,827 square miles and is divided into four topographical zones: the Great Himalayas, the Middle Himalayas, the Outer Himalayas, and the Terai. The highest is the Great Himalayas Zone, in northern Nepal, in which are located most of the world's highest mountains, among them: Mount Everest (29,035 feet), the highest mountain in the world; Mt. Kangchenjunga (28,169 feet); Mt. Lhotse; and Mt. Makalu among others. To the south are located the Middle Himalayas, with peaks averaging less than 9,900 feet, and then comes the zone of the Outer Himalayas, with an average elevation of about 3,300 to 6,600 feet. The most southern part of the country is the Terai zone, a generally flat, fertile lowland.

Because of the shape of its territory and the height changes in every topographical zone, Nepal has tremendous climate variations. The Terai region presents subtropical weather, while the northern and central parts of the country present an alpine climate with cool summers as well as severe winters. Summer (June–August) and late spring (March–May) temperatures range from 83°F in the hill regions to more than 104°F in the Terai. In winter, average minimum and maximum temperatures in the Terai range from 45°F to 74°F. Much colder temperatures prevail at higher elevations. The Kathmandu Valley, situated in the Middle Himalayas zone, ranges between 67°F and 81°F in summer and between 36°F and 68°F in winter. Average annual precipitation ranges from seventy inches in the east to thirty-five inches in the west.

The population is estimated at approximately 24.7 million, with an annual growth rate of 2.2%. As of 2001, the capital city, Kathmandu, has a population of about 800,000. Nepal is mainly a rural country having only 15% urban population. The official religion and language are Hinduism and Nepali, respectively. However, over twenty distinct languages are also spoken, with English also widely understood.

As early as 1790 the Nepali tried to extend their territory into Tibet, but the Chinese invaded the country and the Nepali had to ally with the British to fight the invaders; however, they were defeated. Nepal continued as an ally during other conflicts and after World War I, having fought as soldiers for the British. In 1923 Nepal and Great Britain signed a treaty of friendship, which granted Nepal's independence. In 1948 Nepali Prime Minister Padma Shamsher Rana announced the first constitution of Nepal. Nepal already was a constitutional monarchy.

Until 1951, members of the Rana family held complete control of the government. That year Bisweswore Prasad Koirala became the first non-Rana prime minister for more than one hundred years. In 1959 the first free elections were held and a new constitution inaugurated, although in December 1960 King Mahendra banned all political parties and suspended the Constitution until it was restored in 1962. In 1972 King Mahendra died and was succeeded by Prince Birendra.

In May 1980 a referendum was held to give the people a choice between a reformed version of the existing system or a multi-party-based system, which resulted in the return of the Rashtriya Panchayat. In February 1990 violence erupted over demands by ten thousand civilians for an end to the Rashtriya Panchayat. Police and the Army responded and around fifty people were killed, following which the king announced that a new constitution would be drafted that would allow for a multi-party system of government. A Maoist insurgency, launched in 1996, gained traction and threatened to bring down the regime. In 2001, the crown prince is believed to have massacred ten members of the royal family, including King Birendra and the queen. In October 2002, the new king dismissed the prime minister and his cabinet, after which the Parliament was dissolved and elections could not be held because of the ongoing insurgency. As of this writing, the country is governed by the king, Gyanendra Bir Bikram Shah, uncle of the assassinated Birendra, and his appointed cabinet, which has negotiated a cease-fire with the Maoist insurgents until elections can be held at some unspecified future date.

The Nepali economy has traditionally been based on livelihood and agriculture, mainly in the production of rice, corn, and wheat. The industrial sector is less important but constitutes approximately 20% of the GDP. The primary industries include tourism, and carpet and textile production, along with jute, oilseed, cement, and bricks. However, industry only accounts for 3% of the labour force, while agriculture occupies 80% and 40% of the GDP. The rest of the GDP is from the service sector. The total GDP for the year 2004 was estimated at $38 billion, and per capita income was around $1,400.

Exports consist mainly of carpets, leather, and jute goods; imports consist of petroleum products, machinery, and other equipment. Major trade partners are India, China, and the United States.

The unemployment rate is around 47% and nearly 42% of the total population lives below the poverty line, with further disadvantages experienced by women and people of particular ethnic and socioeconomic groups.

One of Nepal's major social concerns/issues is the serious lack of available health care and poor access to education. According to the United Nations Development Program (UNDP), Nepal is rated as a medium developed country but at the border of becoming a low developed one (UNDP 2004). Nepal's maternal mortality rate supports this fact. It is the highest in the South Asia region at 740 per 100,000 live births (2000). The infant mortality rate has improved considerably in the last three decades. In 1970 it was 165 deaths per one thousand live births but by 2002 it had decreased to sixty-six (UNDP 2004). Consequently, with the improvement in the infant mortality rate, the life expectancy at birth also got better, although nowadays it is one of the lowest in South Asia. It is currently fifty-nine years both for male and female, much better than in the 1970s when it was forty-six and forty-nine, respectively.

The gross school enrollment ratio has also advanced a lot in the last thirty years, changing from 26% of the population in 1975 to approximately 80% as of this writing. However, the adult literacy rate is very low (44%, 2002 est.).

As of 2005, the World Bank has undertaken several financial programs to help the development of the health, education, and economic sectors.

DIEGO I. MURGUÍA

See also Central Asia: History and Economic Development; Central Asia: International Relations; Ethnic Conflicts: Central Asia

References and Further Reading

Blaikie, Piers M., John Cameron, and David Seddon. *Nepal in Crisis: Growth and Stagnation at the Periphery*. New York: Oxford University Press, 1980.
Gimlette, Lieut. Col. G. H. D. *Nepal and the Nepalese*. New Delhi: Anmol Publications, 1993.
Pandey, Ram Niwas. *Making of Modern Nepal*. New Delhi: Nirala Publications, 1997.
Rose, Leo E. *Nepal: Strategy for Survival*. Berkeley, CA: University of California Press, 1971.
Rose, Leo E. and Margaret W. Fisher *The Politics of Nepal: Persistence and Change in an Asian Monarchy*. Ithaca, NY: Cornell University Press, 1970.
Rose, Leo E. and John T. Scholz. *Nepal: Profile of a Himalayan Kingdom*. Boulder, CO: Westview Press, 1980.
Sill, Michael and John Kirkby. *The Atlas of Nepal in the Modern World*. London: Earthscan, 1991.
Vaidya, T. R. *Advanced History of Nepal*. New Delhi: Anmol Publications, 1994.

NETHERLANDS ANTILLES

The Netherlands Antilles *(Nederlandse Antillen)* are five islands in the Caribbean under Dutch control. While they are not a colony in the traditional sense (they are politically autonomous for domestic affairs), their foreign affairs are controlled by the Netherlands, which provides for their defense needs. Until 1986 the Netherlands Antilles also included the island of Aruba, but in that year Aruba became a separate unit (an "autonomous member") of the Kingdom of the Netherlands. The people of the Netherlands Antilles are citizens of the Netherlands, as are residents of Aruba. Curaçao and Sint Maarten are to become independent in this way as well, but dates for their change in status have not been set.

The islands of the Netherlands Antilles are geographically separated into two groups. The western islands, Curaçao and Bonaire, are located approximately 280 kilometers northwest of Caracas, Venezuela. These islands, along with Aruba, are commonly known as the A-B-C islands from the first letters of their names. The geography of these islands is a mixture of their dormant volcanic origins and thousands of years of coral growth, resulting in higher elevations than the other islands in the group. Natural forces have brought an abundance of plant life to these islands, and erosion has created the beaches, which have become part of the attraction for tourists in the modern era.

Prior to the arrival of Spanish explorers at Curacao in 1499, the A-B-C islands were inhabited by the Caiquetios, related to the Arawak Indians of what is now Venezuela. The first Europeans to reach these islands were led by Alonso de Ojeda, whose chief pilot on this voyage was Amerigo Vespucci. The reports of this first voyage contain some contradictions, but in any case the islands were explored to some degree in the summer of 1499. The names of the A-B-C islands changed many times during the first years of their exploration; Curacao had first been reported as the *Isla de los Gigantes* (Island of the Giants) based on Vespucci's reports of the inhabitants (he also noted that the people of Bonaire were tall); later the island was referred to by many derivations, which may have come from the Spanish (*corazón*) or Portuguese (*curazon*) word for "heart." Bonaire was shown on early maps as *Isla de Palo de Brasil* (Brazilwood Island).

Other than brazilwood, which was used by Europeans to create a red dye for cloth, little else considered to be of value was found by the Spaniards. The native populations of Aruba, Bonaire, and Curacao was captured in the early 1500s and taken to the larger Spanish island of Hispaniola as slave laborers, but within a few years some of them were brought back to their native islands to serve as a workforce for the Spaniards who had taken control of these islands. In addition to manipulating the human population of the A-B-C islands, by the 1530s the Spaniards had introduced European work and farm animals (goats, pigs, cattle, and horses) as well as non-native plants for farming.

The smaller islands of Saba, Sint Eustatius, and Sint Maarten (the northern half of which is called St. Martin and is claimed by France as part of the "overseas department" of Guadeloupe) are located approximately 260 kilometers east of Puerto Rico, some eight hundred kilometers northeast of Curaçao. Saba, Sint Eustatius, and Sint Maarten, and are part of the islands known in English as the Leeward Islands of the Lesser Antilles, but are known in Dutch (*de Bovenwinden*) and Spanish (*las Islas de Barlovento*) as the Windward Islands.

Unlike the A-B-C islands, these Leeward Islands were not inhabited when first visited by Europeans. It is believed that the native Arawaks had been conquered by the more warlike Carib Indians. These smaller islands had less attraction to the European colonizers, and rather than living resources (brazilwood or slaves), the first Dutch interest in Saint Martin in 1631 came from the Dutch need for salt, which was used as a preservative by the Dutch fishing fleet. However, this Dutch presence so close to Spanish territories led to a Spanish conquest of Saint Martin in 1633. The Spanish held the island until 1648, and upon their departure the island was retaken by the French on the north and the Dutch on the southern side.

European politics continued to drive Caribbean activities throughout the seventeenth and eighteenth centuries, and those islands with significant populations were fortified. The American Revolution added an additional player in these moves, with the French allying themselves with the Americans and using ports in the Caribbean for their activities. The Americans sought to gain the Netherlands as a European ally as well, and when the British heard of this they sought to end Dutch trade with the Americans. Curaçao and Sint Eustatius had been major trading ports, which provided war supplies for the American revolutionaries, and in 1781 the British fleet attacked the port of Sint Eustatius to end its trade with America. In the years to come, Holland would become America's major source of foreign loans.

The French Revolution led to renewed conflict between England and France, and this affected the Netherlands and its colonies as well. The governments of France and the Netherlands drew closer, but on Curaçao support for the French was seen as a source of potential trouble. The governor of the island chose to remain neutral, placing him at odds with French naval ships in the Caribbean. This led to a French entry into Curaçao's capital city of Willemstad in 1800, but this was ended by a British naval intervention (and French withdrawal), and Curaçao became an English possession for the next three years. The treaty ending the conflict between France and England (the Peace of Amiens) called for Curaçao to be returned to Dutch control. The islands changed hands among the Dutch, the Spanish, and the British over the next several years, with the Kingdom of the Netherlands finally establishing control in 1816.

As with the A-B-C islands, the Leeward Islands changed hands among the French, Dutch, and British in the seventeenth and eighteenth centuries and like with the other islands, Dutch control was established in 1816.

In the nineteenth century the Netherlands Antilles were affected less by European politics than by the increasing influence of Venezuela. Trade in salt continued to be an important source of revenue, and late in the 1800s phosphate was also discovered on two islands. Gold was found on Aruba and mined until the supply was exhausted, and since the end of World War I the Netherlands Antilles have been a major site of oil refining in the Caribbean. Recently, drug trafficking in the Antilles has also increased via passenger flights from the Antilles to the Netherlands.

The Antilles have exercised autonomy in internal affairs since 1945. In 1954, the Netherlands Antilles became a full part of the Kingdom of the Netherlands rather than a colony. The island of Aruba was divided off in 1986. In 1993, the Antilles held a general referendum on the issue of independence; the majority voted to stay a part of the Kingdom. However, in 2000, the island of St. Martin held its own referendum, wherein 69% of the population voted to remain within the Kingdom of the Netherlands, but to become autonomous from the federation of the Antilles. In 2004, a commission confirmed this opinion, recommending that St. Martin and Curaçao be autonomous. No actions, however, had been taken on these recommendations at press time: the Dutch government does not support this division due to fears that St. Martin would not be able to support its own government or infrastructure.

As of 2004 the population of the islands of the Netherlands Antilles was slightly under 220,000 and stable. In addition to petroleum refining, tourism and banking are the major industries of the islands.

THOMAS P. DOLAN

See also Caribbean: History and Economic Development; Caribbean: International Relations

References and Further Reading

Adélaïde-Merlande, Jacques. *Histoire contemporaine de la Caraïbe et des Guyanes: de 1945 à nos jours*. Paris: Karthala, 2002.
Groslinga, Cornelis. *A Short History of the Netherlands Antilles and Surinam*. The Hague: Martinus Nijhoff, 1979.

Hermans, Hans. *Zes Eilanden in de Zon (Six Islands in the Sun)*. Aruba: Uitgave, 1978.

Welling, George M. "The Dutch and the American Revolution." In *From Revolution to Reconstruction*. University of Groningen, 2004.

NEW ECONOMIC POLICY (MALAYSIA)

Malaysia's New Economic Policy (NEP) of 1970–1990 was a successful redistribution of Malaysia's historically high rate of economic growth in order to significantly improve the lives of the impoverished and with a focus on enriching the historically disadvantaged *Bumiputra*. The NEP coupled explicit statistical targets with diverse (and pragmatically flexible) means of attaining them. This bold and long-term vision was a response to the grave May 1969 race riots; the riots resulted in the twenty-one-month suspension of parliamentary democracy and in the 1971 revision of the Constitution so that it became seditious to publically question the necessity for the New Economic Policy.

Bumiputra is defined as the ethnic majority Malay people as well as the diverse indigenous societies in contemporary Malaysia. It literally translates as "sons of the soil." In the 2000 Census, *Bumiputra* are the largest ethnic minority, making up 65% of the population, followed by ethnic Chinese (26%) and Indian (8%). In 1970, relative to the other two ethnic groups, *Bumiputra* had the highest poverty rates (65%) and the lowest average income (2.29 times lower than the average Chinese, and 1.76 times lower than the average Indian).

One of the NEP's two primary objectives was a dramatic reduction of poverty irrespective of race. In 1970 nearly half of all households in Peninsular Malaysia were below the poverty line. By 1990 the official poverty rate was down to 17% in the country. Critics emphasize that the agricultural states with the greatest poverty were largely excluded, that rural development programs and price subsidies were grossly inefficient, and that plantation workers (primarily Tamil-speaking Indians) were almost entirely overlooked by the NEP.

The other primary objective was the restructuring of society to reduce the identification of race with economic occupations. In practice this generally meant improving *Bumiputra* relative to ethnic Chinese. In 1970, two-thirds of all agricultural workers were Malay and only 13% of Malays were in middle-class occupations (professional, technical, administrative, managerial, clerical, or sales jobs). As a result of rapid industrialization and diverse affirmative action programs in both public and private sector businesses as well as university admissions, by 1990 only one-third of agricultural workers were Malays and 27% of Malays were in middle-class occupations.

In Malaysia the restructuring of society is frequently measured in terms of corporate ownership. Malay ownership of the corporate sector rose from 1.5% in 1970 to 20.3% in 1990. This was accomplished by government-engineered mergers and acquisitions of foreign-owned Malaysian companies, the creation of financial trusts to hold corporate equity on behalf of *Bumiputra*, and the creation and promotion of Malay-owned corporations.

The NEP is a critical case in contemporary debates regarding whether a state with a redistributive agenda is capable of generating new industries and an entrepreneurial middle class from a historically disadvantaged class, or whether it merely creates crony capitalists at the expense of others. Especially striking was that Malaysia was capable of this flexible redistributive policy while maintaining an open economy reliant on foreign direct investment. However, two key questions remain. First, have such policies altered the economic structure so that *Bumiputra* are not merely reliant on continuing government subsidies, preferences, and special regulations? Secondly, given that preferential treatment for *Bumiputra* continues throughout every industry in the Malaysian economy, can such preferences be maintained without creating renewed social conflict grounded in racial resentment?

AARON Z. PITLUCK

See also Malaysia

References and Further Reading

Andaya, Barbara Watson and Leonard Y. Andaya. *A History of Malaysia*, 2nd ed. Houndmills, UK: Palgrave, 2001.

Drabble, John H. *An Economic History of Malaysia, c.1800–1990: The Transition to Modern Economic Growth*. London: Macmillan Press, 2000.

Gomez, Edmund Terence and Jomo, K. S. *Malaysia's Political Economy: Politics, Patronage and Profits*, 2nd ed. Cambridge and New York: Cambridge University Press, 1999.

Khan, Mushtaq H. and Jomo, K. S. *Rents, Rent-Seeking and Economic Development: Theory and Evidence in Asia*. Cambridge and New York: Cambridge University Press, 2000.

Searle, Peter. *The Riddle of Malaysian Capitalism: Rent-Seekers or Real Capitalists?* St. Leonards, Australia: Allen & Unwin, 1999.

Shamsul, A. B. "The Construction and Transformation of a Social Identity: Malayness and Bumiputeraness Reexamined." *Journal of Asian and African Studies*, 52 (1996).

NEW INTERNATIONAL ECONOMIC ORDER (NIEO)

In the 1970s developing countries began to challenge the international economic order, under the grounds that the existing economic structures had been strongly stacked against their economic interests. One sign of this was the imbalance in the distribution of international monetary reserves. While the developing world constitutes 70% of the world's population, they received less than four percent of the international reserves of US$131 billion during the first half of the 1970s.

Another sign was the control exerted over how and in what way the value-added products traded internationally were to be distributed. Developing nations usually received only a small fraction of the final price. The processing, shipping, and marketing of the primary products are controlled in the developed countries. Developing countries were sometimes forced to repurchase their own exports at inflated prices because they had been unable to process the raw materials.

Thirdly, developed nations introduced various forms of tariff and non-tariff protections in order to protect their own domestic industries and standards of living.

Fourthly, many developing nations protested that multinational corporations (MNCs) "engineered" their contracts and concessions to their own benefit, but at the expense of host countries. Additionally, because of tax concessions, royalty payments, transfer pricing, and capital allowances, developing countries often received a small fraction of the profits from foreign investments, despite the exploitation of their own natural resources.

Finally, developing countries have been underrepresented in international organizations. Though representing a majority of the world's population, developing countries have an insignificant representation at the World Bank and International Monetary Fund (IMF) as well as at the United Nations.

The UN General Assembly NIEO resolution of April 1974 committed the organization to establishing an order based on equity, sovereign equality, common interest, and cooperation among all states to eliminate the developmental gap. This declaration spawned a series of "programs of action" that avoided new forms of economic colonialism. The NIEO program addressed four fronts including aid and assistance; international trade; industrialization and technology; and social issues.

Aid and development assistance is required to ensure that developed countries set aside a small proportion of their gross national product (GNP) for aid.

All developed countries aimed at increasing assistance to an agreed target of 0.7% of their GNP. International trade issues include redefining the terms of trade and access to markets achieved through the use of a stable foreign currency with prices indexed for certain commodity prices for manufactured goods, to stabilize price fluctuations of primary commodities by establishing buffer stockpiles and preferential treatment of exports from developing countries. Industrialization issues include import-substitution industrialization (ISI), technology transfer, regulating the activities of MNCs, and the improved use of natural resources. In social terms, proposals ensured an equitable distribution of income; the elimination of unemployment; and the provision of health, education, and other cultural services.

NIEO Program for Action

The NIEO Program for Action included re-examining issues of industrialization and technology.

- Objective 15 of the NIEO involves the negotiation for a redeployment of the industrial productive capacity to developing countries. This proposed a shift of the industrial capacity of developed countries to the Third World, especially those high labour content industries, those industries which required natural resources, and industrial processes requiring locally available raw materials.
- Objective 16 establishes a mechanism for the transfer of technology. Developing countries need access to modern technology if they are to achieve their objectives. The NIEO calls for greater access to technology through a review of international patents, the facilitation of access to patented and non-patented technology, the expansion of assistance to Third World countries for R&D programs, and the control of the import of technology.
- Objective 17 relates to the regulation and supervision of the activities of MNCs and the elimination of restrictive business practices. An international code of conduct prevents enterprises from interfering in the internal affairs of countries in which they operate, eliminates restrictive business practices, and requires that more activities conform to national development plans. Also, the proposal encourages MNCs to assist in the transfer of technology and management skills to developing countries, to regulate the repatriation of profits accruing

from off-shore operations, and to promote the restructuring of their profits in developing countries.

A principal weakness among most developing countries is both the lack of access to technology and their poor command of it. However, merely acquiring technology itself is insufficient because it needs the infrastructure to absorb these new ideas—the so-called "absorptive capacity." Technology transfer may involve the sale of patents and equipment, the supply of know-how and processes, and the dissemination of scientific and technological information. The benefits include the reduction of production costs, increases in production efficiency accompanied by the elimination of wastes, the re-allocation of capital resources, and improvements in the use of technology resulting in higher productivity.

But "backwash effects" resulting from the transfer of technology arise through the following:

- The spread of MNC domination in investments in domestic economies;
- The imposition of Western products on fragile Third World markets behind import-substituting tariff barriers that protect the monopolistic practices of MNCs;
- Outmoded and irrelevant systems of education and university training, which engender inappropriate international professional standards;
- The "dumping" of cheap products in markets, thereby upsetting industrial processes in developing countries; and
- Harmful international trade policies that lock Third World countries into primary-product exports.

GEORGE CHO

See also Development History and Theory; Globalization: Impact on Development; International Bank for Reconstruction and Development (IBRD) (World Bank); International Monetary Fund (IMF); Modernization; Multinational Corporations and Development

References and Further Reading

Bhagwatti, J. N., ed. *The New International Economic Order: The North–South Debate.* Cambridge, MA: MIT Press, 1977.

Cho, G. "Global Interdependence and the Developing Economies." In *Vanishing Borders: The New International Order of the Twenty-First Century,* edited by Lee Boon-Thong and Tengku Shamsul Bahrin. Aldershot, UK: 1998, pp. 15–36.

Ekins, P. "A New World Order—For Whom?" *Development Bulletin,* 23:35, 1992.

Laszlo, E. et al. *The Obstacles to the New International Economic Order.* New York: Pageant Press, 1980.

Laszlo, E and J. Kurtzman, ed. *The Structure of the World Economy and Prospects for a New International Economic Order.* Oxford and New York: Pergamon Press, 1980.

Makiyama, H. *A New International Economic Order, Selected Documents, 1977.* New York: UNITAR, 1982.

Moncarz, R. *International Trade and the New Economic Order.* Oxford, UK: Pergamon, 1995.

Singh, J. S. *A New International Economic Order: Toward a Fair Re-distribution of the World's Resources.* New York: Praeger, 1977.

NEW JEWEL MOVEMENT

The New Jewel Movement (NJM) was a Marxist-inspired political party that ruled Grenada from 1979 until 1983. The NJM came into being on March 11, 1973, when Maurice Bishop's Movement for Assemblies of the People (MAP) merged with Unison Whitman's Joint Endeavor for Welfare, Education, and Liberation (JEWEL). Until the 1970s, Grenadian politics had been dominated by Eric Gairy's Grenada United Labour Party (GULP) and the Grenada National Party. The NJM called for a program to raise the standard of housing, living, education, health, food, and recreation for all people. *The Manifesto of the New Jewel Movement* (1973) stated: "The people are being cheated and have been cheated for too long—cheated by both parties, for over twenty years. Nobody is asking what the people want. We suffer low wages and higher costs of living, while the politicians get richer, live in bigger houses, and drive around in bigger cars." The NJM also called for the nationalization of all foreign-owned hotels.

In May 1973, the British government announced that Grenada would receive independence in February 1974. In 1976, Bishop won a seat in the House of Representatives and became leader of the opposition. In 1977, while Gairy established close ties with Chile's Augusto Pinochet, the NJM established ties with Cuba's Fidel Castro. On March 13, 1979, the NJM staged a virtually bloodless revolution and established the People's Revolutionary Government (PRG). One school of thought holds that the charismatic Bishop was merely a figurehead for a group of pro-Soviet sympathizers within the NJM intent on encircling the Caribbean in a communist net, aided by Nicaragua and Cuba. Another school of thought holds that Bishop truly wanted democratic reform, but that hostility from the United States and neighboring Caribbean states pushed him into an alliance with Castro. Although the NJM called for a form of popular socialism based on grassroots democratic local councils, it arrested hundreds of political prisoners, closed newspapers, and rapidly militarized the nation.

On October 18, 1983, the NJM imploded. Minister of Finance Coard, who wanted to pursue a more pro-Soviet, anti-US policy, overthrew Bishop with the support of the army. Bishop and many of his closest associates were arrested and executed the next day. On October 25, US President Ronald Reagan unleashed Operation Urgent Fury, which removed Coard and his supporters from power. Although pro-Bishop survivors of the 1983 coup organized the Maurice Bishop Patriotic Movement (MBPM), the Grenadian political system since 1984 has been dominated by Keith Mitchell's New National Party (NNP) and the National Democratic Congress (NDC), which maintains close ties with members of Coard's faction of the NJM.

MICHAEL R. HALL

See also Bishop, Maurice; Grenada

References and Further Reading

Heine, Jorge, ed. *A Revolution Aborted: Lessons of Grenada.* Pittsburgh, PA: University of Pittsburgh Press, 1991.

Lewis, Gordon K. *Grenada: The Jewel Despoiled.* Baltimore, MD: Johns Hopkins University Press, 1987.

Scoon, Paul. *Survival for Service: My Experiences as Governor General of Grenada.* London: Macmillan Caribbean 2003.

Sinclair, Norma. *Grenada: Isle of Spice.* Northampton, MA: Interlink Publishing Group, 2003.

NEW PEOPLE'S ARMY

The military wing of the Communist Party of the Philippines (CPP), the New People's Army (NPA), is a Maoist group formed on March 29, 1969. The NPA started with sixty fighters armed with only nine automatic rifles and twenty-six inferior arms (single-shot rifles and handguns). Its avowed aim is to overthrow the Filipino government through protracted guerrilla warfare. Like the CCP, it advocated land reform and the establishment of a socialist state.

Jose Maria Sison is both head of NPA and CPP. Sison has been in exile in the Netherlands for the past two decades but he still sets the general direction of the NPA. Because the top leadership is located overseas, local NPA commanders have considerable autonomy. In recent years, there are credible reports that some local NPA cells were involved in kidnapping and ransom activities. There are also reports that some have become killers for hire.

The NPA derives most of its funding from contributions of supporters in the Philippines, Europe, and elsewhere, and from so-called "revolutionary taxes" extorted from local businesses. In the rural areas, most businesses cannot rely on the government to protect them and must pay the NPA.

The NPA grew substantially during the reign of the dictatorial regime of Ferdinand Marcos (1965–1986) when many opposition elements sided or joined the NPA after Marcos suppressed legitimate political opposition. Several priests influenced by liberation theology also joined the NPA. During this period, the NPA also developed strong sympathy from leftist student movements who opposed US bases in the Philippines.

When Marcos was deposed and democracy was restored in 1986, the NPA continued its fight against the administration of Corazon Aquino and subsequent governments. Despite continuous operations by the Philippines armed forces to wipe them out, the NPA has managed to survive. High levels of poverty in the rural areas, no land reform, and corruption among local government officials are the primary reasons why the NPA still enjoys support among the populace.

The NPA strongly opposes any US military presence in the Philippines and attacked US military interests before the US base closures in 1992. In the past, the NPA had claimed responsibility for the assassination of US military personnel. In January 2002, the NPA publicly expressed its intent to target US personnel sent to the Philippines as part of the war against terror.

Although primarily a rural-based guerrilla group, the NPA has active urban cells that conduct assassinations of high-profile individuals such as politicians, military and police officers, judges, government informers, former rebels who wish to leave the NPA, US troops stationed in the Philippines, and so forth.

At present, the NPA is estimated to have slightly more than ten thousand fighters. They operate in sixty of the Philippines' seventy-three provinces. They are most active in the northern islands of the Philippines with limited presence in the South.

JAMES CHIN

See also Aquino, Benigno, and Corazón; Philippines

References and Further Reading

Chapman, William. *Inside the Philippine Revolution.* New York: Norton, 1987.

Jones, Gregg R. *Red Revolution: Inside the Philippine Guerrilla Movement.* Boulder, CO: Westview Press, 1989.

Kessler, Richard J. *Rebellion and Repression in the Philippines.* New Haven, CT: Yale University Press, 1989.

NEWLY INDUSTRIALIZED ECONOMIES (NIES)

Newly Industrialized Economies (NIEs) are defined as: the economies of export-led industrialization.

The World Bank established a GNP per capita threshold to determine which developing countries belonged to this category. At the beginning of the 1980s, the World Bank used the term "newly industrialized economies" for the first time. The Organization for Economic Cooperation and Development (OECD), however, prefers the term "new industrialized countries." But the two international organizations converged regarding their explanation of this category: it involves a scheme of development based on a contribution of industry above 25% to GNP, with exports composing the major part of manufactured products; the developing country has high economic growth and the gap with developed countries is closing. Even if no clear classification is established, the following countries fall into this category: the four dragons of Asia—Singapore, Hong Kong, Taiwan, and Korea; plus, later on, the four ASEAN countries—Thailand, Malaysia, Indonesia, and the Philippines; and a few Latin Americas countries—Brazil, Mexico, Chile, and to some extent Argentina.

The most represented countries were to be found in Asia; during a twenty-five-year period (1965–1990), the export-oriented model was followed by the dragon economies, and exports as a proportion of GDP increased from 27% to 72.1% (Islam and Chowdhury 1997). The World Bank also recognizes that regional integration is one factor of economic growth, along with the development of market-oriented economies in the NIEs at the beginning of the 1980s and the increase of intra-regional trade at the end of the 1980s.

The newly industrialized economies, during their economic takeoff, accepted the challenge of choosing a new direction for their economies and a new way of life for the future. They adapted continually to changes in their economy, which enabled them to have a unique economic success. The means employed by these countries, with exceptional success, can be a model for other developing countries. Their industrial revolution was implemented through export-oriented strategies in order to counterbalance the weakness of their domestic markets (Arrighi, Hamashita, and Selden 2003). These newly industrialized economies recognized their potential for success as part of the new integration to the global economy. However, even with a common economic orientation, the economic systems of the newly industrialized countries present significant differences, which force them to translate their experience to a higher standard of economic growth. These deep economic changes promoted a long-term high growth rate (averaging 8%) for most of these countries during a twenty-year period. Even during the two oil crises of the 1970s, their economic activity remained high.

In the 1970s, various authors elaborated a new approach to international economy. In these new theories they integrated diverse contributions: new microeconomies in the situation of incomplete information, industrial economy in terms of corporate strategy, local economy in terms of agglomeration effects, territoriality and game theory in terms of interactions between strategic players. The structure of imperfect competition of markets and increased output has been favored by the NIFs over local comparative advantages (Hugon 1997).

According to P. Krugman (1991) in his *Geography and Trade,* the production of economic goods appears in a determinate spot and its effects are linked with increasing output, leading to and reinforcing a spill-over, and competitive poles or competitive advantages; thus, it is possible to explain that international specialization develops from territorial specialization.

An Historical Approach of Development and Technological Transfer

From 1965 to 1995, some countries had a remarkable growth rate sustained by low-end industrialization. After the themed-1970s a peak of success was attained in contrast to stagnation in the world economic picture caused by the two oil crises. In the middle of the 1980s, mastery of the industrial process provided a new impetus to the NIEs, which in turn gave them a higher ranking among industrialized countries. They prepared their economic structure for industrial and technological development by choosing an outward-oriented economic development model, which meant increasing exports. Among the NIEs, the Asian NIEs have particularly progressed in this way. Hong Kong has benefited from mainland refugees inspired by a capitalistic spirit. A great number of them came from the Guangzhou area with their know-how and their capitalistic way of managing companies. Concerning Singapore, this state-city benefited from UK aid until 1965, the year of its independence from the Malay Federation. It then adopted the export industrialization strategy and received guidance from its own government. Malaysia also followed the example of Singapore and has adopted the industrial export scheme (Dufour 1998).

Taiwan and South Korea, whose development was turned toward the domestic market in agriculture and textiles, radically changed their approach to economic development at the beginning of the 1970s by concentrating on an industrial and technological strategy turned toward exports. To do this, they abandoned the import-substitution system in favor of export production to other Asian and foreign markets. For South Korea, economic development was assured by enormous US financial assistance during the Korean War and lasting for ten years after the war—a total of about fifteen years of aid.

Then, by the end of the 1960s, the new orientation of the World Bank was "trade, not aid." This new orientation was immediately put into practice with a decrease of US aid to South Korea as well as to Taiwan, and these two countries, later followed by Singapore, Malaysia, and Hong Kong, have acquired a comparative advantage, based on low labor costs, for gaining foreign direct investment. This has resulted in the de-localization of US and Japanese companies. It was the beginning of the transformation of financial flow from foreign aid to foreign direct investment. Then foreign direct investment from the United States and Japan showed exponential growth for about fifteen years, until the end of the 1980s. This foreign direct investment included know-how and transfer of technology, even if in the 1970s, the latter was only intermediate technology, especially from Japan. In the starting phase of industrialization, textiles, garments, and chemical and petroleum derivative products were the main exports. These were highlabor-intensity and low added-value products. During this period the NIEs' success became associated with the image of sweatshop conditions and low salaries.

The NIEs with their export industrialization strategy in the 1970s were classified as the first 10 countries of the Third World for manufactured product exports. During the decade of the 1980s, these countries quadrupled their industrial exports and doubled their share of manufactured products in international trade (Assidon 2000).

As these Asian NIE countries mastered sophisticated technology, high-end semi-conductor activities developed. But this new technology-based economy has drained increasing financial assets of enterprises and caused increased indebtedness.

During the 1980s the NIEs diversified their industrial exports in new sectors, such as electronics and machine tools, which has allowed them to launch new industrial de-localization strategies and increase the dynamics of growth. The transfer of technology was the central question posed by international organizations such as the World Bank, OECD, and the transnational companies. The Asian NIEs and especially South Korea have asked the transnational companies to increase the transfer of technology in the local companies by means of shared know-how and apprenticeship. In the second half of the 1980s, the NIEs were considered as industrialized countries and they upgraded their production methods in, for instance, electronics, automobile industry, and naval construction.

In the mid-1990s, South Korea and Taiwan became principal exporters of semi-conductors. In the same period, Hong Kong developed one of the world's biggest stock exchanges and Singapore had one of the highest levels of ship traffic in the world.

The Process of Economic Liberalization of the NIEs

In the case of the Asian NIEs, through the middle of the 1990s, regional integration came into being through the setting up of regional arrangements. At this point, the concept of open regionalism was on its way, different from the European integration or regional blocs, and having access to the international markets with more trade and foreign direct investments. But in order to set up such regional economic arrangements, liberalization of the economies was a necessity (Garnaut and Drysdale 1994).

All through the different APEC Summits of the 1990s, the recurrent motives were to follow a process of trade liberalization between member countries and to find concrete ways of associating with the business world (Paix and Riviere d'Arc 1997). Then, in 1993, an informal structure was set up: the Pacific Business Forum, which was later replaced by the APEC Business Advisory Council. In this way the principle of open regionalism was adapted, without adding constraints to the diversity of national economies and leaving a large autonomy of decision making to the member countries. An original and flexible institutional framework was on its way to meeting the demands of internationally oriented economic growth (Kagami, Humphrey, and Piore 1998).

The 1993 World Bank report entitled "East Asian Miracle, Economic Growth and Public Policies," explained that in fact it was not a miracle, but that labor and capital increases and technical progress were responsible for this success, aided by strong governmental support given to new industries. If the term "miracle countries" is used, it is because these countries were able to rapidly master industrial processes similar to those of developed countries.

The Asian NIEs began to get richer and their per capita GNP tremendously increased; social indicators progressed in terms of services: drinking water, electricity, sanitary equipment, household appliances, and number of telephones. The NIEs are ranked high in the UNDP's Human Development Index. These successes were possible because of the high literacy rate and the emphasis that was placed on education. And in 1996, South Korea became the first NIE member of the OECD.

The governmental interventionist policies of the NIEs were brought to bear on the economy until the beginning of the 1990s and were beneficial to the companies. But economic reform was retarded by the dominant role of the state and it was necessary to reduce that role in order to liberate the economy. This form of governmental intervention became an impediment to the development of enterprises. Japan was the model for this type of governmental overseeing (Androuais 2002). In the NIEs, the government was never entirely neutral toward the market and its intervention was too strong and of too long a duration.

The brutal 1997 economic crisis forced the newly industrialized economies to change certain orientations in order to take a new direction in their development. The Asian financial crisis of July 1997 started in Thailand when hedge funds dropped their interest in the region because of negative anticipation. This financial crisis had a tremendous negative impact on the Asian economies; it revealed weak factors, such as overcapacity in production, company debt, and the short-term capital financing of long-term capital.

After the Asian crisis, the IMF requested structural reforms at the governmental level and also in the private sector, which would prepare for a greater liberalization of the economy and less state intervention. These policies were widely applied to economic and financial situations, such as uniformity of customs taxes, additional measures to finance the economy, and the reduction of public debt. The main instruments of this liberalization were the deregulation of finances, reforms in public finances, and changes to upgrade the economy. At the beginning of the new millennium, the Asian NIEs started to adopt a postindustrial model, that is to say, a model having a technological services base (Dufour 2000).

ANNE ANDROUAIS

References and Further Reading

Androuais, Anne. "L'Économie Japonaise, Vers un Cercle Vertueux? (The Japanese Economy, Toward a Virtuous Circle?)." In *L'Asie Demain* (Asia Tomorrow). Group Asia 21, Futuribles. Paris: L'Harmattan, 2002.

Arrighi, Giovanni, Takeshi Hamashita, and Marc Selden. *The Resurgence of East Asia, 500, 150 and 50 Year Perspectives.* New York: Routledge, 2003.

Assidon, Elsa. *Les Théories Economiques du Développement* (Economic Theories of Development). Paris: La Découverte, 2000.

———. *L'Asie Emergente Après la Crise: Les Dragons, les Tigres et la Chine* (Asia Emerging After the Crisis: Dragons, Tigers, and China). Paris: EMS, 2000.

Dufour, Jean-François. *Les NPI Asiatiques* (Asian New Industrialized Countries). Paris: Dunod, 1998.

Freeman, Nick. J. *Financing Southeast Asia Economic Development.* Singapore: ISEAS, 2003.

Garnaut, Robert and Peter Drysdale, eds. *Asia-Pacific Regionalism—Readings in International Economics Relations.* Sydney: HarperCollins, 1994.

Hugon, Philippe. *Economie Politique Internationale et Mondialisation* (International Political Economy and Globalization). Paris: Economica, 1997.

Islam, Iyanatul and Anis Chowdhury. *Asia-Pacific Economies.* London and New York: Routledge, 1997.

Kagami, Mitsuhiro, John Humphrey, and Michael Piore. *Learning, Liberalization, and Economic Adjustment.* Tokyo: Institute of Developing Economies, 1998.

Krugman, Paul. *Geography and Trade.* Cambridge, MA: MIT Press, 1991.

Noland, Marcus and Howard Pack. *Industrial Policy in an Era of Globalization: Lessons from Asia.* Washington, DC: Institute for International Economics, 2003.

Paix, Catherine and Hélène Rivière d'Arc. *Esprit d'Entreprise et Nouvelles Synergies de Part et d'autre du Pacifique* (Entrepreneurial Spirit and New Synergies on Both Sides of the Pacific). Paris: Maison-Neuve et Larose, 1997.

World Bank. *East Asia Miracle, Economic Growth and Public Policies.* Washington, DC: Author, 1993.

NICARAGUA

Nicaragua is located in Central America between Costa Rica and Honduras, bordering both the Caribbean Sea and the North Pacific Ocean. It has a coastline of 910 kilometers and is the largest but most sparsely populated country in Central America. The climate is generally warm and relatively humid with some regional variation, mainly a function of altitude—tropical in the lowlands, cooler in the highlands. The Pacific lowlands are generally more fertile than Caribbean ones. Rainfall is periodic, with May through October as the wettest months. The eastern part of the country receives high average annual rainfall, while the west is drier. Precipitation varies between 1,000 and 6,500 millimeters annually. The Caribbean coast is subject to destructive tropical storms and hurricanes from July to October.

Nicaragua has three major geographic regions. The Pacific lowlands or western region is characterized by flat terrain broken by a line of active volcanoes between the Golfo de Fonseca and Lago de Nicaragua paralleling the Pacific coast. East of the volcanoes lies a large structural rift forming a long, narrow, swampy, and indented depression (sixty to one hundred kilometers) from the Caribbean Golfo de Fonseca southeastward—Costa de Mosquitos (the Mosquito Coast). The two largest freshwater lakes in Central America (Lago de Managua and Lago de Nicaragua, connected by the Tipitapa River) are also located in this rift. The eastern Caribbean lowlands region covers about half of the national territory and consists of tropical rain forest and pine savannas crossed by numerous rivers flowing to the Caribbean. Between the Pacific lowlands and the Caribbean lowlands are the central highlands. The highest point is Mogoton, at 2,438 meters. Western Nicaragua is situated at a juncture between colliding tectonic plates, resulting in a high incidence of earthquakes and volcanic activity. The population as of July 2004 is estimated at 5.36 million. The capital and largest city is Managua, with a population of 1.4 million.

Prior to the Spanish colonization, Nicaragua was settled by Indian tribes of Nicarao, from which the country's name is derived, as well as the Misquito, Garotegas, and others. The area was discovered by Europeans in 1502 with the arrival of Christopher Columbus, and twenty years later the Pacific Coast of Nicaragua was absorbed as a Spanish colony. In 1812 a constitutional monarchy was established in Spain, which liberalized colonial rule. The election of town councils in Central America marked the beginning of national political life. The United Provinces of Central American declared independence from Spain in 1821, a result of the War for Independence of the Spanish colonies in America. At first, Nicaragua was part of the short-lived Mexican Empire under General Agustin de Iturbide, later Emperor Agustin I (1822–1823). From 1823–1838, Nicaragua was, together with Costa Rica, Guatemala, Honduras, and El Salvador, part of the United Provinces of Central America. Political conflict and contradictions between federation members and the capital increased from 1829 on. In 1838, the Central American Congress allowed states to leave the federation; Nicaragua, Honduras, and Costa Rica seceded and became separate republics.

For the next century, Nicaragua's politics was dominated by the competition for power between the Liberals, who were centered in the city of Leon, and the Conservatives, localized in Granada. Britain occupied the Caribbean Coast in the first half of the nineteenth century, but gradually ceded control of the region in subsequent decades. In 1856 US mercenary William Walker was hired by a Nicaraguan political party to topple the president, but he took control of the government and set himself up as president. He was ousted the next year and executed in 1860. US marines intervened following the chaos and disorder after ousting the dictator Jose Santos Zelaya in 1909, and they remained there from 1912 to 1933.

In 1927 prospects emerged for a peace agreement among fighting factions in Nicaragua with provisions for ending US occupation and installing subsequent elections. However, General Augusto C. Sandino refused to accept a peace accord and launched a guerrilla war against the US Marines. Five years later an interim president was elected, and General Anastasio Somoza Garcia was named commander-in-chief of the newly established, allegedly non-partisan National Guard in Nicaragua. The US Marines withdrew. The next year Sandino was murdered by members of the Nicaraguan National Guard. In 1937 Somoza became president, and for the next forty-two years Nicaragua was ruled by the Somoza dynasty—Anastasio; his two sons, Luis and Anastasio Jr.; and various figureheads. Its abuses and corruptive practices caused fierce opposition. Somoza Sr. was assassinated in 1956. He was succeeded as president by his eldest son, Luis Somoza Debayle, a United States-trained engineer. His brother Anastasio "Tachito" Somoza Debayle, a West Point graduate, took over leadership of the National Guard, launching a major political repression campaign. Luis Somoza Debayle won the presidency in 1957 with little opposition. During his six-year term, from 1957 to 1963, his government provided citizens with some freedoms and raised hopes for political liberalization. Puppet figures held the presidency from 1963 until 1967. When poor health prevented Luis Somoza Debayle from running, his brother Anastasio won the February 1967 presidential election. Two months later, Luis—who also objected to "Tachito's" rise to power—died of a heart attack. As president, Anastasio Somoza Debayle retained the National Guard directorship, which gave him absolute political and military control over Nicaragua. Corruption and abuses intensified, accelerating opposition from both populist and business groups. When his four-year term was to end in 1971, Anastasio Somoza Debayle amended the constitution to stay in power until 1972. Increasing pressures from the opposition and even from his own party, however, forced the dictator to formally step down and introduce a three-member junta to rule from 1972 until 1974.

Popular discontent grew also in response to deteriorating social conditions. Illiteracy, malnourishment, inadequate health services, and lack of proper housing also ignited criticism from the Roman Catholic Church, led by Archbishop Miguel Obando y Bravo. On December 23, 1972, a powerful earthquake shook Nicaragua, destroying most of the capital city. It left approximately ten thousand dead and some fifty thousand families homeless, and destroyed 80% of Managua's commercial buildings. Immediately after the earthquake, the National Guard joined the widespread looting of most of the remaining business establishments in Managua. When reconstruction began, the government's illegal appropriation and mismanagement of international relief aid, directed by the Somoza family and members of the National Guard, shocked the international community and produced further unrest in Nicaragua. By some estimates, Somoza's personal wealth soared to US$400 million in 1974. As a result, Anastasio Somoza Debayle's support base within the business sector began to crumble. A revived labor movement increased opposition to the regime and to the deteriorating economic conditions. Somoza Debayle's intentions to run for another presidential term in 1974 were resisted even within his own party. Increasing political repression and further censorship of the media and the press was the rebuttal. In September 1974, Anastasio Somoza Debayle was re-elected president. Leftist forces founded the Sandinista Front for National Liberation (FNSL), which initiated armed resistance, reaching dimensions of a civil war. About the end of 1970s, the United States suspended its backing of Somoza. Marxist Sandinistas came to power on July 19, 1979; Somoza fled into exile and was later murdered. The Sandinistas' communist-type regime launched agrarian reform, nationalization of the banks and some industries, and social reforms. The Sandinistas' support for the leftist rebels in El Salvador, backed by Cuba and the USSR, incited the United States to fund anti-Sandinista "freedom fighters," led by conservatives but composed of people representing many political views, during most of the 1980s. When Nicaraguan free elections were held in 1990, 1996, and in 2001, the Sandinistas were voted out of power and yielded to conservatives, who were represented by Chamorro and Aleman. Moreover, in 1997 the transfer of power between the media owner Violeta Chamorro and the former mayor of Managua, Arnoldo Aleman, acted out the very first time in Nicaragua's history that this office was transferred peacefully and democratically from one democratically elected individual to another. This recurred in 2001, when Arnoldo Aleman stepped down to open the way to the newly elected President Enrique Bolaños. In addition to the political turmoil and economic woes, twice during the last century—in 1932 and in 1972—earthquakes led to the devastation of the capital city of Managua. The country slowly rebuilt its economy during the 1990s, but the Atlantic Coast suffered severe damage from hurricanes Juana in 1988 and Mitch ten years later.

Nicaragua is one of the poorest countries in the Western hemisphere. It faces low per capita income, massive unemployment, and huge external debt. Per capita GDP is $2,200, and more than half of the population lives below the poverty line. Distribution of income is one of the most unequal anywhere in the world. This country has made some progress toward macroeconomic stability early in the twenty-first century; however, GDP annual growth of 1.5%–2.5% has been far too low to meet the country's needs. Nicaragua will continue to be dependent on international aid and debt relief under the Heavily Indebted Poor Countries (HIPC) initiative. Donors have made aid conditional on the openness of government financial operation, poverty alleviation, and human rights. A three-year poverty reduction and growth plan (2003–2005), agreed to with the IMF, steers economic policy. The country received immense support from the international community in 2004 when the IMF and World Bank forgave $4.5 billion of Nicaragua's debt.

Relatively smooth democratization of the country has been overshadowed by continuing corruption. Former president Aleman was charged with fraud and embezzlement, and in 2003 was sentenced to twenty years in prison. However, he was released on December 3, 2004, after only six months of incarceration, and the Court of Appeals found that evidence for his indictment was insufficient. Aleman is also suspected of conspiring with Sandinista leader, Daniel Ortega, to make certain amendments in the constitution and to undermine president Bolaños' positions. The country still relies heavily on foreign assistance and aid. During the past two decades, freedoms of press, assembly, and speech have increased, and respect for human rights has improved considerably. Ethnic issues have never been a serious source of strife. There are territorial disputes with Colombia over the Archipelago de San Andres y Providencia and Quita Sueno Bank region, and about the Honduran access to the Pacific at Golfo de Fonseca; and a legal dispute exists over navigational rights of the San Juan border river. Criminal drug smuggling persists—Nicaraguan shores serve as a transshipment point for cocaine destined for the United States, and for arms-for-drugs dealing.

Nicaragua's economic infrastructure leaves still room for improvement and shaping according to the modern standards. Railways are only six kilometers narrow gauge; highways total 19,032 kilometers, of which 2,094 kilometers are paved. There are 2,220 kilometers of waterways, including Lakes Managua and Nicaragua. Airports have eleven total paved runways, of which three are equipped for landing of large air crafts. There are seven maritime and river ports and harbors, but no merchant marine. The educational system is generally underfinanced and insufficient. Access to education improved during the 1980s, with introduction of free education, but a large majority of the population has not completed primary school. A literacy campaign in the 1980s reportedly raised the functional literacy rate from about 50% at the end of the Somoza regime to 67.5%, almost equally distributed for males and females. There are universities at León and Managua. Health indicators are generally poor. Life expectancy at birth was seventy years in 1991; birth rate is 25.5 per 1,000; population growth rate is 1.97% (2004 est.); infant mortality rate 30.1 per one thousand live births. There is a high incidence of malnutrition; a high incidence of infectious diseases, mainly enteritis, malaria, and tuberculosis; and a still relatively low incidence of the HIV virus. The health care system is still inadequate despite modest improvement during the 1980s. There are approximately 85.6 physicians and ninety-two nurses per one hundred thousand population. Welfare indicators are generally poor, too. Nearly 50% of the working force is unemployed or underemployed, there is unsatisfactory access to safe drinking water, and the quality of basic public services is generally poor, especially in rural areas and on the Caribbean coast. Quality of housing is inferior in urban, suburban, and rural areas, with an acute housing shortage in the capital.

STEPHAN E. NIKOLOV

See also Central America: History and Economic Development; Central America: International Relations; Central American Common Market (CACM); Contras; Nicaraguan Revolution; Sandinista National Liberation Front (FSLN); Somoza García, Anastasio; Somoza DeBayle, Anastasio

References and Further Reading

Bermann, Karl. *Under the Big Stick: Nicaragua and the United States Since 1848.* Boston: South End Press, 1986.

Booth, John A. *The End and the Beginning: The Nicaraguan Revolution.* Boulder, CO: Westview Press, 1985.

Brown, Timothy C. *The Real Contra War: Highlander Peasant Resistance in Nicaragua.* Norman: University of Oklahoma Press, 2001.

Castro, Vanessa and Gary Prevost, eds. *The 1990 Elections in Nicaragua and Their Aftermath.* Lanham, MD: Rowman & Littlefield, 1992.

Gilbert, Dennis L. *Sandinistas: The Party and the Revolution.* New York: Basil Blackwell, 1988.

Gutman, Roy. *Banana Diplomacy: The Making of American Policy in Nicaragua, 1981–87.* New York: Simon & Schuster, 1988.

Hodges, Donald Clark. *Intellectual Foundations of the Nicaraguan Revolution.* Austin: University of Texas Press, 1986.

Macaulay, Neill. *The Sandino Affair.* Durham, NC: Duke University Press, 1985.

Miranda, Roger and William Ratliff. *The Civil War in Nicaragua: Inside the Sandinistas.* New Brunswick, NJ: Transaction, 1992.

Stimson, Henry Lewis. *American Policy in Nicaragua: The Lasting Legacy.* New York: Markus Wiener, 1991.

NICARAGUAN REVOLUTION

The Nicaraguan revolution cannot be categorized as peasant, proletarian, or bourgeois like other classic revolutions in Europe, North American, and Asia. The Sandinista Front for National Liberation (FSLN) gathered a broad array of social forces that overthrew the dictatorship of Anastasio Somoza Debayle on July 19, 1979. On that day, it was difficult to find a citizen in the country who did not talk like a revolutionary and claim the vindication of national hero and martyr August César Sandino.

From Sandino to Fonseca

The roots of the Nicaraguan revolution are intertwined with the lives and the deaths of its principal intellectual architects. August César Sandino was born in 1895 as the illegitimate son of Gregorio Sandino, a merchant, and Margarita Calderón, a coffee picker, in the small town of Niquinohomo. He went to Mexico in the early 1920s to work in the oil fields near Tampico and Veracruz. There he absorbed a wide range of revolutionary ideologies from anarchism to communism and participated in radical union organization. This experience influenced his moral outrage at the intervention of the United States in Central American and the Caribbean conflicts. In 1926, Sandino returned to Nicaragua to support the military campaign of Liberal forces against a Conservative government with ties to the administration of Calvin Coolidge. He pledged his loyalty to Liberal general José Moncada, who espoused classical liberal values of the rule of law, respect for private property, and limited republican government. However, a contingent of US Marines maintained a strong presence in the country to defend Conservative politicians and to protect US business interests. When US envoy Henry Stimson arranged a truce between Liberal and Conservative factions in 1927, Sandino decided to form his own army in the northeastern mountains of Nicaragua.

In the village of El Chipote, he promulgated the Articles of Incorporation of the Defending Army of the National Sovereignty of Nicaragua. After nearly five years of sporadic engagement with guerrilla combat units, the administration of Franklin D. Roosevelt withdrew the Marines as part of his Good Neighbor Policy unveiled in 1932. Roosevelt left the responsibility of maintaining order and stability to Anastasio Somoza García, a graduate of the US military academy at West Point, who became the chief officer of the Nicaraguan National Guard. In August 1933, the National Guard attacked a Sandinista camp, which prompted Sandino to request that Liberal President Juan Batista Sacasa declare the Guard unconstitutional. Nevertheless, in February 1934, Sandino agreed to meet with Sacasa and Somoza García in Managua to negotiate a settlement. Upon leaving the presidential headquarters, National Guardsmen kidnapped him, his brother Socrates, and two Sandinista commanders, and executed them in an empty field.

When Somoza García became president in 1937, he began to use state power to repress political opposition and to enrich a small clique of family members and close associates. Through the instrument of the National Guard, he monopolized the security forces and controlled the judicial system, the banks, and the construction industry, and the primary means of national communication and transportation. In September 1956, the assassination of Somoza García by a radical poet, Rigoberto López Pérez, sparked a state of siege and the bogus convictions of university professors and Conservative political leaders. In this atmosphere, a young law student at the National Autonomous University of León, Carlos Fonseca Amador, began to acquire a revolutionary consciousness. In 1957, Fonseca quit a youth organization affiliated with the Conservative Party and joined the Nicaraguan Socialist Party. In June 1959, Fonseca assembled an armed column of students, peasants, and Cuban advisers in southern Honduras to carry out attacks on the National Guard at several points in northern Nicaragua. The Honduran military arrested the group before the plan could be executed, but Fonseca was released less than a week later. This aborted attempt to destabilize the dynasty occurred almost simultaneously with the emergence of a moderate reform movement of Social Christian and Christian Democrats led by Conservative dissident Pedro Joaquín Chamorro.

Fonseca soon realized the futility of agitating within the restrictive ideology of the Socialist Party and started the New Nicaragua Movement, with fellow Socialists Tomás Borge and Silvio Mayorga, in 1960; they created the Sandinista National Liberation Front (FSLN) in July 1961. As the principal thinker behind the organization, Fonseca carefully refined Sandino's socialist and nationalist orientations to address the repressive political climate and the desperate social conditions of the working classes and rural poor. The FSLN advocated cooperation with diverse urban and rural groups and the gradual accumulation of forces. But the Sandinistas' military actions in the 1960s were dismal failures. The National Guard captured Fonseca in 1964 and deported him to Guatemala. He returned clandestinely to Nicaragua to continue the cause, but was later arrested for bank robbery in Costa Rica. Once Fonseca was freed from jail after Sandinista operatives hijacked an airliner, he spent most of his time in Cuba, under the tutelage of Fidel Castro, developing a strategy of prolonged popular war that guided the guerrilla campaign in the 1970s.

By the time that Anastasio Somoza Debayle took control of the state apparatus in 1967, the FSLN had been eclipsed by the rise of other sources of opposition to the dictatorship among Social Christians and other progressive Catholics, and leftist university professors and students. On December 23, 1972, a massive earthquake destroyed Managua. Somoza's blatant misuse of emergency relief funds alienated even some erstwhile supporters and exacerbated unemployment, the lack of social services, and the scarcity of food in the capital. In December 1974, the Sandinistas burst back into the public eye with a dramatic raid on a party at the home of a cabinet minister and took hostage several foreign diplomats and corporate executives.

In 1975, the FSLN divided into three ideological factions. Fonseca led the dominant Prolonged Popular War faction that borrowed heavily from the successful guerrilla strategy promoted by Che Guevara in Cuba. Maoists shaped the Proletarian Tendency based on factory workers and barrio dwellers. Daniel and Humberto Ortega forged the Third (*Tercerista*—"the Third Way") faction that avoided the dogmatic positions of the other groups and sought alliances with businessmen, religious leaders, and professionals. Humberto Ortega had fought alongside Fonseca in the remote mountains during the 1960s, but he wanted to pursue an urban insurrectionary struggle. On November 8, 1976, the National Guard killed Fonseca in an ambush near Matagalpa at the height of ideological competition within the FSLN. While Fonseca is still considered the most prominent historical figure of the Nicaraguan revolution, his death proved advantageous for the Terceristas, who assumed control of the surging revolutionary tide in the late 1970s.

Victory and Revolutionary Government

On January 10, 1978, Pedro Joaquín Chamorro, the leader of the centrist Democratic Liberation Union and the editor of the newspaper *La Prensa*, was assassinated while driving through Managua. Following this event, mass demonstrations, business lockouts, and labor strikes spurred the creation of the Broad Opposition Front that included prominent politicians, intellectuals, entrepreneurs, and clerics. The

Front called for the resignation of Somoza, yet it lacked political leverage and the moral authority of a leader like Chamorro whose anti-Somoza credentials stretched back to the 1950s. Meanwhile, the FSLN organized the United People's Movement around student groups, trade unions, and progressive Christian activists. Several urban guerrilla attacks, the most dramatic of which was the occupation of the National Palace by Sandinista commandos, enhanced the FSLN's popularity. In March 1979, the Sandinista factions united publicly to conduct the final offensive on major urban areas that vanquished the National Guard. On July 20, the FSLN entered Managua accompanied by jubilant crowds to assume political power.

Daniel Ortega became the Sandinista representative on the Governing Junta of National Reconstruction. The Junta immediately nationalized the banking, insurance, foreign commerce, and mining industries and confiscated the substantial property holdings of the Somoza family and its closest associates. After the resignation of Edén Pastora and Violetta Chamorro, two non-Sandinista members of the junta, in April 1980, Ortega and Sergio Ramírez, a university professor and literary figure, became the dominant political figures of the revolution. In coordination with the nine-member Sandinista National Directorate, the junta pursued aggressive policies of literacy, health, agrarian reform, a mixed socialist-capitalist economy, and a nonaligned international status.

Commitments to popular democracy, social justice, and economic transformation punctuated the revolutionary decade of the 1980s. The Sandinista leadership emphasized the redistribution of resources in favor of their constituencies among urban working classes, small farmers, and the poor. The program in agrarian reform focused primarily on land expropriated from the Somoza family and its closest associates in the early 1980s. But the state gradually increased the confiscation of property from other economic elites who remained in the country or went into exile in the United States. The arbitrary application of agrarian reform laws alienated peasants and rural labor and infuriated larger capitalist interests that attempted to operate within contradictory state policies about production and marketing. Agricultural credit and food prices were heavily subsidized to levels that placed great monetary and fiscal pressures on state coffers. Public housing projects and universal health care raised living standards in urban areas, especially in Managua where commercial and industrial labor was concentrated. Primary, secondary, and university education policies delivered on revolutionary promises but also served ideological purposes. The formation of labor and trade unions,

professional organizations, and neighborhood activist groups complemented Sandinista social initiatives in urban slums; isolated rural areas; and among women, youth, and artisans.

However, many middle-class and grassroots elements began to criticize openly the government's heavy-handed vertical administrative style. Although the FSLN dominated the political landscape, other moderate and conservative political parties, business organizations, and non-governmental organizations expressed opposition openly and played critical roles in the representation of non-revolutionary economic and social groups. The newspaper *La Prensa* and the Supreme Council of Private Enterprise (COSEP) were the primary voices for non-Sandinista civil society. The government closed *La Prensa* on several occasions and jailed outspoken COSEP leaders, but never outlawed them.

After the Sandinista ticket of Daniel Ortega and Sergio Ramírez won the national election in November 1984, the government convened a constituent assembly to craft a new constitution. The new constitution that was promulgated in January 1987 reflected the mass appeal of a socialist vanguard party and the desire to consolidate a unique revolutionary experience in Latin America. During this period, Ortega divided his time between the constitutional debate, economic planning, and diplomacy. He traveled widely in Latin America, Europe, and Asia in search of economic and military assistance and international solidarity. He played a key role in the negotiations for a regional peace agreement initiated by former Costa Rican President Oscar Arias in February 1987.

Relations between the United States and Nicaragua deteriorated rapidly after Ronald Reagan became president in 1981. The Reagan administration accused the FSLN of fomenting instability in El Salvador and formed a counterrevolutionary force of Somocista (who followed Anastasio Somoza) exiles under the guidance of the Central Intelligence Agency (CIA). The *Contras*, as they became popularly known, operated from camps in Honduras and Costa Rica to carry out economic sabotage, military incursions, and political intimidation. The CIA mined the Port of Corinto in 1984 and continued to fuel the civil war even after the United States Congress had prohibited any further backing of the *Contras*. In 1985, the Reagan administration imposed a trade embargo and a lending moratorium through the cooperation of the International Monetary Fund and the World Bank. These international conditions hampered the Sandinista government's ability to deliver to its main constituents the promise of revolutionary transformation.

Under the pressures of a deep economic and social crisis in the late 1980s, the Sandinista government implemented a structural adjustment program intended to control hyperinflation, encourage greater productivity in the private sector, and reduce public spending. At the same time, Ortega opened lines of communication with Conservative and Liberal opposition political parties and the business community in anticipation of the 1990 presidential election. The FSLN was contested by a fourteen-party coalition that supported the candidacy of Violeta Barrios de Chamorro, widow of slain newspaper editor Pedro Joaquín Chamorro. Barrios de Chamorro's victory with 52% of the vote to Ortega's 41% demonstrated significant discontent among important sectors of society, including peasants, housewives, and young males. In the wake of defeat, Ortega promised Sandinista stalwarts that the revolution would continue "from below."

The End of the Revolution and Democratization

The Chamorro administration and its legislative majority pursued an agenda of liberal democracy, market economics, and individual rights. Official efforts to reform the state's role in the economy and society targeted the Sandinista state apparatus. The executive bureaucracy used decree powers between 1991 and 1994 to privatize hundreds of public enterprises and return land to original elite owners whose property had been confiscated under the provisions of revolutionary laws governing agrarian reform. In January 1993, the National Assembly launched a comprehensive overhaul of the 1987 constitution that struck at the heart of Sandinista institutions and ideology. The reformed constitution of 1996 placed paramount importance on the individual rights of citizenship and civil liberties, competitive politics, private enterprise, and property ownership. The provisions that governed agrarian reform were altered to emphasize the democratization of property, the fair distribution of land, and the pursuit of sustainable economic development rather than collective justice in the countryside.

Furthermore, the Sandinista officer corps was subordinated to civilian authority, and references to the revolutionary heritage of the Sandinista Popular Army were expunged in favor of the defense of sovereignty, independence, and territorial integrity. The reforms adjusted the relationship between the executive, legislative, and judicial branches of government, thus limiting the decree powers of the president and strengthening the autonomy of legislators and magistrates. The responsibilities of the Supreme Electoral Council were expanded to manage national, departmental, regional, and municipal elections.

Over the course of the 1990s, the FSLN remained the largest single political party in the country, holding approximately 40% of the seats in the National Assembly. However, the Sandinistas reexamined their platform and policies and reorganized their membership and party bureaucracy. Sandinista legislators and party officials supported painful market-oriented economic reforms; drastic cuts in social spending on education, health, and welfare; and the reduction of the army's rank and file from ninety thousand to fifteen thousand soldiers. The negative social impact of the dramatic reduction of state employment, subsidies, and services caused rifts in the party hierarchy and the resignation of several key leaders, including Sergio Ramírez and Humberto Ortega, the chief of the Sandinista Popular Army since 1979. In addition, the popular base of the FSLN eroded in urban neighborhoods and rural communities, and among teachers, students, and professional and labor groups that once exemplified the multi-class character of the revolutionary coalition aligned against the Somoza dictatorship.

During the first half of the 1990s, the FSLN faced a wave of demands from popular organizations to decentralize the party apparatus and implement pluralist and autonomous decision-making practices. Resistance at the pinnacle of the FSLN led to the emergence of factions, including the Sandinista Renewal Movement. The rigors of competitive elections revealed the Sandinistas' weaknesses in the face of new challenges from old sources of Liberal and Conservative political interests. Daniel Ortega's effort to regain the presidency in 1996 ended in defeat at the hands of Arnoldo Alemán and the Liberal Alliance. Alemán enjoyed the support of traditional Liberal families that had long associations with the Somoza family during the dynastic years. The Liberal resurgence in the late 1990s raised optimism among thousands of claimants who wanted to retrieve property that was confiscated by the FSLN during the 1980s. Liberal and Conservative economic elites mounted a legal assault against several Sandinista decrees and laws that remained in effect after 1990 and challenged the validity of executive actions on the property question during Chamorro's term in office. The struggle over property rights rekindled lingering ideological hostilities from the revolutionary past in which the Sandinistas insisted on the defense of acquired rights to land and enterprises.

Daniel Ortega was nominated once again as the FSLN's presidential candidate for the 2001 national elections. Dissident Sandinista groups objected to the party's decision, arguing that Ortega no longer represented the diversity of opinion within the Sandinista movement. The winner, Enrique Bolaños, a Liberal businessman and Alemán's former vice-president, maintains antipathy for the Sandinistas due to the confiscation of his property in the mid-1980s.

MARK EVERINGHAM

References and Further Reading

Babb, Florence. *After the Revolution: Mapping Gender and Cultural Politics in Neoliberal Nicaragua*. Austin, TX: University of Texas Press, 2001.

Booth, John. *The End and the Beginning: The Nicaraguan Revolution* 2nd ed. Boulder, CO: Westview Press, 1985.

Everingham, Mark. "Neoliberalism in a New Democracy: Elite Politics and State Reform in Nicaragua." *Journal of Developing Areas*, 32, no. 2 (1998).

———. *Revolution and the Multiclass Coalition in Nicaragua*. Pittsburgh, PA: University of Pittsburgh Press, 1996.

Gilbert, Dennis. *Sandinistas: The Party and the Revolution*. New York: Blackwell, 1988.

Hodges, Donald. *Intellectual Foundations of the Nicaraguan Revolution*. Austin, TX: University of Texas Press, 1986.

LeoGrande, William. *Our Own Backyard: The United States and Central America, 1977–1992*. Chapel Hill, NC: University of North Carolina Press, 1998.

Macaulay, Neill. *The Sandino Affair*. Micanopy, FL: Wacahhota Press, 1998.

Millett, Richard. *Guardians of the Dynasty: A History of the U.S.-Created Guardia Nacional De Nicaragua and the Somoza Family*. Maryknoll, NY: Orbis, 1977.

Palmer, Steven. "Carlos Fonseca and the Construction of Sandinismo in Nicaragua." *Latin American Research Review*, 23, no. 2 (1988).

Ryan, Phil. *The Fall and Rise of the Market in Sandinista Nicaragua*. Montreal: McGill-Queens University Press, 1995.

Spalding, Rose, ed. *The Political Economy of Revolutionary Nicaragua*. Winchester, MA: Allen & Unwin, 1987.

Walker, Thomas. *Nicaragua in Revolution*. New York: Praeger, 1982.

———, ed. *Nicaragua without Illusions: Regime Transition and Structural Adjustment*. Wilmington, DE: Scholarly Resources, 1997.

Walter, Knut. *The Regime of Anastasio Somoza García and the State Formation in Nicaragua, 1936–1956*. Chapel Hill, NC: University of North Carolina Press, 1993.

Wright, Bruce. *Theory in the Practice of the Nicaraguan Revolution*. Athens, OH: Center for International Studies, Ohio University Press, 1995.

Zimmerman, Matilde. *Sandinista: Carlos Fonseca and the Nicaraguan Revolution*. Durham, NC: Duke University Press, 2000.

NIGER

The Republic of Niger is a land-locked West African country, bordered by Algeria, Libya, Chad, Nigeria, Benin, Burkina Faso, and Mali. The country totals 489,189 square miles with less than 3% arable land. Niger consists primarily of the Sahara Desert, including the partly volcanic Air mountains in the central region, with some flat-to-rolling savanna plains in the south where most of the population resides. The Niger River flows for approximately 310 miles (five hundred kilometers) through the country's southwestern-most corner. From July to September, the river is navigable by small boats and provides irrigation along its immediate banks. The country shares Lake Chad on its southeastern corner with Nigeria, Chad, and Cameroon. Niger contains large quantities of tin, iron ore, copper, phosphates, and uranium. Agriculture, primarily groundnuts, millet, sorghum, cassava, beans, and rice, as well as pastoralism dominate the domestic economy, with some fishing and rock salt mining. Several ethnic groups, including the Hausa (56% of the population), Djerma (or Zerma), Songhai, Fulbe, and Tuareg inhabit Niger, which is about 85% Muslim. French is the official language, with Hausa, Djerma, and Fulbe as national languages. The population totals approximately 11.5 million with almost 1 million people living in the capital, Niger, situated on the Niger River. The country consistently ranks as one of the ten poorest countries in the world, with annual per capita income estimated at less than $800.

The nomadic Tuareg were the first inhabitants of the region, followed by the Hausa and other sedentary groups. About one thousand years ago, Arab traders from North Africa first made contact with the Tuareg and Hausa, introducing Islam and linking the region with the increasing trans-Saharan trade, comprising exchange in supplied salt, metals, and slaves. Parts of the area were loosely incorporated into the great Western Sudanic empires of Mali and Songhai, although the Tuareg in the northern desert regions retained much of their autonomy. After the fall of the Songhai Empire in the late sixteenth century, a series of small political entities and Tuareg confederations emerged, including several Hausa city-states in the extreme south. The Fulbe jihads of the early nineteenth century affected the southern region, which was eventually subsumed into the newly created Sokoto Caliphate where it remained until conquest by the French in the late nineteenth century. Parts of the desert north were not disrupted by the Europeans until well into the twentieth century. Niger became a French colony in 1922, administered from Dakar, Senegal.

The French launched military expeditions into the interior to control and tax trading caravans. The colonial administration also imposed taxes to force people to farm, particularly groundnuts for export. Little was invested in social or infrastructural development. Local government was left in the hands of traditional ruling elites. No Western-educated elite emerged as it did in coastal colonies. In 1946, the peoples of Niger, in common with other peoples in French Africa, were granted French citizenship with limited self-rule, and a small but short-lived political party was formed. In elections in 1958, Hamani Diori won the presidency and he retained this position when the country won independence on August 3, 1960. Close ties were maintained with France, and French advisers and troops remained in the country.

Diori and his elite supporters concentrated on attempts to develop the economy and consolidate their own power. Diori won re-election in 1965 and 1970, but he was overthrown in a military coup in 1974 by Lt. Colonel Seyni Kountche who promised to root out corruption and push for development. He also had strong French support for his proposed reform policies. The Sahelian drought of the late 1970s and early 1980s profoundly affected the country, as did falling uranium prices on the world market after 1979. Kountche confronted growing popular opposition and attempted coups and assassinations with an increasingly authoritarian style. In 1987, Kountche died and was succeeded by Colonel Ali Seybou, who was chosen as president by the Supreme Military Council. Seybou was forced to accept austerity measures and a structural adjustment program consisting of privatization of state enterprises and cuts in student scholarships and civil servant salaries. Seybou also oversaw a transition program to civilian rule, which included a new constitution. A national conference convened in 1991 to draft a new constitution set the stage for multiparty elections in 1993, won by Mahamane Ousmane as president and Mahamadou Issoufou as prime minister. Infighting between the two men, as well as continued drought and declining uranium prices, disrupted the country's stability and economic progress. Issoufou resigned in 1994 and new elections for prime minister were won by opposition leader Hama Amadou. Infighting paralyzed the government, internal unrest among students and northern Tuareg rebels intensified, and bankruptcy loomed. Both Ousmane and Amadou were overthrown in a violent military coup in January 1996 led by Colonel Ibrahim Barre Mainassara who declared himself president of the Fourth Republic of Niger. He was assassinated in early 1999 by the presidential guard whose leader, Major Mallam Daouda Wanke, assumed power briefly. Free elections in late 1999 elevated Mamadou Tandja to the presidency while Hama Amadou was reinstated as prime minister. Tandja signed peace agreements with Tuareg rebels and, although periodically instituting states of emergencies to repress student rebellions in the capital, Niamey, has generally moved toward easing strict security measures. Structural adjustment measures continue to be implemented, albeit slowly.

In addition to the constant threat of rebellions and coups, Niger faces severe economic hardships. The economy is based on uranium mining, totaling over 75% of the country's exports, and subsistence agriculture, practiced by 80% of the population. Desertification, resulting from both natural and human activity, poses a significant and growing problem. The country is heavily dependent on foreign aid, mostly from France. The GDP is estimated at $9 billion with an external debt of over $1.6 billion. Education and health care are sorely lacking. The adult literacy rate is approximately 16%; life expectancy averages forty-two years for men and women. The infant mortality rate is 122 per 1,000 live births and population growth is 2.9% with an 80/20 rural/urban ratio. Niger's future political and economic prospects appear bleak.

ANDREW F. CLARK

See also Ethnic Conflicts: West Africa; West Africa: History and Economic Development; West Africa: International Relations

References and Further Reading

Ajayi, J. and M. Crowder, eds. *History of West Africa*, vol. 2. London: Longman, 1974.

Charlick, Robert. *Niger: Personal Rule and Survival in the Sahel.* Boulder, CO: Westview Press, 1991.

Decalo, Samuel. *Historical Dictionary of Niger.* Lanham, MD: Scarecrow Press, 1989.

Fugelstad, Finn. *A History of Niger, 1850–1960.* Cambridge, UK: Cambridge University Press, 1983.

Gervais, Myriam. "Niger: Regime Change, Economic Crisis, and Perpetuation of Privilege." In J. Clark and D. Gardiner, eds., *Political Reform in Francophone Africa.* Boulder, CO: Westview Press, 1997.

NIGERIA, THE FEDERAL REPUBLIC OF

The Federal Republic of Nigeria is situated in Western Africa, bordering the Gulf of Guinea, between Benin and Cameroon. Nigeria's climate is characterized by strong latitudinal zones, becoming progressively drier as one moves north from the coast. Rainfall is the key climatic variable, and because all of Nigeria is within the tropics, there is a marked alternation of wet and dry seasons in most areas. The wet season takes place between May and September and the dry season between October and April in most of the country; the temperature is always warm. Rainfall varies from more than 130 inches along the coast to less than twenty-six inches along the northern border. Maximum temperatures range from 95°F on the coast, where cloud cover is nearly continuous, to above 105°F in the north. Minimum temperatures range from 72°F in the south to 66°F in the north. The northern part of the country consists mainly of desert, which rises to savanna-covered hills and a central agricultural plateau. The southeastern and southwestern zones consist of savanna and rain forests. Along the coastline are thick mangrove swamps.

Nigeria's population is one quarter of the entire African continent and is Africa's most populated country with an estimated population of about 137 million and an annual growth rate of 2%. Among the most populated countries in the world, it occupies the tenth place. Prior to 1991 the capital city had been Lagos, but from then on Abuja, a much smaller city with 371,674 persons (1991) and located in the geographical centre of the country, has occupied its position.

Nigeria's two main rivers are the Niger River and the Benue River. Nigeria is culturally rich but also diverse and complex. The country has three major ethnic groups (Igbo, Yoruba, and Hausa) and hundreds of ethnic subgroups. There is no single language that can be understood by the masses, but English is the official language followed by the Hausa, Yoruba, Igbo (Ibo), and Fulani in different parts of the country. As for religion, half the population are Muslims, who live mainly in the north; Christians are about 40% and they mostly live in the south; and 10% of people have indigenous beliefs.

As early as 1849 the British had already occupied the cities of Benin and Biafra, developing commercial strategies that mainly consisted of the slave trade. In 1885, British claims to a sphere of influence in that area received international recognition and, in the following year, the Royal Niger Company (RNC) was chartered under the leadership of Sir George Goldie. On January 1, 1901, Nigeria became a British protectorate. In 1914, the area was formally united as the Colony and Protectorate of Nigeria. Following World War II, successive constitutions legislated by the British government moved Nigeria toward self-government on a representative basis. Nigeria was granted full independence in October 1960 under a constitution that provided for a parliamentary form of government.

In October 1963, Nigeria altered its relationship with the United Kingdom by proclaiming itself a Federal Republic, and Nnamdi Azikiwe became the country's first president. However, tensions between ethnic groups grew stronger and conflicts arose. On January 15, 1966, a small group of army officers, mostly southeastern Igbos, overthrew the government

and assassinated the federal prime minister and the premiers of the northern and western regions. This was the beginning of more than thirty years of almost continuous military rule and conflicts in Nigeria until the year 1999.

In 1966, the federal military government that assumed power under General Aguyi Ironsi, was unable to quiet ethnic tensions or produce a constitution acceptable to all sections of the country. In July, a second coup established the leadership of Major General Yakubu Gowon. In May 1967, Lt. Col. Emeka Ojukwu, who emerged as the leader of increasing Igbo secessionist sentiment, declared the independence of the eastern region as the Republic of Biafra. The ensuing Nigerian Civil War was bitter and bloody, ending in the defeat and dissapearance of Biafra in 1970 and a resulting two million casualties.

On July 29, 1975, Gen. Murtala Mohammed staged a new bloodless coup, accusing the military government of Gowon of delaying the promised return to civilian rule and becoming corrupt and ineffective. General Muhammed replaced thousands of civil servants and announced a timetable for the resumption of civilian rule by October 1, 1979. However, Muhammed was assassinated on February 13, 1976, in an abortive coup.

In 1979, five political parties competed in a series of elections in which Alhaji Shehu Shagari was elected president. Again, in December 1983, the military overthrew the Second Republic. Maj. Gen. Muhammadu Buhari emerged as the leader of the Supreme Military Council (SMC), the country's new ruling body. The Buhari government was peacefully overthrown by the SMC's third-ranking member, Maj. Gen. Ibrahim Babangida, in August 1985.

Babangida ruled with military force until the new presidential election was finally held on June 12, 1993. The historic presidential elections indicated that the wealthy Yoruba businessman M. K. O. Abiola had won. However, on June 23, Babangida annulled the election. Without popular and military support, he was forced to hand over to Ernest Shonekan who was supposed to rule until new elections, scheduled for February 1994. But he had to resign his power and deliver it to Defense Minister Gen. Sani Abacha who forced Shonekan's "resignation" on November 17, 1993. In October 1995 Gen. Sani Abacha announced the timetable for a three-year transition to civilian rule. Abacha, widely expected to succeed himself as a civilian president on October 1, 1998, died suddenly of heart failure on June 8 of that year.

He was replaced by General Abdulsalami Abubakar who decided to have elections in 1999. In February 1999, former military head of state Olusegun

Obasanjo ran as a civilian candidate and won the presidential election. The emergence of a democratic Nigeria in May 1999 ended sixteen years of consecutive military rule. Finally, the April 2003 elections marked the first civilian transfer of power in Nigeria's history, with elections won again by Obasanjo.

The Nigerian economy is the largest and most dynamic in Black Africa. In 2004 the GDP was estimated at $114.8 billion. Since the beginning of oil exploitation in the 1970s, Nigeria's unpopular military rulers have failed to make significant progress in diversifying the economy away from overdependence on the oil sector, which provides 30% of GDP, 95% of foreign exchange earnings, and about 80% of budgetary revenues. The United States remains Nigeria's largest customer for crude oil, accounting for 40% of the country's total oil exports; Nigeria provides about 10% of overall US oil imports and ranks as the fifth-largest source for US imported oil.

The oil boom accelerated massive migration to urban centres, which then became crowded with rural migrants who lack jobs and the resources to return to the countryside. This meant increasingly widespread poverty, especially in rural areas, and a collapse of basic infrastructure and social services since the early 1980s. The country's urban population is 45% of the total.

Besides the oil sector, agriculture is an important sector as it employs more than half of the total population, mostly on a subsistence level, but contributes only about 30% of the GDP. The exports consist of rubber, cotton, and palm oil. The country used to be a great exporter of cocoa, but nowadays exports are stagnant at around 180,000 tons annually, whereas twenty-five years ago it was three hundred thousand tons. The leading subsistence crops are yams, cassava, and cocoa in the south; and maize, guinea corn, rice, and millet in the north.

Lake Chad is the prime source of fish. The largely subsistence agricultural sector has failed to keep up with rapid population growth, and Nigeria, once a large net exporter of food, now must import food. Other important industries are textile manufacturing, food processing and brewing, cement production, motor-vehicle assembly, sawmilling, and small consumer-goods manufacturing. The poor infrastructure of the country is a major constraint to economic development with most of the roads and ports in poor shape.

Although Nigeria's GDP is growing, the country is far from being a developed one. Despite having a large GDP, the per capita income has been as low as $900, which makes Nigeria one of the poorest countries worldwide in terms of per capita income. Nigeria has a terribly unequal distribution of resources and

services. Although its territory has many resources, the distribution of those is so unequal that most of its population suffers from economic, health, and educative problems. The constant civil wars from 1966–1999 prevented the country from advancing in its development.

As for the health conditions, Nigeria had 1,170 hospitals in 1994, most of them in poor condition. The number of beds was 46,544, amounting to nearly 1,912 persons per bed. As of the early twenty-first century, around 15% of Nigerian children do not survive to their fifth birthday. The leading causes of child mortality are malaria, diarrhoea, and malnutrition, which contribute to 52% of deaths of children under the age of five. Malnutrition has become commonplace, and infant and maternal mortality rates continue to be among the highest in the world. The under-five infant mortality rate has slightly improved in the last thirty years, passing from an alarming 201 per one thousand live births in 1970, to 183 in 2002. The life expectancy at birth also improved a little, from forty-four years in 1970 to fifty-one in 2002 (UNDP 2004). Despite improving, it still is very low, below the average even for Sub-Saharan countries (forty-six years in 2002).

Less than half of the population has access to safe water and water-borne disease is widespread. Since the beginning of the economic crisis in the 1980s, the health sector has suffered dramatically. Development and recurrent expenditure has declined, resulting in a scarcity of drugs and medical supplies, and the deterioration of facilities.

Similar conditions reign for the education sector. The percentage of the GDP spent in 1990 for education was very low, only 0.9% (UNDP, 2004). Compared to the developed countries, which spend around 7%, this is very low. It is also very low when compared to neighbouring countries with a low human development index. These are all indicators that education is not a national priority in the country.

Six years of primary education are free and compulsory. Secondary-school enrolments are limited. The primary enrolment was only 60% in 1990 and 69% in 1995. At both the primary and secondary level, schools are generally overcrowded, and they lack teachers and basic infrastructure such as buildings, teaching aids, equipment, textbooks, and furniture. At the tertiary level, education has experienced phenomenal expansion without a proportionate increase in funding and facilities. The system suffers from problems such as outdated, dilapidated, or nonexistent infrastructure; poorly stocked libraries, inadequate laboratories and equipment, low staff-student ratio, and poor quality of teaching; as well as low quality of graduates, especially in science and technology. The adult literacy rate improved from being 40% in 1985 to 66% in 2002.

The working conditions are not much better. The unemployment rate is quite high and so is the number of poor people. About 66% of the population now falls below the poverty line of about a dollar a day, compared to 43% in 1985. Although Nigeria's economy is forecast to keep growing, the growth is primarily driven by the energy sectors and is unlikely to feed through to the wider population.

Nigeria's official foreign debt is approximately $31 billion and about 75% is owed to Paris Club countries. As of the early twenty-first century, in the absence of government programs, the major multinational oil companies have launched their own community development programs. A new entity, called the Niger Delta Development Commission (NDDC), has been created to help catalyze economic and social development in the region. Although as of this writing, it has yet to launch its programs, hopes are that the NDDC can reverse the impoverishment of local communities and improve human conditions in the country.

DIEGO I. MURGUÍA

See also Biafra; Ethnic Conflicts: West Africa; West Africa: History and Economic Development; West Africa: International Relations

References and Further Reading

Badru, Pade. *Imperialism and Ethnic Politics in Nigeria, 1960–1996*. Trenton, NJ: Africa World Press, 1998.

Barbour, Kenneth Michael, et al. *Nigeria in Maps*. New York: Africana, 1982.

Dyson, Sally and Alhaji L. A. K Abibi. *Nigeria: The Birth of Africa's Greatest Country: From the Pages of Drum Magazine*. Oxford, UK: Spectrum Books, 1998.

Falola, Toyin. *The History of Nigeria*. Westport, CT: Greenwood Press, 1999.

Forrest, Thomas. *Politics, Policy, and Capitalist Development in Nigeria, 1970–1990*. Boulder, CO: Westview Press, 1992.

Kirk-Greene and D. Rimmer. *Nigeria Since 1970: A Political and Economic Outline*. London: Hodder & Stoughton, 1981.

Metz, Helen Chapin. *Nigeria: A Country Study*. Washington, DC: GPO, 1992.

Morgan, William Thomas Wilson. *Nigeria*. London: Longman, 1983.

Myers, Robert A. *Nigeria*. Oxford, UK; Santa Barbara, CA: Clio Press, 1989.

Nwabueze, Benjamin Obi. *A Constitutional History of Nigeria*. New York: Longman, 1982.

Osaghae, Eghosa E. *Crippled Giant: Nigeria Since Independence*. Bloomington: Indiana University Press, 1998.

United Nations Development Program (UNDP). *Human Development Report 2004. Cultural Liberty in Today's Diverse World*. New York: Hoechstetter, 2004. Available at http://hdr.undp.org.

NIUE

Often said to be "the world's largest uplifted atoll," Niue is oval in shape and has a surface area of one hundred square miles (260 square kilometers). Located in the heart of Polynesia at coordinates 19°02″S and 169°52″W, its nearest neighbours are Tonga, Samoa, and the Cook Islands. Niue's upper plateau is composed of coral rocks interspersed with pockets of soil and a covering of forest and scrub, while rugged limestone cliffs dominate the coastline. Its climate is tropical, with a mean annual temperature of 75.5°F, an average annual rainfall of eighty inches, and trade winds from the southeast. An underground lens of fresh water can be accessed only via deep caves or (in recent decades) piped bores. Droughts and cyclones are a constant threat.

The ancestors of the Niuean people arrived from Tonga about 1,500 years ago. By late traditional times, however, the island was effectively an isolate, due to its singular location, dangerous shores, and fierce warriors. In the 1600s, Niue's population of four thousand was divided into eight districts, each possessing a similar pie-shaped portion of coast and land. Within each district, family groups pursued slash-and-burn horticulture (taro, yam, sugarcane, coconut), along with hunting (fruitbats, birds, landcrabs), gathering (fruits, berries, roots, crustaceans), and fishing (from both reef and canoe). Each area of usable land belonged to a family, while coastal zones and virgin forests were usually controlled by the district. Gender and age constituted the only real divisions of labour, with each co-resident group being materially self-sufficient. Unlike its Polynesian neighbours, Niue had neither hereditary elites nor chiefly institutions.

Contact with whaling ships from the 1820s, and especially the establishment of the London Missionary Society on the island in the late 1840s, triggered major changes. The introduction of steel axes, knives, and fishhooks, in particular, significantly increased productive capacity, which in turn encouraged the export of coconut sennit, copra, fungus, cotton, and handicrafts. But, during the 1860s, Niue was found to have an even more important resource—labour. At any time over the next five decades, two hundred to five hundred men from the island would be absent as indentured workers in plantations, mines, or on ships throughout the Pacific.

During the great territorial carve-ups of the late nineteenth century, Niue's role as a supplier of labour was what most interested the imperial powers. Thus, in 1900 Britain formally annexed Niue, and the following year transferred control of the island to New Zealand. With the formal ending of the indenture system in 1915, the emphasis changed to ensuring the territory's social and economic self-sufficiency. Paternalistic colonial administrations now haphazardly encouraged domestic industry, particularly exportable food crops and traditional handicrafts, though such initiatives invariably were undermined by natural calamity, international conflict, economic depression, and unreliable shipping.

Top-down modernisation arbitrarily imposed on the people of Niue after World War II contributed to the murder of New Zealand's resident commissioner in 1953. Under pressure from the United Nations, New Zealand then began to emphasise decolonisation as much as development. New policies offered unprecedented levels of investment in public service infrastructure and wage employment, especially in the education, health, communications, and administrative sectors. Migration to New Zealand—where there was an ongoing shortage of unskilled labour—also was encouraged, culminating in the opening of Niue's first airport. In 1974, after a United Nations-administered referendum on independence, the island became a self-governing territory constitutionally associated with New Zealand. From then on, an elected assembly, cabinet, and premier were to control its internal affairs, while New Zealand accepted responsibility for international relations and financial supply.

Development plans also were introduced about this time, though their hopes often were not achieved. On the one hand, key indicators such as levels of participation in the formal economy, real incomes, educational attainment, life expectancy, and so on show that basic living standards continued to improve. But such gains were consistently undermined by out-migration, with the resident population falling from a high of 5,200 during the late-1960s, down to around 1,500 in the early twenty-first century. As a result, about twenty thousand persons of Niuean descent now live in New Zealand, where they have automatic citizenship rights, and hundreds of others have moved on to Australia.

Several times over recent decades, New Zealand has reduced its funding to Niue and demanded restructuring of the public sector—always at the cost of jobs. While most households have continued to provide much of their own basic foods through cultivating, fishing, hunting, and gathering, the need for cash income is a constant pressure. Lack of wage employment often triggers emigration, especially for young adults. Different products and services have been variously promoted, often with considerable government support, as "the solution" to Niue's economic problems: fish, coconut cream, taro, lime oil, honey, passion fruit, timber, sewing footballs, philatelics (the production of attractive stamps for sale to collectors), offshore banking, tourism, and the Internet. In each case, however, tangible success has been limited in duration or constrained by actual circumstances. Most often, unreliable airline and shipping connections have undermined the very best efforts at helping Niue escape the aid-dependency trap.

Nature similarly continues to exert its hold on "the world's smallest nation." In January 2004 an unprecedented category-five cyclone devastated Niue and destroyed much of Alofi, its main town. Since then, environmental recovery and material reconstruction have been this microstate's priorities, with considerable help from New Zealand and elsewhere. But a predicted "final exodus" from the island in the wake of Cyclone Heta has so far failed to materialize, suggesting that Niueans always will maintain a core population on their homeland, guaranteeing their unique society and culture an ongoing existence—regardless of ecological and economic uncertainties.

TOM RYAN

See also Ethnic Conflicts: Oceania; Oceania: History and Economic Development; Oceania: International Relations

References and Further Reading

Barker, Judith C. "Hurricanes and Socio-Economic Development on Niue Island." *Asia Pacific Viewpoint*, 41:2, 191–205, 2000.
———. "Niue." *Countries and Their Cultures: Volume 3*, pp.1643–1649, edited by Ember and Carol R. Ember. New York: Macmillan, 2001.
Chapman, Terry M. *The Decolonisation of Niue*. Wellington: Victoria University Press and New Zealand Institute of International Affairs, 1976.
Douglas, Hima. "Niue: The Silent Village Green." *Class and Culture in the South Pacific*, pp. 186–192, edited by Antony Hooper and Steve Briton et al. Auckland and Suva: University of Auckland and University of the South Pacific, 1987.
Kalauni, Solomona, and Ron Crocombe et al. *Land Tenure in Niue*. Suva: Institute of Pacific Studies, University of the South Pacific, 1977.
Ryan, Tom. "Fishing in Transition on Niue." *Journal de la Société des Océanistes*, 72–73: 193–203, 1981.
———. "Niueans." *Encyclopedia of World Cultures Supplement*, pp. 227–230, edited by Melvin Ember and Carol R. Ember et al. New York: Macmillan, 2002.
Vilitama, Hafe and Terry Chapman et al. *Niue: A History of the Island*. Suva: University of the South Pacific and Government of Niue, 1982.

NKRUMAH, KWAME

Kwame Nkrumah (1909?–1972), was a pre-eminent Ghanaian statesman, pan-Africanist, and political philosopher, best known for his fight against colonialism. He was born in Nkroful in the Western Region of

Ghana. (Nkrumah's date of birth is uncertain; however, he used September 21, 1909—a date stipulated on his baptismal certificate by the priest who baptized him into the Roman Catholic Church—in many of his official records). Nkrumah graduated from the prestigious Achimota College in Legon, Accra, in 1930, before leaving for the United States where he earned a B.A. in economics and sociology from Lincoln University in 1939; a B.A. in theology from the Lincoln Theological Seminary in 1942; and completed a Ph.D. candidacy in philosophy at the University of Pennsylvania in 1943. He later moved to London, where he read law at Gray's Inn, and also attended law lectures at the London School of Economics in 1945. While in England, Nkrumah assumed the editorship of the *New African,* a journal of the West African National Secretariat, and also became the joint organizing secretary (with George Padmore) of the Fifth Pan-African Congress in Manchester in 1945. In 1947 he moved to Ghana (then the Gold Coast) to become the general secretary of the United Gold Coast Convention (UGCC)—a nationalist organisation. In 1948, Nkrumah broke away from the UGCC to form the Convention People's Party (CPP) with which he spearheaded the struggle that eventually secured Ghana's independence from Britain in 1957, making Ghana the first independent nation in Black Africa, and Nkrumah its first prime minister.

Even though the practical realities of politics compelled Nkrumah to start his major political activities in his native Ghana, he devoted ample attention to Pan-Africanism. Nkrumah's contribution to development went beyond his native Ghana; it includes his active involvement, leadership roles, and collaborative efforts with such notable Pan-African pioneers as W.E.B. Du Bois, Sékou Touré, Julius Nyerere, and Leopold Sénghor in the formation of the Organization of African Unity (OAU, now African Union [AU]) in particular, and the African liberation struggle in general.

Nkrumah's Development and Political Philosophy

Nkrumah saw development as a multifaceted phenomenon, entailing economic, cultural, social, and political progress. However, he believed in the primacy of politics in the development process. In his words: "Seek ye first the political kingdom and all other things will be added unto it." Nkrumah was an exponent of the dependency theory, which posits that the world system is divided into "'cores'' and "peripheries," with the former exploiting the latter.

Nkrumah contended that the nations of the periphery would remain dependent on those of the core, as the relationship between the two entities is inherently exploitative. Nkrumah saw no better approach to development than socialism; his infatuation with this ideology emanated from his experience with racism and injustice in both United States and Britain, as well as his personal encounter with colonialism in Africa.

The most insightful exposition of Nkrumah's philosophy is in his book, *Consciencism,* where he argues that colonialism entails two forces: positive action and negative action. According to him, the former "is the sum of those forces seeking social justice" while the latter "is the sum of those forces tending to prolong colonial subjugation and exploitation" (Nkrumah 1964, p. 99). According to Nkrumah, negative action always exceeds positive action under colonialism. To him neo-colonialism is a guise adopted by negative action in order to give the impression that it has been outweighed by positive action; thus "neo-colonialism is negative action playing possum" (Nkrumah 1964, p.100). Nkrumah's "consciencism" was couched in socialism, as he was convinced that the traditional African society was essentially egalitarian and communalistic. Nkrumah originally favoured nonviolence. However, after his overthrow in 1966, he became very radical, advocating for violence in several of his publications, notably in *The Struggle Continues* (1973), and *Revolutionary Path* (1973). His position on religion was decidedly ambiguous. He writes in his *Consciencism* that while his philosophy is underpinned by materialism, "it is not necessarily atheistic." Still, he claims in the same book that "religion is an instrument of bourgeois social reaction."

Contributions to National and International Development

After Ghana's independence, Nkrumah sought to centralize power by moving toward a one-party state. He diminished the power of the military and the role of the traditional chiefs, making the latter dependent on his ruling party, the Convention People's Party (CPP), for official recognition. While this helped alleviate tribalism, it also entrenched him in power. Nkrumah launched Ghana's First and Second Development Plans, from 1951–1956 and 1959–1964, respectively. With these D-Plans, he embarked on massive industrialization, using local raw materials and labour to provide employment and to reduce the nation's dependence on imported goods.

Nkrumah built the Volta River Project to provide power for the new industries and for mass electrification. The nation's state farms were established in the 1960s to curb food and raw material shortages; a Workers' Brigade was also created to provide labour for these farms. Nkrumah increased the production of cocoa, the main cash crop, but, unfortunately, the price of cocoa plunged in the world market for the greater part of his time of reign.

The Ghana National Trading Corporation (GNTC) was established to reduce the role of middlepersons and expatriate traders in the distribution of consumer goods. Similarly, the Ghana Commercial Bank and the Black Star Line were founded to compete with the existing foreign banks and shipping lines, respectively. The most enduring legacy of Nkrumah is his policy of free education, which gave Ghana the highest enrolment rate in Africa by 1966. Nkrumah also made the provision of basic health care free across Ghana.

Regarding Pan-Africanism, Nkrumah teamed up with Sékou Touré to form the Ghana–Guinea Union in 1958, as part of his plan to create a Union of African States with one parliament and an All-African Defence Force. Nkrumah organized the first All-African Peoples' Conference (AAPC) in Accra in 1958; this culminated in the formation of a Pan-African Secretariat in Accra. Mali, under President Modibo Keita, joined the Ghana–Guinea Alliance in 1960. However, practical problems of geography, language, and the emergence of competing regional groups with different ideologies (e.g., the Casablanca Group, the Brazzaville Group, and the Monrovia-Lagos Bloc) thwarted Nkrumah's efforts to form a federation of African states. Indeed, some African leaders then, including Milton Obote, Modibo Keita, and Leopold Sénghor, were concerned that Nkrumah might use his Pan-Africanism to interfere with their internal affairs. Nonetheless, initiatives in the early twenty-first century by the African Union (AU) to form an all-African federation not only attest to Nkrumah's prodigious foresight, but they also lend support to Nietzsche's famous aphorism that "some people are born posthumously." Additionally, Nkrumah was actively involved in the nonaligned movement, the United Nations, the Commonwealth, and the international peace movement. In fact, it was during a peace mission to Hanoi that he was overthrown in 1966.

Even though Nkrumah left an enduring positive legacy in Ghanaian and African politics, he was hardly a paragon of virtue. By the time of his overthrow, he was virtually running a one-man regime. Nonetheless, the fact that Nkrumah was a shrewd political leader in Ghana and a pacesetter in the African liberation struggle remains indubitable. His remarkable accomplishments earned him many international awards, including an Honorary Doctorate of Law from London University in 1957 and the International Lenin Peace Prize in 1962. Nkrumah lived in exile in Guinea, following his overthrow in 1966; he died in a hospital in Bucharest, Romania, on April 27, 1972, and was buried in his home town after state funerals in both Guinea and Ghana.

JOSEPH MENSAH

See also All-African Peoples Conference (AAPC); Ghana; Nyerere, Julius; Organization of African Unity (OAU); Pan-Africanism; Sénghor, Leopold; Touré, Sékou

References and Further Reading

Boateng, Charles Adom. *Nkrumah's Consciencism: An Ideology for Decolonization and Development.* Dubuque, Iowa: Kendall/Hunt Publishing Company, 1995.

Bretton, Henry, L. *The Rise and Fall of Kwame Nkrumah: A Study of Personal Rule in Africa.* New York, Washington, and London: Praeger, 1966.

Mbonjo, Pierre Moukoko. *The Political Thought of Kwame Nkrumah: A Comprehensive Presentation.* Lagos, Nigeria: University of Lagos Press, 1998.

McKown, Robin. *Nkrumah. A Biography.* New York: Doubleday, 1973.

Nkrumah, Kwame. *The Autobiography of Kwame Nkrumah.* New York: International Publishers, 1964.

———. *Consciencism: Philosophy and Ideology for Decolonisation and Development with Particular Reference to the African Revolution.* London: Heinemann, 1964.

———. *Revolutionary Path.* New York: International Publishers [posthumous], 1973.

———. *The Struggle Continues.* London: Panaf [posthumous], 1973.

Omari, T. Peter. *Kwame Nkrumah: The Anatomy of an African Dictator*, 2nd ed. New York: Africana Publishing Corporation, 1972.

Smertin, Yuri. *Kwame Nkrumah.* New York: International Publishers 1987; and Moscow: Progress Publishers, 1987.

NONALIGNED MOVEMENT

The end of the Second World War witnessed the polarization of the world into two power blocs—the Communist and the Western—and the beginning of the Cold War. Each bloc engaged in economic, cultural, political, and ideological warfare against the other and tried to draw the newly independent countries of Asia and Africa into its own camp. Owing to a widespread desire on the part of these newly independent countries to keep clear of superpower politics and to work jointly against imperialism and racialism, a movement against alignment developed. The Asian-African Conference held in

Bandung in 1955 may be considered a precursor of nonalignment.

The term "nonalignment" was used first by Jawaharlal Nehru, India's first prime minister and also the foreign minister who shaped India's policy of nonalignment and was a leader of the movement. He believed that India was too large a country to allow herself to be drawn into one or the other hostile camp, and would prefer to judge each issue as it arose on its own merit. Nehru felt this would help in creating an era of peace and preventing another world war. Another essential feature of nonalignment was a resolve to maintain friendly relations with all countries. By being nonaligned, moreover, the doors could be kept open to all possible sources of aid—Western and Soviet.

Western writers in particular have sometimes defined nonalignment as neutralism. In Nehru's view, however, nonalignment is not neutralism as that would mean not having an opinion on any issue and keeping neutral, which certainly India did not intend to do. As has been emphasized by the architects of nonalignment, among others, it goes beyond equidistance from power blocs or neutrality. It stands for a number of things, which it strove actively to promote: anti-imperialism, anti-racism, anti-neocolonialism, and peaceful coexistence of all countries. It also supports the right of every nation, no matter how small, to exist and progress without having to join the big powers. Beginning with the first summit meeting in Belgrade in 1961, the policy of nonalignment was institutionalized into a movement. In its early years, nonalignment was often looked upon with incomprehension and even hostility by the superpowers. But as the Cold War gave way to détente, it began to be viewed with tolerance, even approval, by the United States and the USSR.

The movement did have a regional emphasis, with most of its members from Asia and Africa, though the former Yugoslavia was an important European member country with Marshal Tito as one of the leaders of the movement.

An important development was that the nonaligned countries came to have a two-thirds majority in the United Nations by the 1960s. Given the deadlock in the Security Council as a result of superpower rivalry during the Cold War, the General Assembly (and the nonaligned member states who formed the majority here) was able to play a much greater role in international affairs—including in situations of crisis—than what had been originally envisioned. The nonaligned countries in turn looked upon the United Nations as the most representative forum (its goals also coincided with their own declared objectives) and at successive nonaligned conferences,

reiterated their commitment to upholding its principles and goals. Thus the nonaligned movement, or NAM, came to have a significant impact, even if it was not wholly successful, in resolving the Suez Crisis (1956), the Indochina conflict, and others. Through collective and consistent action in the General Assembly, it also managed to sensitize the world community with regard to a number of issues, including the apartheid system in South Africa.

In the 1970s the economic aspect of independence gained prominence in the NAM in a bid to right the perceived imbalances in the North–South economic relations. The call for a New International Economic Order (NIEO) crystallized in the UN resolution on NIEO in May of 1974. This was a call for restructuring international economic relations, including trade and technology transfer, to lessen the gulf between the developed and developing world. The nonaligned countries tried to achieve their economic goals through the Group of 77 and UNCTAD. Self-reliance and cooperation among countries of the South were emphasized.

The mid-1970s to the late-1980s were the period of the heyday of nonalignment. Starting with twenty-five members at the Belgrade summit in 1961, its membership rose to nearly one hundred. But it also began to appear that its principles were jeopardized due to sheer weight of numbers, as individual members used it to promote their narrow national and ideological interests. On other occasions, during developments in nonaligned countries in the Middle East, the horn of Africa, Afghanistan, and Indochina, these countries have taken distinctly partisan positions and thus revealed the bloc-wise position division within their own ranks.

On the whole, however, the movement was successful in keeping the nonaligned countries insulated from superpower rivalries. They were, over the years, able to strengthen the UN system and make it an important source of public opinion in international affairs.

In the aftermath of the collapse of the Soviet Union in 1989–1991, a development that left the United States at centrestage as the sole superpower, reservations were expressed in several quarters regarding the continued relevance of NAM, with the disappearance of bloc divisions and rivalry. But what must also be noted is that international relations have traveled a long way since the Cold War days. The world has come to have new, autonomous decision-making centers and a new sense of unpredictability permeates it.

At the same time many of the problems that then confronted the nonaligned countries still remain, along with some new ones. Therefore, the reason for continued solidarity also remains, albeit the basis of this may have to be reviewed. Since 1989 a new, cohesive group of fifteen countries (the G-15) has emerged in the NAM. It is meant to function as an institutional mechanism of interaction between the developing countries and the industrially advanced G-7. One of the items on its agenda is to undertake collective negotiations with the G-7, especially in view of the developments during the Uruguay Round of trade negotiations.

AMRITA SINGH

See also: Bandung Conference (1955); Nehru, Jawaharlal; New International Economic Order (NIEO)

References and Further Reading

Bandopadhyaya, J. *The Making of India's Foreign Policy*. New Delhi: Allied Publishers, 1984.
Brecher, Michael. *Nehru: A Political Biography*, 2nd ed. London: Oxford University Press, 1959.
Dutt, V. P. *India's Foreign Policy*. New Delhi: Vani, 1984.
Lyon, Peter Hazelip. *Neutralism*. Leicester, UK: Leicester University Press, 1963.
Nehru, Jawaharlal, *India's Foreign Policy*. Delhi: Publications Division, 1961.

NON-GOVERNMENTAL ORGANIZATIONS (NGOs)

Non-governmental organizations (NGOs) have come to occupy an indispensable position in the realm of development. The presence of NGOs since the Second World War has been conspicuous in most parts of the world. In particular, the growth of the sector has been significant in developing countries. They are known under a variety of names and are broadly grouped as the third sector. Voluntary agencies or organizations, action groups, private organizations, non-profit organizations, people's organizations, grassroots organizations, community organizations, self-help organizations, public service contractors, quasi-autonomous NGOs, and intermediary organizations are some of the popular names of NGOs.

Not only in number but also in terms of coverage, activities, and programmes, the growth of the sector has been quite impressive during the last few decades. NGOs have proven to be both a vital agency and a crucial link between people and development. Rough estimates indicate that NGOs reach 250 million poor people in the developing countries (Streeten 1997) and more than 20% of the official aid for development is now being channelled through NGOs in different countries.

The operations of the NGO sector in some developing countries in Asia and Latin America have achieved remarkable dimensions. In varying degrees of magnitude and activities, NGOs have a presence of their own in all Asian countries. India, for instance, is estimated to have the largest number of NGOs in the world (Lyons and Hasan 2002) with approximately 1.2 million organizations for a population of over one billion. Close to India is China, the most populous county, with about one million registered organizations (Young and Woo 2000, quoted in Lyons and Hasan 2002).

Defining NGOs

Since the coining of the term NGO, for the first time by the United Nations in 1945 and popularized in the following decades, it has undergone extensive changes both in the structure and activities at different levels in disparate locations. For the UN, an NGO is any international organization that is not established by inter-governmental agreement and that accepts members designated by governmental authorities, though such membership does not interfere with the free expressions of the organization. Nevertheless, the basic characteristic pertaining to its governance, which is typified in the name "non-governmental," has remained unchanged for the last 60 years.

Although consensus about an acceptable definition of NGOs is hard to arrive, one can draw at least three important components from the term. They are non-governmental, non-profit making, and voluntary organization. As NGOs are generally organizations that do not include governmental representatives or governments, governmental components are excluded from the definition (Martens 2002). This characteristic of NGOs does not preclude them from seeking some of their funds from government or governmental agencies. Since NGOs are also understood as organizations not seeking governmental power, political parties and organized political groups are excluded from the notion of NGOs (Martens 2002).

Importantly, the second element of non-profit making is rather relative vis-à-vis that of the profit-making corporate sector. This facet of NGOs has been undergoing changes from an exclusively voluntary nature to something more business-like, but not toward making profit from programmes and activities. From organized collectives, meant mostly for voluntary and unpaid services, NGOs have transformed into professionally competent and specialized entities to carry out specific tasks that require skills and expertise by employing paid professionals and experts. This transformation in fact has diluted the purely voluntary character of the NGOs, which was once the hallmark of such organizations. The loss of the purely voluntary nature of the NGOs is partly due to the resultant outcome of the growth that NGOs have been passing through from playing a charity and welfare role to resource providers (Hailey 1999). Members aspiring to join NGOs are now less motivated by their will to contribute to the declared objectives of NGOs on a voluntary basis or their concern for the marginalized and underprivileged sections of the society, but more because of the attractiveness of paid employment.

The most distinguishing feature of NGOs has been the element of voluntarism that motivated people to join such organizations for a specific purpose to achieve, often without the intention of getting paid but with a sense of commitment to the cause of the poor, the neglected, and the marginalized sections of the society. During the course of transformation of such solely voluntary-based organizations into more service-oriented, target-specific, and expert-driven modern NGOs, the spirit of voluntarism has given way to an attitude of pay for the work. NGOs are now service contractors, as Korten (1992) appropriately labels them. Still, they are non-governmental and non-profit organizations with the avowed purpose of providing services but are driven by market considerations rather than values. The new brand of NGOs is like other businesses rather than strictly voluntary organizations that pursue a social mission driven by a commitment to shared values (Korten, 1992). Nevertheless, they remain unique and distinct from the state and organs of the state meant to serve similar purposes.

The third component of "organization" in NGOs signifies that they can be distinguished from other groups or movements of less permanent organizational structure (Martens 2002). NGOs have more or less enduring organizational structures, members, offices, and funds to run them, making them formal institutions of a self-governing nature. Permanence cannot be treated as a universal trait of NGOs as many tend to disappear from the scene after achieving the objectives for which they had been originally formed or when their lifecycle has completed a circle. Sometimes they may take their new incarnation into a different form, or change to a different location with another set of objectives and functions.

Briefly, an NGO is a non-profit, organized group of people who do not seek any governmental office (Willetts 1996), managing with internally or externally raised funds and retaining their commitment to people and society as distinguishable from that of the state and state organizations.

Roles NGOs Play

NGOs have assumed an array of roles in development. They act as advocates, educators, catalysts, monitors, whistle blowers, mediators, lobbyists, activists, mobilizers of people and resources, protectors of human rights, conscientizers (stimulating consciences to correct injustices), animators, and conciliators, responding to the needs of the community and society at large. In developing countries, NGOs undertake initiatives that are often innovative and creative in nature to deal with issues related to poverty, literacy, education, health, unemployment, human rights, empowerment, sustainable development, conservation, the environment, and several other areas. Obviously, NGOs in developing countries have created their own niches, drawing support from the affected population and civil society but not without attracting resistance from the state.

Typology

NGOs are of different kinds. They can be classified into many categories, depending on the basis of the preferred criteria of classification. Based primarily on major functions and activities, they are broadly grouped into consulting NGOs, welfare NGOs, development NGOs, and advocacy NGOs (Bowden 1990). They are also classified as project-based NGOs, national NGOs, international NGOs, and network NGOs (Conyers and Kaul 1990). If origin is the basis, NGOs are either self-initiated or externally supported (Avina 1993). The self-generating ones are usually small organizations that begin with limited internal financing, at least in the initial stages of formation, with moderate goals that are grounded in the immediate needs and resources of the community wherein they are located. In comparison, the externally supported NGOs are built around the locally perceived needs, promoting an externally designed development approach. Organizationally, they benefit from outside technical assistance, field experience of the founding organization, and the political or economic leverage of the founding organization (Avina 1993). In some developing countries, large-scale organizations of the latter kind have outweighed the self-generated ones. There are also cases of self-generated NGOs becoming the second category in the immediate stages of growth due to the availability of and dependency on funds for their activities.

NGOs can be delineated from civil society organizations (CSOs), which inhabits the area between individuals (or families) and the state (Blair 1997). As the UNDP definition goes,

> Civil society is, together with state and market, one of the three "spheres" that interface in the making of democratic societies. The organizations of civil society, which represent many diverse and sometimes contradictory social interests, are shaped to fit their social base, constituency, thematic orientations (e.g., environment, gender, human rights) and types of activity. They include church-related groups, trade unions, cooperatives, service organizations, community groups and youth organizations, as well as academic institutions and others. (Bebbington and Riddell 1997)

In other words, while all CSOs are NGOs, all NGOs are not CSOs (Blair 1997).

Origin, Growth, and Lifecycle

In normal circumstances, the origin, growth, and development of NGOs are determined and facilitated by a set of internal and external factors. External ones are those chiefly rooted in the socioeconomic, cultural, and political settings, whereas the internal ones, which are more relevant in the phases of growth than origin, concern all those factors that fall within the organization. Necessarily, the emergence of NGOs varies from context to context and country to country, influenced by the above internal and external factors.

Importantly, the origin, growth, and development or the lifecycle of NGOs can be portrayed through four stages of startup, expansion, consolidation, and closeout (Avina 1993). All these four stages are not mandatory for the NGOs to follow in a rigid fashion. Some may skip the stages, choosing an entirely different route, while some might follow all the four stages in order. An organization that closes its functioning for some reason may begin its operations later in a different locality. Similarly, an NGO that closes out its operations in one area may start new programmes elsewhere, and thus closing out and starting up would happen simultaneously.

In developing countries, the lifecycle of NGOs generally starts with the attempts of an inspired founder or a group of individuals of similar interests. Focussing on NGOs in India, which has the largest sector of organizations in the world, Radhakrishna (1993) concludes that in the first ten years of existence, the organization struggles hard. If everything goes well, it reaches a plateau or a peak of high quality of work in the second decade. The organization at this stage attracts recognition. At the end of the second decade, as the leadership moves to the next generation, new problems crop up and there are chances for organizational deterioration within the organization. This may be due to several reasons: the expansion of the organization to other geographical spots, proliferation of activities and programmes, the generation gap between the founder leader (or group of leaders) and the current workers, vested interests, alienation between the organization and the community it is meant to serve, increasing bureaucratization within the organization, indifference to the socioeconomic and political changes that happen in the society, increasing demands of the workers for more benefits and unionization, and the pains and pangs of transition. This stage, with the oncoming of organizational difficulties, is a critical period for the life of any organization. Either there is reaffirmation of earlier goals and objectives by the new leadership or redefinition of roles in the changed context. If the opportunities are missed, the graph goes down like an inverted "U" called a hyperbole.

NGOs and Government

NGOs are sometimes viewed in juxtaposition to the state and state agencies, primarily because of the efficiency with which the programmes of NGOs are designed and implemented. Numerous are the advantages for NGOs vis-à-vis that of the state and state agencies. NGOs are known for their proximity to people, responsiveness to needs, sensitivity to the immediate needs, flexibility, micro-based programmes and smaller constituencies of activities, inexpensive strategies that lead to appropriate programmes, people-centeredness, participatory and personalised approach to the problems, and the ability to invent solutions. Compared to the government and other formal agencies, NGOs are more adaptable, sensitive to local conditions, and better suited to work with the poor (Streeten 1997). Within NGOs there is a perceptible lack of bureaucratic rigidity. Flexibility allows NGOs to tailor programmes and services that suit the requirements of the beneficiaries and the communities for whom they are intended for (Salamon 1987). Micro-level operations enable them to define their constituencies and standpoints clearly and work toward innovative solutions to deal with the issues they have chosen to address (Korten 1992). Innovative experiments have often been successfully carried out by NGOs in different locations and in several areas of development that directly affect the lives of the poor and the needy. In community health, indigenous medicine, evolving techniques of delivery of services to the poor in remote destinations (Bhatt 1995), microfinance, and in mobilizing workers in the informal sector, to take a sample, the innovative and creative spirit and strategies of NGOs have been evident.

Placed parallel to NGOs, the state is typified as inefficient, hampered by bureaucracy, and in the control of self-interested politicians (Clark 1997; Robinson 1997). On the other hand, NGOs ensure that the people, the vulnerable groups in particular, are involved in the process of decision making (Clark 1997). Quite often it is the NGOs that begin to venture out into areas where immediate attention is required, even before government agencies start thinking of it (Salamon 1987). NGOs can therefore serve as a test-bed for new ideas and methodologies that are difficult for the government and business sectors to experiment with (Korten 1992). They have successfully acted as a sounding board for government policies and programmes as well. NGOs make use of the scanty resources available at their disposal in a more economic, efficient, and appropriate way than the state tends to do. Due to the talents and expertise that the NGO sector attracts, combined with a heightened sense of commitment among the workers and the staff, the innovative and enterprising spirit for finding solutions to the problems of the society are always kept alive and encouraged. Time and again, the innovative experiments tested and implemented by NGOs have proven to be instrumental in influencing governmental policies in a desirable direction, benefiting the neglected and the marginalized. NGOs do play their advocacy role effectively in areas where interventions are warranted. Illustrations from varied locations are numerous. Naturally, these achievements bring accolades to NGOs as trailblazers, whistle blowers, pioneers, and creative inventors.

NGO-Government Partnership

Individual advantages and disadvantages, merits and demerits, or strengths and weaknesses of NGOs and the government do not necessarily prevent both from entering into partnerships to achieve common goals and objectives of development. Partnership has been promoted as a solution to attaining efficiency and effectiveness (Brinkerhoff 2002). It acts as a mechanism to combine the advantages of both the partners, namely the NGOs and the government, in the delivery of services to the people. Working in collaboration for commonly agreed and accepted objectives through jointly designed strategies and programmes, within the ambience of mutual understanding and recognition of the strengths and weaknesses of the involved partners, NGO–government partnership has

accomplished significant feats in development. The major advantage of this partnership is that it can provide a better service than either partner could provide on its own (Salamon 1987).

NGO–government partnership is apparent in a range of forms: monetary assistance, institutional support, policy formulation, a policy of cooption bringing opposition opinion into the mix, and adoption and application of innovative endeavours. Partnership is bound to be country-specific and subject to societal characteristics as well as the character and nature of NGOs and the government (Clark 1997). The success of NGO–government partnership depends largely on factors such as the attitude of the government officials and the NGOs toward striking such a partnership, the degree of encouragement from both the partners, direction and selection of relevant NGO partners (Clark 1997), and the exigency of needs that necessitate immediate action (such as the united action demanded by unforeseen natural calamities and disasters).

Successful partnership experiences reported from developing countries demonstrate that NGO–government collaboration works effectively with specific programmes that entail some sort of urgency on the part of the people and the state. Time-bound, specific programmes are likely to be more successful under a partnership venture than in a permanent partnership relation within a formal institutional structure. As cases illustrate, adequate financial support from the government motivates NGOs to enter into partnerships and the same monetary supports work as a prerequisite for the successful completion of the ventures undertaken in partnership. NGOs need financial resources, though they have the skills, expertise, and other resources essential for delivering goods efficiently.

Partnership programmes at the same time depend greatly on the government in power, especially its political ideology and commitment to the disadvantaged and deserving sections of the population. Importantly, this political dimension shapes the willingness and cooperation on the part of NGOs who have chosen to work for similar but agreed objectives with the government.

Partnership becomes a positive activity when governmental agencies shed their rigidity and change themselves into a pro-people apparatus, at least for the sake of achieving the agreed objectives with the NGOs. Partly due to the time-bound nature of the programme and the immediate concerns of both the partners, bureaucratic delays give way to expediency. Partnership endeavours should not be restricted to securing financial assistance alone as they also demand participation, sharing, and involvement of the partners in matters of skills, capabilities, and readiness to make the partnership effective and useful for the people.

What benefits do partnerships bring to the partners concerned? Partnership programmes can influence the official structures in bringing about greater transparency, responsiveness (Clark 1997), and enhanced sensitivity of the bureaucracy to the immediate requirements of the people. In return, NGOs gain benefits in the form of better awareness about strategic planning and the macro-level concerns of the government.

Yet, there are imminent strains, difficulties, and dangers in NGO–government alliances. For the NGOs, partnership programmes might create tension and conflict at various levels: between their service role and advocacy role, and between their role as deliverers of government-funded services and their role as critics of government and private policies (Salamon 1987). Salamon (1987) cautions about three potential dangers in this alliance. Heavy reliance on governmental support, firstly, can lead to the loss of autonomy of the NGOs. Secondly, it can lead to "vendorism," or the distortion of the mission of the NGOs in pursuit of governmental support. Finally, there is the danger of bureaucratization and over-professionalization due to government programmes and accounting requirements as the government officials are more concerned about the problems of management supervision, accountability, and authority. The involvement in government programmes impinges on the prominent features of NGOs such as their reliance on volunteers, their sense of independence, and their usual informal and non-bureaucratic character in their dealings with people (Salamon 1987). At the same time, neither the replacement of voluntary sector by the government, nor the replacement of the government by the voluntary sector makes as much sense as their collaboration (Salamon 1987).

Issues

The commendable role played by the NGO sector in developing countries and the recognition it has earned for being influential in the processes of development do not rule out the potential for difficulties and problems that emanate from both within and outside the sector. Internally, NGOs confront problems relating to their objectives (original as well as the added ones in the later stages of growth and expansion), ideology, perceptions on organizational concerns, organizational matters, leadership, management, volunteers, paid workers, staff programmes,

resources, and the like. As NGOs are established with specific goals and objectives, the raison d' être is likely to vary and therefore, the strategies and programmes are bound to differ from NGO to NGO. It is also possible that organizations with similar objectives can have an altogether different orientation and programmes to achieve the same.

The objectives with which NGOs begin to work are often subjected to change when they grow in size, programmes, and institutional complexity. In this process that brings about changes in the originally envisaged objectives, NGOs are likely to miss the link between objectives, programmes, and beneficiaries. When this link is misplaced or lost, incongruity between objectives, programmes, and beneficiaries occurs. If the objectives conceived at the inception of NGOs are not allied with appropriate strategies, there can be problems in achieving their original objectives. More often than not, it is the availability of projects and funds that compels NGOs to deviate from the originally designed goals and programmes, motivating them to take up the new ones in tune with the prescriptions of donors for funded projects. It does not imply that NGOs should keep themselves away from constantly identifying new objectives and programmes during the course of their existence. Any new objective, which may be the result of the understanding of the changing contexts or needs of the people, should seriously take into account the resources available within the organization. Perhaps this incongruity explains why the "implementation gap" between what is planned and what is implemented is very great among the NGOs in developing countries (Turner and Hulme 1997).

NGOs accept projects designed by sponsors (Avina 1993) and statutory agencies, reducing their role to that of an intermediary. More than one-third of the funds of NGOs comes from official donors (Streeten 1997). NGOs look up to the funding agencies for tailor-made programmes by changing themselves into implementing agencies of the donors, or as Korten (1992) calls them, "public service contractors." For a number of reasons, there are regular pressures on the modern NGOs to become public service contractors. Korten's (1992) list includes:

- The fatigue of constantly existing at the margin of financial survival and the attraction of donor funding;
- The strain faced by more activist organizations who must constantly fight established interests, values, and practices;
- The difficulty of maintaining the value consensus and commitment of the organization as the organization grows in size;

- Moral obligation to provide job security for the paid staff of the organization; and
- The belief that contracting will bring in more funds and therefore it will be possible for the organization to do more things.

In these circumstances, the primary concern of the organization shifts from people to the mere survival of the organization with an uninterrupted inflow of funds. NGOs of this kind assume new responsibilities where financial assistance is easy to obtain. When the motive becomes the continued existence of the organizations through a regular flow of funds and new projects, NGOs fail to adopt better management skills for effective functioning. Obsolete management techniques keep the organization at a level from which it cannot grow in tune with the changing times. Tailor-made projects limit the scope for indigenous and innovative strategies as they usually come with a specific package of management guidelines suited only for specific purposes. Programmes and approaches lose urgency and appropriateness as they are planned more in consideration of the source and availability of funds and benefits to the organization than the benefits the projects would bring to the beneficiaries (Sooryamoorthy and Gangrade 2001).

Funded projects and closeness to donors also have consequences on the lifecycle and the functioning of NGOs. Apparently, the birth of NGOs is not always closely linked to the needs of the people or the community where they start their operations. Rather, as is the case in some Asian countries like India, they remain to be self-employment ventures of the founder and his or her team. Easy availability and flow of external funds, in turn, develops problems such as alienation and isolation of organizations, making them more secretive in their nature and function (Radhakrishna 1993). This in due course takes its toll on the transparency and accountability of NGOs. On another front, too, the consequence of this is obvious: well-established NGOs can monopolize the flow of funds to them, limiting the resources for the relatively new and smaller organizations (Salamon 1987).

The shift from people-oriented work to project-oriented activities is more vivid now among the NGOs in developing countries. The dependency of NGOs on government and international donors has not only affected the autonomy of the organizations but has also become counterproductive in their expected role as advocates and lobbyists, leading NGOs to assume the characters of governmental appendages.

On the other hand, an increasing number of organizations in South Asia and Latin America are now diversifying their sources of funding and generating their own income from a mixture of commercial ventures, cost recovery, and local fundraising (Edwards et al. 1999). This kind of change toward resource mobilization would eventually help the NGOs to assume more of the characteristics of a genuine civic actor rather than a service delivery contractor (Edwards et al. 1999).

Structural changes are also part of the consequences of flow of external funds and greater dependency on them. NGOs begin to grow institutionally. Informal type of functioning gives way to a more formalized and complex set of procedures and structures. Presence of professionals and experts in NGOs, predominance of paid workers over volunteers, well-paid staff, and projects designed and supported by donors become the salient characteristics of modern NGOs. Institutionalization correspondingly brings in changes in the approach and attitude of the workers. Although not necessarily stated, new rules and norms are put in place for adherence. The changed setup may require the volunteers and paid workers to work according to a time-bound schedule. Strategies are predesigned and guidelines of the sponsors are followed, undermining the role of the people and the workers in choosing the appropriate ones. As the NGO grows into a more complex institutionalized structure, the workers wish for the NGO to become a permanent body that would protect their interests as workers. In other words, the workers want the NGOs to act more like an employer than an agency that brings developmental opportunities to the people. In India, for instance, there are twenty million paid and voluntary workers in 1.2 million NGOs, contributing 14.8% to the gross national product of the country.

At times NGOs carry on with several programmes simultaneously without considering their structural and functional limitations such as the relevance and usefulness of the programmes, the benefits the programmes could bring to the people, and the infrastructure and resources at their disposal. Efforts are made in such a way that no opportunity to start a new assisted programme is lost. In this process NGOs lose their credibility and efficiency. Empirical studies have revealed that the organizations that undertake and run several programmes concurrently would register a low member-accountability vis-à-vis the organizations that concentrate on a single programme at a time (Smith-Sreen 1995).

Sometimes NGOs are silenced by the mechanism of cooption (Tandon, 1988), particularly when they become critical of governmental policies and programmes, and when they play their advocacy role. Cooption happens in many ways: allocating funds for NGO programmes, and offering respectable positions in government bodies with perks and privileges are some of the means by which NGO workers are coopted. Cooption can come not only from those in power but also from other political actors; including the opposition, as happened in some Arab countries. For them, NGOs are instruments that can be used for the extension of political support and influence.

Conclusion

For the last few decades, NGOs have been playing a very vital but active role in several realms of human life. NGOs have proven to be an indispensable player in developmental programmes affecting the majority of the population scattered in different continents. They have ventured into new areas of activities and have proven themselves to be effective and successful players. This is evident in the growth the sector has achieved over the years. The growth of the sector has been incredible, particularly in some developing countries. For instance, in India and Brazil the number of organizations has grown to one million and 210,000 respectively (Salamon and Anheier 1997). But the spread of NGOs across developing countries is neither uniform nor even. This unevenness, to some extent, is due to reasons of political stability and the presence (or absence) of democracy.

In reality, the roles NGOs take up, variations in contexts and needs notwithstanding, are seldom played in a cordial and complimentary atmosphere, as many of them are critical of state policies that adversely affect the people. Democratic structures and qualities of a nation serve as a determinant factor in providing a conducive and fertile ground for NGOs to take root. African countries in general, for instance, are not offering an encouraging environment for the growth of NGOs, which is attributed to the poor economic performance, limited legitimacy, and cultural heterogeneity that exist in such countries (Dicklitch 1998). In relation to the population, the number of NGOs in most African countries is disproportionate and their role has been confined to filling the gaps left by the withdrawal of the regimes or working in collaboration with the regime to further the objectives of the regime. Although the regimes accept funding from international NGOs, they do not welcome overly political or advocacy-oriented NGOs to their countries. While accepting NGOs as partners in development, the regimes also want to control them through a variety of forms, using their authoritarian, autocratic, and coercive political powers. Things are changing, however, in countries like South Africa where democracy has taken root since 1994.

Despite adverse conditions at the operational level, the element of volunteerism and commitment to social ideals, coupled with innovative programmes and strategies, have enabled NGOs to offer an alternative to the people. In the changing but challenging global situation, the NGO sector will be taking up more and more new roles to serve the people who are sidelined in the process of development and globalisation. Moving from the level of organizations acting at micro levels to dealing with the immediate needs of the society, NGOs are now becoming broad-based organizations. Networking with like-minded NGOs has helped the NGOs to establish links and extend their activities and programmes to new territories. In several developing countries, they are performing more strategic and lobbying functions. This is evident in their lobbying power of the international financial institutions, monitoring of international commitments (like Social Watch), and the democratisation of global economic and other regimes (for example, the WTO) (Edwards et al. 1999). One would naturally hope that in the coming years the NGO sector will be taking over more and more new functions that were hitherto performed by the state, and bring in the fruits of development to the deserving majority.

RADHAMANY SOORYAMOORTHY

References and Further Reading

Avina, Jeffrey. "The Evolutionary Life Cycles of Non-Governmental Development Organisations." *Public Administration and Development* 13, no. 5 (1993): 453–74.

Bebbington, Anthony and Roger Riddell. "Heavy Hands, Hidden Hands, Holding Hands? Donors, Intermediary NGOs and Civil Society Organisations." *In NGOs, States and Donors: Too Close for Comfort?* edited by David Hulme and Michael Edwards. New York: St. Martin's Press, 1997.

Bhatt, Anil. "Voluntary Action in India: Roles, Trends and Challenges." *Economic and Political Weekly* 30, no. 16 (1995): 870–873.

Blair, Harry. "Donors, Democratisation, and Civil Society: Relating Theory to Practice." In *NGOs, States and Donors: Too Close for Comfort?* edited by David Hulme and Michael Edwards. New York: St. Martin's Press, 1997.

Bowden, P. "NGOs in Asia: Issues in Development." *Public Administration and Development* 10, no. 2 (1990): 141–152.

Brinkerhoff, Jennifer M. "Government-Nonprofit Partnership: A Defining Framework." *Public Administration and Development* 22, no. 1 (2002): 19–30.

Clark, John. "The State, Popular Participation and the Voluntary Sector." In *NGOs, States and Donors: Too Close for Comfort?* edited by David Hulme and Michael Edwards. New York: St. Martin's Press, 1997.

Conyers, Diane and Mohan Kaul. "Issues in Development Management: Learning from Successful Experience." *Public Administration and Development* 10, no. 3 (1990): 289–298.

Dicklitch, Susan. *The Elusive Promise of NGOs in Africa: Lessons from Uganda.* New York: St. Martin's Press, 1998.

Edwards, Michael, David Hulme, and Tina Wallace. "NGOs in a Global Future: Marrying Local Delivery to Worldwide Leverage." *Public Administration and Development* 19, no. 2 (1999): 117–136.

Hailey, John. "Ladybirds, Missionaries and NGOs, Voluntary Organizations and Co-Operatives in 50 Years of Development: A Historical Perspective on Future Challenges." *Public Administration and Development* 19, no. 5 (1999): 467–485.

Korten, David C. *Getting to the Twenty-First Century: Voluntary Action and the Global Agenda.* New Delhi: Oxford & IBH Publishing, 1992.

Lyons, Mark and Samiul Hasan. "Researching Asia's Third Sector." *Voluntas* 13, no. 2 (2002): 107–112.

Martens, Kerstin. "Mission Impossible? Defining Nongovernmental Organizations." *Voluntas* 13, no. 3 (2002): 271–284.

Radhakrishna. "Voluntary Agencies in a Critical Decade." *Gandhi Marg* 15, no. 3 (1993): 287–297.

Robinson, Mark. "Privatising the Voluntary Sector: NGOs as Public Service Contractors?" In *NGOs, States and Donors: Too Close for Comfort?* edited by David Hulme and Michael Edwards. New York: St.Martin's Press, 1997.

Salamon, Lester M. "Of Market Failure, Voluntary Failure, and Third-Party Government: Toward a Theory of Government-Non-Profit Relations in the Modern Welfare State." *Journal of Voluntary Action Research* 16, no. 1 and 2 (1987): 29–49.

Salamon, Lester M. and H. Anheier. *The Nonprofit Sector in the Developing World.* Manchester, UK: Manchester University Press, 1997.

Smith-Sreen, Poonam. *Accountability in Development Organisations: Experiences of Women's Organizations in India.* New Delhi: Sage, 1995.

Sooryamoorthy, R. and K. D. Gangrade. *NGOs in India: A Cross-Sectional Study, Contributions in Sociology.* Westport, CT: Greenwood Press, 2001.

Streeten, Paul. "Nongovernmental Organizations and Development." *ANNALS AAPSS* 554 (1997): 193–210.

Tandon, Rajesh. "Growing Stateism." *Seminar*, no. 348 (1988): 16–20.

Turner, M. and D. Hulme. *Governance, Administration and Development: Making the State Work.* London: Palgrave, 1997.

Willetts, P. "Introduction." In *The Conscience of the World: The Influence of Non-Governmental Organizations in the UN System*, edited by P. Willetts, 1–14. London: Hurst, 1996.

NORTH AFRICA: HISTORY AND ECONOMIC DEVELOPMENT

North Africa: The Region

Although there is little consensus on a clear delineation of geographical and political boundaries for the Near East, Middle East, and North Africa, for the purposes of this essay the region of North Africa refers to five countries: Algeria, Egypt, Libya, Morocco, and Tunisia. North Africa is the region north of the Sahara Desert, largely surrounded by water on three sides: the Atlantic Ocean to the west, the Mediterranean Sea to the north, and the Red Sea to the east. The vast Sahara Desert has traditionally separated North Africa from the rest of the African continent. Beginning in the west, the Atlas Mountains run from Morocco to Tunisia. The high peaks of the Atlas produce considerable rainfall. On the northern slopes, flowing rivers produce fertile lands for agriculture and forests. The majority of Moroccans can be found living in the foothills and fertile farmland, valleys, and plateaus stretching from the mountains to the coast. The tallest peak in the Atlas Mountains is Mount Toubkal in southwestern Morocco, reaching a height of 13,665 feet. The mountains are also rich in minerals, including phosphates, lead, zinc, and iron ore. Approximately, 20% of Morocco's land is arable. Earthquakes occasionally strike in the northern mountains. Years of neglect have posed environmental threats of desertification, water supply contamination, and pollution of coastal waters.

Moving eastward to the second-largest country in Africa, we reach Algeria, which comprises a terrain of mostly high plateau and desert. Only about 3% of this country, which is about 3.5 times the size of Texas, is arable. The climate is arid, summers are hot and dry, and winters can be wet and cold. Earthquakes also occur in the mountainous region, and mudslides and floods can strike in the rainy season. Soil erosion, desertification, and industrial pollution have contributed to a neglected ecosystem. Algeria's natural resources include phosphates, iron ore, lead, zinc uranium, petroleum, and natural gas.

Directly east is Libya, which is comparable in size to Alaska. Most of Libya's flat and barren land is inhospitable, given to dust and sand storms. Only 1% of Libya can be farmed. Libya's dry terrain and shortage of fresh water resources have led to the country's investment in the largest water development program in the world, the Great Manmade River Project, designed to tap into ice age water reserves trapped in sandstone beneath the Sahara and pump the water to coastal cities. Oil and natural gas are plentiful in Libya. Like the rest of North Africa, desertification is cause for environmental concern.

In contrast to its two huge neighbors, Tunisia is a tiny country about the size of the US state of Georgia, snuggled in the north between Algeria and Libya on the tip of North Africa, just southwest of Sicily. Approximately 18% of Tunisia's land is arable. Northern Tunisia is mild and rainy in the winter, and hot and arid in the summer. The mountains of the north give way to the Sahara Desert in the south. The land produces phosphates, iron ore, lead, zinc, and petroleum. Improper hazardous waste disposal is now posing health issues. Soil erosion, desertification, and water pollution are additional environmental concerns.

Egypt is the easternmost country in North Africa. The Red Sea, Israel, and Gaza border it on the east, and Sudan on the south. Because over 90% of the country is barren desert, the majority of Egyptians live along the Nile River, which runs south to north and has served as the lifeblood of Egypt for thousands of years. East of the river is the Sinai Peninsula, a huge triangular desert region, home to Mount Sinai and Mount Katherine. The pinnacle of Mount Katherine represents Egypt's highest point at 8,625 feet. Although Egypt is large, about three times the size of New Mexico, less than 3% of the country can be farmed. The land is hot and dry and receives very little rainfall. The winters are moderate with an average temperature during the day of about seventy degrees. Egypt's natural resources are iron ore, phosphates, limestone, gypsum, lead, zinc, natural gas, and petroleum. The country is prone to earthquakes, flash floods, dust storms, and sandstorms. Water pollution from oil, industry, and pesticides now threaten the coastal region. Desertification and soil salination are also environmental concerns.

These five countries all share a common and interlocking heritage, culture, history, and religion. All are Arab countries, meaning the majority of the population speaks a dialect of Arabic. With the exception of Egypt, the Berber language is spoken by some 12 million people across North Africa. The Berbers share an ethnic heritage that stretches back to about 2400 BC, thousands of years before Arabs arrived in the seventh century AD. The newly arriving Arabs of that period brought Arabic and Islam with them. Today the social fabric of North Africa is cut from the cloth of Islamic heritage. Although geographically lying on the African continent, culturally and politically, North Africa is intimately linked with the Middle East and the rest of the Arab world.

History

The modern history of North Africa is closely linked with that of the West and is largely a product of European colonial endeavors in the region.

By the beginning of WWII, tension surfaced between the ruling class of one million European, primarily French, colonists and the nine million Algerian Muslims. The French colonial history of Algeria was characterized by inequality that left the most fertile, and highly coveted, farmland and governing authority in the hands of colonists. This inequality created profound bitterness between the two groups. Algerian nationalism began to take the form of a growing Islamic movement intent on expanding Algerian independence and assimilation. The Algerian masses wanted complete equality with their colonial rulers.

During WWII, many Algerian Muslims fought alongside the French. In 1945 after the war, Algerian nationalists celebrating the Allied victory, displayed an Algerian flag at a city called Setif. A series of ensuing scuffles with the French police soon escalated into a massacre of some ninety colonists. The French military reacted by brutally killing more than 1,500 Algerian civilians. In November 1954, the National Liberation Front (FLN), an indigenous resistance organization, initiated a series of assaults on police and government targets. Within a year, the FLN's membership had swollen from twenty to approximately two thousand. In August of 1955, Algerian Muslims revolted and slaughtered 123 men, women, and children at Phillipville. The French military retaliated by massacring thousands of Algerians. Over the next year in an effort to eliminate the FLN, French authorities launched a campaign of arrests and torture of known Algerian nationalists. As violence escalated in August 1956, the French targeted a bomb factory at 3 Theves Street that killed eighty civilians. The following month, Algerians retaliated by bombing three civilian targets. Far from discouraging extremists, the French actions forced many moderate Muslims to sympathize with the FLN. By 1957, the resistance fighters had risen to nearly twenty-five thousand as violence escalated. Half a million French troops eventually quelled the rebellion and drove a debilitated FLN into rural areas.

The news of French brutalities in Algeria generated a huge anti-war movement at home in 1958, as the French publicly protested these human rights violations. War hero Charles de Gaulle, who was elected president of France in 1959, negotiated a truce in 1962, and Algerians voted for independence in a referendum. De Gaulle proclaimed Algeria an independent nation, and all but thirty thousand Europeans left Algeria over the next year.

Algerian World War II hero and FLN militant leader, Ben Bella, assumed the premiership in 1962 and was elected president the following year. But struggles in Algeria were far from over. Houari Boumedienne, Ben Bella's defense minister, staged a coup against the president in 1965. For the next fifteen years Ben Bella remained under house arrest until he left the country in 1980.

Between 1972 and 1974 the price of crude oil quadrupled from $3 a barrel to $12. Many Arab oil-producing nations reacted to the 1973 War in Israel by placing an embargo on nations that supported Israel. The resulting Arab Oil Embargo produced shortages in supply for those countries. The Iranian revolution further decreased production, driving the price of crude from $14 in 1978 a barrel to $35 in 1981. In the mid-1980s the price of crude oil dropped to below $10.

Algeria as a member of OPEC has the fourteenth largest natural reserves of oil. It ranks fifth in natural gas reserves and is second in natural gas exportation. The oil boom of the 1970s and early 1980s yielded huge profits for Algeria, and as a result it enjoyed a vibrant economy. The plummeting prices in the mid-1980s, however, took their toll on the Algerian economy. In the early 1990s, Algeria's economy improved due to rescheduling of foreign debt and economic policy reforms supported by the World Bank and International Monetary Fund (IMF).

In 1991, an Islamic extremist movement known as the Islamic Salvation Front (FIS) won the first round of general and presidential elections, gaining 188 of the 231 seats in parliament. The military and the FLN—which won only fifteen seats—canceled the second round of elections, banned the FIS, and arrested a number of its members. A backlash of violence broke out and evolved into a civil war in 1992. Islamic extremists assassinated Mohammed Boudiaf, the newly elected president of Algeria, the same year. In 1999 amnesty was granted to many armed militants, and in 2000 the Islamic Salvation Army, the armed wing of the FIS, was disbanded. The civil war claimed an estimated one hundred thousand lives.

Thousands of Italian colonists settled in Libya in the 1930s. Libya became part of Italy in 1939 and served as a major battleground in World War II. The Allied forces defeated and replaced the Axis powers in Libya in 1943. The postwar Libyan economy was broken. The country's infant mortality rate reached 40% while the literacy rate dropped to 10%. Although the United Nations granted Libya independence in 1951, the West continued to exert its influence in Libya.

British-supported King Idris granted the British permission to establish military bases on Libyan soil. The United States began using Wheelus Field as an Air Force base in 1943 after the British 8th Army captured it from the Germans. The United Kingdom of Libya was granted independence in 1951. Libya went on to align itself with the West through the adoption of the Eisenhower Doctrine in 1957. The doctrine, designed to counter the growing expansionist efforts of the Soviet Union, committed the United States to military action to protect allies in the Middle East.

The discovery of oil in Libya in 1958 changed the dynamics between the former Italian colony and the West. Over the next decade, the state's revenue vastly increased as its dependence on foreign subsidies diminished. In 1964 Libya expelled most of the British military although a handful of British and US forces remained. In 1969 Colonel Muammar Qaddafi led a group of military officers in a bloodless coup d'etat to overthrow the monarchy of King Idris. Qaddafi crafted a type of Islamic socialist rule over Libya, which emphasized social services and public-owned industry, on the one hand, and nominal Islamic values—such as proscribing alcohol and gambling—on the other. During the early years of his rule, Qaddafi seemed to pacify Washington with his ardent anti-Soviet policies. In the years to follow, Qaddafi instituted a set of policies on oil, terrorism, Israel, and the Soviet Union that served to alienate Libya from the United States. In 1973 the Libyan leader supported Arab forces in the Arab–Israeli War. After the war, Qaddafi campaigned to impose an oil embargo against Israel's supporters. Qaddafi subsequently supported the Palestinian Liberation Organization (PLO) and sought to warm relations with the Soviet Union. Throughout the 1970s and 1980s, Libya was implicated in a number of terrorist activities, including support for the "Black September Movement" responsible for the massacre at the 1972 Olympics in Munich, Germany.

In 1982 the United States banned the import of Libyan oil and the export of US petrochemical technology to Libya. Accusing Qaddafi of supporting terrorism, US President Ronald Reagan launched a brief bombing campaign against suspected terrorist sites in Tripoli and Benghazi in 1986. The attack killed sixty people including Qaddafi's young daughter. Two years later, Libya was linked to the terrorist bombing of a Pan Am airliner over Lockerbie, Scotland, that killed 270 people. The United Nations imposed sanctions against the North African nation in 1992. Finally in 2003, Libya assumed responsibility for the Lockerbie disaster after two of its government employees were implicated in the bombing. Qaddafi also established a $2.7-billion fund to compensate families of each victim in the Lockerbie bombing. As a result, the UN lifted sanctions in September 2003.

After the fall of Saddam Hussein in 2003, Qaddafi publicly unveiled his nation's weapons of mass destruction program and invited international inspectors to dismantle it. The inspectors subsequently began identifying and destroying Libya's chemical and nuclear weaponry. In light of Qaddafi's recent reversal in position, the United States took steps to normalize relations with Libya in 2004.

During World War II, the British used Egypt as a center of operations in North Africa. The war ended in 1945. Three years later, in May 1948, Egypt sent troops to Palestine to bolster Iraqi, Lebanese, Palestinian, and Syrian fighters in an effort to defeat the newly declared Israeli state in the First Arab–Israeli War. The Israeli troops, primarily comprising Haganah soldiers who had gained experience in WWII, defeated the Arab forces. Egypt succeeded in gaining control over the Gaza Strip.

Against the backdrop of the humiliating Arab defeat in the war and widespread Egyptian discontent with Israel, the West, and Egyptian monarchy, Gamal Abdul Nasser led the Free Officers—a group of revolutionary military officers—in a coup that ousted King Farouk in the Egyptian Revolution of July 1952. Later, Nasser assumed the premiership by arresting General Muhammad Naguib. Two years later, Nasser ran uncontested for the presidency and won. Although Nasser's regime brutally repressed his opponents—most notably, communists and Islamic militants—his popularity in the Arab world soared. Nasser came to represent the epitome of the defiant Arab leader who resisted Western pressure.

Preying on US fears that Egypt would align itself with the Soviet Union, Nasser accepted US support in a project to construct the Aswan High Dam in 1956. The same year, the Egyptian leader later turned to the Soviets for weapons after the United States refused sell Egypt arms. As a result, US President Dwight Eisenhower announced his withdrawal of aid for the dam project. In a speech one week later, Nasser sent the coded message *Ferdinand de Lesseps* to Egyptian troops to seize the Suez Canal. Nasser proceeded to nationalize the canal and oust British officials from the country. British and French powers, seeking to protect their financial investments in the canal, plotted with the Israelis to attack Egypt. In October 1956, the Second Arab–Israeli War erupted when Israel invaded the Sinai. When Nasser refused British and French demands to withdraw troops from the canal zone, the Western powers bombed Egyptian military targets. Moscow and Washington responded by pressuring the invading forces to withdraw, and Nasser surfaced as a champion of the Arab world for his defiance toward the West.

In 1958, Nasser merged Egypt with Syria in an effort to create a Pan-Arab state. Nasser served as president of the new entity, called the United Arab Republic, with Cairo as its capital. Due to internal problems, Syria withdrew in 1961.

Tensions between Israel and her neighbors continued to rise over the next few years. A series of posturing activities led up to the Third Arab–Israel War (also called the Six-Day War or the 1967 War). In 1966, Egypt and Syria signed a defense pact. Border skirmishes escalated. In May 1967, Nasser demanded that UN forces evacuate the Sinai, which had served as a buffer zone between Israel and Egypt. The two nations immediately mobilized troops along the border. Egypt closed the Gulf of Aqaba, obstructing Israel's access to the Port of Eilat. Jordan signed a treaty with Egypt, placing Jordanian troops under Nasser's command. The war officially began on June 6, 1967, when Israel launched a preemptive strike against Egypt. During the first three days of the Six-Day War, Israel seized the Sinai, crushed Egypt's air force, and reached the Suez Canal. On the last three days of the war, Israeli forces captured the West Bank, Jerusalem, and the Golan Heights.

In the humiliation of defeat at the hands of the Israelis and the loss of the Sinai and Gaza Strip, Nasser offered his resignation. The Egyptian people, however, refused. Nasser remained in power until dying of a heart attack in 1970. Nasser was succeeded by Anwar Sadat, an original member of the Free Officers and close associate of Nasser.

President Sadat sought to restore Egyptian prestige and regain the Sinai after the previous military defeats. Sadat's request of US Secretary of State Henry Kissinger to negotiate the return of the Sinai to Egypt was rejected. The Fourth Arab–Israeli War began on October 6, 1973, when Egypt launched a surprise attack against Israeli forces in the Sinai, and Syria attacked Israel from the north. Iraq sent thirty thousand troops to support Syria in addition to eight other Arab nations that joined forces against Israel. A massive airlift of weapons to Israel by the United States saved the Israeli military. The conflict escalated to an international incident when the Soviets countered with an airlift of weapons to Syria and Egypt. Kissinger flew to Moscow to defuse tensions. The UN brokered a cease-fire on October 25, and Egypt succeeded in securing concessions regarding the Sinai from Israel. Sadat addressed the Knesset (Israeli parliament) in 1977. A year later, US President Jimmy Carter hosted a series of peace talks, known as the Camp David Accords, between President Sadat and Israeli Prime Minister Menachem Begin at Camp David, Maryland. In March of 1979, Egypt and Israel signed a peace agreement that ended more than thirty years of conflict. In order to encourage continued peace, the United States promised both nations billions of dollars in military and economic assistance.

For his role in the peace accords, Sadat received the Nobel Peace Prize in 1978. Sadat's foreign policies succeeded in gaining international recognition, regaining the Sinai, securing billions in aid from the United States, and establishing peace in a volatile region. Yet while the peace treaty was applauded in the West, much of the Arab world perceived Sadat as having sold out the Palestinians. Egypt's membership in the Arab League was suspended. In Egypt, a number of violent uprisings erupted. In 1981 during a military parade, Islamic extremists assassinated Sadat.

Hosni Mubarak succeeded Sadat as Egypt's president. Mubarak's foreign policies continued to cultivate good relations with the United States and Israel while seeking to improve relations with the Arab world. Due to a changing political landscape in the region over the next decade, the Arab League reinstated Egypt's membership in 1989. In 1991, Egypt joined the US-led coalition against Saddam Hussein's invasion of Kuwait, and Mubarak helped broker the peace agreement between Israel and the Palestinian Authority in 1993. Intensified struggles with Islamic militants at home plagued Mubarak's government from 1992 through 1997, culminating with a deadly attack on foreign and Egyptian tourists near the Temple of Queen Hatsheput in Luxor in November 1997. During those years, some 1,200 Egyptians, primarily Coptic Christians, were killed in the violence. Mubarak's brutal counterterrorist measures succeeded in reducing violence in the country. The October 2004 bombings of Israeli tourist resorts that killed thirty-four people in the Sinai were the first major terrorist attacks since the Luxor attacks in 1997.

Economic Development

North African nations left with the economic legacy of the past century now face a number of challenges to reform and adapt their economies to the realities of the twenty-first century. Like much of the Arab world, North African economies are characterized by bloated public sectors, excess government spending, and constraints on the private sector and foreign trade. Industrial production is regularly hampered by the small size of Arab markets, uncompetitive Arab economies, and lack of transparency and accountability. Nepotism and corruption traditionally discourage competition. The legacy of traditional agriculture and dependence on oil revenues has presented obstacles for development. Arab economies routinely discourage foreign investment while much-needed Arab capital is often invested in industrialized nations. Government investment in human capital has failed to keep pace with the growing demand,

and the "brain drain" is contributing to what the drafters of the 2003 Arab Human Development Report call "reverse development aid." Talented, educated Arabs regularly leave their homeland for more promising careers in developed nations.

Algeria's capital is Algiers. The nation's current population is 32 million. With a workforce of about 9.6 million people, 32% work for the government, 14% work in agriculture, 13.5% in industry, 14.5% in trade, and 10% in construction and public works. The per capita GDP is $6,000. Like other oil-producing countries in the region, the government has struggled to diversify the economy to become less centered on the energy sector. Hydrocarbons still account for 30% of the nation's GDP and 95% of its export earnings. The country continues to suffer from huge foreign debt (40% of GDP), high unemployment (26%), Berber unrest, and a small-scale armed insurgency that attacks government interests in the south.

The capital of Egypt is Cairo. The economic reforms of the early 1990s orchestrated by the IMF helped to improve Egypt's economy. Solid fiscal and monetary policies contributed to lowering inflation and reducing budget deficits. For her part in the Gulf War in 1991, Egypt was relieved of $7 billion in foreign debt. A bulging public sector, excess spending, and allegations of corruption, however, have contributed to domestic ills. Egypt's per capita GDP is $4,000. The $2 billion in US aid each year serve as a stabilizing force in Egypt's economy. Egypt relies heavily on tourism. The 1997 terrorist attack in Luxor hurt tourism, and the 2004 attacks on Israeli resorts in the Sinai have raised concerns about the future of the tourist industry.

Tripoli is the capital of Libya. The nation's socialist-oriented legacy and heavy reliance on the oil sector characterize the nation's economy. The oil sector represents approximately one-fourth of its GDP. The nation's relatively small population (five million) matched with large oil revenues allow for a high per capita GPD ($6,400), second only to that of Tunisia ($6,900). Nonetheless, unequal distribution of oil wealth and high unemployment (30%) still plague the nation's economy. Libya's poor soil conditions and severe climate restrict agricultural production, and as a result the nation must import three-fourths of its food. Like other nations of North Africa, Libya has taken steps to reform the economy, while political thawing of its foreign policy in recent years has resulted in the UN-lifted sanctions in 2003 and a US move toward normalized relations in 2004.

With Rabat as its capital, approximately one-fourth of Morocco's economy is agriculture-based. Morocco produces grains, citrus, wine, olives, and livestock. Industry accounted for 36% of the economy, producing phosphates, food, leather goods, and textiles. Morocco exports clothing, fish, minerals, fertilizers, and petroleum products. Services represent 42% of the nation's economy, and its per capita GDP is $4,000. Morocco underwent structural adjustment programs—supported by the IMF, World Bank, and Paris Club—and partially privatized the state tobacco company and telecommunications company recently. Morocco also signed a Free Trade Agreement with the United States in 2004, and is seeking to attract foreign investment in an effort to improve the economy and provide jobs.

The Role of Human Development

Economic development in North Africa is inextricably linked to human development. Issues of public education, social and political freedoms, labor markets, gender equality, and human capacity represent dimensions of North African society that impact development in the region. Past experience in the region has demonstrated that investments in industrial infrastructure and fixed capital alone—such as factories and equipment—do not provide the expected social returns. According to the 2002 *Arab Human Development Report,* human development in the Arab world is suffering from three deficits: Freedom, women's empowerment, and human capacity/knowledge relative to income. Regarding freedom, the region scores the lowest in the world. Popular voice in political processes, civil liberties, political rights, and independence in the media are all lagging behind most of the world.

One of the biggest challenges in North Africa is finding effective means to build human capital in such a way that will translate into a productive society that can compete in the twenty-first-century context of globalization. At the very foundation of the human capital-building effort lies education. Strides in the expansion of education have been made in the past thirty-five years. Primary education enrollment reached approximately 90% for boys and 75% for girls a decade ago. Over half of secondary-school-age children are enrolled in school while tertiary enrollment is among the highest in the developing world. Over the past three decades, literacy has expanded significantly. Between 1960 and 1995, illiteracy rates were cut in half while female literacy increased threefold in the Arab world.

Despite these successes, the quality of education in the Arab world is still poor. Many children continue to lack access to basic education. In 2000, enrollment for girls in Morocco was only 45% while class sizes in some rural regions averaged more than forty-five students. Across the region, enrollment in higher education is on the decline, and public expenditures on education have decreased since 1985. Adult illiteracy is still high, with female illiteracy rates the most extreme. North Africa's two largest countries, Morocco (32 million people) and Egypt (76 million people), suffer the lowest literacy rates of men and women over the age of fifteen: 52% and 58%, respectively. Only 34% of Moroccan women can read and write compared with 47% in Egypt. Algeria, also with a population of about 32 million, has a literacy rate of 70% (61% for women), while 74% (64% for women) of Tunisians and 83% (72% for women) of Libyans can read and write.

Aside from mechanical indicators of educational achievement, such as enrollment, completion, and literacy, a more pragmatic issue haunts the region: lack of relevant education. A huge disconnect exists between products (graduates) of Arab education systems and realities of the labor market. In Egypt, the education system does not prepare the average graduate for prospects of increased earnings in the labor market. Parents who allow their children to abandon education at early stages in the Arab world commonly cite school's lack of relevance to their child's future. In a rapidly changing environment of globalization and accelerating technology, existing education systems have been slow to react. Effective links between education and training systems, and realities of the labor market have yet to be established. To address the information gap, the 2002 *Arab Human Development Report* recommended attitudinal changes in knowledge-acquisition strategies, including a greater respect for science and knowledge, greater creativity and innovation, and the application of new discoveries to increasing productivity and income.

Education, economy, and politics are mutually dependent, and therefore the need for education reform is tied to economic and political reform. Improvements in education must prepare students with the technical skills to compete in the labor market while simultaneously developing a workforce that can make economic and political achievements that place a nation in position to compete in an environment of globalization. Equally important as the provision of technical skills, the responsibility of providing the capacity to solve problems, think critically, and demonstrate the cooperation needed to build democracy and civil society falls to education systems.

In many ways, knowledge production and dissemination is stagnant in North Africa. With the exception of Algeria, gaps in scientific knowledge are represented by low enrollment in scientific disciplines in tertiary education. Scientific research and development (R&D) also suffers, while advanced research in information technology and molecular biology is almost nonexistent. Public and private investment in R&D is extremely low, while state spending in R&D barely covers salaries. The number of scientists and engineers who work in R&D in Arab countries is slightly more than one-third of the global rate. Half the full-time researchers in the Arab world work in Egypt, and women are severely underrepresented in R&D. Research conducted in institutions often lacks a clear objective. In recent years, some effort has been made in North Africa to link a number of research projects conducted in institutions of higher education and research centers to the realities of Arab society. Egypt, Algeria, and Tunisia stand out as having the highest number of independent research centers in the Arab world.

Information production through the written word is also dangerously low in the region. While translation from foreign languages serves as a solid medium for information sharing, communication with the rest of the world, and cutting-edge advances, the number of books translated into Arabic in the first five years of the 1980s was slightly more than four books per million people as compared to 519 books in Hungary and 920 in Spain. Given the paucity of translated materials, a lack of clearly-defined policies regarding foreign language instruction within education systems has failed to bridge the gaps. In the postcolonial milieu of North Africa, efforts at Arabization have faced the realities of the prominence of the French language in government school curricula. Still, Algeria begins teaching French only at third grade, while Tunisia and Morocco begin French language instruction at fourth grade.

Access to books is another shortcoming. Although Egypt is one of the two hubs of book production in the Arab world (Lebanon being the other), as a whole Arab countries only produced 1.1% of the world's published books while constituting 5% of the population. Censorship often hampers book production and distribution. Of the total number of published works, 17% of the books are on religion—over three times the number for other parts of the world.

Access to other sources of information and media is also among the lowest in the world. Only fifty-three newspapers were produced per thousand people—less than one-fifth the rate of other developing countries. While limited access to the written word can be partially linked to low literacy rates, there are other indications of sluggish or stagnant development. For instance, there are five times as many telephone lines in other developing nations as there are in the Arab world. In addition, only 1.6% of the Arab population has access to the Internet, and there are only eighteen computers per one thousand people—about one-fourth the global average. Ratios of televisions are also low in the region. Compared with 641 televisions per one thousand people in high-income nations and 275 for middle-income nations, Tunisia has 198 per thousand people and Egypt but 189.

Lack of gender empowerment in Egypt, Tunisia, Algeria, and Morocco is also an obstacle to development. While advances have been made in education for females, particularly in higher education, women's participation in political organizations is still lagging well behind. Politically, women are underrepresented. Few women are found in parliaments and cabinets. In economic terms, women also fare poorly. Arab society as a whole suffers from lower family incomes and standards of living because women do not receive their full legal and citizenship entitlements. Gender inequality is apparent in the workforce as evidenced in employment status, wages, and gender-based occupational segregation. In Tunisia, some progress in bridging the gender gap has been attributed to progressive government initiatives taken in the 1950s, including the adoption of a more liberal interpretation of Islam.

Existing shortcomings in economic and human development have created a labor market in which job creation has been unable to keep pace with the expanding workforce in some cases. Libya's unemployment rate is approximately 30%, Algeria's 26%, Morocco's 20%, Tunisia's 14%, and Egypt's 10%. During the 1990s, Egypt and Tunisia actually experienced slight declines in unemployment as job creation outpaced expansion of the workforce. Algeria, on the other hand, registered the largest increase in unemployment during that period. Job seekers, including an increasing number of women, entered the labor force at a quicker rate than employment opportunities were created. The introduction of pro-employment programs also encouraged more entrants into the job market. In Morocco, urban unemployment drove a slight increase in the jobless rate for the 1990s.

Large public sectors in North Africa serve to absorb workers and offset unemployment. Non-agricultural, public-sector employment in Morocco is 21%, Tunisia 28%, Algeria 39%, and Egypt 70%. Large, sluggish bureaucracies, however, traditionally discourage productivity and efficiency, and serve as a constraint to economic development. Egypt's large agricultural and public sectors contribute to low productivity while Tunisia enjoys the highest in the region.

The bulging youth demographic across North Africa presents further challenges to development through an increased strain on the education systems and economies in a variety of ways, including a higher demand for jobs and public services. Approximately one-third of the population is age fifteen and under. Over the next decade and a half, the population aged fifteen and above will continue to increase at about 2.5% per year. Unemployment rates are highest among first-time job seekers, particularly secondary school graduates. In Morocco, some 40% of college graduates fail to find jobs. Shortcomings in the education systems often prepare graduates for highly coveted public-sector jobs but poorly prepare them for the private sector. Much has been written about the connection between the shifting demographics, disenfranchised youth, unemployment, and Islamic militancy in the Arab world. Future development efforts in the region will necessitate strategically designed programs that nurture the employability of Arab youth.

North Africa faces considerable development challenges over the next decade. Meaningful success will rely on economic, political, and education reform that is carefully crafted in such a way to develop and utilize human capital to meet the needs of the evolving global economy of the twenty-first century. Issues of youth employability, gender empowerment, and relevant education lie at the center of the long-term development strategies.

(Note: The views expressed in this essay are solely those of the author and do not reflect official positions of the US Department of Labor.)

CRAIG DAVIS

See also Algeria; Aswan High Dam and Development in Egypt; Ben Bella, Ahmed; Egypt; Ethnic Conflicts: North Africa; Morocco; Mubarak, Hosni; Nasser, Gamal Abdel; North Africa: International Relations; Organization of Petroleum Exporting Countries (OPEC); Qaddafi, Muammar; Sadat, Anwar; Tunisia; United Arab Republic (UAR); Women: Legal Status; Women: Role in Development

References and Further Reading

Akkari, Abduljalil. "Education in the Middle East and North Africa: The Current Situation and Future Challenges." *International Education Journal* 5, no. 2 (2004): 144–153.

Davis, Craig. *The Middle East for Dummies.* Edited by Inc. Wiley Publishing. Hoboken, NJ: Wiley, 2003.

Encyclopedia Britannica Online. Available from http://www.britannica.com.

Esposito, John L., ed. *The Oxford Encyclopedia of the Modern Islamic World*, 4 vols. New York: Oxford University Press, 1995.

Gardner, Edward. *Creating Employment in the Middle East and North Africa.* International Monetary Fund, 2003.

Hiro, Dilip. *Dictionary of the Middle East.* New York: St. Martin's Press, 1996.

Noland, Marcus and Howard Peck. "Islam, Globalization, and Economic Performance in the Middle East." *International Economic Policy Briefs*, no. Number PB04-4 (2004).

United Nations Development Programme. "Arab Human Development Report 2002: Creating Opportunities for Future Generations," 1–180. Author, 2002.

———. "Arab Human Development Report 2003: Building a Knowledge Society." Author, 2003.

"Unlocking the Employment Potential in the Middle East and North Africa: Toward a New Social Contract," 1–287. Washington, DC: The World Bank, 2004.

Van Donzel, E., ed. *Islamic Desk Reference.* Leiden, the Netherlands: E.J. Brill, 1994.

NORTH AFRICA: INTERNATIONAL RELATIONS

The North African states are Algeria, Tunisia, Morocco, and Libya. The first three are also commonly know as the Maghreb, or Maghreb, countries—the Arabic term for North Africa. This definition actually pertains only to the area between the high ranges of the Atlas Mountains and the Mediterranean Sea. In 1989, Algeria, Libya, Mauritania, Morocco, and Tunisia established the Arab Maghreb Union (UMA) to promote cooperation and integration among the Arab states of North Africa. Often, therefore, the term "Maghreb" includes Libya and Mauritania. During the colonisation period, Algeria, Tunisia, and Morocco shared a common history as French colonies that had been influenced by French culture and political values. Libya was an Italian colony from 1912 to 1951 and was influenced by Italian culture and politics.

Two factors have shaped the international relations of North African states: decolonisation and the relations of the various states with each other. At the end of World War II a growing resentment toward colonial powers characterised all North African states. The upsurge of Arab nationalism, coupled with the establishment of the Arab League (1945), motivated the North Africans to oust colonial powers from their countries. The subsequent struggle for independence, which marked the decolonisation process in the Maghreb states and Libya, shaped North African states' domestic and foreign policies. Despite their geographical homogeneity and cultural similarities, each of the Maghreb countries developed its own unique political identity, which in turn influenced its international relations. Morocco and Tunisia embarked on a moderate path, while Algerian politics have been characterised by radicalism. Libya likewise embraced radicalism. Territorial disputes and political rivalries amongst the North African states themselves have also influenced their domestic and foreign policies.

Morocco

Morocco, a French protectorate since 1912, gained its independence in 1956. France at first strongly resisted the nationalist movement and, in 1953, exiled Sultan Mohammed V after he had joined forces with the nationalists and refused to cooperate with the French government. France tried unsuccessfully to make Thami al-Glaoui, the Berber Pasha of Marrakech, into the new ruler of Morocco. In 1955, facing growing social unrest all over the country, France allowed Mohammed V to return. Although this was a great victory for the nationalist movement, it did not quell the unrest. By November 1954, violent uprisings in neighbouring Algeria, coupled with widespread Marxist insurgency in Southeast Asia, induced France to abandon its struggle against Moroccan nationalists. In March 1956, Morocco became officially independent under the leadership of Mohammed V. Spain followed suit the following April, handing over most of the Moroccan territory that it had colonised.

Relations between Morocco and France were initially tense because the French government maintained a military presence in Morocco. It was only in March 1961 that France withdrew its troops and vacated its military bases. Another bone of contention was the issue of private property owned by the French and European settlers who had left Morocco after independence. The issue of compensation was finally resolved on August 2, 1974, when the Moroccan government agreed to pay the French government a lump sum to compensate the owners for the loss of their properties.

After a difficult start, relations between Morocco and France gradually improved. France, which had envisaged enjoying a special relationship with the Moroccan government, became frustrated when this expectation failed to materialise. Although cultural and commercial ties remained strong (e.g., French language continued to be part of the school curriculum), politically Morocco never granted France special status. France's hopes of entertaining a privileged relationship with Morocco were part of an overall strategy to maintain a strong influence in North Africa, primarily for geopolitical reasons. For example, the North African air corridor was France's gateway to Africa and Paris was determined to ensure that this access was free from any hostile influence.

French interests in North Africa more recently have taken on a predominantly economic focus, for example, securing access to the oil and gas fields of the region (mainly in Algeria) and to North African importers—France's key export partners. Tensions between Morocco and France have become confined to the issue of immigration. Legal and illegal Moroccan immigrants cross into France almost daily. This phenomenon creates ongoing social tension inside France, where significant sectors of society resent North African immigrants. Immigrants consequently feel marginalised and excluded. Attempts to solve this problem have so far had limited success.

Relations with Spain have been equally important for the Moroccan government, because of the close historic ties between the two countries. Spain at one point controlled most of the North African coast, from Tangier to Tunis. There has been an ongoing territorial dispute between the two countries over five small Spanish enclaves—Ceuta, Mellila, Penon de al-Huceima, Penon de Velez, and Islas Chafarinas—on the Moroccan Mediterranean coast. Both countries claim sovereignty over these enclaves. Spain has on the whole kept a low profile in its relations with North African countries, trying to downplay its colonial past and emphasising its economic interests in the region. It was one of the major players in the early phases of the Western Sahara dispute, attempting to mediate between Morocco and Algeria (see below). Morocco's relations with Algeria were initially marked by cooperation; for example, Morocco supported Algeria's war of independence from France. However, relations between the two countries deteriorated over a territorial dispute concerning Mauritania. This dispute motivated Morocco to join the "Casablanca bloc"—a somewhat nebulous radical anti-Western union of Egypt, Ghana, Guinea, and Mali (formed in 1961).

Since independence Morocco has generally adopted a moderate, conciliatory, and pro-Western foreign policy, becoming a member of the United Nations in 1956. Despite establishing diplomatic relations with the USSR and China in 1958, the conservative monarch Mohammed V never sought a close relationship with communist countries. In 1960, however, he requested—and obtained—arms from the Soviet Union, and officially recognised North Vietnam in 1961. Morocco has also looked toward the United States. In general the United States perceives Morocco as a political asset in the region because of its moderate policy toward the Arab–Israeli dispute. Morocco has endeavoured to mediate between the Israelis and the Palestinians. In 1986 King Hassan II took the daring step of inviting Israeli Prime Minister Shimon Peres for talks, thereby becoming the second

Arab leader, after Anwar Sadat, to host an Israeli leader. Morocco has also taken a strong stand against Islamic radicalism and terrorism. One result of the diplomatic dialogue between the United States and Morocco was the signature, in June 2004, of a comprehensive bilateral Free Trade Agreement (FTA)—only The United States' second such treaty with an Arab country (the first being with Egypt).

Tunisia

Tunisia, a French protectorate from 1881, gained independence from France in 1956. On July 25, 1957, the National Assembly overthrew the last vestiges of the monarchy by deposing the Bey, proclaiming Tunisia a republic, and electing Habib Bourguiba as president. France had granted Tunisian independence reluctantly, under mounting pressure from the insurgencies in Southeast Asia and in neighbouring Algeria. Tunisia's relations with France thereafter deteriorated in the late summer and autumn of 1957, and were marred by sporadic clashes between their respective forces along the Tunisian-Algerian border. These clashes occurred when French troops, pursuing Algerian rebels, crossed the border into Tunisia. The Tunisian government strongly opposed the use of French troops, who were still stationed on its soil, against the Algerian rebels. The major bone of contention with France post-independence was therefore the continuing presence of these troops. In 1962, following the intervention of the United Nations, an agreement was reached and France withdrew its forces.

Tunisia has generally adopted a moderate, pro-Western line in foreign policy. However, it has also been careful to maintain an independent stance and to demonstrate to other Arab states that it is not subservient to Western policies. Tunisia supported the development of the Arab Maghreb Union (UMA) along with Algeria, Morocco, Mauritania, and Libya. (Progress on Maghreb integration has, however, been affected both by political instability in Algeria and by Libya's anti-Western stance and perceived support for terrorism.) On the other hand, Tunisia has avoided joining any extreme left-wing blocs such as the "Casablanca bloc." Originally it had forged some links with the Soviet Union and China; however, these relationships deteriorated in the 1960s and were not fully resumed until 1972. Bourguiba's relations with Gamal Abdul Nasser, the Egyptian leader, were somewhat tense in the late 1950s, because of the former's neutral stance towards the Arab–Israeli conflict. At a time when none of the Arab states was willing to recognise Israel, this unusual stand created tensions with several radical Arab states. In the early 1970s, Bourguiba officially advocated the establishment of a Palestinian state to coexist with Israel. Since Bourguiba's replacement as leader in 1989, Tunisia's relations with radical Arab states have improved, though its moderate neutral policy remains unchanged.

Since independence, Tunisia has sought to maintain good relations with its neighbours; however, relations with Algeria have occasionally been tense due to border disputes. In 1993 the two countries reached an agreement to begin cooperating on the construction of a natural gas pipeline across Tunisian territory, to convey Algerian gas supplies to Italy.

Tunisia's relationship with the United States could generally be defined as cordial. In 1957 the United States provided economic and technical assistance to Tunisia under a bilateral agreement. This agreement provided $2.5 billion of development assistance to be deployed over a period of thirty-five years by the United States Agency for International Development (USAID). In 1991, however, Tunisia's stand against the US role in the First Gulf War led to the temporary deterioration of its relationship with the United States and with many Arab states. Thereafter Tunisia has played a moderating role in the negotiations for a comprehensive Middle East peace. In 1993 it was the first Arab country to host an official Israeli delegation as part of the Middle East peace process.

Algeria

The path to Algeria's independence was long and bloodstained. France ruled Algeria, unlike Morocco and Tunisia, as one of its metropolitan departments (*departements*) and not as a protectorate. Since the 1830s this had resulted in significant settlement by French citizens who, after World War II, accounted for about 10% of the Algerian population. These people regarded Algeria as their home. The Algerian War of Independence began in 1954 and lasted until 1962, when Ahmed Ben Bella became the first president of the Algerian Republic. About one million Algerians died in what was one of the most violent and ruthless wars of the postwar decolonisation period.

After independence, Algeria speedily established relations with most Western European countries, although at times these were marked by major disagreements. Algerian policy tended to be uncooperative, and at times even hostile, to Western politics, which it regarded as hegemonic toward African and Arab countries. In 1965, for example, it severed diplomatic relations with the United Kingdom over the issue of

Rhodesia; however, these were restored in 1968. By far the most important relationship of the newly independent country was that with France. Surprisingly perhaps, there were few major bones of contention between the two countries. One such was the question of France's nuclear experiments in the south of Algeria—a region known as the French Sahara. Other problems were the nationalisation of former European property and the position of Algerian workers in France, a very socially disadvantaged group. There was also tension over the exploitation of Algeria's natural resources, such as oil and gas, which were controlled by French companies. In 1970 the Algerian government nationalised the oil industry, a move that created a serious rift with France. The dispute was resolved in April 1987 when the Algerian government agreed to release assets of former French settlers. In return the French government agreed to provide financial assistance to Algeria for a period of three years. By May 1991, two French oil companies had been granted new concessions in the Sahara. Despite these problems, Algeria's relations with France on the whole have been quite satisfactory. France continued to supply economic and technical assistance, including training and equipment, to Algeria's armed forces.

Algerian relations with Spain were until 1986 cool and, at times, even hostile. This was for two reasons: (1) Algeria claimed that Spain supported Morocco in the conflict in Western Sahara; and (2) Spain suspected that Algeria harboured members of the ETA (*Euskadi Ta Askatasuna* in Basque, Basque Fatherland and Liberty)—a leftist group that used terrorism in the hope of forming an independent Basque state in parts of northern Spain and southwestern France. In 1987 the two countries signed a treaty providing for Algerian officials to be stationed in Spain to monitor the activities of Algerian dissidents, in exchange for closer supervision of members of the ETA within Algeria. Since then, and following the reconciliation with Morocco, relations between Algeria and Spain have improved and normal diplomatic exchanges between them, as of this writing, now take place.

Algerian relations with the Arab world have been marked by radicalism. In the first years of independence, Ben Bella joined the more radical section of the non-aligned bloc and took an extremist stance toward the Arab–Israeli conflict and on disputes within Black Africa. He established close relations with Egypt, Iraq, and especially Syria. Algeria refused to accept the cease-fire after the Arab–Israeli Six-Day War of 1967, and rejected UN Security Council Resolution 242 calling for mutual recognition of the rights of Palestinians and the right of Israel to exist, and for the dispute to be resolved by diplomatic means. In the

1970s, Algeria hosted several Arab armed groups. It supported Yasser Arafat in 1971, when Jordan expelled the PLO (Palestine Liberation Organization) from its territory, and severed diplomatic relations with Amman. Algeria was also a prominent supporter of radical factions in disputes within the African continent, providing training bases for several guerrilla movements. Relations with the Soviet Union and Cuba were also close and Algeria was one of the first countries to recognise Communist North Vietnam and North Korea.

After the death in 1978 of President Houari Boumedienne, who had ruled Algeria since 1965, and his replacement by Colonel Chadli Benjedid, Algerian policy became more pragmatic and less driven by ideology. This shift was apparent in its relationship with the United States. After the Six-Day War, Algeria had been critical of the United States and hostile toward its pro-Israeli stance. However, while diplomatic relations may have been tense, economic cooperation remained strong. Algeria's militant line on the Arab–Israeli dispute, and its support for Arab and African armed groups, did not prevent it cooperating economically with Western countries, including the United States. US oil companies invested in Algeria's oil industry and these interests had to be guaranteed. Algeria played a role in the negotiations for the release of US hostages in Iran, leading to their release in 1981. However, diplomatic relations remained overshadowed by US sympathies for Morocco in the Western Sahara conflict. The most important shift in Algeria's stance in international relations came in 1999 when Abdelaziz Bouteflika was elected president. He made two visits to the United States in 2001, heralding a new era in relations between the two countries. This new approach was demonstrated after September 11, 2001, when Bouteflika immediately offered Algeria's support in the "war on terror."

Libya

Libya was an Italian colony from 1912 until 1951, when it gained independence under the leadership of King Idris. Initially, after independence, the country adopted a moderate pro-Western stance. It joined the Arab League in 1951 and in 1955 it became a member of the United Nations. It also participated in the Sterling Zone, a sphere of trade cooperation, and in 1953 signed a pact with Britain that allowed the latter to maintain its military bases in Libya. A similar agreement was reached with the United States in return for US financial aid.

Libya's pro-Western stance provoked tension with Egypt, which took a more radical anti-Western approach. Aware of his vulnerable position, King Idris tried to reinforce the country's neutral policy and to avoid emphasising relations with the West. However, there was growing pressure from the Libyan population to take a less conciliatory and more hostile approach toward the West. There were demands for Britain and the United States to evacuate their military bases (an agreement to this effect had been signed by Britain and the United States in 1964).

On September 1, 1969, Colonel Muammar Qaddafi staged a coup. This event provoked a complete *volte-face* in Libya's political stance. Qaddafi closed US and British bases and partially nationalised all foreign oil and commercial interests inside Libya. He played a key role in the strategy of using oil as a political weapon against the West, participating in the 1973 embargo in retaliation for United States support for Israel. Qaddafi ostensibly rejected both communism and capitalism in favour of a "middle course." Three factors characterised the Libyan revolution: fundamentalism, authoritarianism, and fanaticism. Qaddafi's policy appeared arrogant in its disregard for external considerations; hence, his regime did not establish close ties with any other countries, though formal diplomatic relations with some were maintained. Nonetheless, Western countries tended to treat him with "kid gloves," partly because of Libya's oil resources and partly because of the country's strategic position in the Mediterranean area.

Libya established relations with the USSR, recognised Communist China in 1971, and had full diplomatic relations with East Germany from 1973. It also had relations with Yugoslavia and received arms supplies from the Soviet Union. Despite his friendly relations with the Soviet Union, Qaddafi continued to declare his hatred for communism. Libya's use—and loss—of Soviet-supplied weaponry in its war with Chad was a notable breach of an apparent Soviet–Libyan understanding not to use the weapons for activities inconsistent with Soviet objectives. As a result, Soviet–Libyan relations reached a low level by mid-1987. Libya also took a radical stance in its policy toward the developing world, supporting the guerrilla movement in Chad, giving its leader refuge, and allowing the rebels to launch raids from Libyan territory. In 1980 it even intervened militarily in the dispute. Qaddafi's stance in the Arab world was also regarded as extreme: he seemed willing to support and assist any resistance or terrorist movement, opposed any peaceful solution to the Arab–Israeli conflict, and declared himself in favour of the destruction of the State of Israel.

In addition to using oil as a weapon of foreign policy, Qaddafi at one time sought to destabilise weaker governments and to promote terrorism, providing refuge and finance for groups that shared his revolutionary and anti-Western views, for example, the Japanese Red Army, radical Muslim groups such as the Popular Front for the Liberation of Palestine-General Command, and Abu Nidal's Fatah Revolutionary Council. Relations with the United States became very tense in the 1980s. In 1981, the United States shot down two Libyan aircraft that had challenged its warplanes over the Gulf of Sirte, which Libya claimed as its territory. Then, in 1986, US planes bombed Libyan military facilities, as well as residential areas of Tripoli and Benghazi—including Qaddafi's house—killing 101 people. The United Kingdom broke off diplomatic relations with Libya in 1984 after a British policewoman was shot dead outside the Libyan People's Bureau, or embassy, in London during anti-Qaddafi protests. Tension between Libya and the West reached its apogee after a Pan Am airliner was blown up over the Scottish town of Lockerbie on December 21, 1988, killing 270 people. In 1991, two Libyan intelligence agents were indicted by federal prosecutors in the United States and Scotland for their involvement in this bombing. In January 1992, the UN Security Council approved Resolution 731, demanding that Libya surrender the suspects, cooperate with Pan Am, pay compensation to the victims' families, and cease all support for terrorism. Libya's refusal to comply led to the approval of a further UN Security Council measure, Resolution 748, in March 1992, imposing sanctions designed to bring about Libyan compliance. Continued Libyan defiance resulted in the passage of UN Security Council Resolution 883 (November 1993), providing for a limited freeze of Libya's assets and an embargo on selected oil equipment. However, Libya persisted in its non-compliance until 1999, when it handed over two suspects for trial by a Scottish court convened in the Netherlands. UN sanctions were subsequently suspended, and lifted altogether in September 2003 following an agreement between the United States, the United Kingdom, and Libya over the Lockerbie issue. A shift in Libya's attitude became evident in August 2003, when it sent a letter to the United Nations accepting responsibility for the actions of the Libyan officials involved in the Lockerbie case and agreeing to payment of appropriate compensation, as well as renouncing support for terrorism. Later that year, Libya signed a compensation agreement worth $2.7 billion with lawyers representing families of the Lockerbie/Pan Am victims. In December 2003, Qaddafi further announced his abandonment of programmes to develop weapons of mass destruction. This paved the way for a visit to Libya by British Prime Minister Tony Blair, in March 2004, and for his meeting with Qaddafi at that time.

Relations with the European Union

North African states attach great importance to relations with Europe as a whole, and especially with those bordering on the Mediterranean. Western Europe has traditionally been the greatest trading partner for the Maghreb states, and more recently also for Libya. North African states have regarded France, Italy, and Spain as major gateways for their trade and exports. The foundation, first of the European Economic Community, and later of the European Union with its growing political and especially economic power, has caused the North African states to seek a closer relationship with the European Union. Most of the states manifested an interest in evolving a Mediterranean consensus on various issues. A cooperation agreement between the European Union and the Maghreb countries was signed in April 1976, enabling certain trade provisions to come into effect as early as July 1976. This was followed by a full trade agreement in January 1979, according to which the North African states' industrial products were granted immediate duty-free entry to the European Union, while customs preferences were awarded for certain of their agricultural products. The agreement also included some improvements in conditions for migrant workers from North Africa. However, Morocco's application to join the European Union in 1987 was rejected on the grounds that it is not a European country. The European Union has not hesitated to use its financial leverage on some of the North African countries, for instance, on Morocco in 1992, in protest of Morocco's activities in the Western Sahara; and on Algeria, making financial aid conditional on progress toward democracy. In June 1992, the European Union approved proposals for bilateral relations with the Maghreb countries. Relations with Algeria have, however, been adversely affected by Algeria's internal instability. Tunisia, Morocco, and Algeria are also parties to the Barcelona Declaration of 1995, which aimed to increase Euro-Mediterranean cooperation and agreed to establish a comprehensive partnership amongst the participants by means of political, cultural, and economic ties. An Association Agreement, concluded in February 1996, sets clear targets for the further development of the already close political relations of these states with the European Union, and for a Free Trade area to be established by 2010. The Agreement entered into force on March 1, 2000.

Unlike Algeria, Morocco, and Tunisia, Libya has had no such close relations with the European Union. The European Union's Foreign Ministers have only recently agreed to lift sanctions, including an arms embargo, against Libya. (Italy had argued for the ending of the eighteen-year-old arms ban, so that it could supply Libya with hi-tech equipment intended to curb illegal migration.) Libya now has the opportunity to become a full member of the Barcelona Process if it accepts the Barcelona *acquis*. Several European Union member states already have extensive trade relations with Libya: Italy, Germany, the United Kingdom, and France are Libya's four leading suppliers of manufactured goods and food products.

North African Associations and Inter-State Relations

Despite their geographical and cultural similarities, relationships between these states have not always been easy and have been the subject of frequent disputes. Clear differences exist in the approaches taken by these states toward the West, the developing world, and ideologies such as communism and Islamic fundamentalism.

Relations between Tunisia and Morocco have generally been good as they have no common border, both states tend to adopt moderate policies, and both have at times felt threatened by their more radical neighbours, Algeria and Libya. In the 1950s and 1960s, there was widespread discussion of a so-called Greater Maghreb scheme; this aimed to achieve greater cooperation amongst the states but was hampered by their political differences and economic problems. Each country tended to be suspicious of its immediate neighbour. Relations between Algeria and Morocco have long been characterised by rivalries and occasional hostility. Immediately after Algerian independence, Morocco laid claim to stretches of southern and western Algeria that had been under Moroccan sovereignty before the French gained control over the area in the nineteenth century. In a series of sharp engagements in the disputed territory in October 1963, the Moroccan professional army consistently outperformed Algerian regulars and local guerrillas. Although mediation sponsored by the OAU (Organisation for African Unity) brought an end to the fighting, the success of the Moroccans demonstrated their potential threat to Algerian security in the event of a more serious dispute. In addition to their territorial disputes, both countries vied for primacy in the Maghreb region. Their respective claims were rooted in history and in ideology: Morocco's claim to regional leadership derived from its centuries-old national identity, whereas Algeria's stemmed from the prestige of winning its war of independence from France. The inherent ideological differences between the new socialist republic, on the one hand, and the ancient kingdom, on the other, were sharpened when almost immediately after independence, Ben Bella proclaimed his country's socialist revolutionary doctrines and its opposition to conservative governments such as Morocco's. Relations improved after Boumedienne came to power, as both countries concentrated on their domestic problems. In 1972 a treaty was signed defining the border between them. However, the Moroccan government deferred its official ratification of the treaty until 1989, pending a final resolution of the difficulties over the Western Sahara question.

The dispute over the Western Sahara had originated in 1974, at which time the territory was still under Spanish control and was known as the Spanish Sahara. Morocco began attempts to annex the territory which, after a series of diplomatic initiatives, culminated in a march by 350,000 Moroccans across the territory's northern border. Spain signed a treaty turning over the northern two-thirds of the Western Sahara to Moroccan administration and the rest to Mauritania. By mid-1975 the Algerians were providing supplies, vehicles, and light arms to the Popular Front for the Liberation of Saguia el Hamra and Rio de Oro (Polisario). Polisario was the strongest of several indigenous national liberation movements active in the Western Sahara. Algeria thus became the principal foreign supporter of the Polisario in its long-running desert war to oppose Moroccan control of the disputed area.

Despite their military strength, the Algerians avoided direct confrontation with the more experienced Moroccan troops. However, in January 1976, the Moroccans defeated two battalions of Algerian troops and took prisoners in clashes within the Western Sahara. Following this incident, Algerian regulars refrained from venturing into the Western Sahara (despite Moroccan claims to the contrary) while the Moroccans, for their part, refrained from pursuing rebel troops into Algerian territory. Fighting in the Western Sahara initially featured attacks by Polisario's light mobile forces against isolated Moroccan outposts. By 1982, however, the struggle had shifted in Morocco's favour with the Moroccan military dominating the battlefield. Morocco's military success in the Western Sahara was one factor in the rapprochement between the two nations, achieved in 1988. This followed a twelve-year hiatus in diplomatic relations precipitated by Algeria's recognition of the

Polisario government. By the late 1980s, Algeria was preoccupied with its own internal security problems and was no longer willing to devote arms and support to the independence movement. Algeria's resumption of diplomatic relations with Morocco, accompanied by the opening of borders and a number of joint economic initiatives, eased the security situation on its western flank. Morocco's acceptance of the United Nations peace plan for the Western Sahara, and the conclusion of the UMA treaty in 1989, further helped to abate remaining tensions between the two states.

Whereas Morocco had long been viewed by Algeria as a potential threat, Muammar Qaddafi's Libya was regarded as somewhat more friendly. The Algerian–Libyan security relationship was based on a common antipathy for the Western-dominated economic order and deep hostility toward Israel. However, this relationship suffered several setbacks during the 1980s. In 1984 Morocco and Libya announced that they had secretly negotiated an alliance. Although the alliance's effect was short-lived, Algeria interpreted the agreement as upsetting the strategic balance in the Maghreb. Libya's unilateral annexation of a section of neighbouring Chad, together with its military intervention in Chad, hardened Algerian attitudes against Libya. There were also suspicions that Libya was linked to unrest instigated by Islamist (also seen as fundamentalist) groups in Algeria. Libya's subsequent participation in the UMA, however, appeared to lay the foundation for more stable relationships between itself and Algeria, as well as with the other states of the region.

The 1980s witnessed a successful attempt to bring the countries together. On February 17, 1989, a treaty was signed in Marrakech by the leaders of Algeria, Libya, Mauritania, Morocco, and Tunisia. It was modelled on the European Union and was named the Union of the Arab Maghreb (UMA). Its main aim was to enable its members to negotiate as a bloc with the European Union and to encourage trade, economic cooperation, and freedom of movement across borders. In his efforts to shape a more pragmatic foreign policy, Algeria's Benjedid had succeeded in moderating the stresses in his country's relationships with the West. At the same time, Algeria's concerns shifted in the direction of improving regional stability, which had long been disrupted by the festering disputes with Morocco and Libya. Hence, the formation of the UMA in 1989 heralded a new phase of improved relations between the states of the region. Under important security clauses contained in the treaty, the signatories affirmed that any aggression against one member would be considered as aggression against all the member states. In an apparent allusion to the Western Sahara conflict, member states pledged not to permit any activity or organisation on their territory that could endanger the security or territorial integrity of another member state.

LORETTA NAPOLEONI

See also Algeria; Berbers; Ethnic Conflicts: North Africa; Libya; Maghrib Peoples; Morocco; North Africa: History and Economic Development; Tunisia

References and Further Reading

Abu-Nasr, Jamil M. *A History of the Maghrib*. Cambridge, UK: Cambridge University Press, 1971.
"Algeria—Relations with U.S." GeographyIQ. http://www.geographyiq.com/countries/ag/Algeria_us_relations_summary.htm
Bianco, Mirella. *Gadafi: Voice from the Desert*. New York: Longman, 1975.
Boukhars, Anouar. "A Two-Level Game Analysis of the Complexities of Interstate Rivalry in the Maghreb." *Columbia International Affairs Online*. Department of International Studies, Old Dominion University, http://www.ciaonet.org/access/boa02 (May 2001).
Fernanda, Faria and Alvaro Vasconcelos. "Security in Northern Africa: Ambiguity and Reality." *Chaillot Papers*, http://www.iss-eu.org/chaillot/chai25e.html (September 1996).
"French Decolonisation: Tunisia." http://www.arab.net/tunisia/ta_french.htm (2002).
Joffe, George. *North Africa, Nation, State, and Region*. London, New York: Routledge, 1993.
Lewis, Bernard. *The Arabs in History*. New York: Hutchinson, Row, 1970.
Nellis, John R. "Decentralization in North Africa: Problems of Policy Implementation." In *Decentralization and Development: Policy Implementation in Developing Countries*, edited by G. Shabbir Cheema and Dennis A. Rondinelli, pp. 127–182, Beverly Hills, CA: Sage, 1983.
Parker, Richard. *North Africa, Regional Tensions and Strategic Concerns*. New York: Praeger, 1967.
Samir, Amin. *The Maghreb in the Modern World*. London: Penguin, 1970.
Shimoni, Yaacov. *The Arab States: Their Contemporary History and Politics*. (Hebrew) Tel-Aviv: Am-Oved, 1990.
"The EU's Relations with Libya." *The European Union in the World*. http://europa.eu.int/comm/external_relations/lybia/intro (2004).
"The Middle East and North Africa." *Regional Surveys of the World*, 43rd ed. London: Europa Publications, 1977.

NORTH AMERICAN FREE TRADE AGREEMENT (NAFTA)

The United States, Canada, and Mexico signed the North American Free Trade Agreement (NAFTA) in 1994, following a US–Canada free trade agreement in 1988. In the 1990s, Canada and Mexico were the largest and third-largest US trading partners, respectively (Japan was second). The great benefits predicted by NAFTA supporters did not materialize, but neither did the disasters predicted by opponents.

Mexican Perspective

NAFTA was the culmination of a process set in motion by two Mexican presidents, Miguel de la Madrid Hurtado and Carlos Salinas de Gortari, in response to the Mexican economic crisis of the 1980s. The collapse of world oil prices and the failure of Mexico's long-standing efforts at import substitution had left the country facing a crushing foreign debt, staggering deficits, soaring inflation, high unemployment, and collapsing standards of living. Mexico was effectively bankrupt, and in 1982 announced that it could not pay its foreign debt. In response to this crisis, de la Madrid and his successor, Salinas, strove to liberalize the Mexican economy. Salinas oversaw a radical liberalization of the Mexican economy, above all in international trade. The Mexicans lowered tariff barriers on many products. The maximum tariff rate fell from 100% to 20%; the fraction of imports that required permits had fallen from 93% to less than one quarter. Salinas sold off numerous government-owned enterprises, and signed the General Agreement on Tariffs and Trade (GATT), an international accord aimed at opening the world market. Salinas negotiated debt relief with the United States, cut public expenditures, relaxed laws that had inhibited foreign investment, and privatized the largest Mexican banks. These reforms had succeeded in restoring Mexico to the favor of international investors, who have poured huge sums into the Mexican economy since 1990. But the reform had not yet delivered convincing results where it counts: improved living standards among ordinary Mexicans. After eight years of stagnation, in 1990 the Mexican economy began to grow again. The growth, however, barely kept pace with labor-force expansion. Unemployment remained far higher and real wages lower than in 1980.

For President Salinas, the only way to attract the foreign capital necessary to stabilize the exchange rate and to fund the current account deficit was to provide hesitant potential investors with guarantees of continuity of economic policy and access to the US market through an ironclad agreement with Washington. NAFTA, it was hoped, would satisfy both requirements. The sustained economic growth generated by NAFTA would narrow income differentials by creating jobs. President Salinas' anti-poverty program would ease the transition from stagnation to NAFTA-fueled high growth. Investment from abroad would enable the economy to grow while introducing new technology and efficiency and modernizing Mexican society. Salinas was desperate to attract new foreign investment, and because 85% of Mexico's manufactured exports are shipped to the United States, stable access to the US market became increasingly important to the Mexicans.

In June 1990, President Salinas requested a free trade agreement with the United States. He discarded the national tradition of keeping a suspicious distance from the "colossus of the north." Small-scale industrialists and grain farmers expressed fear that they might be destroyed by US competition, and some intellectuals mourned the imminent demise of the nation's economic sovereignty and cultural pride. However, Salinas stressed his determination to push his country into the first world. NAFTA would be an instrument of economic change and a powerful symbol of the commitment to liberalism that is Salinas' most important legacy.

US Perspective

The first Bush administration (1988–1992) was at first hesitant about free trade with Mexico, but a number of political and economic factors ultimately led the United States to pursue NAFTA. Bush was frustrated with the slow pace of GATT negotiations, wished to do something to address the growing problem of illegal immigration, and had an interest in buttressing liberalizing forces and a friendly president in Mexico. Carlos Salinas de Gortari's government was not a model of democratic virtue. From the US point of view, however, it was the best Mexican government in either nation's history. Salinas' market-oriented reformers had done their best to break with the long tradition of anti-US rhetoric. While Mexico had not had a truly free presidential election, the trend was clearly toward greater openness and democracy. Not long ago, US intelligence analysts worried that a Mexico hammered by the debt crisis and plunging oil prices might become a radicalized national security nightmare.

The health of the Mexican economy is extremely important to the United states. The countries are increasingly interdependent, as was evidenced in 1982 when Mexico's announcement that it could not repay its international debts put seven of the nine largest US banks on the brink of bankruptcy. Bush hoped that the Salinas policy would strengthen the Mexican economy in ways that would avert future crisis, and that economic vitality would buttress political order there. The Bush administration also

wanted to assure the United States of increasing access to petroleum from Mexico, one of the five leading sources of US imports (Mexican shipments in the late 1980s and early 1990s were roughly half as large as those from the topmost source, Saudi Arabia). Furthermore, NAFTA would provide the United States with an important bargaining chip in its trade negotiations with Europe, Japan, and the General Agreement on Tariffs and Trade. Finally, the United States wanted to consolidate diplomatic support from Mexico on foreign policy in general. As demonstrated by disagreements over Central America during the 1980s, this had long been a source of bilateral tension. But with NAFTA in place, Mexico became unlikely to express serious disagreement with the United States on major issues of international diplomacy.

In September 1990, President Bush announced that he would begin talk with the Mexicans. The administration first won "fast-track" authority from Congress, which meant that legislators would have to vote yes or no on the deal as negotiated by the Bush administration and representatives of the Mexican and Canadian governments—members of Congress were prevented from picking apart any trade package to insert exemptions for constituents. The Bush administration claimed that without fast-track, it would have been impossible to negotiate NAFTA, because the Mexicans and Canadians would have feared that the deal would unravel in the legislative process in Washington. The three nations finalized the agreements in August of 1992, laying the foundation for a trading bloc of 358 million citizens and economies with GDPs totaling $6.2 trillion.

The North American Free Trade Agreement, which takes up more than 2,000 pages, established schedules for reducing tariffs and non-tariff barriers to trade over a five- to ten-year period in all but a few hundred of some 20,000 product categories. Despite its length and complexity, NAFTA's goal is very simple: to eliminate or lower barriers to trade in goods and many services, and create a limited common market "from the Yukon to the Yucatan."

Canadian Perspective

The move for Canada to request a comprehensive Free Trade Agreement came from the MacDonald Royal Commission Report in September 1985. Although 85% of Canadian exports were already free of duty, it was recognized that given the dominance of the direction of Canadian exports to the United States, Canada was exposed to the unilateral actions of the application of US trade laws. As a result,

Canada needed a guarantee with respect to continued access to US markets and greater certainty over the conditions of this access.

The Free Trade Agreement represented the further integration of two very close trading partners who experienced significant and ongoing cross-border capital flows and whose capital markets were becoming increasingly aligned. In addition, policy makers expected that the increased specialization, inter- and intra-industry within Canada, would lead to increased competitiveness, not only with respect to the United States, but to redress its large trade imbalance with the rest of the world. NAFTA had the potential to provide greater specialization and efficiency gains.

Canada was at first reluctant to request negotiating status as its trade with Mexico was quite small. Nevertheless, policy makers argued that, if only on defensive grounds, Canada had to seek negotiating status to ensure its continued accessibility to the US market.

The Basics

The agreement has two major elements: it reduces or eliminates US, Mexican, and Canadian tariffs on many goods produced in North America, and facilitates investment across borders on the continent. But it is important to note that NAFTA does not eliminate all trade barriers—the agreement contains provisions protecting economic interests in all three countries against free trade.

First, NAFTA will eliminate tariffs on approximately nine thousand categories of goods sold in North America by the year 2009. Also under NAFTA, many previous restrictions on foreign investments and other financial transactions among the NAFTA countries will end, and investment in financial services operations (such as advertising, banking, insurance, and telecommunications) will flow much more freely across borders. This is particularly important to Mexico. Before NAFTA, Mexico had much higher tariff and non-tariff barriers in place than the United States, so the Mexicans have made far more significant tariff reductions. Beginning in 2000, US banks, which had been virtually banned from operating in Mexico before NAFTA, were able to hold 15% of the Mexican market. Truck and bus companies now have largely unimpeded access across borders, and starting in 2000, US trucking firms were allowed to become majority owners of Mexican trucking companies. While Mexico continued to prohibit foreign ownership of oil fields, in accordance with its constitution, US firms became eligible to compete

for contracts with *Petroleos Mexicanos* (PEMEX) and operate, in general, under the same provisions as Mexican companies.

Only goods adhering to NAFTA's "rule of origin" move across North American borders duty free: goods must be produced in North America to qualify for duty free treatment. Goods that are wholly obtained or produced in North America are considered to originate in North America. Goods containing no North American content, however, must be substantially transformed through further processing in a NAFTA country to qualify for duty free entry. In practice, this means they must undergo a change in tariff classification. Goods containing non–North American content also may be treated as North American if they have sufficient (60%) regional value content, as determined by either the transaction value or the net-cost method. The nationality of a factory's owners is irrelevant under the agreement—Nissan may ship automobiles from its modern Mexican facility to the United States duty free, as long as those cars meet NAFTA's requirements for North American content.

Second, NAFTA protects the property rights of those who invest across borders in North America, and eliminates practices that long discouraged foreign investment in Mexico. NAFTA requires each signatory country to treat foreign investors no differently than domestic investors, and prohibits governments from imposing any special "performance requirements" on foreign investors. For example, before NAFTA, Mexico often required foreign-owned firms to buy certain inputs locally, or to export a specified percentage of their goods. Such requirements, which act as "non-tariff barriers" to trade, violate the free trade agreement; businesses confronting them may appeal to a three-nation panel for damages. Further, in another provision aimed directly at Mexico, NAFTA discourages the nationalization of private enterprises by requiring governments to pay immediate and fair compensation to the nationalized firm's owner. Mexico is hungry for foreign investment, and the protections offered to investors by those provisions will undoubtedly increase investment there.

Again, while NAFTA lowers many trade barriers, it offers protectionist safeguards for certain domestic products in all three countries. First, there are the so-called "snap-back" provisions, which allow governments to impose tariffs temporarily to protect specific economic sectors suffering substantial losses due to import surges. For example, if Mexican tomatoes flood the US market and drive down prices, Washington can throw up tariffs against imported tomatoes while US growers adjust to the new competitive environment. Second, each country insisted on protecting certain domestic industries, and the agreement contains many such arrangements. For example, Mexico protected its oil- and gas-drilling enterprises, and the United States its shipping industry. Third, many protectionist provisions emerged from the political process in the United States. President Clinton made many concessions to individual members of Congress, especially those presenting agricultural interests, and the Mexicans agreed to reinterpret some of the original language of NAFTA to allow those concessions. One such agreement empowered the United States to impose steep tariffs on orange concentrate if Mexican exports rise and the price drops to a specified level for a period of five days. These provisions violate the spirit of free trade, but they were necessary to complete the free trade agreement—legislators withheld support for NAFTA until these arrangements were made.

While these are NAFTA's major elements, the deal has many other crucial components. There are provisions (aimed at Mexico) requiring each country to protect rights in "intellectual property" like copyrights and trademarks, and rules that will allow US and Canadian banks to penetrate the Mexican market for financial services. Perhaps more significantly, the original text of NAFTA, later supplemented by "side agreements" negotiated by the Clinton administration, contained important provisions on health and the environment. NAFTA does not require the three countries to adopt the same regulations protecting the food supply or the environment. The three countries made a nonbinding pledge to seek the "highest standard" of protection, but there is no way to force any country to raise its standards.

Arguments for and Against NAFTA

NAFTA precipitated strenuous debate within the United States. The opponents, including various US labor unions and environmental groups, criticized the low wages and poor labor laws in Mexico, which they feared would drag down US labor standards. Environmentalists similarly criticized Mexico's lax environmental laws and saw NAFTA as giving US corporations licenses to pollute by moving south of the border. In the heart of the 1992 presidential campaign, Democratic candidate Bill Clinton pledged to support NAFTA on condition that there be effective safeguards for environmental protection and workers' rights; by September 1993 the governments reached "supplemental" or side agreements on labor and the environment. As the US Congress prepared to vote on ratification, Texas billionaire Ross Perot led the

charge against the treaty. Perot warned that US workers would hear "big sucking sounds" as their jobs disappeared south of the border. Proponents insisted that NAFTA will make Mexico more appealing to American investors—giving them permanent rights to full control of Mexican subsidiaries and protecting them against any future reversal of Mexican investment rules. Under NAFTA, Mexico would be a better place to do business—with lower financial costs, an improved infrastructure, and a larger pool of trained bilingual personnel. For outside investors, there would also be an intangible comfort factor in knowing that Mexico was somehow legally linked to the United States. In short, NAFTA removes many of the obstacles, perceived or real, that have kept hundreds of companies from ever considering expansion into Mexico.

Disregarding vociferous opposition from unionized labor, a historic bastion of support for Democrats, President Clinton lobbied tirelessly on behalf of the treaty. And after Perot stumbled badly during a memorable television debate with Vice President Al Gore, the House of Representatives finally supported the NAFTA accord by the surprisingly lopsided margin of 234–200; the Senate followed with a vote of 61–38.

Supplemental Agreements

As noted earlier, concerns about the effects of free trade on US labor and environmental standards clouded NAFTA's prospects for acceptance by the Congress. During the 1992 presidential campaign, Governor Bill Clinton endorsed NAFTA, rejected any renegotiation of the text, and enumerated important qualifications. However, he stated his intention to negotiate three supplemental agreements that would be submitted to Congress in parallel with NAFTA implementing legislation. The prospect of supplemental agreements raised hope among US labor and environmental activists that Clinton might push for new international standards in these areas. The supplemental agreements negotiated by the Clinton administration set up new mechanisms to encourage the three countries to enforce existing environmental and labor laws, and to apply sanctions against those that try to use lax enforcement to attract investment and create competitive advantage for their firms.

The first agreement would set up an environmental commission, headed by Vice President Gore, which would have substantial power and resources to prevent and to clean up water pollution; encourage the enforcement of the country's own environmental laws through education, training, and commitment of resources; and provide a forum to hear complaints. The environmental provision strengthened NAFTA and enhanced the protection, conservation, and management of natural resources throughout the region in a manner that would set the standard for future international agreements.

A second supplemental agreement would create a labor commission that would have powers similar to those of the environmental commission to protect worker standards and safety. A Ministerial Council, consisting of the labor ministers of each nation would oversee the activities of the labor commission. They would supervise the implementation of the side accord, including the activities of the International Coordinating Secretariat. They would also establish working groups and committees as deemed appropriate.

Finally, a supplemental safeguards agreement would be negotiated to deal with instances where an unexpected and overwhelming surge in imports from a partner country required temporary protection beyond that provided by the "snap-back" causes enumerated in the NAFTA text. The rationale for such a provision would be to provide an additional avenue for temporary import relief to deal with the aftershocks of regional integration.

President Salinas of Mexico grudgingly agreed to these proposals. The Canadians were a good deal more positive than the Mexicans about the supplemental agreements. They well understood that Canada was not the object of concern.

Assessing NAFTA

NAFTA appeared to achieve the economic goal of expanding commerce. Two-way trade between Mexico and the United States climbed from $83 billion in 1993 to $108 billion in 1995 and $175 billion in 1997. By 1997 the three-way trade of $348 billion represented nearly $1,000 in trade for each of NAFTA's 380 million consumers. Trade among the three partners increased somewhat faster than before the accord. By this time the United States was exporting more to Mexico than to China, Korea, and Singapore combined, and Mexico displaced Japan as the second-largest trading partner of the states (Canada remained in first place). Still, both optimistic and pessimistic forecasts for NAFTA fell short. Few job losses or gains could be traced to NAFTA.

Besides trade and jobs, NAFTA had other effects. Mexico tightened environmental protection while NAFTA was being negotiated and kept the controls in place despite the 1995 financial crisis. The US–Mexico border region flourished following the agreement. Mexican shoppers spent an estimated $22 billion in the United States over the next five years.

Although several US presidents had talked about extending NAFTA to other countries in the Western hemispheric free trade agreement, NAFTA provisions are very vague regarding the requirements countries must meet to become members. Both the lack of clear-cut procedures and making decisions concerning new members by consensus could pose significant obstacles to enlargement. Indeed, the US Congress has been reluctant to give the president fast-track authority in negotiations to extend NAFTA to Chile and other Latin American states.

NASSER MOMAYEZI

See also Free Trade Area of the Americas (FTAA); Maquiladora Program; Mexico: History and Economic Development

References and Further Reading

Cameron, Maxwell A. and Brian W. Tomlin. *The Making of NAFTA: How the Deal Was Done.* Ithaca, NY, and London: Cornell University Press, 2000.

Coffey, Peter, J. Colin Dodds, Enrique Lazcano, and Robert Riley. *NAFTA: Past, Present, and Future.* Boston: Kluwer Academic Publishers, 1999.

DePalma, Anthony. "NAFTA Environmental Lags May Delay Free Trade Expansion." *New York Times*, May 21, 1997, A4.

Grayson, George W. *The North American Free Trade Agreement.* New York: University Press of America, 1994.

Husted, Bryan W. "The Impact of NAFTA on Mexico's Environmental Policy." *Growth and Change*, 28, no. 1 (Winter 1997).

Krugman, Paul. "The Uncomfortable Truth About NAFTA: It's Foreign Policy, Stupid." *Foreign Affairs*, 72, no. 5 (November–December 1993).

Mayer, Frederick W. *Interpreting NAFTA: The Science and Arts of Political Analysis.* New York: Columbia University Press, 1998.

Morales Moreno, Isidro. "Mexico's National Identity After NAFTA." *American Behavioral Scientist*, 40, no. 7 (June–July 1997).

Pastor, Robert A. *Integration with Mexico.* New York: Twentieth Century Fund Press, 1993.

Skidmore, Thomas E. *Modern Latin America.* New York: Oxford University Press, 2005.

NORTH ATLANTIC TREATY ORGANIZATION (NATO)

The North Atlantic Treaty Organization (NATO) is a Brussels-headquartered military and diplomatic alliance of twenty-six countries in Europe and North

America. NATO members attempt to preserve peace and international security around the world. They also collaborate on economic policies in the effort to further economic and political stability. The organization's interest in the developing world began when the collapse of the Soviet Union in 1989 forced NATO, a product of the Cold War created as a safeguard against communism, to find a new reason for its continuing existence.

NATO traces its roots to 1945 when Europe sought to recover from the devastation caused by World War II. The democratic nations of Europe feared that they had been so weakened by the economic and military costs of the conflict that they did not have the strength to fend off an attack by an increasingly aggressive Soviet Union without US assistance. The United States feared that the loss of democratic countries would drastically reduce trade and badly damage the US economy. Europe and US policy makers cooperated to develop an organization that would preserve the stability of the North Atlantic region. This region has its northern boundary at the North Pole, past the Northwest Territories of Canada, while the southern terminus is located at the Tropic of Cancer, which runs between Florida and Cuba.

The treaty establishing NATO was signed in Washington, DC, on April 4, 1949, and then subsequently ratified by its member countries. The NATO signatories agreed that, if an armed attack occurred, each NATO member would assist the victimized state by regarding an attack upon one as an attack upon all. NATO would respond to aggression by taking all necessary actions, including the use of armed force, to restore and maintain international peace and security. The vagueness of the treaty meant that the exact mechanisms of the alliance would develop over time. Policy makers hoped that the threat of US involvement would act as a particularly powerful deterrent to the Soviets.

The collapse of the Soviet Union in 1989 removed the chief reason for NATO's existence. On November 19, 1990, NATO achieved its historic mission when the Charter of Paris formally ended the conflict with the Warsaw Pact. It also offered former Soviet satellite states the opportunity to join the organization. To most countries, European Union membership is the real goal, with NATO membership serving as a proving ground. The members of NATO are: Belgium, Bulgaria, Canada, Czech Republic, Denmark, Estonia, France, Germany, Greece, Hungary, Iceland, Italy, Latvia, Lithuania, Luxembourg, Netherlands, Norway, Poland, Portugal, Romania, Slovakia, Slovenia, Spain, Turkey, the United Kingdom, and the United States. As of this writing, Albania and Macedonia are pursuing membership.

With the Soviet threat gone, NATO began focusing on preserving global security as it struggled to remain relevant. The alliance changed from being a collective defense organization to a self-appointed police officer. Economic, social, and political difficulties, including ethnic rivalries and territorial disputes in Central and Eastern Europe, were identified as likely to cause regional instability and it planned to settle these disputes.

In 1999, NATO sent military forces into action for the first time, in the Kosovo province of Serbia in the Balkans. In Operation Allied Force, the alliance attempted to achieve a political solution to the Kosovo crisis and acted only after negotiations with the Kosovo Serbians and the Kosovo Albanians had failed. Incidents of ethnic cleansing of the Albanian population had already occurred and NATO publicly stated that it feared inaction would lead to a greater humanitarian catastrophe. Additionally, an escalation in the fighting would likely have triggered a massive refugee flow. A great movement of displaced people had the potential to destabilize surrounding countries with a delicate ethnic balance such as Macedonia and Albania. Conflicts between Muslims and Christians might prompt nearby NATO members Turkey and Greece to again come to blows. Regional stability required NATO action but this action came without approval from the Serbian government or the United Nations (UN). NATO violated the provisions of the UN Charter by invading Kosovo without the approval of the UN Security Council.

NATO has subsequently reached outside of its traditional boundaries to protect the North Atlantic region. Since the security of Europe is closely linked to security and stability in the Mediterranean, NATO initiated talks with Algeria, Egypt, Israel, Jordan, Mauritania, Morocco, and Tunisia in the early 1990s. It offered training and technical knowledge but no troops.

The terrorist attacks on the United States in 2001 forced NATO to pay more attention to terrorism. The NATO-Russia Council, established in 2002, is identifying opportunities for joint action in all areas of mutual interest but especially in the use of the military to combat terrorist attacks. In 2004, NATO agreed to send an International Security Assistance Force to Afghanistan to help stabilize the country. Afghan instability is believed to have created a climate in which Islamic nationalist terrorism could develop.

NATO, dominated by the United States, became involved in the US efforts to establish a democratic government in Iraq in 2004. It sent a training mission to help the new government of Iraq address the security needs of the Iraqi people. It did not send troops. Instead, NATO offered training and education and planned to coordinate offers of equipment and help from individual NATO countries. It is not clear how European reluctance to participate in Operation Iraqi Freedom and the subsequent weakening of historic ties between Western Europe and the United States will affect NATO.

NATO has emerged from the Cold War as a global police agency. As the military arm of democratic Western nations, it plans to play an increasing role in establishing and maintaining the security of developing countries. The alliance contends that such activism will fulfill its mission of maintaining North Atlantic stability, but the future of the Atlantic Alliance is in doubt, as it may not have the broad support needed for a radically new agenda.

CARYN E. NEUMANN

See also Afghanistan; Ethnic Conflicts: Central and Eastern Europe

References and Further Reading

Badsey, Stephen and Paul Latawski, eds. *Britain, NATO, and the Lessons of the Balkan Conflicts, 1991–1999.* London: Frank Cass, 2004.

Cook, Don. *Forging the Alliance: The Birth of the NATO Treaty and the Dramatic Transformation of U.S. Foreign Policy Between 1945 and 1950.* New York: Arbor House/William Morrow, 1989.

Hodge, Carl Cavanagh. *Atlanticism for a New Century: The Rise, Triumph, and Decline of NATO.* Upper Saddle River, NJ: Pearson Prentice Hall, 2005.

Kay, Sean. *NATO and the Future of European Security.* Lanham, MD: Rowman & Littlefield, 1998.

NATO. http://www.nato.int/.

Paquette, Laure. *NATO and Eastern Europe After 2000: Strategic Interactions with Poland, the Czech Republic, Romania, and Bulgaria.* Huntington, NY: Nova Science Publishers, 2001.

Park, William. *Defending the West: A History of NATO.* Brighton, UK: Wheatsheaf, 1986.

Schmidt, Gustav, ed. *A History of NATO: The First Fifty Years.* New York: Palgrave, 2001.

NORTHERN SOUTH AMERICA: HISTORY AND ECONOMIC DEVELOPMENT

Northern South America is composed of the independent nations of Colombia, Venezuela, Guyana, and Suriname, plus the French overseas department of French Guiana. Although the region is blessed with rich agricultural land and abundant minerals, the post-1945 period has revealed a number of fundamental flaws in the countries' respective economic systems. After the devastating experience of the Great Depression revealed the negative effects of relying on the liberal, export-led variety of economic development, most of Latin America pursued an economic path based on import-substitution industrialization. Import-substitution industrialization, however, was not the panacea for economic development that its proponents heralded. During the 1980s, while much of North America, Europe, and East Asia was experiencing an economic boom, Latin American nations were experiencing an economic depression that lasted until the end of the decade. As a consequence, most Latin American nations were forced to readjust their economic strategies. They departed from the import-substitution industrialization path, opened their economic systems to free trade, encouraged foreign investment, began the privatization of state-run industries and companies, and pursued the neoliberal, export-led path of economic development. Although most Latin American economies began to revive during the 1990s, social and political instability, coupled with growing economic disparity between the social classes, offset many of the economic gains.

Colombia

The majority of Colombia's people live in the valleys and mountain basins that lie between the ranges of the Andes Mountains. Eleven of Colombia's fourteen major urban centers lie in these valleys. The remaining three urban centers are on the Caribbean coast. Travel between Colombia's centers of population was quite difficult during the colonial period. As such, Colombia's people lived in quite distinctive communities and developed their own specific economic paths based on agriculture, livestock, and mining. Following independence at the beginning of the nineteenth century, Colombia's elites, divided into antagonistic Liberal and Conservative factions, spent most of the century fighting fratricidal civil wars that greatly dislocated the political economy. During the 1880s, the Liberal Rafael Nuñez encouraged the expansion of Colombia's coffee industry. Although production never reached the levels of Brazil's coffee production, the Colombian coffee was of a higher quality and fetched a higher world market price. Nuñez's death in 1899, however, tossed the nation back into the all-too-familiar pattern of civil war. One of Colombia's most destructive civil wars, the Thousand-Day War (1899–1902), ruined the economy, destroyed the nation's infrastructure, left one hundred thousand dead, and weakened the nation to such an extent that the United States was easily able to sever the province of Panama from Colombia. The demoralized Colombians needed a leader capable of reuniting the nation and rebuilding the national economy.

Using dictatorial powers, the Conservative Rafael Reyes (1904–1909) was able to restore fiscal stability, rebuild the nation's infrastructure, and encourage the reorganization of Colombia's nascent coffee industry. Although coffee became the driving force of the Colombian economy, a brief depression hit the nation in the aftermath of World War I. During the 1920s, Colombia's elites began to centralize their power around coffee exports. In 1927, they established the National Federation of Coffee Growers (FNC), a cartel that controlled the export of coffee. Eighty percent of Colombia's coffee was grown by small coffee farmers who sold their coffee to the FNC for marketing. The FNC convinced the government to establish the National Coffee Fund, a state-run agency dedicated to improving coffee production and the transportation network necessary to export Colombia's coffee. While the Colombian elites were investing in coffee production, foreigners, especially the United Fruit Company (UFCO), were establishing export enclaves for banana and oil production. The Great Depression, which caused coffee prices to fall and unemployment to rise, was a direct challenge to elite control of the political economy.

During the 1930s, two outspoken politicians emerged: Jorge Eliécer Gaitán, who represented the radical wing of the Liberals, and Laureano Gómez, who represented the ultra-conservative wing of the Conservatives. Gaitán's assassination in April 1948 ignited a massive riot known as the *Bogotazo*. It unleashed a wave of violence, known as *La Violencia* in Colombia, that took the lives of hundreds of thousands of people and had a negative impact on the development of the national economy. The Conservative Gómez was elected in fraudulent elections in 1950, but was overthrown by former colonel Gustavo Rojas Pinilla in 1953. Rojas Pinilla, who ruled until 1957, encouraged industrialization and developed his own political following. In 1957, Liberal and Conservative elites put aside their differences, established a power-sharing arrangement known as the National Front, and sent Rojas Pinilla into exile. Foreign investment poured into Colombia. Although manufacturing output increased and coffee production also increased with the introduction of new tree varieties, domestic food production declined greatly.

During the 1970s, as demand for Colombian coffee grew and coffee prices rose significantly, international demand for cocaine, especially in North America and Europe, skyrocketed. Although the Colombians are the world's largest producers of cocaine, many of the coca leaves are grown in Ecuador, Peru, and Bolivia. Colombia was flooded with narco-dollars, which drove up the inflation rate. The informal economy, based on the production and smuggling of refined cocaine, generates more wealth than the formal economy based on agriculture. By the 1980s, over 80% of all cocaine consumed in the United States came from Colombia. Farmers gave up planting traditional crops and turned to the more lucrative production of cocaine. With the drug trade came an excessive level of corruption. To make matters worse, a new round of leftist political violence was unleashed during the 1970s. The military, as well as the paramilitary death squads, unleashed a war of retribution against the leftists and drug lords, which left thousands dead. In an attempt to gain popularity, the drug lords offered to pay off Colombia's entire foreign debt. The US government pumped millions of dollars into Colombia to fight the war on drugs. By 1999, the United States was spending almost $300 million annually to combat the drug trade. Meanwhile, the violence continued.

Despite renegotiated debts, new oil discoveries, vast mineral deposits (especially gold, copper, lead, mercury, and uranium), privatization of state-run industries, an expanded flower industry (especially roses), and greatly increased trade with Venezuela (Colombia's second-largest trading partner after the United States), Colombia's economy continued to falter and unemployment increased. By the 1980s, in terms of industrialization and gross national product, Colombia was one of Latin America's wealthiest nations. The wealth, however, was very unevenly distributed. A small group of elites, based on the nineteenth-century families that had made their money in mining, as coffee barons, and merchants, had meshed with a small group of new elites, whose money came from industry, banking, and illegal drug exports. These elites controlled the majority of Colombia's wealth. The lifestyle of the nation's elites is supported by a private security force of over 250,000 armed guards. Colombia's resources are quite capable of supporting its population without the cocaine industry, but numerous problems, especially unequal distribution of wealth and incessant violence, must be dealt with before Colombia can achieve and maintain major economic gains.

Venezuela

Venezuela was an economic backwater until the second half of the eighteenth century when the Bourbon Reforms liberalized trade. During this period, cacao exports were the driving force of the colonial Venezuelan economy. The landed elites, who based their wealth on cacao exports and cattle ranching, imported thousands of slaves from Africa to work on the cacao plantations, which changed the ethnic makeup of the nation. During the nineteenth century, after independence, the elites introduced coffee cultivation in the fertile Andean foothills. Coffee was Venezuela's primary export until the discovery of oil in 1914. Large-scale oil production began in 1922 during the regime of Juan Vicente Gómez (1908–1935). Oil quickly surpassed coffee as Venezuela's major export and provided the financial basis for Gómez's dictatorship. By the 1950s, when oil production reached over one billion barrels per year, Venezuela was the third-largest oil producer in the world. Oil exports turned Venezuela into an urban, semi-industrialized nation.

Gómez received a one-eighth *regalía* (fraction) of the well-head price of crude oil. This was more than enough money to pay off the nation's foreign debt. Creole (a subsidiary of Standard Oil of New Jersey), Shell, Gulf, Texaco, and Mobile dominated the Venezuelan oil industry. The foreign oil companies took millions of dollars in profits out of the Venezuelan economy. The increase in wealth caused by oil production led to the development of a middle class as well as organized labor organizations that challenged the elite's domination of the political economy. After Gómez's death, he was succeeded by two of his cohorts, General Eleazar López Contreras (1935–1941) and Isaias Medina Angarita (1941–1945). These post-Gómez governments allowed a democratic opening in the political sphere, while simultaneously laying the groundwork for diversifying and industrializing the economy. In 1943, Medina Angarita passed a new petroleum law that raised the *regalía* to an amount that equaled 50% of the foreign oil companies' profits. In addition, in 1945 the - Venezuelan government, interested in pursuing the import-substitution industrialization path of economic development, created the *Corporación Venezolana de Fomento,* a government-run development corporation to oversee economic diversification and industrialization projects.

In 1945, a coalition of civilians and young military officers who wanted greater political and economic power staged a successful coup against the Medina Angarita government. The coup was led by Rómulo Betancourt, his supporters in *Acción Democrática* (AD), and a group of young military officers led by Marcos Pérez Jiménez. Betancourt led the civilian-military junta until elections were held in 1947. During this period, AD introduced a controversial 50/50 petroleum law. Betancourt's petroleum plan was actually less radical than Medina Angarita's plan. The new law limited Venezuela's share of the profits to 50%. Regardless, Betancourt was able to call the new legislation nationalistic. However, elites and military generals, fearful of AD's populist rhetoric, overthrew the AD government in 1948. Pérez Jiménez used the oil wealth to fund his dictatorship. His dictatorship was very favorable to US business interests, especially oil interests. Skyscrapers, massive highways, and public housing were built during the oil boom of the 1950s. Oil production doubled during the 1950s and foreign investment dramatically increased. In 1957, an economic recession hit Venezuela when the United States restricted foreign oil imports. A popular civilian-military uprising overthrew Pérez Jiménez. Interim President Admiral Wolfgang Larrazabal increased Venezuela's share of the oil profits to 60% and scheduled democratic elections in December 1958, which were won by Betancourt. Betancourt took over a nation that had both tremendous oil revenue and great economic disparity. Refusing to nationalize the foreign oil holdings in Venezuela, Betancourt initiated gradual economic reforms. In an effort to gain greater control over oil prices, Venezuela was in the forefront of organizing the Organization of Petroleum Exporting Countries (OPEC) in 1960. By 1960, oil exports accounted for over 90% of Venezuela's export earnings. In 1960, however, an economic recession worse than that of 1957 hit Venezuela. Betancourt responded with repression.

In an attempt to deflect criticism of unusually high degrees of corruption, during the 1970s the two main political parties, AD and the Independent Electoral Political Organizing Committee (COPEI), increased their populist rhetoric and actions. The 1973 Arab–Israeli War led to an oil embargo by Arab producers, which resulted in quadrupled petroleum prices in the United States. Although Venezuela did not participate in the embargo, it did benefit from the increased revenue. High prices for oil changed Venezuela's perception of its role in international affairs. In 1975, AD President Carlos Andrés Pérez (1974–1979) nationalized, with compensation, the extensive foreign iron ore holdings in Venezuela. In early 1976, the Venezuelan government nationalized the foreign oil holdings in Venezuela. The foreign oil companies were paid $1 billion. The Venezuelan government established *Petróleos de Venezuela* (PDVSA), a state-run oil company. With the increased petroleum revenue, the Venezuelan government increased educational programs, raised wages, and implemented industrialization projects. In an effort to increase the pace of modernization and economic development, Pérez negotiated high-interest loans based on projected oil revenues. At the end of the 1970s, however, oil prices plummeted, which sent the Venezuelan economy into an economic disaster. During the 1980s, the government implemented International Monetary Fund (IMF) austerity measures, which led to a noticeable decline in the standard of living of many Venezuelans.

Pérez's second term as president (1989–1993) was even more corrupt than his first administration. Pérez discarded his populist rhetoric and implemented neo-liberal economic policies, privatized numerous state-run enterprises, and held wages down. In May 1993, Pérez was impeached by the Senate on charges of embezzling $17 million in government funds. Rafael Caldera, who won the 1993 elections, was unable to pull the nation out of economic chaos. Despite decades of oil revenues, Venezuela was an economic disaster. In the 1998 presidential elections, Hugo Chavez, who had led an abortive coup against Pérez in 1992, promised the voters that he would implement economic reforms that would revitalize Venezuela's faltering economy. Although Chavez promised to re-vamp the political economy and lessen the influence of the United States on Venezuela, over 50% of Venezuela's world trade is transacted with the United States. Oil wealth once gave Venezuela one of the highest standards of living in Latin America, but inflation, corruption, and faulty economic planning have eroded it. Oil wealth brought only temporary prosperity. In 2000, Venezuela had a lower per capita income than it did in 1974. Venezuela did not become a rich country and missed many opportunities to turn its oil wealth into real economic development.

Guyana

The Dutch were the first settlers in what today is known as Guyana. They arrived in 1596 and began to settle along the banks of the Essequibo River. They initiated a land reclamation policy that entailed drain-ing swamps and lagoons, as well as building dikes and canals, which made the land habitable and suitable for agriculture. This narrow band of land, no more than ten miles wide and much of it below sea level, extends along Guyana's entire two hundred-mile coastline. Today, this is the nation's primary agricul-tural area and where most of Guyana's people live. The hinterland, which is sparsely populated and has poor soil, is blessed with significant quantities of dia-monds, gold, and bauxite.

The British took the Dutch lands in 1796 and officially re-named the colony British Guiana in 1831. During the nineteenth century, the British were primarily interested in rice, sugar, and cotton

plantations along the coast, as well as some timber felling in the hinterland. Since the Dutch and British found few Indians to work the plantations, they imported African slaves to work the plantations dur-ing the seventeenth and eighteenth centuries. After slavery was abolished in 1830, the British imported large numbers of people from South Asia. Descen-dants of the Africans tend to live in the urban areas and work as merchants, mechanics, and tradesmen, while the descendants of the South Asians tend to work on the farms and live in the rural areas along the coast. The descendants of these two groups make up the majority of Guyana's population today.

During the nineteenth century, the British devel-oped the nation's infrastructure and attempted to open up the interior for settlement and exploration of minerals. Few people, however, were willing to leave the coastal areas. At the same time, the British began to expand the colony westward, at the expense of Venezuela. In 1899, following the 1895 Venezuelan Boundary Dispute, an international tribunal in The Hague awarded the United Kingdom most of its territorial clams in eastern Venezuela. Today, much to the chagrin of the Venezuelan government and people, that land constitutes half of Guyana's ter-ritory. The fact that much of Guyana's gold is found in this contested region makes the Guyanese govern-ment unwilling to discuss the Venezuelan claim. In 1962, Venezuela declared the 1899 tribunal decision void.

The British began planning for Guyana's inde-pendence in the aftermath of World War II. Self-government, which had been planned for 1962, was postponed until 1966 because of racial tensions be-tween the Indo-Guyanese, led by Cheddi Jagan, and the Afro-Guyanese, led by Forbes Burnham. Burn-ham became the first leader of independent Guyana in 1966. To reduce the mono-cultural dependence on sugar exports, Burnham encouraged the expansion of other agricultural products. In 1970, Burnham began to move ideologically toward the left. He de-clared Guyana a cooperative republic and established over one thousand worker cooperatives. In 1971, he began the process of taking over the nation's foreign-owned bauxite mines, which were incorporated into a state-run enterprise called Guybau. During the 1970s, the Guyanese government nationalized the British-owned sugar plantations. The government also took control of the banking industry, the rum factories, and the insurance companies. By 1980, the govern-ment owned virtually the entire Guyanese economy. Burnham's pro-Soviet rhetoric and dreams of a Soviet-funded socialist experiment in Guyana died with him in a Moscow hospital room in 1985. Soon after, Burnham's vice president, Desmond Hoyte, began the process of privatization and began to court US foreign investment in Guyana.

In 1992, Jagan was elected with a majority of the vote. Jagan, who had discarded his Marxist rhetoric and socialist pretensions from the 1960s, portrayed himself as a moderate progressive dedicated to neo-liberal economic polices and privatization of the state-run industries. Within four years of taking power, Jagan reduced the nation's inflation rate from over 100% to less than 5% a year. He lured foreign investors to Guyana's agricultural, mining, and timber sectors. Following Jagan's death in 1997, his US-born wife, Janet Rosenberg Jagan, was elected president. Despite her life-long devotion to Marxism, Janet Jagan continued Chedi Jagan's privatization plans. At the end of the 1990s, the national airline and the bauxite mines were privatized. The nation's largest gold mine, Omai, is owned by two Canadian companies. Although Guyana's economy rapidly improved during the 1990s, its per capita GDP of less than $500 makes it one of the poorest countries in Latin America.

Suriname

In 1667, the Dutch received Suriname from the United Kingdom in exchange for their colony of New Netherlands (what is today New York). Dutch farmers initiated a land reclamation policy that entailed draining swamps and lagoons, as well as building dikes and canals, which made the land habitable and suitable for agriculture. This narrow band of land, no more than ten miles wide and much of it below sea level, extends along Suriname's entire 230 mile coastline. Today, this is the nation's primary agricultural area and where most of Suriname's people live. The hinterland, which is sparsely populated and has poor soil, is blessed with significant quantities of bauxite and timber.

During the Napoleonic Wars (1799–1815), Suriname was occupied by the British. After Napoleon was sent into exile, the entire region of Guiana, as it was then called, was divided into English, Dutch, and French zones. Following the emancipation of slaves in Suriname in 1863, the Dutch imported people from South Asia and Indonesia. In 1948, the colony became a self-governing component of the Netherlands, responsible for its own internal affairs. In 1975, the Dutch granted independence to Suriname. The Dutch government promised $100 million per year for ten years to help the new nation develop its economy. As aluminum production declined during the first decade of independence, the Dutch annual stipend became

the basis of economic stability in Suriname. Regardless, virtually none of the Dutch aid was used to develop the nation's infrastructure. In 1980, the military overthrew the civilian government and installed Lieutenant Colonel Desi Bouterse as the new leader of Suriname. The Dutch government immediately cut off all economic aid. The situation was further complicated by declining aluminum prices.

In 1988, the Dutch restored aid payments to Suriname, but not enough to suit Bouterse, who continued to govern until the free 1991 election, which greatly diminished the military's power in governing. Bouterse's personal power further fell when it was learned that he engaged in drug trafficking, for which, in 1998, he was sentenced in absentia in the Netherlands for transporting cocaine. By the end of the 1990s, the Dutch had again resumed aid payments, albeit at the diminished amount of $65 million per year. Ronald Venetiaan, who came into power in 2000, initiated an austerity program, raised taxes, and attempted to limit government spending. Regardless, Suriname remains dependent on aluminum exports, which provide over 90% of the government's tax revenues. Notwithstanding nationalist rhetoric, the aluminum industry continued to be owned by Suralco, a subsidiary of Alcoa. Rice remains the chief agricultural crop and food staple. The continued reliance on aluminum exports and foreign aid, coupled with the lack of significant attempts at industrialization or agricultural product diversification, does not bode well for Suriname's political or economic future.

French Guiana

In 1946, after more than three centuries as a French colony, French Guiana was transformed into an overseas department —*département d'outremer*—of France. In theory, French Guiana was to be equal and identical to any other French department. As a result of their non-independent status, the people of French Guiana enjoy a standard of living vastly superior to the people of the former Dutch and British Guianas. The people of French Guiana receive generous social security and medical benefits, wages are higher than in the rest of the Eastern Caribbean, and the infrastructure is vastly superior. With its mineral resources and potential for hydroelectric energy, especially the Petit-Saut dam project on the Sinnamary River, French Guiana has great potential to develop its economy.

The traditional colonial economy was based on gold prospecting, forestry, subsistence agriculture, and sugar production. Gold was discovered in 1853. By 1960, gold accounted for almost 70% of French Guiana's exports. Over 70% of French Guiana is covered with tropical forests, which are mostly owned by the state. By 1960, timber accounted for 20% of French Guiana's exports. There is a limited amount of land along the narrow coast suitable for farming. The traditional method of subsistence agriculture is called *abattis* (cultivation for a few seasons in a forest clearing created by slash-and-burn agricultural techniques). This method is only practical in areas of low population density.

During French President Charles De Gaulle's Fourth Republic, the power of the *Préfet*—the local representative in French Guiana of the central government—was increased, giving the position total responsibility for defense and security, as well as a central role in economic affairs. Thus, beginning in 1958 and culminating in the 1970s, French Guiana underwent a significant economic transformation. The traditional agriculture-based productive economy of the colonial era was replaced by a skewered consumer-oriented economy based on massive cash infusions from France. By 2000, over three-fourths of the population was involved in the service sector. Between 1958 and 1978, food production declined by over 50%. As a result, in later years most foodstuffs were imported. Although cattle-raising and rice cultivation have been introduced, the most dynamic sector of French Guiana's economy is the fishing industry. By 2000, shrimp exports represented 60% of French Guiana's total exports. Gold, timber, and rice exports each account for about ten percent of total exports. Regardless, exports remain minimal when compared to the substantial imports, which has perpetuated a negative trade balance.

MICHAEL R. HALL

See also Betancourt, Rómulo; Chavez, Hugo; Colombia; French Guiana; Guyana; Jagan, Cheddi; Organization of Petroleum Exporting Countries (OPEC); Pérez Jiménez, Marcos; Plan Colombia; Suriname; Venezuela

References and Further Reading

Bergquist, Charles. *Labor in Latin America: Comparative Essays on Chile, Argentina, Venezuela, and Colombia.* Stanford, CA: Stanford University Press, 1986.

Burton, Richard D. E. and Fred Reno. *French and West Indian: Martinique, Guadalupe, and French Guiana Today.* Charlottesville, VA: University of Virginia Press, 1995.

Hoefte, Rosemarijn. *In Place of Slavery: A Social History of British Indian and Javanese Laborers in Suriname.* Gainesville, FL: University of Florida Press, 1998.

Layton, Deborah. *Seductive Poison: A Jonestown Survivor's Story of Life and Death in the People's Temple.* New York: Anchor, 1999.

Redfield, Peter. *Space in the Tropics: From Convicts to Rockets in French Guiana.* Berkeley, CA: University of California Press, 2000.

Rivas, Darlene. *Missionary Capitalist: Nelson Rockefeller in Venezuela.* Chapel Hill, NC: University of North Carolina Press, 2002.

Roldan, Mary. *Blood and Fire: La Violencia in Antioquia, Colombia, 1946–1953.* Durham, NC: Duke University Press, 2002.

Sheahan, John. *Patterns of Development in Latin America: Poverty, Repression, and Economic Strategy.* Princeton, NJ: Princeton University Press, 1987.

Smith, William C., Carlos H. Acuña, and Eduardo A. Gamarra, eds. *Latin American Political Economy in the Age of Neoliberal Reform: Theoretical and Comparative Perspectives for the 1990s.* Miami, FL: University of Miami, 1994.

Van Dijck, Pitou. *Suriname: The Economy—Prospects for Sustainable Development.* Miami, FL: Ian Randle Publishers, 2001.

Wiarda, Howard J. and Harvey F. Kline. *Latin American Politics and Development.* Boulder, CO: Westview Press, 1996.

Wilpert, Gregory. *The Rise and Fall of Hugo Chavez: Revolution and Counter-Revolution in Venezuela.* London: Zed Books, 2004.

NORTHERN SOUTH AMERICA: INTERNATIONAL RELATIONS

Northern South America is composed of the independent nations of Colombia, Venezuela, Guyana, and Suriname, plus the French overseas department of French Guiana. The five states have experienced a number of significant border disputes, many of which are still unresolved. Since 1945, one of the most dramatic changes in the region has been the integration of these nations into the global community. Prior to 1945, foreign relations were dominated by relationships with the United Kingdom and the United States. In the post-World War II world, Canada, Japan, Germany, France, Italy, Spain, and the Netherlands have reinforced their influence in the region through cultural programs, economic aid, and support for political parties allied with their predominant ideologies. Regardless, the United States remains an important trading partner and continues to view the Caribbean Basin as its backyard. This trend has been reinforced by US economic and military aid packages. Notwithstanding continued hegemonic assumptions on the part of the United States, the nations of northern South America have pursued foreign policy initiatives that have been, at times, at variance with US foreign policy goals and objectives.

Colombia

In 1822, Gran Colombia (present-day Colombia, Venezuela, Ecuador, and Panama) was the first Latin American nation to receive US diplomatic recognition. Prior to World War II, however, the most pressing concerns for Colombian diplomats revolved around boundary disputes and territorial integrity. Although Colombia and the United States had cordial and friendly relations during the nineteenth century, the secession of Panama from Colombia in 1903 was a major source of friction in US–Colombian relations during the first two decades of the twentieth century. Despite the US government's support of the Panamanians in their independence from Colombia, economic ties with the United States were of great importance to Colombia even in the early twentieth century, since the United States was the largest importer of Colombian coffee. For over a decade, from 1922 to 1934, Colombia feuded over its common boundary with Peru in the Leticia area. The League of Nations agreement provided for Leticia becoming a permanent part of Peru. Brazil and Colombia agreed to a definitive frontier in 1928. Border disputes with Venezuela, especially over offshore exploratory drilling rights in the Gulf of Venezuela, caused great tension in Colombian–Venezuelan relations during the last quarter of the twentieth century. This tension was heightened by the hundreds of thousands of undocumented Colombians who fled the intense violence in Colombia for the relative safety of Venezuela. The most vociferous dispute, however, involved repeated claims by Nicaragua's Sandinista government concerning ownership of San Andrés Island. During the 1980s, the Sandinistas argued that San Andrés, which lies off the coast of Nicaragua, should be controlled by Nicaragua. The Sandinistas claimed that Nicaragua's acquiescence to Colombian ownership of the island in 1928 was not valid since the agreement was made when US marines were stationed in Nicaragua. The Colombian government considered the 1928 agreement binding.

Colombia broadened its foreign policy initiatives after World War II. It was an active participant in the San Francisco Conference that created the United Nations (UN) in 1945. Colombia also played an important role in creating the Organization of American States (OAS) in Bogotá in 1948. Former Colombian President Alberto Lleras Camargo was the OAS's first secretary general. Colombia's approach to national and international security issues has been characterized by a willingness to settle disputes through regional and international security organizations, rather than resorting to force. Throughout the early Cold War period, Colombia's foreign policy was based on consistent support of the United States against the Soviet Union and its allies. Believing that international communism was partially responsible for the violence unleashed in the wake of the 1948 *Bogotazo* (a civil uprising in the captial city over the assassination of Jorge Gaitan, a popular spokesman for the poor), Colombia severed relations with the Soviet Union. Colombia was the only Latin American nation to contribute militarily to the UN Peacekeeping Force in the Korean War. Although the Colombians only contributed one battalion and one battleship, the *Almirante Padilla,* this symbolic gesture strengthened US–Colombian friendship. In addition, Colombia provided the only Latin American troops to the UN Emergency Force in the Suez conflict. Colombia was thus rewarded with generous US economic and military aid packages.

Colombia voted fairly consistently with the United States in international security forums during the 1950s and early 1960s. Because of Fidel Castro's assistance to the *Ejército de Liberación Nacional* (ELN) guerrillas fighting the Colombian government, Colombia actively supported OAS sanctions against Cuba in 1962 and the expulsion of Cuba from the OAS in 1964. Its willingness to follow the US lead in the inter-American system, however, had diminished by the end of the 1960s. In 1968, diplomatic relations were reestablished with the Soviet Union, and in 1975 President Alfonso López Michelsen resumed diplomatic relations with Cuba. In addition, López Michelsen refused to condemn Castro's intervention in the Angolan civil war. In 1981, López Michelsen's successor, Julio César Turbay Ayala, a fervent anti-communist, broke diplomatic relations with Cuba after Castro admitted supporting the M-19 terrorist group in Colombia. Turbay reestablished close relations with the United States and affirmed President Ronald Reagan's thesis that Cuba and Nicaragua were the principal sources of subversion and turmoil in Latin America. Colombia was one of the few Latin American nations not to support Argentina's invasion of the Falklands in 1982.

Belisario Betancur, who won the 1982 presidential elections, reversed Turbay's anti-Argentine position in regard to the Falklands invasion, supported Bolivia's aspirations for territorial access to the Pacific Ocean, argued that the Sandinistas were not a menace to harmony in Central America, took Colombia out of the pro-Reagan camp, and joined the nonaligned movement. Concerned about the possibility of US military intervention in Central America and the escalation of Central American civil wars, Colombia joined with Mexico, Venezuela, and Panama in

January 1983 to form the Contadora Group to seek a solution to the Central American crisis. Betancur was afraid that Central America was turning into a battleground for the Cold War. Betancur became less sympathetic toward the Sandinistas as a result of their alleged involvement in supporting the M-19's 1985 *Palacio de Justicia* takeover and their renewed campaign to acquire San Andrés. Economic problems at home, coupled with domestic criticism of his foreign policy initiatives, convinced Betancur to move away from his nonaligned movement agenda.

Colombia's most difficult issue in foreign relations concerned drug trafficking. By 1980, Colombia was the major source of illegal cocaine and marijuana smuggled into the United States. The bilateral Extradition Treaty between Colombia and the United States, signed by both countries in 1979, provided for the extradition of suspected drug exporters to the United States. At first, Betancur, flush with his nonaligned movement rhetoric, refused to extradite Colombians as a matter of principle. By 1984, however, Betancur launched a war on the drug cartels and began extraditing drug traffickers—including cartel kingpin Carlos Lehder Rivas—to the United States. The drug lords responded by bribing officials, kidnapping prominent people, killing judges, and funding revolutionary movements. The demand for cocaine in the United States had turned Colombia into the most dangerous place in the world to live during the 1980s. Betancur's successor, Virgilio Barco, also declared war on the drug smugglers. The drug lords did not want to be extradited to the United States; they preferred to stay in Colombia, have a quick trial, and bribe the judges to dole out limited sentences. In 1987, the Colombian Supreme Court declared the law enforcing the extradition treaty unconstitutional. It was not until 1997 that the Colombian government allowed the extradition of suspected drug traffickers to the United States. The Clinton administration rewarded the Colombians by lifting the ban on military aid. In 1998, for the first time in three years, the US government "certified" Colombia as an ally in the war on drugs.

Venezuela

Two themes—oil exports and, to a lesser degree, border disputes—have dominated Venezuelan foreign policy initiatives for most of the twentieth century. Maintaining good relations with the United States has been a crucial part of this agenda. Although Venezuelan governments, such as Hugo Chavez's regime since 1999, have intermittently expressed the desire to create and implement foreign policy independent of that of the United States, they have not deviated significantly from the US agenda nor have they threatened oil exports to the United States. Frequently, Venezuelan governments have looked to the United States for leadership and help in solving their border disputes. Venezuela has long-standing border disputes with Colombia and Guyana, some of whose roots can be traced back to the nineteenth century. The disagreement with Colombia is primarily a maritime dispute over the Gulf of Venezuela. In the late 1980s, Colombian attempts to initiate oil exploration projects in the Gulf of Venezuela led to an impasse in Venezuelan–Colombian relations. Through diplomatic negotiations, and a meeting of the presidents of both nations at the border, the conflict was diffused. As of this writing, Venezuela continues to control the oil rights in the Gulf of Venezuela. The dispute with Guyana is much more problematic. Venezuela claims over half of Guyana's national territory. The dispute has its origins in Britain's attempts to expand its territorial holdings in British Guiana during the nineteenth century. Much to the chagrin of the Venezuelans, in 1899 an international tribunal awarded most of the disputed territory to the British.

During World War II, while Brazil and Mexico formally declared war on Nazi Germany, Venezuela merely broke off diplomatic relations with the Axis powers in 1941. Much more significant, however, is the fact that Venezuela provided a steady flow of petroleum to the United States during the war. In addition, the Venezuelan government froze all German assets in Venezuela. In 1947, as the threat of international communism was gradually revealed, Venezuela, like the rest of independent Latin America, signed the Inter-American Treaty of Mutual Assistance (the so-called Rio Treaty), which committed its members to a joint response should an attack be made against any of them. From 1948 to 1958, the military government in Venezuela was involved in a close relationship with the United States. Marcos Pérez Jiménez was an ardent anticommunist and acted quite favorably toward US business interests. During his dictatorship, foreign oil companies received generous concessions. US support for Latin American dictators, however, greatly decreased during the late 1950s. In 1958, members of Rómulo Betancourt's *Acción Democrática* (AD), Jóvito Villalba's Democratic Republican Union (URD), and Rafael Caldera's Independent Political Organizing Committee (COPEI) met at Caldera's home to sign the Pact of Punto Fijo, a civilian plan to avoid interparty conflicts, strengthen constitutional democracy, and establish a government of national unity to ensure that all political forces (with the notable exception of the communists) were represented in the political system. As such, it was the groundwork for a two-party representative democracy somewhat similar to that in the United States. Venezuela also felt a close political affinity to European democracies. AD governments pursued close ties with the socialist and social-democratic parties and governments in Europe, while COPEI administrations established close ties with the Christian democratic governments of Europe.

The first two presidents of the democratic era, Rómulo Betancourt and Raúl Leoni, were supporters and beneficiaries of President John F. Kennedy's Alliance for Progress. Once Juan Bosch's democratically elected government was overthrown by the Dominican Republic's military in September 1963, Venezuela stood as the brightest beacon of Kennedy's idea of a "showcase for democracy." Betancourt and Leoni, both representing the AD, took aggressive stands against nondemocratic regimes in Latin America. Both presidents were equally critical of Cuba's left-wing totalitarian dictator, Fidel Castro, and the Dominican Republic's right-wing authoritarian dictator, Rafael Trujillo, who plotted to assassinate Betancourt in 1960. Both administrations enforced the Betancourt doctrine, whereby Venezuela refused to maintain diplomatic relations with governments formed as a result of military coups. Unfortunately, during the 1960s and early 1970s, this doctrine gradually isolated Venezuela from the rest of Latin America, which was increasingly dominated by governments that came to power through military coups. During the 1970s, Venezuela abandoned the Betancourt doctrine and even restored diplomatic relations with Cuba in 1974.

Venezuela was in the forefront of organizing the Organization of Petroleum Exporting Countries (OPEC) in 1960. The 1973 Arab–Israeli War led to an oil embargo by Arab producers that resulted in quadrupled petroleum prices in the United States. Although Venezuela did not participate in the embargo, it did benefit from the increased revenue. High prices for oil changed Venezuela's perception of its role in international affairs. During the 1970s, Venezuela provided support to the Sandinistas who struggled to overthrow Nicaraguan dictator Anastasio Somoza Debayle. During the 1980s, Venezuela initiated the San José Accords, an agreement designed to supply oil at greatly reduced prices to economically challenged nations in the Caribbean Basin. In 1982, however, Venezuela suspended the discounted oil sales to the Sandinista government. The suspension was as much a result of the Nicaraguan government's failure to pay its massive oil debt as it was Venezuela's disappointment with the lack of progress toward implementing a democratic government in Nicaragua.

The Venezuelan government was supportive of Violetta de Chamorro when she won the 1990 elections in Nicaragua. The Nicaraguan oil debt to Venezuela was canceled and oil exports were immediately resumed. Venezuela strongly supported (and justified) Argentina's invasion of the Falklands in 1982. Venezuela's government, like most of the Latin American governments who argued for hemispheric solidarity at the time, was critical of the US invasion of Grenada in 1983. In 1983, Venezuela, Colombia, Mexico, and Panama met on the island of Contadora to design a regional strategy to obtain peace in war-torn Central America. Venezuela supported the establishment of democratic systems in the Caribbean Basin as the most beneficial solution for the countries involved as well as for Venezuela's own political and economic interests.

Guyana

Since gaining independence in 1966, Guyana's foreign policy has undergone a series of ideological changes in foreign policy making. From 1964 to 1969, Forbes Burnham's People's National Congress (PNC) was pro-Western. This was in marked contrast to Chedi Jagan's People's Progressive Party (PPP) whose leftist platform had prevailed until Burnham came to power in 1964. Beginning in 1969, Burnham began to move Guyanese foreign policy into the nonaligned camp. He also vocalized support for socialist causes in international forums. Guyana established diplomatic and economic ties with the communist governments in Eastern Europe, China, the Soviet Union, and Cuba. For example, in 1975, China agreed to provide interest-free loans to Guyana and to import Guyanese bauxite and sugar. Nevertheless, when Desmond Hoyte succeeded Burnham in 1985 he began to move Guyana back into the pro-Western camp. The fall of communism in the early 1990s accelerated this trend. In 1992, when Chedi Jagan returned to power, he abandoned his socialist rhetoric and continued the pro-Western approach of the Hoyte administration. Foreign relations with the United States, Venezuela, Suriname, and the English-speaking Caribbean states frequently dominate Guyanese foreign policy making.

US–Guyanese relations have ranged from cool to cordial. From 1964 to 1969, Burnham had the support of the United States. The US government was convinced that Burnham's government had no intention of pursuing Jagan-style socialism or of nationalizing foreign-owned industries. Whereas prior to 1964 the US was concerned that Jagan might transform Guyana into a "second Cuba," the United

States believed, all too simply, that Burnham would continue to follow the pro-Western path in foreign affairs. After 1969, when Burnham began to support socialism both domestically and internationally, relations between the United States and Guyana cooled significantly. When Burnham established a cooperative republic in 1970 and nationalized the sugar and bauxite industries in the mid-1970s, he placed Guyana firmly within the nonaligned movement. To retaliate, U.S. President Ronald Reagan excluded Guyana from participation in the Caribbean Basin Initiative (CBI). Burnham, who had ties to Grenada's New JEWEL Movement, was especially critical of the US invasion of Grenada in 1983. After Burnham's death in 1985, relations with the United States improved. President Hoyte energetically sought Western aid and investment in Guyana.

Venezuelan–Guyanese relations have been dominated by a persistent border dispute that dates back to Guyana's pre-independence period. During the nineteenth century, Guyana's colonial masters, the British, began to expand the colony westward at the expense of Venezuela. In 1899, an international tribunal in The Hague awarded the United Kingdom most of its territorial clams in eastern Venezuela. Today, that land constitutes five-eighths of Guyana's land mass. Complicating the situation is the fact that the disputed region is quite rich in minerals, especially gold. In 1962, Venezuela declared the 1899 tribunal decision void. In 1966, British, Guyanese, and Venezuelan representatives signed an accord that established a new tribunal, consisting of two Guyanese and two Venezuelans, to reevaluate the border dispute. Although the commission failed to reach an agreement, both nations promised to refrain from a violent resolution of the dispute. In 1969, Venezuela supported an ill-fated uprising in the southern sector of the disputed zone. Guyana's military crushed the rebellion and Venezuela was criticized by the other Latin American nations. In 1970, because of international pressure, Venezuela and Guyana signed a twelve-year moratorium on the dispute. The protocol was not renewed by Venezuela when it expired in 1982. Fearful that a precedent would be set, the Guyanese government harshly criticized Argentina's invasion of the Falkland Islands in 1982 and the U.S. invasion of Grenada in the subsequent year. As of this writing, although Venezuela still claims the disputed territory, there is little threat of a Venezuelan invasion.

Guyana's relations with Suriname have also been plagued by a border dispute. In 1969, Suriname sent troops into southeast Guyana to occupy a parcel of disputed territory. After the Guyanese defeated the invaders there were no subsequent attempts to take the disputed territory by force. Another problematic issue in relations with Suriname concerns the forced repatriation of Guyanese people living in Suriname. During the 1980s, Suriname's leader Desi Bouterse blamed Guyanese immigrants for Suriname's economic woes and began the forced repatriation.

Although its relations with Spanish-speaking Latin America are limited, Guyana has encouraged greater unity among the English-speaking Caribbean nations. Guyana is a member of CARICOM (the Caribbean Community) and CARICOM's headquarters are located in the capital of Guyana, Georgetown. By 1991, CARICOM's membership included all independent English-speaking nations in the Caribbean Basin. Relations with CARICOM member states were especially problematic in the aftermath of the US invasion of Grenada. Burnham accused Eugenia Charles, Dominica's prime minister, of complicity in the invasion. Tensions with CARICOM members diminished after Burnham's death in 1985.

Suriname

Since gaining independence in 1975, Suriname's foreign policy has been dominated by a series of conflicts regarding its borders with Guyana, Brazil, and French Guiana. These disputes, which trace their roots back to the colonial period, are exacerbated by the sparse population and lack of natural boundaries in the hinterland regions. Although Suriname has resolved its border dispute with Brazil, the border disputes with Guyana and French Guiana remain unresolved. Relations with the former colonial master, the Netherlands, have played a prominent role in Suriname's foreign relations. The Surinamese government has been dependent on continued infusions of economic aid, often totaling over $100 million annually. The continued flow of economic aid has frequently been conditioned by the actions of Suriname's government at home and abroad. When Suriname became independent, its large Asian population feared that it would lose political and economic privileges to the even larger African population. As a result, about 140,000 people (virtually 25% of the population) fled to the Netherlands. The Dutch government has consistently made the giving of aid conditional on the willingness of the Surinamese government, which is dominated by people of African ancestry, to move steadily along the path toward democracy.

Since independence, the most prominent and controversial figure in Suriname's history has been Desi

Bouterse. In 1980, a group of noncommissioned officers overthrew a civilian government led by Henck Arron. After an initial period of confusion, Lieutenant Colonel Bouterse emerged as the center of power. Bouterse greatly expanded the size of the military and experimented with the idea of forming an alliance with Cuba. Realizing the risks involved in this plan, especially in the aftermath of the US invasion of Grenada in 1983, Bouterse quickly disengaged from his foreign policy initiatives with Cuba. Nevertheless, the Reagan administration was suspicious of Bouterse, and the Dutch government cut off economic aid to Bouterse's increasingly brutal regime. In an attempt to regain the desperately needed Dutch economic aid, Bouterse, with varying degrees of success, worked to construct a veneer of democracy for his regime.

In 1986, Ronnie Brunswijk, who represented about fifty thousand descendants of runaway slaves who lived in the interior of Suriname and who were annoyed by Bouterse's attempts to alter their lifestyles by resettling them in urban areas, launched a civil war. US and Dutch government officials condemned Bouterse's tactics to combat the rebels, but stopped short of imposing further sanctions against Bouterse's regime. Thousands of Brunswijk's supporters fled to neighboring French Guiana, which complicated relations with France. Although the civil war continued, Bouterse's efforts to provide a facade of liberalization of the political system convinced the Dutch to resume economic aid by the end of the 1980s.

In 1990, after large quantities of cocaine began to arrive in the Netherlands, an investigation revealed that Bouterse was involved in the export of Colombian cocaine. Once again, the Dutch suspended their massive aid infusions. In 1991, Dutch economic pressure brought about democratic elections that resulted in the removal of Bouterse as commander of the military. In late 1997, Bouterse was tried *in absentia* in a Dutch court for drug smuggling and found guilty. Regardless, as of 2005, Bouterse remains free in Suriname. Since 2000, the democratically elected government of Runaldo Venetiaan has encouraged more Dutch and U.S. investment in Suriname, especially in the bauxite industry, and Suriname has become an active member of CARICOM (Caribbean Community).

French Guiana

Unlike its independent neighbors, French Guiana is still a part of France. As such, foreign policy emanates from Paris. French Guiana became a French colony in 1667. The colony was best known for its infamous prison on the *Ile du Diable* (Devil's Island), which was eventually closed in 1945. Unfortunately, French Guiana has never fully escaped its negative image as a former penal colony with an unhealthy climate and an impenetrable hinterland. In 1946, French Guiana was transformed into an overseas department—*département d'outremer*—of France. Unlike the peoples of other European colonies in the Caribbean who loudly clamored for independence during the post-1945 era, the people of French Guiana saw the economic benefits of remaining part of the French nation. In 1958, the power of the *Préfet,* the local representative in French Guiana of the central government in Paris, was increased, giving him total responsibility for defense and security. Regardless, foreign policy is still controlled by the French government. Since 1980, the French government has encouraged French immigration to the territory. As of the early twenty-first century, Continental French make up over 30% of French Guiana's population of 140,000 people.

MICHAEL R. HALL

See also Betancourt, Romulo; Chávez, Hugo; Colombia; French Guiana; Guyana; Jagan, Cheddi; Pérez Jiménez, Marcos; Organization of Petroleum Exporting Countries (OPEC); Plan Colombia; Suriname; Venezuela

References and Further Reading:

Abrams, Ovid. *Metegee: The History and Culture of Guyana.* Queens Village, NY: Eldorado Publications, 1998.

Burton, Richard D. E. and Fred Reno. *French and West Indian: Martinique, Guadalupe, and French Guiana Today.* Charlottesville, VA: University of Virginia Press, 1995.

Cockcroft, James D. *Latin America: History, Politics, and US Policy.* Chicago: Nelson Hall, 1996.

Crane, Janet. *French Guiana.* Santa Barbara, CA: ABC-Clio, 1999.

Dew, Edward M. *The Trouble in Suriname, 1975–1993.* New York: Praeger, 1994.

Ewell, Judith. *The Indictment of a Dictator: The Extradition and Trial of Marcos Pérez Jiménez.* College Station, TX: Texas A&M University Press, 1981.

Kelly, Janet and Carlos A. Romero. *United States and Venezuela: Rethinking a Relationship.* New York: Routledge, 2001.

Kryzanek, Michael J. *US–Latin American Relations.* Westport, CT: Praeger, 1996.

Langley, Lester. *America and the Americas: The United States in the Western Hemisphere.* Athens, GA: University of Georgia Press, 1989.

Randall, Stephen J. *Colombia and the United States: Hegemony and Interdependence.* Athens, GA: University of Georgia Press, 1992.

Redfield, Peter. *Space in the Tropics: From Convicts to Rockets in French Guiana.* Berkeley, CA: University of California Press, 2000.

Wilpert, Gregory. *The Rise and Fall of Hugo Chavez: Revolution and Counter-Revolution in Venezuela.* London: Zed Books, 2004.

NYERERE, JULIUS

Julius Nyerere (1922–1999) was president of Tanganyika from 1962–1964 and the co-founder and first president of Tanzania (1964–1985), first president of TANU (Tanganyika African National Union), and the founder and chairman (1977–1990) of the *Chama Cha Mapinduzi* (Revolutionary Party of Tanzania). Nyerere, known as Mwalimu (teacher) in Tanzania, was one of the greatest of the first generation of leaders of independent African states. As president of Tanzania, he directed one of the most widely studied—though little imitated—development efforts in the developing world. While some of the efforts he oversaw bore limited fruit, there is continuing interest in Nyerere's analysis of development issues, and especially in his ideas concerning education in the developing world.

Nyerere thought the goal of development efforts should be "man-centered" (Nyerere 1968). By this he meant that development should be aimed at establishing equity, self-reliant economic growth, and political order. Nyerere held that this would only be achieved through socialist policies. He identified socialism, however, not with specific institutions but with "an attitude of mind" (Nyerere 1968). Attitudes supporting non-exploitive relationships—whether economic, political, or social—should be the motivating force for development plans and reinforcing them should be a major policy goal. This required Tanzania to follow policies aimed at rural development, self-sustaining industrial growth, increased educational attainment, and political democracy within a one-party framework.

The development program was only partially successful. It had two prongs: Increased agricultural production was to take place through concentrating rural populations in so-called "ujamma" (familyhood) villages based on cooperative agriculture and application of agronomic techniques. While the ujamma villages did make delivery of government services more efficient, they were not generally successful. Tanzania has a long tradition of peasant agriculture based on ethnic and clan ties. The exploitation of these cultural bonds by local entrepreneurs and a relentlessly bureaucratic organizational structure combined to produce, at best, mixed success. The second prong was an ambitious industrial development program, based on cash crop agriculture, import substitution industries, and increased infrastructural investment. The failure of the ujamma village scheme, while not fatal to this effort, made it more problematic. Cash crop production never attracted the level of investment to become the engine of development Nyerere envisioned during his lifetime. Resource constraints, especially for petroleum products, had negative effects as well, given Tanzania's meager natural endowments. Finally, the lack of governmental planning capacity was never effectively overcome while Nyerere ruled Tanzania.

Nyerere's legacy has been more favorable in the area of social and human capital. Tanzania's commitment to democracy within a one-party framework was successful and paved the way for the adoption of multi-party democracy in 1995. While occasional human rights abuses have arisen (Saul 2000), the country has maintained political unity and made an easy transition to elective democracy. Tanzania has also managed to avoid the military takeover that has afflicted so much of Africa. Here the experience of the Ugandan War and the subsequent intervention of Tanzania in the insurrection in Mozambique are illustrative. In the course of the war, the Tanzania People's Defense Force (TPDF) transformed itself from five independent battalions to a divisional structure, increasing its size fourfold. The TPDF defeated the Ugandans and their Libyan allies and militarily occupied Uganda for two years. The subsequent demobilization of this force, including the diminution in rank of most of the officer corps, followed by the partial deployment of the TPDF to support the army of Mozambique, speak volumes about the stability and legitimacy of the government Nyerere created.

It is Nyerere's emphasis on educational policy, however, that is his main legacy. He insisted on reforming the education policies inherited from the colonial period to more closely fit the goal of increasing knowledge relevant to individual economic and political self-reliance. This meant attempting to extend primary education to all and reforming it to emphasize economically useful skills. Adult education was to be increased as well and refocused on eradicating illiteracy and, again, teaching useful skills. Secondary and collegiate education was to be reformed to tie advanced degrees to development goals and to eliminate its elite character. While, again, resource constraints have prevented full realization of these ideas in Tanzania, Nyerere's thoughts on these subjects are now received wisdom among development policy makers.

Tanzania is one of the few developing countries that has consistently attempted to promote growth with equity. While remaining poor, the country has created, largely due to Nyerere's influence, an environment (political participation and stability, government capacity, and macroeconomic stability) conducive to sustained, internally directed development (Helleiner 2000). As such, Tanzania and Nyerere's ideas should remain of interest to all concerned with the developing world.

TRACY L. R. LIGHTCAP

See also Tanzania

References and Further Reading

Assensoh, A. B. *African Political Leadership: Jomo Kenyetta, Kwame Nkrumah, and Julius K. Nyerere*. New York: Krieger, 1998.

Bienen, Henry. *Tanzania: Party Transformation and Economic Development*. Princeton, NJ: Princeton University, 1970.

Buchert, Lene. *Education in the Development of Tanzania: 1919–1990*. Athens, OH: Ohio University Press, 1994.

Legum, Colin and Geoffrey Mmari, eds. *Mwalimu: The Influence of Nyerere*. London: Africa World Press, 1995.

Von Freyhold, Michaela. *Ujamma Villages in Tanzania: Analysis of a Social Experiment*. New York: Monthly Review, 1979.

INDEX

A

AAPC (All-African People's Congress), 29–30
Abantu-Botho (newspaper), 10
Abasuma people, 939
Abbagholizadeh, Malboobeh, 1720
Abdali, Ahmad Shah, 3
Abdelrahman Al-Saud, Abdulaziz bin, 1391
Abdel-Razig, Ali, 878
Abduh, Mohammad, 877
Abdullah II, King, 893
Abiola, M.K.O., 1142
Abkhazians, in Georgia, 697
Abkhazia territorial dispute, 87–88, 378, 1533
Aborney, 167
Abortion, 656
    infanticide and availability, 819
    legalization of, 654, 655
    Ronald Reagan and funding of, 1635–1636
    Soviet Union and, 654–655
Abrams, Gen. Creighton, 1668
Absentee voting, 557
Abubakar, Gen. Abdulsalami, 1142
Abu Dhabi Fund for Development, 927
Abu Dhabi Investment Authority, 1595
Abu Dhabi National Oil Company, 1595
Abuja Treaty, 9, 1204
Abu Masa island, 1534
Acción Democrática (Venezuela), 1178, 1259–1260, 1659
Acción Popular (Peru), 1269
Aceh independence, 1455
Aceh people, 618–619
Aceh War, 619
Acidic solutions, 1
Acid precipitation, 1–3, 558, 1289
Acíon Democrática, 1183–1184
ACP (African–Caribbean and Pacific Group), 506
Action Against Hunger, 480
Adams, Grantley, 155
Adams, Tom, 248
Addis Ababa conference, 29–30
Addo Elephants National Park, 1245
Adedeji, Adebyo, 530
Adem, Idris, 577
Adiaphora policy, 51
ADPS (ASEAN Dialogue Partnership System), 115
Adriatic Charter, 411
Afar people, 478–479. *See also* Djibouti
AFDU (*Alliance des Forces Démocratiques pour la Libération du Congo Zaire*), 265
Afghani Communist Party (PDPA), 3–4
Afghanistan, 3–4
    immunization programs, 1330
    Initiative for Strengthening Afghan Family Laws, 1719
    Islam in, 299–300

mujahedin, 1091–1092, 1223, 1520
    opium trade, 489
    Soviet invasion, 303, 416, 1091
    Taliban, 1092, 1224, 1520–1522
    territorial disputes, 1534–1535
    UNICEF in, 1603
    United States and, 307, 1521–1522
    USAID road-building projects, 1636
    women, 1092
Aflaq, Michel, 71, 335
Afobaka Dam (Suriname), 1508
AFRC (Armed Forces Revolutionary Council), 700
Africa. *See also* African *entries and individual countries*
    agricultural privatization, 24
    agricultural water use, 1689
    authoritarian states, 121, 122, 123
    balkanization, 360–361, 500–501, 626–627
    banking in, 149
    caste system, 255
    civic education, 339–340, 342
    colonial legacy, 364–366
    colonial partitioning, 360–361, 500–501, 626–627
    education, 342
    foreign direct investment by, 672
    foreign direct investment in, 671
    global climate change and, 705
    health care systems, 748
    HIV/AIDS, 756–757
    Language Plan of Action for, 940
    legal system, 956
    Lomé Convention, 964–966
    national parks, 1245
    Organization of African Unity (OAU). *See* Organization of African Unity
    poverty in, 1311, 1312
    refugees and decolonization, 1352
    single-party government and, 1415
    Soros foundations in, 1436
    susu groups, 151
    water management, 872
    white colonial administrators, 1705
    white colonists, 1705–1706
    white community in, 1705–1708
Africa Growth and Opportunity Act, 233
African–Caribbean and Pacific Group (ACP), 506
African Central Bank, 9
African Charter on Human and Peoples' Rights, 782
African Committee of Central Bank Governors, 9
African Development Bank (ADB), 4–5, 506, 1608. *See also* Economic Commission for Africa
African Development Bank Group, 151
African Development Fund, 4
African Diaspora, 6–9, 240, 1234
    African independence and, 7–8
    globalization and, 8

African Economic Community (AEC), 1204
African Farmer's Association, 10
African Farmers Union, 1585
African Gender and Development Index, 530
African Growth and Opportunity Act (AGOA), 1700, 1701
African Homelands, 152–154, 979. *See also* Apartheid;
    Native reserves
African independence movements, 7–8
African Investment Bank, 9
Africanists, 11
African Monetary Fund, 9–10
African National Congress (ANC), 59, 61–62, 153, 435, 436,
    989–990, 1440, 1463. *See also* Apartheid; Mandela, Nelson
    Albert Luthuli and, 967
    Bandung Conference, 139–140, 1118, 1234–1235, 1506–1507
    Bishop Desmond Tutu and, 1581
    Thabo Mbeki, 1006–1007
    Zambian, 1752
African Union, 5, 1202, 1700, 1702. *See also* Organization of
    African Unity (OAU)
    global trading patterns and, 1568
Africare, 476
Afrikaner Party, 10, 11
Afrikaners, 57–62, 1439. *See also* Apartheid; South Africa
    Boer War, 58, 622, 1706
    D.F. Malan, 979–980
    Great Trek, 622
Afro-Shirazi Party (ASP), 1197–1198, 1523
AFTA (Asian Free Trade Area), 97
Agency for International Development (AID), 459
Agenda 21, 1510
Agglomeration economies, 1643, 1644. *See also* Urbanization
Aging populations
    United Nations International Institute on Aging, 1624–1625
    Vienna International Plan of Action on Aging, 1625
    World Assembly on Aging, 1625
Agrarian reform, 934–936
    Albania, 26
    Brazil, 1410
    Central America, 934
    Chile, 31, 681, 934
    China, 582, 935
    Cuba, 413
    development and, 1615
    Dominican Republic, 186
    East Asia, 513
    El Salvador, 934
    Gamal Abdel Nasser and, 1102
    global perspective, 935
    Grenada, 720
    Guatemala, 80
    Iraq, 130
    Kenya, 935
    Landless Peoples Movement, 934
    Latin America, 33
    Mexico, 1247
    Nicaragua, 934, 1138
    Peru, 46, 47
    South Africa, 935
    Southeast Asia, 1450
    Southern African controversies, 1466–1467
    South Korea, 935
    Soviet Union, 935
    Suba, 934
    Syria, 130
    Taiwan, 935
    Tanzania, 934–935
    Venezuela, 171, 1660
    Zimbabwe, 935
Agri-business, 17
Agricultural development. *See also* Rural development
    African Development Bank and, 5
Agricultural diversification, in Caribbean, 236
Agricultural globalization, 11–18
    capital concentration and, 14–15
    environmental consequences, 12–13
    future prospects, 17–18
    land ownership and, 14
    political power and, 15–16
    social consequences, 12
    technological innovation and, 17
    trade liberalization and, 13–14
Agricultural pollution, 1284–1288
    air, 1285–1286
    biodiversity and habitat loss, 1286
    haze, 116, 445–446, 1419–1420
    human health and, 1287–1288
    soil degradation, 1286
    water, 1285
Agricultural privatization, 18–25
    into agri-enterprises, 23
    employment and, 24
    land fragmentation and, 19–20, 21–22
    restoration and compensation, 19, 21–22
Agricultural research
    globalization and, 17
    Rockefeller Foundation and, 1367, 1368
Agriculture. *See also specific crops*
    Bangladesh, 141–142
    Central Africa, 261–262
    Central America, 274
    Central Asia, 299
    Consultative Group on International Agricultural Research
        (CGIAR), 852–853
    corporate, 665
    deforestation and, 445–446, 1347
    Equatorial Guinea, 575, 576
    erosion and, 580–581
    Estonia, 583
    Food and Agriculture Organization (FAO), 15, 1692,
        1732–1734
    Gambia, 691
    globalization and, 11–18. *See also* Agricultural globalization
    Green Revolution, 717–719
    Guatemala, 725
    Hong Kong, 765
    international government organizations and, 15
    International Rice Research Institute (IRRI), 852–853
    irrigation, 870–875
    Israeli communal farms, 881
    Malawi, 982
    migrant workers, 194–195
    monoculture, 17, 1347, 1501
    non-governmental organizations (NGOs) and, 16
    non-intensive crop production, 1501
    Oceania, 1193
    peasants, 1256–1258
    privatization of, 18–25. *See also* Agricultural privatization
    rainfed, 870–871, 903
    slash-and-burn. *See* Deforestation; Haze pollution

slavery and, 7
subsistence defined, 12, 21. *See also* Subsistence agriculture
sustainability of. *See* Sustainability
Tonga, 1553
United Nations Food and Agriculture Organization,
    1616–1617
United Nations International Fund for Agricultural
    Development, 1624
virtual water trade, 1671–1672
water usage, 1689
water used by. *See also* Irrigation
women in, 1724–1725
Aguirre Cerda, Pedro, 680
Ahidjo, Ahmadou, 25–26, 217–218, 264, 269.
        See also Cameroon
Ahmed Ali, Abduraham, 1433
AIC (ASEAN Industrial Complementation), 114
AID (Agency for International Development), 459
Aidid, Mohaed Farad, 507
AIDS. *See* HIV/AIDS
AIP (ASEAN Industrial Project), 114
Air and Rain: The Beginnings of a Chemical Climatology
    (Smith), 2
Air pollution
    agricultural, 1285–1286
    from biomass burning, 1286
    dioxins, 1682–1683
    furans, 1682–1683
    industrial, 1289–1290
    smaze, 1419–1420
    TCDD, 1683
Akan peoples, 626, 700
Akayev, Askar, 383
Akhan peoples, 1540
Akoerio Indians, 1507
ALADI (Latin American Integration Association), 945–946
ALALC (*Asociación Latinoamerica de Libre Comercio*), 44
al-Aqsa *intifada*, 861–862, 883–884, 1227. *See also* Intifada
Alarcón, Fabian, 49
al-Assad, Bashar, 1513
al-Assad, Hafiz, 470
Alawi people, 608–609, 632
Alawi religion, 1028
al-Aziz ibn Saud, Abd, 1391
al-Bakr, Ahmad Hasan, 868
Albania, 26–27. *See also* Albanians
    agricultural privatization, 19, 21, 22
    Black Sea Economic Cooperation Organization, 183–184
    Enver Hoxha, 766–768
    international relations, 294–295
    Macedonia and, 972
    political history, 287–288
    Romania and, 1488
    territorial disputes, 1532
Albanians
    in Macedonia, 972
    in Serbia, 138, 1059, 1398
Albert, Zaly, 974
Albright, Madeleine, 772
Alcoholism, 1014. *See also* Substance abuse and dependence
al-Din ibn al-Arabi, Muhyi, 1504–1506
Alemán, Arnoldo, 1135
Alemán Valdés, Miguel, 1017, 1021
Alessandri, Arturo, 31
Alessandri, Jorge, 31

al-Faisal, Toujan, 1720
al-Fatah, 70, 79. *See also* Arafat, Yasser; PLO
Alfonsín, Raúl, 93, 1485
al-Gaylani, Nuri al-Said, 868
Algeria, 27–29
    Ahmed Ben Bella, 165–166, 1157–1158, 1166, 1169
    Arab Maghreb Union (AMU), 67–68, 1165, 1169–1170
    Barcelona Declaration, 1168
    Berbers in, 170
    decolonization, 361–362
    Economic Commission for Africa and, 528–530
    economic development, 1160
    ethnic conflict, 612–613
    French atrocities, 1157
    French nuclear testing and, 1166
    geography and climate, 1156
    Houari Boumédiénne, 191–193
    independence movement, 69
    international relations, 1165–1166
    Islamic Salvation Front, 1158
    Libya and, 1169
    Marxism in, 1001
    Morocco and, 1164, 1168–1169, 1204
    National Liberation Front (FLN), 28, 166, 191–192, 613,
        1157, 1537, 1545
    OAPEC and, 1208
    oil production, 1158
    OPEC and, 1158
    political history, 1157–1158
    populism in, 1305
    Spain and, 1166
    Tunisia and, 193
    unemployment, 1162
    white community, 1707
    women, 1162
Algerians, in Azerbaijan, 127
al-Ghazah, Mohammed, 1504–1506
Alianza Anticomunista Argentina, 82
Alianza para el Desarrollo Sostenible (ALIDES), 280
Alianza Popular Revolucionaria Americana (APRA),
        46, 62–65, 1267
Ali Ato, Osman, 1433
ALIDES (*Alianza para el Desarrollo Sostenible*), 280
Aligarth Muslim University, 36
Ali Jinnah, Azam Mohammad, 1097, 1222
Ali Khan, Liaquat, 35, 36, 1222
Ali Mahdi, Mohammed, 1433
Aliyev, Haidar (Heydar), 127, 382
al-Jazeera television, 1032
Alkaline solutions, 1
Alkali Works Act of 1863, 2
Alkatiri, Mari, 524
All-African People's Congress (AAPC), 29–30, 1147
All-Africa Peoples Organization, 1235
Allende Gossens, Salvador, 30–32, 309, 321, 416, 681, 934,
        1274, 1477, 1484. *See also* Chile
    ECLAC and, 1615
Alliance Congress Freedom Charter (1955), 11
Alliance des Forces Démocratiques pour la Libération du
    Congo Zaire (AFDU), 265
Alliance for Progress, 32–35, 278–279, 732, 1106, 1184, 1635
    historical context, 32–33
    program, 33–34
Alliance for Sustainable Development, 280
All-India Muslim League, 35–36

All-India Muslim Students Federation, 35
All People's Congress (Sierra Leone), 627
Alma-Ata Declaration, 375–379. *See also* Commonwealth
    of Independent States
Alma-Ata health care conference, 749–750
Almond, Gabriel, 459, 460
Almoravid movement, 1004
al-Qadir, Abd, 28
al-Qaeda, 4, 730, 1091, 1264
    in East Africa, 508
    Egypt and, 1089–1090
    Taliban and, 1520–1522
    in Yemen, 1747
al Qawasim tribe, 1595
al-Rimawi, Abdullah, 129
al-Sabah, Sheikh Jaber, 927
al-Said, Nuri, 130
Alsalam Farij, Mohammed Abed, 1096
al-Salim, Abdullah, 925
al-Sistanni, Ayatolla Ali, 870
Altaic languages, 1576
Alternative development, 1592–1593
Alternative energy, 558–561
Alternative technology, 1593
Aluku people, 1507
Aluminum. *See* Bauxite
Alvarez, General Gregorio, 1647
Amadou, Hama, 1141
Amanullah (Afghan king), 3
Amazon rainforest, 1245, 1345–1346, 1474–1475. *See also*
    Rainforest
    biodiversity, 1346
    deforestation, 1345–1349, 1474
    Ecuadoran, 49
    Huaorani Indians, 49
    Kayapó Indigenous Area, 624
    pharmaceuticals from, 179, 1346
    species count, 179
Ambedkar, Bhimrao Ramji, 1640–1641
American Colonization Society, 959
American Convention on Human Rights, 782
American Declaration of Independence, 777, 779
American Declaration of the Rights and Duties of Man, 782
American decolonization, 358–359
American Samoa
    demographics, 1191
    international relations, 1194
American Society of African Culture (AMSAC), 1235
American Wildlife Foundation, Kenyan elephant project, 1711
Americas
    slavery in, 6–7
    water management status, 872
Amerindian peoples, 605–606. *See also specific peoples*
Amid, Idi, 632
Amin, Hafizullah, 4, 1091
Amin, Idi, 36–37, 503, 504, 600. *See also* Uganda
Amin, Qassim, 878
Amin, Samit, 461
Amin Dada, Gerald Idi, 1586
Amin Didi, Maumoon, 984
Amnesty International, 37–38
    Argentina and, 1482
    China and, 519–520
    Equatorial Guinea and, 576
Amoako, K. Y., 530

AMSAC (American Society of African Culture), 1235
Anaconda Copper Corporation, 1484
Anarchy, State and Utopia (Nozick), 798
ANC. *See* African National Congress
Ancient Ghana, 1694–1695
Ancient Mali, 1695
Andean Common Market, 44
Andean Community, 38–39. *See also* Andean South America
Andean Council of Foreign Ministers, 39
Andean Development Corporation, 9, 39
Andean Pact, 39
Andean Regional Initiative, 1277
Andean South America. *See also individual countries*
    Andean Regional Initiative, 1277
    Bolivia, 184–186
    Chile, 320–323
    Cold War and, 40–42
    Colombia, 350–353
    Ecuador, 541–542
    Ecuadorian/Peruvian border conflict, 42–43
    geography and climate, 45–46, 1475
    international relations, 39–45
    Peru, 1267–1270
    Peruvian relations with Chile and Bolivia, 43–44
    political history, 45–51
    regional issues, 44–45
    Uruguay, 1646–1648
    Venezuela, 1658–1661
Andrés Pérez, Carlos, 1178–1179, 1659–1660
Anglican Church, in Barbados, 155
Anglican Communion, 51–52
Anglicization, 1119
Anglo-Boer War, 58, 622, 1706. *See also* Afrikaners
Anglo-Dutch Treaty, 619
Anglo-Iranian Oil Company, 1029, 1085, 1221
Angola, 53–54
    CIA in, 309
    COMESA and, 369
    Cuban invasion, 246, 416
    debt holdings, 370–371
    diamond production, 250
    Economic Commission for Africa and, 528–530
    ethnic conflicts, 623
    independence, 1462
    Movimiento Popular de Libertação de Angola, 1292–1293
    oil industry, 270, 646–647, 649
    South African war with, 60–61, 189
    Southern African Development Community and, 1463
    territorial disputes, 1536
    United Nations Development Program in, 1607
    white community, 1706
Anguilla
    Caribbean Community and Common Market and, 233–235
    Caribbean Development Bank and, 235–237
Animal husbandry. *See* Livestock production
Anopheles mosquitoes, 822
Antall, Jozsef, Visehrad Four and, 1672
Anthropological development theories, 458–459
Antigua and Barbuda
    Association of Caribbean States and, 111
    Caribbean Basin Initiative and, 232–233
    Caribbean Community and Common Market and, 233–235
    Caribbean Development Bank and, 235–237
    Caribbean Free Trade Association and, 237–238, 238
    international relations, 248–249

Antigua Trades and Labour Union (ATLU), 56
Anti-Semitism. *See also* Ethnic conflicts
    in Communist-occupied lands, 592
    in Eastern and Central Europe, 593
    of HAMAS, 741–742
Antonescu, Ion, 1074
Aotcaro, 1195
Apartheid, 10–11, 57–62, 435–436, 957, 980, 1462–1463. *See also*
    Afrikaners; Racial discrimination; South Africa
    Bantustans and, 152–154
    Bishop Desmond Tutu and, 1580–1581
    collapse of, 61–62
    Defiance Campaign, 1440
    demise of formal, 1440–1441
    historical development of, 57–58
    introduction of, 1439–1440
    legacies of, 622–623
    liberation struggle, 59–60
    Organization of African Unity and, 1203–1204
    resistance to, 1440. *See also* African National Congress
    rules and legislation, 58–59
    world community and, 60–61
APEC (Asia–Pacific Economic Cooperation), 108–111, 1450
APEC Energy Initiative, 109
APEC Summit, 1132
Applications of Meteorology Programme (WMO), 1739
APRA (*Alianza Popular Revolucionaria Americana*), 46, 62–65.
    See also Aprismo; Aprista movement
Aprismo, 62–65
Aprista movement, 62–65, 745
Aquatic system, acid precipitation and, 2
Aquifers, 1688. *See also* Water
Aquino, Benigno, 65–66, 977, 996, 1272–1273. *See also* Philippines
Aquino, Corazón, 65–66, 1273, 1349. *See also* Philippines
Arab Bank for Economic Development in Africa, 927
Arab Berbers. *See* Berbers
Arab Economic Unity Council, 67
Arab Fund for Economic and Social Development, 927
Arabian-American Oil Company (ARAMCO), 72–73, 1036,
    1085, 1391–1392
    OPEC and, 1213
Arab–Israeli Wars, 73–78, 1381–1382
    of 1948–1949, 73–75
    First, 1159
    Fourth, 1159
    intifadas and, 71, 80, 741–742, 860–862, 883–884, 1038, 1227,
        1231–1232
    Israel's development and, 882–883
    October (Yom Kippur) War, 77–78, 1038
    Six-Day War, 70, 71, 76–77, 161, 883, 1038
    Suez War of 1956, 17, 75–76, 219–220, 548, 1035–1036, 1059
    United Nations Relief and Works Agency for Palestine
        (UNRAW), 1629–1631
Arab League. *See* League of Arab States
Arab Maghreb Union (AMU), 67–68, 1165
Arab Maritime Petroleum Company, 1208
Arab Monetary Fund, 9
Arab nationalism, 68–72. *See also* Pan-Arabism
    Ba'ath Party and, 71
    early roots, 68
    forums of Arab expression, 71–72
    future of, 72
    Palestine question and, 70–71
    Pan-Arabism and, 69–70
    in 20th century, 69

Arab Petroleum Investments Corporation, 1208
Arab Petroleum Services Company, 1208–1209
Arab Revival Movement, 129. *See also* Ba'ath Party
Arab Revolt, 1226
Arab Shipbuilding and Repair Yard Company, 1208
Arab Socialist Ba'ath Party. *See* Ba'ath Party
Arab Specialized Organizations, 67
Arafat, Yasser, 70–71, 78–80, 861, 883, 884, 1036. *See also*
    Palestine Liberation Organization (PLO)
    Algeria and, 1166
    HAMAS and, 742
    refugee camps and, 1631
Aral Sea
    pollution, 299, 1286, 1374, 1648
    salinization, 1689
    territorial disputes, 1534
Aram, Abbas, 305–306
ARAMCO. *See* Arabian-American Oil Company
Aram-Pegov Agreement, 305–306
Arap Moi, Daniel, 502
Arawak Indians, 131, 154, 586–587, 683, 1083, 1125, 1126,
    1507, 1669
Arbenz, Jacobo, 278, 308, 726, 727, 732
Árbenz Guzmán, Jacobo, 80–81. *See also* Guatemala
Arbitration, of disputes, 837
Archaelogical treasures, Three Gorges Dam and, 1547
Archaeological findings, Papua New Guinea, 1240
Arden-Clarke, Sir Charles, 30
Ardipithecus ramidus, 500
Arendt, Hannah, 1555, 1557–1558
    ideology and, 1558
    social revolution theory, 1421
Arévalo, José, 80
Argentina, 81–83
    agricultural oligarchy, 1476
    arms exports, 96
    banking industry, 149
    Brazil and, 228
    bureaucratic authoritarianism in, 208, 209
    Carlos Menem, 1011–1012
    debt, 223, 439, 441, 442, 1011–1012
    Ejército Revolucionario del Pueblo (ERP), 82, 1363–1364
    erosion control, 582
    ethnic conflicts, 624–625
    financial crises, 150, 1011–1012, 1479
    foreign direct investment, 708
    geography and climate, 1474, 1475
    income inequality, 1311
    international relations, 1481–1482
    Juan Perón, 1260–1261, 1476–1477, 1481
    Justicialist Movement, 1081
    liberal elites, 1481
    Malvinas/Falkland Islands, 83, 986–987, 1487
    Malvinas/Falkland War, 83, 986–987, 1479
    MERCOSUR and, 1472–1474
    Montoneros, 1081–1082
    national parks, 1244
    Nazi Germany and, 1481
    Paraguay and, 1242–1243
    Paraguayan dependence on, 1485
    Partido Revolucionario de Trabajo (PRT), 1363
    Patagonia region, 1475
    Peronistas, 1477
    populism in, 1304
    reforestation, 582

Argentina (*Continued*)
    territorial disputes, 1538, 1647
    transition to democracy, 123
    Treaty of Asunción, 200, 1483
    urban guerilla warfare, 1477–1478
    Uruguayan and, 1647
    War of the Triple Alliance, 1484
    Yungas Biosphere Reserve, 1245
Argentine Institute for the Promotion of Trade, 1260
Arias, Harmodio, 1238
Arias Foundation for Peace and Human Progress, 84
Arias Madrid, Arnulfo, 1237
Arias Peace Plan, 394
Arias Sanchez, Oscar, 84–85, 279, 280, 394, 726. *See also*
    Costa Rica
Arica, 43
Arif, Abd as-Salam, 129
Aristide, Jean-Bertrand, 85–86, 244. *See also* Haiti
    Organization of American States and, 1206
Aristotle, 347
Ariyanattne, A.T., 1489
Armed Forces for National Liberation (FALN), 171
Armed Forces of the People (FAP), 86–87
Armed Forces Revolutionary Council (AFRC), 700
Armenia, 87–88
    agricultural privatization, 21, 23
    Black Sea Economic Cooperation Organization, 183–184
    Black Sea Economic Organization and, 381
    Commonwealth of Independent States and, 375–380
    destruction of Red Kurdistan, 924
    ethnic conflict, 596
    Nagorno-Karabakh dispute, 87–88, 378, 382, 924, 1253, 1533
Armenian National Movement, 382
Armenians, in Georgia, 697
Arms control, 91
Arms embargoes, 90
    Cuba, 159, 887
    Czechoslovakia, 116
Arms industrialization
    development and, 95–96
    international political conditions and, 93
    political aspects, 93–94
    "spin-off" development, 95
Arms industry. *See also* Arms industrialization; Arms transfer
    decline in world market, 96
    market niches and restrictions, 94–95
    motives and goals for establishing, 92–93
Arms transfer, 88–92. *See also* Arms industrialization;
    Arms industry
    to Central Africa, 268
    development and, 91–92
    to East Africa, 600
    to Egypt, 117
    to India, 694
    international system and, 89–90
    to Kosovo Liberation Army, 138
    to Madagascar, 86
    to Nigeria, 628
    recent trends, 90–91
    US to Nicaragua, 394
    volume of, 88
Arosemena Monroy, Carlos Julio, 47–48
Arrhenius, Svante, 703–704
Arron, Henk, 1508
Arsenic poisoning, groundwater and, 1688

Arteaga, Rosalia, 49
Art of War (Sun Tzu), 728
Aruba, 1125, 1126. *See also* Netherlands Antilles
    Association of Caribbean States and, 111
    Caribbean Basin Initiative and, 232–233
Arusha Declaration, 1524
Arusha Peace Accords, 212
ASEAN, 66, 67, 97–98, 112–116, 481, 645
    Asian Financial Institute and, 104–105
    Common Effective Preferential Tariff (CEPT), 97–98
    dispute settlement, 114–115
    evolving issues, 115
    foreign direct investment and, 1530
    formation, 1449–1450
    historical background, 112
    industrial cooperation programs, 1529
    industrial development, 114
    international relations, 1455–1456
    investment development, 114
    margin of preference (MOP), 97–98
    Mekong Basin Development Corporation, 98–100
    Newly Industrialized Economies in, 1131
    Post Ministerial Conferences (PMC), 113
    Preferential Trade Agreement (PTA), 97, 113
    regional security, 114–115
    Singapore and, 1412
    Spratly Islands dispute and, 1241–1243
    structure, 112–113
    trade expansion efforts, 97
    trade policy, 1563–1564
    trade promotion within, 113
    Vietnam and, 1665
ASEAN Declaration, 112
ASEAN Dialogue Partnership System (ADPS), 115
ASEAN Free Trade Area, 113
ASEAN Industrial Complementation (AIC), 114
ASEAN Industrial Joint Venture, 114
ASEAN Industrial Project, 113, 114
ASEAN Regional Forum, 115
Ashante people, 626
Asia
    colonial legacy, 366–368
    countertrade in, 407
    foreign direct investment by, 672
    global climate change and, 705–706
    human rights development, 782
    legal systems, 956
    water management status, 872
Asia-Africa Conference (Bandung), 1506–1507
Asian Development Bank (ADB), 100–101, 151, 1609, 1610
    Japan and, 101
    Kiribati and, 913
    Mekong Basin Development Corporation, 98–100
    Micronesia and, 1026
    reorganization of, 101
    Vietnam Poverty Reduction Partnership Agreement, 1666
Asian Development Fund, 100–101
Asian "economic miracle," 101–103. *See also* Asian Tigers;
    Tiger economies
Asian financial crisis, 102, 109–110, 221, 765
    Malaysia and, 978–979
    Singapore and, 1412–1413
Asian Financial Institute, 104–105
Asian Free Trade Area (AFTA), 97
Asian Monetary Fund, 104–105

Asian Relations Conference, 1442

Asian surveillance, 9

Asian Tigers, 105–108, 463, 816, 917–918, 1450. *See also* Tiger economies

    export-oriented and import-substitution, 105–106, 515

    Hong Kong, 764–765

    language and, 940

    as Newly Industrialized Economies, 1131

    Singapore, 1411–1414

    South Korea as example, 106

    sustaining growth, 106–107

Asian values, 1449

Asia Pacific Economic Cooperation (APEC), 1450

    Singapore and, 1412

Asia-Pacific Economic Cooperation (APEC), 108–111, 1383

    agendas, 109

    annual meetings and institutionalization, 109

    challenges to, 110

    economic reform, 109–110

    future prospects, 110

    origin and evolution, 108–109

Asia-Pacific Economic Forum, 518

As-Khalifa family, 133–134

Aslonov, Kadreddin, 302

Asociación Latinoamerica de Libre Comercio (ALALC), 44

ASP (Afro-Shirazi Party), 1197–1198

Assad, Bashar, 71

Assad, Hafiz, 77, 129

Assassinations. *See also Coups d'etat*

    Abdul Ghassemlou, 921

    Anastasio Somoza Deayle, 1434

    Anastasio Somoza Garcia, 1134

    Anwar Sadat, 70, 220, 1096, 1382

    Archbishop Oscar Romero, 660, 958

    Archduke Franz Ferdinand, 285

    Benigno Aquino, 66, 996, 1273

    CIA, 309

    CIA in, 308

    Count Folke Bernadotte, 74

    Eliécar Gaitán, 1177

    François Tombalbaye, 311

    Gamal Abdul Nasser attempt, 1096

    Imre Nagy, 790

    Indira Gandhi, 1409

    Jigme Wangchuck Dorsi, 174

    Jorge Gaitán, 351

    Martin Luther King, 344

    Maurice Bishop, 232

    Merchior Ndadaye, 212

    Mexico, 1019, 1020, 1024

    Mohandas Gandhi, 344

    Muslim Brotherhood and, 1096

    Nicaragua, 1434

    Palau, 1225

    Patrice Lumumba, 309, 388, 966

    Pedro Joaquin Chamorro, 1137–1138

    Rafael Trujillo, 186, 245, 484

    Rajiv Ghandi, 804

    Richard Ratsimandrava, 973–974

    Samuel K. Doe, 960

    Sassou-Nguesso, Denis, 390

    Thomas Sankara, 211

    Tom Mboya, 906

    Yuschenko attempt, 384

Associated-dependent development, 465

Association, freedom of, 347

Association of Caribbean States (ACS), 111–112, 243

Association of Southeast Asian Nations. *See* ASEAN

Aswan High Dam, 76, 116–119, 1090, 1103, 1159, 1688

Asylum policies, 1353. *See also* Refugees

Atacama Desert, 453

Ataturk, Mustafa Kemal, 920, 1049, 1577

Atlantic Charter, 29

ATLU (Antigua Trades and Labour Union), 56

Atmospheric Research and Environment Programme (WMO), 1739

Atomic energy. *See* Nuclear energy

Atomic weapons. *See* Nuclear weapons

Atrocities

    Balkan Wars, 136–137

    Bosnia, 188

    Bosnia-Herzegovina, 295

    Ciskei, 154

    Dominican Haitians, 484

    East Timor Santa Cruz Massacre, 524

    French in Algeria, 1157

    Ma'alot massacre of school children, 1228

    My Lai, 1668

    partition of India and, 361

    Robert Mugabe accused of, 1090

    in Rwanda, 212

    Soweto Massacre, 1440

    Tiananmen Square massacre, 451, 1549–1551

    Tlatelolco student massacre, 1018–1019, 1022–1023, 1247–1248

    Trujillo against Haitians. *See* Atrocities

    against Uzbeks, 596

    Windhoek massacre (Namibia), 1444

AUC (United Self-Defense Forces of Colombia), 352–353

Aung San Suu Kyi, 119, 344, 1098

Australia

    ASEAN and, 115

    in Asia-Pacific Economic Cooperation, 108

    Camberra Agreement, 1194

    diamond production, 250

    ICSID Implementation Act, 838

    income inequality in, 1311

    International Arbitration Act of 1974, 838

    Marau Peace Agreement, 1431

    Micronesia and, 1026

    mining industry, 648

    national identity, 1195

    national parks, 1244

    SEATO and, 1458

    Tonga and, 1554

    Tuvalu Trust Fund, 1583

    withdrawal from UNIDO, 1621

Australopithecus ananensis, 500

Austria

    Black Sea Economic Cooperation Organization and, 183–184

    Soviet Union and, 288, 1488

Austrian–Hungarian Empire, 284–285. *See also* Habsburg monarchy

    Croatia and, 410

    Czech independence from, 430

    Slovakia and, 1416

Authoritarian Democracy of Pinochet, 1275

Authoritarianism, 119–124

    bureaucratic, 207–209, 1477–1478

    definition and history, 119–120

Authoritarianism (*Continued*)
    ethnic conflicts and, 632–633
    inherited vs. acquired, 121
    Middle East, 1028
    modernization under, 1070–1071
    nationalism and, 122–123
    Southeast Asia, 1448–1449
    varieties of, 120–121
    vs. totalitarianism and democracy, 121
Authoritarian personalities, 121, 573, 1416
Authoritarian state, 120
Avila Camacho, Manuel, 1021
Awami League, 124, 125–126, 141, 1092–1093
Aydid, Hussien, 1433
Aylwin, Patricio, 322, 1275, 1484
Aymara people, 626–627, 685, 958
Ayub Khan, Muhammad, 124–126, 1222. *See also* Pakistan
Ayuh, General, 124
Azcona Hoyo, José, 763
Azerbaijan, 126–127
    agricultural privatization in, 20, 23
    Armenia and, 87–88
    Baku-Thilisi-Ceyhan Pipeline Project, 638, 698
    Black Sea Economic Cooperation Organization, 183–184
    Black Sea Economic Organization, 381
    Caspian Sea and, 305
    Commonwealth of Independent States and, 375–380
    Economic Cooperation Organization and, 304, 537–538
    ethnic conflict, 596
    GUAM group and, 381
    literacy, 543
    Nagorno-Karabakh dispute, 87–88, 378, 382, 924, 1253, 1533
    privatization in, 1323
    territorial disputes, 1534
    Turkic state federation and, 1534
Azerbaijanis, in Georgia, 697
Azikiwi, Benjamin Nnamdi, 127–128, 1142. *See also* Nigeria
Az-Zubarah Island territorial dispute, 1534

B

Ba'ath Party, 71, 129–130, 335, 1037
    Iraq, 71, 129–130, 868, 1598
    Syria, 1038, 1598
Background extinction rate, 179
Badawi, Abdullah Ahmad, 983
Bagaza, Jean Baptist, 212
Baghdad Conference, 1209
Baghdad Pact, 75, 130–131, 310, 868. *See also* Central Treaty Organization
Bagmara Forest (Nepal), 1711–1712
Baguio Conference, 1442
Bahamas, 131–132
    Association of Caribbean States and, 111
    Caribbean Basin Initiative and, 232–233
    Caribbean Community and Common Market and, 233–235
    Caribbean Development Bank and, 235–237
    international relations, 248
Bahrain, 132–134
    OAPEC and, 1208
    oil industry, 646–647
    political and economic reforms, 1032
    territorial disputes, 1339, 1534
Bakhtiar, Shahpur, 910
Bakhtin, Nikhail, 1294

Bakongo people, 53
Baku, 126–127
Baku-Thilisi-Ceyhan Pipeline Project, 638, 698
Balaguer, Joaquín, 186, 245
Balance of Payments and Statistics Yearbook, 1043
Balante people, 734
Balfour Declaration, 69, 134–135, 980, 1226, 1759
Balkanization, 360–361, 500–501, 626–627, 1585
    Africa, 360–361, 500–501, 626–627
    Caribbean region, 239–240
    problems of, 240
Balkan states
    international relations, 294–295
    Soros foundations in, 1436
    Stability Pact, 1436
Balkan Wars, 135–139
    atrocities in, 136–137
    First, 285
    Macedonia and, 971
Baltic states. *See also* Estonia; Latvia; Lithuania
    Commonwealth of Independent Nations and, 382
    Council of Baltic Sea States, 381
    independence, 713
    international relations, 293–294
    peacekeeping, 1253
    privatization, 1324
    Soviet occupation, 592
Banaba Island. *See* Kiribati
Banana exports
    Belize, 164
    Caribbean region, 240–241
    Central Africa, 261
    Central America, 274
    Ecuador, 47
    Guadeloupe, 723
    Guatemala, 725
    Honduras, 762, 763
    Martinique, 999
    Organization of Eastern Caribbean States and, 1211
    St. Lucia, 1494
    St. Vincent and the Grenadines, 1495
Banda, Hastings, 981
Bandaranaike, Mrs. Sirimavo, 1489
Bandaranaike, S.W.R.D., 1489
Bandung (Asia-Africa) Conference, 139–140, 1118, 1234–1235, 1506–1507, 1545
Bangladesh, 140–142
    Asian Development Bank loans, 100–101
    Awami League, 124
    Bhola Cyclone, 1112
    economy, 141–142
    global climate change and, 704
    Green Revolution and, 717–718
    history, 141
    Human Development Index, 658
    South Asian Association for Regional Cooperation and, 1441–1444
    territorial disputes, 1692
    water management, 1688
Bangladore, technology and education, 1529
Bani Yas tribe, 1595
Bank capital, 150
Bank crises. *See* Financial crises
Bank failures, 144
Bank for Credit and Commerce International failure, 144

Bank for International Settlements, 132–145. *See also* Banking
  decision making, 143
  evolution, 144–145
  Nazi transactions, 145
  operations, 143–144
  origin, 142–143
Bankhaus Herstatt failure, 144
Banking, 145–152
  adverse selection, 146
  Bahamas as center of, 132
  credit functions, 150
  depository functions, 146
  in developing countries, 149–151
  direct and indirect finance, 14–146
  discount rate, 147–148
  discount window, 147
  Hong Kong and, 764
  interest income, 146
  Lebanon, 948
  offshore. *See* Offshore banking
  open market operations, 148–149
  Panama, 1236
  regional and international banks, 151
  regulation and central banking, 147–148
  Singapore, 1413
  traditional institutions, 151
  trends in, 151–152
Bank of Credit and Commerce International (BCCI), 398
Banks. *See also individual banks*
  central. *See* Central banks
  deposits, 146
  interest income, 146
  nations having international, 151–152
  regional and international, 151
  runs on, 147
Banque Centrale des États de l'Afrique de L'ouest (BCEAO), 219
Banque des États de l'Afrique Centrale (BEAC), 219
Banque Quest Africaine De Developement (BOAD), 151
Bantu Authorities Act, 11, 152–153, 1462
Bantu-speaking peoples, 500, 621, 1459, 1522–1523
  Angola, 53–54
  Malawi, 981
  South Africa, 59
  Tswana, 190–191
Bantustans, 152–154, 1661. *See also* Native Reserves
Banyarwanda, of Zaire, 590
Banzer Suárez, Hugo, 50, 185
Baqir al-Sadar, Ayatollah Muhhamad, 865
Barak, Ehud, 80
Baran, Paul, 460, 461, 1592
Barbados, 154–156, 720
  Association of Caribbean States and, 111
  Caribbean Basin Initiative and, 232–233
  Caribbean Community and Common Market and, 233–235
  Caribbean Development Bank and, 235–237
  Caribbean Free Trade Association and, 237–238
  international relations, 247–248
Barbados Labour Party, 155
Barbuda, 55–57. *See also* Antigua and Barbuda
Barcelona Declaration, 1168
Barclay, Arthur, 959–960
Bargaining theory, 668. *See also* Foreign direct investment
Barioloche Foundation, 569
Barre, Gen. Mohammed Siad, 501, 505–506
Barre Mainassara, Gen. Ibrahim, 1141

Barrientos, General René, 47
Barrio Village Education Movement, 544
Barter transactions, 406
Bartholomew, Reginald, 92
Barzani, Massoud, 921
Barzani, Mulla Mustafa, 921, 923–924
Basarabia, 1073–1074. *See also* Moldova
Base colonies, 356
Basel Accord on Capital Adequacy, 144
Basel Committee on Banking Supervision, 143, 144
Basel Concordats, 144
Basel Convention on the Control of Transboundary Movements
    of Hazardous Wastes and Their Disposal, 178, 1685
Basel Core Principles for Effective Banking Supervision,
    144–145
Basic Education and Life Skills (BELS) program, 544–545
Basic human needs, 156–158, 1635
  Caribbean Development Bank and, 236
Basic Human Needs Trust Fund, 236
Bassa people, 626
Basutoland. *See* Lesotho
Basuto people, 956–957
Bataka Party, 1585
Batellista economic program, 1647
Batista Sacasa, Juan, 1137
Batista y Zaldivar, Fulgencio, 32, 158–159, 246, 256, 413.
    See also Castro, Fidel; Cuba
  Twenty-sixth of July Movement, 1583–1584
Batlle y Ordóñez, José, 1476, 1486, 1647
Batuta, Ibn, 1695
Batwa people, 1061
Bauxite
  Central Africa, 261
  Guinea, 733
  Guyana, 1185
  Jamaica, 888–889
  producer cartels, 250
  Suriname, 1508
Baya, Paul, 25–26
Bay of Pigs invasion, 308, 414
BCCI (Bank of Credit and Commerce International), 398
BEAC (Central Bank of Central African States), 267
Beblawt, Hazem, patriachal monarch theory, 1075–1076
Bedié, Henri Konan, 403–404
Bedouin societies, 159–160, 1501. *See also* Berbers
Begin, Menachem, 160–162, 220, 549, 882, 1038, 1159,
    1381–1382. *See also* Israel
Behari Vajpayee, Atal, 899
Beijing World Conference on Women, 1626
Beja people, 1503
Belarus, 162–163
  Commonwealth of Independent States and, 375–380
  independence, 290
  privatization, 1323
  territorial disputes, 1533
Belarusian Initiative, 1437
Belaúnde Terry, Fernando, 41, 42, 43, 46, 48, 64, 746,
    987, 1269
Belgian colonies, 29–30, 360–361, 503
  Central Africa, 262
  ethnic conflicts, 589–590
  independence, 269
Belgian Congo, 263, 360–361. *See also* Democratic Republic
    of Congo; Republic of Congo
Belgium, international banks in, 151

Belize
  Association of Caribbean States and, 111
  border conflicts, 283
  Caribbean Basin Initiative and, 232–233
  Caribbean Community and Common Market
    and, 233–235
  Caribbean Development Bank and, 235–237
Bello, Walden, 106
Ben Bella, Ahmed, 28, 165–166, 192, 1157–1158, 1166, 1169
  as populist, 1305
Benedict, Ruth, 458
Benenson, Peter, 37
Benes, Eduard, 286, 1318–1319
Benevides, Gen. Oscar, 745
Bengal. See Bangladesh
Ben-Gurion, David, 166–167. See also Israel
  Golda Meir and, 1008
Benin, 167–168. See also West Africa
  Economic Commission for Africa and, 528–530
  health care, 748
  West African Monetary Union and, 1703–1705
Benjedid, Col. Chadli, 28, 1166
Bentinck, Lord William, 1119
Berbers, 27–28, 29, 168–170, 613
  of Maghreb, 975–976
  in Mauritania, 1004
  in Tunisia, 1574
Berger, Peter, 515–516
Beria, Lavrenti, 455
Berlin Conference, 626–627, 734
Berlin Wall, 170–171, 290, 295, 417, 713, 1656
Bermuda, Caribbean Community and Common Market and, 233–235
Bernadotte, Count Folke, 74
Berryman, Phillip, 334
Betancourt, Rómulo, 171–172, 484, 1178, 1183–1184, 1659, 1660. See also Venezuela
  in Dominican Republic, 1572
Betancur, Belisario, 1182–1183
Betel nuts, 492
Bethlehem, conflict over, 74–75
Beveridge Plan, 1426
Bevin, Ernest, 353
Bharatiya Janata Parishad (Indian People's Party), 857
Bhashani, Maulana Hamid Khan, 124
Bhutan, 173–174
  South Asian Association for Regional Cooperation
    and, 1441–1444
Bhutto, Benazir, 174–175, 878, 1223.
    See also Pakistan
Bhutto, Mir Murtaza, 175
Bhutto, Zulfikar Ali, 125–126, 898, 1222–1223
Biafra, 175–177
  ethnic conflicts, 627
  Organizaioin of African Unity and, 1204
Big emerging markets (BEMs), 1067–1068
Bin Ali, Zine el-Abdin, 193
Bin Ias Al-khalif, Sheikh Saman Bin Hamad, 134
Bin Laden, Osama, 4, 299, 1091. See also Al-Qaeda
  Sudan and, 1503
  Taliban and, 1520–1522
Bin Saud, Abdul Aziz, 73
Biodiversity. See Amazon rainforest
  agricultural, 1286
  agricultural globalization and, 12, 13, 17

conservation, 177–179
deforestation and, 445
Drylands Development Center, 1608
national parks and, 1245
patents on life forms and, 826–827
United Nations Development Program and, 1608
Biodiversity Convention, 1510
Bioengineering, 665
  intellectual property rights and, 826–827
Biological effects, of acid precipitation, 2
Biological waste treatment (composting), 1682
Biomass burning, 1286. See also Haze pollution
Biomass energy, 559–560
Bionf, Abdou, 1395
Biopiracy, 827
Biosphere Reserves
  Central Suriname Nature Reserve, 1508
  Mamiraua Sustainable Development Reserve, 1348
  Manu National Park and Biosphere Reserve (Peru), 1712
  Virgin Islands National Park, 1670
Biotechnology, agricultural globalization and, 17
Bird, Lester, 56
Bird, Vere Cornwall, 56
Birth control. See Family planning
Birth rate. See Population growth
Bishop, Maurice, 179–180, 232, 243, 248, 416, 720–721, 1083.
    See also Grenada; Movement for Assemblies of the People
Bismarck, Otto, health care system of, 747
Bissell, Richard, 308
Biya, Paul, 218, 269
Bizerta naval base, 193
Bizimungu, Pasteur, 1378
Blackbirding. See Slavery; Slave trade
Black Civil Rights Movement, 8, 344
Black Consciousness Movement, 59–60, 153–154
Black Diaspora. See African Diaspora
Black market, 180–184, 223
  Central/Eastern Europe, 289
  communism and, 1429
  economic impact, 182–183
  Myanmar/Thailand, 1098
  size, 181–182
Black Market Peso Exchange, 1077
Black Power movement, 1571
Black reserves. See Apartheid; Native Lands Act; Native Reserves
Black Sea, territorial disputes, 1532
Black Sea Economic Cooperation Organization, 183–184
Black Sea Fleet, 377, 381
Black September Movement, 1158, 1228
Black Tai people, 1540
Blair, Tony, 1167
Blaize, Herbert, 721
Blix, Hans, 1265
Blizzards, 1113
Bloc Populaire Senegalais, 30
Bloemfontain meeting, 10
Boas, Frank, 458
Bodde, Derk, 686
Boers, Trek, 1439, 1706. See also Afrikaners
Boer War, 58, 622, 1706. See also Afrikaners
Boff, Leonardo, 958
Bogra, Muhammad Ali, 125
Bokassa, Col. Jean-Bédel, 264
Bolívar, Simón, 351, 358

Bolivia, 184–186
  Andean Regional Initiative, 1277
  Cold War and, 40–41
  default on debt, 48
  economic stabilization, 50
  Ernesto "Che" Guevara in, 732
  income inequality in, 1311
  MERCOSUR and, 1472–1474
  National Bolivian Revolution, 47
  National Bourgeois Revolution (1952), 46
  Nationalist Revolutionary Movement (MNR), 46, 185
  New Economic Plan, 50
  Peruvian relations with, 43–44
  political history, 46, 48, 50–51
  Sendero Luminoso (Shining Path) in, 44, 48. *See also*
    Sendero Luminoso
  shadow economy, 182
  slavery and emancipation, 7
  territorial disputes, 1473, 1537–1538
  Túpac Amaru Revolutionary Movement (MRTA), 48,
    50, 64, 685
Bolsa Familia, 1410
Bolshevik Revolution, 298–300. *See also* Lenin, Vladimir,
  Soviet Union; Marxism
Bonaire, 1125. *See also* Netherlands Antilles
Bongo, El Hadjy Omar, 265, 589–590
Bophuthstswana Homeland, 153
Bordaberry, Juan Maria, 1486, 1647
Bordatella pertussis, 822
Border disputes. *See* Territorial disputes *and specific countries*
Borge, Tomás, 1137, 1389
Borja, Rodrigo, 49, 542
Borneo, fires, 1112
Bosch, Juan, 186–187, 245, 308–309, 484–485, 1184. *See also*
  Dominican Republic
Bosnia, 287
  independence, 290
    Montenegro and, 1080
    NATO and, 1255
Bosnia-Herzegovina, 135–139, 187–188, 1398–1399,
  1749–1750
  establishment, 135
  ethnic conflicts, 592
  humanitarian relief, 786
  international relations, 294, 295
Botha, P.W., 61, 188–190, 436, 990, 1463. *See also* South Africa
Botswana, 190–191
  Basic Education and Life Skills (BELS) program, 545
  decolonization, 361–362
  Economic Commission for Africa and, 528–530
  ecotourism in, 539
  national parks, 1245
  Sir Seretsa Khama, 907
  South Africa and, 60–61
  Southern African Customs Union and, 1468–1470
  Southern African Development Community and, 1463
Boudiaf, Mohammed, 28
Bouédienne, Houari, 28, 166
Bougainville Copper Mine conflict, 1240
Bougainville ethnic conflict, 615–616
Bougainville Women for Peace and Freedom, 1432
Bougeiois society, 347
Boumédiénne, Houari, 191–193, 1166, 1169, 1305.
    See also Algeria
Boundaries. *See also* Balkanization; Territorial disputes

African and colonization, 500–501
  political vs. indigenous, 500–501
Bourguiba, Habib, 166, 193, 1165, 1574. *See also* Tunisia
Bouteflicka, Abdelaziz, 28–29, 1166
Bouterse, Desi, 1180, 1185, 1186, 1505
Boutros Ghali, Boutros, 395, 1433
Bozizé, General François, 272
Bracero Program, 194–195, 1018
Bradshaw, Robert, 1491
Brahmin caste, 253–254, 255, 1640
Brain drain, 195–198, 222, 1043–1044
  causes, 195–196
  emulation effect, 197
  Migration for Development Program, 850
  national development and, 197–198
  nation-centered model, 196
  North Africa, 1160
  person-centered model, 196
  remittances and, 197
  underdevelopment and, 196–197
Brandt, Willy, 139
Brasilia, 919
Brasilia Protocol, 1472, 1473. *See also* MERCOSUR
Brazauskas, Algirdas, 964
Brazil, 198–201
  agrarian reform, 1410
  agricultural oligarchy, 1476
  agricultural privatization, 20
  Alliance for National Renovation (ARENA), 1414
  Argentina and, 228
  arms industrialization, 93–94, 94–95
  arms transfer, 95, 96
  banking crises in, 150
  banking in, 149
  Bolsa Familia, 1410
  bureaucratic authoritarianism in, 208, 209
  cartel regulation, 251
  Central Unica dos Trabahadores, 1410
  Chaco region, 1475
  coffee cartel, 250
  coffee production, 840
  Cuba and, 1483
  decolonization, 358–359
  environmental problems, 1410
  ethnic conflicts, 624
  Fernanco Henrique Cardoso, 227–229
  financial crises, 222, 1478, 1479
  foreign direct investment, 669
  Friendship Bridge, 1485
  geography and climate, 1474–1475
  Getúlio Vargas, 1476–1477, 1653–1654
  government, 198
  history, 1475
  import substitution industrialization, 1482
  income inequality, 1311
  independence, 198–199
  innovation studies, 1530
  international relations, 1482–1483
  Itaipú Dam, 885–886
  Japan and, 1483
  Juscelino Kubitschek, 919–920
  Kayapó Indigenous Area, 624
  Luíz Inácio "Lula" da Silva, 201, 1409–1411
  Mamiraua Sustainable Development Reserve, 1348
  MERCOSUR and, 1472–1474

Brazil (*Continued*)
  military regime, 200
  MOBRAL education program, 341
  Moviento sem Terra, 1478
  Movimento Brazileiro de Alfabetização, 543–544
  national parks, 1244
  as Newly Industrialized Economy, 1131
  new republic, 200–201
  in nineteenth century, 199
  Paraguay and, 1242–1243
  political history, 1482–1483
  populism in, 1304
  Positivist movement, 1050
  Programa Fome Zero, 1410
  remittances to, 197
  slavery, 7, 1475–1476
  Suriname border conflict, 1185
  territorial disputes, 1538
  transition to democracy, 123
  Treaty of Asunción, 200, 1483
  twentieth century, 199–200
  United States and, 1483
  War of the Triple Alliance, 1484
Brazzaville Twelve, 1202
Breastfeeding, infant mortality and, 818
Breastfeeding initiatives, 818, 1736
Bretton Woods System, 4, 142–143, 459, 828, 832, 846.
      See also World Bank
  Heavily Indebted Poor Countries Initiative (HPIC) and, 836
  trade policy and, 1561
Brewing industry, Central Africa, 262
Brezhnev, Leonid, 78, 289, 911, 1373
  Russian Orthodox Church and, 1377
Brezhnev Doctrine, 294, 1488, 1655
Britain. *See also* United Kingdom
  Beveridge Plan, 1426
  British Overseas Territories Act, 1492
  common law, 952–953
  Commonwealth Immigrants Act 2002, 1492
  in Group of 8, 573
  Guyana and, 887–888
  Hinduism and, 755
  Hong Kong and, 764
  income inequality in, 1311
  Iraq War and, 1265
  Kashmir and, 897
  Kenya and, 903
  Malvinas/Falkland Islands action, 83, 986–987, 1479, 1486–1489
  Middle East policy, 130–131
  in Oceania, 1190
  Palestine policy, 134
  Palestinian mandate, 73–75
  poor laws, 1309
  SEATO and, 1458
  South Africa and, 1439
  Suez War and, 17, 75–76, 117, 219–220, 548, 1035–1036
  Terrorism Act, 1539
  Tripartite Declaration, 75
  Tuvalu Trust Fund, 1583
  withdrawal from UNIDO, 1621
Britain/France Great Game, 1519
British American Council, 92
British colonies, 29–30. *See also individual countries*
  African, 361
  banking in, 149
    slavery and emancipation, 7
    West Africa, 1696
British Commonwealth. *See also* Commonwealth
      of Nations
  Anguilla and, 54–55
  Barbados and, 155
  neocolonialism and, 1120
  renaming of, 372
  South Africa and, 57–58, 1463
British East India Company, 141, 801
  colonialism and, 358
  St. Helena and, 1491–1492
British Empire. *See also* British Commonwealth;
      Commonwealth of Nations
  decolonization in, 366–367
British Gold Coast colony, 29–30
British Guiana, 887. *See also* Guyana
British Honduras. *See* Belize
British Mandate, on Palestine, 1008
  on Palestine, 167, 1226
British Overseas Territories Act, 1492
British Petroleum (BP), 53, 1029
  OPEC and, 251, 1212
British South Africa Company, 1089, 1751, 1757
British Virgin Islands, 1668–1669
  Caribbean Basin Initiative and, 232–233
  Caribbean Community and Common Market
      and, 233–235
  Caribbean Development Bank and, 235–237
British West Indies Federation, 237. *See also* Caribbean
      Free Trade Association
Broederbund (South Africa), 58
Brundtland, Gro Harlem, 569, 574, 1509
Brundtland Report, 465, 569, 574, 1509–1510. *See also*
      Sustainable development
Brunei, 97, 201–203
  ASEAN and, 1456
  Spratly Islands claims, 1241
Bryan, William Jennings, 1303
Bryant, Gyude, 960
Bucaram, Abdalá, 49, 542
Bucarem, Assad, 48
Buddhism, 203–204
  colonialism and, 366
  in Indonesia, 810
  in Malaysia, 982
  nationalism and, 1447
  revitalization movement, 859
  Tibetan, 1548–1549. *See also* Tibet
Budra caste, 253–254
Buenos Aires Consensus, 228
Buenos Aires Protocol, 1205. *See also* Organization of
      American States
Buganda, 1586
Buhari, Muhammadu, 1142
Build-operate-transfer (BOT), 99
Bukoshi, Bujar, 138
Bulganin, Nikolai A., 456
Bulgaria, 204–207
  Black Sea Economic Cooperation Organization,
      183–184
  education, 769–770
  in Grenada, 721
  human resource development, 770
  Macedonia and, 972

political history, 285–288
privatization, 1324
Bulk Terminal Project (Djibouti), 5
Bunche, Dr. Ralph, 74, 207. *See also*
United Nations
Burakumin caste, 1640
Bureaucracy
capitalism and, 227
meritocratic, 515
North Africa, 1162
Bureaucratic authoritarianism, 207–209
Caribbean region, 243
East Asia, 514
Latin America, 1477–1478
Burka, 3, 4
Burke, Edmund, 772
Burki, Shahid, 156
Burkina Faso, 210–211. *See also* West Africa
Berbers in, 170
Economic Commission for Africa and, 528–530
West African Monetary Union and, 1703–1705
Burma. *See* Myanmar
Burma Project/Southeast Asia Initiative, 1437
Burmese caste systems, 255
Burnham, Forbes, 239, 1179–1180, 1184
Burundi, 211–213. *See also* East Africa
Batwa people, 1061
caste system, 255
COMESA and, 369
Economic Commission for Africa and, 528–530
Economic Community of Central African States and, 531–533
ethnic conflict, 264–265
Hutu-Tutsi conflict, 211–213, 244, 264–265, 389–390, 590, 600–601, 630
political history, 503
trusteeship, 1632
United Nations High Commissioner for Refugees and, 1617–1618
Bush, George H. W., 394
abortion funding and, 1636
NAFTA and, 1171
Palestine Liberation Organization and, 1227
Persian Gulf War, 793–794, 869
Tiananmen Square massacre and, 1550
Bush, George W., 80
abortion funding and, 1636
Afghanistan and, 1521–1522
Andean Regional Initiative, 1277
Cuba policy, 418
Free Trade Area of the Americas (FTAA), 1638
Iraq War, 487, 794, 869–870, 1264–1267
Mexico and, 1024
Bush Negroes, 1507–1508
Business Is Calling (Novak), 709
Bustamante, Alexander, 246–247
Bustamante y Rivero, José, 40, 46, 745
Butaritari Islands. *See* Kiribati
Buthelezi, Mangosuthu Gatsha, 154, 212–213, 438
Buyoya, Major Pierre, 212
Buyoya (Uprona), Patrick, 212
Byzantine church, 716
Byzantine Empire, 922
in Libya, 961
Turkey and, 1576

C

Cabañas, Lucio, 1019
CABEI (Central American Bank for Economic Integration), 281–282
Cabral, Amilcar, 215–216, 734
Cabral, Donald Reid, 485
CACM. *See* Central American Common Market
Cadmium, Central Africa, 261
CAFTA, 276, 280
Cairo Agreement, 948
Cairo Declaration on Human Rights in Islam, 782
Cakste, Janis, 946
Caldera, Rafael, 171, 1179, 1659, 1660
Cali drug cartel, 1361
California, shadow economy, 182
Calles, Plutarco, 1246
Camaño Deño, Francisco, 485
Cambodia, 216–217
ASEAN and, 97, 112–116, 1456
China and, 1664
CIA in, 309
colonial legacy, 1454
economy, 98
humanitarian relief, 786
Hun Sen, 787–788
Khmer Rouge, 216–217, 309, 685, 787, 907–909, 1070, 1408, 1449, 1454, 1664
Mekong Basin Development Corporation, 98–100
Norodom Sihanouk, 1407–1408
Pol Pot, 1408, 1664
SEATO and, 1458
telecommunications industry, 99
territorial disputes, 1535
Thailand and, 1456
United Nations Development Program in, 1607
US bombing of, 1407–1408
Cameroon, 217–219
See also West Africa
Amidou Ahidjo and, 25–26
Basic Education and Life Skills (BELS) program, 545
Cameroon National Union, 25
Chad and, 269
Economic Commission for Africa and, 528–530
Economic Community of Central African States and, 531–533
economic development, 267
ethnic conflicts, 589
Lake Chad Basin Commission, 933–934
Ni John Fru Ndi, 1116–1117
oil production, 270
political history, 264, 269
Reuben Un-Nyobe and, 1590
trusteeship, 1632
Union des Populations du Cameroon (UPC), 25
Camp David Accords, 71, 118, 161, 219–221, 549, 861, 882, 1036, 1159, 1381–1382
Cámpora, Héctor, 1261
Canada
in Asia-Pacific Economic Cooperation, 108
Caribbean Development Bank and, 235–237
diamond production, 250
globalization and, 711
in Group of 8, 573
income inequality, 1311
international banks, 151

Canada (*Continued*)
  mining industry, 648
  NAFTA and, 1171–1172
  NAFTA transparency decision, 1570
  national parks, 1244
  natural gas production, 647
  oil production, 646–647
Canada Corps, 221
Canadian International Development Agency (CIDA), 221–222
Canary Islands, indigenous peoples, 975
Canberra Agreement, 1194
Cannabis, 491. *See also* Drug trafficking; Marijuana
Cape-Verde. *See also* West Africa
  Economic Commission for Africa and, 528–530
Capital
  equity, 666–667
  financial, 225–226
  human, 222, 1161
  physical, 225, 226
Capital (*Das* Kapital) (Marx), 1000
Capital accumulation
  civil rights and, 345
  underdevelopment and, 1591–1592
Capital concentration
  agriculture and, 14–15
  privatization and, 20
Capital control, 223
Capital flight, 222–225. *See also* Banking; Capitalist
    Economic Model
  contagion effect, 221–222
  Mexico, 1024
  money laundering and, 1076
  overcoming, 223
  transfer volumes, 223–224
Capital flow. *See also* Foreign direct investment
  to Central America, 282–283
  debt relief and, 444
  Malasia and, 978
  multinational corporations and, 1094–1095
  technology transfer and, 1094–1095
Capitalism and Slavery (Williams), 1713
Capitalist economic model, 225–227. *See also* Free market
  colonialism and, 362–363
  Communist critique of, 386
  contradictions of, 1425
  corruption and, 226, 227
  denial of democracy attributed to, 1425
  dependent, 207–208
  historical roots, 225
  Marxian theory of, 1000
  modern, 225–226
  private property rights and, 1320–1321
  Protestant ethic and, 855–856, 1067
  readjustments of, 1426
  shortcomings, 226–227
  tenets of, 225
Capital mobility, agriculture and, 14–15
Capital resources, 768. *See also* Capital flight; Capital flow
Capitulation agreements, 335
Caracas Declaration, 44, 722
Caracas Plan of Action, 722. *See also* Group of 77
Carbon dioxide, 704, 1289. *See also* Global climate change;
    Greenhouse effect
  deforestation and, 1346–1347

from landfilling, 1683
  as pollutant, 1
  top polluting countries, 564
  from waste incineration, 1682–1683
Carbonic acid, 1
Carbon sequestration, 13
Carbon to nitrogen ratio, of solid waste, 1682
Cárdenas, Cuáuhtemoc, 1248
Cárdenas del Rio, Lázaro, 1018, 1246–1247, 1382
Cárdenas Solórzano, Cuanhtémoc, 1382–1383
Cardenas, Victor Hugo, 50
Cardoso, Fernando Henrique, 227–229, 569, 1410, 1478, 1615.
    See also Brazil
CARE, 229–231, 476
  development programs, 230–231
Cargo cults, 1652
Caribbean, 238–239. *See also individual countries*
  African heritage, 587–588
  Afro-Americans, 606–607
  agricultural imports, 241
  Association of Caribbean States (ACS), 111–112
  banking crises in, 150
  economic, social, and political progress, 241–243
  economic history and industrialization, 240–241
  ethnicity and culture, 240
  European descendants ruling, 606–607
  Free Trade Area of the Americas and, 678
  geography and climate, 238–239
  history and development, 238–243
  independence, 242
  industrialization, 241
  Inter-American Development Bank and, 828–829
  international relations, 243–249
  Latin American Integration Association, 945–946
  Lomé Convention, 964–966
  Organization of Eastern Caribbean States, 1210–1212
  plantation system and Triangle Trade, 357–358, 1696
  political background and balkanization, 239–240
  privatization, 1324
  2807 (9802) provision and, 550–551
  remittances and, 241
  St. Christopher and Nevis, 1490–1491
  susu groups, 151
  Trinidad and Tobago, 1570–1572
Caribbean Basin Economic Expansion Act of 1990, 550. *See also*
    Caribbean Basin Initiative
Caribbean Basin Economic Recovery Act of 1983 (CBERA),
    231, 550. *See also* Caribbean Basin Initiative
Caribbean Basin Initiative, 231–233
  Jamaica and, 247
  807 (9802) provision and, 550–551
  Special Access Program (SAP), 550–551
Caribbean Basin Trade Partnership Act of 2000, 550
Caribbean Community and Common Market (CARICOM),
    132, 155, 164, 233–235, 242, 247, 830, 1185
Caribbean Development Bank (CDB), 55, 235–237
  ordinary and special operations, 236–237
Caribbean Diaspora, 240, 241
Caribbean Food Corporation, 236
Caribbean Free Trade Agreement (CARIFTA), 132, 155,
    237–238, 720
Caribbean Free Trade Partnership Act, 233
Carib Indians, 154, 483, 586–587, 683, 723, 998, 1083, 1494,
    1507, 1570, 1669

CARICOM. *See* Caribbean Community
    and Common Market
CARIFTA (Caribbean Free Trade Agreement), 132, 155,
    237–238, 720
Carmichael, Stokely, 1571
Carpio, Ramiro de Leon, 1206
Carson, Rachel, 574
Cartagena Declaration, 38, 44, 1205, 1353
Cartels, 249–252. *See also* Multinational corporations
    Cali drug, 352, 1361
    coffee producers, 250
    defined, 249
    international producer, 249–250
    Medellin drug, 352–353, 1077, 1361
    private international "hard-core," 251–252
    tin producers, 250
Carter, President Jimmy, 34, 220, 882, 1038
    Camp David Accords, 549, 1381–1382
    Central America and, 279
    Chile and, 1484
    Cuban relations and, 416–417
    human rights and, 772
    Oceania and, 1194
    Panama and, 1236, 1238
    Paraguay and, 1485
Casablanca bloc, 1164, 1165, 1202
Case Concerning Gabcikovo-Nagymaros Project, 1622
Case–Zablock Act, 309
Cash reserves, 147–148
Caspian Flotilla, 377
Caspian Sea, 126, 305–306, 901
Castello Branco, Humberto, 1483
Caste systems
    Bhimrao Ramji Ambedkar and, 1640–1641
    Caribbean, 586
    colonial, 630
    current, 255–256
    features, 253–254
    India, 252–256
    Japan, 1640
    Madagascar, 973
    Mexico, 605
    Oman hierarchy, 1199
    origin, 253
    Sierra Leone, 1406
    Tonga, 1554
    untouchables (Dalits), 1640–1641
    worldwide, 254–255
Castro, Fidel, 32, 123, 159, 256–258, 413. *See also* Cuba;
    Cuban Revolution
    in Central America, 279
    CIA and, 308
    Guyana and, 887
    "History Will Absolve Me" speech, 1584
    invasion of Angola, 246
    invasion of Ethiopia, 246
    26th of July Movement, 1583–1584
    Venezuela and, 171, 1659
Catholic Church
    Maronite, 336
    Roman. *See* Roman Catholic Church
    Uniate Churches, 335
Cato, R. Milton, 1495
Caucasus, territorial disputes, 1533

Caviar production, Central Asia, 299
Cayman Islands, 258–259
    Caribbean Community and Common Market and, 233–235
    Caribbean Development Bank and, 235–237
    Caribbean Free Trade Association and, 237–238
    postage stamp business, 258
Ceausescu, Nicolae, 259–260, 287, 1488, 1656–1657.
    See also Romania
CEDAW (Convention of the Elimination of Discrimination
    against Women), 1717–1718
CEN-SAD (Community of Sahel-Saharan States), 506
Cental banks, as lenders of last resort, 148
Center for International Environmental Law, 638
CENTO (Central Treaty Organization), 94, 130,
    310–311, 1035
Centra Internacional de Maiz y Trigo, 853
Central Africa. *See also individual countries*
    biological resources, 261–262
    colonial legacy, 262–263
    economic development, 267–269
    economy, 261–262
    ethnic conflicts, 589–590
    failures of democracy, 263–264
    geography and climate, 260–261
    geological and hydrological resources, 261
    history and economic development, 260–267
    HIV/AIDS in, 266
    independence, 263
    internal conflicts, 268–269
    international relations, 267–271
    natural resources and development, 271
    recent inter-country conflicts, 269–270
    unending conflict in, 264–265
Central African Peace and Security Council (COPAX), 267
Central African Republic, 271–273
    Economic and Customs Union of Central Africa (ECUCA),
        526–527
    Economic Commission for Africa and, 528–530
    Economic Community of Central African States and,
        531–533
    ethnic conflicts, 589–590
    Lake Chad Basin Commission, 933–934
    political history, 264, 269
    territorial disputes, 1536
Central America
    agrarian reform, 934. *See also individual countries*
    authoritarian states, 121, 122
    CAFTA and, 276–277
    colonial period, 273–274
    contemporary period, 275–276
    debt, 282
    definitions, 273, 277
    economic growth, 274–275
    geography and climate, 273
    history and economic development, 273–277
    international relations, 277–281
        independence through WW II, 277–278
        post-WW II, 278–280
    land distribution, 934
    life expectancy, 276
    lost decade (1980s), 275, 352, 708, 1269, 1563
    Nicaragua, 1133–1136
    poverty rates, 281
    refugees, 1353

Central America (*Continued*)
  remittances, 283
  slavery and emancipation, 7
  United States–Dominican Republic–Central America Free
    Trade Agreement, 1637–1638
Central American Bank for Economic Integration (CABEI),
    281–282
Central American Common Market (CACM), 274, 280, 281–283
  Guatemala and, 725
  Honduras and, 762–763
  members, 281
Central American Free Trade Agreement. *See* CAFTA
Central American Parliament (PARLCEN), 280
Central and Eastern Europe. *See also individual countries*
  agricultural privatization in, 19, 24
  border disputes, 296
  CIA in, 308
  definitions, 290–291
  demographic changes, 770
  ethnic conflicts, 590–593
  European Bank for Reconstruction and Development,
    636–640
  history and economic development, 284–290
  HIV/AIDS, 757
  international relations, 290–297
    evolution and rebellion, 292–293
    post-1989, 293–295
    post-WW II through 1989, 291–292
    return to Europe, 295–296
  political culture, 1281–1282
  single-party governments, 1414
  Soros foundations in, 1436
Central Asia. *See also individual countries*
  Commonwealth of Independent States, 637–638
  economic development, 299–301
  electrification, 300
  ethnic conflicts, 593–596
  European Bank for Reconstruction and Development and,
    637–638
  historical overview, 297–299
  independence, 300
  industrialization, 299–300
  international relations, 302–307
Central Bank of Central African States (BEAC), 267
Central banks, 147–148
  open market operations, 149
Central Eurasia Project, 1437
Central Europe
  agricultural privatization in, 19, 24
  Visehrad Four and, 1672–1673
Central European Free Trade Association (CEFTA), Visehrad
    Four and, 1672
Central European "human face" socialism, 1428
Central European University, 1437
Central Intelligence Agency (CIA), 307–309
  in Afghanistan, 1091
  attempts to rein in, 309
  Bay of Pigs invasion, 246, 414
  in Central Africa, 263
  in Cuba, 414
  in developing world 1950s, 308
  in developing world 1960s, 308–309
  in Ecuador, 308–309
  in Guatemala, 80–81, 1021
  in Indonesia, 1507

  in Laos, 1250
  Mafia and, 308
  in Nicaragua, 392–393, 1138
  Operation Mockingbird, 307–308
  Operation Mongoose, 308
  Operation Phoenix, 309
  prior organizations, 307–308
Central planning. *See also* Socialist economic model
  agriculture and, 18
  Albania, 26
  Caribbean, 241
  China, 326
  dictatorships and, 472
  industrialization and, 814–815
  Mongolia, 1078–1079
  Soviet Union, 1372, 1427
  in state-directed economies, 1496–1497
Central Treaty Organization (CENTO), 94, 130, 310–311, 1035
Central Unica dos Trabahadores, 1410
Centre for International Crime Prevention, 1604
Centre for the Study of Islam and Democracy (ISID), 878
CEPT (Common Effective Preferential Tariff), 113–114
Ceremonial food, 1257
Cerro, Luís Sánchez, 64
Césaire, Aimé, 587, 999
Ceylon. *See* Sri Lanka
CGIAR (Consultative Group for International Agricultural
    Research), 17, 852–853
Chaco region, 1475
Chaco War, 1485, 1497
Chad, 311–312
  Cameroon and, 269
  Economic and Customs Union of Central Africa and,
    526–527
  Economic Commission for Africa and, 528–530
  Economic Community of Central African States and, 531–533
  economic development, 311–312
  ethnic conflicts, 589
  internal and external conflicts, 269
  Lake Chad Basin Commission, 933–934
  Libyan annexation, 269, 1169
  political history, 264
Chaebol conglomerates, 103, 107
Chagas disease (*Trypanosoma cruzi*), 820–821
Chama che Mapinduci (Zanzibar), 1523
Chamar caste, 1640
Chamberlain, H.S., 1593
Chamorro, Pedro Joaquin, 1137–1138, 1139, 1389
Chamorro, Violetta Barrios de, 393, 394, 1135, 1139
Chamorros, 724–725
Chan, Julius, 1240
Chang, P.C., 1639
Charles, Eugenia, 248, 483, 1185
Charriére, Henri "Papillon," 684
Charter of Algiers, 722. *See also* Group of 77
Charter of Paris, 1175. *See also* NATO
Chatham Islands. *See* Kiribati
Chávez, Hugo, 171, 312–313, 1179, 1660. *See also* Venezuela
Chechen wars, 383, 596–599
  September 11 and, 598
Checking accounts (demand deposits), 146
Chen Shui-Ban, 522
Chernobyl disaster, 379, 563, 1373
Chevron Texaco. *See also* Texaco
  in Central Africa, 270

Chewa people, 981
Chiang Ching-kuo, 313–314, 1516. *See also* Chiang Kai-shek
Chiang Kai-shek, 314–315, 451, 761, 1454
   Taiwan and, 1515–1516
Chiapa Indians, 625
Chicago School of economists, 1121, 1275. *See also*
   Neoliberalism
Chico, Frei, 1410
Child labour, 316–317
   education and, 544
Children, 315–320
   child labour, 316–317, 544
   current research, 319–320
   gender differences, 318–319
   in sex work, 317–318
Chile, 320–323. *See* Pinochet, Augusto
   agrarian reform, 934
   agricultural oligarchy, 1476
   Andean Community and, 39
   arms transfer, 96
   Asia-Pacific Economic Cooperation and, 108
   Augusto Pinochet, 1274–1276
   Aymara people, 626–627, 685, 958
   Bolivia and, 184
   Bolivian natural gas pipeline project, 50
   bureaucratic authoritarianism, 208, 209
   Christian Democratic Party, 681
   CIA in, 309
   Cold War and, 41–42
   copper production, 1484–1485
   Cuba and, 416, 1584
   ECLAC and, 1615
   Eduardo Frei, 680–682
   education, 543
   ethnic conflicts, 625
   Falange Nacional, 680–682
   financial crises, 1478
   foreign direct investment, 669, 708
   geography and climate, 320–321, 1474, 1475
   historical overview, 321–322
   international relations, 1483–1484
   Landless Peoples Movement, 934
   life expectancy, 1330
   MERCOSUR and, 1472–1474
   neoliberalism and, 1121
   as Newly Industrialized Economy, 1131
   nitrate production, 1484
   Peruvian relations with, 43–44
   recent socioeconomic development, 322–323
   Rockefeller Foundation and, 1367
   Salvador Allende. *See* Allende Gossens, Salvador
   Seven Modernizations program, 1121
   shadow economy, 182
   slavery and emancipation, 7
   Social Christian Federation, 681
   territorial disputes, 1473, 1537, 1538
Chilembwe, John, 29
Chiluba, Dr. Frederic, 901
China. *See also* East Asia
   agrarian reform, 582, 935
   Agrarian Reform Law, 513
   agricultural privatization, 21
   in Angola, 54
   arms industrialization, 94
   arms transfer, 95, 96

ASEAN and, 1455
Asian Development Bank loans, 100–101
Asia-Pacific Economic Cooperation and, 108
Bandung Conference and, 139–140
boundary agreement with Pakistan, 125
Cambodia and, 908
Caribbean Development Bank and, 235–237
caste system, 520
civic education, 340
Colombo Plan, 353–354
as Communist case study, 386
Confucianism in, 855
Cultural Revolution, 323–325, 327–328. *See also* Cultural
   Revolution; Mao Zedong
currency devaluation, 424
Democracy Wall, 328
democratization, 709
Deng Xiaoping, 328, 450–452, 1755. *See also* Deng Xiaoping
drought-related famine, 1112
earthquakes, 1114
economic rise, 518–519
education, 603
ethnic conflicts, 602–604
Falungong Movement, 774
family planning, 658
female infanticide, 819
Five-Year Plan, 385
foreign direct investment by, 672
foreign direct investment in, 669, 671
founding, 326
Four Modernizations, 328
Fulbright Program and, 686
gaige kaifung policy, 452
geography and people, 510
globalization and, 711
Great Leap Forward, 326–327, 714–715, 991–992
Green Revolution and, 717–718
Group of 77 and, 722
Guangdong Special Economic Zone, 970
Han majority, 602–604
historical background, 325–326
Ho Chi Minh and, 761
human rights and trade self-interest, 774
Import Substitution Industrialization, 515
Indonesia and, 1507
international banks in, 151
irrigated and drained area, 871
irrigation and drainage, 873–874
Islam in, 602, 603
Jiang Zemin, 890–891
Kuwait Fund for Arab Economic
   Development and, 926
legal system, 955–956
Libya and, 1167
Mao Zedong, 729–730, 990–992, 1428–1429
market socialism, 1428–1429
Mekong Basin Development Corporation, 98–100
military-civil relations, 1048
minority issues, 520
monetary policy, 150
Mongolia and, 520–521, 603
Most Favored Nation status, 774
Nationalist, 326. *See also* Chiang kai-Shek
North Korea and, 914
one-child policy, 658

China (*Continued*)
  Peking Diary: A Year of Revolution (Bodde), 686
  People's Republic of, 325–330
  population growth, 658
  pre-Communist, 313–315
  privatization, 1324
  Romania and, 1488
  single-party government, 1414
  socialist economic model and, 1428–1429
  Soviet Union and, 514
  Special Administrative Regions, 969
  Special Economic Zones, 644
  split with Soviet Union, 293, 328, 330
  Spratly Islands claims, 1241
  Taiwan and, 521–522, 1517–1518
  technocratic leadership and reform, 329
  technological capacity growth, 1527–1528
  territorial disputes, 18, 517, 1535
  Three Gorges Dam, 520, 1546–1548, 1688
  Tiananmen Square massacre, 328, 451, 519, 1549–1551
  Tibet and, 520–521, 602, 603, 1548–1549
  tobacco-related deaths, 1331
  trade policy and self-interest, 774
  Ugyhur minority, 603
  World Trade Association and, 890
  World Trade Organization and, 517, 518
  Yangtze River, 1113, 1688
  Yunnan Province, 98–100
  Zhou Enlai, 1754–1755
  Zuang minority, 602–603
China, People's Republic of. *See* China
China, Republic of. *See* Taiwan
Chinese
  Cambodian massacre of, 908
  ethnic (overseas), 620, 632, 982, 983, 1071, 1540, 1570
Chinese Communist Party, 323–324, 326, 329–331, 331–332, 1454
  Jiang Zemin and, 890–891
  Mao Zedong and, 990–992
  Zhou Enlai and, 1754–1755
Chinese Revolution. *See* China; China, People's Republic of;
  Chinese Communist Party; Mao Zedung
Chipko Movement, 446
Chissano, Joachim, 683
Chivambo Mondlane, Eduardo, 682
Chixoy Dam, Mayan population and, 634
Cholera, 821–822
Chomsky, Noam, 939
Christian Democratic Party (Chile), 31
Christian fundamentalism, 858
Christianity, 332–334. *See also Subtopics*
  capitalism and, 858–859
  capitulation (Status Quo) agreements, 335
  civil society and, 348
  colonialism and, 365
  in East Africa, 502
  in Georgia, 698
  Great Schism, 334–335
  Greek Orthodox Church and, 715–716
  Islam and, 335
  Liberation Theology, 85, 333–334, 858–859, 958–959, 1359
  Malaysia, 982
  Middle East, 334–337
  missionaries, 332–333, 365, 1144
  Myanmar (Burma), 619
  populism and, 1302

Christians, caste systems and, 253
Chuan Leekpai, 337–338. *See also* Thailand
Chun Doo Hwan, General, 103
Church, Sen. Frank, 309
Churchill, Winston, 333, 1655
  chemical weapons and, 868
Church of England, 51
  Evangelical Party of ("low church"), 639
Church World Services, 476
CIA (US Central Intelligence Agency). *See* Central
  Intelligence Agency
CIA and the Cult of Intelligence (Marchetti and Marks), 309
CIDA (Canadian International Development Agency), 221–222
CIDI (Inter-American Council for Integral Development), 1205
Cigarette making. *See* Tobacco production
Cinnamon production. *See also* Spice trade
  Central Africa, 261
  colonialism and, 359
CISC (World Confederation of Labour), 1727–1728
Ciskei Homeland, 153
CITES (Convention on International Trade in Endangered
  Species of Wild Animals), 1511
CITES (Convention on International Trade in Endangered
  Species of Wild Flora and Fauna), 178
Cities. *See also* Urbanization
  health advantages of, 1642
  megacities, 1643, 1644
Citizenship education. *See* Civic education
Civic action, by military, 1050–1051
Civic education, 338–343
  Africa, 339–340
  defined, 338–339
  India, 340–341
  Latin America, 341
  national and regional differentiation, 339
  prospects and problems, 341–342
Civil disobedience, 343–344
Civil law system, 951–952
Civil liberties, 344. *See also* Legal systems
  East Asia, 519–520
  European Union (EU), 955
  as measure of development, 467
Civil–military relations, 1046–1048
  commissar system, 1046
  in developing world, 1046
  internal security and, 1047
  military security and, 1047
  models for, 1047–1048
  prospects for, 1048
  revolutions affecting, 1047–1048
Civil religion, 856
Civil rights, 344–345
Civil rights movement, US, 8, 344
Civil servants, corruption of, 396–401. *See also* Corruption
Civil society, 346–348
  East Asia, 515–516
  Middle East, 1032
  Peru, 1269
  Suriname, 1508
  Taiwan, 1516
  UNICEF programs, 1602
Civil society discourse, 347
CLASC (Latin American Federation of Christian Trade
  Unions), 1728
Class struggle concept, 26. *See also* Marxism

CLAT (Latin American Workers Central), 1728
Clausewitz, Karl von, 728–729
Clearing accounts, 407
Climate. *See also* Geography and climate
El Niño, 1687
Inter-Tropical Convergence Zone, 1686–1687, 1694
Inter-Tropical Front, 1694
urbanization and, 1645–1646
World Meteorological Organization (WMO), 476, 705, 1738–1739
Climate change. *See* Global climate change
Climate Convention, 1510
Climatic hazards
blizzards, 1113
droughts, 1112
El Niño (Southern Oscillation), 1113
fire, 1112
floods, 1112–1113
tornadoes, 1113
tropical cyclones (hurricanes), 1111–1112, 1144, 1553
Clinton, President Bill, 418, 861
abortion funding and, 1636
China policy, 774
Export Expansion and Reciprocal Trade Agreements Act and, 679
Free Trade Area of the Americas and, 679
NAFTA concessions by, 1173
nation building and, 1106
Oslo Peace Accords and, 883
Palestinian peace plan of, 80
Plan Colombia and, 1276–1278, 1361–1362
USAID and, 1636
Closed corporate communities, 1256–1257
Clostridium tetani, 821
Club of Rome, 569
Clusters, innovation, 1528–1530, 2643. *See also* Growth triangles
CMEA (Council for Mutual Economic Assistance), 417, 481, 708
CMS (Convention on the Preservation of Migratory Species of Wild Animals), 178
CO_2. *See* Carbon dioxide
Coal combustion, acid precipitation and, 2
Coal production, 562
Coard, Bernard, 179
Coase, Ronald, 675–676
COBAC (*Commission Bancaire d'Afrique Centrale*), 527
Cobb, John B., 1070, 1509
Cocaine manufacture, 493. *See also* Coca production; Drug trafficking
Colombia, 1177, 1361
Cocaine traffic. *See also* Coca production; Drug trafficking
Belize, 164
Jamaica, 247
Coca production
Bolivia, 50, 1177
Colombia, 352–353, 1361
Ecuador, 1177
Peru, 1177
Cocoa production
Central Africa, 261
Ghana, 424, 700, 701
Haiti, 740–741
International Cocoa Organization (ICCO), 838–839
Nigeria, 1143
producer cartels, 250

Coconut oil production, Micronesia, 1025
Coconut production. *See also* Copra production
Central Africa, 261
Micronesia, 1025
Oceania, 1191
CODELCO, 322
CODESA (Convention for a Democratic South Africa), 62, 438
Coffee production
Brazil, 1654
Central America, 274, 275
Colombia, 351, 1177
Equatorial Guinea, 575, 576
Ethiopia, 585–586
Guatemala, 725
Haiti, 740–741
International Coffee Organization, 840–841
Kenya, 906
Rwanda, 1378
St. Helena, 1492
Tanzania, 1523
Venezuela, 1178
Colby, William, 309
Cold War. *See also* Soviet Union; United States
Andean South America and, 40–42
Angola and, 54
Antigua and Barbuda and, 249
arms transfer and, 88–89, 90, 96
Asian "Economic Miracle" and, 102
Central America and, 278
Central and Eastern Europe and end of, 296
corruption and, 398
Cuba and, 257
Democratic Republic of Congo and, 388
domino theory, 485–487
East Africa and, 501, 505–506
East Asia and, 513–514, 516–517
end of, 89–90. *See also* Soviet Union, collapse of
human rights and, 771–772
Iran and, 1221
Jamaica in, 247, 889
Middle East and, 1034–1035
Non-Aligned Movement, 192, 416, 1035, 1147–1149, 1183, 1552, 1749
North Korea and, 913–914
Organization of American States and, 1206
Organization of Eastern Caribbean States and, 1211
Paraguay and, 1242–1243
peacekeeping and, 1251–1252
refugees and, 1353
Republic of Congo and, 269
socialist world revolution and, 1425
Southeast Asia and, 1454
Soviet Bloc in, 1488
Third World and, 1543–1544
US–Latin American relations and, 32–33
West Africa and, 1700–1701
Collectivism, 348–350
definition, 348–349
practical implications, 349–350
theoretical approaches, 349
Collectivization, 162, 1372
Ba'ath Party and, 130
Central Asia, 300
Central/Eastern Europe, 291–292

Collectivization (*Continued*)
  China, 513
  Hungary, 789
  Kyrgyzstan, 928
  Laos, 944
  Mali, 984
  Mongolia, 1078
  Mongolian *negdels*, 1078
  Mozambique, 972
  North Korea, 914
  Soviet Union, 456, 1372
  Turkmenistan, 1579
Collor de Mello, Fernanco, 228, 1410
Colombia, 350–353
  Andean Community and, 39
  Association of Caribbean States and, 111
  Black Market Peso Exchange, 1077
  Bogotazo riot, 1177
  Caribbean Development Bank and, 235–237
  civic education, 341
  coffee production, 351, 840, 1177
  counterinsurgency, 405
  Cuba and, 352, 1182
  drug trafficking, 352–353, 489, 1183
  foreign direct investment in, 669
  Fuerzas Armadas Revolucionarias de Colombia (FARC),
    352, 1277, 1362–1363, 1537
  geography and climate, 1176
  history and economic development, 1176–1177
  internal refugees, 1277
  international relations, 1182–1183
  La Violencia, 351–352, 1177
  "lost decade" and, 352
  Marxist insurgency, 233
  Medellin drug cartel, 1077
  National Federation of Coffee Growers, 1177
  National Liberation Army (ELN), 352–353,
    1110–1111, 1182
  Nevada del Ruiz volcanic eruption, 1115
  Non-Aligned Movement and, 1183
  oil, 351
  Organization of American States and, 1182
  Plan Colombia, 1276–1278
  political history, 350–352, 1176–1177
  populations, 350
  Resolution 1600, 341
  Sendero Luminoso (Shining Path) in, 1077
  slavery and emancipation, 7
  territorial disputes, 1135, 1182, 1537
  United Nations founding and, 1182
  Venezuelan trade, 1177
Colombo Plan, 353–354
Colombo Powers Conference, 1442
Colonialism. *See also* Colonies; Decolonization; Imperialism;
  Neocolonialism; *specific colonies*
  African legacy, 364–366
  American decolonization, 358–359
  Asian legacy, 366–368
  capitalism and, 362–363
  Caribbean plantations and Triangle Trade, 357–358, 1696
  colonies of domination, 359–360
  Cultivation System, 809
  early European expansion, 356
  East Asian development and, 512–513
  economics of, 363

  ethnicity and, 630
  Europe and Indian Ocean, 359
  forms of, 355–356
  history, 355–362
  Landrent System, 809
  Latin American legacy, 363–364
  legacies of, 362–368
  Middle East, 1028
  New World, 356–357
  North American settlements, 357
  partition of Africa and, 360–361
  as predisposing to dictatorship, 470–471
  Southeast Asia, 1446–1447
  territorial disputes and, 500–501, 626–627.
    See also Balkanization
  transportation patterns and, 1697
  West African boundaries and, 1697, 1698–1699
  white community in Africa and, 1705–1708
  World War I and II and, 361–362
Colonies
  base, 356
  of domination, 355, 359–360
  settlement, 355–356
Colonization. *See also* Colonialism
  development and, 458–459
  Paraguayan internal, 1243
  sociopolitical systems following, 459
Colosio, Luis Donaldo, 1020, 1024
Coltan wars, 649
Columbite, 649
Columbo-tantalite, 649
Columbus, Christopher, 356, 483, 723, 888,
  1134, 1490, 1570
Comarca system, Panama, 607–608
COMESA. *See* Common Market for Eastern and
  Southern Africa
Comisión Economica por America Latina (CEPAL). *See* United
  Nations Economic Commission for Latin America and
  the Caribbean
Comisión Permanente del Pacifico Sur, 45
Command economies, 1448–1449. *See also* Communism;
  Socialist economic model
Commissar system, 1047
Commission Bancaire d'Afrique Centrale (COBAC), 527
Commission for Assistance to a Free Cuba, 418
Commission on International Commodity
  Trade, 1604–1605
Committee for Economic Cooperation for Central America
  (CCE), 281
Committee of Central Bank Governors (Africa), 9
Commodity prices, 1604–1605
Common Effective Preferential Tariff (CEPT), 97–98, 113–114
Common External Tariff, 243
Common law, 952–953
Common Marine Fisheries Investment and Management
  Policy, 371
Common Market for Eastern and Southern Africa
  (COMESA), 369–372, 506, 529
  contribution to development, 370–372
  institutions, 370
  objectives, 369–370
Common Market of the South. *See* MERCOSUR
Commonwealth defined, 372–373
Commonwealth Human Rights Initiative, 374
Commonwealth Immigrants Act 2002, 1492

Commonwealth of Independent States, 381, 713, 928
    activities, 376–379
    Agreement on Armed Forces and Border Troops, 377
    Agreement on Strategic Forces, 377
    ethnic conflicts, 596–599
    European Bank for Reconstruction and Development, 637–638
    history and economic development, 375–380
    international relations, 380–385
    Moldova and, 1074
    structure, 376
Commonwealth of Nations. *See also* British Commonwealth
    Barbados and, 247
    St. Vincent and the Grenadines and, 248
Commonwealth Preference agreement, 373
Communidades de base, 958
Communism. *See also* Communist economic model; Communist Party
    authoritarianism and, 120
    black markets fostered by, 1429
    collapse of, 290, 295
    in Cuba, 1428
    in Dahomey, 168
    ethnic conflicts and, 632–633
    Hungarian welfare, 1428
    industrialization under, 814–815
    labor and, 932
    in Middle East, 130
    nation building as opposing, 1104–1105
    in Serbia, 137–138
    single-party government and, 1414–1415
Communist economic model, 385–387
    basic features, 385
    China as case study, 386
    critique of, 386
    ideological origin, 386
    industrialization and, 386
Communist Party
    Afghani (PDPA), 3–4
    Chile, 31–32
    Chinese, 323–324, 326, 329–331, 331–332. *See also* Chinese Communist Party; Mao Zedong
    Cuban, 415. *See also* Cuban Revolution
    Czech, 430
    Hungarian, 789–790
    Indonesian, 809–810, 1506
    Italian, 307
    Kampuchea, 907. *See also* Cambodia
    Kyrgyzstan, 928
    Manifesto of the Communist Party (Marx), 1000
    Middle East, 1035
    Peruvian, 46, 63
    Philippines, 65–66
    Romanian, 287
    South African, 11, 1463
    Vietnamese, 760–761
Communists. *See also* Marxism; Marxists
    Czech, 495–496
Community and Society (*Gemeinschaft und Gesellschaft*) (Tönnies), 349, 1591
Community for Democracies, 1438
Comoros Islands, 387–388
    COMESA and, 369
    Economic Commission for Africa and, 528–530
Compagnie Française des Petroles, 53. *See also* British Petroleum (BP)

Comparative advantage theory, 1671
Compensation form of countertrade, 406
Compeoré, Blaise, 211
Composting, 1682
Compton, John, 1493
Comte, Auguste, 1050
Concertacíon los Partidos por la Democracia, 322
Concerted lending strategy, 442
Conciliation, of disputes, 837
Concini, Sen. Dennis De, 1238
Concordancia (Argentina), 81
Condensation nuclei, 1645
Confederación de Trabajaderes Mexicanos, 1247
Confederación de Trabajadores Peruanos, 63
Confederación Generale de Trabajadores Peruanos, 63
Confederación Nacional de Campesinos, 1247
Conference of Independent African States, 1234–1235
Conflict in World Politics (Harff), 591
Confucianism
    capitalism and, 855
    China, 855
    civil society and, 348
    East Asian development and, 510–511, 515–516
Congo. *See also* Democratic Republic of Congo; Republic of Congo
    UN peacekeeping, 1252
Congo-Brazzaville, 689
Congo Free State, 263, 966. *See also* Democratic Republic of Congo; Republic of Congo
Congress for Mutual Economic Assistance (CMEA), 481
Congressional system, 555
Congress of Democrats (COD), 11
Congress of South African Students, 11
Congress of South African Trade Unions, 11
Conquistadores, 356–357
Conrad, Joseph, 262–263
Consciencism (Nkrumah), 1146
Conservation International (CI), 177
Consociationalism, 189, 632
Constitutional and Legal Policy Institute, 1437
Constitutional government, evolution of, 1075
Constitutionalism
    corruption cleanups and, 400–401
    dictatorship and, 473
    functional definition, 391
    liberal definitions, 391
Constitutional (Tanzimat) Movement, 1049
Constitution of Medina, 68
Consultative Group for International Agricultural Research (CGIAR), 17, 852–853
Contadoras, 279–280
Contagion effect, in capital flight, 221–222
Conté, Lansana, 627, 733
Continental Illinois Bank failure, 144
Contonou Peace Agreement, 1255
Contraception, 656. *See also* Family planning
Contras, 279, 309, 392–395, 763, 1023, 1135. *See also* Iran-Contra scandal; Nicaragua
    end of, 394–395
    Iran-Contra scandal, 394
Convention for a Democratic South Africa (CODESA), 62, 438
Convention Muslim League, 1097
Convention of the Elimination of Discrimination against Women (CEDAW), 1717–1718

Convention on Biological Diversity (CBD), 178
Convention on International Trade in Endangered Species of
    Wild Flora and Fauna (CITES), 178, 1511
Convention on the Elimination of All Forms of Discrimination
    Against Women, 772
Convention on the Preservation of Migratory Species of Wild
    Animals (CMS), 178
Convention on the Protection of the World Cultural and
    National Heritage, 178
Convention on Wetlands of International Importance
    (Ramsar), 178
Convention People's Party, 30, 1146–1147
Convergence effect, of migration, 1041, 1042
Convergence theory, of war and development, 1677
Cook, Robin, 772
Cook Islands, demographics, 1191
Cooperative farms, 162
Cooperative for American Remittances to Europe. See CARE
Cooperative for Assistance and Relief Everywhere. See CARE
Cooperative market socialism, 1428
Cooperative socialism, 239
COPAX (Central African Peace and Security Council), 267
Copper production. See also Extractive industries
    Bougainville, 615
    Central Africa, 261
    Chile, 31, 322, 1484–1485
    nationalization, 31, 681
    Zambia, 1752
Copra production
    Central Africa, 261
    Oceania, 1191
Coptic Orthodox Church, 395–396, 614
Copyright. See Intellectual property rights
Corn production, Central Africa, 261
Corporación Venezolana de Fomento, 1178
Corporación Venezolana de Petróleos (CVP), 171
Corporate agriculture, 665
Corpus Juris Civilis, 951
Corruption, 396–401
    Ali Akbar Rafsanjani and, 1343–1344
    China, 328
    classifications of, 307
    cleanups, 399–401
    constitutionalism and cleanups, 400–401
    Croatia, 411
    Cuba, 417
    definitions of, 396–397
    deforestation and, 1347
    Democratic Republic of Congo, 389
    Equatorial Guinea, 576
    Gambia, 691
    globalization and, 398–399
    Iran, 909–910, 1343–1344
    Kenya, 904–905
    Lithuania, 964
    Macedonia, 971
    Mali, 985
    Mexico City Olympic Games, 1247
    Moldova, 1074
    Myanmar, 1098
    Panama, 1236–1237
    Philippines' Ferdinand Marcos, 995–996
    public sector reform, 1331–1333
    regulatory law and, 397–398
    tactical uses, 226, 227

theory of public choice and, 397–398
    Togo, 1553
    transparency and, 1569–1570
    Venezuela, 1179, 1259
    Zambia, 1753
Corruption Perception Index, 1593
COSEP (Supreme Council of Private Entrepreneurs), 1138
Cossacks, in Ukraine, 1588
Costa Rica, 401–402
    Arias Sanchez, Oscar, 84–85
    Association of Caribbean States and, 111
    Caribbean Basin Initiative and, 232–233
    debt relief, 443
    ecotourism in, 539
    life expectancy, 276
    literacy, 276
Cote d'Ivoire, 402–404. See also West Africa
    coffee production, 840
    Economic Commission for Africa and, 528–530
    ethnic conflict, 628
    Félix Houphoët Boigny, 765–766
    invasion of Liberia, 960
    peacekeeping, 1253
    United Nations Development Program in, 1607
    West African Monetary Union and, 1703–1705
Cotton production
    Bahamas, 131
    Central Africa, 261
    Central Asia, 299
    Paraguay, 1243
    Uzbekistan, 1648
Council for Mutual Economic Assistance (CMEA), 417, 708
Council for Peace and Security in Central Africa
    (COPAX), 532
Council Muslim League, 1097
Council of Baltic Sea States, 381
Council of Europe, antidiscrimination efforts, 1063
Council of Regional Organizations in the Pacific, (CROP),
    1219–1220
Counterinsurgency, 404–406
    defined, 404
    future of, 405
    national security and, 404–405
    strategy and, 405
Counterpurchase, 406
Countertrade, 406–408
    barter transactions, 406
    clearing accounts, 407
    compensation, 406
    counterpurchase, 406
    evaluation, 408
    forms of, 406–407
    mixed agreements, 407
    offsets, 406
    rationales and experiences, 407–408
    switch trading, 407
Coups d'etat, 408–410. See also Assassinations; Military regimes
    Batista, 413
    Brazil, 358–359
    Bulgaria, 290
    Cambodia, 907, 1408
    Cameroon, 269
    Central African Republic, 269, 272
    Chile, 321–322, 1274
    CIA in, 308

Colombia, 351–352
common causes, 409
Cote d'Ivoire, 404
Cuba, 158
Czech Communist, 1318–1319
Dahomey, 167–168
definition, 408
Ethiopia, 1393
Fiji, 662
Ghana, 424
Grenada, 248
Guatemala, 726
Indonesia, 1507
Iraq, 868
Liberia, 626
Libya, 961, 1158, 1167
Mexico, 1022
against Mikhail Gorbachev, 299, 302, 375, 382, 384, 713
Nicaragua, 392–393
Niger, 1141
Nigeria, 1142
Panama, 1236, 1238, 1554
Paraguay, 1243
political development and outcomes, 409–410
Republic of Congo, 265
Seychelles, 1401
Sierra Leone, 1406
Solomon Islands, 1431
South Korea, 917
Suriname, 1508
Thailand, 338, 1540–1541
in Third World politics, 408–409
Turkey, 1577
Venezuela, 313, 1659, 1660
Covenant on Civil and Political Rights, 1639
Covenant on Economic, Social, and Cultural Rights, 1639
Crawling-peg currency regimes, 427
Credit guarantee schemes, 150
Creole language, 7, 155, 737
Haitian, 740
origins, 586–587
Cricket, 155
Crimean peninsula, 381
Criminal activities
Centre for International Crime Prevention, 1604
International Criminal Police (Interpol), 398, 842–843
United Nations Commission on Crime Prevention and
Criminal Justice, 1603–1604
Critical Linguistics Study, 941
Croatia, 187, 287, 410–412. See also Yugoslavia
current economy, 411–412
debt holdings, 412
development after 1945, 410
establishment of, 135
Franjo Tubjman, 1573
independence, 136, 290, 1749–1750
international relations, 294
privatization in, 1324
Serbia and, 1058
Croatian Spring, 1749
Croat-Muslim Federation, 188
CROP (Council of Regional Organizations in the Pacific),
1219–1220
Crop specialization, 12, 13, 14. See also Biodiversity;
Monoculture

Crude oil. See Oil industry
Cuba, 1583–1584
in Africa, 256–257
Algeria and, 1166
in Angola, 416
arms embargoes, 159, 887
arms transfer to, 93
Association of Caribbean States and, 111
Batista y Zaldivar, Fulgencio and, 158–159
Bay of Pigs invasion, 33, 246, 308, 414
boat people and, 418
in Chile, 416
CIA and, 308
in Colombia, 352, 1182
in Dominican Republic, 245
economic sanctions, 1386, 1388
economy, 158–159
El Gran Susto (the Great Fear) of Haiti, 588
in El Salvador, 279
Ernesto "Che" Guevara in, 730–731, 732
in Ethiopia, 416
Family Code, 416
free peasants' markets, 417
in Grenada, 721
in Guatemala, 279
in Guyana, 887
international relations, 245–246
invasion of Angola, 54, 256
invasion of Ethiopia, 246, 256
July 26th Movement, 413
LIBERTAD Act, 1388
Mexico and, 1022
in Nicaragua, 279, 1389
Non-Aligned Movement and, 416
Platt Amendment and, 245–246, 412–413
single-party government, 1414
Soviet Union and, 417
trade unions, 415–416
Twenty-sixth of July Movement, 1583–1584
Venezuela and, 171, 1184, 1659
women's rights in, 416
Cuban Democracy Act of 1992 (Torricelli Bill), 417–418
Cuban exiles, 418
Cuban Liberty and Democratic Solidarity
(LIBERTAD) Act, 1388
Cuban Missile Crisis, 246, 414, 1022
Cuban Revolution, 412–419. See also Cuba
rectification program, 417
reversals, 415
Southern Cone and, 1477
Cultivation System, 809
Cultural cooperation, Alliance for Progress and, 33
Cultural divergence, Oceania, 1192–1193
Cultural effects, of ecotourism, 539–540
Cultural hegemony, 420–421
Cultural initiatives
in Albania, 27
Organization of American States, 1207
Rockefeller Foundation, 1367–1368
Soros foundations, 1437
Cultural perceptions, 419–422
alternative culture–based, 421–422
cultural hegemony, 420–421
culture and development, 419–420
deconstructionism, 421

Cultural Revolution
  China, 323–324, 327–328, 330
  Libya, 962–963, 1305
Culture
  language and, 938–939
  modernization and, 1071
  "noisy music" and popular sectors, 1295–1296
  political, 1281–1283
  population movement and, 1299–1300
Curaçao, 1125. *See also* Netherlands Antilles
Currency, Commonwealth of Independent States, 380
Currency crisis, 227. *See also* Financial crises
Currency depreciation, 422
Currency devaluations, 422–424. *See also* Financial crises;
    Monetary policy
  debt and, 439
  definition, 422
  effects of, 423–424
  Marshall-Lerner conditions for, 422–423
Currency exchange. *See also* Exchange rates
  debt relief and, 441
  Vietnam, 482
Currency pegs. *See also* Monetary policy
  Asian, 104
Currency reform, Mexico, 1248
Currency regimes, 424–427
  crawling-peg, 427
  fixed-rate, 425–426
  free-floating, 426–427
Currency valuation, 846–847. *See also* International
    Monetary Fund
Custodio, General Luther, 1273
CVP (*Corporación Venezolana de Petróleos*), 171
Cyclones
  as climatic hazard, 1111–1112, 1144
  Cyclone Theta, 1144
  Tonga, 1553
Cyprus, 428–429
  Turkish invasion, 1035
  UN peacekeeping, 1252
Czechoslovakia. *See also* Czech Republic
  international relations, 294
  political hstory, 286
  Prague Spring, 1318–1319, 1654–1655, 1656
  Václav Havel, 743–745
  Velvet Revolution, 1654–1655
Czech Republic, 429–432
  ethnic conflicts, 592–593
  human resource development, 770
  Klaus–Meciar confrontation, 430–431
  in NATO, 294
  political history, 430
  privatization, 1324
  Soviet Union and, 430
  Václav Havel, 743–745
  Visehrad Four and, 1672–1673

D

Dacko, David, 264
Dagomba people, 627–628, 1552
Dahik, Alberto, 49
Dahomey, 167–168
  independence movement, 30
Dalai Lama, 1548–1549. *See also* Tibet

Dalits (Untouchables), 1640–1641. *See also* Caste systems
Daly, Herman, 1070, 1509
DALYs. *See* Disability Adjusted Life Years
Dams
  Afobaka, 1508
  Aswan High Dam, 116–119, 1090, 1103, 1159, 1688
  Chixoy Dam, 634
  displacement of indigenous peoples, 625, 634
  gravity, 118
  Itaipú Dam, 885–886, 1485, 1498
  Petit-Saut, 684, 1180
  projected additional life storage, 873
  Three Gorges Dam, 520, 1546–1548, 1688
  water resources and, 1688
  Yacyretá Dam, 1243
Danish colonies, slavery and emancipation, 7
Danish West Indies, 1670
Danish West Indies Company, 1670
Danquah, J. B., 29–30
Danube River, Gabcikovo-Nagymaros Project, 1622
Daoud, Prince Mohammed, 3
Darod clan, 1434
Dar ul Islam, 297–298
Darwin, Charles, 654
Das Kapital (Marx), 1000. *See also* Marxism
Daud, General Mohammad, 1091
Davies, James, J-curve theory of social revolution, 1421–1422
Dawes and Young Plan, 142
Dawn (All-India Muslim League newspaper), 36
DAWN (Development Alternatives with Women for a
    New Era), 433–435
Dayan, Moshe, 76–77
Dayton Accords, 138, 188, 411, 786, 1059, 1573
DDT. *See* Agricultural pollution; Water pollution
Dead Sea Transform, 1114
Death penalty, Amnesty International and, 38
De Beers diamond cartel, 250. *See also* Diamond production;
    Extractive industries
  Sierra Leone, 1406
Debt, 437–440
  Argentina, 1011–1012
  COMESA member nations, 370–371
  Cote d'Ivoire, 403
  deforestation and timber sale and, 446
  Democratic Republic of Congo, 388
  domestic industries and, 438
  East Asian, 515
  Ecuador, 542
  food shortage and, 439–440
  growth and, 437–438
  Heavily Indebted Poor Countries Initiative, 818, 836, 849
  Hungary, 790
  International Development Association (IDA) and, 843–844
  Jamaica, 889
  living standards and, 440
  Mauritania, 1004
  Mexico, 1019
  Morocco, 1084
  Nicaragua, 1135
  Niger, 1141
  Nigeria, 1144
  oil and, 835
  relief efforts, 440–444. *See also* Debt relief; Structural
    adjustment programs

social change and, 440
    trade and, 438
Debt cancellation, 444
Debt relief, 440–444
    austerity measures, 441
    by cancellation, 444
    concerted lending strategy, 442
    market-based reduction, 444
    SAPs (structural adjustment programs), 441, 442, 461, 849,
        904, 928, 1005–1006, 1078–1079, 1178
Debt restructuring, Bank for International Settlements and, 145
Debt service, 439
Déby, Idriss, 264
Decentralization, corruption cleanup and, 400
Decolonization
    American, 358–359
    refugee situation and, 1352
De Concini, Sen. Dennis, 1238
Deconstructionism, 421
Defense economics, 91–92. *See also* Arms industrialization
Defiance Campaign, 10–11, 1440
Deforestation, 444–447
    agriculture and, 445–446
    Amazon rainforest, 1345–1349, 1474
    carbon dioxide pollution and, 1346–1347
    causes, 444–445, 1347
    corruption and, 1347
    debt status and, 446
    desertification and, 453
    environmental effects, 445–446
    erosion and, 580–581
    forest management programs, 1348
    mitigation attempts, 1348
    movements against, 446
    national parks and, 1244, 1245, 1712
    Papua New Guinea, 1240
    privatization and, 20
    smaze and, 1420
    Thailand, 1541
    wood fuel and, 562
De Gaulle, Charles, 28, 30, 389, 403, 613, 684
    Algeria and, 1157
    French Guiana and, 1181
De-industrialization, 814, 1071–1072
    North Korea, 915
De Klerk, Frederik W., 190, 433–435, 435–437, 990, 1441. *See also*
        Apartheid; South Africa
De la Rúa, Fernando, 83
Delayed dependent development, 449
Delayed development, 465
Delta-Nimir oil company, 306–307
Demand deposits, 146
Democracy
    failed in Central Africa, 263–264
    transition to, 122
    vs. authoritarianism, 121
Democracy Wall (China), 328
Democratic Front for the Liberation of Palestine, 1228
Democratic Labour Party, Barbados, 155
Democratic Republic of Congo, 388–389
    COMESA and, 369
    debt, 371, 388
    diamond production, 250
    Economic Commission for Africa and, 528–530
    Economic Community of Central African States and, 531–533

    ethnic conflicts, 589–590, 601
    as failed democracy, 263
    Garamba National Park, 1709
    HIV/AIDS, 371
    Hutu refugees in, 269–270
    independence, 269
    mining industry, 648
    mining industry and civil wars, 649
    political history, 264–265
    UNICEF in, 1603
    United Nations Development Program in, 1607
    Virunga National Park, 1709–1710
Democratic Union (Cameroon), 218
Democratization, 447–450. *See also* Elections
    causes and preconditions, 448
    clash of civilizations and, 449–450
    concomitants and consequences, 449
    definition and dimensions, 447–448
    development and, 459
    end of history concept, 450
    globalization and, 449, 709–710
    human rights development and, 775–776
    of language, 942–943
    liberal conception, 448
    as measure of development, 466–467
    Nicaragua, 1139–1140
    political development and, 449
    problems of, 448–449
Demographic transition theory, 1297–1298
Deng Xiaoping, 330, 450–452, 1755
    Cultural Revolution and, 323–324, 327–328
    Jiang Zemin and, 889–890
    reforms under, 324–325, 328
    Tiananmen Square massacre, 451, 1549–1551
Denmark, Virgin Islands and, 1670
Dependency and Development in Latin America (Cardoso),
        228, 1615
Dependency theory, 460–461, 569, 643–645, 667, 1319–1320,
        1544, 1560–1561, 1592, 1615. *See also* Foreign
        direct investment
    contradiction of, 644–645
    trade policy and, 1561, 1562
Dependistas, 1560–1561
Depository banking functions, 146
Deprivation. *See also* Poverty
    relative and social revolution, 1321
Deregulation, 1064
Desai, Morarji, 804, 1442
Desalinization, 1688–1689
Descartes, René, 1569
Desertification, 261, 452–455. *See also* Deforestation;
        Soil degradation
    causes and consequences, 453–454
    combatiing, 454–455
    Niger, 1141
Desparedicidos, 82
De-Stalinization, 287–288, 914. *See also* Khrushchev,
        Nikita; Russia
Development
    alternative, 1592–1593
    anthropological theories of, 458–459
    arms industrialization and, 95–96
    arms transfer and, 91–92
    associated-dependent, 465
    as compared with growth, 1509

Development (*Continued*)
  debt and, 437–440
  defining of, 463–464
  delayed, 465
  delayed dependent, 449
  democratization and, 459
  dependency theory and Marxism, 460–461
  developmentalism, 459
  dictatorships and, 471–472
  disasters and, 477
  economic, 466
  energy and, 561–567
  globalization and theory, 463–464
  high-income countries, 1594
  history, 458–464
  human, 467–468
  major kinds of, 465–466
  measures of, 464–468. *See also* Development measures
  modernization theory, 459–460
  national characteristics and, 462
  neoclassical liberalism/Washington Consensus and, 461–463
  political, 466–467
  post-colonial context of, 458–459
  as process vs. goal, 1594
  social mobility and, 459
  special-relationship, 465
  special-resource, 465
  sustainable, 468
  theoretical base, 458–459
  of underdevelopment, 465
  uneven, 465
  vs. growth, 1591
Development aid, migration and, 1045
Developmental state theory, 463
Development Bank of South Africa, 4
Development measures, 464–468
  first-world (Global North), 464–465
Devil's Island, 683–684, 1186
Dhuluo language, 939
Diamond production
  Angola, 53
  Botswana, 191
  Central Africa, 261, 271
  Democratic Republic of Congo, 649
  Guinea, 733
  producer cartels, 250
  Sierra Leone, 1406
  South Africa, 1461
Diamond smuggling
  Liberia to Sierra Leone, 960
  Sierra Leone, 1406
Diarrheal diseases, 821–822
Diaspora
  African, 6–9, 240, 1234. *See also* African Diaspora
  Caribbean, 240, 241
  Jewish, 6
  Kurdish, 920
  Palestinian, 1229–1233
  Somali, 1432–1433
  Tibetan, 1548
  Turkish, 1578
  West Indian, 1571
Diaz, Adolfo, 392
Diaz Ordaz, Gustavo, 1022

Dictatorship, 469–474. *See also* Authoritarianism; Military regimes; Totalitarianism
  development and, 471–472
  ending of, 473–474
  maintaining, 472–473
  making of, 469–470
  personal, 196, 473, 1416
  predisposing factors, 470–471
  vs. authoritarianism, 120
Didi, Amin Maumoon, 984
Die Burger newspaper, 979–980
Diem, Ngo Dinh, 1258, 1449, 1664, 1667
Dien Bien Phu, battle of, 1663–1664, 1667. *See also* Indochina; Vietnam; Vietnam War
Digil-Mirifle clan, 1434
Dimitrov, George, 287
Dimli Kurds, 1576
Diori, Hamani, 1141
Dioxins, 1682–1683. *See also* Air pollution; Pollution
Dir clan, 1434
Disability Adjusted Life Years (DALYs), mental illness and, 1012–1016
Disaster Mitigation Facility for the Caribbean, 236
Disaster preparedness, 1115–1116
Disaster Relief, CARE and, 230
Disaster relief, 474–478. *See also* Humanitarian relief projects
  early warning, 476
  globalization and, 477–478
  international assistance network, 475–476
  International Committee of the Red Cross, 841–842
  poverty and, 475
  UNICEF and, 1602
Disasters, development and, 477
Discount rate, 147–148
Discount window, 147–148
Discourse Analysis, 941
Discourse on Method (Descartes), 1569
Discrimination, 7, 1059–1064. *See also* Caste systems; Ethnic conflicts
  colonialism and, 363–364, 365
  defined, 1059–1060
  forms of, 1060–1061
  globalization and, 1061
  means of combating, 1062
  minorities at risk, 1062
  against native peoples, 332
  against peasants, 1256
  prevention of ethnic conflicts, 1062–1063
  racial/color, 1061
Dispute resolution, methods of, 837–838
Distribution of resources. *See also* Income distribution
  Nicaragua, 1138
Disunity, dictatorship and, 471
Divergence effect, of migration, 1041, 1042
Diversity, positive aspects, 633
Djerma people, 1140
Djibouti, 478–479. *See also* East Africa
  Bulk Terminal Project, 5
  colonial history, 501
  COMESA and, 369
  Economic Commission for Africa and, 528–530
  literacy, 543
  Somalians in, 1432
Doba Basin Oil Project, 312

Doctors Without Borders, 476, 480–481
Doe, Samuel Kanyon, 626, 960
Doi moi, 481–482
Dominica, 483–484
    Association of Caribbean States and, 111
    Caribbean Basin Initiative and, 232–233
    Caribbean Community and Common Market and, 233–235
    Caribbean Development Bank and, 235–237
    Caribbean Free Trade Association and, 237–238
    international relations, 248
Dominican Republic, 484–485
    Association of Caribbean States and, 111
    Caribbean Basin Initiative and, 232–233
    food imports, 240–241
    Haiti and, 244, 245
    international relations, 244–245
    Juan Bosch, 186–187
    remittances to, 197
    Trujillo dictatorship, 484, 1572
    United States–Dominican Republic–Central America Free Trade Agreement, 1637–1638
    Venezuela and, 171
Domino effect vs. domino theory, 487
Domino theory, 485–487
Donaldo Colosio, Luis, 1248
Donovan, General William "Wild Bill," 307
Dorji, Jigme Wangchuck, 173, 174
Dos Santos, José Eduardo, 54
Dos Santos, Teodorio, 569
Dostum, Abdul Rashid, 1092
Dracunculuus medinensis (Guinea worm disease), 820
Draft Declaration on the Rights of Indigenous Peoples, 487–488
Dragons in Distress: Asia's Miracle Economies (Bello), 106
Dreyfus, Alfred, 683–684
Dromania
    Nicolae Ceausescu, 259–260, 1656–1657
    political history, 286–287
    territorial disputes, 1532–1533
Droughts, 701, 1112
Drugs
    definitions of, 490–491
    herbal, 491–492
Drug trade, 488–490. *See also* Drug trafficking; Drug use
    legislation, 489
    medicinal drugs, 490
    production, 489
    vs. drug trafficking, 489–490
    war on drugs and, 488–489
Drug trafficking. *See also* Coca production; Drug use
    Black Market Peso Exchange, 1077
    Bolivia, 48
    Colombia, 352–353, 1177, 1183, 1361
    Commonwealth of Independent States and, 379
    Cuba and, 417
    ECOSOC Commission for Narcotic Drugs, 1611
    Guyana, 1180
    Jamaica in, 247
    money laundering and, 1077
    Organization of American States and, 1207
    Paraguay, 1485
    Plan Colombia, 1276–1278
    United Nations International Drug Control Program (UNDCP), 1623
    Yemen, 1746

Drug use, 490–493
    in developing countries, 492–493
    historical perspective, 491–492
    legality and, 492
    ritual and religious, 492
Druze, 493–495, 1028
    in Syria, 609
Drylands Development Center, 1608
Dubcek, Alexander, 294, 430, 495–497, 1319, 1416, 1656. *See also* Czechoslovakia; Slovakia
DuBois, W.E.B., 29, 1234
Dubs, Adolph, 4
Dudaev, Gen. Jokhar, 597
Duddei, Goukouni, 311
Due diligence, 150
Dulles, John Foster, 130–131, 1022
    SEATO and, 1458
Durán Ballén, Sixto, 49, 542
Durand Treaty, 3
Durban strike, 11
Durkheim, Emile, 855, 1071, 1294–1295
Dust Bowl, 453
Dutch colonies. *See also* Afrikaners
    slavery and emancipation, 7
Dutch East India Company, 57
    colonialism and, 359
    South Africa and, 1439
Dutch Guiana. *See* Suriname
Dutch Reformed Church, 58
Dutra, Enrico, 1482
Duvalier, François, 243–244, 497
Duvalier, Jean-Claude, 243–244

E

Earth First!, 572
Earthquakes, 1113–1114. *See also* Disaster relief; Natural disasters
    Nicaragua, 276, 1134–1135
    Turkey, 1575
Earthquake/tsunami of 2004, 811, 985, 1489
Earth Summit, 178, 1509–1510
Earth Summit Declaration, 872
East Africa, 499–504. *See also* Burundi; Djibouti; Somalia; Eritrea; Ethiopia; Kenya; Rwanda; Sudan; Tanzania
    border conflicts and development, 505–506
    countries comprising, 504
    economic bloc formation, tread, and development, 506
    Economic Commission for Africa and, 528–530
    ethnic conflicts, 599–602
    geography and climate, 499–500, 504–505
    international relations, 504–508
    post-Cold War international conflicts, 506–507
    Rift Valley fossils, 500
    strategic issues, 507–508
East African Community (EAC), 504, 508–510
East Asia
    bureaucratic authoritarianism in, 514
    civil society and, 515–516
    debt and financial crises, 515
    economic cooperation, 518
    ethnic conflicts, 602–605
    Exclusive Economic Zones, 518
    explaining development, 512–516
    financial crises, 511–512
    future challenges, 523

East Asia (*Continued*)
 history and economic development, 510–516
 Hong Kong, 764–765
 human rights, 519–520
 import substitution industrialization, 515
 inter-Korean talks, 522–523
 international relations, 516–524
 Japan's legacy in, 522
 military spending, 517–518
 natural resources, 514
 non-governmental organizations, 519
 regional order and security, 516–517
 Shanghai Five summit, 520
 social initiatives, 512
 strategic environment, 517–518
East Asian financial crisis, 221, 427
East Asian Tigers, 105–108, 515, 764, 816. *See also* Asian
  "economic miracle"; Asian Tigers; Tiger economies
East Bengal, 1222. *See also* Pakistan
Easter Island. *See* Rapanui
Eastern and Central Asia, privatization in, 1323
Eastern Europe. *See* Central and Eastern Europe;
  specific countries
East India Company. *See* British East India Company;
  Dutch East India Company
East Pakistan. *See* Bangladesh
East Timor, 524–525. *See also* Indonesia; Timor Leste
 colonial legacy, 1454
 Santa Cruz Massacre, 524
Ebola fever, 5
Ebola virus, 1330
Éboué, Félix, 389
ECA. *See* Economic Commission for Africa
ECCAS (Economic Community of Central African States), 506
Echeverría Alvarez, Luis, 1019, 1022–1023
Eckstein, Harold, 1424
ECO (Economic Cooperation Organization), 304–305
Ecological effects, of agriculture, 12–13. *See also* Environment
Ecology, linguistic, 942–943
ECOMOG (Economic Community of West African States
  Cease-Fire Monitoring Group), 1253, 1699
Economic and Customs Union of Central Africa (ECUCA),
  526–527
 Common External Tariff, 526
 Single Tax, 526
Economic and Philosophical Manuscripts of 1844 (Marx), 1000
Economic asymmetry, 114, 115
Economic Commission for Africa (ECA), 369, 528–530, 534
 accomplishments, 529–530
 African Gender and Development Index, 530
 Gender and Development Division, 529–530
 Preferential Trade Area, 529–530
 program divisions, 528–529
Economic Community of Central African States (ECCAS),
  506, 531–533
Economic Community of the Great Lakes, 531
Economic Community of West African States (ECOWAS),
  5, 526, 529, 533–536, 627, 1204, 1699
 contributions to development, 535–536
 future prospects, 1702
 institutions, 534–535
 Liberian war and, 960
 objectives, 534
 origin, 533–534
 peacekeeping operations, 1254

Economic Community of West African States Cease-Fire
  Monitoring Group (ECOMOG), 1253, 1699
Economic Cooperation Organization (ECO), 304–305, 537–538
Economic development, 466. *See also* Industrialization
 Central Africa, 260–267, 267–269
 Central Asia, 299–301
 spillover effect, 268
Economic Freedom Index, 1593
Economic growth vs. economic progress, 1525–1526
(An) Economic History of Latin America in the 20th Century
  (Thorp), 1615–1616
Economic infrastructure. *See* Infrastructure
Economic linkage theory, 1615
Economic models
 socialist, 1426–1429. *See also individual models*
 state-directed economies, 1496–1497
Economic Partnership Agreements (EPAs), 1701–1702
Economic planning, Latin America, 33
Economic policy, human rights development and, 773–774
Economic rights, 344
Economics, structuralist school, 667, 1319–1320
Economic sanctions, 774, 1386–1388
 against Iraq, 869
 against Socialist Republic of Vietnam, 1664
 South Africa, 1440, 1463, 1581
Economic stagnation, 465
Economic Support Fund, 158
Economic systems
 Capitalist Economic Model, 225–227
 free market economy, 674–677. *See also* Capitalism
 mixed economy, 1064–1066
 Neoliberalism, 1120–1123
 private property rights and, 1320–1321
 socialism, 955–956
Economies of scale, 1615
Ecosystem preservation, 1708–1713. *See also*
  Wildlife preservation
Ecotourism, 538–541
 Belize, 164–165
 cultural impacts, 539–540
 economic inequities and, 540
 environmental issues, 539
 Guyana, 738
 marine, 540
 potential disadvantages, 540–541
 social and economic issues, 539
 Virgin Islands National Park, 1670
ECOWAS (Economic Community of West African States),
  5, 526, 529, 627
Ecuador, 541–542
 Andean Regional Initiative, 1277
 banana boom, 47
 CIA in, 308–309
 Cold War and, 40
 Concentration of Popular Forces (CFP), 47
 debt, 542
 ecotourism in, 539
 Galapagos Islands national park, 1710
 geography and climate, 541
 national parks, 1244
 oil boom, 48–49
 oil production, 541–542
 Peru boundary dispute, 541
 political history, 46–49
 territorial disputes, 39, 42–43, 1537

Edhi, Abdul Sattar, 1224
Edhi Foundation, 1224
Education, 542–547. *See also* Civic education; Literacy
  Africa, 342
  Albania, 27
  Antigua and Barbuda, 56
  Argentina, 81
  Barbados, 155
  Central Africa, 272–273
  Chad, 312
  Chile, 320, 543
  Chinese minority peoples, 603
  civic, 338–343. *See also* Civic education
  colonial, 364
  correspondence programs, 545
  Czech Republic, 432
  economic rationalism, 543
  Fulbright Program, 686–687
  government-sponsored programs, 543–544
  Indonesia, 811
  information technology and, 545–546
  international aid and, 543
  Kenya, 906
  Kuwait, 925
  language and, 543, 942
  Libya, 962
  life expectancy and, 544
  Malawi, 982
  Maldives, 984
  Marshall Islands, 997
  Mauritania, 1004–1005
  migration for, 1299
  mission schools, 332
  moral, 543
  Nepal, 1125
  Nigeria, 1143–1144
  nomadic peoples and, 545
  North Africa, 1161–1162
  nutritional status and, 1722
  Oman, 1199
  Pakistan, 125, 1223
  political stability and, 543
  as poverty measure, 1315
  problems of Western-style, 544–545
  Project Impact, 544
  Qatar, 1339
  Saudi Arabia, 1391, 1392
  Senegal, 1396
  Seychelles, 1302, 1401
  South Africa, 1441
  Sri Lanka, 1489
  St. Helena, 1492
  teacher competence, 545
  technology and, 1527–1528
  United Arab Emirates, 1597
  Vietnam, 1665
  women's rights and, 318–319
  Yemen, 1747
Education and Business Development Program (Soros
    Foundation), 1437
Export-oriented industrialization, 1562–1563
EGP (Guerilla Army of the Poor), 726–728
Egypt, 547–549. *See also* Nasser, Gamal Abdel; Sadat, Anwar
  arms exports, 96
  Aswan High Dam, 116–119, 1090, 1103, 1159, 1688

  in Bandung Conference, 139–140
  Black Sea Economic Cooperation Organization
    and, 183–184
  book production, 1162
  Camp David Accords, 219–221
  Christianity in, 336
  COMESA and, 369
  Economic Commission for Africa and, 528–530
  economic development, 1160
  Emergency Laws, 1089
  ethnic conflict, 612, 613–614
  geography and climate, 116, 547, 1157
  history, 547–548
  Hosni Mubarek, 1088–1089
  Islamic fundamentalism in, 1089–1090
  Kuwait Fund for Arab Economic Development and, 927
  League of Arab States and, 71–72
  literacy, 1161
  Muslim Brotherhood, 1089–1090, 1096–1097
  OAPEC and, 1208
  in Palestinian conflict, 74
  Palestinian refugees in, 1231
  political history, 1159–1160
  population growth, 657
  populism in, 1304–1305
  remittances to, 197, 1043
  shadow economy, 181
  Soviet arms transfer, 75–76
  Soviet Union and, 1381
  Suez War and, 17, 75–76, 117, 219–220, 548, 1035–1036,
    1102, 1159
  territorial disputes, 1536, 1692
  tourism, 548, 1160
  unemployment, 1162
  United Arab Republic (UAR), 69–70, 130, 1103,
    1159, 1597–1598
  US foreign aid to, 1106
  water and, 547
  women, 1162
807 provision, 549–552
  Caribbean Basin Initiative and, 550–551
  controversial aspects of, 551
  regional impact, 549–551
Eisenhower, Dwight D., 278, 1021
  domino theory and, 485
  nation-building in Vietnam, 1105
  OPEC and, 1213
  Panama and, 1238
  SEATO and, 1458
  Vietnam and, 1664, 1667
Eisenstadt, S.N., 1591
Ejército de Liberación Nacrional (ELN), 352–353,
    1110–1111, 1182
Ejército Revolucionario del Pueblo (ERP), 82, 1363–1364
El-Abdin Bin Ali, Zine, 193
Elchibey, Abulfaz, 127
Election campaigns, 556–557
Election monitoring, Organization of American
    States, 1206–1207
Elections, 553–558. *See also* Democratization
  elective procedures, 555–556
  electoral process, 556–557
  functions of, 554–555
  history, 553–554
  observation and monitoring, 557

Elections (*Continued*)
  registration, 557
  types of, 555
  voter turnout, 557
Electoral initiative, 555–556
Electrification. *See also* Hydroelectricity
  Cambodia, 99
  Central Asia, 300
  Kazakhstan, 901
  Kyrgyzstan, 929
Electronics industry, market prospects, 110
Elephants, resolving human/wildlife conflict, 1711
ELF (Eritrean Liberation Front), 576–577
Elías Calles, Plutarco, 1018
Ellacuría, Ignacio, 958
Ellice Islands. *See* Kiribati
ELN (National Liberation Army), 352–353, 1110–1111
El Niño (Southern Oscillation), 1113, 1687
El Salvador, 552–553
  agrarian reform, 934
  Association of Caribbean States and, 111
  Caribbean Basin Initiative and, 232–233
  civil war, 233
  Farabundo Marti Front for National Liberation (FMLN), 405, 553, 660–661, 1364
  foreign direct investment, 552–553
  "Fourteen Families," 552
  Frente Democratico Revolucionaria (FDR), 1364
  Liberation Theology and, 334, 958
  life expectancy, 276
  remittances to, 283
  territorial disputes, 1538
  United Nations Economic Commission for Latin America and, 281
  war with Honduras, 763
Emancipation, 7
Embargoes. *See* Arms embargoes; Economic sanctions
Emigration. *See* Migration
Employment, agricultural privatization and, 24
Employment trends, brain drain, 195–198
Encomienda system, 273–274
Endangered species. *See also* Extinction
  World Conservation Union Red List, 178
Endara, Cuillermo, 1236–1237
Enderbury. *See* Kiribati
Energy
  alternative, 558–561, 566. *See also specific forms*
  biomass, 559–560
  development and, 561–567
  fusion processes, 558
  geothermal, 560
  hydroelectricity, 560–561, 563. *See also* Hydroelectricity
  hydrogen, 561
  importance of renewable, 558–559
  nuclear, 563
  OPEC and, 564–565. *See also* OPEC
  solar, 559
  sources and uses, 562–564
  tidal power, 560
  usage by region and type, 563
  wind, 559
Energy crisis, 72. *See also* OPEC; Petroleum
Energy crops, specialization in, 13
Energy markets, 565–566
Engels, Friedrich, 999–1000

Engels' Law, 1641–1642
  city-driven economic growth, 1642–1643
  overurbanization, 1642
Enlightenment, 1072
  land distribution and, 934
Ennals, Martin, 37
Enriquez, Camilo Ponce, 47
Enron scandal, 226
Entrepreneurs, peasants vs., 1257
Entrepreneurship, 226, 567–569
  colonialism and, 365
  Communist Hungary, 1428
  developing world, 567–568
  implications of, 567
  stimulating, 568
  underdevelopment and, 1591–1592
Environment. *See also* Deforestation; Environmentalism; Pollution; Soil degradation
  agricultural privatization and, 21
  Brazil, 1410. *See also* Rainforest
  Center for International Environmental Law, 638
  dams and, 885
  defined, 573
  deforestation and, 445–446
  developed vs. developing countries, 569
  ecotourism and, 539
  European Bank for Reconstruction and Development and, 638
  extractive industries and, 648
  government policies, 569–572
  Green Revolution and, 718–719
  international institutions and policies, 570–571
  Laos, 944–945
  NAFTA provisions, 1174
  nuclear wastes, 1373–1374, 1685
  present situation, 571–572
  preservation vs. conservationism, 1244
  problems in developing countries, 569–570
  rainforest destruction, 1345–1349
  recommendations, 572
  refugee camp impact on, 1356
  Slovenia, 1419
  Southeast Asia, 1452
  Taiwan, 107
  Three Gorges Dam and, 1547
  Togo, 1552–1553
  Tuvalu, 1582
  United Nations Environment Program (UNEP), 1692
  urbanization and, 1643–1646
  wildlife preservation, 1708–1713
Environmentalism, 572–575
  possible action, 574
  recent history, 573–574
  underdevelopment and, 1592–1593
Environmental legislation, Namibia, 1102
Environmental organizations, 177–179
Epidemiological transition, 1330–1331
EPLF (Eritrean People's Liberation Front), 576
EPRDF (Ethiopian Peoples' Revolutionary Democratic Front), 585
Equatorial Guinea, 262, 575–576. *See also* Guyana
  Economic and Customs Union of Central Africa and, 526–527
  Economic Commission for Africa and, 528–530
  Economic Community of Central African States and, 531–533
  political history, 265
Equity capital, 666–667

Erica oil spill, 648
Eritrea, 479, 576–578, 1536. *See also* East Africa
  colonial history, 501
  COMESA and, 369
  Economic Commission for Africa and, 528–530
  Ethiopia and, 505, 507
Eritrean Liberation Front (ELF), 576–577
Eritrean People's Liberation Front (EPLF), 576
Erosion, 579–583. *See also* Deforestation; Soil degradation
  combating, 581–582
  effects of, 581
  factors influencing, 580–581
  soil composition and, 580
  water, 581
ERP (*Ejército Revolucionario del Pueblo*), 82, 1363–1364
Ershad, General Hussain Mohammad, 141
Erwin, Terry, 179
Escapulas II agreements, 280
Esman, Milton, 629
Esso. *See* Exxon-Mobil
Estonia, 583–584. *See also* Baltic states
  Council of Baltic Sea States and, 381
  independence, 290, 293–294, 382–383
  Isamaa Party, 931
  Maart Laar, 931–932
  privatization in, 1324
  Tiit Väl, 1651–1652
Estrada, Joseph, 1273
Eta caste, 255
Ethiopia, 584–586. *See also* East Africa
  authoritarianism in, 123
  colonization and, 501
  COMESA and, 369
  Cuba and, 416
  Cuban invasion, 246
  debt holdings, 371
  division of, 479
  Economic Commission for Africa and, 528–530
  Emperor Haile Selassie, 1382–1393
  Eritrea and, 505, 507, 1536
  Haile Maryam Mengistu, 739–740
  Human Development Index, 658
  infrastructure, 1393
  partitioning of, 501
  Rastafarianism, 1393
  Somalian invasion, 416
  Somalis in, 1432
Ethiopian Peoples' Revolutionary Democratic Front (EPRDF), 585
Ethnic cleansing. *See also* Genocide
  Democratic Republic of Congo, 390
Ethnic communities, 1061–1062
Ethnic conflicts
  Bougainville Copper Mine, 1240
  Caribbean, 586–589
  Central and Eastern Europe, 590–593
  Central Asia, 593–596
  Commonwealth of Independent States, 596–599
  development and, 628–629, 631–632
  East Africa, 599–602
  East Asia, 602–605
  Fiji, 662
  former Yugoslavia, 1058–1059
  Guyana, 738, 1179–1180
  Kenya, 1002–1003
  Liberation Theology and, 958
  Madagascar, 973, 974
  Malaysia, 983
  Mexico and Central America, 605–610
  Middle East, 609–611, 1027, 1037
  military occupation and, 592
  mitigation of, 632–633
  Moldova, 1074
  Myanmar, 1098
  NATO and, 1173–1176
  Nigeria, 1142
  North Africa, 611–615
  Oceania, 615–618, 1193
  Papua New Guinea, 1240
  Rockefeller Foundation and, 1367
  Senegal/Mauritania, 1395
  Serbia, 1398–1399
  Somalia, 1405
  Southeast Asia, 618–620
  Southern Africa, 620–624. *See also* Afrikaners; Apartheid; South Africa
  Southern Cone (Latin America), 624–626
  Sri Lanka, 1489
  Sudan, 1503
  Sunni–Shi'ia, 1027
  Tanzania, 1524–1525
  Tutsi/Hutu, 211–213, 255, 264–265. *See also* Burundi; Rwanda
  Ukraine, 1587
  Uruguay, 1647
Ethnic Groups in Conflict (Horowitz), 631
Ethnicity, 629–632. *See also* Ethnic conflicts
  colonialism and, 630
  definitions, 629–630
  development and, 633–634
  ethnic groups defined, 1061–1062
  international aid and, 633–634
  language and, 938–939
  Middle East, 1027
  mitigation of tensions, 632–633
  population movement and, 1299–1300
  positive aspects of diversity, 633
  Serbia, 1398
  Sri Lanka, 1489
  St. Lucia, 1494
  United States Virgin Islands, 1670
Ethnic Politics (Esman), 629
Ethnic secessionism, 87–88
Ethnolinguistic vitality, 940
ETZEL (*Ergun Zva'I Le'umi*), 161
EU. *See* European Union
Eugenics, 654–655. *See also* Nazi Germany
Eurocentrism, 634–636
  criticism, 635–636
  definition, 634–635
  origin, 635
Europe
  religion, 1359
  slavery and, 7
  water management status, 872
European Bank for Reconstruction and Development, 636–640
  Commonwealth of Independent States and, 637–638
  Eastern Europe transition policy, 637
  environmental policy, 638
  European Union and, 638–639

European Bank for Reconstruction and Development (*Continued*)
  future of concessional development aid, 639
  Latvia and, 947
  in South East Europe, 637
European Commission, Black Sea Economic Cooperation
    Organization and, 183–184
European Commission of Human Rights, 781
European Community
  arms transfer by, 89–90
  Yugoslavia and, 136
European Convention for the Protection of Human Rights
    and Human Freedoms, 781
European Court of Human Rights, 781
European Development Bank, Caribbean Development
    Bank and, 236
European Economic Union, Vietnam and, 1665
European Payments Union, 9, 144
European Social Charter, 379, 782
European Union (EU)
  acquis communautaire, 638
  agricultural subsidization in, 13
  ASEAN and, 115
  Britain and, 373, 374
  Central and Eastern Europe and, 295–296
  civil liberties, 955
  Commonwealth of Nations and, 373
  Cyprus and, 429
  Czech Republic and, 432
  disaster relief, 476
  Estonia in, 583
  European Bank for Reconstruction and Development
      and, 638–639
  Hungary in, 791
  legal system, 953–955
  Lomé Convention, 964–966
  member countries, 954–955
  MERCOSUR and, 1473
  minorities and discrimination, 1062
  Morocco and, 1085
  neoliberalism and, 1122
  North Africa and, 1168
  rainforest preservation and, 1348
  Roma people (gypsies) and, 1062
  Single European Act of 1986, 955
  Southern Cone nations and, 1480
  St. Lucia and, 1494
  St. Vincent and the Grenadines and, 1495
  trade policy, 1564
  Treaty of Amsterdam, 955
  Treaty of Maastricht, 955
  Tunisia and, 1574
  Turkey and, 920
  Visehrad Four and, 1672
Eutrophication, 1285, 1690
Evangelical Protestanism, 639
  in Guatemala, 725
Evans, Melvin, 1670
Evapotranspiration, 445, 1686
Ewe people, 1552
Exchange rates, 143–144, 422. *See also* Currency devaluations
  debt and, 439
  fixed, 425–426
  flee-float, 426–427
Exclusive Economic Zones, 518
Expert appraisal, 838

Export orientation, 105–106
Export-oriented economies, 641–645. *See also* Dependence theory;
    individual countries
  dependency thesis and, 643–645
  Hong Kong, 642
  market forces and government intervention, 643
  Singapore, 642–643
  South Korea, 642–643
  Taiwan, 642–643
Export replacement. *See also* Import Substitution Industrialization
  foreign direct investment and, 667
Externality, negative and positive, 1065
External threat perception, South Asian nations, 1443
Extinction, 178–179
  background extinction rate, 179
  species, 1708–1713. *See also* Wildlife preservation
Extractive industries, 645–651. *See also specific minerals
    and commodities*
  environmental effects, 648
  Guinea, 733
  Guyana, 738
  illegal in national parks, 1245
  Jordan, 893
  Kyrgyzstan, 928, 929
  Laos, 1250
  Macedonia, 971
  mining, 647–648
  Mongolia, 1079
  natural gas, 647
  Niger, 1140
  Oceania, 1191
  oil, 646–656
  Papua New Guinea, 1191
  sustainable development and, 648–650
  Zambia, 1752
Exxon Mobil, 171, 1029
  in Central Africa, 270
  OPEC and, 251, 1212
Exxon Valdez oil spill, 648
Eyadéma, Gnassingbé, 534
EZLN (Zapatista Army of National Liberation), 608, 1017,
    1024, 1248, 1383, 1753–1754

F

Facilitation, of disputes, 837–838
Failed states
  foreign aid to, 1679–1680
  preservation of peace in, 1680
Faisal II, King, 130
Faith-based organizations, HIV/AIDS and, 759
Falange Nacional, 680–682
FALANTIL, 524, 525
Falkland/Malvinas Islands War, 83, 986–987, 1479, 1486–1489
FALN (Armed Forces for National Liberation), 171
Family farms, 17
  in Russia, 23
Family planning, 653–659
  cultural heritage and, 1300
  current status, 657–659
  demographic challenges and, 653
  in developing countries, 656–657
  ECOSOC Population Commission, 1611
  goals and objectives, 656
  ideological aspect of, 654–655

institutions of, 655–656
International Planned Parenthood Federation, 851–852
methods, 656
nature of, 654
Ronald Reagan and funding of, 1635–1636
Singapore, 950
United Nations Population Fund, 1628–1629
Family Planning Associations, 655
Famine. *See also* Hunger
Biafra, 176–177
East Africa, 504–505
Irish potato, 179
Nigeria, 176–177
Fanon, Frantz, 659–660, 1544–1545. *See also* Martinique
Fante people, 626
FAP (Armed Forces of the People), 86–87
Farabundo Martí National Liberation Front (FMLN), 405, 553, 660–661, 1364
FARC (*Fuerzas Armadas Revolucionarias de Colombia*), 352, 1277, 1362–1363, 1537
Farkas, Mihály, 789
Farm restructuring, 22. *See also* Agricultural privatization
Farouk I, King, 69
Fascism. *See also* Nazi Germany
authoritarianism and, 120
in Brazil, 199–200
Fauji Foundation, 1224
FDN (*Fuerza Democrática Nicaragüense*), 393
Febres Cordero, León, 49, 542
Fedayeen, 1228, 1267. *See also* Palestine Liberation Organization
Federalism, ethnic conflict and, 632
Federal Republic of Germany, 170. *See also* Germany
Federal Reserve Bank. *See* US Federal Reserve Bank
Federation of Cuban Women, 416
Federation of French Equatorial Africa, 689
Federation of French West Africa, 403, 733
Federation of Serbia and Montenegro, 290. *See also* Montenegro; Serbia
Female genital mutilation, 758
Female infanticide, 319, 819
Feminism. *See also* Women
human rights and, 772
Rawls' income distribution theory and, 799
Feminization (political). *See also* Women
of HIV/AIDS, 758
Fernandez Maldonado, Jorge, 41
Fertility. *See* Population growth rate
Fertilizer use
agricultural globalization and, 13
agricultural privatization and, 20
Fierlinger, Zdenek, 1318
Figures, Jose, 84
Fiji, 661–663
demographics, 1191
ethnic conflict, 616–617, 662
women's rights, 1195
Financial Action Task Force on Money Laundering (FATF), 1076
Financial crises
Argentina, 1011–1012
Asian, 515, 978–979
Central America, 275
developing countries and, 150–151
East Asian, 511–512
Latin America, 1478
Latvia, 947

Lithuania, 964
Mexico, 1019
Nicaragua, 1138–1139
Poland, 289
Southeast Asia, 1451–1452
Thailand, 337
Uruguay, 1647–1648
Venezuela, 1659–1660
Financial liberalization, 441–442
Financial Options (Eichengreen), 104
Financial scandals, 226
Financial Stability Forum, 143
Financing for Development and Remittances and Gender, 1626
Finland, Soviet Union and, 288
Firestone, Harvey, 960
First World, 459, 464–465, 1542
trade policies, 1564–1565
First World War. *See* World War I
FIS (*Front Islamique du Salut*), 28
Fisheries, tuna, 1582
Fishing industry
Central Asia, 299
in COMESA nations, 371
Common Marine Fisheries Investment and Management Policy, 371
Gambia, 691
Lake Chad, 1143
Micronesia, 1026
Palau, 1225
Fishing rights, 44–45
Andean nations and, 39
Ecuador and, 47
Guinea-Bissau, 735
Morocco/Spain, 1084
Oceania, 1194
Peru and, 41
Five-Year Plans
Bhutan, 174
China, 385, 714–715
Communist economic model and, 385
concept of, 26–27
India, 35–36
South Korea, 917
Soviet Union, 127, 385, 814–815, 1372–1373, 1427
Yugoslavia, 1080
FLCS (*Front de Libération de la Côte des Somalis*), 479
Fleming, Osborne, 55
FLN (*Front de Libération Nationale*), 28, 166, 191–192, 613, 1157, 1537, 1545
Floods, 1112–1113
urbanization and frequency, 1645
FMLN (Farabundo Martí National Liberation Front), 405, 553, 660–661
Fonseca Amador, Carlos, 1137, 1389
Food and nutrition, 663–666. *See also* Hunger
ceremonial, 1257
in developing countries, 664–665
food sovereignty vs. food security, 664
Food-borne infections, 822
Food for the Hungry, 476
Food imports, Caribbean region, 240, 241
Food processors, globalization and, 14–15
Forces Armées Populaires (FAP), 86–87
Ford, Gerald, Mozambique and, 682
Ford, Henry, 813

Ford Foundation, Green Revolution and, 853
Fordism, 646
Foreign aid
    to failed states, war and, 1679–1680
    Middle East economy and, 1030
Foreign direct investment (FDI), 226, 666–672, 1094
    Argentina, 1481
    definition and terminology, 666–667
    determinants of, 668–669
    globalization and, 710–711
    global trading patterns and, 1567
    growth of, 708
    host country development and, 669–671
    Japanese, 1527
    Newly Industrialized Economies and, 1132
    recent trends, 671–672
    Singapore, 1412
    technology transfer and, 1528
    Thailand, 1541
    theories of, 667–668
        dependency/NeoMarxist school, 667
        integrative school (institutional theories), 668
        modernization school, 667
    Turkey, 1578
    Uzbekistan, 1649
    Venezuela, 1178
    wages and labor standards and, 671
Foreign investment. *See also* Foreign direct investment
    dependency thesis, 643–645
    in El Salvador, 552–553
    in Estonia, 583
    in export-oriented economies, 643
    Vietnam, 482
Forest management programs, 1348
Forestry, privatization in, 20, 22
Former Yugoslav Republic of Macedonia, 970–972.
        See also Macedonia
Fossil fuels, 562–564. *See also* Coal industry; Oil industry
Four Dragons economies, 641–645. *See also* East Asia;
        Hong Kong; Singapore; South Korea; Taiwan
Fox, Vicente, 672–673, 1020, 1024, 1248. *See also* Mexico
Foz de Iguazo Declaration, 1472
Franc de la Communauté Financiére d'Afrique, 1703
France. *See also* French colonies
    arms transfer by, 75, 90–91
    Association of Caribbean States and, 111
    Black Sea Economic Cooperation Organization and, 183–184
    in Chad, 264
    First Indochina War, 1663–1664
    in Group of 8, 573
    Indochina and, 1667
    international banks in, 151
    Iraq War and, 1265
    Moroccan immigrants, 1164
    Napoleonic Civil Code, 951
    Nuclear Tests Case (New Zealand v. France), 1623
    in Oceania, 1190
    Organizasion armeé secrete, 613
    SEATO and, 1458
    Senegal and, 1396, 1397
    Suez War and, 75–76, 117, 219–220, 548, 1035–1036
    Tripartite Agreement and, 75–76
    Tunisia and, 193, 1165
    Tunisian and, 1574
Franco, Generalissimo Franciso, 207

Franco, Itamar, 200, 228
Francophonie Institutionelle, 673–674
Franc Zones, 218–219
Frank, André Gunder, 34, 460, 461, 569, 1546
Franklin National Bank failure, 144
Fraser Institute of Vancouver, 1593
Free Aceh Movement, 619
Freedom House survey, 467
Freedom of association, 347
Free market economic model, 102, 674–677. *See also* Capitalism;
        Capitalist economic model
    assumptions of model, 674–675
    Chile, 322
    economic development and, 676
    externalities and, 675
    gains from trade, 674
    globalization and, 707
    government intervention and, 675–676, 918
    Macau, 969–970
    pollution and, 675–676
    South Korea as contradiction, 917–918
    spillover effect, 675
Free Officers' Revolt, 335
Free Papua Movement, 619
Free Trade Area of the Americas (FTAA), 201, 677–680, 830, 1638
    negotiations, 678–680
    origin, 677
    potential obstacles and prognosis, 679–680
    strategic context, 677–678
Free trade zones, 708. *See also specific countries and agreements*
    Andean, 39
    ASEAN as, 97
    Asia-Pacific Economic Cooperation, 108
    Caribbean Free Trade Association and, 238
    Commonwealth of Independent States, 377–378, 379
    Latin American, 39
Frei, Eduardo, 31, 321, 322, 680–682. *See also* Chile
Frei Montalva, Eduardo, 1484
Frei Ruiz-Tagle, Eduardo, 680
FRELIMO (Front for the Liberation of Mozambique), 682–683,
        972, 1087
French Antilles. *See* Martinique
French colonies, 478–479. *See also individual countries*
    Algeria, 68–69
    Central Africa, 262
    colonial administrators, 1705
    decolonization, 361–362
    independence, 268–269
    independence movements, 29–30
    slavery and emancipation, 7
    white colonists, 1705–1706
French-Davis, Ricardo, 1617
French Declaration of the Rights of Man and of the Citizen
        (1789), 779
French Doctors (*Médicins sans Frontiers*), 480–481
French Equatorial Africa, 263, 311, 389
French Guiana, 683–684, 723, 999, 1180–1181
    Association of Caribbean States and, 111
    Devil's Island, 1186
    international relations, 1186
French *Institute National l'Etudes Demographiques*, 655
French Polynesia, demographics, 1191
French Revolution, 779
    Caribbean and, 1126
    human rights and, 772

French Somaliland, 478. *See also* Djibouti
French Territory of the Afars and Issas, 478. *See also* Djibouti
Frente Amplio, 1647
Frente Democratico Revolucionaria (FDR), 1364
Frent Farabundo Marti de Liberacion Natonal (FMLN), 405,
    553, 660–661, 1364
FRETILIN (Revolutionary Front for Independent
    East Timor), 524
Friedman, Milton, 1121, 1275
Friendship Bridge, 1485
Friends of the Earth, 572
Friends Service Committee, Palestinian refugees and, 75
Frondizi, Arturo, 82
Front de Libération de la Côte des Somalis (FLCS), 479
Front de Libération Nationale (FLN), 28, 166, 191–192, 613,
    1157, 1537, 1545
Fronte Sandinista de Liberacion (FSLN). *See* Sandinistas
Front for the Liberation of Mozambique (FRELIMO), 682–683,
    972, 1087
Front for the Liberation of South Vietnam, 1664
Front Islamique du Salut (FIS), 28
FSLN (*Fronte Sandinista de Liberacíon*). *See* Sandinistas
FTAA (Free Trade Area of the Americas), 201, 830
Fuerza Democrática Nicragüense (FDN), 393
Fuerzas Armadas Revolucionarias de Colombia (FARC), 352,
    1277, 1362–1363, 1537
Fujimori, Alberto, 39, 41, 42, 44, 48, 49–50, 684–686,
    1267–1268. *See also* Peru
    Organization of American States and, 1206
Fukuyama, Francis, 450, 1121
Fulani people, 626, 627
Fula people, 627, 734
Fulbe people, 733, 1140
Fulbright, Sen. William, 686
Fulbright-Hays Act, 687
Fulbright Program, 686–687
Fund of the Americas, 571
Furans, 1682–1683. *See also* Air pollution; Pollution
Fur tribe, 1504
(The) Future of Multinational Enterprise (Buckley and
    Carson), 668

G

Gabcikovo-Nagymaros Project dispute, 1622
Gabon, 689–690
    Ebola virus in, 1330
    Economic and Customs Union of Central Africa and, 526–527
    Economic Community of Central African States and, 531–533
    economic development, 267
    ethnic conflicts, 590
    oil production, 270
    political history, 265
Gaia theory, 573
Gaige kaifung policy, 452
Gairy, Eric, 180, 248, 720, 1129. *See also* Grenada
Gaitán, Jorge Eliécer, 351, 1177
Galapagos Islands (Ecuador), 1710
Galedewos, Idris, 576–577
Galtieri, Gen. Leopoldo, 987
Gama'a al-Islamiya, 396
Gambia, 690–692. *See also* West Africa
    decolonization, 361–362
    Economic Commission for Africa and, 528–530
Gambling industry, Macau, 970

Gandhi, Indira, 692–693, 803–804, 898, 1409
Gandhi, Mohandas K., 35–36, 343, 693–694, 802.
    See also India
    Untouchables and, 1640
Gandhi, Rajiv, 694–695, 804
Ganges River, 1687
    global climate change and, 704
Ganwa people, 211
Ga people, 700
Garamba National Park (Congo), 1709–1710
Garang, John, 1503
Garbage. *See also* Waste; Waste management
    defined, 1681
García Meza, General Luis, 185
Garcia Pérez, Alan, 43–44, 48, 64, 685, 1267
Garifona Indians, 606
Garotega people, 1134
Garvey, Marcus, 29, 1234
Gas, natural, 647. *See also* Oil industry
GATT (General Agreement on Tariffs and Trade), 676, 695–697,
    1739–1741. *See also* World Trade Organization
    Agreement on Agriculture, 16
    agriculture and, 16
    background and evolution, 695
    commodity prices and, 1604–1605
    dependency theory of, 1069
    developing countries and UNCTAD, 1604
    establishment of, 459, 1612
    exceptions in, 1561–1562
    genesis, 1606
    globalization and, 707
    Inter-American Development Bank and, 828, 830
    Mexico and, 1024
    most favored nation concept, 707–708, 1567–1568
    operations, 695–697
    tariff reductions vs. ASEAN's, 113
    Trade-Related Intellectual Property Rights (TRIP) agreement,
        16, 490, 824–825, 827
    Tunisia and, 1574
    Uruguay Round, 13–14, 97, 337, 696–697, 707
Gaviria, César, 352–353
Gayed, Nazir, 396
Gayoom, Maumoon Abdul, 984
Gaza Strip, 71, 75–76, 161, 883, 1229, 1382. *See also*
    Arab-Israeli wars
    HAMAS in, 741–743
    intifadas, 71, 80, 741–742, 860–862, 883–884, 1038, 1227,
        1231–1232
    Palestinian refugees in, 1232
Gbagbo, Laurent, 404
Gemayel, Bashir, 336
Gemeinschaft und Gesellschaft (Tönnies), 349, 1591
Gender and Development Division, Economic Commission for
    Africa, 529–530
Gender Awareness Information and Networking System
    (GAINS), 1626
Gender Empowerment Measure, 1593
    Islam and, 876
Gender-Related Development Index, 1593
General Agreement on Tariffs and Trade. *See* GATT
General Dynamics Corporation, arms transfer and, 90
Generalized reciprocity, 1500
Generalized System of Preferences (GSP), 707–708, 965
Generalized System of Trade Preferences Among Developing
    Nations (GSTP), 722. *See also* Group of 77

INDEX

General Law of Ecological Balance and Environmental
    Pollution (Mexico), 1420
General Treaty of Central American Economic Integration, 281
Genetically modified organisms, 665. *See also* Bioengineering
Genetic engineering, intellectual property rights and, 826–827
Genetics research, Rockefeller Foundation and, 1367
Geneva Convention Relating to the Status of Refugees, 1055, 1352
Genghis Khan, 3, 298, 1518–1519
Genocide
    Bosnia-Herzegovina, 295
    Cambodian Pol Pot regime, 908
    Holocaust, 1034–1035, 1037, 1226, 1638
    against Mayan people, 605–606
    Rwanda, 211–213, 212, 244, 264–265, 389–390, 503–504, 590,
        600–601, 630
Geography and climate, 126
    Albania, 26
    Algeria, 27, 1156
    Andean South America, 45–46
    Anguilla, 54
    Antigua and Barbuda, 55
    Bahrain, 132–133
    Bangladesh, 140–141
    Biafra, 176
    Bosnia and Herzegovina, 187
    Botswana, 190
    Brazil, 1474–1475
    Brunei, 201
    Bulgaria, 204–205
    Cambodia, 216
    Cameroon, 217
    Caribbean, 238–239
    Central Africa, 260–261
    Central African Republic, 271–272
    Central America, 273
    Chad, 311
    Chile, 320
    China, 510
    Colombia, 350, 1176
    Comoros islands, 387
    Costa Rica, 401
    Cote d'Ivoire, 402–403
    Croatia, 410
    Czech Republic, 429
    Democratic Republic of Congo, 388
    Dominica, 483
    East Africa, 499–500, 504–505, 599–600
    Ecuador, 541
    Egypt, 116, 547–548, 1157
    El Salvador, 552
    Eritrea, 576
    Estonia, 583
    Ethiopia, 584–585
    Fiji, 661–662
    Gabon, 689
    Gambia, 690–691
    Georgia, 697
    Ghana, 699–700
    Guadeloupe, 722–723
    Guatemala, 725
    Guinea, 732–733
    Guinea-Bissau, 734
    Guyana, 737–738, 1179
    Haiti, 740
    Honduras, 762
Hong Kong, 764
India, 801
Indonesia, 808
Iran, 862
Iraq, 862, 867
Israel, 880–881
Jamaica, 888
Kazakhstan, 901
Kenya, 902
Kiribati, 911, 912
Kurdistan, 920, 921–922
Kuwait, 924–925
Kyrgyzstan, 927
Laos, 943
Latvia, 946
Libya, 961, 1156
Lithuania, 963
Macedonia, 970
Malawi, 980–981
Mali, 984
Martinique, 998
Mauritania, 1003–1004
Mexico, 1016–1017
Middle East, 1027
Montserrat, 1082
Montenegro, 1079–1080
Morocco, 1156
Mozambique, 1086
Myanmar, 1098
Nepal, 1124
Netherlands Antilles, 1125
Nicaragua, 1133–1134
Niger, 1140
Nigeria, 1141–1142
Niue, 1144
North Africa, 1156–1157
Oman, 1198
Pakistan, 1221–1222
Panama, 1236
Papua New Guinea, 1239
Paraguay, 1242
Peru, 1267
Philippines, 1271
Puerto Rico, 1333–1334
Qatar, 1338–1339
Republic of Congo, 389
Rwanda, 1377–1379
Samoa, 1384–1385
Saudi Arabia, 1390
Senegal, 1395
Seychelles, 1401
Slovakia, 1416–1417
Slovenia, 1418
Somalia, 1432
South Africa, 1438
Southeast Asia, 1446
Southern Africa, 1465
Southern Cone (Latin America), 1474–1475
Sri Lanka, 1488–1489
St. Christopher and Nevis, 1490
Sudan, 1501–1502
Suriname, 1180, 1507
Tajikistan, 1518
Tanzania, 1522
Thailand, 1540

Tibet, 1548
Tonga, 1553
Trinidad and Tobago, 1570
Tunisia, 1156–1157
Tuvalu, 1582
United Arab Emirates, 1596
Venezuela, 1658
Virgin Islands, 1668, 1669
West Africa, 1693–1694
Yugoslavia, 1747–1748
Zambia, 1751
Geography and culture, Maldives, 983–984
Geological resources. *See also* Extractive industries;
     Oil; *specific minerals*
  Central Africa, 261
Geologic hazards, 1113–1115
  earthquakes, 1113–1114
  volcanoes, 1114–1115
Georgia, 697–699
  Abkhazia dispute, 378
  agricultural privatization in, 22
  Armenians in, 87
  Baku-Thilisi-Ceyhan Pipeline Project, 638, 698
  Black Sea Economic Cooperation Organization,
    183–184, 381
  Commonwealth of Independent States and, 375–380
  ethnic conflicts, 596
  GUAM group and, 381
  literacy, 543
  peacekeeping, 1253, 1255
  pipeline routes, 306
  privatization in, 1324
  shadow economy, 181
  territorial disputes, 1533
Geothermal energy, 560
German Civil Code, 951
German colonialism, 360
German Democratic Republic, 170. *See also*
    Berlin Wall; Germany
  in Grenada, 721
Germanium production, Central Africa, 261
German reunification, 713
German Society for Technical Cooperation, 571
German Unification (1871), 360
Germany
  arms transfer by, 90–91
  Berlin Wall, 170–171
  Black Sea Economic Cooperation Organization and, 183–184
  Caribbean Development Bank and, 235–237
  countertrade laws, 408
  East and West, 170
  foreign direct investment, 708
  in Group of 8, 573
  income inequality in, 1311
  international banks in, 151–152
  Iraq War and, 1265
  Kurds in, 920
  Micronesia and, 1025
  partitioning of, 1487
  religion in East vs. West, 1360
  Turkish migration to, 1578
  US nation building, 1104
Gero, Erno, 788
Ghana, 699–702. *See also* West Africa
  Ancient, 1694–1695

authoritarianism in, 123
in Bandung Conference, 139–140
Basic Education and Life Skills (BELS)
    program, 545
civic education in, 342
Cocoa Marketing Board, 424
Convention People's Party, 1146–1147
development experience, 701–702
Economic Commission for Africa and, 528–530
ethnic conflicts, 626, 627–628
health care, 748
Human Development Index, 658
independence, 30
Kwame Nkrumah, 1145–1147
neoliberalism and, 1121
political history, 700
Program of Action to Mitigate the Social Costs of
    Adjustment (PAMSCAD), 701
trusteeship, 1632
Volta River Project, 1147
Ghana-Guinea Union, 1147
Ghannouchi, Rachid, 878
Ghassemlou, Abdul, 921
Ghaznivid dynasty (Afghanistan), 3
Gheorghii-Dej, Gheorghe, 259
Gherogiu-Dej, Gherogliu, 287
Ghiday, Wolfe, 577
GIA (Group Islamique Armée), 28
Giap, General Vo Nguyen, 730, 1663
Giddens, Anthony, 349
Gierek, Eduard, 288
Gilbert Islands. *See* Kiribati
Gillot, Gen. Jacques, 723
Gini index (Mexico), 1017
Girot de Langlade, Paul, 723
Glasnost, 289, 382, 702–703, 712–713. *See also*
    Gorbachev, Mikhail
  Russian Orthodox Church and, 1377
Gligorov, Kiro, 136, 971
Global Alliance for Tuberculosis Drug Development, 1368
Global Burden of Disease study, mental health, 1012–1016
Global Campaign for Secure Tenure, 1600
Global Campaign on Urban Governance, 1600
Global Civil Society yearbook, 347
Global climate change, 703–707. *See also*
    Energy; Environment
  agricultural globalization and, 13
  beneficial effects, 704–705
  deforestation and, 445–446
  effects of, 704–705
  extractive industries and, 648
  forecasting and observation, 705
  industrial pollution and, 1289
  Little Ice Age, 1189
  past extremes, 705
  regional outlooks, 705–706
  sustainable development and, 1510
  water resources and, 1691
Global Environment Facility, 571, 1511
Global integration, Central Africa, 267–269
Globalization, 707–712
  African Diaspora and, 8
  agriculture and, 11–18
  Central and Eastern Europe, 295–296
  Commonwealth of Nations and, 374

Globalization (*Continued*)
  communications, 709
  corruption and, 398–399
  definitions of, 13
  democracy and, 709–710
  democratization and, 449
  developing countries and, 710–711
  development theory and, 463–464
  dictatorships and, 474
  disaster relief and, 477–478
  discrimination and, 1061
  economic sanctions and, 1388
  ethnic conflicts and, 593–594
  income distribution and, 800
  inter-religious relations and, 857
  modernization and, 1072
  public health and, 1329
  refugees and, 1355
  regional integration and, 9
  sustainable development and, 1510
  of trade and finance, 708
Global North. *See* First world
Global trading patterns, 1565–1568
  growth in trade as, 1565–1566
  Multifibre Agreements, 1566
  newly industrialized countries (NICs), 1566
  regionalization and trade regulation, 1567–1568
  spatial/directional, 1566–1567
  transitional economies, 1566
  transnational corporations and, 1567
Global Water Partnership, 1692
GNP (gross national product), 466
Gobi Desert, 453
Godreau, Isar, 587
Goh Chok Tong, 712. *See also* Singapore
Goh Keng Swee, 949
Gold Coast, 29–30
Gold francs, 144
Gold production
  Aruba, 1126
  Bougainville, 615
  Central Africa, 261
  Fiji, 1191
  French Guiana, 1181
  Ghana, 700
  Guyana, 1179
  South Africa, 60, 1461
  West African history and, 1695–1696
  West Papua, 619
Goldring, Natalie J., 92
Gold smugglinng, Suriname, 1508
Gold standard, 845–846
Gómez, Juan Vicente, 1178
Gómez, Laureano, 1177
Gomulka, Wladyslaw, 286, 288, 456
Gonja people, 627–628
Gonzáles, Elían, 418
Gorbachev, Mikhail, 163, 289, 299, 712–714, 911, 1374
  Afghanistan and, 1091
  Annus Mirabilis and, 713
  coup d'etat attempt, 299, 302, 375, 382, 384, 713
  decline of, 1657
  glasnost and *perestroika* and, 289, 596, 702–703, 712–713, 1374
  human-face socialism under, 1428

  Hungary and, 790
  Moldova and, 1074
  nationalism and, 596
  Poland and, 1430
  Russian Orthodox Church and, 1377
  Soviet Bloc and reforms of, 1488
  Tajikistan and, 1519
  Turkmenistan and, 1579
  Velvet Revolution and, 1655
  visit to China, 1550
Gore, Al, 1173–1174
Gorgas, Dr. William Crawford, 1237
Gottvald, Klement, 1318–1319
Goulart, Joáo, 228, 1482
Gouled, Hassan, 479
Governance models
  congressional system, 555
  non-governmental organizations and, 1151–1152
  parliamentary system, 554–555
  partnerships with NGOs, 1152–1153
  single-party states, 1414–1416
  social revolution and, 1420–1424
Governance
  failed states, 1679
  Millennium Development Goals, 1607
Governance models. *See also individual models*
  democratization, 447–450
  monarchy, 1075–1076
  socialism, 1424–1426. *See also* Socialist economic model
  Southeast Asia, 1448–1449
Government corruption. *See* Corruption
Government intervention. *See also* Mixed economy
  in economic inequality, 1065–1066
  forms of, 1064–1065
  free-market economies and, 675–676, 918
  indications and methods, 1065
  market forces, 643
  in monopoly, 1065
  in negative externality, 1065
  neoliberalism and, 1121
  in positive externality, 1065
  tiger economies and, 1070–1071
Government of India Act of 1935, 36
Gowda, D. Deve, 804
Gowon, Gen. Yakubu, 176, 534, 1142
Gqozo, Oupa, 154
Grain production. *See also specific grains*
  Central Africa, 261
Gramsci, Antonio, 1294
Gravity dams, 118
Grazing. *See also* Livestock production
  erosion and, 580–581
Great Britain. *See* Britain; British *entries*
Great Depression, 8, 40, 46
  in Argentina, 81
  Bank for International Settlements and, 142
  bureaucracy and, 209
  socialism and, 1426
Greater Tumb/Lesser Tumb islands, 1534
Great Leap Forward, 326–327, 330, 714–715
Great Man-Made Rivers Project (Libya), 1338
Great Migration, in United States, 8
Great People's Cultural Revolution, 330
Great Proletarian Cultural Revolution, 327–328

Great Silk Road, 1518, 1578

(The) Great Transformation: The Political and Economic Origins of Our Time (Polanyi), 458

Greece
Black Sea Economic Organization and, 381
CIA in, 307
Cyprus and, 428
Macedonia and, 971–972
Turkey and, 1577

Greed, as motive for war, 1678–1679

Greek Orthodox Church
Communist totalitarianism and, 716–717
origin, evolution, and teaching, 716

Greek Uniate Church, 336

Greenhouse gases, 703, 1289. *See also* Global climate change; Industrial pollution
agricultural globalization and, 13
deforestation and, 1347

Greenpeace, 446, 572

Green Revolution, 125, 717–719
ecological impact, 718–719
peasants and, 1256
pollution and, 1287
rice culture and, 853
socioeconomic impacts, 718
technological impacts, 719
trends in yields and production, 717–718

Green World movement, 384

Grenada, 720–721
Association of Caribbean States and, 111
Caribbean Basin Initiative and, 232–233
Caribbean Community and Common Market and, 233–235
Caribbean Development Bank and, 235–237
Caribbean Free Trade Association and, 237–238
education, 543
international relations, 248
New Jewel Movement (NJM), 180, 242, 248, 1129–1130
Souffriere Hills volcanic eruption, 1083
US invasion, 1–83, 232, 248, 278, 417, 720–721, 1185

Grenadines. *See* St. Vincent and the Grenadines

Gross Domestic Product (GDP), 466. *See also* Gross National Product
as development measure, 464, 466
expatriate labor force and, 1041
Human Development Index and, 1028–1029
migration and, 1041
quality of life and, 1340
West Africa, 1697

Gross National Product (GNP). *See also* Gross Domestic Product
as definition of development, 464
as development measure, 466
education and, 543
infant mortality correlation, 817
per capita as poverty measure, 1315

Group Islamique Armée (GIA), 28

Group of 3, 1659

Group of 7 (G7), 1149
in East Africa, 507
Financial Action Task Force on Money Laundering, 1076
trade policy and, 1561

Group of 8 (G8), 573

Group of 10 (G10), 143

Group of 15 (G15), 1149

Group of 77 (G77), 139, 461, 573, 721–722, 835
Non-Aligned Movement and, 1148

Groups Areas Act (South Africa), 58–59. *See also* Bantustans; Native Reserves

Grove, Marmaduke, 30

Growth
as compared with development, 1509, 1591

Growth triangles
Indonesia-Malaysia-Singapore, 1529
Singapore-Johor-Riau, 1529

Grupo Andino, 44

GSTP (Generalized System of Trade Preferences Among Developing Nations), 722. *See also* Group of 77

GTZ (German Society for Technical Cooperation), 571

Guadalcanal, 1431. *See also* Solomon Islands
Honiara Peace Accord, 1431

Guadeloupe, 722–724, 999
Association of Caribbean States and, 111

Guairá Falls, 885

Guam, 724–725
demographics, 1191

GUAM group, 381

Guanche people, 975

Guantanamo Bay naval base, 246

Guarani Indians, 1475, 1498

Guatemala, 725–726
Arbenz Guzmán and, 80–81
Association of Caribbean States and, 111
Caribbean Basin Initiative and, 232–233
CIA in, 308, 1021
Guerilla Army of the Poor (EGP), 726–728
Mayan genocide, 605–606
Mayan Indians, 632, 634
National Revolutionary Unity of Guatemala (URNG), 726–728
Organization of American States and, 1206
private property rights in, 1321
remittances to, 283
territorial disputes, 164, 283
US and, 278

Guaymiés (Ngobe) Indians, 606, 607–608

Guebaza, Armando, 683

Guerilla Army of the Poor (EGP), 726–728

Guerilla movements, 1678–1679

Guerrilla War (Guevara), 730, 731

Guerrilla warfare, 728–731
urban, 728, 730

Guevara, Ernesto ("Che"), 40, 48, 414, 730–731, 732, 1584
foco model, 731
in Guatemala, 727

Guido, Jóse María, 82

Guinea, 732–734. *See also* Equatorial Guinea
ethnic conflicts, 627
independence movement, 30
Rassemblement Democratique Africaine, 1558–1559
Sékou Touré, 1558–1559

Guinea-Bissau, 215, 734–735. *See also* West Africa
Economic Commission for Africa and, 528–530
West African Monetary Union and, 1703–1705

Guinea worm disease (*Dracunculuus medinensis*), 820

Gujetari Indians, 1071

Gujral, Kumar, 804

Gulf Corporation Council, 735–736

Gulf Oil Corporation, 171
OPEC and, 251, 1212

Gulf War. *See* Persian Gulf War

Gum Arabic production, Chad, 261

Gunmede, J. T., 10
Guomindang, 326, 331. *See also* Chiang Kai-shek;
　　China, Nationalist
Gurma people, 1552
Gurr, Robert, social revolution theory, 1421–1422
Gus Dur (Kiai Haji Abdurrahman Wahid), 734–735.
　　See also Indonesia
Gusmáo, José Alexandre "Xanana," 525
Gutierrez, Gustavo, 858–859
Gutiérrez, Lucio, 49, 542
Guyana, 737–738, 1179–1180. *See also* West Africa
　　Association of Caribbean States and, 111
　　banking crises in, 150
　　bauxite production, 1185
　　Caribbean Basin Initiative and, 232–233
　　Caribbean Community and Common Market and, 233–235
　　Caribbean Development Bank and, 235–237
　　Caribbean Free Trade Association and, 238
　　drug trafficking, 1180
　　ethnic conflicts, 738, 1179–1180
　　extractive industries, 738
　　gold production, 1179
　　international relations, 1184–1185
　　Jagan Cheddi, 887–888
　　People's National Congress, 1184
　　People's Progressive Party, 1184
　　sugar production, 1185
　　Suriname border dispute, 1185
　　territorial disputes, 1179, 1183, 1537
Guzmán, Abimael, 685
Guzmán, Antonio, 485
Guzmán, General Leigh, 1275
Guzmán, Jacobo Arbenz, 32
Gypsies (Roma), ethnic conflicts with, 592, 593

H

Habash, George, 335
Habermas, Jurgen, 1569
Habitat loss, 178, 1286
　　agricultural globalization and, 12–13
Habitat preservation, 1708–1713
Habré, Hussène, 264
Habsburg monarchy, 187
　　Hungary and, 788–789
　　Serbia and, 1398
Habyarimana, Juvenal, 601, 1378
Hadendowa people, 1503
Haemophilus influenzae, 821
Haganah, 74
Hague Agreements, Bank for International Settlements and, 142
Haig, Alexander, 279, 987
Haile Maryam, Mengistu, 739–740. *See also* Ethiopia
Haiti, 740–741. *See also* Aristide, Jean-Bertrand
　　arms embargo, 90
　　Association of Caribbean States and, 111
　　banking crises, 150
　　Caribbean Basin Initiative and, 232–233
　　Caribbean Community and Common Market and, 233–235
　　Caribbean Development Bank and, 235–237
　　CIA in, 308
　　Dominican Republic and, 244, 245
　　economic sanctions, 1386
　　ethnic conflicts, 588
　　François Duvalier, 497

international relations, 243–244, 741
Organization of American States and, 1206
peacekeeping in, 1253, 1254
poverty, 241, 242
public health in, 1329
slave revolts, 588
slavery and emancipation, 7
Halaf culture, 922
Hamad al-Thani, Shaykh Skhalifa bin, 1339
HAMAS, 741–743, 1096. *See also* Israel; Palestine
Hamza, 494
Handicap International, 480
Hansen's disease (leprosy), 820
Harare Declaration, 373–374
Harti/Darod clan, 1434
Harvest of Shame (documentary), 194
Hasan Ahmed-al-Bashir, Uman, 1502
Hasemite dynasty, 1598
Hasenfus, Eugene, 394
Hashemite dynasty, 868, 892–893, 1033–1034
Hassan II, King, 743. *See also* Morocco
Hassan Sheikh Adan, Shariff, 1434
Hasyim Asy'ari, KH, 737
Hatta, Mohamad, 1506
Hausa-Falani, 176. *See also* Biafra
Hausa people, 626, 627, 1140, 1141, 1142
Haute Volta, independence movement, 30
Havel, Vaclav, 289, 430, 431, 496, 743–745, 1656. *See also*
　　Czechoslovakia; Czech Republic
　　Visehrad Four and, 1672
Hawar Islands dispute, 1339, 1534
Hawiya clan, 1434
Haya de la Torre, Victor Raúl, 46, 64, 65, 745–746.
　　See also Peru
Hay-Bunau-Varilla Treaty, 1236
Hayek, Friedrich von, 1121
Hays, Rep. Wayne, 687
Hazardous wastes, 1684–1685. *See also* Nuclear waste;
　　Waste management
　　Basel Convention on the Control of Transboundary
　　　　Movements of Hazardous Wastes and
　　　　Their Disposal, 1685
　　radioactive, 1685
　　sources, 1684–1685
　　types, 1684
Haze pollution, 445–446
Health care, 746–761. *See also* Human Development Index;
　　Infant mortality; Life expectancy; Maternal mortality;
　　Public Health
　　Africa, 748
　　Central Africa, 273
　　Chad, 312
　　development of health care systems, 747–748
　　Fiji, 662
　　Gambia, 691
　　HIV/AIDS and, 756–760. *See also* HIV/AIDS
　　indigenous medical practices, 807–808
　　infant mortality and, 817–819
　　integrating traditional medicine, 750
　　Kuwait, 925
　　Laos, 944
　　Latin America, 748–749
　　Libya, 961–962
　　Malawi, 982
　　Maldives, 984

Marshall Islands, 997
mental health, 1012–1016
Nicaragua, 1136
Niger, 1141
Nigeria, 1143
Oceania, 1196
Panama, 1237
perspectives on, 750–751
as poverty measure, 1315
Qatar, 1339
Roemer's four-tier typology, 747
Russian *Zemstvo* system, 747
Rwanda, 1378–1379
Saudi Arabia, 1392
Senegal, 1396
Seychelles, 1302, 1401
Sri Lanka, 1489
Sudan, 1503
United Nations Population Fund, 1628–1629
urbanization and, 1642
women and, 750
Health for All by the Year 2000, 1736, 1737
Heart of Darkness (Conrad), 262–263
Heat, urbanization and, 1645
Heavily Indebted Poor Countries (HIPCs), 439–440, 444, 1004,
    1133–1136. *See also* Debt
    Debt Initiative, 818, 836, 849
Hecksher-Ohlin theorem, 1560
Hegel, Friedrich, 347
Hegemony, cultural, 420–421
Hekmatyar, Gulbuddin, 1092
Helms, Richard, 309
Helms-Burton Bill, 418
Helsinki Final Act on Human Rights, 751–752
Hemp exports, Bahamas, 132
Herb, Michael, 1076
Herbal drugs, 491–492
Herbalism, 808. *See also* Indigenous medical practices
Herding communities, 159–160, 1500–1501. *See also*
    Nomadic societies
    in Kuwait, 925
Herero people, 53
Heroin, 493
Herrera, Enrique Olaya, 351
Hertzog, James Barry, 58, 979–980
Herzl, Teodor, 134, 1758. *See also* Zionism
Hese Note, Kessai, 996
Hezbollah, 752–763, 948
High-income countries, 1594
High-Performing Asian Economies. *See* Asian "economic miracle"
High-yielding varieties (HYVs). *See* Green Revolution
Hima people, 211. *See also* Tutsi people
Hinduism, 754–755
    British codification of, 755
    caste system, 253–254, 1640–1641
    in Indonesia, 810
    in Malaysia, 982
    in Nepal, 1124
HIPCs. *See* Heavily Indebted Poor Countries
Hipólito Igoyen, 81
Hippopotamus, extinction of, 1709–1710
Hirschman, Albert, 755–756, 795, 1600
Hirschman, Robert O., 1615
Hispanidad, 605
Histadrut (General Federation of Jewish Labor), 1008

History
    Brazil, 1475
    British Virgin Islands, 1669
    Caribbean, 238–243
    Central Africa, 260–267
    Central Asia, 297–299
    China, 325–326
    of colonialism, 355–362
    Commonwealth of Independent States, 375–380
    of development, 458–464
    drug use, 491–492
    Egypt, 547–548
    of elections, 553–554
    Eritrea, 576
    Guyana, 1179
    Indonesia, 809–810
    Iran, 863
    Laos, 943–944
    North Africa, 1157–1160
    Poland, 1279
    Seychelles, 1401
    Singapore, 1411
    South Africa, 1439
    Southern Cone (Latin America), 1474–1475
    Sudan, 1502
    Suriname, 1180
    Tanzania, 1522–1523. *See also* Tanganyika; Zanzibar
    Tunisia, 1574
    Turkey, 1576–1577
    Ukraine, 1587–1588
    Uruguay, 1647
    of waste management, 1680–1681
    World Council of Churches, 1728–1729
Hitler, Adolf, 1416. *See also* Fascism; Nazi Germany
HIV/AIDS, 756–760, 821
    Botswana, 191
    Caribbean, 1211
    in children, 318
    in COMESA member states, 370–371
    development and, 756–757
    drug trade and, 490
    East Africa, 504–505
    ethical issues regarding, 758
    Ethiopia, 658
    ethnic conflict and, 628
    family planning and, 654
    feminization of, 758
    Gabon, 690
    gender differences in risk, 319
    Ghana, 658
    Guyana, 737
    human rights and, 757–759
    International Development Association and, 844
    International Planned Parenthood Federation and, 851
    Kiribati, 913
    Laos, 944
    life expectancy and, 1330
    Malawi, 982
    Mozambique, 1087
    Namibia, 1102
    non-governmental organizations and, 759
    Papua New Guinea, 1239
    public health and, 1328–1329
    Rockefeller Foundation and, 1368
    Southeast Asia, 1452

HIV/AIDS (*Continued*)
   Southern African future and, 1467
   Tanzania, 1523
   Thabo Mbeki's denial of, 1007
   Thailand, 337, 1542
   United Nations Population Fund and, 1628
   United Nations Program on HIV/AIDS (UNAIDS), 1629, 1737
   USAID programs, 1636–1637
   WHO and, 1737
   Zambia, 1752
   Zimbabwe, 1756
Hmong people, 1250, 1540
Ho, Edmund, 969
Hobbes, Thomas, 1075
Ho Chi Minh, 730, 760–761, 1662, 1663
Ho Chi Minh Trail, 1250
Hofstadter, Richard, 486–487
Holocaust, 1034–1035, 1037, 1226, 1638
Holper-Samuelson theorem, 1560
Homelands, African. *See* Bantustans; Native Reserves
Honduras, 762–763
   Association of Caribbean States and, 111
   border conflicts, 283
   British. *See* Belize
   Caribbean Basin Initiative and, 232–233
   El Salvadoran war, 763
   life expectancy, 276
   literacy, 276
   territorial disputes, 1538
Honecker, Eric, 1656
Hong Kong, 764–765. *See also* East Asia; Tiger economies
   anti-communism in, 514
   Asian "economic miracle" and, 101
   in Asia-Pacific Economic Cooperation, 108
   banking industry, 764
   civic education, 340–341
   economic development, 511–512
   globalization and, 711
   Import Substitution Industrialization, 515
   as knowledge-based economy, 1529
   as Newly Industrialized Economy, 1131
   shadow economy, 181
   technology transfer, 1131–1132
   tourism, 764
Honiara Peace Accord, 1431
Hon Sui Sen, 949
Hope Dies Last (Dubcek), 496
Hopper, Rex, social revolution theory, 1421
Horn, Gyula, 1655
Horn of Africa, 576
Horowitz, Donald, 631
Horticulture, subsistence living and, 1501
Houphoët-Bouigny, Félix, 403, 765–766
Household farms. *See also* Family farms
   in Russia, 23
Howell, Leonard, 1350–1351
Hoxha, Enver, 26, 27, 287, 766–768, 1487. *See also* Albania
Hoyte, Désmond, 1179–1180, 1184
Hua, Guofeng, 330
Huang He River, 1687
Huaorani Indians, 49
Huguenot persecution and South Africa, 1439
Hukna ng Bayan Laban sa Hapon (Huks), 977, 1272
Human capital, 222, 1161
Human development, 467–468

Human Development Index, 421, 464–465, 467–468, 1310, 1593–1594
   GDP and, 1028–1029
   Guatemala, 725–726
   Islam and, 876
   Mongolia, 1079
   for Newly Industrialized Economies, 1133
   as poverty measure, 1315
   Singapore, 1413
   Taiwan, 1515
   Turkmenistan, 1579
Humanitarian aid, 773, 784–787. *See also* Disaster relief
   complex emergencies and, 785–786
   forms of assistance, 785
   infrastructure problems and, 1618–1619
   principles, 784–785
   United Nations Department of Humanitarian Affairs, 1619
Humanitarian Emergency Grant (Liberia), 5
Human Poverty Index, 1315, 1593
Human resource development, 156, 768–770. *See also* Basic Human Needs; Resources
   change and, 769
   concept, 768
   demographic changes and, 769
   humanitarian approach, 769
   industrialization approach, 769
   internal political changes and, 769
   management changes and, 769
   organic human model, 769
   present status, 768–769
   specifics in developing world, 769–770
Human resources, population growth and, 1296–1297
Human Resources Management, 768
Human rights. *See also* Human rights development; Human rights violations
   Amnesty International and, 37–38, 519–520, 576, 1482
   Commonwealth Human Rights Initiative, 374
   Covenant on Civil and Political Rights, 1639
   Covenant on Economic, Social, and Cultural Rights, 1639
   defined, 771–772, 777
   East Asia, 519–520
   foreign policy aspects, 770–777
   generational/positive vs. negative, 780
   Helsinki Final Act on Human Rights, 751–752
   hierarchy of, 781
   historical documents of, 779
   HIV/AIDS and, 757–759
   human nature and, 778–779
   Inter-American Commission on Human Rights, 1207
   International Bill of Human Rights, 779–780
   military and, 1053–1057
   multinational corporations and, 1095
   natural law justification, 777
   Organization of American States and, 1207
   positivist justification, 778
   refugees and, 1355–1356
   regional developments, 781–782
   religion and, 778
   United Nations and, 779
   United Nations Sub-Commission on the Promotion and Protection of Human Rights, 1627
   Universal Declaration of Human Rights, 37, 771, 777, 779, 1638–1640
   universalism vs. relativism, 781
   war crimes tribunals, 1054–1055

Human rights development
   basic diplomatic relations and, 772–773
   conditionality of aid, 774–775
   democracy and, 775–776
   economic and trade policy and, 773–774
   economic development and, 775
   history of foreign policy and, 772
   humanitarian intervention, 773
Human rights violations, 782–783. *See also* Atrocities;
      Ethnic conflicts
   Argentina, 1481–1482
   Cambodian Pol Pot regime, 908
   Colombia, 1277
   Equatorial Guinea, 576
   Guinea, 733–734
   Nicaraguan Somoza government, 1434
   Peru, 49
   Togo, 1552–1553
Humphrey, John P., 1639
Hundertwasser, Friedensreich, 573
Hungarian Revolution, 293, 456, 788, 790, 1430, 1488, 1655
Hungarians, outside Hungary, 593
Hungary, 788–791
   agricultural privatization, 19
   debt, 790
   ethnic conflicts, 592
   Gabcikovo-Nagymaros Project dispute, 1622
   Guyana and, 887
   human resource development, 770
   international relations, 293
   magyarization policy, 284
   in NATO, 294
   political history, 284, 286, 289
   privatization, 1324
   territorial disputes, 1533
   Velvet Revolution, 1655–1656
   Visehrad Four and, 1672–1673
   welfare communism, 1428
Hunger, 663–666. *See also* Food and nutrition
   International Baby Food Action Network (INFAN), 818
   Nicaragua, 1136
   Nigeria, 1143
   poverty and, 1316
   Rockefeller Foundation and, 1367
   World Food Conference, 1624
   world situation, 663–664
Hun Sen, 216, 787–788. *See also* Cambodia
Huntingdon, Samuel P., 449–450, 459, 460, 857–858, 1071,
      1105–1106, 1421
Hunting/gathering peoples, 1500
   vs. foraging, 1500
Hurricanes, 1111–1112. *See also* Disaster relief; Natural disasters
   Central America, 276
Hurtado, Osvaldo, 49, 542
Husak, Gustav, 430, 1319, 1416
Hussein, King of Jordan, 70–71, 77, 791–792, 893
Hussein, Saddam, 71, 96, 130, 470, 486, 792–794,
      1036–1037, 1262. *See also* Iraq
   invasion of Kuwait, 79
   Iran-Iraq War and, 865
   Kurds and, 611
Hussein, Sharif, 69
Hussein-McMahon Correspondence, 69
Hutu/Tutsi conflict, 211–213, 244, 255, 264–265, 269–270, 389–390,
      503–504, 590, 600–601, 630. *See also* Burundi; Ruwanda

Hu Yaobang, 889
Hydrochloric acid pollution, 1, 2
Hydroelectricity, 560–561, 563. *See also* Dams
   Itaipú Dam, 1485, 1498
   Lesotho Highlands Project, 957
   Petit-Saut dam, 1180
   Slovenia, 1419
   Three Gorges Dam, 520, 1546–1548, 1688
   Volta River Project (Ghana), 1147
   water use, 1690
Hydrogen bomb. *See* Nuclear testing
Hydrogen energy, 561
Hyperinflation. *See* Inflation; Monetary policy

I

IAEA (International Atomic Energy Agency), 831–832
IATA (International Air Transport Association), 830–831
Ibañez del Campo, Carlos, 30, 321
Iberian colonialism, 363–364. *See also* Portuguese colonies;
      Spanish colonies
Ibo people, 176, 626, 627. *See also* Biafra
Ibrahim, Seid Kutub, 1096
IBRD (International Bank for Reconstruction and
      Development), 837
ICARA (International Conferences for Assistance to Refugees
      in Africa), 850
ICCO (International Cocoa Organization), 838–839
ICID (International Commission on Irrigation and
      Drainage), 871
ICO (International Coffee Organization), 840–841
ICSID (International Center for Settlement of Investment
      Disputes), 837–838
IDA (International Development Association), 833–834,
      843–844. *See also* World Bank
Idris, Sheikh Sidi, 961
IFC (International Finance Corporation), 834. *See also*
      World Bank
Igbo people, 1142
Illia, Arturo, 82
Image of the limited good, 1257
Immorality Act (South Africa), 58
Immunization, Rockefeller Foundation support, 1366–1367
IMO (International Maritime Organization), 845
Imperialism. *See also* Colonialism
   decline of, 1075–1076
   East Asia and, 512–513
   Lenin's theory of, 1415, 1423, 1592
Import Substitution Industrialization, 105–106, 209, 458, 461,
      708, 795–797, 1248, 1615
   Brazil, 1482
   Central America, 274
   East Asia, 515
   foreign direct investment and, 667
   Honduras, 762–763
   Mauritius, 1005
   Mexico, 1018
   Peru, 1269
   in practice, 796
   rationale, 795–796
   reconsideration of, 796–797
   structuralist theory and, 1320
   trade policy and, 1562
   Venezuela, 1178
Income distribution, 797–801. *See also* Poverty

Income distribution (*Continued*)
  criticism of Rawls' theories, 798–799
  global distributive justice, 799–800
  globalization and, 800
  government intervention in, 1065–1066
  Southern Cone (Latin America), 1479
  in state-directed economies, 1497
  Tanzania, 1524
  in Western society, 797–798
Income inequality, 1310–1311. *See also* Poverty
Indenture. *See also* Slavery
  African Diaspora and, 6–7
  in Niue, 1144–1145
India, 801–805. *See also* India-Pakistani wars
  agricultural water use, 1689
  All-India Muslim League, 35–36
  arms industrialization, 94
  Asian Development Bank and, 100–101
  Bangladesh and, 141
  Bharatiya Janata Parishad, 857
  Bhutan and, 174
  as British colony, 360
  Buddhism in, 859
  caste system, 252–256, 1640–1641
  Chipko Movement, 446
  civic education in, 340–341
  Dutch East India Company and, 359–360
  earthquake of 1950, 1114
  external threat perception, 1443
  foreign direct investment, 708
  Fulbright Program and, 687
  global climate change and, 704
  Green Revolution and, 717–718
  Hinduism in, 859
  India-Pakistani war, 1093
  infant mortality, 804
  irrigated and drained area, 871
  Jawaharlal Nehru, 1117–1118
  Kashmir dispute, 94, 805–807, 897–899, 1443
  Khalistani (Sikh) movement, 858
  literacy, 804
  Macaulayism and, 1119–1120
  Manas Wildlife Sanctuary, 1710, 1711
  Mohajir migrants, 1222
  Mohandas Ghandi. *See* Ghandi, Mohandas
  neem tree and biopatents, 827
  neoliberalism and, 1121
  Non-Aligned Movement and, 1147–1149
  partitioning of, 802
  population growth, 658
  religious revitalization in, 859
  Rockefeller Foundation and, 1367
  SEATO and, 1458
  secularism in, 859
  Sikhism, 1408–1409
  South Asian Association for Regional Cooperation and, 1441–1444
  Sri Lanka conflict, 804
  telecommunications industry, 804
  territorial disputes, 1535, 1692
  UNICEF in, 1603
  water management status, 872
  in World War II, 361
Indian Congresses, 10
Indian Economic Plan, 1525

Indians. *See also* Indigenous peoples *and specific groups*
  Akoerio, 1507
  Amerindian, 605–606
  Andean, 51
  Arawak, 131, 1093, 1125, 1126, 1669
  Carib, 998, 1083, 1494, 1507, 1570, 1669
  expatriate, 1071
  Guarani, 1498
  Gujetari, 1071
  Tirios, 1507
  Wajana, 1507
Indian–Pakistani wars, 94, 802, 803, 805–807, 897–899
Indigenous medical practices, 807–808
Indigenous peoples
  Aceh, 618–619
  Amerindian, 605–606
  Andean, 51
  Arawak, 131, 154, 586–587, 683
  Arawak Indians, 1669
  Aymara, 626–627, 685, 958
  Balante, 734
  Bantu-speaking, 1522–1523
  Basuto, 956–957
  Bolivian, 45–46
  British Virgin Islands, 1669
  Bumiputra, 1127
  Bush Negroes, 1507–1508
  Carib Indians, 154, 586–587, 683, 723, 1494, 1570, 1669
  Chamorros, 724–725
  Djerma, 1140
  Fula, 734
  Fulbe, 733, 1140
  Garotega, 1134
  Guarani Indian, 1475, 1498
  Hausa, 1140, 1142
  Hmong of Laos, 1250
  Huaorani, 49
  Igbo, 1142
  Kanak, 1194
  Kenya, 939, 1002
  Kono, 1406
  Kpelle, 960
  Kru, 960
  language and, 939
  legal definition of, 1393–1394
  Maghrib, 975–976
  Malasia, 1127
  Malawi, 981
  Malay, 973, 1272
  Mande, 733
  Mandinka, 734
  Maur, 975
  Mayan, 632, 634, 727
  military and, 1050
  Misquito, 1134
  Niger, 1140
  Nigeria, 1142
  Peruvian, 49
  Philippines, 1271–1272
  Songhai, 1140
  Sosso, 733
  Southern Africa, 1459
  subsistence living, 1500–1501
  Sudan, 1503
  Swaziland, 1512

Tamil, 804
Thailand, 1540
Togo, 1552
Tuareg, 975, 1140
United Nations Permanent Forum on Indigenous
  Peoples, 1627–1628
UN Working Group on Indigenous Populations, 1627
Yoruba, 1142
Indochina. *See also* Cambodia; Laos; Vietnam
  authoritarian governance, 1449
  First Indochina War, 1663–1664
  France and, 1662, 1663
  French in, 1667
  Japanese occupation, 1448
  territorial disputes, 1535
Indochinese Wars, 730
Indonesia, 808–812. *See also* East Asian Tigers
  ASEAN and, 97, 112–116, 1455–1456
  in Asia-Pacific Economic Cooperation, 108
  in Bandung Conference, 139–140
  banking in, 149
  CIA in, 1507
  currency devaluation, 424
  earthquake/tsunami of 2004, 811
  East Timor (Timor Leste) and, 1455
  economy of, 98
  education, 811
  ethnic (overseas) Chinese in, 620
  ethnic conflicts, 618–619
  financial crisis, 1451
  foreign direct investment in, 670
  form of government, 810–811
  Guided Democracy, 1506
  Gus Dur (Kiai Haji Abdurrahman Wahid), 734–735
  history, 809–810
  independence, 809
  Independence War, 1506
  Indonesia-Malaysia-Singapore growth triangle, 1529
  invasion of East Timor, 524
  irrigated and drained area, 871
  Islam and, 810
  MAPHILINDO and, 1272
  national parks, 1245
  as Newly Industrialized Economy, 1131
  non-Islamic religions, 810
  Project Impact, 544
  religion and, 1457
  Suharto regime, 1449, 1451
  Sukarno, 1506–1507
  territorial disputes, 1535
  Tesso Nilo National Park, 1712
Indonesia-Malaysia-Singapore growth triangle, 1529
Indonesian Communist Party, 809–810, 1506
Industrialization, 812–817. *See also* Economic development;
    Import Substitution Industrialization; Industry
  African Diaspora and, 7
  Albania, 26–27
  Argentina, 82, 1260
  arms, 92–96. *See also* Arms industry; Arms transfer
  ASEAN and, 114
  Cameroon, 218
  Caribbean, 240–241, 241
  Central Asia, 299–300
  Communist economic model and, 386
  debt and, 438

defining, 812
de-industrialization, 814, 1071–1072
demographic transition theory, 1297–1298
development and, 458–459, 815–816
Dominican Republic, 186
East Asian Tigers, 105–108, 512, 515, 764, 816
export-oriented, 1562–1563
forced of Jungary, 789–790
Gabon, 268
Great Migration and, 8
Guatemala, 80
Kyrgyzstan, 928
migration and, 1040
Peru, 46, 63
progression of, 1067–1068
Puerto Rico, 1334
Russia, 1375
science and technology and, 813–814
secularization and, 857
Singapore, 1411–1412
Soviet and state-sponsored, 814–815
in state-directed economies, 1497
Taiwan, 1516
tobacco use and, 1331
Trinidad and Tobago, 247
Ukraine, 1588
water use and, 1689–1690
Yugoslavia, 1080
Industrial pollution, 1288–1292
  air, 1289–1290
  global climate change and, 1289
  Kyoto Protocol, 1290
  Love Canal, 1290
  Minamata Bay mercury, 1289–1290
  thermal, 1290
  waste disposal and, 1290
  water, 1289–1290
Industrial Revolution, 2, 812–813, 1067
  capitalism and, 225
  colonialism and, 364, 366
  pollution and, 1288–1289
  poverty and, 1310
Industrial wastes. *See* Waste; Waste management
INFAN (International Baby Food Action Network), 818
Infanticide, 819–820
  female, 319
Infant mortality, 817–819
  Antigua and Barbuda, 56
  breastfeeding initiatives, 818, 1736
  Cuba, 241
  Ethiopia, 658
  gender discrimination and, 817. *See also* Infanticide
  Ghana, 658, 700
  GNP correlation, 817
  health care and, 746, 750
  India, 804
  Kenya, 659
  Lebanon, 948
  Libya, 962
  Mauritania, 1005
  modernization and, 1071
  Nepal, 1125
  Nicaragua, 1136
  Niger, 1141
  Nigeria, 1143

Infant mortality (*Continued*)
  Panama, 1236
  Philippines, 659, 1274
  as poverty measure, 1315
  Rwanda, 1379
  Saudi Arabia, 1392
  Sri Lanka, 1489
  St. Helena, 1492
  Sudan, 659
  Tanzania, 1523
  United Nations Convention of the Rights
    of the Child, 818
  Vietnam, 659
  water management and, 1688
  Zambia, 1752
Infectious diseases, 820–824. *See also specific diseases
    and organisms*
  HIV/AIDS. *See* HIV/AIDS
  Nigeria, 1143
  Panama, 1237
  public health and, 1328–1329
  regional patterns in, 823
  USAID programs, 1636–1637
  water-borne, 1691
  water management and, 1688
Inflation, 149–151. *See also* Currency devaluation;
    Currency regimes; Monetary policy
  Argentina, 82–83
  Baku-Thilisi-Ceyhan Pipeline Project, 699
  Brazil, 228
  Gabon, 690
  Jamaica, 889
  neoliberalism and, 1121, 1122
  Peru, 49
  Slovenia, 1419
  Yugoslavian collapse and, 1058
Influenza, 821
Information access. *See also* Internet
  agriculture and, 16
Information age, transparency and, 1569
Information saturation, 1569
Information technology
  COMESA and, 371–372
  corruption and, 398–399
  education and, 545–546
  globalization and, 709
  Jordan, 893
  Malaysia, 983
  Mekong Basin Development Corporation and, 99
  Taiwan, 1517
Infrastructure. *See also* Transportation
  colonialism and West African, 1697
  Ethiopia, 1393
  Gambia, 691
  Guinea, 734
  Guinea-Bissau, 735
  humanitarian aid and, 1618–1619
  Laos, 944
  Libya, 961
  Malawi, 982
  Nicaragua, 1135–1136
  Philippines, 1274, 1349
  population movement and, 1299
  public health and, 1329
  Russia, 1374

Rwanda, 1378–1379
  Senegal, 1396
  Singapore, 1413
  war and, 1677
  Zambia, 1752
Initiative, electoral, 555–556
Initiative for Strengthening Afghan Family Laws, 1719
Inkatha Freedom Party, 212
Innovation, diffusion of, 1069
Innovation clusters, 1528–1530, 1643. *See also* Growth triangles
Inside the Company (Agee), 309
Institute for Management Development, 1593
Institute National l'Etudes Demographiques, 655
Institutional Action Party (*Partido Revolucionario Institucional*,
    PRI), 1017–1019, 1024, 1107, 1246–1249
Institutional FDI fitness theory, 668. *See also* Foreign
    direct investment
Institutionalization
  as measure of development, 467
  of revolution, 1247
INSTRAW (tions International Research and Training Institute
    for the Advancement of Women), 1625–1626
Integrated Regional Information Network, 476
Integrated Water Resource Management, 1692
Integrative theory, 668. *See also* Foreign direct investment
Intellectual property rights, 824–827
  NAFTA and, 1173
  trademarks, 827
  TRIP agreement, 16, 490, 824–825, 827
  World Intellectual Property Rights Organization
    (WIPO), 825–826
Inter-American Commission on Human Rights, 1207
Inter-American Council for Integral Development (CIDI), 1205
Inter-American Declaration on the Rights of Indigenous
    Populations, 1321
Inter-American Development Bank, 40, 151, 571, 828–830, 1206
Inter-American Institute for Social Development, 829
Inter-American Treaty of Mutual Assistance, 1183
Inter-American Treaty of Reciprocal Assistance (Rio Treaty),
    1206, 1482
Inter-Arab Investment Guarantee Corporation, 927
Intergenerational equity, 1622–1623
Intergovernmental Authority on Drought and Development
    (IGAAD), 502
Intergovernmental organizations (IGOs)
  humanitarian relief and, 784–787
  modernization and, 1067–1068
  WHO and, 1735–1736
Intergovernmental Panel on Climate Change, 558
Inter-Korean Joint Declaration, 523
Intermediate development, theory of, 1071–1072
Internal conflicts. *See also* Ethnic conflicts; Political history
  Central Africa, 268–269
Internally Displaced Persons, 1353. *See also* Refugees
International Agency for Research on Cancer, 1737
International Air Transport Association (IATA), 830–831
International Atomic Energy Agency, 831–832
  Iraq and, 1264–1267
International Baby Food Action Network (INFAN), 818
International Bank for Reconstruction and
    Development, 151, 837. *See also* World Bank
International Bill of Human Rights, 779–780
International Business Companies. *See* Multinational corporations
International Center for Settlement of Investment Disputes
    (ICSID), 834, 837–838

International Chamber of Commerce, anti-corruption measures, 398

International Clearing Union, 846

International Cocoa Organization (ICCO), 838–839

International Code of Conduct, political prisoners, 37

International Coffee Organization (ICO), 840–841

International Commission on Irrigation and Drainage (ICID), 871

International Committee of the Red Cross, 475–476, 841–842
  Geneva Conventions, 1055

International Commodity Agreements, 249–250

International Confederation of Christian Trade Unions, 1727

International Conference for Assistance to Refugees in Africa (ICARA), 850

International Conference on Assistance to Refugees, 1618

International Conference on Financing for Development, 1621

International Conference on Human Rights (Tehran 1968), 37

International Conference on Population and Development, 1628

International Conflict Resolution (Azar and Burton), 633

International Council of Voluntary Agencies (ICVA), 476

International Court of Justice (The Hague), 374, 1621–1623

International Covenant on Civil and Political Rights, 1391.
    See also Self-determination

International Covenant on Economic, Social and Cultural Rights, 1393. *See also* Self-determination

International Criminal Court, 771, 1057

International Criminal Police (Interpol), 398, 842–843

International Criminal Tribunal for the Former Yugoslavia, 1055–1056

International Development Association, 833–834, 843–844, 1606.
    See also World Bank

International Development Bank
  Caribbean Development Bank and, 236
  in Central Africa, 270

International Disaster Assistance network, 476

International Energy Agency (IEA), 1209

International Federation of Red Cross and Red Crescent Societies, 475–476, 841

International Finance Corporation, 834, 1606. *See also* World Bank

International governmental organizations, agriculture and, 15–16

International Governmental Panel on Climate Change, 705

International Higher Education Support Program (Soros Foundation), 1437

International Human Rights Day, 37

International law, 950–951. *See also* Legal systems

International Maritime Organization, 845

International Meteorological Organization, 1738. *See also* World Meteorological Organization

International Military Tribunal, 1054–1055

International Missionary Council, 1729

International Monetary Fund (IMF), 9, 10, 506, 832–833.
    See also World Bank
  agriculture and, 15
  Argentina and, 83
  Asian Development Bank and, 100
  Asian loans, 103
  Asian Monetary Fund and, 104
  Balance of Payments and Statistics Yearbook, 1043
  Bolivia and, 185
  Burkina Faso and, 211
  Central Africa and, 267
  Compensatory Financing Facility, 848
  concessionary loans, 1316. *See also* Debt

Cote d'Ivoire and, 403
  debt relief and, 440–441
  Democratic Republic of Congo and, 388
  dependency theory of, 1069
  Dominican Republic and, 485
  evolution, 848–849
  fixed but adjustable system, 846–847
  founding, 845–847
  Gabon and, 690
  Gambia and, 691
  General Arrangements to Borrow, 848
  genesis, 1606
  Ghana and, 503
  Group of 10 and, 143
  Haiti and, 85
  Heavily Indebted Poor Countries Initiative, 818, 836, 849
  institutions, 847
  International Monetary and Financial Committee, 847
  Kyrgyzstan and, 928
  Latvia and, 947
  Madagascar and, 974
  Malaysia and, 978
  Mauritius and, 1005–1006
  member states, 847
  Mongolia and, 1078–1079
  neoliberalism and, 1123
  Nicaraguan debt and, 1135
  Pakistan and, 1223
  petrodollars and, 1270–1271
  political agendas and, 227
  Poverty Reduction and Growth Facility, 848
  privatization and, 1323
  public sector reform and, 1331–1333
  refugee classifications, 1354
  Structural adjustment programs (SAPs). *See* Structural adjustment programs
  Sukarno and, 1507
  trade policy and, 1561–1562
  Tunisia and, 1574
  Uganda and, 503
  US funding of, 1561
  WW II and, 459

International Organization for Migration (IOM), 850–851

International Petroleum Corporation, 41, 46

International Planned Parenthood Federation, 655, 851–852

International Plan of Action on Aging, 1625

International Radiotelegraph Convention, 854

International Red Cross and Red Crescent Movements, 784–785

International Refugee Organization, 1606, 1611, 1616. *See also* United Nations High Commissioner for Refugees

International relations
  Albania, 293
  Algeria, 1165–1166
  Antigua and Barbuda, 248–249
  Bahamas, 248
  Barbados, 247–248
  Brazil, 1482–1483
  Caribbean, 243–249
  Caspian Sea and, 305–306
  Central Africa, 267–271
  Central America, 277–281
  Central Asia, 302–307
  Chile, 1483–1484
  Commonwealth of Independent States, 380–385

International relations (*Continued*)
  Cuba, 245–246
  Czechoslovakia, 294
  Dominica, 248
  Dominican Republic, 244–245
  East Africa, 504–508
  East Asia, 516–524
  Grenada, 248
  Haiti, 243–244, 741
  human resource development and, 769
  Hungary, 293
  Jamaica, 246–247
  Libya, 1166–1168, 1338
  Mexico, 1020–1025
  Middle East, 1033–1039
  Morocco, 1164–1165
  North Africa, 1163–1170
  Northern South America, 1181–1187
  Paraguay, 1484–1486
  Poland, 294
  Romania, 293
  Southeast Asia, 1453–1457
  Southern Africa, 1464–1468
  Southern Cone (Latin America), 1479–1480
  St. Kitts and Nevis, 249
  St. Vincent and the Grenadines, 248
  Trinidad and Tobago, 247
  Tunisia, 1165
  United Arab Emirates, 1596
  Venezuela, 1183–1184
  West Africa, 1698–1703
  Yemen, 1747
  Yugoslavia, 294
International Rice Research Institute (IRRI), 852–853
International Service for National Agricultural
    Research (ISNAR), 17
International Sugar Agreement, 840
International Telecommunication Union (ITU), 854
International Telegraph Convention, 854
International Telephone and Telegraph (ITT), 1484
International Timber Organization (ITTO), 446
International Tin Agreement, 840
International Tin Council, 250
International Union for Conservation of Nature and National
    Resources, 1509. *See also* World Conservation Union
International Union for the Protection of Nature, 1244
International Women's Rights Conferences, 1718
International Youth Internship Program, 221
Internet
  agriculture and, 16
  civil society and, 347
  connectivity and access problems, 546
  education and, 545–546
  globalization and, 709
Interpol, 842–843
  anti-corruption measures, 398
Inter-religious relations, 854–860. *See also* Religion
  defining religion, 854–856
  globalization and, 857
Inter-Tropical Convergence Zone, 1686–1687, 1694
Inter-Tropical Front, 1694
Intervention, government. *See* Government intervention
Intifadas, 71, 80, 741–742, 860–862, 883–884, 1038, 1227,
    1231–1232
  al-Aqsa, 883–884, 1227

Investment development, by ASEAN, 114
Inward FDI index, 669
IOM (International Organization for Migration), 850–851
Iqbal, Mohammad, 36, 877
Iran, 862–865. *See also* Iran-Iraq War
  agricultural privatization, 21, 23–24
  Algiers Agreement, 865
  Ali Akbar Rafsanjani, 1343–1344
  Anglo-Iranian Oil Company, 52–53
  arms transfers to, 95, 96
  Ayatollah Khomeini, 909–910
  Baghdad Pact, 868
  Caspian Sea and, 305
  claim to Bahrain, 133
  Cossack Brigade, 863
  Economic Cooperation Organization and, 304
  economic sanctions, 1386
  geography and climate, 862
  Hezbollah and, 753
  independence, 1034
  Iranian Revolution, 865
  irrigated and drained area, 871
  irrigation and drainage, 874–875
  Islamic Republic of, 864–865, 910
  Kurdistan and, 920, 921
  Kurds in, 920
  languages spoken, 1027
  Mohammed Mossadeq, 1085–1086
  nationalization of oil companies, 1085–1086
  natural gas production, 647
  Nazi Germany and, 909, 1034
  oil industry, 647
  privatization, 1323
  Qajar dynasty, 863
  Regional Cooperation for Development and, 304
  Reuters Concession, 863
  Revolutionary Guards, 864
  Shah Mohammad Reza, 1220–1221
  Soviet Union and, 311
  territorial disputes, 1534
  US downing of Flight 655, 867
  Uzbekistan and, 303
  White Revolution, 864
  women's rights movements, 878
Iran-Contra scandal, 394
Iranian Revolution, 868–869
Iran–Iraq War, 96, 130, 793–794, 864, 865–869. *See also*
    Hussein, Saddam
  Gulf Corporation Council and, 735–736
Iran–Libya Economic Sanctions Act, 1387
Iran–Soviet Memorandum, 305–306
Iraq, 867–870. *See also* Hussein, Saddam; Iran–Iraq War;
    Persian Gulf War (1991); Persian Gulf War (2003)
  aid to PLO, 71
  arms embargo, 90
  arms transfers, 95
  Ba'ath Party, 71, 129–130, 868, 1598
  Baghdad Pact and, 130–131, 310, 868
  Christianity in, 336
  economic sanctions, 1386
  Egyptian Free Officers' Movement and, 868
  fedayeen, 1267
  geography and climate, 867
  Hashemite dynasty, 868
  independence, 1034

Israeli bombing, 161
Kurd Safe Havens in, 1355
Kurds and, 71, 610–611, 794, 868–869, 920, 921, 1254
Kuwait invasion, 79, 89, 486, 793–794, 869, 925, 1037, 1160, 1261–1262. *See also* Persian Gulf War (1991)
League of Arab States and, 71–72
no-fly zones, 869
nuclear development, 161, 1037
OAPEC and, 1208
occupation and reconstruction, 1267
oil-for-food program, 920
oil industry, 647, 868
in Palestinian conflict, 74
privatization, 1323
single-party government, 1414
USS Stark incident, 866
weapons of mass destruction, 1262–1263
Iraq Petroleum Company, 868
nationalization of, 130
Iraq War. *See* Persian Gulf War (2003)
Irish potato famine, 179
Iron
Angola, 53
Central Africa, 261
Guinea, 733
Industrial Revolution and, 813
Iron Curtain, 1488, 1655
Ironsi, Gen. Aguyi, 1142
Irredentism, 1455
IRRI (International Rice Research Institute), 852–853
Irrigated and drained area, ten countries
with largest, 871
Irrigation, 870–875. *See also* Dams; Water *entries*
dams and water resources for, 1688
desertification and, 453–454
Earth Summit Declaration, 872
food production and, 1689
India, 873
International Commission on Irrigation and Drainage (ICID), 871
Kadakum Canal System (Turkmenistan), 1579
soil degradation and, 1286
Water Users Associations, 872
Isamaa Party (Estonia), 931
Isbegovic, Alija, 137
ISID (Centre for the Study of Islam and Democracy), 878
Islam, 875–879. *See also* Islamic fundamentalism; Muslims
agricultural privatization and, 24
Almoravid movement, 1004
basic facts, 875–876
Cairo Declaration on Human Rights in Islam, 782
capitulation (Status Quo) agreements, 335
in Central Asia, 297–298, 299–300
Christianity and, 335
civil society and, 348
Coptic Orthodox Church and, 396, 614
development and, 876
drug use and, 492
in East Africa, 502
HAMAS, 741–743
Hezbollah, 752–763
historical interpretations impeding development, 877
in Indonesia, 810
jihad, 891–892
Kurdish, 920

in Mauritania, 1003–1004
modern interpretation and reform, 877–878
nationalism and, 1447
in Niger, 1140
In North Africa, 611–612
Organization of the Islamic Conference, 1215–1216
organizations contributing to development, 878
populism and, 1302
principles conducive to human development, 876–877
Salafist movement, 1505
Saudi Arabia, 1391
Shar'iah law, 955, 1595
Sharia laws, 1503
Southeast Asian issues with, 1457
Sufism, 1504–1506
theoretical considerations for development, 879
Universal Islamic Declaration of Human Rights, 782
universality of, 68
Uzbekistan, 1649
Women Living Under Muslim Law, 1719–1720
Islamic Democratic Alliance, 1097
Islamic Development Bank, 151, 927
Islamic fundamentalism, 8, 858, 877, 879–880. *See also* Islam; Muslim *entries;* Muslims
al-Aqsa (2000–present), 861–862
Egypt, 1089–1090
first (1987–1983), 860–861
HAMAS, 741–743
Hezbollah, 752–763
jihad, 891–892
West Africa and, 1701
Islamic law (*Shar-iah*), 955
Islamic Salvation Front, 28, 1158
Islamic World Conference on Human Rights, 771
Islam se Tanali Malaya, 1344
Island states, global climate change and, 706
ISNAR (International Service for National Agricultural Research), 17
Israel, 880–885, 1227. *See also* Arab–Israeli Wars; Gaza Strip; Palestine; West Bank; Zionism
Arab nationalism and, 69
arms industrialization, 94
arms industry, 95
arms transfers by, 95
Balfour Declaration, 69, 134–135, 980, 1226, 1759
Bandung Conference, 139–140
Black Sea Economic Cooperation Organization and, 183–184
bombing of Iraq reactor, 161
Camp David Accords, 219–221
creation of, 1034–1035, 1037–1038, 1226
development and Arab–Israeli conflict, 882–883
development towns, 881
Druze in, 495
establishment of, 881–882
geography and climate, 880–881
Golda Meir, 1007–1009
HAMAS and, 741–743
intifadas and. *See* Intifadas
invasion of Lebanon, 161, 753
kibbutzim and *moshavim* (communal farms), 881
Ma'alot massacre of school children, 1228
Oslo Accords, 1227, 1231–1232
Palestinian occupation, 883
Palestinian refugees in, 1231–1232

Israel (*Continued*)
  society, 1027
  territorial disputes, 1534, 1692
  treaty with Jordan, 883
  in twenty-first century, 883–884
  US foreign aid to, 1106
  virtual water trade, 1671–1672
  Zionism, 166–167, 881, 1037, 1758–1759
Israeli Mossad, 1221
Issa people, 478–479. *See also* Djibouti
Itaipú Dam, 885–886, 1485, 1498
Italian colonies, 479, 501
Italy
  autonomous regions, 1394
  Black Sea Economic Cooperation Organization and, 183–184
  Caribbean Development Bank and, 235–237
  CIA in, 307
  in Group of 8, 573
ITTO (International Timber Organization), 446
ITU (International Telecommunication Union), 854
Ivory Coast. *See also* Cote d'Ivoire
  independence movement, 30
Iwokrama rainforest, 738
Izebegovic, Alija, 136, 411, 1059

J

Jagan, Cheddi, 887–888, 1179–1180, 1184. *See also* Guyana
Jagan, Janet Rosenberg, 1180
Jain, Devaki, 434
Jamaica, 888–889
  Association of Caribbean States and, 111
  banking crises, 150
  bauxite production, 888–889
  Caribbean Basin Initiative and, 232–233
  Caribbean Community and Common Market and, 233–235
  Caribbean Development Bank and, 235–237
  Caribbean Free Trade Association and, 237–238
  Cayman Islands and, 258
  debt holdings, 889
  ethnic conflicts, 587
  food imports, 240–241
  international relations, 246–247
  Rastafarianism, 1349–1351
Jammeh, Yaha Abdul, 691
Japan
  ASEAN and, 115, 1455
  Asian Development Bank and, 101
  Asian "economic miracle" and, 101–102
  Asia-Pacific Economic Cooperation and, 108
  Brazil and, 1483
  caste system, 255, 1640
  Colombo Plan and, 354
  "comfort women" sexual slavery, 522
  currency devaluation, 424
  defense and security, 517
  in East Asia, 512–513
  East Asian legacy, 522
  financial crisis, 1451
  fishing rights in Oceania, 1194
  foreign direct investment, 708
  globalization and, 711
  in Group of 8, 573
  income inequality, 1311, 1312
  in Indochina, 1664

  international banks in, 151–152
  Micronesia and, 1025, 1026
  Minamata Bay mercury poisoning, 1289–1290
  mining industry, 648
  nation building in, 1104
  natural gas production, 647
  occupation of Guam, 724–725
  Oceania and, 1240
  Southeast Asia and, 1447–1448
  Southeast Asia and postwar, 1456–1457
  suicide rate, 1015
  Taiwan and, 1515
  territorial disputes, 1535
  US land redistribution, 935
  war crimes tribunals, 1055–1057
  zaibatsu conglomerates, 103
Japan Bank for International Development, 1529–1530
Japanese colonies, 361
Japan International Cooperation Agency, 571
Jarulzelski, Wojchiech, 288, 889–890, 1430. *See also* Poland
Java, Green Revolution/peasants study, 1256
Javier Arana, Francisco, 80
Jayawardene, J.R., 353, 1442
J-curve theory of social revolution, 1421–1422
Jensen, Arthur, 1594
Jerusalem, conflict over, 74–75
JEWEL (Joint Endeavor for Welfare, Education, and
    Liberation), 180, 242, 248, 1129–1130
Jewish Diaspora, 6
Jewish fundamentalism, 858. *See also* Zionism
Jewish refugees, 881
  from Soviet Union, 883
Jews. *See also* Anti-Semitism; Israel
  caste systems and, 253
  under Communism, 592
  ethnicity and, 630
  of Mahgrib, 976
Jiang Qing, 327–328
Jiang Zemin, 329, 890–891
  reforms under, 325
  Theory of the Three Represents, 891
Jihad, 891–892, 1038
  in Algeria, 28
  Egypt and, 1089–1090
Jiménez, Marcos Pérez, 171
Jinnah, Fatima, 125
Jinnah, Mohammad Ali, 35–36, 125
John Frum cargo cult, 1652
Johnson, Chalmers
  social revolution theory, 1420–1421
  social systemic theory, 1422–1423
Johnson, Lyndon B., 34, 186
  Alliance for Progress and, 279
  Dominican Republic and, 245, 485
  Panama and, 1238
  Tonkin Gulf Resolution, 1458, 1667
  Vietnam War and, 1664, 1667
Johnston, Harry, 960
Johnstone, Peter, 55
Joint Declaration of 77 Developing Countries, 721. *See also*
    Group of 77
Joint Endeavor for Welfare, Education, and Liberation
    (JEWEL), 180, 242, 248, 1129–1130
Jordan, 892–894
  Egypt and, 1159

extractive industries, 893
independence, 1033–1034
King Hussein, 791–792
Kuwait Fund for Arab Economic Development and, 927
League of Arab States and, 71–72
Palestine Liberation Organization and, 9277
in Palestinian conflict, 74
Palestinian refugees in, 1230
Persian Gulf War and, 893
political and economic reforms, 1032
Six-Day War and, 77
territorial disputes, 1692
treaty with Israel, 883
virtual water trade, 1671–1672
war with Syria, 70–71
Yasser Arafat in, 79
Jorge Blanco, Salvador, 485
Juárez, Benito, 1017
Juché economic model, 914, 915
Judaism. *See also* Jews
Conservative, 895
historical view, 894
Jewish denominations, 895
Jewish identity in modern Israel, 895
Orthodox, 895
rabbinical view, 894–895
Reconstructionist, 895
Reform, 895
Jujuy people, 625
July 26th Movement, 413, 416
JUNAL (Brazil) National Indian Foundation, 624
Juntas. *See also* Military coups; Military regimes
Argentina, 82, 1082
Ecuador, 47–48
Guatemala, 80–81
Nicaragua, 1389
Venezuela, 171, 1259
Jurrian culture, 922
Jus commune (common law of Europe), 951
Justice Party (Turkey), 1577
Justicialist Movement, 1081
Just War concept, 773
Jute cultivation, Bangladesh, 141

K

Kabila, Joseph, 265, 389, 601
Kabila, Laurent, 388–389, 590
Kabiy people, 1552
Kadakum Canal System (Turkmenistan), 1579
Kádár, János, 288, 788, 790
KADU (Kenya African Democratic Union), 903
Kadyrov, Ahmed, 598
Kagame, Paul, 601, 1378
Kahlistan, 692–693
Kalahari Desert, 190
Kalakhani, Habibullah (Afghan king), 3
Kamkalavan, Wavel, 1401
Kanak people, 1194
KaNgame Homeland, 153–154. *See also* Native Reserves
Kant, Immanuel, 773, 1569
Kanton. *See* Kiribati
KANU (Kenya African National Union), 903–904
Kanyon Doe, Samuel, 626
Karadzic, Radovan, 136, 137

Karen people, 618–619
Karimov, Idom, 1648
Karimov, Islam, 303
Kariuki, J.M., 906
Karl, Terry, 564
Karmal, Babrak, 3–4, 1091
Karzai, Hamid, 1522
Kasavubu, Joseph, 966
Kashmir dispute, 94, 805–807, 897–899, 1443
Kassem, General Abd al-Karim, 308
Katanga, 269
Kaunda, Kenneth, 899–901, 1751–1752. *See also* Zambia
Kavan, Jan, 772
Kayapó Indigenous Area (Brazil), 624
Kayibanda, Gregoire, 1378
Kazakhs, 298
Kazakh Soviet Socialist Republic, 298–299. See also Kazakhstan
Kazakhstan, 126, 901–902
Black Sea Economic Cooperation Organization
and, 183–184
Caspian Sea and, 305
Commonwealth of Independent States and, 375–380
Economic Cooperation Organization and, 537–538
oil, 306
political history, 299, 383
pollution, 1374
territorial disputes, 1534
Keita, Fodebo, 29–30
Keita, Modibo, 984, 1147
Kemal, Mustafa. *See* Ataturk, Mustafa Kemal
Kemalism, 1049
Kenjaev, Safarali, 302
Kennecott Copper Company, 1484
Kennedy, John F., 171
Alliance for Progress and, 33–34, 278–279, 732, 1106,
1184, 1635
Bay of Pigs invasion, 246, 308, 414
Cuban Missile Crisis, 246, 414
Dominican Republic and, 245, 484–485
Haitian aid and, 497
Laos and, 1249
national security intiatives, 404
Samoa and, 1385–1386
USAID and, 1634
Vietnam and, 1105
Kenya, 902–905. *See also* East Africa
agrarian reform, 935
civic education, 342
colonial history, 361–362
COMESA and, 369
decolonization, 361–362
East African Community and, 503, 508–510
Economic Commission for Africa and, 528–530
economy, 904
ecotourism, 539
Human Development Index, 659
independence, 30
indigenous people's languages, 939
Kenya African Democratic Union (KADU), 903
Kenya African National Union (KANU), 903–904, 1415
Marsabit Federal Reserve, 1245
Mau Mau, 502, 906, 1002–1003
National Rainbow Coalition (NARC), 905
Native Reserves, 903, 1002
privatization, 24

Kenya (*Continued*)
  Somalia and, 1204
  Somalis in, 1432
  Structural Adjustment Program (SAP), 904
  Swynnerton Plan, 1003
  white community, 1706, 1707
Kenya African Democratic Union (KADU), 903
Kenya African National Union (KANU), 502,
    903–904
Kenyatta, Jomo, 29, 502, 508, 904–905, 905–907
Kérékou, Mathieu, 168
Keynes, John Maynard, 833, 846. *See also* Bretton
    Woods System
Khader, Asma, 878
Khaldun, Ibn, 1294
Khaldun Center for Development Studies, 878
Khalistani (Sikh) movement, 858
Khama, Sekgoma, 907
Khama, Seretse, 190, 907. *See also* Botswana
Khan, Amanullah (Afghan king), 3
Khan, Ayah, 898
Khan, Genghis, 3, 298, 1518–1519
Khan, Great, 298
Khan, Habibullah, 3
Khan, Irene, 37
Khan, Nadir, 3
Khan, Reza. *See* Pahlavi, Shah Mohammed Reza
Khan, Zahir, 3
Khatami, Muhammad, 306, 864–865, 878
Khilafat Movement, 36
Khlmelnytsky, Bohdan, 1588
Khmer Rouge, 216–217, 309, 685, 787, 907–909, 1070, 1408,
    1449, 1454, 1664. *See also* Cambodia
Khoikoi people, 1459
Khoisan people, 1459
Khomeini, Ayatollah Ruhollah, 793, 858, 864–865,
    909–910, 1220–1221. *See also* Iran
  as populist, 1302, 1306
Khosian language, 53
Khrushchev, Nikita, 287–288, 910–911, 1001–1002, 1373
  Russian Orthodox Church and, 1376–1377
Kibbutzim and *moshavim* (communal farms), 881
Kikungo language, 53
Kikuyu people, 1002–1003
Kimathi, Didan, 906
Kimbundu language, 53
Kim Dae-Jung, 523
Kim Il Sung, 914–915
Kim Jong-Il, 915
Kim Young Sam, 103
Kinfu, Kadane, 577
King, Martin Luther, Jr., 344
Kipochakia, 1534
Kirchner, Néstor, 83
Kiribati, 911–912, 1191
Kirimati (Christmas) Island. *See* Kiribati
Kissinger, Henry, 1159, 1209
  Chile and, 1484
  Israel and, 78
  Mozambique and, 682
Kiswahili language, 500–501, 502, 940
KLA (Kosovo Liberation Army), 138
Klaus, Vaclav, 430–431, 1416
Knowledge-based economies, 1529
Kohl, Helmut, Bishop Desmond Tutu and, 1581

Koirala, Prasad Bosweswore, 1124
Kolingba, André, 264, 272
Kolkhozy, 19, 23, 162, 928, 1579
Komati Accord, 189
Konaré, Alpha Oumar, 985
Konkomba people, 627–628
Kono people, 1406
Korea
  North. *See* North Korea
  South. *See* South Korea
  Syngman Rhee and, 1364–1365
Korean War, 918
  Colombo Plan and, 354
  domino theory and, 486
  economic development and, 511
  Japanese economy and, 102
  South American exports and, 46, 47
  Uruguayan economy and, 1647
Koroma, Major Johnny-Paul, 1406
Kosovo, 137, 138, 1749
  atrocities in, 295
  NATO and, 1175
Kosovo Liberation Army (KLA), 138
Kosygin, A.I., 1373
Kouchner, Bernard, 480
Kountche, Col. Seyni, 1141
Kpelle people, 960
Krahn people, 626
Krakatoa volcanic eruption, 1114
Krenz, Egon, 1656
Kruger, Paul, 1439
Kru people, 626, 960
Kruschev, Nikita, 712
  Cuban Missile Crisis, 246, 414
  de-Stalinization and, 455–456
  Hungary and, 790
  polycentrism policy, 288–289
  Tito and, 1552
  Virgin Lands program, 298
Kshatriya caste, 253–254, 1640
Kuanda, Kenneth
  contribution, 900–901
  political philosophy, 900
Kubitschek, Juscelino, 33, 919–920, 1482. *See also* Brazil
Kucan, Milan, 1419
Kuffour, J.A., 700
Kumanji Kurds, 1576
Kuna Indians, 606, 607–608
Kunayev, Dinmukhamed, 383
Kuomintang, in Taiwan, 1515–1516
Kurdish Autonomous Province (Red Kurdistan), 923–924
Kurdish ethnicity, 630
Kurdish nationalism, 610–611
Kurdistan, 920–921. *See also* Kurds
  history, 921–923
  Iran and, 921
  Iraq and, 921
  territorial disputes, 1533–1534
  Turkey and, 920
Kurds, 921–924
  displaced, 850
  in Georgia, 698
  groups within, 1576
  history, 921–923
  Iranian, 924

Iraqi, 71, 794, 868–869, 1254, 1355
  modern times, 923–924
  Turkey and, 1533–1534
  Turkish, 920, 924, 1576, 1577
Kurili Islands territorial dispute, 517, 1535
Kurmanji language, 920
Kuwait, 924–926. *See also* Persian Gulf War (1991)
  agricultural water use, 1689
  independence, 1034
  Iran-Iraq War and, 866
  Iraqi invasion, 79, 89, 486, 793–794, 869, 925, 1037, 1160, 1261–1262
  OAPEC and, 1208
  oil, 646–647
  OPEC and, 1261–1262
  Palestinian refugees in, 1231
  Saudi Arabian invasion, 925
  United Arab Republic and, 1598
  Yasser Arafat in, 70
Kuwait Fund for Arab Economic Development, 926–927
Kuwait Oil Company, 925
KwaNdebele Homeland, 153. *See also* Native Reserves
Kwasniewski, Aleksander, 1676
Kwinti people, 1507
Kyanasur disease, 1366, 1368
Kyoto Protocol, 446, 574, 1290, 1511
Kyrgyzstan, 299, 927–929
  Commonwealth of Independent States and, 375–380
  Economic Cooperation Organization and, 537–538
  ethnic conflicts, 594–595
  independence, 383
  tourism, 300
Kyrillos VI, 396

L

Laar, Maart, 931–932, 1651. *See also* Estonia
Labor, 932–933. *See also* Organized labor
  cheap and East Asian development, 513–514
  Communist view of, 932
  expatriate workers, 1030–1031
  Maquiladoras Program, 644, 992–995, 1018
  Marxist theory of, 932, 1000
  Middle East, 1030–1031
  multinational corporations and, 1095
  NAFTA and, 1173
  neoliberalism and, 933
  North Africa, 1162
  Puerto Rican industry and, 1201
  social democratic view of, 932
  in state-directed economies, 1497
  United Arab Emirates, 1597
  women's conditions, 1725
  World Federation of Trade Unions (WFTU), 1731–1732
Labour Islamic Alliance, 1096
LAFTA (Latin American Integration Association), 945
Lagos Plan, 529, 1204
Laino, Domingo, 885, 1485
Lake Chad, 1143
Lake Chad Basin Commission, 933–934
Lakes Edward and Albert Fisheries (LEAF) Project (Republic of Congo and Uganda), 5
Lake Titicaca, 43–44
Land Acts (South Africa), 152–154. *See also* Native Reserves
Land and climate. *See* Geography and climate

Land distribution, 934–936. *See also* Agrarian reform
  global perspective, 935
  Latin America, 934
  sub-Saharan Africa, 934–935
Land erosion, 579–583. *See also* Deforestation; Desertification; Erosion
Landfills, 1683–1684
  leachate, 1683
  Observations of Solid Waste Landfills in Developing Countries (Johannessen and Boyer), 1683–1684
  operated dumps, 1683
Land fragmentation, 19–20
  agricultural privatization and, 21–22
Landmines, 230, 1437
  United Nations Development Program project, 1607
Land ownership
  agricultural, 12
  agricultural globalization and, 14
  decolonization and, 367
  Iraq, 130
  Latin America, 34
  Oceanic women's, 1197
Land per capita. *See also* Population density
  West Africa, 1694
Land reform. *See* Agrarian reform
Landrent system, 809
Landsbergis, Vytautas, 937. *See also* Lithuania
Language(s). *See also* Language planning
  African Diaspora and, 7
  Altaic, 1576
  Barbados, 155
  Chomsky's theories of, 939
  decline or obsolescence of, 940
  democratization of, 942–943
  development and, 938
  East Africa, 500–501
  education and, 942
  Georgia, 698
  Indonesia, 808–809
  Kiswahili, 500–501, 502
  Kurdish, 920
  Language Acquisition Device theory, 939
  Linguistic Relativity Hypothesis, 938–939
  Macedonian, 136
  Malaysia, 543
  Middle East, 1027
  Mongolia, 1078
  Niger, 1140
  Nigeria, 1142
  Oceania, 1192
  official, 942
  Palau, 1225
  politics and, 941–943
  power and, 941–942
  Puerto Rico, 1334
  Slovenian, 136
  social prestige and, 940
  Sranan Tongo, 1508
  Sri Lanka, 1489
  Suriname, 1508
  Swahili, 500–501
  Tajikistan, 1518
  thought and culture and, 938–939
  as tool, 941
  Turkmen, 1578

Language(s) (*Continued*)
  Ukraine, 1587
  UN Declaration on the Rights of Persons Belonging to
    National or Ethnic, Religious, and Linguistic
    Minorities, 938
  vs. ethnicity and nationality, 939
Language Acquisition Device theory, 939
Language planning, 939–941
  allocation of function, 940
  status, 940
Language shift, 940
Language skills, North Africa, 1162
Lanuse, Alejandro, 1261
Lao People's Revolutionary Party (LPRP), 1249–1250
Laos
  ASEAN and, 97, 112–116, 1456
  colonial legacy, 1454
  Communist threat in, 1454
  development since 1954, 944
  economy, 98, 944
  ethnic (overseas) Chinese in, 620
  ethnic conflict, 619
  history, 843–944
  Hmong people, 1250
  Mekong Basin Development Corporation, 98–100
  SEATO and, 1458
  telecommunications industry, 99
  territorial disputes, 1535
La Prensa (newspaper), 1137, 1138
Larrazábal, Wolfgang, 171, 1178
Latin America. *See also* South America *and individual countries*
  agrarian reform, 934
  Alliance for Progress, 32–35, 1106
  Andean Community. *See* Andean Community; Andean
    South America
  banking crises, 150
  CIA in, 308–309
  civic education, 341
  decolonization, 358–359
  ethnic conflicts, 624–626
  foreign direct investment, 671
  global climate change and, 706
  health care, 748–749
  import substitution industrialization, 796
  income inequality, 1311
  Inter-American Development Bank and, 828–829
  Migration for Development Program, 850
  military and, 1049–1050
  Organization of American States (OAS), 1205–1207
  populism in, 1302–1304
  private property rights in, 1321
  privatization, 24, 1324
  religion, 1359
  Return of Talent for Latin America, 850
  Structuralist School of Development, 1319–1320
  territorial disputes, 1536–1538
  transition to democracy, 123
Latin American Federation of Christian Trade Unions, 1728
Latin American Free Trade Association (LAFTA), 38, 945.
          See also Latin American Integration Association
Latin American Integration Association, 945–946
Latin American Workers Central, 1728
Latvia, 946–947. *See also* Baltic states
  Commonwealth of Independent Nations and, 382
  Council of Baltic Sea States and, 381

Guntis Ulmanis, 1589–1590
  independence, 290, 293–294
  Latvian Farmers Union, 1589
Law. *See* Legal systems *and specific laws and types*
LDCs (less developed countries), 462
LEAF (Lakes Edward and Albert Fisheries) Project, 5
League of Arab States, 67, 71, 506
League of Nations, 73, 373, 495
  economic and finance organizations, 1606
  Liberia and, 960
  Mandate System, 1631
  refugee programs, 1601
  trusteeships, 1631
League of Red Cross Societies, 841. *See also* International
          Committee of the Red Cross
Leakey, Mary, 500
Least-developed countries (LDCs), 1067
Lebanese Phalange, 336
Lebanon, 947–948
  banking, 948
  book production, 1162
  Christianity in, 335
  civil war in, 71, 79
  confessional politics in, 1027
  ethnic conflicts, 609
  Hezbollah in, 753, 948
  independence, 1033–1034
  Israeli invasion, 79, 161, 753
  Maronite Christians and, 947
  Palestine Liberation Organization (PLO) om, 1630
  in Palestinian conflict, 74
  Palestinian refugees in, 1230
  religion, 1027
  UN peacekeeping, 1252
Lebed, Gen. Alexander, 597
Lebowa Homeland, 153. *See also* Native Reserves
Lechín Oquendo, Juan, 47, 185
Lee Hsien Long, 712
Lee Kuan Yew, 948–949, 1412, 1449, 1450
Lee Teng-hui, 1517
Leeward Islands, 1126, 1668–1669. *See also* Netherlands Antilles
Legal systems, 950–956
  civil law system, 951–952
  common law, 952–953
  customary law, 956
  European Community law, 953–955
  hybrid, 956
  international law, 950–951
  Islamic law (*Shar'iah*), 955, 1595
  Sino-Soviet (socialist) law, 955–956
Le Kha Phieu, 1666
Lenin, Vladimir, 380, 1000–1001, 1495
  imperialist theory, 1069, 1415, 1423, 1592
Leninist model of socialism, 1425–1426, 1427
  single-party government and, 1414–1415
Lenin Peace Prize, Kwame Nkrumah, 1147
Leoni, Raúl, 1184
Leopold II, King of Belgium, 262, 360
Leopoldo Galtieri, General, 83
Leprosy (Hansen's disease), 820
Lernca Indians, 606
Lerner, David, 1069
Lesotho, 956–957
  Economic Commission for Africa and, 528–530
  history and economic development, 1460–1462

as Native Reserve, 1461
Southern African Customs Union and, 1468–1470
Southern African Development Community and, 1463
Lesotho Highlands Project, 957
Less developed countries (LDCs), 439–440, 461, 462
globalization and, 710–711
Lesser Tumb/Greater Tumb islands, 1534
Letanka, D.S., 10
Letsie, King, 957
Liberalization, financial, 441–442
Liberation of Women (Amin), 878
Liberation Theology, 85, 333–334, 858–859, 958–959, 1359
Liberia, 959–960. *See also* West Africa
arms embargo, 90
civic education in, 342
Contonou Peace Agreement, 1255
Economic Commission for Africa and, 528–530
ethnic conflict, 626, 628
Humanitarian Emergency Grant, 5
Kuwait Fund for Arab Economic Development and, 927
literacy, 543
peacekeeping, 1253, 1254, 1255
People's Redemption Council, 960
UNICEF in, 1603
United Nations Development Program in, 1607
Liberian Development Company, 960
Liberians United for Reconciliation and Democracy (LURD), 960
Libermanism, 289
LIBERTAD Act, 1388
Liberterian theory of justice, 798
LIBOR (London Inter-Bank Offered Rate), 437–438
Libya, 961–962. *See also* Qaddafi, Muammar
Algeria and, 1169
annexation of Chad, 264, 1169
Arab Maghreb Union (AMU), 67–68, 1165, 1169–1170
arms embargo, 90
Cultural Revolution, 962–963
Economic Commission for Africa and, 528–530
economic development, 1160
economic sanctions, 1386
ethnic conflicts, 612
European Union and, 1168
geography and climate, 1156
international relations, 1036, 1166–1168, 1338
Lockerbie plane downing, 1158, 1167, 1338
Man Made River project, 962
OAPEC and, 1208
occupation of Chad, 264, 269
oil, 1158, 1167
political history, 1158–1159
Sterling Zone and, 1166
Uganda invasion, 1188
unemployment, 1162
Lien Viet Front, 1662
Life expectancy
Antigua and Barbuda, 56
Azerbaijan, 126
Bangladesh, 658
Benin, 168
Bhutan, 174
Cambodia, 217
Caribbean, 241
Chile, 1330

Costa Rica, 401
Cuba, 241
education and literacy and, 544
Ethiopia, 658
Gambia, 691–692
Ghana, 658
Guatemala, 725–726
health care and, 746
HIV/AIDS and African, 1330
Islam and, 876
Kiribati, 912
Lebanon, 948
Libya, 962
Malawi, 981
Maldives, 984
Mauritania, 1005
as measure of development, 464
modernization and, 1071
Mozambique, 1087
Nicaragua, 1136
Niger, 1141
Nigeria, 1143
Palau, 1225
Panama, 1236
Philippines, 1274
as poverty measure, 1315
public health and, 1330
Rwanda, 1379
Saudi Arabia, 1392
Seychelles, 1302, 1401
Slovenia, 1419
St. Helena, 1492
Tanzania, 1523
Tunisia, 1573
Uruguay, 1646
Lima Conventions, 44
Limann, Hilla, 700
(The) Limits of Growth (Club of Rome), 569
Lim Kim San, 949
Lin Biao, 327
Linguistic Relativity Hypothesis, 938–939
Linguistics. *See* Language(s)
Linz, Juan J., bureaucratic authoritarianism theory, 207–209
Li Peng, 329
Lipset, Seymour Martin, 449, 458, 460
Lissouba, Pascal, 390
Literacy
Algeria, 1161
Botswana, 191
Caribbean, 1211
Central Africa, 272–273
Central Asia, 300
Costa Rica, 276, 401
female and gender discrimination, 817
Fiji, 662
Ghana, 700
Honduras, 276
India, 804
Lebanon, 948
Libya, 1161
Maldives, 984
Mauritania, 1004
as measure of development, 464
Morocco, 1085, 1161
Nepal, 1125

Literacy (*Continued*)
 Nigeria, 1144
 North Africa, 1161
 Oceania, 1192
 poverty and, 1312
 Saudi Arabia, 1392
 Sri Lanka, 1489
 Suriname, 1508
 Tunisia, 1161, 1573
 United Arab Emirates, 1597
 Uruguay, 1646
 Vietnam, 1665
 women, 1161
 Zambia, 1752
Lithuania. *See also* Baltic states
 Commonwealth of Independent Nations and, 382
 Council of Baltic Sea States and, 381
 independence, 290, 293–294
 privatization, 20, 1324
 Sajudis movement, 964
Litigation of disputes, 837
Little Ice Age, 1189
Liu Shaoqi, 327–328
 Cultural Revolution and, 323–324
Livestock production, 580–581. *See also* Herding communities
 agricultural privatization and, 21
 Central Africa, 262
 desertification and, 453
 illegal in national parks, 1245
 Kyrgyzstan, 927
 Mongolia, 1078
 Oman, 1199
 Somalia, 1432
 water use and, 1689
Lleras Camargo, Alberto, 352
Loans. *See also* Banking
 conditionality of, 9
Locke, John, 347, 771, 777, 1075, 1320
Lockerbie plane downing, 1158, 1167
Lomé Accords, 1406–1407, 1701
Lomé Convention, 964–966
London East India Company. *See* British East India Company
London Inter-Bank Offered Rate (LIBOR), 437–438
London Mission Society, 1144
Long, Gov. Huey, 1303
Long March, 331, 1754. *See also* Chinese Revolution; Mao Zedong
Lon Nol, 216, 309, 907–908, 1408
López Contreras, Gen. Eleazar, 1178
López Mateos, Adolfo, 1022
López Michelson, Alfonso, 1182
Lopez Pérez, Rigoberto, 1137, 1435
López Portillo, José, 1019, 1023
Lost decade, Latin America, 275, 352, 708, 1269, 1563
Louisy, Pearlette, 1493
Lovelock, James, 573
Luanda, 53. *See also* Angola
Lucy fossil, 500
Luka, Vasile, 287
Lukashenko, Alexander, 163
Lumumba, Patrice, 263, 308, 309, 388, 589–590, 966–967
Lunda-Chokwe people, 53
Luos people, 939
Lutheran World Federation, 476
Luthuli, Albert, 967
Luxemburg, Rosa, 1425

M

Ma'alot massacre of school children, 1228
Maasai people, 1002–1003
Macapagal, Diosado, 1272
Macapagal Arroyo, Gloria, 1273
MacArthur, Gen. Douglas, 977, 1055, 1104
Macau, 969–970
 gambling industry, 970
Macaulay, Thomas Babington, 1119
Macaulayism, 1119–1120
MacBride, Sean, 37
Macedonia, 287, 970–972. *See also* Yugoslavia
 establishment, 135
 Greece and, 971–972
 independence, 290
 international relations, 294
 peacekeeping, 1253
Macedonian language, 136
Machel, Samora, 682, 683, 972–973. *See also* Mozambique
Machiavelli, Nicolai, 120
Macias Nguema, Francisco, 265, 575
MacIntyre, Alasdair, 798
Madagascar, 973–975
 COMESA and, 369
 debt holdings, 371
 Economic Commission for Africa and, 528–530
 Forces Armées Populaires (FAP), 86–87
 history and economic development, 1462
 UNICEF in, 1603
Madero, Francisco, 1246
Madl, Ferenc, 791
Madrid Hurtado, Miguel de la, 1019, 1023, 1170, 1248
Maga, Hubert, 167
Magellan, Ferdinand, 724
Maghrib peoples, 975–976
Magliore, Paul E., 497
Magna Carta, 779, 953
Magsaysay, Ramon, 977, 1272. *See also* Philippines
Magyarization policy, 284
Mahathir bin Mohamad, Dr. Dato Seri, 978–979.
 See also Malaysia
Maghreb
 Arab Maghreb Union (AMU), 1165
 ethnic conflicts, 613–614
 European Union and, 1168
Mahkamov, Kahar, 302
Mahuad, Jamil, 542
Majlis Al-Shura, 134
Majoritarianism, 621, 633. *See also* Ethnic conflicts
Makarios III, Archbishop, 428
Makonnen, Tafari. *See* Selassie, Emperor Haile
Malaita
 Solomon Islands and, 1431
 Townsville Peace Agreement, 1431
Malan, D.F., 188, 979–980, 1440. *See also* Apartheid
Malaria, 822, 944
 Rockefeller Foundation and, 1366–1367
Malawi, 980–982
 COMESA and, 369
 debt holdings, 371, 444
 decolonization, 361–362
 Economic Commission for Africa and, 528–530
 history and economic development, 1460–1462
 HIV/AIDS in, 371

independence, 30
Southern African Development Community and, 1463
Malawi people, 1507
Malaya, Communist movements in, 1455
Malay people, 618–619, 1272
Malaysia, 982–983
Abdul Tunku Rahman, 1344–1345
agricultural privatization, 20, 24
ASEAN and, 97, 112–116, 1455–1456
in Asia-Pacific Economic Cooperation, 108
colonial legacy, 1454
currency devaluation, 424
economy, 98
education, 543
ethnic (overseas) Chinese in, 620, 632
financial crisis, 1451
foreign direct investment, 670
Indonesia-Malaysia-Singapore growth triangle, 1529
Indonesian migration to, 1456
literacy, 543
MAPHILINDO and, 1272
national parks, 1245
New Economic Policy, 1127, 1450
as Newly Industrialized Economy, 1131
religion and, 1457
Spratly Islands dispute, 1241
territorial disputes, 1535
United Malay National Organization (MNO), 1599
Vision 2020, 983
Malaysian Federation, 1507
Maldives, 983–985
ecotourism, 539
South Asian Association for Regional Cooperation
and, 1441–1444
Malenkov, Georgi, 456, 1373
Mali, 984–985. See also West Africa
Ancient, 1695
authoritarianism in, 123
Berbers in, 170
Economic Commission for Africa and, 528–530
independence movement, 30
West African Monetary Union and, 1703–1705
Malik, Charles, 1639
Malinke people, 626, 627
Malloum, Félix, 264, 311
Malnutrition, 663–666. See also Food and nutrition; Hunger
Malthus, Thomas, 654. See also Family planning
Malvinas/Falkland Islands War, 83, 986–989,
1479, 1486–1489
Mamiraua Sustainable Development Reserve, 1348
Managerial know-how, 226
Managua Agreement, 1205
Manas Wildlife Sanctuary (India), 1710, 1711
Mancham, James, 1401
Manchester Conference, 29
Manda people, 733
Mandela, Nelson, 10, 11, 30, 59, 61–62, 435, 989–990, 1441, 1463
Bishop Desmond Tutu and, 1581
Mandingo people, 626
Mandinka people, 734
Mane, Gen. Ausmane, 735
Manh, Nong Duc, 1666
Manifesto of the Communist Party (Marx), 1000
Manila Declaration, 1610
Manila Pact, 1458. See also Southeast Asia Treaty Organization

Manley, Michael, 239, 247, 889
Man Made River project, 962
Manning, Patrick, 1571
Mano Blanca (White Hand) death squad, 726
Mano people, 626
Man Tran Dan Toc Giai Phong Mien Nam (NLF), 1108–1110
Manu National Park and Biosphere Reserve (Peru), 1712
Mao Zedong, 330, 331–332, 385, 990–992. See also China;
Chinese Communist Party
Cultural Revolution and, 323–324
de-Stalinization and, 456
Great Leap Forward, 326–327, 714–715
Great Proletarian Cultural Revolution, 327–328
guerrilla warfare model, 729–730
Marxist theory and, 991
socialist economic model, 1428–1429
MAP (Movement for Assemblies of the People), 180, 1129–1130
Mapuche people, 625
Maquiladoras Program, 644, 992–995, 1018
Maraita, Marau Peace Agreement, 1431
Marau Peace Agreement, 1431
Marcos, Fernando, 344, 995–996, 1130. See also Philippines
constitutional authoritarianism, 1448–1449
Marcos, Imelda, 1273
Margai, Dr. Milton, 627
Marginal Individual Benefit, 1065
Marginal Individual Cost, 1065
Marginal Social Benefit, 1065
Marginal Social Cost, 1065
Margin of preference (MOP), 97–98
Mariam, Maj. Mengistu Hailie, 501
Marianas Islands, Northern, 724–725. See also Guam
demographics, 1191
Marighella, Carlos, 730
Marijuana
Belize, 164
Jamaica, 247
Marine ecotourism, 540
Maritain, Jacques, 680
Maritime zones, 44–45
Market fundamentalism theory, 1438
Market socialism, 1427–1428
in China, 1428–1429
cooperative, 1428
Maronite Christians, 1028
Maronite Church, 336
Maroons, 7, 588, 1350, 1507. See also Slavery
Marsabit Federal Reserve, 1245
Marshall Islands, 996–998
Compact of Free Association, 996
demographics, 1191
economic development, 997
social developments, 997–998
trusteeship, 1632
Marshall-Lerner conditions, for currency devaluation, 422–423
Marshall Plan, 32, 41, 102, 144, 353, 459, 1104, 1488
Alliance for Progress vs., 1635
Central/Eastern Europe and, 286
Marti, Agustin Farabundo, 660
Martinez de Hoz, José, 82–83
Martinique, 723, 998–999
Association of Caribbean States and, 111
Creole elite of, 587
Frantz Fanon, 659–660
Mt. Peleé eruption, 1114–1115

Marx, Karl, 120, 347, 458, 855
  private property and, 1320–1321
Marxism, 999–1002. *See also* Communism; Communist
    Party; Socialism
  collapse of Soviet Union and, 1001–1002
  in Colombia, 233
  in Democratic Republic of Congo, 270
  development and, 460–461
  as economic model, 1426–1427
  human rights and, 772
  imperialist theory, 1002, 1415, 1423, 1592
  income distribution theory and, 799
  labor and, 932
  legal system derived from, 955–956
  of Lenin, 1000–1001
  Mao Zedong and, 991
  of Marx, 999–1000
  as model of socialism, 1425
  modernization theory, 1069
  New Jewel Movement (NJM), 180, 242, 248,
    1129–1130
  in North Korea, 913–914
  Praxis Group, 1001
  religion and, 855
  single-party government, 1414–1415
  theory of trade, 1560–1561
  vs. Trotskyism, 1001
  Western, 1001
Masaleet tribe, 1504
Masaliyev, Apsamar, 928
Masaryk, Jan, 286, 430
Masaryk, Thomas G., 430, 1416
Massacres. *See* Atrocities
Massamba-Debat, Alphonse, 265, 390
Matabele people, 623
Matanzima brothers, 154
Maternal mortality
  Ethiopia, 658
  Ghana, 658
  health care and, 750
  Kenya, 659
  Nepal, 1125
  Philippines, 659
  Sudan, 659
  Vietnam, 659
Mathathir Mohamad, 1449
Matte, Eugenio, 30
Matthews, Herbert, Fidel Castro and, 413
Mau Mau guerilla movement, 502, 906, 1002–1003
Mauritania, 975, 976, 1003–1005. *See also* West Africa
  Arab Maghreb Union (AMU), 67–68, 1169–1170
  Economic Commission for Africa and, 528–530
  literacy, 543
Mauritius, 1005–1006
  COMESA and, 369
  debt, 371
  Economic Commission for Africa and, 528–530
  history and economic development, 1460–1462
  multiethnicity, 633
Maur people, 975
Mayan Indians, 632, 634, 727
  Guatemalan genocide, 605–606
  as minority, 606
Mazowiecki, Tadeusz, 1676
M'Ba, Léon, 264, 265, 689

Mbeki, Thabo, 1006–1007, 1441, 1463
Mbida, André-Marie, 25
Mbo people, 211
Mboya, Tom, 906
Mbundu people, 53
McDonnell-Douglas Company, arms transfer and, 90
McFarlane, Robert, 394
McNamara, Robert, 91
Mdayizeye, Domitien (Frodebu), 212
Mead, Margaret, 458
Meade, Reuben, 1083
Meadows Report, 569
Measles, 822
Meatpacking, Central Africa, 262
Meciar, Vladimir, 430–431, 1417–1418
Medellin drug cartel, 352–353, 1077, 1361. *See also*
    Drug trafficking
Media. *See also* Television
  as modernization factor, 1069
  oversimplification of ethnic conflicts, 628
Mediation of disputes, 837
Medicinal drugs. *See* Drug trade; Pharmaceutical industry
Médicins sans Frontiers, 480–481
Medina Angarita, Isaias, 1178, 1660
Megacities, 1643, 1644
Meir, Golda, 1007–1009
Mekong Basin Development Corporation, 98–100
Menchu, Roberta, 726
Menchú, Vicente, 1010
Menchú Túm, Rigoberta, 1009–1011
Mende, Brig. Maada-Bio, 1406
Mende people, 627
Menem, Carlos, 83, 1011–1012, 1478. *See also* Argentina
Meningitis, 822
Mental health, 1012–1016
  definitions, 1012
  depression, 1013
  modernization as stress, 1072–1073
  substance abuse and dependence, 1013–1014
  suicide, 1014–1016
MERCODUS (Common Market of the South), 228
MERCOSUR (South American Common Market), 200,
    228, 830, 1480
  Brasilia Protocol, 1472, 1473
  Brazil and, 1483
  foreign direct investment and, 1473
  Foz de Iguazo Declaration, 1472
  Grupos de Tranajo, 1472–1473
  member states, 1472
  neoliberalism and, 1122
  origins, 1472–1473
  Paraguay and, 1486
  trade policy and, 1564
Mercury pollution
  Minamata Bay (Japan), 1289–1290
  United Nations Industrial Development Organization
    and, 1620
Meri, Lennart, 1651
Merina people, 973–974
Merit goods, 1065
Meritocratic bureaucracy, in East Asia, 515
Merwin, John, 1670
Mesa, Carlos, 50
Mesa Gisbert, Carlos, 185
Mesic, Stipe, 411

Methane pollution, 13, 704. *See also* Global climate change; Greenhouse effect
    from landfilling, 1683
    from waste incineration, 1682–1683
Metula oil spill, 648
Mexico
    Amerindian peoples, 605
    Association of Caribbean States and, 111
    Bracero Program, 194–195, 1018
    bureaucratic authoritarianism in, 209
    Caribbean Development Bank and, 235–237
    cartel regulation, 251
    caste system, 605
    closed corporate peasant communities, 1257
    currency reform, 1248
    debt holding, 223
    ethnic conflicts, 605–601, 608, 625
    financial crisis, 222
    foreign direct investment, 669, 708
    General Law of Ecological Balance and Environmental Pollution, 1420
    geography and climate, 1016–1017
    Gini index, 1017
    Green Revolution and, 717–718
    Hidalgo Revolt, 1017
    history and economic development, 1016–1020
    import substitution industrialization, 1248
    income inequality in, 1311
    international relations, 1020–1025
    irrigated and drained area, 871
    Law of State Security, 625
    Maquiladoras Program, 644, 992–995, 1018
    migration from, 1023–1024
    NAFTA and, 283, 1019–1020, 1024, 1170–1171, 1248, 1383
    National Environmental Program, 1420
    natural gas production, 647
    neoliberalism and, 1248
    as Newly Industrialized Economy, 1131
    Partido de Acción Nacional (PAN), 1107–1108, 1247
    Partido Revolucionario Institucional (PRI), 1017–1019, 1024, 1107, 1246–1249
    Petróleos Mexicanos (PEMEX), 1247
    peyote use in, 492
    political history, 1017–1020
    populists in, 1301
    Positivist movement, 1050
    privatization, 1383
    remittances, 197
    slavery and emancipation, 7
    smaze problem, 1420
    suicide rate, 1014
    Tlatelolco student massacre, 1018–1019, 1022–1023, 1247–1248
    transition to democracy, 123
    Vicente Fox, 672–673
    Zapatista Army of National Liberation (EZLN), 608, 1017, 1024, 1248, 1383, 1753–1754
Mexico City, smaze problem, 1420
Mexico City Olympics, 1018, 1022
Mexico City (abortion) policy, 1635–1636
Meztizos, in Nicaragua, 607
MFDC (Movement of Democratic Forces of Senegal), 627
Mfecane (great upheaval), 621–622
Mgoubbí, Marien, 265
Michael, King of Romania, 286–287

Micombero, Captain Michel, 212
Micronesia, Federated States of, 1025–1026
    Contract of Free Association with US, 1025–1026
    demographics, 1191
    trusteeship, 1632
Middle East. *See also individual countries and regions*
    Christianity in, 334–337
    colonialism and, 1028
    dependence on oil revenues, 1031
    economy, 1028–1031
    ethnic conflicts, 609–611
    ethnicity, 1027
    expatriate workers in, 1030–1031
    foreign aid, 1030
    geography, 1027
    history and economic development, 1026–1033
    Human Development Index, 1029
    international relations, 1033–1039
    labor force, 1030–1031
    monarchic government in, 1075
    Non-Aligned Movement and, 1035
    political and economic reforms, 1031–1032
    political systems, 1027
    populism in, 1304
    privatization in, 1323–1324
    society, 1027
    women in, 1032
Midgan caste, 255
MIGA (Multilateral Investment Guarantee Agency), 834
Migrant laborers
    colonialism and, 365–366
    vs. ethnic groups, 1062
    women, 1626
Migration, 1039–1046
    Botswana/South Africa, 191
    Bracero Program, 194–195, 1018
    brain drain, 1043–1044
    case studies, 1045
    classic economic theory of, 1041
    convergence effect, 1041, 1042
    Cuba to US, 246, 418
    development and, 1040–1041, 1045
    direction of, 1041, 1042
    economic theories of, 1041
    as emigration, 1040
    Financing for Development and Remittances and Gender, 1626
    forced of Han Chinese, 520
    GDP and, 1041
    Haitian, 244, 740
    historical overview, 1039–1040
    industrial cycles and, 1040
    International Organization for Migration (IOM), 850–851
    Mexican to US, 1023–1024
    Mohajir from India, 1222
    Morocco to France, 1164
    Nigerian oil boom and, 1143
    from Niue, 1145
    from Oman, 1198
    Palestinian refugees, 1229–1233
    policy measures, 1044–1045
    Puerto Rican to US, 1202
    push-pull relationship, 1298–1299
    remittances and, 1042–1043
    return, 1044

Migration (*Continued*)
  Richmond's theory of multivariate typology, 1354
  to Samoa, 1386
  seasonal vertical (transhumance), 1501
  Senegal, 1396
  sociological theory of, 1040–1041
  into Solomon Islands, 1431
  Southeast Asian, 1456
  to Southern Cone region, 1476
  Turkish to Germany, 1578
  to Venezuela, 1659
  women and, 1725
Mikolajcsk, Stanislaus, 286
Military
  attitudes toward, 1049–1050
  civic action by, 1050–1051
  civilian control, 1046–1048. *See also* Civilian-military
    relations; Military regimes
  development and, 1048–1053
  in economic development, 1051–1052
  human rights and, 1053–1057
  justice and war, 1053–1054
  neoliberal globalization and, 1052
  in World War II, 1054–1055
Military aid. *See also* Arms transfer
  to Bolivia, 40, 47
  to Chile, 41–42
  end of Cold War and, 89
  to Peru, 41
Military coups. *See* Assassinations; *Coups d'etat;*
  Military regimes
Military Observation Mission Ecuador/Peru, 42
Military regimes. *See also* Authoritarianism; *Juntas*
  Argentina, 1082
  Batista, 413
  Brazil, 93–94, 200
  Cuba, 123
  economic performance, 1478
  Ecuador, 542
  Myanmar (Burma), 119
  Paraguay, 1498
  Peru, 63–64, 1269
  Sierra Leone, 1406–1407
  Southern Cone (Latin America), 1477–1478
  Uruguay, 1478, 1647
  Venezuela, 171
Military security, 1047
Military spending, East Asia, 517–518
Military training
  in Bolivia, 46, 47
  French in Madagascar, 86
Milk production, agricultural privatization and, 21
Mill, John Stuart, 773
Millennium Declaration. *See* United Nations Millennium
  Declaration
Millennium Development Goals, 1317, 1607
Millennium Summit, 1607
Millspaugh, Arthur, 863
Milošević, Slobodan, 136, 137, 138–139, 411, 1057–1059,
  1398–1399, 1749
Mindanao, 66, 977
Mindszenty, Cardinal Jozsef, 286, 789
Miners' strikes
  Bolivia, 185
  South Africa, 10

Minimanual of the Urban Guerrilla (Marigella), 730
Mining industry, 647–648. *See also* Extractive industries
  and specific minerals
  Angola, 53
  COMESA area, 370–371
Minorities. *See also* Discrimination
  defined, 1059–1064
  discrimination against, 1059–1064
  ethnic communities and, 1061–1062
Minto, Lord, 36
MINUGUA, 727
Mirabal sisters, murder of, 484
MIRAB economies, 1192, 1582
Misquito people, 1134
Missionaries
  Christian, 332–333
  colonialism and, 365
  to Niue, 1144
  Sierra Leone, 1406
Misuari, Nur, 1349
Mitteleuropa concept, 290. *See also* Central and
  Eastern Europe
Mixed economy, 1064–1066. *See also*
  Government intervention
  advantages, 1066
  deregulation and, 1064
  disadvantages, 1066
  forms of intervention, 1064–1065
  private and public sectors, 1064
Mixed Marriages Act (South Africa), 57
Mjeb-ur-Rahman, Sheikh, 141
MK (Spear of the Nation, *Umkhonto we Sizwe*), 11, 59–60
Mkapa, Benjamin, 503, 1524
Mladic, General Ratko, 136, 137
MLSTP (Movement for the Liberation of São Tomé
  and Princep), 263
MNR (Nationalist Revolutionary Movement), 46, 185
Mobil Oil Corporation. *See* Exxon-Mobil
MOBRAL education program, 341
Mobuta Sese Seko Koko Ngbendu Wa Za Banga, 264. *See also*
  Mobuto, Joseph
Mobuto, Joseph, 264, 270, 469–470, 590
Mobutu, Joseph, 123
Modernity, 1072–1073
Modernization, 1066–1073. *See also* Industrialization
  categories of, 1067–1068
  culture and, 1071
  dependency theories, 1069
  East Asia, 512
  ethnic conflict and, 631
  functionalist intervention and, 1068–1069
  globalization and, 1072
  Human Development Index and, 1071
  nation building and, 1104
  Niue, 1145
  Oceania, 1195
  progression of, 1067–1068
  religion and, 856
  social costs of, 1071–1072
  social revolution and, 1422
  theoretical origins, 1067–1068
  Third-World applications, 1070–1071
  underdevelopment and, 1591
  world-systems theories, 1070
Modernization Theory, 459–460, 1544

Mogae, Festus, 191
Mohajir migrants, 1222
Mohamad, Mahathir, 983
Mohammed, Ali Mahdi, 507
Mohammed, Gen. Murtala, 1142
Mohammed V, King, 1202
Moi, Daniel arap, 502, 904, 905, 906
Moldova, 1073–1074
   agricultural privatization, 20, 22, 23
   Black Sea Economic Cooperation Organization,
      183–184, 381
   Commonwealth of Independent States and, 375–380
   GUAM group and, 381
   independence, 290, 383–384
   peacekeeping operations, 1253
   territorial disputes, 1532
Mole-Dagomba people, 700
Molotov, Viacheslav M., 455, 456
Molucca people, 618–619
Momoh, General Joseph Saidu, 627, 1406
Monarchic governance
   institutions of, 1076
   Middle East, 1028
   Nepal, 1124
   Oman, 1198–1200
   Papua New Guinea, 1239
   patriarch theory of, 1075–1076
   Qatar, 1338–1339
   Saudi Arabia, 1390–1392
   Swaziland, 1512–1513
   Thailand (Siam), 1540–1541
   theories of, 1075
   Tonga, 1195, 1553
Moncada, José, 1136
Mondlane, Eduardo Chivambo, 682
Monetary base, 148
Monetary policy
   agricultural privatization and, 21
   Japan, 104
Money laundering, 1076–1079. *See also* Corruption;
      Offshore banking
   capital flight and, 222, 1076. *See also*
      Offshore banking
   Cayman Islands, 258
   dirty money, 1076
   drug money, 1077
   origins, 1077
   Panama, 1555
   terrorism and, 1076–1077
Money supply, 147–148
Monge, Luis Alberto, 84
Mongol Empire, 297–298
Mongolia, 520–521, 1078–1079
   China and, 603
   Chinese nuclear programs in, 603
   extractive industries, 1079
   single-party government, 1414
   territorial disputes, 1535
Monoculture, 17. *See also* Crop specialization
Monopoly, 1065–1066. *See also* Cartels
   natural, 1065
Monroe Doctrine, 239, 278
Montenegro, 287, 1079–1081
   establishment of, 135
   independence, 290

Montesinos, Vladimiro, 685, 686, 1267–1268
Montoneros, 82
Montreal Protocol on Substances that Deplete the
      Ozone Layer, 1511
Montserrat, 1082–1083
   Caribbean Basin Initiative and, 232–233
   Caribbean Community and Common Market and, 233–235
   Caribbean Development Bank and, 235–237
   Caribbean Free Trade Association and, 237–238
Montsioa, Mangena D., 10
Moody, Dwight L., 639
Moore, Barrington, 449
   social revolution theory, 1422
Morales Bermúdez, Fernando, 1269
Morales Bermúdez, General Francisco, 42, 47
Morán, Rolando, 727–728
Morauta, Mekeré, 1240
Morbillivirus, 822
Morinigo, Higinio, 1485
Morocco, 29, 1083–1085
   Algeria and, 1164, 1204
   Arab Maghreb Union (AMU), 67–68, 1165, 1169–1170
   Barcelona Declaration, 1168
   Berbers in, 170
   Casablanca bloc, 1164
   debt, 1084
   Economic Commission for Africa and, 528–530
   economic development, 1160–1161
   ethnic conflict, 612–613
   France and, 1164
   geography and climate, 1156
   Green March, 743
   international relations, 1164–1165
   Israeli–Palestinian mediation, 1164
   King Hassan II, 743
   literacy, 543, 1161
   migration, 1164
   Moroccanization plan, 1084
   Polisario warfare, 192
   population growth, 657
   religion, 1084
   Spain and, 1164
   Structural Adjustment Plan, 1084
   territorial disputes, 1168–1169, 1532, 1536
   Tunisia and, 1168
   unemployment, 1162
   Water Sector Adjustment Program, 5
   women, 1162
Moro National Liberation Front (MNLF), 1349
Moro people, 618–619
Moros Islands independence, 1455
Mortality
   infant. *See* Infant mortality
   maternal. *See* Maternal mortality
Mosaddeq, Dr. Mohammad, 52–53
Moscoso, Mireya, 1237
Moscoso, Teodoro, 1200–1201, 1334
Moshoeshoe, Chief, 957. *See also* Lesotho
MOSOP (Movement for the Survival of the
      Ogony People), 649–650
Mosquitia, 607
Mossadeq, Muhammad, 308, 863–864, 1085–1086, 1221
Most favored nation principle, 707–708, 1567–1568
Most Favored Nation status, China, 774
Moto, Severo, 575

Mountbatten, Louis, 897
Mouvement Nationale de la Révolution, 390
Movement for a Multiparty Democracy (Zambia), 1751, 1752
Movement for Assemblies of the People (MAP), 180, 1129–1130
Movement for Democracy in Liberia (MODEL), 960
Movement for the Liberation of Angola (MPLA), 53–54, 416, 1536
Movement for the Liberation of São Tomé and Princep (MLSTP), 263
Movement for the Survival of the Ogony People (MOSOP), 649–650
Movement of Democratic Forces of Senegal (MFDC), 627
Moviento de Participación Popular (MPP), 1575
Moviento sem Terra, 1478
Movimiento Brazileiro de Alfabetização, 543–544
Movimiento de Liberación Nacional (Tupamaros), 1486, 1575, 1647
Movimiento Popular de Libertação de Angola, 1292–1293
Movimiento Revolucionario Tupac Amaru, 48, 50, 64, 685, 1575
Movimiento Revolucionario 26 de Julio, 1584
Moyen Congo, 389
Mozambican National Resistance (RENAMO), 682, 683
Mozambique, 1086–1087
    assimilados, 1087
    debt holdings, 444
    Economic Commission for Africa and, 528–530
    ethnic conflicts, 623
    FRELIMO, 682–683, 972, 1087
    humanitarian relief, 786
    independence, 1462
    reforestation, 582
    Resisténica Nacional Moçambicana (RENAMI), 682–683, 972, 1087
    Samora Machel, 972–973
    South Africa and, 60–61, 189
    Southern African Development Community and, 1463
    territorial disputes, 1536
MPLA (Popular Movement for the Liberation of Angola), 53–54, 416, 1536
Msmang, R. W., 10
Mswati, 1512
Mt. Peleé volcanic eruption, 998, 1114–1115
Mtikila, Christopher, 1524
Mubarak, Hosni, 549, 925, 1088–1089, 1160, 1381
Mugabe, Robert, 30, 334, 632, 935, 1089–1990, 1757, 1758
Muhammad, Qazi, 921
Mujahedin, 4, 1091–1092, 1223, 1520–1521
    Algerian, 28
    Soviet invasion and, 1091
Mujeb-ur-Rahman, Sheikh, 125–126, 1092
Mullah Mohammad Omar, 1521
Multiethnic societies. *See also* Diversity
    positive aspects, 633
Multifibre Agreements, 1566
Multilateral Fund for the Implementation of the Montreal Protocol, 571
Multilateral Investment Fund, 829
Multilateral Investment Guarantee Agency (MIGA), 834
Multilateral Treaty of Free Trade and Economic Integration, 281
Multinational corporations (MNCs), 1093–1096
    agriculture and, 14–15
    in Cayman Islands, 258
    in Central Africa, 271
    in Central/Eastern Europe, 289
    corporate agriculture and, 665

    countertrade and, 406–408
    dependency and, 461
    foreign direct investment by. *See* Foreign direct investment
    human rights and, 1095
    Japanese, 103
    labor and, 1095
    market consolidation, 1094
    Mexico, 1383
    mobility of, 1095
    negative aspects, 1095
    origins, 1093
    outsourcing strategy, 1094
    positive contributions, 1094–1095
    privatization and, 1095
    profit-repatriation by, 1095
    relocation of, 106–107
    Singapore, 949
    South Africa, 60
    South Korean *charbols*, 103, 514–515
    strategies for expansion, 1094
    strategies of internalization, 1093–1094
    strategies of penetration, 1093
    structuralist theory and, 1320
    technology transfer and, 1530
    trading patterns and, 1567
Mundt, Rep. Karl F., 686
Munich Olympic Games, terrorism at, 37, 71, 883, 1227
Municipal solid waste, 1681
Muñoz Martin, Luis, 1200–1201, 1334
Murmiao (South African newspaper), 10
Museneni, Yoweri Kaguta, 503, 1586
Musharraf, General Pervez, 898–899, 1223. *See also* Pakistan
Music
    Dominican blues, 587
    "noisy," 1295–1296
Music industry, Barbados, 155
Muslim Brotherhood, 1089–1090, 1096–1097
Muslim League, 124, 1097–1098
    Zanzibar, 1523
Muslims. *See also* Islam
    Cambodian massacre of, 908
    caste systems and, 253
    in India, 859
    Islamic law and, 955
    of Maghreb, 976
    Sri Lanka, 1489, 1490
Muslim women's organizations, 878
Muslim World Leadership Institutes, program on feminism, 1719
Mutalibov, Abulfaz, 127
Mutea II, King, 503
Mvumbi, Albert John. *See* Luthuli, Albert
Mwanawasa, Levy, 1751–1752
Mwinyi, Hassan Ali, 1523
Myanmar (Burma), 1098–1099
    ASEAN and, 97, 112–116, 1456
    Aung San Suu Kyi, 119, 1098
    authoritarian governance, 1449
    in Bandung Conference, 139–140
    civil disobedience in, 344
    colonial legacy, 1454
    economy, 98
    ethnic conflicts, 618–619
    internal politics, 115
    Mekong Basin Development Corporation, 98–100

Open Door policy, 1450
    SEATO and, 1458
    Shan states independence, 1455
    State Peace and Development Council, 1098
Mycobacteria leprae, 820
Mycobacterium tuberculosis, 822, 823
My War with the CIA: Memoirs of Norodom Sihanouk, 1407

N

NAACP (National Association for the Advancement of
        Colored People), 29
Nabiyev, Rahman, 302, 383, 1512
NAFTA (North American Free Trade Association), 200–201,
        645, 708, 830, 1170–1174
    arguments for and against, 1173
    assessment of, 1174
    basic provisions, 1172–1173
    Canadian perspective on, 1171–1172
    Canadian transparency decision, 1570
    Caribbean and, 233
    Central America and, 283
    environmental provisions, 1174
    foreign investors and, 1172
    Free Trade Area of the Americas and, 677
    global trading patterns and, 1568
    intellectual property and, 1173
    labor commission, 1174
    Maquiladoras Program and, 994
    Mexican perspective on, 1170–1171
    Mexico and, 283, 1019–1020, 1024, 1248, 1383
    neoliberalism and, 1122
    organized labor and, 1173, 1174
    Petroleos Mexicanos (PEMEX) and, 1172
    rule of origin, 1172
    snap-back provisions, 1172, 1173
    Southern Cone nations and, 1480
    trade policy and, 1563–1564
    US perspective on, 1171
    US politics and, 1173
Nagorno-Karabakh dispute, 87–88, 127, 378, 382, 924,
        1253, 1533
Nagu, Ferenc, 286
Nagu, Imre, 289
Naguib, General Muhammad, 1159
Nagy, Imre, 456, 790
Najibullah, 4, 1091–1092
Namaliu, Rabbie, 1240
Namibia, 1101–1102
    COMESA and, 369
    diamond production, 250
    Economic Commission for Africa and, 528–530
    ethnic conflicts, 623
    history and economic development, 1460–1462
    national parks, 1245
    South Africa and, 60–61, 189
    Southern African Customs Union and, 1468–1470
    Southern African Development Community and, 1463
    South-West Africa People's Organization (SWAPO), 1101,
            1444–1445
    Soviet Union and, 1445
    white community, 1706, 1707
Nanumba people, 627–628
Napoleonic Civil Code, 951
Narcotics trafficking. *See* Drug trafficking

Nasser, Gamal Abdel, 117, 166, 547–549, 1034, 1035, 1038,
        1102–1103, 1159. *See also* Egypt
    Ba'ath Party and, 130, 1598
    Baghdad Pact and, 310
    in Bandung Conference, 139–140
    Free Officer's revolt, 335
    Muslim Brotherhood and, 1096
    Non-Aligned Movement and, 1552
    populism of, 1304–1305
    Suez War and, 75–76, 117, 219–220, 548, 1035–1036,
            1102, 1159
    United Arab Republic and, 69–70, 1598
    Yemen and, 1746
National Action Party (*Partido Acción Nacional*, PAN),
        672–673, 1024, 1107–1108
National Association for the Advancement of Colored People.
        See NAACP
National consciousness, Oceania, 1196
National debt. *See* Debt
National Endowment for Democracy (NED), 878
National Federation of Coffee Growers, 1177
National Front for the Liberation of Angola (NLA), 53–54
National Indicative Programs (NIPs), 965
Nationalism
    Arab, 68–72. *See also* Pan-Arabism
    authoritarianism and, 122–123
    Cuban, 246
    Kurdish, 610–611, 1577
    migration and, 1044
    Montenegro, 1080
    refugee movements and, 1354
    religious, 857–858
    single-party government and, 1415
    Southeast Asia, 1447–1448
Nationalization
    Algeria, 1166
    Anglo-Iranian Oil Company, 1221
    Argentina, 82
    Belarus, 162
    Central/Eastern Europe, 291–292
    Chile, 31, 681, 1484
    Cuba, 257, 413–414
    Democratic Republic of Congo, 390
    Ecuador, 48
    Gamal Abdel Nasser and, 1102
    Guatemala, 32
    Iran, 863–864, 1085–1086
    Iraq Petroleum Company, 130
    Laos, 944
    Nicaragua, 1138
    North Korea, 914
    Peru, 41, 1269
    Suez Canal, 75–76, 117, 219–220, 548, 1035–1036, 1102
    Syria, 1513
    Trujillo holdings, 186
    Zambia, 1752–1753
National Liberation Army (ELN), 352–353, 503,
        1110–1111, 1182
National Liberation Council (Ghana), 700
National Liberation Front (NLF), 1108–1110
National Liberation Party (NLP), 84
National parks, 1244–1246
    deforestation and, 1712
    future and recommendations, 1245–1246
    Galapagos Islands (Ecuador), 1710

National parks (*Continued*)
  Garamba National Park (Congo), 1709–1710
  international and sustainable development, 1244–1245
  Manas Wildlife Sanctuary (India), 1710, 1711
  Serengeti National Park (Tanzania), 1710
  Tesso Nilo National Park (Indonesia), 1712
  Virunga National Park (Congo), 1709–1710
  in wildlife preservation, 1710–1711
National Party (South Africa), 30, 58, 61–62, 188–191,
    989–990, 1462
National Rainbow Coalition (NARC), Kenya, 905
National Redemption Council (Ghana), 700
National Resistance Council, of Uganda, 503
National Revolutionary Movement (MNR), 46, 185
National Revolutionary Unity of Guatemala
    (URNG), 726–728
National Salvation Council (Somalia), 1433
National security, counterinsurgency and, 404–405
National Security Council, Iran-Contra scandal and, 394
National Security Decision Directive 17, 393
National Union for the Total Independence of Angola
    (UNITA), 53–54, 1293
Nation building, 1103–1107
  Strategic Hamlet Program, 1105
Native Reserves, 332–333, 903, 935, 979, 980,
    1002, 1439–1440
  establishment of, 1462
  Hendrick Verwoerd and, 1661
  Lesotho and Swaziland as, 1461
Natives Land Act, 10, 935, 1439–1440, 1462
Natives Representative Councils, 1462
NATO, 381, 1173–1176
  arms industry and, 94–95
  arms transfer and, 89
  Baltic states in, 294
  Berlin Wall and, 171
  in Bosnia, 1255
  Central and Eastern Europe and, 286, 290, 294, 295
  collapse of Soviet Union and, 1175
  Croatia and, 411
  Czech Republic in, 294
  formation of, 1488
  Hungary in, 294, 791
  Iraq War and, 1175–1176
  in Kosovo, 138, 1253
  North Africa and, 1175
  peacekeeping by, 1253
  Poland in, 294
  Russia and, 383
  Serbia and, 1399
  terrorism and, 1175
  Turkey and, 310
  Yugoslavian no-fly zone and, 137
Natron (sodium carbonate) production, Chad, 261
Natural disasters, 1111–1116. *See also* Disaster relief;
    Natural hazards
  Association of Caribbean States and, 112
  Caribbean Development Bank and, 236
  Central America, 276
  climatic hazards, 1111–1113
  disaster preparedness, 1115–1116
  earthquake/tsunami of 2004, 811, 985, 1489
  Grenadan Souffriere Hills volcano, 1083
  Haitian hurricanes, 741
  Honduras, 763

Maldives, 984–985
  natural hazards vs., 1111
  Organization of Eastern Caribbean States and, 1211
Natural gas, 647
Natural hazards
  climatic, 1111–1113
  geologic, 1113–1115
Natural monopoly, 1065
Natural resources, 768. *See also* Extractive industries
  depletion and deterioration, 769
Nature Conservancy, 1348
Nauru
  demographics, 1191
  trusteeship, 1632
Nawaz Sharif, Mian, 1223
Nazarbayev, Nursultan, 383, 902
Nazi Germany. *See also* Fascism; Hitler, Adolf; Holocaust
  Argentina and, 1481
  Bank for International Settlements and, 145
  eugenics programs, 654–655
  Hungary and, 789
  Iran and, 909, 1034
  Latvia and, 946
  occupation of Ukraine, 1588
  Paraguay and, 1485
  Poland and, 1280
  Slovakia and, 1416
  Soviet Non-Aggression Pact, 288, 963–964, 1496
  sterilization programs, 654, 655
  as totalitarian state, 1555, 1556
  Uruguay and, 1486
  war crimes tribunals, 1054–1055
  Yugoslavia and, 1748
Ndadaye, Melchior, 212
Ndebele people, 1439
Ndi, Ni John Fru, 1116–1117. *See also* Cameroon
Ndjuka people, 1507
Ndluli, Laborsibeni Gwamile, 10
Ndzwani, 387
NED (National Endowment for Democracy), 878
Negdels. See Collective farms; Collectivization
Negrito people, 1271–1272
Negritude literature, 1234, 1396, 1545
Nehru, Jawaharlal, 802–803, 1117–1118. *See also* India
  in Bandung Conference, 139–140
  Non-Aligned Movement and, 1148, 1552
Neisseria meningitidis, 822
Nemeth, Miklós, 790, 1655
Neoclassical liberalism/Washington Consensus, 461–463,
    965, 966
Neocolonialism, 1118–1120
  Kwame Nkrumah and, 1146
Neoliberalism, 1120–1123. *See also* Mixed economy
  backlash against, 1122
  labor and, 933
  Mexico and, 1248
  military and, 933
  trade policy and, 1563
Neo-Marxist theory, 667. *See also* Foreign direct investment
Neostructuralism, 1617
NEPAD. *See* New Partnership for Africa's Development
Nepal, 1123–1125
  Bagmara Forest, 1711–1712
  counterinsurgency in, 405
  national parks, 1245

Rana family, 1124
South Asian Association for Regional Cooperation and, 1441–1444
Netanyahu, Benjamin, 883
Netherlands
    international banks in, 151
    Papua New Guinea and, 1240
    Suriname and, 1185–1186
Netherlands Antilles, 1125–1127
    Association of Caribbean States and, 111
    Caribbean Basin Initiative and, 232–233
    Venezuela and, 1126
Neto, Agostiño, 1292
Neutralism vs. nonalignment, 1148
Nevada del Ruiz volcanis eruption, 1115
Neves, Tancredo, 200
Nevis Reformation Party, 1491
New Caledonia
    international relations, 1194
    Kanak people, 1194
    national identity, 1193–1194
New Economic Policy (Malaysia), 1127
New Guinea trusteeship, 1632
New International Economic Order, 139, 461, 835, 1128–1129
    cartels and, 249–250
    Lomé Convention and, 964–966
    Non-Aligned Movement and, 1148
    Program for Action, 1128–1129
    trade policy and, 1562
New Jewel Movement (NJM), 180, 242, 248, 1129–1130
Newly Emerging Nations, military and, 1050
Newly industrialized countries (NICs), 101–103, 463, 1067, 1546
    export characteristics, 1566
Newly industrialized economies (NIEs), 101–103, 1130–1133
    economic liberalization of, 1132–1133
    foreign direct investment in, 1132
    technology transfer and, 1131–1132
New Partnership for Africa's Development (NEPAD), 5, 1204, 1466, 1700, 1701
New People's Army, 1130
New Zealand
    ASEAN and, 115
    Canberra Agreement, 1194
    Marau Peace Agreement, 1431
    Niue and, 1144–1145
    Nuclear Tests Case (New Zealand v. France), 1623
    Samoa and, 1385
    SEATO and, 1458
    Tonga and, 1554
    Tuvalu Trust Fund, 1583
Nganguela people, 53
Ngobe (Guaymiés) Indians, 606, 607–608
Nguema, Francisco Macías, 264
Nguema Mbasongo, Teodoro Obiang, 265, 575, 576
Ngum people, 1512
Nguyen Al Quoc. See Ho Chi Minh
Ngwane, 1512
Nicaragua, 934, 1133–1136. See also Nicaraguan Revolution
    Anatasio Debayle Somoza, 1434–1435
    Association of Caribbean States and, 111
    Caribbean Basin Initiative and, 232–233
    CIA in, 309
    Contras, 309, 392–395, 1023
    Cuba in, 257
    debt, 1135

democratization, 1139–1140
    earthquake of 1972, 1134–1135
    education, 543
    ethnic conflicts, 607
    history, 1134
    in Honduras, 763
    infrastructure, 1135–1136
    life expectancy, 276
    literacy, 544
    Mexico and, 1023
    Organization of American States and, 1206–1207
    political history, 392–393, 1134–1135
    private property rights in, 1321
    remittances to, 283
    San Andrés Island dispute, 1182
    Sandinistas, 233, 416, 660–661, 763, 1023, 1135, 1389–1390
    Supreme Council of Private Enterprise (COSEP), 1138
    territorial disputes, 283, 1135, 1538
    United Nicaraguan Opposition, 1389–1390
    United States and, 279, 1023
Nicaraguan Revolution, 1136–1137
Nickel production, New Caledonia, 1191
NICs. See Newly industrialized countries
Niger, 1140–1141. See also West Africa
    Berbers in, 170
    debt relief, 443
    Economic Commission for Africa and, 528–530
    ethnic conflict, 628
    extractive industries, 1140
    independence movement, 30
    Lake Chad Basin Commission, 933–934
Niger Delta Development Commission, 1144
Nigeria, 1141–1144. See also West Africa
    Benjamin Nnamdi Azikiwi, 127–128
    Biafra and, 175–177
    civic education, 342
    currency devaluation, 423
    debt, 223, 1144
    decolonization, 361–362
    Economic Commission for Africa and, 528–530
    economy, 1143
    ethnic conflicts, 627, 628–629
    famine, 176–177
    health care, 748
    Lake Chad Basin Commission, 933–934
    Niger Delta Development Commission, 1144
    oil, 270–271, 646, 649–650, 1143
    peacekeeping, 1254
    petroleum royalties, 221
    political history, 1142–1143
    shadow economy, 181
    white community, 1706
    Yoruba people, 1257
Nigerian Trust Fund, 4
Niger River Valley Zone, 582
Nile River, 547, 1157, 1688. See also Egypt
NIPs (National Indicative Programs), 965
Nitric acid pollution, 1, 2
Nitrous oxide pollution, 1, 1289
    agricultural globalization and, 13
Niue, 1144–1145
Nixon, Richard M., 32
    Israel and, 78
Niyazov, Saparmurad, 1579
Niyazov, Saparmyrat, 299

NJM (New Jewel Movement), 180, 242, 248, 1129–1130
Nkomo, Joshua, 30, 334, 1757
Nkoniti Accord on Non-Agression and Good
    Neighborliness, 973
Nkrumah, Kwame, 29, 30, 700, 1145–1147, 1202, 1463.
    See also Ghana
  in Bandung Conference, 139–140
NLA (National Front for the Liberation of Angola), 53–54
NLP (National Liberation Party), 84
Nobel Peace Prize
  Amnesty International, 38
  Arafat/Peres/Rabin, 79
  Bishop Desmond Tutu, 1580, 1581
  De Klerk/Mandela, 438, 990
  Lech Walesa, 1676
  Oscar Arias Sanchez, 84, 280
  Sadat/Begin, 161, 220, 1038, 1159, 1382
  Ximines Bel/Ramos Horta, 525
Nobel Prize, Rockefeller Foundation and, 1366, 1368
Noboa, Gustavo, 49, 542
"Noisy music" and popular sectors, 1295–1296
Nomadic pastoralism, 159–160
Nomadic societies, 1500
  Central Asia, 297, 299
  education and, 545
  Kuwait, 925
  Saudi Arabia, 1391
  Tuareg, 1140
Non-Aligned Movement, 192, 416, 1035, 1147–1149,
    1234–1235, 1545
  Colombia and, 1183
  Gamal Abdel Nasser and, 1552
  Josip Broz Tito and, 1552, 1749
  Norodom Sihanouk and, 1407
  Sukarno and, 1506–1507
  Summit Conference, 1442
  vs. neutralism, 1148
Nong Duc Manh, 1666
Non-governmental organizations (NGOs), 519, 1149–1156.
    See also individual organizations
  agriculture and, 16
  antidiscrimination efforts, 1063
  CARE, 229–231
  Code of Conduct, 784
  DAWN (Development Alternatives with Women for a
    New Era), 433–435
  debt crisis and, 849
  defining, 1149–1150
  against deforestation, 446
  development and, 459
  for disaster relief, 475–476
  environmental, 177–179, 571, 572–575, 1348
  funding, 1153–1154
  government and, 1151–1152
  government or political cooption of, 1154–1155
  government partnership programs, 1152–1153
  health care, 748, 759
  HIV/AIDS and, 759
  humanitarian relief projects, 784–787
  human rights coalition, 37–38
  in India, 1154
  institutionalization of, 1154
  Islamic, 878
  issues confronting, 1153–1155
  management issues, 1154

  modernization and, 1067–1068
  multiple concurrent programmes, 1154
  objectives, 1153
  origin, growth, and life cycle, 1151
  Oxfam, 1217–1218
  in Pakistan, 1224
  people-oriented vs. project-oriented activities, 1154
  of Protestant origin, 639
  risk of vendorism, 1153
  Rockefeller Foundation, 1365–1368
  roles, 1150
  Salvation Army, 1384
  Soros critique of, 1438
  Soros Foundation Network, 1435–1438
  typology, 1150–1151
  voluntarism as characteristic, 1150
  vs. civil society organizations, 1150–1151
  WHO and, 1736
Noriega, General Manuel, 1236–1237
North, Col. Oliver, 309, 394
North Africa. *See also individual countries and regions*
  associations and inter-state relations, 1168–1170
  Economic Commission for Africa and, 528–530
  economic development, 1160–1161
  education, 1161–1162
  ethnic conflicts, 611–615
  European Union and, 1168
  geography and climate, 1156–1157
  history, 1157–1160
  human development, 1161–1163
  international relations, 1163–1170
  literacy, 1161
  monarchic government in, 1075
  NATO and, 1175
  research and development in, 1162
North American Free Trade Association (NAFTA). *See* NAFTA
North Atlantic, sustainable development and, 1510
North Atlantic capitalism, social revolution theory of, 1422
North Atlantic Treaty Organization. *See* NATO
Northern Mariana Islands
  international relations, 1194
  trusteeship, 1632
Northern South America. *See also individual countries
    and regions*
  Colombia, 1176–1177, 1182–1183
  French Guiana, 1180–1181, 1186
  Guyana, 1179–1180, 1184–1185
  history and economic development, 1176–1181
  international relations, 1181–1187
  Suriname, 1180, 1185–1186
  Venezuela, 1177–1179, 1183–1184
North Korea, 913–915. *See also* East Asia
  arms exports, 96
  arms industrialization, 94
  civic education, 340
  economic decline, 915
  economic development, 511, 914–915
  economic sanctions, 1386
  in Grenada, 721
  histography, 913–914
  Import Substitution Industrialization, 515
  Inter-Korean Joint Declaration and, 523
  Japanese rule of, 513
  Juché economic model, 914, 915
  missile program, 517

single-party government, 1414
South Korea and, 522–523
Soviet Union and, 514
territorial disputes, 1535
Novak, Michael, 709
Novotny, Antonin, 496, 1319
Nozick, Robert, 798
NRC (National Redemption Council, Ghana), 700
Ntaryamira, Cyprien, 601
Nuclear development, Iraq, 1037
Nuclear energy, 563
Chernobyl disaster, 379, 563, 1373
International Atomic Energy Agency (IAEA), 831–832
Lithuania, 963
Soviet Union, 1373–1374
Taiwan, 1517
Nuclear technology, 96
Nuclear testing
British near Kiribati, 912
France in Algeria, 1166
Kiribati civil suit, 912
in Micronesia, 1025
Nuclear Tests Case (New Zealand v. France), 1623
in Oceania, 1194
Soviet, 298–299, 902
Nuclear wastes
management of, 1685
Russian, 1373–1374
Taiwan, 1517
Nuclear weapons. *See also* Weapons of mass destruction
International Atomic Energy Agency (IAEC), 1264
Iraqi, 1264
in Mongolia, 603
Soviet Union, 1488
Nuremberg Charter, 1056
Nuremberg Trials, 1055
Nutmeg. *See also* Spice trade
colonialism and, 359
Nutrition. *See* Food and nutrition; Hunger
Nyaneke-Humbo people, 53
Nyanja people, 981
Nyassaland. *See* Malawi
Nyerere, Julius, 30, 37, 180, 502–503, 508, 600, 906, 934, 940, 1188–1189, 1524
Arusha Declaration, 1524
Seychelles *coup d'etat* and, 1401
single-party government and, 1415

O

OAS (*Organisation Armée Secrète*), 28
OAS (Organization of American States). *See* Organization of American States
OAU. *See* Organization of African Unity
Obando y Bravo, Archbishop Miguel, 1134
Obote, Milton, 36, 503, 504, 508, 1147, 1586
Obregón, Alvaro, 1018
Observations of Solid Waste Landfills in Developing Countries (Johannessen and Boyer), 1683–1684
Ocalan, Abdullah, 920
Oceania. *See also* Fiji; Samoa; Tonga
caste/class system, 1194–1195
ethnic conflict, 615–618
France and, 1193–1194
Free Association Contract, 1225

history and economic development, 1189–1190
international relations, 1192–1197
national consciousness, 1196
nuclear testing in, 1194
Pacific Islands Forum, 1219–1220
water management status, 872
whaling industry, 1190
Ochoa Sánchez, Gen. Arnaldo, 417
October (Yom Kippur) War, 77–78, 1038
Odinga, Oginga, 906
O'Donnell, Guillermo, 449, 1477–1478
bureaucratic authoritarianism theory, 207–209
Odría, General Manuel, 40, 41, 46
OECS (Organization of Eastern Caribbean States), 236, 243. *See* Organization of Eastern Caribbean States
Office of Strategic Services (OSS), 307
Offsets, 406
Offshore banking
Angola, 55
Bahamas, 132
Cayman Islands, 258
Dominica, 484
Mauritius, 1006
Panama, 1236, 1555
Vanuatu, 1653
Ogaden National Liberation Front, 585
Ogony people, 649–650
OIC (Organization of the Islamic Conference), 72
Oil-for-food program, 920
Oil industry. *See also* Extractive industries
Algeria, 29, 192, 1158
Anglo-Iranian Oil Company, 52–53
Angola, 53
Arabian American Oil Company (ARAMCO), 2–3, 72–73
Argentina, 82
Azerbaijan, 127
Bahrain, 133
Biafra, 177
Bolivia, 184
Brunei, 202
Caribbean, 241
Central Africa, 261, 270–271
Central Asia, 304–305
Chad, 312
Colombia, 351
debt holdings and, 835
deforestation and, 1347
dependency and, 1031
East Timor, 524–525
Economic Cooperation Organization and, 304–305
Ecuador, 40, 48–49, 541–542
as energy source, 562–563
Equatorial Guinea, 576
as extractive industry, 646–656
Guinea-Bissau, 735
Iran, 863, 1085–1086
Iraq, 868
Kazakhstan, 306, 901–902
Kurdistan, 920
Libya, 1158, 1167
Mauritania, 1004
Middle East economy and, 1029
Netherlands Antilles, 1126
Nigeria, 1143
OPEC and, 563–564, 1212–1215. *See also* OPEC

Oil industry (*Continued*)
Peru, 41
petrodollars, 1270–1271, 1563
pipeline routes, 306, 638, 698
producer cartels, 250. *See also* OPEC
Qatar, 1339
Republic of Congo, 270
Russia, 564
Saudi Arabia, 1391–1392
Suez War and, 76
Syria, 1513–1514
Trinidad and Tobago, 1571
Turkmenistan, 306, 1579
United Arab Emirates, 1595, 1596–1597
Venezuela, 171, 313, 1178
war on terrorism and, 679–680
Oil production, Venezuela, 1658–1659
Oilseed production, Cameroon, 261
Oil spills
Amoco Cadiz, 648
Erica, 648
Exxon Valdez, 648
Metula, 648
Polycommander, 648
Torrey Canyon, 648
Ojeda, Alonso de, 1125
Ojukwu, Emeka, 176, 627, 1142
Okello, John, 1197–1198
Okin, Susan Moller, 799
Oligarchic democracies, 209
Oligarchies
Argentinian, 82
El Salvador "Fourteen Families," 552
Latin American, 1476
Olusuba language, 939
Olympic Games
Mexico City, 1018, 1022, 1247
Munich, 37, 71, 883, 1158, 1227
South Africa barred from, 1204
Oman, 1198–1200
independence, 1034
political and economic reforms, 1032
territorial disputes, 1534
Omar, Mullah Mohammad, 1521
"On the Duty of Civil Disobedience" (Thoreau), 343
OPEC, 1212–1215
Algeria in, 1158
as Arab forum, 72
Arabian American Oil Company
(ARAMCO) and, 1213
as cartel, 251
Ecuador and, 40
founding, 1209
future of, 1215
history, 1212–1215
Kuwaiti defiance of, 1261–1262
Middle East economy and, 1029
natural gas production, 647
oversupply and, 1214–1215
petrodollars, 1270–1271
rise of, 563–564
stagflation and, 1121
Venezuela and, 171, 1184, 1659
World Bank and, 835
OPEC Fund for International Development, 927

Open Society and Its Enemies (Popper), 1435–1436
Open Society Institute, 1437. *See also* Soros
Foundation Network
Operation Bootstrap, 1200–1202, 1334–1335
Operation Desert Storm. *See* Persian Gulf War (1991)
Operation Iraqi Freedom, 1265–1266. *See also* Persian
Gulf War (2003)
Operation Mockingbird, 307–308
Operation Mongoose, 308
OPIC (Overseas Private Investment Corporation), 1216–1217
Orange Revolution (Ukraine), 1589
Organisasion armeé secrete (OAS), 28, 613
Organization for Economic Cooperation and Development
(OECD), 102–103, 1383
anti-corruption measures, 398
Slovakia and, 1417–1418
Organization for Security and Cooperation in Europe,
1063, 1253
Organization of African Unity (OAU), 227, 257, 264, 507,
529, 782, 1202–1205, 1235, 1700. *See also* African Union
Algerian/Moroccan border dispute settlement, 1168–1169
apartheid and, 1203–1204
contributions to development, 1203
Convention on Refugees, 1353
Coordinating Committee for the Liberation of Africa, 1203
global trading patterns and, 1568
institutions, 1203
Language Plan of Action for Africa, 940
peacekeeping by, 1252
Organization of American States (OAS), 33, 40, 278, 571,
1205–1207
anti-corruption measures, 398
charter members, 1205
Cold War and, 1206
Colombia and, 1182
cultural programs, 1207
Dominican Republic invasion and, 485
election monitoring, 1206–1207
Haiti and, 85
human rights and, 782
institutions, 1205–1206
peacekeeping operations, 1254
peacemaking efforts, 1206
terrorism and, 1207
Organization of Arab Petroleum Exporting Countries
(OAPEC), 1207–1210, 1270
impact, 1209–1210
numbers, 1210
structure, 1207–1208
Organization of Eastern Caribbean States (OECS), 236, 243,
248, 1210–1212
Organization of Petroleum Exporting Countries. *See* OPEC
Organization of the Islamic Conference, 72, 1215–1216
Organized labor
African Diaspora and, 8
arguments against privatization, 1326–1327
Cuba, 415–416
NAFTA objections, 1173
Puerto Rican industry and, 1201
South African, 10–11
World Confederation of Labour (CISC), 1727–1728
(The) Origins of Totalitarianism (Arendt), 1555, 1556
Oromo Liberation Front, 585
Ortega, Daniel, 393, 1138, 1139–1140, 1389
Ortega, Humberto, 1139

Orthodox Church. *See also* Religion; Russian Orthodox Church
  Coptic, 396, 614
  Greek, 715–717
  Ukrainian, 384, 1587
Osborne, John, 1083
Oslo Peace Accords, 71, 79, 861, 883, 1036, 1227,
    1231–1232, 1631
Osorio tank incident, 95
Ossetians, in Georgia, 697
Ottoman Empire, 68–69, 87, 284–285
  Britain and France and, 135
  Christianity and, 335
  Constitutional (Tanzimat) Movement, 1049
  Croatia and, 410
  Cyprus and, 428
  Druze religion and, 494–495
  international relations, 1033
  in Iraq, 867–868
  Jordan and, 893
  Kurdistan and, 922–923
  military in, 1049
  Palestine, 1225–1226
  Qatar and, 1339
  Serbia and, 1398
  Turkey and, 1576
Oubangui-Chari. *See* Central African Republic
Oueddei, Goukouni, 264
Our Common Future. See Brundtland Report
Ousmane, Mahamane, 1141
Ovamboland People's Congress, 1444, 1445. *See also*
    South West Africa People's Organization
Ovambo people, 53
Overseas Development Assistance, 1317
Overseas Private Investment Corporation (OPIC), 1216–1217
Ovimbundu people, 53, 54
Owen, Robert, 1592
Ownership, land. *See* Land ownership
Oxfam, 476, 1217–1218
Ozone depletion. *See also* Global climate change; Pollution
  Montreal Protocol on Substances that Deplete the
      Ozone Layer, 1511
  sustainable development and, 1510

P

Pacific Business Forum, 1132
Pacific Economic Cooperation Council, Singapore and, 1412
Pacific Islands Forum, 1219–1220
Pacific Islands Forum Fisheries Agency, 1582–1583
Pacific Rim, Lomé Convention, 964–966
Pacific "Ring of Fire," 1113–1114
Pacto de Punto Fijo, 1183, 1659
Padmore, George, 29
Pahlavi, Shah Mohammad Reza, 863–864, 909–910, 1034,
    1220–1221. *See also* Iran
PAHO (Pan-American Health Organization), 749
Paiewonsky, Ralph, 1670
Pakistan, 1221–1224
  Agha Mohammed Yahya Khan, 1222, 1745–1746
  arms transfers to, 96
  Asian Development Bank loans, 100–101
  Awami League, 124, 1092–1093
  Baghdad Pact, 868
  Bandung Conference, 139–140
  Bangladesh and, 141

Benazir Bhutto, 174–175
  boundary agreement with China, 125
  CENTO and, 311
  Democratic Action Committee, 125–126
  East. *See* Bangladesh
  Economic Cooperation Organization and, 304, 537–538
  economic growth, 125
  Edhi Foundation, 1224
  education, 125, 1223
  external threat perception, 1443
  Fauji Foundation, 1224
  Fulbright Program and, 687
  Green Revolution and, 717–718
  independence, 36
  India's wars with, 94
  irrigated and drained area, 871
  irrigation and drainage, 874
  Islamic Democratic Alliance, 1097
  Kashmir dispute, 94, 805–807, 897–899, 1443
  Mujahedin and, 1091, 1223
  Mukti Sanad (Six-Point Program), 1092
  Muslim League, 1097–1098
  national parks, 1245
  pipeline routes, 306–307
  political history, 1222–1224
  public safety issues, 1223
  Regional Cooperation for Development and, 304
  remittances, 197, 1043
  SEATO and, 1458
  South Asian Association for Regional Cooperation
      and, 1441–1444
  Taliban and, 1521–1522
  territorial disputes, 94, 805–807, 897–899, 1443, 1535
Pakistan Resolution, 36
Paksas, Rolandas, 964
Pakuristan territorial dispute, 1534–1535
Palau (Belau), 1224–1225
  demographics, 1191
  trusteeship, 1632
Palés Matos, Luis, 587
Palestine, 1225–1228. *See also* Arab-Israeli Wars;
    Palestine Liberation Organization
  anti-Zionism, 166–167, 881, 1037, 1758–1759
  Arab nationalism and, 69, 70–71
  Arab Revolt, 1226
  Balfour Declaration, 69, 134–135, 980, 1226
  British Mandate, 167, 1008, 1226
  Christianity in, 336
  creation of Israel and, 1226
  early history, 1225–1226
  intifadas, 71, 80, 741–742, 860–862, 883–884, 1038, 1227,
      1231–1232
  Israeli occupation, 883, 1008, 1037–1038
  Oslo Peace Accords, 1227, 1231–1232
  Sykes-Picot Agreement, 69, 135, 495, 947, 1226
  territorial disputes, 1534
  terrorism and, 1226–1227
  United Nations High Commissioner for Palestine, 1611
  United Nations Relief and Works Agency for Palestine,
      1606, 1611, 1629–1631
  United Nations Relief for Palestine Refugees, 1611
Palestine Liberation Organization (PLO), 37, 883, 927, 1036,
    1228–1229. *See also* Arafat, Yasser
  Algeria and, 1166
  early history, 70–71

Palestine Liberation Organization (PLO) (*Continued*)
  HAMAS and, 742
  in Lebanon, 1630
  Libya and, 1158
  terrorism and, 1226–1227, 1228–1229
Palestinian Authority, 79–80, 1227, 1229, 1233
Palestinian Diaspora, 1229–1233
  right of return and, 1233
Palestinian refugees, 75, 881
Palm kernel production, Central Africa, 261
Pampas, Argentinian, 81
PAN (*Partido Acción Nacional*), 672–673
Pan-African Congress, 11, 436, 1234, 1440, 1463
Pan-African Freedom Movement, 901. *See also*
      Kuanda, Kenneth
Pan-Africanism, 8, 1233–1236
  All-African People's Congress, 29–30, 1147
  branches of, 1235
  Kwame Nkrumah and, 1145–1147
  negative effects of, 1235–1236
  negritude literature, 1234, 1396, 1545
  Rastafarianism and, 1350
Pan-African Union, Jomo Kenyatta and, 906
Pan-African Workers Congress (PAWC), 1728
Panama, 1236–1237. *See also* Panama Canal
  anti-American demonstrations, 32
  Association of Caribbean States and, 111
  Canal Zone, 1237–1238
  Caribbean Basin Initiative and, 232–233
  Comarca system, 607–608
  Hay-Bunau-Varilla Treaty, 1236, 1237
  Liberation Theology and, 334
  Omar Torrijos Hérrera, 1554–1555
Panama Canal, 1237
Panama Canal Treaties, 1237–1239
Pan-American Health Organization (PAHO), 749
Pan-Arabism
  Ba'ath Party and, 129
  nationalism and, 69–70
Panchayat, Rashtriya, 1124
Panchayat caste, 254
Panday, Basdeo, 1571
Paniagua, Valentin, 1267–1268
Pan-Malaysian Islamic Party, 1344
Papa Doc. *See* Duvalier, François
Papaya production, Central Africa, 261
Papua New Guinea, 1239–1240
  demographics, 1191
  education, 545
  ethnic conflict, 615–616
  popular sectors in, 1295–1296
  trusteeship, 1632
Papuan Liberation Organization, 1535
Paracel, 1241–1242
(*The*) *Paradox of Plenty* (Karl), 564
Paraguay, 1242–1243
  agricultural oligarchy, 1476
  Alfredo Stroesser, 1485–1486, 1497–1498
  Chaco War, 1485, 1497
  dependence on Argentina, 1485
  financial crises, 1478
  Friendship Bridge, 1485
  geography and climate, 1474, 1475
  Guairá Falls, 885
  Institute of Rural Welfare, 1243

international relations, 1484–1486
  Itaipú Dam, 885–886, 1485, 1498
  MERCOSUR and, 1472–1474, 1486
  Nazi Germany and, 1485
  Organization of American States and, 1206
  outward-directed development (*desarrollo hacia afuera*), 1243
  Peace Corps in, 1485
  Radical Civic Union, 1485
  single-party government, 1414
  slavery and emancipation, 7
  Treaty of Asunción, 200
  in United Nations, 1485
  War of the Triple Alliance, 1484
  Yacyretá Dam, 1243
Parallel sailing, 724
Paramaka people, 1507
(*The*) *Paranoid Style in American Politics* (Hofstadter), 486–487
Paratyphoid fever, 821
Pariah caste, 1640
Paris Club, 442
Paris Peace Accords, 216, 1250
Park Chung Hee, 94, 102–103, 917
Park systems, national, 1244–1246. *See also* National parks
      and specific parks
PARLCEN (Central American Parliament), 280
Parliamentary system, 554–555
Parsons, Talcott, 458, 1293–1294, 1591
Parsons' structural-functionalist theory, 1069
Parti Congolais du Travail, 390
Partida de Liberacíon Dominicano (PLD), 485
*Partido Africano da Independocia da Guineé Cabo
      Verdw*, 215–216
Partido Aprista Peru, 745
Partido Arnulfista, 1237
Partido de Acción Nacional (PAN), 672–673,
      1024, 1107–1108, 1247
Partido de la Liberación Dominicana (PLD), 186
Partido Justicialista (Argentina), 83
Partido Radical (Chile), 321
Partido Revolucionario de Trabajo (PRT), 1363
Partido Revolucioria Democrático (PRD), 1237
Partido Revolutionario Institucional (PRI), 1017–1019, 1024,
      1107, 1246–1249
Parti Progressiste Tchadien (PPT), 311
Partiya Karkaren Kurdistan (PKK), 920
Pas Estenssoro, Victor, 46, 47, 50
Pashtunistan, 3
Pass Laws (South Africa), 11, 59–60. *See also* Apartheid
Pastoralism, 1500–1501
  nomadic, 159–160
Pastrana, Andées, 1361
Patagonia, 1475
Patassé, Ange-Felix, 269, 272
Patents. *See also* Intellectual property rights
  on life forms, 826–827
Pathet Lao, 1249–1250
Pauker, Ana, 287
PAWC (Pan-African Workers Congress), 1728
Paz Estenssoro, Victor, 185
Paz Zamora, Jaime, 50
Peace Corps, 40, 459
  in Paraguay, 1485
Peacekeeping, 1250–1256
  Chad, 1252
  challenges and future directions, 1255

Commonwealth of Independent States, 378
Congo, 1252
  deployment procedures, 1254–1255
  evolution of operations, 1251–1252
  Lebanon, 1252
  objectives, 1251
  peace building, 1253–1254
  post-Cold War, 1252–1254
  preventive deployment, 1253
  quasi-enforcement, 1253
  Sierra Leone, 1406–1407
  Somalia, 1433–1434
  Suez War, 1252
  traditional roles, 1252
  United Nations, 295, 590, 607, 966, 1103–1104, 1182, 1250–1256
Peanut production, Gambia, 691
Pearling industry, 133
Peasants, 1256–1258
  closed corporate communities of, 1256–1257
  image of the limited good, 1257
  leveling mechanisms, 1257
  weapons of the weak concept, 1257
Pedi people, 622
Pedro I and II (Brazil), 199
Pegov, Nicolai, 305–306
Peking Diary: A Year of Revolution (Bodde), 686
Peña Gómez, Francisco, 485
Pentagon attack (September 11), 300
Peoples, legal definition of, 1393–1394
People's Action Movement (PAM), 1491
People's Action Party (Singapore), 1413
People's Army of Vietnam, 1249
People's Front for Democracy and Justice (PFDJ), 576
People's Front of Azerbaijan, 127
People's Liberation Armed Forces (PLAF), 1258–1259
People's National Congress (Guyana), 1184
People's Progressive Party (Guyana), 887, 1184
People's Republic of China. *See* China
Pepper production. *See also* Spice trade
  Central Africa, 261
  colonialism and, 359
Peres, Shimon, 79–80
Perestroika, 289, 596, 702–703, 712–713, 1374. *See also* Gorbachev, Mikhail
  Russian Orthodox Church and, 1377
Perestroika and New Thinking for Russia and the Entire World (Gorbachev), 712
Pérez, Carlos Andrés, 312
Pérez, Manuel, 1110
Perez, Simon, 1164
Pérez Balladares, Ernesto, 1237
Perez de Cuéllar, Javier, 685
Pérez Jiménez, Marcos, 1178, 1183, 1259–1260, 1659. *See also* Venezuela
Permanent Arab Commission on Human Rights, 782
Perón, Eva, 82, 1260
Perón, Isabel, 82, 988, 1261, 1481
Perón, Juan Domingo, 32, 81–82, 123, 988, 1260–1261, 1476–1477, 1481
  Justicialismo, 1081, 1302, 1304
  Movimiento Peronista Montonero (Montoneros), 1081–1082
  Peronismo, 1081–1082
Perot, Ross, 1173

Persian Gulf War (1991), 79, 382, 869, 925, 1034, 1089, 1160, 1261–1264
  Argentina and, 1482
  arms transfer and, 89–90
  Bahrain and, 133
  causes, 1261–1262
  international response to, 1262
  Iraq and, 793–794
  Jordan and, 893
  Operation Desert Storm, 1262–1263
  peacekeeping operations, 1253–1254
  significance, 1263
Persian Gulf War (2003), 794, 869–870, 924, 1036, 1264–1267
  Argentina and, 1482
  Jordan and, 893
  Mexico and, 1024
  nation building and, 1106–1107
  NATO and, 1175–1176
  Operation Iraqi Freedom, 1265–1266
Persistent Organic Pollutants (POPs), 1286–1287
Personal dictatorships, 196, 473, 1416
Pertussis (whooping cough), 822
Peru, 1267–1270
  Acción Popular, 1269
  agrarian reform, 47
  Alianza Popular Revolucionaria Americana (APRA), 46, 62–65, 1267
  Andean Regional Initiative, 1277
  arms transfer to, 93
  Asia-Pacific Economic Cooperation and, 108
  Bolivian and Chilean relations, 43–44
  Cold War and, 41
  development post-World War II, 1268–1269
  economic reforms, 49–50
  economy, 1268
  ecotourism, 539
  geography and climate, 1267
  historical background, 1267–1268
  import substitution industrialization, 1269
  income inequality, 1311
  lost decade and, 1269
  Manu National Park and Biosphere Reserve, 1712
  military coups, 47
  Organization of American States and, 1206
  political history, 46, 1267–1270
  Sendero Luminoso (Shining Path). *See Sendero Luminoso*
  slavery and emancipation, 7
  territorial disputes, 39, 42–43, 541, 1537
  Víctor Raúl de la Torre, 745–746
  women's rights, 1404
Peruvian Aprista Party, 745
Pesticide use
  agricultural globalization and, 13
  agricultural privatization and, 20–21
Petit-Saut Dam, 684, 1180
Petrescu, Elena, 259
Petrodollars, 1270–1271, 1563
Petróleos de Venezuela (PEDEVESA), 1178–1179, 1659
Petróleos Mexicanos (PEMEX), 1172, 1247
Petroleum. *See* Oil production
Petroleum royalties, Nigeria, 221
Pewenche Indians, 625
Peyote, 492
PFDJ (People's Front for Democracy and Justice), 576
PFI (political freedom index), 467

PFLP (Popular Front for the Liberation of Palestine), 335
PH, of acid precipitation, 1, 2
Phak Pasason Purivat Lao (Pathet Lao), 1249–1250
Pharmaceutical industry, 490. *See also* Drug trade
    cost of exported product, 1565
Pharmaceuticals, from Amazon rainforest, 179, 1346
Phieu, Le Kha, 1666
Philately, Cayman Islands stamps, 258
Philippines, 1271–1274
    ASEAN and, 97, 112–116, 1455–1456
    Asia-Pacific Economic Cooperation and, 108
    Barrio Village Education Movement, 544
    civil disobedience in, 344
    currency devaluation, 424
    economic history, 1450
    economy, 98
    erosion control measures, 582
    ethnic (overseas) Chinese in, 620
    Fidel Ramos, 1349
    financial crisis, 1451
    foreign direct investment, 670
    geography and climate, 1271
    Green Revolution and, 717–718
    Huks, 977, 1272
    Human Development Index, 659
    infrastructure, 1349
    MAPHILINDO and, 1272
    mercury contamination, 1620
    Moro National Liberation Front (MNLF), 66, 1349
    Moros Islands independence, 1455
    National Democratic Front, 66
    as Newly Industrialized Economy, 1131
    New People's Army, 1130
    population growth, 657
    Project Impact, 544
    Ramon Magsaysay, 977
    religion, 1457
    remittances, 197
    SEATO and, 1458
    Spratly Islands claims, 1241
    territorial disputes, 1535
Phoenix Factor theory, of war and development, 1677
Phomvidane, Kaysone, 1250
Phouma, Souvanna, 1249
Phoumasavane, Nouhak, 1250
Pinochet, Augusto Ugarte, 32, 123, 321–322, 934, 1274–1276, 1484
    CIA and, 308
    ECLAC and, 1615
Pinto de la Costa, Manuel, 263
Pipelines
    Central Asian routes, 306
    Chile-Bolivia natural gas pipeline project, 50
    Pakistan, 306–307
    Tanzania–Zambia, 900
    United States routes, 306
Pipil Indians, 606
Pitcairn, demographics, 1191
Plan Colombia, 1276–1278, 1361–1362
Planned economy, 385. *See also* Central planning
Planned Parenthood Federation of America, 655, 852
Plantation system. *See also* Slavery
    British Virgin Islands, 1669
    Caribbean, 357–358
    Guyana, 1179
    Kenya, 1002

    Suriname, 1508
    Tanzania, 1524
    Tobago, 1571
    United States Virgin Islands, 1670
Platt Amendment, 245–246, 412–413
Plaza, Galo, 42, 46–47
PLD (*Partido de la Liberación Dominicana*), 186, 485
PLO. *See* Arafat, Yasser; Palestine Liberation Organization
Pluralism, democracy requiring, 121
Plurality, religion and, 857
Pohamba, Niñkepunye, 1101
Poland, 1278–1281. *See also* Walesa, Lech
    Black Sea Economic Cooperation Organization and, 183–184
    Cardinal Stefan Wyznynski, 1743–1744
    exports, 1279
    financial crises, 289
    Germanization, 1279
    history, 1279
    human resource development, 770
    independence, 1280
    international relations, 294
    Karol Wojtyla (Pope John Paul II), 288, 366, 1375, 1714–1715
    in NATO, 294
    Nazi Germany and, 1588
    political history, 284–285, 286, 288
    Round Table Agreement, 1676
    Rural Solidarity, 1430
    Solidarity Union, 890, 1280, 1429–1431, 1488, 1655, 1676
    Soviet Union and, 889–890
    Visehrad Four and, 1672–1673
    Wojchiech Jarulzelski, 889–890
    Workers' Defense Committee, 1429–1430
Polanyi, Karl, 458
Polar regions, global climate change and, 706
Poliomyelitis, 820
Political culture, 1281–1283
    Eastern Europe, 1281–1282
    factors in, 1281
Political development, 466–467
Political freedom index (PFI), 467
Political history
    Algeria, 1157–1158
    Bulgaria, 284–285, 290
    Central Africa, 262–266
    China, 325–326
    Colombia, 350–352, 1176–1177
    Costa Rica, 402
    Czech Republic, 430
    Democratic Republic of Congo, 388–389
    East Africa, 501–504
    Egypt, 1159–1160
    Ghana, 700
    Hungary, 284, 289
    Iraq, 864
    Libya, 1158–1159
    Marshall Islands, 996–997
    Mexico, 1017–1020
    Nicaragua, 392–393, 1134–1135
    Nigeria, 1142–1143
    Pakistan, 1222–1224
    Poland, 284–285
    Republic of Congo, 389–390
    Sudan, 1502–1503
    Taiwan, 1516–1517

Third World, 1544–1545
United Arab Emirates, 1595
Venezuela, 1659–1661
Yugoslavia, 290
Political Liberalism (Rawls), 798
Political Order in Changing Societies (Huntingdon), 1105–1106
Political prisoners, Amnesty International, 37–38
Political reforms, Alliance for Progress and, 34
Political systems. *See* Governance models
Politics, Personality and Nation-Building: Burma's Search for Identity (Pye), 1104–1105
(The) Politics of Cultural Pluralism (Young), 629
Politics of language, 941
Pollution. *See also* Waste management; *specific types*
   acid precipitation, 1–3
   agricultural, 1284–1288
   agricultural globalization and, 13
   air, 1419–1420
   carbon dioxide, 1346–1347
   Cospa Mica (Romania) toxic waste cleanup, 1620
   deforestation and, 445
   from fossil fuels, 563–564
   free market economy and, 675–676
   haze, 116, 445–446, 1419–1420
   industrial, 1288–1292
   Persistent Organic Pollutants (POPs), 1286–1287
   of poverty, 1510
   from refineries, 648
   in Taiwan, 107
   United Nations Industrial Development Organization and mercury, 1620
   urbanization and, 1645–1646
   from waste incineration, 1682–1683
   water, 13, 1240
Pollution vouchers, 675–676
Pol Pot, 215–217, 787, 1408, 1449, 1664. *See also* Cambodia
Ponce Vaides, Federico, 80
Pondoland Revolt, 11
Pope Bendict XVI, 1714
Pope John Paul II (Karol Wojtyla), 288, 336, 366, 1275, 1375, 1714–1715
Pope Kyrillos VI, 396
Pope Shenouda III, 396
Popper, Sir Karl, 1435–1436
Popular Action Front (Chile), 31
Popular Front for the Liberation of Palestine (PFLP), 335, 1228
Popular Movement for the Liberation of Angola, 53–54, 416, 1292–1293, 1536
Popular sectors, 1293–1296
Popular Unity (Chile), 31–32
Population density
   environment and, 571
   water resources and, 1687
   West Africa, 1694
Population growth rate, 653, 1296–1300. *See also* Family planning
   demographic transition theory, 1297–1298
   Ethiopia, 658
   Gambia, 692
   Ghana, 658, 700
   human resources and, 1296–1297
   Kenya, 659
   Macau, 969
   Mozambique, 1087
   Nicaragua, 1136

Philippines, 659
   Rwanda, 1379
   Slovenia, 1419
   Southeast Asia, 1452
   Sudan, 659
   Tajikistan, 1518–1520
   Togo, 1552
   trends in, 657
   Tunisia, 1573
   United Arab Emirates, 1597
   urbanization and, 1642
   Vietnam, 659, 1665
   world trends in, 657
Population movement, 1298–1299
   ethnicity and cultural heritage and, 1299–1300
   infrastructure and, 1299
Population size, 1297–1298
Populations Registration Act (South Africa), 58, 1440. *See also* Apartheid
Populism, 1301–1306
   Aprista movement and, 64
   Brazil, 1482
   Chiang Ching-Kao and, 314
   Christianity and, 1302
   comparative perspective on, 1302–1306
   definition, 1301–1302
   Mexico, 1019
   nationalism and, 1301–1302
   Progressive Party and, 1303
   Unitarianism and, 1301
Porfirio Diaz, 1017, 1021
Porto-Novo, 167
Portugal, exploration and colonization, 356
Portuguese colonies, 53–54. *See also individual countries*
   Central Africa, 263
   East Timor, 524–525
   independence, 1707
   West Africa, 1695–1696
Positivism, 1050
Postmodernism, 1073
Potato production, Central Africa, 261
Potsdam Conference, 1496
Poultry industry
   Central Africa, 262
   corporate farms, 665
Poverty, 1307–1312. *See also* Human Development Index
   absolute and relative, 1312–1313
   Central America, 281
   as concept, 1307
   Costa Rica, 401
   definitions, 1307–1308, 1312
   deprivation and, 1308
   development and, 1312–1318
   disaster and, 475
   extreme defined, 1311, 1312
   Guatemala, 725–726
   HIV/AIDS and, 757
   Honduras, 763
   human well-being and, 1313–1314
   hunger and, 664, 1316. *See also* Food and nutrition
   income inequality and, 1310–1311
   Kenya, 904
   measurement of, 1308, 1315–1316
   Mongolia, 1079
   moral dimensions, 1316–1317

Poverty (*Continued*)
  multidimensional, 1313, 1315–1316
  Nicaragua, 1135
  Nigeria, 1143
  Organization of African Unity and, 1204
  overpopulation theory and, 1316
  Overseas Development Assistance and, 1317
  pollution related to, 1510
  poverty line, 1308–1309
  public health and, 1330
  quality of life, 1340–1341
  reduction strategies, 1317
  socialistic approach to, 1309
  Tajikistan, 1520
  trends in, 1309–1311
  Uzbekistan, 1648–1649
  Vietnam, 1665
  worldview of, 1307
Poverty-conflict trap theory, of war, 1677, 1678
Poverty Reduction and Growth Facility, of IMF, 848
Poverty Reduction Strategy Papers, of World Bank, 836
Power-conflict theory, of social revolution, 1423
Pozsgay, Imre, 289
PPP (People's Progressive Party), 887
PPT (*Parti Progressiste Tchadien*), 311
Prado Ugarteche, Manuel, 44, 46, 63–64
Pragmatics, 941
Prague Spring, 430, 496, 1318–1319, 1488,
    1654–1655, 1656
Prasad Koirala, Bosweswore, 1124
Praxis Group, of Marxists, 1001
PRD (*Partido Revolucioria Democrático*), 1237
Prebisch, Raúl, 458, 1018, 1319–1320, 1614–1616
Preferential Trade Agreement (PTA), 97, 113
Preferential Trade Areas (PTAs)
  COMESA and, 369
  Economic Commission for Africa, 529–530
Premadasa, R., 1490
Prestes, Luis Carlos, 199
Préval, René, 85
PRI. *See Partido Revolutionario Institucional*
Private property rights, 1320–1321
Private sector development, Caribbean Basin
    Initiative and, 232
Privatization, 1321–1327
  agricultural, 18–25. *See also* Agricultural Privatization
  Belarus, 163
  Bolivia, 185
  case for, 1325–1326
  consumer welfare argument against, 1327
  corruption and, 1343–1344
  debt relief and, 441
  definition and meaning, 1322
  deregulation as panacea argument for, 1325
  efficiency/profitability argument against, 1326
  efficiency/profitability argument for, 1325
  Estonia, 1651
  ethnic/racial discrimination fear against, 1326
  expansion of foreign partnership argument for, 1326
  foreign domination fear argument against, 1326
  growth of private sector argument for, 1326
  Guyana, 1180
  internal factors and, 1324
  logic and scope of programs, 1322–1325
  Mexico, 1383
  mixed economy and, 1064
  Morocco, 1084–1085
  Mozambique, 683
  multinational corporations and, 1095
  neoliberalism and, 1122
  political interference argument for, 1325
  protection of jobs argument against, 1326–1327
  social justice argument against, 1326
  Structural adjustment programs and, 1500–1501
  Venezuela, 1660
  Vietnam, 481–482
Production for use vs. for market, 15
Profit repatriation, 1095
Programa Fome Zero, 1410
Progressive Liberation Movement (Antigua), 56
Progressive Party (US), 1303
Prohibition, Bahamas and smuggling, 132
Prohibition of Mixed Marriages Act, 1462
Project Impact, 544
Proportionality principle, 1054
Protestanism, evangelical, 639
Protestant Ethic, 1067
  capitalism and, 855–856
  population movement and, 1299–1300
(*The*) *Protestant Ethic and the Spirit of Capitalism* (Weber),
    855–856, 1299–1300
Protestant Reformation, 639
Protocols of the Elders of Zion, 742. *See also*
    Anti-Semitism
Provincias Unidas del Centra de América, 277–278
Psychiatric illness. *See* Mental health
Public health, 1327–1332. *See also* Health care
  definition, 1327–1328
  Ebola virus and, 1330
  epidemiological transition concept, 1330–1331
  financial resources and, 1328
  globalization and, 1329
  immunization programs, 1329
  infrastructure and, 1329
  internal political conflict and, 1329
  poliomyelitis program, 1329–1330
  Rockefeller Foundation in, 1366–1368
  scope of, 1329
  Soros Foundation programs, 1437
  tobacco-related illnesses and, 1331
Public sector reform, 1331–1333. *See also* Structural
    adjustment programs (SAPs)
Puerto Rican Reconstruction Administration, 241
Puerto Rico, 1333–1335
  Chardon Sugar Plan, 1200
  ethnic conflicts, 587
  food imports, 240–241
  industrialization, 1334
  migration to US, 1202
  Operation Bootstrap, 1200–1202, 1334–1335
  Organic Act of Puerto Rico, 1200
  promotion of, 1201
  slavery and emancipation, 7
  textile industry, 1201
Punjab territorial dispute, 1535
Purchasing Power Parity measure, 1309
Push-pull relationship, in migration, 1298–1299
Putin, Vladimir, 383, 1375
  Chechen wars and, 597–598
Pye, Lucian, 1104

Q

Qaddafi, Muammar, 961–962, 1036, 1158, 1167, 1337–1338
  Cultural Revolution, 1305
  Libyan Cultural Revolution, 962–963
  populism of, 1302, 1305–1306
Qai (narcotic plant), 1746
Qajar dynasty, 863
Qasim, Abdel Karim, 1598
Qasin, Gen. Abd al-Karib, 868
Qatar, 1338–1340
  geography and climate, 1338–1339
  independence, 1034
  natural gas production, 647
  OAPEC and, 1208
  political and economic reforms, 1032
  territorial disputes, 1534
Quadros, Jánio, 1482
Quajr, Mozaffaredin Shah, 52
Quality of life, 1340–1341
  capability approach, 1340
  GDP as measure, 1340
  as measure of development, 464
Quiroga, Jorge, 50
Quran. *See also* Islamic fundamentalism; Islam; Muslims
  interpretations impeding development, 877
  Islamic law and, 955
Qwa-Qwa Homeland, 153

R

Rabin, Yitzhak, 76, 79–80, 861, 883
Racial segregation. *See also* Apartheid; Caste systems;
    Discrimination
  Kenya, 1002–1003
  in US, 8
Radcliffe, Cyril, 897
Radical Civic Union (Paraguay), 1485
Radioactive wastes, 1373–1374, 1685
Radio Free Europe, Hungarian uprising and, 788
Radium production, Central Africa, 261
Rafsanjani, Ali Akbar Hashemi, 864, 1343–1344
Rahman, Tunku Abdul, 982–983, 1344–1345
Rainfed agriculture, 870–871, 903
  in Kenya, 903
Rainforest
  Amazon. *See* Amazon rainforest
  biodiversity, 1346
  Central African, 260
  definition and status, 1345
  deforestation and, 444–445, 1345–1349, 1420
  extent of destruction, 1345
  Guyana, 738
  Iwokrama, 738
  smaze and, 1420
  species extinction and, 1708
  Suriname, 1508
  Tesso Nilo National Park (Indonesia), 1712
  Trinidad and Tobago, 1570
Rainforest Action Network, 178
Rainforest Preservation Foundation, 1348
Rais, Amien, 735
Rajk, Lázló, 789
Rákosi, Ernesto, 789
Ramirez, Sergio, 1138, 1139

Ramirez de Leon, Ricardo Arnoldo (Rolando Morán), 727–728
Ramos, Fidel V., 66, 1273, 1349. *See also* Philippines
Ramos Horta, José, 524, 525
Ramsar (Convention on Wetlands of International
    Importance), 178
Ranariddh, Prince Norodom, 216, 907–908
Rao, P. V. Marasimha, 804
Rapanui (Easter Island), demographics, 1191
Rassemblement Democratique Africaine, 1558–1559
Rastafarianism, 1349–1351, 1393
  colonial origins, 1350
  development of, 1350–1351
  post-colonial resurgence, 1351
Ratsimandrava, Richard, 973–974
Ratsiraka, Didier, 86, 974
Ratzel, Friedrich, 486
Rawlings, Jerry, 700, 701
Rawls, John, 797–798. *See also* Income distribution
Raznatovic, Zelijko, 138
RCD (Regional Cooperation for Development), 304
Reagan, Ronald, 139, 171
  abortion funding and, 1635–1636
  Bishop Desmond Tutu and, 1581
  Caribbean Basin Initiative and, 232, 247, 550
  Chile and, 1484
  Colombia and, 1182
  development theory and, 462
  Grenada invasion, 417, 720–721, 1185
  Guyana and, 1185
  Iran hostage crisis, 864
  Iranian airliner shooting, 867
  Iran-Iraq War and, 866
  Libyan bombing, 1158
  Mexico City (abortion) policy, 1635–1636
  Micronesia and, 1026
  National Security Decision Directive 17, 393
  neoliberalism and, 1121
  Nicaragua and, 279, 392–393, 1023, 1138,
    1389. *See also* Iran-Contra scandal
  Oceania and, 1194
  Paraguay and, 1485
  Poland and, 1430
Real Plan, 228
Red Cross, International Committee of, 841–842
Red Kurdistan (Kurdish Autonomous Province), 923–924
Reformation, Protestant, 855
Refugee Convention, 1352
Refugees, 1351–1358. *See also* Migration
  adaptation of, 1356
  anthropological study of, 1356
  asylum policies, 1353
  in Azerbaijan, 127
  Bosnian, 137
  Burundian, 1617–1618
  Cambodian, 1454
  Cartagena Declaration, 38, 44, 1205, 1353
  Central America, 1353
  Cold War and, 1353
  Colombian internal, 1277
  decolonization and, 1352
  development and, 1356–1357
  environmental, 1357
  environmental impact of, 1356
  Eritrean, 577
  explaining movements of, 1353–1354

Refugees (*Continued*)
  Geneva Convention for, 1352
  humanitarian aid and, 1354–1355
  human rights and, 1355–1356
  International Conference on Assistance to
      Refugees, 1618
  International Organization for Migration, 850–851
  International Refugee Organization, 1606, 1611
  Jewish, 881
  legal status of, 1352–1353
  Nepalese, 173–174
  Organization of African Unity Convention on
      Refugees, 1353
  Palestinian, 75, 608, 860–862, 881, 1036, 1229–1233
  recent history, 1352–1353
  Richmond's theory of multivariate typology, 1354
  Rwandan, 601, 1617–1618
  socioeconomic impact, 1356
  Soviet Jews, 883
  United Nations and, 1352
  United Nations High Commissioner for Refugees, 475,
      1617–1620, 1629
  United Nations Population Fund and, 1628
  United Nations Relief and Works Agency for Palestine
      (UNRAW), 1629–1631
  United Nations Relief for Palestine Refugees, 1611
  vs. Internally Displaced Persons, 1353
  World War II and, 1352
Regional Cooperation for Development (RCD), 304
Registration, voter, 557
Reinhard, Wolfgang, 355
Religion(s), 1358–1361. *See also specific religions*
  Adiaphora policy, 51
  Africa, 1360–1361
  Afrikaner, 58
  Alawi, 1028
  Anglican Communion, 51–52
  Berbers and, 170
  Buddhism, 203–204, 859
  Byzantine church, 716
  Central Asia, 297–298. *See also* Islam
  Christianity, 332–334
  civil, 856
  civil society and, 348
  Confucianism, 340, 510–511, 515–516
  Coptic Orthodox Church, 395–396, 614
  defining, 854–856
  democratization and, 448
  developing society and, 1358–1359
  development and, 856–857
  drug use as part of, 492
  Druze, 493–495, 1028
  Dutch Reformed Church, 58
  Eastern Orthodox, 336
  East Timor, 524–525
  East vs. West Germany, 1360
  Emile Durkheim on, 855
  Ethiopia, 585
  Europe, 1359–1360
  evangelical Protestanism, 640–641
  future prospects, 862
  Georgia, 698
  Greek Orthodox Church, 715–717
  Guatemala, 725
  Guyana, 738

  Hinduism, 754–755
  Huguenot persecution and South Africa, 1439
  human rights and, 778
  inter-religious relations, 854–860
  involvement in change, 1361
  Islam, 891–892
  Islamic beliefs. *See also* Islam
  Judaism, 894–895
  Latin America, 1359
  Lebanon, 947–948
  Liberation Theology, 85, 333–334, 858–859, 958–959, 1359
  Malaysia, 982
  Maronite Christians, 947, 1028
  Max Weber on, 855–856
  Middle East, 1027. *See also* Christianity; Islam; Islamic
      fundamentalism
  modernization and, 856
  Moldova, 1073
  Mongolia, 1078
  Morocco, 1084
  Mozambique, 1086
  Namibia, 1101
  Nepal, 1124
  Niger, 1140
  Palau, 1225
  plurality and, 857
  Poland, 1278–1279
  Pope John Paul II, 288, 366, 1375, 1714–1715
  revitalization of, 858–859
  Russian Orthodox Church, 1376–1377
  Salvation Army, 1384
  secularization and, 856–857
  Sikhism, 1408–1409
  South Africa, 58
  Southeast Asia, 1457
  Sri Lanka, 1489
  Tajikistan, 1518
  Tewahdo Orthodox Church, 585
  Turkey, 1576
  Ubuntu theology (Desmond Tutu), 1580
  Ukraine, 1587
  Ukrainian Orthodox Church, 384
  World Council of Churches, 1728–1731
  Yugoslavia, 136
  Zimbabwe, 1757
Religious conflict. *See also* Ethnic conflicts
  Tanzania, 1524–1525
Religious conversion, colonialism and, 364
Religious nationalism, 857–858
Remeliik, Haruo, 1225
Remengesau, Tommy Esang Jr., 1225
Remittances, 197
  Caribbean region, 241
  Central America, 283
  Financing for Development and Remittances and
      Gender, 1626
  migration and, 1042–1043
  MIRAB economies, 1192, 1582
  Oceania, 1192
  Senegal, 1396
  Somalia, 1432
  Syria, 1513, 1514
  Tonga, 1553, 1554
  Tuvalu, 1582–1583
RENAMO (*Resisténica Nacional Moçambicana*), 682, 683

René, France-Albert, 1401
Repression, rationales for, 472–473
Republican People's Party (*Cumhurtiyet Halk Partisi*), 1577
Republic of Chad. *See* Chad
Republic of China. *See* Taiwan
Republic of Congo, 265, 389–391
    COMESA and, 369
    Ebola virus in, 1330
    Economic and Customs Union of Central Africa
        and, 526–527
    Economic Commission for Africa and, 528–530
    Economic Community of Central African States
        and, 531–533
    ethnic conflicts, 589
    immunization programs, 1330
    Lakes Edward and Albert Fisheries (LEAF) Project, 5
    oil production, 270
    political history, 269
Republic of the Ivory Coast. *See* Cote D'Ivoire
Research, agricultural, 17
Reservation of Separate Amenities Act (South Africa), 58
Reserve deposit ratio, 147
Resisténcia Nacional Moçambicana (RENAMO), 682–683,
    972, 1087
Resolution 1600 (Colombia), 341
Resources
    capital, 768. *See also* Capital flight; Capital flow
    human, 768. *See also* Human resource development
    natural, 768. *See also* Extractive industries;
        Natural resources
    technological, 768. *See also* Information
        technology; Technology
Respiratory infectious diseases, 764–765, 821, 1452
Return of Talent for Latin America program, 850
Reuters Concession, 863
Revolutionary Armed Forces of Colombia (FARC), 352,
    1277, 1362–1363, 1537
Revolutionary Army of the People (ERP),
    82, 1363–1364
Revolutionary Feminine Unity (Cuba), 416
Revolutionary Front for Independent East Timor
    (FRETILIN), 524
Revolutionary Workers Party (Argentina), 1363
Reyes, Rafael, 1177
Rhee, Syngman, 913
Rhinoceros, extinction of, 1709
Rhodes, Cecil, 1089
Rhodesia, Federation of. *See* Zimbabwe
    decolonization, 361–362
    white community, 1706, 1707
Ricardo, David, 1121, 1559–1560
Rice production
    air pollution from, 1286
    Green Revolution and, 719
    Haiti, 740–741
    International Rice Research Institute (IRRI), 852–853
    Suriname, 1508
Richmond's theory of multivariate typology, 1354
Rift Valley fossils, 500
Rights, definition and type, 344
Rio Declaration on the Environment and Development,
    570, 1510
Rio de Janeiro Conference, 570, 582
Rio de Janeiro Protocol, 42
Rios Montt, José Efrain, 726, 1010

Rio Treaty (Inter-American Treaty of Reciprocal Assistance),
    1206, 1482
Rising expectations theory, of social revolution, 1421–1422
Rivonia Trial, 59
Riyale Kahin, Dahir, 1433
Roberto Flores, Carlos, 763
Roberto Santucho, Mário, 1363
Roca–Runciman Agreement, 81
Rockefeller Foundation, 1365–1368
    Green Revolution and, 717, 853
Rodríguez, Andrés, 1485
Rodríguez Lara, General Guillermo, 48
Roe v. Wade, 655
Rogers, Everritt, 1069
Rojas Pinilla, Gustavo, 352, 1177
Roldós, Jamie, 48–49, 542
Roma (Gypsies)
    in Kosovo, 1253
    Nazi extermination of, 1557
Roman Catholic Church
    Argentina, 1261
    authoritarianism and, 209
    Cardinal Stefan Wyznynski, 1743–1744
    Central/Eastern Europe, 288
    Chile, 320
    Coptic Orthodox Church and, 396, 614
    Croatia, 136
    Cuba, 413
    Czech Community Part and, 1319
    Dominica, 483
    Eastern Orthodox, 336. *See also* Russian
        Orthodox Church
    East Timor, 524–525
    Great Schism, 334–335
    Greek Uniate, 336
    Grenada, 720
    Guatemala, 725
    Indonesia, 810
    Latin America, 1359
    Nicaragua, 1134, 1434
    opposition to family planning, 657
    Pope John Paul II, 288, 366, 1375, 1714–1715
    Slovenia and, 1419
    World Council of Churches and, 1728–1729
Romania
    agricultural privatization in, 18, 19, 20, 24
    Black Sea Economic Cooperation
        Organization, 183–184
    Cospa Mica toxic waste cleanup, 1620
    ethnic conflicts, 592
    independence, 1656–1657
    Moldova and, 384
    nationalist/isolationist socialism, 1428
Roman law, 951
Roma people (gypsies), 1062
Romero, Archbishop Oscar, 334, 660, 958
Roosevelt, Eleanor, 1639
Roosevelt, Franklin D., 333
    Good Neighbor Policy, 1136
    New Deal, 1426
    OSS and, 3407
Rostow, Walt W., 33, 459–460, 1591, 1635
    economic growth model, 815
Rousseau, Jean-Jacques, 1075, 1569
Royal Dutch Shell Company. *See* Shell Oil

Royal Lao Army, 1249
Roye, Edward, 959
Rubber production
    Central Africa, 262
    Liberia, 960
    producer cartels, 250
Rubbish. *See also* Waste; Waste management
    defined, 1681
Rugova, Ibrahim, 138
Ruiz Cortines, Adolfo, 1021
Rumsfeld, Donald, Iran–Iraq War and, 866
Rural development. *See also* Agricultural development
    African Development Bank and, 5
Russia, 1372–1375. *See also* Soviet Union
    agricultural privatization, 18–25
    Armenians in, 87
    arms transfer by, 90–91, 96
    Asia-Pacific Economic Cooperation and, 108
    Black Sea Economic Cooperation Organization and,
        183–184, 381
    Boshevik Revolution, 298–300. *See also* Lenin, Vladimir;
        Marxism
    Caspian Sea and, 305–306
    Central Asia and, 298
    Chechen wars, 596–599
    Commonwealth of Independent States and, 375–380
    Council of Baltic Sea States and, 381
    diamond production, 250
    in East Africa, 507
    foreign direct investment, 1375
    glasnost and *perestroika*, 289, 596, 702–703, 712–713, 1374
    in Group of 8, 573
    health care, 1328
    income inequality, 1311
    industrialization, 1375
    infrastructure, 1374
    Iraq War and, 1265
    irrigated and drained area, 871
    Latvia and, 947
    legal system, 955–956
    natural gas production, 647
    oil production, 564, 646–647
    populists (*Narodniks*) in, 1301, 1302, 1303
    privatization, 1324, 1375
    shadow economy, 181
    Soros foundations in, 1436
    Tajikistan and, 302–303
    territorial disputes, 517, 1533, 1534, 1535
    Zemstvo system of health care, 747
Russian Federation. *See* Russia
Russian Orthodox Church, 1376–1377
    Leonid Brezhnev and, 1377
    Mikhail Gorbachev and, 1377
    Nikita Khrushchev and, 1376–1377
    numbers, 1377
Russians, in Georgia, 697
Russo-Iranian Alliance Treaty, 305–306
Rwanda, 212, 1377–1379. *See also* East Africa
    Batwa people, 1061
    caste system, 255
    COMESA and, 369
    debt holdings, 371
    Economic Commission for Africa and, 528–530
    Economic Community of Central African States
        and, 531–533
    ethnic conflicts/genocide, 211–213, 244, 264–265, 389–390,
        503–504, 590, 600–601, 630, 783
    geography and climate, 1377–1379
    HIV/AIDS in, 371
    infrastructure, 1378–1379
    political history, 503
    refugees, 1355
    trusteeship, 1632
    United Nations Criminal Tribunal for Rwanda,
        1055–1057
    United Nations High Commissioner for Refugees and,
        1617–1618

S

Saba, 1126
Sabotage Act of 1962 (South Africa), 59
SACPO (South African Coloured People's Organization), 11
SACTO (South African Congress of Trade Unions), 11
SACU. *See* Southern African Customs Union
Sadat, Anwar, 70, 118, 220, 336, 549, 882, 1038, 1089, 1159,
    1381–1382. *See also* Egypt
    Muslim Brotherhood and, 1096
SADC (Southern African Development Community), 5, 369
SADCC (Southern African Development Coordination
    Conference), 506
Sahara Desert, 261, 453, 1156, 1693
    in Mauritania, 1003
Sahei desertification, 452–453
Saidu Momoh, Joseph, 627
Sajudis movement, 964
Salafist movement, 1505
Salat Hassan, Abdulkassim, 1433
Saleh, Ali Abdullah, 1746
Saleh Sabbe, Osman, 576–577
Salinas de Gortari, Carlos, 1019, 1024, 1170,
    1248, 1382–1384
Salinization, 1689
Salmonella paratyphii, 821
Salmonella typhii, 821
Salta people, 625
Salt iodization, 818
Salt Satyagraha of Ghandi, 343
Salvation Army, 476, 639, 1384
Samarkand, conquest of, 297
Samoa (Western Samoa), 1384–1386. *See also*
        American Samoa
    demographics, 1191
    international relations, 1194
    trusteeship, 1632
Samphen, Khien, 908
Sampson, Nicos, 428
Sanakoine, Phoui, 1249
Sánchez Cerro, Luis M., 745
Sánchez de Lozada, Gonzalo, 50, 185
Sanctions, economic, 774, 1386–1388
Sandel, Michael, 798
Sandinistas (FSLN), 233, 279, 393, 395, 416, 660–661,
        763, 1023, 1135
    agrarian reform and, 934
    San Andrés Island dispute, 1182
Sandino, Augusto César, 392, 1134, 1136, 1389.
        See also Sandinistas
Sangoulé Lamizana, General, 210
Sanguinetti, Julio Maria, 1486–1487, 1647

Sani Abacha, Gen. Ernest, 1142
Sankara, Thomas, 210–211, 211
Sankoh, Foday, 627
San Martín, Dr. Ramón, 413
San people, 1459
San Remo Conference, 73
Sanskritization, 255–256
SANU (Serbian Academy of Sciences), 137
Sao Tomé and Principe
    Economic Commission for Africa and, 528–530
    political history, 265–266
SAPs. See Structural adjustment programs
Sar, Saloth. See Pol Pot
Sarajevo, 137. See also Balkan Wars
Saramaka people, 1507
Sarney, José, 200
SARS (Severe Acute Respiratory Syndrome), 764–765, 1452
Sartre, Jean-Paul, 1001
Sasanian Empire, 922
SASM (South African Student Movement), 11
SASO (South African Students Association), 59–60
Sassou-Nguesso, Denis, 270, 390
Saudi Arabia, 1390–1392
    aid to PLO, 71
    arms transfer, 90
    Baghdad Pact and, 130–131
    Brazil's tank sale to, 95
    independence, 1034
    Kuwait invasion, 925
    League of Arab States and, 71–72
    natural gas production, 647
    OAPEC and, 1208
    oil, 646–647
    population growth, 657, 1390
    privatization in, 1323
    Taliban and, 1521–1522
    Yemen and, 1746
Sauvy, Alfred, 1542–1543
Savannah
    Central African, 260–261
    fire risk in, 1112
    in Malawi, 981
    Rwandan, 1377–1378
    Suriname, 1507
Save the Children, 476
Savimbi, Jonas, 309
Savings deposits, 146
Scandinavia, family planning in, 655
Schedina, Abdulaziz, 878
Scherbak, Yuri, 384
Schnake, Oscar, 30
Schumacher, E.F., 574
Schumacher's theory of intermediate development, 1071–1072
Schuster, W. Morgan, 863
Scottish Enlightenment, 347
Seaga, Edward, 232–233
SEATO (Southeast Asia Treaty Organization). See Southeast
    Asia Treaty Organization
Seawater distillation, 1670
Sebastian, Cuthbert, 1490–1491
Sebe brothers, atrocities of, 154
Second Treatise of Government (Locke), 347
Second World, 459, 1069, 1542
Secretariat of the Pacific Community, 1219
Sectoral Import Programs (SIPs), 965

Secularization, 856–857
    India, 859
Securities markets, central banks and, 148–149
Security
    internal, 1047
    military, 1047
Segregation. See Apartheid; Discrimination;
        Racial segregation
Sékou Touré, Ahmed, 627
Selassie, Emperor Haile, 576, 577, 585, 739, 1204, 1382–1393.
        See also Eritrea; Ethiopia; Rastafarianism
Self-determination, 1393–1395
Selwyn-Clarke, Percy, 1401
Seme, Pixley Ka Izaka, 10
Sendero Luminoso (Shining Path), 44, 48, 64, 685, 1077,
        1267, 1403–1404
    chronology of movement, 1403
    goals, ideology, and strategies, 1403
    revolutionary activities, 1404
    social appeal, 1404
Senegal, 1395–1396. See also West Africa
    CIDA in, 221
    Economic Commission for Africa and, 528–530
    ethnic conflict, 627
    independence movement, 30
    literacy, 543
    West African Monetary Union and, 1703–1705
Sénghor, Leopold, 29, 1147, 1396–1397. See also Senegal
September 11 terrorist attacks, 880, 1076–1077, 1264
    Chechnya and, 598
    NATO and, 1175
Serbia, 135–139, 287, 1397–1399. See also
        Slobodan Milosevic
    Albanians in, 138, 1059, 1398
    ethnicity, 1398
    independence, 290
    international relations, 295
    NATO and, 1175
Serbia and Montenegro, 1081, 1397
Serbian Academy of Sciences (SANU), 137
Serbian Republic of Karjina, 1058
Serbs, NATO and Albanian, 1175
Serengeti National Park (Tanzania), 1710
Serrano, Jorge, 1206
Settlement colonies, 355–356
Seven Modernizations, 1121
Seven Sisters (oil producers), 251, 1212
Severe Acute Respiratory Syndrome (SARS),
        764–765, 1452
Sewage treatment wastes. See Waste; Waste management
Sex slavery, Sudan and, 1503–1504
Sex tourism, 1399–1400
Sex trade/trafficking, 1399–1401
Sexually transmitted diseases (STDs). See also HIV/AIDS
    syphilis, 822–823
    United Nations Population Fund and, 1628
Sexual slavery, 522
Sex work, child, 317–318
Seybou, Col. Ali, 1141
Seychelles, 1401–1403
    COMESA and, 369
    Economic Commission for Africa and, 528–530
    history and economic development, 1460–1462
Seychelles Democratic Party, 1401
Seychelles National Party (Parti Seselwei), 1401

Seychelles People's Progressive Front, 1401
Seychelles People's United Party, 1401
Shadow economy, 180–184. *See also* Black market
Shadra caste, 1640
Shah, King Zahir, 1091
Shanghai Five summit, 520
Sharecropping, 7
   multiple sources of risk, 1257
Shar'iah (Islamic law), 955, 1595
Sharm el Sheikh, 76, 77
Sharon, Ariel, 80, 861, 1229
Shastri, Lal Behadur, 803
Shehu Shagari, Ahaji, 1142
Shell Oil, 53, 171, 1029
   Caspian Sea and, 305
   in Nigeria, 649–650
   OPEC and, 251, 1212
Shenouda III, 396
Shevardnadze, Eduard, 382
Shigellosis, 821
Shi'ite Muslims, 1027
   in Bahrain, 133
   in Lebanon, 335
Shinawatra, Thaksin, 338
Shining Path (*Sendero Lominoso*). *See Sendero Luminoso*
Shipping industry
   Black Star Line (Ghana), 1147
   flags of convenience, 1006
   International Maritime Organization (IMO), 845
Shiva, Vanadna, 827
Shonekan, Ernest, 1142
Shushkevich, Stanislav, 163
Siad Barre, Gen. Mohammed, 505–506, 1404–1405.
     See also Somalia
SICA (*Sistema de Integracion Centoamericana*), 280
Sierra Leone, 1405–1407. *See also* West Africa
   Basic Education and Life Skills (BELS) program, 545
   caste system, 1406
   diamond production, 250
   Economic Commission for Africa and, 528–530
   ethnic conflict, 627, 628
   Lomé Accord, 1406–1407
   Revolutionary United Front, 1406
Sihamoni, Norodom, 216
Sihanouk, Prince Norodom, 216, 907–908, 1407–1408.
     See also Cambodia
Sikhism, 1408–1409
Sikhs, in India, 692–693
Silent Spring (Carson), 574
Siles Zuazo, Hernán, 46, 48, 50, 185
Silié Valdez, Arturo, 111
Silk production, Central Asia, 299
Silk Road, 126, 299
SILOS (*Systemas locales de salud*) health care
   organizations, 749
Silva, José Ferreira de la, 1410
Silva, Luíz Inácio "Lula" da, 201, 1409–1411, 1478–1479
Silver mining, Central Africa, 261
Sinai Peninsula, 70, 1157, 1382. *See also* Arab-Israeli Wars;
   Israel; Palestine
Singapore, 948–949, 1411–1414
   ASEAN and, 97, 112–116, 1455–1456
   Asian "economic miracle" and, 101
   banking, 1413
   Central Provident Fund, 949

colonial legacy, 1454
Communist movements in, 1455
development and sovereignty quest, 1411–1412
early development, 1450
early poverty, 1411
financial crisis, 1412–1413, 1451
foreign direct investment, 1412
globalization and, 711
Goh Chok Tong, 712
governance, 1413
history, 1411
Human Development Index, 1413
Indonesia-Malaysia-Singapore growth triangle, 1529
infrastructure, 1413
Lee Kwan Yew, 1449, 1450
as market economy, 1412
as Newly Industrialized Economy, 1131
People's Action Party (PAP), 1413
per capita income, 1413
shadow economy, 181
Singapore-Johor-Riau growth triangle, 1529
technology transfer and, 1131–1132
Singapore Declaration, 373–374
Singapore-Johor-Riau growth triangle, 1529
Singh, Dr. Manmohan, 804
Singh, Vishnawanath, 804
Single European Act of 1986, 955
Single-party government
   class analysis and, 1415
   Communism and, 1414–1415
   economic development and, 1416
   nationalism and, 1415
   non-ideological, 1416
   non-Marxist states, 1414
   states having, 1414–1415
Sinhalese people, 1489, 1490
Sino-Soviet (socialist) law, 955–956
Sino-Soviet split, 293, 328, 330
Sint Eustatius, 1126. *See also* Netherlands Antilles
Sint Maarten, 1126. *See also* Netherlands Antilles
SIPR (Stockholm International Peace Research Institute), 90
SIPs (Sectoral Import Programs), 965
Sirte Declarations, 1204
Sisal production
   Bahamas, 132
   Tanzania, 1523
Sislu, Walter, 10, 11
Sison, José Maria, 1130
Sistema de Integracion Centoamericana (SICA), 280
Sisterhood Is Global Institute, 878
Sisulu, Walter, 1463
Sivaraska, Sulak, 859
Six-Day War, 70, 71, 72, 76–77, 161, 883, 1038
Siyad Barre, General Mohammed, 1433
Skate, Bill, 1240
Skoepol, Theda, 1423–1424
Slash-and-burn cultivation, 1474. *See also* Haze pollution
   as subsistence living, 1501
Slavery
   African Diaspora and, 6–7
   Antigua and Barbuda, 56
   Bahamas, 131–132
   Barbados, 155
   Belgian colonies, 262
   Brazil, 1475–1476

Caribbean ethnic conflicts and, 586
Central African Republic, 272
colonialism and, 364, 365
Dominica, 483
East Africa, 500
Ethiopia, 1393
founding of Liberia and, 959
French Guiana, 683
Grenada, 720
Guyana, 1179
Haiti, 588
Maroons, 7, 588, 1350, 1507
Martinique, 998
Mauritania, 1004–1005
Oceania, 1190
as practiced by Africans, 1606
as practiced by Arabs, 1606
Rastafarianism and, 1350
sexual, 522
Sierra Leone, 1405–1406
South Africa, 1439
St. Helena, 1492
St. Vincent, 1494
Sudan, 1501, 1503–1504
sugar cane and, 357–358
Suriname, 1507
Tobago, 1571
Triangle Trade, 357–358, 1696
Trinidad, 1571
United States Virgin Islands, 1670
Virgin Islands, 1669
West Africa, 1695–1696
Slave trade, Oceania, 1190–1191
Slovak Republic, 430, 431, 1416–1418
    Black Sea Economic Cooperation Organization
        and, 183–184
    displaced Hungarians in, 593
    Gabcikovo-Nagymaros Project dispute, 1622
    geography and climate, 1416–1417
    privatization, 1324
    Visehrad Four and, 1672–1673
Slovenia, 187, 287, 1418–1419
    establishment, 135
    independence, 290, 1749–1750
    international relations, 294
Slovenian language, 136
Slovo, Joe, 11
Smallholders. See Peasants
Small Is Beautiful (Schumacher), 574
Smallpox, 820
Smaze (smoke haze), 116, 445–446, 1419–1420
Smith, Adam, 1121, 1559–1560
Smith, Ian, 1090, 1757
Smith, Robert Angus, 2
Smith, Sen. Alexander, 686
Smith-Mundt Act, 686–687
Smithsonian Museum of Natural History, species count, 178–179
Smoking-related illnesses, 1331
Smuggling, during Prohibition, 132
Smuts, Jan, 1440
Snowball Earth period, 705
Sobers, Garfield, 155
Sobhuza II, King, 1512–1513
SoCal, 251, 1029
Socarrá, Carlos Prio, 158

Social Democratic Front (Cameroon), 218
Social Democratic Party (Brazilian), 228
Social initiatives
    Albania, 27
    Alliance for Progress and, 33
    APEC, 109
    Association of Caribbean States, 111
    to Central America, 282–283
    Chile, 322–323
    Costa Rica, 402
    Cuba, 414
    decolonization and, 368
    East Asia, 512
    Kyrgyzstan, 928
    Saudi Arabia, 1392
    Seychelles, 1401
    Somalia, 1405
    Soviet Union, 300
    Turkmenistan, 1579
Socialism, 1424–1426. See also Socialist economic model
    Cold War and, 1425
    collapse of and trade policy, 1563
    contradictions of capitalism and, 1425
    cooperative, 239
    denial of democracy and, 1425
    industrialization under, 814–815
    Julius Nyerere and, 1188
    labor and, 932
    legal system, 955–956
    Leninist model, 1425–1426
    Marxian model, 1425
    military, 1555
    as social order, 1424–1425
    Stalinist model, 1425–1426
    Trotsky's world revolution model, 1425
Socialist economic model. See also Socialism
    Castro's Cuban, 1428
    Central European "human face," 1428
    cooperative market socialism, 1428
    Gorbachev's human-face, 1428
    Lenin's, 1427
    market (Lange) socialism, 1427–1428
    Marxist, 1426–1427
    Romanian isolationist, 1428
    Stalinist, 1427
    standard of living and, 1428
    Tito's cooperative, 1428
Socialist Party (Chile), 31–32
Social Origins of Dictatorship and Democracy (Moore), 1422
Social revolution, 1420–1424
    Arendt's democratic theory, 1421
    definitions, 1420
    evidence of, 1421
    globalization of, 1424
    Gurr's psychological theory, 1421–1422
    Huntingdon's description of, 1421
    internal causality of, 1424
    internal war theory of, 1424
    J-curve theory of Davies, 1421–1422
    Johnson's social systemic theory, 1422
    Johnson's theory of force and violence, 1420–1421
    lag and disharmony theories, 1422
    Marxist-Leninist theory, 1423
    normative and cultural change theory, 1421
    process modeling of, 1422

Social revolution (*Continued*)
  relative deprivation theory, 1321
  rising expectations theory, 1421–1422
  Skoepol's class struggle theory, 1423–1424
  social subversion theory, 1422
  structuralist theories, 1422
  Tilly's power-conflict theory, 1423
  Wolf's North Atlantic capitalism theory, 1422
Social systemic theory, 1422–1423
Society
  civil, 346–348
  defined, 346
Sociolinguistics, 941
Soglo, General Christophe, 167
Soil degradation, 1286
  agricultural globalization and, 13
  agricultural privatization and, 20–21
  Aral Sea, 299, 1286, 1374, 1648
  erosion and, 581
  irrigation and, 1286
  St. Christopher and Nevis, 1490
Soilihi, Ali, 387
Solar energy, 559
Solidarity Movement (Poland), 890, 1429–1431,
      1655, 1676. *See also* Walesa, Lech
  Round Table Agreement, 1676
  Rural Solidarity, 1430
Solomon Island Development Trust, 616
Solomon Islands, 1431–1432
  Bougainville Women for Peace and Freedom, 1432
  demographics, 1191
  ethnic conflict, 616
  Honiara Peace Accord, 1431
  Malaita and, 1431
  Marau Peace Agreement, 1431
  Townsville Peace Agreement, 1431
  women's rights, 1431–1432
Solomon Islands Alliance for Change, 1431
Solow model of economic growth, 1497
Somalia, 1432–1434. *See also* East Africa
  arms embargo, 90
  colonial history, 501
  Economic Commission for Africa and, 528–530
  Ethiopian invasion, 416
  ethnic communities, 1432–1433, 1434
  ethnic conflicts, 1405, 1433
  geography and climate, 1432
  humanitarian relief, 786
  Kenya and, 1204
  peacekeeping, 1254
  remittances, 1432
  social initiatives, 1405
  Soviet Union and, 1405
  Supreme Revolutionary Council, 1405
  territorial disputes, 1536
  trusteeship, 1632
  United States and, 507, 1405
Somalian Salvation Democratic Front, 1433
Somali caste systems, 255
Somali National Movement, 1433
Somali Patriotic Movement, 1433
Somare, Michael, 1240
Somoza, Luis, 392–393
Somoza Debayle, Anastasio, 392–393, 1134, 1137,
      1389, 1434–1435

Somoza Debayle, Luis, 1134–1135
Somoza García, Anastasio, 1134, 1136–1137, 1435
Somoza Garcia, Augusto, 392
Songhai people, 1140
Songhay (Songhai) Empire, 1694–1695
Sorami language, 920
Sorghum production, Central Africa, 261
Soros, George, market fundamentalism theory, 1438
Soros Foundation Network, 1435–1438
  institutions, 1436
  open society alliance, 1437–1438
  open society idea, 1435–1436
  programs and other initiatives, 1436–1437
Sosso people, 733
Sotho people, 1512
Sotho-Tswana people, 1439
Souphanovong, Prince, 1249–1250
South, countries of the. *See* Third World
South Africa, 1438–1441. *See also* African National Congress;
      Afrikaners; Mandela, Nelson
  agrarian reform, 935
  Angola and, 1293
  apartheid, 622–623, 1439
  Bantu Authorities Act, 1462
  barred from sports events, 1204
  Bishop Desmond Tutu, 1580–1581
  Botswana and, 190–191
  COMESA and, 369
  Defiance Campaign, 1440
  Democratic Party, 1463
  Development Bank of, 4
  D.F. Malan, 979–980
  diamond production, 250, 1461
  Die Burger newspaper, 979–980
  Economic Commission for Africa and, 528–530
  economic sanctions, 1386, 1581
  education, 1441
  geography and climate, 1438
  gold production, 1461
  Great Trek, 622. *See also* Afrikaners
  history, 1439, 1460–1462
  Immorality Act, 1462
  independence movement, 30
  Land Acts, 153. *See also* Native Reserves
  Mfecane (great upheaval), 621–622
  mining industry, 648
  national parks, 1245
  National Party, 30, 58, 61–62, 188–189, 190–191, 435–436,
      989–990, 1440, 1462
  National Security Management System, 61, 189
  Native Reserves, 332–333, 903, 980, 1002
  Natives Land Act, 935, 1439–1440, 1462
  Natives Representative Councils, 1462
  Nkoniti Accord on Non-Aggression and Good
      Neighborliness, 973
  Organization of African Unity and, 1203–1204
  Populations Registration Act, 1440, 1462
  private property rights in, 1321
  Prohibition of Mixed Marriages Act, 1462
  Promotion of Black Self-Government Acts, 1440
  provinces of, 1438–1439
  Sauer Report, 980
  shadow economy, 181
  Southern African Customs Union and, 1468–1470
  Soweto Massacre, 1440

Thabo Mbeki, 1006–1007
Tomlinson Report, 980
Tricameral Parliament, 189
wars waged by, 189
white community, 1706–1707. *See also* Afrikaners
South African Coloured People's Organization
  (SACPO), 11
South African Communist Party, 1463
South African Congress of Trade Unions (SACTO), 11
South African National Party, 30, 58, 188–191,
  989–990, 1462
South African Native National Congress, 10
South African Student Movement (SASM), 11
South African Students Association (SASO), 59–60
South America. *See also* Latin America *and*
  individual countries
  Alliance for Progress, 1635
  Andean. *See* Andean Community; Andean
    South America
  arms industrialization, 93–94
  authoritarianism in, 123
  Black Market Peso Exchange, 1077
  bureaucratic authoritarianism in, 208
  development and colonization, 458–459
  Free Trade Area of the Americas (FTAA), 1638
  mining industry, 648
  northern, 1176–1181. *See also* Northern South America *and*
    specific countries
  Organization of American States (OAS), 1205–1207
  slavery and emancipation, 7
South American Common Market. *See* MERCOSUR
South Asia, poverty in, 1311, 1312
South Asian Association for Regional Cooperation
  (SAARC), 1441–1444
  external threat perception and, 1443
  founding nations, 1441–1442
  Kashmir dispute and, 1443
South Asian Regional Cooperation (SARC), 1442. *See also*
  South Asian Association for Regional Cooperation
Southeast Asia. *See also* Tiger economies; *individual nations*
  ASEAN and, 1449–1450, 1455–1456. *See also* ASEAN
  Chinese suzerainty in, 1453
  Cold War and, 1454
  colonialism in, 1446–1447
  colonial legacy in, 1454
  Communist threat to, 1454
  environmental issues, 1452
  ethnic conflicts, 618–620
  financial crisis, 1451–1452
  geography and climate, 1446
  history and economic development, 1446–1452
  international development implications, 1457
  international relations, 1453–1457. *See also* ASEAN
  irredentism and autonomous movements, 1455
  Japan (post-war) and, 1456–1457
  migration issues, 1456
  nationalism in, 1447–1448
  original state formation in, 1453
  population growth, 1452
  post-independence development, 1448–1449
  reform and economic growth, 1449–1451
  Severe Acute Respiratory Syndrome (SARS), 764–765, 1452
South East Asian Centre for Educational Innovation and
  Technology, 545
Southeast Asian Tigers, 1450

Southeast Asia Treaty Organization (SEATO), 94, 1458
  founding members, 1458
  Manila Pact, 1458
Southern Africa
  apartheid and, 1462–1463. *See also* Apartheid;
    South Africa
  countries comprising, 1464
  definition of region, 1459
  democratization, 1463–1464
  diamond production, 1461
  Economic Commission for Africa and, 528–530
  European migration to, 1459
  extractive industries, 1461
  global relations, 1467
  gold production, 1461
  history and economic development, 1459–1464
  HIV/AIDS and, 1467
  indigenous peoples, 1459
  inter-African relations, 1466–1467
  international relations, 1464–1468
  international relations within, 1465–1466
  landlocked countries, 1461
  land reform controversies, 1466–1467
  New Partnership for Africa's Development (NEPAD)
    and, 11466
  precursors of post-1945 development, 1459–1460
Southern African Customs Union (SACU), 1468–1470
  institutions, 1469
Southern African Development Community (SADC), 5, 369,
  1463, 1464, 1470–1471
Southern African Development Coordination Conference
  (SADCC), 506, 1470. *See also* Southern African
  Development Community
Southern Cone (Latin America). *See also* Argentina; Brazil;
  Chile; Paraguay; Uruguay
  countries comprising, 1474
  geography and climate, 1474–1475
  history and economic development, 1474–1480
  international relations, 1479–1480, 1480–1487
  MERCOSUR and, 1472–1474, 1480
Southern Cone Common Market, 39. *See* MERCOSUR
Southern Rhodesia. *See also* Rhodesia
  independence movement, 30
South Korea, 916–919. *See also* East Asia
  agrarian reform, 935
  anti-communism in, 514
  arms exports, 96
  arms industrialization, 94
  arms industry, 95
  ASEAN and, 1455
  Asian "economic miracle" and, 101, 102–103
  banking, 149
  banking crises, 150
  boundary disputes, 18, 517
  chaebol conglomerates, 103, 107, 514–515
  civic education, 340
  culture and economy, 918
  currency devaluation, 424
  democratization, 709
  economic development, 511–512, 916–917
  education, 769–770
  financial crisis, 1451
  globalization and, 711
  Import Substitution Industrialization, 515
  innovation studies, 1530

South Korea (*Continued*)
  Inter-Korean Joint Declaration and, 523
  monetary policy, 150
  as Newly Industrialized Economy, 1131
  North Korea and, 522–523
  Syngman Rhee, 1364–1365
  technology transfer and, 1131–1132
  territorial disputes, 1535
  tiger economy, 106, 917–918
South Ossethia territorial dispute, 1533
South Pacific, demographics, 1191
South Pacific Forum, 1219. *See also* Pacific Islands Forum
South West Africa People's Organization (SWAPO), 1101,
  1444–1445, 1536
Sovhozes (collective farms), 19. *See also*
  Agricultural privatization
Soviet Bloc, 1487–1488. *See also* Central and Eastern Europe;
  Central and Eastern Europe *and individual countries;*
  Cold War; Soviet Union
  arms industry and, 94–95
  arms trade, 78
  Velvet Revolution, 289, 294, 430, 496, 592–593, 713, 1416,
    1654–1657
Soviet-Nazi Non-Aggression Pact, 288–1496, 963–964
Soviet Union. *See also* Russia
  abortion in, 654–655
  Afghanistan invasion, 4, 303, 416, 1091, 1520
  agrarian reform, 935
  Algeria and, 1166
  in Angola, 54
  arms transfer, 41–42, 75, 76, 77
  Aswan High Dam financing, 118
  Austria and, 288
  in Azerbaijan, 126–127
  Basarabia and, 1074
  Belarus and, 162–163
  Berlin Wall, 170–171
  in Central Africa, 263
  Central/Eastern Europe and, 285
  Chechen wars, 596–599
  Chernobyl disaster, 379, 563, 1373
  collapse of, 89, 96, 290, 345, 380–381, 417, 1175, 1375
  Commonwealth of Independent States and, 375–380, 713
  Cuba and, 246, 257, 414, 417
  Cuban Missile Crisis, 246
  Czech invasion, 496
  de-Stalinization, 455–456, 914, 1427
  domino theory and, 486
  in East Africa, 505
  Economic Cooperation Organization and, 304
  economy of Eastern Europe and, 288
  Egypt and, 1381
  in El Salvador, 279
  environmental issues, 2
  Estonia and, 583
  ethnic conflicts, 591
  Finland and, 288
  Five-Year Plans, 385, 1372–1373
  foreign aid expenditures, 1374
  German nonagression pact, 963–964
  glasnost and *perestroika*, 289, 596, 702–703, 712–713, 1374
  in Guatemala, 279
  Ho Chi Minh and, 761
  Hungarian Revolution and, 788
  Indonesia and, 1507

  Iran and, 311
  Kurds in, 920
  Kyrgyzstan and, 928
  Latvia and, 946–947
  Libya and, 1167
  Living Church movement, 1376
  Marxism and, 1001
  Mexico and, 1021
  Middle East and, 130, 1035
  Mongolia and, 1078
  in Nicaragua, 279
  nomenklatura, 703
  Non-Aligned Movement and, 1148
  North Korea and, 914
  nuclear testing, 902
  oil production, 646–647
  Poland and, 889–890, 1280, 1429
  Romania and, 259
  Russian Orthodox Church and, 1376–1377
  social initiatives, 300
  Somalia and, 1405
  South West Africa People's Organization and, 1445
  split with China, 293, 327, 330
  Stalinist model of socialism, 1425
  Syria and, 1513
  Tajikistan and, 302–303, 1519
  as totalitarian state, 1555, 1556
  Turkmenistan and, 1578–1579
  Vietnam and, 760, 1450
  wheat blight, 179
  Zemstvo system of health care, 747
Sovkhosy (collective farms), 23, 162
Soweto Massacre, 11, 60, 1440
Spain
  Algeria and, 1166
  Morocco and, 1164
  territorial disputes, 1532
Spanish-American War, 1200
  Caribbean region and, 245
  Guam and, 724
Spanish colonies, 356–357
  Central Africa, 263
  Central America, 273–274
Spanish Sahara, 29
Spear of the Nation (*Umkhonto we Sizwe*), 11, 59–60, 967
Special Drawing Rights (SDRs), 144, 848
Special Economic Zones, China, 644
Special-relationship development, 465
Special-resource development, 465
Species extinction, 1708–1713. *See also* Wildlife preservation
Spender, Percy, 353
Spice trade
  colonialism and, 359
  Comoros islands, 387
Spillover effects, 268, 675
  of war, 1678
SPLA (Sudanese People's Liberation Army), 502
Spratly Islands, 1241–1242
Sranan Tongo language, 1508
Sri Lanka, 1488–1489
  agricultural privatization, 20
  Asian Development Bank and, 100–101
  in Bandung Conference, 139–140
  education, 545
  ethnic conflict, 1489

Green Revolution and, 717–718
Gum Adava (Village Awakening), 1489
Indian conflict, 804
Liberation Tigers, 694–695
resources, 1489
South Asian Association for Regional Cooperation and, 1441–1444
suicide rate, 1014
tsunami of 2004, 1489
St. Barthéleme, 723. *See also* Guadaloupe
St. Croix, 1670
St. Helena, 1491–1492
St. Kitts and Nevis, 1490–1491
Association of Caribbean States and, 111
Caribbean Basin Initiative and, 232–233
Caribbean Community and Common Market and, 233–235
Caribbean Development Bank and, 235–237
Caribbean Free Trade Association and, 237–238
international relations, 249
Nevis Island Assembly, 1491
People's Action Movement (PAM), 1491
St. Lucia, 1493–1494
Association of Caribbean States and, 111
Caribbean Basin Initiative and, 232–233
Caribbean Community and Common Market and, 233–235
Caribbean Free Trade Association and, 237–238
St. Martin, 723, 1126. *See also* Guadaloupe
St. Thomas, 1670
St. Vincent and the Grenadines, 1494–1495
Caribbean Basin Initiative and, 232–233
Caribbean Community and Common Market and, 233–235
Caribbean Development Bank and, 235–237
Caribbean Free Trade Association and, 237–238
international relations, 248
Stabilization of Export Earnings (STABEX), 965
(The) Stages of Economic Growth: A Non-Communist Manifesto (Rostow), 459–460, 1635
Stagflation, 1121
Stalin, Joseph, 287, 291, 380, 712, 760, 1001, 1372–1373, 1495–1496
de-Stalinization, 455–456, 1427
Nikita Khrushchev and, 910–911
Russian Orthodox Church and, 1376
Soviet-Nazi Non-Aggression Pact, 288, 1496
Tito and, 1551–1552
Stalinist model of socialism, 1425, 1427
Standard Oil of New Jersey, 171
in Peru, 41
Stanger, Margaret, 655
State (political), role of, 16
State-directed economies, 1496–1497
Solow model of economic growth, 1497
State intervention. *See* Government intervention
Statement of Forest Principles, 1510
State of the World's Children Report (UNICEF), 1602
State Peace and Development Council, 1098
States and Social Revolution (Skoepol), 1423–1424
State terror, 473
Steppes, of Central Asia, 297
Sterilization programs, 654–655
Sterling Zone, 1166
Stockholm Declaration on the Human Environment, 570
Stockholm International Peace Research Institute (SIPR), 90
Strasser, Captain Valentine, 1406
Strategic Hamlet Program, 1105
Strategic trade theory, 1560

(The) Strategy of Development (Hirschman), 755
Streeten, Paul, 156
Streptococcus pneumoniae, 821
Strikes. *See also* Organized labor
Chilean, 31–32
Durban, 11
South Africa, 10–11
tactical uses, 227
Stroesser, Adolfo, 1485
Stroesser, Alfredo, 1242–1243, 1485–1486, 1497–1498
Stroesser, Gustavo, 1485
Structural adjustment programs (SAPs), 441, 442, 461, 849, 904, 928, 1498–1500
description, 1498–1499
effectiveness, 1500–1501
Ghana, 701
Mauritius, 1005–1006
Mongolia, 1078–1079
Morocco, 1084
peasants and, 1256
privatization and, 1323, 1500–1501
public sector reform, 1331–1333
trade liberalization, 1500
Turkey, 1577
Uruguay, 1647
Venezuela, 1179
Structural-functionalist theory, 1069
Structuralism, 667, 1319–1320, 1561, 1614–1616. *See also* Foreign direct investment; Neo-Marxist theory
neostructuralism, 1617
Sub-Saharan Africa
banking in, 149
literacy, 543
Subsidization, agricultural, 13, 14
Subsistence agriculture. *See also* Subsistence living
agricultural privatization and, 24
French Guiana, 1181
globalization and, 12
Maldives, 984
Nigeria, 1143
Palau, 1225
privatization and, 21
Rwanda, 1378
Vanuatu, 1653
Subsistence economies, of indigenous people, 625
Subsistence first economic orientation, 1257
Subsistence living
egalitarianism, 1500
foraging, 1500
generalized reciprocity, 1500
horticulture, 1501
pastoralism, 1500–1501
Substance abuse and dependence, 1013–1014. *See also* Drug trafficking
Sudan, 1501–1504. *See also* East Africa
arms embargo, 90
Aswan High Dam and, 117
colonial history, 501–502
COMESA and, 369
debt, 223, 371
decolonization, 361–362
Economic Commission for Africa and, 528–530
geography and climate, 1501–1502
health care, 748
health issues, 1503

Sudan (*Continued*)
  history, 1502
  Human Development Index, 659
  independence movement, 30
  political history, 1502–1503
  Sha'ria laws and, 1503
  slavery, 1501, 1503–1504
  territorial disputes, 1536, 1692
  UNICEF in, 1603
Sudanese People's Liberation Army, 502, 1503, 1536
Suez War, 75–76, 116, 219–220, 548, 612, 1035–1036, 1159.
      See also Egypt
  United Nations Emergency Force in, 1252
  Yasser Arafat in, 79
Sufism, 1504–1506
Sugar production
  Antigua and Barbuda, 56
  British Virgin Islands, 1669
  Central Africa, 261
  Cuba, 159, 257, 414
  Guatemala, 725
  Guyana, 1179, 1185
  Haiti, 740–741
  producer cartels, 250
  Puerto Rico, 1200
  St. Christopher and Nevis, 1490, 1491
  St. Lucia, 1494
  Triangle Trade, 357–358, 1696
  United States Virgin Islands, 1670
Suharto, 619, 810, 1449
  in Bandung Conference, 139–140
Suicide, 1014–1016
Sukarno, 809–810, 1506–1507
  in Bandung Conference, 139–140
  Guided Democracy, 1506
Sukarnoputri, Megawati, 734–735, 810. *See also*
      Indonesia; Sukarno
Sulfur dioxide pollution, 1–2, 1289
Sumatra, Aceh independence, 1455
Sunni Muslims, 1027
  Ba'ath Party and. *See* Ba'ath Party
  in Bahrain, 133
  in Lebanon, 947–948
  in Libya, 961
  in Syria, 609
  in Tajikistan, 1518
Sun Tzu, 728. *See also* Guerrilla warfare
Sun Yat-sen, 326
Supreme Council of Private Enterprise (COSEP), 1138
Suriname, 1180, 1185–1186, 1507–1509
  Caribbean Community and Common Market and, 233–235
  Caribbean Development Bank and, 235–237
  CARICOM and, 1185
  Central Suriname Nature Reserve, 1508
  international relations, 1185–1186
  rainforest, 1508
  slavery, 1507
  territorial disputes, 1185
Sustainability
  agricultural globalization and, 14
  agricultural privatization and, 20
Sustainable Cities Program, 1600
Sustainable development, 468, 1290–1291, 1509–1512
  extractive industries and, 648–650
  growth vs. development, 1509

  intergenerational equity, 1622–1623
  International Court of Justice and, 1622
  international park system and, 1244–1245
  terminology, 1509
  UNICO and, 1620–1621
  water resource, 1672
Sustaining Export-Oriented Development: Ideas from Asia
      (Grilli and Riedel), 643
Susu groups, 151
Svododa, Ludwik, 1319
Swahili language, 500–501
Swahili peoples, 500–501
SWAPO. *See* South West Africa People's Organization
Swaziland, 1512–1513
  COMESA and, 369
  decolonization, 361–362
  Economic Commission for Africa and, 528–530
  history and economic development, 1460–1462
  as Native Reserve, 1461
  Southern African Customs Union and, 1468–1470
Swaziland Independence Constitution, 1512
Sweatshops, 551
Sweden, income inequality in, 1311
Swedish International Development Agency, 1692
Sweezy, Paul, 460, 461
Switch trading, 407
Switzerland, international banks in, 151
Swynnerton Plan, 1003
Sykes, Mark, 135
Sykes-Picot Agreement, 69, 135, 495, 947, 1226
Syngman Rhee, 1364–1365
Syphilis, 822–823
Syria, 1513–1514
  Alawi people, 608–609, 632
  Ba'ath Party in, 71, 129–130, 1038, 1598
  Christianity in, 336
  Druze in, 495, 609
  independence, 1033–1034
  international relations, 1036
  Kurdistan and, 920
  League of Arab States and, 71–72
  OAPEC and, 1208
  occupation of Lebanon, 79
  in Palestinian conflict, 74
  Palestinian refugees in, 1230–1231
  privatization in, 1323
  Six-Day War and, 77, 1038
  Soviet Union and, 1513
  state economic dominance, 1031
  Sunni Muslims in, 609
  United Arab Republic (UAR) and, 69–70, 130, 1103,
      1159, 1597–1598
  war with Jordan, 70–71
SYSMIN, 965
Systemas locales de salud (SILOS) health care
      organizations, 749
System of Central American Integration, 280

T

Tabrizi, Ahmad Kasravi, 878
Tacna, 43
Tadzhik tribe territorial dispute, 1534
Tafari, Ras, 1350. *See also* Rastafarianism
Ta'if Accord, 948

Taiwan, 1515–1518. *See also* East Asia; Tiger economies
  agrarian reform, 935
  agricultural development, 1516
  anti-communism in, 514
  Asian "economic miracle" and, 101, 102–103
  Asia-Pacific Economic Cooperation and, 108
  Chiang Ching-Kuo, 313–314
  Chiang Kai-shek and, 313–315
  China and, 1517–1518
  civil society, 1517
  democratization, 709
  Dominican Republic and, 245
  economic development, 511–512
  GDP per capita, 1515
  geography and climate, 1515
  globalization and, 711
  Import Substitution Industrialization, 515
  indigenous rights movement, 1517
  industrial development, 1516
  information technology sector, 1517
  as Newly Industrialized Economy, 1131
  nuclear energy, 1517
  nuclear wastes, 1517
  political and economic restructuring, 1517
  political history, 1516–1517
  reunification proponents, 1518
  sovereignty issue with China, 521–522
  Spratly Islands claims, 1241
  technology transfer, 1131–1132
  territorial disputes, 1535
  Women's Awakening Foundation, 1517
Tajikistan, 299, 300, 1518–1520
  civil war, 302–303
  Commonwealth of Independent States and, 375–380
  Economic Cooperation Organization and, 537–538
  education, 543
  ethnic conflicts, 594–595
  independence, 383
  international relations, 303
  literacy, 543
  privatization, 1324
  Soviet Union and, 302–303, 1519
  Uzbekistan and, 303
Take Shima (Lioncort Rocks) territorial dispute, 1535
Talabani, Jalal, 923–924
Taliban, 299–300, 381, 489, 1092, 1224, 1520–1522, 1534.
        See also Afghanistan; Islamic fundamentalism
  Pakistan and, 1521–1522
Talmud, 894
Tamanantsoa, Gabriel, 973
Tambo, Oliver, 10, 11, 1463
Tambora volcanic eruption, 704, 1114
Tamerlane, 3
Tamil people, 1489, 1490
Tanganika African National Union (TANU), 1188
Tanganyika, 502. *See also* Tanzania
  independence, 30
  trusteeship, 1632
Tanganyika African Association, 1522–1523
Tanganyika African National Union (TANU), 1415, 1522–1524
Tantalite, 649
Tantulum, 649
Tanzania, 1522–1525. *See also* East Africa
  agrarian reform, 934–935
  arms transfer, 212

  CIDA in, 221
  COMESA and, 369
  debt holdings, 371, 444
  diamond production, 250
  East African Community and, 503, 508–510
  Economic Commission for Africa and, 528–530
  GDP per capita, 1523
  geography and climate, 1522
  history, 1460–1462, 1522–1523
  language planning and, 940
  national parks, 1245, 1710
  neoliberalism and, 1121
  political history, 502–503
  revolt in, 11
  Seychelles *coup d'etat* and, 1401
  Southern African Development Community and, 1463
  Uganda and, 37, 600, 1188
  Ujamaa Vijinji (Socialism in the Village), 1188, 1524
Tanzania–Zambia pipeline, 900
Taraki, Nur Mohammad, 4, 1091
Tariffs. *See also* GATT
  agricultural privatization and, 21
  agriculture and, 13–14
  ASEAN and, 97–98, 113
  Common External Tariff, 243
Tariff Schedule of the United States, classification 807, 549
Tarzi, Mahmud, 3
Tashkent Agreement, 898
Taylor, Charles, 798, 960, 1406
Taylor, Frederick, 226
Tbilisi, territorial disputes, 1533
TCDD, 1683. *See also* Air pollution; Pollution
Tchicaya, Felix, 389
Tea production
  Central Africa, 261
  Rwanda, 1378
Technological innovation. *See also* Technology;
        Technology transfer
  agricultural privatization and, 20
  agriculture and, 17. *See also* Biotechnology
  in Albania, 27
  Southeast Asia, 1450
Technological resources, 768. *See also* Information
        technology; Technology
Technology
  alternative, 1593
  catch-up efforts, 1528
  China and, 1527–1528
  development and, 1525–1531
  as exogenous production factor, 1526
  governments and, 1526
  innovation clusters, 1528–1530, 1643
  Japanese foreign direct investment and, 1527
  learning and educational issues, 1525–1527, 1527–1528
  official development assistance, 1528
  original brand manufacture, 1527
  original design manufacture, 1527
  original equipment manufacture, 1526–1527
  premises of technology transfer, 1525
  transport cost reduction and, 1529
Technology transfer, 1069
  ESCAP and, 1609–1610
  foreign direct investment and, 1528
  Mekong Basin Development Corporation, 99
  multinational corporations and, 1094–1095

Technology transfer (*Continued*)
  Newly Industrialized Economies (NIEs) and, 1131–1132
  Oceania, 1196–1197
  principles of, 1525
Tehran Conference, 1496
Tejudin (Genghis Khan), 3
Telecommunications
  in Cameroon, 219
  India, 804
  International Telecommunication Union (ITU), 854
  Mekong Basin Development Corporation and, 99
  tantulum production and, 649
Television
  al-Jazeera, 1032
  North Africa, 1162
Teller Amendment, 245
Temne people, 627
Temperature, urbanization and, 1645
Temple, Archbishop William, 1729
Tenant farming, 7
Terai Arc Landscape Program, 1711
Territorial disputes, 1531–1538
  Abkhazia, 378
  Africa, 1536
  Algeria/Morocco, 1168–1169
  Argentina/Paraguay, 886
    Itaipú Dam and, 885
  Bolivia/Chile, 1473
  Botswana/Namibia, 374
  Brazil/Paraguay, 885
  Central and Eastern Europe, 296
  Colombia, 1182
  as colonial legacy, 364, 367, 470–471, 626–627, 1585, 1697,
    1698–1699. *See also* Balkanization
  dictatorship and, 470–471
  East Africa, 505
  economic reasons, 1531
  Ecuador/Peru, 42–43, 541
  Ethiopia/Eritrea, 505
  Europe, 1532–1533
  Guatemala/Belize, 164, 283
  Guyana/Suriname, 1185
  Guyana/Venezuela, 1185
  Honduras/Nicaragua, 283
  Kashmir (India/Pakistan), 94, 805–807, 897–899, 1443
  Kuril Islands (China/South Korea), 517
  Latin America, 1536–1538
  Middle East and Asia, 1533–1534
  Nagorno-Karabakh, 87–88, 378, 382, 924, 1253, 1533
  Nicaragua/Colombia, 1135
  Nile Basin, 505
  Pakistan/China, 125
  Peru/Venezuela, 1182
  Qatar/Bahrain, 1339
  religious/ethnic reasons, 1531–1532
  Somalia-Eritrea, 505
  Spratly Islands, 1241
  strategic reasons, 1531
  Timor Sea, 525
  Venezuela/Colombia, 1183
  Venezuela/Guyana, 1179, 1183
  Venezuela/Peru, 1182
  water resources and, 1692
  Western Sahara, 1169
Terror
  state, 473
  totalitarian use of, 1556–1557
Terrorism, 1538–1540
  Afghanistan, 299–300, 307
  Argentina, 1082
  Asia-Pacific Economic Cooperation (APEC) and, 109
  Belgian in Central Africa, 262
  Chechen "black widows," 598
  Commonwealth of Independent States and, 379
  Coptic Orthodox Church and, 396, 614
  East Africa, 507–508
  economic sanctions and, 1386, 1387
  Egypt, 1160
  funding of, 109
  HAMAS, 741–743
  Hezbollah, 752–763
  international, 1540
  as Iraq War rationale, 1264
  legal definitions, 1539
  money laundering and, 1076–1077
  motives for, 1539–1540
  Munich Olympics, 37, 71, 883, 1227
  Muslim Brotherhood, 1096
  National Liberation Army (Colombia), 1110
  NATO and, 1175
  Organization of American States and, 1207
  Palestine, 1226–1227
  Palestine Liberation Organization and, 1228–1229
  September 11, 300, 880
  Shining Path (*Sendero Luminoso*). See *Sendero Luminoso*
  Taliban and, 1520–1522
  tools used by, 1539
  US trade agreements and, 679
  USAID and antiterrorism, 1636
  Yasser Arafat and, 79–80
  Yemen and, 1747
Terrorism Act of 1967 (South Africa), 59
Tesso Nilo National Park (Indonesia), 1712
Tetanus (lockjaw), 821
Tewahdo Orthodox Church, 585
Texaco, 171, 1029
  OPEC and, 251, 1212
Textile industry
  Central Africa, 262
  Honduras, 763
  Industrial Revolution and, 813
  Mauritius, 1005
  Puerto Rico, 1201
  sweatshops, 551
Textron, 1201
Thailand, 1540–1542
  ASEAN and, 97, 112–116, 1455–1456
  Asia-Pacific Economic Cooperation and, 108
  banking, 149
  Burmese refugees and, 1456
  Cambodia and, 1456
  Cambodian refugees and, 1454
  colonial legacy, 1454
  Communist movements in, 1455
  currency devaluation, 424
  economy, 98, 1449–1450
  erosion control measures, 582
  ethnic (overseas) Chinese in, 620

ethnic conflicts, 619
financial crises, 150, 337, 1451
geography and climate, 1540
HIV/AIDS, 1542
income inequality, 1311
indigenous peoples, 1540
irrigated and drained area, 871
Mekong Basin Development Corporation, 98–100
monetary policy, 150
as Newly Industrialized Economy, 1131
Patani independence, 1455
religion and, 1457
SEATO and, 1458
Separatist movement, 1542
State Enterprise Labor Relations Act, 1541
Thais, Cambodian massacre of, 908
Thar Desert, 453
Thatcher, Margaret, 139, 171
    Bishop Desmond Tutu and, 1581
    development theory and, 462
    Malvinas/Falkland Islands action, 83, 986–989
    neoliberalism and, 1121
Theiler, Dr. Max, 1366
(A) Theory of Justice (Rawls), 798. See also
        Income distribution
Thermal pollution, 1290
Third Assessment Report (of IGPCC), 705
Third Universal Theory, 961
Third Wave, 449–450
Third World, 459, 1542–1546
    Cold War and, 1543–1544
    conclusion of, 139–140, 1118, 1234–1235–1246, 1506–1507
    definition, 1542
    dependency theory and, 1544
    development measures, 465–466
    modernization theory and, 1544
    origin of term and alternates, 1542–1543
    political history, 1544–1545
    world system theory and, 1544
Thoreau, Henry David, 343
Thorp, Rosemary, 1615
Three Gorges Dam, 520, 1546–1548, 1688
Three Mile Island nuclear meltdown, 563
Tiananmen Square massacre, 328, 451, 519, 1549–1551
Tibet, 520–521, 1548–1549. See also Bhutan
    Bhutan and, 173
    Buddhism in, 1548–1549
    China and, 602, 603
    earthquake of 1950, 1114
    forced Chinese migration to, 1548
    geography and climate, 1548
    migration to India, 1549
Tidal power, 560
Tiger economies, 105–108, 816, 764, 1450. See also Asian Tigers;
        East Asian Tigers
    as Newly Industrialized Economies, 1131
    Singapore, 1411–1414
Tilly, Charles, power-conflict theory, 1423
Timber products
    Belize, 164
    Central Africa, 261
    deforestation and, 444
    Estonia, 583
    as fuel, 562

Ghana, 701
    illegal in national parks, 1245
    Papua New Guinea, 1239
Time deposits, 146
Timor Leste, 1455
    ASEAN and, 1456
    territorial disputes, 1535
TIPAC (Transport Inter-Etat des Pays d'Afrique
        Centrale), 527
Tirios Indians, 1507
Tito, Josip Broz, 135–136, 188, 1001, 1080, 1551–1552,
        1749–1750. See also Yugoslavia
    Bandung Conference, 139–140
    cooperative socialism, 1428
    Croatia and, 411
    Franjo Tudjman and, 1573
    Non-Aligned Movement and, 1148, 1552, 1749
    Slovenia and, 1418
    Soviet Bloc and, 1487
Tlatelolco student massacre, 1018–1019, 1022–1023, 1247–1248
Tobacco-Free Initiative (WHO), 1331
Tobacco products
    Central Africa, 262
    Tanzania, 1523
Tobacco-related illnesses, 1331
Toba people, 625
Tocqueville, Alexis de, 1294, 1320
Togo, 1552–1553. See also West Africa
    authoritarianism in, 123
    Economic Commission for Africa and, 528–530
    West African Monetary Union and, 1703–1705
Tokelau, 1191
Tokes, Pastor Laszlo, 289, 1657
Tolbert, William R., 626, 960
Toledo, Alejandro, 48, 49–50, 50, 64, 685–686
Tomal caste, 255
Tombalbaye, François, 264, 311
Tonga, 1553–1554
    demographics, 1191
    Niue and, 1144
Tongaland, 1512
Tonga people, 1512
Tonkin Gulf Resolution, 1458, 1667
Torah, 894–895
Tornadoes, 1113
Torrey Canyon oil spill, 648
Torriello Garrido, Jorge, 80
Torrijos Hérrera, Omar, 1236, 1238, 1554–1555.
        See also Panama
Totalitarian Dictatorship and Autocracy
        (Friedrich and Brzezinski), 1556
Totalitarianism, 1555–1558
    mobilization of the masses, 1557–1558
    Nazi and Soviet systems and, 1555, 1556
    six traits of, 1556
    terror tactics, 1556–1557
    Third World similarities, 1555–1556
    transition to democracy, 122
    vs. authoritarianism, 121
Toure, Samori, 733
Touré, Sékou, 29, 30, 733, 1147, 1415, 1558–1559
Tourism
    Angola, 55
    Antigua and Barbuda, 56

Tourism (*Continued*)
 Association of Caribbean States and, 111–112
 Bahamas, 132
 Barbados, 247
 Belize, 164–165
 Cambodia, 217
 Caribbean, 239, 241, 1211
 Cayman Islands, 258
 Central Asia, 300
 Dominica, 483–484
 Dominican Republic, 485
 ecotourism. *See* Ecotourism
 Egypt, 548, 1160
 Fiji, 662
 Gambia, 691
 Grenada, 720–721
 Hong Kong, 764
 Kiribati, 912
 Maldives, 984
 Marshall Islands, 997
 Mexico, 1018
 Oceania, 1191
 Palau, 1225
 Panama Canal, 1237
 sex, 1399–1400
 Seychelles, 1401
 Singapore, 949, 1413
 St. Barthéleme, 723
 St. Christopher and Nevis, 1491
 St. Helena, 1492
 St. Lucia, 1494
 Trinidad and Tobago, 1571
 Uzbekistan's potential for, 1649
Townsville Peace Agreement, 1431
Trade
 comparative advantage theory, 1671
 definition, 1559, 1565
 economies of scale and, 1560
 specialization and, 1560
 virtual water, 1671–1672
Trade embargoes, 1386–1388. *See also* Arms embargoes
 Cuba, 414, 418, 687
Trade liberalization
 Africa and, 9
 agricultural privatization and, 21
 agriculture and, 13–14
 migration and, 1045
Trademarks, 827. *See also* Intellectual property rights
Trade policies, 1559–1565
 collapse of socialism and, 1563
 dependency theory and, 1562
 dependistas, 1560–1561
 export-oriented industrialization and, 1562–1563
 Hecksher-Ohlin theorem, 1560
 Holper-Samuelson theorem, 1560
 human rights development and, 773–774
 import substitution industrialization. *See* Import
  substitution industrialization
 liberal perspective, 1560
 Marxist perspective, 1560–1561
 neoliberalism and, 1563
 New International Economic Order and, 1562
 petrodollars and, 1563
 strategic trade theory, 1560
 structuralist school, 1561. *See also* Structuralism

Trade-Related Intellectual Property Rights (TRIP) agreement,
  16, 490, 824–825, 827
Trade unions. *See also* Organized labor
 in Antigua and Barbuda, 56
 World Federation of Trade Unions (WFTU), 1731–1732
Trading patterns, global, 1565–1568. *See also* Global
  trading patterns
Trajkovki, Branko, 971
Transhumance, 1501
Transjordan. *See* Jordan
Transkei Homeland, 153
Transnational corporations. *See* Multinational corporations
Transnational identities, 8
Transnistria, 1074, 1532–1533. *See also* Moldova
Transoxiana, 297. *See also* Central Asia
Transparency, 1568–1570
 compliance and, 1569–1570
 definition, 1568
 historical development of concept, 1569
 information age and, 1569
Transparency International, 398, 1593
Transportation. *See also* Infrastructure
 Association of Caribbean States and, 111
 Central Africa, 272
 colonialism and West African, 1697
 Guinea, 734
 International Air Transport Association (IATA), 830–831
Transport cost reduction, technology transfer and, 1529
Transport Inter-Etat des Pays d'Afrique Centrale (TIPAC), 527
Transvaal National Party, 189. *See also* South Africa
Transylvania
 displaced Hungarians in, 593
 territorial disputes, 1533
Traoré, Moussa, 984–985
Trash. *See also* Waste; Waste management
 defined, 1681
Treason Trial (South Africa), 59–60
Treaty disputes, International Court of Justice, 1621–1623
Treaty of Amsterdam, 955
Treaty of Asunción, 200, 228, 1483. *See·also* MERCOSUR
Treaty of Chaguaramas, 233, 242
Treaty of Laudanne, 923
Treaty of Maastricht, 955
Treaty of Paris, 358, 723
Treaty of Sévres, 923
Treaty of Versailles, 373, 495
Treaty of Westminster, 357
Trek Boers, 58, 622, 1439. *See also* Afrikaners
Treponema pallidum, 822–823
Triangle Trade, 357–358, 1696
Trianon Peace Treaty, 593
Trinidad and Tobago, 1570–1572
 Association of Caribbean States and, 111
 Caribbean Basin Initiative and, 232–233
 Caribbean Community and Common Market and, 233–235
 Caribbean Development Bank and, 235–237
 Caribbean Free Trade Association and, 237–238
 Eric Willaims, 1713–1714
 food imports, 240–241
 international relations, 247
 People's National Movement, 1571
 United National Congress, 1571
TRIP agreement, 16, 490, 824–825, 827
Tripartite Declaration, 75
Tropical cyclones (hurricanes), 1111–1112, 1144, 1153

Trotsky, Leon, 1001
  world revolution model of socialism, 1425
Trujillo, Rafael, 171, 186, 244–245, 484, 1184, 1572. *See also*
        Dominican Republic
Trujillo (Peru) uprising, 63
Truman, Harry S.
  China and, 326
  CIA and, 307
  Fulbright Program and, 686
  Mexico and, 1021
  Palestine and, 73–74
Truong Vam Cam (Nam Cam), 1666
Trusteeship System, 1631–1633
Trypanosoma cruzi (Chagas disease), 820–821
Tshombe, Moise, 263, 590
Tsirinana, Philibert, 973
Tsunamis, 811, 985, 1114–1115, 1489
  of 2004, 811, 985, 1489
Tsvangirai, Morgan, 1090
Tswana people, 190–191
Tuaregs, 170–171, 628, 975, 1140. *See also* Berbers
Tuberculosis, 822, 823
Tubman, William, 960, 1202
Tudjman, Franjo, 136, 411, 1059, 1573, 1750. *See also* Croatia
Tugwell, Rexford, 1200
Tumb islands, 1534
Tumen River Area Development Plan, 518
Tumen River Economic Development Area, 518
Tuna fishing, Japanese, 1194
Tuna Wars, 40. *See also* Fishing rights
Tunisia, 1573–1575
  Arab Maghreb Union (AMU), 67–68, 1165, 1169–1170
  Barcelona Declaration, 1168
  Black Sea Economic Cooperation Organization and, 183–184
  Economic Commission for Africa and, 528–530
  ethnic conflict, 612–613
  geography and climate, 1156–1157
  history, 1574
  Industrial Promotion Agency, 1574
  international relations, 1165
  Kuwait Fund for Arab Economic Development and, 926
  literacy, 1161
  Morocco and, 1168
  OAPEC and, 1208
  unemployment, 1162
  women, 1162
Tunisian Railway Infrastructure Modernization Project, 5
Tupamaros (*Movimiento de Liberación Nacional*), 1486,
        1575, 1647
Turbay Ayala, Julio César, 352, 1110, 1182
Turkey, 1575–1578. *See also* Ataturk, Kemal
  Armenians in, 87
  Baghdad Pact and, 130–131, 310, 868
  Baku-Thilisi-Ceyhan Pipeline Project, 638, 698
  Black Sea Economic Cooperation Organization and, 183–184
  counterinsurgency in, 405
  earthquakes in, 1575
  Economic Cooperation Organization and, 304, 537–538
  geography and climate, 1575–1576
  Greece and, 1577
  history, 1576–1577
  invasion of Cyprus, 1035
  irrigated and drained area, 871
  Justice Party, 1577
  Kurds and, 920, 924, 1533–1534, 1576

languages spoken in, 1027
  military-civil relations, 1048
  multiethnicity, 1576
  pipeline routes, 306
  Regional Cooperation for Development and, 304
  Republican People's Party (*Cumhurtiyet Halk Partisi*), 1577
  territorial disputes, 1532, 1533–1534
Turkic state federation, 1534
Turkish Republic of Northern Cyprus, 428–429
Turkmenistan, 299, 1578–1580
  Caspian Sea and, 305
  Commonwealth of Independent States and, 375–380
  Economic Cooperation Organization and, 304, 537–538
  failed development, 1579
  oil, 306
  pipeline routes, 306
  privatization, 1324
  Soviet Union and, 1578–1579
  tourism, 300
Turkmen language, 1578
Turks, Ottoman. *See* Ottoman Empire
Turks and Caicos
  Caribbean Community and Common Market and, 233–235
  Caribbean Development Bank and, 235–237
  Caribbean Free Trade Association and, 237–238
Turojonzade, Akbar, 594
Tutsi-Hutu conflict, 211–214, 244, 255, 264–265, 269–270,
        389–390, 503–504, 590, 600–601, 630. *See also*
        Rwanda, Burundi
Tutu, Bishop Desmond, 1580–1581
  apartheid and, 1581
  Ubuntu theology, 1580
Tuvalu, 1581–1583
  demographics, 1191
Tuvalu Trust Fund, 1583
Twa people, 211, 255
26th of July Movement, 1583–1584
Typhoid fever, 821

U

US Federal Reserve Bank, 144
Ubangi-Shari. *See also* Central African Republic
  slavery and, 272
Ubíco, Gen. Jorge, 726
Ubuntu theology, 1580
Uganda, 1585–1586
  colonial history, 502
  COMESA and, 369
  debt, 444
  deportation of Asians, 36–37
  East African Community and, 503, 508–510
  Ebola virus in, 1330
  Economic Commission for Africa and, 528–530
  economy, 36–37
  elections, 1586
  ethnic conflicts, 632
  HIV/AIDS, 371
  independence, 30
  invasion of Tanzania, 37
  Lakes Edward and Albert Fisheries (LEAF) Project, 5
  Libyan occupation, 1188
  National Resistance Army, 1586
  political history, 270, 503
  war with Tanzania, 600

Uganda National Congress, 1585
Uganda National Liberation Army (UNLA), 600
Uganda Peoples Congress, 1586
Uganda Peoples Union, 1586
Ugyhur minority, China, 603
Ujamaa Vijinji (Socialism in the Village), 1188, 1524
Ukraine, 1587–1589
    Black Sea Economic Cooperation Organization,
        183–184, 331
    Commonwealth of Independent States and, 375–380
    Cossack uprisings, 1588
    ethnic conflicts, 1587
    ethnicity, 1587
    geography and climate, 1587
    governance, 1588–1589
    Green World movement, 384
    GUAM group and, 381
    history, 1587–1588
    independence, 290, 384
    natural gas production, 647
    Nazi occupation, 1588
    Orange Revolution, 1589
    privatization, 23
    Rurik dynasty, 1587–1588
    Scandinavian colonization, 1587–1588
    territorial disputes, 1532, 1533
Ukrainian Helsinki Union, 384
Ukrainian Orthodox Church, 384
Ukrainians, in Georgia, 698
Ul-Haq, Zia, 175
Ulmanis, Guntis, 946, 1589–1590
Ulmanis, Larlis, 946
Ul-Mulk, Nawab Viqar, 36
Umbundu language, 53
Umkhonto we Sizwe (Spear of the Nation), 11, 59–60
Um-Nyobe, Reuben, 1590
UNAIDS program, 1608, 1737
Underdevelopment, 1590–1595
    alternative development and, 1592
    capital accumulation and, 1591–1592
    causes, 1591–1593
    contract theory, 1591
    dependency theory, 1592. *See also* Dependency Theory
    early theorists, 1591
    entrepreneurship and, 1591–1592
    high-income countries, 1594
    imperialist theory, 1415, 1423, 1592
    measurement of, 1593
    mechanical/organic solidarity theory, 1591
    modernization theory and, 1591
    origin and evolution of concept, 1590–1591
    populism and, 1592
    racial/cultural theories, 1593–1594
    twenty-first century state of, 1593–1594
    Weber's rationality theory, 1591
    world systems theory, 1592
Underground economy, 180–184. *See also* Black market
UNESCO
    Basic Education and Life Skills (BELS) program, 544–545
    educational effectiveness study, 544
    family planning and, 654
    human rights and, 779
    television education and, 546
    World Experimental Literacy Program, 542–543
Uneven development, 465

Uniate Churches, 335
UNICEF (United Nations Children's Fund), 475, 1601–1603
    civil society programs, 1602
    development activities, 1602
    disaster relief, 1602
    genesis and early years, 1601, 1606
    humanitarian relief projects, 785
    primary health care/health-for-all approach, 749–750
    public health and, 1329
    State of the World's Children Report, 1602
    structure and authority, 1601–1602
    WHO and, 1735–1736
Unidad Popular, 681. *See also* Allende, Salvador
Unión Cívica Radical (Argentina), 81
Union des Populations du Cameroun (UPC), 25
Union Douanière des Etats l'Afrique Centrale, 531
Union for the Conservation of Nature and Natural Resources,
        1244–1245
Union of South Africa. *See* South Africa
Union of Soviet Socialist Republics (USSR). *See* Soviet Union
Unions de Populations du Cameroun (UPC), 218
UNITA (National Union for the Total Independence
        of Angola), 53–54, 309, 1293
Unitarianism, populism and, 1301
United Arab Emirates (UAE), 1595–1597
    creation of, 1034
    economic diversification, 1031
    geography and climate, 1596
    history, 1595–1596
    industry and economy, 1596–1597
    international relations, 1596
    labor market and population, 1597
    OAPEC and, 1208
    oil, 646–647
    political background, 1595
    Shar'iah law and, 1595
    territorial disputes, 1534
    women, 1720
United Arab Republic (UAR), 69–70, 130, 1103, 1159,
        1597–1598. *See also* Egypt; Syria
United Democratic Front (South Africa), 11
United Fruit Company, 80, 634, 762, 1177
United Kingdom. *See also* Britain; British Commonwealth
    arms transfer by, 90
    Caribbean Development Bank and, 235–237
    in Central America, 278
    countertrade laws, 408
    foreign direct investment, 708
    international banks in, 151–152
    invasion of Grenada, 278
    oil production, 646–647
United Malay National Organization, 1599
United Nations. *See also* UN *entries*
    Amnesty International and, 37–38
    anti-corruption measures, 398
    Bahrain declaration, 133
    Black Sea Economic Cooperation Organization and,
        183–184
    Convention of the Elimination of Discrimination against
        Women (CEDAW), 1717–1718
    creation of, 1638–1639
    Criminal Tribunal for Rwanda, 1055–1057
    Decade for Women, 433, 1716–1718
    Dr. Ralph Bunche and, 207
    Earth Summit, 1290

Economic Commission for Africa, 529–530
economic sanctions, 1440, 1463
El Salvador and, 661
family planning and, 654
Group of 77 and, 721
HIV/AIDS and, 1329, 1608, 1737
human rights and, 771, 779
International Bill of Human Rights, 779–780
International Criminal Tribunal for the Former Yugoslavia, 1055–1056
Jerusalem question and, 75
in Kosovo, 138
Millennium Declaration, 1609, 1690
New International Economic Order and. See New International Economic Order
nonaligned majority in, 1148
Organization of African Unity and, 1203
Pan-Africanism and, 29
Refugee Convention, 1352
Somalia and, 1433
South Africa and, 1440, 1463
statement on agricultural pollution, 1284
Sukarno and, 1507
World Food Program, 475, 785, 1606, 1732–1734
World Health Organization and. See World Health Organization (WHO)
World Intellectual Property Rights Organization (WIPO), 825–826
World Meteorological Organization (WMO), 476, 705, 1738–1739
Yasser Arafat legitimized by, 1228–1229
Yugoslavian no-fly zone and, 137
United Nations Advisory Committee on Security Questions in Central Africa, 532
United Nations Center for Human Settlements (UN-HABITAT), 1599–1600
United Nations Charter, 1638–1639
United Nations Children's Fund (UNICEF). See UNICEF
United Nations Commission on Crime Prevention and Criminal Justice, 1603–1604
United Nations Commission on Human Rights, 487–488, 1639
United Nations Conference on Desertification, 453
United Nations Conference on Environment and Development, 178, 446, 582, 1509–1510
United Nations Conference on Trade and Development (UNCTAD), 139, 667, 669, 721, 835, 1148, 1604–1605
United Nations Convention on Biological Diversity, 446
United Nations Convention on the Rights of the Child, 818, 1602
United Nations Declaration of Action for the Establishment of a New Economic Order, 139
United Nations Declaration on the Rights of Indigenous Peoples, 487–488
United Nations Declaration on the Rights of Persons Belonging to National or Ethnic, Religious, and Linguistic Minorities, 938
United Nations Department of Humanitarian Affairs, 475, 1619
United Nations Development Program (UNDP), 15–16, 115, 467–468, 475, 1511, 1592–1593, 1605–1608
genesis, 1606
poverty research, 1308–1312, 1312–1318
programming efforts, 1607
structure and authority, 1606–1607
water management and, 1692
United Nations Disaster Relief Agency, 475

United Nations Economic and Social Commission for Asia and the Pacific (UNESCAP), 1608–1611
evaluation, 1610–1611
history and functions, 1609–1811
overview, 1608–1609
regional institutions, 1610
United Nations Economic and Social Committee for Asia and the Pacific (UNESCAP), 100
United Nations Economic and Social Council (ECOSOC), 37–38, 1611–1613, 1639
Commission on International Commodity Trade, 1604–1605
conference diplomacy, 1612–1613
early initiatives, 1611–1612
future outlook, 1613
trade reforms and controversies, 1605
World Trade Organization and, 1605
United Nations Economic Commission for Latin America and the Caribbean, 281, 458, 1613–1616
current programs, 1614–1616
mission, 1614
structure, 1614
United Nations Educational Scientific and Cultural Organisation. See UNESCO
United Nations Emergency Force, 76–77, 1252. See also Peacekeeping; United Nations peacekeeping
United Nations Environment Program, 453, 571, 1511
water management and, 1692
United Nations Expanded Program of Technical Assistance, 1606
United Nations Food and Agriculture Organization (FAO), 15, 1606, 1612, 1616–1617, 1692, 1732–1734
water management and, 1692
United Nations Framework Convention on Climate Change, 446, 574
United Nations General Assembly
Declaration on Principles of International Law Concerning Friendly Relations and Cooperation among States, 1394
Declaration on the Granting of Independence to Colonial Countries and Peoples, 1393
NIEO resolution, 1128. See also New International Economic Order
Resolution 1080, 1206
Resolution 1514, 987
Resolution 2085, 987
United Nations High Commissioner for Human Rights, 780
United Nations High Commissioner for Refugees, 475, 1352, 1606, 1611, 1617–1620, 1629
aid and development linkages, 1618–1619
International Conference on Assistance to Refugees, 1618
zonal development programs, 1617–1618
United Nations Human Rights Commission, 1063
United Nations Independent Commission on International Development (Brandt Commission), 139
United Nations Industrial Development Organization (UNIDO), 1620–1621
Market Access Initiative, 1621
United Nations International Convention for the Suppression of the Financing of Terrorism, 1539
United Nations International Court of Justice (The Hague), 1621–1623
development issues and, 1622–1623
intergenerational equity cases, 1622–1623
Nuclear Tests Case (New Zealand v. France), 1623
United Nations International Drug Control Program, 489, 491, 1623

United Nations International Fund for Agricultural
Development, 1624
United Nations International Governmental Panel on Climate
Change, 705–706
United Nations International Institute on Aging, 1624–1625
United Nations International Research and Training Institute
for the Advancement of Women (INSTRAW), 1625–1626
United Nations Korean Relief and Reconstruction
Agency, 1612
United Nations Office for the Coordination of Humanitarian
Affairs, 475, 1619
United Nations Palestine Partition Plan, 1226
United Nations peacekeeping, 295, 590, 607, 966, 1103–1104,
1150–1256, 1182. *See also* Peacekeeping
    Balkan states, 295
    Chad, 1252
    Colombia, 1182
    Congo, 590, 966, 1103–1104, 1252
    Cyprus, 295, 1252
    Lebanon, 1252
    Rwanda, 507
United Nations Permanent Forum on Indigenous
Peoples, 1627–1628
United Nations Population Fund, 1628–1629
United Nations Relief and Works Agency for Palestine, 75,
1229, 1606, 1611, 1629–1631
    Peace Implementation Program, 1631
    shelter rehabilitation programs, 1631
    subsidized loan program, 1630
United Nations Relief for Palestine Refugees, 1611
United Nations sanctions
    Iraq, 869
    Libya, 1167
    Yugoslavia, 971
United Nations Security Council
    Resolution 242, 77, 78, 220
    Resolution 338, 78, 220
    Resolution 598, 867
    Resolution 687, 1263, 1264
    Resolution 731, 1167
    Resolution 748, 1167
    Resolution 883, 1167
    Resolution 1306, 1407
    Resolution 1441, 1265
United Nations Special Committee on Palestine, 73
United Nations Special Fund for Economic Development, 1606
United Nations Sub-Commission on the Promotion and
Protection of Human Rights, 1627
United Nations Transitional Authority for East Timor, 525
United Nations Transitional Authority in Cambodia,
216, 217
United Nations Trusteeship Council, 1631–1633
United Nations Trust Territory of the Pacific Islands,
996, 1225
United Nations University, 1633
United Nations Water Conference, 1690
United Nations Working Group on Indigenous
Populations, 1627
United Nations World Heritage Sites, 1710–1711
United Nations World Summit for Children, 1602
United Nicaraguan Opposition, 1389–1390
United Progressive Party (Zambia), 1753
United Provinces of Central America, 277–278, 552
United Self-Defense Forces of Colombia (AUC), 352–353
United Somali Congress–Somali National Alliance, 1433

United States. *See also* US *entries*
    Afghanistan and, 307, 1521–1522
    African Growth and Opportunity Act (AGOA), 1700, 1701
    agricultural subsidization, 13
    Alliance for Progress and, 32–35
    American Society of African Culture, 1235
    Andean South America and, 39–45
    Argentina and, 1481
    arms transfer veto by, 95
    ASEAN and, 115
    Asian Development Bank and, 101
    Asia-Pacific Economic Cooperation and, 108
    Bank for International Settlements and, 142
    Berlin Wall and, 171
    Black Sea Economic Cooperation Organization and, 183–184
    Bracero Program, 194–195, 1018
    Cambodian bombing, 1407–1408
    Christian fundamentalism in, 858
    Colombo Plan and, 354
    corn blight, 179
    countertrade laws, 408
    Cuba and, 416–418
    Declaration of Independence, 777, 779
    Dominican Republic and, 245
    East Africa and, 505–506
    Egypt and, 1106
    foreign aid and Cold War, 1106
    foreign assistance program, 156–158
    foreign direct investment, 667, 708
    Free Association Contract, 1225
    Fulbright Program, 686–687
    globalization and, 711
    Grenada invasion, 232, 248, 278, 720–721, 1185
    in Group of 8, 573
    Guatemala and, 1021–1022
    Guyana and, 887–888, 1184–1185
    Haiti and, 84, 85
    Hay-Bunau-Varilla Treaty, 1236, 1237
    human rights and, 772
    immigration and, 1023–1024
    income inequality in, 1311
    industrialization and Great Migration, 8
    intellectual property rights and, 825–826
    international banks in, 151–152
    International Development Association and, 844
    International Energy Agency, 1209
    Iran hostage crisis, 864
    Iranian airliner shooting, 867
    Iran–Iraq War and, 866
    irrigated and drained area, 871
    Israel and, 1106
    Jamaica and, 247
    Japanese land redistribution, 935
    Kurdistan and, 921
    Kyoto Protocol and, 446, 574
    Laos and, 1249–1250
    Liberia and, 960
    Libya and, 1167
    Malvinas/Falkland Islands action, 83, 986–989
    Maquiladoras Program, 644, 992–995, 1018
    MERCOSUR and, 1473
    Mexico and, 1020–1021
    Micronesia and, 1025–1026
    Middle East policy, 130–131
    mining industry, 648

NAFTA and, 1171
nation building, 1103–1107
natural gas production, 647
Oceania and, 1194
oil production, 646–647
OPEC and, 1209
Operation Bootstrap, 1334–1335
pan-Africanism and, 1235
Panama and, 1236–1237
Panama Canal Treaties, 1237–1239
Paraguay and, 1242–1243
Persian Gulf War of 1991, 925, 1160
Persian Gulf War of 2003 (Iraq War), 794, 869–870, 1036
pipeline routes, 306
Plan Colombia, 1276–1278
Platt Amendment, 245–246
populism in, 1303
Puerto Rico and, 1200–1202, 1333–1335
Samoa and, 1385–1386
SEATO and, 1458
September 11, 1076–1077
Somalia and, 507, 1405, 1433–1434
South Africa and, 60–61
suicide rate, 1015
Taiwan/Chinese disputes and, 521–522
Terrorism Code Title 22, 1539
Tonkin Gulf Resolution, 1458, 1667
Tripartite Agreement and, 75–76
Tunisia and, 1165
Universal Declaration of Human Rights and, 1639
USS Stark incident, 866
withdrawal from UNIDO, 1621
United States Constitution, Thirteenth Amendment, 7
United States–Dominican Republic–Central America Free Trade Agreement, 1637–1638
United States Foreign Assistance Act, 1634–1636
United States Information Agency (USIA), 687
United States Virgin Islands, 1669–1671
Universal Declaration of Human Rights, 37, 771, 777, 876, 1638–1640
private property rights and, 1321
Universal Declaration of Women's Rights, 1715
Universal Islamic Declaration of Human Rights, 782, 876
University of Chicago school of economists, 1121, 1275. *See also* Neoliberalism
University of Tirhana, 27
UNLA (Uganda National Liberation Army), 600
Unocal, 306
Untouchables (Dalits), 1640–1641. *See also* Caste systems
UPC (*Unions de Populations du Cameroun*), 218
Upper Hungary. *See* Slovak Republic
Upper Volta. *See* Burkina Faso
Uranium production
Central Africa, 261
Niger, 1141
(The) Urban Guerrilla (Oppenheimer), 730
Urbanization
deforestation and, 445
development and, 1641–1643
development-driven, 1641–1642
East Asia, 512
Engels' Law and, 1641–1642
environmental impact, 1643–1646
erosion and, 580
health advantages of cities, 1642

hydrologic regime and, 1644–1645
Marshall Islands, 997
measures of, 1641
megacities, 1643, 1644
Urban population, 1644
Uribe Vélez, Alvaro, 1361
URNG (National Revolutionary Unity of Guatemala), 726–728
Ur-Rahman, General Zia, 141
Uruguay, 1646–1648
agricultural oligarchy, 1476
Batellista economic program, 1647
bureaucratic authoritarianism, 208, 209
Colorado/Blanco conflict, 1647
financial crisis, 1647–1648
Frente Amplio, 1647
GDP per capita, 1646
geography and climate, 1474, 1475
history, 1647
IMF Structural Adjustment Program, 1647
international relations, 1486–1487
MERCOSUR and, 1472–1474
Movimiento de Liberación Nacional (Tupamaros), 1486, 1575, 1647
Movimiento de Participación Popular (MPP), 1575
Nazi Germany and, 1486
slavery and emancipation, 7
Treaty of Asunción, 200, 1483
Tupumaros, 1486
urban guerilla warfare, 1477–1478
War of the Triple Alliance, 1484
World War II and, 1647
Uruguay Round of GATT, 13–14, 14, 97, 113, 227, 696–697, 707. *See also* GATT
US Agency for International Development (USAID), 33–34, 275, 475–476, 1634–1635
in Vietnam, 1105
US Arms Control and Disarmament Agency, 88
US Caribbean Basin Trade Partnership Act of 2000, 231. *See also* Caribbean Basin Initiative
US Centers for Disease Control (CDC), HIV/AIDS and, 1329
US Central Intelligence Agency (CIA). *See* Central Intelligence Agency
US Congress, Basic Human Needs legislation, 157
US Foreign Assistance Act, 33
US Freedom of Information Act, 1570
US Military Assistance Command, 1105
USAID Expanded Promotion of Breastfeeding Program, 818
USIA (United States Information Agency), 687
US–Philippines Military Bases Agreement, 66
USSR (Union of Soviet Socialist Republics). *See* Soviet Union
Utilitarians, human rights and, 772
Utopian concepts, Robert Owen, 1592
Utub tribe, 133
Uzbekistan, 300, 1648–1649
Aral Sea disaster, 299, 1286, 1374, 1648
Commonwealth of Independent States and, 375–380
cotton production, 1648
Economic Cooperation Organization and, 304, 537–538
ethnic conflicts, 594–595
independence, 383
international relations, 303–304
poverty, 1648–1649
shadow economy, 181

Uzbekistan (*Continued*)
    Tajikistan and, 303
    territorial disputes, 1534
Uzbek Soviet Socialist Republic, 299. *See also* Uzbekistan

V

Vai people, 626
Vaishya caste, 253–254, 1640
Vajpayee, Atal Behari, 804, 899
Väl, Tiit, 1651–1652. *See also* Estonia
Vanuatu, 1652–1653
    demographics, 1191
    John Frum cargo cult, 1652
    national identity, 1193–1194
    National Planning Office, 1652
    offshore banking, 1653
Vargas, Getúlio, 199–200, 1476, 1482, 1653–1654.
        See also Brazil
Vargas Llosa, Marios, 685
Variola (smallpox) virus, 820
Vas, Zoltán, 789
Vásquez Lajara, Horacío, 1572
Vattimo, Gianni, 1569
Velasco Alvarado, General Juan, 40, 41–42, 47, 1267
Velasco Ibarra, José, 42, 46–48
Velvet Revolution, 289, 294, 430, 496, 592–593, 713,
        1416, 1654–1657
Venda Homeland, 153
Venda people, 1439
Venetiaan, Ronald, 1180, 1508
Venezuela, 1658–1661
    Acción Democrática, 1178, 1183–1184, 1259–1260, 1659
    Andean Community and, 39
    anti-American demonstrations, 32
    Association of Caribbean States and, 111
    coffee production, 1178
    Corporación Venezolana de Fomento, 1178
    debt, 223
    financial crisis, 1659–1660
    foreign direct investment, 669
    import substitution industrialization, 1178
    income inequality, 1311
    Inter-American Treaty of Mutual Assistance, 1183
    international relations, 1183–1184
    Netherlands Antilles and, 1126
    oil, 1178, 1658–1659
    overdependence on petroleum, 1659–1660
    Pacto de Punto Fijo, 1183, 1659
    Petróleos de Venezuela, 1178–1179
    political history, 1659–1661
    slavery and emancipation, 7
    Social Christian Party (COPEI), 1659, 1660
    territorial disputes, 1179, 1185, 1537
Verdan, Marie-Claude, 684
Verreenigde Oost-Indische Compagnie. See Dutch East
        India Company
Verwoerd, Hendrik, 1462, 1661. *See also* Apartheid;
        South Africa
Vibrio cholerae, 821–822
Vicente Gómez, Juan, 1660
Videla, General Jorge Rafael, 82, 1082
Vieira, Gen. Joao, 734–735
Vienna International Plan of Action on Aging, 1625
Viet Cong (People's Liberation Armed Forces), 1258–1259

Viet Minh (Vietnam Independence League), 1662, 1663, 1667
Vietnam, 1663–1666. *See also* Vietnam War
    agrarian reform, 582
    American war. *See* Vietnam War
    ASEAN and, 97, 112–116, 1456
    Asia-Pacific Economic Cooperation and, 108
    Cambodia and, 907–908
    CIA in, 309
    colonial legacy, 1454
    doi moi strategy, 481–482
    economy, 98
    ethnic (overseas) Chinese in, 620
    financial crisis, 1451
    under French. *See* Indochina
    Front for the Liberation of South Vietnam, 1664
    GDR per capita, 1665
    Ho Chi Minh, 730, 760–761
    Human Development Index, 659
    Lien Viet Front, 1662
    literacy, 543
    Mekong Basin Development Corporation, 98–100
    National Liberation Front (NLF), 1108–1110
    nation-building and, 1105
    Pathet Lao and, 1249–1250
    People's Army of Viet Nam, 1664
    Poverty Reduction Partnership Agreement, 1666
    privatization, 21
    Red River flood, 1113
    SEATO and South, 1458
    Soviet Union and, 1450
    Strategic Hamlet Program, 1105
    telecommunications industry, 99
    territorial disputes, 1241, 1535
    Viet Minh (Vietnam Independence League), 1662, 1663, 1667
    Viet Nam Fatherland Front, 1662
    Vo Nguyen Giap, 730
Vietnamese, Cambodian massacre of, 908
Viet Nam Fatherland Front, 1662
Viet Nam Quoc Ddn Dang (Van Dao), 1662
Vietnam War, 1105–1106, 1108–1110, 1666–1668
    arms industrialization and, 93
    Army of the Republic of Vietnam, 1259
    counterinsurgency in, 405
    development theory and, 461–462
    guerrilla tactics in, 730
    Ho Chi Minh Trail, 1250
    international relations and, 1454
    Laos and, 944
    My Lai, 1668
    Norodom Sihanouk and, 1407–1408
    Paris Peace Accords, 1250
    People's Army of Vietnam, 1249, 1258
    People's Liberation Armed Forces (PLAF), 1258–1259
    Tet offensive, 1259, 1664
    Viet Cong (People's Liberation Armed Forces),
        1258–1259
Vike-Freiberga, Vaira, 1589
Villa, Francisco "Pancho," 1246
Villalba, Jóvito, 171
Villalobos, Ruy López, 1224
Viral diseases. *See* Infectious diseases *and specific diseases
    and organisms*
Virgin Islands
    British, 1668–1669
    United States, 1669–1671

Virgin Islands National Park, 1670
Virtual water trade, 1671–1672
Virunga National Park (Congo), 1709–1710
Visehrad Four, 1672–1673
Visser't Hooft, W.A., 1729
Voice of the Arabs, 310
Vojvodina, displaced Hungarians in, 593
Volcanic eruptions, 1114–1115
    acid precipitation and, 1–2
    climate change and, 704
    Krakatoa, 1114
    Matupit Volcano (Papua New Guinea), 1239
    Mt. Peleé, 998, 1114–1115
    Mt. Pinatubo, 2
    Nevada del Ruiz, 1115
    Souffriere Hills (Grenada), 1083
    Tambora, 704, 1114
Volta River Project, 1147
Vo Nguyen Giap, 730
Voorhoeve, J.C.C., 156
Vorster, John, 188, 1581
Voter registration, 557
Vulnerability, as poverty measure, 1315

W

Wade, Abdoulaye, 1395
Wahid, Kiai Haji Abdurrahman (Gus Dur), 734–735, 810.
        See also Indonesia
Wahid Hasyim, K.H., 735–736
Wajana Indians, 1507
Walesa, Lech, 294, 890, 1430, 1488, 1655, 1675–1676.
        See also Poland; Solidarity Movement
    Nobel Peace Prize, 1676
    Visehrad Four and, 1672
Walker, William, 278
Wallenstein, Immanuel, 460, 461, 1070
Wallis and Futuna, 1191
Walsh, Lawrence, 394
Walter, George, 56
WAMU (West African Monetary Union), 1703–1705
War
    casualties in developed vs. undeveloped nations, 1677
    classic theories of development and, 1677
    collective goods theory and, 1678
    conditional theories of development and, 1677–1678
    convergence theory, 1677
    development and, 1676–1680
    discrimination principle, 1054
    domestic vs. international, 1676–1677
    failed states and, 1679
    future of conflict and development, 1679–1680
    Geneva Conventions, 1055
    greed-inspired, 1678–1679
    guerilla movements and, 1678–1679
    infrastructure and, 1677
    military necessity principle, 1054
    Phoenix Factor theory, 1677
    poverty trap theory, 1677, 1678
    proportionality principle, 1054
    rules of, 1053–1054
    spillover effects, 1678
    United Nations Charter and, 1053
    weapons proscribed in, 1054
War crimes, 1054–1055. See also Atrocities

War of the Pacific, 43
War of the Triple Alliance, 1484
War on drugs, 488–489. See also Drug trade; Drug trafficking
Warsaw, Menachem Begin in, 161
Warsaw Pact, 286, 1175, 1487–1488
    Czech invasion and, 1319
    dissolution of, 791
    Poland and, 890
Washington, Booker T., 1234
Washington Consensus, 461–463, 965, 966
Wasmosy, Juan Carlos, 885, 1206
Waste management, 1680–1686. See also Pollution; Wastes
    Basel Convention on the Control of Transboundary
        Movements of Hazardous Wastes and Their
        Disposal, 1685
    biological treatment (composting), 1682
    defining, 1680–1681
    hazardous waste, 1684–1685
    history of, 1680–1681
    integrated, 1684
    landfilling, 1683–1684
    solid waste treatment, 1681, 1682–1684
    by source reduction, 1684
    by source separation, 1684
    thermal treatment, 1682–1683
    three major points of, 1681
Wastes
    agricultural, 1690
    carbon to nitrogen ratio, 1682
    collection of, 1681
    composition and management of, 1681
    incineration, 1682–1683
    municipal solid, 1681
    types considered hazardous, 1684
Water
    agricultural privatization and, 20
    aquifers, 1688
    availability of and settlement patterns, 1687–1689
    chemical pollution, 648
    desalinization, 1688–1689
    in developing countries, 570
    diseases borne by, 1691
    Economic Commission for Africa and, 530
    Egypt, 547–549
    evapotranspiration, 1686
    global climate change and, 1691
    Great Man-Made Rivers Project (Libya), 1338
    groundwater reserves, 1688
    groundwater resources, 1686–1687
    human uses, 1689–1690
    hydrological cycle, 1686–1687
    Integrated Water Resource Management, 1692
    Inter-Tropical Convergence Zone, 1686–1687
    Maldives, 984
    Middle East, 1027
    politics and resources, 1691–1692
    quality, 20, 1690–1691
    resource planning, 1691
    resources and distribution, 1686–1693
    sewage treatment wastes. See Waste; Waste management
    surface water resources and human settlement, 1687–1689
    urbanization and, 1644–1645
    virtual water trade, 1671–1672
    World Water Commission, 1692
Water-borne infectious diseases, 821–822, 1691

Water erosion, 581
Water management
  Gabcikovo-Nagymaros Project (Danube River), 1622
  Lake Chad Basin Commission, 933–934
  Lesotho Highlands Project, 957
  Libyan Man Made River project, 962
  seawater distillation, 1670
  Three Gorges Dam, 520, 1546–1548, 1688
Water pollution
  agricultural, 1285
  industrial, 1289–1290
Water Sector Adjustment Program (Morocco), 5
Water Users Associations, 872
Wazel, Hasina, 141
(The) Wealth of Nations (Smith), 1559–1560
Weapons of mass destruction (WMDs), 1262–1263, 1387
  United Nations Security Council Resolution 1441, 1265
Weather, urbanization and, 1645–1646
Weber, Max, 349, 458, 855–856, 1067, 1299–1300
Weismann, Chaim, 134–135
West Africa
  Cold War and, 1700–1701
  Economic Commission for Africa and, 528–530
  Economic Community of West African
      States and, 533–536
  economic development, 1696–1698
  Economic Partnership Agreements (EPAs), 1701–1702
  ethnic conflicts, 626–629
  ethnic regionalization, 1696
  Euro-centricity and, 1694
  failed states, 1697
  geography and climate, 1693–1694
  global powers and, 1700–1702
  Gross Domestic Product (GDP), 1697
  history, 1694–1696
  international relations, 1698–1703
  intra-Africa relations, 1700
  Lomé agreements and, 1701
  population densities, 1694
  privatization, 1324–1325
  Rassemblement Democratique Africaine, 1558–1559
  slavery, 1695–1696
  subregional relations, 1699–1700
  white community, 1706
West African Development Bank, 151
West African Monetary Union (WAMU), 1703–1705
  currency, 1703
West African National Congress, 29
West Bank, 71, 161, 883, 1229, 1382. See also Arab-Israeli
      Wars; Israel; Palestine
  HAMAS in, 741–743
  intifadas, 71, 80, 741–742, 860–862, 883–884, 1038, 1227,
      1231–1232
  Palestinian refugees in, 1232
Western Christian Civilization concept, 640. See also
      Evangelical Protestanism
Western Europe
  family planning in, 655
  globalization and, 711
  income inequality in, 1311
  mining industry, 648
  oil consumption, 647
  Palestinian migration to, 1232–1233
Western Samoa, 1385. See also American Samoa; Samoa
West Indian Diaspora, 1571

West Indies Federation, 155, 246, 1211, 1493, 1494. See also
      Organization of Eastern Caribbean States
Westmoreland, Gen. William C., 1668
West Papua
  ethnic conflict, 619
  gold production, 619
Weyand, Gen. Fred, 1668
WFTU (World Federation of Trade Unions), 1731–1732
Whaling industry, 1190, 1710
What Is Enlightenment? (Kant), 1569
White, Harry Dexter, 833, 846. See also Bretton Woods System
White, Tim, 500
White African communities, 1705–1708. See also Colonialism
"White man's burden," 360
White Tai people, 1540
Whitman, Unison, 180
WHO Conference on the Rational Use of Drugs, 490
Wichi people, 625
Wiesel, Eli, 136–137
Wilderness Society, 446
Wildlife, agricultural globalization and, 12–13
Wildlife preservation
  causes of extinction, 1709–1710
  connecting corridors and, 1711
  future actions, 1712–1713
  international efforts, 1712
  resolving human/wildlife conflict, 1711–1712
  species extinction and, 1708
  strategies for, 1710–1711
  value systems and, 1708–1709
Williams, Eric, 241, 247, 1571, 1713–1714. See also Grenada
Wilson, Edward O., 177
Wilson, Woodrow, 134, 333, 430
Wind energy, 559
Windward Islands
  St. Lucia, 1493–1494
  St. Vincent and the Grenadines, 1494–1495
Wingti, Paias, 1240
WIPO (World Intellectual Property Rights Organization), 825–826.
      See also Intellectual property rights; TRIP agreement
Witt, Mahuad, 49
Wittfogel, Karl, 120
Wojtyla, Karol (Pope John Paul II), 288, 366, 1375, 1714–1715
Wolde Kahasi, Christian, 577
Wolf, Eric, 1422
Wolf's North Atlantic capitalism theory, 1422
Wolof people, 626
Women
  Afghanistan, 3, 4
  African Gender and Development Index, 530
  in agriculture, 12, 1724–1725
  Amnesty International and, 38
  Argentina, 1260
  Beijing World Conference on Women, 1626
  Bougainville Women for Peace and Freedom, 1432
  Chechen "black widows," 598
  China, 326
  Convention of the Elimination of Discrimination against
      Women (CEDAW), 772, 1717–1718
  Cuba, 416
  current emphases in development, 1724–1725
  DAWN (Development Alternatives with Women for a
      New Era), 433–435
  development and, 1721–1722
  development theory as ignoring, 464–465

directions in theory and practice, 1725–1726
East Asia, 512
education and, 318–319
Egypt, 548
female genital mutilation, 758
female infanticide, 319, 819
Fiji, 662
Financing for Development and Remittances and Gender, 1626
Gender and Development Division of Economic Commission
    for Africa, 529–530
gender and development (GAD) theory, 1723–1724
Gender Awareness Information and Networking System
    (GAINS), 1626
Gender Empowerment Measure, 876
gender issues and development, 1722–1723
gender roles in Oman, 1199
global response to, 758
Green Revolution and, 718
health care and, 750
HIV/AIDS and, 758
identity and roles, 1720–1721
infant mortality and, 817–819
International Women's Rights Conferences, 1718
Iran, 863
Islam and, 878
Japanese "comfort women" sexual slavery, 522
Kuwait, 925–926
labor issues, 1725
legal status of, 1715–1719
Liberation of Women (Amin), 878
Liberation Theology and, 958
literacy, 544, 1161
Marshall Islands, 997
Middle East, 1032
migrant, 1626, 1725
Millennium Development Goals, 1626–1627
Morocco, 743, 1085
Muslim women's organizations, 878
networks and development, 1725
North Africa, 1162
Oceania, 1195–1196, 1196–1197
Peru, 1404
Qatar, 1339
Solomon Islands, 1431–1432
South Africa, 11
Swaziland, 1513
tobacco-related illnesses, 1331
UN Decade for Women, 433, 1716–1718
UN International Research and Training Institute for the
    Advancement of Women, 1625–1626
United Arab Emirates, 1596
United Nations Population Fund and, 1628–1629
women and development (WAD) theory, 1723
Women and Law in the Muslim World Programme, 1719
women in development (WID) theory, 1723
Women Living Under Muslim Law, 878, 1719–1720
Women United Together Marshall Islands, 997
World Conference of the International Women's Year,
    1625–1626
Workers' Defense Committee (Poland), 1429–1430
World Assembly on Aging, 1625
World Bank, 10
    African Development Bank and, 5
    agriculture and, 15
    Argentina and, 83

    Asian Development Bank and, 100
    Basic Human Needs program, 156–158
    Burkino Faso and, 211
    Caribbean Development Bank and, 236
    Cold War and, 40
    concessionary loans, 1316. *See also* Debt
    criticisms of, 836
    debt relief and, 442
    Democratic Republic of Congo and, 388
    dependency theory of, 1069
    East Africa and, 506
    environmentalism and, 650
    foreign direct investment (FDI) study, 670
    genesis of, 1606
    Group of 10 and, 143
    Haiti and, 85
    Heavily Indebted Poor Countries Initiative, 818, 836, 849
    HIV/AIDS and, 1329
    institutions, 833–834
    Inter-American Development Bank and, 828
    International Development Fund, 1612
    Kuwait Fund for Arab Economic Development and, 927
    Latvia and, 947
    Malaysia and, 978
    Mongolia and, 1078
    neoliberalism and, 1123
    Newly Industrialized Economies and, 1131
    Nicaraguan debt and, 1135
    operations, 834–836
    political agendas and, 227
    poverty measures, 1316
    Poverty Reduction Strategy Papers, 836
    poverty studies, 1309, 1310, 1313, 1315
    privatization and, 1323
    public sector reform and, 1331–1333
    Purchasing Power Parity measure, 1309
    refugee classifications, 1354
    structural adjustment programs (SAPs). *See* Structural
        adjustment programs
    Sukarno and, 1507
    trade not aid policy, 1132
    trade policy and, 1561–1562
    US funding of, 1561
    World Development Report, 466
    WW II and, 459
World Commission on Human Medium and Development, 569
World Commission on the Environment and Development,
    573–574
World Competitive Index, 1593
WorldCom scandal, 226
World Confederation of Labour (CISC), 1727–1728
World Conference Against Racism, 1759
World Conference of the International Women's Year,
    1625–1626
World Conference on Women (Beijing), 1626
World Congress on National Parks and Protected Areas,
    1245–1246
World Conservation Strategy, 1509
World Conservation Union, 1245, 1509. *See also* International
    Union for Conservation of Nature and National Resources
World Conservation Union Red List, 178
World Council of Churches, 1728–1731
    history, 1728–1729
    Pan-Africanism and, 30
    political and social issues, 1730–1731

World Council of Churches (*Continued*)
  theological issues, 1729–1730
  Zimbabwe and, 1757–1758
World Declaration and Program of Action on the Survival,
    Protection, and Development of Children, 1602
World Development Report, 466, 1593–1594
World Economic Forum, 1123
  anti-corruption measures, 398
World Employment Program of International Labour
    Office, 1045
World Experimental Literacy Program, 542–543
World Federation of Trade Unions, 1727, 1731–1732
World Food Conference, 1624
World Food Program, 475, 785, 1606, 1732–1734
World Health Assembly, 1734–1735. *See also* World Health
    Organization
World Health Organization (WHO), 1734–1738
  challenges to, 1738
  definition of public health, 1328
  family planning and, 654
  genesis, 748, 1606
  "health for all" strategy, 749–750, 1737–1738
  HIV/AIDS and, 759
  membership and structure, 1734–1735
  mental health and, 1016
  regionalization, 1735
  relations with intergovernmental organizations, 1735–1736
  relations with nongovernmental organizations, 1736
  relations with private sector, 1736–1737
  relations with states, 1735
  statement on agricultural pollution, 1284
  Tobacco-Free Initiative, 1331
  UNICEF and, 1735–1736
World Health Report, 1330
World Heritage Sites, 1710–1711
World Human Rights Fund, 37
World Intellectual Property Rights Organization
    (WIPO), 825–826
World Investment Report, 667
World Meteorological Organization (WMO), 476, 705, 1738–1739
  Applications of Meteorology Programme, 1739
  Atmospheric Research and Environment Programme, 1739
World Nature Letter (1982), 570
World Social Forum, 1123
World Summit for Sustainable Development, 1510, 1621
World systems theory, 1070, 1544
  of underdevelopment, 1592
World Trade Center attack (September 11), 4, 300, 880
World Trade Organization (WTO), 459, 1739–1743.
      See also GATT
  agriculture and, 13–14
  Asia-Pacific Economic Cooperation and, 108
  assessment and future challenges, 1742–1743
  China and, 517, 518
  China in, 329, 890
  closed regionalism policy, 1637–1638
  critics of, 1742
  dependency theory of, 1069
  ECOSOC and, 1605
  Estonia in, 583
  foreign direct investment definition, 666–667
  GATT and, 695, 697
  history, 1740–1741
  Kyrgyzstan and, 928
  Latvia and, 947

Lomé Convention and, 965–966
  Mongolia and, 1078
  most-favored nation principle, 1567–1568
  neoliberalism and, 1123
  non-tariff barriers and, 1741
  origin, 708
  principles, 1741
  protests against, 1565
  Seattle meeting, 14
  Singapore and, 1412
  structure and role, 1741–1742
  trade policy and, 1561–1562
  US funding of, 1561
World Vision, 476
World War I
  Arab nationalism and, 68
  Bahrain and, 133
  British Commonwealth and, 373
  Central/Eastern Europe and, 285–286
  colonialism and, 361
  development and, 459
  financial crises following, 142
  health care system development and, 747–748
  Latvia and, 946
  Micronesia and, 1025
World War II
  African Diaspora and, 8
  Albania and, 26
  Bracero Program, 194–195, 1018
  Brazil and, 200
  CARE and, 229
  Caribbean tourism and, 132
  Central African independence and, 263
  Central America and, 277–278
  Central Asia and, 300
  Central/Eastern Europe and, 286
  colonialism and, 361–362
  Commonwealth of Nations and, 373
  development and, 459
  Dominican Republic and, 1572
  ethnic conflicts following, 591–592
  financial crises and, 142
  Golda Meir and, 1008
  Maquiladoras Program and, 644, 992–995, 1018
  Micronesia and, 1025
  Middle East and, 1033
  NATO and, 1175
  Oceania and, 1191, 1225
  populism and, 1304
  refugees and, 1352
  Samoa and, 1385
  South American authoritarian states and, 123
  Southeast Asian nationalism and, 1447–1448
  UNICEF and, 1601
  Uruguayan economy and, 1647
  Venezuela and, 1183
  war crimes and, 1054–1055
  Yugoslavia and, 1749
World Water Commission, 1692
World Wide Fund for Nature. *See* World Wildlife Fund
World Wide Web. *See* Internet
World Wildlife Fund, 177, 446, 1245, 1712
  Project Tiger, 1245
  Terai Arc Landscape Program, 1711
Worrell, Frank, 155

WTO. *See* World Trade Organization
Wye Peace Agreement, 1631
Wye River Memorandum, 71
Wyznynski, Cardinal Stefan, 1743–1744

X

Xhosa people, 622, 1439
Ximenes Belo, Bishop Carlos, 525
Xindonga people, 53
Xinhai Revolution, 331–332
Xinjiang relocation, 520
Xinjiang Uyghur Autonomous Region, 603
Xosa people, 630

Y

Yahya Khan, Agha Mohammed, 1222, 1745–1746
Yalta Conference, 1496
Yameógo, Maurice, 210
Yangtze River, Three Gorges Dam, 520, 1546–1548, 1688
Yanukovych, Viktor, 384
Yebir caste, 255
Yellowstone National Park (US), 1244
Yeltsin, Boris, 375, 383, 713–714, 1657
    Chechnya and, 597
Yemen, 1746–1747
    independence, 1034
    Kuwait Fund for Arab Economic Development and, 926
    League of Arab States and, 71–72
    oil, 646–647
    territorial disputes, 1534
Yhombi-Opango, Joachim, 265
Y2K, 145
Yoder, Dale, social revolution theory, 1421
Yom Kippur War, 77–78, 1038
Yongchaiyudh, Gen. Chavalit, 337
Yoruba, 176. *See also* Biafra
Yoruba people, 626, 1142, 1257
    in Trinidad and Tobago, 1571
Youlou, Félix, 390
Youlou, Fulbert, 264
Young, Crawford, 629
Youth League, of African National Congress, 10, 11
Yudhoyono, Susilo Bambang, 810
Yugoslavia, 1747–1750. *See also* Tito, Josip Broz
    arms embargo, 90
    in Bandung Conference, 139–140
    collapse of, 295
    cooperative socialism, 1428
    destalinization and, 287–288
    domino theory and, 486
    early history, 1748
    end of, 1750
    geography and climate, 1747–1748
    history 1918–1941, 1748
    International Criminal Tribunal for the Former Yugoslavia, 1055–1056
    international relations, 294
    Macedonia and, 971
    Montenegro and, 1080
    Nazi Germany and, 1748
    Non-Aligned Movement and, 1148, 1749
    political history, 287, 290
    Praxis Group of Marxists, 1001

reestablishment post World War I, 135
    Serbia and, 1397–1399
    Slovenia and, 1418
    Soviet Bloc and, 1487
    in World War II, 1749
Yuschenko, Viktor, 384, 1589
Yusef Ahmed, Abdullah, 1434
Yusof, Mohhamad, 3

Z

Zagawa tribe, 1504
Zahedi, General Zahedi, 52
Zaibatsu conglomerates, 103
Zaire. *See also* Democratic Republic of Congo
    arms transfer, 212
    authoritarianism in, 123
    Banyarwanda of, 590
    Chad and, 264
    Economic Community of Central African States and, 531–533
    independence, 269
Zambia, 1751–1753
    COMESA and, 369
    debt, 371
    decolonization, 361–362
    Economic Commission for Africa and, 528–530
    geography and climate, 1751
    health care, 748
    history and economic development, 1460–1462
    HIV/AIDS, 371, 1752
    independence, 30
    Kenneth Kuanda, 899–901, 1751–1752
    Movement for a Multiparty Democracy, 1751, 1752
    Southern African Development Community and, 1463
    United Progressive Party, 1753
Zambian African National Congress, 1752
Zanzibar. *See also* Tanzania
    Chama che Mapinduci (Revolutionary Party), 1523
    history, 1523
    independence, 30
Zanzibar and Pemba Peoples' Party, 1523
Zanzibar Nationalist Party (ZNP), 1198, 1523
Zanzibar Revolution, 1197
Zanzibaran Civic United Front, 1524
Zapata, Emiliano, 1246
Zapatista Army of National Liberation (EZLN), 608, 1017, 1024, 1248, 1383, 1753–1754
Zapawepwe, Simon, 1763
Zapotocky, Antonin, 1319
Zardari, Asif Ali, 175
Zedillo, Ernesto, 1020, 1024
Zerbo, Colonel Saye, 210
Zero growth, 569
Zero Hunger Program (Brazil), 1410
Zhivkov, Todor, 206, 288
Zhivkova, Ludmilla, 206
Zhosa Homeland, 153. *See also* Native Reserves
Zhou Enlai, 1754–1755
    in Bandung Conference, 139–140
Zhu Rongji, 325, 329. *See also* China
Zia, Khaleda, 141
Zia ul-Haq, Muhammad, 1223, 1756
Ziaur Rahman, 1442

Zimbabwe, 1756–1758
   agrarian reform, 935
   COMESA and, 369
   Economic Commission for Africa and, 528–530
   ecotourism in, 539
   ethnic conflicts, 623, 632
   history and economic development, 1460–1462
   Movement for Democratic Change, 1090
   Robert Mugabe, 1089–1990
   South Africa and, 60–61
   Southern African Development Community and, 1463
   white community, 1706
   World Council of Churches and, 1757–1758

Zimbabwean African People's Union (ZAPO), 1090
Zinc production, Central Africa, 261
Zionism, 134, 166–167, 881, 1037, 1758–1759
   Menachem Begin and, 161
   in Palestine, 73–74
   Teodor Herzl, 134, 1758
Zivilgesellschaft, 347
ZNP (Zanzibar Nationalist Party), 1198
Zolberg, Aristide, 1354
Zuang minority, China, 602, 603
Zulu nation, 438, 621–622, 630, 1439
   African National Congress and, 10
   Mangosuthu Gatsha Buthelezi, 212–214